M.weaver

The Equine Medical Encyclopaedia

The Equine Medical Encyclopaedia

David Ramey DVM

with Peter Rossdale OBE PhD FRCVS
and Joanna Brocklesby MRCVS

J.A. ALLEN
LONDON

© *David Ramey, 2009*

ISBN 978-0-85131-901-8

J.A. Allen
Clerkenwell House
45–47 Clerkenwell Green
London EC1R 0HT

J.A. Allen is an imprint of Robert Hale Limited

www.halebooks.com

The right of David Ramey to be identified as author
of this work has been asserted by him in accordance
with the Copyright, Designs and Patents Act 1988

A catalogue record for this book is available from the British Library

Typeset by Ed Pickford
Line illustrations by Maggie Raynor and Sue Devereux
Printed in the UK by the MPG Books Group

Author's Note

Working in the world of equine medicine, one is always aware of the depth and breadth of knowledge required to perform successfully in the field. In any one day, one may be asked to be a radiologist, a medical specialist, a surgeon, an anaesthesiologist, or an obstetrician. One becomes comfortable with – and perhaps stops appreciating – the fact that diverse skill, and a wide range of knowledge, is essential.

This *Equine Medical Encyclopaedia* is an attempt to summarize the vast skills and knowledge that are needed to be competent in the field. It is by no means totally comprehensive – for example, entire books are devoted to the details of particular surgical techniques, or the interpretations of specific blood panels – but enough detail should be provided so as to give the reader an understanding of many of the basic diseases, pathogens, and therapies that are available to those who endeavour to heal the horse. The book is certainly no substitute for good veterinary advice; however, on the occasions when the book is consulted, perhaps such advice will be rendered a bit more understandable, or a bit less arcane.

Trying to provide a compilation of such knowledge is, then, both exhausting and exhilarating. Exhausting because the mere attempt to try to summarize some of the vast amount of information pertaining to medicine, surgery, reproduction, pharmacology – an encyclopaedic undertaking, to be sure – requires a base of knowledge obtained from years of studying and practising, as well as a systematic combing of academic resources to make sure that knowledge is complete, current and accurate. Exhilarating because completing the task brings a degree of satisfaction obtained both from the refreshment of memory, as well as the acquisition of new knowledge. Furthermore, the thrill obtained merely from finishing months of work (and freeing up a few hours in each subsequent day) simply cannot be overstated.

I owe a great debt of gratitude to my wife, Oryla, for her uncomplaining support and sympathy during those long hours of work. She was a great and patient motivator for my effort. She is a tireless educator in her own right, both of high school students, for whom she provides new and endless opportunities, as well as horses, which she determinedly steers through the inscrutable labyrinth that is dressage. Thanks also to our sons, Jackson, 12, and Aidan, just 10, who had the intellectual curiosity to occasionally read and ask questions (in between baseball and soccer games), as well as the innate emotional sensitivity to keep me company from time to time on the days when the task seemed overwhelming (somewhere around the letter P, as I recall). I am proud to be their father.

Finally, to Cassandra Campbell, tireless editor, and to Joanna Brocklesby, whose initial compilation of equine medical terminology served as an invaluable framework for the book, thank you for your patience, enthusiasm and confidence. To Peter Rossdale, who has almost single-handedly driven the world of equine medical education into the world of science, it is a privilege to have your name associated with any work on which my name also appears. I do think that we've created a unique and valuable resource, and it certainly could not have been done without you.

Glossary of Latin and Greek Terms

a- (see an-)	(G)	negation	caco-	(G)	bad
ab- as- a-	(L)	away from	caput	(L)	head
abdomen	(L)	belly	cardio-	(G)	heart
acere	(L)	to be sour	carpos	(G)	wrist
acro-	(G)	top	cata/e-	(G)	down(ward)
ad- a- ac-	(L)	to	cauda	(L)	tail
af- g-			ceno-	(G)	empty (new)
al- n-			cent-	(L)	one-hundred fold
ap- r-			centri/o	(L/G)	centre
as- t-			cephal(o)-	(G)	head
aden	(G)	gland	cera-	(G)	horn
-aemia	(G)	blood	cerebr(o)-	(G)	brain
-aesthesia	(G)	feeling, sense	cervix	(L)	neck
-algia	(G)	pain	chiro-	(G)	hand
ambi-, amphi-	(L/G)	both (ways)	chole-	(G)	bile
an-, a-	(G)	not	chromo-	(G)	colour
ana-	(G)	again, up, back, anew	chrono-	(G)	time
analgesia	(G)	painlessness	chrys(o)-	(G)	gold
ante-	(L)	before	cine- (kine-)	(G)	motion
anth(o-	(G)	flower	circum-	(L)	around
anti-	(G)	against, opposite	-clonus(ic)	(L/G)	twitch, spasm
apo-	(G)	(derived/away) from	com-, con-	(L)	with, together
arch-	(G)	chief, first	co-, col-, cor-		
arteria	(G)	artery	contra-	(L)	against, opposite
arthr-	(G)	joint	corp-	(L)	body
-asthenia	(G)	weakness	coxa	(L)	hip
atrium	(L)	central part of house	cryo-	(G)	ice, cold
audi/o	(L)	hear	crypto-	(G)	hidden
auris	(L)	ear	cutis	(L)	skin
aut(o)	(G)	self	cyclo-	(G)	circle
axilla	(L)	armpit	-cyte	(G)	cell
baktron	(G)	stick	cyto-	(G)	living (cell)
baro-	(G)	weight, pressure	dakryon	(G)	tear
bene-	(L)	well, good	de-	(L)	down (from), away
bi(n)-	(L)	two, twice, double	deca-	(G)	ten-fold
bilis	(L)	bile	deci-	(L)	one-tenth
bio-	(G)	life	dens	(L)	tooth
-blast	(G)	cell	derma	(G)	skin
blepharon	(G)	eyelid	desmos	(G)	band
brachio-	(G)	arm	di-	(G)	two-fold
brachy-	(G)	short	dia-	(G)	through
bradus	(G)	slow	digitus	(L)	finger, toe
broncho-	(G)	windpipe	dilatare	(L)	to spread out
bursa	(L)	bag	diplo-	(G)	twice

dis-	(L)	negation	hippo-	(G)	horse
dorsum	(L)	back	hist(o)-	(G)	tissue
ducere	(L)	to lead, draw	holo-	(G)	whole
ductus	(L)	leading	homo-	(G)	same
dys-	(G)	bad, abnormal	hormon	(G)	setting in motion
eco-	(G)	habitat	hydro-	(G)	water
-ectasis	(G)	dilation	hygro-	(G)	wet, moist
ecto-, exo	(G)	outside	hyper-	(G)	above, more
-ectomy (see -tomy)			hypo-	(G)	under, less
ego-	(G)	'I'	hyster(o)-	(G)	womb
ektos	(G)	outside	ig-, ir-	(L)	negating
emphusan	(G)	puff up	ikteros	(G)	jaundice
empuein	(G)	to suppurate	il-, im-	(L)	in, into
emulgere	(L)	to milk out	ilium	(L)	entrails, flank
encephalos	(G)	brain	inguen	(L)	groin
-enchyma	(G)	infill	inter-	(L)	between, among
endemios	(G)	native	intra	(L)	inside
endo-	(G)	inside	iso-	(G)	same, equal
entero-	(G)	gut, intestine	-itis	(G)	inflammation
epi-	(G)	on, over	jejunus	(L)	fasting
equi-	(L)	equal	jugulum	(L)	collar bone, throat
equus	(L)	horse	kardia	(G)	heart
erythro-	(G)	red	katabole	(G)	throwing down
espavain	(OF*)	swelling	kentesis	(G)	pricking
ethno-	(G)	nation	khondros	(G)	cartilage
eu-	(G)	well, good	khulos	(G)	juice
ex-	(G)	out of, from	kilo-	(G)	thousand(fold)
facere	(L)	to make	kranion	(G)	head
-facient	(L)	maker	kreas	(G)	flesh
facies	(L)	appearance, face	krinein	(G)	to sift
faeces	(L)	dregs	kustis	(G)	bladder
-ferous	(L)	bearing	lacrima	(L)	tear
-folium	(L)	leaf	lamina	(L)	layer
foramen	(L)	hole, opening	leio	(G)	smooth
galact(o)-	(G)	milk	leuc(o)-	(G)	white
gastere	(G)	stomach	ligare	(L)	to bind
-gen, -ogen	(G)	producer	lipos	(G)	fat
genes	(G)	born	lith(o)-	(G)	stone
-genesis	(G)	production	-logue	(G)	word(s)
ger(onto)-	(G)	old	-logy, -ology	(G)	study
gingiva	(L)	gum	lumbus	(L)	loin
glandula	(L)	throat gland	lusis	(G)	loosening
glotta	(G)	tongue	lympha	(L)	water
glyco-	(G)	sweet	lymphaticus	(L)	mad
gnathos	(G)	jaw	lyo-	(G)	separation
-gram	(G)	written	lyso-	(G)	make loose, split
-graph(y)	(G)	writing	macro-	(G)	large, great
gyn(aeco)-	(G)	female	mal-	(L)	bad
haem-	(G)	blood	malignare	(L)	to contrive maliciously
haplo-	(G)	single			
hemi-	(G)	half	mamma	(L)	breast
hepar	(G)	liver	mandere	(L)	to chew
hernia	(L)	rupture	-mania	(G)	madness
heter(o)-	(G)	different	matri-	(L)	mother

maxilla	(L)	jaw	*-ostomy*	(G)	forming stomata opening
medi(o)-	(L)	middle			
mega-	(G)	big, million	*ourein*	(G)	to urinate
melan-	(G)	black	*ovi-*	(L)	egg (ovum)
meninx	(G)	membrane	*oxy-*	(G)	sharp (sense)
meta-	(G)	among, with	*pan*	(G)	all
metabole	(G)	change	*pan(to)-*	(G)	all
-meter, -metric	(G)	measurer	*panniculus*	(L)	layer of membrane
-metrium	(G)	womb	*papilla*	(L)	nipple
micro-	(G)	small	*para-*	(G)	beside
milli-	(G)	thousand(fold)	*paries*	(L)	wall
-mimetic	(G)	imitating	*parturire*	(L)	to be in labour
mini-	(L)	small	*path-*	(G)	feeling, pity, illness
mono-	(G)	single	*-pathy*	(G)	feeling, suffering (treatment)
morph(o)-	(G)	shape, form			
mukes	(G)	fungus	*pectus*	(L)	chest
multi-	(L)	much, many	*ped-*	(L)	foot
myc(o)-	(G)	fungus	*penia*	(G)	poverty
-myce(te)s	(G)	fungus	*per-*	(L)	through
myel(o)-	(G)	marrow	*peri-*	(L)	around, encircle
myo-	(G)	muscle	*perone*	(G)	fibula
myx(a/o)-	(G)	mucus	*phagia*	(G)	eating
necro-	(G)	death	*phalanx*	(G)	bone of finger or toe
neg-	(L)	not, negation	*pharm(aco)-*	(G)	medicine (poison)
neo-	(G)	new	*pharunx*	(G)	throat
nephro-	(G)	kidney	*pheno-*	(G)	visible
neuro-	(G)	nerve	*-phile*	(G)	love
neuter	(L)	neither	*-phobe*	(G)	dislike
non-	(L)	not, negation	*phon(o)-*	(G)	sound
-nychia	(G)	nail	*phos-, phot(o)-*	(G)	light
-nym	(G)	name	*phragma*	(G)	fence
ob-, oc(c)-	(L)	in the way of	*phren*	(G)	diaphragm
obstetrix	(L)	midwife	*phreno-*	(G)	mind
obturare	(L)	to stop up	*phyllo-*	(G)	leaf
oculus	(L)	eye	*physio-*	(G)	nature
odont(o)-	(G)	tooth	*-phyte*	(G)	plant
-oid	(G)	shape of, like	*planta*	(L)	sole
oidein	(G)	to swell	*plasis*	(G)	formation
olene	(G)	elbow	*-plasty*	(G)	mould (form, make)
olfactus	(L)	smell	*-plegia*	(G)	blow, paralysis
-oma	(G)	swelling, tumour	*pleura*	(G)	side of body
omphalos	(G)	navel	*pneumo-*	(G)	lung, breath(e)
oo-	(G)	egg	*-poeiesis*	(G)	production
ophthalmos	(G)	eye	*poly-*	(G)	many
-opia	(G)	eyes	*post-*	(L)	after, behind
-opthalmi(a,ic)	(G)	eyes	*pre-*	(L)	before
opthalmo-	(G)	eye	*pro-*	(L)	before, forward
optos	(G)	seen	*proto-*	(G)	first
orkhis	(G)	testis	*prurire*	(L)	to itch
ortho-	(G)	straight, correct	*pseud(o)-*	(G)	false
-ose(sis)	(L/G)	state of (disease)	*psych(o)-*	(G)	soul, mind
osmos	(G)	push	*pubes*	(L)	genitals, groin
oss-	(L)	bone	*pulmonarius*	(L)	lung
oste(o)-	(G)	bone	*pulsus*	(L)	beating

8

pupilla	(L)	pupil	*tenon*	(G)	sinew
pyr-	(G)	fire	*teras*	(G)	monster
quad(r)-	(L)	four(fold)	*tetanos*	(G)	muscular spasm
radia/o	(L)	spoke, ray	*thalamos*	(G)	inner chamber
re-	(L)	again, return	*-therapy*	(G)	treatment
renes	(L)	kidneys	*thermo-*	(G)	heat
retro-	(L)	backwards, behind	*thorax*	(G)	thorax, chest
rhegnumi	(G)	burst	*thrombos*	(G)	blood clot
rheum-	(G)	flow	*tomo*	(G)	slice, cut
rhin(o)-	(G)	nose	*-tomy (otomy,*	(G)	cut
-rrhoea	(G)	flow unusually	*-ectomy)*		
rub-	(L)	red	*-tonus*	(G)	spasm
sapro-	(G)	rotten, decayed	*toxo-*	(G)	arrow
sarco-	(G)	flesh	*trans-*	(L)	across, beyond
scler-	(G)	hard	*trauma*	(G)	wound
sebum	(G)	grease	*troph(o)-*	(G)	food
-section	(L)	cut	*tumere*	(L)	to swell
semi-	(L)	half	*tussis*	(L)	cough
semin-	(L)	seed	*ulcus*	(L)	ulcer
skolios	(G)	bent	*ulna*	(L)	elbow
skopein	(G)	to examine	*ultra-*	(L)	beyond
sono-	(L)	sound	*umbilicus*	(L)	navel
sorbere	(L)	to suck in	*un-*	(L)	reversal
sperm-	(G)	seed	*-uria*	(L)	urine
sphuxis	(G)	pulse	*uterus*	(L)	womb
spirare	(L)	to breathe	*vena*	(L)	vein
spondylus	(L)	vertebra	*venter*	(L)	belly
-spore	(G)	seed	*viscera*	(L)	internal organs
squama	(L)	scale	*vita*	(L)	life
steg(an)o-	(G)	hidden, covered	*vivi-*	(L)	alive
steno-	(G)	contracted, narrow	*vulva*	(L)	womb
stoma	(G)	mouth	*xer(o)-*	(G)	dry
stomakhos	(G)	gullet	*zoo-*	(G)	animal
strat-	(L)	layer	*zugon*	(G)	yoke
sub-, suf-, sup-	(L)	under, below	*zygo-*	(G)	joining two similar
super-, supra-	(L)	over, above			things
sur-	(L)	over, above	*zym(o)-*	(G)	ferment (yeast)
syn-, syl-, sym-	(G)	with, together			
tachy(e/o)-	(G)	speed			
tarsos	(G)	flat of foot	*OF = Old French		
-taxis	(G)	turning, arrange			

Pronunciation

Underlined syllable is that which is stressed.
/ indicates break between words.
◀᎓ Speaker symbol denotes pronunciation key.

a   = a as in hat
aw = a as in hall
ā   = a as in hate
ă   = as in pair or dare
ar = a as in car
ang   =   ang as in hang
ch = ch as in chin
čh = ch as in loch
dl = single sound as in saddle
e   = e as in bed
ĕ   = a as in analysis and as in hernia; ar
      as in articular; e as in taken; er as in
      shoulder, o as in staphylectomy and
      histology; or as in factor; ou as in
      squamous; u as in speculum and
      nervous
ē   = ee as in teeth
er = er as in serve
é   = ee as in beer
i   = i as in sit
ī   = i as in wine and synapse
ing= ing as in walking and yn as in
      synchronous
iy = y as in tyre

ks = x as in ataxia
o   = o as in hot
ō   = as in boat and blow
ŏ   = o as in cold
ő   = ow as in how, or ou as in house
oi = oi as in soil
or = or as in horse
ů   = oo as in zoo or ue as in glue
u   = u as in hug
ū   = u as in universe
ŭ   = u as in pull
ŭr = ur as in pure
ü   = u as in put
f   = f as in fix and ph as in photograph
j   = j as in jelly and g as in gem
k   = k as in king or c as in cot
sh = sh as in ship
th = th as in think
th = th as in the
tl = single sound as in perinatal
zh = as in fusion
y   = y as in stallion
z   = z as in zebra and x as in xylazene

A

Ab *abbr.* antibody.

a-, an- *prefix.* without.

ab- *prefix.* away from.

Abaxial *ab aks ē ūl, adj.* situated away from the axis of the body or limb, e.g. abaxial surface of the equine lower limb is on the outside of the limb, away from the middle line of the body.
See Axis.

    A. nerve block *ab aks ē ūl / nerv / blok, n.* local anaesthetic nerve block of the palmar nerves; a regional block used for anaesthesia of structures distal to the fetlock, including the pastern and foot.

Abdomen *ab dē mĕn, n.* the portion of the body lying between the thorax and pelvis. The abdomen contains a cavity (See A. cavity, below) which is bounded dorsally by the spine and back muscles, cranially by diaphragm, and ventrally by the muscles of the abdominal wall. The posterior border, at the pelvic inlet, is incomplete.
See Abdominal, Diaphragm, Spine.

Abdominal *ab do min ūl, adj.* pertaining to abdomen.

    A. abscess *ab do min ūl / ab ses, n.* localized collection of pus, usually caused by bacterial infection, often involving local mesenteric lymph nodes. Many potential causes, including from spread of infection from various tissues, including lungs, as a complication of infection from *Streptococcus equi* ('strangles', 'distemper'); may also be seen in cases of extreme parasitism. Chronic cases may result in formation of adhesions within abdomen, which may lead to further complications, including colic. Clinical signs may include weight loss, intermittent low-grade colic, poor appetite, fever and intermittent diarrhoea. Diagnosis may be supported by complete blood count, rectal palpation, ultrasonography and analysis of fluid from abdominal cavity. Horses with extensive secondary complications may not recover, or may be considered for euthanasia.
See Abscess, Adhesion, Colic, Diarrhoea, Mesentery, Pus, Strangles, Ultrasonography, Worm.

    A. cavity *ab do min ūl / cav it ē, n.* body cavity contained within the abdomen. Lined by thin membrane called peritoneum. Contains many major organs, including: bladder, stomach, small intestine, large intestine, liver, spleen, pancreas.
See Abdomen, Peritoneum, organs under individual entries.

    A. hernia see Hernia

    A. wall *ab do min ūl / wawl, n.* the multi-layered structure made up of skin, subcutaneous tissue, muscle, fibrous tissue (fascia) and peritoneum (thin lining layer) which forms the lateral and ventral borders of the abdomen. Fascia has superficial and deep layers (abdominal tunic). Muscles of the abdominal wall include: obliquus externus abdominis, obliquus internus abdominis, transversus abdominis, and rectus abdominis.
See Fascia, Muscle, Peritoneum.

Abdominocentesis *ab do mi nō sen tē sis, n.* perforation or tapping of the abdominal cavity with a needle or similar device to withdraw fluid from abdominal cavity. Normally performed for diagnostic purposes (e.g. peritonitis, colic); occasionally performed to drain abnormal fluid, as in peritoneal lavage. Normally, the horse's abdominal fluid is watery, clear, and straw-coloured, with low protein levels.
See Colic, Peritonitis.

11

Abducens nerve ◀ᴇ *ab dū sēnz* / *nerv, n.* cranial nerve VI. Supplies muscles responsible for movement of eyeball. With oculomotor (III) and trochlear (IV) nerves is responsible for normal eye position. Normal function allows retraction and lateral movement of eyeball.
See Cranial nerve, Eye, Oculomotor nerve, Trochlear nerve.

Abduct ◀ᴇ *ab dukt, v.* draw away from the median plane; to abduct limb is to move it away sideways from body.
See Axis.

Abiotrophy ◀ᴇ *ā bī ō trō fē, n.* spontaneous premature progressive loss of certain tissues or organs, especially nervous tissue.
See Neuron.

> **Cerebellar a.** ◀ᴇ *se rí be lē* / *ā bīō trō fē, n.* a genetically linked, neurological condition found almost exclusively in Arabian horses. Breeding experiments indicate a recessive mode of inheritance for this condition, that is, a horse can 'carry' the disease gene but not be affected by it. However, when two carrier horses are bred, they will produce an affected foal 25% of the time.

Ablate ◀ᴇ *ab lāt, v.* remove, especially by cutting.

Abnormal behaviour see Behaviour

Abort ◀ᴇ *ēb ort, v.* to check the usual course of a disease. In reproductive medicine, to miscarry foetus before it is able to survive; to terminate pregnancy.
See Foetus, Pregnancy.

Abortifacient ◀ᴇ *ēb ort i fāsh ēnt, n.* drug or other agent causing abortion, e.g. prostaglandin F-2α can cause abortion if given by injection approximately between days 15 and 35 of gestation.
See Abortion, Gestation, Prostaglandin.

Abortion ◀ᴇ *ēb or shun, n.* the premature expulsion from the uterus of the products of conception, including the foetus and foetal membranes. Numerous causes, including elective.

INFECTIOUS CAUSES
- Bacteria: *Brucella abortus* (occasional)
  Ehrlichia spp.
  Escherichia coli (most common at 150–300 days)
  Leptospira spp.
  Klebsiella spp.
  Pseudomonas spp.
  Salmonella abortus equi
  Staphylococcus spp.
  Streptococcus spp. (most common in first 150 days)
- Fungi: *Aspergillus fumigatus*

Fungal infection spreads up from vagina, abortion usually at 200–300 days. Placenta is thickened, brown exudate, abnormal areas seen in liver of foetus. Diagnosis requires demonstration of inflammatory response to fungus.

- Viruses: Equine herpes virus 1 (EHV-1) (sudden abortion in last four months)
  Equine viral arteritis (late gestation)

Diagnose by histopathology (intranuclear inclusion bodies with EHV-1), virus isolation and serology.

NON-INFECTIOUS CAUSES
- Placental insufficiency.
- Twin foals (common, only approximately 11% of mares with twin foals will deliver two healthy foals at term).
- Umbilical cord abnormalities (e.g. long cord may twist and compromise foetal blood supply).
- Uterine body pregnancy – rare; pregnancy loss in the caudal uterine body has been estimated at 83%; preganacy loss in the cranial uterine body has been estimated at 22%.

NOTE: Though commonly diagnosed, insufficient production of progesterone by the ovary in early term has rarely, if ever, been diagnosed. Thus, supplemental progesterone in early pregnancy, though commonly prescribed, is rarely, if ever, indicated.
See Anaplasmosis *Aspergillus, Brucella abortus*, Equine herpes virus, Equine viral arteritis, *Escherichia, Klebsiella* spp., *Leptospira* spp., Pregnancy, Progesterone,

Pseudomonas, *Salmonella*, *Staphylococcus*, *Streptococcus*, Twin, Uterus.

Abortus ◀ *ĕb* *or* *tĕs*, *n.* dead foetus or foetus unable to survive, expelled before natural end of pregnancy.

Abrasion ◀ *ĕb* *rā* *zhĕn*, *n.* the wearing away of a substance or structure, such as skin or teeth, caused by some abnormal mechanical process (e.g. rubbing or scraping).
See Crib-biting, Wound.

Abscess ◀ *ab* *ses*, *n.* localized collection of pus (dead cells, exudate and usually bacteria) buried in tissues, organs, or confined spaces, such as a body cavity. May be acute or chronic. Many causes, including foreign body, infection (bacterial or fungal), larvae of parasites migrating through tissues.
See *Corynebacterium*, Foreign body, Larva, Parasite, Pus, Strangles, and under specific anatomical sites

Absorbent ◀ *ĕb* *zor* *bĕnt*, *n.* able to take in; having tendency to soak up or incorporate.

Absorption ◀ *ĕb* *zorp* *shĕn*, *n.* taking in; passage of fluid or substance into or across tissues, including skin, mucous membrane, intestine, or kidney tubules, and into blood or lymph.
See Blood, Lymph.

Acanthocyte ◀ *ā* *kan* *tho* *sīt*, *n.* also known as 'spur cells', acanthocytes are red blood cells with a few irregular, blunt, finger-like projections. These cells have a decreased survival time and may occasionally be seen in liver disorders or with blood storage. Infrequently seen in horse histopathology.
See Red blood cell.

Acantholysis ◀ *ā* *kan* *tho* *lī* *sis*, *n.* disruption of the connections between keratin-producing cells in outer layer of skin (epidermis), resulting in clefts and blisters (vesicles and bullae). Seen especially in inflammatory, viral and autoimmune skin diseases, e.g. pemphigus.
See Autoimmune disease, Pemphigus foliaceous, Skin.

Acapnia ◀ *ā* *kap* *nē* *ē*, *n.* a deficiency of carbon dioxide in the blood or tissues.
See Carbon dioxide.

Acariasis ◀ *a* *kē* *rī* *ē* *sis*, *n.* infestation with mites (mange) or ticks (arthropod parasites).
See Mange, Tick.

Acaricide ◀ *a* *ka* *ri* *sīd*, *n.* substance/agent used to kill mites or ticks. Permethrin is one of several chemical compounds that may be used in horses.

Accessory carpal bone ◀ *ak* *ses* *ĕr* *ē* / *car* *pŭl* / *bōn*, *n.* one of the seven small bones of the carpus (knee joint) of the equine forelimb; lies on the posterior aspect of the upper row of bones.
See Arthroscopy, Carpus, Radiography, Sesamoid bone.

A.c.b. fracture ◀ *ak* *ses* *ĕr* *ē* / *car* *pŭl* / *bōn* / *frak* *tŭr*, *n.* infrequently occurring fracture, occurring especially during athletic activity. Signs of fracture include lameness, swelling and pain on palpation and carpal flexion; diagnosis usually confirmed by radiography; occult fractures may be revealed with scintigraphy. Prognosis guarded; some cases are amenable to surgical repair.

Accessory ligament ◀ *ak* *ses* *ĕr* *ē* / *lig* *ē* *mĕnt*, *n.* Horses have four ligaments that may be referred to as accessory ligaments. Forelimb accessory ligaments are thought to help dampen the spring in the horse's stride:

- A.l. of the superficial flexor tendon (radial a.l.) attaches the superficial flexor tendon to the posterior distal aspect of the radius. This ligament may be surgically transected to treat some cases of superficial digital flexor tendon injury.
- A.l. of the deep digital flexor tendon (carpal a.l.) attaches the palmar carpal ligament to the mid-body of the deep digital flexor tendon. This ligament may be surgically transected to treat selected cases of flexural deformity ('club foot'), injury, or lameness.

Hind limb:
- A.l. of the distal hind limb is a long, slender, weakly developed structure that arises from the fibrous joint capsule of the hock, and joins the deep flexor tendon near the middle of the distal limb.
- A.l. of the hip helps to stabilize the hip joint. Originates from opposite prepubic tendon of abdominal muscles, enters hip socket (acetabulum) through acetabular notch and attaches to head of thigh bone (femur) inside acetabulum. Only found in horse family.

Accessory nerve ◀ː *ak ses ēr ē / nerv, n.* cranial nerve XI. Has two main branches: internal and external. Internal branch detects sensation and controls movement of pharynx, larynx and oesophagus with glossopharyngeal (IX) and vagus (X) nerves. External branch supplies superficial neck muscles. Assess function by observation of swallowing, endoscopic examination of pharynx and larynx.
See Endoscopy, Glossopharyngeal nerve, Larynx, Oesophagus, Pharynx, Vagus.

Accessory sex gland ◀ː *ak ses ēr ē / seks / gland, n.* supplementary gland of reproductive tract. In stallions are bulbourethral glands, seminal vesicles and prostate; in mares are vestibular glands of vagina and mammary glands.
See Bulbourethral gland, Mammary gland, Prostate gland, Seminal, Vagina.

Acclimatization ◀ː *a klīm ēt īz ā shun, n.* to adjust to a new environment. For example, a horse may have to acclimatize to his surroundings when moved to a new stables.

Acellular ◀ː *ā sel ū lēr, adj.* containing no cells.
See Cell.

Acepromazine maleate ◀ː *ās prō maz ēn mal ēāt, n.* phenothiazine-derivative sedative/tranquillizer. Myriad, dose-dependent uses. Has little or no pain-killing effect. Causes dilation of small peripheral blood vessels; has been prescribed for treatment of laminitis. Potential for causing drop in blood pressure, accordingly should be used with caution in debilitated or anaemic horses, those with heart or blood vessel disease, or those which have low blood volume (hypovolaemia), e.g. from dehydration or severe bleeding, as a pre-anaesthetic, or immediately post-exercise (rapid drop in blood pressure may precipitate fainting). Partial penile paralysis (paraphimosis) is a rare, but potential side-effect in male horses. The drug should be used by, or on the advice of, a qualified veterinarian.
See Anaemia, Heart, Hypovolaemia, Paraphimosis, Phenothiazine, Sedative, Vasodilation.

Acer rubrum see Red maple

Acetabulum ◀ː *a set ab ū lēm, n.* cup-shaped cavity in the lateral aspect of the bony pelvis formed where pubis, ilium and ischium join together. Head of femur fits into acetabulum to form hip joint.
See Hip, Pelvis.

Acetazolamide ◀ː *ē set ē zol ē mīd, n.* a diuretic drug which increases potassium excretion by kidneys (carbonic anhydrase inhibitor). May be used to treat or maintain horses affected with hyperkalaemic periodic paralysis (HYPP).
See Hyperkalaemic periodic paralysis, Potassium.

Acetylcholine ◀ː *a sit īl kō lēn, n.* neurotransmitter substance which acts at the nerve–muscle junctions (myoneural junctions) of striated muscle. Rapidly inactivated by cholinesterase after nerve impulse has passed, thus, has no therapeutic applications.
See Central nervous system, Neurotransmitter, Parasympathetic nervous system, Sympathetic nervous system.

Acetylcholinesterase ◀ː *a sit īl kō lēn ēs trāz, n.* enzyme involved in inactivation of acetylcholine (splits it into choline and acetic acid), e.g. at nerve–muscle junction inactivates acetylcholine after impulse has passed, so stops stimulation of muscle.

Action may be inhibited by some poisons, e.g. organophosphates.
See Acetylcholine, Organophosphate.

Acetylcoenzyme A ◀⧧ *a sit īl kō en zīm / ā, n.* in biochemisty, a molecule important in tricarboxylic acid cycle (Krebs cycle), the final common pathway for the oxidation to CO_2 of all molecules used by the body as fuel.
See Metabolism.

Acetylsalicylic acid ◀⧧ *a sit īl sa li si lik / a sid, n.*(**aspirin**) Non-steroidal anti-inflammatory and pain relieving (analgesic) drug. Used to treat various muscular pains and arthritis, and to reduce fever, although other NSAID drugs may be more effective in horses. May be used in the treatment of blood clots (thrombosis) due to its anticoagulant effects on blood platelets. Has been advocated for the treatment of horses with laminitis. Side effects include gastric and intestinal mucosal ulceration and bleeding, particularly with prolonged or high doses.
See Analgesic, Arthritis, Thrombosis.

Achilles tendon see Gastrocnemius. Achilles was a mythological Greek hero whose mother held him by the heel to dip him in the river Styx.

Acid ◀⧧ *a sid, n./adj.* sour, any of a large class of chemical substances, often represented by the generic formula HA [H^+A^-], traditionally considered to give a solution with a pH less than 7.0 when dissolved in water. Opposite to alkali, with which it reacts to form salts.
Generally, acids have the following properties:

* taste – usually sour;
* touch – strong or concentrated acids commonly produce a stinging or tingling feeling on mucous membranes;
* reactivity – strong acids react strongly with many metals, causing corrosion;
* electrical conductivity – acids are electrolytes;
* litmus paper – acids turn blue litmus paper red.

Acid–base balance ◀⧧ *a sid – bās / bal ēns, n.* equilibrium between acidity and alkalinity of body fluids. Acid–base balance refers to a condition where the net rate of acid or alkali production is balanced by the net rate of acid or alkali excretion. The point of acid–base balance is to maintain a steady state of H^+ ions. Optimum pH of body fluids is 7.4. Mild shifts to either side of optimum can be compensated for by three primary methods of control: 1) chemical (buffer), 2) respiratory, 3) renal.
Acid-fast ◀⧧ *a sid / farst, adj.* descibes bacteria which, when stained, do not readily lose colour in acid, e.g. mycobacteria.
See Bacterium.

Acidosis ◀⧧ *a sid ō sis, n.* an accumulation of acid and hydrogen ions; alternatively, a depletion of the alkaline reserve. Acidosis lowers blood pH, and can be pathological. Most commonly diagnosed by blood gas analysis of arterial blood.
See Blood, pH.
Metabolic a. ◀⧧ *me ta bo lik / a sid ō sis, n.* (bicarbonate concentration reduced) occurs when the acid–base status of the body shifts towards the acid side due to loss of base or retention of acids (as opposed to respiratory acidosis, which is caused by a retention of carbon dioxide). The body has several mechanisms for compensation, including increased breathing rate. Complication of numerous disease processes, including shock (both toxic and from loss of blood), strangulated bowel, diarrhoea, and sometimes peritonitis, ruptured bladder, kidney failure.
See Diarrhoea, Peritonitis, Shock, Sodium bicarbonate.
Respiratory a. ◀⧧ *re spē rē trē / a sid ō sis, n.* (accumulation of carbon dioxide) seen in severe decrease in efficiency of breathing, e.g. pneumonia, obstruction of upper airway. Several methods of compensation, including retention of bicarbonate by kidneys.
See Kidney, Pneumonia.

Aconite ◀⧧ *a kon īt, n.* (*Aconitum napellus,* monkshood, wolfsbane) poisonous plant, generally grown in gardens in UK. 65 cm to 2 m high, yellow or blue flowers, each with a hood-shaped petal. All parts contain poisonous alkaloid, especially roots. In horses, if eaten may cause restlessness, colic, unsteady gait, hind limb paralysis, unconsciousness and death.
See Colic.

Acorn ◄⬧ _ā korn_, _n._ fruit of oak (_Quercus_ spp.). Can cause poisoning, especially seen at end of long dry summer. Contains tannic acid which causes kidney failure and gastrointestinal damage. Clinical signs of poisoning include dullness, loss of appetite, constipation sometimes followed by bloody diarrhoea, pale gums. Inflamed stomach and intestines at post mortem.
See Oak.

Acquired ◄⬧ _ē kwiyd_, _adj._ used to describe a condition which the animal develops during life, as opposed to a congenital condition with which an animal is born.

Acquired defect see Defect

Acriflavine ◄⬧ _a kri flā vin_, _n._ orange–red dye, used as topical antiseptic at 1 in 1,000 dilution.
See Antiseptic.

Acrosome ◄⬧ _a krē zōm_, _n._ cap found at the anterior portion of the nucleus of a sperm cell; contains enzymes for penetration of ovum.
See Fertilization, Sperm.

ACTH see Adrenocorticotrophic hormone

Actinism ◄⬧ _ak tin izm_, _n._ that property of radiant energy which produces chemical changes.

Actinobacillus ◄⬧ _ak tin ō bas il ēs_, _n._ genus of bacteria, Gram-negative, pleomorphic rods.
　　A. equuli ◄⬧ _ak tin ō bas il ēs / ek wē lī_, _n._ causal agent of diarrhoea and septicaemia in foals.
　　See Diarrhoea, Septicaemia, Sleepy foal disease.

Activated charcoal ◄⬧ _ak ti vāt id / char kōl_, _n._ a general term referring to carbon material mostly obtained from charcoal. Under electron microscopy, the structure of activated charcoal resembles crumbled paper ribbons, interspersed with wood chips. This structure contains many nooks and crannies, and these micropores provide an exceptionally high surface area for adsorption. As such, activated charcoal has been used to treat some equine intestinal disorders, especially diarrhoea.

Acupuncture ◄⬧ _a kū pungk tūr_, _n._ a technique of inserting thin needles into the horse's body in an effort to achieve a therapeutic effect. The current practice has roots in China and western Europe, especially twentieth-century France, but no historical precedent. Numerous postulated mechanisms of action, including endorphin release and placebo effect, but none proven. Numerous proposed uses in veterinary medicine, but no reliable evidence of effectiveness yet demonstrated in sound scientific trials.
See Endorphin, Laminitis, Navicular syndrome.

Acute ◄⬧ _ē kūt_, _adj._ sharp; describing condition with a short, often relatively severe course.

Acute arthritis see Arthritis

Acute respiratory distress syndrome ◄⬧ _ē kūt / re spē re trē / dis tres / sin drōm_, _n._ (ARDS) lung injury characterized by damage to the alveoli, pulmonary oedema and respiratory failure. Primary lung injury resulting in ARDS can be caused by aspiration, e.g. iatrogenic administration of medications via nasogastric tube, smoke inhalation, or overwhelming infection. Lung injury may also be secondary to conditions such as anaphylaxis, sepsis, trauma, and embolism. The end result of ARDS is poor gas exchange. Affected horses are in respiratory distress; frothy discharge may be seen in nostrils. Fever may accompany infectious causes. Noises may be heard on auscultation; endoscopic examination may show oedema, necrosis of mucous membranes, or the presence of foreign material. Blood gases show hypoxaemia and hypocapnia. Treatment is supportive; intravenous fluids should be used cautiously owing to pulmonary oedema. Antimicrobials may be indicated; anti-inflammatory agents, especially corticosteroids, may be useful to help decrease inflammation and permeability of lung blood vessels. See Premature, Respiratory, Surfactant.

Acyclovir ◄€ *ā sī klō vér, n.* antiviral agent. The drug has selective activity against herpes viruses by blocking normal DNA formation. In addition to topical usage, e.g. viral keratitis, it has also been used to treat systemic herpes (EHV) infections. See Keratitis, Equine herpes virus.

ad- *prefix.* to, between, in addition to, near.

Adaptation ◄€ *ad apt ā shun, n.* 1) the adjustment of an organism to its environment, or the process by which it enhances such adjustment, e.g. an animal's response to a change in its environment; 2) the normal adjustment of the eye to changes in the intensity of light. See Eye.

Addison's disease see Hypoadrenocorticism

Adduct ◄€ *ē dukt, v.* draw towards median plane; to adduct limb is to move it towards body. See Axis.

Adenitis ◄€ *a dēn ī tis, n.* inflammation of a gland. See Gland, Inflammation.

Adenocarcinoma ◄€ *a dēn ō kars in ō mē, n.* a carcinoma (epithelial cell tumour) derived from glandular tissues or in which the tumour cells form recognizable glandular structures; often malignant. See Gland, Tumour.

Adenoma ◄€ *a dēn ō mē, n.* benign tumour derived from glandular epithelium or which has a glandular structure. See Gland, Tumour.

Adenopathy ◄€ *a dēn o pēth ē, n.* enlargement of gland or lymph node. See Gland, Lymph.

Adenosarcoma ◄€ *a dēn ō sar kō mē, n.* a sarcoma (connective tissue tumour), usually of mixed connective and glandular tissue origin; often malignant. See Connective tissue, Gland, Tumour.

Adenosine ◄€ *a den ō zēn, n.* nucleoside. A component of ribonucleic acid (RNA); its nucleotides, particularly adenosine triphosphate (ATP) play major roles in the reactions and regulation of metabolism. Adenosine triphosphate (ATP) is a nucleotide of adenosine, that is, it is an adenosine molecule linked with a phosphate group. See Deoxyribonucleic acid, Ribonucleic acid.

Adenovirus ◄€ *a dēn ō vī rēs, n.* a DNA-containing virus of the equine respiratory tract that rarely causes problems in horses that have competent immune systems. May cause fatal pneumonia in Arabian foals with combined immunodeficiency syndrome (CID). See Carrier, Combined immunodeficiency.

Adhesion ◄€ *ad hē zhēn, n.* a stable joining of two surfaces that are normally separate, as in wound healing, or as occurs in some disease processes; or fibrous band that joins two surfaces that are normally separate.
  Cervical a. ◄€ *ser vī kēl / ad hē zhēn, n.* fibrous bands in uterine cervix, usually from breeding or following injury at foaling. Interfere with cervical function, may result in uterine fluid accumulation during oestrus. Can be difficult to treat successfully, depending on the degree of cervical abnormality. See Cervix, Pyometra, Uterus.
  Intestinal a. ◄€ *in tes tī nūl / ad hē zhēn, n.* abnormal tissue band between loops of intestine, or loop of intestine and other organ, most commonly following peritonitis or abdominal surgery, especially if infection and damaged tissue present. May cause colic if adhesions constrict or entrap intestine. See Colic, Intestines, Peritonitis.
  Intrauterine a. ◄€ *in trē ū tēr in / ad hē zhēn, n.* abnormal bands between folds of uterine lining, following difficult foaling, uterine infection (endometritis) or administration of

caustic solution into uterus. May cause infertility, collection of pus within uterus (pyometra) or difficulty foaling (dystocia). See Dystocia, Endometritis, Infertility, Pyometra.

Adhesive ◀€ *ad hē siv, n./adj.* An adhesive (n.) is a substance that causes adjoining tissues to stick together. For example, there are adhesives used for gluing shoes to hooves. Adhesive (adj.) means, 'sticky, or tenacious'.

Adipose ◀€ *a di pōz, adj.* fatty, used to describe tissue composed of fat cells (adipocytes). See Fat.

Adjuvant ◀€ *ad jū vĕnt, n.* Adjuvant means 'assisting or aiding'. Any substance which aids another is adjuvant, e.g. putting a bandage on a horse's limb is an adjuvant therapy to stall rest for some injuries. In vaccine technology, an adjuvant is a non-specific stimulator of the immune response, which may be added to some vaccines in order to enhance their effect. See Vaccine.

Ad lib ◀€ *ad / lib, adv.* giving unlimited quantity, e.g. feeding, treatment.

Administer ◀€ *ad min is tĕr, v.* to give or apply. Typically drugs and medications are administered by one or more of several routes, including topical, enteral or parenteral. Enteral routes are typically oral (per os), but can rarely be per rectum. Parenteral routes include intramuscular (IM), intravenous (IV), and subcutaneous (SQ), but can also include intra-articular (IA) and intradermal (ID). Topical application is generally on the skin, but is also inhaled (inhaled medications are considered topical applications to the alveoli and bronchi, with limited systemic effect). See Intra-articular, Intramuscular, Intravenous, Oral, Subcutaneous, Topical.

Adnexa ◀€ *ad nek sē, n.* appendages or adjunct parts. The adnexa of the eye include the eyelids, and the tear apparatus; adnexa of skin include hair, sebaceous glands, sweat glands, etc. See Eye, Skin.

Adrenal exhaustion see Hypoadrenocorticism

Adrenal gland ◀€ *ē drēn ūl / gland, n.* endocrine gland. The horse's adrenal glands, occur retroperitoneally (above the peritoneum) near the cranial and medial portions of each kidney. Consists of inner medulla and outer cortex. Produces hormones: catecholamines (epinephrine and norepinephrine) from medulla, corticosteroids (glucocorticoids e.g. cortisol, and mineralocorticoids e.g. aldosterone) and androgens from cortex. See Aldosterone, Androgen, Catecholamine, Corticosteroid, Cortisol, Epinephrine, Glucocorticoid, Hormone, Mineralocorticoid, Phaeochromocytoma.

Adrenal insufficiency see Insufficiency

Adrenaline see Epinephrine

Adrenergic ◀€ *a dren er jik, adj.* activated by or secreting epinephrine or epinephrine-like substances. Used to describe nerves of sympathetic division of autonomic nervous system which release small amount of norepinephrine when nerve impulse passes. See Autonomic nervous system, Norepinephrine.

Adrenocortical ◀€ *ē drēn ō kor tik ēl, adj.* relating to cortex of adrenal gland. See Adrenal gland.

Adrenocorticotrophic hormone ◀€ *ē drēn ō cor ti cō trō fik / hor mōn, n.* (ACTH, corticotropin) hormone secreted by anterior lobe of pituitary gland in brain. Normally stimulates adrenal gland cortex to produce corticosteroids. ACTH levels may be measured as a single test for equine pituitary pars intermedia dysfunction (PPID: Cushing's disease). ACTH has been illegally administered to show horses as a calming agent; no scientific evidence for such an effect.

See Adrenal gland, Cortisol, Pituitary pars intermedia dysfunction.

Adsorb ◀‹ *ad* zorb, *v.* to attract or retain other material on the surface; activated charcoal or smectite clays may act as intestinal adsorbents.
See Activated charcoal, Smectite.

Adsorption ◀‹ *ad* zorp *shēn, n.* referring to the process of one material attracting and holding molecules of another substance to the surface of its molecules (as distinguished from absorption, whereby atoms or molecules move into a porous or permeable material, such as the absorption of water by a sponge, or of nutrients by the intestines). Adsorbents such as activated charcoal or kaolin are often used in the treatment of diarrhoea or various toxicities. Adsorption is also the first step in the viral infection cycle.
See Activated charcoal, Kaolin.

Adult ◀‹ *ad* ult, *n./adj.* having attained full growth or maturity. Opinions may vary as to when individual horse breeds reach full adulthood.

Adventitia ◀‹ *ad ven* ti *shē, n.* outer connective tissue coat of an organ or blood vessel, or other structure.

Adventitious ◀‹ *ad ven* ti *shēs, adj.* occurring in an unusual place; accidental or acquired (not natural or hereditary).

-aemia ◀‹ *ē mē ē, suffix.* of the blood.

Aerobe ◀‹ *ā rōb, n.* in bacteriology, aerobes are microorganisms that live and grow in presence of oxygen.
See Microorganism, Oxygen.
Facultative a. ◀‹ *fak ūl tē tiv / ā rōb, n.* microorganism that can live in presence of oxygen but does not require it.
Obligate a. ◀‹ *ob lig ēt / ā rōb, n.* microorganism that requires oxygen to survive.

Aerobic ◀‹ *ā* rō *bik, adj.* having molecular oxygen present; growing, living or occurring in the presence of molecular oxygen.
See Microorganism, Oxygen.

Aerophagia ◀‹ *ā rō* fa *jē ē, n.* swallowing of air, aberrant behaviour associated with crib-biting.
See Crib-biting.

Aerosol ◀‹ *ār ō* sol, *n.* a type of solution in which fine particles are suspended in a gas. May be used for administration of drug into airway, or as a spray, e.g. for application to wounds.

Aetiology ◀‹ *ē tē* ol *ē jē, n.* the study or theory of the factors that cause disease or disorder, and the method of their introduction into the host.

Afebrile ◀‹ *ā fē brīl, adj.* without fever, i.e. with normal body temperature.
See Temperature.

Afferent ◀‹ *a* fē *rēnt, adj.* conducting inwards or towards centre, e.g. describes nerves conducting impulses from peripheral nervous system to central nervous system. Opposite: efferent.
See Nerve, Nervous system.

Aflatoxin ◀‹ *a* flē tox *in, n.* group of poisonous metabolites produced by mould (*Aspergillus* spp.) in grains and other feedstuffs. Although rarely reported, toxicosis has developed in horses being fed contaminated feedstuffs. Causes acute and chronic toxicities of the liver, although clinical reports in horses are concerned mainly with acute intoxication. Clinical signs of acute toxicosis include loss of appetite, high temperature, lethargy, convulsions, colic, abdominal straining, subcutaneous bleeding, blood clotting problems (coagulopathy), increased heart rate and respiratory rate, diarrhoea, yellowing of eyes and gums (icterus: jaundice) possible. May be fatal in acute stage. Experimental trials have demonstrated that many horses refuse mould-contaminated grain. Well-fleshed animals may be at a lesser risk of developing aflatoxicosis than unthrifty animals.
See Clotting, Icterus, Liver.

African horse sickness ◀‹ *a* fri kēn / hors / sik *nis, n.* viral infection of horses and horse family (mules and donkeys more resistant than horses; zebras usually have no signs of infection), endemic in sub-Saharan Africa and has also occurred in Middle East, Asia, Spain and Portugal. Orbivirus with nine subtypes, spread by *Culicoides* midges, less commonly mosquitoes and ticks, possibly by contaminated needles or surgical instruments. Virus is found in horse's blood and internal organs. Immunity against one type will not necessarily protect against another. Historically, the disease has been divided into pulmonary, cardiac, mixed and mild forms. Mild forms occur in donkeys, mules and animals that have some resistance to the disease. The 'mixed' form is most common, and typically has cardiac and pulmonary signs (hence, 'mixed'). Pulmonary or cardiac forms are clinical descriptions that depend on which organ loses function first. The terms 'peracute' and 'subacute' are merely terms that refer to the course of the disease.

Four syndromes recognized:
- Peracute form – signs mainly related to lung damage. Incubation period 3–5 days, high temperature (up to 40.5 °C), difficulty breathing, rapid breathing (60–75 breaths per minute) caused by fluid accumulation in lungs, head and neck extended, cough, red gums, yellow/blood-tinged frothy discharge from nose, death within 1–3 days. High mortality (95%).
- Subacute form – signs mainly related to heart damage. Incubation period 7–14 days, high temperature (up to 40.5 °C) develops slowly, red gums, fluid swellings of head, neck and chest, small bruises on tongue and around eyes (conjunctiva), abdominal pain, death may occur in 4–8 days. Mortality 50%.
- Mixed form – most common clinical form. Incubation period 5–7 days, signs of both heart and lung forms, death in 3–6 days. Mortality 50–95%. Often diagnosed only at post-mortem.
- Horse sickness fever – mild fever (up to 39.5 °C), conjunctivitis, mild depression, deep breathing. Recover in 5–8 days. This form seen in donkeys and partially immune horses.

DIAGNOSIS
The clinical signs of African horse sickness are not pathognomonic for the disease, thus, diagnosis based on clinical signs alone may be difficult. Several blood tests have been described. Submitted specimens must include red blood cells (not just serum) because the virus is closely associated with those cells. Virus isolation is possible from blood, spleen, lymph nodes and lungs post-mortem.

CONTROL
No effective treatment.
- Vaccination in endemic areas. Vaccine must include all local strains to be effective, given in spring, 2–3 months before outbreak expected. Mares in advanced pregnancy not vaccinated. Rest horse for 3 weeks after first dose.
- Prevent horses being bitten: keep horses away from low lying wet areas where insects breed, house at night, insect screens, insect repellants, control vector.

LEGISLATION IN UK
The Infectious Diseases of Horses Order 1987. African horse sickness included in Specified Diseases (Notification and Slaughter) Order 1992 which lays down control rules and measures. Imported horses from at-risk countries outside European Union routinely tested for African horse sickness.
See Conjunctiva, *Culicoides*, Immunity, Incubation, Lung, Mortality rate, Serology, Vaccine.

Afterbirth see Placenta

Agalactia ◀ *ā gēl ac tē ē, n.* failure of mammary glands to secrete milk. May be seen in mares with premature or stillborn foals; ergot toxicity (tall fescue toxicosis) in mares in late preganancy reported to cause agalactia in Canada and USA. Domperidone is a drug used to treat this condition.
See Domperidone, Ergot, Mammary gland.

Agammaglobinulaemia ◀ *ā gē mē globin ū lę̄ mē ē, n.* very low levels or absence of

immunoglobulins (antibodies) in blood. Rare condition, reported in male Thoroughbreds and Standardbreds. The condition was first seen in 1976, and has been diagnosed in four males of the Quarter Horse, Standardbred and Thoroughbred breeds. May be linked to X chromosome disorder. Horse presents with severe, recurrent infections as early as two months of age. Lymphocyte count normal, IgM and IgA absent, serum concentrations of IgG decline sequentially, thymus abnormal on histopathology. May see transient response to antibiotic therapy. Clinical management consists of providing antibodies through IV administration of suitably matched plasma or serum, but does not provide a cure or result in a horse with breeding or sport potential. Prognosis grave.
See Immunoglobulin, Thymus.

Agar ◀˦ _ā gar, n._ mucilaginous substance prepared from one of several species of red algae (seaweed). When dissolved in water and allowed to cool forms gel commonly used in culture media for growing bacteria and other micoorganisms in laboratory, as well as many other uses.
  A. **gel immunodiffusion test** ◀˦ _ā gar / jel / im ūn ō di fū zhun / test, n._ diagnostic serological test, identifies presence of antibody and antigen from horse's blood. AGID refers to any technique that involves the diffusion of antigen or antibody through a semisolid medium, usually agar, resulting in a precipitation reaction (bands form where concentrations of antigen and antibody are serologically equivalent). The Coggin's test used to diagnose equine infectious anaemia is one example of an AGID test.
See Antibody, Antigen, Equine infectious anaemia.

Age ◀˦ _āj, n._ time lived. Measured from date of birth, but in some breeds official age taken from arbitrary registration date, e.g. Thoroughbred, 1st January (N hemisphere) or 1st August (S hemisphere). Age is commonly assessed by development and wear of teeth, although studies indicate that this method of aging is not accurate after five years of age. In first year, horse called foal when still nursing alongside mother, or weanling after weaning from mother and prior to one year of age; second year called a yearling.
See Aged, Tooth.

Aged ◀˦ _ā jid, adj._ in horses, a general term referring to an older horse, most typically for a horse in its mid- to late teens, or older, particularly when there are no registration papers to indicate date of birth.

Agenesis ◀˦ _ā jen isis, n._ absence, e.g. of an organ, through failure of development.

Agglutination ◀˦ _a glū tin ā shēn, n._ clumping together; especially bacteria or blood cells. Agglutination may occur with or without the presence of cell surface antibody/antigen reactions. Used in identification of bacteria; shows incompatible blood type in cross-matching. When blood types are incompatible, blood cells from each type clump together.
See Antibody, Antigen, Blood.

Agglutinin ◀˦ _a glū tin in, n._ substance causing agglutination, e.g. antibody in blood which will cause agglutination of invading bacteria.
See Agglutination, Antibody.

Aggression ◀˦ _a gre shēn, n._ a form of behaviour that leads to self-assertion; in horses, such behaviour can be hostile or destructive; however, it is also a healthy self-expressive drive to mastery, such as an aggressive wild stallion's behaviour in protecting or earning his harem.

Agonist ◀˦ _a gēn ist, n._ in anatomy, an agonist is a prime muscle mover. In pharmacology, a drug may be an agonist by acting at receptors normally stimulated by naturally occurring substances.

Agranulocytosis ◀˦ _ē gran ū lō sīt ō sis, n._ a rare condition characterized by marked decrease in granulocytes (white blood cells with cytoplasmic granules).
See Granulocyte.

Air ◀ː *ă, n.* colourless, odourless gaseous mixture surrounding earth and makes up its atmosphere, approx. 20% oxygen, 80% nitrogen, small quantities carbon dioxide, ammonia, argon.

Airway ◀ː *ă wā, n.* passage through which air travels into and out of lungs, includes nasal passages, larynx, trachea, bronchi, bronchioles, ending at alveoli.
See Alveolus, Bronchiole, Bronchus, Lung, Nasal, Trachea.
    A. obstruction ◀ː *ă wā / ob struk shĕn, n.* partial or complete blockage of airway. Many causes, including defect in airway function (e.g. problem with nerve supply to larynx – recurrent laryngeal neuropathy), inhaled foreign body, space-occupying lesion (e.g. laryngeal lymphoma), spasm of small airways (e.g. chronic obstructive pulmonary disease). Clinical signs depend on location and cause of obstruction, include respiratory noise and difficulty breathing (dyspnoea).
    See Laryngeal, Lymphoma, Recurrent airway obstruction.

Ala ◀ː *ā lĕ, n.* (pl. alae) wing; a term used in anatomical nomenclature to describe a winglike structure or process. Paired cartilages which support outer side of nostrils.
• Alar cartilages – paired cartilages which support outer border of nostrils.
• Alar fold – mucous membrane forming medial and lower walls of false nostril. May vibrate during expiration, causing noise while breathing out (high blowing). Excessive enlargement (hypertrophy) of folds may cause noise during inspiration.
See Nostril.

Alanine aminotransferase ◀ː *ā lĕ nēn / ĕ mē no trans fer āz, n.* (ALT) an enzyme normally present in liver and heart cells. ALT is released into blood when the liver or heart are damaged. Some medications can also raise ALT levels. Also known as serum glutamic pyruvic transaminase (SGPT).
See Aminotransferase.

Albinism ◀ː *al bin izm, n.* a general term for a number of congenital abnormalities affecting pigment cells. True albinism is seen in two genetic forms in horses. One is autosomal dominant, the other is autosomal recessive (Lethal white syndrome in Overo Paint horses). White horses with pink skin may be incorrectly called albino; however, they commonly have pigmented (dark) eyes.
See Congenital, Gene, Lethal White Syndrome.

Albino ◀ː *al bē nō, adj./n.* animal affected by albinism.
See Albinism.

Albumin ◀ː *al bū min, n.* water-soluble protein found in animal and vegetable tissues, coagulates when heated. Classified according to source, e.g. egg albumin (albumen; egg white), serum albumin (albumin in blood).
See Protein.
    Serum a. ◀ː *sé rum / al bū min, n.* a large molecular weight protein produced in liver; the major protein of blood plasma, approx. 60% of protein in plasma. As a large particle (colloid), albumin is responsible for much of the colloidal osmotic pressure in blood vessels (a very small percentage of total pressure). However, because colloids cannot cross the capillary membrane easily, osmotic pressure is extremely important in transcapillary fluid dynamics. The primary function of albumin is as a transport protein, and, as such, it carries molecules such as fatty acids, bilirubin, hormones, and drugs.
    See Hypoalbuminaemia, Plasma.

Albuminuria ◀ː *al bū min ŭr ē ĕ, n.* presence of albumin in urine. Sign of kidney disease or damage elsewhere in urinary tract.
See Kidney, Proteinuria, Urinary.

Aldosterone ◀ː *al dō stē rŏn, n.* mineralocorticoid secreted by cortex of adrenal gland, regulates electrolyte balance by causing retention of sodium and bicarbonate, and excretion of potassium and hydrogen ions by the kidney.
See Adrenal gland, Blood, Kidney.

Algae ◀€ *al gē, n(pl).* primitive, single-celled water plants, including the seaweed. Some can be fed to horses, e.g. powdered seaweed, as source of iron and other minerals. However, seaweed can be a source of excessive iodine. See Iodine, Iron.

Algal bloom ◀€ *al gēl / blŭm, n.* blue-green algae (cyanobacteria) may form accumulations (scum) on water surface during periods of high temperature and low water levels, where nutrient levels in water, such as nitrogen or phosphorus, are high. These algae may produce toxins, which can be fatal to horses drinking the water, producing signs of abdominal pain, diarrhoea, muscle tremor, difficulty breathing, prostration, neurological problems, and death, with signs often beginning within a few minutes of ingestion.

Alimentary tract ◀€ *al i ment ē rē / trakt, n.* (alimentary canal, digestive tract, intestine, guts, bowel) passage down which food travels from mouth to anus, in which digestion takes place. Comprised of mouth, pharynx, oesophagus, stomach, small intestine (three divisions: duodenum, jejunem, ileum), large intestine (four major divisions: caecum, large colon, small colon, rectum). Various secretions, including from salivary glands, pancreas, and liver, enter tract to aid digestion. See Anus, Large intestine, Liver, Mouth, Mucous membrane, Oesophagus, Pancreas, Pharynx, Salivary gland, Small intestine, Stomach.

Alkali ◀€ *al kēl ī, n.* substance which neutralizes acid, and forms soaps when combined with fatty acids; turns red litmus paper blue, e.g. bicarbonate. See Acid.
   A. disease ◀€ *al kēl ī / di zēz, n.* a chronic disease of horses associated with low level, long duration intake of selenium, characterized by emaciation, hair loss, hoof abnormalities, depression, and arthritis. Seen in areas of high soil selenium concentration, e.g. western United States.

Alkaline phosphatase ◀€ *al kēl īn / fos fē tāz, n.* an enzyme found throughout the horse's body, especially liver and kidney, responsible for removing phosphate groups from many types of molecules. Important in normal liver function. May be elevated with damage to the liver's biliary system, as well as in many other disease conditions; not specific for diagnosis of liver disease. Levels are higher in foals than in adult horses, due to immaturity of liver.
See Bile, Liver.

Alkaloid ◀€ *al kēl oid, n.* nitrogen-containing, basic substance of plant origin, usually with a very bitter taste. Many alkaloids have strong physiological action. Numerous alkaloid derivatives have pharmacological activity, including atropine, cocaine, digitalis, morphine, pilocarpine. See Atropine, Foxglove, Morphine, Pilocarpine.

Alkalosis ◀€ *al kēl ō sis, n.* a pathological condition that results from an accumulation of base, or from a loss of acid without a comparable loss of base, characterized by a decrease in hydrogen ion concentration. Body fluids have pH above 7.4. Diagnose by blood–gas analysis of arterial blood.
See Acid, pH.
   Metabolic alkalosis ◀€ *me tē bo lik / al kēl ō sis, n.* increase in blood pH and bicarbonate concentration, seen in failure of bicarbonate excretion by kidneys, reflux of stomach contents, severe sweating, excessive bicarbonate administration. Treatment with fluids containing chloride and potassium, which cause increased bicarbonate excretion by kidneys.
   See Bicarbonate, Kidney.
   Respiratory alkalosis ◀€ *re spē rē trē / al kēl ō sis, n.* rare, seen in hyperventilation.

Allantochorion see Allantois, Chorion

Allantoic fluid ◀€ *al ēn tō ik / flŭ id, n.* brown/yellow-brown fluid, formed from the hindgut of the embryonic horse, and containing foetal urine and other metabolic waste products not eliminated by the placenta, which passes from bladder via urachus. Foetus separated from fluid by amnion. Volume: 100 ml at 45 days of

gestation, 2,000 ml at 100 days and 8,500 ml at 300 days. On ultrasound examination, the quality of the allantoic fluid may be a useful guide to foetal well-being. Protects foetus by cushioning, and lubricates passage of foetus at birth. Lost in second stage of labour.
See Parturition, Placenta, Urachus, Uterus.

Allantois ◀ː *al ēn tō is, n.* outgrowth of foetal hindgut, forms bladder and carries blood vessels in umbilicus, becomes large sac which fuses with chorion to form part of placenta (allantochorion). Also may fuse with amnion to form allantoamnion (allantois outside – amnion inside). Cystic adenomatous hyperplasia (nodular growth of glands) of the equine allantois has occasionally been reported, although the cause or significance of such lesions is undetermined. Other allantoic abnormalities, such as allantoic cystic lesions, or tumours originating from the allantoic epithelium, are rare.
See Chorion, Placenta, Umbilicus.

Allele ◀ː *ē lēl, n.* any alternative form of a gene that can occupy a particular locus on a chromosome. Determines alternative inheritable characteristics.
See Gene.

Allergen ◀ː *al ē jēn, n.* substance capable of inducing immediate-type allergic (hypersensitivity) reaction, e.g. dust, mould, or fungal spores. Cause of recurrent airway obstruction.
See Allergy, Antigen, Hypersensitivity, Recurrent airway obstruction.

Allergic ◀ː *ēl er jik, adj.* pertaining to, affected with, or caused by allergy.
See Allergy.

Allergy ◀ː *al ē jē, n.* hypersensitivity reaction to specific allergen (antigen) following second or subsequent exposure. Different types of reaction depending on allergen, including rash or weals on skin, spasm of small airways, or fluid-filled legs and general malaise.
See Allergen, Hypersensitivity.

Allograft ◀ː *a lō grarft, n.* graft (i.e. transplant) of tissue from animal of same species, but not same genotype (i.e. from animal that is not genetically the same).
See Graft.

Alloimmunization ◀ː *a lō im ū nīz ā shēn, n.* development of antibodies to allergens from an animal that is not genetically the same, e.g. in rejection of allograft, or in haemolytic anaemia of newborn.
See Allergen, Antibody, Haemolytic.

Aloe ◀ː *a lō, n.* genus of plants with erect spikes of flowers and bitter juice. Has historically been used as a purgative, given orally, with action on large intestine, where increases movement (peristalsis) and secretions. The sticky juice of various plants has also been used topically as a demulcent to soothe irritated membranes and skin surfaces, and as a treatment for wounds and burns (Aloe vera).
See Large intestine, Peristalsis.

Alopecia ◀ː *a lō pē shē, n.* loss of hair, baldness, may be generalized or localized. May be normal, as with shedding. Also secondary to pruritis (itching), e.g. because of skin irritation, parasites or allergy, autoimmune disease, photosensitization.
See Allergy, Autoimmunity, Photosensitization, Skin.

Alpha ◀ː *al fē,* first letter of Greek alphabet. Used to denote subclass of some substances, e.g. alpha-immunoglobulins, alpha-tocopherol.

Alphavirus ◀ː *al fē vī rēs, n.* virus, belongs to Togaviridae family. Alphaviruses cause Eastern, Western and Venezuelan equine encephalitides.
See Encephalitis.

Alsike Clover see Clover

Alternative therapy ◀ː *awl ter nē tiv / the rē pē, n.* a diverse and unrelated group of therapies that are 1) generally not taught in veterinary colleges, 2) often conducted outside of mainstream veterinary practice, and 3) lacking in proven effectiveness,

in many cases after decades of use and study. Rationale for therapies tends to diverge widely from accepted scientific thought.
See Acupuncture, Chiropractic, Herbal medicine, Homeopathy.

Alum ◄ː *a lĕm, n.* odourless, colourless crystalline substance with styptic (stops bleeding) and astringent properties. Prepared from bauxite (hydrated aluminium oxide) and sulphuric acid, with the addition of ammonium.
    A. root ◄ː *a lĕm / rŭt, n.* a North American herb that has been used in traditional Native American medicine in the treatment of inflammation and haemorrhoids. Grows to about 0.6 m tall with an erect, unbranched stem.
See Astringent, Styptic.

Alveolar ◄ː *al vē ō lĕr, adj.* pertaining to alveolus (dental or pulmonary).
See Alveolus.

Alveolus ◄ː *al vē ō lĕs, n.* small sac-like structure.
    Dental a. ◄ː *den tĕl / al vē ō lĕs, n.* tooth socket.
See Tooth.
    Pulmonary a. ◄ː *pul mĕn rē / al vē ō lĕs, n.* minute terminal air sac, millions at end of airways in lungs. Site where air in lungs comes in direct contact with blood cells; here, oxygen enters blood and carbon dioxide leaves blood.

Ambient ◄ː *am bē ĕnt, adj.* surrounding, i.e. ambient temperature is that of the surroundings.

Ameloblastoma ◄ː *ē mē lō blas tō mē, n.* tumour arising from enamel-forming cells of the teeth. Rare in horses, more prevalent in older horses than other odontogenic tumours (i.e. tumours arising from dental tissue). Causes localized swelling in jaw. Diagnosis by biopsy.
See Biopsy, Enamel (dental), Tooth.

Amelogenesis ◄ː *ē mē lō jen i sis, n.* formation of dental enamel.
See Enamel (dental), Tooth.

Amikacin ◄ː *ē mik ē sin, n.* bactericidal

aminoglycoside antibiotic active against many Gram-negative microorganisms.
See Aminoglycoside, Antibiotic, Bacterium, Gram stain.

Amine ◄ː *ā mēn, n.* organic compound containing nitrogen.

Amino acid ◄ː *ə mē nō / a sid, n.* an organic (carbon-containing) compound, chemically composed of an amino (-NH₂) and a carboxyl (-COOH) group. Certain amino acids may combine in long chains to form proteins. Many amino acids exist; not all are protein-related.
    Essential a.a. ◄ː *i sen shul / ē mē nō / a sid, n.* those amino acids required for protein synthesis that cannot be synthesized by the horse, and so must be obtained in the diet.

Aminoglycoside ◄ː *ē mē nō glī kō sīd, n.* one of class of antibiotics derived from various species of *Streptomyces* bacteria, or produced synthetically. Includes streptomycin, amikacin, gentamycin. This antibiotic inhibits bacterial protein synthesis by binding with the bacterial 30S ribosomal subunit. All aminoglycosides are bactericidal, with primary activity against Gram-negative organisms. Potential for toxicity, especially kidney toxicity, in high doses, in combination with non-steroidal anti-inflammatory drugs, or in young animals with immature kidney function.
See Antibiotic, Bacterium, Gram stain.

Aminophylline ◄ː *a min o fi lēn, n.* a salt prepared from the two drugs theophylline and ethylenediamine. May be used for bronchial dilation. Mild heart stimulant. Has been generally replaced in horses by more effective agents.
See Bronchus.

Aminotransferase ◄ː *ē mē no tranz fer āz, n.* an enzyme that catalyses the transfer of an amino group from a donor molecule to a recipient molecule. The donor molecule is usually an amino acid. Two of the better known aminotransferase enzymes are aspartate aminotransferase (AST – also known as serum glutamic oxaloacetic transaminase (SGOT)) and alanine

aminotransferase (ALT – also known as serum glutamic pyruvic transaminase (SGPT)). Both of these enzymes are normally found primarily in cells in the liver and heart, are released into the blood stream as the result of liver or heart damage, and thus may be used in liver and heart testing.
See Alanine aminotransferase, Amino acid, Aspartate aminotransferase.

Amitraz ◀≀ _am_ i *traz, n.* compound used in treatment of sarcoptic and demodectic mange in dogs, sheep, pigs and cattle. Used as acaricide on horses in S. America but not licensed for this use, and may cause heart problems and fatal impaction of intestines.
See Acaricide, Mange.

Ammonia ◀≀ ẽ _mō_ nē ẽ, *n.* alkaline gas, NH_y with pungent odour. May be released from decomposing manure and urine, and cause respiratory tract irritation and conjunctivitis in horses in poorly ventilated stables and barns. Good ventilation and regular cleaning of stables will reduce build-up of ammonia.
See Conjunctivitis, Ventilation.

Amniocentesis ◀≀ _am_ nē ō sen _tē_ sis, *n.* removal of sample of amniotic fluid from pregnant mare's uterus. Experimentally, transabdominal ultrasound-guided amniocentesis has been used for detection of equine herpes virus 1 (EHV-1)-induced foetal infection in utero. Technique involves significant risk of abortion, so does not have wide clinical application.
See Pregnancy.

Amnion ◀≀ _am_ nē ẽn, *n.* translucent membrane surrounding foetus, contains amniotic fluid; acts as a physical cushion for the foetus. May fuse with allantois to form allantoamnion (allantois outside – amnion inside). Dressings prepared from equine amnion have been employed in equine wound management.
See Pregnancy.

Amniotic fluid ◀≀ am nē _ot_ ik / _flŭ_ id, *n.* fluid surrounding foetus, composed of foetal urine, pulmonary secretions, and secretions of amnion. Volume 3,600 ml by eighth month of gestation.
See Pregnancy.

Amorphous ◀≀ ẽm _or_ fẽs, *adj.* having no definite form; in pharmacology, not crystallized.

Amoxicillin ◀≀ ẽm _oks_ i _si_ lin, *n.* antibiotic, a synthetic derivative of ampicillin. Acts by affecting bacterial cell wall development. May be effective against certain Gram-positive and some Gram-negative aerobic organisms; requires dosing four times daily for effectiveness. Occasionally used in foals, but not widespread. Must be given by intravenous or intramuscular injection; oral penicillins are not used in horses.
See Antibiotic, Bacterium, Gram stain, Penicillin.

Ampicillin ◀≀ _amp_ i _si_ lin, *n.* semi-synthetic and acid-resistant penicillin antibiotic; as with all penicillins, acts by affecting bacterial cell wall devlopment. Broader spectrum of activity than penicillin; may be effective against some Gram-negative bacteria. May be administered to horse by intramuscular or intravenous injection.
See Antibiotic, Bacterium, Gram stain, Penicillin.

Ampoule ◀≀ _am_ pūl, *n.* small sealed glass or plastic container; may be sealed to preserve sterile material for injection.

Ampulla ◀≀ am pŭ lẽ, *n.* flask-like dilation of vessel or duct, e.g. ends of semicircular canals in ear.
A. ductus derefentis ◀≀ am pŭ lē / duc tēs / de fē ren tis, *n.* glandular enlargement at urethral end of vas deferens (duct which carries spermatozoa from testis to urethra).
See vas deferens.

Amputation ◀≀ am pŭ _tā_ shēn, *n.* surgical removal of an appendage, e.g. limb, ear pinna, because of disease or injury. Successful limb amputations have been occasionally reported in horses: in mares, in order to allow them to deliver a full-term foal, and in valuable breeding stallions. These horses are usually also fitted with a limb prosthesis.

Amsinckia see Fiddleneck

Amylase ◄ɛ *a mi lāz, n.* enzyme secreted by pancreas (and salivary glands in some animals, but not horse). Splits starch into simpler compounds. See Digestion.

Amyloid ◄ɛ *a mi loid, n.* starch-like insoluble protein; the pathological, extracellular protein-like substance deposited in amyloidosis.
See Amyloidosis, Protein.

Amyloidosis ◄ɛ *a mi loid ō sis, n.* deposition of amyloid in tissues. Causes tissues to become non-functional. Amyloidosis may be primary or secondary, systemic or localized, immunocytic or idiopathic, and can occur in many tissues and organs. May also be associated with chronic disease or inflammation.
See Amyloid.
　Nasal a. ◄ɛ *nā zēl / a mi loid ō sis, n.* deposition of amyloid in subcutaneous tissues of head and neck, or nasal tissues and bones. May be associated with nose bleeds.

Anabolic ◄ɛ *a nē bo lik, n.* pertaining to anabolism.

Anabolism ◄ɛ *ē na bē lizm, n.* constructive phase of metabolism, conversion of simple substances into complex ones for tissues, etc. Anabolic drugs increase anabolism.

Anaemia ◄ɛ *ēn ē mē ē, n.* a decrease in the mass of circulating red blood cells. Anaemia is not necessarily a 'deficiency' of red blood cells, rather, it is caused by an imbalance in the rate of loss or destruction of red blood cells and the rate of their production in the bone marrow. All anaemias are also classified as regenerative or non-regenerative, based on the response of the bone marrow.
　Normal circulating red blood cell levels for horses may vary depending on age, breed, location (horses at high altitude have a higher concentration of circulating red blood cells than do horses at sea level)

and physical condition. A veterinarian or veterinary reference lab is a good source of information for horses in particular circumstances.
　Anaemia is rarely, if ever, a primary disease in horses. Rather, when it occurs, it is most commonly a haematological abnormality that results from an underlying disease process. In healthy horses, the horse's spleen contains a huge reservoir of red blood cells, so a single blood sample that falls just below laboratory values is most likely not reflective of any underlying disease process. Accordingly, so-called 'haematinics', that is, iron-containing compounds or B-vitamins that may be prescribed to 'build' a horse's blood are almost never indicated.
　Signs of anaemia may include pale mucous membranes, rapid, shallow respiration, and increased heart rate and force of beat.

CAUSES
- Loss of blood (haemorrhage), internal or external.
- Increased destruction of red blood cells, e.g. haemolytic anaemia or other immune-mediated diseases; bacterial infections (*Strep.* or *Clostridium*) species, neoplasia, drug reactions.
- Infections: bacteria, viruses (e.g. equine infectious anaemia), protozoa (e.g. *Babesia*).
- Dietary deficiency reducing red blood cell or haemoglobin production, e.g. lack of iron, copper, cobalt, vitamin B. NOTE: Dietary-related anaemias are extremely rare in horses. Insofar as red blood cells go, most horses do not benefit from supplementation of vitamins and minerals.
- Oxidative injury (phenothiazine, onion, garlic, red maple leaf, familial methaemoglobinaemia).
- Iatrogenic (hypotonic or hypertonic solutions).
- Toxicities (intravenous dimethylsulfoxide, oak).
- Miscellaneous conditions (hepatic disease, disseminated intravascular coagulation).

See *Babesia*, Copper, Equine infectious anaemia, Haematology, Haemoglobin,

Haemolytic, Haemorrhage, Iron,
Vitamin.

Anaerobe ◄⁞ *an ă rōb, n.* a microorganism
that lives in the complete, or almost
complete, absence of oxygen.
See Microorganism.

Facultative a. ◄⁞ *fak ūl tē tiv / an ă rōb, n.*
microorganism that can live with or without
oxygen.

Obligate a. ◄⁞ *ob lig ēt / an ă rōb, n.* microorganism that cannot grow in presence of
oxygen, e.g. *Clostridium tetani.*
See *Clostridium.*

Anaesthesia ◄⁞ *an ēs thē zē ē, n.* loss of
sensation. May be from damage to nerve
or nerve receptor, or from administration
of a drug, or by another medical intervention (e.g. surgical neurectomy).

Epidural a. ◄⁞ *e pi dŭr ūl / an ēs thē zē ē, n.*
regional anaesthesia produced by injection
of anaesthetic agents into the epidural space,
achieved by injection of substances such as
local anaesthetics, xylazine or narcotic
agents into epidural space around spinal
cord. Most commonly injected in the lumbar
space, between first and second coccygeal
vertebrae. May be used for surgery of anus,
perineum, rectum, tail, vagina, vulva, and to
prevent excessive straining in dystocia (difficult birth). Techniques to allow continuous
epidural anaesthesia by leaving a needle or
catheter in place are described to facilitate
longer procedures.

General a. ◄⁞ *jen ē rūl / an ēs thē zē ē, n.*
reversible loss of consciousness, achieved by
administration of general anaesthetic, by
intravenous injection, or by inhalation.
See Anaesthetic.

Intra-articular a. ◄⁞ *in trē ar ti kū lē / an ēs thē
zē, n.* loss of sensation in a joint due to injection of a volume of local anaesthetic within
a joint. Most commonly used in lameness
diagnosis, but has been used unscrupulously to eliminate arthritis-related pain in
performance horses, posing a danger to
horse and rider.

Local a. ◄⁞ *lō kēl / an ēs thē zē ē, n.* loss of
sensation in small area achieved by injection
of local anaesthetic. May be achieved by
injection of local anaesthetic into skin, e.g.
for wound repairs.

Perineural a. ◄⁞ *pe ri nŭ rūl / an ēs thē zē ē, n.*

loss of sensation in an area distal to the injection site over a superficial nerve. Most
commonly used in lameness diagnosis. Also
referred to as a 'nerve block'.

Regional a. ◄⁞ *rē jē nūl / an ēs thē zē ē, n.* loss
of sensation to a region of body achieved
either by injection of local anaesthetic over
nerves supplying that area by injecting local
anaesthetic agents in a diffuse area.
See Nerve block.

Topical a. ◄⁞ *to pi cūl / an ēs thē zē ē, n.* loss of
sensation in an area secondary to direct
application of an anaesthetic agent to the
surface. Used especially to facilitate procedures involving the equine eye.

Volatile a. ◄⁞ *vo lē tīl / an ēs thē zē ē, n.*
general anaesthesia using inhaled anaesthetic agent(s), which are absorbed from the
lungs.
See Anaesthetic.

Anaesthetic ◄⁞ *an ēs the tik, n.* substance
used to achieve anaesthesia.
See Anaesthesia.

A. circuit ◄⁞ *an ēs the tik / ser kit, n.* arrangement of pipes or tubes from anaesthetic
machine to animal, which may include
rebreathing bag, valves to ensure directional
flow of gases, and soda lime canister to
absorb carbon dioxide.

A. machine ◄⁞ *an ēs the tik / mē shēn, n.*
appliance used to administer volatile anaesthesia. Includes cylinder of oxygen,
flowmeter to assess flow of oxygen, anaesthetic gas vaporizer.

Local a. ◄⁞ *lō kēl / an ēs the tik, n.* substance
administered by injection into skin or near
nerves to achieve loss of sensation (e.g
Lidocaine, Mepivicaine).

General a. ◄⁞ *jen ē rūl / an ēs the tik, n.*
substance administered by injection or inhalation to achieve loss of consciousness.

Anaesthetist ◄⁞ *ēn ēs the tist, n.* person
trained in administering anaesthetics.
See Anaesthesia.

Anagen ◄⁞ *an ē jēn, n.* The phase of the
hair cycle during which synthesis of hair
occurs.
See Hair.

Anal ◄⁞ *ā nēl, adj.* pertaining to the anus.
See Anus.

A. sphincter ◀︎ *ā nĕl* / *sfink tĕr, n.* muscular ring surrounding anal opening, composed of inner smooth muscle (not under voluntary control of animal) and outer striated muscle (under voluntary control of animal). Important for faecal continence. See Anus.

Analeptic ◀︎ *a nĕ lep tic, adj.* stimulant drug, such as caffeine or amphetamine.

Analgesia ◀︎ *a nĕl jē zēē, n.* absence of sensitivity to pain; relief of pain without loss of consciousness. See Analgesic.

Analgesic ◀︎ *a nĕl jē zik, adj./n.* relieving pain; not sensitive to pain; an agent administered to provide pain relief, without loss of consciouness. Examples include non-steroidal anti-inflammatory drugs, e.g. phenylbutazone, flunixin, and narcotics, e.g. morphine, pethidine, butorphanol. See Arthritis, Colic, Morphine, Nerve block, Non-steroidal anti-inflammatory drug.

Analysis ◀︎ *ē na li sis, n.* determination of exact composition of substance; separation into component parts.

Anamnesis ◀︎ *an ĕm nē sis, n.* medical case history.

Anamnestic response ◀︎ *an ĕm nes tik* / *ris pons, n.* immunological memory, occurring on second or subsequent exposure to antigen. Anamnestic responses are why vaccines are effective, and why immunity is developed after exposure to certain diseases. More negatively, anamnestic responses are responsible for allergic reactions. See Antigen, Immunity.

Anaphylaxis ◀︎ *a nē fi lak sis, n.* exaggerated immune response (type I hypersensitivity reaction) to second or subsequent exposure to foreign substance, such as may occur following administration of certain drugs or blood products, ingestion of some feed proteins, inhalation of dust and fungal spores. Initially causes urticaria (hives), pruritis (itching), followed by vascular collapse and shock in severe cases, often accompanied by life-threatening respiratory distress. See Allergy, Hypersensitivity, Shock.

Anaplasma phagocytophilum ◀︎ *anē plaz mē* / *fāgē sī to fi lĕm, n.* causitive agent of anaplasmosis (formerly known as *Ehrlichia equi*). See Anaplasmosis.

Anaplasmosis (equine granulocytic anaplasmosis) ◀︎ *anē plaz mē sis (ekwīn* / *gran ūlō sitik* / *anē plaz mē sis), n.* disease caused by the bacterium *Anaplasma phagocytophilum* (formerly *Ehrlichia equi*). Cause of infections in several animal species, as well as humans. Circum-global distribution, especially within the northern hemisphere but also South America. Bacterium shows a host species predilection that varies by the geographic region in which the disease is found. Adaptation by the bacterium to a host species may contribute to various clinical presentations worldwide, and this may also be related to the bacterium's relationship with its tick vectors, all of which belong to the *Ixodes* group. Prevalent in most countries in Europe (it is the most widespread tick-borne infection in animals in Europe), as well as the northern United States and Canada. The clinical signs, and their severity, may vary with the age of the horse and the duration of illness. In mild cases, fever may be the only sign; more severe cases show high fever, depression, oedema of the abdomen and ventral limbs, anorexia, reluctance to move, ataxia and icterus; experimentally infected horses have maintained signs of disease for up to two weeks. Has been associated with rhabdomyolysis in one horse. Seldom fatal unless complicated by other problems; one horse that was experimentally infected died from widespread haemorrhaging in its internal organs, and vasculitis and thrombosis in the kidneys, as typically seen with disseminated intravascular coagulation. Laboratory findings include cytoplasmatic inclusions in phagocytic cells, lymphopaenia, and mild anaemia; results of serum biochemical analyses are

not specific, but may include high bilirubin concentrations from inappetance. Polymerase chain reaction testing can detect *A. phagocytophila* DNA in unclotted blood or buffy coat smears; indirect fluorescent antibody test can detect rising antibody titers to the bacterium. Treatment with tetracycline antibiotics is rapidly curative. Horses with severe ataxia and oedema may benefit from short-term corticosteroid treatment. After recovery, immunity from reinfection lasts at least two years. No vaccine available; tick control measures necessary for disease control.
See Bilirubin, Disseminated intravascular coagulation, Indirect fluorescent antibody, Polymerase chain reaction, Rhabdomyolysis, Tetracycline, Tick.

Anasarca ◀ɛ *a nē sar kē, n.* a generalized massive oedema (swelling); accumulation of fluid beneath skin (subcutaneous oedema), especially ventral wall of chest and abdomen and limbs. Skin retains impression of finger after pressure released (pitting oedema). Associated with heart failure, malnutrition, allergy, vasculitis, lymphoma and septicaemia.
See Allergy, Heart, Lymphoma, Malnutrition, Oedema, Septicaemia, Vasculitis.

Anastomosis ◀ɛ *ē na stēm ō sis, n.* connection between two blood vessels; an opening created by surgical, traumatic or pathological means connecting two spaces or organs that are normally separate.
Intestinal a. ◀ɛ *in tes tī nūl / ē na stēm ō sis, n.* the establishment of a connection between two portions of the intestinal tract. In colic surgery, removal of a diseased portion of intestine may be followed by intestinal a., where healthy cut ends are joined to restore continuity.

Anatomy ◀ɛ *ē na tēm ē, n.* science of body structure, and relationship of body parts.
Comparative a. ◀ɛ *kom pa rē tiv / ē na tēm ē, n.* comparison of body structure of different species.
Developmental a. ◀ɛ *di ve lop men tēl / ē na tēm ē, n.* the field of embryology, concerned with the changes that germ cells undergo as

they develop into offspring; includes prenatal and postnatal development.
Microscopic a. ◀ɛ *mī krō sko pik / ē na tēm ē, n.* histology.
Regional a. ◀ɛ *rē jē nūl / ē na tēm ē, n.* descriptive anatomy arranged according to regions of the body.

Androgen ◀ɛ *an drē jēn, n.* any substance which produces masculinization, e.g. testosterone, nandrolone.
See Androsterone, Hormone, Testosterone.

Androsterone ◀ɛ *an drē sté rōn, n.* androgen degradation product, normally excreted in urine of both sexes.
See Androgen, Libido.

Anechoic ◀ɛ *an ik ō ik, n.* in ultrasonography, absence of internal echoes.
See Ultrasonography.

Anergy ◀ɛ *an ē jē, n.* lack of energy, or passivity; in immunology, a diminished reactivity to antigens.

Aneurysm ◀ɛ *an ŭr izm, n.* dilation of artery, vein, or heart as a result of weakness of wall; may rupture. Can be subsequent to disease; however, it is not known why most aneurysms form.
See Artery.
Verminous a. ◀ɛ *ver min ēs / an ŭr izm, n.* (verminous arteritis) damage caused to intestinal blood vessels by migrating larvae of *Strongylus* spp. worms. Larvae cause arterial walls to thicken, reduce blood flow, and damaged walls develop weakness (aneurysm).
See *Strongylus* spp., Thrombosis.

Angi- (variant angio-) ◀ɛ *an jī* a vessel; especially blood or lymphatic vessel.
See Bile, Blood, Lymphatic.

Angiitis see Vasculitis

Angiogenesis ◀ɛ *an jē ō jen i sis, n.* development of blood vessels; formation of new blood vessels (neovascularization).

Angiography ◀ɛ *an jē og rē fē, n.* radiographic technique, allows visualization of blood flow to and from organ by injection

of contrast medium. Not commonly used in horse; however, some veterinarians feel that angiograms of the feet (venograms) are important in assessing and treating horses with laminitis.
See Laminitis, Radiography.

Angioma ◀︎€ *un jē ō mē, n* benign tumour derived from blood vessels (haemangioma) or lymph vessels (lymphangioma).

Angiotensin ◀︎€ *an jē ō ten sin, n*. hormone which causes constriction of blood vessels. Formed in blood when renin is released by kidneys, in response to low blood pressure. Reduces fluid loss from kidneys and increases blood pressure.
See Hormone

Angle ◀︎€ *ang gūl, n*. the degree of convergence of two intersecting lines.
  A. of jaw ◀︎€ *ang gūl / ov / jor, n*. junction of vertical and horizontal parts (rami) of lower jaw (mandible).
  See Mandible.
  A. of hoof ◀︎€ *ang gūl / ov / hūf, n*. the angle formed by the convergence of the solar surface with the dorsal hoof wall.
  A. of shoulder ◀︎€ *ang gūl / ov / shōl der, n*. most discussions of equine conformation mention shoulder angle, with a sloping shoulder considered desirable for many athletic disciplines. However, poorly defined terms make understanding exactly what is meant by shoulder angle difficult. Measurement techniques include: from the point of the shoulder to the start of the mane hair on the withers, the angle of the joint itself between the scapula and humerus, and the slope of the spine of the scapula. However, these are three very different measurements and can lead to different results.
  Filtration a. ◀︎€ *fil trā shēn / ang gūl, n*. the angle formed between the iris and the cornea, marking the edge of the anterior chamber of the eye; it is the principal site of exit for the aqueous fluid of the eye.

Angleberry ◀︎€ *ang gūl be rē, n*. wart-like growth on skin or mucous membranes, more commonly of cattle.

Angular limb deformity ◀︎€ *ang gū lē / lim / di for mi tē, n*. defect of leg, e.g. at carpal

joint, where leg is not straight, but angles in or out. May be present at birth, associated with joint laxity, or develop as foal grows. Developmental angular deformity in foals may be angled in from midline (varus deformity), or angled out from midline (valgus deformity).
See Growth.

Anhydrosis ◀︎€ *an hī drō sis, n*. inability to sweat, dry coat syndrome. Seen in athletic horses in warm humid climates. Cause is undetermined and the subject of much speculation. Signs include lack of sweating when hot or exercised, decreased athletic performance, rapid breathing, and high body temperature. Acute cases may progress to heat exhaustion and circulatory collapse if not recognized. Horses affected for several months may have a dry flaky coat or loss of hair from the face and body friction areas. Diagnosis from clinical signs, and testing with injections of epinephrine (adrenaline) of differing dilutions (normal horses will produce sweat at all injection sites, anhydrotic horses only produce sweat at site of highest epinephrine concentration). Will generally resolve if horse moved to cooler climate. May be able to manage with cooler housing, avoiding exercise in hottest part of day. No medical or nutritional therapy has been shown to be consistently helpful in any horse with anhydrosis.
See Catecholamine, Epinephrine, Sweat gland, Thermoregulation.

Anhydrous ◀︎€ *an hī drēs, adj*. containing no water.

Animal Health Act, 2002 UK legislation concerned with control of notifiable animal diseases.
See Notifiable disease.

Animal Health Trust UK charity involved in veterinary research, provides specialist veterinary clinical, diagnostic and surgical services.

Animals (Scientific Procedures) Act, 1986 UK legislation concerned with use of animals in scientific experiments.

Aniridia ◀︎ *an i rid ē ē, n.* partial or complete absence of iris in eye. Described once in veterinary literature, in 1955, in a Belgian draught stallion. Affected foals showed a congenital absence of the iris, with secondary cataracts; as a result, most affected animals were blind and not suitable for work. Autosomal dominant gene arising by spontaneous mutation was thought to be the cause; normal sons and daughters of affected animals did not pass on the condition. No longer considered a problem in the Belgian breed.
See Eye, Iris.

Aniso- ◀︎ *an ī zō, prefix.* unequal, dissimilar.

Anisocoria ◀︎ *an ī zō kor ē ē, n.* pupils of unequal sizes; may indicate blindness in one eye; also associated with central nervous system disease.
See Eye.

Anisocytosis ◀︎ *an ī zō sī tō sis, n.* presence in the blood of red blood cells with excessively varying sizes; observed on blood smear.
See Erythrocyte.

Ankylosis ◀︎ *ang ki lō sis, n.* immobility and consolidation of a joint due to disease (as occurs in chronic arthritis), injury or as a desired result of a surgical procedure (see Arthrodesis).
See Arthritis.

Annular ◀︎ *an ū lē, adj.* shaped like a ring.
A. ligament ◀︎ *an ū lē / li gē mĕnt, n.* The annular ligament of the flexor tendons is a thick band of tissue that runs from one proximal sesamoid, over the back of the tendons, to the other sesamoid, around the fetlock joint. This ligament can become inflamed and thickened, or, in horses with injuries to flexor tendons, it can restrict movement of the affected tendon. Treatment for annular ligament problems may involve rest, local anti-inflammatory therapy, or surgery.

Anodyne ◀︎ *a nē dīn, adj./n.* able to relieve pain.

Anoestrus ◀︎ *an ēs trēs, n.* absence of sexual cycle in female, not sexually receptive. Usual in mares in winter (seasonal anoestrus) and pregnancy.
See Oestrous cycle.

Anomaly ◀︎ *a nα mē lē, n.* a marked deviation from normal.

Anophthalmos ◀︎ *an op thal mos, n.* congenital absence of eye. May affect one eye (unilateral) or both (bilateral). Rare. May occasionally have very small, imperfect eye(s) (microphthalmos).
See Eye.

Anoplocephala ◀︎ *a nō plō sef ē lē, n.* genus of tapeworms. Generally asymptomatic but may occasionally cause colic. Tapeworms are most commonly associated with intussusceptions (telescoping) of the bowel, which requires surgical correction. Tapeworms that affect horses include:
- *Anoplocephala perfoliata* – tapeworm of horses. Found in lower small intestine and caecum.
- *Anoplocephala magna* – tapeworm of horses and donkeys. Found in small intestine.
See Colic, Tapeworm.

Anorchid ◀︎ *an or kid, adj./n.* uncastrated male without testes in scrotum.
See Cryptorchid, Testes.

Anorexia ◀︎ *a nor reks ē ē, n.* absence of appetite.

Anovular ◀︎ *an ov ū lē, adj.* not accompanied by the discharge of an ovum (release of egg). Mare's oestrous cycle may appear normal, but ovulation does not occur.
See Oestrous cycle, Ovulation.

Anoxia ◀︎ *an oks sē ē, n.* absence of oxygen.
See Hypoxia, Oxygen.

Antacid ◀︎ *ant a sid, n.* substance given to counteract excess acid in digestive system, usually in the stomach.

Antagonism ◀︎ *an tag ēn izm, n.* active

opposition, e.g. muscles which act against each other (one flexing a joint and the other extending it) are antagonistic. Drugs are described as antagonistic if one decreases activity of other.

Antagonist ◀᠅ *an tag ĕn ist, n.* something that opposes or acts against another thing, e.g. drug, muscle.
See Antagonism.

Ante- ◀᠅ *an tē, prefix.* before.

Antebrachiocarpal joint ◀᠅ *an tē brā kē ō kar pūl / joint, n.* joint between the radius and the proximal row of carpal joints; also known as the radiocarpal joint.

Antebrachium ◀᠅ *an tē brā kē ĕm, n.* the part of the equine forelimb between the carpus (knee) and the elbow.

Ante-mortem ◀᠅ *an tē / mor tēm, adj.* before death.

Ante-natal ◀᠅ *an tē / nā tl, adj.* before birth.

Anterior ◀᠅ *an tér rē ē, adj.* to the front or forwards in position. Used to describe parts of body, e.g. anterior aspect of limb is that facing forwards.
A. enteritis see Duodenitis-proximal jejunitis

Anterior segment dysgenesis ◀᠅ *an tér rē ē / seg mĕnt / dis je ni sis, n.* a congenital, non-progressive syndrome of anomalies of the eye that commonly afflicts, but is not restricted to, Rocky Mountain Horses with a chocolate coat colour and a white mane and tail color. Most common signs are uveal cysts and retinal lesions, but not blindness. Horses with only one defective gene (heterozygous) are more mildly affected than are horses with two defective genes (homozygous). Homozygous horses typically have a wider array of abnormalities, including a large, protruding cornea (megalocornea), pupillary abnormalities (small pupil, abnormally shaped pupil, and a pupil that fails to dilate), and/or cataract formation; however, the homozygous condition is relatively uncommon. Because the gene

for ASD is widespread in the Rocky Mountain Horse population, horses with cysts are still usually bred; other breed registries may be less tolerant.

Anthelmintic ◀᠅ *an tēl min tik, n.* drug used to control helminths (intestinal parasites; 'worms'). Various drugs used in horses: benzimidazoles (e g, fenbendazole, mebendazole), ivermectin, moxidectin, praziquantel, pyrantel. Usually given as paste, drench, via nasogastric tube, or in feed.
See Anthelmintic resistance (below), Parasite.
A. resistance ◀᠅ *an tēl min tik / rez is tēns, n.* ability of parasitic worms to be unaffected by anthelmintics. Seen especially with benzimidazole group of drugs. Once resistance achieved, ability passed genetically to later generations of worms.
See Anthelmintic (above), Parasite, Resistance.

Anthrax ◀᠅ *an thraks, n.* infection with *Bacillus anthracis*. Usually acute and rapidly fatal. *B. anthracis* can form itself into extremely resilient spores, may survive in soil many decades. Infection generally by direct contact with, or inhalation of, spores. Zoonosis. Notifiable disease. Uncommon.

SIGNS
• Acute disease: high temperature (up to 41.6°C). The most prominent clinical feature is usually colic. Large oedematous swellings, especially in the cervical area, may occur. Death may occur within hours of the onset of clinical signs. The carcass autolyses very quickly, and blood may be present at body orifices. Post-mortem lesions include an enlarged, friable spleen and multiple swollen, oedematous, haemorrhagic lymph nodes.
• Subacute disease: signs of colic, large spleen (palpable by rectal examination), red patches on mucous membranes, muscle rigidity, lameness, swellings on neck and lower abdomen, terminal difficulty breathing, blue colour to gums, coma, death in up to 8 days.

- Cutaneous disease: lesions similar to malignant pustule in human caused by inoculation of skin wound with *B. anthracis*.

TREATMENT
Although usually the disease is rapidly fatal, the anthrax organism is extremely sensitive to penicillin.

DIAGNOSIS
NB Notifiable disease: permission to test animal for anthrax should be received from DEFRA before blood smear taken. Blood smear from dead animal (ear vein), identification of chains of square-ended bacilli, with capsules. Post-mortem should not be carried out if anthrax suspected.
See Antibiotic, *Bacillus*, Notifiable disease.

Anti- ◀﹦ *an tē, prefix.* against.

Antiarrhythmic ◀﹦ *an tē ā rith mik, n.* preventing or alleviating abnormalities of heart rhythm.
See Arrhythmia, Dysrhythmia.

Antibacterial ◀﹦ *an tē bak té rē ūl, adj./n.* killing or suppressing growth of bacteria; substance which kills or suppresses growth of bacteria.
See Antibiotic.

Antibiotic ◀﹦ *an tē bī o tik, n.* destructive of life; chemical substance, derived from microorganism (generally fungus), which has the ability, in dilute solutions, to destroy or suppress growth of or to kill other microorganisms (usually bacterium). Antibiotics are sufficiently non-toxic so that they are used as chemotherapeutic agents in the treatment of infectious diseases by microorganisms. Synthetic derivatives of antibiotics are also manufactured.
See Infection, Microorganism, and specific antibiotic types.
A. resistance ◀﹦ *an tē bī o tik / rez is̱ tēns, n.* genetic adaptation whereby bacteria that were previously sensitive to an antibiotic become unaffected by that same antibiotic, either by genetic mutation or plasmid

transfer (transmissible drug resistance). Incidence of a. resistance may increase with widespread use of a.s at low doses. More common with some classes of a., and serious threat to successful treatment of some infections when present.
See Resistance.
A. sensitivity ◀﹦ *an tē bī o tik / s̱en si ti̱ vi tē, n.* laboratory test carried out to determine which drug might best treat a bacterial infection. Bacteria isolated from infection grown in laboratory and then tested with different antibiotics to see which antibiotic best stops or reduces bacterial growth.
See Antibiotic, Bacterium.
Bacteriocidal a. ◀﹦ *bak té rē ō s̱i dēl / an tē bī o tik, n.* a. which kills bacteria.
Bacteriostatic a. ◀﹦ *bak té rē ō s̱ta tik / an tē bī o tik, n.* a. which reduces growth and reproduction of bacteria.

Antibody ◀﹦ *an tē bo̱ dē, n.* a protein molecule produced in body by cells of the lymphoid series in response to antigen. Reacts specifically with that antigen. Part of immune response. Also called immunoglobulin, classified as IgA, IgD, IgE, IgG, IgM.
See Antigen, Immunity, Immunoglobulin.

Anticholinergic ◀﹦ *an tē kō lin e̱r jik, adj.* describes substance which blocks transmission of impulses along parasympathetic nerves, e.g. atropine.
See Parasympathetic nervous system.

Anticoagulant ◀﹦ *an tē kō a̱g ū lēnt, n.* substance which prevents or delays blood clotting. May be used in tubes for blood collection (e.g. EDTA, heparin), in collection of blood for transfusion (sodium citrate), in treatment of thrombosis.
See Blood, Transfusion, Thrombosis.

Anticonvulsant ◀﹦ *an tē kēn vul sēnt, n.* substance which stops or relieves convulsions (seizures, fits).
See Seizure.

Antidiarrhoeal ◀﹦ *an tē dī ē re̱ ūl, n.* substance given to control diarrhoea. Various mechanisms of action, depending on substance used.
See Diarrhoea.

Antidiuretic hormone ◀╎ _an_ tē dī ŭr _et_ ik / _hor_ mōn, n. (ADH, vasopressin) hormone secreted by posterior pituitary gland. Myriad important functions in the horse's body. Stimulates contraction of capillaries and arterioles, raising blood pressure; promotes contraction of intestinal musculature; specific effects on kidney tubules to stimulate resorption of water and hence increase urine concentration. Helps maintain fluid balance.
See Diabetes, Kidney, Pituitary.

Antidote ◀╎ _an_ tē _dōt_, n. substance which neutralizes effect of poison, either by rendering poison harmless, or by causing body reaction which neutralizes the poison.
See Poison.

Antifungal ◀╎ _an_ tē _fung_ gēl, adj./n. substance which kills fungi or inhibits their growth. May be used topically (e.g. miconazole) or systemically (e.g. griseofulvin, ketoconazole) to treat fungal infections.
See Fungus, specific antifungal types.

Antigen ◀╎ _an_ ti jēn, n. substance which stimulates production of an immune response and a specific antibody. Stimulus may be microorganism, virus, blood product, foreign protein, toxin, etc., or small part of any of these.
See Antibody, Immunity.

Antigenic drift ◀╎ _an_ tē jēn _et_ ik / drift, n. changes in genes of antigens (e.g. viruses) caused by mutations. Animals which were exposed to the original antigen may not mount an effective immune response to the changed viruses. In horses, this is of major importance in equine influenza, as new viral strains arise.
See Equine influenza, Immunity, Virus.

Antihistamine ◀╎ _an_ tē _his_ tē mēn, n. drug that counteracts effects of histamine. Numerous examples.
See Histamine.

Anti-inflammatory ◀╎ _an_ tē in _flam_ ē trē, adj./n. reducing inflammation; drug or process which reduces inflammation.
See Inflammation.

Antimicrobial ◀╎ _an_ tē mī _krō_ bē ēl, adj./n. killing or reducing growth of microorganisms; substance which kills or reduces growth of microorganisms.
See Antibiotic, Antibacterial, Microorganism.

Antineoplastic ◀╎ _an_ tē nē ō _plas_ tik, adj./n. inhibiting growth or replication of tumour cells; substance which inhibits growth or replication of tumour cells.
See Neoplasia, Tumour.

Anti-oxidant ◀╎ _an_ tē _oks_ si dēnt, adj./n. substance that inhibits oxidation of other compounds. Used in feeds to prevent fats becoming rancid. Some vitamins act as anti-oxidants in some circumstances, e.g. vitamin E. Therapeutic value unclear.
See Vitamin E.

Antipruritic ◀╎ _an_ tē _prü_ ri tik, adj./n. reducing itching (pruritus); substance or process which reduces itching (pruritus).
See Pruritus.

Antipyretic ◀╎ _an_ tē pī re tik, adj./n. reducing pyrexia (fever); agent or process which reduces pyrexia (fever), e.g. hosing with cold or tepid water, anti-inflammatory drugs, e.g. phenylbutazone.

Antiseptic ◀╎ _an_ tē sep tik, adj./n. preventing sepsis; agent or process which prevents sepsis. A substance that inhibits the growth and development of microorganisms without necessarily killing them. Various antiseptic substances may be employed, e.g. they may be applied to horse's skin to clean it thoroughly before surgical operation, or others might be useful in helping to clean a hospital floor.
See Sepsis.

Antiserum ◀╎ _an_ tē _sé_ rum, n. serum that contains antibodies. Prepared by injecting horse or other animal with specific antigen, which stimulates production of specific antibodies required. Blood contains high levels of these antibodies, samples are purified, then can be used to provide antibodies to ill animal, e.g. in treatment of tetanus.
See Antibody, Antigen, Antitoxin, Tetanus.

35

Antispasmodic ◄⁝ _an_ tē spaz _mod_ ik, adj./n. preventing spasm; substance which prevents spasm.
See Colic.

Antitoxin ◄⁝ _an_ tē _toks_ in, n. antibody produced in response to toxin.
See Tetanus, Toxin.

Antitussive ◄⁝ _an_ tē _tu_ siv, n. substance or process which reduces or prevents coughing.
See Cough.

Antivenin ◄⁝ _an_ tē _ven_ in, n. proteinaceous material used in the treatment of poisoning by animal venom, e.g. crotalid snake bites.
See Snake bite.

Antiviral ◄⁝ _an_ tē _vī_ rūl, adj./n. destroying viruses or preventing their replication; a substance which has such activity against viruses, e.g. aciclovir, interferon.
See Acyclovir, Interferon, Virus.

Anuresis ◄⁝ an ŭr _ē_ sis, n. retention of urine in bladder.
See Bladder, Urine.

Anuria ◄⁝ an ŭr _ē_ ē, n. complete suppression of urinary secretion. May be caused by lack of production by kidney, urinary tract blockage, bladder rupture.
See Bladder, Kidney, Urinary.

Anus ◄⁝ _ā_ nēs, n. terminal opening of alimentary tract. Surrounded by muscular ring (sphincter) which is generally tight, so maintains faecal continence.
See Alimentary tract, Sphincter.

Anxiety ◄⁝ ang _zī_ it ē, n. state of uneasiness.

Anxiolytic ◄⁝ ang zī ō _li_ tik, n. medication which relieves anxiety, e.g. mild sedatative.

Aorta ◄⁝ ā _or_ tē, n. the main trunk from which the systemic arterial system proceeds; arises from left ventricle of heart.
See Artery, Aneurysm.

Aortic ◄⁝ ā _or_ tik, adj. pertaining to aorta.
A. arch ◄⁝ ā _or_ tik / arch, n. that part of aorta that gives rise to the brachiocephalic trunk, and the carotid and subclavian arteries.
See Aorta.
A. insufficiency see Insufficiency
A. rupture ◄⁝ ā _or_ tik / _rup_ tŭr, n. rupture may occur as sequel to aneurysm or degenerative changes to arterial wall, or arterial ring where aorta connects with heart. Most frequently seen in aged breeding stallions.
A. valve ◄⁝ ā _or_ tik / _valv_, n. valve at entrance to aorta from left ventricle of heart, composed of three semilunar cusps. Valve opens during contraction of heart, so blood flows into aorta, then closes as heart relaxes so blood does not flow back into heart. Closure of valve makes second of four possible equine heart sounds. Insufficiency of valve may occur due to damage to cusps. These lesions may be degenerative, inflammatory, or due to bacterial endocarditis. Valve cusps may also tear, causing acute insufficiency. In addition, there is a decrease in contractile function of the aortic valve with age, sometimes resulting in aortic valve disease. A reliable diagnosis of aortic insufficiency can be made with the detection of bounding arterial pulses, along with a holodiastolic murmur with maximal intensity over the aortic valve area, and may be confirmed by echocardiography.
See Aorta, Auscultation, Echocardiography, Electrocardiography, Heart.

Aorto-cardiac fistula see Fistula

Aorto-iliac thrombosis ◄⁝ ā _or_ tō / _i_ lē ak / throm _bō_ sis, n. blood clot formation in terminal aorta and/or iliac artery; cause generally unknown. Embolus may break off and block blood vessel in leg. Signs include lameness, abdominal pain, worsening with exercise and improving after rest. Affected leg is cool and pulse is faint beyond obstruction. Diagnosis involves rectal palpation (can sometimes feel altered pulse), ultrasonography, scintigraphy.

Aperture ◄⁝ _a_ pē tŭr, n. opening in the body.

Apex ◄⁝ _ā_ peks, n. top; pointed end of a conically shaped organ, e.g. of heart or lung.

Aphagia ◀﹦ *ē fā jē ē, n.* the refusal or inability to swallow. See Dysphagia.

Apical ◀﹦ *ā pik ēl, adj.* of apex; situated at tip.

Aplasia ◀﹦ *ē plā zē ē, n.* failure of development, causing absence or inadequate development of organ or tissue.

Aplastic anaemia ◀﹦ *ā plas tik / ē nē mē ē, n.* anaemia seen in bone marrow suppression or failure, where there is failure of development of all blood cell types. May be secondary to viral or bacterial infection, administration of certain drugs, neoplasia; hereditary or of unknown cause; may possibly occur as autoimmune condition. See Anaemia, Autoimmunity, Blood, Bone.

Apnoea ◀﹦ *ap nē ē, n.* cessation of breathing. May be seen in newborn foal or anaesthetized animal especially after it has taken several deep breaths.
> **Terminal a.** ◀﹦ *ter min ūl / ap nē ē, n.* heart beating but horse not breathing. Fatal in few minutes unless emergency measures implemented.

Apocrine ◀﹦ *a pō krīn, adj.* type of glandular secretion where products concentrate at free end of secreting cell and then are cast off with portion of cytoplasm, e.g. milk from mammary gland. Other types of gland include holocrine and merocrine. See Gland, Mammary gland.

Aponeurosis ◀﹦ *a pō nŭr rō sis, n.* a white, flattened or ribbon-like tendon expansion that serves mainly to connect a muscle with the part that it moves, e.g. abdominal aponeurosis is the conjoined tendons of abdominal muscles on the abdomen. See Linea alba.

Apophysis ◀﹦ *ē po fi sis, n.* a normal bony outgrowth that has never been entirely separated from the bone of which it forms a part, e.g. process or tuberosity.

Apoptosis ◀﹦ *a pop tō sis, n.* a pattern of cell death affecting single cells; a mecha-nism of cell deletion in the regulation of certain cell populations; often called 'programmed cell death'.

Apparatus ◀﹦ *a pē rā tēs, n.* arrangement of number of body parts to make a system, e.g. copulatory apparatus, stay apparatus. See Stay apparatus.

Appendage ◀﹦ *ē pen dij, n.* thing or part appended, as a limb; something attached, outgrowth, e.g. tail.

Applanometer ◀﹦ *ē plan ō mē tē, n.* instrument used to determine pressure within eyeball in diagnosis of glaucoma (measures how much pressure is needed to flatten a small area of cornea); applanation tonometer. See Eye, Glaucoma, Tonometry.

Apposition ◀﹦ *a po zi shēn, n.* placement of structures so they come into juxtaposition or proximity to each other.

Aprosopia ◀﹦ *a prō sō pē ē, n.* (facelessness) partial or complete absence of all or part of the face; rare congenital condition where eyes, nostrils and mouth have not formed. Foal dies at birth.

Aqueous ◀﹦ *āk wē ēs, adj.* containing water; watery.
> **A. humour** ◀﹦ *āk wē ēs / hū mē, n.* clear fluid in anterior chamber of eye. Produced by ciliary body and drains through corneoiridial angle (filtration angle). Provides nourishment for lens and cornea and maintains intraocular pressure. Disturbance of drainage causes glaucoma. See Eye, Glaucoma.

Arachidonic acid ◀﹦ *ē ra ki do nik / a sid, n.* essential fatty acid from which prostaglandins and other chemicals involved in inflammation are derived. Important in platelet aggregation in blood clotting and control of tone of blood vessels. See Inflammation, Platelet, Prostaglandin.

Arachnida ◀﹦ *ē rak ni dē, n.* class of Arthropoda, includes spiders, ticks, mites and scorpions. Important in equine

medicine are ticks (e.g. *Ixodus, Rhipicephalus*) and mites (e.g. *Sarcoptes, Demodex, Chorioptes*).
See *Chorioptes, Demodex*, Mange, Mite, *Sarcoptes scabei*, Tick.

Arachnoid membrane ◀ *ē rak noid / mem brān, n.* one of the thin layers of tissue covering brain and spinal cord.

Arbovirus ◀ *ar bō vī rēs, n.* virus which replicates in arthropod (e.g. insect or tick), arthropod acting as vector, transmitting virus to host, e.g. equine encephalitis.

Arc ◀ *ark, n.* in geometry, an arc is a structure or projected path having a curved or bowlike outline. In physics, it is a visible electrical discharge, usually taking a curved path. In neurology, it is a pathway of neural reactions.
   Reflex a. ◀ *rē fleks / ark, n.* pathway of nerves followed in reflex action: from sensation along afferent nerves to a nerve centre, then outward from the centre along efferent nerves to an effector organ or part.
   See Nerve, Reflex.

Arcade ◀ *ar kād, n.* a series of arches. In dentistry, the upper and lower arcades are the rows of teeth.

Arch ◀ *arch, n.* anatomical term for structure with curved or bow-like shape, e.g. aortic arch.
See Aorta.

Arecoline ◀ *ē rek o lēn, n.* alkaloid derived from nuts of betel nut tree (*Areca catechu*). Causes contraction of smooth muscle, e.g. in intestines, contracts pupils. In past was used as purgative to treat impacted colic; an ingredient of the anthelmintic drobarbil.

Areolar connective tissue ◀ *a rē ō lē / cē nek tiv / ti shū, n.* type of connective tissue made up of interlacing fibres; also called loose connective tissue; found between muscles or under skin.

Arrhythmia ◀ *ā rith mē ē, n.* irregular heart beat, any variation from normal rhythm of the heart beat. Diagnosis by auscultation and electrocardiography.

See Auscultation, Dysrhythmia, Electrocardiography, Heart.
   Sinus a. ◀ *sī nēs / ā rith mē ē, n.* normal cyclic variation in heart rate, related to impulses from vagus nerve to pacemaker area (sinoatrial node) of heart. Not common in resting horse, but seen frequently after exercise.

Arsenic ◀ *ar sēn ik, n.* chemical element, in past was used as medication for various conditions, including as an appetite stimulant. Signs of acute toxicity secondary to intentional poisioning with lead arsenate included watery diarrhoea, excessive salivation, muscle tremors, ataxia and depression. By the time that clinical signs are recognized, significant toxicity has already occurred, and successful treatment outcome is unlikely.

Arterial ◀ *ar té rē ēl, adj.* pertaining to artery or arteries.
See Artery.

Arteriole ◀ *ar té rē ōl, n.* A minute branch of an artery, especially leading to a capillary.
See Artery.

Arteriovenous ◀ *ar té rē ō vē nēs, adj.* pertaining to or affecting both artery and vein.
See Artery, Vein.
   A. anastomosis ◀ *ar té rē ō vē nēs / ē na stēm ō sis, n.* direct communication between artery and vein. Seen where large volumes of blood needed intermittently, e.g. intestines. In the horse, arteriovenous anastomoses are extremely important in the normal physiology of the hoof, for tolerance of cold, as well as in laminitis.
   A. fistula ◀ *ar té rē ō vē nēs / fis tū lē, n.* abnormal connection between artery and vein. May occur e.g. in heart defects, in liver.

Arteritis ◀ *ar tē rī tis, n.* inflammation of artery.
See Equine viral arteritis.

Artery ◀ *ar tē rē, n.* blood vessel, muscular tube which carries blood from heart to tissues. Has elastic wall with three layers: outer (tunica adventitia), middle (tunica

Artery	Tissue to which artery transports blood	Notes
Aorta	Whole body, except for lungs	Aorta leaves left ventricle of heart, carrying oxygenated blood. Branches from aorta form the major arteries of the body, excepting pulmonary artery, supplying all organs with oxygen
Brachial	Front limb	
Carotid	Head, neck, brain	Inadvertent injections have caused death
Coronary	Muscle of heart	
Femoral	Hind limb	
Hepatic	Liver	
Iliac	Hind limb	Femoral artery is a branch of iliac artery
Mesenteric	Intestines	May be affected by *Strongylus* worms
Pulmonary	Lungs	Take deoxygenated blood from right side of heart to lungs
Renal	Kidney	

media) and inner (tunica intima). Blood is under relatively high pressure. Arteries branch and divide as travel away from heart, eventually becoming arterioles and then capillaries. See Table of major arteries. See Arteriole, Capillary, Circulation.

Arthr- ◀ *arthr, prefix.* joint.

Arthritic ◀ *ar thri tik, adj.* Pertaining to or affected with arthritis, as in an arthritic joint.
See Arthritis, Joint.

Arthritis ◀ *ar thrī tis, n.* inflammation of joints; myriad causes, including, but not limited to, infection and trauma. Any joint may be affected. Characterized by inflammation of joint lining (synovial membrane) and joint structures which may also cause changes in joint fluid (synovial fluid). Swelling within and around joint, pain, lameness, and heat may be features of the disease, but signs vary in individual cases. See Joint, Osteoarthritis.

> **Acute a.** ◀ *ē kūt / ar thrī tis, n.* arthritis marked by pain, heat, redness, and swelling; due to inflammation, infection or trauma.
> **Degenerative a.** see Osteoarthritis.
> **Infectious a.** ◀ *in fek shēs / ar thrī tis, n. a.* caused by infection of a joint with a microorganism, either as part of generalized infection or in one joint only.
> See Septic arthritis (below).

> **Proliferative a.** ◀ *prō li fer ē tiv / ar thrī tis, n.* arthritis with proliferation of the synovium.
> **Septic a.** ◀ *sep tik / ar thrī tis, n.* bacterial infection within joint; the term is usually used to refer to an acute, highly inflammatory process characterized by purulent effusion. Bacteria involved usually coliforms, *Staphylococcus aureus*, *Streptococcus* spp. In foals also *Salmonella*, *Rhodococcus equi* and *Actinobacillus*. In adult horses usually caused by penetrating wound in or near joint, or by joint injection. In foal (joint ill) often spreads via blood stream from umbilicus (navel), pneumonia or intestinal infection (enteritis). Articular cartilage rapidly damaged, causes lameness, joint swelling, heat and pain, may also be inflammation of soft tissues around joint area (cellulitis). Diagnosis by synovial fluid analysis and radiography.
> See Cellulitis, Joint, Pneumonia, Umbilicus.
> **Traumatic a.** ◀ *tror mat ik / ar thrī tis, n.* inflammation of joint caused by either isolated incident or long-term repetitive trauma. Chronic traumatic arthritis is thought to predispose to the development of osteoarthritis.
> See Osteoarthritis.

Arthrocentesis ◀ *ar thrō sen tē sis, n.* Puncture and aspiration of a joint. Fluid can be obtained for diagnostic purposes, or may simply be removed prior to injection (joint injections appear to be more effective when fluid is withdrawn first). See Synovial.

Arthrodesis ◀⁞ _ar thrō dē sis, n._ the surgical fixation of a joint by a procedure designed to accomplish fusion of the joint surfaces, with aim of pain-free, stable joint. Several methods are described, depending on joint and preference of the veterinary surgeon.
Chemical a. ◀⁞ _kem i kal_ / _ar thrō dē sis, n._ chemical arthrodesis, using injections of substances to destroy joint cartilage and encourage subsequent fusion, has been described. Sodium monoiodoacetate was promoted in the late twentieth century, but this technique was subsequently abandoned due to extreme pain and discomfort in some treated horses. The most recent substance tried for chemical arthrodesis is ethyl alcohol.
See Osteoarthritis.

Arthrography ◀⁞ _ar thro grē fē, n._ radiography of a joint after injection of an opaque contrast material.

Arthropathy ◀⁞ _ar thrō pē thē, n._ any joint disease.
See Arthritis, Osteoarthritis.

Arthropoda ◀⁞ _ar thro pēdē, n._ phylum of animal kingdom, includes Insecta and Arachnida classes. Bilaterally symmetrical animals with hard exoskeleton, segmented body, paired jointed legs. Important in horse medicine as may cause and spread disease; e.g. mites, ticks, midges.

Arthropod ◀⁞ _ar thrē pod, n._ an animal belonging to the Arthropoda.

Arthroscope ◀⁞ _ar thrē skōp, n._ an endoscope for examining the interior of a joint and for carrying out diagnostic and therapeutic procedures within a joint.
See Endoscope.

Arthroscopy ◀⁞ _ar thro skē pē, n._ use of arthroscope to examine inside joint for diagnostic and therapeutic purposes.

Arthrosis ◀⁞ _ar thrō sis, n._ arthropathy.

Arthrotomy ◀⁞ _ar thro tēm ē, n._ surgical opening of joint, e.g. to drain fluid or gain access for surgery.

Arthus reaction ◀⁞ _ar thēs_ / _rē ak shēn, n._ local hypersensitivity reaction, where antigen–antibody complexes which fix complement are deposited in small blood vessel walls and cause acute inflammation. (Named after Nicolas Maurice Arthus French physician– 1862–1945)
See Allergy, Antibody, Antigen, Complement, Hypersensitivity.

Articular ◀⁞ _ar tik ū lē, adj._ of or pertaining to a joint.
A. cartilage ◀⁞ _ar tik ū lē_ / _kar ti lij, n._ smooth hyaline cartilage covering the ends of bones that meet in joints. Cushions ends of bones and facilitates a nearly frictionless joint movement.
See Cartilage.

Articulation ◀⁞ _ar tik ū lā shēn, n._ any place of junction between two different parts or objects. A synovial articulation is a joint. The teeth also articulate – the articulation is the contact relationship of the teeth while they are in action.

Artifact ◀⁞ _ar ti fakt, n._ artificial product. Histological artifacts are features that are introduced by processing that are not part of the examined tissue. In radiology, an artifact is an image that is not part of the living tissue being examined, produced during the imaging process.

Artificial insemination ◀⁞ _ar ti fi shēl_ / _in se min ā shēn, n._ the transfer of a stallion's semen into a mare's uterus by artificial means, with aim of achieving pregnancy. Fresh, cooled extended, or thawed frozen semen may be used.

Artificial respiration ◀⁞ _ar ti fi shēl_ / _re spi rā shēn, n._ assisting breathing by means of mechanical ventilation (moving chest wall, pumping rebreathing bag from anaesthetic machine) and/or providing oxygen via tube in windpipe (endotracheal tube) or mask.

Artificial vagina see Vagina

Aryepiglottic fold ◀≋ *a rē e pi glo tik / fōld, n.* fold of lining of larynx, which joins epiglottis to arytenoid cartilage, forms wall of laryngeal vestibule. May collapse inwards during exercise (can be observed during endoscopy of larynx with horse on treadmill) and cause harsh noise when horse breathes in.
See Arytenoid cartilage, Endoscopy, Larynx.

Arytenoid cartilage ◀≋ *a ri tē noid / kar ti lij, n.* one of pair of cartilages in top part of larynx. Provides attachment for muscles of vocal cords and forms dorsal edge of laryngeal opening (rima glottis).
See Larynx.
  A. chondritis see Chondritis

Ascaridae ◀≋ *as ka ri dē, n.* class of parasitic intestinal roundworms, includes genera *Ascaris* and *Parascaris*, members of which can affect horses.
See *Parascaris equorum*.

Ascending ◀≋ *ē sen ding, adj.* having an upwards course in anatomy, e.g. ascending aorta is that part rising from heart towards spine.

Ascites ◀≋ *ē sī tēz, n.* effusion and accumulation of serous fluid in abdominal cavity. Seen in various conditions, including abdominal neoplasia, obstruction to liver blood flow, septicaemia, and low blood serum protein levels.
See Anaemia, Hypoalbuminaemia, Septicaemia.

Ascorbic acid ◀≋ *as kor bik / a sid, n.* vitamin C, can be synthesized by horse, so not essential part of diet.

-ase ◀≋ *āz, suffix.* denotes enzyme.
See Enzyme.

Asepsis ◀≋ *ā sep sis, n.* freedom from infection, or prevention of contact with microorganisms.
See Antiseptic, Disinfect.

Ash ◀≋ *ash, n.* used on feed labelling to mean that part which would be left after combustion, the minerals in a diet are included in that residue.

Aspartate aminotransferase ◀≋ *ē spar tāt / a mē nō trans fer āz, n.* (AST) An enzyme that facilitates the conversion of aspartate and alpha-ketoglutaric acid to oxaloacetate and glutamate. Low levels of AST are normally found in the blood. When body tissue or an organ such as the liver is diseased or damaged, additional AST is released into the bloodstream. The amount of AST in the blood is directly related to the extent of the tissue damage. (Formerly known as SGOT – serum glutamic oxaloacetic transaminase).

Aspergillus ◀≋ *as pē ji lēs, n.* genus of fungi, some members of genus may cause disease, e.g. *Aspergillus fumigatus* may cause abortion in mares, or fungal infections in ulcerated eyes; allergy to *Aspergillus fumigatus* spores can contribute to chronic obstructive pulmonary disease; others produce toxins which can contaminate feed. These fungi are not inherently toxic, but under conditions of adequate temperature and humidity, the fungi can grow rapidly and elaborate toxins. Signs of acute aflatoxicosis include anorexia, fever, increased heart and respiratory rates, convulsions, icterus, colic and death, among others.
See Abortion, Aflatoxin, Recurrent airway obstruction.

Aspermatogenesis ◀≋ *ā spē ma tō jen ē sis, n.* failure of sperm production.
See Sperm.

Asphyxia ◀≋ *as fik sē ē, n.* suffocation, lack of oxygen in inspired air which will cause death if not corrected.
  Neonatal a. ◀≋ *nē ō nā tl / as fik sē ē, n.* deprivation of air to foetus during birth. If uncomplicated, normal breathing will occur if foal stimulated or artificial respiration given.
See Artificial respiration.

Aspirate ◀≋ *a spi rāt, v.* suck up fluid, e.g. remove fluid from operation site by suction. As a noun, an aspirate refers to the substance which is obtained by aspiration.

Aspiration ◀≋ *a spi rā shēn, n.* inhalation, especially of fluids, mucus or vomit, into respiratory tract; removal of fluid by suction from a body cavity; to obtain specimens for biopsy by suction.

A. biopsy see Biopsy

A. pneumonia ◀ᵉ *a spi r̲a̲ shēn / nū m̲o̲ nē ē*, *n.* inflammation and infection of lung caused by inhalation of foreign material, e.g. food inhaled when horse has difficulty swallowing (dysphagia), or material deposited in lung by improper placement of nasogastric tube. Can cause death of lung tissue (necrosis). See Dysphagia, Pneumonia.

Aspirin see Acetylsalicylic acid

Assay ◀ᵉ *a̲ sā, n.* determination of content of substance; determination of the biological or pharmacological potency of a drug.

Asthenia ◀ᵉ *as t̲h̲ē̲ nē ē, n.* lack or loss of strength or energy; weakness.

Dermal a. ◀ᵉ *d̲e̲r̲ mēl / as t̲h̲ē̲ nē ē, n.* Hereditary equine regional dermal asthenia (HERDA) belongs to a group of inherited, congenital connective tissue dysplasias usually described as hyperelastosis cutis, cutaneous asthenia, dermatosparaxis, or Ehlers–Danlos-like syndrome. Inherited skin problem; disorder of collagen synthesis. Affected horses have bilateral asymmetrical lesions of the trunk and lumbar regions, with hyperextensible skin. Handling of the skin elicits a painful response and superficial trauma leads to skin wounds. The skin is thinner than normal in the affected areas, with thickened borders and harder fibrotic masses (pseudotumours). The histopathological findings include thinner and smaller collagen fibrils, and a loose arrangement of collagen fibres in the middle, adventitial and deep dermis. Pedigree charts support an autosomal recessive type of inheritance. NOTE: The condition may take months to years before becoming clinically apparent to the owner. Reported in American Quarter Horse foals, Paints and Appaloosas, as well as Arabian crossbreeds. See Collagen, HERDA, Skin.

Asthma ◀ᵉ *as̲ mē, n.* condition of the airways characterized by difficulty breathing (dyspnoea) and wheezing, caused by spasm of bronchioles (small airways). Usually an allergic reaction to inhaled allergen. An analogous condition is chronic obstructive pulmonary disease (COPD), but there are great differences between human asthma and equine COPD. Horse owners may call COPD equine asthma, but it is not the same thing. See Allergy, Recurrent airway obstruction.

Astragalus see Locoweed, Milkvetch

Astringent ◀ᵉ *ē s̲t̲r̲i̲n̲ jēnt, adj./n.* causing contraction; usually refers to a local tissue shrinkage effect after topical application. True indications are rare in equine medicine, but astringents find common application in many topical liniment preparations sold to horse owners. See Proud.

Astrocyte ◀ᵉ *as̲ trō sīt, n.* star-shaped nerve cell found in brain tissue.

Asymmetry ◀ᵉ *ā̲ s̲i̲m̲ ē trē, n.* a lack or absence of symmetry; e.g. asymmetry of face when one side of face is swollen.

Asymptomatic ◀ᵉ *ā̲ simp tēm a̲ tik, adj.* not showing or causing symptoms or signs of condition.

Asystole ◀ᵉ *ā̲ s̲i̲s̲ tē lē, n.* absence of heart beat, complete lack of cardiac electrical and mechanical activity. No heart beat on auscultation, flat line on electrocardiograph. Emergency, requiring immediate resuscitation. See Auscultation, Cardiac, Electrocardiography, Heart, Resuscitation.

Ataxia ◀ᵉ *ā̲ t̲a̲k̲ sē ē, n.* failure of muscular coordination. Ataxic horses will often have wide-based stance, hindquarters may sway at walk or trot, movements are not smooth, toes may be dragged on floor. If more severe, horse may stumble. Various causes, including fever, neurological disease, and congestive heart failure. See Brain, Paresis, Proprioception, Spinal.

Atelectasis ◀ᵉ *ā̲ tē l̲e̲k̲ tē sis, n.* collapse, incomplete expansion, or failure of inflation of lungs or part of lung.

Foetal a. ◄≋ *fē tl / ā tē lek tē sis, n.* failure of lungs to expand at birth.

Atheroma ◄≋ *a thē rō mē, n.* a tumour of granuline matter. In horses, normally used to describe a sebaceous cyst of the false nostril. Treatment is surgical removal; injection of formalin has also been described. See Nostril, Sebaceous.

Atlantal ◄≋ *at lan tēl, adj.* of the atlas. (In Greek mythology, Atlas was the titan who held the universe on shoulders.) See Atlas.
A. bursa see Bursa

Atlantoaxial ◄≋ *at lan tō ak sē ūl, adj.* of the joint between atlas and axis. See Atlas, Axis.
A. joint ◄≋ *at lan tō ak sē ūl / joint, n.* joint between first and second cervical vertebrae. Peg-and-socket joint, allows side-to-side movement of head.

Atlanto-occipital ◄≋ *at lan tō ok si pi tēl, adj.* of the joint between atlas and skull (occipital bone).
A.-o. joint ◄≋ *at lan tō ok si pi tēl / joint, n.* joint between atlas and skull (occipital bone). Allows head to move up and down.
A.-o. malformation ◄≋ *at lan tō ok si pi tēl / mal for mā shēn, n.* congenital malformation of a.-o. joint in horses has been described, primarily Arabian horses, but also Appaloosa and Quarter Horses. Affected horses commonly have abnormal head and neck carriage since birth; neurological deficits may not become evident clinically until later. Palpation and manipulation of the base of the skull and cervical area are useful diagnostically; typically, in comparison with clinically normal horses, the range of dorso-ventral motion at the atlantoaxial joint is increased. Alternate subluxation and relocation of this joint may generate audible clicking sounds. Radiography typically reveals symmetrical atlanto-occipital fusion, with modification of the atlas, atlantoaxial joint, and axis.

Atlas ◄≋ *at lēs, n.* first bone of spine, cervical vertebra, has joint with skull. Modified shape compared with other vertebrae, allows large range of movements. See Vertebra.

Atony ◄≋ *ā tē nē, n.* lack of normal tone or strength.

Atopy ◄≋ *ā tē pē, n.* inherited allergic condition involving itchy skin, often associated with inflammation of eyes (conjunctivitis) or nose (rhinitis) or gastrointestinal signs. Hypersensitivity reaction involving IgE, to allergens such as dust, pollen, feathers, mites, etc. Signs can be seasonal or non-seasonal. Allergen may be identified using intradermal skin testing; serum testing is also employed, however the test lacks sensitivity according to scientific studies.
See Allergen, Hypersensitivity.

Atraumatic ◄≋ *ā tror ma tik, adj.* not causing injury.

Atresia ◄≋ *ā trē zē ē, n.* absence of or closure of normal body opening or tubular organ.
A. ani ◄≋ *ā trē zē a / ā nī, n.* absence of anus or part of rectum may be seen as congenital condition in foal.

Atrial ◄≋ *ā trē ēl, adj.* of the atrium. See Atrium, Heart.
A. fibrillation ◄≋ *ā trē ēl / fi bri lā shēn, n.* condition where walls of atria contract rapidly and ineffectually, resulting in irregular heart beat. Common dysrhythmia in horse, especially racing horses. May occur on its own, or secondary to condition causing atrial enlargement. Associated with poor performance.
A. septal defect ◄≋ *ā trē ēl / sep tul / dē fekt, n.* congenital problem of heart where wall between left and right atria is incomplete, allowing mixing of oxygenated and non-oxygenated blood. Signs will depend upon size of defect.

Atrioventricular ◄≋ *ā trē ō ven tri kū lē, adj.* (AV) of both atrium and ventricle of the heart.
See Atrium, Heart, Ventricle.
AV block ◄≋ *ā trē ō ven tri kū lē / blok, n.* heart problem where there is slowing or failure of conduction of impulses through av. node. May be caused by fibrosis at node, or with some drugs, e.g. halothane. Varying degrees of severity, most common is second degree block, where failure of conduction is inter-

mittent; considered normal in resting horses, conduction failure is thought to be due to the large size of the equine heart; second degree AV block is also associated with the use of alpha blockers, such as xylazine or detomidine. Third degree block is complete blockage, and atria and ventricles beat independently. Diagnosis by auscultation, electrocardiography.
See AV node (below), Electrocardiography, Heart, Sinoatrial node.

AV. insufficiency ◀ *ā trē ō ven tri kū lē / in sē fi shēn sē, n.* damage to atrioventricular valve (right or left) which allows blood back from ventricle to atrium when heart contracts. Causes murmur. Right av. insufficiency may be asymptomatic, but can cause poor performance if severe. Left av. insufficiency can cause fluid in lungs (pulmonary oedema) and respiratory problems, often associated with poor performance. Diagnosis by echocardiography and electrocardiography.
See Echocardiography, Electrocardiography, Heart.

AV. node ◀ *ā trē ō ven tri kū lē / nōd, n.* heart muscle fibres (Purkinje fibres) which transmit impulses from sinoatrial node to muscle of ventricles, so that ventricles contract.
See Sinoatrial node.

AV. valve ◀ *ā trē ō ven tri kū lē / valv, n.* valve between atrium and ventricle. Two in horse heart, left (mitral, bicuspid) and right (tricuspid).
See AV. insufficiency (above), Heart, Valve.

Atrium ◀ *ā trē ēm, n.* chamber; one of two first chambers of heart, where blood from veins enters. Left atrium receives oxygenated blood from pulmonary veins, right atrium receives blood from venae cavae, returning from body. Blood then passes from atrium to ventricle.
See Heart.

Atrophy ◀ *a trē fē, n./v.* a wasting away; a reduction in the size of a cell, tissue, organ or part; causes include lack of nourishment or lack of use.
Muscle a. ◀ *mu sēl / a trē fē, n.* wasting of muscle due to lack of use or damage to nerves serving it.

Atropine ◀ *a trē pēn, n.* alkaloid drug; synthetic derivative of nightshade (*Atropa*

belladonna), henbane and thornapple. Blocks transmission of impulses from parasympathetic and cholinergic sympathetic nerves to muscles; anticholinergic and antispasmodic. Systemic atropine is rarely used therapeutically in the horse because it can cause a fatal ileus (colic). In ocular medicine, atropine causes prolonged dilation of pupil and is thus used therapeutically to treat cases where eye inflammation is a feature, and to reduce the pain of iris spasm associated with uveitis and corneal ulceration. Also causes bronchodilation. Some veterinarians have injected atropine into synovial swellings in an effort to reduce them (e.g. idiopathic joint effusion, 'windpuffs').
See Parasympathetic nervous system, Pupil, Sympathetic nervous system.

A. poisoning ◀ *a trē pēn / poi sēn ing, n.* overdosage with atropine in horses typically causes intestinal ileus (failure of intestinal movement), with subsequent colic, and, if irreversible, death.

A. test ◀ *a trē pēn / test, n.* intravenous administration of atropine can dramatically reduce bronchospasm within 15 minutes, and has been used as a test for COPD in horses.

Attenuation ◀ *ē ten ū ā shēn, n.* making thin; weakening; in the sense of weakening, the word is used to describe process of altering virulence of virus or microorganism for vaccine production by repeated passage through host or growth media.
See Vaccine.

Attrition ◀ *ē tri shēn, n.* gradual wearing away, caused by friction. Seen in teeth as they rub against each other.

Atypical ◀ *ā ti pi kēl, adj.* not conforming to normal pattern, unusual.

Auditory ◀ *or di tē rē, adj.* pertaining to sense of hearing or ear.
A. nerve see Vestibulocochlear nerve
A. tube diverticulum see Guttural pouch

Aural ◀ *or ūl, adj.* of the ear.
See Ear.
A. plaque ◀ *or ūl / plak, n.* a condition seen in the ears of horses older than 1 year, char-

acterized by small, raised, depigmented papules on the inner surface of the ear. Lesions typically progress, especially in summer time when biting flies are active. No treatment has been shown to be consistently effective, but treatments include topical steroid administration. Fly repellents, masks and insecticidal sprays may help in fly management.

Auricle ◀ᴇ *o ri kĕl*, *n.* external ear, pinna; and appendage to the atrium (first chamber of heart) in some individuals. See Atrium, Ear.

Auricular cartilage ◀ᴇ *o ri kū lĕ / kar ti lij*, *n.* one of three cartilages supporting structure of external ear: conchal (funnel-shaped, gathers sound waves), annular (ring-shaped surrounding external meatus) and scutiform (attachment of muscles which move ear). See Ear.

Auscultation ◀ᴇ *ors cĕl tā shĕn*, *n.* listening to sounds produced within body, as aid to diagnosis, e.g. cardiac auscultation is listening to heart sounds. Usually performed with stethoscope. See Borborygmus, Heart, Respiratory, Stethoscope.

Auto- ◀ᴇ *or tō, prefix.* self.

Autoclave ◀ᴇ *or tō klāv*, *n.* apparatus used for sterilizing surgical instruments, swabs. Uses high temperatures, and produces steam under pressure. See Sterilization.

Autogenous See Autologous

Autoimmune disease ◀ᴇ *or tō i mūn / di zĕz*, *n.* condition where animal produces antibodies against its own cells, immune system fails to recognize body's own structures and treats them as foreign, e.g. pemphigus foliaceus. See Autoimmunity, Bullous pemphigoid, Discoid lupus erythematosus, Pemphigus foliaceus.

Autoimmunity ◀ᴇ *or tō i mū ni tē*, *n.* condition characterized by a specific immune response against constituents of the body's own tissues.

Auto-infection ◀ᴇ *or tō-in fek shĕn*, *n.* spread of infection within body from one part to another.

Autologous ◀ᴇ *or tol ĕg ĕs, adj.* self-produced, originating within animal's own body, e.g. autologous skin graft uses skin taken from another part of the patient's body. Also called *autogenous* or *autogenic*. See Graft.

    A. vaccine ◀ᴇ *or tol ĕg ĕs / vak sĕn, n.* a vaccine produced from a portion of the horse's own body, in an effort to stimulate an immune response, e.g. an autologous vaccine is available for the treatment of melanoma (no proven effectiveness).

Autolysis ◀ᴇ *or to li sis, n.* destruction of cells by their own enzymes. Generally occurs after death.

Autonomic nervous system ◀ᴇ *or tē no mik / ner vĕs / sis tĕm, n.* part of nervous system which regulates actions not under voluntary control, e.g. dilation of pupil, intestinal peristalsis, heart rate, secretion from glands. Has two divisions, sympathetic and parasympathetic. See Nervous system, Parasympathetic nervous system, Sympathetic nervous system.

Autopsy ◀ᴇ *or top sē, n.* post-mortem inspection of the human body, including internal organs, by dissection, so as to determine the cause of death or the nature of pathological changes. In animals, the procedure is normally referred to as *necropsy.* See Necropsy.

Avermectins ◀ᴇ *ā ver mek tinz, n.* group of chemical compounds derived from fungus (*Streptomyces avermitilis*), with strong antiparasitic activity. Used against various internal parasites and certain external parasites.

Avulsion ◀ᴇ *ē vul shĕn, n.* injury or surgery involving tearing or pulling away.
    A. fracture ◀ᴇ *ē vul shĕn / frak tŭr, n.* an indirect fracture caused by avulsion or pull of a

ligament, such as may be seen at the origin of the suspensory ligament, or associated with the navicular bone.

Awn ◀ᴇ *orn, n.* slender bristle projecting from some seeds, especially grasses. May penetrate skin and cause abscess, or enter ear canal or eye and cause irritation and/or infection.

Axial ◀ᴇ *ak sē ūl, adj.* relating to an axis, denoting relationship to the axis of a structure or part; pertaining to second cervical vertebra (axis).
See Axis.

Axilla ◀ᴇ *ak zi lē, n.* area between forelimb and chest (equivalent to human armpit), through which pass vital arteries and nerves supplying front leg.

Axis ◀ᴇ *ak sis, n.* a line around which specified parts of the body are arranged; also, a line about which a revolving body turns, or about which a structure would turn if it did revolve. Second cervical vertebra, has modified shape to allow articulation with atlas.
See Atlas.

Axon ◀ᴇ *ak son, n.* that part of a neuron by which impulses travel away from the nerve cell body. Impulses pass along axon away from cell body, branches at end of axon have junctions (synapses) with other nerve cells or other effector organs, such as muscle cells.
See Nerve.

Azalea ◀ᴇ *ē za lē ē, n.* garden shrub, contains cardiac glycosides, may cause sudden death if eaten.

Azoospermia ◀ᴇ *ā zū ō sper mē ē, n.* absence of sperm in semen.
See Semen, Sperm.

Azotaemia ◀ᴇ *ā zō tē mē ē, n.* increased level of serum urea nitrogen and/or other nitrogenous compounds in the blood; also called *uraemia.*
See Creatinine, Kidney, Urea, Uraemia.

Azoturia see Exertional rhabdomyolysis

B

B lymphocyte (cell) ◀⁞ *bē* / *lim fō sīt, n.* lymphocyte derived from haematopoietic tissue (primarily bone marrow in adult; foetal yolk sac, liver and spleen) involved in antibody production (humoral immunity). Activated by binding to antigen, cell multiplies, these cells mature to plasma cells, interact with T helper lymphocytes and macrophages. B lymphocytes secrete antibodies (immunoglobulins) specific to antigen which previously bound to original B lymphocyte.
See Antibody, Antigen, Immunity.

Babesia ◀⁞ *ba bē zē ē, n.* genus of protozoan parasite (piroplasm). Pear-shaped organisms occurring as a single or paired parasite and found within red blood cells of various vertebrates. Two species, *Babesia caballi* and *Babesia equi,* are widely distributed and transmitted primarily by ticks of various genera.
See Babesiosis.

Babesiosis ◀⁞ *ba bē zē ō sis, n.* (biliary fever, piroplasmosis) any of a variety of diseases caused by infection with *Babesia caballi* or *Babesia equi*; spread primarily by ticks, but also potentially by contaminated needles or surgical instruments, or contaminated blood transfusions. The disease occurs in tropical, subtropical and some temperate regions of the world; it is estimated that only 10% of the world's horses live in regions that are free of babesiosis. Infection leads to destruction of red blood cells.

CLINICAL SIGNS
Signs include fever, depression, pale or yellow (jaundiced) mucous membranes, bloody ocular discharge, swelling around the eyes, loss of appetite, haemoglobinuria (red urine), fluid swelling (oedema) of ventral abdomen, anaemia, and abortion in pregnant mares. Urine may be red due to presence of haemoglobin from destruction of red blood cells. Mortality may be high.

DIAGNOSIS
Diagnosis is based on typical clinical signs, and confirmed by demonstration of parasites within red blood cells on stained blood smear. Serological or PCR testing is available, and may be required for regulatory purposes. The complement fixation (CF) test was the previous official standard test for equine babesiosis worldwide, but the regulatory test for horses entering the United States of America is the capture ELISA test. The indirect immunoflurorecent antibody test (IFAT) is more sensitive than the CF test, and has been used as an additional test when CF testing is inconclusive. Polymerase chain reaction tests (PCR) are primarily used for research at this time.

TREATMENT
Treatment of horses with babesiosis has variable success. Treatment aims may include supporting the acutely infected horse, or trying to eliminate the parasite entirely (may not be possible). Imidocarb is usually the drug of choice; toxicity of imidocarb has been described. Other pharmaceuticals employed for treatment have included diminazene, amicarbalide, and acridine dyes, such as euflavine. Effective measures to prevent abortion or stillbirth have not been described.

PREVENTION
At present, no successful immunization strategies have been developed. Control largely depends on pharmacological therapy, tick control, and restricted movement of infected horses.

SIGNIFICANCE
Economic losses associated with babesiosis are considerable and include treatment costs, loss of animals, and restrictions on horse movement. Horses affected with *B. equi* remain carriers for life, regardless of whether clinical signs resolve (naturally or with treatment); horses affected with *B. caballi* may relapse even after signs resolve, suggesting that they may also harbour lifelong infections. Carrier horses are a reservoir for maintenance and spread of the disease.

Also known as piroplasmosis, equine malaria, equine biliary fever, or horse tick fever.

See Babesia, Complement, ELISA, Tick.

Bacillus ◄ *bē si lēs, n.* genus of Gram-positive rod-like bacteria which form spores. Most members except *B. anthracis* do not cause equine disease.
See *B. anthracis* (below), Gram.

> **B. anthracis** ◄ *bē si lēs / an thrā kis, n.* Gram-positive, rod-shaped organism, causes anthrax. Under adverse conditions can form into spores. Spores have been found in bone meal, blood fertilizers, wool, hides, feeds. Bacillus comparatively fragile, killed by ordinary disinfectants.
> See Anthrax, Disinfectant, Gram stain.

Bacillus ◄ *bē si lēs, n.* any rod-shaped bacterium (as opposed to a coccus, which is round); an organism of the genus *Bacillus*. Many examples, including *Escherichia coli* (normally found in faeces, may also cause diarrhoea), *Klebsiella pneumoniae* (causes a form of equine venereal disease), *Pseudomonas mallei* (causes glanders), etc.
See Diarrhoea, *Escherichia*, Glanders, *Klebsiella* spp., *Pseudomonas*, Venereal.

Bacitracin ◄ *ba si trā sin, n.* antibacterial polypeptide produced by the growth of a Gram-positive, spore-forming organism, *Bacillus subtilis*. Interferes with bacterial cell wall synthesis; has activity against Gram-positive bacteria. Commonly used in equine medicine in topical preparations for the eye (with neomycin and polymixin B) or in dermatological preparations.
See Antibiotic.

Back ◄ *bak, n.* (dorsum) part of the trunk, from withers to tail; the area of horse anatomy where the saddle goes.

> **B. at the knee** see Calf knee
> **Broken b.** ◄ *brō kĕn / bak, n.* fracture of one or more vertebrae; severity depends on location of fracture; severe cases that involve the spinal cord with resultant incoordination and/or paralysis carry a grave prognosis. See Fracture, Paralysis, Spinal, Vertebra.
> **Cold b.** ◄ *kōld / bak, n.* colloquial term describing a horse that resents saddling and girth tightening. Normally, this is a behavioural aberration, but may occasionally be due to back pain or poorly fitting tack.
> **Hollow b.** ◄ *ho lō / bak, n.* (dipped back) exaggerated concave shape of back behind withers. These horses tend to have higher head carriage due to higher set necks coming out of the shoulders.
> **Sway b.** see Hollow back (above)

Backbone ◄ *bak / bōn, n.* spine or vertebral column, composed of 54 bones (vertebrae) which are aligned into continuous row from neck to tail, provides support for limbs and ribs and bony housing for spinal cord.
See Spinal, Spine, Vertebra.

Backflow ◄ *bak / flō, n.* flow of fluid in a direction the reverse of that normally taken; e.g. in heart with a damaged valve, blood can backflow from second chamber (ventricle) to first chamber (atrium).
See Heart.

Backing ◄ *bak ing, v.* going backwards, especially as part of training or while being ridden. Horse will have difficulty with backing in conditions which cause incoordination or ataxia, e.g. 'wobblers'.
See Ataxia.

Backraking ◄ *bak / rā king, v.* manual removal of faeces from rectum; archaic term describing an attempt to evacuate the bowels in the treatment of colic.
See Rectal.

Bacteraemia ◄ *bak tē rē mē ē, n.* presence of bacteria in blood.

Bacteria ◀ᛊ *bak té rē ē, n.* plural of bacterium.
See Bacterium.

Bacterial ◀ᛊ *bak té rē ēl, adj.* pertaining to or caused by bacteria; e.g. a bacterial infection is an infection caused by bacteria.
See Bacterium.

Bactericidal ◀ᛊ *bak té ri sī dl, adj./n.* destructive to bacteria.
See Bacterium.
 B. antibiotic see Antibiotic

Bacterin ◀ᛊ *bac tē rin, n.* vaccine made from killed bacteria.
See Bacterium, Vaccine.

Bacteriostasis ◀ᛊ *bak té rē ō stā sis, n.* inhibition of bacterial growth or multiplication by chemical or biological materials; bacteria not killed.
See Bacterium.

Bacteriostatic ◀ᛊ *bak té rē ō sta tik, adj./n.* inhibiting bacterial growth or multiplication; an agent which inhibits bacterial growth or multiplication.
See Bacterium.
 B. antibiotic see Antibiotic

Bacterium ◀ᛊ *bak té rē ēm, n.* (plural bacteria) microscopic single-celled organism, multiplies by simple division (fission). Important in many disease processes (infections: see table below). The resident bacteria of the equine digestive tract (flora) are critical for normal digestion; bacterial action in large intestine breaks food down into absorbable molecules. Classified according to:

- Shape: rods, cocci (round), filamentous, comma-shaped, etc.
- Staining: take up different stains according to structure, e.g. Gram-positive, Gram-negative, acid-fast, etc.
- Size: range between 1μm and 8μm.
- Spore formation: some will form resistant spores, e.g. *Bacillus anthracis*, *Clostridium tetani*.
- Motility: whip-like processes (flagella) on some bacteria allow movement if bacteria suspended in fluid.
- Arrangement: may form chains or clump together.
- Growth requirements: e.g. requirement for oxygen (aerobic) etc.
- Capsules: some are surrounded by layer of gelatinous material.

Cultivation in laboratory requires special substances (media) in which bacteria will grow, and may need special conditions of temperature, presence or absence of oxygen, etc.

EXAMPLES OF BACTERIAL DISEASES

Disease	Causal bacterium
Anthrax	*Bacillus anthracis*
Botulism	*Clostridium botulinum*
Brucellosis	*Brucella abortus*
Glanders	*Pseudomonas mallei*
Leptospirosis – numerous species, including:	*Leptospira pomona* *Leptospira sejroe*
Lockjaw, tetanus	*Clostridium tetani*
Salmonellosis	*Salmonella* Typhimurium *Salmonella* Abortus equi *Salmonella* Agona *Salmonella* Anatum *Salmonella* Enteritidis
Sleepy foal disease	*Actinobacillus equuli*
Strangles	*Streptococcus equi*
Tuberculosis	*Mycobacterium tuberculosis*
Ulcerative lymphangitis	*Corynebacterium pseudotuberculosis*

Any bacterium may cause disease under conditions that are optimum for the growth of that bacteria. A number of diseases are associated with one or more of several species of bacteria, e.g. abscess, neonatal septicaemia, joint-ill, meningitis, pneumonia, uterine infection.
See Gram stain, Infection, Stain, and under specific conditions.

Bag ◀≀ *bag, n.* mammary glands (colloquial term).

Balance ◀≀ *bal ēns, v./n.* the harmonious adjustment of parts; the harmonious performance of functions; equilibrium.
See Ear.
> **Acid–base b.** see Acid
> **Dietary b.** ◀≀ *dī ē tē rē / bal ēns, n.* balanced diet is one where all nutrient requirements are adequately satisfied, but not to excess.
> **Fluid b.** ◀≀ *flŭ id / bal ēns, n.* the state of the body in relation to ingestion and excretion of water and electrolytes.
> **Hoof b.** ◀≀ *hŭf / bal ēns, n.* a poorly defined and controversial term, referring to the orientation of the hoof in three dimensions. In general, hoof balance describes a combination of toe length, hoof angle, and mediolateral (side to side) symmetry, and how they relate to one another. Many performance problems are attributed to problems with hoof balance. However, hoof imbalance, even in an extreme presentation, may not cause any apparent problems.
> **Nitrogen b.** ◀≀ *nī trē jēn / bal ēns, n.* the state of the body in regard to ingestion and excretion of nitrogen.
> **Postural b.** ◀≀ *pos tŭr ūl / bal ēns, n.* the horse's bodily equilibrium; position of the horse's body in space. Maintained by complex connections of the horse's nervous system. Often said to be impeded by poor riding technique.

Balanic ◀≀ *bē la nik, adj.* of glans penis or glans clitoridis.
See Penis.

Balanitis ◀≀ *ba lē nī tis, n.* inflammation of glans penis.
See Penis.

Balanoposthitis ◀≀ *ba lē nō pos thī tis, n.* inflammation of glans penis and prepuce.
See Penis, Prepuce.

Bald ◀≀ *bawld, adj.* lacking, wholly or partially, a usual covering (of hair). In horse may see bald patches where has rubbed coat, or in skin diseases or injury. Also, white or light colour on a horse's head from poll to nose, including around the eyes. Overo is the name of a coloration pattern in American Paint Horses in which the horse's head is bald or nearly bald.
See Alopecia.

Baleri ◀≀ *ba lǎ ri, n.* disease caused by infection with one of several species of *Trypanosoma*, as described in Sudan. Trypanosomiasis causes fever, weakness, body swelling, and lethargy, which lead to weight loss and anaemia; in some animals the disease is fatal unless treated. Spread by biting insects, especially flies. Affects horses, sheep, goats and cattle.
See Nagana, *Trypanosoma*.

Ball ◀≀ *bawl, n.* spherical mass; formerly, a medicinal formulation in a roughly spherical mass, administered orally, sometimes with the assistance of a balling gun; not commonly used today.

Ballotment ◀≀ *ba lot mēnt, n.* (also spelt ballottement) diagnostic technique used to determine presence of organ or other body suspended in fluid. In equine pregnancy diagnosis, presence of foetus may sometimes be established by pushing fist into flank of mare, foetus can be felt to rise and then fall, in the manner of a heavy body in water (not a reliable test).
See Pregnancy.

Band ◀≀ *band, n.* an object or appliance that confines or restricts; a strip that holds together or binds two or more separate objects or parts, (e.g. a band of fibrous tissue, the frenulum of the tongue, the taenia of the equine colon; an elongated area with parallel, or roughly parallel, borders that is distinct from the surrounding surface by colour or texture (e.g. a chromosome band).
> **B. keratopathy** ◀≀ *band / ◀≀ ke rē tō pēth ē, n.*

a linear opacity seen on the surface of the eye in some normal horses.

B. neutrophil ◀ *band / nū tro fil, n.* immature neutrophil (white blood cell) released into blood stream in response to high demand (e.g. in infection).
See Frenulum, Leukocyte, Neutrophil, Taenia

Bandage ◀ *ban dij, n./v.* strip of material for wrapping or binding any part of the body; used in wound management, to provide 'support' for limb, protection during travelling, etc.; to apply bandage. Many types of bandage are available, including:

• Adhesive b. – a bandage affixed to a fabric or film coated with a pressure-sensitive adhesive.

• Cold b. – a bandage used to apply cold temperature; various methods of application, including ice, and chemical packs; generally used immediately after some injuries in an effort to reduce swelling.

• Crepe b. – a traditional cotton crepe bandage provides padding and protection to the bandaged area, but stretches. Thin, disposable crepe bandages are commonly used to bandage horse limbs.

• Elastic b. – elastic bandages come in many different sizes and lengths. These bandages are sometime called elastic 'roller' bandages, and are sold under various brand names. Elastic bandages typically come in rolls with metal clips, tape, or Velcro® to fasten them in place.

• Esmarch's b. – a rubber bandage applied around the limb from distal to proximal in order to expel blood from it; used to facilitate standing surgery of the distal limb; also known as Esmarch's tourniquet.

• Exercise b. – a bandage applied to the limb of a horse prior to exercise, usually to either protect the limb from hoof trauma (interfering), or to provide 'support' to the limb, in an effort to reduce tendon or ligament fatigue.

• Self-adherent b. – a bandage material that holds fast or sticks to itself but without the use of an adhesive, e.g. self-adherent gauze bandages.

• Spider b. – a bandage made of material that is sliced in on both sides toward the center to leave a series of ties. These ties are then fastened around the affected part. Spider bandages are used to cover areas that bend, such as the knee or hock joints.

• Stable b., aka, Standing b. – stable bandages are often applied to horse limbs overnight, especially after a horse has undergone exercise or competition, usually in an effort to prevent limb swelling.

Care should always be taken to ensure any bandage is not too tight.
See Wound.

Bar ◀ *bar, n.* **1)** rectangular piece of rigid material; **2)** part of upper gum behind incisors (front teeth), where there are no teeth; **3)** part of hoof, where wall of hoof is reflected at heel to run parallel to frog, part of weight-bearing surface.
See Foot.

B. shoe ◀ *bar / shū, n.* special horseshoe with metal bar, either in the heel region or over the frog; variety of applications, mostly for heel-related soreness, or in horses with low heels, where heels may be injured by contact with ground.

Heart b. shoe ◀ *hart / bar / shū, n.* special horseshoe with a metal bar placed over the axis of the frog; has been advocated in the treatment of laminitis, or for conditions where weight redistribution is desired.

Barbiturate ◀ *bar bi tŭr ĕt, n.* drug derived from barbituric or thiobarbituric acid; classified according to duration of action; therapeutic uses in equine veterinary medicine as sedative or anaesthetic agents, include pentobarbital (pentobarbitone), phenobarbital (phenobarbitone), thiopental (thiopentone). Also used as anti-convulsant agent, in the treatment of seizures. Poisoning or overdose causes shallow breathing, lethargy, absence of normal reflexes, coma, death from respiratory failure. High doses may be used for euthanasia (but not if meat is to be used as food, e.g. for hounds).
See Anaesthetic, Euthanasia.

Barker ◄‡ *bar kē, n.* (barker foal) foal suffering from neonatal maladjustment syndrome (Hypoxic ischaemic encephalopathy (HIE)). As classically described, an HIE foal appears normal at birth and progressively loses interest in its surroundings, stops suckling, becomes recumbent, seizures, and may start vocalizing. The vocalization, often accompanied by strenuous respiratory effort, has been described as that of a barking dog, hence the term 'barker' foal.
See Hypoxic ischaemic encephalopathy.

Barley ◄‡ *bar lē, n.* cereal of genus *Hordeum*; the most widely cultivated cereral grain in the world. Barley grain looks similar to, but is harder than, oats. When fed to horses, it is often rolled or crimped first, to rupture case around grain; however, this does not increase feeding value for horses with normal teeth, so benefit of such processing is questionable. Barley tends to be less palatable to horses than oats or corn, so it is commonly used in a grain mix, frequently with added molasses. Barley straw may be used as bedding.
See Grain, Straw.

Baroreceptor ◄‡ *ba rō ri sep tē, n.* sensory nerve ending, stimulated by changes in pressure, e.g. in blood vessel walls.
See Nerve.

Barren ◄‡ *ba rĕn, adj.* infertile, unable to produce young. Barren mare is a mare that is not pregnant after attempts to breed.

Barrier ◄‡ *ba rē ĕ, n.* obstruction.
Blood–brain b. ◄‡ *blud / brān / ba rē ĕ, n.* barrier system separating the blood and the tissues of the central nervous system. Consists of unique endothelial cells having tight junctions and with few structures for fluid transport. Permeable to water, oxygen, carbon dioxide, non-ionic solutes (e.g. glucose, general anaesthetics), but not all drugs or substances can pass from blood into central nervous system.
Gastric mucosal b. ◄‡ *gas trik / mū kō zēl / ba rē ĕ, n.* the physiological property of the lining of the stomach which renders it relatively impermeable to ions. Function is impaired by non-steroidal anti-inflammatory drugs, organic acids, and shock, stress or trauma.
Placental b. ◄‡ *pla sen tēl / ba rē ĕ, n.* placental separation of foetal from maternal blood and bloodborne materials; prevents certain drugs or substances from passing from mare's blood to foetus, or vice versa.

Basal ganglion see Ganglion

Base ◄‡ *bās, n.* lowest part or foundation of anything; in biochemistry, non-acid part of a salt. Presence of bases in blood, and equilibrium with acids, important to maintain normal function. Excessive levels of bases cause alkalosis.
See Acid, Alkalosis.
B. narrow ◄‡ *bās / na rō, n.* describes forelimb conformation where the feet are closer together and more under the body than the shoulders.
B. wide ◄‡ *bās / wīd, n.* the horse stands with its feet placed wider at the shoulders, often associated with a narrow chest; less common than base narrow.
B. of skull ◄‡ *bās / ov / skul, n.* part of skull nearest to junction with neck (cervical vertebrae). Consists mainly of occipital bone and basisphenoid. Fracture may occur in this region following trauma, clinical signs may include head tilt, facial paralysis, depression, incoordination.

Basement membrane ◄‡ *bās mĕnt / mem brān, n.* a sheet of extracellular material on which the basal surfaces of epithelial cells rest; associated with various cells in the body. Of particular interest in the pathology of equine laminitis; it is felt that the first changes associated with laminitis occur in the basement membrane.
See Laminitis.

Basidiobolomycosis ◄‡ *ba si dē ō bo lō mī kō sis, n.* an ulcerative, granulomatous skin disease caused by the fungus *Basidiobolus haptosporus*, a member of class of parasitic fungi called Zygomycetes. No seasonal, age, breed or sex predilections. Occurs in tropical and subtropical areas of the world. Causes large ulcerative skin masses.
See Skin, Ulcer, Zygomycosis.

Basilar sesamoid bone fracture ◀⑤ *ba si lē / se sē moid / bōn / frak tŭr, n.* a fracture through the distal part of one or both of the paired proximal sesamoid bones, behind the equine metacarpophalangeal (fetlock) joint. More common in racing horses.

Basophil ◀⑤ *bā sō fil, n.* white blood cell type, has granular cytoplasm and two-lobed nucleus. Stains with basic dyes. Increased in allergic, inflammatory, and some neoplastic diseases.
See Leukocyte.

Basophilia ◀⑤ *bā sō fi lē ē, n.* an abnormal increase in number of basophils, determined by analysis of blood sample.

Bastard strangles ◀⑤ *bar stēd / strang gŭls, n.* a perhaps unfortunate and archaic term that has become embedded in the veterinary literature, first having appeared in the early nineteenth century. Refers to strangles (infection with *Streptococcus equi*) that has disseminated to lymph nodes throughout the body, especially abdominal lymph nodes, but also brain, lungs, liver, muscle.
See Strangles, *Streptococcus*.

Bay ◀⑤ *bā, adj.* coat colouring, any shade of brown with black mane and tail, and often black lower legs.

Bear's foot ◀⑤ *băz / fŭt, n.* colloquial term used to describe a plant of hellebore family (Green hellebore – *Helleborus viridis*). Hellebores are widely grown in European gardens for decorative purposes, as well as for their purported medicinal abilities and uses in witchcraft. Can cause poisoning if eaten. Signs include tremors, abdominal discomfort, diarrhoea, poor coat, breathing difficulty. NOTE: As per many common plant names, the term 'bear's foot' may not be restricted to a specific species of plant. In this case, at least one member of *Aconitum* spp. is called by the same name; it is also toxic in sufficient dose.

Beat ◀⑤ *bēt, n.* a throb or pulsation, especially of heart or artery; caused by contraction of heart muscle, which propels blood through arteries, causing them to expand in a pulsitile fashion; can be felt, or heard by auscultation.
See Auscultation, Heart.

Bedding ◀⑤ *be ding, n.* material placed in stable or shelter to provide soft, dry lying area, insulate from cold, help keep stable clean. Straw (especially wheat straw), peat moss, sand, wood shavings, rice hulls, shredded paper may be used, among other materials.

Beet pulp (sugar beet pulp) ◀⑤ *bēt / pulp, n.* after sugar is extracted from beets, the remaining pulp may be dried and used as horse feed. Dried beet pulp may be fed by itself, or it can be blended with other substances, such as molasses, to increase the energy content. It may be used as a replacement for grain in the horse's diet. Its energy and fibre content are between, and its protein content similar to, grains and good quality grass hay. It is high in calcium but low in phosphorus and B-vitamins. It is generally fed wet; an association between feeding dry beet pulp and oesophageal obstruction ('choke') has been asserted, but not confirmed.

Behaviour ◀⑤ *bi hā vŭr, n.* deportment or conduct; the way in which horse acts. Much normal horse b. relates to how horses are observed to behave as undomesticated animals; the behaviour of domesticated horses may be affected by housing and confinement, style of management, and handling. General behaviour may be, in part, inherited trait.
Abnormal b. ◀⑤ *ab nor mēl / bi hā vŭr, n.* (also known as vices, but this name suggests fault with horse, whereas most are due to management or training) includes crib-biting, wind-sucking, weaving, rearing, bucking, biting, etc.
See under separate headings.
Eating b. ◀⑤ *ē ting / bi hā vŭr, n.* feral horses graze for a large proportion of a day. Stabled horses should be fed at least twice daily; no advantage has been demonstrated from feeding more than three times daily.
Mating b. ◀⑤ *mā ting / bi hā vŭr, n.* normal: colt may show erection and mounting

behaviour at 6–8 months, but unlikely to successfully mate before 2 years old. Stallion will try to establish that mare is receptive (generally in oestrus) by smelling vulva, curling upper lip (Flehmen reaction). When erection complete, mounts mare from behind, and ejaculates shortly after intromission. If mare not receptive she may kick, bite, etc.
See Oestrus, Pheromone.

Resting b. ◀ res ting / bi hā vūr, n. normal: horse dozes/sleeps for several hours of day, may doze standing up or lying down; for true rapid eye movement (REM) sleep, horse must be lying down. If horse has difficulty lying or rising, or is bullied by other horses in group, resting behaviour may be affected.

Social b. ◀ sō shūl / bi hā vūr, n. normal: herd animal, social interaction important in learning of behaviour. Horses will establish social hierarchy within group. Horses kept in isolation may develop behavioural abnormalities.

Belch ◀ belch, v. eructation; to expel gas from stomach via mouth. Horses do not commonly belch, for two reasons. First, the musculature around the oesophagus as it enters the stomach is quite thick. This band effectively operates as a one-way valve, allowing food to pass down the oesophagus into the stomach as the valve relaxes but the valve squeezes down the opening and cuts off the passage for food going back up. Also, the oesophagus meets the stomach at an angle, which becomes more acute when the horse's stomach is bloated with food or gas.

Belladonna ◀ be lē do nē, n. a perennial plant, 'deadly nightshade', 'death's herb', (Atropa belladonna). Indigenous to central and southern Europe, and cultivated in North America. Contains a variety of anticholinergic alkaloids, including atropine, hyoscyamine, and scopolamine, which have medicinal uses. Ingestion of plant can cause anticholinergic poisoning.
See Atropine, Deadly nightshade.

Belly see Abdomen

Benign ◀ bi nīn, adj. not malignant; not recurrent; favourable for recovery. Term used to describe growths which will not recur once removed, do not infiltrate locally or spread to distant parts of the body. Opposite is malignant.
See Malignant, Tumour.

Benzalkonium chloride ◀ ben zēl kō nē ēm / klor īd, n. ammonium-based compound, used in solution with water or alcohol as surface disinfectant, detergent, and topical antiseptic for preoperative sterilization of hands and arms. Also used as an antimicrobial preservative in ophthalmic solutions.
See Disinfectant, Sterilization.

Benzathine penicillin ◀ ben zē thēn / pe ni si lin, n. combination of penicillin and benzathine, an ammonium-based compound. Marketed as a 'long lasting' penicillin; however, studies have shown that benzathine penicillin offers no therapeutic advantage over the more commonly prescribed procaine penicillin G, either in effectiveness, or dosing frequency.
See Long, Penicillin.

Benzimidazole ◀ ben zi mi dā zōl, n. group of compounds used as anthelmintics, i.e. to treat intestinal worms, e.g. fenbendazole, mebendazole. All of these drugs act in the same fashion, by interfering with the energy-generating mechanisms of the parasites. The drug kills parasites over a two- to three-day period. In increased doses, benzimidazoles also kill parasite larvae (as does ivermectin, another deworming agent). Killing the immature larvae before they reach the adult stage in the intestines is of obvious benefit. Thiabendazole at ten times the normal dose for two days, fenbendazole at one and a half times the normal dose for five days, and oxfendazol at five times the normal dose once have all demonstrated the ability to kill parasite larvae.These drugs have an extremely wide margin of safety and have been tested at up to forty times overdose. Given orally as paste or granules, or as a drench via nasogastric tube. Parasite resistance to benzimidazoles is a problem, especially in Strongylus spp.

See Anthelmintic, *Strongylus* spp.

Benzodiazepine ◄⁞ *ben* zō dī *a* zē pēn, *n.* any of a group of minor tranquillizers with a common molecular structure, and having antianxiety, sedative, hypnotic, and muscle relaxing effect. Diazepam (Valium™) is occasionally used in preanaesthetic drug combinations for horses, but the drugs do not otherwise find wide clinical application in horses.
See Diazepam.

Benzyl benzoate ◄⁞ *ben* zīl / *ben* zō āt, *n.* clear, colourless, oily liquid with a variety of uses; as an antiparasitic insecticide, sometimes used to treat mange, and in an effort to prevent 'sweet itch' (equine allergic dermatitis).
See Mange, *Culicoides* spp.

Benzylpenicillin ◄⁞ *ben* zīl /pe ni si lin, *n.* (penicillin G) crystalline form of penicillin. Penicillin G is typically given by a parenteral route of administration (not orally) because it is unstable in the hydrochloric acid of the stomach and because oral penicillins are not well absorbed by the horse.
See Penicillin.

Bermuda grass ◄⁞ *bē mū dē / grars, n.* a grass used for production of hay. Well adapted to sandy soils; one of the most heavily produced hay crops in the southern United States. High yielding, but loses nutritional value when overly mature.

B.g. impaction ◄⁞ *bē mū dē / grars / im pak shēn, n.* feeding Bermuda grass hay has been associated with a risk of ileal impaction in horses; quality of the hay appears to be a factor, as well.

Beta ◄⁞ *bē tē, β,* second letter of Greek alphabet, used to denote subclass of some chemicals etc., e.g. betaglobulin.
See Globulin.

B. adrenergic receptor ◄⁞ *bē tē / a dren er jik / ri sep tē, n.* adrenergic receptors that respond to epinephrine; divided into β_1 receptors (cardiostimulation) and β_2 receptors (bronchodilation and vasodilation).

B. blocker ◄⁞ *bē tē / blo kē, n.* a class of drugs used for various indications, but particularly for the management of cardiac arrhythmias and cardioprotection after myocardial infarction in humans. A drug that blocks effect of epinephrine on beta-adrenergic receptors in heart muscle and bronchial/blood vessel smooth muscle. Causes slow heart rate and contraction of smooth muscle. Little therapeutic indication in horses. In race horses, beta blockers have been used illegally to alter race outcomes; in horses, running horses would appear normal, but when the heart rate did not increase with exercise, the horses would stop.
See Epinephrine.

B.-carotene ◄⁞ *bē tē / ka rō tēn, n.* beta-carotene is a vitamin A precursor that has been recommended by some as a vitamin A supplement in pregnant mares; however, research suggests that supplemental beta-carotene does not affect the reproductive function of mares fed adequate dietary carotene (green forage or pasture).

B. haemolysis ◄⁞ *bē tē / hē mo li sis, n.* breakdown of red blood cells in culture media by certain *Streptococcus* bacteria, seen as zone of clear growth medium around colony of *Streptococcus* when cultured on blood agar. Used to identify the type of bacteria.
See *Streptococcus.*

Betadine see Povidone-iodine

Betaglobulinaemia ◄⁞ *bē tē glo bū li nē mē ē, n.* increase in beta fraction of globulins in blood. May be seen during serum protein electrophoresis testing in horses with parasitic infections caused by both large strongyle and *Cyathostomum* worms.
See Cyathostome, Globulin.

Betamethasone ◄⁞ *bē tē me thē zōn, n.* potent anti-inflammatory corticosteroid used by intravenous, intramuscular injection or injection directly into a joint (intra-articular), also available as eye drops. For uses and side effects see corticosteroid.
See Anti-inflammatory, Corticosteroid.

Bethanecol ◄⁞ *be than i kol, n.* a cholinergic agonist used to stimulate smooth muscle contraction in the bladder and gastrointestinal tract; has found occasional use in the treatment of oesophagitis, urinary incontinence, gastroduodenal ulcers, and for stimulation of GI motility post-surgery.

Bi- ◀⁞ *bī, prefix.* two, twice or double.

Bicarbonate ◀⁞ *bī kar bĕn āt, n.* any salt containing HCO_3; blood bicarbonate levels are an indication of the alkali reserve and are useful in determining acid–base balance.
B. of soda see Sodium bicarbonate (below).
Sodium b. ◀⁞ *sō dē ĕm / bī kar bĕn āt, n.* $NaHCO_3$; base used in the treatment of a variety of equine disorders, including chronic renal failure, congestive heart failure, and metabolic acidosis. Was once a first line treatment for equine exertional myopathy ('tying up', rhabdomyolysis) because of a perceived lactic acidosis, but, in fact, affected horses have been shown to have a metabolic alkalosis with this condition. Thus, administration of sodium bicarbonate to horses with exertional myopathy is unwise unless the acid–base status of the horse has been determined. 'Milkshakes' of sodium bicarbonate and other substances have been administered to horses prior to racing, in an effort to buffer lactic acid as it appears in the blood as a result of muscle metabolism. This practice has not been shown to affect performance, but the practice is dangerous, and has been outlawed in many racing jurisdictions.
See Acid, Acidosis.

Biceps ◀⁞ *bī seps, n.* muscle with two heads.
B. brachii ◀⁞ *bī seps / brā kē ī, n.* two-headed muscle of forelimb, runs from scapula to radius, causes flexion of elbow joint.
B. femoris ◀⁞ *bī seps / fe mĕr ris, n.* two-headed muscle of hind limb, one of hamstring muscles at caudal part of thigh. Runs from sacrum and pelvis to tibia, causes flexion of stifle joint.
See Pelvis, Stifle, Tibia.
B. tendon ◀⁞ *bī seps / ten dĕn, n.* tendon of origin of biceps brachii muscle, runs through intertubercular groove at shoulder end of humerus, and is protected from rubbing on

bone here by a fluid-filled sac, the bicipital bursa.
See Biceps brachii (above), Bicipital bursa, Bursa, Humerus, Tendon.

Bicipital bursa ◀⁞ *bī si pi tēl / ber sĕ, n.* a bursa occurring under the tendon of the biceps brachii muscle on the central ridge of the bicipital groove of the humerus; bursa extends around tendon.
See Bursa.
B. bursitis ◀⁞ *bī si pi tēl / ber sī tis, n.* inflammation of bicipital bursa. Caused by trauma or infection. Uncommon cause of forelimb lameness; signs include pain, especially on direct palpation, and on flexion of shoulder, short stride, stumbling. The bursa can be imaged ultrasonically to assist in diagnosis. Treatment options include rest, cold therapy, local injection, and surgery.
See Bursa.

Bicuspid ◀⁞ *bī kus pid, adj.* having two projecting points or cusps; e.g. bicuspid (mitral) valve of heart (between left atrium and left ventricle); premolar teeth in humans.
See Heart, Tooth.

b.i.d. *abbr. bis in die* (Latin), twice a day. Used in prescriptions, to indicate a dose should be given twice daily.

Big head see Nutritional: N. secondary hyperparathyroidism

Big leg see Lymphangitis

Bilateral ◀⁞ *bī la tĕr rūl, adj.* with two sides, or affecting both sides, e.g. a bilateral eye condition affects both eyes.

Bile ◀⁞ *bīl, n.* green–yellow or brown fluid secreted by liver, passes along bile ducts to small intestine. Horse has no gall bladder (unlike other domestic animals), so bile not stored. Main constituents include bile salts (taurocholate, chenodeoxycholic acid, glycocholic acid), bile pigments (bilirubin, biliverdin), cholesterol, phospholipids, electrolytes. Important digestive functions:
• bile salts play an essential role in fat absorption by dissolving the products

of fat digestion into water soluble colloid particles called *micelles*, which can then be absorbed;
- alkalinizes the intestinal content;
- aids absorption of fat and fat-soluble vitamins.

See Bilirubin, Biliverdin, Digestion, Peristalsis.

B. acids ◄⁞ *bīl / a̱ sids, n.* bile acids produced by liver cells act as a biological detergent. In the duodenum, bile acids help allow for fats to be made soluble, digested, and absorbed. In a liver that is functioning normally, bile acids are continually recycled via the *enterohepatic* circulation. If any part of this recycling loop is disrupted, there will be a change in the levels of circulating bile acids. Bile acids can be helpful in detecting a number of conditions, including identifying chronic liver damage prior to the onset of icterus, monitoring returning hepatic function after liver disease has occurred, and for assessing the severity of acute hepatic injury. If the horse is already showing signs of severe liver disease, with icterus (jaundice), bile acids will not provide any additional information, however. Once the animal is showing signs of icterus, bile acids will be elevated, as well.
See Enterohepatic circulation, Icterus.

B. duct ◄⁞ *bīl / dukt, n.* tube which carries bile from liver, opens into small intestine. Within liver, small bile canaliculi drain into bile ductules, which in turn drain into hepatic ducts. These unite at the porta hepatis (fissure on surface of liver, where hepatic blood vessels enter/leave) to form bile duct.
See Liver.

Biliary ◄⁞ *bi lē ē rē,* adj. pertaining to bile or bile ducts.

B. atresia ◄⁞ *bi lē ē rē / ā tre̱ ze̱ ē, n.* bile ducts do not form properly, very rare congenital condition.

B. calculus ◄⁞ *bi lē ē rē / ka̱l kū lēs, n.* (cholelith, gallstone) rarely occurring condition. In horses, biliary calculi are mostly composed of calcium bilirubinate. Typically, they are associated with inflammation of the bile ducts (cholangitis), which accounts for the fever that typically accompanies the condition. If the calculi obstruct bile flow, they also cause increased biliary pressure,

which presents as colic. If long-standing, this pressure can cause liver cell death and liver fibrosis. Biliary calculi should be considered as a possible diagnosis in horses with a history of fever, icterus and abdominal pain, especially if accompanied by signs of hepatic disease. Ultrasound of the liver is helpful in securing a diagnosis; however the site of obstruction usually cannot be seen by ultrasound, thus, the calculi are generally only found by palpation at surgery. Obtaining a liver biopsy is useful for diagnostic, therapeutic and prognostic purposes.
See Colic, Liver, Ultrasonography.

B. fever see Babesiosis

B. tract ◄⁞ *bi lē ē rē / trakt, n.* the organs and ducts involved in production and transport of bile, i.e. liver and bile duct. Damage or obstruction usually causes increased enzyme levels on serum chemistry tests, especially gamma glutamyl transferase (GGT) and alkaline phosphatase.
See Alkaline phosphatase, Enzyme, Gamma, Liver.

Bilirubin ◄⁞ *bi lē ru̱ bin, n.* bile pigment; formed primarily from breakdown of haemoglobin when red blood cells are destroyed by cells in liver. Most excreted in faeces, and a little in urine (as urobilinogen). High concentrations of bilirubin result in icterus (jaundice).
See Bile, Haemoglobin, Icterus.

Bilirubinaemia ◄⁞ *bi lē ru̱ bin e̱ mē ē, n.* presence of bilirubin in blood. If biliary tract damaged or obstructed, or excessive destruction of red blood cells occurs, increased levels of bilirubin may be found, resulting in clinical signs of icterus (jaundice).
See Bile, Red blood cell.

Fasting hyperb. ◄⁞ *fa̱rs ting / hī per bi lē ru̱ bin e̱ mē ē, n.* in horses that have been without feed, bilirubin levels normally rise to above normal ranges. Exact cause unknown; appears to be of hepatic origin.

Bilirubinuria ◄⁞ *bi lē ru̱ bin ŭr rē ē, n.* presence of bilirubin in urine, indicates liver disease.
See Liver.

Biliverdin ◀╎ *bi lē ver din, n.* the initial green bile pigment from the catabolism of haemoglobin; converted to bilirubin in liver.

Bioassay ◀╎ *bī ō a sā, n.* method of determining strength of drug by comparing its effect in an animal or isolated organ preparation with that of standard preparation of drug.

Biocide ◀╎ *bī ō sīd, n.* substance that destroys living organisms.

Biological ◀╎ *bī o lo ji cūl, adj.* pertaining to biology; also, a term generally used to describe medicines prepared from living organisms or their products, especially vaccines or antitoxins.

Biometry ◀╎ *bī o m e trē, n.* the science of the application of statistical methods to biology and medicine.

Biopsy ◀╎ *bī op sē, n.* removal and examination (microscopic) of tissue from living animal, for diagnostic purposes.
- Aspiration b. – biopsy in which the tissue is obtained by applying suction through a needle that is attached to a syringe.
- Core b. – biopsy with a large, hollow needle that extracts a core of tissue.
- Excisional b. – biopsy of tissue removed by excision; biopsy of an entire lesion, usually including some normal tissue (as in cancer diagnosis).
- Punch b. – biopsy in which skin is obtained using a sharp circular punch.

Biotin ◀╎ *bī ē tin, n.* member of vitamin B complex (sometimes called vitamin H). Important in formation of keratin (protein in skin, hair and hooves), dietary supplementation may be of benefit in horses with weak, crumbly, cracked hooves. Initial investigations in pigs concluded that biotin supplementation improved hoof quality in that species. Subsequently, a few studies in the 1980s, done in horses, suggested that biotin could help improve the resilience and quality of the hoof in that species. Since hoof grows from the coronary band down to the ground, and biotin is only incorporated into growing hoof, it may be several months before any effect from biotin supplementation is seen in the horse's hoof, if an effect is seen at all. Neither biotin toxicity nor biotin deficiency have been reported in horses.

Birdsville horse disease ◀╎ *berdz vil / hors / di zēz, n.* condition seen in desert areas of Australia, caused by eating poisonous plant, *Indigophera* spp. (*linnaei, dominii, enneaphylla*). The plant contains a toxic amino acid, indospicine, an analogue of the amino acid arginine. Disease causes primarily neurological symptoms: circling, dramatic incoordination, somnolence and toe-dragging; affected animals may lift and extend their front legs in an exaggerated fashion. May progress to convulsions and death. Horses need to graze the plant for about 10 days before clinical signs appear. May be prevented by feeding arginine-rich diet, e.g. peanut meal, alfalfa.
See *Indigofera.*

Birth see Parturition

Birth canal ◀╎ *berth / kē nal, n.* route foetus passes along from uterus through cervix, vagina, vulva, to outside. Contained within pelvis of mare.

Birth defect see Defect

Bishop ◀╎ *bi shēp, v.* after five years, the age of a horse can only be guessed at by examination of the teeth. Deceitful individuals may 'bishop' the teeth of older horses, that is scoop out the incisors, in order to imitate the cups that occur in the incisors of young horses.

Bismuth compounds ◀╎ *biz mēth / kom pōnds, n.* (subsalicylate, carbonate, etc.) bismuth compounds are found in commonly used antacids and antidiarrhoeal products. In horses, such compounds have been used for the treatment of conditions including gastric ulceration, intestinal parasitism, non-steroidal anti-inflammatory drug toxicity, and salmonellosis. Since bismuth compounds are messy, and large doses of bismuth compounds are generally prescribed at frequent intervals in horses, their use in the horse is often limited due to the time, expense and mess involved with treatment. Bismuth pastes are also available, but their dose is almost certainly too small to have any significant treatment effect.

Bisphosphonate ◀╏ *bī fos fen āt, n.* bisphosphonates (also called diphosphonates) are drugs that inhibit the resorption of bone. The drugs were first developed in the nineteenth century, but it was not until the 1960s that they were first investigated for use in disorders of human bone metabolism; their mechanism of action was not demonstrated until the 1990s. In Europe, the bisphosphonate drug tiludronate is approved for the treatment of navicular syndrome in horses.
See Navicular syndrome, Tiludronate.

Bit ◀╏ *bit, n.* the usually metal part of bridle which fits in mouth, over tongue. Allows control of horse via reins.
   B. resentment ◀╏ *bit / rē zent mēnt, n.* behaviour seen when horse will not cooperate when bit is placed in mouth. May be behavioural; also associated with dental disease or other painful conditions of mouth.

Bite ◀╏ *bīt, v./n.* the forceable closure of the upper teeth against the lower teeth; the measure of that closure; a morsel of food; a wound or puncture caused by teeth.
See Tooth.

Black locust ◀╏ *blak / lō kĕst, n.* Black locust grows as a tree or shrub in open woods, waste places, and along fence rows throughout the midwestern United States. Several toxic compounds are found in black locust sprouts, leaves, bark, flowers, and seed pods, including a glycoside (robitin) and phytotoxins (robin and phasin). Horses are most susceptible to the effects of black locust. Poisoning and death have been reported for horses consuming bark, leaves, or sprouts. Affected animals often stand with feet spread apart. Other signs include depression (often extreme), diarrhoea, anorexia, weakness, posterior paralysis, colic, pupil

dilation, coldness of extremities, laminitis, weak pulse, and rapid, irregular heart beat. In severe cases, death can result from cardiac failure.

Black walnut ◀╏ *blak / wawl nut, n.* Black walnut is a large tree growing in rich forest soils. The toxic phenolic compound juglone is found in the bark, wood, nuts, and roots of black walnut. Horses are primarily affected when exposed to shavings that contain black walnut wood. Shavings contaminated with black walnut can cause poisoning in 24 hours. Affected horses exhibit depression, lethargy, laminitis, distal limb oedema, and increased temperature, pulse, respiration rate, abdominal sounds, digital pulse, and hoof temperature. Consumption of the shavings may also cause signs of mild colic. Signs usually disappear within a few days after shavings are removed.
See Laminitis.

Bladder ◀╏ *bla dē, n.* any membranous sac, such as one serving as a receptacle for a secretion; usually refers to urinary bladder, a hollow distensible sac within pelvic cavity.
See Urinary tract, Urine.
   B. calculi ◀╏ *bla dē / kal kū lī, n.* (cystic calculi) bladder calculi ('stones'), primarily formed of calcium carbonate. May form in any part of the urinary tract, but are most commonly found in the bladder. The factors responsible for calculi formation are not well understood, but include urine pH; formation is favoured under alkaline conditions and with inadequate water intake. There appears to be no breed or sex predilection. Affected horses urinate frequently, with straining or dribbling of urine. Diagnosis may involve rectal palpation, urinalysis, catheterization or endoscopy. Surgical removal is the only effective method of treatment for large stones. Preventive measures include acidification of the diet, control of dietary minerals, and adequate sources of drinking water.
   B. distension ◀╏ *bla dē / dis ten shĕn, n.* overfilling of bladder, so that wall is stretched. May occur if urethra blocked by calculus (stone); can cause abdominal pain with colic-like signs.

B. incontinence ◀˧ _bla dē / in kon tin ēns, n._ inability to control the excretory functions of the bladder; rare problem in horses, usually with a neurological cause, including from lumbosacral trauma, equine herpes virus 1 myeloencephalitis, and Sudan grass toxicity. Treatment is supportive; often accompanied by recurrent infections. Can recover gradually, especially if a specific cause can be determined and treated.

B. infection ◀˧ _bla dē / in fek shēn, n._ infections of the bladder may occasionally develop as a result of colonization of infectious bacteria in the urethra or bladder. The bacteria can proliferate rapidly, because the bladder does not have a protective bacterial flora. Antibiotic therapy (sulfas, penicillins) is usually highly effective at eliminating the problem, although recurrent infections can be problematic. Relatively uncommon in horses.

B. neoplasia ◀˧ _bla dē / nē ō plā zē ē, n._ tumour of bladder wall, rare in horse. May be diagnosed by cystoscopy (examination of inside of bladder with fibreoptic endoscope).
See Endoscope, Tumour.

B. rupture ◀˧ _bla dē / rup tŭr, n._ tearing of bladder wall; most commonly seen in foals (primarily male foals) after parturition, possibly associated with birth trauma, or because of congenital abnormality of bladder development. Occasionally occurs in adult horses, in mares during foaling, or in male horses through blockage of urethra by calculus (stone). Causes uroperitoneum (bladder in abdominal cavity), distended abdomen, pain may cause loss of appetite, rapid breathing and heart rate, may strain to pass urine. Diagnosis by sampling peritoneal fluid (high in creatinine), ultrasonography, dye placed in bladder recovered from peritoneal fluid, radiography.
See Peritoneal, Radiography, Ultrasonography.

Urinary b. ◀˧ _ŭr in ēr ē / bla dē, n._ urine travels from kidneys, down ureters into bladder, where stored until voided by contraction of muscular bladder wall and relaxation of bladder sphincter. Bladder may hold up to 5 litres urine. Bladder wall has inner mucous membrane, loose submucosal tissue, thick muscular layer and incomplete peritoneal covering. Sphincter is muscular ring at exit of bladder into urethra.

Blasto- ◀˧ _blas tō, prefix._ Denoting a relationship to bud, or budding. Often used in terminology describing early stages of embryo development.
See Embryo.

Blastocyst ◀˧ _blas tō sist, n._ early embryo, consisting of cell mass and fluid-filled cavity.
See Embryo.

Blastula ◀˧ _blas tū lē, n._ very early stage of development of embryo, formed from dividing, fertilized ovum. Consists of blastoderm (cell mass) and blastocoele (fluid-filled cavity).
See Embryo.

Bleb ◀˧ _bleb, n._ small amount of fluid under skin; a blister; e.g. small amount of local anaesthetic under skin.

Bleed ◀˧ _blēd, v._ to emit or lose blood; to escape oozing or flowing, as from a wound. May also be used to describe taking a blood sample (to 'bleed' a horse).
See Haemorrhage.

Bleeder ◀˧ _blē dē, n._ term for horse that develops clinical signs of nosebleeds (epistaxis). Blood most commonly originates from lungs (exercise-induced pulmonary haemorrhage), but may also come from auditory tube diverticulum (guttural pouch), nasal passages or throat. Common problem in high performance horses, e.g. Thoroughbred racehorses.
See Epistaxis, Exercise-induced pulmonary haemorrhage.

Blepharitis ◀˧ _ble fē rī tis, n._ inflammation of eyelids. Numerous causes, including injury, bacterial infection (e.g. _Moraxella equi_), parasites (e.g. _Onchocerca, Habronema_), allergic reactions, flies and other biting insects, radiation from sun (in horses with unpigmented eyelids).
See _Habronema, Moraxella equi, Onchocerca._

Blepharospasm ◀˧ _ble fē rō spazm, n._ tonic muscular contraction of eyelid muscles, producing more or less complete closure of the eyelids. Seen especially in painful conditions of eye (e.g. corneal ulceration, uveitis). Often accompanied by lacrimation. See Eye, Eyelid.

Blind ◀◜ *blīnd, adj.* not having the sense of sight, in reference to scientific trials, blinding refers to being done without knowledge of particular information that could cause bias, e.g. researchers may be *blind* as to whether a procedure was performed before attempting to determine the outcome of that procedure.

Blind staggers ◀◜ *blīnd / sta gerz, n.* colloquial term, used to describe the appearance of horses exposed to certain toxic plants, especially members of *Astragalus* and *Oxytropis* spp., and from chronic ingestion of selenium-accumulating plants. Affected animals wander aimlessly, circle, and appear to be blind, sometimes even bumping into objects in their way. See Locoweed, Selenium.

Blindfolding ◀◜ *blīnd fōld ing, v.* diagnostic technique in horses with suspected vestibular disease (relating to the inner ear); horses that have compensated for their disease will show a head tilt and ataxia when blindfolded. Also used as a method of overcoming fear in horses; nervous or anxious horses may follow a handler if the horse is blindfolded; technique has been used in emergency situations (e.g. stable fire) or to facilitate trailer loading. See Vestibular disease.

Blindness ◀◜ *blīnd nis, n.* inability to see, may be unilateral (one eye) or bilateral (both eyes), sudden or gradual in onset. Many causes including:
- head trauma;
- chronic uveitis (inflammation of the middle layer of the eye, consisting of the iris, ciliary body and choroid coat);
- inflammation of optic nerve (optic neuritis);
- trauma to eye;
- retinal detachment.
See Eye, Optic, Retinal, Uveitis.

Blister ◀◜ *blis tē, n.* a fluid-filled elevation of the epidermis. Also, an irritant ointment applied to horse's leg with the intention of producing healing of tendons or joints. Numerous studies have demonstrated that the technique is ineffective and not capable of being effective; causes no changes in target tissues; humane concerns have been raised.

Blister beetle ◀◜ *blis tē / bē lel, n.* beetles in the Coleoptera family Meloidae are commonly known as blister beetles. They are known as 'blister beetles' because they secrete cantharidin, a poisonous chemical causing blistering of the skin and painful swelling. Several common species feed on alfalfa plants used for hay crops; beetles may get crushed during the haymaking process and baled in hay. Cantharidin is very stable and remains toxic in dead beetles. The substance is comparable to cyanide and strychnine in toxicity. Animals are poisoned by ingesting beetles in cured hay. If eaten by horses cantharidin is absorbed through the intestine and can cause clinical signs such as inflammation, colic, straining, elevated temperature, depression, increased heart rate and respiration, dehydration, sweating, and diarrhoea. In the first 24 hours after ingestion horses urinate frequently, accompanied by inflammation of the urinary tract. This irritation may also result in secondary infection and bleeding. Blood calcium levels may be dramatically lowered and heart muscle tissues destroyed. Affected animals can die within 72 hours; there is no effective treatment. The best way to deal with blister beetles is through management practices to keep fields from being attractive, and by use of haymaking practices that avoid crimping. See Calcium, Cantharidin, Colic.

Bloat ◀◜ *blōt, v.* abdominal distension due to excessive gas formation; usually accompanied by colic signs. Numerous causes, including simple obstruction of the intestines; grain overload; exhaustion, with secondary intestinal shutdown; secondary to diarrhoea. See Colic, Diarrhoea.

Block ◀﹦ *blok, n.* obstruction; regional anaesthesia.

Heart b. ◀﹦ *hart / blok, n.* impairment of conduction of an impulse in heart excitation, either permanent, or transient, due to an anatomical or functional impairment; e.g. second degree atrioventricular blocks in normal resting horses.
See Heart.

Joint b. ◀﹦ *joint / blok, n.* local anaesthesia caused by injecting a volume of local anaesthetic into joint space, removing sensation from joint; diagnostic technique in equine lameness evaluation.
See Joint.

Nerve b. ◀﹦ *nerv / blok, n.* regional anaesthesia caused by making an injection of local anaesthetic in close proximity to a nerve whose conductivity is to be cut off; diagnostic technique in equine lameness evaluation.
See Nerve block.

Blood ◀﹦ *blud, n.* red fluid circulating through the heart, and in arteries, capillaries and veins. Carries oxygen and nutrients to tissues, and metabolites away from tissues for excretion; transports hormones. Composed of plasma, a pale yellow, protein-rich fluid, approx. 65%, which carries the microscopically visible components of blood, and cells (approx. 35%), made up of erythrocytes (red corpuscles), leukocytes (white corpuscles) and platelets.
See Erythrocyte, Leukocyte, Plasma, Platelet.

B.–brain barrier see Barrier

B. cell ◀﹦ *blud / sel, n.* one of the formed elements of the blood; erythrocyte, leukocyte, or platelet.
See Erythrocyte, Leukocyte.

B. count ◀﹦ *blud / cônt, n.* Analysis of cellular elements of blood; a common diagnostic test for many diseases and infections. Usually given as number of cells per millilitre of blood.
See Erythrocyte, Leukocyte.

B. culture ◀﹦ *blud / kul tūr, n.* test to determine presence of bacteria in blood (bacteraemia), by incubating a blood sample in appropriate medium (usually broth). Test may lack sensitivity, and bacteraemia is frequently intermittent, so often several samples must be taken at intervals.
See Bacterium.

B. dyscrasia see Dyscrasia

B. flow ◀﹦ *blud / flō, n.* passage of blood through vessels. In arteries is pulsatile, blood is pushed by contraction of heart. In veins is dependent on muscular movement, respiration and arterial pressure. Normal blood flow in large vessels is laminar (concentric laminae that slide over each other, middle moving fastest). Turbulent blood flow causes murmur (e.g. in heart defect).
See Heart.

B. gas analysis ◀﹦ *blud / gas / ē na li sis, n.* measurement of oxygen and carbon dioxide levels in blood. Performed on arterial blood; useful in monitoring critically ill foals, in assessment of metabolic status; can assist in diagnosis of respiratory conditions, especially of lower respiratory tract; used to monitor animals under general anaesthesia. Also used to assess acid–base balance. Sample collected into lithium–heparin-coated syringe, with all air bubbles removed. Needle capped with rubber stopper, and sample analysed within 30 minutes (or 2 hours if kept on ice).
See Acid.

B. poisoning ◀﹦ *blud / poi zēn ing, n.* lay term for presence of pathogenic microorganisms or their toxins in blood (septicaemia).
See Septicaemia.

B. pressure ◀﹦ *blud / pre shē, n.* the pressure of blood against the walls of any blood vessel, usually measured in mm of mercury (Hg); dependent on the energy of the heart action, the elasticity of the walls of the arteries, and the volume and viscosity of the blood. During contraction of heart (systole), arterial pressure is high (approx. 120 mmHg), during relaxation of heart (diastole) arterial pressure is lower (approx. 80 mmHg). Venous pressure generally only about 5 mmHg. Blood pressure generally not routinely evaluated in horse. Arterial blood pressure may be monitored during anaesthesia. There are two arterial blood pressures:

- Systolic b.p. – the pressure of blood inside walls of arteries when the blood is being driven by a contracting heart (systole).
- Diastolic b.p. – the pressure of blood inside walls of arteries when the heart is at rest (diastole).

See Heart.

B. sample ◀ *blud / sarm pel, n.* small volume of blood, generally collected from superficial vessel, for analysis. Blood usually collected into hypodermic syringe or special vacuum tube. Blood may be collected into plain tube, or one containing anticoagulant, depending on what is to be analysed. Anticoagulants used include:

- EDTA – blood counts
- lithium–heparin – plasma biochemistry, e.g. proteins, urea, creatinine
- sodium citrate – blood clotting tests
- fluoride oxalate – blood glucose.

Advice from laboratory analysing blood samples should be followed as regards which samples should be collected and how they should be treated (e.g. separation of plasma/serum from cells).

B. supply ◀ *blud / se pli, n.* volume of blood carried in vessels to an organ. If blood supply is cut off, organ may undergo destruction through lack of blood (ischaemic necrosis).

See Ischaemia.

B. test ◀ *blud / test, n.* Any one or more of a number of analyses of a blood sample; used in diagnosis of diseases, pregnancy, immune status, etc. Many different tests may be performed, depending on information needed, including:

- complete blood count: red blood cells, white blood cells, platelets;
- red blood cells: total count, haemoglobin, haematocrit (packed cell volume), mean corpuscular volume (MCV), mean corpuscular haemoglobin (MCH), mean corpuscular haemoglobin concentration (MCHC);
- total and differential white blood cell count: neutrophil, eosinophils, basophils, monocytes, lymphocytes;
- blood biochemistry: serum proteins, blood urea nitrogen (BUN), various enzymes, creatinine, sodium, potassium, calcium, phosphate, glucose, glycerol, bilirubin;
- other: e.g. hormones, pregnancy diagnosis, immune status, blood clotting.

See tests under individual entries.

B. transfusion see Transfusion

B. type ◀ *blud / tip, n.* (blood group) red blood cells and serum proteins have hereditary antigen characteristics which allow blood to be divided into types or groups.

- Red blood cell groups: A, C, D, K, P, Q, T and, U; can be further divided into factors. These are similar to A, B, AB, and O groups found in humans. However, unlike human blood groups, each of the equine blood groups can exist in one of several forms. For example, a horse that has type A blood may mean type aA1, type aA', type aH, type aA'H, or type a. And, in addition to having a blood type from the A family, a horse may also have a type from each of the other seven groups. Over 30 different erythrocyte antigens have been identified in horses.
- Serum protein systems: albumin (AL), transferrin (TF), esterase (ES), PR, 6PGD and PGM, can be further divided into factors.

Combination of systems and factors can help establish parentage of horse.

Blood typing is especially important in human blood transfusions, where blood of donor must be tested with that of recipient (cross-matching), to ensure that antigens of blood type are compatible, and that donor blood will not cause adverse reaction in recipient; however, in horses, the first transfusion to a recipient that has not received prior blood transfusion (or had an incompatible pregnancy) is generally well tolerated because antibodies to foreign blood cells in normal horses are generally rare and react weakly. In lieu of testing in a life-threatening situation, a one- or two-year-old horse of either sex, with no history of blood transfusion or plasma therapy, is likely to be the best potential donor.

See Transfusion, Cross-matching, Neonatal.

B. urea nitrogen see BUN

B. vessel ◀ *blud / ve sel, n.* any of the vessels through which blood travels round body: artery, arteriole, capillary, vein, venule.

See Artery, Capillary, Vein.

B. volume ◀ *blud / vo lum, n.* the plasma volume added to the volume of blood cells; total quantity of blood in body. Relatively constant; affected by regulatory mechanisms of fluid exchange at capillaries and hormonal control of fluid excretion in kidneys.

See Kidney, Shock.

B. worm ◀ *blud / werm* (also, bloodworm), *n.* lay term for intestinal parasites with larval stages that migrate in, and sometimes cause

damage to, blood vessels, e.g. *Strongylus vulgaris, S. edentatus, S. equinus.*
See *Strongylus.*

Bloodroot ◀ᴇ *blud / rŭt, n. (Sanguinaria canadensis)* bloodroot preparations in low concentrations have been used as a mouthwash in humans. Sanguinarine, the primary compound food in bloodroot, appears to have antimicrobial, antifungal, anti-inflammatory, and antihistamine activity. In horses, a product said to be useful in the treatment of skin cancers is available. However, this product also contains high concentrations of zinc chloride, a caustic chemical (see zinc chloride). There is no evidence that bloodroot alone has any effectiveness in the treatment of cancer. Indeed, during the mid-1800s, topical preparations of bloodroot extracts were used unsuccessfully for treatment of human breast tumours.

Bloodstock ◀ᴇ *blud / stok, n.* a special variety of domesticated animals within a species; especially as applied to horses bred and kept for racing; especially Thoroughbreds and Standardbreds.

Blowfly ◀ᴇ *blō flī, n.* fly of Calliphoridae family. Larvae of most species are scavengers of carrion and faecal material, and most likely make up the majority of the maggots found in such material. Some species may lay eggs on wounds, and maggots may develop in tissue (blowfly strike). The primary screwworm, a type of blowworm, once was a major pest in the southwestern United States, but has been eradicated by the release of huge numbers of sterilized males. Blowfly maggots have been employed successfully in wound management, as they debride necrotic tissue. The name blowfly comes from an older English term for meat that had eggs laid on it, which was said to be fly blown.

Blue-green algae ◀ᴇ *blŭ-grēn / al gē, n.* blue-green algae (one of eleven groups of algae) are microscopic plants that grow mainly in brackish ponds and lakes throughout the world. Of the more than 1500 known species, some are useful as food, while others have been reported to cause gastroenteritis and hepatitis. Various products are available, with claims that they were effective against a wide range of health problems. These claims are unsupported by any good research in horses. See Algal bloom.

Body condition ◀ᴇ *bo dē / kon di shēn, n.* a subjective assessment of the horse's overall appearance and health. Body condition scoring systems have been developed in an effort to provide a standard scoring system which can be used across breeds and by all horse people, as opposed to vague words such as 'good', 'fair', 'bad', or 'poor'. Most popular systems assign a score to a particular body condition, from 1 (poor) to 9 (extremely fat).

Body weight ◀ᴇ *bo dē wāt, n.* weight of animal, important in calculation of dosage of medication. Average adult horse approx. 450 kg (but obviously great variability according to breed and body condition).

Bog spavin ◀ᴇ *bog / spa vin, n.* old term describing fluid swelling in hock joint; acute or chronic; fluid visible most easily as fluctuant swelling in front of joint. Lameness may be present, depending on cause. Many causes, including injury, infection, osteochondrosis.
See Hock, Osteochondrosis.

Boil ◀ᴇ *boil, n.* a painful, swollen nodule formed in the skin by localized inflammation of skin tissues or hair follicle.
   Shoe b. ◀ᴇ *shŭ / boil, n.* a swelling on the point of the elbow, traditionally thought to occur from trauma occurring due to contact with the branches of a horseshoe when the horse lies down.

Bolus ◀ᴇ *bō lēs, n.* a rounded mass of food which is ready to swallow; a pharmaceutical preparation for swallowing.

Bone ◀ᴇ *bōn, n.* hard form of connective tissue which makes up the majority of the skeleton. Composed of organic component (collagen matrix and cells), and mineral, principally calcium phosphate (85%) and calcium carbonate (10%). Mineral provides bone with its rigidity.

Covered by a tough outer membrane (periosteum). Calcium phosphate component constantly replaced (about every 200 days). Structure arranged as series of fine canals (Haversian canals) which contain blood vessels and nerves. Two main types of bone structure:

- Compact bone – consists of closely packed structural units called osteons or Haversian systems. This unit is made up of a central canal called the osteonic (Haversian) canal, which is surrounded by concentric rings (lamellae) of collagen matrix. The bone cells (osteocytes) are located in spaces called lacunae, between the matrix rings. In compact bone, the osteons are packed tightly together to form what appears to be a solid mass, penetrated only by interconnected blood vessels which communicate with vessels on the surface of the bone. In long bones, compact bone forms a strong tube with central cavity filled with bone marrow.
- Cancellous (spongy) bone – is lighter and less dense than compact bone. Spongy bone consists of plates (trabeculae) and bars of bone next to small, irregular cavities that contain red bone marrow. These cavities connect to the adjacent cavities to receive their blood supply (instead of to a central canal). The plates are organized to provide maximum strength similar to braces that are used to support a building. The trabeculae of spongy bone follow the lines of stress and can realign if the direction of stress changes. Short bones (e.g. facial bones) and the ends of long bones are made up of cancellous bone. See Bone marrow (below).

B. cyst ◀ *bōn / sist, n.* although not technically a cyst, by strict definition (there is no secreting epithelial lining), bone cysts are abnormal fluid-filled cavities in bone, usually occurring just under articular cartilage (i.e. in subchondral bone). Any number of joints may be affected, including medial femorotibial (in stifle joint), carpus, pastern, elbow, shoulder, hock. Mostly thought to occur as abnormality of cartilage development; perhaps because of injury to articular cartilage or underlying bone. Often causes lameness, depending on lesion site and size; diagnosed by radiography. See Cartilage, Cyst, Radiography.

MAJOR BONES *(horses usually have 205 bones)*

Forelimb – typically, 20 bones
Scapula
Humerus
Radius and ulna
Carpus (knee) normally contains seven small bones; an eighth is present in some individuals
Metacarpus (cannon bone) – III metacarpal bone; splint bones are II and IV (medial and lateral respectively) metacarpal bones
1st, 2nd and 3rd phalanx bones (digit)

Hind limb – typically, 19 bones
Pelvis (ilium, ishium and pubis)
Femur
Tibia and fibula
Metatarsal (cannon bone) – III metatarsal bone; splint bones are II and IV (medial and lateral respectively) metatarsal bones
1st, 2nd and 3rd phalanx bones (digit)

Axial skeleton
Skull (34 bones, main ones: frontal bone, nasal bone, maxillary bone, parietal bone, temporal bone, mandible)
Vertebrae (cervical, thoracic, lumbar, sacral, caudal)
Ribs and sternum

B. graft ◀℥ *bōn / grarft, n.* bone tissue transplanted from one site to another; usually performed to aid healing, e.g. in repair of fractures. Bone usually from same animal (autogenous graft), from various sites.

B. marrow ◀℥ *bōn / ma rō, n.* soft material in cavities of bones, two types: yellow (mostly fatty tissue) and red (blood vessels, connective tissue, fat and blood-producing cells). Site of formation of red bood cells (erythrocytes), platelets (thrombocytes), and many white blood cells (B lymphocytes, monocytes and other leukocytes). Blood cells at all stages of development are present in bone marrow. Production of cells increased when demand is high: infection will cause increased production of white cells; blood loss will cause increased production of red blood cells.
See Erythrocyte, Leukocyte.

B. m. biopsy ◀℥ *bōn / ma rō / bī op sē, n.* sample of bone marrow obtained by aspiration (sucked up in a needle) or as a core (cut with large gauge needle). Sampling sites include sternebrae (ventral midline between forelimbs), tuber coxae of pelvis or ribs. Histological examination of bone marrow used for diagnostic purposes; aspirated material can be used to make smears for cytological analysis; core biopsies are typically fixed and stained.
See Cytology, Histology.

B. m. suppression ◀℥ *bōn / ma rō / sē pre shēn, n.* failure of production of all cell lines (i.e. red blood cells, white blood cells and platelets). May be seen in aplastic anaemia, phenylbutazone toxicity, haematopoietic neoplasia (i.e. cancer of blood cell precursors).
See Aplastic anaemia, Phenylbutazone.

B. plate ◀℥ *bōn / plāt, n.* surgical tool used to assist in the healing of fractured bones. Fractures are first set, then held in place using titanium and stainless steel plates screwed into the bone while healing occurs.

B. scan see Scintigraphy

B. screw ◀℥ *bōn / scrū, n.* surgical tool used to assist in the healing of fractured bones. Bone screws may be used to hold bone plates in place, or may be used by themselves to stabilize fractures or perform surgical arthrodesis of bones of the lower limb.
See Arthrodesis.

B. spavin ◀℥ *bōn / spa vin, n.* bony swelling of medial hock joint caused by osteoarthritis. Normally causes lameness; usually exacerbated after hind limb flexion (spavin) test (this flexion test is not specific for this condition). Horses with palpable bone spavin may also be sound if the fusion has resulted in ankylosis of the affected joint(s). Diagnosis by radiography.
See Hock, Osteoarthritis, Radiography.

Booster ◀℥ *bûs ter, n.* second or subsequent dose of an immunizing agent; given to prolong protection against disease.
See Vaccine.

Boot ◀℥ *bût, n.* an enclosing or protective casing or sheath; protective material (often leather or polyurethane) affixed to lower limbs to protect against injury, e.g. brushing boot strapped to cannon bone/ fetlock to reduce injury from hoof of opposite leg, or to provide 'support' (e.g. to attempt to reduce lower limb extension). An almost unlimited number of boots available, mostly named according to the anatomical part over which they fit (e.g, hock boot, splint boot) or their purpose (e.g. shipping boot).

Borborygmus ◀℥ *bor bor rig mēs, n.* a rumbling noise caused by the propulsion of gas, fluid or food in intestines. Can be heard with stethoscope, or sometimes with naked ear. May increase or decrease in a variety of conditions; not specifically diagnostic, however.
See Diarrhoea, Colic.

Bordetella spp. ◀℥ *bor dē tel ē / spē shēs, n.* a Gram-negative bacterium that occasionally infects primarily the lower airways in horses.

Boric acid ◀℥ *bor rik / a sid, n.* white crystalline acid. Solution obtained from its salts and used occasionally as a weak antiseptic on intact skin, mucous membranes, and cornea. Poisonous when ingested.

Borium ◀℥ *bor rē ēm, n.* a generic name for tungsten carbide crystals which have been embedded in a carrier material. Borium is sometimes applied to horseshoes in an effort to provide traction. Borium usually is found as steel or brass tubing with a matrix of tungsten carbide crystals in it, and in some horseshoe nails. The element boron is called borium in a number of languages; it is a different material entirely.

Borna disease ◀℥ _bor_ nē / di zēz, _n_. an intectious neurological disease, originally identified in sheep and horses in Europe. The name comes from the town of Borna, in Saxony, Germany, which suffered an epidemic of the disease in horses in 1885. The virus occurs in a wide range of warm-blooded animals and has been found in Europe, Asia, Africa, and North America. It is the most important viral disease of the central nervous system of German horses.

INFECTION
It is generally assumed that the virus enters the horse's body by intranasal infection, through olfactory (smell) nerve endings. After an incubation period, during which the virus disseminates throughout the central nervous system, an immune-mediated meningitis and encephalitis develops. Clinical signs vary but can include excitation or depression, 'pipe smoking' (hay in mouth, but no chewing), ataxia, excessive movement, unusual ear positions, and abnormal posture. Natural infection can result in peracute, acute, or subacute disease, which leads to death in 1 to 4 weeks after the onset of clinical signs. Mortality rates in horses are in excess of 80%.

TREATMENT
There is no specific therapy available for the treatment of horses with Borna disease. One report recommended use of the antiviral drug amantadine sulphate; however, this is controversial. Filtration of cerebrospinal fluid was used to successfully treat two horses.

PREVENTION
Vaccination was practised for many years in Germany; however, the efficacy of the vaccine was questionable, and vaccination was generally abandoned. Newer vaccine technology is being investigated.

Bot ◀℥ _bot_, _n_. The horse bot is a honey bee-sized fly that glues its tiny yellow eggs (nits) to body hairs of horses, donkeys and mules. The larvae of flies of four major species: horse bot fly, _Gasterophilus intestinalis;_ nose bot fly, _Gasterophilus haemorrhoidalis;_ throat bot fly, _Gasterophilus nasalis_, and rarely, in Europe, _Gastrophilus pecorum_. Flies active beginning in early summer, and into autumn, in temperate regions. Female flies lay up to 1500 eggs, primarily on hairs of horse's forelegs; eggs stimulated to hatch by self-grooming of horse. Larvae penetrate mucosa of mouth and migrate to stomach where live for 10–12 months. Third stage larvae passed in faeces in spring, pupate on ground, adult flies emerge after 1–2 months.

CLINICAL SIGNS
Flies can cause nuisance when laying eggs – horses may react frantically, possibly from noise. Small numbers of bots may not cause health problems, but increasing populations cause gastrointestinal problems. Infestations can produce signs such as: irritation of stomach membranes; stomach ulceration; peritonitis; perforating ulcers; colic; mechanical blockage of stomach with stomach rupture; and squamous cell tumours. First stage larvae migrating in the tongue and gums have been shown to cause pus pockets in the mouth. The larvae developing in the stomach can also cause anaemia. Rarely may get aberrant migration, e.g. to central nervous system. See Migration, Stomach.

Botryomycosis ◀℥ _bo_ trē ō mī kō sis, _n_. an infectious bacterial skin granuloma; uncommon disease caused by bacteria which are usually inoculated into wound at time of injury; the organism elicits a response from the host, but the host is only able to contain the organism, not eradicate it. Characterized by non-healing chronic granulomatous lesions at site of wound (especially on leg or at site of castration). Diagnosis confirmed by skin biopsy; the causative organism is identified by bacterial or fungal culture. Surgical excision or wide debulking followed by long-term anti-microbial therapy has been most successful. The term botryomycosis

is technically wrong; the disease is not normally caused by a fungus.
See Castration, *Staphylococcus*.

Botulism ◀ː <u>bo</u> tū lizm, n. disease caused by ingestion of toxin from *Clostridium botulinum*, which may be present in decaying vegetable matter (e.g. spoiled big bale silage) and animal carcasses (e.g. feed contaminated with carcass). More rarely, *C. botulinum* may be ingested and produce toxin as part of infection. Also known as 'shaker foal syndrome'.

CLINICAL SIGNS
Toxin blocks neuromuscular junction, i.e. stops impulses travelling from nerves to muscles. Clinical signs variable: sudden death, acute onset of flaccid paralysis, trembling, progressive weakness, pharyngeal paralysis causing difficulty with swallowing, flaccid tail and tongue, recumbency, respiratory difficulty; death is almost always from respiratory failure. Clinical diagnosis is usually made by history and clinical signs after exclusion of other possibilities. Definitive diagnosis may be made based on identification of toxin in serum, faeces, gastrointestinal contents, or feed. Electrophysiological testing may be helpful, but equipment is rarely available and interpretation of results requires considerable experience.

TREATMENT
An antitoxin against *C. botulinum* toxin is available and clearly effective if administered early in the course of disease. Polyvalent and monovalent antitoxins are available. Antimicrobial treatment is usually not required. Respiratory support (ventilation, oxygen) may be required in foals. Nutritional support is often indicated. Survival rate in treated foals approaches 90%; in adults, horses that remain standing have a good prognosis for recovery, although full recovery may take months. Adult horses that become recumbent have a poor prognosis, due to secondary effects of prolonged recovery on the musculoskeletal and respiratory systems.

PREVENTION
Appropriate vaccination is thought to be almost 100% effective in adult horses; foals may get disease in spite of vaccination, if infection overwhelms the available immunity (foals have immature immune systems at birth, and may not respond well to early vaccination).
See *Clostridium*.

Bowed tendon ◀ː bōd / <u>ten</u> dēn, n. lay term for injury to deep and superficial flexor tendons and/or their sheaths (tendonitis, tenosynovitis) of forelimb. Seen as swelling and pain on palpation in tendon area behind cannon bone.
See Tendinitis, Tendon, Tenosynovitis.

Box ◀ː boks, n. (*Buxus sempervirens*) ornamental shrub or hedge; originally European, but widely grown in North America. Contains poisonous alkaloid, with as yet undetermined mode of action. Most poisonings occur when clippings are fed to animals, or if box hedges are placed around horse enclosures. Approximately 1.5 pounds of green leaves may be fatal to horse. If eaten may cause severe enteritis, colic, haemorrhagic diarrhoea, pain, and convulsions can be expected. In acute toxicity, death results from respiratory failure.

Bowel ◀ː bōl, n. intestines.
See Small intestine, Large intestine.

Brace ◀ː brās, n. liniment; 'bracing', in the sense of invigorate or freshen.

Brachial ◀ː <u>brā</u> kē ūl, adj. related to the foreleg.
    B. plexus ◀ː brā kē ūl / <u>plek</u> sēs, n. important group of nerves, originating from last four cervical and first thoracic spinal nerves, contains principal nerves supplying shoulder and foreleg.
    See Nerve.

Brachy- ◀ː <u>bra</u> kē, prefix. short.

Brachygnathism ◀ː <u>bra</u> kig <u>nā</u> thizm, n. (parrot mouth, overshot mouth) short mandible, causes upper incisor teeth to lie in front of lower incisors, and may affect ability to graze if severe. May make wear of cheek teeth uneven, and may cause sharp hooks to form on teeth.
See Tooth.

Brachytherapy ◀ *bra kē the rē pē, n.* form of radiotherapy, where source of radiation is implanted in animal, e.g. as seeds or needles. Sources for irradiation include radioactive gold, cesium, cobalt and iridium.
See Radiotherapy.

Bracken fern ◀ *bra kēn fern, n.* (*Pteridium aquilinum*) ubiquitous fern plant contains toxin (thiaminase), causes poisoning if eaten from chronic thiamine deficiency. Horses may eat bracken if other forage is scarce or poor quality (e.g. late summer) or if bracken fern used for bedding. Clinical signs often not seen until plant has been eaten for several months. Toxin causes degeneration of myelin coating of peripheral nerves.

CLINICAL SIGNS
Initially, bracken fern-induced thiamine deficiency is characterized by a noticeable loss of body condition and weight, in spite of a good appetite, and incoordination. If not treated, the disease will progress, and the horse will display a crouching stance, and lose muscular control; it may lie down, become recumbent, and seizure. Ultimately, death follows, in several days to several weeks after the onset of clinical signs.

TREATMENT
For successful treatment, signs must be recognized early. At this point, removing the bracken fern may be enough. Aggressive thiamine administration may be helpful.

PREVENTION
The best method of prevention is to keep good pastures, eliminate bracken fern from fields, and check to make sure that bracken fern is not present in hay.
See Nerve, Vitamin B-1.

Bradycardia ◀ *bra dē kar dē ē, n.* relatively slow heart rate; may be pathological or physiological.
See Heart.

Bradykinin ◀ *bra dē kī nin, n.* peptide released in damage to tissue, acts to dilate blood vessels (vasodilator), constrict smooth muscle, stimulate pain receptors.

Brain ◀ *brān, n.* part of central nervous system contained within cranium; weight approx 650 g in adult horse. Made up of grey and white matter, generally with grey matter on surface. Grey matter composed largely of nerve cells and blood vessels. White matter contains nerve fibres which connect to nerve cells in grey matter. Brain covered by meninges, three layers of membrane: pia mater, arachnoid, dura mater (latter lines bones of cranium). Small amount of fluid (cerebrospinal fluid) lies between arachnoid and pia mater. Main segments of brain:

- Cerebrum – largest part, composed of two hemispheres joined by corpus callosum, the most important line of union for left and right cerebrocortical cross-talk; outer layer of grey matter (cortex; this area is responsible for sensory perception, issuing motor commands, and generating thought). Each hemisphere divided into lobes. Olfactory bulb at front of each hemisphere, carries impulses about smell from nose. Hemispheres contain basal ganglia, thalamus, hypothalamus, pituitary. Cerebrospinal fluid contained within lateral ventricles (cavities within hemispheres).
- Brainstem – nerve tissue at base of brain, includes midbrain, pons, medulla oblongata.
- Cerebellum – composed of two hemispheres. Responsible for regulating skeletal muscle activity to produce smooth, accurate movements.

B. abscess ◀ *brān / ab ses, n.* localized collection of pus within brain tissue. Very rare. Rarely a primary disease, rather, associated with extension to brain from primary infection site, such as in strangles (*Streptococcus equi*) or glanders (*Pseudomonas mallei*), or from extension from other structures in the head (e.g. sinuses, middle ear infection, trauma, tooth root abscess). Signs variable, caused by septic meningitis or pressure on brain from expanding abscess, include fever, depression, head pressing, circling, wandering, blindness (on opposite side from lesion), excitement. Diagnosis from history, clinical signs, neurological examination, with goal of neuroanatomic localization of

lesions, blood tests (neutrophilia, hyperfibrinogenaemia), cerebrospinal fluid analysis (changes can be minimal or non-specific). There are at least two reports of magnetic resonance imaging (MRI) being used for diagnosis of brain abscesses in horses. Early recognition, long-term anti-microbial therapy, anti-inflammatory therapy, and surgical intervention have been common features in horses that have survived.
See Abscess, Cerebrospinal, Glanders, Pus, Strangles.

B. disease see Encephalitis, Meningitis

B. haemorrhage ◀፥ *brān* / *he mē rij, n.* bleeding within brain tissue, associated with injury, e.g. kick, rearing into ceiling, running into tree, etc.
See Brain trauma (below).

B. trauma ◀፥ *brān* / *tror mē, n.* (concussion) injury to brain tissue, caused by kick, running into obstacle, etc. Signs seen depend on which part of brain damaged, include coma, depression, walking in circles, head tilt, seizures, blindness, weakness.

B. tumour ◀፥ *brān* / *tū mē, n.* cancer (neoplasia) within brain. Very rare in horse; may rarely cause blindness, due to pressure on optic nerves, located just above pituitary gland, and depression. Note: Cushing's disease, enlargement of the pituitary gland, is not a neoplastic process.
See Pituitary pars intermedia dysfunction.

Bran ◀፥ *bran, n.* outer coat (husk) of cereal grain; wheat bran most commonly fed to horses. Included in horse diet as source of fibre, as a palatable treat, or as a remedy for colic. First introduced to horses as a possible hay substitute in the nineteenth century; diets too high in bran may affect bone (nutritional secondary hyperparathyroidism; 'Big head') because bran is low in calcium, high in phosphorus.
See Diet, Nutritional.

B. disease see Nutritional

Branch ◀፥ *brarnch, n.* division or offshoot from main stem; in anatomy describes blood vessels, nerves, etc.

Break see Fracture

Breakover ◀፥ *brāk ō vē, n.* that time during the horse's stride when the heels leave the ground and start to rotate around the toe of the hoof, which is still in contact with the ground. Initiated by the deep digital flexor muscle, in conjunction with various ligaments. Many shoeing and trimming techniques purport to affect breakover; little evidence that any are effective.

Breast ◀፥ *brest, n.* anterior aspect of the thorax; front part of chest, in front of forelegs (pectoral region).

B. bone ◀፥ *brest* / *bōn, n.* sternum. Keel-shaped bone runs along centre of chest.
See Sternum.

Breath ◀፥ *breth, n.* air taken into lungs during inspiration, and pushed out of lungs in expiration.

Bad b. ◀፥ *bad* / *breth, n.* (halitosis) unpleasant smell of breath; subjective; may be sign of colic, constipation, sinusitis, guttural pouch problem, tooth problem, pneumonia.
See Colic, Pneumonia, Sinusitis, Tooth.

B. sounds ◀፥ *breth* / *sōnds, n.* normal breathing sounds are produced by turbulent airflow in the trachea and bronchi. They vary in intensity depending on the portion of the lung that is being auscultated; they are often heard more easily on the right side of the horse than on the left. Sounds increased with intensity of breathing (after exercise, with fever) or in thin animals (less fat cover to muffle sounds). Abnormal breathing sounds – or absence of breathing sounds – associated with various diseases of the respiratory tract, e.g, wheezing and crackling with chronic obstructive pulmonary disease (COPD), or friction rubs with pleuropneumonia.

Breathing ◀፥ *brē thing, v.* alternate taking in and expulsion of air through expansion and contraction of chest (thorax) and diaphragm; ventilation.
See Respiration.

Breech ◀፥ *brēch, n.* abnormal presentation of foal at birth; posterior presentation, with hips flexed, and buttocks or hocks arrive first.
See Dystocia.

Breed ◀╎ *brēd, n./v.* group of animals within species, presumably related by descent from common ancestors, which are similar enough to produce similar-looking offspring when mated with each other; to propagate sexually, and usually under controlled conditions; reproduce. See Behaviour, Reproduction.

Breeder's stitch ◀╎ *brēd ēs / stitch, n.* a single, large diameter, suture, often of umbilical tape, placed near the ventral limits of the dorsal vulvar aperture to protect the vulva from tearing at breeding. Suture material and position is designed to protect the stallion's penis from injury, as well.

Breeding ◀╎ *brē ding, v.* mating.
  B. hobble ◀╎ *brē ding / hob ūl, n.* hind leg hobbles used in breeding that prevent mare from kicking stallion.
  See Hobble.
  B. management ◀╎ *brē ding / ma nij mēnt, n.* breeding of horses often intensively managed, especially where horses not naturally bred; date of breeding important for certain breeds (e.g. Thoroughbred).
  See Behaviour, Oestrus, Reproduction.
  B. roll ◀╎ *brē ding / rōl, n.* a long padded cylinder, often with a leather cover, placed dorsal to a stallion's penis at intromission to prevent complete entry of the entire length of the penis (and subsequent injury to the mare).
  B. season ◀╎ *brē ding / sē zĕn, n.* mares have a season in which they can be successfully bred. In spring, increasing daylight stimulates receptors in the brain, which stimulate production of reproductive hormones that initiate regular periods of oestrus ('heat'). These periods continue through the summer, but normally cease with decreasing daylight in autumn or early winter.

Bridle ◀╎ *brī dl, n.* headgear used for control of horse, made up of reins, headstall and bit. May occasionally cause injury, especially if too tight or if chafes skin.

Brisket ◀╎ *bri skit, n.* area of chest over sternum (breast bone).

Broken wind see Recurrent airway obstruction

Brome grass ◀╎ *brōm / grars, n.* a cool season, perennial, smooth bladed pasture grass, drought resistant, on well drained soils of silt/clay basis. Used for early pastures and haying. Does particularly well when seeded with alfalfa.

Bromocryptine ◀╎ *brō mō krip tēn, n.* an ergot alkaloid dopamine agonist. Slows dopamine turnover and inhibits prolactin secretion. Has been used in horses to encourage cessation of lactation; as a treatment for equine pituitary pars intermedia dysfunction (PPID, Cushing's disease).
See Dopamine, Ergot, Pituitary pars intermedia dysfunction, Prolactin.

Bromosulphthalein ◀╎ *brō mō sulf thā lēn, n.* BSP; phenolphthalein dye used to assess liver function. Clearance (i.e. rate its level falls in blood) prolonged in liver disease. Because pharmaceutical grade BSP is no longer commercially available, test is limited to research institutions.
See Liver.

Bronchi ◀╎ *brong kē, n.* plural of bronchus.
See Bronchus.

Bronchial ◀╎ *brong kē ūl, adj.* pertaining to bronchus.
See Bronchus.

Bronchiectasis ◀╎ *brong kē ek tar sis, n.* chronic dilation of the bronchi, characterized by bad breath, coughing, and mucopurulent excretions.

Bronchiole ◀╎ *brong kē ōl, n.* small branch of bronchus within lung.
See Bronchus, Lung.

Bronchiolitis ◀╎ *brong kē ō lī tis, n.* inflammation of bronchioles, small airways fill with fluid and inflammatory cells. Associated with infections by various microorganisms.
See Bronchiole, Cough, Equine herpes virus.

Bronchitis ◄⁞ *bron kī tis, n.* inflammation of a bronchus or bronchi; may be associated with inhalation of dust/smoke, or infection with microorganisms. May occur as acute or chronic condition:

- Acute – associated with viral infections, recurrent airway obstruction (RAO), or allergic reactions; signs of infection include high temperature, nasal discharge, loss of appetite, rapid breathing, and cough; COPD or allergic reactions typically not accompanied by fever or loss of appetite.
- Chronic – bronchitis marked by long duration, by frequent recurrence over a long time, and often by slowly progressing seriousness. Associated especially with recurrent airway obstruction (RAO). Signs include coughing, sometimes in spasms, nasal discharge, weight loss.

See Bronchus, Cough, Recurrent airway obstruction.

Bronchoalveolar lavage ◄⁞ *brong kō al vē ō lē / lav arzh, n.* (BAL) technique for obtaining samples of secretions from lower airways. A process whereby a sterile tube is passed through one nostril of the horse into the peripheral airways; a large volume of sterile saline is quickly injected and withdrawn from the air passages through the tube. This sample is then analysed microscopically for both the total number of cells present and the number and percentage of each cell type present (i.e. macrophages, lymphocytes, neutrophils, eosinophils, and mast cells); results of BAL analysis reflect the type of disease process.
See Alveolus, Bronchus, Recurrent airway obstruction, Cytology.

Bronchoconstriction ◄⁞ *brong kō kon strik shūn, n.* constriction or narrowing of the air passages, most commonly as a result of bronchial smooth muscle contraction.

Bronchodilator ◄⁞ *brong kō dī lā tē, n.* drug which causes bronchi to dilate (open up); e.g. epinephrine, clenbuterol: causes smooth muscle in bronchial walls to relax. Bronchodilators may be used in treatment of chronic obstructive pulmonary disease,

or in any condition where improved airway mechanics is a goal of therapy.
See Bronchus, Recurrent airway obstruction, Clenbutarol, Epinephrine.

Bronchopneumonia ◄⁞ *brong kō nū mō nē ē, n.* inflammation and infection of bronchi and lungs, which typically become clogged with exudates; occurs with infections of the respiratory tract. Signs include rapid breathing, cough, wheezes heard on auscultation.
See Auscultation, Bronchus, Cough, Equine influenza, Pneumonia.

Bronchoscopy ◄⁞ *brong kos kē pē, n.* examination of bronchial tree with endoscope. Horse may be sedated, endoscope passed through nose to larynx, and then down trachea to bronchi. Bronchoscopy can be used to ascertain whether discharge is unilateral or bilateral, in diagnosis of inflammation, collapse, foreign bodies, lungworms (*Dictyocaulus arnfieldi*), tumours. Diagnostic samples may be obtained through endoscope.
See Bronchus, *Dictyocaulus arnfieldi*, Endoscopy.

Bronchus ◄⁞ *brong kēs, n.* any of the larger air passages of the lungs. A main bronchus enters each lung and divides further into smaller bronchi (form bronchial tree), which divide into bronchioles (terminate in alveoli). Bronchus has wall of smooth muscle with cartilage plates, lined by ciliated mucous membrane which contains mucus-producing goblet cells.
See Cilium, Lung, Mucus, Trachea.

Broodmare ◄⁞ *brūd măr, n.* female horse kept for production of foals.
See Breeding, Reproduction.

Brown-Adson forceps ◄⁞ *brōn / ad sēn / for seps, n.* a thumb forceps used to facilitate tissue handling in surgery.

Brucella abortus ◄⁞ *brū se lē / ē bor tēs, n.* Gram-negative rod bacterium. Causes brucellosis. Zoonosis. Has been eradicated from Britain. (Named after Sir David Bruce, bacteriologist.)
See Brucellosis.

Brucellosis ◄≀ *brŭ si lō sis, n.* infection with *Brucella abortus*, rare in horses. May cause abortion; naturally occuring infections of the carpal bursa and withers have also been described ('Fistulous withers'), associated with fever, stiffness and lethargy.
See Abortion, *Brucella abortus*, Fistulous withers.

Bruise ◄≀ *brŭz, n./v.* an injury transmitted through unbroken epidermal tissue to underlying tissue, which causes rupture of small blood vessels and escape of blood into the tissue; discoloration may result depending on skin colour and location of injury; to cause a bruise to form.

Bruised sole ◄≀ *brŭzd / sōl, n.* contusion (bruising) of the solar cushion and corium (the soft tissues between the sole of the hoof and the third phalanx (coffin bone)). Causes rupture of local small vessels, resulting in haematoma, inflammation and pain. Sole bruises are a commonly diagnosed cause of lameness; clinical signs include variable degrees of sudden lameness, heat in the foot, or increased character of the digital pulses (felt at the digital arteries behind the pastern). Sole bruising is often associated with riding, especially on hard or rocky ground, and frequently attributed to the horse stepping on stones or rocks (stone bruise). Aggressive trimming of the protective horn tissue may make the foot vulnerable to bruising, and poorly fitted horseshoes may increase pressure on the sole. Heavier horses may be more prone to bruising than lighter horses. Bruising is also commonly seen in association with chronic cases of laminitis. Examination of a bruised sole with hoof testers will yield a painful response; the sole is then examined for areas of discoloration, or for abscesses, with a hoof knife. Radiographs may show underlying pathology (e.g. rotation of the third phalanx in laminitis). Treatment is often no more than allowing a few days for the pain to resolve; additional treatments, such as soaking the foot, poulticing, etc., may not provide any real therapeutic advantage. Horses that bruise their soles chronically may benefit from a protective pad interposed between the sole and the horseshoe.
See Foot.

Bruit ◄≀ *brŭ it, n.* any of several abnormal sounds or noises heard during auscultation.
See Auscultation, Heart.

Brush ◄≀ *brush, v.* strike medial side (inside) of fetlock and coronet with hoof of opposite leg; interfere. Can cause injury, can protect against injury by use of protective boots strapped to legs.
See Boot, Gait, Interfering.

Brush border ◄≀ *brush / bor dē, n.* specialized surface of some cells made of minute finger-like processes, which greatly increases cell surface area for absorption. Seen in intestines, and convoluted tubules of kidney.

Buccal ◄≀ *bu kēl, adj.* pertaining to, or directed towards, the cheek.

Buccotomy ◄≀ *bu co tē mē, n.* surgical incision of cheek. May be performed to gain access to cheek teeth, e.g. for extraction of tooth. Also, an old and rejected method of treating cribbing in horses, consisting of the surgical creation of a permanent buccal fistula.

Buck ◄≀ *buk, v.* spring into the air with arched back. Performed by horse, often in an attempt to unhorse rider.

Bucked knee ◄≀ *bukt / nē, n.* deformity of knee joint (carpus), knee is displaced forwards (i.e. appears constantly flexed). Severity varies considerably. Numerous causes, including congenital, and post-trauma (usually one leg only). May be seen in foals, mild cases will often resolve spontaneously by 6 months of age. In more severe cases, splinting, casting, oxytetracycline administration, or surgery (especially check ligament desmotomy or transaction of ulnaris lateralis and flexor carpi ulnaris tendons) may be required. In mild cases, prognosis favourable; in more severe cases, prognosis is guarded for athletic performance.

Bucked shin ◀ *bukt / shin, n.* (sore shins) stress damage to dorsal (anterior) cannon bone (third metacarpal bone) associated with stress caused by intense exercise; seen mainly in young Thoroughbred racehorses in training (2–5 years old). Dorsal cortex of bone suffers compression and undergoes microfractures and callus formation. Area of front of cannon bone is painful, swelling may be felt and horse may be lame.

TREATMENT
Mild cases respond to rest, with gradual return to exercise. Chronic cases can be more difficult, and may require extended rest (4–6 months), or various surgeries (e.g. dorsal cortical drilling). The myriad other treatments available (e.g. electrical stimulation, 'shock wave' therapy, freezing, pinfiring, blistering, steroid injection, etc.) reflect both the fact that many cases resolve spontaneously (in spite of treatment), and others may not respond well to any treatment.

PREVENTION
Distinct training strategies have been described that greatly reduce the incidence of bucked shins, with recommendations to focus training efforts more on short-distance breezing and less on long-distance galloping.
See Callus, Cannon, Fracture.

Buckwheat ◀ *buk wēt, n.* (*Fagopyrum* spp.) cereal plant. Can sometimes cause photosensitization: substances in plant enter skin after absorption from intestines, and when sunlight interacts with these substances, the skin is damaged. Signs include redness and swelling of unpigmented skin, which may blister and slough. Horse will recover if removed from source of plant and kept out of sun.
See Photosensitization.

Buffer ◀ *bu fẽ, n.* a chemical system that prevents change in the concentration of another chemical substance; e.g. the bicarbonate ions and dissolved carbon dioxide in the horse's body, which helps determine the pH of the blood.

Buffy coat ◀ *bu fẽ / kōt, n.* the superficial layer of yellowish or buff coagulated plasma seen in blood samples from which the erythrocytes have separated; the layer of blood cells in a separated, anticoagulated blood sample that contains leukocytes.

Bulbourethral gland ◀ *bul bō ŭr rē thrēl / gland, n.* male accessory sex gland, one of two glands at the level of the pelvic inlet in male horse. Size: 4 cm x 2.5 cm. Secretes seminal plasma, which lubricates and provides nourishment for sperm, into urethra.
See Semen, Sperm, Urethra.

Bulb of heel ◀ *bulb / ov / hēl, n.* two oval bulges on posterior of the hoof at the coronary band, above where frog joins to walls of hoof. May be bruised or lacerated in horse that over-reaches (i.e. hind hooves hit fore hooves in gait).
See Foot.

Bulla ◀ *bū lē, n.* large (>5 mm) raised skin lesion containing watery fluid.
See Blister.

Bull-nosed foot ◀ *būl–nōzd / fũt, n.* foot with hoof rasped at front, so toe is short and squared in appearance.
See Foot.

Bullous pemphigoid ◀ *bū lēs / pem fi goid, n.* rare autoimmune skin disease, i.e. caused by autoantibodies produced by horse against own skin and mucous membranes. Causes large blisters (bullae) in mouth, junctions between skin and mucous membrane, skin (especially axilla and inguinal region). Pain, itching, inappetence, fever and salivation are common. Diagnosis by biopsy of lesions. Long term corticosteroid therapy has been employed in treatment.
See Autoimmune, Biopsy, Bulla, Pemphigous foliaceus.

BUN *abbr.* blood urea nitrogen (also termed SUN, serum urea nitrogen). A blood serum test that measures the amount of urea nitrogen (a breakdown product of protein metabolism) in the blood. Levels typically elevated in kidney disease; may also elevate in dehydration.
See Kidney.

Bundle ◄ *bun dūl, n.* group of muscle or nerve fibres; e.g. muscle bundle is one of the primary subdivisions of a muscle, made up of muscle fibres and separated from other muscles by fascia. See Heart.

Burn ◄ *bern, n./v.* injury to tissues caused by contact with dry heat (fire), moist heat (steam or hot liquid), electricity, certain chemicals (especially corrosive substances), friction, or radiation; to cause damage to tissues by heat, etc. Classification:
- First-degree: affects only top-most layers of skin, causes reddening, layers affected may be lost by sloughing, but are quickly replaced from below.
- Second-degree: involves epidermal layer and some of underlying dermis, other structures within skin affected, e.g. sweat glands, hair follicles.
- Third-degree: extending through the skin and nerves and including vascular tissue. Full thickness skin sloughs.

Extensive burns can cause severe fluid loss and shock; burn infections can be quite serious and may progress to septicaemia.
See Graft, Shock, Skin, Toxaemia.

Bursa ◄ *ber sē, n.* fluid-filled sac or sac-like cavity, situated at places in tissues where friction might otherwise occur; e.g. allows tendon to move smoothly over bone. Many around body; of particular note in horse:

Atlantal b. ◄ *at lan tēl / ber sē, n.* bursa between ligamentum nuchae and rectus capitis dorsalis major muscle; when inflamed or infected, described as 'poll evil'.

Bicipital b. ◄ *bī si pi tēl / ber sē, n.* (intertubercular bursa); bursa located between the tendon of origin of the biceps brachii muscle and the tubercles of the cranioproximal aspect of the humerus.

Cunean b. ◄ *kū nē ēn / ber sē, n.* bursa located between the medial tendon of the tibialis cranialis muscle (cunean tendon) and the distal tarsal bones.

Navicular b. ◄ *na vi kū lē / ber sē, n.* bursa between the navicular bone and the deep digital flexor tendon, in the horse's foot.

Olecranon b. ◄ *o le kra nēn / ber sē, n.* bursa located over olecranon tuberosity; when infected or inflamed, described as 'capped elbow'.

Subcutaneous calcaneal b. ◄ *sub kū tā nē ēs / kal sā nē ūl / ber sē, n.* bursa above tuber calcis, on the point of the hock; when infected or inflamed, described as 'capped hock'.

Supraspinous b. ◄ *sup rē spīn ēs / ber sē, n.* bursa over the spinous processes of the withers; can become inflamed, or infected ('fistulous withers').

Bursitis ◄ *bē sī tis, n.* inflammation of bursa.
See Bursa.

Buscopan® ◄ *bus kē pan, n.* (n-butylscopolammonium bromide) an antispasmodic drug used to relieve colic pain that is caused by painful spasms in the muscles of the gastrointestinal or genitourinary tract. In horses, the drug has been approved for use in Europe for more than 20 years. It was approved for use in horses in the United States in 2005. Buscopan® works by relaxing smooth muscle that is found in the walls of the stomach, intestines and bile duct (gastrointestinal tract) and the reproductive organs and urinary tract (genitourinary tract). If the muscles go into spasm, such as can occur in certain types of colic, this can cause pain. Buscopan® stops the spasms in the smooth muscle by preventing the neurotransmitter acetylcholine from acting on the muscle. It does this by blocking the receptors on the muscle cells on which the acetylcholine would normally act. By preventing acetylcholine from acting on the muscle in the GI and genitourinary tracts, Buscopan® reduces the muscle contractions, spasms, and cramps. By relaxing intestinal muscles, Buscopan® may also be used to help make it easier to do rectal exams on reluctant horses. Smooth muscle is also found in the iris, or coloured portion, of the eye, and administration of Buscopan® can cause the eye to dilate, facilitating a visual examination of the back of the eye.
SIDE EFFECTS: Buscopan® also usually causes a temporary increase in the heart rate for about an hour after administration. This is not harmful to the horse.
See Colic.

Butorphanol ◀⊱ *bū* <u>tor</u> *fē nol, n.* Butorphanol is a synthetic opioid analgesic (pain-relieving) drug for the horse. It comes as a sterile solution that is most commonly used intravenously. Butorphanol has been shown to be effective for the relief of pain arising from colic in experimental situations, with relief lasting up to four hours. Butorphanol is not as effective as the sedative-analgesic drugs xylazine or detomidine at relief of abdominal pain; however, it has little sedative effect, so it is sometimes combined with the other drugs to provide increased analgesic effects. Clinical experience suggests that this combination of drugs also tends to reduce the horse's reaction to external stimuli when compared with the sedative effects of xylazine or detomidine alone. There are no controlled studies on the use of butorphanol in breeding horses, weanlings or foals. Toxic effects of butor-phanol are not seen until the dosage is exceeded by twenty times.
See Colic, Sedation.

Button ◀⊱ *bu tĕn, n.* knob-like structure; e.g. used in equine anatomy to describe distal ends of splint bones (2nd and 4th metacarpal and metatarsal bones).
See Splint bone.

Buttress foot ◀⊱ *bu trĕs / fŭt, n.* a deformity of the hoof and an alteration in the normal angle of the distal interphalangeal (coffin) joint; a condition of periostitis and osteitis in the region of the pyramidal process of the os pedis, usually preceded, but sometimes followed, by fracture of the process; causes enlargement at front of foot at coronary band.
See Foot, Third: T. phalanx.

Buxus sempervirens see Box

C

Cachexia ◀⋲ _kē kek sē ē, n._ profound debility, general ill health, wasting. May be seen in association with malnutrition or chronic disease, e.g. cancer.
See Chronic, Malnutrition.

Cadmium ◀⋲ _kad mē ēm, n._ poisonous heavy metal, may rarely produce toxicity in horses grazed near smelting plants. Signs of unthriftiness, lameness, swollen joints, osteoporosis, proteinuria, and nephrocalcinosis.
See Diarrhoea, Kidney.

Caecum ◀⋲ _sē kēm, n._ large comma-shaped, blind-ended sac of alimentary canal, between small intestine and colon. In adult horse approx. 1.25 m long, with capacity of 25 litres, lies under right flank. Important in digestion as a chamber for fermentation of cellulose; holds 19–38 litres of ingesta. May become impacted, especially if horse fed coarse roughage and there is an underlying motility problem, causing colic. Diagnosis of impaction from clinical signs, including pain (pawing, lying down, flank watching), peritoneal fluid analysis and rectal palpation.
See Alimentary tract, Colic.

Caesarian section ◀⋲ _si ză rē ēn / sek shēn, n._ surgical incision of the walls of the abdomen and uterus for delivery of foetus. Not frequently indicated in mares, but may be needed if foetal malpresentation (dystocia) cannot be corrected through vagina, or in life-threatening emergencies such as uterine torsion. General anaesthesia required. Abdominal wall cut in midline, uterus opened along greater curvature, contents drained away from abdomen, and foal removed and placed alongside mare with umbilical cord intact until breathing on its own. Postoperative complications may include metritis, peritonitis, laminitis, retained placenta, adhesions. (Julius Caesar, Roman emperor is said to have been delivered by such an operation.)
See Adhesion, Dystocia, Laminitis, Peritonitis, Placenta, Umbilical, Uterine, Uterus.

Caffeine ◀⋲ _ka fēn, n._ substance obtained from coffee, tea and guarana plants. Central nervous system stimulant, increases muscle efficiency, diuretic. Use as a stimulant for competition horses is prohibited.

Calcaneus ◀⋲ _kal kā nē ēs, n._ (fibular tarsal bone, os calcis) large bone at the back of the tarsus (hock); points upward and can be palpated easily (point of the hock).
See Tarsus.
   Calcaneal bursa see Bursa

Calcareous ◀⋲ _kal kă rē ēs, adj._ of or containing calcium carbonate, e.g. calcareous deposits in ligaments which form in chronic inflammation.
See Calcium, Ligament.

Calciferol see Vitamin D

Calcific band keratopathy ◀⋲ _kal si fik / band / kerē top ēth ē, n._ a degenerative ocular condition in which calcium crystal is deposited in the basement membrane of the cornea. Associated with uveitis. Crystals appear as white plaques in the corneal stroma. Can cause ulceration if lesions become dense enough to lift the corneal epithelium. Cause unknown. Treatment by keratectomy. Prognosis

guarded, particularly if underlying problem cannot be eliminated.
See Corneal, Keratectomy, Uveitis.

Calcification ◀£ _kal_ si fi _kā_ shēn, n. deposition of calcium salts, e.g. in bones, where cartilage matrix is hardened by calcification. Also, abnormal deposition of calcium salts within tissue.
See Bone, Calcium.

Calcinosis circumscripta ◀£ kal _sin_ ō sis / _ser_ kēm scriptē, n. (tumorous calcinosis) deposition of calcium in subcutaneous tissues, often near joints or tendon sheaths. Seen especially on lateral side of stifle joint, closely associated with joint capsule; horse presents with firm, unsightly swelling of subcutaneous tissue. May cause lameness; surgical removal has been described, but surgery should only be performed if lesion is confirmed as cause of lameness due to morbidity associated with surgery and proximity to joint.

Calcitonin ◀£ _kal_ si _tō_ nin, n. hormone involved in calcium homeostasis (regulation). Produced by C-cells of thyroid gland in response to high level of calcium in blood (hypercalcaemia), and reduces resorption of calcium from bone and in kidney tubules, tending to lower blood calcium levels.
See Calcium, Hypercalcaemia.

Calcium ◀£ _kal_ sē ēm, n. metallic element, present in body tissues, especially high levels in bones and teeth. Essential for blood clotting, neuromuscular activity, permeability of membranes and muscle contraction. Present in blood either as complexed form, bound to protein (albumin) or ionized (biologically active form). Balance of calcium and phosphorus in diet is important for normal formation of bones and teeth; horses tolerate a relatively wide ratio of calcium:phosphorus, up to 7:1, although most dietary recommendations are for a much narrower range, from 1–2:1. Regulation and balance of levels of calcium in body is controlled by three substances:

• Parathyroid hormone – acts to increase vitamin D production, mobilizes calcium from the bone, increases calcium absorption from intestine, increases calcium resorption in the kidney (so it is not lost in urine) when level of calcium in blood is low (hypocalcaemia). Also increases urinary phosphate excretion.

• Vitamin D – stimulates absorption of calcium from small intestine and release of calcium from bone.

• Calcitonin – reduces resorption of bone in kidney and from bone when level of calcium in blood is high (hypercalcaemia).

See Bone, Calcitonin, Hypercalcaemia, Hypocalcaemia, Parathyroid, Phosphorus, Tooth, Vitamin D.

  C. borogluconate ◀£ _kal_ sē ēm / _bo_ rē _glŭ_ kē nāt, n. calcium compound used as an injectable solution in treatment of low calcium level in blood (hypocalcaemia, e.g. lactation tetany) and some poisonings (e.g. chloroform, carbon tetrachloride).
  See Hypocalcaemia, Lactation.

Calculus ◀£ _kal_ kū lēs, n. abnormal concretion of mineral salts (often calcium) occurring within the body; may form in bladder, kidney, bile duct, salivary gland ('stones').
See Biliary, Enterolith, Salivary gland, Urolith.

  Dental c. ◀£ _den_ tal / _kal_ kū lēs, n. a hard concretion that forms on the teeth, primarily incisors or canines; associated with gingival inflammation.

Caley pea ◀£ _kā_ lē / pē, n. (Singletary pea, _Lathyrus hirsutis_) a legume with winged stems that grow from 25–100 cm long. The vegetation of the plant is not toxic and is highly nutritious, but the seeds contain toxic amino acids. Lathyrism, the neurological syndrome produced by chronic consumption of the seeds, can affect all species including humans, but horses are the most sensitive. Horses are usually affected by hay containing intact pods with seeds. Signs include sudden, transient laryngeal paralysis with dyspnoea, degenerative changes to nerves and muscles, stringhalt-like gait, and inflammation of liver and spleen.

Calf knee ◀︎ _karf_ / _nē_, _n._ conformation term; the knee inclines backward, behind a plumb line dropped from the middle of the forearm to the fetlock. Also, 'back at the knee'.

Calkin ◀︎ _kal_ kin, _n._ any of several types of projections which may be forged or welded onto a horseshoe. Calkins are used in an effort to increase traction, alter move ment, or adjust stance; whether they actually do what they are intended to do has not been demonstrated. A.k.a: Caulk; calk.

Calliphora ◀︎ ka _li_ fĕr rē, _n._ genus of blow-flies, lay eggs in wounds and decaying flesh. Not common in horses.

Callus ◀︎ _ka_ lēs, _n._ woven bone laid down at site of fracture (break) of bone as bone heals, replacing the original fibrin clot; may be felt under skin as hard bony swelling, e.g. in fractured splint bone. Also, localized hyperplasia of the epidermis, from friction or pressure. See Bone, Fracture.

Calor ◀︎ _ka_ lĕr, _n._ heat, one of the cardinal signs of inflammation. See Inflammation.

Calorie ◀︎ _ka_ lē rē, _n._ unit of heat or energy; in chemistry, the amount of heat required at a pressure of one atmosphere to raise the temperature of one gram of water one degree Celsius – abbreviation _cal_; called also _gram calorie_, _small calorie_; in nutrition, the amount of heat required to raise the temperature of one kilogram of water one degree Celsius, that is equal to 1,000 gram calories – abbreviation _Cal_; called also _kilocalorie_, _kilogram calorie_, _large calorie_. Used to denote energy content of food and in study of metabolism. Nutritional calories are not measured amounts of energy, but are calculated from food composition.

Camped (out) ◀︎ _camt (öt)_, _adj._ conforma-tion term; in hind limb, refers to cannon bone and fetlock joint being 'behind' a plumb line dropped from point of buttock (camped out behind); in forelimb, refers to the entire forelimb being too far forward when viewed from the side, e,g. as seen in laminitis. See Conformation.

Camphor ◀︎ _kam_ fĕr, _n._ a waxy, white, or transparent solid with a characteristic, pungent odour; applied topically to the skin as an anti itch and anti-infective; found in some liniments.

Canal ◀︎ _kē_ nal, _n._ relatively narrow tubal passage in body, e.g. alimentary canal. Many examples in anatomy, including:
- Alimentary c. – digestive tract.
- Birth c. – the canal through which the foetus passes at birth.
- Carpal c. – the canal through which tendons pass at the posterior aspect of the carpus.
- Teat c. – the canal leading from the mammary gland to the exterior of the gland.

Canaliculus ◀︎ ka nē _li_ kū lēs, _n._ extremely narrow channel in body, e.g. lacrimal duct, in bone, bile canaliculi. See Bile, Eye, Lacrimal apparatus.

Cancellous ◀︎ _kan_ si lēs, _adj._ having a spongy or lattice-like structure. Used to describe bone tissue, especially in short bones and at ends of long bones. See Bone.

Cancer ◀︎ _kan_ sē, _n._ uncontrolled growth of cells; neoplastic growth, especially that which is malignant (i.e. will invade locally, regrow if removed or spread to remote parts of body by metastasis). Two broad categories: carcinoma and sarcoma. Not frequently diagnosed in horses. See under separate organs or neoplastic conditions, Malignant, Metastasis, Neoplasia, Tumour.

Candida ◀︎ _kan_ di dē, _n._ genus of yeasts, commonly part of normal flora of mouth, skin, intestine and vagina. Can cause opportunistic infections, especially of skin and ears.
   C. albicans ◀︎ _kan_ di dē / _al_ bi _kanz_, _n._ the most significant member of the genus _Candida_. Extremely rare cause of infection in

horse. One report of cutaneous skin nodules. Has caused white–grey lesions in mouth of immunodeficient foals. Vulvovaginal infection was reported in six Thoroughbred mares after administration of oral progestin. Potentially seen after prolonged antibiotic therapy if balance of normal flora is upset by antibiotics; however, this does not appear to be a common occurrence in horses.

Canine ◀⁞ *kā nīn, n./ adj.* of dog, dog-like. **C. tooth** ◀⁞ *kā nīn / tŭth, n.* (tush, tusk) generally only present in adult male, one on each side of upper and lower jaw, between incisors and cheek teeth, generally erupt by 4 years of age. Mares may have small canine teeth on the lower jaw. Large tooth, approximately 70% of which is a long root. See Dentition, Tooth.

Canker ◀⁞ *kang ker, n.* chronic infectious condition of foot, characterized by the development of a chronic hypertrophy of the horn-producing tissues, generally originates in the frog; may remain focal, but has the capacity to become diffuse and invade the adjacent sole, bars and hoof wall. Aetiology uncertain; traditionally thought to be caused by standing in unhygienic conditions, but canker is seen in well cared for horses. Signs include foul smell, caseous white exudate ('cottage cheese'), tattered appearance of frog. May cause lameness in advanced cases. Clinical diagnosis may be confirmed by biopsy; lesion is described as a chronic, hypertrophic, moist pododermatitis. The treatments described have consisted of debridement and the application of topical medications including antibiotics, astringents, antiseptics, and caustic powders; cryosurgery of affected area has been described. No treatment is consistently effective; prognosis guarded. After treatment, daily foot care is crucial for successful outcome. See Foot.

Cannon ◀⁞ *ka nĕn, n.* bone between carpus (knee) and metacarpophalangeal joint (fetlock) in forelimb (third metacarpal bone) or between tarsus (hock) and metatarsophalangeal joint (fetlock) in hind limb (third metatarsal bone).

Cannula ◀⁞ *ka nū lē, n.* small tube which can be inserted into vessel, duct, or cavity for infusion or drainage of fluid. See also: Catheter.

Cannulate ◀⁞ *ka nū lāt, v.* to insert cannula into body, e.g. into blood vessel, body cavity, etc.

Canter ◀⁞ *kan tē, n.* a three-beat gait in which the horse's hooves strike the ground in the order: hind foot, contralateral hind foot and ipsilateral forefoot together, contralateral forefoot; this sequence is followed by a brief period of suspension during which all four feet are momentarily off the ground. See Gait.

Cantharidin ◀⁞ *kan tha ri din, n.* a poisonous chemical compound obtained from blister beetle or dried Spanish fly; after mating, female beetle covers eggs with it to discourage predators. Causes skin irritation and blistering. Has been used to treat warts in people. Ingestion of crushed beetles in hay causes toxicosis. See Blister beetle.

Canthus ◀⁞ *kan thēs, n.* angle at either end of the opening of eyelids, where upper and lower lids meet. Each eye has a lateral and a medial canthus. See Eye.

Capacitation ◀⁞ *kē pa si tā shun, n.* the last step in maturation of spermatozoa of mammalian species. Capacitation is a biochemical event that renders sperm capable of fertilizing an oocyte. Capacitation occurs after ejaculation, and typically occurs in the female reproductive tract. See Fertilization.

Capacity ◀⁞ *kē pa si tē, n.* power or ability to hold, contain, or the ability to absorb; e.g. cranial c. is amount of space in skull; total lung c. is volume of air held in lungs at end of maximal inspiration, etc. Measured in litres (l) and millilitres (ml).

Capillary ◀⁞ *kē pi lē rē, n.* any of the minute vessels between arteriole and venule. Comprised of thin wall of endothelial cells which allows transfer of gases, nutrients and waste products between blood and tissues.

C. refill time ◀︎ _kē pi̱ lē rē / re̱ fil / tïm, n._ time taken for normal pink colour to return to mucous membrane of gums after blanching by applying pressure from finger. Normal is 1–2 seconds. Delayed c. r. t. indicative of dehydration; if excessively prolonged, and accompanied by discoloured mucous membranes, of shock.
See Dehydration, Shock.

Capped ◀︎ _kapt, adj._ said of a fluid swelling, especially occurring over an anatomical prominence.
See Bursitis.

C. elbow ◀︎ _kapt / eḻ bō, n._ fluid swelling over point of elbow (olecranon) caused by inflammation of bursa or bruising of soft tissues. May be caused by ipsilateral fore or hind foot hitting elbow when horse rises from lying position ('shoe boil').
See Olecranon.

C. hock ◀︎ _kapt / hok, n._ fluid swelling over olecranon, caused by inflammation of either or both of two bursae (one between skin and tendon, other between tendon and bone).
See Subcutaneous.

Capsaicin ◀︎ _kap̱ sī sin, n._ an irritating alkaloid, found in hot peppers. Topical application has been used as a topical analgesic to reduce pain sensitivity, probably due to depletion of substance P, a short-chain polypeptide that stimulates nerve endings at an injury site and within the spinal cord, causing increased sensations of pain; irritating to skin.

Capsule ◀︎ _kap̱ sūl, n._ a fibrous or membranous anatomical structure which encloses an organ or body part; numerous examples, including hoof, kidney, joint, or lens of eye. Some bacteria have a capsule of polysaccharide or polypeptide, an envelope of gel which surrounds the bacterial cell.

Capsulitis ◀︎ _kap̱ sū li̱ tis, n._ inflammation of capsule.

Carbachol ◀︎ _kaṟ bē kol, n._ substance which stimulates parasympathetic nervous system, including the smooth muscle of

the alimentary tract. Used in past to treat mild colic and ileus; no longer used because contractions are uncoordinated.
See Parasympathetic nervous system.

Carbamate ◀︎ _kaṟ bam āt, n._ group of substances used as agricultural pesticides; readily absorbed through lungs, GI tract, and skin. May cause poisoning in horses by blocking enzymes which help regulate autonomic nervous system. Signs include uneasiness, severe colic with GI hypermotility, sweating, salivation, laboured breathing, muscle tremors. May cause collapse and death from respiratory failure in severe cases. Treatment with atropine sulphate; oral adsorbents, such as activated charcoal, may be useful in binding ingested toxin.
See Adsorption, Atropine, Autonomic nervous system.

Carbohydrates ◀︎ _kaṟ bō hī̱ drāts, n._ group of organic compounds containing carbon, hydrogen and oxygen; the most abundant of the four major classes of biomolecules, which also include proteins, lipids and nucleic acids. The basic carbohydrate unit is called a monosaccharide, e.g. glucose. Linking monosaccharides results in additional carbohydrate compounds:

- Disaccharides, two joined monosaccharides, e.g. sucrose, lactose.
- Three to six monosaccharide units are termed oligosaccharides.
- Anything larger is a polysaccharide. Polysaccharides, such as starch, glycogen, or cellulose (the primary carbohydrate in the cell wall of plants), can reach thousands of units in length.

Nutritionists commonly classify carbohydrates as simple (monosaccharides and disaccharides) or complex (oligosaccharides and polysaccharides). Carbohydrates provide energy for the body. Complex carbohydrates must be broken down by bacteria in the large intestine before they can be absorbed and used by the horse. Carbohydrates can be stored as glycogen in the body, primarily in muscle tissue or, in excess, may be converted to fat. Genetic defects in carbohydrate metabolism have been identified in horses.
See Polysaccharide storage myopathy.

Carbon ◄⁞ _kar_ _bĕn_, _n._ chemical element, present in all organic compounds. The presence of large amounts of carbon in the universe, as well as the unique polymer-forming ability of carbon-based compounds at the Earth's usual temperatures, make carbon the basis of the chemistry of all known life.

Carbon dioxide ◄⁞ _kar_ _bĕn_ / _dī_ _ok_ _sīd_, _n._ CO_2; composed of two oxygen atoms covalently bonded to a single carbon atom. Colourless, odourless gas, produced in body during metabolism, as an end product of the processes that produce energy (cellular respiration). Removed from tissues by blood; most of it (about 80–90%) is converted to bicarbonate ions HCO_3^- in red blood cells, and is crucial for regulating blood pH; 5–10% is dissolved in the plasma and expelled from lungs on expiration; and 5 –10% is bound to haemoglobin as carbamino compounds (percentages vary, depending on whether the blood is arterial or venous). Present as 0.03% of normal air. See Ventilation.

Carbon fibre ◄⁞ _kar_ _bĕn_ / _fī_ _bĕ_, _n._ synthetic fibre made of carbon filaments; high tensile strength. Has been previously used as implant for repair of soft tissues, e.g. tendons and ligaments; however, tendons and ligaments repaired with c. fibre have failed to demonstrate an advantage in such surgeries; in addition, the fibres have the potential to become infected and be rejected by the horse's body. Such problems have essentially eliminated its use in equine surgery. See Ligament, Tendon.

Carbon tetrachloride ◄⁞ _kar_ _bĕn_ / _te_ _trĕ_ _klor_ _rīd_, _n._ fumigant, propellant, and solvent; chemical used in distant past as anthelmintic but no current therapeutic indications. Death from toxicosis either peracute, from severe pulmonary oedema, or in 3–7 days as a result of kidney and liver failure. No antidote. See Anthelmintic.

Carbuncle ◄⁞ _kar_ _bung_ _kĕl_, _n._ a painful, localized purulent inflammation of the skin and deeper tissues; usually discharging pus, with necrosis and sloughing of dead tissue; generally associated with _Staphylococcus_ spp. bacterial infection. See Abscess, _Staphylococcus._

Carcinogen ◄⁞ _kar_ _si_ _nĕ_ _jĕn_, _n._ any substance which causes cancer.
- Epigenetic c. – an agent that does not damage DNA, but causes alterations, such as immunosuppression, that predispose to cancer.
- Genotoxic c. – carcinogen that reacts directly with deoxyribonucleic acid (DNA), or with molecules that then react with DNA, and alters its normal functions.

See Cancer, Deoxyribonucleic acid, Neoplasia.

Carcinoma ◄⁞ _kar_ _si_ _nō_ _mĕ_, _n._ malignant tumour of epithelial origin, which tends to infiltrate surrounding tissues and give rise to metastases; most common equine carcinoma is squamous cell carcinoma, seen especially on pink skin, especially of vulva or prepuce, and in eye. See Squamous, Tumour.

Cardiac ◄⁞ _kar_ _dĕ_ _ak_, _adj._ about or of the heart; pertaining to the orifice between the oesophagus and the part of the stomach immediately next to and surrounding the orifice. See Heart.

    C. arrest ◄⁞ _kar_ _dĕ_ _ak_ / _ĕ_ _rest_, _n._ sudden stoppage of effective heart action. May be from failure of normal impulses for contraction or fibrillation of ventricles of heart. See Heart.

    C. index ◄⁞ _kar_ _dĕ_ _ak_ / _in_ _deks_, _n._ cardiac output divided by the body surface area. A measurement of heart dynamics based on the cardiac output, which is the amount of blood the left ventricle ejects into systemic circulation in one minute, measured in litres per minute (l/min). The cardiac index relates heart performance to the size of the individual. The unit of measurement is litres per minute per square metre.

    C. insufficiency see Insufficiency

    C. murmur see Heart

    C. output ◄⁞ _kar_ _dĕ_ _ak_ / _ōt_ _püt_, _n._ volume of blood pumped by heart in a minute. It is equal to the heart rate multiplied by the stroke volume. See Stroke volume.

C. tamponade ◀⁞ *kar dē ak / tam pon ard, n.* mechanical compression of the heart by large amounts of fluid or blood within the pericardial space; limits the normal range of motion and function of the heart. Common cause of death in horses with rupture of aortic root. See Aortic.

Cardiology ◀⁞ *kar dē o lē jē, n.* study of heart, its action, and heart diseases. See Heart.

Cardiomegaly ◀⁞ *kar dē ō meg ēlē, n.* an abnormal enlargement of the heart, e.g. as may be seen in congestive heart failure, due to weakening and dilation of cardiac muscle, or can be associated with various types of cardiomyopathy. See Cardiomyopathy, Congestive heart failure.

Cardiomyopathy ◀⁞ *kar dē ō mī o pē thē, n.* a primary non-inflammatory disease of heart muscle, and not the result of ischaemia. Reduces pumping function of heart. Cause usually not determined. Most affected horses deteriorate after diagnosis, and must be euthanized. Diagnosis by cardiac ultrasound; cardiac enlargement, with dilation of atria and ventricles typical. Seen with vitamin E and selenium deficiency in foals from mares living in selenium-deficient areas (white muscle disease); foals usually less than six months old with weakness, respiratory distress, murmurs, arrhythmias, and pulmonary oedema. Has also been reported in aged horses. May present as exercise intolerance in younger horses; aged horses have been presented with lethargy, blindness, head pressing, ataxia, and circling, as a result of secondary congestive heart failure. See Heart.

Cardiopulmonary resuscitation ◀⁞ *kar dē ō pul mon rē / rē su si tā shēn, n.* (CPR) an emergency medical procedure for treatment of cardiac arrest. The size of the adult horse generally precludes effective CPR. Neonatal foals may require CPR immediately after birth or after cardiac arrest from progression of a disease process such as severe sepsis or septic shock. Initial CPR treatment is aimed at establishing an airway, usually via a tracheal tube, and providing ventilation. Circulatory support is provided by closed-chest compressions. Placement of an intravenous catheter is important to provide intravenous fluid and pharmacological therapy for cardiovascular support. Asystole and cardiovascular collapse are most frequently encountered problems. Successful outcome requires trained personnel, proper supplies, and team cooperation. Most of the information used for CPR in neonatal foals is derived from human medical research and clinical medicine.

Cardiovascular ◀⁞ *kar dē ō vas kū lē, adj.* pertaining to heart and blood vessels.
 C. system ◀⁞ *kar dē ō vas kū lē / sis tēm, n.* the heart and blood vessels, by which blood is pumped and circulated through the body.

Caries ◀⁞ *kă rēz, n.* decay, e.g. of bone or teeth, whereby the tissues become soft, discoloured, and porous.

Carotid ◀⁞ *kē ro tid, n.* pertaining to the principle artery of neck.
 C. body ◀⁞ *kē ro tid / bo dē, n.* small collection of specialized cells situated at bifurcation of common carotid arteries able to detect changes in levels of oxygen and carbon dioxide in blood, helps to regulate respiration.
 C. sinus ◀⁞ *kē ro tid / sī nēs, n.* region of carotid artery sensitive to changes in blood pressure, helps regulate heart rate and blood pressure.

Carpal ◀⁞ *kar pūl, adj.* of the carpus joint (knee of horse's forelimb). See Carpus.
 C. bones ◀⁞ *kar pūl / bōnz, n.* seven or eight bones arranged in two rows: proximal (radial c.b. [scaphoid], intermediate c.b., ulnar c.b., accessory c.b.) and distal (2nd, 3rd and 4th c.b.s; 1st c.b. present as pea-sized bone in medial ligament in approx. 10% of horses). Any of c.b.s may fracture, most common in radial, accessory and third. Usually caused by trauma: signs include heat, pain, swelling, lameness. Diagnosis by radiography from several angles. See Accessory carpal bone.

C. bone hypoplasia ◀᠄ _kar pūl_ / _bōn_ / _hi pō plaz ēē, n._ failure of development of carpal bones; seen most commonly in premature or dysmature foals. Foal usually presents with carpus valgus and hyperextension. If the limb is unprotected by splint or casting, the immature bones will be crushed, and will mature in abnormal shapes, resulting in a permanent deformity. The causes of the condition are poorly understood, and genetics and external forces such as the environment in the mare's uterus, nutrition of the foal and mare are suspected influences.

C. canal ◀᠄ _kar pūl_ / _kēn al, n._ bony and fibrous tissue canal through which flexor tendons and median nerve pass, on rear (caudal) side of carpus. Formed by carpal bones and deep fascia (flexor retinacula).

C. canal syndrome ◀᠄ _kar pūl_ / _kēn al_ / _sin drōm, n._ compression of flexor tendons within carpal tunnel, as result of trauma or space-occupying lesion (e.g. osteochondroma of distal radius). Causes fluid swelling of carpal sheath, pain on flexion of carpus and reduced range of movement. Pulse in leg below carpus is reduced.

C. flexion test ◀᠄ _kar pūl_ / _flek shēn_ / _test, n._ a lameness test, involving holding the carpus in flexion for a period of time (often 60 seconds), before trotting the horse away immediately. Lameness suggests various problems in the carpal region, including, but not limited to, carpal arthritis, or suspensory ligament desmitis. See Osteoarthritis, Suspensory ligament.

C. joint see Carpus

C. tunnel see Carpal canal (above)

Carprofen ◀᠄ _kar prō fen, n._ a non-steroidal anti-inflammatory drug (NSAID) approved for use in horses in Europe, but not the United States. While carprofen is not a selective inhibitor of cyclooxygenase (COX) isoenzymes, the drug is a more selective inhibitor of COX-2 than is phenylbutazone (PBZ) or flunixin meglumine (FM). The drug has a longer half-life than other NSAID drugs, and can be given once daily. Carprofen has been shown to reduce prostaglandins in inflammatory exudates, to reduce neck swelling in an experimental model in ponies, to relieve skin pain for 24 hours in another experi-

mental model, and to be equally effective as PBZ or FM for analgesia post-surgery. Dosing intervals for carprofen that are used in horses may not be appropriate for use in donkeys.
See Cyclooxygenase, Flunixin meglumine, Phenylbutazone.

Carpitis ◀᠄ _kar pī tis, n._ (popped knee) inflammation of carpus. Signs include swelling of joint, pain on movement and reduced range of movement.
See Arthritis, Carpus, Osteochondrosis.

Carpus ◀᠄ _kar pēs, n._ (knee, carpal joint) joint of forelimb, equivalent of human wrist. Complex joint (see Carpal bones), divided into three main joints which contain approximately 26 individual articulations:

- Antebrachiocarpal (radiocarpal) – between radius and proximal row of carpal bones.
- Midcarpal or intercarpal – between proximal and distal rows of carpal bones.
- Carpometacarpal – between distal row of carpal bones and metacarpal bones (cannon and splint bones). This joint is capable of very little movement due to tight ligamentous attachments.

Two separate synovial cavities:

- Antebrachiocarpal.
- Combined midcarpal and carpometacarpal.

The carpus is a common site of injury in racing horses. Joint may be affected by arthritis or various fractures, all of which may cause lameness, swelling, pain on flexion, reduced range of movement of joint to some degree. Diagnosis of carpal problems is commonly by radiography; several angles are required to evaluate various bone joint surfaces.
See Arthritis, Carpal, Osteoarthritis.

C. valgus ◀᠄ _kar pēs_ / _val gēs,n._ conformational term, primarily applied to foals: the proximal forelimb deviates toward the midline and the distal limb deviates outward. This creates the appearance that the limbs are bent inward, under the horse; 'knock-kneed'.
See Valgus.

C. varus ◀᠄ _kar pēs_ / _var ēs,n._ conformational

term, primarily applied to foals: the proximal forelimb deviates away from the midline and the distal limb deviates inward. This creates the appearance that the limbs are bent outward; 'bow-legged'. See Varus.

Carrier ◀﹦ *ka rē ê, n.* animal which has disease-causing agent in body without signs of disease; can transmit agent to other animals, and so cause disease in them. Seen especially with strangles; equine infectious anaemia. See Equine infectious anaemia, Strangles.

Cartilage ◀﹦ *kar ti lij, n.* dense connective tissue, composed of collagen and elastin, containing cells called chondrocytes that are embedded in a firm ground substance called the matrix. Contains no nerves or blood vessels; nutrients diffuse from the joint fluid through the cartilage matrix. Numerous functions, including:

• Providing a framework upon which bone deposition begins; forms skeleton of embryo, and this is gradually replaced by bone.
• Supplies smooth surface for movement of bones in joints.
• In growing horse, cartilage at growth plates (epiphyseal cartilages – between shaft and ends of bone) is where increase in length of bone occurs.

Cartilage occurs in many places in the horse's body, including joints, ribs, ear pinnae, hoof (collateral cartilages), the trachea and bronchial tubes, intervertebral discs, and as shock-absorbing discs (menisci) in some joints.

Numerous disease conditions involve cartilage, including arthritis of all types, osteochondrosis, and infection. Cartilage generally has very limited capacity to repair itself after injury. Because cartilage lacks blood supply, and because cartilage cells are bound in the matrix, they cannot easily migrate to new areas (unlike epithelium). Damaged cartilage is usually replaced by fibrocartilage scar tissue or proliferative bone.

There are three main types of cartilage:

• Elastic c. (yellow c.) – found mainly in ear pinnae, Eustachian tubes, larynx, and epiglottis. Similar in composition

to hyaline cartilage (see below) but contains bundles of elastin throughout the matrix that makes tissue stiff, but still elastic.

• Fibrocartilage (white c.) – a specialized cartilage occurring in areas that need support or high tensile strength, such as intervertebral discs, the pubic symphysis of the hip, sites connecting tendons and ligaments to bone, and joint menisci. When joint hyaline cartilage is damaged, it is often replaced by fibrocartilage, which does not function as well.

• Hyaline c. – the most abundant cartilage. Avascular, found covering the ends of bones in joints (articular cartilage), and inside bones, serving as a centre for bone growth. Hyaline c. forms most of the skeleton of the embryo.

See Arthritis, Bone, Costal, Growth, Larynx, Joint, Meniscus, Trachea.

Caseation ◀﹦ *kā zē ā shēn, n.* type of necrosis where tissue becomes dry and cheese-like. See Abscess.

Casein ◀﹦ *kā zēn, n.* primary protein in milk.

Caslick ◀﹦ *kaz lik, n.* (vulvoplasty) operation performed to prevent air entering vagina (pneumovagina), to reduce contamination of vagina in older mares with poor vulvar conformation (tipped vulva), and as part of the repair of perineal lacerations. Local anaesthetic required. Lips (labia) of upper part of vulva are trimmed, then stitched together. Mare that has had operation must be cut prior to foaling (episiotomy); may be resutured after foaling or subsequent breeding. (Named after E. A. Caslick, American veterinarian.) See Pneumovagina.

Cassette ◀﹦ *ka set, n.* container used to hold film for radiography. Prevents exposure to light, but X-rays can pass through. May contain intensifying screen which enhances quality of radiograph. See Radiography.

Cast ◄꞉ *karst, v./n.* **1)** to force an animal to lie down for surgical procedures using ropes, not often used currently as anaesthetic/sedative techniques improve; **2)** to become cast is to be recumbent and unable to rise because of being trapped in position, as in the corner of a stall; **3)** stiff dressing, e.g. of plaster of Paris or polyurethane resin, used to hold part of body immobile, such as in repair of fractures; urinary cast may occur in urinary sediment, a mould of renal tubule usually in waxy material.

Castor bean ◄꞉ *kars* ter / bē, *n.* (*Ricinus communis*) plant grown in southern USA for oil (castor oil). Contains a toxin, ricin, which can cause anaphylaxis and shock. Horses are poisoned by eating seeds; as little as 0.01% of body weight can cause poisoning. Signs of poisoning include incoordination, muscle spasms, sweating, fast heart rate, fast respiratory rate, colic, diarrhoea, death within a few days. Castor oil is safe; the ricin toxin is insoluble in the oil. Castor oil is a potent purgative.

Castrate ◄꞉ *kas* trāt, *v.* (cut) remove gonads from animal, rendering it sterile. In horses, used generally to mean removal of testicles from male animal; geld.

Castration ◄꞉ *kas* trā shĕn, *n.* (orchidectomy, cutting, gelding, emasculation) surgical removal of one or both testes from male animal. Removal of both testes renders animal sterile and largely eliminates masculine behaviour. Horses can be castrated at any age, and procedure is generally well tolerated. Is more easily performed in horses less than 1 year of age, but commonly performed between 1 and 2 years of age when behaviour becomes intolerable. Occasionally one testis may be removed (unilateral castration), e.g. in cases of testicular tumour, testicular trauma, inguinal hernia. Anaesthesia is legal requirement in UK; operation performed either under sedation and local anaesthesia or under general anaesthesia. There are three techniques:

- Open – parietal tunic of each testis opened, testis is completely freed from

tunic, and testis removed, leaving tunic in horse.
- Closed – each testis removed within parietal tunic.
- Half-closed – tunic opened and testis and cord isolated, but then tunic and testis are removed separately.

Closed and half-closed techniques are said to decrease the incidence of post-operative complications related to the parietal tunic, such as hydrocoele, and are preferred for surgical treatment of disease conditions that may involve the tunic, such as neoplasia.
See Testes.

Catabolism ◄꞉ kē ta bo lizm, *n.* destructive metabolic process, whereby organisms convert substances into excreted compounds; e.g. in loss of muscle through malnutrition.
See Metabolism.

Cataplasm ◄꞉ ka tē plazm, *n.* poultice or soft external application; often medicated.
See Poultice.

Cataplexy ◄꞉ ka tē pleks ē, *n.* a condition characterized by abrupt attacks of muscular weakness; associated with narcolepsy.
See Narcolepsy.

Cataract ◄꞉ ka tē rakt, *n.* a partial or complete opacity (cloudiness) of lens of eye, or lens capsule. May be classified according to cause, age of onset, location within lens and degree of maturity. Many cataracts in horses cause no significant effect on vision. Congenital cataracts uncommon; have been reported in Quarter Horses, Belgian, Arabian, Rocky Mountain, and Morgan horses. Acquired cataracts may be caused by trauma, inflammation (especially uveitis). Senile cataracts may occur in aged horses, but are uncommon, and rarely interfere with vision.
See Eye, Uveitis.

Catarrh ◄꞉ kē tar, *n.* inflammation of mucous membrane, e.g. in nose or alimentary tract, with free discharge of mucoid or mucopurulent fluid.

Catecholamine ◀ᑉ _ca_ tĕ kol _ā_ mēn, *n.* substance which stimulates sympathetic nervous system, e.g. epinephrine, nore-pinephrine, dopamine. Released by body in response to stress.
See Autonomic nervous system, Sympathetic nervous system.

Catgut ◀ᑉ _kat gut,_ *n.* material prepared from sheep's intestines, used for stitching wounds, ligating blood vessels, etc. Absorbable (i.e. dissolves within animal's body), not of very high strength. May be impregnated with chromium trioxide (chromic catgut). Largely replaced today by synthetic materials.

Cathartic ◀ᑉ _kĕ thar_ tik, *n.* purgative, i.e. causes passing of faeces.

Catheter ◀ᑉ _ka_ thē tĕ, *n.* flexible tube, usually Teflon™ or nylon, introduced into a cavity or vessel, either for removal of fluids from body (e.g. urinary c. used to remove urine from bladder) or for admin-istration of fluid (e.g. intravenous c. used to give fluids into blood stream; uterine c. used to administer treatment directly into infected uterus).
    Foley c. ◀ᑉ _fō_ lē / _ka_ thē tĕ, *n.* catheter with a balloon tip, inflated with air or liquid, designed to remain in place (indwelling). (Named after F.E.B. Foley, American urolo-gist.)
    Indwelling c. ◀ᑉ _in dwe_ ling / _ka_ thē tĕ, *n.* catheter intended to remain in place within body for some time, e.g. stay within urethra or bladder to allow drainage of urine.

Catheterization ◀ᑉ _ka_ thē tĕ rī _zā_ shĕn, *n.* insertion or use of catheter.
See Catheter.

Cation ◀ᑉ _kat īen_, *n.* an ion carrying a posi-tive charge; opposite of anion.

Cauda ◀ᑉ _kor_ dĕ, *n.* general anatomical term for a tail or tail-like structure.
    Cauda equina ◀ᑉ _kor_ dĕ / ek _wīnē_, *n.* the collection of spinal roots descending from the lower part of the spinal cord.
    C.e. syndrome ◀ᑉ _kor_ dĕ / ek _wīnē_ /sin drŏm, *n.* neurological condition caused by numerous infectious, inflammatory, and/or traumatic factors, with neurological signs apparent in hind limbs stemming from damage to the cauda equina. Signs include tail paralysis/weakness, poor or no anal muscle tone, rectal and bladder paralysis or weakness, and relaxation and protrusion of the penis in males. Skin sensation of the tail, anus, and perineum may be lacking. Coccygeal muscles may atrophy. If anterior aspect of the cauda equina is damaged, hind limb weakness and ataxia may be seen. Other signs might include reproduc-tive dysfunction such as impotence, urospermia (urine ejaculated in semen), and, in mares, urine pooling. Trauma to the sacral/coccygeal area is the most common cause, resulting from falls, backing under a closed top door in a stall, or from tail pulling (such as when the tail is used to help pick up a horse that is down). Various infectious causes, e.g, equine herpes virus, equine protozoal myelitis. Prognosis is largely dependent on the initial cause.

Caudal ◀ᑉ _kor_ dl, *adj.* anatomical term, denoting a position towards tail or rear end.
    C. aortic thrombosis ◀ᑉ _kor_ dl / _ā_ _or_ tik / throm _bō_ sis, *n.* see Aorto-iliac thrombosis.
    C. maxillary sinus ◀ᑉ _kor_ dl / mak _zi_ lē rē / _sī_ nẽs, *n.* air-filled space within maxilla bone of skull. Other sinuses drain into c.m.s., which itself drains into nasal cavity. Roots of upper cheek teeth lie within maxillary sinuses.
See Sinus, Sinusitis, Skull, Tooth.

Cause ◀ᑉ _korz_, *n.* process or thing that brings about a condition or effect.

Caustic ◀ᑉ _kos_ tik, *adj.* able to burn or corrode organic tissue; e.g. silver nitrate is a caustic substance used to reduce size of warts or proud flesh.

Cauterization ◀ᑉ _kor_ tĕ _rīz_ _ā_ shĕn, *n.* burning of skin with hot iron, electric current or caustic chemical to stop bleeding, remove small skin mass, etc.

Cava see Vena cava

Cavity ◀ᑉ _ka_ vi tĕ, *n.* hollow place or space or potential space within body or in one of its organs; e.g. thoracic cavity, abdominal cavity.

CBC see Complete blood count

Ceftiofur ◀ǂ *sef tē ō fer*, *n*. third-generation cephalosporin antibiotic developed for veterinary use. Comes as powder, which must be reconstituted prior to use. See Cephalosporin.

Cell ◀ǂ *sel*, *n*. microscopic fundamental structural unit of all living organisms. Basic structure is cell wall or membrane surrounding cytoplasm (water, proteins, salts, etc.) and nucleus (contains chromosomes, genetic material of cell). Not all cells have nuclei, e.g. red blood cells (erythrocytes) have no nucleus when mature; bacteria also have no nucleus, although nucleoproteins and genes are present. Within cytoplasm are also organelles, e.g. mitochondria (contain enzymes and responsible for energy production), ribosomes (granules of ribonucleic acid [RNA]), Golgi apparatus (area of protein production), etc. Nucleus surrounded by nuclear membrane; cell may also contain nucleoli, a sub-organelle of the nucleus. Chromosomes of each cell contain all genes of that organism, but cell function is determined by which genes are expressed in each individual cell. Structure of individual cells varies enormously depending on function – innumerable types described.
See Chromosome, Cytoplasm, Gene, Nucleus.

Cellophane tape test ◀ǂ *se lō fān* / *tāp* / *test*, *n*. preferrred test for detection of pinworms (*Oxyuris equi*). Ova stick to perineum; rarely seen in faecal analyses. Tape is wrapped around fingers and pressed against perineum, then placed on glass slide for examination under microscope.
See *Oxyuris equi*.

Cellulitis ◀ǂ *se lū lī tis*, *n*. acute, diffuse, spreading, oedematous, suppurative inflammation of connective tissues and sometimes muscle or tendon sheaths. Generally caused by bacterial infection, often from introduction into wound. Aggressive treatment required to prevent permanent limb distortion with scar tissue.

Cellulose ◀ǂ *se lū lōs*, *n*. the most abundant polysaccharide in nature, forming the skeleton of most plant structures and plant cells.
See Carbohydrates.

Celsius ◀ǂ *sel sē ēs*, *n*. (abbr. C) scale of measurement of temperature, where zero degrees is freezing point of water, and 100 degrees is boiling point of water. (Named after Swedish scientist, Anders Celsius.)

Cementum ◀ǂ *si men tēm*, *n*. the bone-like rigid connective tissue covering the tooth root; serves as attachment for periodontal ligament.

Centesis ◀ǂ *sen tē sis*, *n*. 1) puncture of body cavity and withdrawal of fluid; 2) a suffix: - centesis, denoting a perforation or tapping operation, with the part on which the centesis is performed indicated by the root to which the suffix is attached; e.g. abdominocentesis, thoracocentesis.
See Abdominocentesis, Thoracocentesis.

Central nervous system ◀ǂ *sen trēl* / *ner vēs* / *sis tēm*, *n*. – the largest part of the nervous system; includes brain and spinal cord. Protected by bony shell: the brain within the cranium and the spinal cord within the vertebral column. Covered by meninges.
See Brain, Spinal.

Centre ◀ǂ *sen tē*, *n*. middle point; collection of nerves concerned with a certain function, e.g. respiratory centre controls breathing.

Centrifuge ◀ǂ *sen tri fūj*, *v./n*. spin a solution extremely quickly to cause any solids in suspension (e.g. blood) to settle and form a sediment, using centrifugal force; machine which is used to spin a suspension for separation of solids (centrifugation). Process may be used to separate blood cells from serum/plasma, or to separate sediment in urine sample.

Cephalic ◀ǂ *si fa lik*, *adj*. relating to the head, or towards head end of body.

Cephaloridine ◀ǂ *se fē lo ri dēn*, *n*. a first-generation cephalosporin, effective against

a range of Gram-positive and some Gram-negative bacteria. Generally not used in horses because of nephrotoxicity.
See Cephalosporin.

Cephalosporin ◀ *se fē lo spor rin, n.* any of a group of broad-spectrum β-lactam antibiotics originally derived from a species of the fungus *Emericellopsis minimum,* isolated in 1945 from the sea near a sewage outlet on the coast of Sardinia, Italy. Related to penicillins in both structure and mode of action. Relatively penicillinase-resistant; inhibit cell wall manufacture in susceptible bacteria. Those used today are semi-synthetic derivatives of the original natural cephalosporin. Several generations of cephalosporin antibiotics have been developed, each with a broader range of Gram-negative bacteriocidal activity than previous generations, and greater resistance to β-lactamase enzymes.
See Antibiotic.

Cerebellar ◀ *se ri be lē, adj.* pertaining to the cerebellum.
See Cerebellum.
 C. abiotrophy see Abiotrophy

Cerebellum ◀ *se ri be lēm, n.* region of the brain, situated on back of brainstem, that helps integrate sensory perception and motor function. The cerebellum sends information to the muscles to help them move, and gets feedback as to where the horse's body is in space (proprioception). The cerebellum constantly fine-tunes the body's movements.
See Brain.

Cerebral ◀ *se rē brēl, adj.* pertaining to brain, or specifically, to cerebrum.
See Cerebrum, Brain.
 C. haemorrhage ◀ *se rē brēl / he mē rij, n.* bleeding within brain. Occurs most commonly in premature or dysmature foals. 'Stroke', as occurs from c. haemorrhage in humans, has not been recognized in adult horses.
See Brain.
 C. ischaemia ◀ *se rē brēl / isk āmiē, n.* loss of blood supply to brain; usually transient, resulting in syncope (fainting).

C. oedema ◀ *se rē brēl / i dēmē, n.* swelling of brain and cerebrum; most commonly seen in premature or dysmature foals.

Cerebrospinal ◀ *se ri brō spī nēl, adj.* pertaining to the brain and spinal cord.
 C. fluid ◀ *se ri brō spī nēl / flū id, n.* fluid which surrounds brain and spinal cord. Lies in subarachnoid space, within ventricles of brain and in central canal of spinal cord. Produced continuously by choroid plexus within ventricles, and absorbed by arachnoid villi. May be sampled by inserting needle into cisterna magna (atlanto-occipital space) at base of skull (general anaesthesia required) or lumbosacral space (can be performed in standing horse). May be analysed for bacteriology, cytology, protein content, antibodies, etc.
See Brain, Cytology, Spinal.

Cerebrum ◀ *se rē brēm, n.* the larger anterior portion of the brain, consists of two hemispheres and connecting structures; considered to be the seat of conscious mental processes.
See Brain.

Cerumen ◀ *si rū mēn, n.* earwax, secretion of glands of external ear.
See Ear.

Cervical ◀ *sē vī kēl, adj.* pertaining to neck (e.g. cervical vertebrae are bones of neck) or cervix.
 C. adhesion see Adhesion

Cervical vertebral stenotic myelopathy ◀ *sē vī kēl /ver tib rūl / sten ot ik / mī ēl op athē, n.* a neurological syndrome produced by spinal cord compression at the cervical (neck) level, characterized by an abnormal gait in the front and/or hind legs. Referred to as 'wobbler' syndrome; the horse may seem wobbly when walking or exercising. The severity of clinical signs depends on the degree of spinal cord involvement, from stiff neck, weakness and stumbling to difficulty rising, or falling easily. When running, horse may appear 'drunk', from lack of perception of where limbs are (proprioception).
 The spinal cord compression can be dynamic or static. In a dynamic stenosis,

compression only occurs when the horse bends or extends its neck; most commonly recognized affecting the intervertebral spaces between the third and fourth cervical vertebra (C3–C4) and C4–C5 in young animals (yearlings). In static stenosis, compression is constant and irrespective of neck position, most commonly between C5–C6 and C6–C7 in older animals, often associated with vertebral osteoarthritis. Numerous postulated causes, including osteochondrosis and nutritional factors; genetic factors have been debated, but not established. No single cause of the condition has been identified.

DIAGNOSIS
Typical clinical signs give clue to problem. Affected animals may be reluctant to turn neck. Clinical signs may worsen with neck flexion; in older animals, may be seen as hind limb lameness under saddle. Radiographs may be diagnostic; myelogram of the spinal canal required to show compression (dye column is pinched in restricted areas).

TREAMENT
Rest may provide some short-term improvement but is not curative. Corticosteroids may help relieve oedema around spinal cord in older animals and result in clinical improvement. Intra-articular facet injections may help relieve spinal cord arthritis in older animals. Surgery to fuse vertebral bodies involved in compression has been successful in returning some animals to full function. See Myelography, Osteoarthritis.

Cervicitis ◀ᛗ _ser vi sī tis_, *n.* inflammation of cervix, caused by injury, infection (e.g. endometritis), irritants (e.g. air/urine in vagina).

Cervix ◀ᛗ _ser viks_, *n.* narrow muscular neck of uterus, where opens into vagina. May be inspected through vaginal speculum; changes (e.g. colour, degree of moisture) seen at different stages of oestrous cycle or pregnancy. Swab may be taken from cervical canal prior to mating for examination for fungi or bacteria which may affect fertility or be transmis-

sible to stallion. Presence of neutrophils in smear made from swab may indicate inflammation of uterus. Post-foaling injury to cervix may result in infertility. See Fertile, Inflammation, Neutrophil, Uterus.

Cestode ◀ᛗ _ses tōd_, *n.* tapeworm: flat, segmented, internal parasite belonging to class *Cestoda*. See Tapeworm.

Chaff see Straw

Chamber ◀ᛗ _chām bē_, *n.* enclosed space or cavity, e.g. the anterior chamber of the eye is that part in front of iris; chambers of heart are the atria and ventricles. See Eye, Heart.

Champignon ◀ᛗ _shom pē nyon_, *n.* (funiculitis) postoperative complication of castration, abscess of stump of spermatic cord caused by infection with *Streptococcus* spp. A common complication prior to the invention of the emasculator; importance now is mostly historical. See Castration, Funiculitis, *Streptococcus*.

Character ◀ᛗ _ka rik tē_, *n.* nature of organism or object. In genetics is used to describe the expression of the phenotype of a gene or group of genes. See Gene.

Charcoal, activated ◀ᛗ _char kŏl, ak ti vā tid_, *n.* charcoal is almost pure carbon. It is the residue of burning wood in the presence of air. Charcoal is generally treated by a number of chemical processes to increase its ability to adsorb (attract and retain material on its surface) various substances. This process is referred to as activation. Activated charcoal is most commonly given orally, to help adsorb toxins after poisonings. Charcoal has no recognized value in the treatment of diarrhoea, although it has been used for that.

Chasteberry see *Vitex agnus castus*

Check ◀ᛗ _chek_, *v.* control or restrain; as applied to equine anatomy, to restrain or diminish the action or force of [a tendon].

C. apparatus ◀€ *chek / a pē rā tēs, n.* the check ligaments of the limb; important part of stay apparatus, supporting lower leg and preventing overextension.
See Check ligament, Stay apparatus.

C. ligament ◀€ *chek / li gē mēnt, n.* band of tough connective tissue forming part of stay apparatus. In foreleg c.l.s are superior and inferior check ligaments (accessory ligaments) which contribute to the stay apparatus, in conjunction with superficial and deep flexor tendons; in hind leg tarsal check ligament contributes to stay apparatus with deep digital flexor tendon.
See Accessory ligament, Stay apparatus.

Cheek ◀€ *chēk, n.* (bucca) skin on side of face, below eye, and to the side of the mouth. More broadly: the side of the face.

C. tooth ◀€ *chēk / tūth, n.* premolar or molar tooth, i.e. those along side of mouth, rather than across the front.
See Tooth.

Chelate ◀€ *kē lāt, v.* to combine with a metal in chemical complexes.

Chelating agent ◀€ *kē lā ting / ā jēnt, n.* substance (e.g. ethamine diamine tetraacetic acid [EDTA]) which can bind certain metal ions to form stable compounds. Used in treatment of poisoning with some metals, e.g. lead, where the compound formed is non-toxic.
See Lead.

Chemical arthrodesis see Arthrodesis

Chemical ejaculation see Ejaculate/ejaculation

Chemistry ◀€ *kem is trē, n.* science of elements and their compounds; numerous chemistry disciplines. Also, chemical properties of a substance; e.g. blood chemistry is analysis of the chemical compounds of blood.

Chemoreceptor ◀€ *ke mō ri sep tē, n.* specialized nerve receptor which is excited by chemical substances, e.g. the olfactory receptor; a sense organ which is sensitive to chemical changes in the blood stream;

e.g. cells in carotid body which detect level of oxygen and carbon dioxide.
See Carotid.

Chemosis ◀€ *kē mō sis, n.* severe oedema (fluid swelling) of conjunctiva, e.g. in conjunctivitis.
See Conjunctiva, Conjunctivitis.

Chemotherapy ◀€ *kē mō the rē pē, n.* treatment of disease with chemical agent(s).

Cherry ◀€ *che rē, n.* (genus *Prunus*) type of fruiting tree. Leaves of some species toxic, containing amygdalin, a material that converts to cyanic or prussic acid as leaves are crushed or wilt; causes cyanide poisoning when ingested. May cause poisoning when a tree or branch falls into a horse pasture; the branch wilts, and the horses eat the bark or leaves. Cyanide prevents oxygen uptake by tissues. Signs of poisoning include difficulty breathing, trembling, incoordination, recumbency.
See Glycoside, Oxygen.

Chest see Thorax

Chestnut ◀€ *ches nut, n.* **1)** small horny outgrowth just above inside of carpal (knee) joint and below inside of each hock, probably vestiges of carpal and tarsal pads; **2)** coat colour of reddish brown, can vary in shade.
See Coat colour.

Chewing ◀€ *chūw ing, v.* (mastication) movement of lower jaw from side to side so food is ground between upper and lower teeth and mixed with saliva. Problems may occur in painful conditions of teeth or tongue.
See Tooth, Tongue.

C. disease see Nigropalladial encephalomalacia

Chigger ◀€ *chi gē, n.* six-legged larva of mites of genus *Trombiculidae*; common species of mite in Northern America is *Trombicula alfreddugesi*; in the UK the most prevalent mite is *Trombicula autumnalis*, harvest mites. Can occasionally cause irritation of skin in horses.

Chip fracture ◀ᯅ *chip* / *frak tŭr, n.* small piece(s) of cartilage and bone, usually broken through repetitive trauma; thought to be the result of chronic damage to a joint surface. In racing horses, chip fractures of carpal bones and metacarpophalangeal (fetlock) joint are common; cause pain, lameness and swelling. Diagnosis by radiography. Normally treated by arthroscopic removal at the time of injury, although many older, retired horses are recognized to have had chip fractures, and seem to have no ill effects from their presence.
See Carpal.

Chiropractic ◀ᯅ *kī rō prak tik, n.* controversial field founded in United States in late nineteenth century, on the premise that all disease occurs as a result of misalignment of vertebrae (subluxation). Animals are diagnosed and treated based on perceived joint misalignments, including back, pelvis and ribs, based on the philosophy and practice of the individual practitioner. There are no objective standards for diagnosis, treatment, or recovery; not recognized as a speciality field in veterinary medicine by any veterinary organization.
See Spine.

Chloramphenicol ◀ᯅ *klor rēm fe ni kol, n.* broad-spectrum bacteriostatic antibiotic originally derived from the bacterium *Streptomyces venezuelae*; the first antibiotic mass-produced on a large scale. Effective against Gram-negative (e.g. *Salmonella*) as well as Gram-positive organisms. An effective medication, but unpredictable human side-effect of aplastic anaemia has limited drug's use. Estimates of rate of complications vary from 1:24,000 to 1:225,000. Cannot be used in animals intended for human consumption. Most commonly used in ophthalmic ointments for treatment of eye problems, including conjunctivitis.
See Antibiotic, Conjunctivitis.

Chlorhexidine hydrochloride ◀ᯅ *klor hek si dēn* / *hi drō klor rīd, n.* topical antiseptic; available as surgical scrub for preparation of skin prior to surgery and cleaning skin wounds, in liquid for topical disinfection, and ointment, for wound application.

Chloride ◀ᯅ *klor rīd, n.* an ion formed when the element chlorine picks up one electron; Cl^-. Chloride ions have important physiological roles, e.g. the chloride–bicarbonate transport protein increases the blood's capacity to carry carbon dioxide, in the form of the bicarbonate ion. Depletion of chloride ions causes muscle dysfunction, e.g. after prolonged exercise with ion loss in sweat.

Chlorinated hydrocarbon ◀ᯅ *klo ri nā tid* / *hī drō kar bĕn, n.* group of organic pesticide compounds, e.g. DDT. Use is discontinued or severely restricted because of persistence in environment and incorporation into the food chain. May cause accidental poisoning if animal exposed. Signs include nervous symptoms: excitability, muscle spasms, seizures. No specific antidote; treatment symptomatic.
See Insecticide.

> **C.h. toxicity** ◀ᯅ *klo ri nā tid* / *hī drō kar bĕn* / *tok sis it ē, n.* pesticide; causes stimulation or depression of central nervous system, depending on dose. No specific treatment; supportive care is given (controlling seizures; activated charcoal to adsorb toxins). The use of chlorinated hydrocarbon pesticides is being phased out, or severely restricted because of environmental concerns.

Chloroform ◀ᯅ *klo rē form, n.* colourless liquid, used in past as general anaesthetic, but now superseded by more satisfactory anaesthetic agents.
See Anaesthetic.

Choanal stenosis see Stenosis

Choke ◀ᯅ *chōk, n.* obstruction of oesophagus/pharynx by foreign body or dry food material, e.g. inadequately soaked sugar beet pulp or hay pellets (NB lay term referring to oesophageal obstruction, not obstruction of airway). Causes distress, arching neck, drooling of saliva/ food from nostrils and mouth. May resolve spontaneously, but often relieved by passing nasogastric tube. Occasionally

associated with aspiration pneumonia if saliva and feed are aspirated into lungs. Can be recurrent, particularly if previous episodes have resulted in oesophageal scarring, with constriction of oesophageal lumen (stricture).
See Oesophagus, Pharynx, Stricture.

Chol- ◄ː *kōl-, prefix.* relating to bile or bile ducts.
See Bile.

Cholangiohepatitis ◄ː *kō lan jē ō he pē tī tis, n.* inflammation of bile ducts and liver. May occur from reflux of intestinal contents into common bile duct. Diagnosis by blood examination, with typical liver enzyme elevations; elevating of white blood cell count suggests infection, and antimicrobial therapy may be indicated. Supportive care indicated in most cases. Diagnosis by biopsy; prognosis depends on the degree of liver damage.
See Bile, Duodenum, Liver.

Cholelithiasis ◄ː *kō lē lith ē āsis, n.* the formation of biliary calculi ('stones'). Occasional cause of liver disease. Most common in adult, middle-aged horses; broodmares may have increased incidence. Signs include icterus, colic, fever, depression, and weight loss. Blood tests show liver involvement, but not specific; gamma glutamyl transferase (GGT) levels usually greatly elevated. May have increased abdominal fluid. Diagnosis by hepatic ultrasound or hepatic biopsy. General supportive care and long-term antimicrobials may be curative in some cases, continuing until GGT is normal. Surgery is possible, and there is a report of successful treatment, but there is no presurgery test to determine the extent of biliary tract obstruction. Prognosis depends on the extent of secondary liver damage, severity of clinical signs, and the number and location of the choleliths.

Cholesterol ◄ː *ko les tē rol, n.* fat-like substance present in most body tissues, in cell membranes, myelin nerve sheaths, precursors of bile acids.
See Bile, Myelin.

C. granuloma ◄ː *ko les tē rol / gra nū lō mē, n.* cholesteatoma; rare growth, sometimes found in the choroid plexus of the brain of old horses. Usually cause no signs, but large c.g.s may cause blindness, circling and depression.
See Choroid.

Choline ◄ː *kō lēn, n.* organic compound, usually grouped with B vitamin group. Found in cell membranes, and as important neurochemical for transmission of nervous impulses (acetylcholine). Choline deficiencies are unknown in horses.
C. chloride ◄ː *kō lēn / klor rīd, n.* dietary supplement; common in over-the-counter products for sale to horse owners. Has been added to the diets of horses with chronic obstructive pulmonary disease; no scientific reports of beneficial effect for any condition.

Cholinergic ◄ː *kō lin er jik, adj.* term to describe nerve fibres which release acetylcholine at synapses (junctions) when impulse is transmitted; substance which simulates the nerve receptors of parasympathetic nervous system.
See Acetylcholine, Choline, Parasympathetic nervous system, Nerve.

Chondritis ◄ː *kon drī tis, n.* inflammation of cartilage.
See Cartilage, Inflammation.
Arytenoid c. ◄ː *arē tēn oid / kon drī tis, n.* inflammation of one or both of the arytenoid cartilages, in the larynx. Usually diagnosed in young horses that perform at high speeds, particularly racing Thoroughbreds. Most often the disease is associated with respiratory noise and exercise intolerance. Diagnosed by endoscopic examination. Antibiotic therapy may help in some cases; many require surgery. Complications associated with surgical treatment include inspiratory obstruction, most likely a result of collapse of the unsupported adjacent soft tissues. Some horses will develop a cough when eating; aspiration of food particles may result in pneumonia. Only approximately 50% of horses treated surgically will return to their previous level of athletic performance.

Horses in which both arytenoids are affected usually do not return to competitive racing ability. Many horses with mineralization of the laryngeal cartilages fail to return to previous levels of performance.
See Cartilage, Inflammation.

Chondro- ◄∈ *kon drō, prefix.* relating to cartilage.
See Cartilage.

Chondroblast ◄∈ *kon drō blarst, n.* immature cell which produces cartilage.
See Cartilage.

Chondrocyte ◄∈ *kon drō sīt, n.* mature cartilage cell, lies in lacuna in cartilage matrix.
See Cartilage.

Chondroid ◄∈ *kon droid, adj./n.* resembling cartilage; mass which resembles cartilage, e.g. solid concretion formed in guttural pouch after infection and chronic accumulation of pus.
See Guttural pouch.

Chondroitin sulphate ◄∈ *kon droi tin / sul fāt, n.* important structural component of cartilage; provides much of its resistance to compression. Common dietary supplement for the prevention and treatment of osteoarthritis; commonly derived from bovine trachea. Little scientific support for effectiveness as dietary supplement.

Chondroma ◄∈ *kon drōmē, n.* benign tumour-like growth, composed of granulation tissue; occasionally seen in Thoroughbred and Standardbred racehorses as a mass from the surface of one or both of the arytenoid cartilages. Associated with respiratory noise at exercise; prognosis good for recovery after surgery.
See Arytenoid cartilage.

Chorda ◄∈ *kor dē, n.* cord, sinew, thin length of tough fibrous tissue.
   C. **tendina** ◄∈ *kor dē / ten di nē, n.* cord which connects cusp of atrioventricular valve to heart muscle. Several cordae tendinae are attached to each cusp.
   See Heart.

Chorion ◄∈ *ko rē ēn, n.* outermost foetal membrane, fuses with allantois to form foetal part of placenta between days 30 and 40; allantochorion.
See Allantois, Placenta.

Chorionic ◄∈ *ko rē o nik, adj.* pertaining to the chorion.
See Chorion, Placenta.
   C. **girdle** ◄∈ *ko rē o nik / ger dl, n.* the progenitor tissue of the endometrial cups. Appears around day 25 after ovulation.
   C. **gonadotrophin** ◄∈ *ko rē o nik / gō na dō trō fin, n.* see Equine chorionic gonadotrophin.

Chorioptes (bovis, equi) ◄∈ *ko rē op tēz (bōvis / e kwī), n.* non-burrowing mite, causes chorioptic mange, common dermatitis of horses; no age, breed, or sex predilection. Commonly seen on lower limbs of horses, especially those with heavily feathered legs; tail also affected. Mange more common in cold weather, causes stamping of feet, rubbing lower limbs, matting of hair with dried exudate, scaly skin patches if severe. Definitive diagnosis based on examination of skin scrapings. Ivermectin marginally effective, since parasite spends time off host; topical treatment with insecticides at one to two week intervals is ideal. Disinfection of grooming tools, and thorough cleaning of stables recommended.
See Mange, Mite.

Chorioretinitis ◄∈ *ko rē ō re ti nī tis, n.* inflammation of choroid and retina in eye; may be the result of equine recurrent uveitis or a manifestation of systemic disease such as equine infectious anaemia, adenovirus, West Nile virus, ehrlichiosis, and many others. The most common abnormality of the equine fundus. Active lesions appear with oedema and haemorrhage of retina; retinal detachment, if severe. Inactive lesions, chorioretinal scars, may be seen as incidental finding in examination of eye as hyperreflective or hyperpigmented areas; classic scar is called a 'butterfly' lesion. Effect on vision will depend on extent of lesion and cause. No specific medical or surgical therapy; underlying cause must be treated.
See Choroid, Eye, Retina.

94

Choristoma see Dermoid (d. cyst)

Choroid ◀⁃ _ko_ roid, adj./n. resembling chorion, especially in having lots of blood vessels; middle of three tunics which make up the eye, contains many blood vessels. See Chorion, Eye.

    C. plexus ◀⁃ _ko_ roid / _plek_ ses, n. network of blood vessels in ventricles of brain, site of production of cerebrospinal fluid. See Brain, Cerebrospinal.

Chromatography ◀⁃ _krō_ mē _to_ grē fē, n. a process in which a chemical mixture carried by a liquid or gas is separated into components; various techniques.

Chromomycosis see Phaeohyphomycosis

Chromosome ◀⁃ _krō_ mē zōm, n. coiled strand of deoxyribonucleic acid (DNA) in nucleus of cell which transmits genetic information. Each cell of animal contains same number of chromosomes, arranged in pairs, and these contain all genetic material for that individual. Each equid species has constant number of chromosomes: horse has 64; donkey has 62; mule has 63; zebra, depending on species, has between 44 and 62; onager has 56. See Deoxyribonucleic acid, Nucleus.

    Sex c. ◀⁃ seks / _krō_ mē zōm, n. one pair of chromosomes in each nucleus, determine gender of individual: XY in male, XX in female. Occasionally may have variation on this, e.g. XXY or XYY, or XY and XX both present in different cells of one animal. These abnormalities may result in intersex animals. See Intersex.

Chronic ◀⁃ _kro_ nik, adj. lasting for a long period, e.g. chronic disease (opposite is acute).

Chronic inflammatory bowel disease ◀⁃ _kro_ nik / in _fla_ mē tē rē / bōwl / di zēz, n. group of proliferative or inflammatory intestinal disorders characterized by malabsorption, poor body condition, weight loss; other signs may include diarrhoea, loss of appetite, intermittent colic, fever, fluid swelling of extremities or ventral abdomen. Conditions include lymphosarcoma, granulomatous enteritis,

eosinophilic gastroenteritis, lymphocytic–plasmocytic enterocolitis, and proliferative enteropathy. Ante-mortem diagnosis is often by process of elimination and commonly only confirmed on post-mortem exam. Diagnosis suggested by clinical signs; blood test findings (including hypoalbuminaemia, anaemia, neutrophilia) generally non-specific. Rectal palpation may reveal enlarged lymph nodes or abdominal masses. Abdominocentesis or rectal mucosal biopsy may be of diagnostic value. Rectal mucosal biopsy may be diagnostic; surgical biopsy of intestine requires general anaesthesia and is rarely performed. Treatment largely unsuccessful, except proliferative enteropathy of foals.
See Anaemia, Biopsy, Colic, Diarrhoea, Enteritis, Enteropathy, Granulomatous, Hypoalbuminaemia, Lymphocytic–plasmocytic enterocolitis, Neutrophilia.

Chronic interstitial nephritis see Nephritis

Chronic obstructive pulmonary disease see Recurrent airway obstruction

Chrysotherapy ◀⁃ _krī_ sō _the_ rē pē, n. treatment (as for pemphigus folliaceous) by injection of gold salts.

Chyle ◀⁃ kīl, n. lymph that is milky from fat absorption; characteristically present in the lymphatic lacteals of the intestines after a meal. Travels in thoracic duct to drain into veins in thorax.
See Lymphatic, Thoracic.

Chyloperitoneum ◀⁃ _kī_ lō _pe_ ri to _nē_ ēm, n. presence of chyle in abdominal cavity. May rarely develop secondary to tearing of mesenteric adhesions and rupture of mesenteric lymphatic vessels, or secondary to large colon torsion; has been seen in foals with congenital failure of development of lymphatics (lymphangiectasia).

Chylothorax ◀⁃ _kī_ lō _thor_ raks, n. presence of chyle in thoracic cavity, caused by rupture of thoracic duct. Rare in horse; has been reported with thoracic haemangiosarcoma;

in foals in association with meconium impaction and congenital diaphragmatic defects.
See Thoracic.

Cicatrix ◀€ _si kĕ triks, n._ a scar resulting from formation and contraction of fibrous tissue as wound heals.
See Wound.

Cicuta ◀€ _si kū tē, n._ genus of plants of Umbelliferae family; known as water hemlock and cowbane, both highly poisonous. One of the most toxic plants in the United States; very little of it needs to be eaten to cause death. Humans have been killed after only one or two bites of what they thought were 'parsnips' (water hemlock root resembles a parsnip). Cattle are the primary species affected, hence the name 'cowbane'. Animals have been poisoned by drinking water that had been contaminated with trampled water hemlock roots. Signs of poisoning include muscle twitching, dilation of pupils, difficulty with breathing, incoordination, convulsions, rapid death. Uncommon problem in horses.
See Cowbane, Water hemlock.

Ciliary body ◀€ _si lē ērē / bo dē, n._ the circumferential tissue inside the eye composed of the ciliary muscle and ciliary processes; part of the uveal tract.

Cilium ◀€ _si lē ĕm, n._ (plural: cilia) eyelash; tiny hair-like structure on surface of some cells, e.g. in lower respiratory tract. Beat rhythmically to move material over surface of cells, e.g. the cilia of the respiratory tract work to move mucus upwards to pharynx.

Cimetidine ◀€ _sī me tē dēn, n._ histamine H_2 receptor antagonist, drug which inhibits action of histamine in stomach and reduces secretion of acid. Has been used in the treatment of gastric ulcers in foals and adults; some reports of usefulness in treating cutaneous melanoma (estimated 20–30% response).
See Ulcer, Histamine, Melanoma.

Circulation ◀€ _ser kū lā shĕn, n._ orderly movement through a circuit or path; in reference to the body, may refer to movement of fluid through vessels, e.g. blood through blood vessels, lymph through lymphatics. Flow; e.g. describes movement of air within building.
See Blood, Heart, Lymph.

Cirrhosis ◀€ _si rō sis, n._ diffuse infiltration of normal liver tissue by fibrosis, with areas of regeneration; caused by various chronic progressive conditions affecting the liver; e.g, cholelithiasis. Diagnosis by hepatic biopsy. Signs include chronic loss of weight. Prognosis poor.
See Liver.

Cisapride ◀€ _si sĕ prīd, n._ drug which increases motility of stomach and intestines, may be used to treat ileus (loss of intestinal movement) after intestinal surgery (e.g. surgery for colic). Dosages and routes of administration are variable; little evidence of efficacy.
See Colic, Ileus.

Cisplatin ◀€ _sis pla tin, n._ platinum-containing compound used in treatment of cancer. Cisplatin acts by cross-linking DNA in several different ways, making it impossible for rapidly dividing cells to duplicate their DNA for mitosis. May be used in horse to treat sarcoid and other cutaneous tumours. Commonly given as injection of suspension in oil; implantable cisplatin beads are also available.
See Cancer, Equine sarcoid.

Cisterna ◀€ _sis ter nĕ, n._ A fluid-containing sac or cavity in the body of an organism.
    C. magna ◀€ _sis ter nĕ / mag nĕ, n._ large subarachnoid space between the caudal part of the cerebellum and the medulla oblongata; space at base of skull from which cerebrospinal fluid may be aspirated.
    See Cerebrospinal.

Citrate ◀€ _si trāt, n._ ionic form of citric acid; important in metabolism. Citrate compounds are used as anticoagulants in collection of blood, e.g. acid citrate dextrose, citrate phosphate dextrose.

Works by binding calcium, but not as strongly as EDTA.
See Anticoagulant, EDTA.

CK see Creatine kinase

Clamp ◀ᴇ *klamp, n./v.* any of a number of instruments or devices for holding or compressing something; especially, an instrument used to hold, compress, or crush vessels and hollow organs, and to aid in surgical excision, e.g. a clamp used for compressing a blood vessel during surgery to prevent bleeding; as verb, to use a clamp to hold something tightly.

Claudication ◀ᴇ *klor di kā shēn, n.* pain, fatigue or weakness in the limbs; limping.
> **Intermittent c.** ◀ᴇ *in tēr mi tēnt / klor di kā shēn, n.* episodic pain, weakness and lameness in hind legs, seen especially after exercise, e.g. as caused by blood clot in iliac artery.
> See Aorto-iliac thrombosis.

Cleft palate see Palate

Clenbuterol ◀ᴇ *klen bū tē rol, n.* β_2-adrenergic agonist drug which causes bronchodilation; used in treatment of recurrent airway obstruction. Typically used orally. Also causes increase in muscle mass through partitioning effect and has been used in past as growth promoter in cattle (now illegal for such purposes).
See Recurrent airway obstruction.

Clinical diagnosis see Diagnosis

Clip ◀ᴇ *klip, n/v.* 1) a flat projection, usually triangular or round, extending upward from the outer edge of a horseshoe, fitted flat against, or set into, the outer surface of the hoof wall. Clips may be drawn from the metal of the shoe or welded on. Used to prevent the shoe from shifting on the hoof, to stabilize the hoof wall, or sometimes as a purely cosmetic touch; 2) to trim hair; to cut off the outer part of, as in clipping a foot while running.

Clitoral fossa ◀ᴇ *kli tē rūl / foss ē, n.* depression in ventral vulva housing clitoris; site of persistent infection for contagious equine metritis; mares can harbour organism in clitoral fossa without signs of disease. Swabs may be taken from clitoral fossa for examination for disease-causing organisms before mare is used for breeding, or prior to export.
See Breeding, Contagious equine metritis.

Clitoris ◀ᴇ *kli tē ris, n.* small organ of erectile tissue on the ventral aspect of the vulva; in female, homologous structure to male penis.

Clostridial ◀ᴇ *klo stri dē ēl, adj.* pertaining to or caused by genus of bacteria, *Clostridium*.

Clostridium ◀ᴇ *klo stri dē ēm, n.* genus of anaerobic bacteria, Gram-positive, rod-shaped, form spores. Many species part of normal body bacterial flora; associated with numerous disease conditions including infectious myositis, acute diarrhoea and colic, botulism, tetanus. Examples:
- *C. botulinum* – causing botulism.
- *C. chauvoei* – associated with acute muscle infections (gas gangrene; infectious myositis).
- *C. difficile* – implicated in acute infectious diarrhoea and antibiotic associated diarrhoea; diagnosis by identification of toxin in faecal samples.
- *C. novyi* – associated with infectious myositis; infectious necrotic hepatitis (rare).
- *C. perfringens* – cause of acute infectious diarrhoea and antibiotic associated diarrhoea; acute muscle infections (gas gangrene; infectious myositis).
- *C. piliformis* – cause of Tyzzer's disease.
- *C. septicum* – associated with acute muscle infections (gas gangrene; infectious myositis).
- *C. tetani* – elaborates exotoxin causing tetanus.

Care for various clostridial diseases varies depending on aetiology and clinical signs. Antibiotic therapy indicated for muscle infections, but rarely for other clostridial infections. Supportive care crucial; may include fluid therapy (enterocolitis), sedation (tetanus), or anti-inflammatories. Vaccines available for prevention of *C.*

botulinum and *C. tetani* infections; vaccines produced for prevention of diarrhoea in other species not available for horses. See Botulism, Gangrene, Myositis, Tetanus, Tyzzer's disease.

Clot ◀≀ *klot, n/v.* coagulated mass produced by clotting of blood; to undergo a sequence of complex chemical and physical reactions that convert blood into a coagulum. Sequence involves loss of blood; release of thromboplastin from blood platelets and injured tissues; heparin inactivation by thromboplastin, which allows calcium ions in the blood plasma to convert prothrombin to thrombin; interaction of thrombin with fibrinogen to create a fibrin network that traps plasma and blood cells, and contraction of the clot to squeeze out excess fluid; coagulation. Compared to humans, the most striking features of the equine clotting system are the greatly prolonged clotting time (12–15 minutes), poor clot retraction in spite of a platelet count within normal human limits, and a prolonged one-stage prothrombin time. See Blood, Clotting.

Clotrimazole ◀≀ *klō tri mē zōl, n.* antifungal agent used by topical application. Has been used to treat mycotic keratitis (fungal infection of cornea of eye) in horse, with 50% success in one report; efficacy of drug in routine clinical setting is unknown. See Keratitis.

Clotting ◀≀ *klo ting, n.* coagulating. See Haemophilia, Warfarin.

　C. factor ◀≀ *klo ting / fak tē, n.* any of several components of plasma (such as fibrinogen, prothrombin, and thromboplastin) that are involved in the process of clot formation. See Haemophilia, Warfarin.

Clover ◀≀ *klō vē, n.* pasture plant, high in protein. Some types of clover may be associated with photosensitivity (damage to skin caused by sunlight acting on chemicals absorbed from plants); mouldy clover may be associated with presence of dicoumarol (chemical that can interfere with blood clotting).

Alsike c. ◀≀ *al sīk / klō vē, n.* (*Trifolium hybridum*) 'dew poisoning, trifoliosis'; common cause of photosensitivity in horses, especially in the northwest United States and Canada. As little as 20% alsike clover in the diet causes poisoning; clinical signs appear 2–4 weeks following poisoning. Clinical signs of photosensitivity include sunburn of non-pigmented skin and mucous membranes of the mouth, eyes, and vulva. In more severe cases, signs of liver disease occur, including progressive weight loss, inappetance, depression, icterus, circling, yawning, colic, recumbency, and eventually coma and death. The toxin responsible for the liver disease associated with alsike clover poisoning is unknown. Diagnosis based on presence of clover in the diet, detection of the fungus *Cymodothea trifolii* on the clover, elevated liver enzymes, and the presence of photosensitization. Horses not severely affected will recover if they are removed from the clover and kept out of the sun until the liver enzyme profile returns to normal. See Clotting, Photosensitization.

　Red c. ◀≀ *red / klō vē, n.* (*Trifolium praetense*) 'slobbers'; black patch fungus on leaves of plant causes disease characterized by excessive salivation; in severe cases, can cause dehydration. See Slaframine.

　White c. ◀≀ *wīt / klō vē, n.* (*Trifolium repens*) herbaceous, perennial legume plant widely grown as a pasture crop.

Club foot ◀≀ *klub / fūt, n.* deformity of foot and lower limb; angle of wall of hoof to ground is greater than 60°, with dished hoof wall. Various causes, including contracture of flexor tendons, as congenital defect, as result of nutritional deficiency or through injury. May be bilateral or unilateral. May respond to farrier care; some cases require surgery, commonly desmotomy of the inferior check ligament. See Check, Congenital, Flexor.

Coagulant ◀≀ *kō ag ū lēnt, n.* something which causes formation of clot in blood. See Clot, Clotting.

Coagulation ◄≦ *kō ag ū lā shēn, n.* formation of clot in blood.
See Clot, Clotting.

   C. disorder ◄≦ *kō ag ū lā shēn / dis ordē, n.* a disturbance in normal clotting function; e.g. haemophilia, dicoumarol poisoning.

   C. factors see Clotting

   C. test ◄≦ *kō ag ū lā shēn / test, n.* test to evaluate clotting capability of blood. Several tests used including prothrombin time, activated partial thromboplastin time, platelet count. Fibrin degradation products tests for breakdown of fibrin: increased in disseminated intravascular coagulation.

   C. time ◄≦ *kō ag ū lā shēn / tīm, n.* time for stable clot to form; horse's longest of domestic mammals, 12–15 minutes.
See Clot, Clotting, Disseminated.

Coat ◄≦ *kōt, n.* hair covering horse's body; outer layer covering organ.
See Hair.

Coat colour ◄≦ *kōt / ku lē, n.* colour of horse's hair, inherited characteristic, although some colours will change with age (e.g. grey horse may be born black and coat colour lightens as horse gets older). Some breed societies only recognize animals of specific colour(s). Specific colours recognized in horses include:
- Bay – brown with black mane and tail, often black points.
- Black – black body and mane and tail, white markings allowed.
- Brown.
- Chestnut – reddish brown, no dark points, mane or tail.
- Cream – very pale coat, including muzzle, mane and tail (unusual).
- Dun – yellow, darker mane and tail, with brown stripe along back from withers to top of tail.
- Grey – grey all over, including points. Variations, e.g. steel grey has black points, silver grey has white mane and tail.
- Palomino – golden with white mane and tail.
- Piebald – large irregular patches of black and white.
- Roan – uniform mixture of white and coloured hairs, e.g. red roan, blue roan.
- Skewbald – large irregular patches of any colour but black, and white.

Cocaine ◄≦ *kō kān, n.* alkaloid obtained from leaves of coca plants, used in past as topical anaesthetic, but now superseded by other products because of human addiction. Controlled drug; has been used illegally as stimulant in horses.

Coccidia ◄≦ *kok si dē e, n.* group of microorganisms, parasites of epithelial cells of intestine; uncommon cause of disease in horses.

Coccidioides immitis ◄≦ *kok si dē oi dēz / i mi tis, n.* soil fungus, may rarely cause disease if inhaled or absorbed through skin. Found in specific geographical locations, from 40 degrees latitude south to 40 degrees latitude north, e.g. South and Central America, southwestern USA.
See Coccidioidomycosis, Fungus.

Coccidioidomycosis ◄≦ *kok si dē oid ō mī kō sis, n.* fungal disease most commonly caused by inhalation of fungal spores (arthroconidia). Wide range of manifestations and severity. Pulmonary infections most common, but can be spread through lymphatic system to various sites, cause abortion, or, rarely, cause local skin infections after wound inoculation. Granulomas of nasal passages also reported. Clinical signs vary with site of disease, but include fever, weight loss, cough, increased respiratory sounds in pulmonary form. Other signs reflect the system involved, e.g. draining tracts in skin infection. Blood tests non-specific. Affected horses tend to be young to middle aged, from endemic areas. Diagnosis from typical signs in endemic area, demonstration of organism on smears (e.g. tracheobronchial aspirates), and culture. Serum antibody testing indicates exposure; rising titres on subsequent tests indicate worsening disease, whereas decreasing titres indicate improvement. Therapy may be supportive in mild cases, involve surgical incision in others, or require antifungal therapy, e.g. amphotericin B or ketoconazole. Antifungal therapy prolonged, often several months. Prognosis related to extent of initial infection.

Coccus ◄ɛ _ko_ _kĕs_, _n._ spherical bacterium, e.g. _Staphylococcus_, _Streptococcus_. See Bacterium.

Coccygeal ◄ɛ _kok_ _si_ _jē_ _ēl_, _adj._ of the tail, e.g. coccygeal vertebrae are bones of the tail.

   C. fracture ◄ɛ _kok_ _si_ _jē_ _ēl_ / _frak_ _tŭr_, _n._ break of one or more bones of tail. May heal with kink in tail, or tail may be left permanently flaccid.

Coeliac ◄ɛ _sē_ _lē_ _ak_, _adj._ abdominal; e.g. coeliac artery.

Coeliotomy ◄ɛ _sē_ _lē_ _ot_ _ēmē_, _n._ an incision into the abdominal cavity; laparotomy.

Coffin bone ◄ɛ _ko_ _fin_ / _bōn_, _n._ distal phalanx (3rd phalanx), contained within hoof.

Coffin joint ◄ɛ _ko_ _fin_ / _joint_, _n._ joint between 2nd and 3rd phalanges; distal interphalangeal joint.

Coggins test ◄ɛ _ko_ _ginz_ / _test_, _n._ test used for diagnosis of equine infectious anaemia, detects antigen and antibody in horse's blood by agar-gel immunodiffusion. (Named after Dr Leroy Coggins, American veterinarian, who developed the test.)

Coital exanthema ◄ɛ _kō_ _i_ _tēl_ / _ek_ _zan_ _thē_ _mē_, _n._ infectious venereal disease caused by equine herpes virus 3. See Equine herpes virus, Venereal, Vesicle.

Coitus ◄ɛ _kō_ _i_ _tēs_, _n._ mating, sexual intercourse.

Cold ◄ɛ _kōld_, _n._/_adj._ general term describing disease of upper respiratory tract; in horses, characterized by coughing and discharge from nose, generally with fever.

Cold back see Back

Cold-blooded ◄ɛ _kōld-blu_ _did_, _adj._ referring mainly to draught breeds, e.g. Clydesdale, Percheron, Shire, etc. Opposite is hot-blooded, e.g. Arabian and Thoroughbred horses.

Colibacillosis ◄ɛ _kō_ _lē_ _ba_ _si_ _lō_ _sis_, _n._ disease caused by infection with _Escherichia coli_, e.g. _E. coli_ septicaemia and diarrhoea in foals.

Colic ◄ɛ _ko_ _lik_, _n._ acute abdominal pain, not a specific disease. Wide range of signs, loosely related to severity of underlying problem:

- Mild – pawing ground, turning head towards flank, stretching out, lying down.
- Moderate – pawing, kicking at abdomen, rolling, turning head to flank, keeps moving.
- Severe – sweating, violent rolling, continuous movement.

Colic has many causes but cases can be roughly divided into two groups: medical colics, i.e. those that respond to medical treatment, and surgical colics, i.e. those that require surgical correction. Various other terms have been used to describe colic, mostly based on clinical signs or aetiology, e.g. alimentary colic, biliary colic, renal colic, but such descriptive terms are of little practical use. Common descriptions of colic include:

- Spasmodic – thought to be common; however, muscular 'spasm' as a cause of colic has never been demonstrated objectively.
- Impaction – intestine blocked with food, sand, foreign body (e.g. baling twine), enterolith, etc. Can potentially occur at any location, but most common at narrowings or turns, such as the pelvic flexure or ileocaecal junction, or in the blind sac that is the caecum. When a horse has colic as a result of an impaction, the clinical signs are usually more moderate and their onset is more gradual when compared to those colics that directly compromise blood supply to the intestines.
- Flatulent – build-up of gas in intestine from various causes, including proximal to impactions (fermentation continues, but gas cannot pass), displacement of gut, ileus (failure of peristalsis, e.g. after anaesthesia), stress, pain, feeding highly fermentable food. Frequently dramatic clinical signs, as distension of the bowel is very painful.

- Strangulation/obstruction – blockage of intestine by twist (volvulus), strangulation, intussusception (telescoping of bowel). Normally causes more dramatic signs; often rapid onset, rapid heart rate and breathing, severe sweating, pale mucous membranes, shock.

Other causes of abdominal pain include enteritis (inflammation of small intestine), idiopathic (cause unknown), intestinal parasites (e.g. *Strongylus vulgaris*), and grass sickness.

DIAGNOSIS
The most important decision to be made in colic management is whether the problem can be managed medically, or will require surgery. Various clinical signs and diagnostic techniques assist in diagnosis of colic.

a. Heart rate – elevates with pain and with onset of shock. Heart rate above 60 beats per minute associated with a greater likelihood of surgical colic.

b. Body temperature – fever is negatively associated with the likelihood that a horse will require surgery, that is, if the horse has a fever, it is less likely that it will need surgery than if its temperature is normal.

c. Mucous membranes – mucous membrane colour is a relatively insensitive indicator of whether a horse requires colic surgery, unless shock has begun.

d. Rectal examination – relatively insensitive; only 40% of abdomen can be examined rectally. When problem can be detected, diagnostic accuracy is fairly good, but many problems escape detection.

e. Nasogastric intubation – reflux on nasogastric intubation may indicate obstruction, or medical problem such as enteritis. Reflux not commonly obtained; if reflux present, must be interpreted along with clinical signs.

f. Complete blood count – helpful in assessing body's response to colic problem, but cannot be performed in field, so of limited diagnostic value.

g. Abdominal auscultation – lack of gut sounds is associated with a need for surgery; however, many medical colics have decreased abdominal sounds,

while virtually no surgical colic has abdominal sounds.

h. Abdominocentesis – when changes in abdominal fluid occur, the disease process is usually well established. Can give hint as to causes of colic not directly related to intestinal problem, e.g. neoplasia.

i. Radiography – fairly sensitive indicator of radio-opaque material causing obstruction, e.g. sand or enterolith.

j. Ultrasound – sensitive indicator of problems in bowel; can see distension, ileus, and some cases of obstruction/strangulation.

See Abdominocentesis, Auscultation, Grass sickness, Ileus, Rectal, Shock, Spasm, Nasogastric, *Strongylus* spp.

False c. ◄ₑ *fawls / ko lik, n.* signs of abdominal pain not caused by gastrointestinal disorder, e.g. severe distension of bladder, thrombosis of iliac artery, pregnant mare with uterine torsion, acute exertional rhabdomyolysis (horse may suddenly drop to ground during exercise, sweat, kick out).
See Exertional rhabdomyolysis, Thrombosis, Uterine.

Medical c. ◄ₑ *med ik ēl / ko lik, n.* a colic that is amenable to resolution with medical therapy alone. Prognosis usually good.

Surgical c. ◄ₑ *ser ji kēl / ko lik, n.* a colic which requires surgical treatment, e.g. untwisting, removal of damaged bowel, etc. Prognosis varies depending on type and duration of colic, and the extent of secondary changes.
See Obstruction.

Coliform ◄ₑ *ko li form, adj.* relating to Gram-negative bacilli from intestine, e.g. *Escherichia coli, Klebsiella, Enterobacter.*

Colitis ◄ₑ *ko lī tis, n.* inflammation of colon and caecum with the presence of large numbers of inflammatory cells. Causes acute diarrhoea, with endotoxaemia and leukopenia, colic, rapid and severe dehydration, and death. Can affect horses of all ages, but more common in horses between 2 and 10 years. Sudden onset and rapid progression; definitive diagnosis only made in 20–30% of cases. Several causes including bacterial infection (*Salmonella, Clostridium*), antibiotic

therapy, non-steroidal anti-inflammatory drug therapy. Successful treatment requires administration of large amounts of polyionic fluids until condition resolves; other treatments include electrolyte and protein replacement, therapy to combat the effects of endotoxin, and, when indicated, antimicrobial therapy (most horses with colitis do not benefit from antimicrobial therapy).
See Colic, Diarrhoea.

Colitis X ◀⁞ *kō lī tis / eks, n.* peracute colitis of unknown cause with diarrhoea, colic and dehydration. Archaic term; modern terminology attemps to reflect possible aetiologies.

Collagen ◀⁞ *ko lē gen, n.* primary protein found in connective tissue, skin, tendons, cartilage, etc. Consists of strong fibres, primarily in connective tissue but relatively ubiquitous, e.g. small network of collagen fibres in vitreous humour of eye.

Collapse ◀⁞ *kēl laps, v./n.* enter state of extreme depression, prostration, with failure of circulation; circulatory collapse. To fall helpless or unconscious.
See Heart.

Collateral ◀⁞ *ko la tē rēl, adj.* relating to or being branches of a bodily part, e.g. collateral ligament; a small side branch, e.g. collateral circulation.

C. cartilages ◀⁞ *ko la tē rēl / kar til lij is, n.* two flattened cartilage plates, one each on medial and lateral side of foot, above coronary band. Covered by venous plexus, slightly overhanging the 3rd phalanx (coffin bone). Below and behind, the cartilage is tied to the digital cushion. Ossification of the collateral cartilage is called sidebone; infection of the collateral cartilage is called quittor.
See Quittor, Sidebone.

C. circulation ◀⁞ *ko la tē rēl / ser kū la shĕn, n.* circulation of blood that is established when a major vessel is functionally obstructed; occurs by enlargement of minor vessels and anastomosis of vessels with those of adjacent parts; the vessels through which such circulation occurs. Horses have a good deal of collateral circulation to vital organs, and so are not thought to suffer from events related to blood vessel obstruction (primarily cardiac arrest and stroke).

C. ligament ◀⁞ *ko la tē rēl / lig ē ment, n.* any of various ligaments on one or the other side of a hinge joint, e.g. as occur in the coffin joint or stifle.

Colloid oncotic pressure see Pressure

Colloid osmotic pressure see Pressure

Coloboma ◀⁞ *ko lē bō mē, n.* congenital defect of eye in which portion of normal ocular tissue is missing. Can be unilateral or bilateral, alone or with other congenital abnormalities, and can affect virtually any structure except the cornea. Severe colobomas have been associated with vision defects; no treatment. Breeding from affected animals should probably be avoided.
See Eye, Iris, Uvea.

Colon ◀⁞ *kō lon, n.* part of intestine from caecum to rectum (large intestine). Composed of:
1. Caecum: cul-de-sac pouch, about 1.2 m long, that holds approx 36 litres of semi-liquid material. It contains bacteria that digest cellulose plant fibre through fermentation.
2. Large colon, 3–3.6 m long, holds up to 90 litres of semi-liquid material. Site of gas production and elimination, microbial digestion of food, and carbohydrate and volatile fatty acid absorption. Large colon is further divided into:
   • right ventral (lower) colon
   • left ventral (lower) colon
   • left dorsal (upper) colon
   • right dorsal (upper) colon
   • transverse colon.
   Spatial organization quite complicated in horse, forming an uncoiled loop bent over on itself several times).
3. Small colon, 3–3.6 m in length and holds approximately 23 litres of material. Most of water in the horse's diet is absorbed here; the place where faecal balls are formed.

Colorado strangles see *Corynebacterium pseudotuberculosis*

Colostrum ◀⁞ *kē lo strēm, n.* first milk secreted by mammary glands after giving

birth. Thick, yellow, rich in maternal anti-bodies which are absorbed across foal's intestine in first 24 hours of life; confer initial immunity on foal. If foal does not suckle or mare does not produce colostral antibodies (e.g. premature birth), foal will be predisposed to infections due to failure of passive transfer.
See Immunity, Mammary gland, Milk, Passive transfer.

Colour see Coat colour

Colpotomy ◄⁝ *kol po̱ tē mē, n.* surgical cutting of vaginal wall. May be performed in operation to remove ovaries (e.g. to correct behavioural problem caused by female hormones); allows operation to be performed without general anaesthesia.
See Ovary.

Colt ◄⁝ *kolt, n.* young entire (i.e. not castrated) male horse; age arbitrarily designated as up to 4 years of age.

Coma ◄⁝ *ko̱ mē, n.* state of prolonged unconsciousness; may occur in terminal stage of severe disease, from injury, or from toxicity.

Comatose ◄⁝ *ko̱ mē tōz, adj.* in state of coma.
See Coma.

Combined immunodeficiency ◄⁝ *kom bi̱nd / i̱ mū no di fi̱ shēn sē, n.* hereditary defect of Arabians and Arab cossbreeds, where there is failure of maturation of B and T cells, so immune system does not function. Foals appear normal at birth, but suffer opportunistic infections and usually die by 5–6 months of age. Autosomal recessive trait; both parents are carriers and should not be used for breeding again.
See B lymphocyte, Hereditary, Opportunistic, T lymphocyte.

Commensal ◄⁝ *ko men sēl, n./adj.* organism which benefits from living on or in another organism. Host does not benefit, but is not harmed (unlike with parasite), e.g. bacteria which live on horse's skin.
See Parasite.

Comminuted ◄⁝ *ko̱ mi nū tid, adj.* broken into small pieces.
C. fracture ◄⁝ *ko̱ mi nū tid / fṟak tŭr, n.* breakage of a bone resulting in many bone fragments; usually as result of severe trauma, e.g. fall, road traffic accident. Prognosis for repair guarded, depending on extent of fracture; prognosis for return to athletic soundness generally poor if joint involved.
See Fracture.

Commissure ◄⁝ *ko mi su̱r, n.* point where two parts join; e.g. where upper and lower lips join at sides of mouth; nerve fibres which join two halves of brain.

Common digital extensor ◄⁝ *ko mēn / dij it ēl / ex ten sē, n.* referring to a mechanism of action that is involved in straightening (extending) the horse's lower limb (digit); the mechanism is shared by multiple anatomical structures (i.e. it is common to all of them).
C.d.e. muscle ◄⁝ *ko mēn / dij it ēl / ex ten sē / mu sēl, n.* large muscle of forelimb, origi-nating from the humerus and travelling distally, to become the common digital extensor tendon. Second part originates from the lateral radius, and joins the tendon. This muscle extends the carpal, pastern, and coffin joints.
C.d.e. tendon ◄⁝ *ko mēn / di ji tēl / ek sten sē / ten dēn, n.* tendinous part of common digital extensor muscle, originating at the bottom third of the radius of the forearm; facilitates muscle action. At the knee, tendon sheath may be injured or infected, resulting in swelling and lameness and soreness on carpal flexion. Rupture of the tendon in neonatal foals, especially Arabians, Quarter Horses and Arabian–Quarter Horse cross-breds may be present at birth or immediately after birth. May have accompanying birth defects, such as carpal hypoplasia. Associated with flexural deformity of the carpus, but it is generally not known whether the rupture precedes the flexural deformity, or whether the flexural deformity comes first. Treatment varies; if no flexural deformity is present, bandaging the limb to protect the dorsal fetlock from abrasion may be all that is required. If carpal bone prob-lems are present, casting or splinting of the

limb is required. Prognosis depends on degree of flexural deformity and severity of associated birth defects.
See Fetlock, Tendon.

Communicable ◀≀ *kom ū nik ēbūl, adj.* capable of being transmitted from one individual to another, as in disease.

Comparative anatomy see Anatomy

Compartmental syndrome ◀≀ *kom part men tēl / sin drōm, n.* rare condition, most commonly seen in forearm, in which high pressure develops in a fascial space, such as a muscular sheath; pain results from compression of tissues within space. Common causes include trauma and falling. Typically, horses are lame starting a few hours after a traumatic event. Affected area may seem swollen, hard, painful on palpation, and warm. Clinical signs usually sufficient for diagnosis. Most cases resolve with cold therapy, non-steroidal anti-inflammatory drugs, and rest for 4–5 days; cases that do not respond may require cutting of the fascial space (fasciotomy) to release pressure; relief usually seen immediately. Prognosis generally good, whether the condition is managed conservatively or by surgery, unless muscle fibrosis occurs.

Compensation ◀≀ *kom pen sā shēn, n.* correction of a fault or defect by excessive development or by increased functioning, either of another structure, or by normally functioning parts of the same structure; e.g. heart beats faster if blood oxygen is low; heart muscle grows thicker and stronger to cope with faulty heart valves; horse bears more weight on one limb to compensate for lameness in another limb. See Heart.

Complement ◀≀ *kom pli mēnt, n.* complex proteins present in serum, important in body's defence against disease. Combines with antibody–antigen complex and brings about destruction of antigen.
See Antibody, Antigen.
   C. fixation test ◀≀ *kom pli mēnt / fik sā shēn / test, n.* laboratory test used to identify presence of specific antibody or antigen in blood

serum. In the test a serum sample is exposed to a particular antigen and complement in order to determine whether or not antibodies to that particular antigen are present, i.e. to determine whether or not there has been an immune response to disease; e.g. in diagnosis of glanders, brucellosis.

Complementary medicine see Alternative therapy

Complete blood count ◀≀ *kom plēt / blud / kōnt, n.* (CBC) an analysis of the cellular components of blood; includes separate counts for red and white blood cells, and platelets. Also known as a Differential blood count.

Complex ◀≀ *kom pleks, n.* a chemical association of two or more molecules, e.g. antigen–antibody complex; the sum of the factors (such as clinical signs and lesions) characterizing a disease, e.g. navicular disease complex.

Compound ◀≀ *kom pōnd, n.* substance made up of chemical union of two or more materials or elements.
   C. fracture ◀≀ *kom pōnd / frak tŭr, n.* break in bone in which skin is pierced by bone fragment(s); has implications for treatment as infection may enter the fracture site through the broken skin. Also known as open fracture.

Compress ◀≀ *kom pres, v.; kom pres, n.* as verb, to press or squeeze together; as noun, pad of soft material (hot or cold) applied with pressure to stop bleeding or reduce inflammation.

Computed radiography ◀≀ *kom pū tid / rā dē og rēf ē, n.* radiographic technique employing a plate with a phosphor screen instead of radiographic film. The plate is inserted in a machine that reads the information and displays it on a computer screen, eliminating need for darkroom development.
See Radiography.

Computed tomography ◀≀ *kom pū tid / to mo grē fē, n.* method of imaging body tissues. Specialized X-ray equipment used to get images from many different angles around a single axis; computer then used to combine images to give cross-sectional picture of tissues. Expense of equipment limits availability. Has been used in diagnosis of conditions of lower legs, skull, and sinuses. See X-ray.

Concentrate ◀ᴊ _kon sen trat, n._ less dilute; e.g. a strong solution, i.e. little water or other dilutent present relative to active ingredient; refers also to grain ration in diet (i.e. there are more calories concentrated in grain than in forage).

Conception ◀ᴊ _kĕn sep shĕn, n._ beginning of pregnancy, including fertilization of ovum, and/or when viable blastocyst implants in uterine wall.

Concha ◀ᴊ _kon chĕ, n._ shell; in anatomy, shell-shaped, e.g. concha of nasal passages; ethmoturbinate bones (internal structure of nasal passages).
See Nasal.

    Conchal sinuses ◀ᴊ _kong kĕl / sĭ nĕs iz, n._ two small sinuses, dorsal and ventral, medial to orbit of the eye. May be invaded with ethmoid haematoma or dentigerous cyst; occasional site of infection.
    Ear c. ◀ᴊ _ér / kon chĕ, n._ the largest and deepest concavity of the external ear.

Concussion ◀ᴊ _kĕn ku shĕn, n._ impact, as in concussion on hoof or limb from exercise activity; injury that results from violent blow, especially to brain.

Condition ◀ᴊ _kĕn di shĕn, n._ something essential to the appearance or occurrence of something else, e.g. moist condition of a stall is conducive to the development of lower limb dermatitis; a state of health, usually defective, e.g. a lameness condition; physical fitness, e.g. the horse is in good physical condition.
    C. score see Body condition

Condom ◀ᴊ _kon dom, n._ technique for collection of stallion semen where a sheath (condom) is placed over penis of stallion.

Condyle ◀ᴊ _kon dīl, n._ rounded prominence at end of bone; used primarily to describe a matched pair of prominences that resemble a pair of knuckles, e.g. condyles of distal humerus at the articulation of the radius/ulna in elbow joint.

Conformation ◀ᴊ _kon for mā shĕn, n._ the shape and proportionate dimensions of a horse; refers to general appearance of animal, including symmetry, shape and size of different areas of body. People attempt to judge a horse's suitability for athletic performance based on a conformation 'ideal'. Examples of 'poor' conformation of legs of horse include feet too close together or too wide apart, pasterns too upright, legs set too close together or too far apart on body, etc. Common wisdom holds that less than ideal conformation may cause problems, e.g. sprains, strains, and bone injuries; however, such associations are generally not supported by scientific evidence, and many horses seem to be unaware of their conformation problems and perform well in spite of them.

Congenital ◀ᴊ _kĕn je ni tĕl, adj._ present at or dating from birth. Conditions such as cleft palate, ventricular septal defect, or umbilical hernia may be seen when a foal is born. May be hereditary or occur as result of outside influences (disease, toxicity, etc.) during development in womb; the aetiology of many congenital conditions is unknown.
See Hernia, Palate, Ventricular, and other defects under individual entries.

Congestion ◀ᴊ _kĕn jes chĕn, n._ an excessive accumulation, especially of blood or mucus; e.g. congested mucous membranes as a result of shock.

Congestive heart failure ◀ᴊ _kĕn jes tiv / hart / fā lŭr, n._ (CHF), a condition in which the heart cannot pump enough blood to the body's other organs. Rare in horses. When seen, clinical findings include heart murmur, tachycardia, enlargement and distension of the jugular veins, jugular pulse (where the beating of the heart can be seen in the jugular veins because of blood being pushed backwards by the heart), coughing, tachypnoea, exercise intolerance, intermittent collapse, and swelling of the ventral abdomen and lower limbs. Various causes, insufficiency of mitral valve being common. Diagnosis by clinical signs and echocardiography; echocardiogram usually shows enlarged heart. Prognosis poor; most horses are euthanized or die shortly after diagnosis. See Compensation, Heart.

Conidiobolomycosis ◀ː *ko ni̱ dē ō bō̱ lō mī kō̱ sis, n.* rarely diagnosed fungal infection (*Conidiobolus coronatus*) of nasal passages. Seen in southern USA and Mexico, causes granulomatous lesions in nasal passages. Successful treatment has been reported with a combination of surgical removal of lesions and antifungal medication (amphotericin B).

Conium maculatum see Water hemlock

Conjunctiva ◀ː *con jungk ti̱ vē, n.* mucous membrane lining the inner surface of the eyelids and continuing over the forepart of the eyeball.
See Eye.

Conjunctival ◀ː *con jungk ti̱ vēl, adj.* pertaining to conjunctiva.
See Conjunctiva.

  C. graft ◀ː *con jungk ti̱ vēl / grarft, n.* technique for repair of ocular defects, e.g. in large corneal ulcers not responding to treatment, or in corneal perforation. A piece of healthy conjunctiva is raised as a flap, rotated to cover the defect and sutured into place.

  C. neoplasia ◀ː *con jungk ti̱ vēl / nē ō plā zē ē, n.* tumour of conjunctiva. Most common is squamous cell carcinoma, especially in unpigmented areas where conjunctiva joins skin. Rarely, may see haemangioma and melanoma. Diagnosis by histopathology.
See Haemangioma, Histopathology, Melanoma, Squamous cell carcinoma.

  C. pseudotumour ◀ː *con jungk ti̱ vēl / sū dō̱ tū mē, n.* nodular lymphocytic conjunctivitis; flat or nodular masses of the conjunctiva of the eye, third eyelid and cornea. Nodules typically composed of lymphoid components and lymphocytes; diagnosed by histology. Suspected immune-mediated problem. Treatment by surgical

excision and topical and intralesional corticosteroids.

Conjunctivitis ◀ː *cēn jungk ti̱ vī tis, n.* inflammation of conjunctiva, may affect one or both eyes. Conjunctiva is very reactive because of high concentration of blood vessels and lymphatic tissues. Signs include discomfort of eye (spasm and closure of eyelids; blepharospasm), discharge (tearing and mucoid discharge), redness (hyperaemia), chemosis (swelling, oedema of conjunctiva). Causes include irritants, allergies, parasites (e.g. *Onchocerca*), bacteria (e.g. *Moraxella equi*), viral infection (e.g. equine influenza). Diagnosis involves bacterial culture and sensitivity, and cytology of conjunctival scrapings. Viral isolation or fungal culture may be performed if agents suspected as cause. Other causes of disease should be investigated in chronic cases, as conjunctivitis is sometimes a secondary problem. Corneal ulceration should be ruled out in all cases.

Connective tissue ◀ː *kē nek tiv / ti̱ sū, n.* a tissue consisting primarily of various cells (especially fibroblasts) and interlacing protein fibres (especially collagen) in a carbohydrate ground substance. Connective tissue supports, encases, and binds together other tissues; various types, including loose forms (e.g. adipose tissue), dense forms (e.g. tendons, ligaments, and aponeuroses), and specialized forms (e.g. cartilage and bone).

Constipation ◀ː *kon sti pā̱ shēn, n.* delayed or infrequent passage of faeces. Faeces hard and dry as fluid has been absorbed because of slow passage through colon; impaction. May be primary problem (e.g. lack of water consumption) or secondary feature of some clinical diseases; impaction.

Constitution ◀ː *kon sti tū shēn, n.* the physical make-up of the body; made up of genetic information influenced by the environment.

Contact dermatitis see Dermatitis

Contagious ◄⁞ *kēn tā jĕs, adj.* able to be spread from animal to animal, either directly (by contact between animals) or indirectly (e.g. spread by contaminated equipment).

Contagious equine metritis ◄⁞ *kēn tā jĕs / e kwīn / me trī tis, n.* (CEM) highly contagious veneral disease of horses caused by infection with one of two strains of *Taylorella equigenitalis,* a Gram-negative bacterium. The organism localizes around the external genital openings of stallions and mares. First reported in England in 1977. Venereal transmission; bacteria may be carried by stallions and in clitoral sinuses of mares. Infected stallions do not show clinical signs. Infected mares show variable clinical signs; disease may be clinically inapparent, or present as a severe and purulent inflammation of the uterus lining, short oestrous cycles in mare, and temporary infertility. Controlled in Thoroughbreds in GB by code of practice: swabs taken from urethra, urethral fossa, penile sheath and pre-ejaculatory fluid of stallion before start of breeding season. If causal agent of bacterial venereal disease is isolated, stallion may not be used for breeding until treated and three sets (at least 7 days apart) of negative swabs have been obtained. Breeding animals intended for international shipment must be tested and certified free of disease prior to shipment.

Contra- ◄⁞ *kon trē, prefix.* against.

Contraceptive ◄⁞ *kon trē sep tiv, n/adj.* an agent that diminishes the likelihood of, or prevents, conception; the action of such an agent. Methods of equine contraception include hormone therapy, intrauterine marbles, and ovariectomy.
See Marble, Ovariectomy, Progesterone.

Contract ◄⁞ *kēn trakt, v.* to draw together so as to become diminished in size, as in wound contraction; action of muscle to thicken and become shorter, allows movement of part of body.

Contracted ◄⁞ *kēn trak tid, adj.* shortened or drawn together.

C. heels ◄⁞ *kēn trak tid / hē lz, n.* condition where heels of foot are too close together, frog is small; associated with various causes of lameness. Various farriery techniques are attempted to spread heels.
See Heel.

C. tendons ◄⁞ *kēn trak tid / ten dēnz, n.* condition most frequently seen in newborn foals and growing horses. May be congenital, of unknown cause; causes of acquired contractures in growing horses somewhat speculative, but include bones growing faster than tendons, and nutritional factors. May be acquired in older horses subsequent to severe limb injury, if horse refuses to bear weight on limb. Results in flexion (knuckling) of fetlock and sometimes knee (carpus). Horse may walk on front of fetlock in severe cases. Neonatal cases often treated with oxytetracycline (thought to bind calcium ions and relax muscle, allowing relaxation of muscle/tendon unit); splinting or supportive hoof care may be required. More severe cases may require surgery, e.g. inferior check ligament desmotomy. Contracted tendons of older horses have more guarded prognosis because of permanent changes in connective tissue.
See Flexural deformity, Tetracyclines.

Contraindicated ◄⁞ *kon trē in di kā tid, adj.* inadvisable; usually in terms of a treatment which should not be used, perhaps in a certain medical condition or age of animal; e.g. the quinolone antibiotic enrofloxacin is contraindicated in neonatal foals because it has been found to cause damage to articular cartilage.

Contrast agent ◄⁞ *kon trarst / āj ēnt, n.* a substance (e.g. iodine solution or suspension of barium sulphate) which is opaque to X-rays compared to surrounding tissues. Typically introduced into the body by injection or intubation. Used to highlight and contrast an internal part (for example, the oesophagus, bladder, blood vessels, or draining tracts) from its surrounding tissue in radiographic examination; also known as contrast medium, or contrast material.

Contusion ◄⁞ *kon tū zhēn, n.* tissue injury, usually secondary to trauma, that occurs without laceration; bruise.

Convalescence ◀ᴇ _kon vē le sēns, n._ period of recovery from operation, illness, injury, etc.

Convolution ◀ᴇ _kon vē lū shēn, n._ fold or twist, especially folding of structure in upon itself, e.g. any of the irregular ridges on the surface of the brain.

Convulsant ◀ᴇ _kēn vul sēnt, n._ producing or causing convulsions.
See Convulsion.

Convulsion ◀ᴇ _kēn vul shēn, n._ series of violent involuntary contractions of muscles, causing jerky, incoordinated movement (e.g. seizure associated with some poisonings) or spasm (e.g. in tetanus). Often used in plural (convulsions).
See Seizure, Spasm, Tetanus.

Cool ◀ᴇ _kūl, v._ to reduce temperature, either of animal as a whole, e.g. when fevered, or after exercise (cool down), or of specific area in inflammation, e.g. hosing of inflamed tendon.

Coombs' test ◀ᴇ _kūmz / test, n._ one of two clinical blood tests used in immunohaematology and immunology; sometimes used in diagnosis of conditions suspected to have an immune component, such as haemolytic anaemia:
- Direct Coombs' test detects antibody and/or complement on surface of red blood cell; used to test for immune system diseases.
- Indirect Coombs' test detects anti-red blood cell antibodies in unbound blood; commonly performed on blood prior to transfusion.

Coon-footed ◀ᴇ _kūn / füt ed, adj._ conformation term. Coon-footed horses have a hoof wall steeper than the pastern (as in club foot), but with long, sloping pasterns. Often seen in rear feet. Conformation may develop with suspensory ligament degeneration in certain breeds (Paso Fino) or aged horses.
See Suspensory ligament.

Coordination ◀ᴇ _kō or di nā shēn, n._ movement of parts of body in smooth harmonious fashion.

Copper ◀ᴇ _ko pē, n._ red–brown metal element; a trace mineral. An essential part of many of the systems of the horse's body. Functions include ionic form in several enzymes, bone and blood formation, and skin pigmentation. Relationships exist between levels of copper and zinc, as well as levels of copper and molybdenum. Copper is also important for the normal absorption of iron. Most equine diets have adequate levels of copper, and copper deficiencies are rarely heard of in adult horses. It was suggested by some researchers in the 1980s that increasing levels of dietary copper in young horses may be useful in helping to prevent the occurrence of osteochondrosis, a disease that results in abnormal cartilage development in growing foals; hence, it found widespread use for a time, but the suspected link has not been proven. Copper supplementation has also been recommended for the treatment of loss of skin pigment (vitiligo) that occurs in some horses, although there are no reports that copper supplementation has been a successful treatment for this condition. Copper is also the stuff of some equine lore and legend. Tying copper wire around the tail was once used as a treatment for exercise-induced pulmonary haemorrhage (ineffective). Copper wire put in a water bucket also allegedly prevents oestrus (also ineffective).
See Osteochondrosis, Vitiligo.

C. naphthenate ◀ᴇ _ko pē / nap thēn āt, n._ ingredient in a number of preparations for the treatment of thrush, an infectious condition of the horse's hoof; a caustic chemical that dries the hoof tissue and destroys the infectious agents. Contact with sensitive skin tissues should be avoided.
See Thrush.

C. sulphate ◀ᴇ _ko pē / sul fāt, n._ blue crystalline copper salt; caustic chemical. Found in a number of preparations sold for wound treatment in the horse. It causes local tissue destruction; advocated by some for the treatment of exuberant granulation tissue ('proud flesh'). As a wound treatment, copper sulphate causes a hard scab to form on tissue. It causes surface proteins to come out of solution (to 'precipitate'). While copper sulphate does kill bacteria directly, the growth of bacteria may even be favoured

underneath the protection of the chemically caused scab. The treatment of wounds with harsh caustic substances is also generally not recommended.
See Granulation, Proud.

C. toxicity ◄⁑ <u>ko</u> pē / tok <u>si</u> si tē, n. poisoning caused by eating copper-containing materials, e.g. grazing pasture naturally rich in copper. Copper may be stored in liver, and plants causing liver damage may cause sudden release of copper. Signs include haemolysis, jaundice.
See Mineral.

Coprophagy ◄⁑ ko <u>pro</u> fa gē, n. habitual eating of dung (faeces); may be normal in foal at 2–5 weeks of age that eats mare's faeces (possibly to seed intestines with bacteria to aid digestion). May serve to transmit parasites but otherwise harmless. Assertions that coprophagy occurs because of lack of dietary nutrients are unsupported by scientific evidence.

Cor ◄⁑ kor, n. the heart.
C. pulmonale ◄⁑ cor / <u>pul</u> mē <u>nar</u> lā, n. enlargement of right ventricle of heart associated with disease of lung; results from increase in heart workload secondary to increased vascular resistance in the lungs, or from pulmonary hypertension. Normally progresses to right-sided heart failure. Has been reported in horses as a result of recurrent airway obstruction, and with granulomatous pneumonia.
See Heart, Recurrent airway obstruction.

Cord ◄⁑ kord, n. slender, flexible anatomical structure:
• Spermatic cord.
• Spinal cord.
• Umbilical cord.
• Vocal cord.
See under separate entries.

Core biopsy see Biopsy

Corium ◄⁑ <u>kor</u> rē ēm, n. the sensitive vascular layer of dermal tissue; in horses, especially as applied to the sensitive tissue inside horn of hoof, rich in blood vessels and important in nourishment of horn. Commonly referred to by its anatomical location, e.g.

• Perioplic c. – narrow band, merges with skin above coronary border.
• Coronary c. – forms coronary band with perioplic c., responsible for growth of horn.
• Laminar c. – has sensitive laminae (sheets) which bind to lamellae in hoof wall.
• Frog c. – provides nourishment to frog.
• Sole c. – supports horn of sole, attached to lower surface of pedal bone.
See Foot, Hoof.

Corn ◄⁑ korn, n. **1)** the seeds or grain of an important cereal grass; maize. **2)** contusion (bruise) between sole of foot and sensitive laminae, commonly occurring in heel area, where the hoof joins the bar. Associated with foot trauma from various causes; results in lameness, pain when pressure applied to bruised area; red spot often visible at affected spot. Generally treated by protecting the affected area with shoe or pad, following trimming to try to relieve pressure on corn.

Cornea ◄⁑ kor <u>nē</u> ē, n. transparent layer at front of eye, part of fibrous tunic surrounding eye. Has outer epithelium and inner endothelium, with stroma between, composed of layers of protein fibres and water. No blood vessels present in normal cornea. Common conditions affecting cornea include (but are not limited to) inflammation (keratitis), ulcer, abscesses, neoplasia, and foreign body.
See Corneal, Eye, Keratitis.

Corneal ◄⁑ kor <u>nē</u> ūl, adj. pertaining to cornea.
C. degeneration ◄⁑ kor <u>nē</u> ūl / <u>dē</u> jen er <u>ā</u> shun, n. a general term for breakdown of the cornea. The root causes and development of corneal degeneration are largely unknown. Some degenerations may result from irregularities within corneal fibroblasts, others can result from corneal injuries or inflammation (keratitis), or from accidental injuries such as chemical burns.
See Band, Endothelial degeneration.
C. epithelium ◄⁑ kor <u>nē</u> ūl / ep ith <u>ē</u> lēēm, n. the surface cells of the cornea; function to protect the eye from trauma and from infec-

tion, and to help prevent the excess uptake of water by the stroma.

C. neoplasia ◀ *kor nē ūl / nē ō plā zē ē, n.* neoplasia of cornea; diagnosis by biopsy, impression smear or scraping. Corneal neoplasms of horse include, haemangioma, haemangiosarcoma, lymphosarcoma, melanoma, and squamous cell carcinoma.

C. oedema ◀ *kor nē ūl / i dē mē, n.* a condition in which the cornea becomes overly hydrated. In order to remain transparent, the cornea is normally kept relatively dry through oxygen supplied in tears and the draining of water by the corneal endothelium. Any changes to the dehydration process or an influx of fluid can impede the process and allow fluid to accumulate. When fluid accumulates, the cornea swells and turns an opaque blue–white colour. Common feature of equine recurrent uveitis, corneal degeneration, or corneal ulcer.

C. reflex ◀ *kor nē ūl / rē fleks, n.* the blink reflex; an automated involuntary blinking caused by contact with the cornea (e.g. touching). Protects the eyes from foreign bodies (e.g. dirt, insects); corneal reflex is one of the last bodily functions to disappear at death.
See Reflex.

C. stromal abscess ◀ *kor nē ūl / strōmēl / ab ses, n.* occasional sequel of healing corneal ulcers or defects; results from bacteria or fungal organisms (or both) being trapped within the corneal stroma after healing. Seen as an opaque spot in corneal stroma, accompanied by keratitis and blood vessel growth across cornea (neovascularization); uveitis also common. Treatment with long-term topical and occasional systemic antibiotics, eye-dilating agents, and topical and systemic non-steroidal anti-inflammatory drugs; surgical removal of the abscess followed by corneal graft may be required in severe or refractory cases.

C. ulcer ◀ *kor nē ūl / ul sē, n.* superficial injury to cornea, caused by trauma, foreign body, or exposure (such as improperly functioning eyelid); or from bacterial, viral, or fungal infections. Ulcers caused by viruses are most often caused by the equine herpes virus (viral keratitis). Causes pain, blepharospasm, tear production (lacrimation). Ulceration may lead to corneal scarring if chronic.
See Eye.

C. wound healing ◀ *kor nē ūl / wûnd / hē ling, n.* after corneal injury or ulceration, corneal cells enlarge and the sheet of epithelial cells begins to migrate to cover the defect. The initial covering may be only one cell thick, but mitosis of the cornea restores thickness. Full replacement can occur within 2 weeks.

Coronary ◀ *ko rēn rē, adj.* encircling, crown-like; term may be applied to vessels, nerves, ligaments, etc., but most commonly pertaining to heart, and in horses, hoof.

C. artery ◀ *ko rēn rē / ar tē rē, n.* one of two arteries, left and right, which branch off aorta and supply heart muscle with blood.

C. band ◀ *ko rēn rē / band, n.* thickened band of highly vascular tissue that lies at the dorsal border of the horse's hoof wall. Area from which horn of hoof grows.
See Corium.

C. thrombosis ◀ *ko rēn rē / throm bō sis, n.* blood clot in coronary artery, may occur in young horses associated with infestation with *Strongylus vulgaris* (intestinal worm); associated with presence of focal ischaemic lesions in heart muscle.
See *Strongylus* spp.

Coronavirus ◀ *ko ronē vī rēs, n.* family of viruses that have been demonstrated as causing respiratory and gastrointestinal diseases in many animal species. Suspected cause of foal diarrhoea, but not directly demonstrated; virus is difficult to isolate and culture. The role of coronaviruses in equine enteric disease is unclear.

Coronet see Coronary

Coronoid process ◀ *ko rē noid / prō ses, n.* topmost part of mandible (jaw bone), a flattened projection where temporal muscle attaches; prominence on ulna, forms part of articulation with humerus at elbow joint.

Corpora nigra ◀ *kor pēr rē / nī grē, n.* black masses in horse's eye on border of pupil. Present in most horses, formed from layer of cells at back of iris; may act as a light barrier.
See Eye.

Corpus ◀╪ _kor_ pēs, _n._ the main part or body of a bodily structure or organ; body, usually used in describing a discrete structure.

    C. callosum ◀╪ _kor_ pēs / kē lō̲ sēm, _n._ the large band of fibres crossing to unite the cerebral hemispheres.

    C. haemorrhagicum ◀╪ _ku̲r_ pēs / _hom̲_ ā̲ rɑj ik um, _n._ a ruptured ovarian follicle containing a blood clot; forms immediately after ovulation. Blood clot is absorbed as the cells lining the follicle form the corpus luteum.

    C. luteum ◀╪ _kor_ pēs / lū̲ tē̲ ēm, _n._ (yellow body) glandular mass in ovary formed within wall of ovarian follicle after ovulation (shedding of egg). Secretes progesterone. If mare does not become pregnant, c.l. lasts 15–17 days then regresses and new follicle forms for next oestrous cycle. If mare is pregnant c.l. and secondary c.l.s form, and last about 180–200 days (at some point, placenta becomes main source of progesterone).

    Secondary c. luteum ◀╪ _se kēn drē_ / _kor_ pēs / lū̲ / tē̲ / ēm, progesterone-secreting structures that appear on the ovary at approximately day 40 of gestation, increasing to approximately day 140, and regressing by day 180–200. Formation of these structures is a unique feature of the mare; probably responsible for progesterone rise during days 60–90 of gestation.

See Oestrous cycle, Ovary, Ovulation, Pregnancy, Progesterone.

Corpuscle ◀╪ _kor_ pu sēl, _n._ a living cell, especially in reference to cells not part of tissues, such as erythrocytes, leukocytes, and cells of cartilage or bone.

See Blood.

Cortex ◀╪ _kor_ teks, _n._ outer layer of organ or structure, e.g. adrenal cortex is outer layer of adrenal gland, renal cortex is outer layer of kidney, cerebral cortex is outer layer of brain, etc.

See Adrenal gland, Kidney.

Cortical ◀╪ _kor_ ti kēl, _adj._ pertaining to cortex (outer layer) of an organ or bone.

Corticosteroid ◀╪ _kor_ ti kō sté̲ roid, _n._ a class of hormones produced by the two small adrenal glands. The drugs are important in many physiological systems,

including stress and immune responses, regulation of inflammation, metabolism of carbohydrates. Two basic groups:

- Glucocorticoids: affect carbohydrate metabolism, anti-inflammatory by several mechanisms; e.g. cortisol.
- Mineralocorticoids: affect salt/mineral and water balance, primarily by promoting sodium retention in the kidney; e.g. aldosterone.

THERAPEUTIC USES

Various synthetic hormones have been produced; they are a part of medical therapy for many conditions. The most important effects of the corticosteroids in medicine are anti-inflammatory, reducing inflammation of a variety of tissues and combating allergic reactions. Various corticosteroid preparations are given intravenously, in the muscle, orally, into joints and on the surface of the body, as well as both on and in the eye. The drugs are also used in the treatment of early stages of shock.

TYPES OF CORTICOSTEROID

Many types of corticosteroid exist. Various agents differ in potency and duration of action, but selection of various corticosteroid drugs is largely a matter of veterinarian preference and cost. There is no consensus in the veterinary community as to which steroid is the 'best' for use in any condition. (See Betamethasone, Dexamethasone, Prednisolone, Prednisone, Triamcinolone.)

INDICATIONS

Corticosteroids do not cure any disease process. Their anti-inflammatory effects can quiet a variety of inflammatory conditions, and allow healing, but if the underlying condition is unresolved (e.g. osteoarthritis), relief is usually only temporary. Similarly, corticosteroids can control the abnormal responses seen with allergic reactions (urticaria; 'hives') but they do not desensitize the horse to whatever it is that it is allergic to. Corticosteroid ointments can be applied to skin wounds to help control the growth of granulation tissue. A few days after a wound on the skin, corticosteroid ointments applied to the wound surface have no adverse effect on healing. (See Granulation tissue, Osteoarthritis, Urticaria.)

DOSING CONSIDERATIONS

Corticosteroid drugs should be used with caution in the face of infection. Inflammation is an important and necessary response of the body, helping to combat infection. If the inflammatory response is suppressed, infections may be able to spread more easily. Furthermore, while corticosteroid agents suppress the immune system, e.g. helping to control allergies, this effect is not desirable when the body is trying to fight off an infection. Corticosteroids should also not be given at the same time as vaccines, so as to avoid impeding the normal immune response to vaccination.

Because corticosteroids can induce labour in some species, some people have advised caution in giving corticosteroids to mares late in their pregnancy. In scientific studies, pregnant mares have not been shown to abort their foetuses when given corticosteroids, however.

Steroidal anti-inflammatory drugs have also been accused of accelerating joint destruction in horses, especially those that have pre-existing arthritis. The medical studies are far from clear on this point. Corticosteroids impede normal tissue metabolism, and, in a joint, this effect would tend to retard or prevent the normal processes, including the process of repair of damaged tissue. Theoretically, then, this impedance would allow destruction of the joint, i.e. the so-called steroid arthropathy.

However, many arthritic joints benefit from the relief of inflammation, even if only temporarily. In fact, there is some good evidence that the drugs, when used appropriately, actually protect joint cartilage. There is, in fact, little experimental information regarding the effects of injection of corticosteroid anti-inflammatory agents into previously damaged or arthritic joints. Indeed, considerable evidence exists that injection of steroids into normal joints is not harmful.

CONTRAINDICATIONS

Corticosteroid preparations should never be used to treat an eye that has an ulcer on its surface. Corticosteroids retard or prevent healing of the ulcerated surface of the eye. (See Corneal ulcer.)

Although no direct causal link has been established, the use of corticosteroid drugs has occasionally been associated with the onset of laminitis. High doses and prolonged use of longer-acting systemic corticosteroid products are reportedly risk factors for causing laminitis. Under any circumstances, it is generally considered that corticosteroids should not be used in the treatment of laminitis because they help decrease the flow of blood to the hoof. (See Laminitis.)

SIDE EFFECTS

Naturally occurring levels of corticosteroids are carefully controlled by a complex mechanism. Corticosteroids are synthetic drugs that mimic the effects of the natural hormones. If the drugs are administered regularly and in high enough doses, the body may not feel the need to produce its own corticosteroids, relying instead on the drug from the outside. This is loosely referred to as drug dependence. Once the drug is removed, the body may not be ready to produce the required 'natural' amounts of the hormone. For this reason, it is commonly recommended in most species that corticosteroids be withdrawn from the body slowly, with a decreasing dosage over a period of time.

Prolonged corticosteroid therapy in dogs or humans also commonly produces a whole host of other side effects, such as weight gain, increased appetite, increased thirst, increased urination, gastrointestinal ulceration and tissue wasting. For some reason, however, horses seem to be particularly insensitive to the negative effects of corticosteroids and of drug dependence. Horses seem to tolerate relatively large doses of these drugs for prolonged periods of time with few adverse effects and little need for slow withdrawal. Many veterinarians prefer, however, to withdraw horses slowly from corticosteroid therapy just in case negative effects might be seen.

Repeated injections of corticosteroids into the skin, such as to treat skin lesions, can cause thinning of the skin and hair loss.

See Adrenal gland.

Corticotrophic ◀€ _kor_ ti kō _trō_ fik, adj. having stimulating effect on adrenal cortex, increasing secretion of corticosteroid(s), e.g. adrenocorticotrophic hormone.
See Adrenal gland, Adrenocorticotrophic hormone.

Corticotropin see Adrenocorticotrophic hormone

Cortisol ◀€ _kor_ ti zol, n. (hydrocortisone, 17-hydroxycorticosterone) glucocorticoid hormone, $C_{21}H_{30}O_5$. Secreted by adrenal cortex upon stimulation by adrenocorticotrophic hormone (ACTH). Has anti-inflammatory and immunosuppressive properties; levels in the blood may rise in response to stress.
See Adrenal gland, Corticosteroid.

Cortisone ◀€ _kor_ ti zōn, n. glucocorticoid secreted by adrenal cortex, $C_{21}H_{28}O_5$. Also has mineralocorticoid activity. Synthetic analogues are most commonly used as replacement therapy for deficient adrenocortical secretion. Also used as common term for any corticosteroid.
See Adrenal gland, Corticosteroid

**Corynebacterium** ◀€ ko _rī_ nē bak _té_ rē ēm, n. genus of Gram-positive bacteria.

  C. pseudotuberculosis ◀€ ko _rī_ nē bak _té_ rē ēm / _sū_ dō tū _ber_ kū _lō_ sis, n. Gram-positive, rod-shaped, facultatively anaerobic, soil-borne bacterium with worldwide distribution. In North America, most prevalent in southwestern United States. Portal of entry is thought to be via wounds or abrasions on skin or mucous membranes. Insects may act as vectors; may be predisposed by dermatitis of the ventral midline. Transmission may be horse-to-horse or from vectors or contact with contaminated soil. Seasonal; most disease occurs during dry months. Diagnosis by bacterial culture; blood work and blood chemistry may help confirm an infectious process, and serology will support diagnosis. Ultrasonography useful in establishing location of abscesses. Low incidence in horses less than 6 months of age, and in horses that are stabled, instead of being outside. Incubation period of 7–28 days. Bacterium elaborates an exotoxin, which plays a role in the virulence of the organism. Recovery from disease usually in 2–4 weeks, with long-lasting subsequent immunity. Bacteria susceptible to most antimicrobials used in the horse; choice of antimicrobials generally based on practitioner experience and culture/sensitivity. Good sanitation measures may help prevent infection and spread; no vaccine is available for horses.
In horses, infection with _C. pseudotuberculosis_ causes:

- Internal infection – rare, but when occurs can be fatal due to localization of organism in a specific organ. Clinical signs include fever, lethargy, weight loss, and signs of respiratory or abdominal discomfort. Abdominocentesis frequently abnormal.

- External abscesses ('pigeon fever', so called because infected pectoral muscles swell up like a pigeon's breast; 'dryland distemper'; Colorado strangles) – well encapsulated abscesses in large muscle groups, prepuce, mammary glands, and axillary area. Involvement of joints and bone has been reported. In addition to swelling, signs include oedema, fever, lameness, weight loss, and non-healing wounds. Horses recover quickly once abscesses are drained, but drainage can be difficult because of depth of abscesses. Ultrasonography may assist in finding abcesses.

- Ulcerative lymphangitis – least common form of infection; involves lymphatic vessels of limbs. Causes severe cellulitis, with swelling, painful nodules which ulcerate and discharge. Long-term antimicrobial therapy required; limb scarring a frequent sequel.

- Skin infections – bacterial folliculitis and furunculosis; treatment includes topical antimicrobial shampoos, systemic antimicrobial agents, and thorough grooming.

See Ulcerative.

Coryza ◀€ kē _rī_ zē, n. obscure general term for diseases characterized by inflammation of, and discharge from, the mucous membranes of the upper respiratory tract, sinuses, and eyes.
See Nose.

Costal ◀⁙ _kos tēl, adj._ of a rib or ribs.
See Rib.

    C. cartilage ◀⁙ _kos tēl / kar ti lij, n._ band of cartilage attached to rib, joins rib to breastbone (sternum) for ribs 1–8. Costal cartilages of ribs 9–18 do not attach directly to sternum, but fuse to form costal arch which joins on to costal cartilage of rib 8. By their elasticity, the c. cartilages permit movement of the chest in respiration
    See Rib.

Cough ◀⁙ _kof, v./n._ to expel air from lungs suddenly with sharp noise; sudden expulsion of air from lungs with sharp noise. Usually occurs as reflex response to irritation of larynx or lower airways, secondary to infection (bacterial, viral, fungal) or inflammation (e.g. recurrent airway obstruction). Coughs may be productive (producing mucus) or non-productive; productive coughs more typical of infection. Obvious pain on coughing may indicate pleuropneumonia.
See Emphysema, Larynx, Pleuritis/ Pleuropneumonia, Trachea.

    C. reflex see Reflex

Coumarin ◀⁙ _kŭ mēr in, n._ anticoagulant commonly used in rodenticides; occasionally ingested, causing toxicity. Acute onset of signs includes bleeding, anaemia, weakness, haematoma formation and ecchymoses on mucous membranes. Diagnosis by evidence of exposure, and prolonged clotting times. Vitamin K_1 is specific antidote.

Count ◀⁙ _kŏnt, n._ term for numerical analysis, e.g. blood count (number of blood cells in given volume of blood sample), egg count (number of parasite eggs present in given weight of dung sample), sperm count (number of viable sperm in a given volume of semen sample).

Counter-irritant ◀⁙ _kŏn tē - i ri tēnt, n._ substance which produces inflammation or irritation of skin; many chemical compounds are capable of providing counter-irritation. As originally conceived, inflammation of skin would theoretically relieve inflammation elsewhere, e.g. preparation put on skin to cause blistering

used in past to treat inflamed tendons of horses' legs. No scientific support for such a concept. Some counter-irritants can serve as anti-itch preparations.

Cover ◀⁙ _ku vē, v._ in breeding: to serve, mate; to bring stallion together with mare.

Cowbane ◀⁙ _kŏ bān, n._ (_Cicuta virosa_) plant of umbelliferae family, poisonous if eaten. Signs of poisoning include dilated pupils, colic, convulsions, death.
See _Cicuta_.

Cow hocks ◀⁙ _kŏ / hoks, n._ conformation term pertaining to hind limbs; indicates hocks close together and feet further apart.
See Bog spavin, Conformation.

COX see Cyclooxygenase

Coxa ◀⁙ _kok sē, n._ hip, hip joint (joint between pelvis and femur at top of hind leg).
See Hip.

Coxitis ◀⁙ _kok sī tis, n._ inflammation of hip joint.
See Hip.

Coxofemoral joint ◀⁙ _koks ō fem ērel / joint, n._ hip joint; head of femur articulates with bone of the pelvis in acetabulem.

Crackle ◀⁙ _kra kēl, n._ short non-musical noises, heard primarily during inhalation on auscultation of lungs; rale. Sign of some lung diseases, including pneumonia or recurrent airway obstruction.
See Auscultation, Pneumonia, Rale, Recurrent airway obstruction.

Cranial ◀⁙ _krā nē ūl, adj._ pertaining to head, skull or cranium; describing position of part of body as that part towards or near the head.

Cranial nerve ◀⁙ _krā nē ūl / nerv, n._ Paired nerves originating directly from brain; in contrast to spinal nerves which emerge from segments of the spinal cord. Arranged symmetrically in twelve pairs.

CRANIAL NERVE	FUNCTION
1 Olfactory	Smell
2 Ophthalmic	Sight
3 Oculomotor	Movements of eyeball, constriction of pupil
4 Trochlear	Movements of eyeball
5 Trigeminal	Sensation of side of face, chewing
6 Abducens	Movements of eyeball
7 Facial	Sensation of tongue, muscles of face (expression)
8 Vestibulocochlear	Balance and hearing
9 Glossopharyngeal	Sensation and movements of pharynx and larynx
10 Vagus	Essential for normal function of respiratory tract and gastrointestinal tract
11 Accessory	Movements of pharynx and muscles around shoulder
12 Hypoglossal	Movements of tongue

Craniotomy ◀ _krā nē o tē mē, n._ surgical opening of the skull.

Cranium ◀ _krā nē ēm, n._ skull, particularly that part enclosing brain.

Creatine ◀ _krē ē tēn, n._ a substance that is normally found within the cells of the horse's body. Creatine's role within the cell is to rapidly make ATP (energy) available during times of high energy consumption, such as exercise. Creatine has been promoted as a supplement for horses engaging in heavy exercise. However, in the only large study to date, it was not possible to show any beneficial effect from creatine on the skeletal muscle characteristics examined. The lack of benefit from creatine supplementation is not unexpected; from a physiological standpoint, horses are nearly perfect athletes, and appear to have little room for improvement.

Creatine kinase ◀ _krē ē tēn / kī nāz, n._ (CK, creatine phosphokinase) enzyme present in brain and heart and skeletal muscle. Level in blood may rise (peak at 6–12 hours) following muscle or brain damage, usually returns to normal in 3–4 days, depending on extent of initial insult. Used in diagnosis of muscle damage, e.g. exertional rhabdomyolysis.
See Exertional rhabdomyolysis.

Creatinine ◀ _krē a ti nēn, n._ nitrogenous compound, a breakdown product of crea-

tine phosphate in muscle, excreted in urine. Ordinarily produced at a fairly constant rate. Neonatal foals normally have levels 30–50% higher than adult horses, but return to normal levels, or levels slightly lower than adults, within the first 3–5 days of life. Elevated levels may indicate kidney impairment; may also elevate with non-renal causes, such as fasting, dehydration, exertional rhabdomyolysis, and heavy exercise.

C. clearance test ◀ _krē a ti nēn / klér ēns / test, n._ test that provides a reasonable estimation of glomerular filtration rate (GFR). A decrease in c. clearance indicates a decrease in GFR, but it cannot differentiate causes of decreased GFR. A properly performed creatinine clearance test is more sensitive than simply checking creatinine levels in detecting loss of renal function. Test involves a measurement of the starting serum creatinine concentration, complete evacuation of the bladder, collection of all urine created in a set amount of time (ideally, 24 hours) and determination of a final serum creatinine concentration. The urine creatinine value is determined. The test is then computed based on the following calculation:
Creatinine clearance = [urine creatinine (mg/dl) x urine volume (ml/min) ÷ serum creatinine (mg/dl)] ÷ body weight (kg)
See Glomerular filtration rate, Glomerulus, Kidney.

Creep feeding ◀ _krēp / fē ding, v._ providing supplemental nutrition to growing foals; when foal is with dam, or

115

other horses, feed is placed on one side of a barrier (creep feeder) small enough to allow only young horse's muzzle to get access to feed.

Crepitation/Crepitus ◀≡ *kre pi tā shĕn / kre pi tus, n.* grating or crackling sound or sensation, e.g. as produced by ends of fractured bone rubbing against each other, around lungs, e.g. in advanced cases of pleuropneumonia, or on palpation of tissue with subcutaneous emphysema. Crepitus in a joint can occasionally be felt in cases of severe osteoarthritis.
See Arthritis, Auscultation, Pleuritis/ Pleuropneumonia, Osteoarthritis.

Crest ◀≡ *krest, n.* a process or prominence on the body, e.g. the upper curve or ridge of a horse's neck; a neck with excessive fat deposition is said to be 'cresty'. Also, in anatomy, describes a ridge, especially on a bone, e.g. tibial crest.

Cretinism see Hypothyroidism

Crib-biting ◀≡ *krib - bī ting, v.* (cribbing, wind-sucking) repetitive behaviour in which horse grasps fixed object (e.g. manger, stable door) between front teeth and arches neck, often making a sound. Arching of neck forces air from pharynx into oesophagus; air does not enter stomach, but returns to pharynx when muscles relax. Can cause abnormal wear of incisor teeth; an association has also been made between crib-biting and epiploic foramen entrapment; otherwise, little evidence of harm from behaviour. May develop in response to management conditions which do not allow expression of normal behaviour of horse; however, behaviour is also seen in feral horses. No evidence that horses that crib-bite will teach other horses this behaviour. Numerous devices and surgeries have been devised to attempt to 'correct' behaviour, but most meet with little success.
   C. collar ◀≡ *krib - bī ting / kolē, n.* any one of a number of devices designed to restrict expansion of muscles of the neck when horse crib-bites.
   See Wind-sucking.

Cricoid ◀≡ *krī koid, n.* ring-shaped cartilage, one of several cartilages comprising larynx; articulates with the lower cornua of the thyroid cartilage; arytenoid cartilages articulate with it.
See Larynx.

Crofton weed ◀≡ *krof tēn / wēd, n.* (*Eupatorium* spp.) Native Central American plant, introduced to Australia in 1875 as an ornamental plant, where it soon spread out of control. Causes poisoning if leaves or flowers of plant are eaten. Coughing, rapid heaving respiration, decreased exercise tolerance and loss of condition are seen in affected horses. In long-standing cases fibrosis, alveolar lining cell proliferation, oedema, neutrophil infiltration and abscessation are seen. In some cases vascular thrombosis and infarction occur in the lungs. Condition known as Tallebudgera Horse Disease.

Cromolyn sodium ◀≡ *krō mō lin / sō dē ĕm, n.* usually marketed as the sodium salt sodium cromoglycate; this drug prevents the release of inflammatory chemicals such as histamine from mast cells; mechanism of action by blocking chloride channels. Was shown to be effective in prevention of recurrent airway obstruction in one study; limited use in treating the disease once it has occurred.
See Mast cell, Recurrent airway obstruction.

Cross-firing ◀≡ *kros - fī ring, n.* problem of gait, where inside of hind foot hits opposite forefoot.
See Gait.

Cross-matching ◀≡ *kros - ma ching, v.* testing blood from one horse with that from another to determine suitability for blood transfusion. Compatability shown by absence of clumping together of cells (agglutination) or cell breakdown (haemolysis).
See Transfusion, Blood.

Crotalaria see Rattlepod

Croup ◀≡ *krŭp, n.* area of hindquarters from highest point to top of tail.

Crown ◀﹦ *kr ŏn, n.* top part of organ or structure, e.g. top of head, enamelled part of tooth.

Cruciate ◀﹦ *krŭ sh āt, adj.* cross-shaped.

C. **ligaments** ◀﹦ *krŭ sh āt / li gē mēnts, n.* pair of fibrous bands (anterior and posterior cruciate ligaments; aka cranial and caudal cruciate ligaments) which span stifle joint in X-shape and provide crucial support and stability to the joint. May be injured, typically during athletic activity, although injury is relatively uncommon; diagnosis of sprains is difficult. Clinical signs of cruciate ligament injury include lameness and joint swelling; horses may resent limb flexion or have lameness made worse after limb flexion. Radiography may show avulsed fragment of bone in severe injuries; scintigraphy may localize joint inflammation; ultrasonography occasionally helpful, particularly in evaluating concurrent meniscal tears; arthroscopy usually required to confirm diagnosis of tear or rupture. Prognosis for complete tear is usually poor; secondary osteoarthritis usually develops as a result of chronic joint instability. Rest is mandatory for possible recovery; the more intact the injured ligament, the better the prognosis.
See Stifle.

Crus see Gaskin

Crust ◀﹦ *krust, n.* a hard, dry surface mass, composed of varying amounts of keratin, serum, cellular debris, and, commonly, microorganisms. Further described as serous, haemorrhagic, cellular, serocellular, and palisading (alternate rows of keratine, cellular debris and pus), depending on composition.

Cryosurgery see Cryotherapy

Cryotherapy ◀﹦ *krī ō the rē pē, n.* therapeutic use of cold; cryosurgery. At freezing temperatures, ice crystals form in cells, which destroy cells. Additional damage is caused when blood vessels supplying tissues freeze, depriving tissues of circulation. Two common methods of application are use of liquid nitrogen sprayed, dabbed or poured on diseased tissue, or by use of a metal cryoprobe. In horses, has most commonly been used in treatment of superficial tumours, e.g. tumours of cornea, sarcoids, to desensitize inflamed areas, such as splints (also known as 'freeze firing'), and to temporarily desensitize nerves ('cryoneurectomy'). The term cryotherapy is also used to describe use of icepacks or other source of cold to reduce inflammation, e.g. in trauma to limb.

Crypt ◀﹦ *kript, n.* in anatomy, a pit, depression, or invagination; e.g. glands opening into intestinal lumen.

Cryptococcus neoformans ◀﹦ *krip tō ko kēs / nē ō for mēnz, n.* uncommon and sporadic disease-causing agent of horses; a ubiquitous budding yeast; causes cryptococcosis. Respiratory and nervous system diseases are most common clinical manifestations, showing nasal discharge, cough, and weight loss, and dementia, head tilt, and ataxia, respectively. Cases have been clustered primarily in Australia; eucalyptus trees there harbour organism. Initial exposure occurs by ingestion, through injured skin, or by inhalation of spores. Disease onset often slow and gradual; infection usually well established when signs present. Diagnosis by identification of large numbers of fungi in tracheal aspirate, or by endoscopy and tissue biopsy; serum antigen titres also helpful. Few reports of successful treatment, however antifungal therapy may be useful in selected cases.
See Pneumonia.

Cryptorchid ◀﹦ *kript or kid, n.* (rig) male animal in which one or both testes have not descended into scrotum. Testis may be in abdomen or inguinal canal. Higher temperature than in scrotum prevents formation of viable sperm, although male hormones will be produced. Has hereditary component; considered undesirable by some breed organizations. Several techniques for castration described, including laparoscopic.
See Castration, Testes.

Cryptosporidium ◀﹦ *krip tō spēr ri dē ēm, n.* coccidian parasite, infects intestinal epithelial cells in many species, including horses. Horses become infected by ingesting oocysts of parasite; incubation in 3–7 days, with disease characterized by dehydration, weakness, and death if untreated. Cause of severe infection in foals with combined immunodeficiency. Serum titre surveys suggest subclinical infection may be common. No known specific therapy; supportive care, as appropriate. Potential zoonotic disease. See Diarrhoea, Immunodeficiency.

Cubital joint ◀ *kŭ bit ēl / joint, n.* joint between forearm and upper arm; elbow.

Cuboidal bone disease ◀ *kŭ boi dēl / bōn / di zēz, n.* cuboidal bones are the small, roughly cube-shaped, bones of the carpus (knee) or tarsus (hock). Cuboidal bone disease is most commonly seen in premature foals. In these foals, abnormal bone development can result in bones developing in a wedge-shaped form. This usually appears clinically as an angular limb deformity of the carpus in the forelimb, or in a sickle hock conformation in the case of tarsal bone collapse of the hind limb. Diagnosis is confirmed radiographically.

Cuboni test ◀ *kŭ bō nē / test, n.* pregnancy test, involves detection of oestrogens in urine by fluorescence. May be used in mares after 5 months gestation. (Named after F. Cuboni, Italian veterinarian.)

Culex spp. ◀ *kŭlex / spē shēs, n.* a genus of mosquito; several species act as vectors of important equine diseases, including West Nile virus and viral encephalitis. See Encephalitis, West Nile virus.

Culicoides spp. ◀ *kū li koi dēz / spē shēs, n.* genus of biting midges, over 1,000 species across world ('no-see-ums'). Life cycle is egg to larva to pupa to adult; complete cycle can occur in 2–6 weeks, depending on the species and environmental conditions; larvae cannot develop without moisture. Primarily associated with culicoides hypersensitivity and resultant dermatitis. Also involved in spread of some diseases, e.g. African horse sickness.

Culicoides hypersensitivity ◀ *kū li koi dēz / hī pē sen si ti vi tē, n.* (sweet itch, Queensland itch) itchy allergic reaction to bite of *Culicoides* midge. Itchy patches especially at root of tail, croup and base of mane. Rubbing by horse may break hairs and cause patchy hair loss. May also be associated with secondary skin infections. *Culicoides*-related problems may be managed by:

- Medical therapy – usually corticosteroid or antihistamine therapy, especially hydroxyzine, in individual animals.
- Environmental control – reduction of biting insect populations, e.g. insect repellents, moving horses away from wet areas, stabling at dawn and dusk.
- Barriers – masks, blankets (rugs), stall screens, etc., may be helpful in providing a physical barrier to the insect bite.
- Nutritional supplements – many have been advocated, including fatty acids, garlic, and B vitamins; most have been proven ineffective.
- Immunotherapy – a variety of techniques have been tried for desensitization, including canine flea antigen and commercial serums; none have proved successful.
- 'Alternative' therapies – an almost limitless number of suggestions, including herbal, homeopathic, and acupuncture, all with no proven effectiveness.

See Allergy.

Culture ◀ *kul tŭr, n./v.* the act or process of growing of cells or microorganisms on special media, e.g. for diagnosis of disease, production of vaccines; to grow cells or micororganisms on special media.

Cunean ◀ *kū nē ēn, adj.* pertaining to the cunean tendon region of the tarsus (hock).

C. bursa ◀ *kū nē ēn / ber sē, n.* the bursa interposed between the cunean tendon and the tarsal bones on the medial aspect of the tarsus.
See Bursa, Bursitis.

C. tendon ◀ *kū nē ēn / tēn don, n.* the medial branch of the insertion of the tibialis cranialis muscle in the hind limb.

C. tenectomy ◀ *kū nē ēn / ten ek tēmē, n.* surgical transection or excision of a portion of the cunean tendon; ordinarily performed

as a treatment for tarsal osteoarthritis (bone spavin). Procedure has generally failed to alleviate problem.
See Bone, Osteoarthritis.

Curb ◀€ *kerb, n.* firm swelling at back of cannon bone below point of hock, caused by inflammation of plantar ligaments or superficial flexor tendon. May be result of trauma or strain (associated with poor conformation), often associated with inflammation and lameness in acute stages; horse may stand resting heel of affected limb. If traumatic in origin, and severe, periostitis of underlying bone may occur. If septic, is associated with significant limb swelling, lameness, and pain on palpation. Chronic cases may result in a permanent enlargement of the area, but usually not lameness. Diagnosis by clinical signs; ultrasonography can confirm; radiographs may show bone changes. Must be differentiated from other causes of swelling in area, such as superficial digital flexor tendinitis. Treatment may include rest, cold therapy, and topical or systemic anti-inflammatory therapy; extracorporeal shock wave therapy, firing, blistering have also been advocated, with no demonstrable results. Prognosis generally favourable, unless continuing injury occurs with exercise.

Curettage ◀€ *kŭr ret arj, n.* use of curette (spoon-like instrument) to scrape or clean surface of organ or tissue, e.g. the removal of infected bone in deep wounds.

Curette ◀€ *kŭr ret, n.* surgical instrument with a scoop, loop, or ring at its tip; used to perform curettage.

Cushing's disease see Pituitary pars intermedia dysfunction

Cusp ◀€ *kusp, n.* rounded or pointed projection, e.g. on tooth; fold or flap of heart valve.
See Heart.

Cut ◀€ *kut, n./v.* **1)** to penetrate with a sharp instrument; to operate on in surgery. **2)** to castrate. **3)** the emergence of a tooth through the gum (cut a tooth).

See Castration.
C. proud see Proud

Cutaneous ◀€ *kū tā nē ĕs, adj.* relating to or affecting skin.
See Skin.

C. asthenia ◀€ *kū tā nē ĕs / as thē nē ĕ, n.* (Ehler-Danlos syndrome, hyperelastosis cutis, cutis hyperelastica) congenital problem, inherited disorder of collagen production. In horses, onset is later than in other species with similar problems; the lesions are usually well circumscribed, consisting of hyperextensible, very elastic, and somewhat fragile skin, which is easily torn; sometimes joints are overly flexible. Reported in American Quarter Horse and Arabian cross foals.
See Collagen, HERDA, Skin.

C. habronemiasis ◀€ *kū tā nē ĕs / ha brō nē mī ĕ sis, n.* granulomatous skin condition of wounds and moist areas, especially around eyes and genitalia. Seen in USA, caused by larvae laid by feeding flies of horse stomach worm, *Habronema*. Diagnosis based on clinical signs of non-healing skin granulomas that often contain yellow, calcified material the size of rice grains; cause can be confirmed histologically. Control by topical or systemic anti-inflammatory corticosteroids, often in proprietary combinations of medication including dewormers and dimethylsulfoxide; systemic deworming agents (especially ivermectin) often used; however, inflammatory response generally kills parasite. Surgical removal of excessive tissue may be necessary in some cases.

C. lymphoma ◀€ *kū tā nē ĕs / lim fō mē, n.* nodular masses under skin caused by tumours of lymphoid tissue; slowly progressive. Diagnosis by aspiration of mass, or biopsy. Can remain stable for several years, even without treatment. Several forms of treatment, including systemic chemotherapeutic agents, although use of such agents is limited by cost and possible toxicity concerns. Corticosteroids may help reduce the size of the tumours and also reduce secondary problems. Surgical removal of individual tumours may be warranted, depending on area and morbidity. Least common form of lymphoma in horses.
See Lymphoma.

119

C. onchocerciasis ◀ᴇ *kū tā nē ēs* / *ong kō sē kī ē sis, n.* skin lesions caused by allergy to immature forms of parasite *Onchocerca cervicalis* in skin. Microfilariae typically are most concentrated in the skin of the ventral midline of all horses, but cause dermatitis in susceptible animals. Lesions include scaling, crusting, ulcers, hair loss, and depigmentation of ventral midline, head, neck, and sometimes limbs; often pruritic. Treatment with microfilarial drugs (e.g. ivermectin, moxidectin) generally results in dramatic improvement; dead and dying microfilariae may temporarily worsen problem. Diagnosis may be based on typical lesions, response to treatment, or skin biopsy. Rare in UK.

Cutis ◀ᴇ *kū tis, n.* skin.
See Skin.

C. hyperelastica see Cutaneous, HERDA

Cyanide ◀ᴇ *sī ē nīd, n.* any chemical compound that contains the cyano group (C≡N); cyanide specifically is the anion CN⁻. Cyanides are produced by certain bacteria, fungi and algae and also occur as cyanogenic glycosides in a number of foods and in over 1,000 different species of plants (e.g. oleander, hemlock, larkspur, Johnson grass, yew, Death Camas, avocado, Sudan grass, some cherry species). Many cyanide-containing compounds are highly toxic, but many are not. Cyanide is an irreversible enzyme inhibitor. Tissues dependent on aerobic respiration, such as the central nervous system and heart, are particularly sensitive to the effects of cyanide. Cyanide ion also binds to iron in haemoglobin, resulting in bright red mucous membranes in acute poisonings, but unavailability of oxygen to tissues. Can cause rapid death by respiratory failure if eaten in large quantities, even though haemoglobin is saturated with oxygen. Chronic toxicity results in signs of neurological disease. Treatment with intravenous sodium nitrite or sodium thiosulphate has rarely been successful.

Cyanobacteria see Blue-green algae

Cyanosis ◀ᴇ *sī ē nō sis, n.* bluish colour of skin or mucous membranes caused by low oxygen level in blood (haemoglobin with no oxygen has a blue colour). Most easily seen in gums of horse. May be seen in pneumonia, heart failure.
See Haemoglobin, Heart, Pneumonia.

Cyathostome ◀ᴇ *sī a thō stōme, n.* member of one of several genera of roundworms (small strongyles) found in large intestine of horses, may cause clinical signs in heavy infestation (cyathostomosis). Larvae may have period of arrested development in large intestine for up to 3 years.

Cyathostomosis ◀ᴇ *sī a thō stē mō sis, n.* heavy infestation with cyathostome (small strongyle) larvae. The typical patient is young; signs often seen between late autumn and early spring. Causes the gradual wasting of the affected animal, much as do other chronic inflammatory bowel conditions of unknown aetiology. Causes chronic diarrhoea, weight loss, intermittent colic, fluid swelling of limbs and ventral abdomen. Laboratory findings include hypoalbuminaemia, neutrophilia, anaemia, and hyperglobulinaemia. Abdominocentesis and rectal palpation are typically normal; parasite control history is usually adequate. Diagnosis can be difficult, as faecal egg counts may be zero in the patient since the causative parasites are immature and not producing eggs.
See Diarrhoea, *Strongylus* spp.

Cycle ◀ᴇ *sī kēl, n.* a recurring series of events; a series of stages of development which an organism tends to pass through in a fixed order, e.g. life cycle; a series of physiological, biochemical, or psychological stages that occur regularly in an individual, e.g. oestrous cycle.

Cyclitis ◀ᴇ *sī klī tis, n.* inflammation of ciliary body of eye.
See Eye, Iridocyclitis.

Cyclooxygenase (COX) ◀ᴇ *sī klō oksē jēn āz, n.* an enzyme that catalyses the conversion of arachidonic acid to prostaglandins; involved in the cascade of events producing the pain and inflammation of arthritis and other inflammatory conditions. COX is inactivated by aspirin and other non-steroidal anti-inflammatory drugs with a similar mechanism of action (e.g. phenylbutazone, flunixin meglumine).

Cyclosporine ◀ *sī klō spor ēn, n.* immunosuppressive agent sometimes prescribed for treatment of equine recurrent uveitis. Cyclosporine helps stop T lymphocytes from producing antibodies that attack the eye.
See Equine recurrent uveitis.

Cynoglossum officinale see Hound's tongue

Cyproheptadine ◀ *sī prō hep tē dēn, n.* drug that is antihistaminic and antiserotonergic (counteracts effects of serotonin, a neurotransmitter). Acts as a receptor antagonist and also blocks calcium channels. Has been used in treatment of pituitary pars intermedia dysfunction (Cushing's disease), in an effort to reduce secretion of adrenocorticotrophic hormone by pituitary tumour. Poor clinical efficacy.
See Pituitary pars intermedia dysfunction.

Cyst ◀ *sist, n.* a closed sac, with a distinct membrane, and often filled with fluid or cellular debris. Develops abnormally in a body cavity or structure. Usually harmless (e.g. atheroma), but may cause problems if grows large or becomes infected.
> **Bone c.** ◀ *bōn / sist, n.* cystic abnormality typically occurring at ends of long bones, as a manifestation of osteochondrosis.
> See Osteochondrosis.
> **Uterine c.** ◀ *ū ter īn / sists, n.* cystic uterine structures; of two embryological origins. Cysts may interfere with foetal implantation, or may prevent placental absorption of nutrients. Many treatments have been attempted, including cyst rupture and removal; the number reflects the inability of any treatment to be consistently successful.
> See Atheroma.

Cystic ◀ *sis tik, adj.* containing cysts; pertaining to a cyst; relating to urinary bladder or gall bladder.

> **C. calculi** ◀ *sis tik / kal kū lī, n.* bladder stones.
> **C. ovaries** ◀ *sis tik / ōv arēs, n.* enlargement of ovaries with cystic structures, as in granulosa cell tumour; common problem in cattle, but different condition and treatment. Terminology may incorrectly be applied to anovulatory follicles.
> See Follicle.
> **C. urolithiasis** ◀ *sis tik / ŭr rō li thī ē sis, n.* a condition characterized by the formation or presence of calculi in the bladder.
> See Urolith.

Cystitis ◀ *sis tī tis, n.* inflammation of urinary bladder. Rare in horse, may be associated with bladder stones (urolithiasis). Causes frequent passing of urine which may be red-coloured from blood. When present in horse population, more common in mares.
See Urolith.

Cystoscopy ◀ *sis to skē pē, n.* examination of inside of bladder by use of fibre-optic scope passed up urethra. Useful in diagnosis of urolithiasis, bladder tumour.
See Bladder, Urolith.

Cytokine ◀ *sītō kīn, n.* any of a group of immunoregulatory proteins and peptides, including interleukin, tumour necrosis factor, and interferon, that are secreted especially by cells of the immune system, and allow one cell to communicate with another. Each cytokine binds to a specific cell-surface receptor. This binding triggers cascades of intracellular events that subsequently alter cell functions.

Cytology ◀ *sī to lē jē, n.* study of cell function and structure; analysis of cell type and numbers in sample of blood, fluid, aspirate from growth, etc., for determining the presence or absence of a disease condition.
See Cell.

Cytopenia ◀ *sī tō pē nē ē, n.* deficiency of cells in blood; especially deficiency of a specific element (as lack of white blood cells in leukocytopenia).

Cytoplasm ◄⁞ _sī tō plazm, n._ material, other than nucleus, including the cytosol and membrane-bound organelles, contained within cell.

Cytotoxic ◄⁞ _sī tō tok sik, adj._ poisonous to cells; may be used to describe drugs which are used to treat cancer by killing cells of a tumour. Cytotoxic agents may be injected, or applied topically, as in cytotoxic creams.

D

Dacryo- ◀ _da_ krē ō, *prefix.* part of word concerning tears (of eye).
See Eye, Lacrimal apparatus.

Dacryocyst ◀ _da_ krē ō _sist_, *n.* (lacrimal sac) widened end of nasolacrimal duct, opened into by lacrimal ducts.
See Eye, Lacrimal apparatus.

Dacryocystitis ◀ _da_ krē ō sis _tī_ tis, *n.* inflammation of lacrimal sac. May be caused by infection, foreign body, parasites, etc.; can result in narrowing or blockage of lacrimal drainage system.
See Eye, Lacrimal apparatus.

Dacryocystorhinography ◀ _da_ krē ō _sis_ tō rī _no_ grē fē, *n.* radiography of nasolacrimal duct used in investigation of problems with drainage of tears. Often done under general anaesthesia. Iodine-based contrast medium injected through cannula placed in nasolacrimal duct; radiographs taken show problems with passage of contrast medium through duct.
See Eye, Lacrimal apparatus.

Dallis grass ◀ _da_ lēs / grars, *n.* (*Paspalum dilatatum*) pasture plant, may be infected with ergot fungus, *Claviceps paspali*. If eaten, fungal toxins can cause 'Dallis grass staggers', characterized by incoordination, tremors, stiff gait, falling.

Dalric shoe ◀ _dawl_ rik / shŭ, *n.* a glue-on horseshoe sometimes used in foals, to assist in correction of various problems, including club feet, flexor tendon laxity, and varus or valgus deformities.

Damalinia equi ◀ _da_ mē _li_ nē ē / _e_ kwī, *n.* biting louse, commonly infests horses. Feeds on the most superficial layers of the skin and skin exudate, which results from the irritant effect of the parasite. Usually they cause little harm, and only occur in small numbers. If large infestations skin damage may occur through heavy grooming by the host; causes dry scaly coat, itching, especially on back, head and neck. If very severe may cause loss of condition. Signs seen especially in winter and early spring. Diagnosis by identification of lice and eggs in coat.

Dandy-Walker syndrome ◀ _dan_ dē-_waw_ kē / _sin_ drōm, *n.* a rare brain defect, reported in Thoroughbred and Arabian foals, characterized by a midline defect of the cerebellum and cystic dilation of the fourth ventricle; foals are neurologically abnormal from birth, and head may be enlarged. Diagnosis usually post-mortem, although a case of ante-mortem diagnosis with computed tomography has been reported.

Dantrolene ◀ _dan_ trō lēn, *n.* drug used as relaxant of skeletal muscles; works by binding to a receptor and decreasing intracellular calcium concentration. In horses, has been most commonly used as a treatment of equine rhabdomyolysis syndrome, or for postanaesthetic myositis.
See Myositis, Exertional rhabdomyolysis.

Darling pea ◀ _dar_ ling / pē, *n.* (*Swainsona* spp.) Australian plant; contains toxic alkaloid (swainsonine) which can cause poisoning if plant eaten. Poisoning primarily affects nervous system, and signs include incoordination, aggression, extreme sensitivity to stimuli. More common in sheep.

Darnel ◀ _dar_ _nel_, *n.* (*Lolium temulentum*) grass often found as weed in cereal crops;

also called ryegrass. Seeds and seed heads are considered poisonous; associated parasitic fungus living in seed head (*Endoconidium temulentum*) is also poisonous. Rare cause of poisoning; incoordination, dilation of pupils, and convulsions and death if large quantities eaten.

Data ◀ː *dā tē, n.* (plural of datum) information, facts and statistics on which a discussion or an inference is based.

Dead space ◀ː *ded spās, n.* a space left in the body, usually as the result of a surgical procedure.

Deadly nightshade ◀ː *ded lē / nīt shād, n.* (*Atropa belladonna*) poisonous bushy plant with drooping purple flowers and black berries, contains atropine. May be eaten by horses if present in hay. Signs of poisoning include dilated pupils, difficulty breathing, tremors, weakness, colic, diarrhoea. See Atropine, Colic.

Deafness ◀ː *def nis, n.* lack or significant deficiency in the sense of hearing. Extremely rare in horses, although this may be due to difficulty of diagnosis.

Death ◀ː *deth, n.* end of life and cessation of all vital bodily functions. Signs of death include no heart beat or breathing, no movement from eyelids, no bleeding from artery if cut.
  D. camas ◀ː *deth / ka mēs, n.* (*Zigadenus* spp.) horses eating approx. 4 kg of this plant salivate and develop colic; death within several days. Several toxic alkaloids in plant, especially in bulb.
  Programmed cell d. ◀ː *pro gramd / sel / deth, n.* the theory that particular cells are programmed to die at specific sites and during specific stages of development. See Apoptosis.
  Sudden d. ◀ː *su dēn / deth, n.* death of animal without previous clinical indication. Not common, may be associated with heart failure, lightning strike, electric shock, clostridial infection, anthrax. See Anthrax, *Clostridium*, Heart.

Debridement ◀ː *di brīd mēnt, n.* removal of devitalized, infected, contaminated or damaged tissue and foreign material from or adjacent to a traumatic wound or infected lesion, until surrounding healthy tissue is exposed. Encourages healing.

Debulking ◀ː *dē bulk ing, v.* removal of the major portion of the material that makes up a lesion, as in surgically debulking a cancerous tumour, leaving a smaller portion for subsequent treatment.

Decalcification ◀ː *dē cal si fi kā shēn, n.* loss of calcium salts from bone or tooth; also, in histology, the process of removing calcium from tissue, so as to facilitate examination under a microscope.

Decay ◀ː *di kā, v./n.* rot, decompose; gradual process of decomposition of organic matter. Also a term for radioactive disintegration.

Deciduous ◀ː *di sid ū ēs, adj.* falling off or shed at maturity; the term is most commonly used to designate the teeth of the first dentition.

Decompresssion ◀ː *dē kom pre shēn, n.* removal of pressure within organ; e.g. gastrointestinal decompression may be required during surgery for obstructive colic, achieved by removing gas or fluid from bowel through large-gauge needle attached to suction pump. See Colic.

Decongestant ◀ː *dē kon jes tēnt, n.* medication used to reduce swelling or congestion, most commonly used as term for drug used to reduce nasal congestion. Steam or volatile inhalations may occasionally be used as nasal decongestants in horses.

Decubital ulcer ◀ː *dē kū bi tēl / ul sē, n.* open sore (ulcer) on skin caused by lying for long periods, generally form over bony prominences, e.g. elbow, point of hip, prominences of head. See Ulcer.

Deep ◀ː *dēp, adj.* situated far beneath the surface; not superficial.
  D. digital flexor tendon ◀ː *dēp / di ji tūl / flek sē / ten dēn, n.* the primary tendon of the

deep digital flexor muscle; little anatomical difference between fore and hind limbs. The tendon inserts on the third phalanx (coffin bone) and is primarily responsible for flexing the digit during the stride. Numerous important pathologies and interventions involve this tendon.
See Bowed tendon, Club foot, Laminitis, Tendinitis.

D. heat ◄⁞ *dēp / hēt*, *n.* use of heat to treat soft tissue injuries, e.g. sprains and strains, or muscle injuries deep in the tissues.
See Physiotherapy.

D. infection ◄⁞ *dēp / in fek shēn*, *n.* infections, usually of internal organs; e.g. fungal infections of internal organs that may secondarily spread to the skin via the blood. Rare.

D. skin scraping ◄⁞ *dēp / skin / skrāp ing*, *v.* scraping skin deeply until capillary bleeding is obtained, for diagnostic purposes, especially mites.

Defecation ◄⁞ *de fē kā shēn*, *n.* elimination of undigested food and waste matter from rectum; passing of faeces.
See Faeces.

Defect ◄⁞ *dē fekt*, *n.* imperfection, failure or absence.
Acquired d. ◄⁞ *ē kwiyrd / dē fekt*, *n.* a non-genetic imperfection as result of disease or trauma occurring after birth.
Birth d. ◄⁞ *berth / dē fekt*, *n.* a defect present at birth.
Congenital d. ◄⁞ *kon je ni tūl / dē fekt*, *n.* a structural or chemical imperfection present at birth. May be genetic; other factors include disease or nutritional problem of mare while pregnant.
Septal d. ◄⁞ *sep tūl / dē fekt*, *n.* a defect occurring in the heart wall.

Defibrillation ◄⁞ *dē fi bri lā shēn*, *n.* stopping of atrial or ventricular fibrillation, usually by administration of electric shock which disrupts electrical circuits in heart muscle and allows heart pacemaker to regain control. Can only be used in foals and small ponies due to physical mass of adult horse, and resultant difficulties in transmission of electrical impulse.
See Atrial, Heart, Ventricular.

Deficiency ◄⁞ *di fi shēn sē*, *n.* lack or defect, e.g. a dietary deficiency is related to a lack of a specific nutrient in diet, e.g. lack of specific vitamin or mineral.
See Immunodeficiency, Vitamin, and individual entries under nutrients.

Deficit ◄⁞ *de fi sit*, *n.* lack or deficiency, e.g. an oxygen deficit during intense exercise.

Definitive ◄⁞ *di fi ni tiv n.* established with certainty.
D. host ◄⁞ *di fi ni tiv / hōst*, *n.* in parasitology, animal in which parasite undergoes sexual reproduction (c.f. intermediate host).
See Parasite.

Deformity ◄⁞ *di for mi tē*, *n.* distortion of body or part of body caused by abnormal development or injury; malformation.
See Defect.
Angular limb d. ◄⁞ *ang gū lē / lim / di for mi tē*, *n.* deformity of the lower limb, usually in foals, characterized by abnormal lateral or medial position of the lower limb relative to the upper limb (valgus or varus deformity, respectively).
Flexural d. ◄⁞ *flek shūr rūl / di for mi tē*, *n.* deformity of the lower limb, most commonly in foals, thought to be caused by tendon or ligament contracture.

Degeneration ◄⁞ *di je nē rā shēn*, *n.* deterioration; especially of cells or tissue, leading to loss of function, or death of cells or tissue. Numerous types of cellular degeneration are described in various tissues.

Degenerative arthritis see Arthritis

Degenerative joint disease see Osteoarthritis

Degenerative suspensory ligament disease ◄⁞ *dij en ē rē tiv / su spen sē rē / li gē mēnt / di zēz*, *n.* **(DSLD)** debilitating disorder thought to be limited to suspensory ligaments of a certain number of breeds, including Peruvian Pasos, Peruvian Paso crosses, Arabians, American Saddlebreds, American Quarter Horses, Thoroughbreds, and some European breeds. DSLD is thought to run in families

and is somewhat similar to some hereditary diseases that affect connective and musculoskeletal tissues in humans (e.g. Marfan's syndrome, Ehlers-Danlos syndrome). DSLD frequently leads to persistent, incurable lameness, especially of the hind limbs. Affected horses are often ultimately euthanized owing to limb breakdown. Treatment is primarily based on empirical concepts of supporting the limb by various shoeing and bandaging techniques, but ultimately it is not effective in stopping disease progression. Diagnosis of DSLD is from family or breed history, clinical examination and ultrasonography of the affected ligament(s); the diagnosis can be definitively confirmed post-mortem. DSLD appears to be a systemic disorder involving many tissues and organs, with significant connective tissue component. As the disease is systemic, and not confined solely to the suspensory ligament, the disease is now called equine systemic proteoglycan accumulation (ESPA).
See Suspensory ligament.

Degloving ◀ː *dē gluv ing*, *n.* describing an injury to the horse's lower limb; skin and subcutaneous tissue is rolled off the bone as if removing a glove from a hand.

Deglutition ◀ː *dē glŭ ti shēn*, *n.* swallowing.
See Swallow.

Degree ◀ː *di grē*, *n.* extent, measure, or scope; unit of measurement of angle or temperature; academic qualification from university.

Dehiscence ◀ː *dē hi sēns*, *n.* splitting open; e.g of wound after suture repair.

Dehydration ◀ː *dē hī drā shēn*, *n.* excessive loss of body water (e.g. through sweating, breathing, urination, blood loss, diarrhoea). Depending on degree of dehydration, clinical signs are variable, but may include loss of elasticity of skin (if skin is pinched up it stays raised instead of returning to normal position; test is quite variable, and not sensitive), eyeball sinks back into socket, weight

loss, faeces become small and dry, decreased production of urine, mucous membranes become dry or pale, capillary refill time is prolonged. Diagnosis from clinical signs; blood tests help determine degree of dehydration, especially packed cell volume (haematocrit) and total protein.
See Diarrhoea, Faeces, Sweat, Urine.

Delivery ◀ː *de li vē rē*, *n.* process of expelling or extracting neonate, including foetal membranes; giving birth, parturition.
See Parturition.

Delphinium spp. ◀ː *del fin ē ēm / spē shēs*, *n.* a genus of plants, including the larkspurs and delphinium, which contain delphinine and other toxic alkaloids; cause of poisoning in some areas of North America.

Demodex ◀ː *de mō deks*, *n.* genus of mite; normal resident of skin in horse. Rare cause of mange in horses, mostly in association with long-term corticosteroid therapy; characterized by patchy hair loss and scaly skin.
See Mange.

Demulcent ◀ː *di mul sēnt*, *adj.* soothing or bland; describes medicine (especially cream or lotion) which relieves inflammation of inflamed or abraded surfaces.

Demyelination ◀ː *dē mī ē li nā shēn*, *n.* loss or destruction of myelin sheath of nerve.
See Myelin, Nerve.

Dendrite ◀ː *den drīt*, *n.* extension of nerve cell; conducts impulses towards cell body.
See Nerve.

Denervate ◀ː *dē nē vāt*, *n.* deprive of nerve supply; e.g. in horse, may cut palmar digital nerves (neurectomy) to reduce pain of navicular disease; the area distal to the surgery is partially denervated.
See Navicular syndrome, Neurectomy.

Dental ◀ː *den tl*, *adj.* relating to tooth or teeth.
See Tooth.
    D. alveolus see Alveolus
    D. calculus see Calculus

Dentigerous ◀ᴊ *den ti jĕ rĕs, adj.* having teeth.

D. cyst ◀ᴊ *den ti jĕ rĕs / sist, n.* an epithelial-lined cavity containing one or more dental elements. The dental structures in the cyst may be unattached within the cyst or firmly attached to underlying bone. Typically, the cyst occurs as a firm, non-painful swelling on the side of the head below the ear. Often, there is a draining tract associated with the swelling. The swelling is usually present at birth and enlarges during the first few weeks after foaling. A definitive diagnosis is made by the use of radiography. Treatment consists of surgical removal of the contents of the cyst, and must be done under general anaesthesia, due to the many nerves and blood vessels in the area. The prognosis is good for cure.

Dentine ◀ᴊ *den tĕn, n.* hard calcified substance which forms bulk of tooth. Covered by layer of enamel or cement. See Tooth.

Dentistry ◀ᴊ *den ti strĕ, n.* the field of medicine concerned with the teeth, oral cavity, and associated structures.

Dentition ◀ᴊ *den ti shĕn, n.* arrangement of teeth in species or in individual. In horse are temporary (deciduous) teeth, which emerge from birth to 3½ years (though many horses have complete temporary dentition in wear by 10 months), and permanent teeth, which emerge from 9 months to 4½ years. See tables below.

DENTITION OF HORSE

Temporary teeth				
	Incisors	Canines	Premolars	Molars
Upper jaw	3	0	3	0
Lower jaw	3	0	3	0

Permanent teeth				
	Incisors	Canines	Premolars	Molars
Upper jaw	3	1*	3–4**	3
Lower jaw	3	1*	3–4**	3

*Usually not present in mares, but may be small ones present on lower jaw. **Not every horse has first premolar (also called wolf tooth); more common in upper jaw, may be shed at about 3 years of age.*

APPROXIMATE AGE OF ERUPTION OF TEETH IN HORSE

Approximate age tooth is present	Incisors			Canines*	Premolars				Molars		
	1	2	3		1	2	3	4	1	2	3
Birth–7 days	□										
4–7 weeks	□	□			□	□	□				
9 weeks	□	□			□	□	□				
6–7 months	□	□	□		■	□	□	□			
9 mos.–1 year	□	□	□		■	□	□	□	■		
1½ years	□	□	□		■	□	□	□	■		
2 years	□	□	□		■	□	□	□	■	■	
2½ years	■	□	□		■	■	□	□	■	■	
3 years	■	□	□		■	■	■	□	■	■	
3½ years	■	■	□		■	■	■	□	■	■	■
4 years	■	■	□	■	■	■	■	■	■	■	■
4½ years	■	■	■	■	■	■	■	■	■	■	■

Often not present in mares; may be small ones present on lower jaw;

□ = temporary tooth; ■ = permanent tooth.

Teeth may also be identified by modified Triadan system, in which each tooth is given a three digit number. Mouth divided into four quadrants and first digit of Triadan number denotes quadrant (for permanent teeth, right upper = 1, left upper = 2, left lower = 3, right lower = 4). Remaining two digits give tooth position within quadrant, always numbered from midline, e.g. permanent left upper first incisor is 201. If a deciduous tooth is being referred to, then a different number is used: upper right, 5; upper left; 6; lower left; 7; lower right, 8.
See Tooth.

Deoxyribonucleic acid ◀፪ *dē ok sē rī bō nū klā ik / a̱ sid, n.* (DNA) nucleic acid, present in nucleus of cells, and forming the primary genetic material of all cellular organisms and the DNA viruses. Strands of DNA are twisted to form a double helix, and are antiparallel. Duplicated by replication. DNA carries the genetic information that encodes proteins and enables cells to reproduce and perform their functions.
See Amino acid, Nucleus, Protein.

Depigmentation see Vitiligo

Depo-Medrol™ ◀፪ *dē po-med rŏl, n.* trademark for a preparation of methylprednisolone acetate; used especially in treatment of joint problems in horses.
See Methylprednisolone.

Depo-Provera™ ◀፪ *dē po-prō va̱r ē, n.* trademark for a preparation of medroxy-progesterone acetate for intramuscular injection; has been advocated for control of oestrus in mares; little evidence of efficacy for such purposes.

Deposit ◀፪ *di po̱ zit, n.* sediment; accumulated matter in tissues, cavity, or viscus.

Depot ◀፪ *de po, n.* a body area in which a substance, especially a drug, can be deposited and from which it can be distributed to the rest of the body; especially pertaining to some intramuscular drug formulations, e.g. progesterone in oil.

Depression ◀፪ *di pre̱ shēn, n.* hollow or downwardly or inwardly displaced area on body or on surface of organ. Decrease in activity, dullness, decrease in response to stimuli; as such, may be seen in horse as result of illness.

Derm- ◀፪ *derm, combining form.* relating to skin; also seen as derma- or dermato-. As suffix (–derm), relating to an embryological germ layer.

Dermacentor ◀፪ *der mē se̱n tē, n.* genus of tick, *D. reticulatus* and *D. nitens.*
See Tick.

Dermal asthenia see Asthenia

Dermatitis ◀፪ *der mē tī tis, n.* inflammation of skin. Many causes, including, but not limited to:
- Allergic d. – due to atopy, or allergic contact.
- Atopic d. – chronic dermatitis seen in those with an inherited susceptibility to itching; often accompanied by other signs of allergy.
- Contact d. – acute or chronic dermatitis caused by materials or substances coming in contact with the skin; may involve allergic or non-allergic mechanisms.
- Irritant d. – a non-allergic form of contact dermatitis due to exposure to a substance that damages the skin.
- Pastern d. – dermatitis of the pastern, commonly the posterior aspect; often a problem in draught horses, especially those with feathers. Many causes, including fungal and bacterial infections. Initially, there is reddening, swelling and scaling, which progresses to hair matting and crusting. Secondary bacterial infection is a frequent complication; can become chronic. In chronic cases, the skin may develop tissue reactions such as granulation tissue formation, or granulomatous reactions; lameness, swelling and draining tracts may develop. Treatment successful when administered early, and may require environmental change, removal of hair, antimicrobial therapy, or even surgical excision in chronic cases.

- Perivascular d. – skin inflammation centred around the superficial and deep blood vessels; usually caused by hypersensitivity reactions, parasitism, infections or contact dermatitis.
- Photoallergic d. – skin response to light allergy; e.g. as seen due to light interaction with bile pigments in liver disease.
- Pustular d. – dermatitis characterized by small collections of pus in the epidermis.
- Ventral midline d. – inflammation of skin, with crusting and hair loss along ventral midline of abdomen, associated with bites of flies or midges (*Haematobia irritans, Culicoides*).
- Vesicular d. – dermatitis with small, fluid-filled elevations; as seen in vesicular stomatitis. See Vesicular.
- Viral papular d. – dermatitis characterized by the formation of firm nodules, often with a dry crust that ultimately detaches; may leave depigmented area. See Aural, Wart.

Signs vary depending on cause and severity, and may include heat, swelling, redness, itching, blisters, oozing, scaliness, loss of hair.

Dermatology ◀ː *der mē to lē jē, n.* branch of medicine concerned with skin and skin diseases.

Dermatomycosis see Dermatophytosis

Dermatophilosis ◀ː *der mē to fi lō sis, n.* (many names, mostly reflecting obsolete ideas about the aetiological agent, including mud fever, rain scald, rain rash, and rain rot) infection of skin with Gram-positive bacterium, *Dermatophilus congolensis*. Commonly occurs in horses and ponies kept outside in wet or muddy conditions; however, there are many factors that are probably required for an infection, and to consider only one in isolation is unrealistic. Skin damage and moisture seem to be common features, however, as it is almost impossible to establish infections in intact skin. Signs include hairs matted together by fluid oozing from skin to form tufts ('paint-brush' appearance), crusty scabs often with greenish pus underneath, usually not itchy. If infection on legs is severe, may cause limb swelling and lameness. Diagnosis from clinical signs, skin biopsy, and identification of causal organism by bacterial culture. Treatment may include: 1) keeping skin dry, 2) removing crusts, 3) topical treatments, 4) systemic antimicrobial therapy, usually penicillin, especially if severe. There is no significant immunity to reinfection.

Dermatophyte ◀ː *der ma tē fīt, n.* any of a group of fungi that are parasitic on keratinized tissue (hair, skin, or hoof), commonly including the genera *Microsporum* and *Trichophyton*.

Dermatophytosis ◀ː *der mē tō fi tō sis, n.* (ringworm) common skin condition caused by fungal infection of hair. Most common causal fungi are *Trichophyton equinum, Trichophyton mentagrophytes* and *Microsporum equinum*. Higher incidence in hot, humid climates than in cold, dry climates. Incubation period in natural infection is 1–6 weeks. Spread by direct contact between animals, or indirectly via grooming equipment, tack, contaminated stable, etc. Most commonly affects young horses, as resistance builds up with exposure; differences in skin and skin secretions, hair growth and replacement, and age-related physiology may also be factors in the relative resistance of older animals. Can spread to humans (zoonosis). Signs include loss of hair in areas rubbed by saddle or reins, redness, crusty skin, generally not itchy. Diagnosis by microscopic examination of hair (can see fungus within hair shaft) and identification of fungus in culture (has to be grown on special media). Many cases resolve spontaneously; there is a virtually unlimited number of therapies available for treatment, accordingly. Many topical antifungal products exist; none has been shown to be a treatment of choice. Systemic antifungals are rarely, if ever, indicated. However, topical treatment of all horses in contact with infected horses, as well as environmental treatment with sodium hypochlorite (bleach) solutions, is

probably helpful in controlling herd infections.
See Fungus, Zoonosis.

Dermatosis ◄⁞ _der_ mē _tō_ sis, n. any skin disease, especially one not involving inflammation.

Dermis ◄⁞ _der_ mis, n. layer of skin deep to epidermis. Consists mainly of network of collagen fibres containing nerves and blood vessels.
See Skin.

Dermoid (dermoid cyst) ◄⁞ _der_ moid (_der_ moid) / sist, n. a rarely described epidermal cyst made up of thick-walled sac lined with epithelium and filled with a thick fluid and hair shafts; cyst wall may contain hair follicles, or glands. In horses, has been reported as a congenital problem occurring along the back, and behind the eye, and requiring surgical removal for elimination. Asymptomatic cases may be observed.

Derris ◄⁞ _de_ ris, n. insecticide powder made from roots of tropical plant (_Derris elliptica_), contains rotenone. However, due to studies revealing its extreme toxicity, as well as due to the concentration of rotenone in refined powder, many experts in ecological and organic growing no longer consider it ecologically sound. Has been used for treatment of lice.

Descemetocoele ◄⁞ _dez_ mē _tō_ sēl, n. condition of eye, herniation of Descemet's membrane, the basement membrane that lies between the corneal stroma and endothelium of cornea, due to corneal ulcer or injury. (Named after Jean Descemet, French physician, 1732–1810.)
See Corneal ulcer, Eye.

Desensitization ◄⁞ _dē_ sen si tī _zā_ shēn, n. the prevention or reduction of hypersensitivity (allergic) reactions by administration of reduced or attenuated doses of allergen. Also, in behavioural management, the treatment of anxieties by exposing the horse to the distressing stimuli.

Desmitis ◄⁞ _dez_ _mī_ tis, n. inflamed ligament. Commonly due to trauma, either

acute or chronic. Signs include lameness, pain, heat and swelling over affected ligament. Often confirmed by ultrasound examination.
See Ligament, Ultrasound.

Desmoid ◄⁞ _dez_ moid, n. rare benign growth, most commonly occurring in large muscle groups. Histopathological features include proliferation of fibroblasts and cells expressing muscle actin (myofibroblasts), with extensive dissecting fibrosis within muscle; features are similar to human condition known as musculoaponeurotic fibromatosis. Tumours are probably traumatic in origin, possibly occurring at sites of injections or bursal rupture. Surgical excision curative, unless size of tumour precludes complete removal.

Desmopathy ◄⁞ _dez_ _mo_ pē thē, n. any disease of a ligament.

Desmotomy ◄⁞ _dez_ _mo_ tē mē, n. surgical cutting or division of ligament, e.g. desmotomy of annular ligament of fetlock may be performed to treat chronic inflammation of digital synovial sheath; desmotomy of check ligament (accessory ligament) may be used to treat deformity of fetlock joint.
See Fetlock, Ligament.

Desquamation ◄⁞ _de_ skwē _mā_ shēn, n. shedding of superficial layers of skin as scales; e.g. seen in dermatophytosis.
See Dermatophytosis.

Detomidine ◄⁞ _de_ _to_ mi dēn, n. potent alpha₂-adrenergic agonist sedative drug with strong analgesic properties in gastrointestinal pain (colic); may be given by intravenous or intramuscular injection to sedate horse to facilitate handling, e.g. for endoscopy, radiography, or wound repair, or to relieve painful colic signs. Sedation typically lasts for 45–60 minutes, depending on dose. Side effects include sweating and urination. Also used in some protocols for chemical ejaculation in stallions.

Development ◄⁞ _di_ _ve_ lop mēnt, n. process of growth and differentiation.

Developmental anatomy see Anatomy

Developmental orthopaedic disease ◀< _di ve_ lop _men_ tēl / _or_ thō _pē_ dik / di zēz, _n._ general term, coined in 1986, to include all orthopaedic problems seen in growing horses; the term is non-specific. Conditions involved include osteochondrosis, acquired angular limb deformities, inflammation of growth plate (physitis), subchondral cystic lesions of bone, flexural deformities, juvenile degenerative joint disease and cervical vertebral malformations ('wobbler syndrome').
See Cervical vertebral stenotic myelopathy, Flexural deformity, Osteochondrosis, Physitis, Valgus, Varus.

Dexamethasone ◀< _dek_ sē _me_ tha zōn, _n._ corticosteroid drug. Used topically, orally, intravenously and intramuscularly as an anti-inflammatory and immunosuppressive drug, e.g. in treatment of urticaria. May have other uses, including in the dexamethasone suppression test, as an aid in the diagnosis of pituitary pars intermedia dysfunction (Cushing's disease). Some also feel that dexamethasone is a calming agent, and, as such, it has been used illegally in competitions where calmness is a desired attribute in the competing horse.
See Corticosteroid, Pituitary pars intermedia dysfunction, Urticaria.

Dextran ◀< _deks_ trēn, _n._ large molecule glucose polymer; in humans, used as blood volume expanders, e.g. in shock caused by loss of blood, septic shock. Cost prohibitive in horses.
See Shock.

Dextrose ◀< _dek_ strōz, _n._ D-glucose monohydrate; the biologically active stereoisomer of glucose, the chief source of energy in the body. Used primarily as a fluid and nutrient replacement, primarily in intravenous fluids, or in combination with other agents for various clinical purposes.
See Glucose.

Deworm ◀< dē _werm_, _v._ to eliminate internal parasites by use of an anthelmintic agent.

Dhobie itch ◀< dō bē / ich, _n._ insect hypersensitivity; secondary to biting midges. See Hypersensitivity.

Diabetes ◀< _dī_ ē _bē_ tēz, _n._ term for condition characterized by increased urine production. Two main types: D. insipidus, D. mellitus.

    D. insipidus ◀< _dī_ ē _bē_ tēz / in _si_ pi dēo, _n._ rare condition characterized by excessive urination (polyuria) and drinking (polydipsia). Cause may be neurogenic or nephrogenic. Neurogenic d. insipidus, resulting from a deficiency of vasopressin, has been described; in one case, the cause was unknown and in the other, d. insipidus was acquired following encephalitis. Nephrogenic d. insipidus results from resistance of the kidney to the action of vasopressin; in humans, it is a hereditary condition, and it has been seen in sibling Thoroughbred colts. Nephrogenic d. insipidus may also potentially be acquired secondary to drug therapy, or a variety of metabolic or infectious disorders. Diagnosis by water deprivation test – specific gravity (measurement of urine concentration) does not increase as horse is given no water. Treatment is directed at managing the polyuria and polydipsia; hormone replacement may be needed in neurogenic cases. Hormone replacement is ineffective in nephrogenic cases, so treatment of these cases has generally been to restrict water and sodium intake and to administer diuretics.
See Antidiuretic hormone, Pituitary pars intermedia dysfunction, Specific gravity.

    D. mellitus ◀< _dī_ ē _bē_ tēz / _me_ li tēs, _n._ rare condition characterized by high blood glucose level, which causes increased urine production, glucose in urine (glucosuria) and thirst. In humans is often due to failure of production of insulin by pancreas, (type 1 diabetes); the horse most often has normal to high insulin levels but their tissues are insensitive to insulin (insulin resistance). The most common cause of d. mellitus in horses is pituitary pars intermedia dysfunction (Cushing's disease). In Cushing's, elevated plasma cortisol levels appear to work against the effects of insulin.
See Hyperglycaemia, Insulin, Pituitary pars intermedia dysfunction.

Diagnose ◀ *dī ēg nōz, v.* to make a diagnosis of a disease or condition.

Diagnosis ◀ *dī ēg nō sis, n.* the determination of the nature of a case of disease; the art of distinguishing one disease from another.
> **Clinical d.** ◀ *kli ni kēl / dī ēg nō sis, n.* diagnosis based on clinical signs and laboratory findings of disease.
> **Differential d.** ◀ *di fē ren shēl / dī ēg nō sis, n.* determination which of several diseases may be causing signs; may also be used as term for list of possible diagnoses which must be considered from presenting signs.
> **Laboratory d.** ◀ *lē bo rē tē rē / dī ēg nō sis, n.* diagnosis based on tests and analysis performed on samples from animal.

Diagnostic ◀ *dī ag nos tik, adj.* relating to diagnosis, e.g. diagnostic test is one carried out to aid diagnosis; may also describe sign which is characteristic of particular condition, such that it points to a specific diagnosis.

Diaphragm ◀ *dī ē fram, n.* any separating membrane or structure, especially the muscular partition between thoracic and abdominal cavities. Attached to ribs, sternum and lumbar spine, and is dome-shaped into thorax. Aorta, oesophagus and large vein (posterior vena cava) pass though diaphragm. Contraction of d. increases volume of thoracic cavity, lowers pressure in lungs, so air is drawn in (inspiration); as relaxation of diaphragm occurs, carbon dioxide and other respiratory gases leave lungs (expiration).
See Respiration.

Diaphragmatic ◀ *dī ē frē ma tik, adj.* of or pertaining to diaphragm.
> **D. flutter** see Synchronous diaphragmatic flutter
> **D. hernia** see Hernia
> **D. rupture** ◀ *dī ē frē ma tik / rup tŭr, n.* rent of diaphragm resulting in incomplete partition between thoracic and abdominal cavities. Rare. May be caused by trauma; also rarely seen as congenital defect. May allow passage of abdominal contents into thorax (herniation). Often accompanied by history of recent thoracic trauma. Signs include colic, bowel

obstruction and respiratory difficulties; rapid death has also been reported from d. rupture, presumably from shock.

Diaphysis ◀ *dī a fi sis, n.* the elongated, cylindrical shaft of a long bone.

Diarrhoea ◀ *dī ē rē ē, n.* abnormal frequency and/or liquidity of faeces. Associated with abnormal fluid dynamics in intestine; numerous causes, including infection (bacterial, viral, fungal), diet (sudden change may affect normal bacteria), use of antibiotics (affect normal bacteria), intestinal parasites, intestinal irritants (e.g. sand diarrhoea), neoplasia, poisons, etc. May be acute (sudden onset) or chronic (long-term), may be associated with weight loss and dehydration. Idiopathic diarrhoeas of unknown origin are not uncommon in adult horses, and are usually not accompanied by any associated pathology. Diagnosis is usually clinically obvious; other techniques, including analysis of faecal samples, blood samples, rectal biopsy, etc., may be required to establish a cause.
See *Clostridium.*

Diastole ◀ *dī a stē lē, n.* the dilation, or period of dilation, of heart between beats; period when ventricles fill with blood.
See Heart.

Diathermy ◀ *dī ē ther mē, n.* electrically induced heat in body tissues. Diathermy has been used to treat muscle and tendon inflammation in horses; objective evaluations of outcomes from such treatment have not been conducted.
> **Surgical d.** ◀ *ser ji kēl / dī ē ther mē, n.* diathermy used for electrocoagulation of tissues during surgery; uncommon in equine surgery.

Diazepam ◀ *dī a zē pam, n.* anxiolytic and skeletal muscle relaxing drug; has especially been used to reduce anxiety in humans. In horses may be used in pre-anaesthetic regimens to relax skeletal muscles, e.g. to prevent or relieve laryngeal spasm; also has been used in treatment of tetanus to relieve muscle spasms.
See Tetanus.

Dichlorvos ◀ *dī klor vēs, n.* organophosphorus insecticide compound, previously used primarily for control of bots. Superseded by safer and more satisfactory compounds today.
See Bot.

Diclofenac ◀ *dik lō fen ak, n.* unique non-steroidal anti-inflammatory drug, available as topical cream that is rubbed directly onto inflamed or sore areas. Mechanism of action by reducing hormones that cause inflammation and pain in the body. In one study, diclofenac liposomal cream was shown to reduce lameness as graded by owners and veterinarians, regardless of the severity or duration of the clinical condition. Another study suggested that the cream may be effective for reducing subcutaneous inflammation in horses. Urine and serum concentrations of diclofenac have been detected following topical administration of 1% liposomal diclofenac cream for 10 days at the labelled dose and at 2X and 4X the labelled dose. The drug is slowly absorbed and eliminated when placed on the skin. As such, the product should be used with caution before a competition in order to prevent an inadvertent positive drug test. It has been reported that veterinary diclofenac use in India has caused a crash of the vulture population, with major ecological consequences. Diclofenac causes kidney failure in vultures that eat treated domestic animals.

Dicoumarol ◀ *dī kū mē rol, n.* anticoagulant compound (affects blood clotting). May be present in mouldy hay made from sweet clover; also present in some rodent poisons.

Dictyocaulus arnfieldi ◀ *dic tē ō cor lēs / arn fē ūl dī, n.* horse lungworm. Main host is donkey where even heavy infections only cause mild clinical signs, but can infect horses and cause chronic cough, increased respiratory rate, and nasal discharge. Lungworm eggs or first stage larvae are passed in faeces, and larvae moult twice before becoming infective, in about 6 weeks. Larvae may be eaten by horse, and migrate from intestine, to local lymph nodes, to lungs. Foals generally show few signs of infection, but heavy worm burdens are associated with significant mortality in horses of all ages. Diagnosis by history and signs, endoscopy (may see larvae or adult worms in trachea and bronchi), high levels of eosinophils in bronchoalveolar lavage fluid, and by identification of eggs and larvae in faeces.
See Bronchoalveolar lavage, Cough, Endoscopy.

Diet ◀ *dī ĕt, n.* customary amount and type of food horse eats. Should be specifically planned to be appropriate for activity of horse, e.g. high in energy if doing heavy exercise.

Dietary balance see Balance

Diethylcarbamazine ◀ *dī eth il kar ba mē zēn, n.* a synthetic organic anthelmintic drug that is highly specific for several parasites, most particularly *Onchocerca* spp. Has been investigated for other uses in horses, especially chronic obstructive pulmonary disease, with little evidence of efficacy.
See *Onchocerca*.

Differential blood count see Complete blood count

Differential diagnosis see Diagnosis

Diffuse ◀ 1) *di fūs, adj.* not localized to one area of body, not concentrated; 2) *di fūz, v.* to pass through or spread widely through a tissue or structure.

Digestibility ◀ *dī jes ti bi li tē, n.* digestibility refers to the amount of ingested nutrients that can be absorbed from the digestive tract. For example, high fibre foods have relatively low digestibility.

Digestion ◀ *dī jes chēn, n.* breaking down of food in alimentary tract into molecules which can be absorbed into blood stream and assimilated into tissues of body. In mouth food is chewed and mixed with saliva. Acid and enyzmes in stomach aid initial digestion; additional digestion in horse occurs in caecum and large intestine, where microorganisms break down complex carbohydrates into simpler sugars.

Digit ◀️ _di_ jit, _n._ any of the divisions in which the limbs of most vertebrates end; most mammals have five digits; typically digits have a series of phalanges bearing a nail, claw, or hoof at the tip. In horse there is only one digit on each limb.

Digital ◀️ _di ji tēl, adj._ of digit.
    D. cushion ◀️ _di ji tēl / kŭ shēn, n._ wedge-shaped pad beneath the rear part of the sole, in hoof. Made of fibrous and elastic fibres, with some fat and cartilage. Lies deep to frog and acts as shock absorber. In the adult horse, the digital cushion tends to become stiffer with age; in diseased hoof, it appears to lose much of its cushioning function. See Foot.
    D. synovial sheath ◀️ _di ji tēl / sī nō vē ŭl / shēth, n._ fluid-filled sleeve surrounding flexor tendons at back of fetlock joint. Fluid allows smooth movement of tendons over the bending joint as digital flexor muscles contract. Wounds to back of fetlock area or caudal third of sole of foot may penetrate sheath and cause infection and inflammation; chronic inflammation of the sheath may be a problem in horses performing in some athletic disciplines.

Digitalis see Foxglove

Digitoxin ◀️ _di ji tok sin, n._ cardiac glycoside present in foxglove (_Digitalis_); toxicities reported when ingested. No clinical usage. See Heart.

Digoxin ◀️ _di jok sin, n._ cardiac glycoside present in foxglove (_Digitalis_); in synthetic form, has been used in treatment of various heart conditions, including congestive heart failure and atrial fibrillation. The main effects of digoxin on the heart are a decreased conduction of electrical impulses through the A-V node (which makes it useful for controlling heart rate) and an increased force of contraction of the heart muscle (which makes it useful for the treatment of heart failure). Digoxin also increases activity of

the vagus nerve, which also helps decrease heart activity. See Heart.

Dilation ◀️ _dī lā shēn, n._ stretching, opening up, or enlarging a part of the body. Can be used to describe widening of blood vessels, opening up of pupil, widening of birth canal, etc.

Dilatation ◀️ _dī lē tā shēn, n._ the condition of being stretched beyond normal size. Seen especially as a result of overwork or disease, e.g. dilatation of the heart in congestive heart failure.

Dimethylglycine ◀️ _dī mē thīl glī sin, n._ DMG is a dietary supplement present in many foods. It is supposed to increase the utilization of oxygen and decrease the production of lactic acid by the muscles during high-intensity exercise. In horses, DMG has most commonly been promoted as a substance to help reduce the incidence of acute or chronic equine exertional rhabdomyolysis, also known as 'tying up', myositis or azoturia. There is no scientific evidence to suggest that DMG actually would do this. Furthermore, the mechanism by which it would exert its effect is somewhat unclear, as lactic acid production (as measured in the blood) does not appear to be a feature of rhabdomyolysis in the horse.

Dimethylsulphoxide ◀️ _dī mē thīl sul fok sīd, n._ (DMSO) chemical solvent that has been credited – legitimately or not – with over thirty properties for the treatment of disease. Used in a wide variety of applications in the horse. DMSO is available in a gel or in a liquid form. The liquid form can be given orally, intravenously (when diluted) or applied on top of the skin; the gel is always used topically. As a therapeutic agent, DMSO is used primarily as an anti-inflammatory agent. There are a variety of ways that DMSO might exert its effect as an anti-inflammatory, of which the most important seems to be the neutralization of some of the destructive substances that are produced by the process of inflammation. In addition to this, DMSO has some of the same

DIPTERA

anti-inflammatory properties as the corticosteroids. In experimental settings, DMSO helps protect tissues from injury induced by a lack of blood (ischaemia). DMSO is unique in that it can go through the skin and mucous membranes without disrupting them. Because of this property, it can be used as a carrier of other substances through the skin. Because it can go through the skin, people who use DMSO report tasting it after they put it on (or in) their horse.

INDICATIONS
There are an almost innumerable variety of conditions for which DMSO has been advocated, including topically to treat swellings; injecting it into joints; using it systemically for muscle soreness, disease of the nervous system and treatment of colic and its associated effects; in the reproductive tract of the mare; for skin conditions; to accelerate wound healing; to prevent blood clotting and for laminitis (to name but a few). Because of its ability to penetrate membranes, DMSO is also commonly employed to help get drugs into areas that are hard to reach, such as the brain or the chest cavity.

DOSING
There are no standard doses that have been generated for DMSO. In the treatment of most medical conditions for which it is used in the horse, no controlled studies have been done to establish how well DMSO works in treating those conditions. Fortunately, and especially so considering how widely it is used, DMSO is fairly benign and has a very low toxicity.

Dimorphism ◀ *dī mor fizm, n.* having two different forms.
> **Sexual d.** ◀ *sek sū ūl / dī mor fizm, n.* having characteristics of both genders (hermaphrodite).
> See Hermaphrodite.

Dioctyl sodium sulphosuccinate ◀ *dī ok tīl / sō dē ēm / sulfo suk si nāt, n.* (DSS) surface tension reducing agent sometimes used for the treatment of colic. By reducing surface tension, DSS is supposed to allow water to more easily penetrate masses of faecal matter. In addition, DSS

causes the intestine to secrete fluid and electrolytes. As such, it can function as a stool softener and laxative. DSS is a liquid that is diluted with water and given by nasogastric intubation; it can also be diluted with water and given in an enema to foals for treatment of retained meconium. Theoretically, DSS should not be given at the same time as mineral oil. DSS has the potential to break down mineral oil into small enough globules that it can be absorbed into the circulation. DSS has the potential to be irritating to the intestinal tract. Overdosage of DSS can create diarrhoea and make horses feel quite ill. Recommended doses of DSS should probably be repeated only every 48 hours, accordingly.

Diode laser ◀ *dī ōd / lā zēr, n.* a device that cuts tissue by the energy of laser light. Used occasionally in equine surgery, especially in palmar digital neurectomies and vascular surgery. YAG and CO_2 lasers are most commonly used.
See Laser.

Dioestrus ◀ *dī ēs trēs, n.* period in oestrous cycle between 'heats', when corpus luteum is present in ovary and progesterone is secreted by corpus luteum. Mare rejects stallion, and progesterone stimulates changes in lining of uterus to make suitable environment for embryo. Last 15–16 days.
See Corpus, Oestrous cycle.

Diphenhydramine hydrochloride ◀ *dī fen hī drē mēn / hī drō klor rīd, n.* antihistamine drug; has been used in treatment of allergies, or in the treatment of side effects associated with the antipsychotic drug fluphenazine.

Diploid ◀ *di ploid, adj.* describes cell which contains two sets of chromosomes, one from each parent, as normally found in higher organisms. Horse cells usually contain 32 pairs of chromosomes.

Diptera ◀ *dip tē rē, n.* order of insects with two wings, includes flies, mosquitoes, midges. Some transmit disease to horses.

135

Dipyrone ◀≀ *dī pī rōn, n.* (metamizole) mild anti-inflammatory, antipyretic (for control of fevers) and analgesic. Chemically related to phenylbutazone and works in the same fashion. Supplied as a sterile solution for IM, IV or subcutaneous administration; most commonly used for the control of abdominal pain (colic) in the horse. However, experiments showed that the drug is certainly not very potent. The United States Food and Drug Administration (USFDA) Center for Veterinary Medicine issued a 'CVM UPDATE' on December 6, 1995 announcing that dipyrone products had not been the subject of an approved New Animal Drug Application (NADA), and that the agency would no longer grant regulatory discretion for the marketing of these products. Currently, dipyrone is not approved for any use in animals in the United States, accordingly. If dipyrone is given for a prolonged period, problems with decreased white blood cells may be seen. The drug should not be used at the same time as barbiturate agents (commonly used to induce anaesthesia in the horse). It should be used with care in horses with heart disease. Overdosage of dipyrone can cause seizures. In Europe, used in treatment of spasmodic colic as combination drug with butylscopolamine (Buscopan compositum).

Dirofilaria immitis ◀≀ *dī rō fil ar ē ē / imi tis, n.* dog heartworm; the most important filarioid parasite of animals in North America. Parasites in the lungs of a young Quarter Horse stallion have been diagnosed; migration of the parasites through the eye of the horse has also been reported, with successful removal from the anterior chamber. Much less commonly reported in horses than in carnivores.

Dirty ◀≀ *der tē, adj.* lay term describing mare that has vulvar discharge, or bacterial uterine infection.

Disc ◀≀ (spelled also disk) *disk, n.* flat circular plate, e.g. optic disc is circular part of back of eye where optic nerve enters; intervertebral disc is somewhat round

cartilagenous pad between bones of spine.
See Intervertebral, Optic.

Discharge ◀≀ *dis charj, v./n.* an excretion or substance passed from body, e.g. from nose or vulva; to pass a liquid substance from body. Discharge may be clear and watery, mucous (thicker), mucopurulent (thick and cloudy), purulent (thick, cloudy, offensive smell), sanguineous (bloody), etc., depending on cause. Also, the passing of an action potential through a nerve or muscle fibre.

Discoid lupus erythematosus ◀≀ *dis koid / lŭ pēs / e ri thē mē tō sēs, n.* rare immune-mediated dermatosis; no systemic involvement. Lesions appear on the lips, nostrils, or around the eyes, may spread to the ears, neck, shoulders, or perineal areas. They appear as circular to oval areas of redness, scaling or crusting, and alopecia with varying degrees of patching and white hairs. Generally not painful nor itchy. Diagnosis by histopathological examination; immunohistochemical staining or immunofluorescence is diagnostic.
See Autoimmune disease.

Discospondylitis ◀≀ *dis kō spon di lī tis, n.* inflammation of intervertebral discs in spine; not commonly recognized in horse; clinical signs may be vague, or affected horses asymptomatic. Various imaging modalities may assist in diagnosis. Radiographic findings include arthritis of vertebral endplates, vertebral misalignment, and ventral spondylosis. Ultrasound examination may confirm vertebral alignment problems, and also highlight disc abnormalities. Scintigraphy may show inflamed areas. One case of bacterial discospondylitis has been reported; that horse returned to normal function with antimicrobial therapy. Note: the term 'discospondylitis' is used essentially interchangeably with 'discospondylosis'.
See Intervertebral.

Disease ◀≀ *di zēz, n.* disorder of structure or function of part, organ or system of animal. Generally has characteristic signs; however, the pathogenesis may or may not be known.

Dish ◀ *dish, v.* fault of gait, where foreleg below carpus is thrown outwards; a shallow vessel, usually of glass or plastic, for laboratory work, e.g. Petri dish for bacterial culture.

Dished ◀ *dishd, adj.* curved in; concave, e.g. a dished hoof, seen in a horse with a club foot.
See Club foot.

Disinfect ◀ *di sin fekt, v.* to kill or remove disease-causing organisms, or render them inert. It may be advisable to disinfect stable, horse tack, surgical instruments, hands of surgeon, etc. Helpful in reducing spread of disease, in enabling surgery to be carried out without introduction of bacteria into wound, etc.

Disinfectant ◀ *di sin fek tent, n.* freeing from infection; substance or agent which destroys disease-causing organisms, e.g. heat, steam, chemicals such as sodium hydroxide, chlorine-based compounds, ammonium-based compounds, etc., especially applied to agents used on inanimate objects.

Dislocate ◀ *dis lō kāt, v.* (luxate) disrupt normal arrangement of part of body, e.g. a dislocated shoulder, but especially as pertains to normal connections with a bone at a joint, e.g. a dislocated fetlock. Uncommon; usually associated with trauma. Results in bones not articulating as normal and causes obvious lameness; may be associated with injury to other tissues. Joints most commonly affected are fetlock or pastern; prognosis may be good, depending on extent of injury.
See Fetlock, Pastern.

Dislocation ◀ *dis lō kā shĕn, n.* (luxation) displacement of any part, especially of a bone.
See Dislocate, Luxation.

Disodium cromoglycate see Cromolyn sodium

Disorder ◀ *dis or dĕ, n.* a derangement or abnormality of function, e.g. an intestinal disorder.

Dispense ◀ *dis pens, v.* to distribute medicines according to veterinary prescription.

Displacement ◀ *dis plās mĕnt, n.* malposition.
See Dorsal.

Disseminated *di se mi nā tid, n.* distributed over a considerable area.

D. intravascular coagulation ◀ (DIC) *di se mi nā tid / in trĕ vas cū lē / cō a gū lā shĕn, n.* bleeding disorder characterized by abnormal reduction in the elements involved in blood clotting due to their usurpation in widespread intravascular clotting. Blood coagulation cascades are initiated inappropriately and cause small blood clots which may block vessels and cause organ damage through lack of oxygen. Depletion of clotting elements causes profuse bleeding in late stages. Associated with any number of disorders, including toxins produced by Gram-negative bacteria in sepsis or gastrointestinal infection, burns, disease of major organs (e.g. kidney, liver), etc. Signs will depend on underlying cause, include small haemorrhages (e.g. on gums), bleeding after blood sample is taken, signs of organ damage. Blood tests show clotting abnormalities. Usually fatal.
See Clot, Sepsis.

Distal ◀ *dis tēl, adj.* remote; farther from any point of reference; as opposed to proximal.

D. axonopathy ◀ *dis tēl / ak sĕn o pĕ thē, n.* degeneration of nerve fibres, starting centrally, and proceeding distally. In horses, this occurs to nerves supplying larynx in recurrent laryngeal neuropathy (laryngeal paralysis), in stringhalt, in equine motor neuron disease, and as an idiopathic peripheral neuropathy characterized by knuckling and stumbling.
See Equine motor neuron disease, Recurrent laryngeal neuropathy, Stringhalt.

D. impar sesamoidean ligament ◀ *dis tēl / im par / sē sa moid ē ĕn / li ga mĕnt, n.* ligament connecting the distal border of the navicular bone to the ventral (solar) surface of the third (distal) phalanx. This strong ligament permits relatively little motion between the navicular bone and the distal phalanx. Can be injured; may result in chronic lameness that can be confused with disease of the navicular bone.

D. interphalangeal joint ◀⧽ _dis_ tēl / in tē fa _lan_ jē ēl / joint, n. the joint occurring between the second and third phalanges; coffin joint.

D. intertarsal joint ◀⧽ _dis_ tēl / in tē tar sēl / joint, n. one of the multiple joints of the hock, a low motion joint proximal to the third metatarsal (cannon) bone. Osteoarthritis of this joint may be seen as part of 'bone spavin'.

D. phalanx see Coffin bone, Third: (T. phalanx).

D. sesamoid bone see Navicular

Distemper see Strangles

Dryland d. see _Corynebacterium_

Distension ◀⧽ _dis_ _ten_ shēn, n. the state of being unduly enlarged or stretched out, e.g. a distended abdomen.

Distress ◀⧽ _dis_ _tres_, n. state of physical or mental anguish or suffering, e.g. respiratory distress, or mental distress.

Diuresis ◀⧽ _dī_ ūr _rē_ sis, n. increased excretion of urine.

Diuretic ◀⧽ _dī_ ūr _re_ tik, n./adj. causing increased excretion of urine, e.g. diuretic medication. Used to remove accumulations of fluid, e.g. in congestive heart failure. Examples of diuretic drugs include furosemide, spironolactone. Most commonly used diuretics in horses work by inhibiting sodium and chloride reabsorption in kidney tubules. By disrupting the reabsorption of these ions, loop diuretics prevent the urine from becoming concentrated.
See Heart, Kidney.

Diurnal ◀⧽ _dī_ _er_ nēl, adj. of the day, during daytime (c.f. nocturnal). Also, having a daily cycle, e.g. diurnal rhythm, occurring every 24 hours.

Diverticulum ◀⧽ _dī_ vē _ti_ kū lum, n. a mucous membrane-lined pouch or sac of variable size, occurring normally, e.g. auditory tube diverticulum (guttural pouch), or created by herniation, e.g. oesophageal or ileal diverticula of mucous membrane through the muscular wall; associated with colic and may be corrected surgically.
See Guttural pouch.

DMSO see Dimethylsulphoxide

Dobutamine ◀⧽ _dō_ _bū_ tē mēn, n. a drug that increases cardiac contractility and output; primary activity results from simulation of beta-adrenoreceptors of the heart. May also be used as supportive therapy to maintain blood pressure in long surgical operations (e.g. colic surgery).

Docking ◀⧽ _do_ king, v. removal of part of tail. Customary in many draft horse breeds in North America; may have arisen out of concern for tail getting caught in traces. Illegal in horses in GB unless tail is removed because of disease.

Dog's mercury ◀⧽ _dogz_ / _mer_ cŭ rē, n. (_Mercurialis perennis_) spring flower found across continental Europe in shady forest areas; found in abundance in soils with high calcium content (e.g. Yorkshire). May cause diarrhoea, colic and blood-stained urine if eaten. In spite of its dangers, dog's mercury has been used as a medicinal herb. According to legend, the medicinal benefits of this plant were revealed by the god Mercury.

Dominant ◀⧽ _do_ mi nēnt, adj. exerting most influence. In genetics refers to trait or gene which will be expressed in offspring even if inherited from only one parent.

Domperidone ◀⧽ _dom_ pe ri dōn, n. domperidone is a dopamine receptor antagonist most often used to treat fescue grass toxicosis and agalactia (lack of milk production). It is generally used within two weeks pre-foaling or up to five days post-foaling to treat agalactia in mares. A domperidone response test has also been developed for the diagnosis of equine pituitary pars intermedia dysfunction.
See Agalactia, Pituitary pars intermedia dysfunction.

Dopamine ◄⁞ *dō pē mēn, n.* catecholamine that acts as neurotransmitter (i.e. helps transmission of impulse from one nerve to next) in central nervous system.
See Central nervous system.

    D. agonist ◄⁞ *dō pē mēn / a gēn ist, n.* an agent that increases the influence of dopamine, e.g. pergolide. Used primarily in the treatment of equine pituitary pars intermedia dysfunction.

    D. antagonist ◄⁞ *dō pē mēn / an tag ēn ist, n.* an agent that works against the influence of dopamine, e.g. domperidone.

Dopaminergic ◄⁞ *dō pē mēn er jik, n.* activated or transmitted by dopamine; relating to tissues or organs affected by dopamine.

Doppler ◄⁞ *do pler, n.* Doppler ultrasonography; one of a variety of ultrasonic imaging techniques used to measure the velocity of moving objects; used to examine blood flow. (Named after Johann Christian Doppler, Austrian physicist.)
See Ultrasonography.

    D. effect ◄⁞ *do pler / i fekt, n.* the change in frequency and wavelength of a wave as perceived by an observer moving relative to the source of the wave, e.g. the siren on a passing emergency vehicle will start out higher than its stationary pitch, become lower as the vehicle passes, and continue lower than its stationary pitch as it moves away from the observer.

Dorsal ◄⁞ *dor sēl, adj.* relating to back, or describing side of organ or part of body more towards the back surface; e.g. the dorsal side of the forelimb is the side that is highest when the limb is swung forward.

    D. cortical stress fracture ◄⁞ *dor sēl / kor ti kēl / stres / frak tŭr, n.* one of several diseases of the dorsal surface of the third metacarpal bone; most commonly seen in 2–3-year-old fast-gaited horses, such as racing Thoroughbreds. Training regimens to reduce occurrence have been described, particularly by Dr David Nunamaker of the University of Pennsylvania. Many therapies, including rest, various surgeries, blistering, and extracorporeal shock wave therapy; particular choice depends mostly on the experience of the examining veterinarian, as no therapy has been proven to be superior to others.
See Blister, Extracorporeal shock wave therapy.

    D. displacement of soft palate ◄⁞ *dor sēl / dis plās mēnt / ov / soft / pa lēt, n.* the elongated soft palate of the horse is a muscular structure that forms the division between the oral and nasal portions of the pharynx. During normal breathing, its posterior border lies underneath the epiglottis. In this position, there is maximum air flow. Except when swallowing, the free border of the soft palate remains under the epiglottis. When the horse cannot maintain the palate in the proper position during exercise, airway function is impaired, the horse may perform poorly (exercise intolerance) and a characteristic loud guttural noise may be heard on expiration, caused by the free border of the palate fluttering in the airway. This condition is known as intermittent dorsal displacement of the soft palate (DDSP). Optimum treatment is controversial; both surgical and medical solutions have been described, with an approximately 60% success rate being commonly claimed for any of them.

    D. laminectomy ◄⁞ *dor sēl / lam in ek tomē, n.* a surgical procedure that involves removal of the caudal aspect of the dorsal part of one vertebra, and the cranial part of the vertebra behind it. Performed for decompression of spinal cord, as in some cervical vertebral malformations.

    D. root ganglion see Ganglion

    D. spinous process ◄⁞ *dor sēl / spī nēs / prō ses, n.* bony protuberance from top part of vertebra.
See Vertebra.

Dorsum ◄⁞ *dor sēm, n.* the aspect of a body part or structure corresponding to the back of animal; upper surface of part of body.

Dosage ◄⁞ *dō sij, n.* the determination and regulation of the size, frequency and number of doses [of medication].

Dose ◄⁞ *dōs, n./v.* quantity of drug to be administered at one time; to administer medicine. In radiology, the amount of radiation absorbed per unit mass of tissue.

Double ◀: *du būl, adj.* having a twofold relation or character.

    D. blind ◀: *du būl / blīnd, adj.* pertaining to a clinical trial or experiment where neither the subject (or, in the case of the horse, the subject's owner) nor the person administering treatment is aware of the treatment that the subject is being given. Performed so as to attempt to avoid bias in interpretation of experimental results.

    D. expiratory effort ◀: *du būl / eks pi rē trē / e fert, n.* intense respiratory effort; sign seen in, e.g., chronic obstructive pulmonary disease, when horse breathes out and pushes out air at end of expiration with lift of abdominal muscles.

See Recurrent airway obstruction.

    D. ovulation ◀: *du būl / o vū lā shēn, n.* release of two ova at ovulation. Occurs in approx 16% of equine ovulations; may result in twin pregnancy.

Dourine ◀: *dor rēn, n.* sexually transmitted disease; caused by infection with the protozoan parasite *Trypanosma equiperdum*. Organisms are present in the urethra of infected stallions and in vaginal discharges of infected mares. Foals born to infected mares may be infected, although it is not clear if infection in foals occurs in utero or during birth. Different strains of the parasite vary in their disease-causing ability. Other names by which the disease is known include Slapsiekte, el Dourin, Mal de coit, Beschalseuche, and Covering disease.

CLINICAL SIGNS

Clinical signs vary, depending mostly on the virulence of the infecting strain and the general condition of the infected animal. In mares, a small amount of vaginal discharge is usually the first sign of infection, with swelling and oedema of the vulva developing and extending later in the course of disease. Other signs include vulvitis, vaginitis, polyuria and other signs of discomfort such as an elevated tail. Abortion may or may not be a feature of infection, depending on the strain.

In stallions, the first signs are oedema of the prepuce and penis, which spreads over the ventral aspect of the horse's body and may wax and wane. Conjunctivitis and keratitis may be observed as well. Paraphimosis may be observed. Vesicles or ulcers on the genitalia may heal and leave permanent white scars (leukodermic patches). 'Silver dollar plaques' on the skin characterize the disease in some areas; when they occur, they are pathognomonic.

Nervous system complications may follow the genital manifestations by weeks or months. The first signs of nervous system involvement are restlessness and weight shifting, followed by progressive weakness and incoordination, and finally by paralysis and the inability to rise. Anaemia and weight loss may be seen, in spite of a good appetite. These signs may be cyclical in some horses; some horses have lived for 10 years after experimental infection.

DIAGNOSIS

Diagnosis on physical signs may be unreliable because many animals develop no signs. The complement-fixation test has been the foundation for the successful eradication of dourine from many parts of the world.

TREATMENT

There are reports of successful treatment with trypanocidal drugs such as suramin or quinapyramine dimethylsulphate, particularly when the disease is caused by more virulent (European) strains of the parasite. In general, treatment is not recommended for fear of continued dissemination of the disease by treated animals. No vaccination exists. The most successful prevention and eradication programmes have focused on serological identification of infected animals. Infected animals should be humanely destroyed or castrated to prevent further transmission of the disease.

CONTROL

All equids in an area where dourine is found should be quarantined and breeding should be stopped for 1 to 2 months while testing continues. Sanitation and disinfection are ineffective means of controlling the spread of dourine because the disease is normally spread by coitus. Has been eradicated from many countries; seen in Africa, Asia, Central and South America, south-eastern Europe. Notifiable disease in European Union and United States; imported horses must be certified free of infection.

Doxycycline ◀ࣿ *dok sē sī klēn, n.* a semi-synthetic member of the tetracycline antibiotics group; commonly used to treat a variety of infections, including Lyme disease and anaplasmosis ('Potomac horse fever'). Works by interfering with the ability of some growing or multiplying bacteria to make proteins, thereby inhibiting their growth. Doxycycline is an inhibitor of enzymes known as matrix metalloproteinases, and as such has been tried in the treatment of laminitis. See Anaplasmosis, Laminitis, Lyme disease.

Drain ◀ࣿ *drān, v./n.* remove fluid completely, as in draining an abscess; to give passage to a bodily fluid, e.g. the Eustachian tube drains the middle ear. Tube or cylinder used to drain fluid, e.g. tube placed below skin during surgery or wound repair to prevent accumulation of subcutaneous fluid.
See Pus.

***Draschia* spp.** ◀ࣿ *dras kē ē / spē shēs, n.* a genus of the worm family of Habronematidae; includes *D. megastoma.* Found in nodules in the stomach wall of infected horses. Rarely causes clinical signs; heavy infestations can occasionally rupture and cause peritonitis. The antiparasitic agent ivermectin provides control.
See Ivermectin.

Dressing ◀ࣿ *dre sing, n.* covering of bandage, gauze, pad, etc. applied to wound. Many types of dressings available, primarily for application to wounds.

Dropped ◀ࣿ *dropt, adj.* in describing anatomical position, means lower than usual.
> **D. elbow** see Elbow
> **D. sole** ◀ࣿ *dropt / sōl, n.* horn of ground surface of hoof becomes flat rather than normal concave shape. May occur in laminitis.
> See Hoof, Laminitis.

Dropsy ◀ࣿ *drop sē, n.* (oedema) accumulation of fluid in abdominal cavity or in tissues. Archaic.
See Oedema.

Drown ◀ࣿ *drō n, v.* to suffocate in water or some other liquid. Rare in horses, but may occur if horse being exercised in water or secondary to nasal intubation, with inadvertent placement of medication into the lungs.

Drug ◀ࣿ *drug, n.* medicine, chemical used to treat, diagnose or prevent illness.

Dry ◀ࣿ *drī, adj.* lack or absence of secretions, effusions, or other forms of moisture.
> **D. coat** see Anhydrosis
> **D. cough** ◀ࣿ *drī / kof, n.* not accompanied by the raising of mucus or respiratory secretions.
> **D. eye** ◀ࣿ *drī / ī, n.* (keratoconjunctivitis sicca) deficiency of watery part of tears. Rare in horses, may be caused by injury to lacrimal gland or damage to facial nerve. Causes thick discharge, pain in eye, dullness and opacity of cornea, and corneal ulceration. Diagnose using paper strip (Schirmer tear test) which measures tear production. In dry eye, readings are <10 mm, often 0 mm.
> See Cornea, Eye, Lacrimal apparatus.
> **D. gangrene** see Gangrene
> **D. matter** ◀ࣿ *drī / ma tē, n.* in feed analysis, the concentration of each nutrient in the diet if it did not contain any moisture; allows comparison of feeds on an identical moisture basis.

Dryland distemper see *Corynebacterium*

Ductus ◀ࣿ *duk tēs, n.* vessel or tube in body; a body passage that occurs within well-defined walls.
> **D. arteriosus** ◀ࣿ *duk tēs / ar té rē ō sēs, n.* arterial duct; blood vessel which connects pulmonary artery to aorta in foetus, allows circulation to bypass lungs as they are not used for respiration in foetus. Usually closes by 4 days of age. If stays open, is termed patent d.a., causes heart murmur, and may cause clinical signs. Rare in horses.

D. deferens ◀€ _duk_ tēs / de fē rēnz, _n._ (vas deferens) duct which carries sperm from testis, joins excretory duct of seminal vesicle and becomes ejaculatory duct.
See Testes, Vas deferens.

D. nasolacrimalis ◀€ _duk_ tēs / _nā_ zō _la_ kri _marl_ is, _n._ nasolacrimal duct; conducts tears from eye to opening in nostril; can become obstructed and cause excessive tearing; in some animals, may not form due to congenital defect.

D. venosus ◀€ _duk_ tēs / ve nō sēs, _n._ part of foetal circulation, a blood vessel which allows circulation to bypass liver. Usually closes by fourth month of foetal life.

Salivary d. ◀€ sē _li_ vē rē / _duk_ tēs, _n._ duct that carries saliva.

Dull ◀€ _dul, adj._ lacking in resonance on chest percussion; having diminished response to external stimuli, lacking brightness or energy, a common sign in many diseases.

Dummy ◀€ _du_ mē, _n._ (dummy foal, post-partum asphyxia syndrome), neonatal maladjustment syndrome, wanderer, barker); all causes of condition have not been identified, but seem to relate to insufficient oxygen delivery to the central nervous system around birth. Affected foals may wander, stare upwards, be blind, may not suckle normally. Signs may develop up to 48 hours of age.
See Hypoxic ischaemic encephalopathy.

Dung ◀€ _dung, n._ faeces, undigested food and body waste passed from rectum.

Dunkop ◀€ _dun kop, n._ pulmonary form of African horse sickness.
See African horse sickness.

Duodenitis–proximal jejunitis (DPJ) ◀€ _dū_ ō di _ni_ tis – _prok_ si mēl / je jü _ni_ tis, _n._ a condition characterized by inflammation of the small intestine, with excessive electrolyte and fluid secretion and gastric reflux. Also known as anterior enteritis or proximal enteritis. Horses present with colic pain, and large volumes of foul smelling, orange–brown fluid on nasogastric intubation. Differentiation between DPJ and small intestinal obstruction may be difficult. Other signs include mild fever, injected mucous membranes, absence of intestinal sounds, prolonged capillary refill time and increased heart rate. Laboratory findings generally reflect dehydration. Abdominocentesis may reveal abdominal fluid with increased protein and elevated numbers of white blood cells. No specific aetiological agents have been identified in most cases. Since a specific cause is rarely known, treatment is largely supportive, and includes intravenous fluid therapy, frequent decompression of stomach, nutritional support, non-steroidal anti-inflammatory drugs. Attention should also be paid to the feet of horses with DPJ, because laminitis is a frequent complication. With appropriate treatment, most horses with DPJ recover, assuming that they do not develop secondary complications.
See Abdominocentesis, Laminitis.

Duodenum ◀€ _dū_ ō _dē_ nēm, _n._ first (proximal) portion of small intestine, extending from the pyloric outlet of the stomach to the jejunum. Bile duct (from liver) and pancreatic ducts open into duodenum. Approximately 3–7 m in length.
See Bile, Pancreas.

Dura mater ◀€ _dŭ_ rē / _ma_ tē, _n._ tough, fibrous membrane; forms outermost layer of meninges covering brain and spinal cord.
See Meninges.

Dynamic ◀€ _dī_ _na_ mik, _adj._ pertaining to, or manifesting, physical force or energy.

D. compression plate ◀€ _dī_ _na_ mik / kom pre shēn / plāt, _n._ bone plate used in fracture repair. Plate applies compression to fracture site by eccentric insertion of screws. The slot for the bone screw has a sloping surface at one end; when the spherical head of the screw is tightened, it slides down the slope and the plate moves away from the fracture, thereby compressing fracture line.

Dys- ◀€ _dis, prefix._ bad, painful, abnormal, difficult; the opposite of eu-.

Dysautonomia ◀︎ _dis_ or _tō_ _nō_ _mēē_, _n._ dysfunction of autonomic nervous system. Grass sickness is a dysautonomia of the gastrointestinal tract; disease causes a marked depressive effect on gastrointestinal tract.
See Grass sickness.

Dyschondroplasia ◀︎ _dis_ _kon_ _drō_ _plā_ _zē_ _ē_, _n._ (osteochondrosis) abnormal cartilage development.
See Osteochondrosis.

Dyscrasia ◀︎ _dis_ _crā_ _zē_ _ē_, _n._ abnormal state, roughly synonymous with disease; term was formerly used to indicate an abnormal mixture of the four humours of Galenic medicine.
> **Blood d.** ◀︎ _blud_ / _dis_ _crā_ _zē_ _ē_, _n._ a pathological condition of blood, usually of the cellular elements.

Dysfunction ◀︎ _dis_ _fungk_ _shēn_, _n._ disturbance, impairment or abnormal function of an organ.

Dysgerminoma ◀︎ _dis_ _jer_ _mi_ _nō_ _mē_, _n._ rare, malignant tumour of ovary. Tends to metastasize rapidly, poor prognosis. Has been reported in a yearling Arabian filly with a history of weight loss, profound anaemia, and peritoneal effusion. At necropsy, a neoplastic mass was found to have replaced the left ovary. Diagnosis was made by histology.
See Ovary.

Dysmaturity ◀︎ _dis_ _mē_ _tŭ_ _ri_ _tē_, _n._ disordered development; signs of prematurity or immaturity in foal born after more than 320 days of gestation. Normal gestation period is 320–360 days. Signs of dysmaturity include small size, lax joints, incoordination, poor suckle reflex, etc.
See Premature.

Dysphagia ◀︎ _dis_ _fā_ _jē_ _ē_, _n._ difficulty in swallowing; many causes, including grass sickness, foreign body in throat or oesophagus, trauma, neoplasia, or pain. Problems resulting in dysphagia can occur anywhere in the upper alimentary tract; in oral cavity (e.g. tooth problems, foreign body, tongue injuries), pharynx

(e.g. paralysis caused by nerve damage, cysts, abscesses) or oesophagus (e.g. grass sickness, obstruction, strictures, tumours).
See Grass sickness, Oesophagus, Pharynx, Strangles, Tooth, Tongue.

Dysplasia ◀︎ _dis_ _plā_ _zē_ _ē_, _n._ abnormality of development, or abnormal size or shape of adult cells.

Dyspnoea ◀︎ _dis_ _nē_ _ē_, _n._ difficulty breathing, distressed breathing. Various causes, including many primary respiratory diseases.
See Breathing.

Dysrhythmia ◀︎ _dis_ _rith_ _mē_ _ē_, _n._ abnormality of rhythm, especially that of heart. Common in horse, may be physiological (occurs in normal hearts, e.g. second degree atrioventricular block, sinus arrhythmia) or pathological (indicates disease of heart muscle, e.g. atrial fibrillation, ventricular tachycardia, ventricular fibrillation). Many causes, including toxins, viral infection, lack of oxygen, electrolyte disturbances, anaesthetics.
See Arrhythmia, Atrial, Atrioventricular, Ventricular.

Dystocia ◀︎ _dis_ _tō_ _kē_ _ē_, _n._ abnormality or difficulty in giving birth. Not common in horse (about 4% of births).
• Foetal dystocia: related to problems with foetus, e.g. head turned back, backward presentation, large size, foetal abnormality, etc.
• Maternal dystocia: related to problems with mare, e.g. lack of uterine contractions, vaginal stricture, etc.
See Parturition.

Dystrophic ◀︎ _dis_ _tro_ _fik_, _adj._ characterized by dystrophy.

Dystrophy ◀︎ _dis_ _trē_ _fē_, _n._ any disorder arising from defective or faulty nutrition; also, any condition with muscle-related atrophy.
> **Muscular d.** ◀︎ _mus_ _cū_ _lē_ / _dis_ _trē_ _fē_, _n._ wasting of muscles, may be related to lack of vitamin E or selenium (white muscle disease

of foals); congenital and acquired myogenic muscular dystrophies are rarely reported in horses.

See Selenium, Vitamin E, White muscle disease.

Dysuria ◀ᴈ _dis_ ŭ _rē_ ē, _n._ difficulty in passing urine. May especially be caused by bladder stones (urinary calculi, urolithiasis) or urethritis.

See Urethritis, Urolithiasis.

E

Ear ◀€ *ér*, *n*. organ of hearing and equilibrium.

E. concha see Concha

E. drum see Tympanic

E. fistula see Fistula

External e. ◀€ *eks ter nĕl* / *ér*, *n*. (auricle, pinna) funnel-shaped organ on top of head, composed primarily of skin and cartilage. Gathers sound waves and transmits them through external ear canal to ear drum (in middle ear). Horse can move external e. to pick up sounds from specific direction, express anger, aggression, etc. Diseases include ear mites, foreign bodies, neoplasia (sarcoids, squamous cell carcinoma, adenoma, melanoma), otitis externa (inflammation usually associated with infection).

Middle e. ◀€ *mi dĕl* / *ér*, *n*. composed of ear drum (tympanic membrane) and three small bones (auditory ossicles: malleus, incus, stapes) in air cavity. Sound waves cause ear drum to vibrate, movement passes along chain of auditory ossicles to inner ear. Eustachian tube (auditory tube) connects middle ear to throat – air is admitted through tube to keep pressure equal either side of ear drum. Auditory tube diverticulum (guttural pouch) is sac-like enlargement of this tube. Diseases include otitis media (inflammation usually associated with infection), diseases of auditory tube diverticulum (guttural pouch).

See Guttural pouch, Temporohyoid osteoarthropathy.

Inner e. ◀€ *i ner* / *ér*, *n*. composed of two parts:

- Membranous saccule which contains cochlea; this has sensitive cells which transmit sound to brain via auditory nerve.
- Fluid-containing semicircular canals which are concerned with balance.

Diseases of inner ear include otitis interna (inflammation usually associated with infection – results in disturbance of balance).
See Balance, Otitis.

Eastern equine encephalitis ◀€ *ēs tĕn* / *ek wīn*/ *en ke fa lī tis*, *n*. alphavirus infection of brain and other nervous tissue. Occurs in western hemisphere; birds, rodents and reptiles act as reservoirs; often spread by mosquitoes. In most cases, peak incidence occurs during the height of the mosquito season. Causes mild to severe fever, depression, anorexia, stiffness; nervous system signs include incoordination, head pressing, blindness, circling, excitability, and aggression. Paralysis of the pharynx, larynx and tongue is common. Recumbency for 1–7 days precedes death. Zoonotic disease: can also cause encephalitis in humans. Clinical diagnosis based on clinical findings and typical epidemiology (no vaccination, typical seasonal occurrence). Diagnosis confirmed by serology and necropsy evaluation. There is no known effective treatment; supportive care may rarely allow animal to eventually clear virus, with gradual improvement over weeks to months; most horses that survive have residual neurological deficits. In USA, vaccination has made disease less common than previously, but sporadic outbreaks occur yearly. Environmental management to reduce insect burden (eliminate standing water, insecticides, screened stalls) can assist in prevention.
See Venezuelan equine encephalitis, Western equine encephalitis.

Eating behaviour see Behaviour

Ecchymosis ◀€ *e ki mō sis*, *n*. blue or purple spot in skin or mucous membrane caused by bleeding. May be seen on mucous membranes in a variety of conditions, including allergic reaction and infection. Larger than a petechial haemorrhage. See Petechiae.

ECG see Electrocardiography

Echinococcus granulosus equinus ◀ᴇ *e kī nō ko kēs / gra nū lō sēs / e kwī nēs, n.* small tapeworm of dog; causes hydatid disease. Horses and other equids are intermediate host. Larvae may develop in horse's liver and lungs and cause cysts, which are not associated with disease. When clinical signs do occur, they are often related to pressure from the growing cysts on adjacent organs. Occasionally cysts may occur in or near eye, and exophthalmos, blindness and head-shaking have been reported when cysts occur behind the eye. Endemic disease in western Europe, the Middle East and Africa. Correlated with the feeding of raw or improperly cooked viscera and trimmings from slaughtered horses to dogs; dogs are definitive host. See Hydatid cyst, Tapeworm.

Echocardiography ◀ᴇ *e kō kar dē o grē fē, n.* a method of recording the position and motion of the structures of the heart using ultrasound waves directed through the chest wall. In horses, is technique of choice for investigation of heart murmurs. Three types of echocardiography used (often in combination):
- Two-dimensional (gives 'slice' view through heart, can see specific lesions, e.g. thickening of valve).
- M mode (gives graph showing changes in structures of heart against time).
- Doppler (shows speed and direction of blood flow).
See Heart, Ultrasound.

Eclampsia ◀ᴇ *i klamp sē ē, n.* (lactation tetany) rarely seen in horses, used to be more frequent when draught horses were in common use. Seen in mares producing large quantities of milk in early postpartum period or after weaning; associated with low serum levels of calcium, and occasionally magnesium. Signs include stiff gait, rapid breathing, muscle tremors and diaphragmatic flutter. Without treat-

ment, tetanic convulsions occur, resulting in death in 24–48 hours. Treatment is with calcium-containing solutions. See Calcium.

E. coli see *Escherichia*

Ecraseur ◀ᴇ *ā kra zer, n.* surgical instrument containing a chain or cord that is looped around a part and tightened in order to remove the part contained in the loop; e.g. may be used in removal of ovary from mare, whereby chain loop is placed over ovary and crushes pedicle and associated blood vessels.

Ectoderm ◀ᴇ *ek tō derm, n.* outermost layer of developing embryo. Skin and associated structures (hair, hooves, glands), nervous system, external sensory organs develop from it. See Embryo.

Ectoparasite ◀ᴇ *ek tō pa rē sīt, n.* parasite which lives on outside of the body of the host, e.g. louse, mite (c.f. endoparasite). See Parasite.

Ectopic ◀ᴇ *ek to pik, adj.* out of usual position, especially if congenital.
E. ureter(s) ◀ᴇ *ek to pik / ŭr et ē, n.* rare problem where ureter is not connected normally to the kidney. Clinical signs are of urinary incontinence. Diagnosis can be confirmed by ureterography, or endoscopic visualization of the ectopic ureteral openings. Ultrasound of the kidneys helps evaluate associated kidney pathology. Unilateral nephrectomy may be necessary, assuming normal function of the other kidney. Successful surgery to reunite the ureter with the bladder has been described (ureterovesicular anastomosis).

Ectropion ◀ᴇ *ek trō pē ēn, n.* eyelid turned outwards, away from eyeball. Rare in horses: may occur in old age or as result of scarring.

Eczema ◀ᴇ *ek zē mē, n.* general term for skin inflammation, involving redness, itchiness, scaling; lesions become scaly, crusted and hardened.
Summer e. see *Culicoides* spp., Dermatitis

Edema see Oedema

EDTA ◀€ *abbr.* ethylenediamine tetra-acetic acid. Anticoagulant contained in some tubes used for collection of blood samples where cellular components of blood are to be examined. Used in treatment of lead poisoning (rare); chemical chelates heavy metals.
See Anticoagulant, Lead.

Efferent ◀€ *e fē rēnt, adj.* leading away from central area. Efferent nerve conducts impulses away from central nervous system to peripheral nerves. Opposite: afferent.
See Nerve.

Effusion ◀€ *i fū zhēn, n.* the escape of fluid into a part, cavity, or tissue, e.g. thoracic effusion (in chest) or peritoneal effusion (in abdomen). Typically characterized according to the protein content, as an exudate or a transudate. May occur for several reasons:
• Low plasma oncotic pressure, allows fluid to be lost from capillaries.
• Increased pressure of fluid within vessels, pushes fluid out.
• Increased permeability of blood vessels, allows fluid to leak out, as with inflammation.
• Blockage of lymphatic vessels which normally drain fluid from cavity.
Determine type and cause of effusion by examining fluid sample and blood and serum parameters.

Egg ◀€ *eg, n.* in mammalian physiology, ovum, female reproductive cell at any stage prior to fertilization; contains genetic material and combines with sperm to form embryo; also, some eggs are complete reproductive bodies, e.g. parasite eggs contain fertilized ovum which can develop into parasite larva.
See Ovum.

Egg bar shoe ◀€ *eg / bar / shŭ, n.* a horse-shoe with metal bar extending behind the heels, giving an oval ('egg') shape appearance to the shoe. Prescribed by some veterinarians and farriers for the treatment of such conditions as heel lameness,

deep digital flexor tendinitis, or navicular syndrome.
See Bar, Deep: (D. digital flexor tendon), Navicular syndrome.

Ehrlichia equi see Anaplasmosis.

Ejaculate/ejaculation ◀€ *i ja kū lāt / i ja kū lā shēn, v./n.* expel suddenly, especially semen from penis.
See Behaviour (mating), Penis, Semen.
  Chemical e. ◀€ *kem ik ēl / i ja kū lā shēn, n.* the induction of ejaculation using pharmaceuticals. Various protocols; most include drugs such as imipramine, xylazine or detomodine. Used e.g. when stallions are unable to mount, or have sustained injury to penis.

Ejection fraction ◀€ *ē jek shēn / frak shēn, n.* pertaining to the physiology of the cardiovascular system, the fraction of blood that is pumped out of the ventricle with each heart beat.

Elastic ◀€ *i la stik, adj.* able to return to original form after being stretched or distorted.

Elastin ◀€ *i la stin, n.* an essential component of connective tissue, especially those tissues that are required to maintain their shape after stretching. Found especially in arteries, but also in lung, ligament, skin, the bladder, and certain types of cartilage.

Elastrator ◀€ *i las trā tē, n.* instrument that stretches strong elastic rubber ring so it can be placed over tissue and cut off blood supply. Used in castration of lambs and calves; has also been used for closure of umbilical hernia in foals.
See Hernia.

Elbow ◀€ *el bō, n.* hinge joint in forelimb between humerus and radius/ulna.
  Capped e. see Capped.
  Dropped e. ◀€ *dropt / el bō, n.* elbow held in lower than normal position; horse is normally unable to extend forelimb, e.g. as seen with fracture, radial nerve paralysis.
  See Paralysis, Radial.

E. cyst ◀≀ *el bō / sist, n.* rare manifestation of osteochondrosis in elbow joint. See Osteochondrosis.

E. fracture ◀≀ *el bō / frak tŭr, n.* fracture of olecranon process of ulna; variable prognosis, depending on involvement of joint surfaces. Typically caused by trauma, e.g. kick or fall. Horse is lame, with dropped elbow, and pain and swelling around elbow. Cannot keep joint extended when bearing weight. Surgical repair of fracture may be necessary – however, conservative management results in successful outcomes in selected cases. See Olecranon.

E. hitting ◀≀ *el bō / hit ing, n.* when the horse hits the elbow with the horseshoe on the foot of the same limb; rare, unless horse wears weighted shoe.

E. luxation ◀≀ *el bō / luks ā shĕn, n.* dislocation of elbow; usually accompanied by damage to collateral ligaments and fracture of radius, ulna or olecranon.

Electrocardiography ◀≀ *i lek trō kar dē o grē fē, n.* recording of records of the variations in electrical potential caused by the electrical activity of heart muscle as it beats. Impulses are recorded by electrodes attached to the skin, which transmit information to electrocardiograph. Trace of impulses is produced on a moving sheet of paper; electrocardiogram. Recording of arrhythmias which occur at exercise or intermittently may be achieved by radiotelemetric e. (transmits ECG to remote receiver) or ambulatory e. (records ECG over 24 hours on magnetic tape which can be analysed later). See Arrhythmia.

Electrocautery ◀≀ *i lek trō kor tē rē, n.* cautery (burning or searing of tissue) with a metal wire which becomes extremely hot when electric current is applied to it. Typical use to control bleeding during surgery. See Cauterization.

Electrocution ◀≀ *i lek trō kū shĕn, n.* death caused by electric current passing through body, e.g. lightning strike, accidental contact with live electric wires, etc.

Electrode ◀≀ *i lek trōd, n.* a medium used between an electric conductor and the object to which the current is being applied; in electrodiagnosis, a needle, clip or plate used to stimulate or record electrical activity of tissue, e.g. electrode used in electrocardiography conducts electrical impulse from body to electrocardiogram (also known as a lead). See Electrocardiography.

Electroencephalograph ◀≀ *i lek trō en ke fē lō grarf, n.* instrument used to record electrical impulses in brain by means of electrodes attached to skin over head; origin of brain electrical impulses is not known. Has limited application to equine medicine; little work has been done in the horse.

Electrolyte ◀≀ *i lek trō līt, n.* substance which, when dissolved in water, separates into ions and so can conduct electricity. Most important ions in body fluids are sodium (Na^+), potassium (K^+), calcium (Ca^{2+}), magnesium (Mg^{2+}), chloride (Cl^-), bicarbonate (HCO_3^-), phosphate (PO_4^{3-}). Various electrolyte solutions are used in treatment of colic, shock, dehydration, etc. Commonly given as dietary supplements to horses that exercise heavily, or live in hot climates; the necessity for electrolyte supplementation in most horses is questionable.

Electromagnetic ◀≀ *i lek trō mag net ik, n.* involving both electricity and magnetism; electromagnetic devices are made by passing an electric current through a wire coil.

E. therapy ◀≀ *i lek trō mag net ik / the rĕp ē, n.* electromagnetic field therapy is typically applied to horses with boots or blankets. Some of the variables of the magnetic field generated, such as the amplitude and frequency of the signal, can be controlled using this form of magnetic therapy. Explanations that magnetic fields 'increase circulation', reduce inflammation', or 'speed recovery from injuries' are simplistic and are not supported by the weight of experimental evidence. Although the therapies appear to be harmless, that does not also mean that they are useful.

Electromyography ◄€ *i lek̲ trō mī o̲ grē fē, n.* recording of extracellular electrical activity in skeletal muscle at rest, during contractions, or during stimulation by means of a variety of surface electrodes, usually a needle inserted into muscle, e.g. to determine status of nerve supply to muscle.

Electrophoresis ◄€ *i lek̲ trō fē rē̲ sis, n.* movement of charged solutes within fluid or gel when electric current passed through it. Enables separation of particles for analysis.

ELISA *abbr.* (enzyme-linked immunosorbent assay) immunological test used to determine presence of an antibody or antigen. In ELISA testing, an unknown amount of an antigen is fixed to a surface, such as a plate, and then an antibody to that antigen is washed over the surface. That antibody, which is linked to an enzyme, binds the antigen. In the final step of the test, a substance is added that the enzyme converts to something that can be detected, such as in fluorescent antibody testing, where the antigen–antibody complex fluoresces, and the amount of antigen can thereby be measured. Used in diagnosis of some equine viral diseases. Specific types of ELISA tests include direct, indirect, and capture ELISA.

Emasculate ◄€ *i mas̲ kū lāt, v.* to castrate, remove the testicles from a male animal.
See Castrate.

Emasculator ◄€ *i mas̲ kū lā tē, n.* instrument used for horse castration (open technique) which crushes blood vessels to limit bleeding at same time as cutting spermatic cord. Various models; used according to preference of veterinary surgeon.
See Castration.

Embolism ◄€ *em̲ bē lizm, n.* sudden obstruction of artery by blood clot, air bubble, fatty material. In horse, may occasionally be seen in branch of anterior mesenteric artery which supplies small intestines, secondary to heavy parasitic damage by *Strongylus* worms.
See Artery, *Strongylus* spp.

Embolus ◄€ *em̲ bē lēs, n.* mass, brought by the blood stream through the blood vessels, which lodges in a vessel that is too small to allow passage, which obstructs the circulation; most commonly blood clot or fatty material.
See Artery, Embolism.

Embryo ◄€ *em̲ brē ō, n.* in animals, the derivative of the zygote that ultimately develops into a new organism, during the period of most rapid development, before it develops major structures (at approx 40 days it becomes foetus).
See Foetus, Placenta, Zygote.

    E. transfer ◄€ *em̲ brē ō / tranz̲ fer, n.* collection of embryo from uterus of mare (donor) and implantation in other mare (recipient). Involves medical synchronization of oestrous cycles of donor and recipient, or use of ovariectomized recipient mare whose pregnancy is then managed with hormones. Donor mare mated at oestrus, and uterus flushed 7–8 days after ovulation. Embryo identified microscopically and placed in uterus of recipient by pipette, or surgically. May be used in transfer of embryo from high-performing mare to recipient so that donor mare can remain in training, or to transfer embryo from mare unable to carry foal for full pregnancy. More than one embryo may be collected from valuable mare in one breeding season in breeds whose societies allow the procedure.

Embryotomy see Foetotomy

Emetic ◄€ *i me̲ tik, adj.* describes drug or substance that causes vomiting. Not used in horses, as horses cannot vomit.

Emollient ◄€ *i mō̲ lē ēnt, adj.* describes substance which soothes and softens skin.

Emphysema ◄€ *em fi se̲ mē, n.* pathological accumulation of air in tissues.
    Pulmonary e. ◄€ *pul̲ mē nē rē / em fi se̲ mē, n.* In humans with chronic respiratory disease, walls of air sacs in lungs may break down, causing increased size of the alveoli. Was formerly thought to occur in chronic obstructive pulmonary disease; in fact, is rare (most common problem is bronchiolitis).

See Bronchiolitis, Recurrent airway obstruction.

Subcutaneous e. ◀ᴇ *sub kū tā nē ēs / em fi sē mē, n.* air in subcutaneous tissues, e.g. from damaged airway (e.g. trachea, nasal sinus wall), or skin wound through which air is drawn in by movement of muscles, or gas-producing bacteria in tissues (e.g. *Clostridia*).
See *Clostridium.*

Empyema ◀ᴇ *em pī ē mē, n.* accumulation of pus (abscess); commonly occurs in body cavities, e.g. pleural cavity or auditory tube diverticulum (guttural pouch). Generally caused by bacterial infection.
See Guttural pouch.

Emulsion ◀ᴇ *i mul shēn, n.* fine droplets of one liquid dispersed through other liquid with which it will not mix (e.g. oil and water, when shaken).

Enamel (dental) ◀ᴇ *i na mēl (den tēl), n.* white, hard calcified substance which covers dentine of tooth and protects it. Uneven wear of teeth can result in sharp e. points; these points may need to be removed by rasping (tooth floating), particularly if secondary oral trauma is seen.
See Tooth.

Enarthrodial joint ◀ᴇ *e nar thrō dē ēl / joint, n.* ball-and-socket type joint; allows movement in any direction, e.g. hip. Full movement of these joints in horse may be limited by muscle mass.

Encephalitis ◀ᴇ *en ke fē lī tis, n.* inflammation of brain, may be caused by bacteria (e.g. *Streptococcus equi*, strangles), or viruses (e.g. Eastern equine encephalitis, Western equine encephalitis, Venezuelan equine encephalitis), or parasites (not common, may be caused by *Strongylus vulgaris, Hypoderma*). Signs depend on area of brain affected, include signs of brain dysfunction, e.g. incoordination, head-pressing, circling, paralysis, seizures.
See Eastern equine encephalitis, *Hypoderma* spp., Strangles, *Strongylus* spp., Venezuelan equine encephalitis, Western equine encephalitis.

Encephalo- ◀ᴇ *en ke fē lō-, prefix.* relating to the brain.

Encephalomyelitis ◀ᴇ *en kē fa lō mī ē lī tis, n.* inflammation of both brain and spinal cord. Clinically indistinguishable from encephalitis; terms tend to be used interchangeably.
See Encephalitis.

Encephalopathy ◀ᴇ *en ke fē lō pē thē, n.* a disease of the brain, especially one involving changes in brain structure.
Hepatic e. see Hepatic

End stage ◀ᴇ *end / stāj, n.* the last phase in the course of a progressive disease, e.g. end-stage liver disease, end-stage kidney disease, etc. 'End stage' is commonly used instead of 'terminal', most likely because it seems less depressing.

Endarteritis ◀ᴇ *end ar tē rī tis, n.* inflammation of inner surface of wall (tunica intima) of artery. In horse, may be caused by migrating larvae of *Strongylus* worms.
See Artery, *Strongylus* spp.

Endemic ◀ᴇ *en de mik, adj.* describes disease which is prevalent in a population of animals at all times; may clinically affect only a small proportion of that population at any particular time.

End(o)- ◀ᴇ *en dō, prefix* denoting an inward situation; within.

Endocarditis ◀ᴇ *en dō kar dī tis, n.* inflammation of inner lining membrane of heart (endocardium). Occurs most commonly around heart valves, and causes proliferative growths around valves, particularly the aortic or mitral valves, which can affect valve function. May occur as a primary disorder, or as a complication of another disease, such as bacterial infection (e.g. *Streptococcus* spp.) or immune complex disease. Clinical signs vary, but usually include history of intermittent fever, weight loss, depression, anorexia, and lethargy. Lab results often non-specific; occasional positive bacterial blood cultures may be obtained, especially with serial samples. Valvular lesions may be sometimes seen

ultrasonographically. Treatment is with high levels of antibiotics. Uncommon.
See Heart, *Streptococcus*.

Endocardium ◀ː *en do kar dē ēm, n.* lining membrane of heart and valves.

Endochondral ossification ◀ː *en do kon drŭl / os if ik ā shēn, n.* one of two types of bone formation; the process responsible for the majority of bone growth in vertebrates (including horses), particularly in the long bones. Occurs mainly by replacement of hyaline cartilage; defects result in bone and cartilage disease, e.g. osteochondrosis.
See Osteochondrosis.

Endocrine ◀ː *en dō krin, adj.* secreting internally; opposite is exocrine. Applied to organs and structures (e.g. glands) that release their products directly into blood or lymph, and also to substances (hormones) that specifically affect other organs.
See Adrenal gland, Exocrine, Gland, Hormone, Pituitary, Thyroid.
    E. disorder ◀ː *en dō krin / dis or dē, n.* abnormality of some part of the endocrine system.
    E. system ◀ː *en dō krin / sis tēm, n.* the system of glands and other structures that produce hormones which influence metabolism and other body processes, e.g. the pituitary gland, thyroid gland, and adrenal glands.

Endocrinology ◀ː *en dō kri no lē jē, n.* study of hormones, the endocrine system, and their function in the body.

Endoderm ◀ː *en dō derm, n.* innermost layer of developing embryo. Develops into epithelium of digestive tract, respiratory tract, bladder, urethra and pharynx.
See Embryo.

Endogenous ◀ː *en do ji nēs, adj.* growing from within; describes something developing from or produced within an animal, or arising from causes within the animal (c.f. exogenous).

Endometrial ◀ː *en dō mēt rē ēl, adj.* pertaining to the endometrium, the inner mucous membrane lining of uterus.
See Endometrium, Uterus.
    E. biopsy ◀ː *en dō mēt rē ēl / bī op sē, n.* biopsy of the uterine endometrium. Tissue samples obtained are submitted for histological evaluation of normal tissue architecture; observed uterine pathology may help predict likelihood that mare will carry a foal to term.
    E. cup ◀ː *en dō mēt rē ēl / kup, n.* shortly after pregnancy is established in equids, high concentrations of the hormone equine chorionic gonadotropin (eCG) appear in the mare's serum (also sometimes called pregnant mare's serum gonadotropin, or PMSG). This is produced by a structure derived from the foetus, and associated with the placenta, called an endometrial cup. E. cups form several weeks into gestation, and are immunologically destroyed 2 to 3 months later.

Endometritis ◀ː *en dō mi trī tis, n.* inflammation of lining of uterus (endometrium). Common cause of poor fertility in mares. Normally, mares can rid themselves of uterine contamination but some mares are unable to clear their uterus, and may develop chronic inflammation or infection. Associated with numerous causative organisms, including *Escherichia coli*, *Klebsiella*, *Pseudomonas*, *Streptococcus*, yeasts and fungi. Pathogenic organisms may be introduced into uterus during mating, at foaling, during veterinary examination or because of pneumovagina. May cause uterine discharge and infertility. Typically diagnosed by a combination of signs, including presence of fluid in uterus on ultrasound, bacterial culture, cytology, (analysis of smear from endometrial fluid), or biopsy sample.
See Infertility, Pneumovagina, Uterus.

Endometrium ◀ː *en dō mē trē ēm, n.* inner mucous membrane lining of uterus.
See Uterus.

Endophthalmitis ◀ː *end of thal mī tis, n.* severe inflammation of eye and adjacent structures. May be caused by trauma or injury to eye; painful, eye is typically cloudy with marked redness of conjunctiva.
See Eye.

Endophyte ◀ *en dō fīt, n.* a parasitic plant organism, usually a fungus. Broodmares consuming endophyte-infected tall fescue grass during late gestation may experience prolonged gestation (as long as 13 to 14 months), dystocia or foaling difficulty, thickened placenta ('red bag' foal) or agalactia (a decrease or absence of milk production), and reduced breeding efficiency following parturition.

Endorphin ◀ *en dor fin, n.* opioid compounds, polypeptides produced by the pituitary gland and the hypothalamus. They act in the same manner as opiate drugs in that they produce analgesia and a sense of well-being. Endorphin release typically accompanies stressful situations, e.g. transport; stereotypical behaviours, e.g. crib-biting, are also accompanied by endorphin release.
See Opiate, Opioid.

Endoscope ◀ *en dō skōp, n.* instrument used for looking within hollow organs or cavities of body. Endoscopes may be specialized for examining specific areas, e.g. bronchoscope, arthroscope, gastroscope. All have viewing tube with lens and light source. Tube may be flexible or rigid. May also have additional accessories, e.g. for taking biopsy samples, suction, cautery, etc.

Endoscopy ◀ *en do skē pē, n.* examination of inside of body cavities or hollow organs by use of endoscope. Used in diagnosis of disease, especially in examination of airway in horse, but also bladder (cystoscopy) and uterus (hysteroscopy).

Endothelial degeneration ◀ *en dō thē lē ēl / di jen ē rā shēn, n.* eye disease of horses; commonly appears as a grey–blue band in the cornea which can progress to total corneal opacity. Typically non-painful early in the course of disease, but may be painful with progression. Endothelial damage results in inability of cornea to control its water content; blue colour results from corneal swelling. Causes not well understood, but include aging, genetic tendency, viral infections, or immune-mediated conditions. Treatment with hypertonic saline ointments may help control swelling in initial stages. Prognosis is guarded; tends to be progressive.
See Endothelium.

Endothelium ◀ *en dō thē lē ēm, n.* layer of cells lining blood vessels, body cavities, heart, and lymphatic vessels. Can also be used to describe internal lining of other organs, such as eye. Derived from mesoderm layer of embryo.

Endotoxaemia ◀ *en dō tok sē mē ē, n.* presence of endotoxins in blood; may result in shock.
See Endotoxin.

Endotoxic shock ◀ *en dō tok sik / shok, n.* septic shock resulting from release of endotoxins by Gram-negative bacteria into blood. Clinical signs include dilation of peripheral blood vessels and drop in blood pressure. Mucous membranes are congested, heart rate is increased, temperature drops and muscles are weak. Prognosis guarded, even with aggressive treatment. Laminitis is a common sequel.
See Endotoxin, Gram stain, Laminitis, Shock.

Endotoxin ◀ *en dō tok sin, n.* stable toxin associated with the outer membranes of certain Gram-negative bacteria; released only when bacteria disintegrate. Mostly produced by bacteria found in intestines (enteric bacilli, Gram-negative cocci, *Pasteurella, Brucella*). If released in sufficient quantities cause haemorrhagic shock and severe diarrhoea, blood vessel dilation and increase in permeability.

Endotracheal ◀ *en dō tra kē ūl, adj.* within the trachea.
See Anaesthesia.
> **E. tube** ◀ *en dō tra kē ūl / tūb, n.* a rubber or plastic tube that is typically placed through the mouth or nostrils (e.g. in foals, or miniature horses), in order to maintain patency of the air passages and to make sure that air can reach the lungs. Allows administration of gaseous anaesthetics, oxygen, etc. to animal. Usually has a cuff on outside of tube which can be inflated once tube has been

placed in trachea; this fills space between outside of tube and tracheal wall and prevents movement of air around outside of tube.

Enema ◄⁞ *e ni mē, n.* introduction of fluid into rectum, typically to help passage of faeces. Commonly used in foals for treatment of meconium retention, using warm saline solution or soapy water introduced through soft, blunt rubber tube. Routinely administered in some foaling barns, with no apparent problems.
See Meconium.

Energy ◄⁞ *e nē jē, n.* the capacity to operate, to work, to produce motion, or to effect physical change. Horse derives energy from food; important dietary energy-providing constituents are carbohydrate and fat, and to a lesser degree, protein. These constituents are metabolized within cells to produce energy. Food energy measured in calories; in all other areas, typically measured in joules.
See Carbohydrates, Fat, Metabolism, Protein.

Enilconazole ◄⁞ *e nil co nē zōl, n.* antifungal drug, used topically to treat fungal infections of nasal sinuses and dermatomycosis (ringworm) in the UK; not currently available in the United States.
See Dermatophytosis, Rhinitis.

Enophthalmos ◄⁞ *en of thal mos, n.* backward displacement (recession) of eyeball into orbit. Several possible causes including dehydration, extreme weight loss (loss of fat behind eyeball), Horner's syndrome (accompanied by drooping of eyelid), injury to bones of orbit, pain; may be a feature of tetanus where the recession of the eyeball causes the 3rd eyelid to protrude.
See Dehydration, Eye, Horner's syndrome, Orbit, Tetanus.

Enostosis ◄⁞ *ē nō stō sis, n.* a bony growth developed within a bone cavity, on the inner surface of the bone cortex. In horses, occasionally seen in the tibia of horses from 3–10 years of age. Causes lameness; diagnosis by scintigraphy or radiography.

Treatment is rest; lameness typically resolves in 2–6 months.

Enrofloxacin ◄⁞ *en rē floks ē sin, n.* a broad-spectrum antibiotic used to treat infections caused by susceptible bacteria. Enrofloxacin belongs to a general class of antibiotics known as fluoroquinolones; it is thought to inhibit the synthesis of DNA within the bacteria, resulting in bacterial death.

Enter/Entero- ◄⁞ *en tē, en ter rō, prefix.* pertaining to intestines.

Enteral ◄⁞ *en tē rūl, adj.* pertaining to the small intestine.
See Enteric.
   E. feeding ◄⁞ *en tē rūl / fē ding, n.* the state of being fed by a feeding tube; sometimes necessary for nutritional support in the treatment of debilitated animals. Various feeding solutions and protocols described.

Enteric ◄⁞ *en te rik, adj.* occurring in or pertaining to small intestines.
   E. bacteria ◄⁞ *en tē rik / bak tēr ia, n.* bacteria typically living in the small intestines, e.g., *Escherichia coli, Enterobacter.*
   E. neoplasms ◄⁞ *en tē rik / nē ō plazmz, n.* cancers of the small intestines; most common is lymphosarcoma. Causes weight loss, malabsorption and anaemia. Uncommon.
   E. nervous system ◄⁞ *en te rik / nerv ēs / sis tēm, n.* the network of neurons in the body that allow for control of motility of the gastrointestinal tract.

Enteritis ◄⁞ *en tē rī tis, n.* inflammation of intestines (especially small intestine). Various causes, including dietary, infectious and inflammatory. Signs include fever, diarrhoea, and inappetence. Treatment dictated by underlying cause.
See Diarrhoea.

Enterobacteriaceae ◄⁞ *en tē rō bak té rē ē sē ē, n.* family of Gram-negative, facultatively anaerobic (i.e. the bacteria can live with or without oxygen), rod-shaped bacteria, includes *Escherichia, Enterobacter, Klebsiella, Proteus, Salmonella, Yersinia.* Found in soil, water, plants, and animals.

Enterohepatic circulation ◀ᴇ *en tē rō hi pa tik / sir kū lā shēn, n.* the circulation of bile from the liver, where it is produced, to the small intestine, where it aids in digestion of fats and other substances. Ninety-five per cent of the bile is reabsorbed and sent back to the liver.

Enterolith ◀ᴇ *en tē rō lith, n.* a hard concretion produced by the concretion of mineral salts; 'stone'. Develops within intestine, formed from layers of salts (especially ammonium magnesium phosphate). Occur in adult horses and can cause obstruction of large intestine (colon), resulting in colic. When sufficiently large to cause obstruction, require surgical removal. Arabian horses are over-represented; an association has been made between an alkaline pH in the intestine and enterolith formation, particularly in horses with a high percentage of alfalfa hay in diet, or restricted access to pasture grass. Prognosis for recovery after surgery generally good. See Colic.

Enteropathy ◀ᴇ *en tēr o pē thē, n.* any disease or pathology of the intestinal tract.

Proliferative e. ◀ᴇ *prō lif ēr at iv / en tēr o pē thē, n.* disease of intestinal tract characterized by proliferative lesions, especially of small intestines. Seen especially in foals, secondary to infection with *Lawsonia intracellularis*.
See *Lawsonia intracellularis*.

Protein-losing e. ◀ᴇ *prō tēn - lū sing / en tēr o pē thē, n.* any condition of the gastrointestinal tract that results in a net loss of protein from the body, through damaged intestinal wall, e.g. in salmonellosis, toxicity of non-steroidal anti-inflammatory drugs. Low protein results in lowering of osmotic pressure of blood, resulting in fluid leaving blood stream and collecting as oedema (swelling), typically in legs and under abdomen. Horses typically lose weight rapidly.
See Blood, Intestine, Osmosis, Salmonellosis.

Enterotomy ◀ᴇ *en tē ro tē mē, n.* incision into the intestines. May be performed in colic surgery, e.g. in removal of obstruction, or for evacuation of bowel.
See Colic.

Enterotoxaemia ◀ᴇ *en tē rō tok sē mē ē, n.* a disease attributed to absorption of a bacterial toxin from the intestine, e.g. *Clostridium perfringens* or *Escherichia coli*. Rarely occurs in foal, causes acute diarrhoea (sometimes with blood) or sudden death.
See *Clostridium*, Diarrhoea, *Escherichia*.

Enthesophyte ◀ᴇ *en the zō fit, n.* bone formation at attachment of tendon, joint capsule, or ligament to bone; 'spur'. Associated with instability, but may also occur as a normal aging change; distinct from osteophyte, which is associated with the joint surface or margin. Rarely of clinical significance.
See Arthritis, Carpus, Osteophyte.

Entrapment ◀ᴇ *en trap mēnt, n.* the state of being trapped, or as if caught in a trap.

Epiglottic e. ◀ᴇ *ep i glo tik / en trap mēnt, n.* the epiglottis is trapped by the arytenoepiglottic fold; causes failure of normal respiratory function. Affected horses show exercise intolerance, noisy breathing, and coughing; the entrapped epiglottis has a characteristic appearance on endoscopy. Condition usually treated surgically.
See Epiglottis.

Intestinal e. ◀ᴇ *in tes tin ūl / en trap mēnt, n.* intestine that becomes caught up in abdominal adhesions or peritoneal ligaments, e.g. the nephrosplenic ligament. Obstruction of intestinal flow, with or without compromise of the intestinal blood supply to the incarcerated loop, follows. Causes colic. Occasional cases may be managed medically; many cases require abdominal (colic) surgery.
See Colic, Nephrosplenic.

Entropion ◀ᴇ *en trō pē ēn, n.* inversion, turning in of eyelid; may allow lashes to rub on eyeball. May occur in one or both eyes, as congenital defect or acquired because of injury to eyelid. Congenital problem in foals usually affects lower lid and can result in discomfort, ocular discharge and damage to cornea. Most cases of congenital entropion can be managed conservatively, or by infiltration of eyelid; acquired cases may require surgical correction.
See Eye.

Enuresis see Incontinent

Environment ◀€ *en vīr ēn mēnt, n.* the combination of physical, chemical, and biotic factors (climate, soil, and feed, living things) that directly influence the horse and help determine health and survival. All good equine medicine considers the horse in the context of its environment.

Enzyme ◀€ *en zīm, n.* complex organic substances produced by animal's cells which act as catalyst for (i.e. speed up) biochemical reactions; e.g. digestive enzymes (pepsin, amylase, lipase, etc.) are secreted into digestive tract and break down food into simpler molecules which can then be absorbed. Level of some enzymes in blood samples can be used in diagnosis, e.g. glutamate dehydrogenase is released into blood when liver cells are damaged, creatine kinase released when skeletal muscle damaged.
See Creatine kinase, Digestion.

Enzyme-linked immunosorbent assay see ELISA.

Eosin ◀€ *ē ō sin, n.* red fluorescent dye, $C_{20}H_8Br_4O_5$, used for staining histological sections and blood smears, especially with haematoxylin (= H&E).
See Haematoxylin and eosin staining.

Eosinophil ◀€ *ē ō zi nō fil, n.* type of white blood cell, has granules in cytoplasm which stain readily with eosin, lobulated nucleus. Numerous functions, e.g. prominent in allergic reactions, and fighting viral and parasitic infections.
See Leukocyte.
    Eosinophilia ◀€ *ē ō zi nō fil ēa, n.* increase in numbers of eosinophils in blood.
    See Leukocyte.

Eosinophilic ◀€ *ē ō zi nō fil ik, n,* characterized by eosinophilia.
    E. dermatitis ◀€ *ē ō zi nō fil ik / der mēt īt is, n.* uncommon, idiopathic disease characterized by mouth ulcers, wasting, skin exfoliation and eosinophil infiltration of skin. Most common in winter. Diagnosis based on history and biopsy; must be distinguished from horses with pemphigus. Occasional horse responds to systemic corticosteroids, but overall, prognosis poor.

See Pemphigus foliaceous.
E. gastroenteritis ◀€ *ē ō zi nō fil ik / gas trō en tē rī tis, n.* infiltration of the small intestinal wall with eosinophils. Causes malabsorption, diarrhoea and weight loss. Uncommon.
E. granuloma ◀€ *ē ō zi nō fil ik / gran ū lō mē, n.* common skin disease; most common non-cancerous nodular skin disease of horse. Single or multiple lumps, commonly on back or in girth area, but can occur anywhere on body; no other significant clinical signs. Skin biopsy provides definitive diagnosis. Sub-lesional injections of corticosteroids may provide relief; diffuse cases may respond to systemic therapy. Lesions tend to wax and wane; observation without treatment may be preferable to intervention. Various names, including nodular collagenolytic granuloma, nodular necrobiosis, or acute collagen necrosis.
E. keratoconjunctivitis ◀€ *ē ō zi nō fil ik / ke ra tō kon jungk tiv īt is, n.* an uncommon condition that affects the horse's cornea. Initially, the edge of the cornea is involved; progressive. Signs include squinting, redness, ulcers and mucous discharge from the eye. Cytology of the cornea shows many eosinophils. Cause unknown; possible allergic basis. Therapy with prolonged corticosteroid treatment (in spite of ulcers), and systemic non-steroidal anti-inflammatory drugs.
See Allergy, Eosinophil, Leukaemia.

Epaxial ◀€ *e paks ēūl, adj.* located above or on the dorsal side of an axis; normally used in reference to the musculature of the equine back, e.g. epaxial muscles.

Epicardium ◀€ *e pi kar dē ūm, n.* innermost layer of pericardium (membrane which surrounds heart).
See Pericardium.

Epicondyle ◀€ *e pi kon dīl, n.* a prominence on the distal part of a long bone serving for the attachment of muscles and ligaments, e.g. lateral e. of humerus. Does not form part of joint surface.
See Condyle.

Epidemic ◀€ *e pi de mik, n./adj.* affecting an unusually large number of individuals in a population at the same time, especially widespread occurrence of infectious disease.

155

Epidemiology ◀ *e pi dē mē o lo jē, n.* study of incidence, distribution, and control of diseases within populations.

Epidermal ◀ *e pi der mēl, adj.* pertaining to epidermis (outermost layer of skin). See Epidermis.

Epidermis ◀ *e pi der mis, n.* outermost layer of skin. Has no blood supply. Composed of four, and sometimes five, layers:
- Basal layer (innermost) – columnar cells.
- Spinous layer – flattened cells which have spiny processes.
- Granular layer – flattened granular cells.
- Clear layer – may be absent in thinner epidermis.
- Horny layer – flattened hard cells without nuclei.

Cells move up from basal layer, maturing gradually into horny cells of outer layer, which are shed continually.
See Skin.

Epididymis ◀ *e pi di di mis, n.* long, convoluted tube along posterior border of testis, connecting testis to vas deferens; provides for storage, maturation, and transit of spermatozoa. The epididymis is further subdivided into a head, a body, and a tail.
See Sperm, Testes.

Epididymitis ◀ *e pi di di mī tis, n.* inflammation of epididymis. Rare in horse, may be seen in association with inflammation of testis (orchitis).
See Epididymis, Orchitis.

Epidural ◀ *e pi dūr ēl, adj.* on or around the dura mater of spinal cord.
See Dura mater.
    E. anaesthesia see Anaesthesia

Epiglottic entrapment ◀ *e pi glo tik / en trap mēnt, n.* a relatively common disorder in the throat of the horse. Can produce an obstruction to airflow, resulting in a respiratory noise when the horse exercises, and exercise intolerance; may be accompanied by displacement of soft palate. Diagnosis by endoscopy. The abnormality occurs when a membrane, the aryepiglottic fold, that normally lies under the larynx becomes dislocated to lie over the epiglottis. Several surgeries described, including use of a special hook knife, and surgical laser.
See Soft palate

Epiglottis ◀ *e pi glo tis, n.* lid-like cartilagenous flap which covers entrance to larynx (and airways) when horse swallows, so that food and drink go down oesophagus.
See Soft palate.

Epilepsy ◀ *e pi lep sē, n.* any group of conditions characterized by abnormal brain function that, in horses, may result in seizures or loss of consciousness. May be inherited or acquired; true inherited epilepsy most likely does not occur in horses.
See Seizure.

Epinephrine ◀ *e pin ef rēn, n.* hormone secreted by medulla of adrenal gland; also, a neurotransmitter involved in regulation of sympathetic division of autonomic nervous system. Released in response to stress, hypoglycaemia and other stimuli. It is a potent stimulator of the sympathetic nervous system and a powerful cardiac stimulant. Increased when horse highly stimulated, e.g. by fear, to prepare body for vigorous action. Constricts blood vessels (vasopressor), dilates pupils, increases heart rate and cardiac output, promotes glycogenolysis, which increases blood glucose. Used as a drug to constrict blood vessels and reduce bleeding, and in combination with local anaesthetic to prevent local bleeding at wound or surgical site. Administered intravenously to treat low blood pressure in shock or anaphylaxis. Also called adrenaline. See Anaesthetic, Anaphylaxis, Autonomic nervous system, Shock.

Epiphora ◀ *e pi for ē, n.* abnormal overflow of tears down face, e.g. as seen with obstruction of lacrimal drainage system.
See Lacrimal apparatus.

Epiphyseal plate ◀ *e pi fi sēēl / plāt, n.* growth plate; the cartilage plate in the

long bones of growing horses (and all juvenile mammals). Bones lengthen primarily from growth that occurs at these plates. Fractures of the epiphyseal plate are occasionally seen in young animals (Salter-Harris fracture).
See Salter-Harris fracture.

Epiphysis ◀≣ *e pi fi sis, n.* the end part of a long bone; ossifies separately and later becomes fused with the main part of the bone. Located in the epiphysis is the epiphyseal plate ('growth plate').
See Bone.

Epiphysitis see Physitis

Epiploic foramen see Foramen

Episiotomy ◀≣ *e pi si ot ēmē, n.* surgical enlargement of the vulval orifice; required to open vulvar aperture reduced by Caslick's operation prior to parturition.
See Caslick.

Epistaxis ◀≣ *e pi stak sis, n.* bleeding from nose. Blood in nasal passages may arise from nasal mucosa, auditory tube diverticulum (guttural pouch), throat or lungs. Commonly associated with blood-clotting problems, infection, tumour, foreign body, exercise-induced pulmonary haemorrhage, or injury. May be seen at rest or at exercise (especially when lowering head).
See Clotting, Guttural pouch, Exercise-induced pulmonary haemorrhage.

Epitheliogenesis imperfecta ◀≣ *e pi thē lē ō je ni sis / im pē fek tē, n.* (aplasia cutis) a hereditary skin disease, with large blisters (bullae) in skin and separation of epidermis and dermis. Condition characterized by missing patches of epithelium of the skin and oral mucosa as well as dental abnormalities. First reported in draught horses in Germany in 1913; has more recently been described in newborn American Saddlebred foals.

Epithelium ◀≣ *e pi thē lē ūm, n.* the covering of internal and external surfaces of body, including the lining of vessels. Encloses and protects the other parts of the body,

and produces secretions and excretions, among many functions. Epithelia differentiated according to one of three shapes, one of three stratifications (layering), and specialization of cells; differentiation appears to be closely linked to function.

SHAPES
- Squamous e. – flattened cells, normally occurring in a single layer. Line alveoli of the respiratory membrane, and the endothelium of capillaries, among many other areas. Normally associated with the diffusion of water, electrolytes, and other substances.
- Columnar e. – tall rectangular cells, e.g. lining portions of digestive tract.
- Cuboidal e. – square cells, e.g. covering ovaries, lining nervous system.

STRATIFICATIONS
- Simple – a single layer of cells.
- Stratified – more than one layer of cells.
- Pseudostratified, with cilia – cells have tiny hair-like projections (cilia) which can move in a wave action, e.g. lining airways; action of cilia moves material away from lungs.

SPECIALIZATIONS
- Keratinization – containing keratin, a tough protein. Keratinized epithelium occurs mainly in the skin, but is also found in the mouth and nose; provides a tough, impermeable barrier.
- Ciliation – hair-like extensions that can beat rhythmically to move mucus or other substances through a duct. Cilia are common in the respiratory system and the lining of the oviduct.
- Other types of epithelium occur, named depending on form and function, e.g. the transitional epithelium of the bladder.

Epizootic ◀≣ *e pi zŭ o tik, adj.* describes disease which affects many animals in population at same time.

Epizootic lymphangitis ◀≣ *e pi zŭ o tik / lim fan jī tis, n.* fungal infection with *Histoplasma farciminosum*. Primarily occurs in Africa, Asia, eastern Europe. Clinical signs include nodules affecting the skin and/or lymphatic vessels, which develop into large, draining ulcers, conjunctivitis, and respiratory tract problems. Chafing the legs together, uneven shoeing, and improper harnessing have been considered to be predisposing factors. Biting insects serve as vectors. No apparent age, breed or sex predilection; cases appear in autumn and winter. Culture of organism is difficult; cytological or histological examination of tissue or exudates are more reliable means of diagnosis. Low mortality, but loss of function and economic impact are considerable. No effective treatment. See Fungus.

Epsom salts see Magnesium

Equidae ◀⁞ *e kwi dē, n.* the family of horse-like animals, order Perissodactyla, genus *Equus*; the horse family. Apart from the horse, other extant equids include the donkey, the four zebras and the onager. All have single supporting digit on each limb (although two other digits remain as splint bones).

Equilin ◀⁞ *e kwi lin, n.* a horse oestrogen; chemical name 3-hydroxyestra-1,3,5,7-tetraen-17-one. Equilin is one of the oestrogens present in the mixture of oestrogens isolated from horse urine. No therapeutic use in horses; widely prescribed in post-menopausal human females. Not produced by other species.

Equine ◀⁞ *e kwīn, adj.* relating to, derived from, or affecting horses or members of horse family.

Equine chorionic gonadotrophin ◀⁞ *e kwīn / ko rē o̱ nik / gō na dō trō̱ fin, n.* hormone secreted by endometrial cups of pregnant mare's uterus. Predominant effect is to stimulate follicles, but hormone also possesses a luteinizing fraction. Detection of hormone can be used for serum diagnosis of pregnancy from approximately days 40–120, but false positive tests are problematic, as positive test indicates presence of endometrial cups, not viable foetus.
See Endometrial, Pregnancy.

Equine degenerative myeloencephalopathy ◀⁞ *e kwīn / di je̱ nē ri tiv / mī̱ ē lō en kef ē lo̱ pē thē, n.* (EDM) a diffuse, degenerative neurological disease of unknown cause, characterized by ataxia, weakness and hypometria, often beginning in the pelvic limbs and progressing. No cranial nerve involvement, muscle atrophy or changes in skin sensation occur. Seen in young equids of many breeds, including Mongolian wild horses and Grant's zebras, and both sexes. Most commonly manifested at less than 6 months of age, but can show as late as 20 years. Signs include progressive symmetrical incoordination, stumbling, may be unable to back or turn sharply. Characterized at post-mortem examination by degeneration and demyelination (loss of fatty covering) of spinal cord. Diagnosis mainly by clinical signs, and by ruling out other conditions which cause ataxia; low vitamin E in serum sample may help support a diagnosis. There is no specific treatment; some horses may benefit from vitamin E supplementation, particularly if treated early in the disease.

Equine ehrlichiosis see Anaplasmosis

Equine gastric ulcer syndrome (EGUS) ◀⁞ *e kwīn / ga̱s trik / u̱l sē̱ / sin drōm, n.* ulceration of the stomach; many causes and complicated in nature. It has been estimated that 25% to 50% of foals and 60% to 90% of adult horses may be affected by gastric ulcers. Gastric ulcers can occur in any part of the stomach, but are most commonly located in the non-glandular region. Two clinical syndromes have been described, one in foals less than 9 months of age, and the other in horses greater than 9 months of age. Although the ulcers themselves are similar in both groups, the syndromes may have different causes and may produce different clinical signs. In foals, and to a lesser extent in adult horses, EGUS may also be complicated by duodenal ulcers, which delay emptying of the stomach, and lead to gastric and esophageal ulcers.

CAUSES
The horse's stomach continuously secretes varying amounts of digestive

juices, including hydrochloric acid. This secretion of acid occurs whether or not there is feed present in the stomach. EGUS appears to be related to an imbalance between the digestive juices (hydrochloric acid, pepsin, bile acids, organic acids) and the substances that ordinarily protect the lining of the stomach from those juices (mucus, bicarbonate). Factors that cause such an imbalance include:

- Prolonged exposure to the digestive juices, (as occurs in gastroesophageal reflux disease in humans) from:
  o fasting;
  o feed deprivation;
  o timing of feeding – horses fed continuously have less stomach acidity than those who are fasted;
  o type of hay – alfalfa (lucerne) hay, with higher protein and calcium concentration, helps buffer the stomach better than does grass hay;
  o percentage of roughage in diet – more roughage produces more saliva, which is high in bicarbonate, possibly providing more buffering of stomach acids than occurs with grain-rich diets;
  o infrequent nursing in foals;
  o problems that interfere with stomach movement and emptying (e.g. colic, frequent lying down in foals);
  o composition of the gastric juice, especially increased acidity. Diet appears to be a significant factor, i.e. roughage is better than grain, alfalfa hay is less ulcerogenic than is grass hay;
  o strenuous athletic performance:
    • prolonged exercise may interfere with emptying of the stomach, and increase exposure of stomach to digestive juices;
    • high carbohydrate diets fed to racehorses may increase the production of volatile fatty acids in the stomach, which can directly injure the stomach lining.
- Impaired blood flow, and decreased mucus and bicarbonate secretion, as occurs in some cases of chronic administration of non-steroidal anti-inflammatory drugs, due to their inhibition of prostaglandins.
- Stress – training or stall confinement may cause excessive release of plasma cortisol, which can interfere with prostaglandin synthesis.

DIAGNOSIS
Based on the presence of typical clinical signs. Affected foals may show signs of colic, especially after nursing or eating, frequent lying down, especially lying down on their backs, irregular or interrupted nursing, diarrhoea, loss of appetite, grinding of teeth (bruxism), and excess salivation (ptyalism). Affected adult horses may have a poor appetite, show lethargy, or have decreased performance, poor body condition and hair coat, weight loss, or show mild colic signs. Clinical diagnosis is confirmed by endoscopic examination of the stomach.

TREATMENT
Involves inhibiting gastric acid secretion so that the stomach lining can heal. Dietary and management changes may be sufficient to treat some cases of EGUS. Such changes would include increased roughage in diet, increased alfalfa (lucerne) hay in diet, decreasing grain concentrates in diet, or increasing turnout. Pharmacological strategies for management include omeprazole, ranitidine, and cimetidine – omeprazole is the best studied, and appears to be the most effective, pharmacological option. Omeprazole given at one-half of the treatment dose may be used for prevention of EGUS.

Equine granulocytic anaplasmosis see Anaplasmosis

Equine herpes virus ◀ꜰ *e kwīn / her pēz / vī rēs, n.* (EHV) the most successful viral pathogen of equidae worldwide. Nine EHVs have been characterized; five cause disease in the domestic horse, and four are associated with infections in wild equids. Sophisticated life cycles involve infection of many cell types in many different tissues, and different means of avoiding the host immune response. Central to their successful survival is the ability of the virus to lie quiet for prolonged periods (latency), which allows virus to avoid immune system, and to allow for a reservoir of transmissible infection. The most important and most studied EHVs are EHV-1 and EHV-4. Different strains of EHV vary widely in virulence. The EHVs of domestic horses are:

EHV-1 – spread in air, infection typically by inhalation; replication in upper respiratory tract. Virus replicates and enters blood stream (viraemia).

- Respiratory disease – high temperature, nasal discharge, coughing, generally worse in young animals (up to 3 years).
- Abortion – in late pregnancy, may follow respiratory infection. Virus moves from circulation into placental unit and induces lesions in the uterine blood supply. Stables may suffer 'abortion storm', with many mares aborting.
- Neonatal disease – foals may rarely be affected by virus. It is not clear whether affected foals are infected in uterus or if infection is acquired immediately after birth. Affected foals are sick at birth, or develop an infection within 1–2 days after birth; may survive for up to two weeks, but eventually die from respiratory disease and other complications.
- Stallion disease – stallions may occasionally develop oedema of the scrotum, loss of libido, and poor sperm quality, and may shed virus through the semen. It is not known if virus shedding in this manner helps spread disease.
- Neurological disease – virus causes inflammation, thrombus formation, and ischaemia of blood vessels supplying spinal cord following infection of endothelial cells; nervous system signs results from ischaemic death of nervous system tissue. Horse develops incoordination of hind legs, urinary incontinence; may progress to recumbency and death.

EHV-2 – appears to be primarily important as ocular pathogen.
See viral keratitis.

EHV-3 (coital vesicular exanthema) – an uncommon venereal pathogen; virus causes pustular blisters on vulva and penis. Does not affect fertility, but stallion with severe lesions may not be able to cover mares.

EHV-4 (rhinopneumonitis) thought to be similar in pathogenicity to EHV-1; however, the details of the pathogenesis are not yet worked out. Causes similar clinical signs to EHV-1, including respiratory disease and abortion; no neurological form as yet identified.

EHV-5 – clinical importance not clearly defined; in certain situations, may be important as respiratory or ocular pathogen (as per EHV-2).

DIAGNOSIS
Clinical exam is usually insufficient to establish diagnosis in EHV infections; no particular signs are pathognomonic. Direct demonstration of virus by various means (e.g. virus isolation), or indirect demonstration by serology, is required to confirm EHV infection.

TREATMENT
Animals with respiratory infections are contagious and should be isolated. Affected horses should not work until one week after clinical signs have resolved. Infection is generally mild and self-limiting. Abortion cannot be prevented or treated. Ocular disease has been treated with antiviral compounds, especially idoxuridine and acyclovir. Neurological cases have been treated with acyclovir.

PREVENTION
Efforts to prevent EHV infections have centred primarily on vaccination; as EHV-2, 3, and 5 are rarely identified, no vaccine is available for prophylaxis against these strains. The inactivated EHV-1/4 vaccines appear to reduce the chance of EHV-1 abortion, as well as the severity and duration of respiratory disease of EHV-1 and EHV-4 after experimental challenge; nevertheless, individual animals may still become infected in spite of vaccination. In addition, if the dose of virus is high, or if management is inappropriate, vaccine prophylaxis is likely to be insufficient to prevent infection. The studies on which vaccination recommen-

dations are made all have problems with design, and it is difficult to make reliable recommendations for vaccine prophylaxis based on those studies. No published studies evaluate the effectiveness of EHV-1 vaccination in prevention of EHV-1 neurological disease, and no commercially available vaccines have been shown to prevent neurological disease.

Equine infectious anaemia ◀€ _e kwīn / in fek shēs / ē nē mē ē, n._ ('swamp fever') notifiable disease caused by retrovirus (can copy viral RNA as complementary DNA which can be inserted into host's DNA and so persist). Transmitted by biting flies, or by use of contaminated needles, etc. Characterized by recurrent episodes of high temperature, loss of appetite, depression, anaemia, lack of platelets (thrombocytopenia), epistaxis (nosebleed), and fluid swelling of ventral abdomen or legs. Some horses may be subclinical carriers and some may develop chronic disease, with weight loss, anaemia, depression and death; the clinical course varies depending on the dose and virulence of the strain of virus, and the susceptibility of the horse. Clinical disease appears to be less severe in donkeys and mules. Diagnosis by haematology (anaemia, thrombocytopenia), serology (agar gel immunodiffusion Coggins' test and ELISA). Early diagnosis can be difficult because seroconversion may not occur for up to 45 days. There is no specific therapy; most affected horses are euthanized. Environmental control to reduce insects helpful; needles and syringes should never be used to inject more than one horse so as to prevent iatrogenic transmission.
See Agar, Anaemia, ELISA, Retrovirus, Thrombocytopenia.

Equine influenza ◀€ _e kwīn / in flū en zē, n._ acute respiratory disease caused by influenza A virus (several subtypes); the most frequently diagnosed and economically significant viral respiratory disease of the horse throughout world. All ages and breeds of horses may be affected. Spread in air as aerosol from coughing horses.

Signs seen as soon as 24–48 hours after exposure, and initially include fever, which can be quite high, lethargy, and inappetence. Coughing and nasal discharge (watery initially but becomes mucopurulent) follow. May also see rapid breathing, stiffness, red eyes, and lymph node swelling. Pneumonia a common secondary problem from secondary bacterial infection; rarely, myocarditis seen.

DIAGNOSIS
A presumptive diagnosis is often made from clinical signs and the rapid spread through a population. However, to confirm the diagnosis, serology, fluorescent antibody, or ELISA testing are required; virus can sometimes be isolated from nasal swabs.

TREATMENT
No specific therapy is available. Non-steroidal anti-inflammatory drugs can help control fever and improve appetite. If signs persist beyond 10 days, it suggests that there are secondary complications, such as pneumonia. A period of rest should be given before horses return to athletic activity; recommendations have been made for up to 100 days following infection.

PREVENTION
Isolation of newcomers for 3 weeks prior to introduction into herd provides some protection; good ventilation of stabling helps with general airway health. Although equine influenza vaccines have been in use for several decades, the effectiveness of the vaccines has rarely been tested in field conditions, and such tests have been disappointing. In spite of aggressive vaccination strategies, equine influenza has spread virtually worldwide. While vaccination may help reduce clinical signs in individual animals, elimination of virus shedding is a goal of vaccination that has, so far, not been achieved. Further, the influenza virus can undergo changes in antigenic structure such that vaccinated animals are not immune to new strains, making elimination of the disease unlikely for the foreseeable future.
See Vaccine.

Equine motor neuron disease ◀≲ *e kwīn /* *mō tē / nŭr ōn / di zēz, n.* (EMND) disease first recorded in 1990 in New York, USA. Most commonly reported in northeast USA and Canada, but has been recorded elsewhere. Exact cause is unknown; oxidative stress arising from chronic vitamin E deficiency has been suspected of playing a major role. Signs initially include weight loss, excessive recumbency and/or trembling. Other clinical diagnostic signs include constant weight shifting of the hind limbs, abnormally low head carriage and muscle tremors. Appetite is not affected; marked coprophagia in some cases. Some horses may have high serum concentration of muscle-derived enzymes. Diagnosis from clinical signs; confirmed by muscle or nerve biopsy. The most commonly identified environmental risk factors for a horse having EMND are absence of grazing for more than a year and provision of poor quality hay. Usually progressive, may occasionally stabilize; acute cases may respond to vitamin E supplementation, or fresh grass pasture.

Equine protozoal myeloencephalitis ◀≲ *e kwīn / prō tē zō ēl / mī ē lō en kef ē lī tis, n.* (EPM) disease caused by protozoan parasite *Sarcocystis neurona*; infection of central nervous system, occurs mostly in N. America. Horse is aberrant host; parasite normally passes from opossum to birds; muscle tissue of bird is definitive host. Horses ingest eggs of parasite from feed contaminated with opossum faeces (from opossum scavenging horse feed). Many horses exposed; few develop disease. Signs of disease include progressive hind limb lameness and incoordination, limb weakness, and muscle wasting; horse may be unable to back up and sink on hind limbs; problems with cranial nerves may develop. Signs usually asymmetrical.

DIAGNOSIS
Clinical signs indicate neurological abnormality. Diagnosis may be difficult to confirm, as a majority of horses in the United States appear to have been exposed. Serology confirms exposure, not disease;

negative titres are fairly reliable in confirming absence of disease. CSF titres confirm disease; however, samples are easily contaminated by blood, confounding results.

TREATMENT
Numerous treatment protocols have been devised, with all reporting some success, including sulphur drugs plus pyramethamine, ponazuril, and nitazoxanide.

PREVENTION
Keeping feed secure, and free from scavengers, is best preventive measure. Vaccine available; efficacy unproven and doubtful. Vaccine causes seroconversion which can confuse interpretation of serological results.

Equine recurrent uveitis ◀≲ *e kwīn / ri ku rēnt / ū vē ī tis, n.* (ERU, recurrent iridocyclitis, lunar blindness, moon blindness – the syndrome was thought by the Romans to be caused by changes in the moon, periodic ophthalmia) immunemediated inflammation of uveal tract of eye (iris, ciliary body, choroid); response may be related to genetic make-up of the animal. The most common cause of blindness in horses. Can affect horses of any age, but initial episode usually occurs between 4 and 8 years. Associated with various antigens, especially *Leptospira* spp. Many other causes, including bacterial, viral, protozoan, parasitic and non-infectious (e.g. secondary to trauma or ulceration). ERU is not one single disease entity; rather, it is a whole complex of diseases related to various causes and presenting signs.

CLINICAL PRESENTATION
Many descriptions of clinical condition, including:
- Acute u. – active pain and visible internal inflammation.
- Anterior u. – affecting primarily the iris, ciliary body, and anterior chamber.
- Classic ERU – characterized by active episodes of inflammation, with periods of minimal inflammation; attacks become increasingly severe.
- End-stage u. – chronic disease with

severe secondary changes that often result in blindness.

- Insidious ERU – low-grade inflammation without outward signs of pain, but leading to chronic clinical signs; especially as seen in Appaloosas and draught horses.
- Panuveitis – inflammation in both anterior and posterior chamber of eye.
- Posterior u. – affecting primarily the vitreous, retina, and choroid.
- Quiescent u. – no visible signs of discomfort, but ongoing inflammation.

Clinical signs vary depending on the acuteness of the disease, whether there are pre-existing changes in the eye, the type of inflammation, and the location of the inflammation. May affect one or both eyes, depending on cause; can recur, often with increasing severity, resulting in chronic damage to eye. Signs of acute condition include pain, often so severe as to preclude routine examination without sedation, swelling of eyelids and conjunctiva, squinting, spasm of eyelids, dislike of bright light (photophobia), lacrimation, redness of eye, dull cornea, constriction of pupil (miosis), poor vision. Chronic changes include poor vision or blindness, cloudy anterior chamber, irregular shape of pupil, cataract, lens luxation, shrinkage of eyeball.

Chronic, recurrent episodes are thought to occur because:

1. The infectious agent or antigen may become incorporated into the uveal tract.
2. Antigen–antibody complexes may be deposited in the uveal tract, which later cause inflammation.
3. Sensitized T lymphocytes may remain in uveal tract that reactivate when exposed to an antigen.

DIAGNOSIS

Based on characteristic clinical signs and history of previous episodes. Thorough examination of the eye required to evaluate primary problems that result in secondary uveitis.

TREATMENT

If a primary cause is identified (ulcer, corneal trauma, etc.), treatment is aimed at eliminating that problem. If no primary cause, treatment is directed at treating signs and reducing inflammation in the eye. To reduce pain and discomfort, agents that dilate the eye (e.g. atropine ophthalmic ointment; phenylephrine) are used. To decrease inflammation, corticosteroids and non-steroidal anti-inflammatory drugs, both topically and systemically, may be employed. Initial therapy lasts for at least 2 weeks, and should be continued for at least 2 weeks after clinical signs have resolved. Sustained release medication devices or implants have been successfully employed in management. In Germany, surgical vitrectomy has been used in over 1,000 eyes to treat selected cases of ERU with reported 98% per cent success from one group of surgeons. However, the procedure has not achieved widespread acceptance, nor the same level of success in other settings.

PREVENTION

Environmental management to reduce allergens, and eliminate potential sources of trauma to the eye are likely to be useful in helping reduce incidence. Routine health care, such as vaccination and parasite control, may help minimize infectious disease occurrence that may predispose to ERU. Vaccination of horses against *Leptospira* spp. has been proposed – however, no vaccine has been tested on horses.

See Eye.

Equine rhinovirus ◀ *e kwīn / rī nē vī rēs, n.* picornavirus, genus *Rhinovirus*; two types, equine rhinitis virus A and B. Has been isolated from nasal swabs taken from horses with acute febrile respiratory disease. High rates of seroprevalence; uncommonly diagnosed as cause of disease, possibly because of dominant status of equine herpes virus and equine influenza virus. Spread through nasal secretions and urine aerosol. Causes mild to severe respiratory disease; infection may often be subclinical. Treatment is symptomatic and supportive (e.g. control fever, provide clean water and food until signs pass). No vaccine available.

Equine sarcoid ◀€ *e kwīn* / *sar koid, n.* common, locally aggressive, fibrous tumour of skin; the most common skin neoplasm of the horse. Thought to be viral in cause, possibly bovine papillomavirus, but transmission to other sites and other horses has not always been successful, so the importance of the virus as a possible cause is still speculative. Appaloosas, Arabians, Quarter Horses, and especially geldings of those breeds, appear to be at increased risk; Standardbreds appear to be at decreased risk. Most common in young to middle-aged horses on head, axillae, around girth, ventral abdomen, around genitalia or on legs; may have multiple locations. May also occur under skin or growing along lymphatic vessels. Variable appearance, but four broad categories are described:

1. Verrucous (wart-like).
2. Fibroblastic (like proud flesh).
3. Mixed verrucous and fibroblastic.
4. Occult (flat, circular area of hair loss, often with scaly skin).

All four types may have satellite lesions around primary lesion.

Diagnosis is by histopathology of biopsy specimen. Biopsy may exacerbate lesion, so may be discouraged by some veterinarians if clinically obvious.

Many treatments described, reflecting fact that no treatment is uniformly successful. Treatments include surgical excision, cryosurgery, radiation therapy, hyperthermia, laser therapy, chemotherapy (e.g. cisplatin, 5-fluorouracil), immunotherapy (e.g. injectable mycobacterial cell wall fraction), or topical caustics (e.g. zinc chloride), alone or in combination. Often recurs if removed surgically: does not metastasize to other parts of body. Small tumours that do not cause discomfort may be observed, and do not necessarily grow or spread.

Equine systemic proteoglycam accumulation (ESPA) See Degenerative suspensory ligament disease

Equine viral arteritis ◀€ *e kwīn* / *vī rēl* / *ar tē rī tis, n.* an infectious disease of equids caused by the equine arteritis virus; first identified in Ohio, USA, in 1953, but noted more than 100 years previously. Worldwide distribution based on seroprevalence studies (except Iceland and Japan). Transmission either by venereal route, mainly in the semen of acutely or chronically infected stallions, or respiratory route, as aerosol in air from nasal discharge or in aerosolized urine. Persistently infected carrier stallions serve as the main reservoir in the equine population. Mares that become infected during natural or artificial breeding can transmit disease. Rarely, newborns can be infected by transplacental transmission and develop overwhelming, fatal infections. Clinical signs and severity vary greatly. Most infections are subclinical, especially in mares that have been infected by stallion. Disease outbreaks are characterized by one or more of the following: acute upper respiratory tract infection, including cough, nasal discharge, and fever; depression; stiffness; conjunctivitis; abortion; enteritis and diarrhoea; urticaria, lymphadenopathy, and peripheral oedema, including fluid swelling of face, ventral abdomen and limbs. Stallions can undergo a temporary period of subfertility after infection; semen quality is generally normal in carrier stallions. Most horses recover fully; carriers are a significant problem (especially stallions).

DIAGNOSIS
Clinical signs alone are suggestive, but not diagnostic. Blood examination of acute cases typically shows leukopenia. Laboratory diagnosis is most commonly based on any combination of virus isolation, serology, and antigen detection. Appropriate samples are nasal or conjunctival swabs or EDTA blood samples.

TREATMENT
There is no specific antiviral treatment for EVA. Nearly all infected horses recover uneventfully. Symptomatic support may be required in more severely affected individuals.

PREVENTION
Natural infection provides a long-lasting immunity. Vaccination strategies are based on use of formalin inactivated and live attenuated vaccines, with a geographical

split in their use between Europe and Japan (inactivated) and North America (live attenuated). New experimental DNA and protein subunit vaccines are also being developed. Good efficacy data exists for the live attenuated MLV vaccine, particularly in preventing the carrier state in vaccinated colts; however, safety concerns regarding inducing clinical disease in vaccinated animals, as well as occasional problems involving the use of the vaccine in late-term pregnant mares, has limited its use in some areas. There is less clear-cut evidence to suggest that inactivated vaccines are truly effective. In the face of outbreaks, stalls and equipment on affected premises should be decontaminated with disinfectants. EVA is a notifiable disease in some countries.
See Carrier.

Equine viral encephalitis see Eastern equine encephalitis, Western equine encephalitis and Venezuelan equine encephalitis

Equine viral papillomatosis ◀╪ _e kwīn_ / _vī rēl_ / _pa pi lō mē tō sis_, _n._ common skin growth of young horse caused by papilloma virus; 'warts'. Usually seen on muzzle and lips; less often on eyelid, genitalia, and distal limbs. Grey to pink to white growths up to 2 cm diameter, usually resolve spontaneously after 2–3 months. Numerous treatments described to help speed regression; none proven more effective than waiting for spontaneous resolution.

Equine viral papular dermatitis ◀╪ _e kwīn_ / _vī rēl_ / _pa pū lē_ / _der mē tī tis_, _n._ (Uasin Gishu disease) infectious skin disease caused by pox virus. Direct transmission, or indirect by biting insects, occurs in Africa, Australia, New Zealand, USA; causes fever and circular papules with hair loss (0.5–2 cm) over body (not head). No systemic signs; papules resolve spontaneously after 4–6 weeks.

Equisetum arvensae see Horsetail

Erection ◀╪ _i rek shēn_, _n._ rigidity, elevation and swelling of penis as blood flows into spongy sinuses, usually as result of sexual stimulation. Enables intromission to occur. Failure to achieve erection may be result of local damage to nerves or blood vessels or psychogenic factors.
See Behaviour.

Ergot ◀╪ _er got_, _n._ **1)** small horny protuberance concealed by hair behind fetlock, probably vestigial digital pad; **2)** type of fungus which can infect cereal grains, e.g. _Claviceps purpurea_ infects rye, can cause poisoning in horses; signs include lethargy, sweating, low temperature, slow breathing and heart rate, coma and death, milder cases may show diarrhoea, colic, abortion.

Erosion ◀╪ _ir ō shēn_, _n._ an eating away, or destruction of the surface of a tissue or structure, such as tooth or skin.

Eruption ◀╪ _i rup shēn_, _n._ a break out, as in eruption of the teeth; visible skin lesions caused by disease.
> **Drug e.** ◀╪ _drug_ / _i rup shēn_, _n._ is an adverse skin reaction produced by the use of a drug.

Erythema ◀╪ _e ri thē mē_, _n._ redness of the skin; seen especially with inflammation.

Erythrocyte ◀╪ _i ri thrō sīt_, _n._ red blood cell. Most numerous cell type in blood, contains haemoglobin which transports oxygen around body to where it is needed. Haemoglobin combined with oxygen is red, which gives cells their colour. Erythrocytes develop in bone marrow, near maturity they lose nucleus (at this stage called reticulocyte), and are released into blood stream once haemoglobin is fully formed. Last approximately 150 days in blood, cannot reproduce (as have no nucleus), old red blood cells removed by liver, spleen, bone marrow and replaced by new cells from bone marrow. Lack of red blood cell production or loss of red blood cells, through bleeding or destruction of cells, will result in anaemia.
See Anaemia, Bone, Haemoglobin, Liver, Spleen.
> **E. index** ◀╪ _i ri thrō sīt_ / _in deks_, _n._ measurements calculated from blood sample testing that describe the size and haemoglobin

content of red blood cells. The indices are used to help in the differential diagnosis of anaemia in most species; limited utility in horses, as anaemia is an uncommon condition in the species.

E. sedimentation rate ◀ᛒ *i ri thrō sīt / se di men tā shēn /rāt, n.* a blood test that measures the speed at which red blood cells settle on the bottom of a test tube; high sedimentation rate signals possible inflammatory or immune-mediated disease. Horse's blood tends to have a high sedimentation rate normally, so the test is not considered useful in this species.

Erythrocytosis ◀ᛒ *e ri thrō sī tō sis, n.* abnormal increase in red blood cell count especially resulting from a known stimulus. Has been reported in horses secondary to various neoplasias.
See Erythrocyte, Polycythaemia.

Erythromycin ◀ᛒ *e ri thrō mī sin, n.* antibiotic, bacteriostatic or bacteriocidal depending on dose and susceptibility of bacteria. Active against some Gram-positive cocci, Gram-positive bacilli and some Gram-negative bacilli; antimicrobial spectrum similar to or slightly wider than that of penicillin. Used on foals in treatment of some cases of pneumonia, especially *Rhodococcus equi,* and infectious arthritis (joint-ill). Has also been used to stimulate bowel motility in post-surgical ileus.
See *Rhodococcus equi.*

Erythropoiesis ◀ᛒ *e ri thrō pō sis n.* the production of erythrocytes.

Erythropoietin ◀ᛒ *e ri thrō poi ē tin, n.* a hormone, secreted primarily by the kidney, that stimulates erythropoiesis. Synthetic erythropoietin was developed for treatment of life-threatening anaemia in humans with kidney failure, and has been used illegally in human athletes looking to gain a performance advantage; one study concludes that synthetic erythropoietin enhances aerobic capacity and exercise performance. However, synthetic human erythropoietin can cause severe non-regenerative anaemia, and even death in horses because the horse's immune system recognizes the human hormone as foreign, and responds by producing antibodies to destroy it. These antibodies also destroy the horse's own erythropoietin.

Escherichia ◀ᛒ *e shē ri shē, n.* genus of Gram-negative, rod-shaped, facultatively anaerobic bacteria found mostly in the large intestine of warm-blooded animals.
E. coli ◀ᛒ *e shē ri shē / kō lī, n.* the principal species of the genus, makes up large proportion of normal intestinal bacteria. Mostly non-pathogenic, but pathogenic strains can cause diarrhoea, septicaemia, urinary tract infections, etc.

Esmarch bandage ◀ᛒ *es march / ban dij, n.* tight rubber bandage used as tourniquet to drive blood out of a limb, and prevent further bleeding, prior to surgery. Applied from distal to proximal. (Named after Johannes von Esmarch, German surgeon, 1823–1908.)

Esophagus see Oesophagus

Essential amino acid see Amino acid

Esterase ◀ᛒ *es tē rāz, n.* enzyme which catalyses reaction of breakdown of esters (esters are compounds formed from an organic acid and an alcohol) into the component alcohol and acid; e.g. cholinesterase breaks down acetylcholine.

Estrogen see Oestrogen

Ether ◀ᛒ *ē thē, n.* diethyl ether; volatile, highly flammable liquid, used in past as inhalation anaesthetic, now superseded by more effective and safer drugs. Has been applied topically as a solvent, or has formerly been used in various liniment preparations.

Ethmoid ◀ᛒ *eth moid, adj./n.* relating to, adjoining, or being one or more bones of the walls and septum of the nasal cavity; bone of skull at base of nose, has cribriform plate, a sieve-like structure through which olfactory nerves pass from nasal passages to olfactory bulb of brain.
E. haematoma ◀ᛒ *eth moid / hē mē tō ma, n.* a

progressive, and locally destructive growth of the ethmoturbinate bones of the horse's nasal passage. The cause and origin are unknown. The growth resembles a bloody tumour, but it is not neoplastic. Clinical signs are mild, intermittent, spontaneous nose bleeding; most often one side only. Diagnosis by endoscopy. Surgical removal often difficult and incomplete, with regrowth common; injection of formalin into mass causes shrinkage and can effect a cure without the morbidity of surgery.

Ethology ◀€ *ē tho lē jē*, *n.* study or science of animal behaviour under natural conditions; study of human character and its formation and evolution.

Eupatorium rugosum see White snake-root

Eustachian tube ◀€ *ū stā shēn / tūb*, *n.* (auditory tube, pharyngotympanic tube) narrow tube which connects middle ear with pharynx, so that pressure either side of ear drum (tympanic membrane) can be equalized. Guttural pouch is outpocketing of tube. (Named after Bartolemo Eustachio, sixteenth-century Italian anatomist.) See Ear, Guttural pouch.

Euthanasia ◀€ *ū thē nā zē ē*, *n.* humane killing of animal, performed to relieve suffering. In horse, most commonly achieved by intravenous injection of drug (e.g. pentobarbital); humane killer (e.g. captive bolt pistol) which fires bolt into brain, or bullet may be used, but proper positioning is crucial (important: should be at intersection of two diagonal lines from base of ear to opposite eye). See Pentobarbital.

Euthyroid sick syndrome ◀€ *ū thī roid / sik / sin drōm*, *n.* low thyroid hormone concentrations in animal caused by condition unrelated to thyroid gland. By down-regulating the thyroid gland, the body tries to lower the metabolic rate and conserve energy and calories. Resting thyroid hormone levels are low, although the thyroid gland itself is normal. Can cause misdiagnosis of hypothyroidism in horses. See Hypothyroidism, Thyroid.

Evisceration ◀€ *i vi sē rā shēn*, *n.* extrusion of viscera outside the body; may be seen as congenital abnormality where abdominal wall does not form properly and abdominal contents are not contained. Rare post-castration complication.

Ewe-neck ◀€ *ū - nek*, *n.* neck with concave topline when viewed from side. Seen in any breed, especially in long-necked horses, e.g. Arabian and Thoroughbred horses. Considered poor conformation. See Conformation.

Examination ◀€ *ig za mi nā shēn*, *n.* investigation, inspection, especially with aim of diagnosing disease. Techniques include palpation, auscultation, percussion; often further qualified according to the method employed; examples below.

- Breeding soundness e. – examination to help determine likelihood that an animal is fertile. In mare, may include genital examination, rectal palpation, speculum examination, bacterial culture, uterine biopsy or ultrasound examination. In stallion, may include genital examination, rectal palpation, and evaluation of semen.
- Cardiac e. – may include listening to heart rate, rhythm, etc. before and after exercise (auscultation) and electrocardiography. Some methods of electrocardiography allow recordings to be taken during exercise.
  See Auscultation, Electrocardiography, Heart.
- Clinical e. – (physical e.) general diagnostic examination of horse. Best if performed according to routine, so as to reduce possibility of missing an abnormality. Includes observing behaviour; recording heart, pulse and breathing rate and rectal temperature; examination of mucous membranes of mouth and eye and inspection of rest of mouth; auscultation of thorax and abdomen; feeling for any abnormalities of muscles, limbs, withers; watching movement as horse walks and trots.
- Genital e. – in mare, inspection of vulva, vagina and cervix using speculum, and rectal palpation of ovaries and uterus. In stallion, external examination of

penis, prepuce, scrotum and testicles and rectal palpation of urethra and accessory sex glands.

- Insurance e. – inspection of horse for insurance company to assess health and fitness for insurance, or to assess its situation (e.g. whether able to work) in event of insurance claim.
- Laboratory e. – any test conducted in a laboratory setting. Includes tests on blood, biopsy samples, discharges, exudative fluids, faeces, urine, etc.; performed to confirm or establish clinical diagnosis. Also may include bacteriology, biochemistry, haematology, histopathology.
- Ophthalmic e. – examination of eye and associated structures. Minimum examination involves use of focused light source; many specialized ophthalmic instruments are available, as well.
- Post-mortem e. – inspection of carcass to establish cause of death. Involves examination of internal organs and laboratory examination of samples from carcass.
- Pre-purchase e. – (soundness e.) examination by veterinarian to establish condition of horse at that time, e.g. before sale. Protocol may vary depending on veterinarian, or protocol of overseeing veterinary body or insurance company. May include any or all of a number of diagnostic tests, including, but not necessarily limited to, clinical or laboratory examination, observation while trotting in hand, during exercise, at lunge and/or under saddle, radiographs, endoscopic examination, and foot examination. Veterinarian typically gives opinion as to the condition of the horse at the time of examination.

Exanthema ◀∈ *eks an thē mē, n.* rash or eruptive condition, e.g. coital vesicular exanthema is a venereal disease caused by equine herpes virus 3.
See Equine herpes virus (EHV-3).

Excipient ◀∈ *ek si pē ēnt, n.* inert substance added to drug to give it a suitable form or consistency for administration.

Excise ◀∈ *ek sīs, v.* to cut out or off.

Excisional biopsy see Biopsy

Excitation ◀∈ *ek sī tā shēn, n.* stimulation, e.g. excitation of a nerve; responding to the addition of energy.

Excrete ◀∈ *eks krēt, v.* to throw off or eliminate by normal discharge. In horses, metabolic waste is excreted as urine and faeces.
See Metabolism.

Exercise-induced pulmonary haemorrhage ◀∈ *ek sēr sīz - in dūst / pul mēn rē / he mē rij, n.* (EIPH) bleeding into lungs which occurs during heavy exercise (e.g. racing), probably in most horses if exercise is of sufficient intensity. Most commonly observed when horse presents with nosebleed (epistaxis) but most horses with EIPH do not show overt signs; depending on extent of injury, bleeding can be severe, even fatal. Caused by rupture of capillary walls, may occur from areas of lung damage from previous disease, but often seen with no pre-existing pathology. Common cause of poor performance, particularly if severe. Diagnosis by endoscopy. Literally dozens of treatments are described, most with little or no proven efficacy. The diuretic drug furosemide is probably the most commonly prescribed drug, but it does not work consistently, and it is banned in some countries. Racehorses in Australia and New Zealand that suffer an attack of EIPH following a race are banned from racing for three months; a further episode results in a lifetime ban.

Exertional rhabdomyolysis ◀∈ *ek ser shēn ēl / rab dō mī ō lī sis, n.* (ER, azoturia, tying up, Monday morning disease) historically, there are many descriptions of what appeared, at the time, to be a single condition. However, it is now clear that there are many different causes that result in a similar clinical presentation. Both acquired and inherited forms of ER exist. Acquired causes are related to over-exertion; inherited causes include defects of muscle calcium regulation and abnormal muscle polysaccharide accumulation.

Clinical signs of acute ER include rapid heart rate, stiff, painful gait, unwillingness to move, sweating, and pain on muscle palpation. Horses may pose as if to urinate or exhibit signs of colic. If damage is more severe, dark, pigmented urine (myoglobinuria) may be seen. If muscle involvement is widespread, horse may become recumbent. If horse is exhausted, high fever may be present; severe signs may include shock and disseminated intravascular coagulation. Secondary renal complications may follow from myoglobinuria.

DIAGNOSIS
History and clinical signs are generally sufficient to establish a clinical diagnosis. History of acquired ER typically includes horse having been rested for few days with grain feeding, horse given sudden increase in work after prolonged rest. Routine changes in all cases include elevations of muscle enzymes creatine kinase (CK) and aspartate aminotransferase (AST). Electrolyte abnormalities, synchronous diaphragmatic flutter, and myoglobinuria may accompany more severe cases and may give clues as to inherited forms of ER.

TREATMENT
Exercise should be stopped immediately on recognition of the condition. Intravenous fluid therapy important in more severe cases, with dehydration, and with myoglobinuria. If there is no urine seen during fluid administration, diuretics may be helpful to stimulate urination. Non-steroidal anti-inflammatory analgesic drugs may be helpful, but should be used with caution in cases of suspected renal damage. Acepromazine has been used for its vasodilatory effects, but should be used with caution in horses with hypovolaemia, and with elevated blood pressure (rapid decrease in blood pressure can cause fainting). Dantrolene may be useful in cases associated with abnormal calcium regulation, such as post-anaesthetic myopathy. Prognosis for full recovery is good in mild–moderate cases; poor for horses with shock or renal failure.

PREVENTION
In acquired cases, prevention centres on regular exercise and feeding schedules, with no rapid or extreme changes. High fat diets may be advocated. Investigation of cases of ER may determine genetic factors that result in management changes appropriate for specific conditions.
See Electrolyte, Enzyme, Hyperkalaemic periodic paralysis, Ischaemia, Muscle, Myoglobin, Polysaccharide storage myopathy, Post-anaesthetic myopathy.

Exhausted horse syndrome ◀ *ig zor stid / hors / sīn drōm, n.* condition seen in horses that perform sustained endurance activities, after prolonged exercise. Clinical signs include depression, high fever, persistent elevated heart rate, muscle tremors and soreness, short, stiff gait and prolonged capillary refill time, synchronous diaphragmatic flutter, and other signs consistent with dehydration. Intravenous and oral fluid therapy is the cornerstone of treatment, with focus on correcting fluid and electrolyte abnormalities, along with aggressive measures to reduce body temperature (cycles of hosing and scraping, judicious use of non-steroidal anti-inflammatory drugs). Prognosis good for mild to moderately affected horses; severely affected horses may die in spite of intensive treatment. Prevention by good training regimen and early recognition of signs of exhaustion.

Exocrine ◀ *ek sō crīn, adj.* producing, being, or relating to a secretion that is released outside its source, e.g. pancreatic secretion of digestive enzyme (trypsin) into small intestine, salivary gland secretion into mouth.

Exogenous ◀ *ek so ji nēs, adj.* developed or originating outside the animal, c.f. endogenous.

Exophthalmos ◀ *ek sof thal mos, n.* (proptosis) forward displacement or abnormal protrusion of eyeball. Various causes, including space-occupying lesion (e.g. tumour or cyst inside or outside orbit), injury to orbit, or sinus problem (injury, cyst, sinusitis), glaucoma.
See Eye, Glaucoma, Orbit, Sinus.

Exostosis ◄⁞ *eks os tō sis, n.* benign outgrowth from bone; may be capped by cartilage, as with osteochondroma; may develop following inflammation of bone. Seen in splints, where exostoses form between splint bones (2nd and 4th metacarpal or metatarsal bones) and can cause irritation to ligaments between these bones and cannon bones. A rare hereditary condition (hereditary multiple exostoses) causes development of exostoses on long bones, ribs and pelvis.
See Osteochondroma, Splint.

Exotoxin ◄⁞ *ek sō tok sin, n.* toxic protein substance formed and released by certain species of living bacteria, e.g. *Clostridium botulinum* and *tetani,* causing botulism and tetanus, respectively.
See Botulism, *Clostridium,* Tetanus.

Expectorant ◄⁞ *ek spek tē rēnt, n.* substance administered to stimulate removal of mucus from respiratory tract by coughing. Unknown efficacy in horse.

- Liquifying e. – acts by decreasing viscosity of mucus, e.g. fluid therapy.
- Stimulant e. – acts by stimulating respiratory muscles.

See Cough.

Expiration ◄⁞ *ek spi rā shēn, n.* breathing out. Generally a passive act as intercostal muscles and diaphragm relax, and size of thoracic cavity is reduced, so air is pushed out of lungs. In respiratory disorders, an expiratory effort may be seen, e.g. in chronic obstructive pulmonary disease, where abdominal and intercostal muscles help to push air out of lungs.
See Recurrent airway obstruction.

Expression ◄⁞ *ek spre shēn, n.* appearance of face, conveying pain, fear, contentment; expression of a gene is presence of heritable trait in individual that carries gene for that trait.
See Gene.

Extension ◄⁞ *ek sten shēn, n.* movement which straightens a joint, or increases the angle between the bones or parts of the body.

Extensor ◄⁞ *ek sten sē, n.* general term for muscle, or related tendon, which straightens a joint, or causes extension when it contracts. Opposite: flexor.

E. muscle ◄⁞ *ek sten sē / mu sēl, n.*muscle that causes extension.

E. tendon ◄⁞ *ek sten sē / ten dēn, n.*any of several tendons which connect extensor muscles to bone, facilitating extension of a limb.

E. process ◄⁞ *ek sten sē / prō ses, n.* proximal part of anterior 3rd phalanx (coffin bone); point of insertion of main digital extensor tendon. Can be fractured; most fractures appear to be the result of a developmental disorder of cartilage (osteochondrosis), with fracture through abnormal tissue. Fractures typically cause chronic lameness; joint surfaces (between 2nd and 3rd phalanges) are commonly affected; over time, such horses may develop a visible enlargement of the anterior aspect of the coronary band (buttress foot). Typical treatment involves removal of smaller fragments by arthroscopy; lag screw fixation of larger fragments has been described.
See Osteochondrosis.

External ear see Ear

Extirpation ◄⁞ *ek ster pā shēn, n.* complete removal or eradication of a tissue or organ; excision; resection.

Extracorporeal shock wave therapy ◄⁞ *ek strē cor por ēēl / shok / wāv / ther ē pē, n.* (ESWT) a non-invasive surgical procedure that uses sound waves ('shock waves') to treat a number of equine physical disorders, including, but not limited to, navicular syndrome, osteoarthritis, dorsal cortical metacarpal fractures, tendon and ligament disease, and back pain. 'Extracorporeal' means 'outside of the body' and refers to the way the therapy is applied. In spite of extensive use for several years in equine surgery, medicine and rehabilitation, there still seems to be no consensus as to what the treatment actually does, or if, and for what conditions, the treatment is truly effective. The therapy does seem to cause temporary analgesia of some treated areas in some horses; consequently, horses that have received the therapy may be prohibited from performing in certain racing jurisdictions for a period of time after treatment.

Extrasystole ◀€ *ek strē sis tē lē*, *n*. premature contraction of heart occurring out of normal rhythm; results from impulse from some part of heart other than controlling sinoatrial node. Diagnosed by electrocardiography.
See Heart.

Extravasation ◀€ *ek strē va zā shēn*, *n*. escape of fluid (e.g. blood, lymph) from vessel into tissues.

Extremity ◀€ *ek stre mi tē*, *n*. general term describing the furthest or most remote part, especially of an elongated or pointed structure, e.g. hoof, limb, tail.

Exudate ◀€ *ek sū dāt*, *n*. material, such as fluid, cells, or cellular debris, that has escaped from blood vessels and been deposited in tissues or on tissue surfaces; usually accumulates as result of inflammation. Fluid may also contain microorganisms (bacteria, fungi) as result of wound, surgery, etc. (septic exudates). Non-septic exudate may arise from tumour, inflammation of organ (e.g. liver) or presence of irritant (e.g. urine from ruptured bladder).
See Inflammation.

Eye ◀€ *ī*, *n*. organ of vision. The horse has the largest eye of almost any mammal, with a diameter about twice that of humans. Eye designed to help horse avoid becoming prey; close to 350 degree field of monocular vision, good visual acuity, some ability to see colour, relatively poor depth perception because of extensive monocular vision (horse lowers or raises head to assist depth perception). One eye on either side of head, contained within bony orbit which protects the delicate structure. Eyeball (globe) is complex structure made up of three tunics. Those tunics, including their major components, are:
1. Nervous tunic (retina) – made up of cells that are extensions of the optic nerve of the brain. Contains rods, which are light sensitive, and cones, which are responsible for colour vision and visual acuity. The optic disc is the visible white area of central retina where optic nerve leaves retina.
2. Vascular tunic (uvea) – made up of the choroid, the ciliary body, and the iris. Choroid is heavily pigmented and made almost totally of blood vessels; choroid contains the tapetum lucidum, which amplifies light in dark conditions, gives horse superior night vision, and is responsible for the bright colour reflection seen when light is shone into a horse's eye at night. Ciliary body attaches lens to vascular tunic; contains muscles to shape lens to focus light on retina; secretes the liquid aqueous humour. Muscles are relatively weak, compared to other species, so horse tilts head slightly to focus on close objects. Iris is a pigmented band, generally golden to dark brown, but also blue, white, or mixture of colours. Granular corpora nigra arise primarily from the dorsal border of the iris, and may act as a light barrier. Iris is the sphincter muscle around the pupil, the contractile opening in the iris that allows light passage to retina; horse's pupil is horizontally oval in shape, becoming more circular on dilation.
3. Fibrous tunic – made up of the sclera and cornea. The sclera is the tough outer protective coat of eye (includes white of eye), made of dense fibrous collagen and elastin. The cornea is the clear connective tissue covering of the anterior portion of the eye.

Additional important structures of the eye are:

- Aqueous humour – transparent, watery fluid filling the space between the lens and the cornea (anterior chamber). Nutritive to cornea; constantly secreted by ciliary body and drained away into veins.
- Lens – biconvex layered structure which focuses light on to retina.
- Vitreous humour (vitreous body, vitreous) – the clear, colourless transparent jelly that fills the eyeball posterior to the lens and which maintains shape of eyeball. Also believed to function as a barrier to the forward

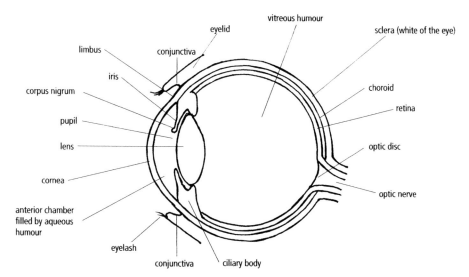

Vertical section through a horse's eye

diffusion of oxygen from the retinal blood supply, to prevent oxidative damage to lens.

Associated structures of eye (adnexa) include eyelids, eyelashes, lacrimal system (see under separate entries).

Eyelash ◀€ *ī lash, n.* (cilium) short hair growing on edge of eyelid.

Eyelid ◀€ *ī lid, n.* upper and lower eyelids are folds of skin lined with conjunctiva, move across eye to protect front of eyeball. Horses also have 3rd eyelid (nictitating membrane) which moves across from inner corner of eye (medial canthus).

F

Face ◀€ *fās*, *n.* front of head, including the mouth, nostrils, cheeks, eyes, and the forehead.

Facial ◀€ *fā shēl*, *adj.* of the face, affecting the face.

    F. nerve ◀€ *fā shēl / nerv*, *n.* cranial nerve VII, supplies muscles of facial expression (muscles in skin which move ears, eyelids, etc.), also innervates some taste buds and salivary and lacrimal glands.
See Cranial nerve.

    F. nerve paralysis ◀€ *fā shēl / nerv / pē ra li sis*, *n.* (facial palsy) paralysis of facial muscles caused by defect in facial nerve, may result in abnormal facial expression, flaccidity of nostril, drooping lip, eyelid, ear, inflammation of cornea (keratitis) through inability to blink. May occur secondary to trauma, surgery (e.g. dental extraction), guttural pouch mycosis, or disease (e.g. rabies). Depending on cause, recovery often occurs spontaneously (depending on site of damage, more likely to recover if distal nerve is damaged), but can be slow.

Facultative ◀€ *fa kēl tē tiv*, *adj.* not obligatory but instead capable of adapting to different conditions; e.g. facultative anaerobe is a microorganism which does not have to live without oxygen, but can do so.

    Facultative aerobe see Aerobe
    Facultative anaerobe see Anaerobe

Faecal ◀€ *fē kēl*, *adj.* of faeces.
See Faeces.

Faecal analysis ◀€ *fē kēl / ē na li sis*, *n.* laboratory examination of faeces, various tests performed:
- Gross examination
  - Presence of worms may be noted.

- Thick mucous strands can indicate delayed faecal passage.
- Blood can be observed
  - Fresh blood indicates source close to rectum;
  - Dark blood indicates digestion, and source from higher in GI tract;
  - Faecal occult blood testing may be performed, but is not a sensitive indicator of disease.
- Faecal flotation – several techniques, using different solutions (sodium nitrate, zinc sulphate, sucrose, sodium chloride). Can help identify parasitic ova or larvae, including nematodes, tapeworms, flagellate cysts, and parasitic mites that have been ingested while grooming or itching.
- Faecal culture – incubation of faecal matter on nutrient base; can help establish parasite species; serial bacterial cultures may help identify bacterial pathogens, e.g. *Salmonella*.
- Faecal sedimentation –fluke eggs (*Fasciola hepatica*) do not rise on faecal flotation tests; sedimentation helps concentrate such ova. Solution is dilute, soapy water; sample poured through gauze in serial steps and evaluated under microscope.
- Direct faecal smear – can identify flagellated and ciliated protozoa (protozoa normally present in horse faeces after 2 weeks of age).
- Baermann procedure – to detect nematode larvae or small adult nematodes. Technique involves placing gauze-wrapped faeces in solution and letting stand; examination of contents of solution in 2–12 hours may show parasites.
- McMaster procedure – used to estimate level of faecal contamination; often

used to determine if an anthelmintic treatment was successful. Uses sodium nitrate solution and special counting chamber. Gives an estimate of eggs per gram of faeces.

- Faecal virus detection – faecal samples may be submitted for detection of suspected viral pathogens, using techniques such as:
  o ELISA
  o Polymerase chain reaction (PCR)
  o Virus isolation.

See *Clostridium*, Cyathostome, ELISA, *Fasciola hepatica*, Lungworm, Nematode, *Parascaris equarum*, Polymerase chain reaction, *Salmonella, Strongyloides, Strongylus* spp., Tapeworm.

Faeces ◄⋮ *fē sēz, n.* (stool, excreta, dung) waste matter, mostly composed of undigested food matter, discharged through anus. Consistency may vary according to state of health and diet, e.g. diarrhoea may indicate infection, hard dry faeces may indicate low intake of water.

Faecolith ◄⋮ *fē kō lith, n.* very hard ball of faeces; may cause obstruction, and therefore colic, and require surgical removal. See Colic.

Fahrenheit ◄⋮ *fa rēn hīt, adj.* (F) a thermometric on scale where water boils at 212°F and freezes at 32°F; commonly used in United States. Normal rectal temperature of horse 99.5–101.0°F. (Named after Gabriel Daniel Fahrenheit, German physicist.)

Failure of passive transfer see Passive transfer

Fallopian tube see Oviduct

False colic see Colic

False negative see Negative

False rig ◄⋮ *fawls / rig, n.* male horse which has been castrated, but which still shows stallion-like behaviour. Almost undoubtedly this is simply a behavioural issue, most likely part of normal social interaction between horses. Approximately 20–30% of castrated horses will continue

to display sexual interest in mares postcastration, and approximately 5% will continue to display aggression towards people. Assertions that false rigs are caused by incorrect castration, with failure to remove epididymal tissue, continued production of testosterone (male hormone) by other tissue, e.g. adrenal cortex or embryonic testicular tissue developed at another site have never been shown to cause stallion-like behaviour; surgery to remove stumps of the spermatic cord in such horses is unadvisable, accordingly. Limiting social contact with other horses, or providing stricter discipline, are most likely to result in more desirable behaviour.

Family ◄⋮ *fa mi lē, n.* in taxonomy, group of animals related to each other; in classification, family (e.g. Equidae) is intermediate between order (e.g. Perissodactyla) and genus (e.g. *Equus*).

Faradism ◄⋮ *fa rē dizm, n.* the application of a faradic (induced) current of electricity, typically for therapeutic purposes. Technique used in physiotherapy, where rhythmic electrical stimulation applied locally to muscles. Various rationales for application; no scientific support for claims in horses. (Named after Michael Faraday, English physicist 1791–1867.) See Physiotherapy.

Farcy ◄⋮ *far sē, n.* cutaneous form of glanders. See Glanders.

Farrier ◄⋮ *fa rē ē, n.* person who makes and fits horseshoes. Training strictly controlled in UK, includes 5 years' training and examination set by Worshipful Company of Farriers. No such standards in United States.

Fascia ◄⋮ *fā shē ē, n.* the soft tissue component of the connective tissue system; functions include maintaining structural integrity, providing support and protection for tissues and organs, and acting as a shock absorber. Essential role in various body functions, and provides the framework for intercellular communication. Fascia is also the body's first line of defence against infectious agents. The fascia creates an environment for tissue repair post-injury. There are three types:

- Superficial f. – found under the skin in most regions of the body.
- Deep f. – dense fibrous connective tissue that surrounds muscles, ligaments, and bones, e.g. tendon, ligament, and periosteum.
- Visceral f. – tissue that suspends the organs in the thorax or abdomen and covers them in membranous layers of connective tissue.

F. lata ◀€ _fa_ shē ē / lar tar, n. the deep fascia of the horse's thigh.

Fasciola hepatica ◀€ _fa_ sē ō lē / he _pa_ ti kē, n. liver fluke, infection rare in horse, may be seen more in donkeys. Adult liver flukes lay eggs in the bile, which pass into the intestine and exit in the faeces. Immature fluke penetrates a snail after hatching to continue life cycle, and multiplies. Flukes leave snail and encyst on grass, where they are eaten by grazing horses. Young parasites penetrate the gut and pass to the liver. Animals experience anaemia, weight loss, decreased growth, and oedema. Severe infestation causes damage to liver, liver scarring, and possible liver failure. Diagnosis confirmed by demonstration of fluke eggs in faeces. Flukes may be found in lungs after aberrant migration of larvae. Control by draining standing water from pasture to control snails, and by applying copper sulphate to the pasture. Infected animals may be treated with a flukicide.

Fasciotomy ◀€ _fa_ sē _o_ tē mē, n. incision of fascia; important in treatment of bacterial myositis, e.g. as caused by *Clostridium* spp.; fasciotomy of the tissue surrounding palmar digital nerves has been performed for treatment of navicular syndrome, without success; fasciotomy of the tissue surrounding the suspensory ligament has been reported as a successful treatment for hind limb suspensory ligament desmitis.
See *Clostridium*, Navicular syndrome, Suspensory ligament.

Fasting hyperbilirubinaemia see Bilirubinaemia

Fat ◀€ _fat_, n. **1)** adipose tissue, composed of fatty acids combined with glycerol, which is deposited in various locations and provides a store of energy for animal; also serves as an important endocrine organ; **2)** a major class of energy-providing foods, any of the many compounds of carbon, hydrogen, and oxygen that are glycerides of fatty acids, and as dietary sources for horses are found in numerous plants; needed in horse's diet for the absorption of fat-soluble vitamins; **3)** obese.

Fatigue ◀€ _fē_ tēg, n. **1)** weariness or exhaustion, often accompanied by significant losses in water, energy and electrolytes (exercise fatigue); **2)** the temporary loss of ability to respond to a stimulus in a sensory receptor or motor end organ caused by continued stimulation (e.g. nerve fatigue); **3)** the tendency of a material to break down under repetitive stress (e.g. tendon fatigue as a predisposing cause for tendon injury).
See Tendon.

Fatty acid ◀€ _fa_ tē / _a_ sid, n. major component of fat, organic molecule composed of long chain (length of which varies between types of fatty acid) of carbon, with hydrogen and oxygen; occur naturally, most commonly in fats, waxes, and essential oils. Deficiencies of fatty acids are unknown in horses.

Volatile f.a. ◀€ _vo_ lē til / _fa_ tē / _a_ sid, n. fatty acids with a carbon chain of six carbons or fewer. Created by bacterial fermentation in the large colon of the horse, and important source of energy.

Feathers ◀€ _fe_ thēz, n. long hairs around pastern, seen especially in draught horses and some ponies. May predispose to pastern dermatitis, especially in moist conditions.
See Dermatitis.

Febrile ◀€ _fē_ brīl, n. having a fever, pyrexic, temperature above 38°C (101°F).
See Fever.

Feces see Faeces

Feed ◀╎ *fēd*, *n./v.* food; give food to animal.

Fell Pony immunodeficiency syndrome ◀╎ *fel / pō nē / i mū nō de fi shen sē / sin drōm*, *n.* syndrome of anaemia, immunodeficiency, and peripheral ganglionopathy, first described in the 1990s in Fell Pony (hardy pony native to north England) foals in England, and more recently in Holland. Foals are normal at birth, but begin showing clinical signs of disease at 2–4 weeks.
Signs include unthriftiness, anaemia (often severe due to undeveloped bone marrow), respiratory infection and diarrhoea. Genetic defect with autosomal recessive transmission. No treatment, any affected foal dies by 3 months of age.

Femoral ◀╎ *fe mē rūl*, *adj.* of the femur or thigh region.
See Femur.

> **F. nerve** ◀╎ *fe mē rūl / nerv*, *n.* nerve which innervates major muscles at front of thigh, especially quadriceps femoris. Damage to nerve causes inability to bear weight or extend and fix stifle.

Femoropatellar joint ◀╎ *fe mē rō pa te lē / joint*, *n.* one of the joints of the stifle; the articulation between the kneecap (patella) and the femur.

Femorotibial joint ◀╎ *fe mē rō ti bi ūl / joint*, *n.* one of the joints of the stifle; the articulation between the femur and the tibia. Complex joint, with medial and lateral sacs, two menisci, and anterior and posterior cruciate ligaments between sacs.
See Cruciate, Meniscus.

Femur ◀╎ *fē mē*, *n.* thigh bone, forms hip joint at top (proximal) end with pelvis, and stifle joint at lower (distal) end with tibia and patella. At proximal end is the head of the femur ('ball'), which articulates with the acetabulum of the hip bone (formed where the three bones of the hip, the ilium, the ischium, and pubis, meet; 'socket'). Prominences on the lateral aspect of the femur (greater, lesser and third trochanters) serve as attachments for

muscle and tendon; greater and third can be felt on lateral thigh. At distal end, lateral and medial condyles form stifle joint, and create a groove (trochlea) for the patella. Lateral condyle can be felt on outer side of stifle joint.
See Hip, Patella, Stifle.

Fenbendazole ◀╎ *fen ben dē zōl*, *n.* anthelmintic of benzimidazole group, used primarily to treat strongyles, pinworms and ascarids. The normal dose of fenbendazole is 5 mg/kg bwt; however, higher doses are safe. In foals, weanlings and yearlings, fenbendazole can be dosed at 10 mg/kg for higher efficacy. For control of fourth stage (migrating) larvae of *Strongylus vulgaris* and/or encysted early L3, late L3 and L4 cyathostome larvae, the dose is 10 mg/kg daily for 5 consecutive days, with approximately 75% efficacy according to one study.
See Anthelmintic, Benzimidazole.

Fenestra ◀╎ *fe nes trē*, *n.* small pores in epithelial cells that allow rapid exchange of molecules between blood vessels and tissues, which can enlarge and contract in response to various stimuli; in anatomy, the term refers to natural window-like openings in the skull or bones, e.g. openings in inner wall of middle ear.

Fermentation ◀╎ *fer mēn tā shen*, *n.* breakdown of carbohydrates by bacteria and yeasts, most importantly into volatile fatty acids and methane gas. Essential part of digestion in horse; allows for efficient digestion of complex carbohydrates. Occurs primarily in caecum and colon.
See Digestion.

Ferritin ◀╎ *fe ri tin*, *n.* form of iron (iron–apoferritin); an iron-storage protein in body.

Fertile ◀╎ *fer tīl*, *adj.* capable of reproduction, e.g. of conceiving young or producing viable sperm.

Fertilization ◀╎ *fer ti lī zā shen*, *n.* (conception) process in which gametes fuse, i.e. the male's capacitated spermatozoon fuses with female's egg (oocyte) to produce single-celled zygote. Occurs in oviduct of mare. Sperm and egg are both haploid (have unpaired chromosomes – 32 in horse), once joined they form a normal diploid cell with normal complement of paired chromosomes (32 pairs in horse; total of 64). Once one sperm has fused with egg, the egg's cell membrane changes, which prevents other sperm penetrating it (the process is called egg activation).

Fescue grass ◀≷ *fes cū / grars, n.* (*Festuca* spp.and *Vulpia* spp.) narrow-leaved grass, present in some pastures; suitable pasture grass. However, if infested with ergot fungus, and eaten by mare in late pregnancy, can cause lack of milk production, retention of placenta and weak foal.
See Ergot.

Fetlock ◀≷ *fet lok, n.* joint between cannon bone (third metacarpal or third metatarsal bone) and first (proximal) phalanx, in front and hind legs. Proximal sesamoid bones are located at back of joint. Disease conditions affecting fetlock joint include fractures (of first phalanx, proximal sesamoid bone or distal part of cannon bone), luxation (disruption of ligaments allowing displacement of joint), osteochondrosis, sesamoiditis, deformity (angular or flexural), osteoarthritis.
See conditions under separate headings.

Fever ◀≷ *fē vē, n.* (pyrexia) elevated body temperature, above 38°C (101°F). Generally associated with infections of various causes. Besides elevated body temperature, other indications of fever include sweating, fast breathing (tachypnoea), fast heart rate (tachycardia), thirst, poor appetite.

Fibre ◀≷ *fī bē, n.* thread-like anatomical structure, e.g. processes of nerve cells, components of muscles; dietary fibre is any of the complex carbohydrates of plants which cannot be broken down by animal's digestive enzymes. Dietary fibre is composed of cellulose, the 'skeleton' of plants, hemicellulose, gums, lignin, pectin and other carbohydrates, which are digestible by Equidae from fermentation in colon and caecum.

Fibrillation ◀≷ *fi bri lā shēn, n.* a small, local, involuntary contraction of muscle, resulting from the action of single muscle cells or muscle fibres that have been deprived of their nerve supply, e.g. atrial or ventricular fibrillation of heart as individual heart muscle fibrils contract in uncoordinated fashion; in osteoarthritis, describes the first degenerative changes in articular cartilage, characterized by softening of cartilage and the development of clefts between groups of cartilage cells.
See Atrial, Cartilage, Ventricular.

Fibrin ◀≷ *fi brin, n.* insoluble protein formed in blood clotting by action of thrombin on fibrinogen. Forms a structural mat of fibres in which blood cells, platelets, etc. are caught to form a clot.
See Clotting.

> **F. degradation products** ◀≷ *fi brin / de grē dā shēn / pro dukts, n.* (FDPs) the substances left behind when clots dissolve. High levels of FDPs may be found in disseminated intravascular coagulation and hepatic disease, for example.
> See Disseminated.

Fibrinogen ◀≷ *fi bri nō jēn, n.* plasma protein formed mostly in liver, essential in blood clotting, where thrombin converts soluble fibrinogen into insoluble fibrin. Fibrinogen levels increase with inflammatory conditions, such as peritonitis and pleuropneumonia, and may be monitored to assess recovery.
See Clotting, Fibrin, Peritonitis, Pleuritis/Pleuropneumonia.

Fibroblast ◀≷ *fi brō blarst, n.* a connective tissue cell; differentiates into various structural cells that form the fibrous, supporting and binding tissues of the horse's body.

Fibrocartilage see Cartilage

Fibroma ◀≷ *fi brō mē, n.* benign tumour made up of fibrous tissue; also called fibroid or fibroid tumour.

> **Ossifying f.** ◀≷ *os i fi ing / fi brō mē, n.* develops from intramembranous bone of jaw (mandible), especially in young horses;

may occur secondary to trauma in some horses. Signs relate to location and size of the tumour, but may include difficulty with prehension, chewing, lymphadenopathy, and oral mucosal bleeding; tumour is often large before clinical signs seen because of adaptation of oral cavity. Complete surgical excision of mass is curative, but cosmetic outcome should be discussed prior to surgery.

Fibronectin ◄⊰ *fi brō nek tin, n.* protein produced by fibroblasts, and epithelial and endothelial cells. A crucial part of early wound healing process. Acts as a physiological adhesive among components of wound healing.

Fibrosis ◄⊰ *fi brō sis, n.* formation of fibrous tissue; normally occurs as part of the repair process of organs and tissues, e.g. as a wound scar, or after chronic inflammation of an organ, (e.g. hepatic fibrosis following chronic hepatitis, fibrosing alveolitis of chronic lung inflammation).
See Fibrous tissue.

Fibrotic myopathy ◄⊰ *fi bro tik / mī o path ē, n.* cause of hind limb gait abnormality due to fibrous tissue in large muscle groups from muscle or nerve damage. Usually secondary to limb trauma, such as kick, slipping, or trailering accident. Affected legs have a short, 'stabby' action with little or no bend in the hock and stifle. The horse often 'slaps' the ground at the walk, pulling the hoof back several inches at the end of the forward swing phase of the stride before slapping the hoof on the ground. Signs dependent on degree of muscle involvement. Affected horses may not show obvious lameness, and may not require further intervention; however, successful surgeries to remove the fibrous tissue causing the problem have been described.

Fibrous dysplasia ◄⊰ *fi brēs / dis plā zē ē, n.* benign condition of bone where there is proliferation of fibrous tissue; not unlike ossifying fibroma, and perhaps part of the same process. Has been described in sinuses, jaw bone (mandible), and acces-

sory carpal bone (causing severe lameness) of horses. Depending on location, surgical excision is curative.

Fibrous tissue ◄⊰ *fi brēs / ti sū, n.* connective tissue of the body, composed of fibres (primarily collagen), produced by fibroblast cells. Strong tissue, makes up tendons, ligaments, bone matrix (before it is calcified), basis of cartilage, holds muscle fibres together, etc. For the most part, fibrous tissue does not contain living cells; the tissue is mainly composed of polysaccharides, proteins and water. Laid down as scars where tissues are healing. Some fibrous tissue has greater concentrations of elastin fibres, which are elastic, and supplies flexibility to tissues that need to expand, e.g. in walls of arteries and in some ligaments.

Fibula ◄⊰ *fi bū lē, n.* small bone, somewhat vestigal, lies roughly parallel to tibia in hind leg, fused to lateral side of tibia at top and bottom.

Fiddleneck ◄⊰ *fi dl nek, n. (Amsinckia)* N. American plant; gets name from flower stems, which have many small flowers, and curl over at the top in a manner that looks like a violin. Seeds are the most toxic part of plant. Poisonings result from feeding seed-contaminated grain or hay containing dried fiddleneck plants. Inadvertent consumption in lush pasture is also possible. Normally unpalatable but may be eaten if withered, e.g. in hay. Contains pyrrolizidine alkaloids which can cause liver failure. Clinical signs vary, and may include behavioural changes, such as dullness, depression, and wandering, head pressing, photosensitization, weight loss, bleeding disorders, and jaundice. Blood tests and liver biopsy are useful in diagnosing liver toxicity.
See Pyrrolizidine.

Filaria ◄⊰ *fi lǎ rē ē, n.* very thin, threadlike nematode worms of family Filaroididae; adults are parasites in the blood or tissues, and larvae usually develop in biting insects; e.g. *Onchocerca*.
See *Onchocerca*.

Filariasis ◀ᴇ *fi lĕ rī ĕ sis, n.* disease caused by infestation with filarial nematode worms.

Film ◀ᴇ *film, n.* **1)** thin layer, e.g. blood film is a very thin layer of blood smeared over a microscope slide for examination of cells; **2)** thin flexible transparent sheet with a radiation-sensitive emulsion for making radiographs, e.g. X-ray film; **3)** an abnormal growth on or in the eye.

Filtration angle see Angle

Fine needle aspirate ◀ᴇ *fin / nēd l / as pi rāt, n.* diagnostic procedure, most commonly used in the diagnosis of superficial skin lumps or masses. To perform the procedure, a thin, hollow needle is inserted into the mass, and cells are aspirated with a syringe. The cells are then examined under a microscope.

Firing ◀ᴇ *fi ĕ ring, v.* archaic veterinary treatment for injury and inflammation, e.g. of tendons of lower limb. Skin burnt by application of red-hot iron; forced horse to rest. Considered unethical by RCVS; no scientific basis for use.

First aid ◀ᴇ *ferst / ād, n.* emergency care given to injured or ill animal before full veterinary care can be given. Useful items in a first aid kit may include emergency telephone numbers (veterinary surgeon, doctor), torch (flashlight), antiseptic wound cleaner, bandages, dressings, cotton wool, thermometer.

First phalanx ◀ᴇ *ferst / fa langks, n.* (long pastern bone, proximal phalanx) bone of lower leg, forms fetlock joint with cannon bone proximally and pastern joint with second phalanx distally. Conditions which affect bone include fractures and osteoarthritis, accompanied by varying degrees of pain, lameness, swelling. Diagnosis of conditions involving the first phalanx includes physical examination, diagnostic anaesthesia, and radiography.
See Cannon, Fetlock, Pastern.

Fissure fracture ◀ᴇ *fi shĕ / frak tŭr, n.* longitudinal crack in a bone which does

not go through full thickness of bone. Cause of lameness; if condition not recognized, can progress to more severe fracture, e.g. fissure fracture of third carpal bone may progress to slab fracture.

Fistula ◀ᴇ *fis tū lĕ, n.* abnormal passage between two organs or between organ and skin; abnormality may be congenital, or acquired secondary to injury. Such passages have also been created surgically for experimental studies of digestive secretions.
    Aorto-cardiac f. ◀ᴇ *ā or tō - kar dē ak / fis tū lĕ, n.* arising from the right aortic sinus, especially in middle aged to older stallions.
    Ear f. see Dentigerous
    Oesophageal f. ◀ᴇ *e so fĕ jē ŭl / fis tū lĕ, n.* fistula from oesophagus to skin; may occur secondary to oesophagotomy incision, or from perforation (wound, foreign body).
    Rectovaginal/Rectovestibular f. see Rectovaginal
    Salivary duct f. ◀ᴇ *sĕ lī vĕ rē / duct / fis tū lĕ, n.* from the parotid salivary duct to the skin; treated by surgical repair of the duct, translocation of the duct, or chemical ablation of the gland.

Fistulography ◀ᴇ *fis tū lo grĕ fĕ, n.* injection of radio-opaque contrast material into a fistula in an effort to determine point of origin, or the presence of foreign bodies, e.g. as performed in the evaluation of draining wound tracts.

Fistulous withers ◀ᴇ *fis tū lĕs / wi thēz, n.* discharging sinus(es) at top of withers region. Often caused by bacterial infection and chronic inflammation in supraspinous bursa (fluid-filled membranous sac which lies over dorsal spinous processes of thoracic vertebrae). Most commonly associated with *Brucella abortus* and *Actinomyces bovis.*

Fixation ◀ᴇ *fik sā shēn, n.* holding or fastening in fixed position.
    Complement f. test see Complement
    Internal f. ◀ᴇ *in ter nēl / fik sā shēn, n.* open reduction and stabilization of fractures using devices implanted in bone, such as bone screws and wires.

Fixative ◀ː *fĭk sē tiv, n.* **1)** chemical, or groups of chemicals, used to preserve biopsy specimens for histological or cytological examination, e.g. formalin; **2)** photographic chemical used to preserve picture (e.g. in radiograph development). See Formalin.

Flail cusp ◀ː *flāl / kusp, n.* torn leaf of heart valve, may occur in aortic or pulmonic valve. Causes acute insufficiency of affected valve, with heart murmur and blood flow in wrong direction. Diagnosis by echocardiography.
See Echocardiography, Heart.

Flap ◀ː *flap, n.* mass of tissue, usually including skin, which is partially detached from one part of body. May be caused by injury, or created surgically to be used as skin or conjunctival graft, in which case blood supply must be preserved.

Flatulence ◀ː *fla tū lēns, n.* excessive production and accumulation of gas in intestines.

Flatus ◀ː *flā tēs, n.* gas produced in intestines, and expelled through rectum; produced during digestion by fermentation of food.

Flatworm ◀ː *flat werm, n.* internal parasite with a flattened cross-section (c.f. roundworms): examples are liver fluke (e.g. *Fasciola hepatica*) and tapeworms (e.g. *Anoplocephala* spp.).
See *Anoplocephala, Fasciola hepatica.*

Flavivirus ◀ː *fla vē vī rēs, n.* a family of viruses with three genera, containing some of the most important human pathogens in the world. Disease carried by vectors (especially mosquitoes), and transmits naturally between the blood of avian and mammalian hosts; iatrogenic infection also possible. In horses, flaviviruses cause Japanese B encephalitis and West Nile virus disease.
See Japanese B encephalitis, West Nile virus.

Flax ◀ː *flaks, n.* (*Linum* spp.) plant grown as crop (for linseed oil); contains cyano-genic glycosides and can cause poisoning if eaten.

Flaxseed see Linseed

Flea ◀ː *flē, n.* small parasitic insect, sucks blood. Common fleas in USA and UK do not commonly affect horses, but are not host specific, and large infestations have been occasionally reported with various species, including the cat flea (*Ctenocephalides felis*), sticktight flea (*Echidnophaga gallinacea*, found in tropical areas, where usual host is chicken) and jigger flea (*Tunga penetrans*, found in tropical areas of Africa and America). Environmental control (stripping stable and spraying stable and barn) is critical for successful treatment, since fleas spend most of their time off the horse.

Flehmen ◀ː *flā mēn, n.* (Flehmen response) behavioural action performed by stallion and other mammals, involving stretching the neck, raising the head, and rolling the upper lip back towards the nostrils. Thought to facilitate transfer of pheromones and smells to the vomeronasal organ, a chemoreceptor organ which is thought to have to do with the perception of such information. Also may be shown in colic and by mare in early stage of foaling.

Flexion ◀ː *flek shēn, n.* the act of bending, or being bent, normally of leg or joint.
　　F. test ◀ː *flek shēn / test, n.* test performed to help diagnosis of lameness, or in the performance of a purchase examination, especially of fetlock joint or hind limb ('hock flexion'). Area in question is held flexed for a period of time and with an applied force customary for the examiner (there is no standard), then released. Immediately after release, horse's gait is watched to check for differences between gaits before and after flexion. Test is extremely non-specific; every structure in the forelimb from hoof to carpus has been reported to respond positively to a flexion test. Furthermore, it can be difficult to flex only one joint, especially in the hind limb. Finally, several studies have shown that flexion tests have no predictive value in sound horses, that is, a positive flexion test cannot predict the occurrence of lameness in the future.

Flexor ◀€ _flek_ sē, _adj_. causing flexion; any muscle which flexes a joint when the muscle contracts.

> **F. tendon** ◀€ _flek_ sē / _ten dĕn, n_. any tendon which facilitates the action of a flexor muscle on a bone or joint, e.g. superficial digital flexor tendon, deep digital flexor tendon. Common area of injury to performance horses.
> See Tendon.

Flexural deformity ◀€ _flek_ shē _rūl / di for mi tē, n_. limb abnormality where the soft tissue structures on the forelimb, and less commonly the hind limb, cause the bones of the affected limb to align in varying degrees of flexion. Although there is much speculation, the pathogenesis of flexural deformities remains unknown. May be congenital or acquired problem. Factors involved in congenital deformities may include malpositioning in utero, ingestion of toxins by the pregnant mare, such as locoweed or Sudan grass, genetic collagen defects, and most likely many as yet unidentified predisposing genetic factors. Multiple factors may be involved in a given case. Acquired deformities show themselves differently depending on the age of the horse. As with congenital deformities, there are many potential causes, including factors important in the development of osteochondrosis. Common features of acquired deformities include fast growing individuals on a high plane of nutrition; foals who have previously been on a poor plane of nutrition may develop a flexural deformity when placed on a higher quality diet. Acquired deformities may develop secondary to limb pain from a variety of causes, including trauma, osteochondrosis, physitis, and joint infection, all of which may result in an altered stance and flexion withdrawal of the limb. If the altered stance persists, soft tissues can contract, and a flexural deformity will result. Two age groups most commonly develop acquired flexural deformities: deformities of the coffin (distal interphalangeal) joint occur relatively early, usually at 1–4 months of age; deformities of the fetlock (metacarpo- or metatarsophalangeal) joint are usually seen later, at 12–14 months of age. Among the reasons

for the age difference is that the growth of the distal limb is mostly finished by three months of age, but the upper limb continues to grow for much longer. If the deep digital flexor tendon is involved, a flexural deformity affecting the foot will result, because this tendon attaches to the coffin bone (distal phalanx). When the superficial flexor tendon is involved, the deformity will appear at the level of the fetlock joint. Severity varies from only occasional knuckling when weight bearing, to permanently knuckling over. Treatment may involve oxytetracycline administration in early cases; splinting of limbs, shoeing methods, or various surgeries may be employed.

Floated heel see Heel

Floating ◀€ _flō_ ting, _v_. rasping molar teeth to remove sharp points; floating in this case is defined in the sense of making level and smooth. Rasp used for this purpose called a float.
See Tooth.

Floppy valve see Valvular

Flu see Equine influenza

Fluconazole ◀€ _flŭ con ē zōl, n_. antifungal drug used in the treatment and prevention of superficial and systemic fungal infections. Inhibits important fungal enzyme activity. Primarily fungistatic (controls growth but does not kill fungus, except at high doses). In horses, has been primarily used to treat fungal keratitis.

Fluid ◀€ _flŭ_ id, _n./adj_. substance which can flow, i.e. liquid or gas, although in medicine, primarily used in reference to liquids.

> **Amniotic f.** ◀€ _am_ nē _ot_ ik / _flŭ_ id, _n_. the watery fluid within the foetal amnion in which the embryo and foetus is suspended. See Pregnancy.
> **Cerebrospinal f.** see Cerebrospinal
> **F. balance** ◀€ _flŭ_ id / _ba_ lĕns, _n_. the concept that the amount of fluid lost from the horse's body should be equal to the amount of fluid taken in. Fluid is lost through sweating, urination, respiration, defecation, as part of

normal body metabolic processes; fluid is taken in primarily through eating and drinking. If either too much fluid is lost, or too much is taken in, there are physical consequences.

F. therapy ◄⁞ _flŭ id_ / _the rē pē, n._ administration of fluid to treat dehydration, acid–base imbalances, shock, blood loss, etc. Fluid may be given intravenously or orally, depends on condition and type of fluid. Type of fluid used and route of administration varies depending on condition treated. Commonly contains electrolytes; less commonly dextrose (glucose). Fluid may be hypotonic (less concentrated than blood), hypertonic (more concentrated than blood) or isotonic (same concentration as normal blood). Hypotonic fluids, e.g. water, are given orally, to prevent blood cell lysis. Isotonic fluids, e.g. lactated Ringer's solution, are most commonly used to provide intravenous fluid support for a variety of conditions. Hypertonic solutions, e.g. hypertonic saline, may be used in treatment of acute shock; the fluids tend to hold water in the system until large volumes of isotonic fluids can be provided. Other types of fluids used in therapy include blood transfusion in cases of severe blood loss, bicarbonate-containing and dextrose-containing fluids for foals with severe diarrhoea which have low blood pH (acidosis) and low blood sugar (hypoglycaemia), or plasma transfusions in cases of failure of passive transfer.

Synovial f. ◄⁞ _sı nō vē ūl_ / _flŭ id, n._ thick, transparent fluid secreted by membrane of a joint, bursa, or tendon sheath; lubricates and provides nutrition.

Fluke ◄⁞ _flŭk, n._ parasitic flatworm, often leaf-like in shape, e.g. liver fluke (_Fasciola hepatica_).
See _Fasciola hepatica._

Flunixin meglumine ◄⁞ _flŭ nik sin_ / _meg lŭ mēn, n._ non-steroidal anti-inflammatory drug, analgesic, antipyretic, and antiendotoxic; cyclooxygenase inhibitor. Commonly prescribed for treatment of colic, although limited evidence that it is more effective than other drugs of same type. Available as solution for injection, granule, or paste. Side effects as per other drugs of this type, including gastric ulcer-

ation, particularly at high, sustained doses. The use of flunixin is prohibited or restricted by many equestrian organizations under their rules of competition.
See Colic, Cyclooxygenase.

Fluorescein ◄⁞ _flor ē sēn, n._ orange dye with yellow–green fluorescence, seen especially with ultraviolet light. Used as topical eye stain to detect corneal ulcers (ulcer stains green; normal cornea does not stain). Had been previously used in an effort to determine viability of intestine during surgery for colic: injected intravenously, fluorescein is rapidly distributed, and fluorescence can be seen with ultraviolet light. It was hoped that if area of intestine had poor blood supply, e.g. because it had been strangulated, there would be no or poor fluorescence; however, studies showed that the predictive value of the technique was only about 50%, so its use has been generally abandoned.

Fluorquinolone see Enrofloxacin

Fluoroscopy ◄⁞ _flor ro sko pē, n._ use of fluorescent screen to capture real-time X-ray images, which can then be viewed on monitor or printed as hard copies. May be used instead of traditional X-ray machine, but more expensive, resolution not as good, and higher radiation exposure. Has been used to observe movement of body structures (e.g. joints) and dynamic body functions (e.g. swallowing – also involves use of contrast medium such as barium), especially in human medicine. Can also be used intraoperatively to check on placement of implants. In equine medicine, largely replaced by digital radiographic machines.

Fluorosis ◄⁞ _flor rō sis, n._ condition caused by eating excessive amounts of fluorine, in horses may be caused by contamination of pasture or water from manufacturing or mining operations. Horses are most commonly affected during growth. Signs include mottled teeth, stiffness, bony outgrowths on bones, especially cannon bone. Diagnosis can be difficult, because of extended time period between ingestion and appearance of clinical signs.

Diagnosis based primarily on history of exposure and typical lesions. Radiography, which may show bony outgrowths or osteoporosis, can be supportive. The effects of fluorosis are not reversible.

Fluphenazine ◄€ *flŭ fen ē zēn, n.* fluphenazine is an antipsychotic drug used to treat psychoses in people, such as schizophrenia or bipolar depression. Chemically, it is distantly related to acepromazine; however, it is much more potent. Fluphenazine has gained some popularity in show horse circles as a long-term calming agent. There is no information available as to how well the drug works, nor have standard doses been established in horses. Severe side effects are occasionally reported in horses given fluphenazine, including progressive agitation and unusual repetitive motions. These usually resolve with treatment over a few days.

Flurbiprofen ◄€ *fler bi prō fen, n.* a non-steroidal anti-inflammatory drug; in horses, most commonly used topically, for the treatment of inflammatory eye conditions such as uveitis or keratitis, especially where corticosteroid therapy is contraindicated.

Fluticasone dipropionate ◄€ *flŭ ti ka zōn / dī prō pe o nāt, n.* fluticasone is an inhaled corticosteroid drug, used with inhalers designed for horses in the treatment of airway problems such as recurrent airway disease. Inhaled steroids are a very effective treatment for inflamed air passages; the inhaled route of administration is considered a topical application of the drugs. Because fluticasone is applied topically, the dose of steroids is quite low, compared to what is necessary when steroids are given by other routes of administration for the treatment of airway disease. A lower dose is typically associated with fewer side effects in the administration of any drug.

Fly ◄€ *flī, n.* member of group of insects which belong to order Diptera (two-winged flies). A large order that contains an estimated 240,000 species of mosquitoes, gnats, midges and others, with less than half of those having been identified.

Extremely important, both in terms of ecology and medicine; in medicine, especially as disease vectors. Several may affect horses, e.g. the mosquitoes (*Culicidae*), which spread diseases such as viral encephalitis, equine infectious anaemia, and West Nile virus; *Culicoides* spp. (midges) can spread disease, and allergy to bites causes sweet itch; *Stomoxys* spp. (stable fly) bites horses and is intermediate host of *Habronema microstomum* (stomach worm, occurs in US); *Haematobia* spp. (horn fly) has painful bite; *Gastrophilus* (horse bot) larvae develop in horse stomach; *Hypoderma* (warble fly) intestinal parasite, larvae migrate and can cause abscesses in back; *Tabanus* spp. (horse fly) has painful bite, etc. Control by environmental management, e.g. general cleanliness, removal of standing water sources; use of insect repellents often helpful in individual animals.
See Bot, Encephalitis, Equine infectious anaemia, Warbles, West Nile virus.

Foal ◄€ *fōl, n./v.* 1) newborn horse of either gender, term may be used to 1 year of age, or until weaning; 2) to give birth to a foal.
  F. heat ◄€ *fōl / hēt, n.* oestrus 7–9 days after foaling; normal in post-partum mares. Mares may be bred at this heat, but pregnancy rates are generally lower than at later oestruses.
  F. heat diarrhoea ◄€ *fōl / hēt / dī ē rē ē, n.* commonly observed period of transient diarrhoea at foal heat. Has been previously attributed to migrating parasites; however, more likely because at that time foal's gastrointestinal tract is undergoing normal changes.
See Oestrus.

Foaling see Parturition

Focal ◄€ *fō kēl, adj.* occurring in a small area, e.g. a disease which is not spread throughout body. A focal chorioretinopathy is a small area of loss of pigment in fundus of eye, not believed to affect vision.

Focus ◄€ *fō kēs, n.* a point at which rays of light converge; a localized area of disease or the chief centre of a generalized disease, e.g. the focus of an infection.

Foetal atelectasis see Atelectasis

Foetotomy ◀⟨ *fē to tē mē*, *n.* cutting apart of foetus in utero. May be required to save mare in difficult foaling (dystocia) or in cases of foetal death; generally Caesarian section is preferred, if possible, as it allows for possibility of saving foal in dystocia, and lessens chance of uterine injury in other circumstances.
See Dystocia.

Foetus ◀⟨ *fē tēs*, *n.* unborn foal, from day 40 of pregnancy until birth. Up to day 40 is called embryo.

Foley catheter see Catheter

Folic acid ◀⟨ *fō lik / a sid*, *n.* a water-soluble vitamin of the B group, occurring naturally in feed. Folate is necessary for the production and maintenance of new cells. Although commonly supplemented in prepartum human females to assist normal foetal development, research suggests folic acid supplementation is not necessary in normal mares. However, mares receiving long-term sulphadiazine, sulphamethoxazole-trimethoprim, or pyrimethamine during gestation (e.g. for equine protozoal myelitis) may be at risk for having foals with congenital defects related to folic acid deficiency; this deficiency is not prevented by supplementation.

Follicle ◀⟨ *fo li kēl*, *n.* sac or small cavity, e.g. hair follicle is sheath surrounding root of hair; ovarian follicle is sac of fluid containing egg (ovum), develops in response to hormonal stimuli and ruptures at ovulation to release egg.
  F. stimulating hormone ◀⟨ *fo li kūl / sti mū lā ting / hor mōn*, *n.* (FSH) hormone produced by anterior lobe of pituitary gland in brain. Stimulates growth of ovarian follicle in mare; normally, works to achieve final maturation and ovulation of follicle. In mares, FSH surges late in oestrus and peaks early in dioestrus, then drops slightly; a second surge starts in mid-dioestrus, peaking in late dioestrus. Therapeutically, FSH has been used to induce follicular development in transitional mares and problem mares who are not cycling, as well as to superovulate cycling mares. Thought to stimulate testicular function in stallion.

Follicular ◀⟨ *fo li kū lē*, *adj.* of a follicle, either hair follicle, or especially ovarian follicle.
  F. cyst (ovary) ◀⟨ *fo li kū lē / sistē (o vē rē)*, *n.* abnormally large, fluid-filled structure on ovary that may persist despite treatment, or occasionally regress spontaneously. May interfere with oestrous cycle. Draining the cyst has been reported as successful treatment.
See Cyst.
  F. cyst (skin) ◀⟨ *fo li kū lē / sist (skin)*, *n.* uncommon skin problem, classified according to their epithelial lining; cause unknown. Most occur on head or distal limbs as well-defined cystic lesions. Cysts usually contain a mucus-like filling. F. cysts may be observed (no treatment) or removed surgically.
  F. dysplasia ◀⟨ *fo li kū lē / dis plā zē ē*, *n.* congenital defect characterized by patches of short, brittle, dull hair, which usually develop to areas of little hair cover. Diagnosis by biopsy; no effective treatment. May be more common in curly coated horses.

Folliculitis ◀⟨ *fo li kū lī tis*, *n.* inflammation of follicles, usually in reference to hair follicles; often seen on back. May be caused by bacterial infection (*Staphylococcus aureus*, *Rhodococcus equi*); often associated with poorly fitting tack, external parasites, or lack of grooming.

Fomite ◀⟨ *fō mīt*, *n.* an object, such as a feeder, blanket, brush, or water bucket, that is not in itself harmful, but which can harbour or transmit pathogenic microorganisms, and in so doing can serve to perpetuate disease outbreaks.

Foot ◀⟨ *füt*, *n.* the keratin covered termination of the limb. In horse this includes (working from outside in):
• Hoof – modified skin which grows from coronary corium, forms hard wall for foot. Base of wall is the weight-bearing surface of foot with frog. Grows approx 4–8 mm per month. Underside of hoof made of concave sole, bars and central, wedge-shaped frog.

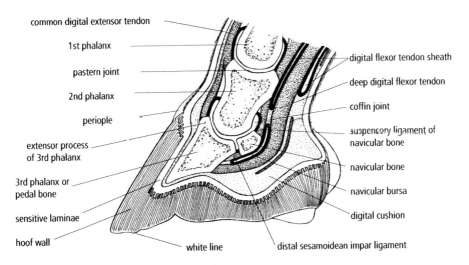

common digital extensor tendon
1st phalanx
pastern joint
2nd phalanx
periople
extensor process of 3rd phalanx
3rd phalanx or pedal bone
sensitive laminae
hoof wall
white line
digital flexor tendon sheath
deep digital flexor tendon
coffin joint
suspensory ligament of navicular bone
navicular bone
navicular bursa
digital cushion
distal sesamoidean impar ligament

Internal structure of the foot

- Laminae – sensitive epidermal structures which form attachment of hoof to underlying tissues.
- Bones – third phalanx (coffin or pedal bone) and navicular bone (distal sesamoid bone). These two form distal interphalangeal (coffin) joint with second phalanx.
- Digital cushion – shock-absorbing fibrous pad, below coffin bone, above frog.
- Blood supply from two palmar digital arteries.

Numerous conditions affect foot; approximately 70% of all equine lameness can be attributed to conditions involving the foot and related structures. These conditions include abscess (e.g. from puncture wound), arthritis of distal interphalangeal joint, bruising of sole, canker, cracks in hoof, fracture of third phalanx or navicular bone, laminitis, navicular disease, and thrush.

See conditions and parts under individual headings.

Foot flight ◀⧸ *füt / flīt, n.* the path that the foot traces in the air during the stride; the sum of all of the joint movements in the limb. Typically described as an arc, foot flight is actually a more complicated biphasic pattern, with the highest point occurring soon after the foot leaves the ground, and a second, smaller elevation at the time that the limb has reached its maximum forward position. Foot flight may be altered by various shoeing and trimming techniques, and lameness.

Forage ◀⧸ *fo rij, n.* food for animals; the leaves, stems, and stalks of plants. May be applied to dried food, e.g. hay, silage, or fresh pasture.

F. poisoning ◀⧸ *fo rij / po i zē ning, n.* illness caused by eating forage which contains toxin, e.g. botulism caused by toxin of *Clostridium botulinum,* or from ingestion of mycotoxins, such as from *Fusarium* spp.
See Botulism, *Fusarium* spp.

Foramen ◀⧸ *fo rē mēn, n.* small hole, or opening, e.g. an opening in bone e.g. holes in skull through which cranial nerves pass.

Epiploic f. ◀⧸ *ep ē plō ik / fo ra mēn, n.* the only opening between the omental bursa and the general peritoneal sac; small intestine may become entrapped. Two studies have suggested that there is an association between crib-biting and epiploic foramen entrapment.
See Colic, Crib-biting.

F. magnum ◀⧸ *fo rē mēn / mag nēm, n.* hole at base of skull, through which spinal cord passes.

F. ovale ◀⧸ *fo rē mēn / ō var lā, n.* opening

185

between atria in foetal heart (allows blood to bypass foetal lungs), normally closes at birth. Failure to close causes atrial septal defect.
See Heart.

Force plate ◀€ *fors / plāt, n.* an instrument, usually mounted into a concrete runway on which a horse can be trotted in hand, used to measure the force a horse exerts on the ground while moving. Has been used in numerous lameness and biomechanical studies; weakness of technique is that usually only a single footfall can be measured.

Forcell's procedure (modified) ◀€ *for sels / prō sē dŭr, n.* surgical treatment for cribbiting, whereby a section of the spinal accessory nerve is removed bilaterally, followed by sections of the omohyoideus, sternohyoideus and sternothyroideus muscles. Procedure causes inability of horse to perform characteristic behaviour; however, results may only be temporary.

Forceps ◀€ *for seps, n.* a surgical instrument used for grasping, holding, or exerting traction, especially on tissue.

Forebrain ◀€ *for brān, n.* (prosencephalon) the anterior of the three main divisions of the vertebrate brain; comprised of cerebral hemispheres, thalamus and hypothalamus. The main control centre for sensory, visceral, and voluntary motor functions. Injury to this area is uncommon, as horse brain is well protected by skull. If forebrain is injured, e.g. from trauma, severe neurological signs result. Prognosis for return to normal function from such injuries is poor.
See Brain.

Foreign body ◀€ *fo rin / bo dē, n.* a mass or particle of material that is not normal to the place where it is found; may cause reaction (see below). Examples of commonly occurring foreign bodies in horses include piece of wood under skin of horse (e.g. from getting caught on fence post), hypodermic needle broken during injection, grass seed in eye, etc. Signs associated with foreign body will depend on material it is made of, site in body, presence of infective microorganisms, etc.

    F.b. reaction ◀€ *fo rin / bo dē / rē ak shun, n.* chronic inflammation and granuloma formation around irritating foreign bodies.

Forelimb ◀€ *for lim, n.* front leg.

Forging ◀€ *for jing, v.* a problem in gait where the hind limb interferes with movement of the forelimb, e.g. the toe of back leg touches heel of front leg on same side. Commonly causes a clicking sound when back foot hits shoe of front foot; can cause injury, e.g. scalping wound of the heel, or tripping and subsequent injury.

Formaldehyde ◀€ *for mal di hīd, n.* colourless gas with strong smell, made by oxidation of methanol. Classified as human carcinogen.
See Formalin.

Formalin ◀€ *for mē lin, n.* aqueous solution of formaldehyde in water, containing a small amount of methanol. Used for preserving tissue specimens (e.g. for histopathology). Powerful disinfectant, but rarely used for this purpose as it gives off irritant gas.
See Fixative, Formaldehyde.

Foxglove ◀€ *foks gluv, n.* (*Digitalis purpura*) common wild flower, contains cardiac glycosides (digoxin, digitoxin) which affect heart. Native to Europe, western and central Asia, and northwestern Africa, but use as ornamental plant caused widespread dissemination in North America. Eating plant may cause sudden death, or diarrhoea and colic. Synthetic glycosides used as heart medications.
See Digitoxin, Digoxin.

Fracture ◀€ *frak tŭr, n./v.* the separation of bone into two or more pieces as a result of stress or trauma, e.g. fall, road traffic accident, running into object, etc; break. There are many ways to describe fractures; the description should give a good idea of the type of treatment required. Fractures are first described by dividing into one of two groups:

- Open fractures – means that part of the bone is sticking through the skin.
- Closed fractures – means that there is no break in the skin.

Next, fractures are described as to their physical character:

- Complete, where the bones are broken totally apart into two or more pieces. Complete fractures may be further subdivided into more specific groups, based on their configuration, which include:
  - o Transverse fracture, when the break is straight across the bone
  - o Spiral fracture, when the break travels around the bone
  - o Oblique fracture, when the break is diagonally across the bone
  - o Comminuted, when the break has crushed or shattered part of the bone.
- Incomplete, where the bones are only cracked or partially broken (also sometimes described as a 'hairline' fracture).

Additional information about fractures may come from a description of their anatomical location, e.g. articular (involves joint), diaphyseal (in shaft), physeal (growth plate), skull, etc.

CLINICAL SIGNS

Signs of fracture depend on type and location, but typically include pain, swelling, loss of normal function, abnormal shape of affected area, grating feeling or sound (crepitus), and if in a limb, extreme lameness.

PROGNOSIS

The prognosis for recovery from fracture depends on many factors, especially including the anatomical location of the fracture and the extent of the trauma. Articular fractures carry a guarded prognosis because osteoarthritis is common as a result of the disruption of joint surfaces. Other mitigating factors include age of the horse, value of the horse, and future intended use, e.g. a chronically lame horse may be an acceptable outcome for a broodmare, but not for an animal in whom athletic performance is desirable. The size of the horse may also preclude successful repair; for healing to occur, fracture site needs to be stable; unfortunately, this is not achievable in all fracture types, e.g. fracture of femur or humerus in adult horse. Regrettably, some fractures will result in euthanasia as the only treatment option.

See also Chip fracture.

Free radical ◀ _frē / ṛu di cāl_, n. an atomic or molecular species with unpaired electrons. Such compounds are usually highly chemically reactive. Play important role in physiology, e.g. free radicals regulate many biological processes, including the control of vascular tone; in the process of inflammation, they also help in the intracellular killing of bacteria by white blood cells. However, because the compounds are so reactive, the same free radicals that are of benefit to the body can also cause unwanted side reactions that result in cell damage. The body has devised many strategies to prevent or limit such damage. Unfortunately, in human medicine, supplementation with free radicals (e.g. vitamin E) has been shown to be largely ineffective at preventing or improving any disease condition.

Freeze-branding ◀ _frēz - bran ding_, n. marking of animal by application of metal instrument made cold by a coolant such as dry ice or liquid nitrogen. Technique kills pigment-producing cells; hair grows white at branded site after 2–3 weeks, and mark is permanent. In light horses, instrument may be left in place for longer and this then kills hair-producing cells so that a hairless mark is made. Freeze brands generally cause less damage to the skin, are less painful, and result in a more obvious mark than do hot branding techniques.

Freeze-firing see Cryotherapy

Fremitus ◀ _fre mi tēs_, n. vibration which can be felt, e.g. can occasionally feel fremitus caused by heart murmurs by laying hand on chest wall.

Frenulum ◀ _fre nū lēm_, n. small fold of mucous membrane that restricts movement of organ, e.g. frenulum under tongue which attaches it to floor of mouth.

Frog ◀€ *frog, n.* raised V-shaped area on bottom of horse's foot, comprised primarily of keratin. Weight-bearing surface of foot, and acts as shock-absorber. Some farriery techniques attempt to divert weight to the frog so as to lessen pressure on other structures (e.g. in a horse with sore heels). See Foot.

    F. wedge test ◀€ *frog / wej / test, n.* test occasionally performed to assist in the diagnosis of navicular syndrome and heel-related lameness. A wooden wedge is placed under the posterior frog, and the contralateral limb is lifted, forcing the horse to stand on the wedge. After a period of time (usually 60 seconds), if the lameness is made worse, problem may be above wedge. Test is fairly sensitive, that is, it helps detect local soreness, but not specific for any structure.

Frontal ◀€ *frun tēl, adj.* relating to the frontal bone; as an anatomical direction, parallel to the main axis of the body and at right angles to a sagittal plane.

    F. bone ◀€ *frun tēl / bōn, n.* large bone of skull, two frontal bones join to form forehead of horse.

    F. (supraorbital) nerve ◀€ *frun tēl / (sŭ prē or bit ēl) / nerv, n.* nerve emerging from above eye, through the supraorbital foramen; mostly sensory to the eye, but also provides some function for eyelid muscles.

    F. nerve block ◀€ *frun tēl / nerv / blok, n.* local anaesthetic block of frontal nerve. Partially prevents movement of upper eyelid; facilitates eye examination.

    F. sinus ◀€ *frun tēl / sī nēs, n.* hollow cavity below frontal bone; connects with nasal cavity. Ethmoid haematomas may extend into f. sinus. Can be drained or tapped in standing horse for diagnostic purposes. See Sinus.

Frostbite ◀€ *frost bīt, n.* superficial or deep freezing of tissues; occasionally occurs with prolonged exposure to cold temperatures. Treatment goals are to prevent infection and to reduce tissue loss; rapid thaw of affected tissues is desirable. Uncommon in horses; circulation of foot is well adapted to tolerate cold.

Fundus ◀€ *fun dēs, n.* the bottom or base of something; part of hollow organ furthest

from opening (e.g. fundus of uterus); back of eye opposite pupil.

Fungal ◀€ *fung gēl, adj.* related to, or caused by, a fungus.

Fungicide ◀€ *fung gi sīd, n.* substance which kills fungi or inhibits their growth. Agents used to treat fungal infections are also called antifungal agents. See Antifungal, Fungus.

Fungus ◀€ *fung gēs, n.* (pl. fungi) general term for any of the kingdom Fungi; saprophytic and parasitic organisms that produce spores; includes moulds, rusts, mildews, smuts, mushrooms, and yeasts. Some fungi may cause disease in horses, e.g. ringworm (dermatophytosis, caused by *Trichophyton equinum, Trichophyton mentagrophytes* and *Microsporum equinum*), histoplasmosis (occurs in Africa, Asia, eastern Europe, nodules in skin caused by *Histoplasma farciminosum*), *Aspergillus* spp. can cause lung, ocular, and nasal infections, *Coccidiodes immitis* and *Cryptococcus neoformans* can cause pneumonia.

Funiculitis ◀€ *fū ni kū lī tis, n.* inflammation and infection of spermatic cord; typically following castration. May be associated with use of contaminated instruments, use of suture material for ligation, or extension from infection of scrotum. Signs, which may not appear until months after operation, include high temperature, scrotal swelling, fever, and discharge. Chronic infection may be called schirrous cord. Treatment is by long-term antibiotic therapy; surgical removal of the infected mass may also be indicated.

Furacin see Nitrofurazone

Furazolidone see Nitrofurazone

Furosemide ◀€ *fŭr ō ze mīd, n.* diuretic drug (increases urine production), therapeutic indications include for the reduction of excess fluid in heart failure. In horses, most commonly prescribed as a preventive treatment for exercise-induced pulmonary haemorrhage. Usage in racing horses is over 90%, according to some reports. Although the medication is widely used and, according to published research, it also results in horses performing better, it is not clear whether the effect on performance is due to improvement in EIPH or because treated horses lose weight (5–10 kg).

Furunculosis ◄⁞ *fü rung kü lō sis, n.* infection of hair follicles (folliculitis) that has extended into the surrounding subcutis and dermis. Clinical signs of nodules, draining tracts, skin ulceration, and crusting, often accompanied by oedema in severe cases. Associated with *Staphylococcus aureus.* Treatment by local antibacterial shampoos and systemic antibiotics.
See Folliculitis.

Fusarium spp. ◄⁞ *fü sär ē ēm / spē shēs, n.* fungal species; toxin causes leukoencephalomalacia; occasional cause of fungal keratitis.
See Keratitis, Leukoencephalomalacia.

189

G

Gag 🔊 *gag, n.* device placed in mouth to hold jaws open so that mouth and teeth can be examined; also occasionally used to open mouth to allow placement of endotracheal tube in anaesthesia. Various types available.

Gait 🔊 *gāt, n.* style of movement. In horses, there are four primary gaits: walk, trot, canter, gallop. Other gaits or variations may be shown by specific breeds; some gaits are inherited, e.g. in Paso Fino horses with their natural four-beat ambling gait. Lameness diagnosis involves evaluation of gait at various speeds. Abnormality of gait may result from lameness, incoordination (ataxia, e.g. in disease affecting central nervous system), poor conformation.
See Ataxia, Canter, Conformation, Force plate, Gallop, Lameness, Trot, Walk.
    G. analysis 🔊 *gāt / ēn al i sis, n.* analysis of how a horse moves; in scientific investigations, gait analysis has been performed using devices such as:
- Implanted strain gauges to measure the force applied to various tissues at exercise.
- High speed cinematography and videography to capture limb movements, often assisted by markers placed at anatomical landmarks, which enable computer analysis.
- Force plates, treadmills, or instrumented shoes to measure such things as strain and vertical ground forces.

    G. defect 🔊 *gāt / dē fekt, n.* an abnormality in movement that can be seen consistently, especially at work.

Gall 🔊 *gawl, n.* **1)** localized skin lesion or swelling, typically developed by rubbing or friction; **2)** bile.
    Girth g. 🔊 *gerth / gawl, n.* pressure or rub sore that develops in girth area, typically treated by changing or padding girth; chronic cases may develop pyoderma.

Gallop 🔊 *ga lĕp, n./v.* fastest gait of horse; to move at fastest speed. Order of limbs touching ground is hind, contralateral hind, ipsilateral fore, contralateral fore, followed by a moment of suspension, where all four feet are out of contact with ground.
See Gait.

Gallstone see Biliary

Galvayne's groove 🔊 *gal vānz / grŭv, n.* vertical groove in lateral surface of upper corner incisor tooth of adult horse. Commonly used as guide to horse's age: said to appear at gum margin at 10 years of age, halfway down tooth at 15 years, all the way down tooth at 20 years, not at top of tooth at 25 years, grown out completely at 30 years. Research has demonstrated that this method of age determination is extremely inaccurate. (Named after Sydney Galvayne, nineteenth-century Australian horse trainer.)
See Dentition, Tooth.

Gamete 🔊 *ga mēt, n.* one of two germ cells (male = spermatozoon, female = ovum) which fuse in fertilization to form new individual; sex cell.
See Fertilization.

Gamma 🔊 *ga mē,* third letter of Greek alphabet, γ, used to denote subclass of some molecules.
    G.-aminobutyric acid 🔊 *ga mē - ē mē nō but i rik / a sid, n.* inhibitory neurotransmitter; levels thought to decrease in seizure activity (increased activity of brain); levels thought

to decrease in hepatic encephalopathy.

G. globulin ◀€ *ga mē / glo bū lin, n.* (immunoglobulin) class of proteins present in blood which act as antibodies.
See Antibody.

G.-glutamyl transferase ◀€ *ga mē - glū tē mīl / tran sfer iūz, n.* enzyme involved in the transfer of amino acids across the cellular membrane; present in liver and kidney, but kidney GGT is released into urine, so not measured in blood. Increased levels in blood are generally considered specific for liver disease, including necrosis of liver cells and obstruction of bile duct (levels also appear to elevate during right dorsal colon displacement because of bile duct compression). Foals 2–4 weeks of age may have higher levels than adults. GGT levels may be normal in horses with chronic, non-active liver fibrosis, or focal liver disease.

G.-linoleic acid ◀€ *ga mē - li nō lā ik / a sid, n.* fatty acid, found in oils such as evening primrose, borage and blackcurrant. Occasionally supplemented in horses with allergy; studies have failed to show benefit from such supplementation.
See Bile, Liver.

Ganglion ◀€ *gan glē ēn, n.* **1)** mass of nerve tissue, containing the cell bodies of neurons, located outside central nervous system; provide relay points and intermediary connections between different neurological structures in the body; **2)** specific mass of grey matter within central nervous system (e.g. basal ganglia); **3)** a cystic swelling, occurring close to a joint or tendon sheath. Surgery is curative, but complete excision may be difficult, and rarely required for other than cosmetic reasons.

Basal g. ◀€ *bā sēl / gang glē on, n.* mass of grey matter (brain tissue) in cerebral hemisphere; functions include responsibility for coordination of muscular activity.
See Brain.

Dorsal root g. ◀€ *dor sēl / rūt / gang glē ēn, n.* a ganglion on the dorsal root of a spinal nerve; often occur as a series of ganglia, and contain sensory neuron cell bodies.

G. cyst see Ganglion

Ganglionopathy ◀€ *gang glē ēn o pēth ē, n.* disease of a ganglion; feature of Fell Pony immunodeficiency syndrome.

See Fell pony immunodeficiency syndrome.

Gangrene ◀€ *gang grēn, n.* death of tissue, usually in large mass(es); associated with failure of blood supply, bacterial invasion, and decomposition. Uncommon, but numerous causes, including pressure, severe oedema, burns, venomous snake bite, vasculitis, ergotism, or infections. Treatment involves removal of affected tissue and identifying and treating the primary cause. Diagnosis by biopsy.

Dry g. ◀€ *drī / gan grēn, n.* occurs when arterial blood supply is lost but lymphatic or venous drainage is unaffected. Affected areas become leathery, cold, discoloured, and dry.

Gas g. ◀€ *gas / gang grēn, n.* infection of tissue with bacteria, especially *Clostridium* spp., which causes death of tissue and production of gas in tissue. Typically occurs following wounds, with bacterial contamination, and following castration, birth trauma, and intramuscular injections. Tends to be rapidly progressive, and affected animals may become very ill very quickly. Typified by painful swellings; crepitation may be felt under skin. Diagnosis by clinical signs and history; treatment must be very aggressive, and includes high doses of antibiotics, typically including penicillin and metronidazole. Surgical treatment to remove devitalized tissue also critical. Supportive therapy (e.g. intravenous fluids and analgesics) may be required. Prognosis in most horses is poor.
See *Clostridium*, Crepitation/crepitus, Metronidazole, Myositis, Penicillin.

Wet g. ◀€ *wet / gang grēn, n.* occurs when venous and lymphatic circulation is also impaired, with secondary bacterial invasion and tissue decomposition (putrefaction). Lesions are typically moist, swollen, and smell bad.

Garlic ◀€ *gar lik, n.* the common seasoning bulb garlic is also reported to have antibacterial, antiparasitic, antiviral, expectorant, and immunostimulant effects, among others. In horses, and other animals, garlic is most commonly given to try to keep flies and other insects away; there is no evidence that garlic is effective for such purposes. Horses eating garlic may also smell of garlic. There is much variation in content among garlic products on the human market; equine products have never been tested. Some odourless garlic preparations for people may not contain active compounds at all. Research has shown that, on their own, horses will consume enough garlic to cause a condition known as Heinz body anaemia (a problem where the blood cells have a characteristic of having certain microscopic features that indicate that they have been injured). The potential for garlic toxicosis exists when horses are chronically fed garlic. Hives have also been reported in one horse fed garlic. The safe dietary dose of garlic in horses is not known.

Gas ◀€ *gas, n.* elastic fluid in which molecules are separated from each other, allowing molecules to have free paths and fill available space. In horse may also be used as a colloquial term for methane gas produced during digestion and fermentation (see Flatus); intestinal gas may accumulate with certain colics that prevent normal passage of ingesta, and cause pain by distending intestines (see Colic).

G. gangrene see Gangrene

Gaskin ◀€ *gas kin, n.* muscular part of horse's hind leg between stifle and hock; crus.

Gastric ◀€ *gas trik, adj.* pertaining to, affecting, or originating in the stomach.

G. dilatation ◀€ *gas trik / dī lē tā shĕn, n.* abnormal accumulation of fluid, gas, and ingesta. Results in signs of acute colic. May occur as primary problem, due to rapidly fermentable feed (grain) or ingestion of feeds that swell with moisture (e.g. sugar beet pulp), or as secondary problem, e.g. following obstructive small intestinal lesions.

G. distension ◀ € *gas trik / dis ten shĕn, n.* (gastric dilatation) overfilling of stomach with food/fluid contents associated with intestinal stasis (ileus) in some colics (especially associated with anterior enteritis – inflammation of small intestine). May result in regurgitation of stomach contents through nose or rupture of stomach. See Colic, Ileus.

G. fluid ◀€ *gas trik / flŭ id, n.* contents of stomach, includes ingested food and water, saliva and secretions of stomach wall (pepsin, hydrochloric acid). Normal pH 3–6. pH higher in intestinal obstruction (6–8).

G. impaction ◀€ *gas trik / im pak shĕn, n.* abnormal, usually dry, accumulation of ingesta in the stomach. Clinical signs include bruxism (from pain), anorexia, and mild colic. True causes unknown, but associated with poor quality feed, irregular feeding, and pyloric stenosis. Stomach cannot be palpated per rectum, so condition is difficult to identify clinically. Stomach can be lavaged in standing horse, massaged and emptied at surgery, or emptied via gastrotomy incision at surgery.

G. mucosal barrier see Barrier

G. reflux ◀€ *gas trik / rē fluks, n.* backward flow of material from stomach; may be seen spontaneously with obstruction of gastric outflow, enteritis, or gastric dilatation, or following passage of nasogastric tube during colic treatment.

G. rupture ◀€ *gas trik / rup tŭr, n.* occasional sequel of horses with colic.

G. tumours ◀€ *gas trik / tū mĕs, n.* relatively uncommon tumours of horse's stomach. Squamous cell carcinoma is most commonly reported; others include leiomyosarcoma and adenocarcinoma. Signs include weight loss, anorexia, lethargy, fever, anaemia, and diffuse oedema. Rectal palpation may show metastasis; abdominocentesis diagnostic in approximately 50% of cases; gastric endoscopy definitive. Successful treatment has not been described.

G. ulcer see Ulcer

Gastritis ◀€ *gas trī tis, n.* inflammation of stomach.

Gastro-, *prefix.* a relationship to the stomach.

Gastrocnemius ◀€ *gas tro nē mē ĕs, n.* muscle in hind leg, extending from the distal third of femur to the point of the hock; extends the hock and flexes the stifle joint (but not at the same time). Arises from two heads which join to a single tendon in mid-tibial region.

G. muscle rupture ◀€ *gas tro nē mē ĕs / mu sĕl / rup tŭr, n.* rupture or tearing of the muscle occurs rarely in newborn foals, usually associated with flexural deformities or dystocias, and adult horses, possibly as a result of excessive tension caused by slipping or falling. Prognosis for neonates is usually grave; adult horses may recover, but may not return to full athletic function.

G. tendinitis ◀ː *gas tro nē mē ēs / ten di nī tis, n.* inflammation of tendon of g. muscle; can affect performance horses of any discipline. Horses are typically short-strided; local swelling and pain on palpation may be noted. Treatment with rest and anti-inflammatory therapy; prognosis is fair, especially if condition recognized early; chronic lesions may heal poorly.
See Tendon, Ultrasonography.

Gastroduodenal ulcer see Ulcer

Gastroenteritis ◀ː *gas trō en tē rī tis, n.* general term for inflammation of lining of stomach and small intestine. Often seen in foal; signs include diarrhoea.

Gastrointestinal ◀ː *gas trō in test in ēl, adj.* pertaining to the stomach and intestine. Numerous gastrointestinal disorders occur in horses.
See individual topics.

Gastrophilus **spp.** see Bot

Gastrotomy ◀ː *gas tro tē mē, n.* incision into stomach.

Gauze ◀ː *gorz, n.* light open-weave fabric of muslin, cotton, or similar material, used for surgical sponges, bandages, and dressings. May be sterile or non-sterile, depending on use.

Gelding ◀ː *gel ding, n.* male horse that has been castrated.
See Castration.

Gene ◀ː *jēn, n.* distinct sequence of DNA on chromosome which determines or contributes to certain characteristic in animal (some characteristics are determined by single gene, some by many genes). Chromosomes are paired (diploid) so there are two copies of each gene in each cell, one from each parent; these will differ slightly and expression of them will affect physical and behavioural characteristics of animal.
See Chromosome.

General anaesthesia see Anaesthesia

General anaesthetic see Anaesthetic

Generic ◀ː *ji ne rik, adj.* non-proprietary; describes a drug not protected by a trademark (a 'brand name' drug). For example, in equine medicine, flunixin meglumine is the generic name for a non-steroidal anti-inflammatory drug; brand names include Finadyne™ in UK and Banamine™ in US.

Genetic ◀ː *ji ne tik, adj.* of genes or heredity; pertaining to birth, origin or reproduction. The study of genes and their heredity is the field of genetics.

Genital ◀ː *je ni tēl, adj.* relating to reproduction; pertaining to the genitalia.

Genitalia ◀ː *je ni tā lē ē, n.* reproductive organs.

Female g. ◀ː *fē māl / je ni tā lē ē, n.* reproductive organs of mare, components include:
- Ovaries – two, produce eggs and hormones (oestrogen, progesterone). Egg released during oestrus.
- Oviduct (fallopian tube) – collects egg when released, where fertilization takes place.
- Uterus (womb) – foal develops here, with nutrition supplied by placenta.
- Cervix (neck of uterus) – generally closed except at oestrus and foaling.
- Vagina – passage from uterus to outside.
- Vulva – end of vagina, prevents air from entering vagina.

See also under separate headings.

Male genitalia ◀ː *māl / je ni tā lē ē, n.* reproductive organs of stallion, include:
- Testes – two, produce sperm and male hormone, testosterone.
- Scrotum – protects testes and holds them away from heat of body.
- Epididymis – vas deferens, spermatic cord: series of strcutures that transport sperm and semen to urethra.
- Urethra – transports semen through penis into female genital tract, and urine from urinary bladder to exterior.

- Penis – erectile organ which inserts into female vagina during mating, and through which urine passes.
- Prepuce – protective covering for penis.
- Bulbourethral gland, prostate gland, seminal vesicle – accessory sex glands that add components to sperm to form semen.

See under individual entries.

Genome ◀ᴇ *jē nōm, n.* all the genes of an organism, contained in a set of chromosomes. The first draft of the horse genome sequence was deposited in public databases, and is freely available for use by biomedical and veterinary researchers, in February 2007. Efforts to improve the accuracy of the draft are ongoing.

Genotype ◀ᴇ *jē nō tīp, n.* all the genetic material of an individual; may be used in comparison with phenotype (how characteristics develop in an individual as a result of genotype and environment).

Gentamicin ◀ᴇ *jen ta mī cin, n.* (gentamycin) aminoglycoside antibiotic active against many Gram-negative (e.g. *Pseudomonas*) and some Gram-positive bacteria; kills bacteria by interfering with mechanisms involved in bacterial reproduction. Comes as a sterile solution that can be administered by IM or IV injection for the treatment of a variety of infections; commonly also infused into the uterus of mares to treat intrauterine infections. Gentamicin solutions and ointments are available for treatment of conditions of the horse's eye. Finally, numerous combinations of gentamicin and corticosteroid products available to treat infections accompanied by inflammation of the eye, ear and skin. While generally safe and effective, aminoglycoside antibiotics such as gentamicin have two primary side effects. First, they can damage the centres of hearing and balance. Second, they may impair function of the kidneys. Horses that have suspect kidney function, such as those that are dehydrated, or very young with immature kidneys, should be monitored closely if this drug is chosen to treat an infection. Care should be taken when gentamicin is used with non-steroidal anti-inflammatory drugs because of the increased potential for kidney-related side effects. It should be used in pregnant mares with caution, due to the potential for kidney impairment and toxicity to the nerves of hearing of the foetus. Because only certain bacteria are killed by gentamicin, it is generally recommended that an attempt be made to isolate the bacteria causing the infection to ensure that gentamicin therapy is appropriate.

Gentian violet ◀ᴇ *jen shēn / vī ē lēt, n.* (crystal violet, methyl violet) synthetic purple dye with antibacterial and antifungal properties, derived from triphenylmethane. May be used for topical treatment of skin infections or wounds. Although gentian violet is effective at killing surface bacteria and fungi, it is messy, and it turns the horse purple where it is applied, usually staining the hands and clothes of the owner at the same time.

Genu see Stifle

Geriatric ◀ᴇ *je rē a trik, adj./n.* referring to aged horses, usually over 20 years.

Germ ◀ᴇ *jerm, n.* microorganism which causes disease; small mass of living substance able to develop into an organism or one of its parts.
>   **G. cell** ◀ᴇ *jerm / sel, n.* an egg (ova) or spermatozoan cell, or a cell which gives rise to eggs or sperm.

Germicidal ◀ᴇ *jer mi sī dēl, adj.* describes substance which destroys disease-causing microorganisms.

Gestation ◀ᴇ *jes tā shēn, n.* period of development in uterus (womb), from fertilization to birth. In mares this gestation is approximately 11 months.
See Pregnancy.

Getah virus ◀ᴇ *gē tē / vī rēs, n.* Alphavirus reported in Japan, Hong Kong, Southeast Asia and India. Arthropod-borne virus; infection from mosquito bite. Life cycle has not been fully determined; virus may be amplified in other mammalian hosts.

May spread by horse-to-horse contact, as well. Disease characterized by fever, limb swelling and stiff gait; skin eruptions and lymph node involvement reported in some animals. Routine blood tests are not diagnostic; diagnosis by combination of clinical signs and virus isolation from blood, or seroconversion. Treatment is supportive care; affected horses should be isolated. Killed vaccine available in Japan, often combined with vaccine against Japanese B encephalitis.
See Japanese B encephalitis.

Giant cell tumour see Histiocytoma

***Giardia* spp.** ◀︎ *jē ar dē ē / spē shēs, n.* protozoan parasite; infrequent cause of diarrhoea and colic in horses. Cysts may be detected on faecal flotation. Treatment with anti-protozoal agents such as metronidazole has been reported effective. (Named after Alfred Mathieu Giard, 1846–1908, French biologist.)

Gingiva ◀︎ *jin ji vē, n.* gum; the part of the oral mucosa associated with the teeth; supporting structure for oral tissues, immovably attached to bone.
See Gum.

Gingivitis ◀︎ *jin ji vī tis, n.* inflammation of gingivae (gums). Increasingly recognized problem in horses, associated with various dental abnormalities such as broken, loose, or infected teeth. Can develop into periodontitis (inflammation of bony attachments of tooth) and cause tooth to become loose.
See Periodontitis, Tooth.

Ginglymus ◀︎ *gin gli mēs, n.* hinge joint, e.g. elbow. Allows movement in only one plane.
See Elbow.

Girdle ◀︎ *ger dēl, n.* encircling structure or part, e.g. pelvic girdle.

Girth ◀︎ *gerth, n.* a measure around a body. In horses, typically taken behind the withers. Girth measurements can be used in estimation of horse's weight.
    G. itch see Dermatitis

Gland ◀︎ *gland, n.* a cluster of cells which secretes or excretes substance unrelated to its normal metabolic needs.
- Endocrine gland – gland with no duct that secretes specific substances (hormones) directly into blood to influence metabolism or other body processes, e.g. adrenal, pituitary, or thyroid glands.
- Exocrine gland – gland that secretes through a duct, secretes on to body surface or into lumen of organ, e.g. mammary, salivary, sweat.
NOTE: Pancreas has both endocrine (secretes insulin) and exocrine (secretes digestive enzymes) glandular parts. Lymph nodes have been called glands, but they are not secretory organs so this is not an accurate name for them.
See Endocrine, Exocrine, Lymph, glands under individual entries.

Glanders ◀︎ *glan dēz, n.* (farcy, enzootic lymphangitis) one of the oldest recorded diseases of horses. Caused by infection with *Burkholderia mallei* (formerly *Pseudomonas mallei*). Transmissible to humans with approximately 95% mortality; considered a significant potential agent for bioterrorism. Geographical distribution restricted to eastern Europe, N. Africa, Asia; considered endemic in Iraq, Turkey, Pakistan, India, Mongolia, and China. No naturally occurring cases have been seen in North America for more than 60 years; the last animal case in the United States was in 1942. Bacterium does not live outside the horse; organism is thought to enter through oral mucous membranes, by ingestion of contaminated feed or water. Horses with subclinical infection spread disease; poor sanitation, crowding and parasitism are considered to increase risk of infection. Incubation period varies from days to months.

CLINICAL SIGNS
Three forms of the disease are generally recognized:
- Cutaneous (farcy) – infectious skin nodules develop into exudative ulcers. Lymphatic vessels swell, ulcerate and drain.
- Nasal – nodules on the nasal septum

develop into ulcers known as stellate scars, accompanied by nasal discharge. Ulcers enlarge and obstruct airway, resulting in dyspnoea, and lymph nodes enlarge. Liver and spleen may become congested; orchitis may be seen in stallions.

- Pulmonary – high fever, septicaemia and bronchopneumonia. Small nodules develop in lungs. High mortality.

Horses with glanders either die quickly or live for several years with chronic abscesses. Some people have suggested that the disease is more severe in donkeys and mules than in horses.

DIAGNOSIS

Typically, a polysaccharide extract of *B. mallei,* mallein, is injected into the skin of the neck or eyelid and the horse is observed for hypersensitivity reaction; mallein test. Other serological tests are also available, although false positive and false negative tests are problematic. Bacteria may also be cultured.

TREATMENT

Euthanasia is recommended, and may be mandatory in some countries. Organism appears to be resistant to many commonly used antibacterial agents.

PREVENTION

The disease has been successfully eliminated from most countries through slaughter of horses with positive mallein test. Various national and international regulations exist pertaining to glanders. No vaccine is available.
See Lymph, Lymphatic.

Glandular ◀ᴷ *glan dū lē, adj.* relating to gland, affecting gland.

Glans ◀ᴷ *glanz, n.* small rounded mass.
   G. clitoris ◀ᴷ *glanz / kli to ris, n.* erectile tissue on end of clitoris.
   G. penis ◀ᴷ *glanz / pē nis, n.* rounded end of penis.

Glaucoma ◀ᴷ *glō kō mē, n.* increased pressure within eye; disorder of outflow of aqueous humour. Rare in horse as primary disease, but may be seen in older horses; more commonly occurring secondary to

uveitis, e.g. from scarring or damage in ciliary body, which prevents normal drainage of aqueous humour; also secondary to lens luxation, intraocular neoplasia, or intraocular infection. Clinical signs are often not obvious, particularly in acute stages, but may include dilated pupil (mydriasis), mild to severe corneal oedema causing cloudiness which may be focal or diffuse, spasm of eyelid (blepharospasm), enlargement of eyeball, or poor vision; signs typically become more severe with chronic disease, and pressure usually ultimately results in optic nerve damage, and blindness. Diagnosis confirmed by measurement of intraocular pressure (tonometry). Treatment goals are to reduce intraocular pressure (e.g. with the β-adrenergic agent, timolol), to reduce aqueous humour production (e.g. with carbonic anhydrase inhibitors such as dorzolaminde or acetazolamide), and to suppress inflammation in eye (e.g. with topical and systemic corticosteroid and non-steroidal anti-inflammatory agents, such as dexamethasone or flurbiprofen). Short term response to medical treatment is usually good, however, long-term prognosis is guarded. Surgical options are also available. Eyes that have been ruined by glaucoma should be enucleated, be replaced by a prosthesis, or made inactive by injection of gentamicin.
See Eye.

Glenoid (cavity) ◀ᴷ *gle noid / (ka vi tē), n.* pit or socket; especially used to describe cavity in scapula (shoulder blade) into which top of humerus fits to form shoulder joint.
See Joint, Shoulder.

Globe ◀ᴷ *glōb, n.* spherical body; eyeball.
See Eye.

Globulin ◀ᴷ *glo bū lin, n.* one of two types of serum protein; the other is albumin. Heterogeneous group with many functions, including carrier proteins (e.g. transferrin carries iron), clotting factors, components of complement, and immunoglobulins (antibodies).
See Antibody, Clotting, Complement, Inflammation.

Glomerular filtration rate ◀︎⁞ *glo me rŭ lē / fil trā shēn / rāt, n.* (GFR) measurement of kidney function; it measures how efficiently the kidneys are filtering waste from blood. Estimated using serum creatinine levels, or most accurately by comparing level of serum creatinine with urine creatinine. Usually expressed in ml/min.
See Creatinine, Glomerulus, Kidney.

Glomerulonephritis ◀︎⁞ *glo me rŭ lō ne frī tis, n.* inflammation of kidney, accompanied by inflammation of the capillary loops in the glomerulus of the kidney; rare in horses. May be caused by production of antibodies against basement membrane of glomerulus or laying down of antibody–antigen complexes on basement membrane (these complexes typically occur from infection elsewhere in body, e.g. streptococcal infection of upper respiratory tract or equine infectious anaemia). Usually causes acute kidney failure. Most common clinical signs are dehydration, depression and inappetence; weight loss, thirst (polydipsia), decreased urination (oliguria), colic, and laminitis may be seen as well. Signs of encephalopathy may be seen with severe azotaemia. Diagnosis by blood samples (increased blood urea nitrogen and creatinine), urine sample (protein in urine), ultrasonography. Kidney biopsy is described; however, severe haemorrhage is reported complication, so technique is rarely performed.
See BUN, Creatinine, Glomerulus, Kidney.

Glomerulus ◀︎⁞ *glo me rŭ lēs, n.* part of nephron (urine-producing unit) of kidney. Made up of mass of capillaries enclosed in Bowman's capsule. Blood is filtered through basement membrane of glomerular capillaries, allowing excretion of waste products and ions (e.g. sodium, potassium). Components of filtered blood needed by animal are reabsorbed. Plasma proteins and blood cells are too large to pass through normal membrane.
See Capillary, Glomerulonephritis, Kidney.

Glossitis ◀︎⁞ *glo sī tis, n.* inflammation of the tongue.

Glosso- ◀︎⁞ *glo sō-, prefix.* of the tongue.
See Tongue.

Glossopharyngeal nerve ◀︎⁞ *glo sō fa rin jē ēl / nerv, n.* cranial nerve IX. Innervates pharynx, larynx and oesophagus, in conjunction with vagus (X) and accessory (XI) nerves. Deficit causes difficulty in eating/swallowing; may be associated with severe disease of auditory tube diverticulum (guttural pouch), rabies, lead poisoning, botulism.
See Cranial nerve.

Glottis ◀︎⁞ *glo tis, n.* part of larynx containing vocal cords and the narrow space between them.

Glucagon ◀︎⁞ *glŭ kē gon, n.* hormone produced by endocrine pancreas when blood glucose levels low, acts to release glucose from glycogen stores in liver and to increase production of glucose (gluconeogenesis).
See Gluconeogenesis, Glucose, Glycogen.

Glucocorticoid ◀︎⁞ *glŭ kō kor ti koid, n.* any of the corticosteroid substances produced by adrenal cortex that regulate carbohydrate, protein, and lipid metabolism, and also inhibit the release of adrenocorticotrophic hormone (ACTH). Glucocorticoids affect microcirculation and muscle tone, help maintain arterial blood pressure, inhibit inflammatory compounds, and perform many other vital functions, e.g. cortisol, cortisone. Synthetic glucocorticoids are drugs used to reduce inflammation, e.g. prednisolone, dexamethaxone.
See Adrenal gland, Dexamethasone, Gluconeogenesis, Glucose, Inflammation, Prednisolone.

Gluconeogenesis ◀︎⁞ *glŭ kō nē ō je ni sis, n.* production of glucose from non-carbohydrates, e.g. amino acids, glycerol. Occurs mostly in liver, as response to corticosteroid and glucagon stimulation.

Glucosamine ◀︎⁞ *glŭ ko sa mēn, n.* amino sugar; part of what makes up the backbone of joint cartilage. Popular supplement, obtained primarily from marine exoskeltons, such as crab shells; marketed to horse owners primarily for prevention or treatment of joint problems in horses. Glucosamine preparations are of one of two salts, hydrochloride or sulphate; the salt may have something to do with their purported activity. Glucosamine is often combined with chondroitin sulphate (see Chondroitin sulphate); however, it is not apparent that the combination is any more effective than the individual ingredients.

Numerous studies have been conducted evaluating glucosamine. The results of those studies are conflicting. Trials sponsored by the glucosamine industry tend to be uniformly positive; trials that are independently funded are generally negative. In the largest trial to date, in 1583 human patients with osteoarthritis, no overall reduction in knee pain was found between the groups using placebo, glucosamine, chondroitin sulphate, or combination therapy. From a biological standpoint, glucosamine is unlikely to have any significant biological activity. At the currently recommended doses, even if the substance were completely absorbed, distributed throughout the horse's body, and not metabolized, it is extremely unlikely that useful concentrations could reach the horse's joints. It is also questionable whether a significant amount of glucosamine gets into the systemic circulation following oral ingestion. Studies in horses have demonstrated that the oral availability of glucosamine in horses is less than 6%, that is, less than 6% of any dose is available to be used by the horse. Furthermore, according to the current understanding of the metabolic pathways involved, glucosamine should be metabolized rapidly by the liver or incorporated into glycoproteins. Contrary to what is often stated, glucosamine is not ordinarily available in the circulation as a source of components for building cartilage; cartilage uses glucose for this purpose. That is to say that glucosamine is *not* essential for the biosynthesis of cartilage molecules.

PRODUCT CONTENT

Two studies have looked at the amount of glucosamine in glucosamine preparations for horses. Both have demonstrated tremendous variations in the quality of glucosamine preparations, with many products containing substantially less than label claims. It has been suggested that an average sized mature horse should get approximately 10 grams per day of oral glucosamine if there is a chance for it to be effective; most products recommend far less than that. Questions of effectiveness aside, the combination of inadequate dose and poor quality control makes it essentially impossible for horse owners or their veterinarians to select a 'proper' glucosamine supplement. Glucosamine appears to be safe and well tolerated by horses.

Glucose ◀𝄇 *glǔ kōz, n.* simple carbohydrate (monosaccharide); one of the most important carbohydrates in biology. All major dietary carbohydrates in the horse's diet contain glucose, either as a building block, e.g. as in starch, or combined with another monosaccharide, as in sucrose and lactose (milk sugar). In the small intestine, complex carbohydrates are broken down to simple sugars by enzymatic action; glucose is then transported across the intestinal wall into the blood. Some of the glucose directly fuels cells, while the surplus is stored in the liver and muscles as glycogen, as well as in fat cells, where it can be used to power reactions which synthesize some fats. Glucose is also a metabolic intermediate. Level in blood regulated by hormones, especially insulin (secreted by pancreas, acts to decrease blood glucose) and glucagon (secreted by pancreas, acts to increase blood glucose). Other hormones (corticosteroids, growth hormone, oestrogen, progesterone) may affect blood glucose concentrations by affecting the body's response to insulin or increasing glucose release from liver.
See Glucagon, Glycogen, Insulin, Insulin resistance, Pituitary pars intermedia dysfunction.

    G. absorption test ◀𝄇 *glǔ kōz / ab sorp shēn / test, n.* test useful in determining malabsorption of carbohydrates from the small intestine. Horse is fasted, the glucose solution is administered by nasogastric tube. Blood is collected to measure glucose concentrations; malabsorption is determined when peak glucose level is significantly less than resting levels.

G. tolerance test ◀⧸ *glŭ kōz / tol ē rĕns / test, n.* oral or intravenous test that may be used to help confirm diagnosis of pituitary pars intermedia dysfunction (PPID; Cushing's disease), insulin resistance, or possible pancreatic disease. Glucose solution is given, and insulin and glucose concentrations are measured in blood. In diseased horses, glucose concentration return to baseline may be delayed.

Glucosuria ◀⧸ *glŭ kō zŭr ē ē, n.* presence of glucose in urine, usually secondary to high level of glucose in blood. Unusual finding in horse urine.
See Diabetes, Glucose.

Glutamate ◀⧸ *glŭ tē māt, n.* most common neurotransmitter in brain; prolonged exposure of glutamate brain receptors to ammonia in hepatic encephalopathy may contribute to clinical signs.
See Encephalopathy, Hepatic.

Glutamine ◀⧸ *glŭ tē mīn, n.* the most abundant naturally occurring, non-essential amino acid. Circulates in the blood as well as being stored in the skeletal muscles. Plays major role in DNA and protein synthesis. Glutamine accumulation is a major cause of brain cell swelling and cerebral oedema in acute liver failure.

Glutaraldehyde ◀⧸ *glŭ tē ral di hīd, n.* colourless oily liquid used as disinfectant, for cold sterilization of some equipment which cannot be sterilized by heat (e.g. endoscopes), and for fixation of tissues for electron microscopy. Toxic.

G. coagulation test ◀⧸ *glŭ tē ral di hīd / cō ag ū lā shŭn / test, n.* precipitation test occasionally performed on foal's serum to check for adequacy of passive transfer.

Gluteal ◀⧸ *glŭ tē ĕl, adj.* describes region of hindquarters (i.e. top of hind leg). Three gluteal muscles (superficial, middle and deep) act to extend, abduct and rotate hip joint.

G. muscle biopsy ◀⧸ *glŭ tē ĕl / mus ĕl / bī op sē, n.* biopsy, commonly obtained from middle gluteal muscle; assists in diagnosis of disorders of skeletal muscle. Obtained standing under local anaesthesia; various techniques described.

G. rise ◀⧸ *glŭ tē ĕl / rīs, n.* observation in hind limb lameness diagnosis; the horse is viewed from behind, and symmetry and duration of the lifting of the gluteal muscles on each side are compared. Rise is seen on the swing phase of the stride. Rise may be depressed with lameness involving swing phase, or with muscle atrophy; may be increased with lameness involving support phase, in an effort to get off the affected limb ('hip hike').

Glycaemia ◀⧸ *glī sē mē ē, n.* presence of glucose in blood.
- Hyperglycaemia – elevated blood glucose. May be seen in primary or secondary [to pituitary pars intermedia dysfunction] diabetes mellitus, or in cases of insulin resistance.
- Hypoglycaemia – decreased blood glucose. May be seen in times of high glucose demand, e.g. septicaemia.

See Diabetes, Insulin resistance, Pancreas, Pituitary pars intermedia dysfunction, Septicaemia.

Glycerin/Glycerine see Glycerol

Glycerol ◀⧸ *gli sē rol, n.* thick, colourless, odourless liquid; commonly used in pharmaceutical preparations, also known as glycerin or glycerine. Sugar alchohol, pleasant-tasting and with low toxicity. Glycerol is also a moistening agent (humectant). It tends to attract water; as such, it is a frequently used emollient for the skin. Many liniment, cough and poultice preparations made for the horse contain glycerol for these reasons. Glycerol is frequently applied to the legs of the horse in so-called sweat wraps. Finally, glycerol finds use in solutions for cryopreservation of equine semen.

Glyceryl trinitrate ◀⧸ *gli sē ril / trin i trāt, n.* ('Nitroglycerine'; GTN) substance has been used to treat heart pain and heart failure in people for over 130 years; works by causing blood vessel dilation. GTN has been recommended for use in the treatment of horses with laminitis because of vessel dilating effect, in hopes that local application of GTN gel will cause dilation of blood vessels to the feet, and possibly help improve the circulation of blood in that area. Unfortunately, at least two studies have shown that increased blood flow to the feet does not occur after such treatment; usefulness in this regard is questionable.

Glycogen ◀≗ *glī kō jēn, n.* cardohydrate (polysaccharide) formed in liver and muscles as energy store of glucose. Hormonal control of metabolism; stored in response to insulin; released in response to glucagon. Abnormally accumulates in polysaccharide storage myopathy.
See Glucagon, Glucose, Insulin, Polysaccharide storage myopathy.

   G. branching enzyme deficiency ◀≗ *glī kō jēn / brarn ching / en zīm / di fi shēn sē, n.* (GBED) heritable disorder described in humans, cats, and horses (only Quarter Horse and Paint breeds affected to date). Cause of abortion; affected newborn foals present for sepsis, prematurity and failure of passive transfer. May have elevated liver and muscle enzymes, and persistent hypoglycaemia. Muscle biopsy shows complete lack of glycogen on staining. Pedigree and genotype analyses support the hypothesis that GBED is inherited as a simple recessive trait from a single founder. A DNA-based test is available to assist in determining specific diagnoses, as well as in choosing matings that avoid conception of a GBED foal.

Glycogenesis ◀≗ *glī kō jēn i sis, n.* the formation and storage of glycogen.
See Glucagon, Glucose, Insulin, Polysaccharide storage myopathy.

Glycoprotein ◀≗ *glī kō prō tēn, n.* type of protein which has a carbohydrate group attached. Examples of glycoproteins include antibodies, structural proteins of connective tissue, and important hormones, such as follicle stimulating hormone (FSH) and luteinizing hormone (LH).
See Antibody, Connective tissue.

Glycopyrrolate ◀≗ *glī kō pir o lāt, n.* anticholinergic drug, used primarily in emergency situations for bronchodilation (in acute airway distress), and in treatment of heart conditions such as bradycardia. May cause colic due to ileus, as per atropine.

Glycosaminoglycan ◀≗ *glī kō sa mi nō glī kēn, n.* (GAG) long, unbranched polysaccharides consisting of a repeating disaccharide unit; an important component of connective tissues, especially joint tissues and cartilage. Important GAGs in joints are chondroitin sulphate, keratin sulphate, and hyaluronan. Oral GAG products are available as joint supplements for horses, but lack convincing evidence of utility.

Glycoside ◀≗ *glī kō sīd, n.* organic compound, composed of a simple sugar attached to another component. Many plants store chemicals in the form of inactive glycosides; when these chemicals are required, the glycosides contact water and enzymes, and the sugar part is broken off, which makes the chemical available for use. Many plant glycosides are used as medications; many are toxic, e.g. digoxin (cardiac glycoside), cyanogenic glycosides. Compounds are thought to exist as a defence mechanism for plant.
See Digoxin.

GnRH see Gonadotrophin

Gnat see *Culicoides* spp.

Goitre ◀≗ *goi tē, n.* swelling of neck as result of enlarged thyroid gland. May be seen in foal as result of iodine deficiency or excessive iodine intake in mare. Feeding excessive amounts of iodine to foals will also produce condition (has been seen in rations supplemented with kelp).
See Iodine, Thyroid.

Gomen disease ◀≗ *gō mēn / di zēz, n.* progressive, degenerative cerebellar condition recognized in the northwest part of New Caledonia; causes mild to severe ataxia. Only occurs in horses that roam free; horses eventually die or are euthanized. Cause unknown; possible toxicity. No effective treatment.

Gonad ◀〜 *gō nad, n.* organ that produces gametes, i.e. testis (produces spermatozoa) and ovary (produces ova).
See Ovary, Testes.

Gonadotrophin ◀〜 *gō na dō trō fin, n.* (gonadotropin) hormone produced by pituitary gland, stimulates gonads, i.e. follicle-stimulating hormone, luteinizing hormone.
See Follicle, Luteinizing hormone, Pituitary.

   G. releasing hormone ◀〜 *gō na dō trō fin / ri lē sing / hor mōn, n.* (GnRH) hormone produced in hypothalamus, stimulates secretion of gonadotrophins (especially luteinizing hormone) by pituitary; sometimes used in reproductive medicine in an attempt to bring non-cycling mares into heat. Unfortunately, the hormone has a very short half life in the horse's system; thus, proper use requires either multiple injections or mini-infusion pumps. Also used in stallion management; given prior to breeding, it appears to help problem breeders ejaculate more easily. Has also been used in an effort to cause one or both retained testicles to drop into the scrotum in cryptorchid horses. In some countries, a GnRH vaccine has been used in an effort to prevent unwanted heat behaviour in mares. The effectiveness of the treatment is reportedly quite variable. The vaccine has also been used in an effort to suppress testicular function and male hormone secretion in stallions; however, as with mares, there seems to be a significant amount of individual variation in the responses among stallions and libido is not totally suppressed.
See Gonadotrophin, Hypothalamus, Pituitary.

Gonitis ◀〜 *go nī tis, n.* non-specific term for inflammation of stifle joint.

Graafian follicle ◀〜 *grar fē ēn / fo li kēl, n.* mature ovarian follicle. (Named after R. de Graaf, Dutch anatomist.)
See Follicle, Ovary, Ovum.

Graft ◀〜 *grarft, n.* any tissue or organ implanted or transplanted surgically. Examples include:

- Allograft – tissue graft between individuals of same species but different genotype; e.g. bone from cadaver for grafting (see Bone graft under Bone).
- Autograft – a tissue or organ that is transplanted from one part to another part of the same body.
- Bone g. – bone transplanted from one site to another; e.g. cancellous bone graft in fracture repair; allograft of bone for surgical stabilization of cervical vertebrae.
- Conjunctival g. – graft of bulbar conjunctiva or eye, usually to assist in healing of corneal ulcers.
- Free g. – graft of tissue completely freed from its circulatory bed; rarely performed in horses because thickness of tissue impedes re-establishment of blood supply prior to tissue death.
- Mesh g. – a split-thickness skin graft in which many tiny splits are made to allow the tissue to expand, cover a large area, and allow wound fluids to seep out between openings.
- Pinch/Punch g. – skin grafting technique where plugs of skin are taken and placed in granulating tissue bed. Done in an effort to speed epithelialization of large wounds.
- Xenograft – tissue transplanted between animals of different species. Not performed in horses.

Graft-versus-host disease ◀〜 *grarft / ver sēs / hōst / di zēz, n.* immune-mediated condition where immune cells from donated tissues (the graft) attack the body of the transplant patient (the host); common problem with bone marrow transplantation in humans. Rare in horses, but has been reported in horses given liver or thymic cells from foetuses, or blood lymphocytes from unrelated horses.

Grain ◀〜 *grān, n.* seed of cereal plant, e.g. wheat, barley, oat, maize (corn). Low fibre content, compared to forages; high in energy, so often used to supply additional calories in diets of horses doing hard work. Overfeeding of grain (e.g. more than 2.5 kg of grain in a single feeding) can cause digestive problems, e.g. diarrhoea and colic, and laminitis. Grains may be fed whole, or are often processed (cooked, cracked, flaked, ground, etc.); horses tend to prefer processed grains when offered. In general, processing large kernel grains such as maize, oats or barley does not improve their digestibility or feeding value, but it may help decrease the risk of digestive problems by allowing for more starch digestion in the small intestine, thereby preventing excessive fermentation in the large intestine. Digestion of small kernel grains, e.g. wheat, rye and milo, can be improved by 10–15% by processing, but added cost should be considered.

Gram ◀ *gram, n.* basic metric unit of weight, one thousandth of 1 kilogram, the weight of 1 millilitre of water at 4°C.

Gram stain ◀ *gram / stān, n.* procedure for staining material smeared on microscope slide, involves staining with crystal violet, treating with iodine, decolorizing with alcohol and counterstaining with another dye. Enables differentiation between types of bacteria into two large groups:
- Gram-negative – describes bacteria whose cell walls do not retain the violet stain of Gram's staining method, but take up counterstain; includes *Salmonella, Escherichia coli.*
- Gram-positive – describes bacteria whose cell walls retain the violet stain of Gram's staining method, includes *Staphylococcus, Streptococcus.*

(Named after Hans C.J. Gram, nineteenth-century Danish physician.)

Granulation ◀ *gra nū lā shĕn, n./adj.* formation of small masses of vascular tissue in wounds during healing; describes tissue which forms in wounds during healing.
See Wound healing.
  G. tissue ◀ *gra nū lā shĕn / ti shū, n.* newly formed small masses of vascular tissue which form in healing wounds that have not been closed by suturing; composed of loops of new blood vessels and connective tissue;

ultimately helps form scar. In horses overgrowth of granulation tissue (exuberant granulation tissue) can be problem in wounds in areas with little subcutaneous tissue (e.g. front of cannon bone), or in wounds in which skin is lost; can form swollen, proliferative mass above level of skin if unattended (proud flesh).
See Wound healing.

Granule ◀ *gra nūl, n.* small particle, e.g. those seen in cytoplasm of some white blood cells (basophils, eosinophils, neutrophils).
See Basophil, Eosinophil, Neutrophil, Leukocyte.

Granulocyte ◀ *gra nū lō sīt, n.* any cell which has granules in its cytoplasm, especially leukocytes, i.e. basophil, eosinophil, neutrophil.
See Basophil, Eosinophil, Neutrophil, Leukocyte.

Granuloma ◀ *gra nū lō mĕ, n.* an imprecise term, applied to any tumour-like growth composed of inflammatory cells and granulation tissue, with varying amounts of fibrosis. Associated with chronic inflammation, e.g. may develop in stump of spermatic cord of male horse as complication after castration, as a response to fungal infections of the skin, etc.
  Collagenolytic g. see Nodular skin disease

Granulomatous ◀ *gra nū lō mĕ tĕs, adj.* containing granulomas.
  G. disease ◀ *gra nū lō mĕ tĕs / diz ēz, n.* rare skin disease characterized by diffuse skin involvement, with scaling, fever, crusting and hair loss, wasting, difficulty in breathing, poor appetite, and granulomatous inflammation of multiple organs. Also called Equine sarcoidosis. Cause unknown; may be an immune-mediated reaction, or an abnormal proliferation of cells. Definitive diagnosis by skin biopsy. Large doses of corticosteroids may be beneficial in treatment, especially early in disease, but prognosis is poor. Spontaneous remissions have been reported.
  G. enteritis ◀ *gra nū lō mĕ tĕs / en ter ī tis, n.* inflammatory bowel disease. Cause of chronic wasting and rapid weight loss, often

in spite of good appetite; diarrhoea, depression and fever occasionally seen. Seen in 1–6-year-old horses, primarily reported in Standardbred breed. Blood work nonspecific; diagnosis by malabsorption tests; rectal mucosal biopsy occasionally helpful. Successful treatment with corticosteroid drugs has been reported, another horse responded to surgical removal of affected segment of intestine.

G. inflammation ◀♦ _gra nū lō mē tēs / in flē mā shŭn, n._ pattern of tissue reaction seen in response to various disease agents or as idiopathic condition; macrophage is predominant cell type. Can be nodular or diffuse.

Granulosa-theca cell ◀♦ _gra nū lō zē / thē kē / sel, n._ (commonly known as granulosa cells) epithelial cells which line ovarian follicle and are responsible for oestrogen production.
See Ovary.

G.-theca c. tumour ◀♦ _gra nū lō zē / thē kē / sel / tū mē, n._ tumour in equine ovary formed from cells which line ovarian follicle. Most common ovarian tumour in mare. Reported in all ages and breeds, as well as in pregnant mares, but are most common in 5- to 10-year-olds. Mares with GCTs usually exhibit one of three types of behaviour depending upon the type and amount of hormones produced by their tumour. These are 1) prolonged anoestrus, 2) persistent or intermittent oestrous behaviour (nymphomania), or 3) stallion-like behaviour. Mares exhibiting the latter may also have a crested neck and enlarged clitoris. Diagnosis by serum hormone analysis (elevated testosterone), and rectal palpation or ultrasound of enlarged ovary; opposite ovary generally small due to hormonal inhibition of growth. Surgical removal of the affected ovary is curative. Most mares have normal oestrous cycles within 6–8 months following the surgery; normal fertility once oestrous cycles have returned.
See Ovary.

Grass ◀♦ _grars, n._ predominant plant of most pastures with long narrow leaves and spikes of small wind-pollinated flowers; grasses are suitable forage for grazing animals, such as horses.

G. founder ◀♦ _grars / fōn dē, n._ founder (laminitis) induced by consumption of pasture grass. Common cause of laminitis; causal factors include high sugar content of fresh grass and low fibre content.
See Laminitis.

G. staggers/G. tetany ◀♦ _grars / sta gēz / grars / tet ē nē, n._ tetany (hyperexcitability of nerves and muscles) as a result of low blood magnesium (hypomagnesaemia); relatively uncommon. Affected horses show muscle tremors, rapid heart rate, stiff gait, and reluctance to move; horses become recumbent and die if severe. May occur when horses are grazing pasture that has low available levels of magnesium.

Grass sickness ◀♦ _grars / sik nis, n._ (equine dysautonomia) acquired disease characterized by degeneration of nerves of autonomic nervous system and nerves of intestines: affects motility of intestines. Cause unknown, may be due to environmental toxin. Occurs in UK, Europe, S. America, and Australia; so far the disease has not been recognized in North America. More common in horses which are grazing and do not receive supplementary food; true cause is unknown. Affected horses are usually between 2 and 12 years of age, with horses from 3–5 years at greatest risk. Three forms are recognized:

- Acute form – signs are related to acute ileus of gastrointestinal tract; course of disease is less than 2 days. Colic, often severe, is caused by distension of bowel, which can be felt on rectal examination. Affected horses are hypovolaemic, which may cause death from heart failure. Other signs include fever, muscle tremors, difficulty swallowing, and patchy sweating; may get reflux of stomach contents following nasogastric intubation.
- Subacute form – course of disease is 3–7 days, with less severe clinical signs. Typically develop impactions of large colon, with intermittent colic signs and patchy sweating.
- Chronic form – course of disease is weeks to months. Most prominent clinical feature is severe weight loss, with little feed material in gastrointestinal tract. Other signs include sweating,

muscle tremors, stiff gait, and accumulation of dry material in nasal passages; coat abnormalities may be seen in later stages.

There are no definitive ante-mortem diagnostic laboratory tests for grass sickness. Clinical signs, radiography (especially using barium to show very slow passage through oesophagus), endoscopy (may show oesophageal ulcers or megaoesophagus), and rectal mucosal biopsy may assist in presumptive diagnosis; ileal biopsy, taken at surgery, is also diagnostic. Diagnosis is usually confirmed post-mortem. No effective treatment; disease is usually fatal in acute or subacute cases. Some chronically affected horses have been successfully treated; however, survivors commonly have residual abnormalities, such as difficulty swallowing, sweating, or coat changes.

Gravel ◀ _gra_ vĕl, _n._ colloquial term for draining tract emerging at coronary band secondary to hoof abscess; very small stones (calculi), e.g. in kidney or bladder.
See Abscess, Calculus, Coronary.

Gravid ◀ _gra_ vid, _n._ pregnant.

Greasy heel see Dermatitis, Pastern

Greenstick fracture ◀ _grēn_ stik / _frak_ tŭr, _n._ incomplete break of bone; similar to crack seen when a green stick is snapped. May occur in foals.
See Fracture.

Grey ◀ _grā_, _adj._ coat colour made from a mixture of dark and white hairs on dark skin. In foal coat will be dark with just a few light hairs (with dark legs) and coat gets greyer (lightens) as horse gets older. Grey horses are prone to development of melanomas (tumours of pigment-producing cells) in middle to old age.
See Melanoma.

Griseofulvin ◀ _gri_ zē ō _fŭl_ vin, _n._ antibiotic produced by _Penicillium griseofulvum_ or by synthetic means; sometimes prescribed for the treatment of dermatophytosis (e.g. ringworm). Griseofulvin is incorporated into the skin layers as the skin cells grow and replace themselves. Thus, the skin becomes toxic to any fungus that is living on it. Unfortunately, the correct dosage of griseofulvin for horses has never been adequately determined and its effectiveness is unknown. Experience in other species would suggest that for griseofulvin to be effective it should be given for thirty to sixty days. Some practitioners give large weekly doses; most authorities feel that this is inappropriate. Should not be given to pregnant animals; premature delivery and congenital defects have been described in one foal of a griseofulvin-treated mare, and similar defects have been described in other species that have received the drug during pregnancy. Gloves should be worn when handling drug, special care should be taken by women of child-bearing age.
See Dermatophytosis.

Growth ◀ _grōth_, _n._ normal process of increase in size of an organism; an abnormal formation, such as tumour, neoplasia or other masses; the proliferation of cells, such as in a bacterial culture.
See Tumour.

    G. hormone ◀ _grōth_ / _hor_ _mōn_, _n._ any of several substances produced by pituitary gland, controls growth of body tissues and involved in regulation of carbohydrate, protein and fat metabolism.
See Pituitary, Somatotropin.

    G. plate ◀ _grōth_ / _plāt_, _n._ (physis) area of long bone where lengthening occurs. Each long bone typically has growth plate near each end. Cartilage cells form plate; cartilage cells multiply and bone cells (osteoblasts) move in and turn the cartilage matrix to bone. This process continues until the horse has fully grown; at this time, growth plate is replaced by bone.
See Bone, Physis.

Guaifenesin ◀ _gwī fen e sin_, _n._ centrally acting muscle relaxant. Has been used to provide muscle relaxation during anaesthesia; may be used in treatment of seizures or conditions characterized by tetany, e.g. tetanus, and strychnine toxicosis.

Guarana ◀ _gwa_ _rar_ nē, _n. Paullinia cupana_, a climbing plant native to the Amazon basin. Seeds contain approximately three times more caffeine than coffee beans. Caffeine is a stimulant of the central nervous and respiratory systems, and cardiac muscle. Has been used as an illegal stimulant in racing horses; can be detected on drug screenings.

Guard hair see Hair

Gubernaculum ◀∈ *gŭ bē na kū lĕm, n*. piece of connective tissue attached to epididymis of testis and base of scrotum; acts to guide foetal testis into scrotum as it descends from abdomen. Persists as scrotal ligament in adults.
See Scrotum, Testes.

Gullet see Oesophagus

Gum ◀∈ *gum, n*. gingiva. Colour of gums (e.g. pale in early stages of shock; bluish in lack of oxygen, etc.) and capillary refill time (normal is approximately 2 seconds), can be helpful in diagnosis of illness.
See Anaemia, Capillary, Gingiva.

Gut ◀∈ *gut, n*. colloquial term for intestines; alimentary tract, bowel.

Guttural ◀∈ *gu tē rĕl, adj*. of the throat.

Gutteral pouch ◀∈ *gu tē rĕl / pŏch, n*. (auditory tube diverticulum) one of two large sacs connected to auditory (Eustachian) tube, which runs from ear to throat; framed by the base of the skull at the top, the pharynx and oesophagus at the bottom, and the salivary glands and mandible on the sides. Opens into pharynx through a narrow slit; internal and external carotid arteries, five cranial nerves, lymph nodes, and some delicate bones and joints are located in or traverse pouch. Lined by ciliated mucous membrane. Pouches are separated from each other by thin layer of connective tissue medially. Diagnosis of conditions by endoscopy and radiography. The guttural pouches surround the internal carotid arteries, which supply blood to the brain. Horses apparently use their guttural pouches to cool these arteries during exercise, keeping the brain from overheating. Affected primarily by one of three conditions:

- G. p. empyema – pus in the guttural pouch; usually secondary to upper respiratory tract infections, although it can develop as a complication of other guttural pouch diseases, local treatment with irritating drugs, or birth defects. Clinical signs include intermittent nasal discharge, often unilateral, swollen lymph nodes or salivary glands; dyspnoea and dysphagia may occur in severe cases. Diagnosis of this disease is confirmed by endoscopy; radiographs of the area and bacterial culture and sensitivity testing of the discharge might provide additional useful information. Treatment involves daily flushing of the guttural pouches to dislodge and remove dead cells, debris, infectious organisms, and other materials, for a period of days to weeks. Antibiotics may not reach sufficient concentration to eliminate problem, so should only be administered in conjunction with flushing. Other medications may be given if warranted by the individual horse's clinical signs and condition.
- G. p. mycosis – fungal infection of g.p. Occurs most often during warmer months in stabled horses. Although caused by a fungus, especially *Aspergillus*, the pathogenesis of the disease is unknown. Most common clinical sign is epistaxis (nose bleed) not related to exercise, secondary to fungal erosion of the wall of the internal carotid artery. Local nerves may also be damaged by infection, resulting in dysphagia (difficulty swallowing). Diagnosis confirmed by endoscopy. Disease is potentially life-threatening if fungal erosions rupture internal carotid artery; referral to a hospital after diagnosis is recommended. Surgery to find and block off the affected artery is the treatment of choice. Medical treatment includes topical antifungal agents; response is highly variable.
See Cranial nerve, Epistaxis.
- G. pouch tympany – entrapment of air within guttural pouch (air gets in but

cannot get out). Age- and gender-related; develops in foals shortly after birth and for up to one year of age; fillies more commonly affected than colts. Several causes suspected but none proven; suspected causes include congenital defects or local tissue swelling from a previous respiratory infection. As with other conditions affecting the guttural pouches, history and clinical signs are suggestive, but the diagnosis is confirmed by endoscopic examination and radiographs. Surgery is the most satisfactory treatment. Surgery involves opening a window (fenestration) in the membrane that separates the affected guttural pouch from the normal one. By so doing, air in the abnormal guttural pouch can pass to the normal side and be expelled into the pharynx. Prognosis following surgery is good.

H

H&E Staining see Haematoxylin and eosin staining

H₂ Blocker see Antihistamine, Cimetidine, Ranitidine

Habronema ◀ᴇ *ha* brō *nē* mē, *n.* equine stomach worm; nematode parasite (roundworm). First stage larvae of mature worms passed in faeces and ingested by fly maggots. Adult flies deposit third stage larvae on mouth and in feed of horses; larvae are ingested and life cycle completed. Normal life cycle rarely causes disease, unless large numbers cause ulceration of stomach or gastritis.
See Habronemiasis.

Habronemiasis ◀ᴇ *ha* brō nē *mī* ē sis, *n.* (summer sore; cutaneous habronemiasis) skin disease that occurs when infective *Habronema* larvae are inadvertently deposited on wounds or other moist body areas (e.g. conjunctiva, penis, prepuce, and vulva). Ulcerative granulomas develop at site of larval deposition; probably hypersensitivity reaction. Especially common in spring and summer. Diagnosis by clinical appearance; blood work often shows high levels of eosinophils. Diagnosis confirmed by biopsy or deep skin scraping. Many medical therapies have been described including ivermectin deworming (may not be necessary, as inflammatory reaction kills larvae), and topical anti-inflammatory agents (e.g. corticosteroid creams or ointments; DMSO; topical dewormers). Surgical debulking of large granulomas may be indicated to reduce size of lesion and facilitate treatment. Regular deworming with ivermectin will kill adult worms and may help prevent larval contamination of faeces.
See *Habronema*.

Haem- ◀ᴇ *hēm-*, prefix. Relating to blood. See Blood.

Haem ◀ᴇ *hēm*, *n.* (heme) non-protein, iron-containing part of haemoglobin. Responsible for carrying oxygen and gives haemoglobin its colour.
See Haemoglobin.

Haemagglutination ◀ᴇ *hē* mē *glŭ* ti *nā* shēn, *n.* clumping together of red blood cells, caused by antibody–antigen reaction. Used in various diagnostic tests, primarily for two purposes, blood typing and the quantification of virus dilutions. The presence of specific antibodies to red blood cells (e.g. as occurs in neonatal isoerythrolysis) or viral antigens in serum can be detected by their clumping effect on red blood cells.
See Antibody, Antigen, Erythrocyte, Neonatal isoerythrolysis.

Haemangioma ◀ᴇ *hē* man jē *ō* mē, *n.* benign growth composed of new blood vessels; in horses, most often occurs in skin, spleen or eye. May be excised for cosmetic reasons; prognosis good with complete excision.

Haemangiosarcoma ◀ᴇ *hē* man jē ō *sar* kō mē, *n.* rare neoplasm; malignant growth composed of vascular endothelial cells. Metastasize readily and bleed profusely if cut. May be seen in various locations, including lungs and pleura, spleen, pericardium, muscles, and bones. Clinical signs include dyspnoea (difficulty breathing), subcutaneous or muscular swelling, nosebleed (epistaxis), and lameness. In disseminated cases, heart and respiratory rates are usually increased and mucous membrane colour is frequently pale or icteric; anaemia, leukocytosis, and thrombocytopenia are also common. Prognosis generally poor; however, remission has been reported in a few cases; when the horse is medically stable, and quality of life is acceptable, a period of observation may be in order.

Haemarthrosis ◀ː *hē mar thrō sis, n.* presence of blood in joint; most commonly follows injury or surgery.

Haematinic ◀ː *hā mē tin ik, n.* 'blood builder', any one of a seemingly endless number of compounds containing such things as iron and B vitamins, purported to increase the volume of red blood cells. No evidence for effectiveness of such products in healthy horses, or any reason why they should be effective.

Haematobia ◀ː *hā mē tō bē ē, n.* horn fly; blood-sucking small black fly, occasional cause of skin irritation and dermatitis in horses.
See Dermatitis.

Haematocele ◀ː *hē mē tō sēl, n.* bleeding into tunic of testis after injury to blood vessels, usually after trauma; rare. Can cause permanent damage to testis as temperature of testis is kept too high by insulating properties of clot and resultant fibrous tissue. Fertility returned in one horse after unilateral castration of affected testicle.
See Testes.

Haematocrit ◀ː *hē ma tō krit, n.* (Packed cell volume; PCV) percentage, by volume, whole blood occupied by red blood cells. Traditional technique involves blood sample taken into anticoagulant and placed in a narrow capillary tube and centrifuged to separate cells and plasma; with modern laboratory equipment the haematocrit is calculated by an automated analyser and not measured directly. Elevated in conditions such as dehydration (less fluid in blood, so percentage of cells higher); decreased in conditions such as anaemia (fewer cells per volume of blood).
See Packed cell volume.

Haematogenous ◀ː *hē mē to ji nēs, adj.* originating in the blood, or carried around body in blood stream, e.g. haematogenous spread of bacterial infection, where bacteria are spread through body in blood; concerned with blood production, or the production of one or more of its components, e.g. the haematogenous functions of the liver.
See Blood.

Haematology ◀ː *hē mē to lo jē, n.* branch of medicine or area of study concerned with blood and blood-forming organs; includes diagnostic testing of blood (cell counts, etc.).
See Blood.

Haematoma ◀ː *hē mē tō mē, n.* swelling filled with blood, usually clotted; forms in a tissue, organ, or body space as a result of a broken blood vessel. Commonly caused by trauma. Will often resolve spontaneously; will also generally respond to surgical drainage in suitable areas (e.g. pectorals, hindquarters). Frequent occurrence in horses with HERDA.
See HERDA.

Haematopinus asini ◀ː *hē mat ō pī nēs / ass ē nē, n.* horse-sucking louse.
See Louse.

Haematoxylin and eosin staining ◀ː *hē mēt oksi lin / and / ē ō sin / stā ning, n.* the most widely used stain in medical tissue diagnostics (histopathology). Involves use of haematoxylin, a basic blue dye, and eosin Y, a bright pink dye. Structures that contain nucleic acids, such as a cell nucleus, stain blue; intracellular and extracellular proteins, such as are found in cell cytoplasm, stain pink. Red blood cells stain intensely red.

Haematuria ◀ː *hē mē tŭr rē ē, n.* presence of blood in urine. Various causes, including kidney infection (pyelonephritis), bladder inflammation (cystitis), bladder stones (urolithiasis), tumour of urogenital tract, injury, problems with blood clotting.
See Cystitis, Pyelonephritis, Urolithiasis.

Haemoconcentration ◀ː *hē mō kon sēn trā shēn, n.* increase in blood cell concentra-

tion, usually as result of decrease in plasma volume, e.g. in dehydration.
See Blood, Dehydration.

Haemodynamic ◀ː _hē mō dī na mik, adj._ relating to the properties of, or flow of blood within blood vessels.
See Blood.

Haemoglobin ◀ː _hē mō glō bin, n._ (Hb) iron-containing oxygen-transport metalloprotein composed of protein attached to iron-containing haem; present in red blood cells. Carries oxygen in blood from lungs to tissues as oxyhaemoglobin, a bright red compound (hence colour of arterial blood). Reverts to darker-coloured haemoglobin (or deoxyhaemoglobin) when gives up oxygen in tissues (hence darker red colour of venous blood).
See Blood, Iron, Oxygen.

Haemoglobinaemia ◀ː _hē mō glō bi nē mē ē, n._ presence of excessive haemoglobin in blood plasma, seen in conditions where red blood cells are damaged within blood vessels, e.g. intravascular haemolysis. Plasma appears pink when separated from blood cells, e.g. when centrifuged.
See Haemoglobin, Haemolytic.

Haemoglobinuria ◀ː _hē mō glō bin ŭr ē ē, n._ presence of excessive haemoglobin in urine; turns urine red/pink. Can be differentiated from haematuria because red/pink colour stays in solution if sample left to stand (in haematuria, red blood cells sink to the bottom of solution). Seen in conditions where red blood cells are damaged within blood vessels, e.g. intravascular haemolysis. Can lead to acute renal failure.
See Haemoglobin, Haemolytic, Urine.

Haemolysis ◀ː _hē mo li sis, n._ destruction, rupture of red blood cells and release of haemoglobin into circulation. Occurs in several conditions, e.g. neonatal isoerythrolysis (where foal's red blood cells are destroyed by antibodies produced by mare), immune-mediated haemolytic anaemia (antibodies are produced which destroy red blood cells, may be caused by drug reaction, infection, or be autoim-

mune where horse produces antibodies against own red blood cells for unknown reason), transfusion reactions, infusion of hypertonic solutions (e.g. dimethyl sulphoxide), equine infectious anaemia, babesiosis, etc. If uncontrolled, horse becomes anaemic; haemoglobin will be present in plasma and urine samples.
See Babesiosis, Equine infectious anaemia, Erythrocyte, Haemolytic, Neonatal.

Haemolytic ◀ː _hē mō li tik, adj._ related to destruction of red blood cells.
See Haemolysis.

H. anaemia ◀ː _hē mō li tik / ē nē mē ē, n._ anaemia (decrease in red blood cells) caused by rupture or destruction of cells. Various causes, including:
1. Infectious diseases – e.g. equine infectious anaemia, babesiosis.
2. Immune mediated – when antibodies are produced that attach to the surface of blood cells.
3. Oxidative damage – e.g. from ingestion of onion, or red maple leaves.
4. Iatrogenic – e.g. from administration of intravenous dimethyl sulphoxide, or hypotonic solutions.
5. Toxicities – e.g. from bacterial toxins, such as _Clostridium_ spp.
6. Secondary to primary disease – e.g. from liver or kidney disease, or disseminated intravascular coagulation.

Clinical signs of h.a. will reflect primary disease process, or cause. Horses with h.a. will typically be weak and lethargic, with rapid heart and breathing rates and pale mucous membranes; urine will be discoloured. Diagnosis depends on specific blood tests and presence of haemoglobin in urine and plasma samples. Therapy may involve treatment of primary disease, blood transfusions, intravenous fluids to help maintain kidney function, and corticosteroids. Prognosis is guarded, but recoveries do occur.

Immune-mediated h. anaemia ◀ː _im ūn - mē dē ā tid / hē mō li tik / ē nē mē ē, n._ develops when antibodies are produced that attach to the surface of blood cells. Rare in adult horses. May be described as:
1. Primary – an autoimmune process, when horse produces antibodies against itself. Uncommon.

2. Secondary – More common than primary disease; antibodies produced for one of three reasons:
   a. Changes in red blood cell membranes secondary to a primary disease, e.g. viral or bacterial infection.
   b. Antigen–antibody complexes that are deposited on the surface of red blood cell membranes, e.g. neonatal isoerythrolysis.
   c. Drugs that cause immunoproteins to react with red blood cells, e.g. penicillin.

H. jaundice ◀€ *hē mō li tik / jorn dis, n.* jaundice (icterus) caused by an increased production of bilirubin from degradation of red blood cells. Causes yellow discoloration of mucous membranes (e.g. in mouth) and whites of eyes.
See Bile, Haemolysis, Icterus.

Haemophilia ◀€ *hē mō fi lē ē, n.* hereditary condition, an X-linked recessive trait, in which blood does not clot properly; the most commonly reported defect of haemostasis in horses. Caused by deficiency of factor VIII, part of the blood clotting cascade (haemophilia A). Has been diagnosed in Arabian, Thoroughbred, Quarter Horse and Standardbred colts. Clinical signs include severe bleeding from minor traumatic or surgical wounds, or spontaneous bleeding with no obvious cause. Diagnosis by specific blood clotting tests (activated partial thromboplastin [APTT] time increased, factor VIII activity low). The severity of the disease is inversely proportional to the activity of factor VIII; severely affected horses may have only 10% of normal activity. No cure exists. Deficiencies of other clotting factors have been reported in an Arabian foal with factor VIII deficiency.
See Blood, Clotting, Coagulation.

Haemopoiesis ◀€ *hē mō pōi ē sis, n.* (haematopoiesis) formation of blood cellular components; occurs chiefly in bone marrow.
See Blood, Bone, Platelet.

Haemorrhage ◀€ *he mē rij, n.* bleeding; discharge of blood from damaged blood vessel. May be external (e.g. in skin wound), internal (e.g. in damage to organ,

such as spleen where blood collects in abdominal cavity), or into tissues (e.g. bruise). Arterial haemorrhage is bright red and spurts; venous haemorrhage is darker red and is lost as a steady flow.
See Blood.

Haemorrhagic ◀€ *he mē ra jik, adj.* characterized by bleeding (haemorrhage).
See Blood.

Haemospermia ◀€ *hē mō sper mē ē, n.* presence of blood in semen, believed to be cause of infertility in stallion, but has not been proven. Causes include bacterial infection (especially *Pseudomonas aeruginosa*), habronemiasis of urethral process, and injury to urethra or penis. Resting the stallion to allow healing is typical treatment; additional therapy as warranted by primary cause.
See Habronemiasis, Semen, Seminal, Urethra.

Haemostasis ◀€ *hē mō stā sis, n.* stopping of bleeding. Occurs naturally by spasm of blood vessel and blood clotting; may also be performed artificially, e.g. during surgery by compression, application of a surgical instrument (e.g. haemostat), or tying suture material around bleeding vessel (ligation).
See Blood, Clotting, Ligate.

Haemothorax ◀€ *hē mō thor raks, n.* presence of free blood in chest cavity; rare in horse. Has been reported after lung biopsy, and following strenuous exercise, with thoracic trauma, e.g. fractured rib, neoplasia in lung or pleura, or with clotting disorders such as haemophilia. Traumatic cases usually resolve spontaneously.
See Blood, Thorax.

Hair ◀€ *hă, n.* thin, filamentous protein outgrowth which only grows from skin of mammals. Grows from follicle within dermis of skin, and is formed from specialized protein material, keratin. Provides a layer of insulation to help maintain body temperature.
See Keratin, Skin, Thermoregulation.

Guard h. ◀€ *gard / hă, n.* the longest, coarsest hairs of the coat; protect undercoat. Water repellent; add sheen to horse's coat. Provide nervous input to skin (e.g. as when flies land on horse).

H. cycle ◀ᴇ *hă/ sīk ēl*, *n.* hair grows in repeated cycles. Each cycle is independent of neighbouring hairs, and is divided into three phases: anagen, the growth phase (most hairs are always growing), catagen, the transitional phase, and telogen, the resting phase, when hair is normally shed.

H. follicle ◀ᴇ *hă/ fol ikēl*, *n.* skin part that grows hair. Attached to follicles are glands, muscle fibres to erect hair, and stem cells from which hair grows.

Hairy vetch ◀ᴇ *hă rē / vech*, *n.* (*Vicia villosa*) native European and western Asian plant; widespread in North America. Possible cause of generalized granulomatous disease in horses, with severe dermatitis, weight loss, fever and peripheral lymph node enlargement; rare in horses, more common in cattle. Disease occurs when the plant is a major component of the forage or when the plant is reaching maturity (mid to late spring). The plant is less likely to cause a problem in hay or when made into silage.

See Granulomatous, Sarcoidosis.

Half-life ◀ᴇ *harf-līf*, *n.* time taken for concentration of drug in animal's body to be reduced by half; written as $t_{1/2}$. Drugs that have shorter half-lives, that is, that are cleared from the blood rapidly, need to be given at more frequent intervals than drugs that have longer half-lives to build up and maintain a high enough concentration in the blood to be therapeutically effective. As doses of a drug are given repeatedly, its concentration in the blood plasma builds up and reaches a steady state (when the quantity of drug in the plasma is of sufficient concentration to be therapeutically effective). As long as regular doses are given, the drug will continue to be active, even though the drug is also being cleared by the body. The time taken to reach the steady state is usually about five times the half-life of a drug. Concept started in the study of radioactive materials, describing exponential decay.

Half-round horseshoe ◀ᴇ *harf-rŏnd / hors shŭ*, *n.* horseshoe in which the ground surface of the outside and inside edges of the shoe are rounded. Supposedly allows a horse to break over more easily, in whichever direction the horse chooses. See Breakover.

Half-shoe ◀ᴇ *harf / shŭ*, *n.* horseshoe made from the toe portion of a shoe; protects toe in cases where horse wears toe excessively (such as incessant pawing); can also be used to elevate toe in horses with short toes and long heels (rare).

Halicephalobus **spp.** ◀ᴇ *ha li ke fē lō bēs / spē shēs*, *n.* soil nematode, can gain entry to the horse's body through damaged mucosal tissues, and migrate, occasionally causing ocular and neurological disease. Ivermectin treatment may be curative if secondary complications are not severe.

Halicephalobus deletrix ◀ᴇ *ha li ke fē lō bēs / de lē triks*, *n.* helminth worm, usually found in decaying plant matter. *H. deletrix* is considered the most important cause of verminous meningoencephalitis in horses. Initially lesions may appear as oral granulomas or facial swelling; parasite larvae may migrate within horse and cause damage to various body systems, most notably the central nervous system. Neurological disease has been reported in foals as young as three weeks of age. Parasitic lesions have also been detected in equine kidneys, with associated urinary tract abnormalities, and in equine eyes, typically accompanied by uveitis, and the male reproductive tract, accompanied by testicular enlargment. Clinical signs reflect the system affected; e.g. brain or spinal cord damage will result in incoordination or circling, etc. Diagnosis is confirmed by demonstration of the parasite larvae, e.g. in biopsied lesions, semen samples, or urine sediment.

See Central nervous system, Cerebrospinal, Eosinophil, Helminth, Meningoencephalitis.

Halitosis ◀ᴇ *ha li tō sis*, *n.* foul-smelling breath. May occur in conditions such as food stuck in mouth, tooth decay, sinusitis, lung disease, or gum disease (gingivitis).

Halothane ◀﹕ *ha lō thān, n.* volatile inhalational general anaesthetic; systematic name 2-bromo-2-chloro-1,1,1-trifluoroethane. Older anaesthetic agent, first used clinically in 1956, in humans. As with all such agents, halothane requires an anaesthetic machine with a special vaporizer, and is administered to the horse along with oxygen, via tube in trachea or face mask.
See Anaesthesia.

Hamartoma ◀﹕ *ham ẽ tō mē, n.* a proliferation of normal or embryonic cells, occurring in any tissue or organ, especially skin. Vascular hamartomas have been found in horse's limbs, and are reported as a cause of lameness; congenital ovarian hamartomas have also been described. Several types of hamartoma appear to be unique to horses.

Hartman's solution see Lactated Ringer's solution

Harvest mite see *Trombicula*

Hay ◀﹕ *hā, n.* herbage, including grasses, legumes, or other pasture plants, which has been cut and dried, and used as animal fodder. Implicated in numerous toxicities, nutrition-related problems, and some diseases, especially if contaminated, poorly processed, or poorly kept. Types include:
- Grass h. – hay made from grasses, such as orchard grass, Timothy grass, coastal Bermuda grass, etc. Tends to be high in fibre and lower in calories than legume hays.
- Haylage – grass or legume; forage plants that have been converted into feed by anaerobic acid fermentation. Higher in moisture than hay, so more feed required to get equivalent calories.
- Legume h. – hay made from leguminous plants (the roots of legumes contain nitrogen-fixing bacteria), such as alfalfa (lucerne), or clover. Tends to be low in fibre, higher in calcium, and higher in calories than grass hays.

Head ◀﹕ *hed, n.* the anterior part of horse's body, containing brain, mouth and important sense organs (eyes, ears, nose). Major bony part of head is called the skull, composed of several bones joined together. See Skull.

Head-shaking ◀﹕ *hed / shā king, n.* disorder featuring persistent or occasional, usually repetitive, movements of the head and neck. Affected horses shake or jerk their heads with no obvious stimulus. Often accompanied by snorting or sneezing. May have seasonal occurrence in some horses; occurs more commonly in Thoroughbreds and geldings in some studies. Has been divided into five classifications:
- Grade 1 – mild and intermittent facial muscle-twitching and mild head-shaking; horse still can be ridden.
- Grade 2 – signs as above, but more intense and more frequent.
- Grade 3 – horse is hard to control.
- Grade 4 – horse is not able to be ridden.
- Grade 5 – horse is dangerous, with bizarre behaviour patterns.

Many proposed causes; one study of 100 horses could identify cause in only 11 horses, and only 2 horses returned to normal after removal of cause. Most recent theories are that behaviour is either caused directly by pain (neuralgia) in the trigeminal nerve, or triggered by light, which results in a referred stimulus to the trigeminal nerve. Diagnosis of an underlying cause can be unrewarding, in spite of thorough physical examination of the skull and mouth, laboratory work, and endoscopy or radiography. Cyproheptadine, an antihistamine drug, has been tried with some success; carbamazepine, a drug used for treating trigeminal neuralgia in humans has been unpredictable. Other therapies, including 'alternative' therapies, have been uniformly unsuccessful. Therapies that try to decrease the stimulus may be successful, such as riding at night, or using nosebands or nets to guard the nose. Horses have also been successfully treated with a permanent tracheostomy, which presumably helps air bypass the nose.

Heal ◄€ *hēl, v.* restoration of structure and function of tissue that has been damaged by disease or injury; to cure disease or injury.

Heart ◄€ *hart, n.* hollow, muscular organ, pumps blood around circulatory system by alternately contracting and relaxing and thereby acting as a force-pump. Composed of two halves, each with two chambers:

- Right side receives venous blood (low in oxygen) from general circulation into right atrium; blood is first pumped into right ventricle and then pumped into pulmonary artery. Blood then travels to lungs and becomes oxygenated.
- Left side receives oxygenated blood from pulmonary vein into left atrium; this is pumped into left ventricle, and is then pumped into aorta. Blood then travels around body, giving up oxygen to tissues.

Outflow of each chamber has a valve which prevents blood flowing back. Heart muscle (myocardium) contains natural pacemaker which stimulates heart to contract regularly, and can respond to differing needs of animal, e.g. beats faster during exercise.

H. block see Block

H. failure ◄€ *hart / fā lŭr, n.* inability of heart to function adequately, so blood does not circulate as well as it should. May be related to problem with valve, heart muscle, inflammation, etc. Signs will depend upon which chamber(s) of heart are affected, failure can be right-sided (i.e. blood is not being pumped to lungs adequately, right ventricle does not empty fully, so blood from major veins and tissues cannot get in and fluid builds up in tissues) or left-sided (i.e. blood is not being pumped to body adequately, left ventricle does not empty fully, so blood from lungs cannot get in, and fluid builds up in lungs). Congestive h.f. is where poor blood flow results in fluid build-up in tissues (oedema) and body cavities (ascites), tissues do not get enough oxygen, and animal is very unwell.

H. murmur ◄€ *hart / mē mer, n.* heart sound detected on auscultation, caused by turbulence of blood flow. Commonly detected in horse, may be normal or associated with congenital heart problem, e.g. hole between ventricles or atria (ventricular or atrial septal defect), leaking heart valve. Echocardiography may be used to evaluate severity of problem.

See Auscultation, Ductus, H. valve (below).

H. rate ◄€ *hart / rāt, n.* number of heart contractions in a set time, usually given as beats per minute (bpm). In normal adult, resting rate is 32–40 bpm; may be lower in very fit individuals. In newborn foal, initially 40–80 bpm, rising to 130–150 bpm as foal attempts to stand. Over the subsequent days, resting rate is typically 70–100 bpm. H. r. increases with exercise, excitement, pain (e.g. colic), high temperature.

The heart rate of the foetus can be determined in utero by electrocardiography or ultrasound. Used for twin detection, for a measure of foetal viability, and to monitor distress at parturition. Foetal h. beat slows from approximately 110 bpm at 150 days gestation, to 60–80 bpm at the end of gestation.

See Anaemia, Colic.

H. score ◄€ *hart / skor, n.* an electrocardiographic measurement of the QRS complex, which is purportedly related to heart mass; heart mass is directly related to performance. Heart score does tend to be heritable; however, its link to performance has not been firmly established.

H. sound ◄€ *hart / sōnd, n.* noise made by heart, and detected on auscultation, associated with closure of heart valves. In humans, two heart sounds are usually described; however, in horses, it is common to hear as many as four:

- First heart sound: the start of ventricular contraction (systole), caused mainly by closure of valves between atria and ventricles (mitral and tricuspid valves).
- Second heart sound: aortic and pulmonic valve closure; associated with the end of systole and beginning of diastole.
- Third heart sound: associated with rapid filling of ventricle in early diastole; occurs as dull thud immediately after second sound.
- Fourth heart sound: associated with atrial contraction; commonly heard immediately before the first heart sound.

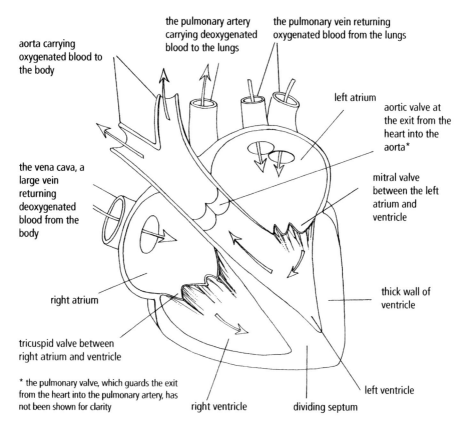

aorta carrying oxygenated blood to the body

the pulmonary artery carrying deoxygenated blood to the lungs

the pulmonary vein returning oxygenated blood from the lungs

left atrium

aortic valve at the exit from the heart into the aorta*

the vena cava, a large vein returning deoxygenated blood from the body

mitral valve between the left atrium and ventricle

right atrium

thick wall of ventricle

tricuspid valve between right atrium and ventricle

* the pulmonary valve, which guards the exit from the heart into the pulmonary artery, has not been shown for clarity

right ventricle

dividing septum

left ventricle

The horse's heart

Most common sequence is 4-1-2-3; sound described as 'du LUBB DUP boo'. Variations of 4-1-2, 1-2, and 1-2-3 are also common. Heart sounds may be heard most clearly in different areas of chest wall, this may be important in diagnosis of conditions of heart or thorax. See H. valve (below).

H. valve ◄€ *hart / valv, n.* one of four structures in heart which, when closed, ensure blood flows in correct direction. Composed of flaps of fibrous tissue covered in endocardium, held in place by chordae tendinae which stop flaps being pushed in wrong direction.

- Mitral valve: left atrioventricular valve, between left atrium and left ventricle.
- Tricuspid valve: right atrioventricular valve, between right atrium and right ventricle.
- Aortic valve: semilunar valve, between left ventricle and aorta.

- Pulmonary valve: semilunar valve, between right ventricle and pulmonary artery.

Disease of valve tissue (e.g. in endocarditis), rupture of chorda tendinae, valvular prolapse (cusp of valve flops in wrong direction), tear in cusp, etc., will cause valve to allow some blood to flow in wrong direction, and heart murmur may be heard. Severity of signs seen will depend on how leaky valve is and which valve is affected: may be no signs, poor performance, heart failure. Echocardiography useful in assessment of valve problems.
See H. murmur (above).

Heart-bar shoe see Bar

Heat ◄€ *hēt, n.* lay term for oestrus; form of energy that raises temperature when transferred from one system to another.

See Oestrus, Temperature.

H. cycle see Oestrous cycle

H. stroke ◀€ *hēt / strōk, n.* condition in which animal's systems to control body temperature fails to keep temperature within normal levels, and temperature becomes abnormally high. Horse's ability to cool itself is relatively limited, compared to other species, and is made more difficult by large body mass. May be seen in conditions of excessive or prolonged heat, such as when horse is transported in hot weather in poorly ventilated vehicle or does too much work in hot, humid conditions. Can be exacerbated by circumstances that insulate horse, such as being overweight, having a long coat, or wearing heavy blankets in inappropriate conditions. Signs related to the extent of the condition; horse may initially show lethargy, rapid heart rate (tachycardia), rapid breathing (tachypnoea), inappetence, unwillingness to perform, and mild fever; if unrecognized, affected horses become dehydrated from loss of sweat, which further exacerbates inability to lose heat. Many horses fail to sweat when overheated; failure to sweat is classic sign of anhydrosis. (see Anhydrosis) If temperature becomes too high, 41.5–42°C, horse can sustain neurological damage, or collapse, and die. Treatment is by providing rapid cooling, including ice water baths, cold water by nasogastric intubation, and evaporative measures (e.g. fan). Prevention is the best option; horses should be ridden when temperatures are not extreme, or, if riding under conditions of extreme heat, their body temperatures should be monitored regularly, and ample water should be provided. See Sweat, Thermo regulation.

H. therapy ◀€ *hēt / the rēpē, n.* the use of heat for the treatment of various conditions. Localized application of heat, either direct, via hot water, or induced, such as induced by ultrasound diathermy, may be used in the treatment of muscle soreness, strains, or sprains; hyperthermia probes are used to treat various neoplasms, e.g. equine sarcoid.

Heave line ◀€ *hēv / līn, n.* line of muscle enlargement seen on abdominal wall of horses with severe recurrent airway obstruction, as result of muscles of abdomen being used to push air out of lungs.
See Recurrent airway obstruction.

Heaves ◀€ *hēvz, n.* lay term for recurrent airway obstruction.
See Recurrent airway obstruction

Heavy metal ◀€ *he vē / me tl, n.* any of a number of metals with higher atomic weights. Horses require trace amounts of some heavy metals, e.g. copper, zinc and iron; however many heavy metals are poisonous in excessive quantities, e.g. lead, cadmium, mercury, arsenic, zinc, copper. See under separate entries.

Heel ◀€ *hēl, n.* back part of foot; includes two soft, rounded 'bulbs' one each side of midline at coronary band, hoof wall, and associated structures. Important area; area of hoof from which lameness commonly originates, and to which numerous shoeing and trimming modifications are applied.
See Foot.

    Contracted h. ◀€ *kon trak tid / hēl , n.* heel conformation characterized by a shift of the hoof wall, resulting in the narrowing of the foot at the heels. Considered undesirable, and predisposing to heel-related lameness.

    Floated h. ◀€ *flō tid / hēl, n.* trimming the heel so that it is not in contact with the shoe. Commonly done in an effort to relieve stress, e.g. in the treatment of hoof cracks. Trimming often done in conjunction with bar shoe.

    H. caulks see Calkin

    H. pain ◀€ *hēl / pāne, n.* lameness caused by pain coming from the heel. Includes lameness from many underlying pathologies, including tendon and ligament injuries, bruising, navicular syndrome, inadequate hoof care, abscess, etc. Diagnosis of heel pain can usually be confirmed by careful physical examination and local anaesthesia, especially palmar digital nerve block; determination of true underlying cause somewhat more problematic, even with advanced diagnostic imaging techniques.

    H. wedge ◀€ *hēl / wej, n.* a device, usually made out of synthetic material, placed between the heel and the shoe, which elevates the heel. Used for the treatment of a variety of conditions in horses, albeit with some controversy in particular applications.

Underrun h. ◀⊱ *undē run / hēl* , n. (also 'underslung') a description of hoof conformation, whereby the angle formed by the intersection of a line drawn along the hoof wall at the heel and the ground is more acute, rather than more vertical. Conformation often accompanied by a long toe. Considered undesirable, and implicated in many lameness conditions. Can be difficult to manage; correction is unreported in veterinary literature.

Height ◀⊱ *hīt*, n. measurement from ground to top of withers (highest part of shoulders). Traditionally given in hands (1 hand = 4 inches = 10.16 cm).
See Withers.

Heinz body ◀⊱ *hīntz / bo dē*, n. inclusions in red blood cells composed of denatured haemoglobin; usually formed as a result of oxidative damage to haemoglobin. May be seen in anaemia caused by red maple, garlic, or onion, associated with diseases such as lymphosarcoma, or toxicities such as those caused by phenothiazine drugs. (Named after Robert Heinz, German pathologist, 1865–1924.)
See Anaemia, Erythrocyte, Red maple.

Helicobacter **spp**. ◀⊱ *hel ēko bak tē / spē shēs*, n. bacterium associated with gastric ulceration in humans; polymerase chain reaction testing has identified bacterial fragments in horses' stomachs, but no association with gastric ulcers in horses has been made.

Helminth ◀⊱ *hel minth*, n. parasitic worm, includes roundworms (nematodes), tapeworms (cestodes) and flukes (trematodes).
See Fluke, Roundworm, Tapeworm.

Hemiplegia ◀⊱ *he mi plē jē ē*, n. paralysis of one side or part of body, e.g. laryngeal hemiplegia.
See Laryngeal.

Hemisphere ◀⊱ *he mi sfér*, n. half of spherical structure or organ; e.g. cerebral h. is one half of cerebrum.
See Brain.

Hemlock ◀⊱ *hem lok, n.* (*Conium maculatum*) poisonous plant native to Europe, especially the Mediterranean region; now widely distributed. May be mistaken for parsley, or fennel. Smooth green stem, usually spotted or streaked with red or purple on the lower half. Contains coniine, a neurotoxin, which causes problems in central nervous system. Horses may eat plant in spring (later in year, is not palatable), rapidly causes incoordination of hind legs, trembling, may lead to recumbency and coma. Name hemlock can be confusing, as it is applied to other plants, e.g. water hemlock (*Cicuta maculata*) and hemlock water-dropwort (*Oenanthe crocata*). These are also poisonous.
See Hemlock water-dropwort, Water hemlock.

Hemlock water-dropwort ◀⊱ *hem lok / wor tē / drop wert*, n. 'Horsebane', 'Dead Tongue' (*Oenanthe crocata*) poisonous plant, with toxin in roots. Common in England, especially in the southern counties, but not occurring in Scandinavia, Holland, Germany, Russia, Turkey or Greece. May occasionally be eaten by horses when it has been dug up as ditches are cleared. Causes convulsions and death.
See Hemlock, Water hemlock.

Hendra virus ◀⊱ *hen drē / vī rēs*, n. a member of the Paramyxovirus family, first recognized in 1994; caused fever, acute respiratory distress, and death in 14 of 21 affected horses in Hendra, a suburb of Brisbane, in Australia. Serious zoonotic disease; two humans died in Australian outbreak, one of respiratory disease, and one of encephalitis. Natural host is fruit bat; camping under trees or buildings where bats roost should be avoided. Virus attacks endothelial cells, causing pulmonary oedema and haemorrhage, pneumonia, and pericardial effusion. No treatment should be attempted, because of zoonotic potential. No vaccine available.

Heparin ◀⊱ *he pē rin*, n. highly sulphated glycosaminoglycan with wide use as an injectable anticoagulant; naturally occurring, released by mast cells and basophils, and present especially in liver and lungs. In body, acts as anticoagulant and involved in metabolism of fats. Clinical uses include conditions associated with coagulation problems, such as disseminated intravascular coagulation, endotoxaemia, and acute diarrhoea; to prevent adhesions, in peritonitis; has been used in treatment of laminitis, in an effort to prevent the formation of small blood clots in the vasculature of the feet (heparin has no demonstrable effectiveness in preventing or treating laminitis). Overdose causes haemorrhage and anaemia. Heparin salts are used in some blood sampling tubes (blue top and green top) to prevent clotting.

Hepatic ◄⁞ _hi pa tik, adj._ of the liver.
See Liver.

    H. encephalopathy ◄⁞ _hi pa tik / en ke fa lo pē thē, n._ abnormal mental state that can occur in conjunction with severe liver disease of any type, including ingestion of certain toxic plants, e.g. ragwort (_Senecio jacobaea_) poisoning in UK and Europe, fiddleneck (_Amsinckia_ spp.), rattlebox (_Crotalaria_ spp.) and groundsel (_Senecio vulgaris_) throughout the world). H. encephalopathy causes progressive neurological dysfunction, characterized by head pressing, ataxia, wandering and yawning in early stages; late stages show aggressive behaviour, stupor, coma, and death. Pathogenesis unclear; probably many factors involved; however, oldest and most popular hypothesis pertains to high levels of ammonia in blood as a result of insufficient metabolism in dysfunctional liver, resulting in abnormal brain function. H. encephalopathy must be differentiated from many other viral, toxic, and traumatic neurological diseases; successful treatment related to ability to address primary cause.
See Ragwort.

    H. insufficiency see Insufficiency

Hepatitis ◄⁞ _he pē tī tis, n._ inflammation of liver. Various causes, including infectious (bacteria, viruses), and plant toxins (e.g. ragwort). Clinical signs seen include weight loss, icterus, loss of appetite, dullness, colic, skin signs (photosensitization), behavioural changes (hepatic encephalopathy), diarrhoea. Initial diagnosis by clinical signs and blood work; serum chemistries may show elevations of liver enzymes such as aspartate aminotransferase (AST), alanine aminotransferase (ALT) gamma glutamyltransferase (GGT) and alkaline phosphatase (see specific entries). More precise diagnostic information may be obtained by percutaneous liver biopsy, and/or ultrasound. Abdominocentesis occasionally helpful. Treatment directed towards inciting cause (e.g. antibiotics for bacterial hepatitis); may offer dietary changes or vitamin supplementation in an effort to reduce metabolic workload of liver. Prognosis depends on cause and extent of damage.
See Colic, Gamma, Hepatic, Liver, Photosensitization.

Hepatopathy ◄⁞ _he pē top ē thē, n._ any liver disease or disorder, including from various toxins or infectious agents. Plants that contain pyrrolizidine alkaloids cause a megalocytic hepatopathy (enlargement of liver cells seen on liver biopsy).

Herbal medicine ◄⁞ _her bēl / med i sin, n._ the use of plants, in whole or in part, as medicine. As far back as evidence can be gathered, humans used various plants to treat their ailments, and, presumably, those of their animals. However, doses were arbitrary, many of the remedies simply did not work, and some were harmful or even deadly. True plant identities are doubtful in regard to genus and species, both in terms of which plants were used in the past, and which plants are contained in current preparations, and prescriptions varied depending on the prescribing person (there were no standards for such prescription). As a result, herbal medications lost popularity in modern civilizations because they could no longer match the advances of science and the resulting public trust that accompanied those advances until the recent revival of interest in their use.

    Herbal and botanical sources form the origin of as much as 30% of all modern pharmaceuticals. However, the fact that herbal products were used throughout history, or that they may have pharmacologically active ingredients, may also overlook real problems. These include ingestion of non-essential compounds (e.g.

tannins in willow bark cause intestinal upset), the natural variation of constituent substances in plants, between plants, and between species of the same plant, unknown potency and rate of decomposition of active substances, and unknown rates of absorption from the gastrointestinal tract.

In laboratory settings, plant extracts have been shown to have a variety of pharmacological effects, including anti-inflammatory, vasodilatory, antimicrobial, anticonvulsant, sedative, and antipyretic effects. This should not be surprising, as many plants contain pharmacologically active ingredients, some of which are highly toxic. From an evolutionary standpoint these sorts of substances are thought to be defence mechanisms for survival of the plant. Whether the actions of plants or extracts that have been shown to have pharmacological effects can be safely or effectively used as medicines is another question, and one that largely has yet to be answered. Indeed, controlled studies on the clinical effects of herbal or botanical preparations in horses are virtually non-existent.

As a result, popular herbalism appears to have abandoned most of the obvious pharmacologically active herbs to the pharmaceutical industry, since their therapeutic window is so narrow and misuse can be deadly. Those that remain in more common use are likely to be neither very potent nor very toxic. Indeed, many of the popular herbal products intended for use in horses contain ingredients with no recognized therapeutic value at all.

Herbal products may be prescribed for reasons that diverge from known medical practice. That is, treatments may be prescribed or based on vague rationales for which there is no proof, or which make no sense. For example, observations such as 'underfunctioning of a patient's systems of elimination' or 'an accumulation of metabolic waste products' make no medical sense whatsoever.

Finally, because some herbal remedies contain multiple biologically active constituents, interaction with conventional drugs is also a concern. Allergic reactions, toxic reactions, adverse effects related to a herb's desired pharmacological actions, and possible mutagenic effects have been identified. Herbal products may also be contaminated, adulterated, or misidentified. Numerous reports of outright fraud.

HERDA *abbr.* (Hereditary equine regional dermal asthenia; hyperelastosis cutis) hereditary skin disease of Quarter Horses or horses with Quarter Horse ancestry. Pedigree evaluation supports an autosomal recessive mode of inheritance, linked to the Quarter Horse sire Poco Bueno. Clinical findings in affected horses include seromas and haematomas, non-healing wounds, sloughing skin, and loose skin that, when pulled up into a tent, does not return to its initial position. Histology is suggestive but not definitive for diagnosis; diagnosis based on combination of pedigree analysis, clinical presentation and histopathological lesions. There is no cure, and carriers cannot yet be identified by genetic analysis. Managed breeding strategy by pedigree analysis is currently the only option for reducing the incidence of HERDA. Affected horses can live to a fairly old age, but they are not suitable as riding animals, and are easily subjected to skin trauma and sunburn.
See Dermal.

Hereditary ◄⁞ *hi re di trē, adj.* describes condition or characteristic passed from parents to offspring or descendants, through the information contained in chromosomes.
See Chromosome, Gene.
> **Hereditary equine regional dermal asthenia**
> see HERDA

Heredity ◄⁞ *hi re di tē, n.* transmission of characteristics or condition via genes from one generation to next.
See Chromosome, Gene.

Heritable ◄⁞ *he rit ēbēl, adj.* capable of being passed on by inheritance.

Hermaphrodite ◄⁞ *her ma frō dīt, n.* animal with both female (ovarian) and male (testicular) gonadal tissue. Not common in horse. Pseudohermaphrodites occur more commonly: these have gonads of one sex, but with various combinations of internal reproductive organs or external genitalia.
See Pseudohermaphrodite.

Hernia ◀︎ _her_ nē ē, n. protrusion of all or part of organ through connective tissue or a wall in which it is normally contained. Hernias may be characterized in various ways:

- May be congenital, e.g. scrotal hernias in newborn colts, or acquired, e.g. diaphragmatic hernias of foaling mares, or trauma.
- Complete or incomplete, depending on whether all or part of an organ has herniated.
- Internal, e.g. herniation of small bowel through the mesentery of the small intestines, or external, where the herniated parts herniate outside the body, e.g. scrotal hernia.
- Reducible, i.e. contents can easily be pushed back to where they belong (but can protrude again), or irreducible, i.e. contents cannot easily be pushed back. Irreducible hernias are at risk of serious complications, such as strangulation, where blood vessels supplying herniated organ(s) get compressed and so organ(s) damaged through lack of oxygen, no removal of waste products, etc. or obstruction, when bowel contents cannot pass through the herniated part. Common causes of colic.

See Colic, Obstruction, Strangulation.

Abdominal h. ◀︎ ab _do_ mi nēl / _her_ nē ē, n. (ventral hernia) protrusion of abdominal contents through abdominal wall, especially after abdominal surgery, or injury. Seen as swelling on ventral abdomen, depending on degree of herniation. Depending on size, requires surgical closure; some defects require synthetic mesh to assist closure. Post-surgical abdominal hernias may not need repair, i.e. studies have shown that most animals do well and do not suffer serious complications; cosmetic issue. Theoretical cause of entrapment or obstruction, in which case signs of colic will occur.

Diaphragmatic h. ◀︎ _di_ ē frē _ma_ tik / _her_ nē ē, n. tear in diaphragm; may allow abdominal organs to pass into thorax. Uncommon; may be caused by trauma, be congenital, or especially in post-foaling mares, where the force of abdominal contractions at parturition tears diaphragm. Clinical signs depend on degree of organ compromise; e.g. may result in intestinal obstruction and colic, or difficulty breathing if lungs compressed. Auscultation of chest may reveal reduced lung sounds or increased intestinal sounds, but such sounds are not diagnostic; fluid sample from chest may be useful to detect devitalized organs; radiography and ultrasonography are diagnostic. Surgical treatment is sometimes successful, depending on extent of tear.

See Auscultation, Diaphragm, Omentum.

H. clamp ◀︎ _her_ nē ē / _klamp_, n. surgical device, usually made of metal or wood, used to close umbilical hernia without surgical incision. Works by compressing the sides of the hernia with enough pressure to disrupt circulation, causing the clamped skin hernia to slough, while the hernia heals underneath the clamp. The foal must be monitored during the process, which can take several weeks, as numerous complications, including evisceration, have been reported if clamp repair is unsuccessful.

Inguinal h. ◀︎ _in_ gwi nēl / _her_ nē ē, n. abdominal contents (e.g. omentum, loop of intestine) pass through inguinal canal (in groin) and into vaginal sac (peritoneum which lines inguinal canal and scrotum), may reach scrotum. May be congenital (in foal, large inguinal ring at entrance to inguinal canal) or acquired (tear in muscle at inguinal ring, in stallions during exercise or after mating). Acquired hernias often become strangulated and require surgery to replace intestines; congenital hernias are usually repaired when recognized. Castration of affected side, with closure of inguinal ring, prevents further problems.

See Inguinal, Omentum, Scrotum, Strangulation.

Scrotal h. ◀︎ _skrō_ tēl / _her_ nē ē, n. inguinal hernia in which inguinal ring or tear at inguinal ring is large enough to allow loop of intestine to reach scrotum.

See Inguinal h. (above), Scrotum.

Strangulated h. ◀︎ _strang_ gū lā tid / _her_ nē ē, n. h. whose contents cannot be reduced, resulting in compromise of blood supply (strangulation) to contents. Causes signs of colic. Immediate surgical correction, with removal of compromised part, is required; without treatment, contents rapidly become gangrenous.

See Gangrene, Strangulation.

Umbilical h. ◀︎ƚ *um bi li kēl* / *her nē ē, n.* herniation of intestinal contents through umbilical remnant. Abdominal contents can pass through hole into hernial sac (out-pocketing of peritoneum); contents vary, depending on size of hernia. Appears to be more common in fillies than colts. Occasional cause of intestinal entrapment or incarceration; if bowel entrapped, signs of pain (colic), fever, and depression may be seen, requiring surgical treatment. Uncomplicated hernias may resolve spontaneously if small enough (usually, two fingers or less fitting into the hernia); closure will usually occur by one year of age; regular monitoring of hernia, with reduction of contents into abdomen, is important to monitor condition, and may help stimulate closure by inciting inflammation. Larger hernias usually repaired by 6–12 months of age; both external techniques (e.g. elastrator, hernia clamp) and surgical techniques are employed; both require anaesthesia.
See H. clamp (above), Umbilicus.

Ventral h . ◀︎ƚ *ven trēl* / *her nē ē, n.* an opening or weakness in the muscular abdominal wall, generally accompanied by protrusion of abdominal contents through the opening (but not through skin), not including umbilical or inguinal hernias. May be caused by injury, e.g. kick, getting caught on gate, or from muscle damage during late-term pregnancy or foaling. Often requires surgical repair, to prevent strangulation of intestine in hernia wall.

Herpes see Equine herpes virus

Hetastarch ◀︎ƚ *hetē starch, n.* synthetic colloid starch, sometimes used to increase colloid oncontic pressure (pressure in blood plasma exerted by tissue fluid proteins) in cases of severe protein loss, such as in acute diarrhoea.
See Pressure.

Heterochromia iridis ◀︎ƚ *hetē rō krō miē* / *ir idis, n.* iris with mix of blue and brown colours; normal variation of iris colour.

Heterotopic polydontia see Dentigerous

High-blowing ◀︎ƚ *hī-blō ing, n.* noise made during expiration (breathing out) when alar folds of false nostrils vibrate. Often occurs during cantering.
See Ala, Nostril.

High flanker ◀︎ƚ *hī* / *flang kē, n.* colloquial term for cryptorchid horse.
See Cryptorchid.

High nail ◀︎ƚ *hī* / *nāl, n.* horseshoe nail placed close to, or into, sensitive structures of hoof. Cause of lameness, and may result in abscess if not recognized immediately.

High performance liquid chromatography ◀︎ƚ *hī* / *per form ēns* / *krō mēt og raf ē, n.* (HPLC) analytical laboratory technique; may be used to separate chemical compounds, such as bile acid fractions, in laboratory diagnostic testing.

High ringbone ◀︎ƚ *hī* / *ring bōn, n.* osteoarthritis of the proximal interphalangeal joint.
See Osteoarthritis.

High suspensory disease ◀︎ƚ *hī* / *sēs pen sēr ē* / *di zēz, n.* inflammation of the proximal suspensory ligament.
See Suspensory ligament.

Hilum ◀︎ƚ *hī lēm, n.* notch or depression in surface of organ, e.g. kidney, lung, spleen, especially where blood vessels, ducts, and nerves enter and leave.

Hind limb ◀︎ƚ *hīnd* / *lim, n.* back leg.

Hip ◀︎ƚ *hip, n.* region of body formed by the lateral parts of the pelvis and upper part of the femur, the joint, and the fleshy parts (including muscle, tendon, ligament and connective tissue) covering them.
See H. joint (below).

H. joint ◀︎ƚ *hip* / *joint, n.* ball-and-socket articulation between pelvis and femur (i.e. joint attaching hind limb to body). Head of femur is 'ball-shaped' area which fits into acetabulum, the socket in the pelvis. Two ligaments help to hold joint in place: round ligament (short, strong band of fibrous tissue which attaches to head of femur and acetabulum) and accessory femoral ligament (longer, runs from femoral head through acetabulum to prepubic tendon). Conditions

which may affect hip joint include osteoarthritis (rarely recognized), fracture, and dislocation (luxation, rare).
See Dislocation, Femur, Ligament, Osteoarthritis, Pelvis.

Hippo- ◀⁞ _hi pō, prefix._ denoting relationship tō a horse.

Hippocampus ◀⁞ _hi pō kam pŭs, n._ area deep in the forebrain, on the floor of each lateral ventricle, that helps regulate emotion, learning and memory.

Hippomane ◀⁞ _hi pō mān, n._ small, round, flat, brownish body, made up of layers of cellular debris, which is ordinarily found associated with the placenta of some postpartum mares. In ancient times, it was used as a love charm.

Hirsutism ◀⁞ _her sū tizm, n._ abnormal hairiness; abnormally long haircoat. Classic sign of horses with Pituitary pars intermedia dysfunction (Cushing's disease).
See Pituitary pars intermedia dysfunction.

Histamine ◀⁞ _his tē mēn, n._ organic compound, $C_5H_9N_3$ found especially in mammalian tissues and cells, especially basophils and mast cells. Once produced from the amino acid histidine, histamine is either stored or rapidly inactivated. Histamine acts at specific receptors on cells in various sites of body to cause capillary dilation, smooth muscle contraction, increased secretion of gastric acid by the stomach, and increased heart rate. Released during the process of inflammation, especially allergic reactions (e.g. urticaria, recurrent airway obstruction). Drug to counter effects of histamine (antihistamine) may be used to treat various conditions in the horse, most with underlying immunological basis, e.g. dermatitis, allergic reactions, recurrent airway obstruction; effects are highly variable, presumably because many other inflammatory mediators are involved in these reactions.
See Allergy, Recurrent airway obstruction, Urticaria.

Histiocytoma ◀⁞ _his tiō sī tōmē, n._ rare neoplasm of skin (a.k.a. giant cell tumour). Cause unknown; no age, sex or breed predilection. Causes single raised, firm nodules, typically on neck, thigh, back and stifle. Surgical excision must have wide margins to be curative, but regrowth common. Does not metastasize.

Histology ◀⁞ _his tō lē gē, n._ study of anatomy at a microscopic level, dealing with structure and function of tissues.

Histopathology ◀⁞ _his tō pē thol ējē, n._ the study of diseased tissues, performed under a microscope.

Histoplasma ◀⁞ _his tō plaz mē, n._ genus of disease-causing fungi; disease uncommon in horses, although serological studies suggest that exposure is common in endemic areas. Three varieties are identified:
1. _H. capsulatum_ var. _capsulatum_ causes histoplasmosis in horses and especially humans. Common in USA east of the Mississippi River area, and in parts of Central and South America. Most horses affected have pulmonary disease, but cases of gastrointestinal disease and one case of central nervous system disease have been reported. Has also caused abortion in mares. Clinical signs of disease include chronic weight loss, depression, pyrexia, dyspnoea, loss of appetite, oedema, and diarrhoea. Radiography may assist diagnosis; yeast cells may be seen on transtracheal aspiration biopsy or bronchoalveolar lavage. Serology may be helpful (complement fixation test). Treatment of affected horses has rarely been attempted because disease has been severe on presentation; one horse was successfully treated with the antifungal agent amphoterin B.
2. _H. capsulatum_ var. _duboisii_, which causes African histoplasmosis in people.
3. _H. capsulatum_ var. _farciminosum_ causes epizootic lymphangitis in horses, a nodular skin condition seen especially in Africa, Asia and eastern Europe.
There is one report of a horse with _H._ spp.

keratitis. It was successfully treated with topical antifungal drops.
See Epizootic lymphangitis, Fungus, Pneumonia.

History ◀︎ *his tērē, n.* an account of a patient's past and present health, usually taken at the time of clinical examination; often gives important clues as to the aetiology of the condition being examined.

Hobble ◀︎ *hob ŭl, n.* device, usually made of leather, which fastens together the horse's legs (usually both forelimbs) and prevents the horse from wandering. Several different configurations of hobbles, and techniques for hobbling, are described.

Hobday procedure ◀︎ *hob dā / prō sēd ŭr, n.* (ventriculectomy) operation to treat recurrent laryngeal neuropathy (laryngeal paralysis). (Named after Sir Frederick Hobday, British veterinary surgeon, 1870–1939.)
See Recurrent laryngeal neuropathy, Ventriculectomy.

Hock ◀︎ *hok, n.* tarsus, joint of hind limb, equivalent of human ankle.
See Tarsus.
> **Cow h.** ◀︎ *cō / hok, n.* describes hind limb conformation where the hocks are pointed inward, towards midline (as opposed to being each on a sagittal plane). Typically accompanied by toe-out conformation of lower limb. Various maladies described as a result of such conformation have not been confirmed scientifically.
> **H. flexion test** ◀︎ *hok / flek shēn / test, n.* lameness test whereby hind limb is held in flexion for a time depending on the examiner, often approximately 90 seconds. Horse is examined for lameness at the trot immediately upon release of limb. Non-specific, as horse cannot independently flex hock joint, and test also stresses soft tissues of limb.
> See Flexion.
> **Sickle h.** ◀︎ *si kĕl / hok, n.* describes hind limb conformation where horses hocks are more acutely angled than is considered desirable. Some people prefer this conformation as it is said that such horses are easier to collect; others express concerns that

this predisposes to uneven hoof wear, and hock and back problems. Neither the alleged benefits or maladies described have been confirmed scientifically.

Hollow back see Back

Holocrine ◀︎ *ho lo krin, adj.* describes gland in which secretion is made up from lysed cells of the gland, e.g. sebaceous gland.
See Gland, Sebaceous.

Homeopathy ◀︎ *ho mē op ĕth ē, n.* in the late eighteenth century, a German physician named Samuel Hahnemann rebelled against the current medical practices of his day, which included bleeding, burning and administering near-toxic doses of mercury. Hahnemann devised a system of medicine based on the belief that medicinal substances had 'vital force' that acted 'spiritually'on the causes of disease (which he did not know). Hahnemann took substances that he thought to be medicinal – things like poison ivy, crushed bees, or duck liver – and diluted them far past the point at which a single molecule of the original substance existed, those molecules being dispersed with each subsequent dilution. He shook the substances up between dilutions, banged them against a leather book, and pronounced them to be powerful medications. He called his approach to medicine homeopathy. Over the years, and with the advent of modern medicine, homeopathic remedies ultimately declined in popularity. However, with the rise of 'alternative' approaches to medicine in the late twentieth century, homeopathic remedies became more readily available. As one might be inclined to suspect, since the system is based on the practice of diluting a substance to a point at which it is effectively water (or water placed on a sugar tablet), it has been essentially impossible to show that homeopathic remedies have any relevant therapeutic effect. Indeed, in 2005, in the largest analysis to date, of 110 trials of homeopathy, an article published in the prestigious British medical journal *The Lancet* concluded that: '… the clinical effects of homoeopathy are placebo effects'. Some homeopathic preparations may be given to horses. No homeopathic remedy has ever been shown to be effective for any condition in sound scientific trials, in horses, or in any other species.

Homeostasis ◀﹕ *hō mē ō stā sis, n.* maintenance of stable physiological conditions under changing environmental conditions. Within horse's body many biological systems are constantly adjusting to changing conditions, e.g. level of glucose in blood, which varies as horse eats and exercises, but which is also kept within quite strict limits which are optimal for life.

Hoof ◀﹕ *hŭf, n.* hard, horny covering of horse's foot.
See Foot.

    H. avulsion ◀﹕ *hŭf / ēv ul shĕn, n.* hoof injury whereby a part of the hoof wall is torn away; result of trauma.

    H. balance see Balance

    H. crack ◀﹕ *hŭf / krak, n.* a narrow break in the hoof wall. H. cracks may originate from ground surface or from coronary band. May be a cause of lameness, especially if crack extends into sensitive tissue, e.g. the coronary band. Various repair techniques described for severe cracks, usually in conjunction with alterations in hoof balance, and horseshoe changes (e.g. bar shoe).

    H. pad ◀﹕ *hŭf / pad, n.* a thin, flat mat or cushion, made out of a variety of materials, including plastic, leather, and synthetic materials, interposed between hoof and horseshoe to cushion force on the hoof, or to shield the hoof against impact. Various configurations may also attempt to alter hoof balance or limb mechanics (e.g. wedge pad).

    H.–pastern axis ◀﹕ *hŭf / pas tĕn / aksis, n.* a measure taken to determine appropriate hoof trimming; describes the relationship between a line drawn along the dorsal hoof wall and a line drawn along the dorsal surface of the pastern region; considered ideal when those lines are parallel. Club-footed horses have an upright h.–pastern axis; horses with underrun heels generally have a broken-back h.–pastern axis.

    H. protractor ◀﹕ *hŭf / prō trakt ē, n.* device used to measure the angle of the horse's foot. Flat plate is placed on the ground surface of the hoof; arm of device is applied to hoof

wall. Device measures angle of hoof wall, determined at the intersection of the two arms of the device.

    H. tester ◀﹕ *hŭf / tes tē, n.* device used in lameness examination; applies pressure to points of the hoof selected by examiner. Positive response is when horse withdraws limb after application of h. testers to a sensitive point. Many different designs. Much variability to response based on operator.

    H. wall ◀﹕ *hŭf / wawl, n.* the part of the hoof that can be seen when the horse is standing on the ground; covers the third phalanx, navicular bone, and associated structures. Comprises toe (front), quarters (sides) and heel.

Hook ◀﹕ *hük, n.* large, curved, protruding points of enamel on chewing surface of teeth, typically the second premolar or the third molar, caused by uneven wear of teeth.
See Tooth.

Hormone ◀﹕ *hor mōn, n.* a chemical messenger produced by a gland or organ; carries a signal from a cell (or group of cells) in one part of the body to a cell (or group of cells) in another part of the body where it causes an effect. The action of hormones is determined by the pattern of secretion and the response of the target tissue to the hormonal stimulus. Numerous examples in mammals, e.g. insulin, produced by pancreas, has effects in liver and many other tissues where it affects metabolism by regulating the storage or use of glucose; growth hormone, produced in pituitary gland in brain, affects growth of the organism.
See hormones under individual entries, Gland.

    Hormonal ◀﹕ *hor mōn ĕl, adj.* of, relating to, or affected by hormones.

Horn ◀﹕ *horn, n.* hard protein substance of which hoof is made: keratin.

    H. spur ◀﹕ *horn / sper, n.* an epidermal spur that sometimes develops as a result of avulsion of hoof wall; cause of lameness, usually requires surgical removal.

Horner's syndrome ◀﹕ *hor nēz / sin drŏm, n.* uncommon neurological syndrome

223

characterized by drooping of eyelid on affected side, constricted pupil, sweating on one side of the face, protrusion of the third eyelid (nictitating membrane), increased temperature on the affected side of the face, and hyperaemia of the mucous membranes. Causes include perivascular injection, with nerve damage, infection in the guttural pouch, or damage to sympathetic nerves in the vagosympathetic trunk. Prognosis depends on cause. (Named after Johann Friedrich Horner, Swiss ophthalmologist, 1831–1886.)
See Autonomic nervous system, Eye, Guttural pouch, Sympathetic nervous system.

Horny layer ◄ؤ *hornē / lā ē, n.* the outer layer of epidermal tissue; stratum corneum.

Horse chestnut ◄ؤ *hors / ches nut, n.* (*Aesculus* spp.) species of deciduous trees and shrubs native to Northern Hemisphere. Contain auesulin, a toxic glycoside. Colic and diarrhoea are the primary problems after ingestion; treatment is supportive.

Horse fly see *Tabanus*

Horsepox ◄ؤ *hors poks, n.* a rare disease, reported to date only in Europe, caused by a poxvirus in the genus *Orthopoxvirus*. Causes typical pox lesions (pustules and crusting, with the development of scarring as lesions heal), especially on the lower limbs, on the vulva of female horses, or around the muzzle. Diagnosis based on history and clinical signs; confirmed by histology. Disease is self-limiting, in 2–4 weeks; lifelong immunity after infection. Zoonotic disease – can also affect cattle.

Horseshoe ◄ؤ *hors shŭ, n.* protective or therapeutic device for the horse's hooves; most commonly 'U' shaped. Horseshoes are typically made from steel or aluminium, but specialized shoes may be made from substances such as rubber, plastic, or other metals. Horseshoes are applied to the horse's hoof most commonly by nails, but also by various glues. Horseshoes aid in protecting horse's feet from wear; innumerable configurations

have been created to assist with hoof-related problems.

Horsetail ◄ؤ *hors tāl, n.* (*Equisetum arvense* (USA), *E. palustre, E. sylvaticum* (Europe), mare's tail, fox tail's) plant which has been reported to cause neurological signs when horse consumes sufficient quantities in hay over a period of time (20% horsetail over 2 weeks in experimental situations). Uncommon problem; last reports are from the mid twentieth century. Contains enzyme which destroys thiamine; affected horse may develop thiamine deficiency, which results in damage to nerves. Signs of thiamine deficiency include incoordination, weakness, depression, diarrhoea, and muscle tremors; affected horses are treated with large doses of thiamine.
See Vitamin B1.

Host ◄ؤ *hōst, n.* animal on, or in which, another organism (parasite) lives. Several types of host:
- Accidental host – a host that harbours an organism which usually does not infect it, e.g. equine protozoal myelitis. Parasite is generally not able to complete stage of life cycle in accidental host. See Dead end host.
- Definitive (primary) host – one in which parasite is an adult and reproduces sexually.
- Dead end host – host from which parasite cannot be transmitted and in which parasite cannot reproduce, e.g. cutaneous habronemiasis.
- Intermediate (secondary) host: host which is normally used by a parasite in its life cycle; parasite may multiply asexually in intermediate host (e.g. larval stages), but not sexually.
See Larva, Parasite.

Hound's tongue ◄ؤ *hŏndz / tung, n.* (*Cynoglossum officinale*) pyrrolizidine alkaloid containing weed; if eaten, causes weight loss, poor appetite, and specific signs of liver failure. Uncommon.
See Liver.

Hulls ◄ؤ *hulz, n.* the outer coverings of grains or seeds, e.g. soyabean, sunflower, or almond. Can be fed to horses to replace all or some of the forage in a horse's diet. Lower in energy, and higher in fibre, than forages. May also be available in pelleted form. Rice hulls reportedly cause oral irritation because of their sharp edges, but have been used as stable bedding.

Human chorionic gonadotrophin see Equine chorionic gonadotrophin

Humeral ◀ _hū mē rūl, adj._ pertaining to the humerus.
See Humerus.

    H. fracture ◀ _hū mē rūl / frak tŭr, n._ breaking of humerus bone. Fractures typically difficult to repair, but may be managed conservatively, depending on type of fracture. Prognosis guarded; numerous complications pertaining to contralateral limb breakdown, radial nerve paralysis, and persistent pain reported.

Humerus ◀ _hū mē rĕs, n._ long bone of upper forelimb, forms shoulder joint with scapula at top end and elbow joint with radius and ulna at lower end.
See Elbow, Fracture, Shoulder.

Humoral immunity ◀ _hū mē rūl / i mū ni tē, n._ ability of animal to combat infection or deal with foreign material (immunity); associated with circulating antibodies (i.e. in blood stream rather than in cells) produced by B lymphocyte cells. Antibodies secreted by B cells bind to antigens on the surfaces of invading microbes (such as viruses or bacteria), and target the microbes for destruction
See Antibody, Antigen, B lymphocyte, Immunity.

Humour ◀ _hū mē, n._ fluid or semi-fluid in body, generally used to describe fluids in the eye: aqueous h. and vitreous h. In ancient physiology, health was said to be determined by a balance of four bodily humours.
See Eye.

Hunter's bump ◀ _hun terz / bump, n._ positional displacement of the tuber sacrale of the hip, typically occurring following injury to the sacroiliac joint (subluxation), usually from repeated trauma, but occa-sionally from single injury (fall or slip). Most commonly seen in jumping horses, trotters, carriage horses, and some endurance horses. Extended rest usually allows body to re-establish a stable sacroiliac joint, but bump usually remains. Nevertheless, even a well-healed injury in this area is more likely to recur than the same injury to a normal pelvis
See Lumbar, Sacral, Vertebra.

Hyaline ◀ _hī ē lin, adj._ describes type of cartilage; predominant type in joints.
See Cartilage.

    H. membrane disease ◀ _hī a lin / mem brān / di zēz, n._ a progressive respiratory failure of newborn foals characterized by rapid breathing, dark mucous membranes, and difficulty on expiration. Cellular debris accumulates within the alveoli of affected foals, resulting in lung oedema and collapse. Normally occurs as part of respiratory distress syndrome in foals.
See Cartilage, Respiratory.

Hyaluronan ◀ _hī ē lūr on ĕn, n._ **(hyaluronic acid)** large disaccharide molecule; naturally occurring substance in the horse's body, and is found in particularly high concentrations in joints, tendon sheaths and the eye. Synthetic hyaluronan derived from purified rooster combs is used in the treatment and control of joint inflammation in the horse. It is available as a sterile solution for injection into the joint and for intravenous administration; oral pastes are also available. For the treatment of tendon and ligament injuries, injection both into and beside these structures has been suggested. In joints, naturally occurring hyaluronic acid functions as a 'boundary' lubricant, at the boundary between the soft tissue of the joint and the joint cartilage as the joint bends and moves. Theoretically, synthetic forms of hyaluronic acid have a number of beneficial effects for joints. Joint lubrication is immediately improved after IA injection of hyaluronic acid. However, the product is also rapidly removed from joints, so it does not have a long duration of action. Because of its molecular size, hyaluronan can apparently impede the movement into the joint of inflammatory compounds by crowding them out (steric hindrance). Hyaluronic acid has a direct anti-inflammatory effect caused by picking up and removing by-products of inflammation and by an anti-prostaglandin effect (as per the non-steroidal anti-inflammatory drugs). Finally, in the laboratory (but not in the live horse), hyaluronic acid has been demonstrated to stimulate the production of more normal joint fluid by inflamed cells from the joint membrane.

There are differences among the various hyaluronic acid products used in joints (of which there are many), the chief ones being cost and molecular weight. The two differences seem to be directly related to each other, that is, the higher the molecular weight of the product, the more it costs. However, most clinical studies have been unable to demonstrate significant differences between the higher and lower molecular weight compounds; some studies have not been able to demonstrate any significant effect at all. Injected into the joint, hyaluronic acid is quite safe and no adverse effects are seen at five times overdose.

The intravenous preparation of hyaluronic acid was approved for use in the horse in 1993. Unlike the preparations for use in the joint, the hyaluronic acid in this preparation comes from a microbial source, rather than rooster combs. In the clinical study done to test the drug, 46 horses with lameness of the fetlock or knee joints (metacarpophalangeal and carpal joints, respectively) were treated with intravenous hyaluronic acid. One, two or three injections were given. Improvement was reported in 90% of the cases. Some surgeons prefer to use this form of the drug immediately post-surgery, rather than direct injection into the joint. However, how, why or if intravenous hyaluronan is consistently effective for treatment of joint inflammation in the horse is not apparent at this time. One study showed no effect of IV hyaluronan in preventing racehorse joint injuries. The fact that hyaluronic acid is removed from the circulation within a few minutes also makes it hard to understand how the product *could* be effective.

PRECAUTIONS
After injection of hyaluronan, either in the joint or in the vein, resting the horse may be recommended prior to gradually resuming normal athletic activity. Injection of hyaluronan into a joint may cause acute inflammation of the joint (joint flare). Signs of joint flare include heat, swelling and pain of the affected joint. This effect is usually temporary but it must be distinguished from a joint infection, a serious result that is possible following injection of any substance into a joint. Injection of any foreign substance into a joint should be preceded by proper procedures to ensure cleanliness and help prevent infection. No adverse side effects were reported in the clinical trials of horses receiving the intravenous preparation of hyaluronan.

Hydatid cyst ◀ː *hī da tid / sist, n.* fluid-filled sac formed around tapeworm larva, especially of species *Echinococcus granulosus equinus*.
See Cyst, *Echinococcus granulosus equinus*, Eye, Tapeworm.

Hydrangea ◀ː *hī drān jē, n.* (*Hydrangea* spp.) group of plants which contain cyanogenic glycosides. If eaten can cause poisoning by disruption of oxygen uptake by tissues, similar to cyanide toxicity. Apparently rare; no reports in horses for several decades. Plant has unpleasant taste, so excessive ingestion is uncommon; mild toxicities have been reported in horses ingesting tender buds. Signs of poisoning include diarrhoea, difficulty breathing, and colic.

Hydration ◀ː *hī drā shēn, n.* the quality of having adequate fluids in body tissues; the introduction of additional water-containing fluids into the body.

Hydrocephalus ◀ː *hī drō ke fē lēs, n.* abnormal accumulation of cerebrospinal fluid within ventricles of the brain. Rare in horse; more common in pony breeds and miniature horses. May occasionally be seen as congenital condition, where head of foal is abnormally large and domed at birth (may cause problem with foaling).

Foal is unable to live. Thought to result from genetic mutation, rather than being a heritable condition. Theoretically, hydrocephalus can also occur as acquired condition where normal circulation of cerebrospinal fluid is prevented, e.g. following meningitis or as result of tumour, but reports of acquired condition are lacking in horses.
See Brain, Cerebrospinal, Congenital, Meningitis.

Hydrocoele ◀≶ *hī drō sēl*, *n.* collection of fluid in scrotum; occasionally seen after castration. Generally painless. Diagnosis confirmed by ultrasound; surgery curative.
See Castration, Scrotum.

Hydrocortisone ◀≶ *hī drō kor ti zōn*, *n.* synthetic form of cortisol, $C_{21}H_{30}O_5$. Name occasionally used to refer to general corticosteroid administration; 1% hydrocortisone ointments, typically combined with antibiotics, are available for topical use on the equine eye. Skin preparations are also available.
See Cortisol.

Hydrogen ◀≶ *hī dri jĕn*, *n.* (H) the most abundant and lightest chemical element, widespread in nature as part of water molecules (H_2O), as well as in organic compounds, such as carbohydrates, proteins, fats.

H. cyanide see Cyanide
H. peroxide ◀≶ *hī dri jĕn / per oks īd*, *n.* (H_2O_2) compound used in solution as antibacterial and cleansing agent in veterinary practice. Within body it is produced in cells as by-product of normal cell function. It is a highly reactive substance which is normally neutralized by specific enzymes, so as to prevent damage to cell membrane. Studies have shown that h. peroxide is toxic to cells and can interfere with wound healing. Infusion of h. peroxide has been suggested as a treatment for mares with uterine infections caused by *Pseudomonas aeruginosa*.

Hydrophilic ◀≶ *hī drō fil ik*, *adj.* a term that refers to a physical property of a molecule, one that allows the molecule to bond transiently with water (H_2O) through

hydrogen bonding, allowing it to dissolve more easily in water than hydrophobic molecules.
Psyllium h. mucilloid see Psyllium

Hydrophobia ◀≶ *hī drē fō bē ē*, *n.* fear of water; old name for rabies. Probably refers to difficulty swallowing, which occurs in later stages of the disease.
See Rabies.

Hydrophobic ◀≶ *hī drē fō bik*, *adj.* a term that refers to a physical property of a molecule that is repelled from a mass of water. Hydrophobic compounds include oils and fats.

Hydrops ◀≶ *hī drops*, *n.* abnormal accumulation of fluid within a hollow organ. Typically used to describe excessive buildup of fluid in foetal membranes during pregnancy. Rare condition of gestating mare, no age or breed predilection. Seen as:
• Hydrops allantois: abnormal accumulation of fluid within the allantois, seen at 8–11 months of gestation, abdomen of mare becomes very swollen.
• Hydrops amnion: abnormal accumulation of amniotic fluid. Less common of the two abnormalities.
Both conditions are associated with abnormality of foetus. Treatment is directed at aborting the foetus, usually by rupture of foetal membranes. Cause unknown; as heritability is possible, and normal pregnancies have been reported following those terminated because of hydrops, affected mares should probably be put to a different stallion on subsequent occasion.

Hydrosalpinx ◀≶ *hī drō sal pingks*, *n.* uncommon condition characterized by distension of the uterus with fluid; usually occurs secondary to some external pressure that obstructs the uterine lumen; one case of cystic hydrosalpinx has been reported.

Hydrotherapy ◀≶ *hī drō ther ēpē*, *n.* water therapy. Hot and cold applications of water are commonly used for the treatment of equine limb injuries; used in management of wounds, to clean debris, especially in areas where bandaging is impossible.

Hygroma ◀ᴇ *hī grō mē, n.* a watery tumour; term typically used to describe the presence of fluid under the skin of the dorsal carpus (carpal hygroma). Usually associated with a history of trauma; affected horses may become lame if hygroma becomes infected. Non-septic cases can be treated with rest, bandaging, and non-steroidal anti-inflammatory drugs; some cases may be treated with corticosteroid injection after drainage. Septic hygromas often require surgery for resection of infected tissue, with post-operative antibiotics and bandaging.
See Carpus.

Hymen ◀ᴇ *hī mĕn, n.* membranous fold which partially or completely covers entrance to vagina.
See Vagina.

    Persistent h. ◀ᴇ *per sis tĕnt / hī mĕn /, n.* most frequently observed developmental abnormality of mare's genital system, especially in Arabian horses. Caused by complete or partial failure of the caudal reproductive tract of the mare to open. May trap uterine secretions, or prevent intromission of penis by stallion. Usually not observed until first breeding. Surgical treatment to open hymen is curative; surgery usually releases accumulated fluid from the vagina and/or uterus.
    See Vagina.

Hyoid ◀ᴇ *hī oid, adj.* U-shaped; relating to hyoid bones.
    H. apparatus ◀ᴇ *hī oid / a pē rā tĕs, n.* structures which support tongue and larynx, composed of single basihyoid bone, paired ceratohyoid, epihyoid, stylohyoid and thyrohyoid bones, and tympanohyoid cartilages. Connected to skull by cartilage. May be damaged by trauma or if horse has inflammation of middle ear (otitis media) (connection to skull fuses in inflammation and stylohyoid bone breaks as tongue moves). Depending on the location of the disease and the nerves affected, clinical signs of disease of the h. apparatus vary between horses. Affected horses have been presented with complaints such as head-

shaking, head tilt, facial muscle paralysis, difficulty swallowing, ear infections, and corneal ulceration.
See Ear, Larynx, Tongue.

Hyper- ◀ᴇ *hī pĕ-, prefix.* above, beyond, or more than normal; excessive.

Hyperaemia ◀ᴇ *hī pē rē mē ē, n.* increase of blood in part of body; congestion, engorgement. May be active, resulting from dilation of arterioles (e.g. in response to inflammation) or passive (e.g. as result of obstruction to blood drainage, as in strangulation/obstruction of the bowel).

Hyperaesthesia ◀ᴇ *hī pē ris thē zē ē, n.* excessive sensitivity to stimuli, e.g. to sudden noise, touch, sudden bright light. Seen in some diseases, e.g. tetanus, rabies, West Nile virus.
See Rabies, Tetanus.

Hyperammonaemia ◀ᴇ *hī pē rē mō nē mē ē, n.* higher than normal level of ammonia in blood. Ammonia is produced in metabolism of proteins, usually converted to urea in liver. High level of ammonia indicates inability of liver to convert it or that blood is not getting to liver (e.g. in congenital abnormality such as portosystemic shunt). High levels of ammonia are associated with abnormal brain function (hepatic encephalopathy).
See Ammonia, Hepatic, Liver, Portosystemic shunt.

Hyperbaric oxygen ◀ᴇ *hī pē bar ik / ok si jĕn, n.* (HO) the medical use of oxygen at a higher than atmospheric pressure. In humans, HO is used routinely in the treatment of decompression sickness and air embolism in underwater divers. However, numerous investigations into the use of HO for disease therapy have been conducted, because the partial pressure of oxygen in tissues, as well as the oxygen transport capacity of blood, is increased with HO therapy. HO therapy is conducted in a pressurized chamber; such chambers have been built for horses, and have been used for the treatment of non-healing wounds, post-colic surgery, in efforts to keep intestinal tissue perfused, in muscle and connective tissue infections, among many others. Unfortunately, there is as yet no consensus as to whether HO therapy has consistent benefits for the treatment of any other condition besides decompression sickness in humans.

Hyperbilirubinaemia ◀< *hī pē bi li rŭ bi nē mē ē, n.* abnormally high level of bilirubin in blood. Bilirubin is a bile pigment, usually excreted down bile duct into intestine. High levels can occur in normal or diseased horses that have not eaten, or elevations in bilirubin may indicate damage to liver, especially secondary blockage of bile duct, e.g. by stones (biliary calculi), or hepatic fibrosis.
See Bile, Biliary, Bilirubin, Liver, Pancreas.

Hypercalcaemia ◀< *hī pē kal sē mē ē, n.* abnormally high level of calcium in blood. May be seen especially in chronic renal (kidney) failure, some plant poisonings (e.g. wild jasmine, found in southern USA, Hawaii, and India), and rarely as result of some cancers (humoral hypercalcaemia).
See Jasmine, Kidney.

Hypercapnia ◀< *hī pē kap nē ē, n.* abnormally high level of carbon dioxide in blood; may be seen in lung diseases, where gas exchange is impaired.

Hyperechoic ◀< *hī pē e kō ik, adj.* term used in ultrasonography to describe a region in an ultrasound image in which the echoes are stronger than normal or stronger than those which occur in surrounding structures. Seen as bright area on scan, e.g. in scanning of healing tendon, fibrous tissue is hyperechoic compared to normal tendon.
See Ultrasonography.

Hyperelastosis cutis see HERDA

Hyperextension ◀< *hī pē iks ten shēn, n.* to extend the angle between bones of a joint beyond normal; to extend a body part beyond the normal range of motion. Hyperextension can result in damage to ligaments or bones, either acutely, e.g. hyperextension of distal interphalangeal joint, which may result in fracture of

extensor process of third phalanx, or chronically, e.g. chronic hyperextension of the carpal joints in racing horses, resulting in bone damage and chip fracture.
See Chip fracture, Extension, Third: T. phalanx.

Hyperfibrinogenaemia ◀< *hī pē fi bri nō je nē mē ē, n.* abnormally high level of fibrinogen in blood. Fibrinogen is a plasma protein (important in blood clotting); high levels may be found in inflammation, cancer and infectious diseases (i.e. not a specific finding in a blood test).
See Fibrinogen.

Hyperflexion ◀< *hī pē flek shēn, n.* to bend a joint so that the angle between the bones of the joint is smaller than normal; fetlock joints are routinely hyperflexed in forelimb flexion tests.
See Flexion.

Hyperglobulinaemia ◀< *hī pē glo bū li nē mē ē, n.* abnormally high level of globulins in blood. Globulins are largely antibodies produced in immune response, so high levels may be found in infectious or inflammatory conditions.
See Globulin.

    Hypergammaglobulinaemia ◀< *hī pē gama glo bū li nē mē ē, n.* an excess of gamma globulins in the blood; frequently seen in chronic disease.
    See Globulin.

Hyperglycaemia ◀< *hī pē glī sē mē ē, n.* abnormally high level of glucose in blood. May be seen in pituitary pars intermedia dysfunction (secondary diabetes mellitus), or tumour of adrenal gland (phaeochromocytoma).
See Adrenal gland, Diabetes, Phaeochromocytoma, Pituitary pars intermedia dysfunction.

Hypericum perfortum see St John's wort

Hyperimmune plasma ◀< *hī pē im ūn / plas mē, n.* blood plasma taken from horses that have been heavily vaccinated against a multitude of diseases, or from horses that have been exposed to a particular disease, so that high concentrations of specific antibodies occur in the plasma and get passed on to the plasma recipient. Has been used especially in foals in an effort to prevent infection with *Rhodococcus equi*; results of studies on this practice have been mixed. However, since the procedure is safe, and the disease is difficult to manage in stables where it is endemic, practice appears to be fairly widespread. The ideal protocol for administration is not known.

Hyperinsulinaemia ◀ɛ *hī pē in sū li nē mē a, n.* abnormally high level of insulin in blood; may be seen in pituitary pars intermedia dysfunction or insulin-resistant horses.
See Insulin, Insulin resistance, Pancreas, Pituitary pars intermedia dysfunction.

Hyperkalaemia ◀ɛ *hī per ka lē mē ē, n.* abnormally high level of potassium in blood, may be seen in conditions such as bladder rupture of foals, (potassium in urine is reabsorbed from abdominal cavity into blood stream), acute or chronic renal failure, poor kidney function (leading to reduced removal of potassium from blood into urine), severe skeletal muscle cell damage (rhabdomyolysis).
See Kidney, Muscle, Potassium.

Hyperkalaemic periodic paralysis ◀ɛ *hī pē ka lē mik / pé rē o dik / pē ra li sis, n.* (HYPP) inherited disease of Quarter Horses, Paint Horses and Appaloosas with bloodlines that can be traced back to the famous Quarter Horse sire, 'Impressive'; inherited as an autosomal dominant trait. Abnormality in the permeability of cell membranes, which results in altered electrochemical gradients, resulting in abnormal muscle excitability. Signs include episodes of intermittent weakness, muscle tremors, sweating, or shivering in less severely affected cases; respiratory distress, resulting from spasm of upper airway musculature and pharyngeal collapse, and recumbency or acute death may occur in more severely affected animals. Diagnosis by clinical signs and elevated potassium levels (hyperkalaemia) during episodes; potassium levels are normal when horse does not show signs.

Treatment depends on severity of episode. Mildly affected horses may respond to light exercise, however, collapse is a potential risk. Feeding a readily absorbed carbohydrate, such as a sugar syrup, promotes insulin-induced potassium uptake in cells. During more severe episodes, administration of 5% dextrose solutions with sodium bicarbonate, or calcium gluconate diluted in 5% dextrose, helps decrease serum potassium. Potassium leaching diuretics, such as acetazolamide, may be beneficial in treatment, and are commonly used in prevention. Dietary management includes oats or timothy hay, instead of alfalfa (lucerne) hay, to decrease total potassium intake; feeding salt (NaCl) or grain on a regular basis may also be helpful (grain is relatively low in potassium). Regular exercise may also be of benefit. Abnormal gene may be identified by DNA testing of mane hair sample; blood test also available.
See Gene, Potassium, Sodium.

Hyperkeratosis ◀ɛ *hī pē kerē tō sis, n.* increased thickness of the outer layer of epidermis (stratum corneum). Various histological characterizations; may be seen in conditions such as dermatitis, certain nutritional deficiencies, various endocrine diseases, and some developmental abnormalities of the skin.

Hyperlipaemia ◀ɛ *hī pē lī pē mē ē, n.* abnormally high level of lipid (fat) in blood. Seen primarily as a condition of ponies and miniature horses. Complex pathogenesis; when caloric demands exceed the calories supplied, (e.g. poorly fed, heavily producing milk, pregnant), when the horse is obese, or when the horse is under stress, the horse's body may start to move fatty acids out of fat stores (adipose tissue). This leads the liver to increase synthesis of triglycerides (hypertriglyceridaemia), and the liver becomes infiltrated with fat. It is the overproduction of triglycerides that causes the problem. Signs of hyperlipaemia include depression, anorexia, ataxia, and icterus. Blood is often visually shiny, from fat globules. Blood tests may indicate liver disease; glucose tolerance tests may be

abnormal because of insulin insensitivity. Liver biopsy or ultrasound may show fatty infiltration of the liver. Treatment includes addressing underlying liver disease, improved caloric intake (intravenous dextrose or parenteral feeding if anorexic), eliminating stress (e.g. weaning foals), treating any other disease, and attempting to inhibit fat mobilization from adipose tissue while increasing triglyceride uptake by the tissues (concurrent carbohydrate and insulin therapy). Heparin therapy has also been used, with questionable benefit. Prognosis is generally poor. Prevention, by appropriate feeding and attention to proper body condition, is the best approach.
See Fat, Insulin, Lipid.

Hyperlipidaemia ◀≡ *hī pē lī pid āe mē ē, n.* increased blood lipids without concurrent liver disease. Associated with stress, obesity, inadequate energy intake, and hormonal imbalances; seen primarily in ponies and miniature horses.

Hypermagnesaemia ◀≡ *hī pē mag nē zē mē ē, n.* abnormally high level of magnesium in blood. Rare in horse; most commonly associated with iatrogenic overdose, e.g. after oral administration of Epsom salts (MgSO$_4$), or to patients with kidney disease. May also be seen after severe rhabdomyolysis. Signs of overdose include sweating, muscle tremors, tachycardia, and flaccid paralysis. Treatment of overdose includes calcium gluconate solutions and intravenous fluids.
See Magnesium.

Hypermetria ◀≡ *hī pē me trē ē, n.* abnormality of movement where movement is exaggerated, and longer than necessary or intended. May be seen in disorders of central nervous system, especially conditions which affect cerebellum, e.g. cerebellar abiotrophy, or conditions affecting transmission of impulses about positioning of limbs (proprioception) up spinal cord to brain, e.g. cervical vertebral malformation.
See Cerebellum, Gait, Proprioception.

Hypernatraemia ◀≡ *hī pē na trē mē ē, n.* abnormally high level of sodium in blood.

May be seen in dehydration, or following administration of saline solution, in lieu of balanced electrolyte solutions.
See Dehydration, Sodium.

Hyperparathyroidism ◀≡ *hī pē pa rē thī roid izm, n.* excess production of parathyroid hormone (PTH) in the parathyroid gland. Parathyroid hormone is involved in maintenance of calcium balance in body; high levels result in resorption of calcium from bone and cause enlargement of bones, especially facial bones, lameness, and poor body condition. Several possible causes:

1. Primary h.– from tumour or hyperplasia of parathyroid gland.
2. Secondary h. – excessive PTH production secondary to other causes, including:
   - Renal s.h. – some horses with chronic renal failure have elevated levels of PTH; uncommon.
   - Nutritional s.h. – from diets high in phosphorus and low in calcium. Uncommon in developed countries; was previously associated with feeding excessive amount of wheat bran, when bran was thought to be a substitute for forage (bran disease, 'Big head'). Addition of calcium-containing supplements may be helpful in recovery.
   - Excessive ingestion of vitamin D.
     See Hypervitaminosis D.

Secretion of a PTH-related protein is seen with some neoplastic conditions. (See Pseudohyperparathyroidism.)
See Calcium, Nutritional, Parathyroid.

Hyperperistalsis ◀≡ *hī pē pe ri stal sis, n.* excessively active intestinal movements (peristalsis); may be associated with signs of colic, from various causes.
See Colic, Peristalsis.

Hyperphosphataemia ◀≡ *hī pē fos fāt ām ēē, n.* increased levels of phosphorus in the blood.
See Hypervitaminosis D.

Hyperplasia ◀≡ *hī pē plā zē ē, n.* proliferation of cells of a tissue or an organ beyond normal. Hyperplasia is a physiological response to a stimulus, and, unlike neoplasia (cancer) hyperplastic cells are still controlled by regulatory mechanisms of the body. Numerous causes, both in normal and diseased states, including increased demand, chronic inflammation (resulting in hyperplasia of inflammatory cell lines), hormonal events, or in response to damage or disease, e.g. liver cells attempting to compensate for liver disease. Cells of the mammary glands normally become hyperplastic under hormonal influences occurring prior to parturition.

Hyperpnoea ◀⁚ *hī perp nē ē, n.* abnormal increase in depth and rate of breathing.

Hypersensitivity ◀⁚ *hī pē sen si ti vi tē, n.* exaggerated reactions produced by the normal immune system. Typically classified into four types (and sometimes five, in humans):

• Type 1: Immediate h. – provoked by an antibody response to a specific antigen. Specific antibodies are attached to basophils or mast cells; when these antibodies bind to the antigen, cells release pharmacologically active substances such as histamine, prostaglandins, and leukotrienes that cause vasodilation and smooth-muscle contraction in surrounding tissues. Type 1 reactions can be local or systemic; signs range from hives (urticaria) to anaphylactic shock. Treatment often involves corticosteroids, epinephrine (especially in emergencies), and antihistamines.
See Anaphylaxis, Atopy.

• Type 2: Antibody-dependent h. – antibodies bind to the horse's own cells, resulting in cell destruction, e.g. in blood transfusion reactions, pemphigus, neonatal isoerythrolysis. Reaction typically takes hours, or days, to occur.

• Type 3: Immune-complex h. – antigen–antibody complexes form in the blood and are deposited in tissues; complexes can cause tissue damage, e.g. deposition of immune complexes in the horse's kidneys following purpura haemorrhagica.

• Type 4: Delayed h. – not mediated by antibodies. T cells react with antigens and release chemicals which cause inflammation usually at least 24 hours after exposure to antigen. Considered to be possible cause of recurrent uveitis; may be important in certain cases of contact dermatitis.
See Allergy, Anaphylaxis, Antibody, Antigen, Atopy, Dermatitis, Immunity, Inflammation, Neonatal isoerythrolysis, Pemphigus foliaceous, Purpura haemorrhagica, Urticaria, Uveitis.

Hypertension ◀⁚ *hī pē ten shēn, n.* high arterial blood pressure. May occur in severe pain, e.g. laminitis. Not recognized as a primary disease in horses.
See Blood, Exercise induced pulmonary haemorrhage, Laminitis.

> **Persistent pulmonary h.** ◀⁚ *per sis tēnt / pul mēn ē rē / hī pē ten shēn, n.* circulatory abnormality of newborn foal, resulting from failure of foetus to make successful transition from uterus to external environment. Causes hypoxia; treatment by providing oxygen and correcting accompanying acidosis.

> **Pulmonary h.** ◀⁚ *pul mōn a rē / hī pē ten shēn, n.* increased pressure in the pulmonary arteries. Has been suggested as a cause of exercise-induced pulmonary haemorrhage, as a result of increased cardiac output, lack of sufficient vessel dilation, and increased blood viscosity that occur with exercise.

Hyperthermia ◀⁚ *hī pē ther mē ē, n.* elevated core body temperature. Seen in conditions such as heat stroke, exertional myopathy, certain drug reactions, or anhydrosis.
See Anhydrosis, Heat, Muscle, Temperature.

> **Malignant h.** ◀⁚ *mēl ig nant / hī pē ther mē ē, n.* a disorder of muscle calcium metabolism. In horses, condition is most commonly caused by inhalant anaesthetics. Signs include tachycardia (fast heart rate), sweating, very high temperature, and muscle twitching, in anaesthetized animal; affected animals may develop severe muscle necrosis and may die.
See Anaesthetic, Anhydrosis, Heat, Muscle, Temperature.

> **Radiofrequency h.** ◀⁚ *rā dēō frē kwen sē / hī pē ther mē ē, n.* use of a radiofrequency electric current (2 MHz) to cause heat to be

produced in tissue. Most commonly used in treatment of superficial tumours of the eye or eyelids.

Hyperthyroidism ◀ _hī pē thy roi dizm, n._ excessive secretion of thyroid hormones by thyroid gland. Rare in horse; may occur with tumour of thyroid gland. Signs include weight loss, fast heart rate, excitability, good appetite. Surgery may be curative in selected cases. Potential risk for secondary hyperthyroidism from exposure to excessive amounts of iodine. See Thyroid.

Hypertonic ◀ _hī pē to nik, adj._ describes fluid which has a higher osmotic pressure than fluid to which it is compared, e.g. hypertonic saline (see Saline); also used to describe excessive muscle tone.

    H. saline ointment ◀ _hī pē to nik / sā lin / oint ment, n._ ophthalmic ointment, usually 5% NaCl. Absorbs fluid from cornea owing to its hypertonicity. May be recommended in the treatment of corneal oedema, e.g. in cases of uveitis or endothelial dystrophy (see entries). See Pressure.

Hypertriglyceridaemia see Hyperlipaemia

Hypertrophic osteopathy ◀ _hī pē tro fik / os tē o pē thē, n._ (Marie's disease) bone disease affecting horses, often secondary to another disease process. Affected animals present with bilaterally symmetrical limb swellings, typically involving both fore- and hind limbs, stiffness, lameness and weight loss. Radiographs show new bone formation over the diaphyses and metaphyses of affected bones, most commonly the metacarpal and metatarsal bones; joint surfaces are usually unaffected. In most cases that have been described, intrathoracic disease has been identified, especially granulomatous inflammation. Most horses identified with the condition are euthanized for humane reasons; horses can recover if primary disease process can be identified and treated.

Hypertrophy ◀ _hī per tro fē, n._ increase in size of organ or part caused by enlargement of existing cells, e.g. muscle hypertrophy is enlargement of muscle mass occurring as a result of individual muscle cells becoming larger, e.g. through training or use (e.g. hypertrophy of neck musculature that may accompany crib-biting).

Hypervitaminosis D ◀ _hī pē vitē min ō sis / dē, n._ condition caused by ingestion of vitamin D_2 (ergocalciferol) or vitamin D_3 (cholecalciferol); results in abnormalities of calcium and phosphorus metabolism. Various plants have vitamin D-like compounds, including _Solanum_ spp., ('enteque seco' in Argentina; 'espichamento' in Brazil), _Cestrum diurnum_ (jessamine, a common shrub in the southern United States) and _Trisetum flavescens_ (yellow oat grass; causes enzootic calcinosis in Europe). Condition caused by increased intestinal absorption of phosphorus, with hyperphosphataemia. Affected horses lose weight, and are anorexic, lame, painful, and reluctant to move; may drink and urinate excessively (polyuria and polydipsia). Cardiac failure secondary to excessive calcium may result in acute death. Mineral deposition in kidneys may result in renal failure. Bones may be grossly enlarged, and new bone deposition can be seen on radiographs; lameness is associated with mineral deposition in tendons and ligaments. Prognosis is poor; treatment with corticosteroid drugs has had varied results.

Hypha ◀ _hī fē, n._ a long, branching filamentous cell of a fungus; the main mode of vegetative growth of fungi. May be seen in impression smears of suspected fungal infections, e.g. fungal keratitis.

Hyphaema ◀ _hī fē mē, n._ presence of blood in anterior chamber of eye; may be seen in uveitis, trauma. Blood typically pools at base of anterior chamber. See Eye, Uveitis.

Hypo- ◀ _hī pō, prefix._ under, below normal.

Hypoadrenocorticism ◀ _hī pō ē drē nō kor ti kizm, n._ (adrenal exhaustion, steroid letdown syndrome) lower than normal

secretion of cortisol by cortex of adrenal gland. Rare in horses. The few cases that have been documented have followed prolonged administration of corticosteroid drugs. Corticosteroids result in reduced adrenocorticotrophic hormone (ACTH) secretion from pituitary gland; in chronic cases, adrenal atrophy has been reported. Signs include depression, poor appetite, exercise intolerance, poor hair coat, lameness, and weight loss. Diagnosis by blood tests (serial plasma cortisol levels; ACTH stimulation test). Treatment involves rest and supplementation with corticosteroid drugs; short-acting drugs, such as prednisolone, appear to be preferable to longer-acting drugs such as dexamethasone or triamcinolone. Drugs are withdrawn slowly, in hope that adrenal gland will resume normal production.
See Adrenal gland, Adrenocorticotrophic hormone, Corticosteroid, Cortisol, Pituitary.

Hypoalbuminaemia ◀ _hī pō al bū mi nē mē ē_, n. abnormally low level of albumin in blood. May be associated with liver or kidney disease, intestinal disease (e.g. protein-losing enteropathy), or starvation. Signs include fluid accumulation in abdominal cavity (ascites) or pleural cavity, diarrhoea, or ventral subcutaneous oedema.
See Albumin, Enteropathy.

Hypocalcaemia ◀ _hī pō kal sē mē ē_, n. abnormally low level of calcium in blood, associated with many different disease conditions. When calcium levels decrease, nerve fibres become excitable, resulting in muscle tremors, spasms, and, in severe cases, tetany. Increased heart rate and cardiac arrhythmias may occur in mild cases; more severe cases result in slow heart rate, owing to decreased cardiac muscle contraction. Intestinal ileus and seizures are also seen in some cases. Conditions associated with hypocalcaemia include: synchronous diaphragmatic flutter ('thumps'), lactation tetany, transit tetany, retained placenta, hypoparathyroidism (primary or secondary), pseudohyperparathyroidism, sepsis, pancreatic necrosis, some poisonings (e.g.

oxalate), exertional rhabdomyolysis, and iatrogenic causes, such as prolonged diuretic therapy (especially furosemide), and administration of tetracylines.
See various disease entries; Calcium, Exertional rhabdomyolysis, Furosemide, Oxalate, Tetany.

Hypochloraemia ◀ _hī pō klor ām ēē_, n. abnormally low blood levels of circulating chloride. Seen mostly when horses have exercised heavily, with chloride loss in sweat; also feature of electrolyte profiles of foals with ruptured bladder.

Hypoderma spp. ◀ _hī pō der mē / spē shēz_, n. genus of warble fly. Cattle are normal hosts; horses are occasional accidental hosts. Cutaneous nodules are reported; larvae may sometimes migrate into central nervous system (larval migrans); neurological signs may result, depending on the number and size of the larvae and the location of the migration. Signs of migration into brain include head tilt, circling, blindness, ataxia, head pressing, etc. Signs of migration into spinal cord include ataxia, weakness, poor tail tone, or paraparesis. Disease must be differentiated from other neurological diseases. Cerebrospinal fluid abnormalities are common but not specific; a polymerase chain reaction test has been developed based on amplification of parasite DNA in the blood. Treatment with anti-inflammatory and anti-parasitic compounds is usually unrewarding because of permanent damage caused by migrating larvae.
See Warbles.

Hypodermic ◀ _hī pō der mik_, adj. beneath the skin; used mainly to describe needle used to inject drugs beneath the skin.

Hypoechoic ◀ _hī pō e kō ik_, adj. term used in ultrasonography to describe tissues which reflect relatively few of the ultrasound waves directed at them. Seen as dark area on scan, e.g. in ultrasound scan of injured tendon, hypoechoic areas might represent fluid or granulation tissue disrupting normal tendon fibre alignment.
See Ultrasonography.

Hypoflexion ◀︎ *hī pō flek shēn, n.* condition in foal where joints of limbs do not flex as much as normal; joints are typically hyperextended, with fetlocks near ground and foals walking on the backs of their heels. Cause unknown. Mild cases may resolve with exercise; may require heel extensions for limb support.

Hypogammaglobulinaemia ◀︎ *hī po ga mē glo bū li nē mē ē, n.* abnormally low levels of gamma globulins (primarily immunoglobulins). Most commonly seen in failure of passive transfer; congenital abnormalities reported (e.g. combined immunodeficiency). First indications of problem are various foal infections; diagnosed by quantification of specific immunoglobulins. Treatment by plasma transfusion in failure of passive transfer; congenital defects in immunoglobulin production are not compatible with life.
See Antibody, Colostrum, Gamma, Immunity, Passive (immunity) transfer.

Hypoglossal nerve ◀︎ *hī pō glo sūl / nerv, n.* cranial nerve XII. Supplies muscle of tongue. If damaged may see change in size of tongue through muscle atrophy, or deviation of tongue (protrudes towards side of injury to nerve); uncommon problem.
See Cranial nerve, Tongue.

Hypoglycaemia ◀︎ *hī pō glī sē mē ē, n.* abnormally low level of glucose in blood, typically as a result of increased glucose demand. May occur in foals with septicaemia, owing to increased energy requirements to fight infection. In adult horse may be associated with overexertion, cancer of pancreas (insulinoma) or liver, other liver disease, or after providing parenteral nutrition, without subsequent adequate caloric intake. Signs include weakness, incoordination, and seizures if severe. Treatment is by administration of glucose-containing solutions, by oral or intravenous administration.
See Glucose, Insulin, Pancreas.

Hypokalaemia ◀︎ *hī pō ka lē mē ē, n.* abnormally low level of potassium in blood. May be seen in some cases of colic, diarrhoea, heavy exercise, renal tubular acidosis, and in ionophore toxicity (e.g. monensin). Clinical signs related to hypokalaemia alone are relatively uncommon; generally occurs in association with other electrolyte abnormalities.
See Electrolyte, Monensin, Potassium, Renal.

Hypomagnesaemia ◀︎ *hī pō mag ne zē mē ē, n.* abnormally low level of magnesium in blood. Recognition of the importance of the condition appears to be increasing; has been associated with abnormalities such as gastrointestinal disease, infectious disease of the respiratory system, surgical colic, and postoperative ileus; horses with low magnesium levels tend to have longer stays in hospital than horses with normal levels. Hypomagnesaemia also typically occurs with hypocalcaemia, and may be seen with sepsis, or secondary to aminoglycoside antibiotic administration; may also be associated with transit, stress, or dietary deficiency. Signs include nervousness, incoordination, muscle weakness, trembling, seizures, and tetany; cardiac abnormalities and ileus may occur in postcolic surgery cases. Diagnosis by serum testing; depending on severity of condition, treatment is by oral magnesium sulphate (Epsom salts; $MgSO_4$) or intravenous infusion.
See Magnesium.

Hyponatraemia ◀︎ *hī pō na trē mē ē, n.* abnormally low level of sodium in blood. May be seen in kidney disease; may be a feature of conditions with significant electrolyte loss, such as after severe sweating, or in enterocolitis.
See Sodium.

Hypophosphataemia ◀︎ *hī pō fos fē tē mē ē, n.* abnormally low level of phosphate in blood. Most commonly seen in chronic renal failure; can be seen in cachexia owing to starvation.
See Kidney, Phosphorus.

Hypophysis see Pituitary

Hypopigmentation ◀︎ *hī pō pig men tā shēn, n.* a lack of pigment, in skin or hair, in areas that should normally have

pigment. Various causes, including from destruction of pigment cells, e.g. cryosurgery or freeze branding; from inflammation, trauma, infection, burns, or irradiation; from congenital conditions such as albinism, or lethal white syndrome; and from genetic defects such as vitiligo. Sun exposure can also bleach hair coats.
See Leukoderma, Leukotrichia, Vitiligo.

Hypoplasia ◀⁞ *hī pō plā sē ē, n.* incomplete development or underdevelopment of an organ or tissue. Various tissues may be affected, including cerebellum (especially of foals), optic nerve, kidney, and gonads. Signs of dysfunction relate to organ or tissue involved.

Hypoproteinaemia ◀⁞ *hī pō prō ti nē mē ē, n.* abnormally low level of protein in blood. May be low albumin (hypoalbuminaemia) or low globulin (hypogammaglobulinaemia), or both. Commonly associated with intestinal disease (protein-losing enteropathy), including duodenitis–proximal jejunitis, and endotoxaemia, and in cantharidin toxicosis.
See Cantharidin, Hypoalbuminaemia, Hypogammaglobulinaemia, Peritonitis, Protein, Enteropathy.

Hypopyon ◀⁞ *hī pō pī on, n.* the presence of leukocytes in the anterior chamber of the eye.

Hypotension ◀⁞ *hī pō ten shĕn, n.* low blood pressure. Most commonly associated with severe disease states such as shock or systemic anaphylaxis; transient hypotension resulting from the administration of tranquillizers with vasodilating effects, e.g. acepromazine, can result in fainting or falling.
See Blood, Shock.

Hypothalamus ◀⁞ *hī pō tha lē müs, n.* part of brain; lies below thalamus at base of cerebrum. Controls and integrates many autonomic functions in body, e.g. regulation of body temperature, water balance, control of thirst and hunger, sleep. Controls secretion of hormones from pituitary gland; may have importance in the pathogenesis of pituitary pars intermedia dysfunction (Cushing's disease).

Hypothalamic–pituitary–adrenal axis ◀⁞ *hī pō tha lē mik–pit ū it a rē–ad rē nal / ak sis, n.* set of feedback interactions between the hypothalamus, the pituitary gland, and the adrenal gland. Interactions between these structures make up a major part of the neuroendocrine system; controls reactions to stress and regulates various body functions including digestion, the immune system, and energy usage.

Hyopthalamic–pituitary–ovarian axis ◀⁞ *hī pō tha lē mik–pit ū it a rē–ōv ar ē an / ak sis, n.* set of feedback interactions between the hypothalamus, the pituitary gland, and the ovary. Ovarian cycle is directed by the pituitary secretion of gonadotrophins; the pituitary gland is under control of the hypothalamus.
See Gonadotrophin, Pituitary, Ovary, Thermoregulation.

Hypothermia ◀⁞ *hī pō ther mē ē, n.* abnormally low body temperature. May be seen in premature foals, in foals with congenital hypothyroidism, or in terminal stages of disease, e.g. septicaemia, or shock, especially in foals. Adult horses generally tolerate low environmental temperatures well; hypothermia is rarely reported in adult horses, but has been reported, e.g. in a horse that was found in a Canadian pond in winter (the horse recovered).
See Hypothyroidism, Premature, Septicaemia, Temperature.

Hypothyroidism ◀⁞ *hī pō thī roi dizm, n.* lower than normal secretion of thyroid hormones by thyroid gland. May be seen as congenital condition in foals born to mares with iodine deficiency (see congenital form, below). Primary hypothyroidism in adult horses, where pituitary gland does not secrete thyroid stimulating hormone (TSH), is extremely rare. Secondary hypothyroidism, as indicated by low circulating levels of thyroid hormones, may occur as a result of other problems, e.g. administration of phenylbutazone, or pituitary pars intermedia dysfunction (equine Cushing's). In adult horse, signs of hypothyroidism, as diagnosed by single tests of circulating thyroid

hormone levels, have been implicated in many conditions, including laminitis, obesity, infertility, and poor performance; however, most studies indicate that such conditions are *not* associated with under-function of the thyroid gland. Thyroid hormone levels vary throughout the day, affected by such things as changes in daylight hours and ambient temperature, and a single blood test is not diagnostic; i.e. a single test of blood thyroid hormone levels cannot tell if true thyroid illness is present. Unfortunately, assessing the true status of a horse's thyroid gland is diffi-cult. The preferred test for diagnosis of hypothyroidism in other species is called the thyroid releasing hormone (TRH) stimulation test. However, equine TSH is not commercially available.
See Hypothermia, Laminitis, Premature, Thyroid.

> **Congenital h.** ◀₹ *con gen i tĕl / hī pō thī roi dizm, n.* (in humans, hypothyroidism occur-ring during infancy or early childhood is termed cretinism) lack of growth and mental development associated with lack of thyroid hormone, may be result of iodine deficiency in mare. Affected foals born weak and usually die shortly after birth.
> See Thyroid.

Hypotonic ◀₹ *hī pō ton ik, n./adj.* a fluid with a lower osmotic pressure than the medium that surrounds it, or a fluid to which it is being compared. Water, which contains no dissolved salts, is hypotonic when compared to blood plasma.

Hypotrichosis ◀₹ *hī pō trī kō sis, n.* congenital lack of hair development. A single case in a Percheron foal has been reported, with the foal showing patchy, progressive areas of hair loss on the trunk and legs; skin biopsy showed severe follicular hypoplasia, but other structures were normal. Horse was small in stature, but otherwise normal.

Hypoventilation ◀₹ *hī pō ven ti lā shĕn, n.* deficient circulation of air by the lungs; results in reduced oxygen content or increased carbon dioxide content of the blood, or both. Seen in premature foals, and in end-stage disease, especially sepsis.

Hypovolaemia ◀₹ *hī pō vo lē mē ē, n.* abnor-mally low volume of blood plasma circulating in blood vessels, e.g. as result of severe bleeding or severe dehydration. May lead to hypovolaemic shock.
See Dehydration, Haemorrhage, Shock.

Hypoxaemia ◀₹ *hī pok sē mē ē, n.* low level of oxygen in arterial blood; typically assessed by blood gas analysis. May be seen in severe respiratory disease, heavy exercise, post-anaesthesia, or some plant poisonings, e.g. plants containing cyano-genic glycosides. Gums may appear bluish from lack of haemoglobin-bound oxygen.
See Anaemia, Blood, Oxygen.

Hypoxia ◀₹ *hī pok sē ē, n.* lower level than normal of oxygen within tissues or avail-able for tissues. May be related to low level of oxygen in blood (hypoxaemia), loss of blood, poor blood supply to tissues (e.g. shock), immature lungs (e.g. prema-ture foals), certain plant toxicities, or abnormality of tissues (e.g. oedema) which prevents oxygen uptake. If prolonged, hypoxia results in cell death in affected tissues.
See Anaemia, Hypoxaemia, Oedema.

Hypoxic ischaemic encephalopathy ◀₹ *hī pok sik / is kā mik / en ke fē lop athē, n.* (HIE) condition of newborn foals, whereby inad-equate oxygen supply causes damage to the cells of the brain and spinal cord. Affected foals may be normal at birth, but begin showing signs of abnormalities of the central nervous system shortly there-after. Clinical signs range from mild depression and loss of the suck reflex, to grand mal seizures. HIE may be associ-ated with foaling problems such as dystocia and premature separation of the placenta; however some foals have no such foaling problems, suggesting some sort of problem occurred in utero. Therapy for HIE involves control of seizures, using agents such as diazepam (seizures increase oxygen use by a factor of five); correction of metabolic abnormalities, such as acidosis; maintenance of normal arterial blood gas values, typically by administra-tion of oxygen; maintenance of tissue perfusion and renal function, typically by administration of intravenous fluids; and correction of secondary problems, such as gastrointestinal dysfunction and infections. Prognosis fair, depending on extent and duration of condition.

Hysterectomy ◀≀ _his tē rek tē mē, n._ surgical removal of (womb) uterus. Uncommon surgery in horse; indications are uterine neoplasia, pyometra which does not resolve medically, uterine rupture, with extensive damage, or segmental aplasia with accumulation of secretions (very rare). Removal of one horn of uterus (partial hysterectomy) has also been reported.

See Uterus.

Hysteroscopy ◀≀ _his tē ros kēpē, n._ endoscopic examination of the saline-distended uterus; may be performed as part of examination of mare's reproductive tract, and can help examiner visualize uterine defects, or find focal areas of pathology or infection.

I

Iatrogenic ◀ ī at rō jen ik, adj. resulting from the activity of the doctor (veterinarian); any adverse condition occurring as a direct result of treatment by the doctor, especially to infections acquired during the course of treatment.

Ichthammol ◀ ik tha mŏl, n. a dark brown or black ointment, with a strong, characteristic tarry odour, obtained from the processing of bituminous schists (shale). Used as a local emollient, disinfectant, hoof hardener, and anti-infective.

Icteric ◀ ik te rik, adj. affected with jaundice.
See Icterus, Liver.

Icterus ◀ ik tē rēs, n. jaundice; yellowing of skin, whites of eyes, gums, by abnormally high levels of bile pigments (hyperbilirubinaemia). May result from:
- Increased production of bilirubin – due to haemolysis (haemolytic icterus).
- Impaired uptake or metabolism of bilirubin – most commonly due to acute liver disease (hepatic icterus); does not normally occur with chronic disease of liver cells. May also be seen with certain drugs, as a result of anorexia, and in prematurity (all impede bilirubin metabolism in an otherwise normally functioning liver).
- Impaired excretion of bilirubin (regurgitation icterus), due to blockage of bile flow. Seen in many chronic liver conditions, such as cholangitis, neoplasia, cholelithiasis, or biliary fibrosis.
See Bile, Liver.

Idiopathic ◀ i dē ō pa thik, adj. of unknown cause, i.e. an idiopathic disease is one for which the cause is not known.

Idiosyncracy ◀ i dē ō sin krē sē, n. abnormal susceptibility of an individual to a drug; a quality of the body that is peculiar to that individual (e.g. an idiosyncratic reaction).

Idoxuridine ◀ ī dok su ri dēn, n. antiviral agent; occasionally used in treatment of inflammation of cornea (keratitis) caused by viruses, especially equine herpes virus. See Equine herpes virus, Eye, Keratitis.

Ig (G, M, E) see Immunoglobulin

Ileocaecal ◀ i lē ō sē kēl, adj. relating to the connection between the ileum and caecum.
See Caecum, Ileum.
> **I. valve** ◀ i lē ō sē kēl / valv, n. a functional one-way valve resulting from the fact that the ileum is partially telescoped into the caecum, so that the opening is surrounded by a fold of mucous membrane, which encloses a thick, circular muscular layer (the ileal sphincter).
> See Caecum, Ileum.

Ileocolonic ◀ i lē ō cē lo nik, adj. relating to ileum and colon, e.g. ileocolonic aganglionosis, a fatal congenital condition with abnormalities of nerves supplying ileum and colon associated with the lethal white syndrome of overo Paint horses.
See Colon, Ileum, Lethal white syndrome.

Ileum ◀ i lē ēm, n. final part of small intestine, between jejunum and caecum.
See Small intestine.

Ileus ◀ i lē ēs, n. obstruction or impaction of intestines caused by failure of effective intestinal contractions (peristalsis). No intestinal sounds can be heard. Occasional,

and sometimes serious, problem in horses during recovery from operations for colic; cause is often not known. Various treatments including, but not limited to, erthryomycin and intravenous lidocaine.
See Colic, Intestines, Peristalsis.

Iliac ◀ *i lē ak, adj.* relating to ilium (bone of pelvis).
See Ilium.
   I. artery ◀ *i lē ak / ar tē rē, n.* blood vessel, branch of aorta, passes near ilium of pelvis. Can be affected by blood clot.
   See Aorto-iliac thrombosis, Clot, Rectal, *Strongylus* spp., Thrombosis, Ultrasonography.

Ilium ◀ *i lē ēm, n.* paired bone of pelvis, each has attachment to sacrum of spine (sacroiliac joint); fused with other bones of the bony pelvis.
See Pelvis.

IM see Intramuscular

Imbalance ◀ *im ba lēns, n.* lack of balance or equilibrium; e.g. acid–base imbalance occurs in acidosis and alkalosis.
See Acid.

Imidocarb ◀ *im id ō karb, n.* current drug of choice for treating *Babesia* spp. infections in horses.
See Babesiosis.

Imipramine ◀ *im ip ra mēn, n.* one of several drugs commonly used in protocols for pharmacologically induced ejaculation in stallions; the drug most commonly used for the control of equine narcolepsy.
See Narcolepsy.

Immature ◀ *i mē tūr, adj.* not fully developed; e.g. immature skeleton is one where bones are not fully grown and growth plates have not closed.
See Bone, Growth plate.

Immobilization ◀ *im ō bil īz ā shēn, n.* the act of rendering immovable, generally by cast or splint.

Immune ◀ *i mūn, adj.* protected from an infectious disease as result of presence in body of specific or non-specific mecha-nisms, including antibodies or protective white blood cells.
See Antibody, Immunity, Leukocyte.
   I.-mediated ◀ *i mūn / mē dē ā ted, adj.* characterized by abnormal activity of the immune system in which the body's immune system either overreacts (e.g. immune-mediated contact dermatitis) or starts attacking the body itself (e.g. immune-mediated haemolytic anaemia).
   I.-mediated haemolytic anaemia see Haemolytic
   I. response ◀ *i mūn / rē spons, n.* a physiological response that defends the body against the introduction of foreign material.

Immunity ◀ *i mū ni tē, n.* the condition of being immune; resistance to or protection against infectious disease conferred either by the immune response (generated by immunization or previous infection) or by other non-immunological factors.
- Acquired i. – immunity obtained by natural infection, vaccination, or by transfer of antibodies or lymphocytes from an immune donor (e.g. the passive transfer of immunity from mare to foal via colostrum).
- Cell-mediated i. – immunity mediated by T lymphocytes; includes certain hypersensitivity reactions.
- Herd i. – resistance of a group to attack by disease because a large proportion of the group is immune; lessens the likelihood that an individual susceptible member will come in contact with an affected individual.
- Humoral i. – immunity mediated by antibodies.
- Nonspecific i. – immunity that does not involve the recognition of antigen and the mounting of a specific immune response; e.g. the protection offered by interferon, or anatomical barriers to infection.
- Passive i. – immunity acquired by transfer from an immune donor, e.g. from serum transfusion or maternal colostrum.
See Antibody, Antigen, Colostrum, Lymphocyte, Vaccine.

Immunization ◀ *i mū nī zā shēn, n.* the induction of immunity; may be either:

- Active i. – stimulation of the immune system to protect animal from disease; e.g. by vaccination.
- Passive i. – providing specific immune reaction in previously non-immune individuals by giving sensitized material from other individuals; e.g. serum transfusion.

See Immunity, Vaccine.

Immunoassay ◀ *i mū nō as ā, n.* any of several techniques for the quantitative determination of chemical substances that employ highly specific binding between an antigen and an antibody; e.g. radioimmunoassay, enzyme-linked immunoassay (ELISA).
See ELISA.

Immunodeficiency ◀ *i mū nō di fi shĕn sē, n.* deficiency of immune response, or a disorder characterized by a deficient immune response; e.g. through failure to produce antibody or appropriate lymphocyte, which renders animal susceptible to infection; e.g. in foals where colostrum (first milk) is not suckled, so foal has low level of antibodies from mother in first weeks of life (failure of passive transfer) or in combined immunodeficiency in Arabian foals (CID).
See Antibody, Antigen, Colostrum, Combined immunodeficiency, Immunity, Lymphocyte.

Immunofluorescent antibody assay (IFA) ◀ *i mū nō flor e sĕnt / an tē bo dē / ass ā, n.* a test using antibody labelled with a fluorescent dye; this technique is often used to visualize the occurrence and distribution of biomolecules of interest, such as in testing for equine herpes virus 1.

Immunoglobulin ◀ *i mū nō glo bū lin, n.* (antibody) protein produced by B lymphocytes following exposure to antigen; function is to combine with infectious agent or foreign material (antigen) and neutralize it so that disease does not occur. Types include:

- IgA – an antibody that plays a vital role in the immunity of mucosal surfaces.
- IgE – a class of antibody, which has only been found in mammals, that plays an important role in allergy; especially associated with type 1 hypersensitivity.
- IgG – the most abundant immunoglobulin. It can bind to many kinds of pathogens, and thereby protects the body against them by a variety of mechanisms.
- IgM – binds to specific antigens, even in the absence of prior immunization. For this reason IgM has sometimes been called a 'natural antibody'. IgM is by far the physically largest antibody.

See Immunity.

Immunology ◀ *i mū no lĕ jē, n.* branch of biomedical science concerned with the response of organisms to antigenic challenge.
See Immunity.

Immunomodulator ◀ *i mū nō mod ū lā tē, n.* a chemical agent that modifies the immune response or the functioning of the immune system.

Immunosuppression ◀ *i mū nō sē pre shĕn, n.* prevention or reduction of immune response; can be done with drugs, e.g. in treatment of purpura haemorrhagica, where antibody–antigen complexes cause damage to blood vessels. Corticosteroids, some chemotherapeutic agents used for treatment of cancer, and radiation have immunosuppressive effects.
See Corticosteroid, Immunity, Purpura haemorrhagica.

Immunotherapy ◀ *i mū nō ther ē pē, n.* therapy incorporating active and passive immunity, involving treatment with agents intended to affect the immune system.

Impaction ◀ *im pak shĕn, n.* condition of being lodged or wedged; e.g. food may be impacted into dental spaces; impaction of intestine occurs when colon is blocked by a mass of faecal material.
See Colon, Ileus.

Impar ligament see Distal: D. impar sesamoidean ligament

241

Implant ◄﹔ *im plarnt, n./v.* an object or material partially or completely inserted into the body, primarily for therapeutic purposes; e.g. an implant to repair a fracture. To fix object or tissue within body, e.g. fertilized egg is implanted in wall of uterus when pregnancy is established. Term also used for fixing of artificial materials in body, e.g. carbon fibre was once implanted to repair damaged tendons. See Fertilization, Tendon.

Implantation ◄﹔ *im plarnt ā shēn, n.* attachment of the embryonic blastocyst to the lining of the uterus; occurs in mares at approximately day 16 of pregnancy.

Impotence ◄﹔ *im pēt ēns, n.* inability of stallion to maintain penis in erect state in order to mate successfully with mare; often behavioural (e.g. from previous breeding shed trauma, or due to having been otherwise frightened by the mare). Term may also be used for other conditions where stallion is unable to copulate because of leg or back problems, management problems which deter desire to mate (e.g. improper temperature of an artificial vagina), etc. See Breeding.

Impression ◄﹔ *im pre shēn, n.* a slight indentation; an effect produced by some external stimulus; a copy produced from a material impressed on a surface.
> **I. material** ◄﹔ *im pre shēn / mat ēr ēēl, n.* used in the dental profession, dental impression material is soft material, such as sodium alginate, agar, and silicone, which is used to make a model of the dentition. In hoof care, impression material may be used to provide padding or cushion for a horse's hoof.
> **I. smear** ◄﹔ *im pre shēn / smér, n.* technique for collection of cells and other material from surface of lesion, e.g. skin growth. Clean glass slide pressed against surface of growth and allowed to dry in air, then stained and studied under microscope.

Imprinting ◄﹔ *im prin ting, n.* rapid learning of behaviour patterns that occurs with exposure to stimulus early in life. Especially foal imprinting, as popularized by Dr Robert Miller, as a method to try to introduce tolerance and submissiveness to various stimuli in neonatal horses. Several studies have questioned the necessity for, or utility of, procedure.

Impulse ◄﹔ *im puls, n.* a sudden, pushing force.
> **Cardiac i.** ◄﹔ *kar dē ak / im puls, n.* the palpable or recorded movement of the chest wall caused by the beating heart.
> **Nerve i.** ◄﹔ *nerv / im puls, n.* the electrochemical process which passes along nerve; the processes by which information is transmitted from nerves to brain (e.g. about pain, heat, hunger, position, etc.) and instructions from brain are transmitted to muscles, glands, etc.
> See Nerve.

Impulsion ◄﹔ *im pul shēn, n.* in reference to the horse's gait, and a rider's description thereof, impulsion describes the powerful thrust from the hindquarters; the surge that occurs when the horse's hindquarters push off the ground.

Incarcerated ◄﹔ *in kar sē rā tid, adj.* imprisoned; constricted; used to describe a situation where a loop of intestine is trapped, and passage of food through the loop is blocked, such as may occur in herniations of various structures; blood supply to intestinal wall is usually normal in early stages. See Hernia.

Incidence ◄﹔ *in si dēns, n.* rate at which an event occurs in a population; for example, the disease incidence may be measured as number of new cases of disease occurring during a certain period.

Incision ◄﹔ *in si zhēn, n.* a surgical cut, or wound, usually made with scalpel or other sharp instrument.

Incisor ◄﹔ *in sī zē, n.* front tooth, has narrow edge designed for biting off food (e.g. grass) during prehension. Horse has 12 incisors in the front of the mouth; 6 on the top (premaxilla) and 6 on the bottom (mandible). See Dentition, Tooth.

Incompetence see Insufficiency

Incontinent ◀⁈ *in con ti nēnt, adj.* lacking normal control over urination and/or defecation; e.g. may be seen in polyneuritis equi, or other conditions affecting the equine nervous system.
See Defecation, Polyneuritis equi, Urinary.

Incoordination ◀⁈ *in kō or di nā shēn, n.* failure of organs to work in a coordinated fashion.
See Ataxia.

Incubation ◀⁈ *in kū bā shēn, n.* the maintenance of an environment with controlled temperature, humidity and/or oxygen; development of infectious disease within animal from the time of infection until the time that clinical signs are seen.
　I. period ◀⁈ *in kū bā shēn /pér ēēd, n.* length of time from entry of pathogen (bacterium, virus, fungus, etc.) until signs of disease are seen; varies a great deal between diseases, e.g. incubation period for equine influenza 1–3 days, that for rabies may be several weeks to months.
　See Equine influenza, Pathogen, Rabies.

Indigofera ◀⁈ *in dī gō fērē, n.* a genus of legumes in the Fabaceae family of plants; some species contain a liver toxin, indospicine, a toxic amino acid.
See Birdsville horse disease.

Indolent ◀⁈ *in dō lēnt, adj.* causing little pain, as with an indolent lesion, e.g. an indolent ulcer of the eye; slow growing, as in an indolent tumour.

Induction ◀⁈ *in duk shēn, n.* bringing about; e.g. induction of parturition is the process of getting foaling started by administration of drugs, e.g. oxytocin or prostaglandin. NOTE: dystocias are reportedly more common in mares following induction of parturition than in mares not induced. In addition, foal survival may be poorer following induction compared with normal foaling.
See Oxytocin, Parturition, Prostaglandin.

Indurated ◀⁈ *in dǔr ā tid, adj.* hardened, e.g. an indurated mass of tissue.

Indwelling ◀⁈ *in dwe ling, adj.* pertaining to a catheter that is fixed in body; e.g. indwelling intravenous catheter is a tube which is held in place in blood vessel (e.g. for administration of drugs) by stitch or adhesive bandage. Foley catheter is a specialized indwelling catheter with an inflatable cuff.
See Catheter.

Infarct ◀⁈ *in farkt, n.* small area of necrotic tissue, resulting from failure of blood supply owing to obstruction of local circulation, most commonly from a thrombus or embolus. In horse, small intestine may develop infarct(s) where larvae of worms (*Strongylus vulgaris*) cause blood clots in arteries supplying intestine wall.
See Embolus, *Strongylus* spp, Thrombus.

Infection ◀⁈ *in fek shēn, n.* invasion of body by microorganisms (e.g. bacteria, viruses, fungi) and their multiplication in tissues. May be localized, if the body's defence mechanisms are effective (i.e. confined to specific area, e.g. abscess), or generalized if those defence mechanisms are overwhelmed (systemic, spread through body affecting several organs, e.g. septicaemia). A local infection may become systemic when the microorganisms gain access to the blood or lymphatic system.
See Abscess, Microorganism, Septicaemia.

Infectious ◀⁈ *in fek shēs, adj.* describes disease which is caused by or capable of being communicated by infection; e.g. an infection with a microorganism.
See Infection.
　I. arthritis see Arthritis

Inferior check ligament see Accessory ligament

Infertility ◀⁈ *in fē ti li tē, n.* diminished capability or inability to reproduce, especially as result of inability to conceive or carry foal to term; as opposed to losing foetus through abortion. Myriad causes:
• Mare – abnormality of uterus (e.g. adhesions), certain drugs, abnormal ovaries (e.g. ovarian hypoplasia), infectious diseases (e.g. contagious equine metritis), etc.

- Stallion – impotence, certain drugs, damage to testes (e.g. trauma, infection causing heat), poor sperm quality, failure to ejaculate, etc.

See Adhesion, Contagious equine metritis, Impotence, Ovary, Sperm, Testes, Uterus.

Inflammation ◀ *in flē mā shēn, n.* localized protective tissue response to injury or destruction of tissues, aimed at destroying, diluting or walling off the factor causing the injury, as well as the injured tissue itself. Many causes, including heat, cold, physical trauma, chemicals, radiation, sunlight, infectious microorganisms (e.g. bacteria, viruses, fungi), etc. Complex cascade of reactions occurs which produces classical signs of inflammation: heat (from increased blood flow in area as blood vessels dilate), redness (same cause as heat), swelling (blood vessels become leaky and lose fluid into tissues), pain (nerves are stretched by tissue swelling), and loss of function (tissues cannot work normally while there is extra fluid present). Chemicals released during the process of inflammation attract white blood cells to area, which clean away damaged tissues and infectious agents by phagocytosis. Various types of inflammation:
- Acute – inflammation of sudden onset, such as from injury.
- Chronic – inflammation of slow progression, marked chiefly by the formation of new tissue; usually causes permanent tissue damage.
- Diffuse – inflammation spread over a large area.
- Granulomatous – inflammation, usually chronic, characterized by the formation of granulomas.
- Subacute – inflammation between acute and chronic.
- Suppurative – inflammation characterized by pus formation.
- Traumatic – inflammation caused by trauma.

See Microorganism, Phagocytosis.

Inflammatory ◀ *in flā mē trē, adj.* pertaining to or characterized by inflammation.
See Inflammation.

Influenza see Equine influenza

Infrared ◀ *in frē red, n.* light with wavelength greater than that of red light, used e.g. in heat lamps for warming foals. Infrared rays emanating from tissues are the basis for thermography.
See Thermography.

Infundibulum ◀ *in fun di bū lum, n.* anatomical term describing any funnel-shaped part of body. Horses' teeth have an infundibulum, which is a cementum-filled indentation of the chewing surface.
See Tooth.

Inguinal ◀ *in gwi nūl, adj.* of the groin.
  I. canal ◀ *in gwi nūl / kē nal, n.* passage through abdominal wall in groin region of horse. Spermatic cord passes through in male. Hernia can occur in inguinal canal; loop of intestine may pass thorough canal into scrotum.
  See Hernia, Scrotum, Spermatic cord.
  I. hernia see Hernia

Inheritance ◀ *in he ri tēns, n.* characteristics of animal passed on from parents.
See Heredity.

Inhibitor ◀ *in hib it ē, n.* any substance that interferes with a chemical reaction, growth, or other biological activity.

Inject ◀ *in jekt, v.* to administer a substance into the body; e.g. a drug may be injected using a syringe and needle.
See Injection, Syringe.

Injection ◀ *in jek shēn, n.* forced administration of liquid into tissues by syringe and needle; can be given by several routes: subcutaneous (under skin), intramuscular (into muscles), intravenous (into vein), intraperitoneal (into abdomen), intradermal (into skin), intrathecal (into spinal canal), etc.
See Syringe.

Injury ◀ *in jē rē, n.* physical wound or damage, especially that caused by an external force, e.g. by blow, knife, kick, chemicals, burn, radiation, etc.

Inoculate ◀ᕽ *i no kū lāt*, *v.* to communicate a disease by inserting a causative agent; vaccinate; also used in microbiology where growth media are inoculated with samples of infected material in order to see which microorganisms are present.
See Vaccine.

Insect ◀ᕽ *in sekt*, *n.* any individual of the class Insecta. Many important insects affect horses, including flies, mosquitoes, midges (e.g. *Culicoides*), lice.
See *Culicoides* spp., Fly, Louse.

Insecticide ◀ᕽ *in sek ti sīd*, *n.* substance which is poisonous to insects. Some insecticides, e.g. organophosphates and carbamate, can be poisonous to horses.
See Carbamate, Insect, Organophosphate.

Insemination ◀ᕽ *in se mi nā shēn*, *n.* depositing of semen within cervix or vagina, as during sexual intercourse.
See Artificial insemination.

Insertion ◀ᕽ *in ser shēn*, *n.* in anatomy, point where muscle attaches to the bone that it moves.
See Bone, Muscle.

Inspiration ◀ᕽ *in spi rā shēn*, *n.* breathing in; inhalation.

Inspissated ◀ᕽ *in spi sā tid*, *adj.* being thickened or dried; e.g. inspissated pus.

Insufficiency ◀ᕽ *in su fi shēn sē*, *n.* inability of organ to perform normally. Examples include:
- Adrenal i. – abnormally decreased activity of the adrenal gland.
  See Hypoadrenocorticsm.
- Aortic i. – defective function of the aortic valve.
- Cardiac i. – failure of heart to pump blood as required.
  See Heart.
- Hepatic i. – inability of the liver to perform its normal functions.
- Renal i. – insufficient kidney function, as demonstrated by quantitative tests.
- Respiratory i. – a condition in which the lungs cannot provide sufficient oxygen or eliminate sufficient carbon dioxide.

Insulin ◀ᕽ *in sū lin*, *n.* hormone secreted into blood by pancreas (by beta cells of islets of Langerhans). Essential in maintenance of glucose balance within body: secreted when blood glucose levels rise and acts to promote storage of glucose, e.g. as glycogen, and transport of glucose out of blood into cells. Lack of insulin secretion or overproduction of other hormones which counteract the function of insulin can cause diabetes mellitus.
See Diabetes, Glucose.

Insulin resistance ◀ᕽ *in sū lin / riz is tēns*, *n.* condition in which cells become resistant to the glucose uptake action of insulin. Initially, more insulin is required to keep blood glucose concentrations within normal limits after feeding. If severe, blood glucose may also be abnormally high. Insulin resistance may ultimately result in muscle loss, lack of endurance, or laminitis.

CAUSES
The exact cause of insulin resistance is unknown. Several contributing factors include:
- Diet – horses have increased insulin resistance when fed high sugar/starch feeds compared to high fibre and fat rations, especially when they are not obese.
- Obesity – overweight horses tend to be insulin resistant, as are 'good doers' ('easy keepers'), even if they are not obese.
- Age – old horses (>20 years) seem to be more prone to insulin resistance, possibly as a result of pituitary dysfunction (Cushing's disease).
- Breed – ponies tend to have higher degrees of insulin resistance than horses. Breeds that are prone to developing cresty necks and obesity may be more likely to develop the problem.

DIAGNOSIS
A single blood sample drawn within 60 to 90 minutes of eating a grain feed is a quick screening test for hyperinsulinaemia. If this test is abnormal, more reliable tests, such as a glucose tolerance test, may be performed.

TREATMENT
Treatment is designed to control weight and decrease sugar intake. If an animal is

obese, appropriate diet and exercise regimens should be followed, on the advice of a veterinarian. Grain and high-sugar feeds should be eliminated. Grass hays, such as Bermuda grass, or feeding beet pulp that does not have added molasses, are good dietary choices. Fat horses, with or without laminitis, should have limited access to fresh grass.

DIETARY RECOMMENDATIONS:

- Feed primarily grass or legume mix hay or pasture in appropriate amounts.
- Feed no grain.
- Use feed products with a low glycaemic index. Oats are commonly used as the standard, with an index of 100. Plain beet pulp has the lowest index. Barley has the lowest index of the commonly fed grains.
- Test pastures and dry forages for amounts of sugars present.
- Soak high-sugar hay in hot water for 30 minutes or cold water for 60 minutes.
- Restrict grazing if grass is lush.
- Add fat and fibre to the diet.

Interfering ◀ _in_ tē _fé_ ring, _v._ a general term, in reference to the foot of one limb interfering with movement of the contralateral limb (analogous limb on the other side of the body).
See Speedy-cutting.

Interferon ◀ _in_ tē _fé_ ron, _n._ non-specific antiviral protein-based molecule released by cells infected by viruses; interferes with virus replication. Three basic types associated with specific producer cells and functions (α, β, γ).
See Virus.

Interleukin ◀ _in_ tē lŭ kin, _n._ a generic term for a non-antibody protein that acts as a mediator of inflammation; important in numerous inflammatory processes, especially arthritis.

Interleukin receptor antagonist protein
◀ _in_ tē lŭ kin / ri sep tē / ant ag on ist / prō tēn, _n._ (IRAP™) IRAP is a serum made from the horse's own blood, intended for use in the treatment of joint disease in the horse. The serum contains anti-inflamma-tory proteins that block interleukin-1, an inflammatory substance that has been shown to be important in the progression of osteoarthritis of the horse's joint, by accelerating the destruction of cartilage. The serum is obtained by drawing a 50 ml blood sample from the horse being treated, using a special syringe containing special treated glass beads. The blood mixes with the glass beads during a 24-hour incubation process. The blood is then spun in a centrifuge to separate the serum from the red blood cells. The serum so-treated contains high amounts of a protein that blocks the effects of interleukin-1. Once enriched, the serum is divided into three to five treatments of 4–5 ml each. It is then injected into the horse's affected joint once a week. Because the serum sample is derived from the horse's own blood, it carries minimal risk of adverse reaction. The serum has also been used for the treatment of tendon and ligament injuries in horses by some veterinarians, although no studies have apparently been done investigating its use for such purposes.

Intermittent claudication see Claudication

Intermittent positive pressure ventilation ◀ _in_ tē _mi_ tēnt / _po_ zi tiv / _pre_ shēr / ven ti _lā_ shēn, _n._ artificial respiration, i.e. administration of oxygen when animal cannot breathe for itself. Oxygen is pushed into respiratory tract, usually from anaesthetic machine, and then pressure is released to allow removal of carbon dioxide. Repeated several times per minute to mimic respiration. May be part of cardiopulmonary resuscitation.
See Cardiopulmonary resuscitation, Oxygen.

Internal ◀ in ter nŭl, _adj._ situated or occurring within, or on the inside.

    I. carotid artery ◀ in _ter_ nŭl / kē rot id / _ar_ tē rē, _n._ a branch of the carotid artery; one of two arteries that supply blood to the brain. Visible within the guttural pouch. Occlusion of the internal carotid artery has been used as a treatment for horses with nosebleed (epistaxis) caused by guttural pouch mycosis.

I. ear see Ear

I. fixation see Fixation

I. haemorrhage ◄፥ *in ter nūl* / *he mē rij, n.* bleeding within body, e.g. into chest or abdomen as result of damage to large blood vessel or injury to organ with rich blood supply, e.g. liver or spleen.
See Liver, Spleen, Thrombocytopenia.

Interosseous ◄፥ *in tēr os ē ēs, adj.* between bones.

    I. ligament ◄፥ *in tēr os ē ēs* / *lig ē mēnt, n.* various interosseous ligaments occur in the horse's body, especially the ligaments connecting the 2nd and 4th metacarpal and metatarsal bones to the 3rd metacarpal and metatarsal bones, respectively. The suspensory ligament of the metacarpus and metatarsus is also called the interosseous ligament.
    See Suspensory ligament.

Intersex ◄፥ *in tē seks, n.* horse with some characters of each sex; hermaphrodite. Intersex animal may have gonads and external genitalia partly from one sex and partly from the other; results from XXY chromosome zygote or XXX trisomy.
See Chromosome, Hermaphrodite, Pseudohermaphrodite.

Interstitial ◄፥ *in tē sti shūl, adj.* pertaining to or situated between small spaces or gaps in a tissue or structure; e.g. the tissue which supports the nephrons of the kidney, the cells which lie between the seminiferous tubules of the testis or the cells which support the alveoli of the lungs. Interstitial disease affects this tissue.
See Kidney, Lung, Testes.

Intertarsal joints ◄፥ *in tē tar sūl* / *joints, n.* the small joints that occur in the distal equine tarsus (hock). Osteoarthritis of these joints is commonly called 'bone spavin'.
See Bone.

Intervertebral ◄፥ *in tē ver ti brūl, adj.* situated between two adjacent vertebrae.
See Cartilage, Spine, Vertebra.

    I. disc ◄፥ *in tē ver ti brūl* / *disk, n.* pad of tissue which lies between adjacent vertebrae of spine, made up of fibrous cartilage ring, with softer central part. Acts as shock absorber and allows smooth movement of spine. Intervertebral disc prolapse or rupture has occasionally been reported in horses.
See Cartilage, Spine, Vertebra.

    I. injection ◄፥ *in tē ver ti brūl* / *in jek shēn, n.* injection technique occasionally used for the treatment of osteoarthritis of the cervical spine.
See Cartilage, Spine, Vertebra.

Intestinal ◄፥ *in tes ti nūl, adj.* relating to the intestines.
See Intestines.

    I. adhesion see Adhesion

    I. anastomosis see Anastomosis

Intestines ◄፥ *in tes tinz, n.* lower part of alimentary tract, long muscular tube which runs from the pyloric opening of the stomach to the anus. Made up of small intestine (has three parts, duodenum, jejunum, ileum) and large intestine (caecum, colons and rectum). Important in digestion of food, absorption of nutrients, electrolytes and water, and to move along and store faecal wastes until they are eliminated. Also known as *bowel* and *gut*.
See Large intestine, Small intestine.

Intra- ◄፥ *in trē, prefix.* within, into, or during.

Intra-articular ◄፥ *in trē ar ti kū lē, adj.* into or within a joint, e.g. intra-articular injection is one given directly into joint space.
See Joint.

    I-a. anaesthesia see Anaesthesia

Intrabursal ◄፥ *in trē ber sūl, adj.* within a bursa. Intrabursal injections may be given in the forearm (bicipital bursa) or foot (navicular bursa).

Intracellular ◄፥ *in trē sel ū lē, adj.* within a cell.

Intralesional ◄፥ *in trē lē zhē nūl, adj.* into or within a lesion, e.g. intralesional injection is one given directly into a lesion, such as a skin nodule.

Intramammary ◄፥ *in trē ma mē rē, adj.* into or within mammary gland (udder).
See Mammary gland.

Intramuscular ◀€ *in* tre *mus* cū lē, *adj.* into or within muscle, e.g. intramuscular injection is one given into a muscle.
See Muscle.

Intranasal ◀€ *in* tre *nā* zēl, *adj.* into the nose, e.g. intranasal vaccines are squirted onto the mucous membranes of the nasal passages.

Intratendinous ◀€ *in* tre *ten* din ēs, *adj.* within a tendon.

Intrathecal ◀€ *in* tre *the* kēl, *adj.* within a sheath; especially into the subarachnoid space of the spinal canal.

Intrauterine adhesion see Adhesion

Intravascular ◀€ *in* tre *vas* cū lē, *adj.* into or within blood vessel, e.g. disseminated intravascular coagulation is a condition where blood clotting occurs within blood vessels.
See Blood, Disseminated.

Intravenous ◀€ *in* tre *ve* nēs, *adj.* into or within a vein, e.g. intravenous injection is one given directly into a vein.
See Vein.

Intubation ◀€ *in* tū *bā* shēn, *n.* insertion of a tube into a body canal or cavity; e.g. placement of tube into windpipe (trachea) during general anaesthesia; nasogastric intubation ('stomach tube') to pass medication into the stomach.
See Anaesthesia.

Intussusception ◀€ *in* tē sē *sep* shēn, *n.* inversion of part of intestine into adjacent part; causes blockage of intestine, and blood supply to inverted part can be cut off so that tissue suffers lack of oxygen and cells die. Occurs mostly in small intestine. May occur following increased motility of intestine, e.g. diarrhoea; more common in foals than adults. Associated especially with tapeworm infestation. Causes severe pain, colic.
See Colic, Diarrhoea, Small intestine, Tapeworm.

In utero ◀€ *in* / *ū* tē rō, *adj./adv.* within the uterus, used e.g. to describe conditions

inside the mare's uterus, especially as pertaining to developing foal.
See Uterus.

In vitro ◀€ *in* / *ve* trō, *adj./adv.* in a glass, or test tube. Used to describe a test or procedure which happens in a laboratory; e.g. in vitro fertilization is where an egg and sperm are brought together in a laboratory under conditions which allow fertilization to take place.
See Fertilization.

In vivo ◀€ *in* / *ve* vō, *adj./adv.* in a living thing; e.g. used to describe a test or procedure performed in a living animal, as opposed to in a laboratory.

Involuntary ◀€ *in* *vo* lēn tē rē, *adj.* without conscious control, e.g. movements of muscles or actions of nerves which happen without animal having voluntary control over them. Mostly applies to smooth muscle (e.g. muscle of intestine, airways, etc.) and autonomic nervous system.
See Autonomic nervous system, Muscle.

Involution ◀€ *in* *ve* *lū* shēn, *n.* shrinkage or rolling up of organ; e.g. involution of uterus is where it shrinks back to normal size after parturition.
See Uterus.

Iodine ◀€ *ī* o dēn, *n.* (I) chemical element, essential in diet in small amounts, important in thyroid gland and in thyroid hormones. Iodine-containing compounds are used as disinfectants (e.g. povidone–iodine). Some iodine salts are used as contrast agents in radiography, as they can be injected into the body and show up as white on radiographs. Iodine is a component of various liniment and hoof preparations, where its particular effects are unknown. Iodine also reportedly tends to help dry the hoof and many horse owners use it to toughen horses' soles. When it is applied to the horse's foot, care must be taken to avoid getting excessive amounts on and around the coronary band, since it can irritate and inflame this area. Iodine is also a component of some over-the-counter medications sold for the treatment of thrush.

See Contrast agent, Disinfectant, Hypothyroidism, Radiography, Thrush, Thyroid.

Ion ◀╎ *ī on, n.* atom or group of atoms that has a positive charge (cation) or negative charge (anion) as result of losing or gaining electron(s). Substances that form ions are called electrolytes.
See Electrolyte.

Ionophore ◀╎ *ī onē for, n.* any of a number of organic compounds that facilitate the transport of ions across the cell membrane. Ionophore antibiotics inhibit the growth of some gram positive bacteria, and promote growth in ruminants, esp. cattle. Toxic to horses.
See Monensin

Iridocyclitis ◀╎ *i ri dō sī clī tis, n.* inflammation of iris and ciliary body of eye, i.e. uveitis.
See Eye, Iris, Uveitis.

Iris ◀╎ *ī ris, n.* circular, coloured membrane in eye behind the cornea; forms elliptical ring around pupil and can be moved by muscles of ciliary body to enlarge or constrict pupil according to amount of light. Conditions which can affect iris include inflammation (fairly common condition of horse as part of the syndrome of uveitis), prolapse, attachments of persistent pupillary membranes (harmless remnants of blood vessels from developing eye); part of iris may be missing (coloboma), injury from direct wound, etc.
See Coloboma, Eye, Persistent: P. pupillary membrane, Prolapse, Uveitis.

Iritis ◀╎ *ī rī tis, n.* inflammation of iris of eye.
See Eye, Iris, Uveitis.

Iron ◀╎ *ī ēn, n.* (Fe) metallic element, essential in diet and present in body in haemoglobin, myoglobin and in some enzymes. Stored as transferrin in blood. Iron is an essential element for oxygen transport by the horse's body. The highest levels of iron are found in the body's red blood cells. Iron supplements are commonly given to horses to act as 'blood

builders', that is, in an effort to increase the production of red blood cells by the horse's body. However, it is virtually impossible to create a diet in horses that is deficient in iron. Additional dietary iron does not stimulate the production of red blood cells nor of haemoglobin, the protein in red blood cells that carries oxygen. Iron supplementation is of little value in the horse. Neither iron deficiencies nor toxicities seem to be a common problem. However, excessive iron intake can occur in foals, causing damage to liver – signs include dullness, icterus (jaundice), nervous signs, coma, death.
See Anaemia, Haemoglobin, Liver, Myoglobin.

Irradiation ◀╎ *i rā dē ā shēn, n.* exposure to radiation for diagnosis or treatment, e.g. X-rays, radiotherapy.
See Radiography, Radiotherapy.

Irrigation ◀╎ *i ri gā shēn, n.* washing out wound or cavity with a stream of fluid; lavage.

Irritant ◀╎ *i ri tēnt, adj./n.* giving rise to irritation; an agent that produces irritation.

Irritation ◀╎ *i ri tā shēn, n.* the act of stimulating; soreness, roughness, or inflammation of a body part.

Ischaemia ◀╎ *is kē mē ē, n.* lack of blood in part of body, as result of blood vessel being blocked (e.g. by blood clot in aorto-iliac thrombosis) or constricted (e.g. from outside pressure).
See Aorto-iliac thrombosis, Blood.

Ischium ◀╎ *i shē ēm, n.* paired curved bone of pelvis, has depression (acetabulum) which forms socket for hip joint.
See Pelvis.

Iso- ◀╎ *ī sō, prefix* or combining form meaning equal, alike, the same, or uniform.

Isoerythrolysis ◀╎ *ī sō erē thrō lī sis, n.* destruction of a body's own blood cells. Caused when the mare produces antibodies against the foal's red blood cells and transfers those antibodies to the foal

through colostrum during the early stages of lactation and nursing.
See Neonatal.

Isoflurane ◀€ *ī sō flē rān, n.* an inhalational anaesthetic sometimes used for the induction and maintenance of general anaesthesia in horses.

Isotonic ◀€ *i sō to nik, adj.* equal tonicity. Describes solution which has electrolytes in same concentration as another fluid with which it is compared; often used to describe fluids which have same concentration or osmotic pressure as blood. An isotonic fluid can be given into vein and will not dilute or concentrate the electrolytes of blood, nor lyse blood cells. Also, involving muscular contraction in which tension is constant while length changes (as occurs in most exercise).
See Electrolyte, Pressure.

Isoxsuprine ◀€ *i zok sū prēn, n.* drug which stimulates nerve receptors of autonomic nervous system (parasympathetic nervous system) to cause widening (dilation) of peripheral blood vessels in humans. In the horse, isoxsuprine has been very popular for the treatment of navicular disease. It was initially prescribed because some veterinarians felt that navicular disease was a result of problems with the circulation to the navicular bone. However, more recent studies have concluded that navicular disease is *not* primarily a circulatory problem. Isoxsuprine is also prescribed by some veterinarians for the treatment of laminitis in the horse, although no studies have been performed to evaluate the effectiveness of isoxsuprine for the treatment of laminitis. However, recent work has suggested that isoxsuprine *cannot* be effective in the horse. The drug is poorly available to the horse orally (only about 2.2% of orally administered drug is available to the horse) and most of that is removed very quickly by the horse's liver. Nor have any significant pharmacological effects of oral isoxsuprine been demonstrated in the horse. Accordingly, the use of isoxsuprine for treatment of navicular syndrome or laminitis – or for any condition – is questionable at best. It is generally felt that isoxsuprine should not be used immediately after foaling in the mare nor should it be given during bleeding episodes. This is because, if the drug were effective, one would presumably not want to dilate blood vessels where the danger of bleeding already exists.
See Blood, Laminitis, Navicular syndrome, Parasympathetic nervous system.

-itis ◀€ *-ī tis, suffix.* inflammation.

IV ◀€ *ī vē, abbr.* intravenous.

Ivermectin ◀€ *ī vēr mek tin, n.* broad-spectrum anthelmintic drug used in horses for treatment of intestinal worms. Effective against many internal parasites, e.g. *Strongylus, Oxyuris, Parascaris,* lungworms, bots). Also has an effect against other parasites, e.g. mange mites, but is not licensed for treatment of these conditions in horses in UK.
See Anthelmintic, Bot, Lungworm, *Oxyuris equi, Parascaris equorum, Strongylus* spp.

Ixodes ◀€ *ik sō dēz, n.* genus of tick. *Ixodes ricinus* can be found on horses and may spread disease, e.g. Lyme disease, anaplasmosis.
See Lyme disease.

J

Jack ◀≀ *jak, n.* male donkey.

Jackson-Pratt drain ◀≀ *jak sēn-prat / drān, n.* small fenestrated drain made from silicone rubber; can be placed in small spaces, such as joints, to facilitate drainage, e.g. from infection.

Japanese B encephalitis ◀≀ *ja pē nēz / bē / en ke fē lī tis, n.* viral disease of humans and horses, widely distributed in eastern Pacific Rim. Caused by flavivirus, spread by mosquitoes (*Culex* spp.). Horse is dead-end host; normal life cycle involves humans, mosquitoes and pigs; wading birds are major wild hosts. Signs vary widely. Mild signs – fever, lethargy, loss of appetite, petechiae, and icterus (jaundice); more severe signs – paralysis, blindness, muscle tremor, incoordination and coma often precede death. Milder cases usually recover completely in 5–10 days. Diagnosis by serology and virus isolation. Treatment is supportive. Vaccine is available.
See Encephalitis, Flavivirus, Icterus, Serology, Virus.

Jasmine ◀≀ *jaz min, n.* (*Cestrum diurnum*) tropical plant, widely cultivated as ornamental plant in southern United States; also in Hawaii and India. Horses show signs of weight loss and increasing degrees of lameness after eating plant for several weeks. Plant contains steroid glycoside with vitamin D-like activity. Consumption results in excessive calcium and phosphorus reabsorption: dystrophic calcification and osteoporosis result. Hypercalcaemia and kidney dysfunction may be apparent on blood tests. No known treatment.
See Dystrophic, Glycoside, Osteoporosis, Vitamin D.

Jaundice see Icterus

Jaw ◀≀ *jor, n.* one of two bony structures at front of head, bearing teeth and used for biting food (prehension) and chewing it (mastication). Horse has fixed upper jaw (maxilla) and movable lower jaw (mandible) which can move up and down and sideways (but usually only rotating in one direction). Upper and lower jaws joined at temporomandibular joint.
See Enteritis, Mandible, Maxilla, Temporomandibular joint, Tooth.

Jejunitis-duodenitis proximal see Enteritis

Jejuno- ◀≀ *je jūn ō, adj. suffix,* pertaining to the jejunum.
See Jejunum.

Jejunocaecal intussusception ◀≀ *je jūn ō sē kēl / in tēs sē sep shēn, n.* intussusception (telescoping) of jejunum and ileum into caecum. Typically treated by removal of affected portion (jejunocaecostomy).

Jejunocaecostomy ◀≀ *je jūn ō sek os tom ē, n.* surgical procedure joining jejunum and caecum; indicated when all or part of ileum is devitalized.

Jejunocolostomy ◀≀ *je jūn ō kol os tom ē, n.* surgical procedure joining jejunum and colon; performed when a complete bypass of distal small intestine is necessary, and caecum possibly compromised.

Jejunoileostomy ◀≀ *je jūn ō ilē os tom ē, n.* surgical procedure joining jejunum and ileum, after removal of portion of diseased ileum.

Jejunojejunostomy ◀ƹ *je jŭn ō je jŭn os tēm ē, n.* removal of a portion of the jejunum, followed by anastomosis of the remaining segments.

Jejunum ◀ƹ *je jŭ nēm, n.* middle part of small intestine, between duodenum and ileum.
See Small intestine.

Jennet ◀ƹ *je nit, n.* (Jenny) female donkey, sometimes called mare in UK.

Joint ◀ƹ *joint, n.* point at which two or more bones of the skeleton are joined.
Joints are primarily classified according to structure and function. Structural classification is determined by how the bones connect to each other, while functional classification is determined by the degree of movement between the articulating bones. In practice, there is significant overlap between the two types of classifications. Structurally, joints may be:

- Fibrous and relatively immovable – bones connected by dense connective tissue. Divided into three types:
  1. Sutures – as found between bones of the skull.
  2. Syndesmosis – found between long bones, e.g. between radius and ulna, or between metacarpal/metatarsal bones and splint bones.
  3. Gomphosis – joint between tooth and tooth sockets.
- Cartilagenous
  1. Primary cartilaginous joints (synchondrosis), e.g. growth plates.
  2. Secondary cartilaginous joints – allow little movement. Also known as symphyses (e.g. the pubic symphysis of the hip).
- Synovial – joints with a space between bones to allow for movement; space filled with synovial fluid.

Functionally, joints may be classified by the degree of mobility they allow:
1. Synarthrosis – little or no mobility. Further subdivided by how the two bones are connected.
   a. Synchondrosis – two bones are connected by a piece of cartilage, e.g. joint between sternum and ribs.
   b. Synostosis – bones that are initially separated but eventually fuse, becoming one bone, e.g. sutures of the bones of the cranium.
2. Diarthrosis – allow many different movements, e.g. flexion, extension, adduction. All synovial joints are diarthrodial; surrounded by joint capsule (see J. capsule below); ends of bone in diarthrodial joints are usually covered with layer of hyaline cartilage which allows movement to be smooth and cushions the ends of the bones. Examples of diarthrodial joints are:
   a. Ball and socket – e.g. hip joint. End of one bone has a cup-shaped depression into which ball-shaped end of other bone fits. Allows movement in many directions (although in horse these joints do not have such a wide range of movement as they do in human).
   b. Hinge – (ginglymus) e.g. elbow joint. Allows movement in one plane only.
   c. Gliding – e.g. intervertebral joints, some carpal and tarsal joints. Two adjoining bone surfaces are almost flat and bones glide sideways.

Finally, joints are named anatomically, according to the bones that meet at the joint, e.g. tarsometatarsal joint (joint between the hock and cannon bone in hind limb), or metacarpophalangeal joint (joint between cannon bone and long pastern bone in the forelimb; fetlock joint).

Many conditions affect joints, including osteoarthritis, bone cysts, dislocation (luxation and subluxation), fracture of bone involving part of joint, osteochondrosis, etc.

See Joints under separate entries, Arthritis, Bone, Cartilage, Fracture, Luxation.

J. angle ◀ƹ *joint / ang gŭl, n.* the angle formed between the longitudinal axes of two adjacent bones. Joint angles are commonly measured in biomechanical studies; dramatic changes in joint angle can occur from lameness.

J. block see Block

J. capsule ◀ƹ *joint / kap sŭl, n.* the tissue envelope that surrounds joints, consisting of an outer fibrous layer and an inner layer, usually called the synovial membrane, which secretes joint fluid.

J. fluid see Synovial

J. space ◄⁞ *joint* /spās, *n.* radiolucent area between bones seen on radiographs of joints. Not actually a space; rather composed of joint cartilage interposed with a thin layer of synovial fluid. Joint space tends to be consistent throughout joint; narrowing of space on radiographs is a sign of osteoarthritis.
See Osteoarthritis, Osteochondrosis, Subluxation.

Joint-ill ◄⁞ *joint-ill, n.* orthopaedic infection of neonatal foal, caused by bacterial infection, usually spread via circulation. Infected navel (umbilicus) commonly thought to be the origin; however, the gastrointestinal and respiratory tracts are likely to be equally responsible; rarely from trauma and subsequent contamination. Infections result in joints, tendon sheaths, bursae, and bones. Infections predisposed to by failure of passive transfer, pneumonia, and enteritis. Many common bacteria implicated. Infection may also spread to other parts of body (neonatal septicaemia). Signs include swollen joints, lameness, pain on joint palpation, stiffness, depression, and high temperature. Complete blood count may show elevated white blood cell count and fibrinogen. Arthrocentesis confirms diagnosis; bacterial culture/sensitivity helps determine appropriate antibiotic therapy (systemic and/or local). Joint lavage important to remove bacteria and inflammatory by-products. Regional limb perfusion may be helpful. Radiographs may help determine extent of damage; however, even in the face of extensive joint damage, defects can heal, and foals can return to normal.
See Arthritis.

Jones test ◄⁞ *jōnz / test, n.* test for patency of nasolacrimal duct. Fluorescein dye is placed in lower puncta of the eye; normally appears in the nostrils in 5–20 minutes.

Test may be falsely negative owing to large volume of duct, but failure to see dye should prompt irrigation of duct.
See Fluorescein, Nasolacrimal duct.

Joule ◄⁞ *jûl, n.* unit of energy; may be used to describe energy content of feed, as per calories. (Named after James P. Joule, English physicist 1818–1889)

Jugulans nigra see Black walnut

Jugular ◄⁞ *ju gū lē, n.* paired large vein of neck, carries blood from head towards heart. Can be seen in jugular groove on either side of neck. Frequently used for injections where drug is given directly into blood stream (i.e. intravenous injection) or for obtaining blood samples.
See Vein.
  J. compression manoeuvre ◄⁞ *ju gū lē / kom presh ēn / mēn û vēr, n.* occlusion of jugular veins; increases pressure in cerebrospinal fluid to help facilitate collection of fluid or to help diagnose compressive lesions in spinal cord.
  J. pulse ◄⁞ *ju gū lē / puls, n.* rhythmic pulsing of jugular vein with beat of heart; reflects blood being pushed back up vein. May be postural (head down) in some horses; seen in various conditions related to cardiac insufficiency (e.g. shock, valvular problems, congestive heart failure).

Junctional epidermolysis bullosa ◄⁞ *jungk shēn ūl / e pi dē mō lī sis / būl ōsē, n.* hereditary skin disease, primarily reported in Belgian and American Saddlebred horses. Characterized by the formation of blisters following minor trauma, and well-defined ulcers, that may appear within the first two days of life on coronary band, anus, vulva, eyelids, and over areas of bony prominences. Crusting and exudation are prominent features. No effective treatment; affected foals become depressed, lose weight, and eventually become septicaemic and/or are euthanized.

K

K-Pen see Penicillin, Potassium.

Kanamycin ◄⧏ *kan ẽ mī sin, n.* aminoglycoside antibiotic; expense typically limits use to treatment of corneal ulcers caused by gentamicin-resistant *Pseudomonas* bacteria.
See Aminoglycoside.

Kaolin ◄⧏ *kā ō lin, n.* fine powdered clay; a hydrated form of aluminium silicate. Used as an intestinal adsorbent, often combined with pectin, a plant polysaccharide used mainly as a gelling agent. May be given as liquid by mouth, or used as paste in poultice.

Karyotype ◄⧏ *ka rē ō tīp, n.* full number of chromosomes in nucleus of animal's cells. Determination of karyotype may be needed to determine gender in intersex animal.
See Chromosome, Intersex.

Keratan sulphate ◄⧏ *ke rēt in /sul fāt, n.* proteoglycan (glycosaminoglycan linked to a protein) that is an important structural component of cartilage. Included in some oral joint supplements; no known therapeutic value.

Keratectomy ◄⧏ *ke rē tek tom ē, n.* surgical removal of part of cornea; may be required as part of treatment of ocular squamous cell carcinoma. Surgical site may need to be supported by conjunctival graft.
See Graft, Squamous.

Keratin ◄⧏ *ke rē tin, n.* specialized protein, primary component of outer layer of skin, horn of hoof, hair.
See Hair, Hoof, Skin.

Keratinization ◄⧏ *ke rē tin iz ā shẽn, n.* conversion into keratin or keratinous tissue; e.g. as occurs following injuries to hoof wall, prior to replacement from new horn growing from coronary band.
See Hair, Hoof, Skin.
  K. defect ◄⧏ *ke rē tin iz ā shẽn / dē fekt, n.* defects in formation of keratin; these defects alter the surface appearance of skin.
  See Seborrhoea.

Keratitis ◄⧏ *ke rē tī tis, n.* inflammation of cornea of eye; may be caused by injury, by various infectious agents (bacteria, viruses, or fungi), or those agents in combination. Signs include excessive tear production (epiphora), spasm of eyelids (blepharospasm), cloudy appearance of cornea (from corneal oedema), redness and swelling of conjunctiva, ocular pain, papillary constriction (miosis), new blood vessel growth on cornea (neovascularization). May also be ulcerative or non-ulcerative. Typically responds to medical therapy that:
1. Attempts to eliminate causative agent (e.g. antibiotic, antiviral or antifungal agents).
2. Controls pain (e.g. atropine, to dilate pupil, systemic and/or topical pain medications.
3. Reduces inflammation (systemic and/ or topical anti-inflammatory agents, which may also help relieve pain). If keratitis cases do not respond to medical therapy, or if problem extends deep into corneal stroma, surgical procedures (various grafting techniques, debridement, keratectomy, etc.) may be required.
Specific types of keratitis are:
• Bacterial k. – corneal inflammation complicated by bacterial infection. Treatment with topical antibiotic

agents, ideally based on culture and sensitivity.

- Fungal k. – corneal inflammation complicated by fungal infection. Not common in United Kingdom, more common in warmer areas. Treatment with topical antifungal agents.
- Non-ulcerative k. – relatively uncommon condition; most cases in southeastern United States. Corneal stroma becomes infiltrated with cells, with intact corneal epithelium. Neovascularization common, with marked uveitis. Cause unknown. Suppression of inflammation is critical, however, and this condition must be diagnosed accurately prior to treatment, because agents used to treat non-ulcerative k., especially topical corticosteroids, can be detrimental to the body's attempt to heal other conditions.
- Ulcerative k. – keratitis in conjunction with corneal ulceration; most common eye problem of horses. Secondary to foreign bodies, lacerations, trauma, etc. May become secondarily infected with pathogenic agents.
- Viral k. – corneal inflammation most commonly induced by equine herpes virus. Signs include multiple small areas of corneal opacity, spasm of eyelids and ocular discharge. Usually only one eye affected. Typically responds to antiviral therapy.

See Conjunctiva, Cornea, Corneal, Eosinophilic, Equine herpes virus, Eye, Uveitis.

Keratocoele see Descemetocoele

Keratoconjunctivitis sicca ◀ː *ke ra tō con jungk ti vī tis / si kē, n.* 'dry eye'. Very uncommon in horses; all reported cases have been associated with trauma, especially to cranial nerves V or VII, but also secondary to fractures of the mandible and stylohyoid bone. Causes inflammation of cornea and conjunctiva of eye related to lack of tear production. Signs include thick, sticky discharge from eye, cloudy cornea, pain, spasm of eyelid, keratitis, and corneal ulceration; secondary bacterial infection common. Diagnosis involves testing of tear production by Schirmer tear test. Treatment with antibiotic ointments to control infection; application of artificial tear ointments are required several times a day to keep cornea moist. Many acute cases will resolve as primary problem is corrected. In chronic cases, cases that do not respond to treatment, or do not resolve on their own, enucleation (removal) should be considered owing to progressive deterioration of eye.

See Conjunctiva, Cornea, Eye, Facial, Lacrimal apparatus, Schirmer tear test.

Keratolytic ◀ː *ke rē tō lit ik, n.* an agent that helps soften the surface layers of the skin, allowing for removal of scale and surface cells (such agents do not dissolve keratin). Keratolytic agents include sulphur, tar shampoos, benzoyl peroxide, and selenium sulphide.

Keratoma ◀ː *ke rē tō mē, n.* uncommon hoof problem characterized by keratin-containing tissue growing between the hoof wall and the coffin bone (third phalanx). Not related to neoplastic process; most cases caused by trauma or chronic irritation; however, in many cases, cause cannot be determined. Tissue causes pressure inside hoof. Signs include insidious onset of intermittent lameness, abnormalities of hoof wall and coronary band, and thickening of hoof visible at white line. In some cases, draining tracts develop, as per hoof abscesses. Diagnosis from clinical signs of lameness and response to pressure from hoof testers; radiography may show discrete semicircular areas of bone resorption in the coffin bone, as a result of pressure from growth. Treatment involves complete surgical removal; recurrence common if tissue not completely removed. Surgery may be performed in standing horse or under general anaesthesia. Hoof wall stabilization may be required post-surgery with special shoe (e.g. bar shoe). Prognosis for soundness is good with complete removal.

See Foot, Hoof.

Keratomalacia ◀ː *ke rē tō mēl ā shē ē, n.* corneal melting; occurs secondary to severe corneal infections and secondary to bacterial enzymatic action against collagen (e.g. collagenase, such as that elaborated by *Pseudomonas* spp.). Rapidly progressing; antibiotics of choice typically have activity against *Pseudomonas*, e.g. tobramycin, ciprofloxacin. Topical anticollagenase therapy includes acetylcysteine and blood serum. Topical tetracycline ointments may also help interfere with enzyme action. Surgical treatment (debridement and grafting) may be indicated in severe cases, or cases that do not respond to medical therapy.

Keratopathy see Band

Keratosis ◄⁞ *ke rē tō sis, n.* disease of the skin marked by overgrowth of horny tissue. Two types:
   Cannon k. ◄⁞ *ka nēn / ke rē tō sis,* plaques of scaling, crusting, hyperkeratosis, and hair loss on anterior surface of cannon bone. Must be differentiated from infectious conditions; persists for life. Not caused by urination on cannon bones, as commonly believed. No treatment is necessary, but keratolytic ointments or creams may help control, if applied regularly.
   Linear k. ◄⁞ *li nē ē / ke rē tō sis,* rare, possibly heritable, dermatosis of unknown aetiology. Most commonly seen in Quarter Horses, Thoroughbreds and Standardbreds; appears as vertical bands of hyperkeratosis and hair loss on neck, shoulder and thorax. Diagnosis by biopsy. Treatment is not needed, but keratolytic shampoos, ointments or creams may help control.

Keratotomy ◄⁞ *ke rē tot ēmē, n.* a surgical incision into the cornea.
   Grid k. ◄⁞ *grid / ke rē tot ēm ē, n.* procedure to stimulate ingrowth of corneal cells; typically employed in treatment of indolent (non-healing) ulcers. Fine gauge needle is traced across anaesthetized cornea in a grid pattern; corneal cells follow grid marks across cornea.

Kerosene ◄⁞ *ker ō sēn, n.* flammable hydrocarbon liquid; has been used as irritant therapy for treatment of endometritis for many years. Recovery from inflammation in 14–21 days post-infusion of 50 ml commercial grade kerosene. One experi-

mental study has suggested that uterine gland activity is improved following kerosene infusion, and high pregnancy rates followed after kerosene infused mares were bred. If performed, infusion most commonly done during dioestrus, with closed cervix, to prevent reflux of kerosene into vagina.

Ketamine ◄⁞ *ke tē mēn, n.* commonly used short-term injectable dissociative anaesthetic drug (reduces or blocks signals to the conscious brain); first developed in 1962. Often used in combination with other drugs in intravenous anaesthetic protocols, or as inducing agent prior to gas anaesthesia. Very safe; little cardiovascular or breathing depression, unlike other anaesthetic agents.
See Anaesthetic.

Ketoconazole ◄⁞ *kē tō con ēz ol, n.* synthetic antifungal drug used to prevent and treat fungal infections, especially of skin. Inhibits sterol formation in fungal cell membrane. Poorly available orally, but availability increased when the drug is acidified.

Ketone ◄⁞ *kē tōn, n.* (ketone body) organic compounds, including acetone, acetoacetate, and beta hydroxybutyrate. Generated from carbohydrates, fatty acids and amino acids in most vertebrates. The pathway for ketone formation is not well developed in horses. Most commonly produced in liver insufficiency, when the body is mobilizing triglycerides and fatty acids to support the body; levels increase if the liver is not performing its normal clearance functions efficiently. Ketones may be measured in blood or urine.

Ketoprofen ◄⁞ *kē tō prō fen, n.* non-steroidal anti-inflammatory drug; comes as a sterile solution for intravenous administration. Intramuscular administration has been reported with no adverse effects. Ketoprofen is recommended used for the relief of pain and inflammation associated with diseases of the musculoskeletal system. The effects of the drug appear to be maximal at about 12 hours and last for up to 24 hours. One study in 1995 suggested that ketoprofen is more effective than phenylbutazone at relieving some types of musculoskeletal pain; however, the expense of the drug may limit its widespread use. Ketoprofen appears to be very safe in the horse unless extreme overdoses are given. Precautions similar to those for other non-steroidal agents would be appropriate. The effects of ketoprofen on fertility, pregnancy and foetal health have not been studied.

See Aspirin, Non-steroidal anti-inflammatory drug.

Kidney ◀ _kid_ nē, _n._ paired organs that filter wastes from the blood and excrete them, along with water, as urine; situated near lumbar spine, outside peritoneal cavity.

FUNCTIONAL STRUCTURE

Main functional unit of kidney is nephron; each kidney has more than 1 million nephrons, which eliminate wastes, regulate blood volume and pressure, control levels of electrolytes and metabolites, and regulate blood pH. Nephron functions are regulated by the endocrine system via hormones such as antidiuretic hormone, aldosterone, and parathyroid hormone. Nephron consists of two parts: one to filter and one to collect. Initial filtering structure is the renal corpuscle, which consists of a glomerulus, a cluster of blood vessels where blood is filtered (proteins and cells stay in blood vessels, water and electrolytes pass through), and a Bowman's capsule which collects the filtered blood. Collecting structure is the long, U-shaped renal tubule, a structure that is specialized for reabsorption and secretion of salts and other ions. Collecting duct collects everything which has not been reabsorbed and passes this fluid (urine) into ureter.

ORGANIZATIONAL STRUCTURE

Outer portion of kidney is the renal cortex, which lies immediately beneath the connective tissue capsule. Deep to the cortex is the medulla; medulla is divided into renal pyramids. Each pyramid forms a renal lobe, along with the overlying cortex. The tip of each renal pyramid (papilla) empties into a calyx; each calyx

empties into the renal pelvis. The pelvis connects to the ureter, which takes urine to the bladder. Blood supply to kidney is by the renal artery.

KIDNEY DISEASE

Conditions affecting kidney include damage to tubules caused by toxins (e.g. various drugs), lack of blood supply (e.g. in endotoxaemic shock), bacterial infection (e.g. septicaemia in foal), glomerulonephritis. Kidney problems may be acute or chronic. Clinical signs of disease may not be seen until 75% of kidney tissue has stopped working, although decreased function may be detected earlier using kidney function tests.

K. biopsy ◀ _kid_ nē / _bī_ op sē, _n._ biopsy of kidney, assisted by ultrasound guidance. Somewhat controversial technique, as severe haemorrhage usually follows; should only be performed if results would change therapeutic plan or prognosis.

K. function tests ◀ _kid_ nē / _fungk shēn_ / _tests_, _n._ various tests measure how well the kidney is performing its vital functions. Function tests include:

1. Clearance tests (e.g. glomerular filtration rate, creatinine clearance test), a measure of the volume of plasma cleared of a substance during a measured time period.
   See Glomerular filtration rate, Creatinine.

2. Urinalysis – analysis of the urine for cells, substances (e.g. protein or glucose), and concentration.
   See Urinalysis.

3. Water deprivation test – tests whether urine is dilute because of a behavioural problem (e.g. psychogenic drinking) or because of a nephrogenic problem (e.g. diabetes insipidus).
   See Water.

4. Blood tests – blood may be tested for substances filtered by the kidneys, including blood urea nitrogen (BUN), creatinine and electrolytes.
   See individual entries.

See Glomerulonephritis, Kidney failure, Septicaemia, Shock.

Kidney failure ◀ _kid_ nē / _fā lŭr_, _n._ (renal failure) condition where kidneys fail to perform normal functions, including a failure to remove waste efficiently from body, resulting in such wastes (e.g. blood urea nitrogen, creatinine) accumulating in blood stream (azotaemia; more broadly, uraemia). Occurs when 65–75% of kidney nephrons are not working. Typically classified as acute renal failure (ARF) or chronic renal failure (CRF). Diagnostic techniques include various kidney function tests (see entry), rectal examination, ultrasonography, radiography in foals or miniature horses, endoscopy, and scintigraphy.

ACUTE RENAL FAILURE

Syndrome associated with a rapid decrease in glomerular filtration rate, resulting in azotaemia, and problems with fluid, electrolyte and acid–base balance. Occurs from:

1. Decreased perfusion (pre-renal ARF), e.g. severe diarrhoea, shock, prolonged exercise without adequate water.
2. Problem with urinary outflow (post-renal ARF), e.g. nephrolith, neoplasia; uncommon, except with ruptured urinary bladder in foals.
3. Ischaemic or toxic damage, e.g. non-steroidal anti-inflammatory drugs, aminoglycoside antibiotics, myoglobinuria following exertional rhabdomyolysis, ingestion of red maple leaves. Typically causes necrosis of renal tubules.

Signs of acute kidney failure often reflect the primary problem, e.g. diarrhoea or rhabdomyolysis. Primary signs of kidney involvement include dehydration, mild colic, loss of appetite, weakness, dullness; urine production varies. Treatment focuses on removing the underlying cause and correcting imbalances in fluids and electrolytes. Prognosis depends on the cause, duration of the problem (the longer the problem has been going on, the less likely horse will respond to treatment), initial response to treatment, and the development of secondary problems such as colic, laminitis, or colitis.

CHRONIC RENAL FAILURE

A gradual and progressive loss of the ability of the kidneys to perform their functions; less common cause of kidney failure than ARF. Final stages of CRF typically referred to as end-stage kidney disease. May be congenital (e.g. failure of normal kidney development, or polycystic kidney disease) or acquired; acquired disease presents with insidious onset and condition may result from an insult (i.e. a preceding event that caused damage) that occurred years previous to presentation, and may result from progression of acute form. Causes of CRF include:

1. Glomerular injury (chronic glomerulonephritis) – including ischaemia, immune-mediated causes, toxic insults, and infection, which lead to renal tissue injury.
2. Chronic interstitial nephritis – chronic kidney disease characterized by damage from inflammatory cells; refers more generally to causes of CRF besides glomerular failure.
3. Chronic obstructive lesions – urolithiasis, nephrolithiasis.
4. Pyelonephritis – kidney infection, usually from ascending urinary tract infection (rare).

Signs of chronic kidney failure reflect the effects of accumulated wastes on cell metabolism and function; disease onset is usually insidious. Horses typically show weight loss, poor appetite (most likely resulting from accumulation of wastes), dullness, excessive drinking (polydipsia) and excessive urination (polyuria). Ventral oedema may occur, with loss of blood proteins through kidneys. Diagnosis suggested by typical clinical signs and inability of kidneys to concentrate urine. Rectal examination may show small or irregular left kidney (cannot palpate right kidney). Renal function tests abnormal; anaemia may be a feature in chronic disease; hypercalcaemia frequently seen owing to impaired renal excretion. Urine tests may show high protein levels; water deprivation test will show failure to concentrate urine, but must be conducted with caution, as horses need water to compensate for disease.

See Azotaemia, Exertional rhabdomyolysis, Glomerulonephritis, Kidney, Nephrolithiasis, Pyelonephritis, Uraemia, Urinalysis, Urolithiasis.

Kimberly horse disease see Pyrrolizidine, Seneciosis

Kimzey leg saver splint™ ◀: *kim zē / leg / sāv er / splint, n.* popular emergency first aid splint, made of aluminium with foam lining, for stabilization of severe injuries including fractures of the sesamoids, long and short pastern bones, and cannon bone, and failure of the suspensory apparatus.

Kinematic gait analysis ◀: *kını ma tık / gāt / ē na li sis, n.* analysis of the horse's way of going concerned with the study of the description of motion. Kinematics evaluates motion characteristics spatially (for example height or displacement) and temporally (for example duration or rate) without direct reference to forces.
See Gait.

Kinetic gait analysis ◀: *kin et ik / / gāt / ē na li sis, n.* analysis of the horse's way of going concerned with the study of the action of forces; attempts to define and measure the forces causing a particular movement.
See Gait.

Kissing spines ◀: *ki sing / spīnz, n.* condition of back allegedly caused by touching or overriding of adjacent spinous processes of vertebrae of spine; controversy exists as to whether this is a real condition in horses. More commonly diagnosed in Europe than United States; condition was previously diagnosed in humans, but diagnosis was subsequently abandoned. Thoracic vertebrae said to be most commonly affected, especially in saddle area; pressure on spine said to result in bony changes of spinous processes. Signs attributed to condition include gradual change in behaviour, unwillingness to jump. Diagnosis by clinical signs; assisted by radiography. Treatment with rest; surgery to remove the dorsal spines of adjacent vertebrae has been described.
See Spine, Vertebra.

***Klebsiella* spp.** ◀: *kleb sē e lē / spē shēs, n.* genus of Gram-negative bacteria, can cause variety of diseases in horse. Many *Klebsiella* spp. may be part of normal genital flora in some animals; however, *Klebsiella pneumoniae* is considered pathogenic. *K. pneumoniae* endometritis is

considered to be a venereal disease, because it can be spread by breeding, by insemination with infected semen, and by handling of genitalia, but it can cause endometritis (uterine infection), preventing conception, and placentitis, which can cause abortion. Can cause septicaemia, pneumonia, and diarrhoea in foals, has also been implicated in bacterial infections of corneal ulcers. Other *Klebsiella* spp. may be associated with infections of burns, and infections of the urinary bladder. Treatment with appropriate antimicrobial therapy; appropriate hygiene measures to prevent venereal transmission should be practised routinely.
See Diarrhoea, Metritis, Septicaemia.

Knee ◀: *nē, n.* carpus. Analogous to human wrist. (Note: stifle joint of horse is analogous to the knee of human). Various associated conditions, including:
• Bench k. – cannon bone is shifted toward the outside of the carpus.
• Bucked k. (goat knee, over at knee) – knee inclines forward when viewed from the side, in front of a plumb line from the middle of the forearm to the fetlock.
• Calf k. (back at knee) – knee inclines backward when viewed from the side, behind a plumb line from the middle of the forearm to the fetlock.
• K. hitting – interference where knee hits contralateral forelimb; seen mostly in racing Standardbred horses.
• Knock k. – one or both knees deviate inward toward each other, with the lower leg angled out, resulting in a toed-out stance (see C. valgus).
See Carpal, Carpus, Stifle.

Knuckling ◀: *nuk ling, v.* bending over forwards at fetlock joint, may be caused by damage to extensor tendons, short or contracted flexor tendons.
See Contracted.

Kunjin virus ◀: *kun jin / vir ēs, n.* a flavivirus, first isolated from *Culex* mosquitoes in north Queensland, Australia in 1960; name from a nearby Aboriginal clan. The virus is endemic in the tropical north of Australia; has cycles of infection between birds and mosquitoes. Closely related to West Nile virus. Mild form is clinically inapparent; severe form causes infections of central nervous system. Treatment is supportive. No vaccine available, but environmental management may help control mosquitoes.

Kyphosis ◀ɕ *kī fō̱ sis, n.* (roach back) abnormally increased concavity of thoracic spine. Occasionally seen as congential abnormality in neonates; in weanlings during periods of growth, sometimes associated with orthopaedic abnormalities, such as osteochondrosis; may be seen as postural adjustment to musculoskeletal injury, or, in adult horses, secondary to certain diseases affecting the musculoskeletal system, e.g. tetanus.

See Osteochondrosis, Spine, Tetanus.

L

Labium ◄€ _lā_ bē ēm, _n_. (plural labia) anatomical term for lip-like structure, e.g. of mouth or of vulva.
See Lip, Vulva.

Laboratory ◄€ lē _bo_ rē trē, _n_. place specially equipped for the carrying out of diagnostic tests or experiments. Many clinical diagnoses are confirmed by various laboratory tests.
   L. diagnosis see Diagnosis

Labour ◄€ _lā_ bēr, _n_. process of foaling; parturition.
See Parturition.

Laburnum ◄€ lē _ber_ nēm, _n_. genus of two species of small trees, native to the mountains of southern Europe from France to the Balkan Peninsula. May cause poisoning if any part of the plant is eaten. Signs of poisoning include excitability, incoordination, sweating, convulsions, and coma. May be fatal.

Labyrinth ◄€ _la_ bē rinth, _n_. general term for a system of interconnecting canals and cavities, especially:
   Ethmoid l. ◄€ _eth_ moid / _la_ bē rinth, _n_. the thin bony structures of the ethmoid bone, of the upper nostrils; help filter air.
   Osseous l. ◄€ _o_ sē ēs / _la_ bē rinth, _n_. bony canals and cavities which form inner ear. Consist of cochlea (concerned with hearing) and vestibule and semicircular canals, (concerned with balance).
   See Ear.

Laceration ◄€ _la_ sē _rā_ shēn, _n_. tear in skin or other tissue; wound caused by tearing or other trauma; cut (as opposed to incision).
See Wound.

Lacrimal ◄€ _la_ kri mūl, _adj_. (lachrymal) concerned with tears, especially secretion of tears.

Lacrimal apparatus ◄€ _la_ kri mūl / a pē _rā_ tēs, _n_. system responsible for production and drainage of tears. Includes lacrimal glands, lacrimal ducts, eyelids and nasolacrimal duct. Lacrimal gland surrounds base of the third eyelid, and secretes watery tears; other glands, e.g. Meibomian glands, glands of third eyelid, goblet cells of conjunctiva, all contribute secretions that add to the composition of tears. Tears are spread across eye by eyelids. Drainage of tears is through two holes (lacrimal puncta) in the margins of the upper and lower eyelids, at the medial canthus of eye. A little duct (canaliculus) leads from each punctum to the beginning of the nasolacrimal duct, a 22–30 cm long duct, which opens out in nose (at junction of skin and mucous membrane on floor of nasal cavity). Failure of the lacrimal apparatus causes keratoconjunctivitis sicca; other conditions affecting lacrimal apparatus include congenital failure of development of a part of the tear drainage ducts, narrowing of the drainage ducts, e.g. by tumour pressing on duct, or obstruction by dried mucus or other debris.
See Eye, Keratoconjunctivitis sicca, Tear.

Lactam ◄€ _lak_ tam, _n_. β-lactam antibiotics are among the most commonly used antibiotics in equine practice; include penicillins and cephalosporins.
See Cephalosporin, Penicillin.

Lactate ◄€ _lak_ tāt, _v./ n_. to secrete milk from mammary glands, especially in order to feed foal; any salt of lactic acid. Lactate

261

levels are elevated in several conditions of the horse, e.g. in colic with poor tissue perfusion; however, lactate tests are not routinely available in most laboratories thus, test is rarely performed. Contrary to popular belief, increased concentration of blood lactate does not directly cause acidosis, nor is it responsible for muscle soreness, as seen in exertional rhabomyolysis.
See Lactic acid, Mammary gland, Milk.

Lactate dehydrogenase ◀€ _lak_ tāt / dē hī _dro_ ji nāz, n. (LDH) enzyme present in many tissues of the horse's body, including striated muscle, liver, heart muscle, kidney and red blood cells. Level in blood is raised if any of these tissues are damaged, e.g. in rhabdomyolysis; however, test is not specific for any condition. Various LDH enzyme isoforms can be isolated by further testing (electrophoresis). Rarely used as a diagnostic test in horses.
See Enzyme, Exertional rhabdomyolysis.

Lactated Ringer's solution ◀€ _lak_ tā tid / _ring_ ēz / sē _lŭ_ shēn, n (LRS; Hartmann's solution) an isotonic fluid most commonly used for intravenous administration, containing sodium, potassium, calcium, chloride and lactate; lactate acts as a buffer for acid in system. Composition varies slightly between manufacturers, so there is no precise formulation. LRS is used for fluid resuscitation associated with blood loss, from hypovolaemia associated with shock or diarrhoea, and for the treatment of dehydration and heat stroke. (Named after Sidney Ringer, British physiologist 1835–1910.)
See Ringer's solution.

Lactation ◀€ _lak_ tā shēn, n. secretion of milk from mammary gland. Stimulated by the hormone prolactin, produced from late pregnancy, and also by suckling of foal. Also, refers to the complete period during which the mare is nursing the foal, from about the time of parturition to weaning.
See Mammary gland, Milk, Prolactin.

    L. tetany ◀€ _lak_ tā shēn / _te_ tē nē, n. rare condition sometimes seen in heavily lactating mares, especially draught breeds,

in first few days after foaling or at weaning. Associated with stress, such as hard work or transport. Caused by low level of calcium in blood (hypocalcaemia), and occasionally low levels of blood magnesium (hypomagnesaemia). Signs include rapid breathing, thumping sounds from chest (spasms of diaphragm), sweating, stiff gait, incoordination; muscle tremors are related to degree of hypocalcaemia. May progress to convulsions and collapse if untreated; treatment with calcium gluconate solutions results in rapid recovery. Re-treatment may be necessary in some cases.
See Hypocalcaemia, Foal.

Lactic acid ◀€ _lak_ tik / _a_ sid, n. a chemical compound that plays a role in several biochemical processes; in solution, loses a protein to produce lactate ion. Produced in muscle tissue during exercise, from breakdown of glycogen in anaerobic metabolism. Theoretically, animals that are more fit will shift to anaerobic metabolism later than less fit animals; attempts have been made to correlate fitness in performance horses with blood lactic acid; however, so far, the results of such tests have not been consistent. Furthermore, fitness may not necessarily correlate with racing performance.
See Exertional rhabdomyolysis, Glycogen, Lactate, Muscle.

    L. acidosis ◀€ _lak_ tik / _a_ sid _ō_ sis, n. acidosis caused by accumulation of lactic acid more rapidly than it can be metabolized.
    See Acidosis.

**Lactobacillus** ◀€ _lak_ tō bē _si_ lēs, n. genus of non-pathogenic bacteria found in high concentrations in the normal equine stomach. _Lactobacillus_-containing products, e.g. over-the-counter pastes, or yogurt, have been used in foals and adult horses as probiotics, especially in the treatment of diarrhoea of various causes, in hopes that it will replace disease-causing bacteria with bacteria normally found in intestines.
See Probiotics.

Lactose ◀€ _lak_ tōz, n. disaccharide that makes up a major portion of equine milk, as well as the milk of most other mammals.

Lag screw ◀ *lag / skrǔ, n.* technique of bone screw application used for repairing broken bones, e.g. in repair of slab fracture of carpal bone. Broken fragment has a hole drilled through it which is wider than the threaded screw; main part of bone has smaller hole drilled in it in which thread of screw will catch. Screw passes through broken fragment; as screw is tightened, fragment is pulled tightly against main part of bone.
See Bone, Fracture.

Lamellar ◀ *lam el ē, adj.* arranged in thin plates.
L. bone ◀ *lam el ē / bōn, n.* bone that forms the major portion of cancellous and cortical bones; makes up the major portion of the equine skeleton.
L. corium ◀ *lam el ē / kor rē ēm, n.* lamellae that interlock with the epidermal lamellae of the inner hoof wall and bars of the hoof.
L. keratectomy ◀ *lam el ē / ke rē tek tēm ē, n.* surgical removal of layers of cornea, most commonly for removal of corneal tumours.
L. keratoplasty ◀ *lam el ē / ke rē tō plas tē, n.* partial thickness graft of layers of autogenous corneal tissue, from same eye or opposite eye; occasionally recommended to treat large corneal defects.

Lameness ◀ *lām nēs, n.* disturbance of normal gait, resulting in abnormal locomotion. Common cause for examination of domestic horses; may be as result of pain (horse trying to avoid pain by reducing amount of weight put on painful leg, caused e.g. by abscess in hoof, broken bone, laminitis, strained tendon, arthritis, etc.), 'mechanical' problem, resulting in inability of limb to function normally (e.g. contracture of tendon), damage to nerve supply, etc. Diagnosis involves watching horse in motion, looking for asymmetries of motion (e.g. at trot, head characteristically goes up when weight is taken on sore front leg, and head will go down when weight taken on sound leg), palpation of foot and limb (feeling for heat, swelling, noting if horse reacts to area being touched, etc.), hoof testing with metal pincers (hoof testers), and manipulation (moving joints and assessing response). Clinical diagnosis

assisted by various techniques, including radiography, ultrasonography, assessment of fluid from joint (synovial fluid), nerve block, scintigraphy, magnetic resonance imaging (MRI), etc.
See Abscess, Arthritis, Laminitis, Magnetic resonance imaging, Nerve block, Radiography, Scintigraphy, Synovial, Tendon, Ultrasonography.

Lamina ◀ *la mi nē, n.* (pl. laminae) thin, flat layer or plate of tissue. **1)** The corium (or, as it is commonly called, the 'quick') is a highly vascularized and well-innervated layer of dermis and epidermis that lies between the hoof wall and the coffin bone. The corium nourishes the hoof, and its connective tissue connects the bone of the hoof (coffin bone) to the hoof wall, and thereby suspends the bone from the inner wall of the hoof capsule. All parts of the corium, except for the corium that interlocks with the inner hoof wall and bars (known as the lamellar corium, or lamina), have small projections (papillae) that fit tightly into the holes in the adjacent hoof. However, the lamellar corium is structured differently; it has parallel layers (the vascular 'sensitive' laminae) that interlock with corresponding layers of the hoof itself (the avascular 'insensitive' laminae). Normal laminar connection is vital to the strength and health of the hoof. **2)** The broad plates of bone that form the dorsal surfaces of the vertebrae.
See Foot, Hoof, Lamellar.

Laminectomy ◀ *lam in ek tomē, n.* excision of the vertebral lamina. Was formerly a commonly used surgical treatment for cervical stenotic myelopathy in foals and adult horses; today interbody fusion of the vertebrae is considered safer, and is more commonly used.
See Cervical vertebral stenotic myelopathy.

Laminitis ◀ *la mi nī tis, n.* (founder) acute or chronic disease condition of horse's feet; numerous underlying causes result in disturbance of blood flow to sensitive laminae of the feet. Many conditions can result in laminitis, e.g. infection of uterus, overfeeding on grain or rich pasture, obesity, following colic operation, prolonged exercise on hard surface, pituitary pars intermedia dysfunction (equine Cushing's), overload of one limb due to excessive weight bearing, such as might occur due to severe pain in a contralateral limb (e.g. following a fracture), etc. Exact pathogenesis is unknown. Blood flow alterations result in lack of oxygen to tissues (hypoxia), and may result in damage to laminar attachments of the hoof. If damage is severe or prolonged, attachments of third phalanx to hoof wall may be lost, and coffin bone may change position inside hoof. This commonly happens in toe area and third phalanx may tip down inside hoof, causing rotation of the third phalanx relative to the long axis of the limb; if damage is very severe, laminar attachments are broadly destroyed, the whole bone sinks ('sinker'). Front feet more commonly affected than back feet, probably because the horse bears the majority of its weight on the forelimbs.

CLINICAL SIGNS
Signs of laminitis are primarily of forelimb lameness, with severity depending on the degree of initial insult and laminar damage. Signs of acute laminitis may include lameness, varying from mild soreness at turns, to a general reluctance to move and recumbency; soreness to application of hoof testers, especially over sole, heat in affected feet; increased character of the pulses in the digital arteries; abnormal stance with forelegs held out in front and hind legs held under body (trying to take weight off forefeet). In chronic laminitis, secondary changes to the hoof occur, such as various hoof deformities, flattening of the sole, or bulging of the sole with extreme rotation of third phalanx. Rotation of bone may penetrate sole in severe cases.

DIAGNOSIS
Primarily from typical clinical signs. Radiography is important to assess the third phalanx for degree of rotation or sinking, which may be helpful in establishing treatment and/or prognosis. Venograms of the distal limb are advocated by some veterinarians to evaluate circulation to the foot; however, the true utility of the procedure has not been well described.

TREATMENT
Myriad treatments for laminitis reflect the fact that the pathogenesis of the condition is not well established; success of any one treatment may depend more on the degree of initial insult and subsequent tissue impairment than any other factor. Treatment of any primary disease condition is of paramount importance. Numerous hoof trimming and horse-shoeing techniques may be recommended, depending on stage of disease and preference of the treating veterinarian, including (but not necessarily limited to) lowering heel; raising heel; removal of devitalized tissue; applying frog pressure, via pad or heart-bar shoe; glue-on shoe; wooden shoe; reverse shoe; sole casts; barefoot deep sand bedding. Local therapies include application of cold (e.g. ice water baths, which appear to interfere with enzyme activity that disrupts laminar connections, or standing in cold, flowing stream), or warm water baths (to help improve circulation). Pharmacological management varies widely but may include pain relief, especially using non-steroidal anti-inflammatory drugs and also dimethyl sulphoxide; agents to preserve or increase circulation, e.g. acepromazine, pentoxifylline, glyceryl trinitrate patches, isoxsuprine hydrochloride; drugs to counteract effects of enzymatic degradation of laminae, e.g. tetracycline antibiotics.

PREVENTION
Appropriate dietary management is mandatory to prevent some cases of laminitis, especially when horses have uncontrolled access to lush grass pasture; such pasture is low in fibre, and high in readily digestible carbohydrates, and consumption of such a diet is a known cause of laminitis. Unfortunately, many cases cannot be effectively prevented due to primary underlying disease.
See Foot, Hoof, Lamina, Radiography.

Lampas ◀ *lam pēs, n.* soft swelling of the mucosa of the hard palate, just behind upper front teeth. Normal feature of young horses, but treated as disease a century ago. Does not cause problems; no treatment required.
See Palate.

Lancefield antigens ◀€ *larns fēld / antī jēnz, n.* classification of antigens of *Streptococcus* spp. proposed by American bacteriologist Rebecca Lancefield in 1928. *Streptococcus* spp. important in equine medicine are primarily Lancefield group C, and include *S. equi* subsp. *equi* and *S. equi* subsp. *zooepidemicus.*
See Strangles, *Streptococcus.*

Laparoscopy ◀€ *la pē ro sko pē, n.* use of laparoscope (fibreoptic device) to look inside abdominal cavity, to inspect surface of organs, take biopsy specimens, etc. Endoscope inserted through small incision in flank. Some surgical procedures may also be able to be performed via laparoscopy, e.g. cryptorchid castration, ovariectomy.
See Biopsy, Endoscope.

Laparotomy ◀€ *la pē ro tē mē, n.* surgical cutting of abdominal wall, e.g. in surgery for colic.
See Colic.

Large intestine ◀€ *larj / in tes tin, n.* part of intestines (tubular portion of the digestive tract), lying between small intestine and anus. In horse, consists of colon, caecum and rectum; primary site for fibre digestion and water absorption in horse. Digestion in the large intestine occurs mainly by bacterial breakdown; water is absorbed from ingesta through the intestinal wall as it moves through colon, ultimately resulting in formed faecal balls that are pushed into rectum. Many enteric diseases affect the large intestine, including various colics (e.g. caused by obstruction, displacement, strangulation), colitis (inflammation of colon, e.g. resulting in infection with *Clostridium* bacteria), etc.
See Caecum, *Clostridium*, Colic, Colitis, Colon, Rectum.

Larva ◀€ *lar vē, n.* (plural larvae), immature form(s) of insect or worm, not capable of reproduction. Larvae of parasites (e.g. worms, bots, warbles) may be involved in causing disease, e.g. larvae of *Strongylus* worms may damage blood vessels in large intestine (verminous arteritis).
See Bot, *Strongylus* spp., Warbles.

Larval migrans ◀€ *lar vēl / mī grans, n.* disease that results from aberrant migration of larval nematodes, e.g. disease caused by *Echinococcus granulosus equinus.*
See *Echinococcus granulosus equinus.*

Laryngeal ◀€ *la rin jē ūl, adj.* of the larynx.
See Larynx.

L. hemiplegia ◀€ *la rin jē ūl / he mi plē jē ē, n.* (recurrent laryngeal neuropathy) condition where muscles of one side of larynx do not hold the arytenoid cartilage of that side open on inspiration; passage of air is partially obstructed. Usually left side of larynx affected as result of degeneration of nerve fibres of recurrent laryngeal nerve (the left side of which is markedly longer than the right). May also be caused by trauma to nerve, injection of irritant substance near nerve, infection (e.g. strangles), etc. During exercise, affected horse makes roaring or whistling sound while breathing in. May cause poor performance, although some affected horses perform normally. Diagnosis may involve palpation of larynx: it may be possible to feel atrophy (wastage) of muscles on affected side. Endoscopy of the upper airway can allow for visualization of the asymmetrical movement of laryngeal cartilages on inspiration. Withers slap test, evoked by slapping the saddle region just caudal to the withers, may be abnormal; however, test lacks sensitivity and specificity. Treatment is typically by 'tie-back' operation of the affected side of the larynx; placement of suture to mimic pull of abductor muscles of affected side opens airway and facilitates breathing.
See Endoscopy, Laryngoplasty, Larynx, Slap test.

L. paralysis ◀€ *la rin jē ūl / pē ra lis is, n.* paralysis of both arytenoid cartilages. May be seen with organophosphate toxicity, and diseases of the central nervous system, such as equine protozoal myelitis (EPM).

L. reinnervation ◀€ *la rin jē ūl / rē in er vā shēn, n.* surgical procedure for the treatment of laryngeal hemiplegia, whereby a nerve muscle pedicle graft from the first cervical nerve is transposed to the laryngeal cartilage. It is not clear how widely this procedure is performed; a prosthetic laryngoplasty appears to be preferred by most surgeons.

Lateral l. ventricles ◀╎ *lat rēl / la rin jē ūl / ven trik ēls,* n. pair of small pouches behind larynx; can become distended with air in cases of laryngeal paralysis. May be removed in conjunction with laryngoplasty operation for laryngeal hemiplegia to help reduce soft tissue collapse in airway; not recommended for sole treatment of condition, as was done previously.

Laryngitis ◀╎ *la rin jī tis,* n. inflammation of larynx. Signs include cough, discomfort on swallowing, pain and cough on palpation of larynx. Many causes, including infection (e.g. equine influenza) or from upper airway irritation, e.g. from environmental dust.

Laryngoplasty ◀╎ *la rin jō plas tē,* n. operation to treat laryngeal hemiplegia; prosthetic ligature placed between the cricoid and arytenoid cartilages of larynx in order to achieve some amount of permanent abduction of the paralysed cartilage, so that airflow is not obstructed at exercise, but not so much as to allow aspiration of saliva, food, and water while swallowing. See Laryngeal, Larynx.

Laryngotomy ◀╎ *la rin go tē mē,* n. surgical incision into larynx; performed to allow access to larynx for procedures such as partial resection of the soft palate (staphylectomy), or ventriculectomy. See Laryngeal, Larynx, Staphylectomy, Ventriculectomy.

Larynx ◀╎ *la ringks,* n. (voice box) modified upper part of respiratory tract. Short tubular structure consisting of a complex arrangement of several cartilages and muscles, which allow limited motion; lined by mucous membrane. Lies at anterior end of windpipe (trachea), behind base of tongue. Contains vocal cords, vibrations of which allow vocalization as air passes. During breathing, muscles pull laryngeal cartilages outwards so that passage for air is widened. Conditions affecting larynx include arytenoid chondritis, laryngeal paralysis, laryngitis. See Chondritis, Laryngeal, Laryngitis, Respiratory tract.

Laser ◀╎ *lā zē,* n. mechanical device that produces a narrow beam of coherent light radiation, in the infrared, ultraviolet, or visible spectra.

L. photoablation ◀╎ *lā zē / fō tō ēb lā shēn,* n. surgical technique using hot surgical laser to remove or destroy tissue, e.g. for the treatment of fungal granulomas, in hope of killing hyphae at surgical margins.

L. surgery ◀╎ *lā zē / ser jē rē,* n. surgery using an intensely hot, precisely focused beam of light to remove or vaporize tissue and control bleeding by cauterization. May be employed in equine surgery for various procedures, including surgical neurectomy.

L. therapy ◀╎ *lā zē / the rēp ē,* n. laser devices with far lower powers than surgical lasers (*milli*watts, rather than watts) have been used since the late 1960s in an effort to reduce pain and improve healing in various applications in horses, such as to joints, tendons, or wounds. Little scientific support for their use.

Lateral ◀╎ *la tē rūl,* adj. at or towards side or outside, away from midline or median plane. Indicates anatomical position of various structures, including many bones, ligaments, nerves, muscles, and blood vessels.

Latex agglutination test ◀╎ *lā teks / ag lū tin ā shēn / test,* n. laboratory test most commonly used for identification of fungal antigens; antigen is adsorbed onto *latex particles* which then clump in the presence of antibody specific for the adsorbed antigen.

Lathyrism ◀╎ *la thi rizm,* n. poisoning caused by Caley pea (*Lathyrus hirsutis*). See Caley pea.

Lavage ◀╎ *la varzh,* n. washing out, e.g. to remove debris, as from wounds, to remove infectious material, or for obtaining diagnostic samples for laboratory analysis. See Bronchoalveolar lavage, Peritonitis, Uterus

Lavender foal syndrome ◀╎ *lav ind ē / fōl / sin drōm,* n. rare inherited condition of Arabian horses. Foals have a bluish skin at birth and various neurological abnormalities. Fatal.

Lawsonia intracellularis ◀€ *lor sō nē ē / in trē sel ū lar is, n.* bacterium first identified in mid 1990s; bacteria live in intestinal cells, and cause proliferative enteric disease in horses. Source of initial infection is unknown; contact with porcine faeces suspected in some cases. Severity of infection depends on number of organisms ingested. Infection of intestinal cells, most commonly in weanling foals, results in decrease of digestive and absorptive capabilities of intestines. Clinical signs include depression, fever, diarrhoea, weight loss, and colic. Blood work typically shows severe hypoproteinaemia. Diagnosis based on clinical signs and blood work; confirmed by serology and/or polymerase chain reaction testing of faeces. Treatment is with antimicrobials that have good penetration into intestinal cells, such as erythromycin, chloramphenicol, and tetracycline. Affected foals should be isolated to prevent transmission of disease; vaccine available in pigs, but not horses.

Laxative ◀€ *lak sē tiv, n.* an agent that acts to promote evacuation of the bowel or soften faecal material, so as to enable horse to pass faeces. Laxatives are often used in treatment of colic, especially colic related to faecal impaction. Examples of commonly used laxatives in horses include liquid paraffin, and dioctyl sodium sulphosuccinate.
See Colon, Dioctyl sodium sulphosuccinate, Faeces, Liquid paraffin.

Lead ◀€ *led, n.* (Pb) soft, heavy, toxic metal element. May cause poisoning in horses though licking old paint, ingesting water contaminated by leaking old car batteries, greases, etc., or from industrial contamination of pasture. Acute and chronic forms occur, depending on the amount of lead ingested and the time period over which it was ingested. Numerous avenues of toxicity; peripheral nerve toxicity thought to result from demyelination. Signs of lead poisoning are dysfunction of peripheral motor nerves, and include dullness, weakness, paralysis of lips, difficulty in chewing or prehending food, paralysis of larynx or pharynx (horse cannot swallow or vocalize normally), stiffness, and incoordination. Terminal cases may show seizures, be unable to eat or drink, and may be completely uncoordinated. Inability to swallow may cause food to be regurgitated down nose, or to be inhaled, resulting in pneumonia. Diagnosis based on blood or tissue lead concentrations. Calcium disodium EDTA is the treatment of choice; medication chelates lead so that it can become soluble and be excreted by kidneys. Removal from exposure to lead is mandatory.
See Laryngeal, Pneumonia.

Lead ◀€ *lēd, v./n.* to guide, usually by means of some physical connection; an insulated conductor connected to, or leading out from, an electrical device, e.g. an electrocardiograph or electroencephalograph.
See Electrocardiography.

Legume ◀€ *lā gūm, n.* any of a large family (Leguminosae syn. Fabaceae, the legume family) of plants that have nodules on the roots that contain nitrogen-fixing bacteria; for horses, legumes such as alfalfa (lucerne) and clover are commonly used forages.

Leiomyoma ◀€ *līī ō mī ō mē, n.* benign tumour of smooth muscle, may occur in uterus or intestines. Often no clinical signs.

Leiomyosarcoma ◀€ *līī ō mī ō sar kō mē, n.* malignant tumour of smooth muscle origin. Leiomyosarcomas have been reported in horse's intestines, causing signs of colic. Guarded prognosis with surgical removal.

Leishmaniasis ◀€ *līsh mā nī ēs is, n.* nodular skin disease caused by an intracellular protozoan parasite. *Leishmania braziliensis* occurs primarily in South America, but has been reported in the United States; *Leishmania infantum* infection has been described in horses in Europe. Diagnosis by histopathology of skin biopsy specimen. Immune response of host may be responsible for relatively infrequent occurrence; few reports of successful treatment.

Lens ◀﹦ *lenz, n.* transparent convex structure within eye, which lies between and divides the anterior and posterior chambers. Focuses light onto retina at back of eye. Surrounded by capsule. Conditions which affect lens include cataract (cloudiness of lens), or subluxation or luxation (e.g. is dislodged from normal position as result of trauma).
See Cataract, Eye.

***Leptospira* spp.** ◀﹦ *lep tō spī rē / spē shēs, n.* genus of elongated, spirally shaped bacteria. *Leptospira* bacteria survive in environment in warm, moist conditions, and are excreted continuously in the urine. Contact with infected urine or contaminated water can result in infection.
See Abortion, Uveitis.

Leptospirosis ◀﹦ *lep tō spi rō sis, n.* disease caused by infection with various species of *Leptospira* bacteria. Route of infection is most commonly by penetration of mucous membranes, or by contact with moist or abraded skin, or through open wounds. Outcome of exposure depends on dose, virulence, and susceptibility of host. *Leptospirosis* has been associated with uveitis and abortion in horses, and may more rarely cause liver or kidney disease. Diagnosis can be difficult, because organism is hard to culture; many horses are exposed without contracting disease, thus, serology is of limited value. Bacteria may be seen with dark-field microscopy of various body fluids; polymerase chain reaction testing may help establish diagnosis. Penicillin and many other antibiotics are effective treatments for systemic disease. Recurrent uveitis cases can be difficult; vitrectomy and replacement of the vitreous humour has been reported to be effective in some cases. Porcine vaccines have been used for prevention, as well as in treatment of uveitis; however, data do not support their use in horses. Prevention is by limiting exposure of horses to stagnant water, and to other livestock that may be potential carriers of the bacteria.
See *Leptospira* spp.

Lesion ◀﹦ *lē zhen, n.* area of damage to any tissue or organ caused by disease or injury, especially one that is well circumscribed.

Lethal white syndrome ◀﹦ *lē thal / wīt / sīn drōm, n.* (LWS) a genetic condition that occurs in newborn foals of various breeds, including Paint Horses, Miniature Horses, Arabian part-breds, Thoroughbreds, and foals born to registered Quarter Horse parents that have too much white to qualify for registration with the American Quarter Horse Association; genetic carriers are most commonly overo white patterned horses. LWS foals have blue eyes and are completely or almost completely white at birth. These foals initially appear normal except for their unusual colouring; however, signs of colic soon occur. LWS foals have underdeveloped intestines caused by a failure of the embryonic cells that form nerves in the gastrointestinal system; these cells also play a role in determining skin colour. There is no treatment for LWS, and surgery to bypass the intestinal damage has never been successful because of the extensive intestinal involvement. Breeders can eliminate the possibility of the birth of an LWS foal by genetic testing of breeding stock.

Leucinosis toxicity ◀﹦ *lū sin ō sis / toks is it ē, n.* toxicity resulting from ingestion of plants of genus *Leucaena,* distributed in southern United States, Hawaii, and northern South America. Ingestion of plant results in gradual loss of tail, mane and fetlock hairs owing to toxic amino acid; laminitis and abnormal hoof growth have been reported. Treatment by removal from plant source; ferrous sulphate, 1%, added to feed has been reported to help limit hoof damage.

Leukaemia ◀﹦ *lū kē mē ē, n.* cancer of the blood or bone marrow; characterized by an abnormal proliferation of blood cells, especially white blood cells (leukocytes).

Rare in horses; no effective treatment.
See Bone, Leukocyte.

Leukocyte ◀᛬ _lū_ kō sīt, n. white blood cell, colourless cell of blood, cells of the immune system which defend the body against both infectious disease and foreign materials. Two types, based on presence of granules in cell cytoplasm:
- Granulocytes, contain granules in cytoplasm: neutrophils, eosinophils, basophils.
- Agranulocytes, no granules in cytoplasm: lymphocytes, monocytes, macrophages.

See Basophil, Eosinophil, Lymphocyte, Macrophages, Monocyte, Neutrophil.

Leukocytosis ◀᛬ _lū_ kō sī tō sis, n. increase in number of white blood cells, e.g. as seen in bacterial infection.

Leukoderma ◀᛬ _lū_ kō _der_ mē, n. acquired loss of pigment from skin, e.g. following burn or other injury.

Leukoencephalomalacia ◀᛬ _lū_ kō en _ke_ fē lō mē _lā_ shē ē, n. (mouldy corn poisoning) degeneration of white matter of cerebral hemispheres of brain; may occur in horses, ponies, donkeys and mules as result of eating mouldy feed. Fungi of genus _Fusarium_ produce toxin. Signs include blindness, circling, incoordination, muscle tremors, sleepiness. Progresses to coma and death. No specific treatment is available.

Leukopenia ◀᛬ _lū_ kō _pē_ nē ē, n. abnormally low level of white blood cells, e.g. seen in conditions of overwhelming need for leukocytes, such as acute infections of various causes, in endotoxaemia, and in bone marrow suppression.
See Bone, Endotoxaemia, Leukocyte.

Leukotrichia ◀᛬ _lū_ kō _tri_ kē ē, n. acquired loss of pigment from hair following injury or inflammation of skin.

Leukotriene ◀᛬ _lū_ kō trī ēn, n. naturally occurring lipid mediators of inflammation; may be responsible for many of the effects of allergies and recurrent airway

obstruction. Produced as part of a complex response to allergens that includes the production of histamine.
See Histamine, Recurrent airway obstruction.

Levamisole ◀᛬ _lev_ _am_ is ol, n. synthetic antibiotic originally used as an anthelmintic to treat worm infestations in both humans and animals, but has limited efficacy and narrow dose range before toxicity occurs. Has been used as an immune stimulant in horses; however, no published studies have shown levamisole's value in this regard. If horses experience signs of toxicity (muscle tremors, hyperexcitability, sweating and lacrimation) signs will resolve if lower than lethal dose has been administered.

Leydig cell ◀᛬ _lā_ dig sel, n. steroid hormone-secreting cell (including testosterone) of the equine testis, found next to the seminiferous tubules. Production of steroid hormones under control of hypothalamus.
See Hypothalamus.

Libido ◀᛬ li _bē_ dō, n. sexual drive. In stallions, libido may be affected by hormonal factors, management factors, pain or discomfort associated with mating (e.g. arthritis), or previous bad experiences mating (e.g. being kicked by mare).

Lice see Louse

Lidocaine ◀᛬ _lī_ dō kān, n. (lignocaine) local anaesthetic drug, commonly used to temporarily block sensation in skin (e.g. before stitching wound); acts by blocking sodium (Na⁺) channels in the cell membrane. Numerous uses, both injected and topical, including spraying into larynx to allow passage of endoscope, nerve blocks, topical anaesthesia of the eye, in enema, to facilitate rectal examination, etc. Some preparations have epinephrine added, which acts to constrict blood vessels around the injection site and control haemorrhage. Also used in intravenous infusions as treatment for some heart dysrhythmias, e.g. ventricular tachycardia, ventricular fibrillation, and as a

prokinetic agent to stimulate intestinal motility, e.g. for the treatment of ileus after colic surgery.
See Anaesthetic, Heart, Ileus, Ventricular.

Ligament ◀≀ _li gē mĕnt_, _n._ term used in anatomy to describe one of three types of structure:
1. Fibrous tissue that connects a bone to a bone; also known as articular ligaments, or true ligaments (most common use).
2. A fold of membranous tissue, such as peritoneum, e.g. the broad ligament of the uterus, the suspensory ligament of the ovary, or the hepatoduodenal ligament surrounding the portal vein and other blood vessels travelling from the duodenum to the liver.
3. A remnant of a foetal structure, e.g. the ligamentum arteriosum, which is the remnant of the foetal ductus arteriosus.

Joint ligaments are short, tough, slightly elastic fibrous bands composed mostly of collagen. They tend to limit the mobility of joints and/or provide joint stability, e.g. the cruciate ligaments of the femorotibial (stifle) joint, which together prevent the joint from moving in an anterior-to-posterior direction, collateral ligaments, which prevent side-to-side movements, or capsular ligaments of the joint capsule that act as mechanical reinforcement for the joint. Damage to a ligament is called a sprain; inflammation of a ligament is called desmitis.
See Desmitis, Sprain.

Ligate ◀≀ _lī gāt_, _v._ to tie off, usually as pertains to a suture placed around a blood vessel to prevent bleeding.

Ligature ◀≀ _li gē tŭr_, _n._ suture or other material used in surgery to tie off a blood vessel or other tissue, or to assist in holding a piece of tissue in place.

Light see Photoperiod

Lignocaine see Lidocaine

Limb ◀≀ _lim_, _n._ any one of the four appendages of the horse's body, concerned primarily with movement; horse has two forelimbs and two hind limbs. Also, a branch or arm of another structure, e.g. the descending limb of the loop of Henle, in the kidney.

Limbus ◀≀ _lim bĕs_, _n._ edge or margin, distinguished by colour or structure. Used especially for edge of cornea in eye, where it joins the white sclera.
See Eye.

Lime sulphur ◀≀ _līm_ / _sul fer_, _n._ a mixture of calcium polysulphides formed by reacting calcium hydroxide with sulphur and a small amount of surfactant. Sometimes used in the treatment of dermatophyte infections. Thought to be the earliest synthetic chemical used as a pesticide, in 1840s in France, to control grape mildew.
See Dermatophyte.

Linea alba ◀≀ _li nē ē_ / _al bē_, _n._ fibrous structure at the midline of the abdominal wall, composed of white collagen, formed at the junction of the abdominal muscles. Typical site of surgical incision into abdomen.
See Abdomen.

Linear keratosis see Keratosis

Lingual ◀≀ _ling gwūl_, _adj._ relating to, or lying next to, the tongue.
See Tongue.

Liniment ◀≀ _li ni mĕnt_, _n._ oily liquid preparation for topical use on the skin, generally containing various combinations of alcohol, camphor, green soap, iodine, menthol, and many other substances. As a general rule, liniments produce local skin irritation. When the skin is chemically irritated, surface blood vessels dilate. In humans, this brings a feeling of warmth to the area and helps to relieve muscle and joint stiffness and soreness. Commonly rubbed on horse skin to treat perceived muscle stiffness or strains. Claims that liniments 'increase circulation' to areas are not supported by any research. As a practical matter, increased circulation has not been demonstrated as a result of any therapy. Nor has any study been done to show that if circulation could be increased, it would somehow improve or speed up healing.

Linseed ◀≷ _lin_ sēd, _n._ (_Linum_, flax) seed of a variety of common flax, _Linum usitatis-cimum_, widely grown for fibre (flax), linseed oil, or meal. Often fed to horses out of belief that it promotes coat health, or acts as a faecal softener. Seeds and plants contain cyanogenic glycosides and enzymes which allow the plants to release cyanide when damaged. However, the enzymes are destroyed by stomach acids, as well as by heat processing. Cyanide is also volatile, so it does not persist in feed. Accordingly, toxicity from linseed is unreported in the horse, and it can be safely used as horse feed, e.g. as linseed cake.

Lip ◀≷ _lip_, _n._ **1)** either of two fleshy folds defining the edge of the mouth, important in prehension of small pieces of food. Upper and lower lips join at commissures. Lips may droop following damage to facial nerve (cranial nerve VII) or in generalized conditions affecting nerves, e.g. botulism; **2)** an edge of a wound; **3)** an anatomical part or structure resembling a lip, e.g. a labium.
See Botulism, Facial nerve, Labium.

Lipid ◀≷ _li_ pid, _n._ term that broadly describes any fat-soluble, naturally occurring, molecule; more specifically, the term refers to fatty acids and derivatives, such as mono-, di-, and triglycerides, as well as other fat-soluble compounds, such as cholesterol. Many functions, including as nutrients, energy storage, structural components of cell membranes, and as signalling molecules. Types of lipid include:
- Fats and oils (oils are liquid fat).
- Phospholipids, an important component of cell membranes.
- Steroids, lipids with a carbon skeleton.
- Waxes, fatty acids and alcohol.

Lipidosis (hepatic lipidosis) ◀≷ _lip_ id _o_ sis (_hip at_ ik / _lip_ id _o_ sis), _n._ infiltration of liver with fat.
See Hyperlipaemia.

Lipoma ◀≷ _lī pō_ mē, _n._ benign tumour made up of fat cells. In horse, may occur in abdomen of middle-aged and older horses and ponies; castrated male Saddlebred and Arabian horses older than 14 years have been identified as being at risk, especially if they are overweight. Pedunculated lipomas (lipoma on a stalk) can get wrapped around intestine and cause strangulation/obstruction. Signs of strangulating lipomas are of severe colic pain, and surgical correction must be performed promptly for successful outcome; prognosis guarded, according to literature.
See Colic.

Lipopolysaccharide ◀≷ _lī_ pō pol _ē_ sak _ēr_ īd, _n._ (LPS) large molecule made up of a lipid and a polysaccharide (carbohydrate) joined by a covalent bond. LPS is a major portion of the structural and protective cell membrane of Gram-negative bacteria. It is also an endotoxin, and induces strong inflammatory responses from the horse when absorbed systemically, e.g. in diseases such as enterocolitis.
See Enterotoxaemia, Gram stain.

Liquid paraffin ◀≷ _li_ kwid / _pa_ rē fin, _n._ (mineral oil) transparent, colourless oily liquid, has no taste or smell. Used in equine medicine as laxative in an effort to ease passage of faeces in colic caused by impaction of intestine contents, and as an additive in some pharmaceutical products.
See Colic, Laxative.

Listeria monocytogenes ◀≷ lis _tér_ rē _ē_ / _mo_ nō sī _tō_ jēnz, _n._ Gram-positive, facultative anaerobic bacterium; ubiquitous in environment. Organism grows well in a variety of conditions; growth in poorly stored silage results in 'silage disease' in ruminants, and perhaps horses. Faecal contamination thought to be the most common source of organism. Route of infection is ingestion, though other routes are possible. Rarely reported cause of disease in horses; has caused septicaemia in foals, abortion in mares, and bacterial ulcerative keratitis. Diagnosis by bacterial culture; organism is usually susceptible to most commonly prescribed antibiotics and affected horses have responded to treatment. Zoonotic potential. See Abortion.

Lithiasis ◀€ *li thī ē sis, n.* formation of stony concretions ('stones'; calculi) within body, e.g. urolithiasis is formation of stones in urine (in ureter or bladder), cholelithiasis is formation of gall stones in bile duct, enterolithiasis is the formation of intestinal stones, etc.
See Biliary, Calculus, Urolithiasis.

Liver ◀€ *li vē, n.* solid, lobed, dark red organ in anterior abdomen, lying against diaphragm. Structure is made up of hexagonal lobules which are composed of sheets of liver cells (hepatocytes) radiating out from a central vein. Branches of major blood vessels (hepatic artery and vein) lie between lobules, as do tiny tubes (canaliculi) which collect bile. These tubes come together to form bile duct. Liver plays a major role in metabolism, storage, digestion, detoxification and elimination of various substances from the body.
See Bile, Digestion, Metabolism.

L. **disease** ◀€ *li vē / di zēz, n.* broad term describing any number of pathological conditions affecting liver; includes various plant poisonings, parasites (e.g. liver fluke), biliary calculi, portosystemic shunt, cirrhosis. Liver has a large reserve capacity (i.e. can still perform all functions when a significant portion of the organ is diseased); extensive regenerative capacity allows for repair after acute injury or disease in some cases. Signs of liver disease related to failure to perform its varied functions include weight loss, dullness, icterus (jaundice), diarrhoea, hepatic encephalopathy, photosensitization, bleeding disorders, etc. Diagnosis may require blood tests (e.g. enzyme assays indicating liver cell damage, bilirubin and bile acid levels, albumin levels, etc.), liver biopsy, ultrasonography.
See Albumin, Bile, Biopsy, Cirrhosis, Diarrhoea, Fluke, Hepatic, Icterus, Photosensitization, Portosystemic shunt, Ragwort, Ultrasonography.

L. **enzymes** ◀€ *li vē / en zīmz, n.* under normal circumstances, liver enzymes are found within the cells of the liver, and assist in normal metabolic functions, e.g. aminotransferase enzymes catalyse chemical reactions in the cells in which an amino group is transferred from a donor molecule to a recipient molecule. When the liver is injured, these enzymes are spilled into the blood stream. Among the most sensitive and widely used of these liver enzymes are aspartate aminotransferase (AST or SGOT), alanine aminotransferase (ALT or SGPT), and gamma glutamyl transferase (GGT).
See Albumin, Fibrinogen, Glycogen, Photosensitization, Prothrombin.

Loading dose ◀€ *lō ding / dōs, n.* initial dose of some drugs; loading doses are usually higher than doses required for maintenance of drug levels. Loading doses are given to rapidly establish a therapeutic drug level before dropping to a lower dose that can maintain those initial levels.

Lobe ◀€ *lōb, n.* portion or division of an organ, often roundish in shape and divided from other portions of the organ by a cleft. In horse, the brain and liver are lobed organs.

Local ◀€ *lō kūl, adj.* relating to a small or restricted part of the body.
L. **anaesthesia** see Anaesthesia
L. **anaesthetic** see Anaesthetic

Lochia ◀€ *lō kē ē, n.* brownish discharge from uterus after foaling. May be normally present for a few days after delivery. Made up of blood and uterine fluids; expelled by process of uterine involution.
See Involution, Parturition, Uterus.

Lockjaw see Tetanus

Locomotion ◀€ *lō kō mō shēn, n.* the act or the power of moving from one place to another; progressive movement [of the body].

Locoweed ◀€ *lō kō wēd, n.* (*Astragalus, Oxytropis*) common name used to describe two different genera of legume plants found in midwestern and western USA; can cause poisoning when consumed over a period of weeks, and toxic level is reached. Contains addicting alkaloid, swainsonine, which affects central nervous system, causing incoordination, high-stepping gait, head-bobbing, excitement, and violent reaction to stimuli. Chronic cases lose weight through inability to eat. Horses may recover if condition is recognized early and if they are removed from plant source, but chronically affected horses will be permanently impaired. No specific treatment.

Long ◀⊱ *long, n.* having greater length than usual; especially as applied to describe various ligaments, tendons and muscles; of greater duration than standard.

> **L.-acting** ◀⊱ *long - ak ting, adj.* term used to describe medication which has prolonged duration of action after administration.
>
> **L. bone** ◀⊱ *long / bōn, n.* any of the elongated bones of the equine limb, e.g. the humerus or metatarsus; long bones have an essentially cylindrical, hollow shaft that contains bone marrow; ends of long bones articulate with other bones.

Lordosis ◀⊱ *lor dō sis, n.* inward curvature of part of the vertebral column; sway-back. Commonly seen in older horses.

Lotion ◀⊱ *lō shēn, n.* a liquid medicinal preparation, usually of an aqueous base, that contains one or more insoluble substances and which is usually applied to the skin, e.g. calamine (mixture of zinc oxide or zinc carbonate with a small amount of ferric oxide) lotion for treatment of skin inflammation associated with *Culicoides* hypersensitivity (sweet itch). See *Culicoides* spp.

Louping ill ◀⊱ *lō ping / il, n.* disease caused by flavivirus infection spread by ticks. Found throughout upland areas of Scotland, Northern Ireland, and Wales; seasonal occurrence. Commonly affects sheep; rare in horses. Most cases are apparently subclinical in horses, but can result in inflammation of central nervous system, with typical disease signs.

Louse ◀⊱ *lŏs, n.* host-specific parasitic insect that spends entire 20–40 day life cycle on host, although non-host-specific lice can occasionally feed on ectopic host (e.g. poultry lice on horses). Lives on skin and in hair coat, flat body with no wings. Transmission by direct contact, and via fomites, such as brushes or tack. Two main species affect horses:

- *Damalinia equi* ('biting louse'), prefers to live on the dorsolateral trunk, where it feeds on shedding epithelial cells and skin debris.
- *Haematopinus asini* ('sucking louse'), prefers the mane, tail, and fetlocks, where it feeds on blood and tissue fluids.

Clinical signs of disease are most common in winter, with varying degrees of itching, scaling, and hair loss. Common external parasite in UK; less common in USA. Heavy infestation with *Haematopinus asini* may result in anaemia through loss of blood if untreated. Treatment is usually easy, and effective, using insecticidal shampoos or pour-on products.
See Anaemia.

Low ◀⊱ *lō, adj.* marking a distal or bottom portion.

> **L. palmar nerve block** ◀⊱ *lō / par mē / nerv / blok, n.* (low four-point block) local anaesthetic block used in diagnosis of lameness; performed by placing anaesthetic over the palmar nerves and palmar metacarpal nerves, at the level of the distal end of the splint bones. Removes sensation to limb distal to block, although fetlock joint retains sensation.
>
> **L. ringbone** ◀⊱ *lō / ring bōn, n.* osteoarthritis of the distal interphalangeal (coffin) joint.

Lower ◀⊱ *lō wē, adj.* relatively move ventral in position; towards the end of a series of anatomical structures.

> **L. limb** ◀⊱ *lō wē / lim, n.* distal part of fore- or hind limb, i.e. cannon (metacarpus, metatarsus), fetlock, pastern and foot.
> See Cannon, Fetlock, Foot, Pastern.
>
> **L. motor neuron** ◀⊱ *lō wē / mō tē / nŭr ōn, n.* the motor neurons that connect the brainstem and spinal cord to muscle fibres. Motor neurons bring nerve impulses from the upper motor neurons to the muscles. The axon of a lower motor neuron travels through a vertebral foramen and ends on an effector muscle that performs the motor

function (e.g. moving a limb). Lower motor neuron disease is characterized by muscle problems or ataxia, and frequently accompanied by muscle atrophy.

L. respiratory tract ◀≋ *lō wē / re spē rē trē / trakt, n.* larynx, trachea, and lungs (and associated structures).
See Alveolus, Bronchiole, Lung.

Lucillia cuprina ◀≋ *lū sil iē / kū prē nē, n.* Australian blowfly.
See Blowfly.

Lumbar ◀≋ *lum bē, adj.* of the loins or lower back, i.e. the part of the back behind the horse's saddle area, between the thoracic vertebrae and sacrum.

Lumbosacral ◀≋ *lum bō sāk rūl, adj.* pertaining to the area where the lumbar and sacral regions of the horse's back meet. Occasional area of disease and injury to the horse's back, including fractures (especially in foals), osteoarthritis, and soft tissue injury.
> **L. tap** ◀≋ *lum bō sak rūl / tap, n.* collection of cerebrospinal fluid in standing horse, via insertion of long spinal needle into subarachnoid space between vertebrae, into a spot on the midline, perpendicular to a line drawn from the posterior aspect of the tuber coxae.

Lumen ◀≋ *lū mēn, n.* cavity within a hollow tubular organ or structure, e.g. lumen of blood vessel is the part where the blood flows; intestinal lumen allows for passage of ingesta.

Lung ◀≋ *lung, n.* organ of respiration. Horse has two lungs, one in each side of chest. Unlike other mammals, horse's lungs are not clearly divided into lobes; they are covered by a thin, membranous layer of pleura. When horse breathes in (inspiration), air travels to lung in tubes called bronchi which branch off windpipe (trachea). Bronchi split into smaller bronchioles, which end in an alveolus, a tiny air sac that is surrounded by a network of delicate capillaries, where the actual gaseous exchange of respiration takes place. Oxygen from air is absorbed into blood in alveoli and carbon dioxide passes from blood into alveoli. When horse

breathes out, air (containing less oxygen and more carbon dioxide than the air breathed in) is pushed out of the respiratory tract (expiration).

Many disease conditions affect the lungs of horses including recurrent airway obstruction, lungworms, pneumonia, bronchopneumonia, pleurisy, tumours, fluid in lungs (pulmonary oedema). Signs of lung disease depend on cause, but include difficulty breathing, rapid breathing, cough, blue tinge to gums (cyanosis), nasal discharge, high temperature, etc. Diagnosis of lung disease involves clinical examination, auscultation, percussion, blood analysis, endoscopy, bronchoalveolar lavage, transtracheal aspiration biopsy, radiography, ultrasonography; lung biopsy may be occasionally indicated, but at risk of significant haemorrhage.
See Alveolus, Auscultation, Biopsy, Bronchiole, Bronchoalveolar lavage, Bronchopneumonia, Bronchus, Cyanosis, Endoscopy, Lungworm, Percussion, Pleura, Pleuritis/Pleuropneumonia, Pneumonia, Pulmonary, Radiography, Recurrent airway obstruction, Trachea, Ultrasonography.

Lunge ◀≋ *lunj, v.* to exercise horse on long rein; horse moves in large circle around trainer. May be used in assessment of horse; e.g. lungeing in tight circle may be used to demonstrate mild lameness.

Lungworm see *Dictyocaulus arnfieldi*

Lupine ◀≋ *lū pin, n.* (Bluebonnet) herbaceous perennial plant with wide distribution in United States; a leading cause of livestock poisoning in the western USA and Canada. Toxicity in lupine is believed to result primarily from the alkaloid D-lupanine. Signs of lupine poisoning are related to the amount and time period ingested. Clinical signs are related to the nervous system, including twitching, nervousness, depression, difficulty in moving and breathing, and loss of muscular control. If large quantities were consumed, convulsions, coma, and death by respiratory paralysis may occur. No specific antidote or treatment.

Lupus erythematosus ◀┊ *lū̲ pēs / e rith̲ ēm at ō̲ sēs, n.* rare, multisystemic immune system disease. In horses, clinical signs are typically of severe lymphatic oedema of the lower limbs. Treatment with high doses of corticosteroids; prognosis grave. The discoid form is an autoimmune skin disease; has been reported in a single horse with scaling, crusting, and hair loss. Controlled with corticosteroids, topically and systemically; avoid sun exposure.

Luteal ◀┊ *lū̲ tē ēl, adj.* relating to, or involving, the corpus luteum or its formation.
See Corpus.

> **L. cyst** ◀┊ *lū tē ēl / sist, n.* condition commonly seen in cattle, and commonly misdiagnosed in horses. May be mistaken for large, persistent, or multiple ovarian follicles, or ovarian haematoma.
> See Corpus, Cyst, Follicle.

Luteinizing hormone ◀┊ *lū̲ ti nī zing / hor̲ mōn, n.* (LH) glycoprotein hormone secreted by pituitary gland. In mare, acts with follicle-stimulating hormone (FSH) to stimulate release of egg from ovary (ovulation); after ovulation, stimulates formation of corpus luteum in ovary and the secretion of progesterone. In stallion, LH stimulates interstitial Leydig cells of testis to produce testosterone.
See Corpus, Follicle, Hormone, Ovary, Ovulation, Pituitary, Testes, Testosterone.

Luxation ◀┊ *luk sā shēn, n.* complete dislocation of a part.

- Joint l. – complete dislocation of a joint, usually because of severe trauma, and often accompanied by damage to supporting ligaments or tendons. Prognosis for normal movement depends on the degree of damage and location of injury, e.g. fetlock luxation may carry a more favourable prognosis than hip luxation.
- Lens l. – total displacement of lens of eye may very rarely occur in horses, e.g. following chronic uveitis, glaucoma, or cataract formation, or possibly from trauma to head with fibres which hold lens in place being

torn; prognosis for vision retention is usually poor.
See Eye, Joint, Ligament, Tendon.

Lyme disease ◀┊ *līm / di zēz, n.* controversial condition caused by infection with one of at least three strains of spirochaete organism, *Borrelia burgdorferi*. Infection spread between ticks (commonly, *Ixodes* spp.) and mammals, especially deer and mice. Horses in eastern half of the United States appear to be commonly exposed. Horses are infected by feeding tick. Many different clinical signs of Lyme disease have been described, but cause and effect are often difficult to prove. Commonly reported signs include low-grade fever, stiffness, swollen joints, muscle soreness, lethargy and changes in behaviour, e.g. irritability; controversy exists over importance of the organism because disease cannot be reliably reproduced by experimental infection, and because many seropositive animals do not demonstrate clinical signs. Most common treatment is intravenous tetracycline, or oral doxycycline antibiotic; metronidazole may be indicated to treat encysted forms. Prevention is by reducing exposure to ticks; no vaccine currently available for horses. Adult ticks feeding on horses are unlikely to infect humans.

Lymph ◀┊ *limf, n.* transparent clear fluid that moves from intercellular spaces of body tissues into lymphatic vessels that ultimately discharge into blood. Similar in composition to blood plasma, i.e. contains water, electrolytes, plasma proteins and some leukocytes (mostly lymphocytes), but few blood cells and no platelets.
See Lymphatic, Lymphocyte, Plasma.

> **L. node** ◀┊ *limf / nōd, n.* (lymph gland) collection of specialized tissue present at intervals along lymphatic vessels, surrounded by connective tissue; filters lymph. Important as part of defence of body against disease: removes foreign material as part of reticuloendothelial system, produces lymphocytes and is involved in formation of antibodies. Lymph nodes are distributed around body; those that can most easily be felt in the horse are just inside lower jaw (submandibular) and in front of shoulder

(prescapular). May also be able to feel parotid (near ear), pharyngeal (at throat) and femoral (inside thigh). Lymph nodes may be enlarged because of infection or tumour.
See Antibody, Lymph, Lymphocyte, Reticuloendothelial system.

Lymphadenitis ◀ *lim fa de nī tis, n.* inflammation of lymph node. Clinically, lymphadenitis results in painful enlargement of node; common sign of many infectious diseases, especially *Streptococcus equi* ('strangles') infection.
See Lymph, Strangles.

Lymphangioma ◀ *lim fan jē ō mē, n.* rare, benign neoplasm of the skin arising from lymphatic vessels. Most are noted within the first six months of life; nodular, poorly circumscribed lesions can be up to 30 cm in diameter, accompanied by oedema and enlarged lymphatic vessels, especially in inguinal and axillary regions. Wide surgical excision may be curative, but extensive involvement of subdermal tissues may preclude successful removal.

Lymphangitis ◀ *lim fan jī tis, n.* (sporadic lymphangitis, ulcerative lymphangitis, Monday morning disease) inflammation of lymphatic vessels. In horses, term is commonly used to describe any acute limb infection with swelling, lameness and fever; cause is often unknown, but may result from local trauma or wound infection. Lymphatic vessels become inflamed and flow of lymph is restricted, fluid builds up in leg and it swells up. Horse is lame, shows high temperature, fluid may ooze through skin if severe. Treatment involves aggressive antibiotic and anti-inflammatory therapy. Constant nursing care to encourage fluid movement in limb, such as exercise, bandaging, massage, or hydrotherapy may be beneficial. If condition does not resolve quickly, significant subcutaneous fibrosis may occur, which impedes normal lymphatic flow, causes limb disfigurement, and predisposes to re-infection. Specific causes of lymphangitis include glanders and epizootic lymphangitis.
See Epizootic lymphangitis, Glanders, Lymphatic.

Lymphatic ◀ *lim fa tik, n./adj.* thin-walled vessel which carries lymph from tissues back to blood. All vessels drain into lymphatic ducts, which drain into subclavian veins on either side of chest.

L. duct ◀ *lim fa tik / duct, n.* any of the lymphatic vessels that collect lymph from the lymphatic capillaries and discharge it into the circulatory system.

L. system ◀ *lim fa tik / sis tēm, n.* the part of the circulatory system that scavenges fluids and proteins that have escaped from cells and tissues and returns them to the blood, removes cellular debris and foreign material, and provides immune responses. L. system overlaps and parallels the blood circulatory system and shares some constituents with it. L. system is made up of the thymus (in immature animals), the spleen, lymph, lymph nodes, lymphatic vessels, lymphocytes, and bone marrow (bone marrow is where stem cells differentiate into the precursors of B and T cells).

Lymphocyte ◀ *lim fō sīt, n.* white, nucleated blood cell of the equine immune system. Two subdivisions: B lymphocyte (B cell) and T lymphocyte (T cell), responsible for humoral and cellular immunity, respectively.
See B lymphocyte, Immunity, T cell.

Lymphocytic–plasmocytic enterocolitis ◀ *lim fō sit ik – plas mō sī tik / en ter ō kol ī tis, n.* rare, infiltrative disease of the equine colon. Cannot be definitively differentiated from other causes of inflammatory disease of the colon ante-mortem. Causes malabsorption of nutrients; clinical signs of wasting and diarrhoea. Prognosis is poor; treatment has been unsuccessful, possibly because the condition is rarely recognized early.

Lymphocytosis ◀ *lim fō sī tō sis, n.* higher than normal lymphocyte count in blood sample. Many causes, including excitement, epinephrine administration, leukaemia, long-term stimulation of immune system.
See Epinephrine, Immunity, Leukaemia.

Lymphoid ◀ *lim foid, adj. n.* referring to lymphocytes; also refers to tissue in which lymphocytes develop (lymphoid tissue). See Lymphocyte, Lymphoma, Lymphosarcoma.

L. hyperplasia see Pharyngitis

Lymphokine ◀ ≥ *lim fo kīn, n.* hormone-like molecule that is secreted from cells; functions to communicate with lymphocytes, affecting their growth, differentiation, and activation. See Cytokine.

Lymphoma ◀ ≥ *lim fō mē, n.* cancerous disease of any lymphoid tissue; uncommon; however, the most common malignant neoplasm of horses. Clinical signs of lymphoma are variable, depending on the location of the tumour, but commonly include weight loss, subcutaneous oedema, lymphadenopathy, fever, anorexia, and depression. Five typical presentations in horses, alone or in combination:

- Generalized or multicentric – most common form of lymphoma; approximately 50% of lymphoma cases. Affected horses have generalized lymph node involvement, and cancer infiltrates internal organs, e.g. liver, spleen, kidneys or lungs.
- Gastrointestinal – affecting primarily the small intestine and regional lymph nodes; affected horses show clinical signs such as diarrhoea, colic, and weight loss.
- Mediastinal – lymphoma of the thoracic lymph nodes; causes fluid build-up within the thorax, dyspnoea, and tachypnoea.
- Extranodal – lymphoma not involving the lymph nodes; tumour development can occur in skin, upper respiratory tract, eyes or adnexal structures of the eyes, and the central nervous system.
- Cutaneous lymphoma (lymphoma of the skin) – occasionally seen, primarily in older horses. Affected horses develop progressive, well-circumscribed, non-painful masses in the skin or subcutaneous tissue; masses tend to enlarge with time, and may wax and wane. Overlying skin is often normal, but may also lack hair or ulcerate; seen especially in the shoulder area, around the anus, or on the chest. Biopsy of mass is diagnostic. Additional diagnostic work, such as rectal palpation, blood work, aspirates of enlarged lymph nodes, or evaluation of thoracic and/or abdominal fluid may be warranted to rule out internal malignancy. If there is no internal organ involvement, cutaneous lymphoma can remain stable for several years, even if untreated.

Several forms of treatment have been used for equine lymphoma, including systemic chemotherapeutic agents. Selected cases have been treated with chemotherapeutic agents, and remission has been reported in one horse. Corticosteroids may help reduce the size of the tumours and help maintain quality of life.

Lymphopenia ◀ ≥ *lim fō pē nē ē, n.* lower than normal circulating lymphocyte count, as measured in blood sample. May be related to stress, viral infection, failure of immunity (e.g. combined immundeficiency of Arabian foals). See Lymphocyte.

Lymphosarcoma ◀ ≥ *lim fō sar kō mē, n.* See Lymphoma. In the past, the terms lymphoma and lymphosarcoma have been used somewhat interchangeably, but the preferred term is lymphoma; no benign form of the disease exists.

Lysis ◀ ≥ *lī sis, n.* destruction at a cellular level, disintegration of cell.

Lyssavirus ◀ ≥ *li sē vī rēs, n.* genus of virus that includes virus causing rabies. See Rabies.

M

M-mode echocardiograph ◀⁓ _m_-mōd / _ek_ ō _kar_ dē og _raf,_ n. use of ultrasound to image the beating heart (echocardiography); M-mode echocardiography provides a one-dimensional moving image of the heart. The waves seen on the ultrasound scan show structures in the heart, such as the valves, chambers and walls; images used can help assess cardiac function and disease, e.g. valvular insufficiency.

Macromineral ◀⁓ _mak_ rō _min_ er ēl, n. dietary minerals that are required in relatively large amounts (as distinct from trace minerals). Such minerals include calcium, sodium, chlorine, potassium, phosphorus, sulphur, and magnesium.
See individual entries.

Macrophages ◀⁓ _ma_ krō fāj iz, n. cells present in tissues, originating from white blood cells called monocytes, which form part of body's defence system against foreign pathogens; they engulf, and then digest, foreign material (phagocytosis). Macrophages also interact with lymphocytes to stimulate production of lymphocytes and other immune cells.
See Antibody, Lymphocyte, Monocyte, Phagocytosis.

Maggot ◀⁓ _mag_ ēt, n. larval stage of a fly life cycle, known especially for eating decomposing flesh. Maggots have been used therapeutically for debriding wound tissue since at least the mid nineteenth century. In controlled settings, maggot therapy has been used to treat non-healing wounds in humans; in horses, has been described for the successful treatment of hoof conditions such as canker, and in the treatment of serious, non-healing wounds.

Magnesium ◀⁓ _mag_ _nē_ zē ēm, n. (Mg) metallic chemical element, essential in the diet. Magnesium ions are essential to nucleic acid chemistry of life; in addition, many enzymes require magnesium ions for their action. Hypomagnesaemia has been occasionally reported in lactating mares (lactation tetany), and in horses in stressful situations (e.g. transport). Lack of magnesium can result in signs of nervous system dysfunction, including muscle twitching, over-excitability, incoordination, seizures; most frequently misdiagnosed as colic.

> **M. hydroxide** ◀⁓ _mag_ _nē_ zē ēm / hī droks īd, n. antacid; has been used for the treatment of gastic ulcer syndrome in horses. Effect is short-lived; may affect the availability of concurrently administered medications.
> **M. oxide** ◀⁓ _mag_ _nē_ zē ēm / oks īd, n. supplemental source of magnesium in horses requiring additional dietary magnesium; has also been given to excitable horses in an effort to calm or sedate them.
> **M. sulphate** ◀⁓ _mag_ _nē_ zē ēm / sul fāt, n. Epsom salts; readily available salt with many uses in horse, including therapeutic water baths (soaking), especially of the hoof, as applied in a paste for disinfection of hoof wounds or cracks, or as administered via nasogastric tube for the treatment of impaction type colics ($MgSO_4$ is administered, sometimes concurrently with intravenous fluids, in an effort to bring water into the intestinal lumen). Oral administration of magnesium sulphate must be monitored so as to avoid magnesium toxicity.

See Hypomagnesaemia, Lactation.

Magnet ◀⁓ _mag_ nit, n. material that produces a magnetic field (a ubiquitous force that, among other properties, affects electrical charges). Attempts to use magnets as therapy are centuries old; various arrays of magnets have been applied to horses in a variety of ways, and for a variety of conditions, with no demonstrable effects.

Magnetic resonance imaging ◀ *mag net ik / reʒ ēn ōns / im ij ing, n,* (MRI) imaging technique that uses the electrical charge of tissue atoms to produce an anatomical image of the area being examined. An applied magnetic field forces hydrogen atoms in the horse's body to line up in a certain way (similar to how the needle on a compass moves when you hold it near a magnet). When radio waves are sent towards the lined-up hydrogen atoms, they bounce back, and a computer records the signal. The computer then produces an image that represents the hydrogen and water content of the scanned tissue. Allows examination of structures in greater detail than with any other imaging modality. MRI units are available for standing examinations of the equine lower limb; larger units are also available, but require general anaesthesia of the horse.

Malabsorption ◀ *mal ēb sorp shēn, n.* difficulty in the digestion or absorption of nutrients from food. Various conditions of the equine digestive tract result in malabsorption, especially infiltrative diseases of the intestinal tract, and enterocolitis. Signs of malabsorption include weight loss and diarrhoea.
See Diarrhoea, Enteropathy.

Maladjustment ◀ *ma lē just mēnt, n.* failure to adapt to environment or to changes in circumstances; especially as applied to the failure of a newborn foal to adapt to the environment out of the uterus, e.g. Hypoxic ischaemic encephalopathy.
See Hypoxic ischaemic encephalopathy.

Malassezia sympodialis ◀ *mal as ēz ē ē / sim pō dī āl is, n.* yeast found on normal horse's skin; has been associated with crusting and scaling dermatophyte infection in horses.
See Dermatophyte.

Malformation ◀ *mal for mā shēn, n.* abnormal development of an organ or part of the body, e.g. cleft palate.

Malignant ◀ *mē lig nēnt, adj.* tending to get progressively worse, ultimately resulting in death. Used to describe tumour which grows rapidly, grows into surrounding tissues, and spreads to other parts of the body (metastasis); benign tumours tend to be non-invasive and slower-growing. Studying cells of biopsy specimen under microscope (histopathology) gives an indication of the aggressiveness of the growing cells, and, by inference, the prognosis.
See Benign, Metastasis, Tumour.
  M. hyperthermia see Hyperthermia
  M. oedema ◀ *mē lig nēnt / i dēmē, n.* rapidly progressing muscle infection typically associate with infection by *Clostridum* spp.; associated most commonly with injections and puncture wounds. Term more generally applied to ruminants.
  See Gangrene, Myonecrosis, Myositis.

Mallein ◀ *mal ān, n.* concentrate prepared from cultures or extracts of the bacterium responsible for glanders, *B. mallei*. Used in skin testing for the diagnosis of glanders in horses.
See Glanders.

Malleolus ◀ *mal ē ō lēs, n.* a rounded process of bone, especially the rounded protuberances on either side of the tibia, in the tibiotarsal joint of the hock. Can be affected by fracture or osteochondrosis.
See Fracture, Osteochondrosis.

Malnutrition ◀ *mal nū tri shēn, n.* general term for a medical condition caused by or associated with an improper or insufficient diet. Signs include weight loss, tiredness, weakness. The vast majority of horses are well adapted to fulfil their nutritional requirements on a diet of high-quality forage and water.

Malocclusion ◀ *mal ok lū shēn, n.* malposition and contact of the teeth of the upper and lower arcades that may occasionally interfere with the efficiency of mastication or the ability to prehend food.

Malposition ◀ *mal pē zi shēn*, *n.* abnormal position, especially of foetus within uterus or birth canal at or near to foaling. May be cause of problems with foaling (dystocia); foetal malposition in utero is often blamed for congenital limb abnormalities, such as flexural deformities.
See Dystocia, Flexural deformity, Parturition.

Mammary gland ◀ *ma mē rē / gland*, *n.* modified cutaneous glandular structure which contains the elements to produce milk for nourishment of the foal. Mare has two mammary glands located between hind legs (udder); milk is secreted into lactiferous sinus, a collecting chamber for the milk. Sinus opens into a teat, which has muscular sphincters to prevent milk leaking out. Mammary glands normally enlarge in pregnant mare as mammary cell division increases owing to the influence of progesterone, 2–4 weeks before foaling. A few days prior to foaling, first milk (colostrum) may accumulate on the teats, giving the teats a waxy appearance (waxing). Conditions affecting mammary glands include mastitis (inflammation and infection) and neoplasia.
See Gland, Mastitis, Parturition, Pregnancy.

Mandible ◀ *man di būl*, *n.* lower jaw bone; largest bone of the face. Horse's mandible has two halves, which unite during the second or third month after birth at front of jaw (mandibular symphysis). Carries lower teeth in bony sockets in the body of the bone. Behind the teeth, the vertical ramus allows for attachments of the powerful muscles of mastication; ramus articulates with the temporal bone of the skull to form the temporomandibular joint.
See Jaw, Temporomandibular joint, Tooth.

Mandibular ◀ *man di bū lē*, *adj.* of the lower jaw, the mandible.
See Mandible.

Manganese ◀ *mang gan ēz*, *n.* (Mn) dietary trace mineral, needed for metabolism of carbohydrates and lipids, and for normal cartilage formation. Actual dietary requirements for Mn are unknown; naturally occurring deficiencies or toxicities have not been reported; a single case of Mn deficiency in an adult horse was thought to be associated with excessive lime being added to the soil.

Mange ◀ *mānj*, *n.* a parasitic skin infestation. Signs include hair loss, itching and inflammation. All mange infestations are caused by microscopic mites, e.g. *Chorioptes, Demodex, Psoroptes, Sarcoptes, Otodectes*. Diagnosis involves identification of mite in skin scraping or ear wax. Treatment includes ivermectin, topical insecticides, bathing, grooming, and environmental management, e.g. cleaning stables. Favourable prognosis.
See *Chorioptes (bovis, equi)*, *Demodex*, Mite, *Psoroptes*, *Sarcoptes scabei*.

Mannitol ◀ *man it ol*, *n.* a sugar alcohol, used for the treatment of central nervous system oedema in horses, especially after trauma. Mannitol is hyperosmotic, and reduces CNS swelling by drawing water to it.

Manual/Manipulative therapy ◀ *man ūl / man ip ūl ēt iv / thē rēp ē*, *n.* physical methods of treating injuries of the horse, real or perceived. Include chiropractic, massage, stretching, trigger point therapy, etc. Claims of effectiveness of such therapies have not been substantiated in horses.
See Chiropractic, Massage.

Maple see Red maple (*Acer rubrum*).

Marble (intrauterine) ◀ *mar būl (in trē ū tē rīn)*, *n.* method of oestrus control in mares. One study has found that placing a 35 mm sterile glass marble into a mare's uterus kept 40% of the studied mares from cycling for 3 months, with no adverse affects on fertility. Additional studies needed to confirm.

Mare ◀ *mǎ*, *n.* adult (3–5 years of age, depending on breed definition) female horse.

    Mare reproductive loss syndrome ◀ *mǎ / rē prō duk tiv / los / sin drōm*, *n.* (MRLS) outbreak of foetal death and abortion in mares in Kentucky, USA, in 2000 and 2001, estimated to have cost the equine industry approximately $500 million. Associated with heavy infestation of Eastern tent caterpillars. These other syndromes occurred concurrently: fibrinous pericarditis, a unilateral panophthalmitis and encephalitis caused by *Actinobacillus* spp. Rigorous epidemiological investigation has concluded that MRLS results from penetration of the intestines by fragments of barbed hairs from the exoskeleton of the caterpillar (setae). These fragments, and associated bacteria, especially *Actinobacillus* spp., then penetrate blood vessels and spread via the circulation as septic emboli, contaminating distant tissues and, in the case of pregnant mares, causing foetal loss. Control of caterpillars via direct application of abamectin (a drug in the same drug class as ivermectin) to trees on which caterpillars live, or by spraying with leaf sprays that kill caterpillars, may be recommended in endemic areas.

Marestail see Horsetail

Marie's disease see Hypertrophic osteopathy

Marrow see Bone

Massage ◀ *mas arj*, *n*. the manual manipulation of muscle and connective tissue. Various unsupported therapeutic claims for the benefits of massage have been made, including increasing circulation, removing lactic acid, preventing muscle soreness, etc. True therapeutic benefits are unknown in horses; procedure should be considered palliative.

Mass spectrometry ◀ *mas / spek trom ēt rē*, *n*. analytical technique used especially in drug detection. Samples isolated from blood serum or urine are bombarded with an electron beam that breaks sample into smaller molecules that are then accelerated through a magnetic field and focused into an analyser. Analyser measures the mass to charge ratio (ratio defines how a particle will respond to an electric or magnetic field) and amount of each ion; the amount versus mass to charge ratio is the mass spectrum. Each drug or medication has its own unique mass spectrum.

Mast cell ◀ *marst / sel*, *n*. cell present in connective tissue throughout body. Contains granules of heparin and histamine which are released from cell in some allergic reactions (type 1 hypersensitivity).
See Connective tissue, Heparin, Histamine, Hypersensitivity.

    M. c. tumours ◀ *marst / sel / tū mērz*, *n*. benign nodules composed mostly of mast cells. These tumours typically occur as a solitary growth of the skin of the head, neck, trunk, or limbs; may also present as a diffuse swelling of the lower limb, with areas of soft tissue mineralization. Rare in horses and usually benign. Arabian horses seem to be predisposed; especially uncommon in Thoroughbreds. Two types, hyperplastic and neoplastic: hyperplastic more common. Diagnosis by skin biopsy. Surgical excision may be curative; treatment with injection of corticosteroids or cryosurgery has also been described. Some cases resolve spontaneously.
See Benign.

Mastitis ◀ *mas tī tis*, *n*. inflammation and infection of mammary gland, usually caused by bacterial infection (most often *Streptococcus* or various Gram-negative species). Not a common problem in mares. One or both glands may be affected. Signs include firm swelling of gland, heat, pain, prominent regional lymphatic vessels, and fever. Milk from affected udder is abnormal (lumpy, discoloured, watery). Diagnosis involves isolation of bacteria from milk. Cytology of milk samples typically shows large numbers of neutrophils, and occasionally bacteria. Gram-negative species have been shown to account for as much as 42% of mastitis infections in some studies. Treatment involves systemic and/or intramammary infusion of antibiotics, frequent milking, hot packs and/or hydrotherapy.
See Lymphatic, Mammary gland, Milk, *Streptococcus*.

Mastocytoma see Mast cell: M. c. tumours

Masturbation ◄⁑ *mas tē bā shēn, n.* self-stimulation of the genital organs by stallion. Has previously been considered a vice, and discouraged by devices such as stallion rings. However, masturbation appears to be normal behaviour for stallions, and occurs regardless of environmental conditions (e.g. frequency of covering). Rarely accompanied by ejaculation, so does not affect fertility or libido. Attempts at control may result in injury to stallion and abnormal behaviour.

Mater see Dura mater, Pia mater

Maternal ◄⁑ *mē ter nēl, adj.* relating to female parent, e.g. maternal antibodies. See Antibody, Colostrum, Immunity.

Mating behaviour see Behaviour

Matrix ◄⁑ *mā triks, n.* substance which surrounds cells in a tissue, e.g. bone matrix is a supportive structure made of collagen. See Bone.

    M. metalloproteinase ◄⁑ *mā triks / met al ō prō tin āz, n.* a protease enzyme, capable of degrading all kinds of extracellular matrix proteins. Especially important in the pathogenesis of inflammatory conditions such as laminitis, where the enzyme degrades the connections between the hoof and the sensitive structures of the foot, and osteoarthritis, where the enzyme degrades joint cartilage. M. metalloproteinase inhibitors, such as tetracycline antibiotics, can reach therapeutic levels, and have been used for the treatment of laminitis, with no published reports of outcome.

Mature ◄⁑ *mē tŭr, adj./v.* having completed natural growth and complete development; may refer to small part of body, e.g. egg (ovum) is released from follicle when it is mature, or to animal as a whole, e.g. sexual maturity. See Ovum.

Maxilla ◄⁑ *mak zi lē, n.* paired principal bone of upper jaw. Forms lower part of eye socket (orbit), side and base of nasal cavity and contains teeth of upper jaw; forms lateral wall of maxillary sinus. See Nasal, Orbit, Sinus.

MCH ◄⁑ *em sē āch, abbr.* (**mean corpuscular haemoglobin**) erythrocyte index measurement (measurement that describes the size and haemoglobin content of red blood cells) calculated from blood sample testing; indicates average weight of haemoglobin in each red blood cell. The formula for this index is the sum of the haemoglobin multiplied by 10 and divided by the red blood cell count. MCH values usually rise or fall as the mean corpuscular volume (MCV) is increased or decreased. See Anaemia, Erythrocyte, Haemoglobin, Iron.

MCHC ◄⁑ *em sē āch sē, abbr.* (**mean corpuscular haemoglobin concentration**) erythrocyte index measurement (measurement that describes the size and haemoglobin content of red blood cells) calculated from blood sample testing; measures the average concentration of haemoglobin in a red blood cell. This index is calculated by dividing the haemoglobin by the haematocrit. MCHC relates to the colour of the cells. Anaemias are categorized as hypochromic or normochromic according to the MCHC index. See Anaemia, Erythrocyte, Haemoglobin, Iron.

McMaster's technique ◄⁑ *mēk mar stēs / tek nēk, n.* method used for demonstrating and counting helminth eggs in faecal samples. The technique uses a counting chamber, enabling a known volume of faeces, suspended in solution, to be examined microscopically. If the weight of the faeces and the volume of flotation fluid used to prepare the suspension are known, then it is possible to calculate the number of eggs per gram of faeces. Unfortunately, the number of eggs is not necessarily indicative of the number of worms present, for a variety of reasons, including weight of the parasite eggs, and the fact that egg production is not continuous through the day (intraday variation).

MCV ◄⁑ *em sē vē, abbr.* (**mean corpuscular volume**) erythrocyte index measurement (measurement that describes the size and haemoglobin content of red blood cells) calculated from blood sample testing;

measures the average volume of a red blood cell. Calculated by dividing the haematocrit by the RBC count. The MCV categorizes red blood cells by size. Cells of normal size are called normocytic, smaller cells are microcytic, and larger cells are macrocytic. May help characterize certain anaemias.
See Anaemia, Erythrocyte, Iron.

Mean arterial pressure ◀ *mēn / art ér iēl / pre shūr, n.* (MAP) the average arterial pressure from one heartbeat to the next. Commonly measured during anaesthetic procedures, MAP reflects the blood perfusion to the organs of the horse's body. If MAP falls too low, generally below 75 mmHg, for too long a time, organs will not get enough blood, resulting in ischaemia; various methods described to increase MAP during surgery include lightening anaesthetic depth, or infusion of vasoactive substances, e.g. dopamine.
See Dopamine, Ischaemia.

Mean corpuscular haemoglobin see MCH

Mean corpuscular haemoglobin concentration see MCHC

Mean corpuscular volume see MCV

Meatus ◀ *mē ā tēs, n.* opening, canal, or passage; e.g. external auditory meatus is the external ear canal.
See Ear.

Mebendazole ◀ *me ben da zōl, n.* broad-spectrum anthelmintic of benzamidazole group. Given as oral paste to horse for treatment of main intestinal worms, e.g. *Strongylus, Oxyuris, Dictyocaulus, Parascaris,* etc. Slowly immobilizes and kills parasites by keeping the worm from absorbing glucose. However, parasite resistance is common with this class of drugs.
See Anthelmintic, Benzamidazole, *Dictyocaulus arnfieldi, Oxyuris equi, Parascaris equorum, Strongylus* spp.

Meclofenamic acid ◀ *mek lō fen ēm ik / as id, n.* oral non-steroidal anti-inflammatory drug, occasionally used for the treatment of lameness in horses. As opposed to the several hours required for the effects of other non-steroidal anti-inflammatory drugs to take effect, meclofenamic acid takes from 36 to 96 hours to begin working; some studies suggest that meclofenamic acid is more effective than phenylbutazone for relief of lameness. When doses of meclofenamic acid are increased above the recommended levels, however, the number of red blood cells in the circulation is observed to reduce; blood may also appear in the faeces. Horses with infestations of bots should be given meclofenamic acid with caution. Mild colic and a change in the consistency of the manure have been seen in horses that were heavily infested with bots and have been given meclofenamic acid.

Meconium ◀ *me kō nē ēm, n.* brown–green faeces present in rectum of newborn foal, composed of materials ingested during the time the foal spends in the uterus, including intestinal epithelial cells, mucus, amniotic fluid, bile, and water. Usually passed within hours after birth. Sometimes foal cannot pass meconium (meconium retention). Signs of retention are of mild colic, including straining to pass faeces, discomfort, and restlessness. Usually resolves with carefully delivered enema.
See Faeces, Placenta, Uterus.

Medial ◀ *mē dē ūl, adj.* situated towards the midline or middle. In anatomical descriptions, term applied to various structures, including tendons, ligaments, and portions of bones, e.g. the medial femoral condyle.

Mediastinum ◀ *mē dē ē stī nēm, n.* a partition; division between two lungs in middle of chest. Contains heart, oesophagus, trachea, nerves, blood vessels, thoracic duct, thymus (in immature animal), lymph nodes. In the horse, the caudal part of the mediastinum is usually open, allowing communication of the two pleural cavities through it.
See organs under individual entries.

Medical colic see Colic

Medication ◀︎ː _med_ ik ā shēn, n. a substance used in an attempt to cure disease or relieve pain.

Medicine ◀︎ː _med_ sēn, n. **1)** substance or preparation given to treat disease; **2)** the science and art dealing with the maintenance of health and the prevention, alleviation, or cure of disease; **3)** science of non-surgical treatment of disease.

Medulla ◀︎ː me _du_ lē, n. distinct inner part of organ, e.g. inner part of kidney, adrenal gland, bone.
See Adrenal gland, Bone, Kidney.

> **M. oblongata** ◀︎ː me _du_ lē /ob long art ē, n. the lowermost portion of the horse's brainstem, continuous with the spinal cord. The medulla oblongata controls respiration, circulation, and certain other bodily functions.
> See Adrenal gland, Bone, Kidney.

Mega- ◀︎ː _me_ gē, prefix. large size; enlargement.

Megalocornea ◀︎ː _me_ gē lō kor nē ē, n. enlarged cornea on an otherwise normal globe. Seen as part of anterior segment dysgenesis, especially of Rocky Mountain Spotted Horses.
See Anterior segment dysgenesis.

Megaoesophagus ◀︎ː _me_ gē _iso_ fi gēs, n. rare condition of horse, usually congenital, where oesophagus is dilated and loses muscle tone. May occur as result of stricture of oesophagus; a case of megaoesophagus secondary to a persistent right aortic arch has also been reported. Cause most often unknown. Food collects in dilated oesophagus. Signs include coughing, difficulty swallowing, food appearing at nostrils; aspiration pneumonia is a common sequel. Diagnosis by radiography, including using contrast material to highlight lumen of oesophagus.
See Lumen, Oesophagus, Radiography, Stricture.

Meibomian gland ◀︎ː mī _bō_ mē an / gland, n. one of several small glands in the eyelids that make a lubricant called sebum; sebum is discharged through the glandular openings in the edges of the lids. (Named after a seventeenth-century German anatomist, Heinrich Meibom.)

Melanin ◀︎ː _me_ lē nin, n. dark brown pigment present in hair, skin, iris of eye, retina of eye. Dermal melanin is produced by melanocytes, which are found in the stratum basale of the epidermis.
See Pigment.

Melanoma ◀︎ː _me_ lē _nō_ mē, n. tumour of melanin-producing cells (melanocytes). Most commonly seen in white or grey horses, but can affect horses of any colour. More common in aged horses; research suggests that up to 80% of grey or white horses will develop melanomas by 15 years of age. Most common tumour locations are under the tail and around the anus, in the prepuce of male horses, in the groin, and in the neck at the site of the parotid salivary glands. The underlying cause of these tumours is unknown; genetic mutations linked to coat colour are being investigated as a cause. Local removal is effective – if untreated, tumours can become quite large, and may metastasize. The extent of systemic involvement is often difficult to determine; although metastasis appears to be more common in melanomas of non-grey horses, it may occur in any horse afflicted with the condition. Small, local tumours are usually not a functional problem, but if large, they may interfere with functions such as defecation. Early treatment of small lesions, before extensive growth occurs, is ideal if such lesions are to be controlled locally. Not all melanomas are benign, and biopsy is necessary for accurate diagnosis and planning of treatment. Surgical excision is locally curative. Cimetidine therapy has been reported to cause remission in a small percentage of affected grey horses; other therapies that are available (e.g. autogenous vaccine) have had no documented success.

Melatonin ◀︎ː me lēt _ō_ nin, n. hormone that communicates information about environmental light conditions to various parts of the body; important effects on biological (circadian) rhythms, and on reproductive function of the horse. Derived from the neurotransmitter serotonin, from the amino acid tryptophan. The effects of melatonin on reproductive systems are anti-gonadotropic, that is, melatonin inhibits the secretion of luteinizing hormone (LH) and follicle stimulating hormone (FSH) from the anterior pituitary gland.

Membrane ◀€ _mem brān_, _n_. thin, flexible layer of tissue which forms a covering or lining of an organ, structure, or region, or separates such structures; the surrounding layer of a cell.
See Mucous membrane.

Menace response ◀€ _me_ nis / ris _pons_, _n_. (eye preservation reflex, menace reflex) test of reflex of eye; finger or hand is moved rapidly towards eye (but care must be taken not to cause an air current near eye). Normal response is closure of eyelids. Lack of response indicates defective vision (e.g. from optic nerve degeneration), paralysis of the eyelids (e.g. from facial nerve paralysis), or serious depression of consciousness. May not be fully developed in foal until several weeks of age.
See Cranial nerve, Facial, Optic, Reflex.

Meningeal ◀€ _me_ nin _jē ūl_, _n_. relating to the meninges.
See Meninges.

Meninges ◀€ _me_ _nin_ _jēz_, _n_. the collective term for the three membranes which cover and protect brain and spinal cord: dura mater (outer), arachnoid membrane (middle), and pia mater (inner). More commonly referred to as dura, arachnoid, and pia.

Meningitis ◀€ _me_ nin _jī_ tis, _n_. inflammation of meninges; commonly implicated causes include bacterial, viral or fungal infection. Most common in foals with septicaemia; rare in adult horses. Signs include fever, stiff neck (reflex spasm of neck muscles caused by inflammation of cervical nerve roots), dullness, loss of appetite, incoordination, blindness, head

pressing, circling, seizures. Diagnosis involves history of infection, analysis of blood and cerebrospinal fluid samples, blood or urine culture, and MRI. Electroencephalography (EEG) can indicate intracranial disease, but is not readily available. Treatment is directed at eliminating the pathogens, usually with specific agents (antibiotics, antifungals, etc.), and controlling the inflammatory response to them; the inflammatory response can be as big a problem as the infection itself. Prognosis for survival is fair to poor; prognosis is better with early diagnosis, but signs are often vague, and disease may not be recognized until it is too late for treatment to help.
See Cerebrospinal, Meninges, Septicaemia.

Meningoencephalitis ◀€ _me_ nin _jō_ en ke _fē_ _lī_ tis, _n_. inflammation of the brain and spinal cord and their meninges. Signs may be indistinguishable from meningitis; signalment, diagnosis, treatment, and prognosis identical.
See Meningitis.

Meniscus ◀€ _me_ _nis_ _cēs_, _n_. crescent-shaped piece of fibrous cartilage which lies within stifle joint; provides shock absorption and stability to the joint, and reduces friction. Each stifle joint has two menisci. Most commonly damaged by trauma to stifle, often with damage to stifle ligaments. Signs include hind limb lameness, joint swelling, and lameness after hind limb flexion. Diagnosed locally by clinical signs and intra-articular anaesthesia. Radiography may reveal associated joint damage. Ultrasound may help image damaged meniscus. Diagnosis confirmed, and treatment possibly by, arthroscopy. Prognosis depends on the extent of injury.
See Arthroscopy, Cartilage, Ligament, Stifle.

Mepivicaine ◀€ _mep_ _iv_ ik _ān_, _n_. a local anaesthetic, with a medium duration of action, often used as an alternative to lidocaine for various types of veterinary anaesthesia.

Mercury ◄€ _mer kŭ rē, n._ (Hg) liquid metal, poisonous. Mercury compounds were used in the past as a seed preservative to treat grain to prevent fungal growth and this has resulted in poisoning in horses; most recent reports involve acute poisoning secondary to ingestion of mercury-containing counterirritants used for treatment of musculoskeletal conditions (blisters). Signs of poisoning all include some form of kidney dysfunction, including depression, oliguria, and azotaemia. Ingestion may cause oral ulceration, or irritation of stomach and intestines, with secondary colic signs. Neurological dysfunction may follow chronic toxicities. Horses should be removed from sources of mercury. Dimercaprol may be used to inactivate circulating mercury, and adsorbents (e.g. activated charcoal) may help acute toxicities, but treatment is otherwise supportive, and directed at maintaining kidney function. Prognosis for acute toxicity depends on dose; prognosis for chronic toxicity is grave.

Merocrine ◄€ _me rē krin, adj._ describes most common form of glandular secretion whereby cells of gland remain intact, and product is secreted directly into the lumen of the gland; e.g. salivary gland, pancreas (c.f. holocrine).
See Gland, Holocrine, Pancreas, Salivary gland.

Mesencephalon see Midbrain

Mesenteric ◄€ _mē zēn te rik, adj._ relating to a mesentery, most commonly the mesentery of the abdominal cavity.
See Mesentery.

Mesentery ◄€ _mē zēn trē, n._ membranous sheet, derived from peritoneum, in which small intestines are suspended; originates from upper (dorsal) wall of abdomen. Blood vessels run through it to the stomach and intestine. Also, term can be applied to other folds of supporting membranes that are not a part of the digestive tract, e.g. the broad ligament of the uterus.
See Abdomen, Peritoneum, Small intestine, Stomach.

Mesh ◄€ _mesh, n._ a woven or knotted material, or pattern, of an open texture with evenly spaced holes.
> **M. graft** ◄€ _mesh / grarft, n._ skin grafting technique to expand skin coverage of large, open wounds. Patterned stab incisions are made in skin; when pulled to cover the defect, the skin stretches and holes in the skin (the mesh) allow drainage of wound fluids.
> **M. implant** ◄€ _mesh / imp larnt, n._ technique for hernia repair, especially incisional hernia post-colic surgery. Polypropylene mesh is most commonly used; piece is cut to cover defect and sutured in place. Most serious complication is post-surgical infection; most horses do not need such repair.

Mesoderm ◄€ _mē zō derm, n._ middle layer of developing embryo (between ectoderm and endoderm). It differentiates to give rise to a number of tissues and structures including those of musculoskeletal, blood, vascular and urinogenital systems, to connective tissue (including that of dermis) and contributes to some glands.

Mesorchium ◄€ _mē zor chi ēm, n._ the fold of peritoneum which attaches the testis to the dorsal wall of the body cavity or scrotal sac.

Mesothelioma ◄€ _mē zō thē lē ō mē, n._ tumour of cells lining pleura, peritoneum or pericardium. One case reported in horses: resulted in massive effusion of fluid. No treatment.
See Pleura.

Mesotherapy ◄€ _mē zō thē rēp ē, n._ technique for treatment of back soreness, involving multiple intradermal injections of lidocaine and corticosteroids. Mechanism is unknown; no published studies of effectiveness.

Metabolic ◄€ _me tē bol ik, adj._ relating to metabolism.
> **M. acidosis** see Acidosis
> **M. alkalosis** see Alkalosis

Metabolism ◄€ _me ta bo lizm, n._ chemical processes that occur within living organism; necessary for maintaining life. Metabolism involves both the breakdown of substances to yield energy, e.g. nutrients absorbed from food, as well as the synthesis of other substances.

Metabolite ◀℈ *me ta bo līt, n.* substance produced by processes of metabolism; a substance necessary for or taking part in a particular metabolic process.
See Metabolism.

Metacarpals ◀℈ *me tē kar pūlz, n.* bones lying between carpus and fetlock of the forelimb. The horse has three metacarpal bones, the medial and lateral splint bones (MCII and MCIV, respectively) and the cannon bone (MCIII).

Metacarpophalangeal ◀℈ *me tē kar pō fal an jē ūl, adj.* relating to the metacarpus and the phalanges, especially the articulation between the cannon bone (MCIII) and the proximal phalanx (fetlock joint).

Metamizole see Dipyrone

Metastasis ◀℈ *me ta stē sis, n.* spread of disease from one part of body to another. Term is only used to describe one of two situations: 1) in infectious disease (e.g. by spread of bacteria through blood stream) or, 2) in spread of malignant tumours. Tumour cells may metastasize via various routes, including in blood, lymphatics, along tissue planes (e.g. between sheets of muscle) or even along incisions made during operations to perform biopsy or remove tumour.
See Malignant, Tumour.

Metatarsals ◀℈ *me tē tar sūlz, n.* bones lying between hock (tarsus) and fetlock of the hind limb. The horse has three metatarsal bones, the medial and lateral splint bones (MTII and MTIV, respectively) and the cannon bone (MTIII).

Metatarsophalangeal ◀℈ *me tē tar so fal an jē ūl, adj.* relating to the metatarsus and the phalanges, especially the articulation between the cannon bone (MTIII) and the proximal phalanx (fetlock joint).

Metered dose inhaler ◀℈ *mē tēd / dōs / in hā lē, n.* pressurized, hand-held devices that use propellants to deliver doses of medication to the lungs of a patient. In horses, metered dose inhalers are most commonly used to deliver bronchodilating drugs, or corticosteroid drugs, to the lungs of horses affected with recurrent airway obstruction.
See Recurrent airway obstruction.

Methaemoglobin ◀℈ *me thē mō glō bin, n.* a form of haemoglobin, in which the iron in the haem group is in the Fe^{3+} state, not the Fe^{2+} of normal haemoglobin. Methaemoglobin is unable to carry oxygen. Normally, only a very small percentage of the horse's total haemoglobin is circulating as methaemoglobin.

Methaemoglobinaemia ◀℈ *mef thē mō glō bin ēm iē, n.* abnormally elevated levels of methaemoglobin in the blood circulation. May be seen as a result of various toxicities, e.g. Red maple toxicity, or diseases, especially renal disease.
See Kidney, Methaemoglobin, Red maple.

Methionine ◀℈ *me thē ō nēn, n.* sulphur-containing amino acid, found especially in high levels in the hoof. Accordingly, a variety of hoof supplements have been devised which include methionine, apparently in the belief that if some methionine is needed for the normal hoof, additional amounts will make the hoof even better. However, methionine deficiencies have not been demonstrated in the horse. Supplementation with methionine to improve hoof quality has largely been disappointing.

Methocarbamol ◀℈ *me thō kar bēm ol, n.* drug that depresses the central nervous system, occasionally prescribed for muscle problems in horses (e.g. rhabdomyolysis) and has been used to help maintain relaxation in horses afflicted with tetanus. Methocarbamol is *not* a muscle relaxant, however. Available as a sterile solution for intravenous injection in horses. An oral tablet is also commonly given to horses; however, no studies have been done on horses to determine what, if any, dose of methocarbamol given orally is effective.

Methocarbamol has the potential to cause sedation in the horse. Because of this effect, the drug has been used in an effort to calm horses, particularly those used for performance. The use of methocarbamol is therefore controlled by organizations that oversee competitions. Intravenous methocarbamol should not be given to horses with kidney failure because the vehicle in which the drug is carried in solution can be potentially harmful if kidney function is impaired. Few adverse side effects of methocarbamol are reported. Methocarbamol appears to be quite safe and nontoxic. The drug appears safe at up to eight times overdose. Salivation, weakness and stumbling are reported effects in small animals.

Methylprednisolone ◀ _mē thīl pred ni so lōn_, _n._ corticosteroid-type drug; considered medium- to long-acting. Comes as a sterile suspension for injection. The drug can also be injected into inflamed areas for reduction of local swelling and inflammation, or for long-term control of allergic reactions where the allergen cannot be eliminated (such as fly allergies). Commonly injected into joints for the treatment of arthritis; after injection into joints, drug levels have been found for up to 39 days. Steroidal anti-inflammatory drugs such as methylprednisolone have been accused of accelerating joint destruction in horses with pre-existing arthritis. In joints, corticosteroids have been demonstrated to decrease the metabolism of cartilage cells. However, there is little experimental information regarding the effects of injection of steroidal anti-inflammatory agents such as methylprednisolone into previously damaged or arthritic joints, and concerns about steroids causing extreme joint destruction, which have been expressed in past years, appear to have been overblown. Considerable evidence exists that injection of corticosteroids into normal joints is not harmful to the joint surfaces, although cartilage metabolism may be affected for up to 16 weeks after injection.

While there are strong and conflicting opinions, there is currently no strong information available to suggest that one particular steroid is the 'best' steroid for joint injection. Nor has the optimum dose of a particular steroid been determined. Research suggests that effective doses of methylprednisolone may be lower than previously prescribed.
See Anti-inflammatory, Corticosteroid, Prednisolone.

Methylsulphonylmethane ◀ _mē thī sul fō nīl mē thān_, _n._ (MSM) a dietary supplement for which there have been many claims made, for the treatment of such diverse conditions as osteoarthritis and allergy. MSM is a naturally occurring compound found in some green plants, certain species of algae, fruits, vegetables, grains, and both bovine and human adrenal glands, milk, and urine. MSM is also an odourless by-product of the chemical breakdown of dimethyl sulphoxide (DMSO) by the body. Because of this, many people have promoted MSM as a 'dietary form' of DMSO. There is no scientific evidence to support claims that MSM has this effect. It may be claimed that MSM is a good source of the mineral, sulfur. However, this claim is unsupported by published research, and research in other species would suggest that MSM's contribution to sulphur metabolism is likely to be negligible in the horse. There is little published scientific research to support its use, in people or in horses.

Metoclopramide ◀ _me tō klō pra mīd_, _n._ a dopamine receptor antagonist; has been used for its prokinetic properties in horses, i.e. it stimulates emptying of stomach and muscular action (peristalsis) in intestines. May be used after colic surgery to try to prevent or treat development of ileus.
See Colic, Ileus, Peristalsis.

Metritis ◀ _me trī tis_, _n._ inflammation of the uterus.
See Contagious equine metritis, Endometritis, Uterus.

Metronidazole ◀ _me tro nī da zōl_, _n._ antibiotic drug, particularly effective against anaerobic bacteria. Anaerobic infections are most commonly seen in the horse's chest: pleuropneumonia or 'shipping fever'. The drug is usually used along with other antibiotics. It has also been

advocated for the treatment of diarrhoea of unknown cause in adult horses. One report advocates the use of a paste made from metronidazole for the treatment of 'canker'. There are no reported precautions or side effects accompanying the use of metronidazole in the horse.
See Anaerobe, Peritonitis.

Miconazole ◀€ *mī ko na zōl, n.* anti-fungal drug; has been used as a topical treatment for fungal eye infections in horse (i.e. mycotic keratitis).
See Keratitis.

Micro- ◀€ *mī krō, prefix.* small.

Microbe ◀€ *mī krōb, n.* microorganism, especially a disease-causing bacterium.
See Bacterium, Microorganism.

Microbiology ◀€ *mī krō bī o lo jē, n.* study of microscopic forms of life, i.e. bacteria, fungi, protozoa, viruses.

Microcornea ◀€ *mī krō kor nē ē, n.* abnormally small, flat, thin cornea. Normally recognized as a congenital ocular defect in foals, along with other ocular problems. Has rarely been recognized in surveys of adult horses with otherwise normal globes, and is usually not a cause of visual impairment in these horses.

Microfilaria ◀€ *mī krō fil ar ē ē, n.* the tiny larval form of a filarial (thread-like) worm, e.g. *Onchocerca cervicalis, Setaria equina*.
See *Onchocerca, Setaria* spp.

Micron ◀€ *mī kron, n.* one millionth of a metre (one thousandth of a millimetre); abbreviated μm.

Micronema deletrix see *Halicephalobus deletrix*

Microorganism ◀€ *mī krō or gē nizm, n.* an organism that can only be seen through a microscope. e.g. bacterium, virus, fungus, protozoon, rickettsia, etc.

Microphthalmos ◀€ *mī krof thal mēs, n.* small, abnormal eye; usually the result of a congenital defect. Prognosis for vision

depends on severity of the problem, as well as the presence of other ocular defects.

Microscopic anatomy see Anatomy

***Microsporum* spp.** ◀€ *mī krō spor ēm / spē shēs, n.* species of fungus; one of the four common dermatophytes in horses (causes ringworm).
See Dermatophyte, Saprophyte.

Micturate ◀€ *mik tū rāt, v.* urinate, pass urine.
See Urine.

Midbrain ◀€ *mid brān, n.* (mesencephalon) part of brainstem, contains nerves which link left and right sides of brain, and centres for reflexes concerned with vision and hearing. Portions of the midbrain are associated with motor system pathways; dopamine production occurs in the midbrain.
See Brain, Reflex.

Middle ◀€ *midl, adj.* not being at either extreme; a central position.
M. carpal joint ◀€ *midl / kar pūl / joint, n.* the middle of the three joints of the equine knee (carpus); always communicates with carpometacarpal joint. Common site of fracture, especially in racing animals.
M. ear see Ear
M. phalanx ◀€ *midl / fal anks, n.* (short pastern bone) the middle of the three bones of the distal limb. Enclosed distally in the hoof, where it articulates with the coffin bone (distal phalanx); articulates proximally with the proximal phalanx. Many tendons and ligaments attach to the bone; common site of fracture, especially in hind limbs, associated with quick turning (e.g. cutting or reining horses).

Midge ◀€ *mij, n.* small, two-winged fly; the term encompasses a variety of biting flies that cause dermatitis and allergic reactions in horses.
See *Culicoides* spp.

Migration ◀€ *mī grā shēn, n.* movement from one place to another, e.g. movement of parasites within body, such as larvae of *Strongylus vulgaris*, which migrate through intestinal wall into arteries, larvae of bot fly, which migrate from lining of mouth to horse's stomach, etc. Migration can result in signs of disease, depending on which tissue is damaged by the parasite. Foreign bodies, e.g. plant material, can also migrate in subcutaneous tissues.

The term aberrant migration is used to describe the pathological abnormal migration of a parasite, especially when parasite migration causes clinical disease, e.g. *Halicephalobus deletrix* in central nervous system.

See Bot, *Halicephalobus deletrix*, Parasite, *Strongylus* spp.

Milk ◀ *milk, n.* opaque white fluid produced by female mammals for nourishment of young. Secreted by mammary gland under influence of hormones, especially prolactin and oxytocin. Contains water, protein, fat, vitamins. First milk (colostrum) contains antibodies from mare which are important for protecting foal against disease for first weeks of life.

See Antibody, Colostrum, Mammary gland, Oxytocin, Prolactin.

Milkshake see Bicarbonate

Milkvetch ◀ *milk vech, n. Astragalus* spp. plants growing in the rangelands of the western United States, Canada, and Mexico. May contain nitroglycosides or nitrotoxins that can result in poisoning of central nervous and respiratory systems; clinical signs of breathing problems, incoordination, depression and ataxia are typical. Affected horses may recover if removed from plant source.

See Locoweed.

Milkweed ◀ *milk wēd, n. (Asclepias* spp.) group of perennial herbs with broad-veined or narrow linear leaves; most species contain copious amounts of milky white sap. May contain cardiac glycosides and can cause poisoning if eaten. Plants can be highly toxic, and ingestion of relatively small quantity of plant can cause acute toxicity and death. Signs of poisoning with sublethal doses include diarrhoea, loss of appetite and colic.

Mineral ◀ *mi nē rūl, n.* naturally occurring inorganic substance with definite and predictable chemical composition and physical properties; term is often used for inorganic substances which need to be present in diet (often in small quantities) for normal function of body, e.g. iron, selenium, zinc, etc.

Mineralocorticoid ◀ *mi nē rūl ō kor ti koid, n.* class of steroid hormones characterized by their influence on salts (sodium, chloride and potassium) and water balance in body fluids. All mineralocorticoids are similar to aldosterone, which is produced by cortex of adrenal gland.

See Adrenal gland, Aldosterone.

Mineral oil see Liquid paraffin

Minimum inhibitory concentration ◀ *min im ēm / in hib it rē / con cēn trā shēn, n.* (MIC) lowest concentration of an antimicrobial that will inhibit the visible growth of a microorganism after the microorganism is incubated in the presence of that antimicrobial. Minimum inhibitory concentrations are important in diagnostic laboratories to confirm the sensitivity of microorganisms to a particular antimicrobial agent, to establish proper drug dosages, and also to help establish the activity and usefulness of new antimicrobial agents.

Miosis ◀ *mī ō sis, n.* excessive contraction of pupil of eye. Seen e.g. in uveitis, corneal ulceration, or other painful conditions of the horse's eye.

See Eye, Uveitis.

Mite ◀ *mīt, n.* tiny insect of subclass Acarina (also known as Acari) and the class Arachnida, with four pairs of legs. Over 45,000 species of mite exist; only a few mites are parasitic, e.g. *Sarcoptes, Psoroptes, Demodex, Otodectes, Chorioptes*. Various parasitic species cause mange.

See under individual entries, Mange.

Mitosis ◀ *mī tō sis, n.* process of cell division, results in formation of two cells, each of which have same chromosome make-up as the original cell. In multicellular organ-

isms, such as horses, the somatic cells undergo mitosis.
See Chromosome.

Mitral valve see Atrioventricular

    M.v. insufficiency ◀ *mī* trēl / *valv* / *in sēf ish ēn sē*, *n.* abnormality of the mitral valve; can result in left atrial enlargement and elevated pressure of pulmonary artery. This heart valve abnormality is the one most likely to cause decreased athletic performance.

Molar ◀ *mō lē*, *n.* the rearmost tooth in most mammals; cheek tooth. Adult horse has three upper and three lower molars on each side of the mouth, which have ridged surfaces designed for grinding food. Equine molars are covered with much enamel and dentine above the gum line and at the top of the pulp, to protect them from wear.
See Dentition, Tooth.

Molybdenum ◀ *mo lib de nēm*, *n.* (Mo) trace element, important in several enzyme systems in horse's body. Neither toxicities nor deficiencies of molybdenum have been reported in horses. Excess intake is associated with malabsorption of copper in other species, but has not been seen to occur naturally in horses.
See Copper.

Monday morning ◀ *mun dā* / *mor ning*, *n.* apparently, a particularly bad time for horses in terms of occurrence of disease. Two diseases have been associated with Monday morning, the diseases in question being seen after a weekend of rest.

    M.M. disease ◀ *mun dā* / *mor ning* / *di zēz*, *n.* an infectious thickening of one or more limbs, identified especially on Monday morning in cart horses that remained in their stalls over a weekend. The term M.m. disease has also been used somewhat interchangeably with M.m. sickness (see below).
See Lymphangitis.

    M.M. sickness ◀ *mun dā* / *mor ning* / *sik nis*, *n.* condition first associated with working horses following a day of rest, as well as a normal grain ration, on Sundays. When put back to work on Monday morning, such horses showed signs such as muscle stiffness, sweating, cramping, rapid breathing (tachypnea), and a reluctance to move.

See Exertional rhabdomyolysis, Polysaccharide storage myopathy.

Monensin ◀ *mo nen sin*, *n.* ionophore antibiotic; a mycotoxin produced by *Streptomyces* spp. Used to increase feed efficiency and growth rate, and to treat and prevent coccidiosis, in poultry and ruminants, but extremely poisonous to horses. Most horses will not eat grains with added monensin; reluctance to eat grain mixes in healthy horses indicates something is wrong. Toxicity is typically acute; signs include loss of appetite, weakness, incoordination, difficulty breathing, shock, and death. Chronic toxicities may be seen; signs include limb oedema, loss of condition, depression, poor exercise tolerance, heart damage, and nervousness on handling. No specific antidote; treatment for acute toxicity is directed at speeding the passage of ingested feed, and supportive care, e.g. intravenous fluids, as needed. Affected feed must be removed. Even if horses survive acute poisoning, heart damage may cause death during subsequent physical exertion. Affected horses should be rested for a minimum of 6 weeks following apparent recovery to allow time for heart and skeletal muscle to heal prior to resuming exercise.
See Ionophore.

Monocyte ◀ *mo nō sīt*, *n.* a type of leukocyte, with oval nucleus. Originates in bone marrow, protects against blood-borne pathogens and moves quickly to sites of infection in the tissues. Blood monocytes may also move into tissues, where they become macrophages.
See Bone, Leukocyte, Macrophage.

Monorchid ◀ *mo nor kid*, *adj.* having only one testis descended into scrotum. May be developmental (e.g. cryptorchidism) or as a result of failure of development of one testicle (rare).
See Cryptorchid, Testes.

Moon blindness see Uveitis

Moraxella equi ◀ *mo rak se lē* / *ek wī*, *n.* small rod-shaped Gram-negative bacterium. Part of normal flora of equine eye;

has been associated with bacterial conjunctivitis in horses.
See Bacterium, Conjunctivitis.

Morbidity ◀€ *mor* <u>bi</u> *di tē, n.* being diseased; used in discussion of disease as the incidence or prevalence of a disease or of all diseases in a population.

Morbillivirus see Hendra virus

Morphine ◀€ <u>*mor*</u> *fēn, n.* narcotic pain-relieving drug, generally not used in horses, as has undesirable effects on motility of intestine and often causes uncontrollable excitement.

Mortality rate ◀€ *mor* <u>ta</u> *li tē / rāt, n.* used in discussion of disease, as the ratio of the total number of deaths to the total population. Can also refer to the rate of death from a particular disease, e.g. rabies has an almost 100% mortality rate.

Mosquito ◀€ *mos* <u>kē</u> *tō, n.* insects which make up the family Culicidae, with scaled wings, slender body, and long legs. The females of most mosquito species suck blood from other animals, which makes them one of the most important vectors of disease known, e.g. in conditions such as encephalomyelitis or West Nile virus infection.
See Encephalomyelitis, West Nile virus.

Motor ◀€ *mō tē, n.* causing motion; involving muscular movement.
    M. end plate ◀€ *mō tē / end / plāt, n.* the spot at which the axon of a motor nerve terminates on a muscle fibre.
    M. neuron ◀€ *mō tē / nŭ rōn, n.* a neuron that conducts nervous impulses from the central nervous system or a ganglion towards or to a muscle, resulting in movement.
    M. unit ◀€ *mō tē / ū nit, n.* a motor neuron and the muscle fibres which are affected by it.

Mouldy ◀€ <u>*mōl*</u> *dē, adj.* having a growth of fungi on surface, e.g. mouldy feed.
    M. corn poisoning ◀€ <u>*mōl*</u> *dē / korn / poi zēn ing, n.* central nervous system toxicity associated with ingestion of corn contaminated

with fungal toxin, e.g. *Fusarium* spp. and leukoencephalomalacia.
See Fungus, Leukoencephalomalacia.

Mouth ◀€ *mŏth, n.* oral cavity, anterior opening of digestive tract, where food is taken in and chewed. Contains tongue, teeth, gums, openings of salivary glands, etc. Lined by mucous membrane. Myriad conditions affect the horse's mouth, including tooth problems, trauma (e.g. penetrating wounds to cheeks), congenital problems (e.g. cleft palate), foreign bodies (e.g. brambles caught at back of mouth), and neoplasia. Signs that the mouth may be the source of a problem include difficulty eating, dropping food from mouth, reflux of food down nostrils.
See Gum, Palate, Salivary gland, Tongue, Tooth.

Moxidectin ◀€ *moks ē* <u>*dek*</u> *tin, n.* an antiparasitic agent available as a 2% equine oral gel. Acts by interfering with the transmission of nervous impulses in the parasite, resulting in paralysis and elimination of the parasite. Though closely related chemically to avermectins, moxidectin's primary claim to superiority is based on the assertion that it is superior to other deworming products at controlling the mucosal stages of small strongyles (encysted cyathostomes), and thereby also useful in reducing the frequency of treatment required for successful strategic equine parasite control. However, several studies suggest that moxidectin is only moderately effective at removing the mucosal stages. Moxidectin may be combined with praziquantel in order to assist in removing tapeworms. Compared to other commonly used deworming agents for horses, moxidectin has a rather narrow margin of safety. This is a particular problem in foals and other young horses, and miniature horses. Moxidectin should also not be used in sick, debilitated, or underweight horses. Reported signs of moxidectin toxicosis include coma, difficulty breathing, depression, incoordination, tremors, seizures, or weakness. Signs of toxicity are seen within 6–22 hours and last for 36–168 hours. With treatment, horses that have moxidectin toxicosis can recover fully.

Mucin ◀⁞ _mū_ sin, _n._ any of a group of mucoproteins found in various secretions and tissues, e.g. in saliva, in the stomach lining and in the skin. Mucus, produced by glands of mucous membranes, is especially rich in mucin.
See Gland, Mucous membrane, Mucus.

Mucocilliary clearance ◀⁞ _mū_ ko sil ē arē _klēr_ ans, _n._ the removal of mucus and other materials from the airways by the cilia of the epithelial cells. A feature of the normally functioning equine respiratory tract.
See Cilium.

Mucoid ◀⁞ _mū_ koid, _adj._ resembling mucus, e.g. used to describe a slimy discharge.
See Mucus.

Mucosa ◀⁞ _mū_ _kō_ zē, _n._ mucous membrane.
See Mucous membrane.

Mucous membrane ◀⁞ _mū_ kēs / _mem_ brān, _n._ epithelial tissue which lines all body passages that communicate with the exterior, e.g. the respiratory, genitourinary, and alimentary tracts. Mucous membranes are comprised of cells and have associated glands that secrete mucus.

Mucus ◀⁞ _mū_ kēs, _n._ slimy substance secreted by mucous membranes, consists of mucin, dissolved salts, cells lost from surface of membrane and water. Secreted as a protective lubricant coating by the cells and glands of the mucous membranes.
See Leukocyte, Mucin, Mucous membrane.

Mud fever see Dermatitis, Pastern

Mule ◀⁞ _mūl_, _n._ offspring of a female horse and male donkey; usually infertile.

Multiparous ◀⁞ _mul_ ti _par_ rēs, _adj._ used to describe mare which has given birth two or more times.

Murmur see Heart

Murray Valley fever ◀⁞ _mu_ rē / _val_ ē / _fē_ vē, _n._ _Flavivirus_ infection; geographically limited sporadic occurrences in the South Pacific. Water birds serve as a reservoir of infection; transmitted by bite of infective mosquitoes. Causes neurological signs, e.g. circling, ataxia. No specific treatment; no vaccine available.

Musca spp. ◀⁞ _mu_ skē / _spē_ shēs, _n._ flies. Flies are an annoying part of life for horses and horse owners. They do not bite, but feed on wounds and body secretions. Eggs are laid in faeces or decaying matter. Life cycle varies from 7–14 days. Can be a nuisance, affecting performance, or a vector for disease, e.g. as carriers of _Habronema_ spp. Control is by keeping environment clean, or repellent sprays; fly masks protect face from fly strikes; wounds and cuts should be bandaged to prevent fly strikes and _Habronema_ infection.
See _Habronema._

Muscle ◀⁞ _mu_ sēl, _n._ tissue made up of specialized cells containing protein fibres which are capable of contraction. Contraction may be voluntary, as in skeletal muscles that respond to a nervous impulse to move, or involuntary, as with the muscles of respiration, of the gastrointestinal tract, or of the heart, the movement of which is stimulated by internal pacemaker cells which regularly contract and stimulate contractions in other muscle cells with which they are in contact. All skeletal muscle and many smooth muscle contractions are facilitated by the neurotransmitter acetylcholine. Bundles of muscle fibres (fascicles) are enclosed in a sheath of fibrous tissue. Muscle spindles (nerve–muscle bundles) are distributed throughout the skeletal muscles and provide sensory feedback information to the central nervous system. Muscle tissue has an abundant blood supply.
Three types of muscle are found in the horse's body:
- Smooth muscle – present in areas where contraction is involuntary, e.g. oesophagus, stomach, intestines, respi-

ratory tract, uterus, bladder, or blood vessel.

- Striated (skeletal) muscle – present in muscles of limbs, back, abdominal wall, etc., which are under voluntary control of animal and used consciously (e.g. for movement), or unconsciously (e.g. to maintain posture). Most are attached to bones by tendons; some are attached to other muscles, or to skin. Striated muscle is further subdivided into:
  - ○ Slow twitch (Type 1) – dense capillaries, and abundant myoglobin and mitochondria. Carries much oxygen and primarily responsible for sustained aerobic activity.
  - ○ Fast twitch (Type 2) – fast twitch fibres contract faster and with more force than slow twitch fibres, but they can sustain only short bursts of anaerobic activity before muscle becomes fatigued and painful.
- Cardiac muscle – specialized muscle, more closely resembling striated muscle histologically, but found only in the heart.

Conditions which affect muscle include inflammation (myositis), rhabdomyolysis, rupture or tearing, bacterial infection (e.g. *Clostridium*), atrophy (most commonly associated with damage to nerve supplying that muscle), etc.

See Acetylcholine, *Clostridium*, Exertional rhabdomyolysis, Myositis, various body systems.

M. atrophy see Atrophy

M. biopsy ◀ *mu sēl / bī op sē, n.* surgical removal of a piece of muscle for histological examination. Used as a diagnostic tool for conditions affecting muscle, such as polysaccharide storage myopathy, or equine motor neuron disease.

See Equine motor neuron disease, Polysaccharide storage myopathy.

M. dystrophy see Dystrophy

M. relaxant ◀ *mu sēl / rē laks ēnt, n.* a drug which affects skeletal muscle function and decreases the muscle tone. Two major therapeutic groups:

- Neuromuscular blockers, e.g. succinylcholine, interfere with nerve transmission at the motor end plate. They can cause temporary paralysis, and are seldom used in equine medicine.

- Spasmolytics, e.g. methocarbamol, depress the central nervous system and are more commonly employed than neuromuscular blockers. Thus, while they are commonly used for muscle soreness, they do not directly relax muscles, and the depression of the central nervous system also finds application in behaviour modification.

Musculoskeletal system ◀ *mus kū lō skel it ēl / sis tēm, n.* the body system that gives horses the ability to move physically, by use of the muscles and their actions on the skeletal system.

Mycobacterium **spp.** ◀ *mī ko bak tē rē ēm / spē shēs, n.* a large bacterial group of aerobic, non-spore forming rods. Slow-growing; may take as long as 60 days to detect in bacterial culture. In horses, disseminated disease with *Mycobacterium avium* subsp. *avium* is rarely reported in North America and Europe; abortions and subcutaneous infections have rarely been described. Infection causes tissue destruction from granulomatous inflammation; clinical signs are non-specific, including depression, weight loss, chronic diarrhoea, or intermittent fever. Culture or cytology of affected tissues may be diagnostic in selected cases; special culture techniques are required to grow the bacterium successfully. Unfortunately, diagnosis is usually made after the disease has become well established, with disease courses of 2–12 months; thus, disseminated infections have been uniformly fatal. Environmental control strategies are unlikely to be helpful in containing the bacterium, since the organism is ubiquitous in the environment.

Mycoplasma **spp.** ◀ *mī kō plaz mē / spē shēs, n.* a genus of bacteria that lack cell walls. Occasionally implicated in equine infections, e.g. inflammation of the heart sac (pericarditis), inflammation of the placenta (placentitis), and in pneumonias of foals and adult horses. Antibiotics that target cell wall synthesis, e.g. penicillin, are not effective; other broad-spectrum antibiotics, e.g. tetracyclines, must be used for treatment.

Mycosis ◀⊰ *mī kō sis, n.* disease caused by infection with fungus.
See Fungus.

Mycotic ◀⊰ *mī ko tik, adj.* of, relating to, or caused by fungal infection.
See Fungus.

Mycotoxin ◀⊰ *mī ko toks in, n.* a poisonous substance produced by a fungus, especially moulds.
See Aflatoxin.

Mydriasis ◀⊰ *mi drī ē sis, n.* excessive or prolonged dilation of pupil of eye, e.g. after application of atropine ophthalmic ointment to the eye.
See Atropine, Eye.

Mydriatic ◀⊰ *mi drē a tik, adj./n.* causing or involving dilation of pupil of eye; e.g. atropine ophthalmic ointment is a mydriatic agent.
See Atropine, Eye.

Myectomy ◀⊰ *mī ek tē mē, n.* surgical removal of a part of a muscle, e.g. removal of a portion of strap muscle of throat may be used as treatment for dorsal displacement of soft palate.
See Soft palate.

Myelin ◀⊰ *mī i lin, n.* fatty substance which forms a thick sheath around some nerves, especially cranial nerves, spinal nerves and white matter of central nervous system; important for normal transmission of nervous impulses in these nerves.
See Nerve.

Myelography ◀⊰ *mī i lo gra fē, n.* radiographic visualization of spinal cord, obtained by using contrast medium injected into space around spinal cord (subarachnoid space) at the atlanto-occipital junction at the base of the skull. Technique is typically performed under general anaesthesia; standing myelograms have been described, but the technique is thought to be less accurate than that which is performed under general anaesthesia. Technique is commonly used to look for compressive lesions of the spinal cord that could be affecting the horse's neurological function, resulting in clinical signs such as stumbling and stiffness.
See Contrast agent, Radiography, Spinal, Spine.

Myeloma ◀⊰ *mī i lō mē, n.* cancerous proliferation of plasma cells in bone marrow, spleen, liver, or lymph nodes. Rare in horses. Signs include weight loss, oedema, fever, and renal failure. Laboratory findings include anaemia, hypercalcaemia, and hyperproteinaemia, with an abnormal increase in gamma globulins (gammopathy). Successful treatment has not been reported.
See Bone.

Myo- ◀⊰ *mī ō, prefix.* muscle.
See Muscle.

Myocarditis ◀⊰ *mī ō kar dī tis, n.* inflammation of heart muscle. Can be a complication of equine influenza infection and strangles; however, it is virtually impossible to make a definitive diagnosis because it is not possible to obtain biopsies of heart muscle. Signs of myocarditis, or any myocardial disease, can vary tremendously, but may include loss of stamina, irregular heart beat, congestive heart failure, or even collapse and death.
See Equine influenza, Heart, Strangles.

Myocardium ◀⊰ *mī ō kar dī ēm, n.* muscle tissue of the heart.
See Heart, Muscle.

Myoglobin ◀⊰ *mī ō glō bin, n.* a protein pigment in muscles containing red iron; the primary oxygen-carrying pigment of muscle. Similar to haemoglobin, but binds more oxygen.

Myoglobinuria ◀⊰ *mī ō glō bin ŭr ēē, n.* the presence of myoglobin in the urine, e.g. as may be seen after exertional rhabdomyolysis.
See Exertional rhabdomyolysis.

Myometrium ◀⊰ *mī ō mē trē ēm, n.* muscular layer of the uterus; composed of smooth muscle. The myometrium stretches during pregnancy to allow for foetal growth, and contracts in a rhythmic, coor-

dinated fashion during foaling in response to hormonal stimulus, especially to oxytocin. After foaling, the myometrium contracts to expel the placenta and reduce blood loss.
See Muscle, Oxytocin, Parturition, Uterus.

Myonecrosis ◀﹕ *mī on ē krō sis, n.* death of muscle tissue; seen as a feature of muscle infections, especially those associated with *Clostridium* spp.
See *Clostridium*.

Myopathy ◀﹕ *mī o pē thē, n.* disorder of muscle or muscle tissues. Most myopathies of the horse share many clinical similarities, including muscle soreness, lameness, and muscle enzyme abnormalities; thorough clinical evaluations, including blood work, history, muscle biopsy and environmental history are often necessary to obtain a definitive diagnosis. Many different conditions result in myopathies in horses, and several classification systems have been suggested, e.g. according to pathophysiology, clinical presentation, or cause. Causes of equine myopathies include:
- Neurogenic – related to primary disease involving the nervous system, e.g. *Clostridium botulinum* infection, or tetanus.
- Myogenic – arising from the muscle. Various causes include:
  - ○ Trauma – e.g. fibrotic myopathy.
  - ○ Infection – e.g. myonecrosis, as caused by *Clostridium* spp. or *Staphlococcus* spp. infections.
- Inflammatory – e.g. from muscle injury.
- Toxic – e.g. from white snakeroot, or monensin toxicity.
- Circulatory – e.g. postanaesthetic myopathy, where muscles are damaged from prolonged recumbency, with constriction of muscle circulation, or from inadequate circulation resulting from low blood pressure.
- Genetic – e.g. mitochondrial myositis, a rare muscle disease associated with dysfunction of the power sources of cells (mitochondria), polysaccharide storage myopathy, hyperkalaemic periodic paralysis, or glycogen branching enzyme deficiency (mitochondria).

- Nutritional – e.g. Vitamin E deficiency (equine motor neuron disease), selenium deficiency.
- Exercise-related – e.g. exhausted horse syndrome.
- Cachexia – following chronic disease.
- Neoplasia – tumours of muscle.
See *Clostridium*, Fibrotic myopathy, Muscle, Exertional rhabdomyolysis, various conditions.

Myositis ◀﹕ *mī ō sī tis, n.* inflammation of muscle. Commonly used as alternative name for exertional rhabdomyolysis.
See Exertional rhabdomyolysis.

> **Infectious m.** ◀﹕ *in fek shēs / mī ō sī tis, n.* myositis as a result of invasion by an infectious agent, e.g. infections caused by *Clostridium* spp.
> See *Clostridium*.

Myosis see Miosis

Myotomy ◀﹕ *mī o tēm ē, n.* incision or division of a muscle. Commonly performed in the treatment of muscle infections associated with *Clostridium* spp.

Myotonia ◀﹕ *mī ō tō nē ē, n.* disorder involving abnormal electrical conduction across the cell membranes of muscle, typically characterized by involuntary spasm of muscles after local stimulation (such as a flick of the finger). Rarely seen congenital condition of Quarter Horses. Three syndromes of varying severity have been described: 1) abnormal EMG findings with no obvious muscle problems, 2) progressive loss of muscle function, starting at about 6 months of life, and 3) severe, progressive muscle function abnormalities starting at about 4 weeks of age. Clinical signs vary depending on severity of disease; include stiffness of hind legs, hypertrophy of muscles of rump, spasm of muscle on percussion. Diagnosis is based on clinical signs, muscle biopsy changes, and abnormal electromyography (EMG) findings. Various treatments have been described, e.g. phenytoin, but none have apparently been successful. Most clinically affected horses are euthanized.
See Muscle, Spasm.

N

N-butylscopolammonium bromide see Buscopan®

Nailbind ◀┊ *nā ūl bīnd*, *n.* (in US, 'hot nail') lameness caused by nail being driven in too close to sensitive tissues of the hoof, thereby putting pressure on delicate tissues. Signs include lameness and increased pulse to the foot, often within a few days after shoeing.
See Foot, Lamina.

Nagana ◀┊ *nag ar nē*, *n.* disease found primarily in sub-Saharan Africa, caused by various *Trypanosoma* spp., which are transmitted by tsetse flies. The trypanosomes infect the blood of the vertebrate host, causing fever, weakness, and lethargy, leading to weight loss and anaemia; in some animals the disease is fatal unless treated. This disease is the animal counterpart of human sleeping sickness. The nagana pest disease has had a significant effect on African history, by keeping horses and camels (and thus cavalry and mounted knights and mounted messengers) out of much of Africa; the disease has been credited with stopping the southward advance of Islam at the northern limit of tsetse fly country.
See *Trypanosoma*.

Naloxone hydrocholoride ◀┊ *nal oks ōn / hī drō klor īd*, *n.* a narcotic antagonist. The mechanism of action is not fully understood, but most evidence suggests that the drug competes for opiate receptor sites. The drug causes contraction of the caecum, and so has been used for the treatment of gastrointestinal ileus; it also increases blood pressure, and has been used in the treatment of hypoxic–ischaemic encephalopathy in foals.

Nandrolone ◀┊ *nan dro lōn*, *n.* anabolic steroid drug; has been used in treatment of conditions where tissue healing or weight gain is considered desirable, although limited scientific evidence supports its use. Has also been used as a performance- enhancing agent, although most evidence suggests that it is not effective in this regard for horses.
See Anabolism.

Napier grass ◀┊ *nā pē ē / grars*, *n.* (*Pennisetum* spp., elephant grass, mission grass). Grass species native to Africa, but cultivated in the southern US as a fodder plant. Can accumulate harmful amounts of oxalate.
See Oxalate.

Naproxen ◀┊ *nap roks en*, *n.* a non-steroidal anti-inflammatory agent that has been used for the treatment of musculoskeletal disorders in the horse. It is no longer manufactured specifically for use in the horse, but a generic pill form is available. It was previously available specifically for horses in a sterile solution for intravenous administration and in a powder for oral administration. Naproxen is from the same class of drugs as aspirin and phenylbutazone, but is reportedly superior to either of these drugs in its anti-inflammatory effect. Naproxen is most commonly used in the treatment of muscle soreness in the horse, such as that seen after intense exertion or associated with exertional rhabdomyolysis, and has been asserted to be the drug of choice for back pain by some veterinarians. The margin of safety of naproxen is good. Precautions and side-effects are similar to those of aspirin or other non-steroidal anti-inflammatory agents.

Narcolepsy ◀ɛ <u>nar</u> ko lep sē, *n.* uncommon, incurable sleep disorder, where horse has uncontrolled periods of sleep or muscle relaxation. Described in many different horse breeds. May be hereditary in Suffolk Punch and Shetland pony foals. Signs vary from mild muscle weakness to collapse; pony breeds may lie down. Horses can be aroused from attacks. Diagnosis is based on history, clinical signs, and provocative testing with physostigmine salicylate. Atropine sulphate may be used to treat attacks; however, horses given the drug must be monitored for colic and ileus. Imipramine, an antidepressant drug, is most commonly used for control, but results are inconsistent. Prognosis varies; affected young horses may recover, but adult-onset horses, and those with a possible hereditary predisposition, are likely to be permanently affected. Horses that show signs of drowsiness with a slow head drop to near collapse, but which catch themselves before hitting the ground more commonly suffer from sleep deprivation (e.g. in late-term pregnancy); a diagnosis of narcolepsy should not be made unless all the criteria necessary to make this diagnosis have been fulfilled.

Nares ◀ɛ nă rēz, *n.* nostrils, openings of nasal cavity.
See Nasal, Nostril.

Nasal ◀ɛ <u>nā</u> zūl, *adj.* relating to the nose.
See Nose.

N. amyloidosis see Amyloidosis
N. cavity ◀ɛ <u>nā</u> zūl / <u>ca</u> vi tē, *n.* first part of the respiratory tract, the passage through the nose from the external nares to the pharynx, between the floor of the cranium and the roof of the mouth. Incompletely divided into left and right sides by nasal septum; walls are lined with ciliated, vascular mucous membrane. The nasal cavity warms, humidifies and filters inhaled air; each half contains ethmoturbinate bones that facilitate this action. Contains sensory epithelium in the upper olfactory part that allows for the sense of smell. Divided into dorsal, middle and ventral meatuses. Conditions affecting nasal cavity include

infections (viral, bacterial, fungal), foreign bodies, progressive ethmoid haematoma, tumour.
See Cilium, Ethmoid, Meatus, Mucous membrane, Nares, Nose, Pharynx.
N. discharge ◀ɛ <u>nā</u> zūl / <u>dis</u> charj, *n.* fluid released from nostrils, usually a sign of disease within respiratory tract. Type of discharge varies depending on cause, e.g. serous (watery), mucous, mucopurulent, sanguinous (blood). Food discharged through the nasal passage indicates choke.
See Choke, Guttural pouch, Larynx, Lung, Nostril, Pharynx, Purulent, Sinus.
N. passages ◀ɛ <u>nā</u> zūl / <u>pa</u> si jiz, *n.* passages through which air moves throughout the anterior portion of the respiratory tract, through the nasal cavity.
See N. cavity (above).
N. septum ◀ɛ <u>nā</u> zūl / <u>sep</u> tēm, *n.* division between left and right halves of nasal cavity, made of bone and cartilage, covered in mucous membrane.
N. shedding ◀ɛ <u>nā</u> zūl / <u>she</u> ding, *n.* transmission of pathogen via nasal secretions, e.g. as occurs in viral or bacterial respiratory infections.
See Mucous membrane, N. cavity (above).

Nasogastric ◀ɛ nā zō <u>gas</u> trik, *adj.* referring to the passage from the nose to the stomach.
See Colic, Nasal, Oesophagus, Pharynx, Stomach.
N. intubation ◀ɛ nā zō <u>gas</u> trik / in tū <u>bā</u> shĕn, *n.* passage of a tube through nasal cavity and pharynx, into oesophagus and then down into stomach. Used for administration of medicines or fluids into stomach, or relief of pressure within stomach in some cases of colic. Requires care to ensure turbinate bones of nose are not damaged, and that tube does enter stomach, not windpipe (trachea).
See Colic, Nasal, Oesophagus, Pharynx, Stomach.
N. reflux ◀ɛ nā zō <u>gas</u> trik / <u>rē</u> fluks, *n.* a flowing back; *n.* when nasogastric reflux is seen after passage of a nasogastric tube, it may indicate the presence of a stomach or small intestinal obstruction, or enteritis, e.g. anterior enteritis.
See Enteritis.
N. tube ◀ɛ nā zō <u>gas</u> trik / tūb, *n.* rubber or

silicone tube passed through the nasal passage into the stomach.
See N. intubation (above).

Nasolacrimal duct ◀ *nā zō la̲ kri mēl / dŭkt, n.* narrow tubular canal which carries tears away from the eye, exiting at the mucocutaneous junction on the nasal floor of the external meatus of the nose.
See Lacrimal apparatus.

Nasopharynx ◀ *nā zō fa̲ ringks, n.* musculomembranous tubular structure between the nasal septum and the larynx; functions during breathing, swallowing and vocalizing. Defined dorsally by the floor of the cranium, and ventrally by the soft palate, which contacts with the larynx to form a sealed passage during normal breathing.
See Pharynx.

Natal ◀ *nā̲ tēl, n.* relating to birth, i.e. foaling, or parturition.
See Parturition.

Natamycin ◀ *na ta mī̲ sin, n.* antifungal drug; dilute washes may occasionally be used as topical treatment for fungal skin disease, e.g. dermatophytosis (ringworm), or fungal keratitis.
See Dermatophytosis, Keratitis.

Navel see Umbilicus

Navel-ill see Omphalitis, Omphalophlebitis, Septicaemia, Umbilical.

Navicular ◀ *na vik̲ ū lē, adj.* boat-shaped.
  N. bone ◀ *na vi̲ kū lar / bōn, n.* distal sesamoid bone; bone shaped like a boat's keel, located in horse's foot on distal surface of the distal interphalangeal (coffin) bone. Bone is covered in smooth, hyaline cartilage; deep digital flexor tendon runs over the flexor surface of the bone, separated from it by a fluid-filled bursa. Proximal surface of bone forms part of distal interphalangeal joint. Bone held in place by suspensory ligaments proximally and distally (distal ligament is also called the impar ligament). N. bone can be affected by fractures, infection of the bursa, bursitis, and especially navicular syndrome.

See Bursa, Bursitis, Cartilage, Foot, Ligament, Navicular syndrome, Tendon.
  N. bursa see Bursa.
  N. bursitis see Bursitis
  N. disease see Navicular syndrome

Navicular syndrome ◀ *na vi̲ kū lē / sin̲ drōm, n.* condition of horse's foot causing lameness, usually bilateral, and involving navicular bone and its cartilage, the navicular bursa, the ligaments of the navicular bone, and the deep digital flexor tendon. Cause unknown; most prominent theory is thought to relate to degenerative changes, similar to osteoarthritis, possibly caused by mechanical pressure on area. Previously thought to be caused by disturbances to blood supply to area; this theory has been generally discredited. Commonly seen in horses of all breeds, especially Quarter Horse, Thoroughbred, and Warmbloods, usually at 7–11 years of age. Signs include gradual development of forelimb lameness, often intermittent at first, usually worse on hard ground, usually both sides affected; other signs include stiff gait, stumbling, and pointing toe at rest. Lameness usually made worse following fetlock flexion test or other stress tests (e.g. wedge test). Pressure from hoof testers may reveal soreness, especially in response to pressure over the frog. Degree of lameness is related to extent of bone disease and associated pathology. Diagnosis involves regional nerve block, radiography (changes to bone with altered shape, lucent areas, calcification of soft tissue), scintigraphy, magnetic resonance imaging. Prognosis relates to extent of tissue damage; rest may allow for bone remodelling in young horses in early stages of disease. Treatment with various horseshoes, e.g. egg bar shoe, and non-steroidal anti-inflammatory drugs. Various vasoactive drugs, e.g. isoxsuprine, pentoxyphylline, have been commonly used, although success is limited, and circulatory problems do not appear to be associated with development of the disease. Chronic cases that do not respond to therapy, and which have been appropriately diagnosed, may be candidates for bilateral palmar digital neurectomy.
See Egg bar shoe, Flexion, Isoxsuprine,

Magnetic resonance imaging, Navicular, Nerve block, Neurectomy, Radiography, Scintigraphy.

Neck ◀ᴇ *nek, n.* part of body which connects head to the body. Supported by seven cervical vertebrae and strong musculature. Oesophagus and windpipe (trachea) run along ventral side of neck. Term also used for narrow part of organ suggestive of a neck, e.g. neck of bladder is the narrow part where it enters the urethra.
See Bladder, Oesophagus, Trachea, Vertebra.

Necrobiosis ◀ᴇ *nek rō bī ō sis, n.* death of a cell or group of cells within a tissue. Nodular necrobiosis is one term used to describe an idiopathic inflammatory skin disease, most commonly occurring in the horse's back or girth area.
See Nodular skin disease.

Necropsy ◀ᴇ *nek rop sē, n.* a post-mortem examination performed on an animal.
See Post-mortem.

Necrosis ◀ᴇ *ne krō sis, n.* death of living tissue, as result of disease, lack of blood supply, injury, etc.

Necrotic ◀ᴇ *ne kro tik, adj.* describes tissue where cells are dead or dying; affected with, characterized by, or producing necrosis.
See Necrosis.

Necrotizing ◀ᴇ *ne kro tī zing, adj.* causing, associated with, or undergoing necrosis, e.g. muscle infections with *Clostridium* spp. are characterized by a necrotizing myositis.
See *Clostridium*.

Needle ◀ᴇ *nē dl, n.* slender, pointed metal object. Three main types in veterinary medicine:
- Biopsy n. – slender needle used for removing fluid or tissue samples from the body.
- Hypodermic n. – slender, hollow needle used to introduce medication or withdraw fluids from the body, e.g. for

diagnostic analysis (needle aspiration). Available in many diameters and lengths
- Suture n. – small, slender, steel instrument designed to carry sutures when sewing tissues in surgery and wound repair. Many different shapes and sizes available, some with suture material attached. May have sharp triangular cross-section (cutting needle) which makes it easier to push through tough tissues (e.g. skin), or tapered, round in cross-section, which causes less tissue damage and can be used for suturing less dense, deeper tissues (e.g. muscle, intestine wall, etc.)
See Suture.
N. holder ◀ᴇ *nē dl / hōld ē, n.* surgical instrument, used to hold suture needle.

Negative ◀ᴇ *neg ē tiv, adj.* expressing, containing, or consisting of a negation, refusal, or denial.
False n. ◀ᴇ *fawls /neg ē tiv , n.* a test result that is negative, but actually fails to reveal an existing situation, e.g. disease. For example, a particular test designed to detect equine protozoal myelitis is negative (no evidence of exposure to the disease-causing organism), but the horse does have equine protozoal myelitis.
Gram-n. see Gram stain
N. feedback loop ◀ᴇ *neg ē tiv / fēd bak / lŭp, n.* a biological pathway whereby the presence of adequate amounts of a particular hormone inhibits production of the hormones that control the formation of that particular hormone, e.g. in regulating the thyroid gland, or various reproductive hormones.
N. predictive value ◀ᴇ *neg ē tiv / prid ik tiv / val ŭ, n.* the probability of a negative test result being truly negative; that is, the probability that a horse that tests negative for a disease will actually not have the disease for which it is being tested. Negative predictive value is one assessment of the reliability of a test; the higher the negative predictive value, the lower the number of false negative results. The negative predictive value is calculated as NPV = TN / (TN + FN), where TN and FN are the number of true negative and false negative results, respectively. For example, the Western blot test for equine protozoal myelitis has a high negative predictive value.

Nematode ◀ː *ne mē tōd*, *n.* member of the class Nematoda which includes 12,000 species of unsegmented, worm-like organisms that have a round body and are pointed at both ends; includes the parasitic roundworms of horses, e.g. *Strongylus*, *Oxyuris*, *Parascaris*, etc. See worms under individual entries.

Neomycin ◀ː *nē ō mī sin*, *n.* aminoglycoside antibiotic with bactericidal activity against Gram-negative bacteria; found in many topical medications for horses, such as creams, ointments and eyedrops. Has occasionally been used in foals and adult horses to treat bacterial enteritis; however, significant potential for kidney toxicity limits its enteral use generally.
See Aminoglycoside, Antibiotic, Bactericidal, Bacterium, Enteritis, Gram stain.

Neonatal ◀ː *nē ō nā tl*, *adj.* relating to foal in first month after birth.

N. asphyxia see Asphyxia

N. isoerythrolysis ◀ː *nē ō nā tl / ī sō e ri thrō lī sis*, *n.* (isoimmune haemolytic anaemia, NI) uncommon condition of newborn foals where mare develops antibodies against foal's red blood cells.

CAUSE
NI may occur when the blood type of the mare is different from that of the stallion and the foal inherits the sensitizing red blood cell type from the stallion. Mares become sensitized from foetal blood that is incompatible with the mare's blood type, e.g. secondary to placentitis, difficult birth, or from a previous blood transfusion. Mares usually do not develop sufficient amount of antibodies to cause NI in their foal during the first pregnancy. However, the risk increases with subsequent pregnancies from covering by the same stallion, or by another stallion with the same red blood cell factor. When the foal ingests colostrum that contains antibodies to red cell factors, the antibodies are absorbed into the foal's blood. The antibodies attach to antigens on the foal's red blood cells, and cause rupture of the foal's red blood cells (erythrocyte lysis, which describes the syndrome's medical name, neonatal isoerythrolysis).

CLINICAL SIGNS
Affected foals are normal at birth, but become weak, lethargic, jaundiced, with rapid breathing and heart rate, and may develop seizures.

DIAGNOSIS
Confirmed by a Coombs' test, which shows antibody on the surface of the foal's red cells, and is supported by the presence of anti-red cell antibodies in the mare's colostrum or serum.

TREATMENT
Mild cases of NI may resolve spontaneously; in more severe cases, supportive therapy for the foal is required, which may include blood transfusion until the foal can produce more blood on its own, intravenous fluids, nutritional support, antibiotics and corticosteroids. The foal should be kept in a warm, dry environment that is free from stressful influences, and activity should be limited until recovery is complete. Prognosis varies depending on the extent of the antigen–antibody reaction.

PREVENTION
NI can be treated in two ways. Colostrum may be withheld from the foal of a mare with antibodies to the red cell factors of her foal. The foal is muzzled and the mare's udder is milked out for 24–48 hours. An alternate source of colostrum must be given to the foal to allow for protective antibodies to be absorbed. NI can also be prevented by sending mares only to stallions with compatible blood types, or to stallions that have red cell factors to which the mare is unlikely to develop antibodies, as determined by antibody screening tests.
See Antibody, Antigen, Colostrum, Erythrocyte, Icterus, Seizure.

N. maladjustment syndrome (barker, dummy, wanderer) see Hypoxic ischaemic encephalopathy

N. septicaemia ◀ː *nē ō nā tēl / sep ti sē mē ē*, *n.* sepsis of the newborn foal; especially seen in foals which have not taken in enough colostrum, such as premature foals. *Escherichia coli* has been implicated as the most common organism isolated from septic foals in most recent studies. However, many bacteria have been implicated in neonatal septicaemia; the geographical location appears to be a factor in the occurrence of specific bacteria, and the bacteria involved are often those found normally in the environment or on foal or mare. Risk factors include prenatal risks, e.g. dystocia, premature placental separation, placentitis, prolonged gestation, and colic; postnatal risks include failure of passive transfer, poor hygiene, improper care of the umbilicus, and infections in other areas (e.g. patent urachus). Infection may occur through respiratory tract, intestines, or umbilicus; the idea that the umbilicus is the most important site of entry for infection is questionable. Signs may be vague initially, but include weakness, failure to suckle, and lethargy (e.g. foal spends excessive time lying down). The mare's udder may be full, indicating a failure to nurse; dehydration and hypoglycaemia may become problems owing to lack of intake of milk. Fever may be seen in initial stages of infection; however, the lack of a fever does not mean that a foal is not septic; low temperature is common in septic shock. Mucous membranes in early stages may be red (injected) with decreased capillary refill time; in later stages, membranes may be cyanotic and dark-coloured, with increased refill time. Infection may be found in many body tissues, including lungs (pneumonia), joints (arthritis), brain (meningitis), umbilicus (navel-ill, omphalophlebitis), etc. Diagnosis should be based on history and clinical signs; culture of bacteria from blood confirms clinical diagnosis, but blood cultures are not always positive, even if there is a bacteraemia, and waiting for the culture results prior to treatment may lead to death of the foal. Samples from other tissues (e.g. from joints, windpipe, cerebrospinal fluid, etc.) may also be taken for culture. Blood tests may show elevated or low white blood cell counts (low may indicate infection is overwhelming the foal's ability to make white blood cells), low blood glucose (hypoglycaemia), electrolyte abnormalities and kidney function impairment. Antibiotics are the cornerstone of therapy for neonatal septicaemia; fluid therapy is crucial to provide cardiovascular support. Therapies used to combat endotoxaemia, e.g. flunixin meglumine, must be used with caution in septic foals because they are potentially toxic to the kidneys of foals that may already have renal impairment. Gastric ulceration is common, and can be treated with appropriate agents (e.g. ranitidine, omeprazole); respiratory system impairment often necessitates supplemental oxygen. Other clinical conditions, e.g. diarrhoea, meningitis, septic arthritis, corneal ulceration and coagulopathies, may require specific therapies. Despite aggressive care, foals can deteriorate rapidly; survival rates commonly range from 50–60%. Prevention efforts should be directed at ensuring the mare is healthy, having good hygiene at foaling (e.g. cleansing the mare's udder to reduce bacterial ingestion, proper umbilical care, ideally using chlorhexidine solutions), and ensuring that foal has taken in enough colostrum.

See Arthritis, Bacterium, Cerebrospinal fluid, Colostrum, Glucose, Meningitis, Neutrophil, Respiratory tract, Shock, Umbilicus, Uveitis.

Neonate ◀ _nē_ ō nāt, n. newly born foal, usually up to 1 month of age.

Neoplasia ◀ nē ō _plā_ zē ē, n. abnormal and uncontrolled cell growth; may occur as discrete entities (e.g. tumour) or be disseminated through the horse's system, e.g. lymphoma.
See Lymphoma, Tumour.

Neoplasm ◀ nē ō _plazm_, n. tumour; abnormal growth involving rapid, uncontrolled cell multiplication.
See Tumour.

Neorickettsia risticii ◀ nē ō rik _et_ sēē / ri _sti_ kē ī, n. bacterial species causing Potomac horse fever; Gram-negative coccus.
See Potomac horse fever.

Neospora spp. ◀ nē ō _spor_ ē / spē shēs, n. protozoan organism; has been associated with abortion in mares in US and France. The role of this organism in equine abortions has not been well established.

Neostigmine ◀ nē ō stig mēn, n. drug that blocks the active site of acetylcholinesterase so the enzyme can no longer break down acetylcholine molecules before they reach the acetylcholine receptors. Rapidly metabolized; frequent doses are necessary. May be used in the diagnosis of narcolepsy, to rule out other conditions that cause muscle weakness. May also be used in an effort to stimulate bowel motility, especially after abdominal surgery; in this regard, neostigmine appears to be most useful for conditions of the large intestine, especially for large colon problems.

Neovascularization ◀ː *nē ō vas kū lē rīz ā shēn, adj.* proliferation of blood vessels in tissue not normally containing them, e.g. as in some cases of keratitis or chronic corneal ulceration; term may also be used to describe re-growth of blood vessels in skin grafting.

Nephrectomy ◀ː *nif rek tēmē, n.* surgical removal of a kidney; has been occasionally used as a treatment for ectopic ureter in horses.
See Ureter.

Nephritis ◀ː *ni frī tis, n.* inflammation of kidney. May be acute or chronic; can result in kidney failure if not responsive to treatment. Clinically difficult to distinguish from other causes of acute renal disease, e.g. renal tubular necrosis or glomerulonephritis.
See Kidney, Kidney failure.

> **Chronic interstitial n.** ◀ː *kro nik / in tē stish ūl / ni frī tis, n.* chronic inflammation of the tissues between the tubules of the kidney; can be the long-term result of acute damage to kidney, e.g. from ischaemia, toxins, sepsis, or endotoxaemia. In practice, the term is used to describe essentially all causes of chronic kidney failure in horses other than those related to the glomerulus; confirmed diagnosis can only be made histologically. Treatment is generally unrewarding because of chronic, irreversible changes in kidney tissue.

Nephrolithiasis ◀ː *ne frō li thī ā sis, n.* formation of stones in kidney. Inciting cause may not be known; formation in some cases may be triggered by kidney disease, but then kidney can be damaged further by presence of stone(s). Generally asymptomatic unless stones cause renal obstruction. When clinical signs occur,

signs of poor performance, depression, weight loss and loss of appetite are more common than signs of obstruction, e.g. straining to urinate, blood in urine, or colic. Can result in chronic kidney failure if obstruction unrecognized. Dilated ureters can be recognized on rectal palpation; ultrasound investigation of kidney confirms presence of stones. Most horses in which diagnosis of nephrolithiasis is made are also in chronic renal failure, so successful treatment is rarely possible. If condition is unilateral, nephrectomy may be curative; lithotripsy, using shock waves to fracture the stone, has been described in one horse.
See Kidney, Kidney failure.

Nephron ◀ː *ne fron, n.* any of the many filtering units of the horse's kidney that remove waste material from the blood.
See Kidney.

Nephrosplenic ◀ː *ne frō splen ik, adj.* related to the kidney and spleen.

> **N. entrapment** ◀ː *ne frō splen ik / ēn trap ment, n.* entrapment of the large colon over the nephrosplenic ligament; cause of colic. Horses of all ages and breeds are susceptible; some have suggested that large geldings may be more at risk. Some horses have been managed by sedation and rolling, or administration of phenylephrine to cause splenic contraction; other cases require surgical correction.

> **N. ligament** ◀ː *ne frō splen ik / lig ē mēnt, n.* ligament that suspends the spleen in the abdominal cavity.

Nephrotic syndrome ◀ː *ne frō tik / sin drōm, n.* a group of clinical signs that characterize some cases of kidney disease; protein loss from damaged kidney results in a combination of low blood protein, protein in urine and fluid swelling of limbs or under belly (peripheral oedema: from fluid leaking out of blood vessels owing to reduced colloid osmotic pressure).
See Kidney, Kidney failure, Oedema, Pressure, Protein.

Nephrotoxin ◀ː *ne frō tok sin, n.* substance which is specifically damaging to kidney cells, e.g. plants (red maple, oak), mercury, non-steroidal anti-inflammatory drugs (e.g. phenylbutazone), and some antibiotics (e.g. aminoglycosides).

Nerium oleander see Oleander

Nerve ◀▥ *nerv, n.* a bundle of fibres that receives and sends messages between the body and the brain. The messages are sent by chemical and electrical changes in the cells that make up the nerves (neurons). Some nerves are enclosed within a sheath of protective material called myelin.

Nerve fibres can be classified in a number of fashions:
- Afferent nerves carry impulses from body to central nervous systems, e.g. information about heat, pain, position of legs, etc.
- Sensory nerves are afferent nerves that receive sensory stimuli, such as how something feels, or if something is painful. There are several types of sensory nerve fibres, e.g. mechanoreceptor fibres sense body movement and pressure; nociceptor fibres sense injury and pain.
- Efferent nerves carry impulses from central nervous system to body, e.g. motor nerves which carry impulses that make muscles contract.
- Motor nerves are efferent nerves that allow the central nervous system to send impulses to tissues and organs, e.g. to send impulses that allow for muscle contraction.
- Mixed nerves contain both sensory and motor fibres, e.g. the vagus nerve (10th cranial nerve).

Nerves are also named according to anatomical location, e.g. cranial nerve, radial nerve, palmar digital nerve, etc. Numerous conditions affect nerves, including injury, toxicities (e.g. tetanus), tumours of nerve sheath.
See Central nervous system, Neuron.

Nerve block ◀▥ *nerv / blok, n.* injection of local anaesthetic in the vicinity of a nerve so that the area it supplies loses sensation. May be used to allow surgical operation on an area, e.g. stitching wound, skin biopsy, or for diagnostic purposes, e.g. in examination of the eye, or in diagnosis of lameness, where local anaesthesia of peripheral nerves supplying a painful area may temporarily resolve lameness, indicating area from which pain originates.

Nerve conduction velocity ◀▥ *nerv / con duk shēn / vel os it ē, n.* a test of the speed of signals through a nerve; can indicate nerve damage. Nerve conduction studies are difficult to perform in horses, and are not normally done. When performed, they must be done under general anaesthesia. May be helpful in diagnosis of injuries to major nerves, including facial nerve, radial nerve, or median nerve.

Nerve sheath tumour see Schwannoma

Nervous system ◀▥ *ner vēs / sis tēm, n.* the system of cells, tissues and organs that regulates the body's responses to internal and external stimuli. In horses, and all vertebrate animals, the nervous system consists of the brain, spinal cord, nerves, ganglia and parts of the receptor and effector organs. The three basic functions of the nervous system are:
1. To receive sensory input from, and sense changes in, both internal and external environments. Sensory input can be in many forms, including pressure, taste, sound, light, blood pH, or hormone levels; these inputs are converted to a nervous signal and sent to the brain or spinal cord.
2. Integrate the input. In the sensory centres of the brain or in the spinal cord, the input is integrated and a response is generated
3. Respond to stimuli. The response is a nervous signal that is transmitted to an organ or tissue that then converts the signal into some form of action, e.g. movement, changes in heart rate, release of hormones, etc.

Typically the nervous system is divided into two major components:
- Central nervous system – brain and spinal cord.
- Peripheral nervous system – the nerves extending beyond the central nervous system, serving the limbs and organs,

unprotected by a bony structure (vertebrae or skull). The peripheral nervous system is typically subdivided into two parts:

1. Somatic nervous system – associated with voluntary control of body movements, and receiving various stimuli. In the somatic nervous system:
   - Motor nerves send impulses from the brain and spinal cord to all of the muscles in the body. This permits horses to walk, trot, canter, jump, etc.
   - Sensory nerves send messages in the other direction, i.e. from the muscles back to the spinal cord and the brain. Special sensors in the skin and deep inside the body help the horse tell if an object is sharp, if it's hot or cold, or whether its body is standing still or in motion.
2. Autonomic nervous system – controls involuntary or semi-voluntary functions, such as heart rate, blood pressure, digestion, and sweating.

See Autonomic nervous system, Brain, Cranial nerve, Spinal cord, Spinal nerve.

Nettle ◀≡ *netl*, *n.* the common name for any of between 30 and 45 species of flowering plants, distributed mainly in temperate areas. Most prominent member is the stinging nettle, *Urtica dioica*, native to Europe, North Africa, Asia, and North America. The plants have large green leaves, and stinging hairs. Stinging nettle root has been used as a medicinal plant, for conditions such as internal bleeding, asthma and cancer, as an astringent, and for topical aches and pains, where it presumably acts as a counter-irritant. Stinging nettle leaf has been used as a diuretic and laxative since the time of the early Greeks.

N. rash see Urticaria

Neural ◀≡ *nŭ rŭl*, *adj.* relating to nerves or nerve cells.
See Nerve, Neuron.

Neuralgia ◀≡ *nŭ ral jē*, *n.* pain along the path of a nerve or nerves. Trigeminal neuralgia is thought to be a cause of head-shaking in some horses.
See Head-shaking.

Neurectomy ◀≡ *nŭ rek tē mē*, *n.* surgical removal of all or part of a nerve, e.g. palmar digital nerves may be cut as a treatment to temporarily relieve lameness associated with navicular syndrome.
See Navicular syndrome, Nerve.

Neurofibroma see Schwannoma

Neurological ◀≡ *nŭ rē lo jikēl*, *adj.* relating to the brain, spinal cord, and nerves.

N. disorder ◀≡ *nŭ ro lo jik ēl / dis or dē*, *n.* a disturbance in the structure or function of the nervous system; may occur as a result of a developmental abnormality, e.g. cervical vertebral malformation, disease, viral encephalomyelitis, injury or toxin, e.g. as elaborated by *Clostridium botulinum.*

N. examination ◀≡ *nŭ ro lo jik ēl / ig za mi nā shēn*, *n.* a systematic examination that surveys the functioning of nerves of both the peripheral and central nervous systems. Comprehensive neurological examinations involve examination of body movement, posture and postural adjustments, responses to stimuli, etc.

N. system see Nervous system

Neurology ◀≡ *nŭ ro lē jē*, *n.* branch of medicine concerned with the diagnosis and treatment of disorders of the nervous system.
See Nervous system.

Neuroma ◀≡ *nŭ rō mē*, *n.* disorganized mass of nerve cells and nerve fibres; occasional complication of surgical neurectomy. Painful; may be cause of lameness and require local anti-inflammatory injection, or surgery, for resolution.

Neuromuscular ◀≡ *nŭ rō mus kū lē*, *n.* relating to both nerves and muscles.

N. pedicle graft ◀≡ *nŭ rō mus kū lē / ped ikēl / grarft*, *n.* treatment for laryngeal hemiplegia. Technique involves implanting a strip of neuromuscular tissue into the affected muscle, in an attempt to reinnervate the paralysed cartilage.

Neuron ◀╎ *nŭ rōn, n.* nerve cell; one of the electrically active cells that transmit signals within the brain or nervous system. Neurons are like other cells, in that they have cell membranes, organelles, and carry out basic cellular processes, but they are unlike other cells because they can communicate with each other by electrochemical processes, via specialized structures, and with specialized chemicals (i.e. neurotransmitters). Made up of cell body and one or more processes (extension of cytoplasm); dendrites bring information to the neuron and axons take information away from the neurons. Three types of neuron occur.
- Sensory neurons typically have a long dendrite and short axon, and carry messages from sensory receptors to the central nervous system.
- Motor neurons typically have a long axon and short dendrites and transmit messages from the central nervous system to the muscles (or to glands).
- Interneurons are found only in the central nervous system, where they connect neuron to neuron.

See Brain, Cytoplasm, Nerve, Spinal.

Neuropathy ◀╎ *nŭ rop athē, n.* any and all diseases or malfunction of the nerves.

Neurotoxin ◀╎ *nŭ rō tok sin, n.* substance toxic to nerves: a substance that damages, destroys, or impairs the functioning of nerve tissue, e.g. lead.
See Lead.

Neurotransmitter ◀╎ *nŭ rō trans mit ē, n.* a chemical substance that transmits nerve impulses across a synapse, e.g. acetylcholine or dopamine.
See Acetylcholine, Dopamine.

Neutralization test see Serum neutralization test

Neutropenia ◀╎ *nū trō pē nē ē, n.* abnormally low level of neutrophils in blood, usually seen as result of neutrophils moving from blood to tissues in case of infection or inflammation, e.g. septicaemia, viral infection, etc.
See Neutrophil, Septicaemia.

Neutrophil ◀╎ *nū trō fil, n.* type of white blood cell, produced in bone marrow, with granules in cytoplasm and a segmented nucleus with 3–5 lobes; immature neutrophils have a band-shaped nucleus (they are often called bands). Neutrophils contain tiny sacs of enzymes that help kill and digest microorganisms they have engulfed by phagocytosis. The neutrophil has a lifespan of about 3 days. Important in response to and control of various infectious disease processes. Decayed neutrophils are a major component of pus.

Neutrophilia ◀╎ *nū trō fi lē ē, n.* increase in level of neutrophils in blood. Common in infectious or inflammatory conditions, especially acute bacterial infections; may also be seen in stress, excitement ('stress leukogram'). Neutrophilia with a 'left shift' is where there is an increased level of immature neutrophlils ('bands') that have been released from bone marrow into blood stream in response to demand.
See Neutrophil.

Nevus ◀╎ *nē vēs, n.* a local developmental defect of the skin, with hyperplasia of skin components. May or may not be congenital. Lesions are solitary, and often present at birth, and may appear on any skin surface. Surgical excision is curative.

Newborn ◀╎ *nū born, adj.* describes foal in first week of life.
See Neonate.

Newmarket cough see Equine influenza

Niacin ◀╎ *nī ēs in, n.* vitamin B3 important for energy production in all cells of the horse's body. As with all B vitamins, there appears to be no reason to provide supplementation with niacin; the horse's normal intake and the production by intestinal bacteria appear to provide vast amounts. Niacin can also be manufactured from the amino acid tryptophan in the horse's tissues. Specific deficiencies or toxicities have not been reported in the horse.

Nictitating membrane see Third: T. eyelid

Nidus ◄⁊ *nī dēs, n.* a place or substance in tissue where organisms originate, lodge, and/or multiply, e.g. the umbilicus is a nidus of infection in neonatal horses.

Night blindness ◄⁊ *nīt / blīnd nis, n.* bilateral, congenital, non-progressive retinal disease occurring in Appaloosa horses. Thought to be an autosomal recessive genetic disease. Signs vary depending on severity, from apprehension to total blindness in the dark. Diagnosis based on history, breed, clinical signs. Fundic exam of the retina is usually normal; diagnosis must be confirmed by electroretinography. No treatment.

Nightshade see Deadly nightshade

Nigropalladial encephalomalacia ◄⁊ *nī grō pē lā dē ūl / en ke fō lē mē lā shē, n.* ('chewing disease'). Neurological disorder caused by ingestion of Russian knapweed or yellow star thistle. Toxicity results in necrosis of the substantia nigra and globus pallidus of the brain. Incurable.
See Russian knapweed, Yellow star thistle.

Nitazoxanide ◄⁊ *nīt az oks an īd, n.* an antiprotozoal drug formulated as oral paste, designed to kill the single-celled protozoan parasite *Sarcocystis neurona*, which causes equine protozoal myelitis (EPM). The treatment regimen lasts 28 days. The drug is reportedly 70–80% effective, which is similar to the effectiveness reported with other treatments such as ponazuril or sulphur/pyramethamine. Nitazoxanide is a member of a class of drugs (pyruvate:ferredoxin oxidoreductase inhibitors) that block an enzyme essential for energy production in the parasite. In safety trials, about 25% of horse owners reported one or more suspicious adverse reactions to nitazoxanide. The most commonly experienced adverse effects were fever, reduced appetite, and lethargy/depression. Some of the horses experienced stocking up in the limbs (filling of the limbs) if they were not allowed to exercise. Other, less-reported side effects included worsening of neurological signs, anorexia, diarrhoea, stiffness, and colic. As with some antibiotics, nita-zoxanide can disrupt the normal microbial flora of the gastrointestinal tract and lead to enterocolitis and even death. Nitazoxanide is excreted in faeces, urine and sweat and can cause pale yellow discoloration of urine and sweat in some cases. This is an indication that the drug is being absorbed. With overdoses, nitazoxanide can cause loose stools, decreased appetite, and lethargy. Therefore, accurate dose calculations are essential. Nitazoxanide is not licensed for use in breeding animals.

Nitrate ◄⁊ *nī trāt, n.* salt of nitric acid, commonly used compound in fertilizers. Excessive applications or improper timing of commercial fertilizer or animal wastes on pastures can lead to excessive nitrate levels in grass pastures or the hay produced from it. Naturally occurring nitrate accumulation in water in dry lake beds has also caused death in wild horses. Nitrates interfere with the horse's ability to carry oxygen in the blood. Excessive nitrates in forages can cause reduced feed consumption and growth rates. Nitrate-poisoned horses show clinical signs of suffocation, including laboured breathing, lack of coordination, and blue mucous membranes. The most reliable symptom of nitrate toxicity is a chocolate-brown coloration of the blood. Other signs include diarrhoea, frequent urination and frothing at the mouth. Mildly affected animals can recover spontaneously; methylene blue may be used to treat more severely affected horses (helps reduce methaemoglobin to haemoglobin), along with supportive treatment, e.g. intravenous fluids, blood transfusion, and oxygen therapy.

Nitrofurazone ◄⁊ *nī trō fū rē zōn, n.* one of the most commonly used antibacterial preparations for the treatment of, and control of infections in, wounds of the horse. It is available in an ointment, a liquid, or a powder. A related compound, furazolidone, is available in a spray that is applied to wounds. The presence of blood, plasma or pus on a wound decreases the ability of nitrofurazone to kill bacteria. Some experimental evidence suggests that

nitrofurazone delays the rate of wound healing by 24%. Nitrofurazone cannot be used systemically; that is, it cannot be given orally or by injection because of a wide variety of side effects. Nitrofurazone-based ointments are also commonly used in 'sweat wraps', applied to affected legs in an effort to reduce swelling. The nitrofurazone ointment can be used alone, or is commonly mixed with corticosteroids and/or dimethyl sulphoxide, theoretically to increase the antiinflammatory effect. After the ointment is applied, the limb is wrapped in plastic wrap, covered with a bandage and left for at least 24 hours. The observed effects of the sweat wrap may only be a consequence of the fact that the ointment occludes the skin. There is some concern as to nitrofurazone's ability to cause cancer in laboratory animals. From the fact that there has been long-term and widespread use of the drug with few reported problems, there certainly would appear to be little reason for deep concern over the use of this drug. However, its cancer-causing potential is being investigated.
See Antibiotic.

Nitrogen ◀ː _nī_ trĕ jĕn, _n._ colourless, odourless, tasteless and mostly inert element; makes up 78.1% by volume of Earth's atmosphere. Nitrogen is a constituent element of all living tissues and amino acids. Many important compounds, such as ammonia, nitric acid, and cyanides, also contain nitrogen.
    N. balance see Balance

Nocardia **spp**. ◀ː _nō_ _kar_ dē ē /spē shēs, _n._ a soil saprophyte; rare cause of suppurative or granulomatous tissue infections in horses, most commonly occurring in horses that are immunosuppressed. Common signs include pulmonary and pleural disease, and nodular and ulcerative skin disease. Bacteria have been reported as part of the normal genital flora, and have also been rarely associated with abortion and placentitis in mares. Diagnosis is by cytological and bacteriological examination of samples. Treatment of infections is by drainage of suppurative

lesions and appropriate antimicrobial therapy, especially sulphur drugs.

Nociception ◀ː nok is _ep_ shĕn, _n._ the perception of pain.

Node ◀ː nōd, _n._ small knob, especially a discrete mass of one kind of tissue enclosed in tissue of a different kind, e.g. lymph node, atrioventricular node.
See Lymph.

Nodular skin disease ◀ː _nod_ ū lē / skin / di zēz, _n._ disease of the skin characterized by raised small masses of rounded or irregular shape (nodules). Myriad causes, including neoplasia, e.g. mast cell tumour, parasitic (e.g. cutaneous habronemiasis), viral, bacterial (e.g. glanders), fungal (e.g. dermatophytosis) and idiopathic (e.g. nodular necrobiosis, eosinophilic granuloma).
See individual conditions.

Non-protein nitrogen ◀ː non-_prō_ tēn / _nī_ trĕ jĕn, _n._ (NPN) dietary sources of nitrogen other than protein, e.g. from urea. Unlike ruminants, horses cannot use NPN for protein synthesis. Feed rations containing NPN will have lower-than-expected protein concentrations when fed to horses, since the nitrogen is not available for microbial protein synthesis. NPN does not cause harm to the horse unless fed at extremely high concentrations.

Non-steroidal anti-inflammatory drug ◀ː non-sté _roi_ dl / an tē-in _fla_ mĕ trĕ / drug, _n._ (NSAID) since the early 1970s, when it was discovered how aspirin works, literally hundreds of structurally different compounds collectively referred to as non-steroidal anti-inflammatory drugs have been synthesized. These drugs are generally both anti-inflammatory and analgesic (pain-relieving); they also can be used to control fever. NSAID drugs commonly used in horses include aspirin, phenylbutazone, flunixin meglumine, ketoprofen, diclofenac, meclofenamic acid and naproxen. Most non-steroidal anti-inflammatory drugs commonly used in the horse act in a similar fashion, i.e. they block the conversion of a naturally occurring substance called arachidonic acid to another group of chemicals called prostaglandins. Among their many effects, prostaglandins are important mediators of pain and inflammation in the horse's body. The side effects of non-steroidal anti-inflammatory drugs are also most likely related to their effect on prostaglandins, which are among the most widely occurring chemical compounds in the body. Although rare, side effects are most commonly seen in the gastrointestinal and renal (kidney) systems of the horse; the drugs should be used with caution in horses affected with diseases of these systems. Side effects also occur more commonly in ponies and foals than in adult large-breed horses, and more commonly with oral, as opposed to intravenous, administration. However, given the widespread use of such drugs, the relative lack of problems is a rather remarkable testimony to their overall safety when used appropriately. Importantly, the adverse effects of these drugs are cumulative; that is, using various members of this class of drugs together will increase the potential for adverse effects. Combination therapies of these drugs should be avoided in horses. See Acetylsalicylic acid, Flunixin meglumine, Inflammation, Ketoprofen, Naproxen, Phenylbutazone, Prostaglandin, Stomach.

Norepinephrine ◀⅀ *no rē pin ē frin, n.* (noradrenaline) chemical released from the adrenal medulla of the adrenal glands as a hormone into the blood in response to stimulation by sympathetic nervous system: results in increased heart rate and constriction of blood vessels. Also serves as a neurotransmitter in the central nervous system and sympathetic nervous system. As a drug, norepinephrine increases systolic and diastolic pressure and so is used in critical care units, especially in the treatment of foals affected with neonatal septicaemia (must be closely monitored). See Adrenal gland, Sympathetic nervous system.

Nose ◀⅀ *nōz, n.* the organ of smell and entrance to the respiratory tract. Opens to outside at nostrils. As air passes through nose, it is warmed, moistened and filtered by mucous membrane lining of nose. See Nasal, Nostril.

No-see-um see *Culicoides*

Nosocomial ◀⅀ *nōz ō kōm ē ūl, adj.* term applies to any disease contracted by a patient while under medical care, especially in a hospital setting.

Nostril ◀⅀ *nos tril, n.* either one of the two external openings to the nasal cavity in the nose. Horse has two nostrils, one on each side of nose. Nostrils supported by alar cartilage.
>   **False nostril** ◀⅀ *fawls / nos tril, n.* blind pouch of skin dorsal to the true nostril in the horse; also called the nasal diverticulum.

Notifiable disease ◀⅀ *nō ti fi ē būl / di zēz, n.* disease which, if suspected, must be reported immediately to the relevant government authority. Notifiable diseases vary between countries. In the UK the relevant government authority is the Divisional Veterinary Manager of the Department for the Environment, Food and Rural Affairs. Notifiable diseases of horses in UK are:
- African horse sickness (has never occurred in UK).
- Anthrax (last occurred in UK in 2002).
- Aujeszky's disease (really a disease of pigs – last occurred in UK in 1989).
- Contagious equine metritis (last occurred in UK in 2003).
- Dourine (has never occurred in UK).
- Epizootic lymphangitis (last occurred in UK in 1906).
- Equine viral arteritis (last occurred in UK in 2004).
- Equine viral encephalomyelitis (has never occurred in UK).
- Equine infectious anaemia (last occurred in UK in 1976).
- Glanders and farcy (last occurred in UK in 1928).
- Rabies (last occurred in UK in 1970).
- Vesicular stomatitis (has never occurred in UK).
- West Nile virus (has never occurred in UK).

NSAID see Non-steroidal anti-inflammatory drug

Nuchal ◀ɛ *nū kĕl, adj.* relating to top (dorsum) of the neck.
See Ligament, Neck.

    N. ligament ◀ɛ *nū kĕl / li gĕ mĕnt, n.* strong, fibrous elastic ligament which joins the back of the skull to the withers, allows head to be supported without major muscular effort. See Ligament, Neck.

Nuclear medicine see Scintigraphy

Nucleus ◀ɛ *nū klĕ ĕs, n.* the large, membrane-bound, usually spherical protoplasmic structure within a living cell, containing the cell's hereditary material (as chromosomes), which controls a cell's metabolism, growth, and reproduction.
See Cell, Chromosome.

Nurse mare ◀ɛ *ners / măr, n.* lactating mare who has lost a foal, then used to suckle a foal who has lost its mother.

Nutraceutical ◀ɛ *nū trĕ kū tik ĕl, n.* food or dietary supplement that is believed or purported to provide health benefits. The word was coined in 1989, combining the words 'nutrition' and 'pharmaceutical', in an obvious attempt to attribute drug-like properties to such substances. The benefits of such products have largely failed to be demonstrated in independent scientific investigations, especially in horses.

Nutrition ◀ɛ *nū tri shĕn, n.* process of taking in the food or other substances necessary for growth, health and good body condition. Horses are remarkably adapted to fulfilling their nutritional requirements under normal conditions with access to good quality forage, and clean water.

Nutritional ◀ɛ *nū tri shĕ nŭl, adj.* relating to nutrition.
See Nutrition.

    N. disorder ◀ɛ *nū tri shĕ nŭl / dis or dĕ, n.* disturbance of normal function related to nutrition. Although nutritional disorders do occur, as long as adequate caloric intake is assured they are uncommon. General

malnutrition will result in manifestations of disease of various systems.

N. muscular dystrophy ◀ɛ *nū tri shĕ nŭl / mus kū lĕ / dis trō fĕ, n.* term sometimes applied to muscle degeneration of nutritional cause (see below). The term is inappropriate, as muscular dystrophies in humans are genetically determined.

N. myodegeneration ◀ɛ *nū tri shĕ nŭl / mī ō dĕ je nĕ ră shĕn, n.* (white muscle disease) condition related to dietary deficiency of vitamin E and/or selenium; typified by extensive muscle damage to heart and skeletal muscles. Typically recognized in foals of both sexes, less than 2 months of age, and of any breed. Disease may appear acutely, from cardiac arrhythmias in damaged heart and respiratory muscles, resulting in death from heart and respiratory failure. In older animals, death may occur post-exercise. In less acute cases, skeletal muscle damage results in stiffness, lethargy, swollen painful muscles, weakness, and difficulty swallowing. If heart or respiratory muscles are damaged, rapid breathing and heart rate may be seen. Blood tests typically show muscle enzyme elevations. Diagnosis is based on clinical signs, blood tests, decreased blood selenium levels, and response to vitamin E and selenium administration. For chronic cases, injections of vitamin E and selenium are required, by various routes. Nasogastric feeding and fluid supplementation may be required in affected foals. Prognosis is guarded, especially if foal is recumbent, or condition chronic. Prevention is by assurance of adequate nutritional status of mares, especially in geographical areas where selenium and vitamin E are known to be deficient. Foals in such areas may be given prophylactic injections of vitamin E and selenium.
See Muscle, Selenium, Vitamin E.

N. secondary hyperparathyroidism ◀ɛ *nū tri shĕ nŭl / se kon drĕ / hī pĕ pa ra thī roi dizm, n.* (big head, bran disease, miller's disease) condition where young horse is fed diet high in phosphorus, low in calcium, or both. Parathyroid gland secretes parathyroid hormone to try to raise blood calcium levels, and this stimulates calcium resorption from bone. Signs seen in horses under 2 years of age include thickened bones of skull ('big head'), intermittent lameness, pain in joints,

stiff gait, difficulty chewing. Diagnosis involves analysis of diet, blood tests, radiography. Uncommon in developed countries.
See Calcium, Parathyroid, Phosphorus, Radiography

N. support ◀ *nū tri shē nŭl / sup ort, n.* nutritional intervention in the treatment of disease conditions. Helps to prevent nutrient depletion, promote tissue repair, reduce secondary complications, and increase the chances of successful recovery. Nutritional support is delivered in addition to other necessary therapies. Support may be enteral if disease has not affected the absorptive capacity of the digestive tract; formulas for feeding through nasogastric tubes have been developed. Aspiration pneumonia is an occasional complication. Parenteral feeding, by intravenous infusion, may be required if the gastrointestinal tract is unable to function normally. Sick foals may require nutritional support with mare's milk, or milk substitute (e.g. powdered milk replacement or goat's milk), in addition to other needs.

Nymphomania ◀ *nim fō mā nē ē, n.* excessive sexual desire by a female of a species. True nymphomania does not exist in horses; however, the term has been used to describe conditions where mare remains in heat (oestrus) for longer than normal, e.g. transitional oestrus in early breeding season, aggressive behaviours characterized by sexual behaviour (e.g. squirting urine, or squealing), or behavioural changes caused by hormonal abnormalities associated with ovarian tumours (especially granulosa-theca cell tumour).
See Ovary.

Nystagmus ◀ *ni ctng mēs, n.* rapid, rhythmic involuntary movements of eyeballs. Both eyeballs move together, usually quickly across in one direction and then more slowly back the other way. Two forms:

- Physiological n. – involuntary eye movement induced by sideways movement of the head (oculocephalic reflex).
- Pathological n. – a clinical sign of a lesion in the cerebellum of the brain or the vestibular system, including diseases of the inner ear or vestibulocochlear nerve (cranial nerve VIII). Pathological nystagmus usually only lasts a few days until the brain compensates.

See Cerebellum, Ear, Vestibulocochlear nerve.

Nystatin ◀ *ni stat in, n.* antifungal agent, most commonly used in diluted aqueous solution for the treatment of intrauterine infections caused by fungi.

O

Oak ◀€ *ōk, n.* (*Quercus*) tree, common in UK, acorns or leaves may be eaten by horses when there is little grazing available; most horses appear to not like the taste of oak if adequate forage is available. Digallic acid is the major active metabolite produced by tannins in acorns, stems, buds and leaves; may rarely cause poisoning in horses. Signs of toxicity are dose dependent: include acute, mild to severe colic, straining to defecate, haemorrhagic diarrhoea, elevated heart and respiratory rates, haemoglobinuria, and increased intestinal sounds; sudden death may occur with heavy ingestion. Laboratory findings include azotaemia, hypoproteinaemia, and blood and protein in urine. No specific treatment is available; supportive treatment, including intravenous fluids and evacuation of the gastrointestinal tract, is recommended. Affected horses should be removed from access to oak.

Oat hay ◀€ *ōt / hā, n.* oat plants mowed and dried for use as fodder. Suitable hay for horses; more fibre, less energy and less protein, when compared to legume hay.

Oats ◀€ *ōts, n.* (*Avena sativa*) the most popular cereal grain fed to horses. Higher in fibre and lower in calories than other grains, making them somewhat safer for horses; higher fibre content and lower energy density (on a volume basis, they contain about half that of other grains) makes oats less likely to cause digestive problems or laminitis. Various cooking methods, as well as processing, e.g. rolling or crimping, are of little value to digestibility, except possibly for foals and older horses with poor dentition. 'Heavy' oats contain less foreign material than regular oats; hull-less oats are higher in energy density, but contain less fibre, and are thus less safe to feed.

Obel grade ◀€ *Ō bel / grād, n.* a forelimb lameness scoring system, developed by Niles Obel in the 1940s, that is sometimes used to rate lameness, especially that associated with laminitis, in four different grades.

- Obel Grade 1 horses show frequent shifting of weight between the feet, but no visible lameness at the walk, and lameness in both forelimbs when trotting.
- Obel Grade 2 horses do not resist having a foreleg lifted, nor do they resist walking, but they do show lameness at the walk.
- Obel Grade 3 horses object to the foreleg being lifted, and are reluctant to walk.
- Obel Grade 4 horses will only walk if they are forced to do so.

See Laminitis.

Obese ◀€ *ō bēs, adj.* excessively overweight; the condition of having excessive amounts of body fat. Overfeeding is the most common cause in horses, and the easiest to correct; stabled horses also commonly do not received adequate exercise. Ponies seem to be particularly susceptible, perhaps because their smaller size makes it easier for them to be overfed. In addition, ponies are somewhat different from horses metabolically, which may also predispose them to obesity. Pregnancy causes mares to gain weight, and should be investigated as a possible cause of obesity in mares. Obesity is commonly associated with hypothyroidism; however, horses that have had their thyroid glands

surgically removed get thin, not fat. Other causes of abdominal distension, e.g. bloat, rupture of the abdominal wall, are acute, and easily distinguished. Obesity is not healthy for horses, and can predispose to or aggravate other diseases, including laminitis, hyperlipaemia, colic, osteoarthritis, etc.
See Diabetes, Hyperlipaemia, Hypothyroidism, Laminitis, Osteoarthritis.

Obligate ◀⁇ *ob* lig āt, adj. restricted to a particular set of living conditions, without which an organism cannot survive, e.g. an obligate parasite can survive only by parasitic dependence upon another organism.

   O. aerobe see Aerobe

   O. anaerobe see Anaerobe

Obstetric ◀⁇ *ob* ste trik, adj. relating to a branch of veterinary science that deals with birth, and with the events preceding and following birth; obstetrical procedures are used to help in difficult foalings (dystocia).
See Dystocia, Parturition.

Obstruction ◀⁇ *ob* struk shēn, n. an impediment to passage, operation, or function. Some obstructions that may impact on the horse's well-being include:
- Airway o. – clogging or blocking of the airways. May be as a result of excessive mucus production or bronchospasm, e.g. as with recurrent airway obstruction, or by changes in the physical nature of the airway, e.g., dorsal displacement of the soft palate, or laryngeal hemiplegia (dynamic airway obstruction). See Laryngeal hemiplegia, Recurrent airway obstruction, Soft palate.
- Biliary o. – clogging of the common bile duct, e.g. as seen with cholelithiasis or colonic displacement. Causes icterus, colic, and increase in bile acids. See Bile, Cholelithiasis, Colic, Icterus.
- Intestinal o. – a group of intestinal disorders characterized by interference with the normal passage of ingesta. (Simple obstructions do not interfere with blood flow to the intestines.) Various causes; sometimes

divided into small and large intestinal causes. Causes of intestinal obstruction include impactions with masses of parasites, feed, sand, enteroliths, intestinal masses (e.g. leiomyoma), or adhesions (e.g. as seen from previous colic surgery). Prognosis for recovery from simple obstructions is generally good, whether treatment required is medical or surgical. See various conditions.
- Oesophageal o. – see Choke
- Tracheal o. – airway obstruction caused by disorders of the windpipe (trachea). Inflammatory conditions, compressive lesions (e.g. neoplasia, abscess, especially as occurs with *Streptococcus equi* infection), or foreign bodies may obstruct air passage through the trachea. Treatment is directed at the primary cause.
- Urinary o. – clogging of the urinary tract. Most common cause is urolithiasis; other causes include neoplasia and trauma. Can result in difficulty in urination or signs of colic; complete obstruction can cause bladder rupture. See Urolith.

Obturator ◀⁇ *ob* tŭr ā tē, adj/n. relating to, or near, the obturator foramen (see below). Also, a prosthesis used to close an opening.

   O. foramen ◀⁇ *ob* tŭr ā tē / fo rā mēn, n. large opening in pelvis between pubic bone and ischium, through which muscles and nerves pass.
See Pelvis.

   O. paralysis ◀⁇ *ob* tŭr ā tē / pē ra lis is, n. paralysis of muscles of the hind limb, usually associated with difficulties in foaling (dystocia). Foaling may damage muscles and/or nerves in the pelvic area, resulting in the inability to adduct the limbs. Usually transient; affected horses commonly recover with time.
See Pelvis.

Occipital ◀⁇ *ok* si pi tŭl, adj. related to, near, or within the occipital bone, located towards back of head; e.g. occipital lobe is the hindmost part on each side of brain, occipital bone is an unpaired bone at the back of the skull.
See Brain, Skull.

Ocular ◀⧏ o̱ kū lē, *adj.* relating to the eye. See Eye.

    O. discharge ◀⧏ o̱ kū lē / dis charj, *n.* matter emitted from the eye; commonly accompanies inflammatory conditions of the eye, e.g. corneal ulcer or keratitis.

    O. examination ◀⧏ o̱ kū lē / ig za mi na̱ shēn, *n.* inspecting the eye for disease or abnormality; visual examination may be assisted by various techniques and/or instrumentation, including fluorescein dye, ophthalmoscope, etc.

    O. trauma ◀⧏ o̱ kū lē / tror mē, *n.* injury to the eye.

Oculomotor nerve ◀⧏ o̱ kū lō mo̱ tē / nerv, *n.* paired cranial nerve III. Supplies muscles responsible for movement of eyeball (with cranial nerves IV and VI) and stimulates constriction of pupil (parasympathetic fibres). Damage to nerve(s) may result in abnormal pupillary light reflex or deviation of eye from normal position (strabismus).
See Cranial nerve, Eye, Parasympathetic nervous system, Reflex.

Odontogenic tumour ◀⧏ ō doṉ tō je nik / tu̱ mē, *n.* growth developing from any of tissues which make up tooth, e.g. odontoma arises from dentine, ameloblastoma arises from enamel. Signs include swelling of jaw. Diagnosis involves biopsy and radiographs; treatment involves surgery. Uncommon.
See Biopsy, Tooth, Tumour.

Odontoma ◀⧏ ō̱ don to̱ mē, *n.* a rare, non-neoplastic malformation, consisting at least partially of tooth material, including enamel, dentine and cementum; e.g. dentigerous cysts. Most common in young horses. Signs include swelling of jaw. Diagnosis involves biopsy; treatment involves surgery.
See Biopsy, Dentigerous, Dentine, Enamel, Teratoma, Tooth.

Oedema ◀⧏ i de̱ mē, *n.* abnormal accumulation of watery (serous) fluid in body cavities (ascites) or within connective tissue spaces. Oedema is not a primary disease – rather, it occurs secondary to other problems. Causes include increased permeability (leakiness) of blood vessels (e.g. as caused by inflammation or various toxicities). low blood protein (results in low osmotic pressure of plasma, so fluid is not held within blood vessels and leaks out), obstruction of vein(s), heart failure (resulting from inefficiency of the cardiac pump, with fluid backup), obstruction of flow of lymph (fluid not drained from tissues), etc. Associated clinical signs depend on the underlying pathology, e.g. pulmonary oedema may cause difficulty in breathing. Specific types of oedema include:

- Cerebral o. – swelling of the brain, e.g. as seen with trauma, or hypoxic–ischaemic encephalopathy.
- Malignant o. – an acute, often fatal infection, usually following infection of wound or injection site by an anaerobic toxin-producing bacterium of the genus *Clostridium.*
- Pitting o. – accumulation of serous fluid in connective tissues, whereby tissues develop soft swelling below skin which will retain imprint from finger pressure.
- Pulmonary o. – abnormal accumulation of fluid in the lungs, e.g. as seen secondary to heart failure.

See Heart, Inflammation, Lymph, Pressure, Pulmonary.

Oesophageal ◀⧏ ē so̱ fē je̱ ūl, *n.* relating to the oesophagus.

    O. fistula see Fistula

    O. stricture ◀⧏ ē so̱ fē je̱ ūl / strik tūr, *n.* abnormal narrowing of the oesophagus, commonly as a result of injury. Cause of choke in some horses.
    See Choke, Oesophagus.

Oesophagoscopy ◀⧏ ē so̱ fē go̱ sko pē, *n.* inspection of inside of oesophagus using endoscope. Food should be withheld before procedure. Flexible endoscope is passed thought nostril, through pharynx into oesophagus. May be used to assist in diagnosis of conditions characterized by difficulty in eating, swallowing (dysphagia), or cases of recurrent choke.
See Choke, Endoscope.

Oesophagus ◀⧏ ē so̱ fē gēs, *n.* (gullet)

muscular tube which runs from throat (pharynx) to stomach, dorsal to the trachea, lined by mucous membrane. At lower end a muscular sphincter prevents food from passing from stomach back up oesophagus. Conditions affecting oesophagus include megaoesophagus, inflammation (oesophagitis), stricture, obstruction (choke).
See Choke, Megaoesophagus.

Oestradiol ◀ *ē strĕ dī̄ el, n.* female steroid hormone, the main oestrogen in cycling mares; estradiol 17β is one most commonly measured. Produced by mature follicle of ovary and adrenal gland; stimulates receptive behaviour seen in mare in oestrus. Oestradiol begins to rise about 6 days prior to ovulation, close to the beginning of oestrus. It reaches its peak approximately 2 days before ovulation, and then levels fall. Oestradiol levels are low throughout most of dioestrus. Surges of oestradiol in dioestrus, beginning at about day 6 post-ovulation, are linked to the development of secondary ovarian follicles.
See Adrenal gland, Follicle, Oestrogen, Oestrus, Ovary.

Oestrogen ◀ *ē strē jĕn, n.* group of sex steroid hormones produced by ovary, named for their importance in the oestrus cycle. Produced in ovarian follicle in all mares, and the foeto-placental unit in pregnant mares; specific compounds include oestradiol (most active in non-pregnant mare), oestriol and oestrone sulphate (most active in pregnant mare). Responsible for development of secondary female sex characteristics in developing mares; helps stimulate receptive behavioural displays at oestrus (e.g. winking, urinating) and stimulates cervical relaxation; acts on female reproductive tract to make a suitable environment for fertilization, implantation and development of embryo.
See Adrenal gland, Embryo, Fertilization, Oestrus, Ovary, Placenta.

Oestrone sulphate ◀ *ē strōn sul făt, n.* one of the oestrogen hormones. Main oestrogen produced in pregnant mare,

by developing gonads of foetus. Detection of increased level of oestrone sulphate in serum can be used as pregnancy test from day 70 onwards as a reliable indicator of foetal viability; level of oestrone sulphate drops rapidly following foetal failure.
See Oestrogen, Pregnancy.

Oestrous cycle ◀ *ē strēs / sī kĕl, n.* sexual cycle of mare, recurs approximately every 21 days during breeding season (spring and summer in northern hemisphere). At oestrus, mare is receptive to stallion, will stand to be mated; this period of sexual receptivity may last from 5–7 days. Mare will ovulate in the last 24–48 hours of that period. Ovulation releases the ovum (egg) from the ovarian follicle for possible fertilization. This begins the period of dioestrus, when mare typically rejects stallion's attempts at mating, lasting until the next oestrus. The ovulated follicle leaves a blood-filled cavity, the corpus haemorrhagicum, which then becomes the corpus luteum (CL) as a result of luteinizing hormone (LH) produced by the pituitary gland. About 5 days post-ovulation, the CL actively secretes progesterone, which maintains dioestrus, or, if the ovum is fertilized, maintains pregnancy; this is called the luteal phase of the oestrous cycle. Another hormone produced in the pituitary gland, follicle-stimulating hormone (FSH), normally acts early in dioestrus to produce another ovarian follicle, which commonly regresses. If the mare is not pregnant, around 13 days after ovulation the endometrium of the uterus secretes PGF2α which lyses (destroys) the CL; this allows for oestrous behaviour to resume. FSH activity again increases late in dioestrus, and causes the selection of one or two dominant follicles. These follicles, which are under the influence of increasing levels of oestrogen, will ovulate at the end of the next cycle. When the mare is out of breeding season there is a period where there is no oestrus cycle; anoestrus.
See Anoestrus, Dioestrus, Follicle, Luteinizing hormone, Oestrogen, Ovary, Pituitary, Progesterone.

Oestrus ◄≶ *ē strēs, n.* (heat) period of female sexual cycle when mare is receptive to stallion's mating advances. Signs include frequent urination, lifting of tail, swollen, raised clitoris, or swelling and winking of vulva. Various behavioural changes have been associated with oestrus in mares, and efforts to control such behaviour via hormone therapy are common, especially in performance horses.
See Oestrous cycle.

Oil ◄≶ *oil, n.* liquid fat; common dietary energy supplement for horses. May be added to horse's diet to decrease dust, bind various additives to feed (e.g. vitamins and minerals), or to increase the caloric density of the ration, especially in times of increased caloric requirements, e.g. exercise or pregnancy. Oils provide roughly three times the calories of an equal weight of grain. Also, commonly given to increase lustre of the hair coat; limited evidence for such an effect.

Ointment ◄≶ *oint mēnt, n.* semi-solid preparation, with an oil base, usually containing a medicine, and typically applied topically to the skin or eye as a medicinal remedy or for soothing an irritation, e.g. as in dermatitis or keratitis, respectively.
See Dermatitis, Keratitis.

Oleander ◄≶ *o lē an dē, n.* (*Nerium oleander*) plant common in southern USA and southern Europe. Oleander contains a cardiac glycoside, causing arrhythmia and cardiac arrest. Highly toxic; just 28 g of oleander leaves can kill a 450 kg horse. Signs of poisoning include dullness, dilation of pupils, severe diarrhoea, colic, sweating, heart rhythm disturbances, coma, death. The effects are reversible and the horse may recover if it has ingested a less-than-lethal dose.

Olecranon ◄≶ *ō le krē non, n.* large, curved bony prominence at top of ulna, where it articulates with the humerus; can be felt in horse as point of elbow.
   O. bursitis see Bursa, Bursitis
   O. fracture ◄≶ *ō le krē non / frak tūr, n.* frac-ture of the point of the elbow. Occurs especially in foals; associated with trauma (e.g. being kicked), or falling. Prognosis for repair is generally good, depending on extent of injury. Conservative management, i.e. box rest and full leg splinting, may be suitable for non-articular, non-displaced fractures; others, with more extensive injury, may require surgical repair with bone plates and bone screws.

Olfactory ◄≶ *ol fak trē, adj.* pertaining to the sense of smell.
   O. nerve ◄≶ *ol fak trē / nerv, n.* cranial nerve I. Responsible for sense of smell. Nerve fibres run from lining of nose through the bony cribriform plate at back of nasal cavity to olfactory bulb of front of brain. Damage to olfactory nerve would cause loss of sense of smell, but would be difficult to assess in horses.
   See Brain, Cranial nerve.

Oligodontia ◄≶ *o li gō don shē ē, n.* rare congenital absence of some teeth, most commonly the incisors; may also be seen after trauma or infection to dental germ buds. Diagnosis confirmed by radiography.
See Tooth.

Omega-3, Omega-6 fatty acids ◄≶ *ō mē ga-3(6) / fa tē / as ids, n.* organic molecules composed of long chain (length of which varies between types of fatty acid) of carbon, with hydrogen and oxygen; considered essential fatty acids, because they cannot be made within the horse. A number of studies have shown fatty acid supplementation to be beneficial for pruritic skin conditions in dogs and cats, especially those arising from hypersensitivity reactions; such studies are lacking in horses. May also be recommended for the treatment of renal failure (supplementation may decrease production of fatty acid metabolites during inflammation); have been experimentally evaluated for the treatment of endotoxaemia.
See Fatty acid.

Omentum ◄≶ *ō men tēm, n.* fold of peritoneum (thin membrane which covers organs of abdomen and lines abdominal wall), connects stomach to other organs within abdomen, and provides support for blood vessels. Has lace-like appearance. Divided into two sections:

- Greater o. – the part of the omentum attached to the stomach and to the colon and covering the intestines.
- Lesser o. – the part of the omentum attached to the stomach and liver and supporting the hepatic vessels.

Omeprazole ◀ *ō me pra zōl, n.* chemical that helps prevent the secretion of acid by the horse's stomach. Omeprazole, like other drugs that, collectively, are known as proton-pump inhibitors, blocks the enzyme in the wall of the stomach that produces acid. By blocking the enzyme, the production of acid is decreased, and this allows the stomach to heal. A number of horses in race or show training have been shown to have gastric ulcers. Omeprazole, which is provided in a paste formulation for horses, has been shown to be effective in assisting in healing of these ulcers. For prevention of gastric ulcers, lower doses of omeprazole than are prescribed for treatment appear to be effective. Omeprazole must be specially formulated for horses so that it is not broken down in the stomach and so that it is absorbed in the intestine.
See Equine gastric ulcer syndrome, Stomach.

Omphalitis/Omphalophlebitis ◀ *om fē lī tis /, om fē lō fleb īt is, n.* (navel-ill) infection of remnants of umbilical cord (omphalitis) or the umbilical remnants and associated blood vessels (omphalophlebitis). Occurs in newborn foals, caused by bacterial infection, or occurs along with a more generalized infection. Infection may spread from umbilicus to other areas of body, e.g. joints; joint infection may be the first indication of infection. Signs include swelling of umbilicus, possibly discharge from umbilicus, high temperature and signs of infection elsewhere. Diagnosis involves blood tests (high number of neutrophils), ultrasonography. Although the umbilicus has traditionally been considered as the source of infection in most cases of neonatal septicaemia, most current indications are that the gastrointestinal tract may, in fact, be the most important route of entry. Treatment involves systemic antibiotics and supportive care; surgery to remove the infected umbilical remnants may be indicated in some cases.
See Abscess, Neutrophil, Ultrasonography, Umbilical.

Onchocerca ◀ *ong kō ser kē, n.* (neck threadworm) genus of parasitic worms. *Onchocerca cervicalis* affects horses and causes onchocerciasis. Adult worms live in ligament of neck (ligamentum nuchae); larvae (microfilariae) migrate to skin and cause allergic reaction which can result in itching, hair loss and scaly skin. Transmitted by biting midges (*Culicoides*); microfilariae live under the horse's skin and are picked up by the biting midge when it feeds on the horse. Microfilariae develop into infective larvae in the midge's mouth and are passed when the midge bites a horse. Most horses which have the parasite will not develop the skin condition (onchocerciasis).
See Onchocerciasis.

Onchocerciasis ◀ *ong kō sē kī ē sis, n.* (cutaneous onchocerciasis) skin condition caused by allergic reaction to larvae of *Onchocerca* worms; characterized by hair loss, especially along neck and ventral midline, and itching (pruritis).
See *Onchocerca*.

Onion ◀ *un yēn, n.* plant of the genus *Allium*. Garden onion is *Allium sepa*. Poisoning with wild onions has been a rare cause of haemolytic anaemia in horses.

Oophorectomy see Ovariectomy

Open ◀ *ō pĕn, adj.* not covered (e.g. by a bandage), enclosed, or scabbed over; an operation or surgical procedure whereby the tissues and organs are fully exposed, e.g. an open abdomen during colic surgery.

   O. fracture see Compound fracture

   O. wound ◀ *ō pĕn wŭnd, n.* a wound that is not covered by a bandage; also, a fresh wound.

Ophthalmology ◀€ _of_ thal _mo_ lē jē, _n._ branch of medicine concerned with the anatomy, functions, pathology, and treatment of the eye.
See Eye.

Ophthalmoscope ◀€ _of_ _thal_ mē skōp, _n._ lighted instrument used for examining the inside of the eye. Bright light shines into eye and eye structures are seen by veterinarian, either viewed directly, or through a lens. Two types:

- Direct o. – Most common o. used in veterinary practice; held close to eye, contains light source and has range of small lenses which can be selected in turn to allow the veterinarian to focus on structures at different levels in the eye. Produces magnified image, but has small field of view.
- Indirect o. – uses a convex lens to examine horse's eye, with separate light source held at a distance. Produces less magnified, inverted image; has larger field of view than direct ophthalmoscope. Used primarily for retinal examination.

See Eye.

Opiate ◀€ _ō_ pē āt, _n._ any of various sedative narcotic agents that contain opium or one or more of its natural or synthetic derivatives (e.g. morphine, codeine). Used clinically in the treatment of pain, cough, and acute diarrhoea in humans, but rarely used in horses because of undesirable side effects (e.g. excitement), and short duration of action.

Opioid ◀ € _ō_ pē oid, _n._ a drug or substance that has some properties that are characteristic of opiate narcotic agents, but that is not derived from opium. Specific opioid receptors exist in the horse's body, being found principally in the central nervous system and the gastrointestinal tract. Three types of opioids are naturally produced in the horse's body (e.g. β-endorphin). Use in horses is limited by undesirable side effects and short duration of action; examples of opioid drugs that have been used in horses are butorphanol tartrate (especially for treatment of colic and for

sedation) and fentanyl (especially for treatment of laminitis).
See Endorphin.

Opisthotonus ◀€ o pis _tho_ tō nēs, _n._ a condition of spasm of the back muscles in which head and tail bend backwards and back arches forward. May occur in some conditions affecting brain, e.g. encephalitis or end-stage toxicities, e.g. from bracken fern ingestion.
See Bracken fern, Encephalitis.

Opportunistic ◀€ _o_ por tū _nis_ tik, _adj._ used to describe microorganism (e.g. bacterium, fungus) which does not normally cause disease, but may do so in certain situations, especially when the host's resistance to disease is somehow impaired; e.g. secondary infections in immunocompromised Fell ponies, or infections secondary to placement of catheters or surgical drains.
See Fell pony immunodeficiency syndrome.

Optic ◀€ _op_ tik, _adj._ relating to the eye or vision.
See Eye.

O. disc ◀€ _op_ tik / disk, _n._ approximately circular whitish area in retina at back of eye, where optic nerve enters eye.
See Eye, O. nerve (below).

O. nerve ◀€ _op_ tik / nerv, _n._ paired cranial nerve II. Only has sensory fibres, responsible for vision, transmitting information from retina to brain. Enters skull at optic foramen. Fibres from each optic nerve reach each eye. Damage to, or hypoplasia or degeneration of nerve results in loss of vision; may be assessed by lack of menace response, reduced pupillary light reflex, or fundic examination.
See Cranial nerve, Eye, Menace response, Reflex.

O. neuritis ◀€ _op_ tik / nŭr ī tis, _n._ inflammation or infection of the optic nerve. May be primary, or secondary to other diseases that affect the central nervous system, e.g. parasitism, viral infection, or neoplasia. Treatment and prognosis depends on the underlying cause and the extent of the injury to the nerve.

O. neuropathy ◀€ _op_ tik / nŭr op ēth ē, _n._ rare

proliferative disease, characterized by a mass attached to the optic disc. No effect on vision reported; can be differentiated from other diseases, e.g. neoplasia, by lack of progression, or from infectious conditions, e.g. optic neuritis, by lack of associated clinical signs.

Oral ◀≋ *or rūl, adj.* relating to the mouth. An oral examination is a careful inspection of the oral cavity, including teeth, tongue and associated structures. Complete oral examination usually involves sedation, and the use of an oral speculum.
See Mouth.

Orbit ◀≋ *or bit, n.* eye socket; bony cavity of skull in which eye sits. Muscles which control movement of eye attach to bones of orbit.
See Eye, Skull.

Orbital ◀≋ *or bi tēl, adj.* relating to the eye socket, orbit, e.g. orbital neoplasia is a tumour within the eye socket; orbital abscess is abscess within eye socket.
See Eye.

Orbivirus ◀≋ *or bē vī rēs, n.* one of nine genera in the family Reoviridae, distinguished from the other members of the family by their protein structure and arthropod transmission cycles. Cause of African horse sickness.
See African horse sickness.

Orchitis ◀≋ *or kī tis, n.* inflammation of testis. May be result of injury or, more commonly, the result of infection, e.g. bacterial infection spread in the blood, or autoimmune reaction, e.g. to semen that has been exposed to the immune system secondary to testicular trauma. Signs include pain on palpation, heat from testis, some swelling; diagnosis assisted by ultrasonography. Treatment depends on underlying cause, and typically involves antibiotics and/or anti-inflammatory agents. If condition is not addressed rapidly, loss of testicular function may occur. Unilateral orchitis may be treated by unilateral castration in some cases.
See Testes.

Organophosphate ◀≋ *or ga nō fos fāt, n.* term used to refer to any of a group of chemicals commonly used as insecticides, rodenticides, fungicides, or herbicides; can cause accidental poisoning in horses from absorption through gastrointestinal tract, skin, or lungs. Organophosphates act to inhibit cholinesterase activity, allowing for acetylcholine to accumulate at neuromuscular junctions. Clinical signs are of over-stimulation of the parasympathetic nervous system, skeletal muscles, and the central nervous system; they include salivation and lacrimation, abdominal pain, diarrhoea, sweating, slow heart rate, difficulty breathing, muscle tremors, stiff gait, anxiety, hyperactivity. Can be fatal with sufficient exposure; affected animals can recover from sublethal doses without permanent consequence. Diagnosis by history of exposure, and demonstration of depressed cholinesterase activity in blood. Treatment involves use of atropine sulphate and supportive therapy, e.g. fluids, laxatives, etc., as indicated.
See Acetylcholine, Atropine.

Oropharynx ◀≋ *or ō fa ringks, n.* part of pharynx between back of tongue and epiglottis, bordered dorsally by the soft palate, which contacts the base of the larynx to separate oropharynx from nasopharynx.
See Nasopharynx, Pharynx.

Orphan ◀≋ *or fēn, n.* foal that has lost its mother, e.g. through foaling death or colic. Orphan foals require continuous monitoring, feeding and care, especially during the first month of life. May be managed with a nurse mare, if available.
See Nurse mare.

Orthomyxovirus ◀≋ *or thō miks ō vīr ēs, n.* family of viruses that includes equine influenza virus.
See Equine influenza.

Orthopaedic ◀≋ *or thō pē dik, adj.* pertaining to the musculoskeletal system, i.e. the muscles, bones and joints. Orthopaedic surgery is surgery to this system and its component parts.

Osmolality/Osmolarity ◀ぅ *os mō lal it ē / os mō lar it ē, adj.* terminology associated with calculated and measured osmotic activity; unfortunately, this terminology is often confusing and is not consistent in the medical literature. The selection of which term to use (osmolality or osmolarity) depends on how the concentration was derived.

- Osmolality is a measure of the amount of chemical compounds per litre of solution; as pertains to medicine, especially the concentration of particles in the blood. Plasma osmolality is a measure of the concentration of substances such as sodium, chloride, potassium, and glucose in the blood. Osmolality of serum can be helpful in the diagnosis of medical conditions such as dehydration and shock.
- Osmolarity is a measure of the amount of chemical compounds per kilogram of solvent.

Numerous equations have been used to calculate osmolality or osmolarity and controversy exists in the scientific literature as to which is most accurate. If the concentration of the measured compounds is very low, osmolality and osmolarity are generally considered equivalent.

Osmosis ◀ぅ *oz mō sis, n.* spontaneous net movement of liquid passing though a semi-permeable membrane from a more concentrated solution to a less concentrated solution; osmosis is a physical process that does not require the expenditure of energy. Semi-permeable membranes do not allow movement of the molecules dissolved in the liquid, but allow for free passage of the liquid itself. This process is very important in the balance of fluids in the body, because many biological membranes are semi-permeable. Osmosis provides the primary means by which water is transported into and out of cells, and helps maintain the concentrations of fluid within cells and outside cells within ranges that are compatible with life.

Osmotic ◀ぅ *oz mot ik, adj.* having to do with osmosis.

    O. diuretic ◀ぅ *oz mot ik / dī ūr ret ik, n.* diuretics tend to increase the flow of urine.

When the kidney filters large amounts of a substance that cannot be reabsorbed by the nephrons, e.g. glucose, an osmotic movement of water follows the substance.
See Diuretic.
O. pressure see Pressure

Oncotic pressure see Pressure

Osselets ◀ぅ *o sē lets, n.* colloquial term for inflammation of the periosteum on the dorsal distal surface of the cannon bone (third metacarpal bone) and the joint capsule of the fetlock, sometimes also involving the proximal end of the first phalanx. Most commonly seen in young racing horses as a result of repetitive stress. Signs include swelling of fetlock joint, pain, especially when joint flexed, gradual onset of lameness. Diagnosis is confirmed by radiography. Treatment involves rest, local and systemic anti-inflammatory medications; surgery may be recommended in some cases, if there are associated osteochondral fragments.
See Arthritis, Conformation, Fetlock, Radiography.

Ossification ◀ぅ *o si fi kā shēn, n.* the process of the formation of bone, or conversion into bone, e.g. cartilage undergoes ossification during development of bones. Involves mineral deposition so that tissue is structurally capable of supporting the body. Ossification may also be pathological, and may occur after inflammation of various soft tissues.

Ossifying fibroma see Fibroma

Osteitis ◀ぅ *os tē ī tis, n.* (ostitis) inflammation of bone; often as a result of infection, trauma, or degeneration.
See Bone, Fracture, Pedal.

Osteoarthritis ◀ぅ *os tē ō ar thrī tis, n.* (OA; also sometimes called degenerative joint disease, although osteoarthritis is the preferred term) is joint disease characterized by progressive and permanent loss of cartilage, and characterized clinically by progressive loss of joint function; it is the end result of most severe joint injuries, or joint diseases that have not been, or cannot be, treated adequately. As the disease

advances, soft tissues of the joint (e.g. the joint capsule and synovial membrane), become affected, and the tissue becomes progressively stiffer. As the disease becomes advanced, cartilage loss is seen as a loss of 'joint space' on radiographs; bone spurs (osteophytes) and mineralization of the joint capsule (enthesophytes) may also develop in response to chronic inflammation of the affected tissues. May occur as an idiopathic primary condition; secondary disease to many conditions, including inflammation of the synovial membrane (synovitis) and joint capsule (capsulitis), joint sprain, joint luxations, intra-articular trauma (e.g. chip fractures, joint fractures), osteochondrosis and joint infections. Inflammation within joint causes release of inflammatory mediators, including collagenase, proteinases, prostaglandins and free radicals; many of these substances are released by cytokines. These mediators degrade cartilage and make it easily damaged. Clinically, OA is characterized by lameness in the affected limb, and pain on palpation or manipulation, with reduced movement of the affected joint in more advanced cases. Flexion tests often result in exacerbation of the observed lameness. Clinical diagnosis may be confirmed by radiography, scintigraphy, magnetic resonance imaging; analysis of synovial fluid may be helpful in selected cases. Treatment may involve rest; limiting or altering exercise regimen; cold therapy; injections of the joint with various substances, including corticosteroids, hyaluronan, polysulphated glycosaminoglycan, and interleukin receptor antagonist protein (IRAP™) or stem cells; or systemic administrations of agents such as non-steroidal anti-inflammatory drugs, hyaluronan, and polysulphated glycosaminoglycan. Selected cases may be candidates for surgical arthrodesis. The existence of so many treatment options suggests that none of them is uniformly successful.
See Arthritis, Arthrodesis, Bone, Cartilage, Joint, Lysis, Magnetic resonance imaging, Osteochondrosis, Osteophyte, Radiography, Scintigraphy, Synovial.

Osteoarthropathy ◀ː *os tē ō ar thro pē thē*, *n.* any disorder involving joint and bone, e.g. osteoarthritis.
See Osteoarthritis.

Osteochondritis ◀ː *os tē ō kon drī tis*, *n.* inflammation of bone, joint and cartilage as a result of failure of normal cartilage ossification, resulting in cartilage fragments being retained in the joint, or at the ends of bone.
See Osteochondritis dissecans, Osteochondrosis.

Osteochondritis dissecans ◀ː *os tē ō kon drī tis / di si kanz*, *n.* condition resulting from failure of cartilage to develop normally at junction between articular cartilage and the underlying bone (osteochondrosis). Cartilage becomes thickened and cells within cartilage are cut off from blood supply, so they die. Cracks form in cartilage and bits of cartilage may form into 'flaps', or osteochondral fragments. Part of a group of diseases known together as developmental orthopaedic disease, which also includes wobbler syndrome and flexural deformities.
See Arthroscopy, Cartilage, Cervical vertebral stenotic myelopathy, Developmental orthopaedic disease, Flexural deformity, Joint, Osteochondrosis, Phosphorus, Radiography.

Osteochondroma ◀ː *os tē ō kon drō mē*, *n.* benign growth of bone and cartilage, commonly occurring near the end of long bones. In horses, the term osteochondroma is commonly, albeit improperly, used to refer to outgrowths of bone and cartilage (exostoses) seen most commonly at the caudal cortex of the distal end of the radius, at the level of the closed physis; these growths may be associated with effusion in the carpal canal, pain on carpal manipulation, and lameness. Regional perineural anaesthesia, or intrathecal anaesthesia of the carpal synovial sheath, commonly resolves lameness. Radiography shows exostoses; arthroscopy confirms diagnosis and allows for removal of exostoses, which may penetrate the carpal synovial sheath or impinge on the deep digital flexor tendon. Surgical removal is generally curative. May occasionally occur as features of a rare hereditary condition, hereditary multiple exostosis (HME) where many such growths develop on bones, especially long bones, ribs, and pelvis.

See Benign, Bone, Cartilage.

Osteochondrosis ◀¿ *os tē ō kon <u>drō</u> sis, n.* failure of cartilage to undergo normal development into bone. It is a failure of endochondral ossification, affecting the cartilage of the articular physis or growth plate. In osteochondrosis, failure of normal ossification results in cartilage fragments being retained. Osteochondrosis may result in inflammation of the affected tissues (osteochondritis). When osteochondrosis results in a crack or flap in the joint cartilage, the condition may be referred to as osteochondritis dissecans (OCD); osteochondrosis may also cause bone cysts at the ends of affected bones. Cause of condition not well understood; may involve hereditary factors, rapid growth, dietary imbalances, lack of exercise, or joint injury. Most commonly seen in young horses, especially males. Signs include lameness, fluid swelling in affected joint. Diagnosis includes flexion test (lameness more pronounced after affected joint has been held bent in flexion), radiography, arthroscopy. Surgical treatment may be curative, depending on extent and location of lesion.

See Cyst, Osteochondritis, Osteochondritis dissecans.

Osteodystrophia fibrosa see Nutritional

Osteoma ◀¿ *os tē <u>ō</u> mē, n.* benign tumour of bone. In horses, most commonly seen in jaw bones and sinuses. Clinical signs relate to impingement and swelling caused by tumour, e.g. may block normal drainage from sinus, affect tooth root, push up into eye socket, etc. Surgical removal is generally curative.

See Bone, Sinus, Tooth.

Osteomyelitis ◀¿ *os tē ō mī ē <u>lī</u> tis, n.* inflammation of bone involving outer cortex and inner medullary cavity; usually caused by bacterial infection. Infection may enter bone through penetrating wound, contamination during surgery to repair broken bone, bacteria in blood (especially in foals, e.g. in septicaemia), etc. Signs include lameness, pain, purulent discharge from wound, non-healing wound; horse may occasionally have fever. Diagnosis involves radiography, isolation of causative bacteria from discharge. Treatment involves rest, antibiotics, systemically or locally, and sometimes surgery to remove dead bone tissue.

See Bacterium, Bone, Septicaemia.

Osteopathy ◀¿ *os tē op ē thē, n.* any disease of bone. Also, originally a nineteenth-century system of medicine first proposed by Andrew Taylor Still based on the theory that problems with the musculoskeletal system affect other body parts, and thus cause many disorders that can be corrected by various manipulative techniques. (A similar definition may be also applied to chiropractic, although the particulars of the therapies may differ considerably.) As human medical science developed, osteopathy gradually incorporated all its theories and practices, and discarded its original theories.

See Hypertrophic osteopathy.

Osteopenia ◀¿ *os tē ō pen ēē, n.* a generalized loss of bone; determined radiographically. Most commonly seen with limb disuse, e.g. after prolonged immobilization of limb post-fracture repair, in chronic lameness conditions, or in association with severe neurological damage, e.g. radial nerve paralysis. Decreased weight-bearing causes increased bone resorption and decreased bone formation. Typically worse in younger animals. Rarely results in a clinical problem; bone returns to normal as normal limb use resumes. Generalized osteopenia may rarely be seen, most commonly associated with nutritional disorders, e.g. diets low in calcium, high in phosphorus, or low in vitamin D.

Osteophyte ◀¿ *os tē ō fīt, n.* a small outgrowth of bone which forms around joints or at other sites where there is dete-

rioration of cartilage; secondary problem, formed in response to chronic inflammation. Commonly seen in later stage osteoarthritis, in association with reduced range of joint motion. Diagnosed by radiography.
See Joint, Osteoarthritis, Radiography.

Osteoporosis ◀€ _os_ tē ō por _rō_ sis, _n_. loss of bone mineral matrix, causing bone to become less dense, more fragile, and prone to fracture. Generalized osteoporosis, as seen in postmenopausal women, is not recognized in horses, and the condition is rarely recognized clinically. In general, the term osteopenia is preferred when describing bone loss in horses.
See Bone, Calcium, Osteopenia, Radiography.

Osteosarcoma ◀€ _os_ tē ō sar _kō_ mē, _n_. malignant tumour of bone. Rare in horse, most commonly reported in jaw bones and sinuses. Signs related to tissue destruction and swelling caused by tumour; may invade surrounding tissues and spread by metastasis to other tissues of body. Surgical excision has been attempted, but is rarely successful. Most cases ultimately result in euthanasia.
See Bone, Malignant, Metastasis, Sinus.

Otitis ◀€ ō _tī_ tis, _n_. inflammation of ear. Different parts of the ear may become inflamed; different conditions are described, accordingly.

- O. externa – inflammation of outer ear and external ear canal; may be related to ticks, insect bites, or bacterial infection. Signs include abnormal position of ear, e.g. drooping ear, swelling around base of ear, smell from ear, waxy material discharging from ear or from skin at base of ear, or rubbing ear. Diagnosis of underlying cause may involve examination of ear, including otoscopy, identification of insects in otic discharge, or bacterial culture.
- O. media–interna – inflammation of middle, or middle and inner, ear; disease of adult horses, with no age, breed, or sex predilection. Usually associated with bacterial infection. Unlike other species, spread of infection from outer ear though ruptured ear drum is uncommon in horses; also not commonly associated with guttural pouch infection, although extension of fungal infections (guttural pouch mycosis) has been reported. The origin of middle and inner ear infections is generally unknown, but blood-borne infections, or migration of bacteria up the Eustachian tube are possible culprits. Infection becomes established, and then tends to spread ventrally, which creates chronic inflammation of the tympanic bulla and the stylohyoid bone. This inflammation causes proliferation of bone, with loss of joint space and fusion. Ultimately, the inflamed and infected bone can fracture, and include bones of the hyoid apparatus, resulting in damage to nerves and bleeding into the middle and inner ears. If inflammation extends through the acoustic meatus, meningitis may develop. Signs depend on the extent of involvement, and when the condition is recognized. Unfortunately, many horses are asymptomatic until neurological problems such as loss of balance, head tilt, walking in circles, or repeated flicking of eyes (nystagmus), are recognized. Affected horses may occasionally rub their ears, toss their heads, or show pain on palpation of the ears. Diagnosis may be complicated. Radiographs of the skull may show proliferation of bone, or bone sclerosis of the petrous temporal or stylohyoid bones; however, disease of acute onset may not show radiographic changes. Scintigraphy of the skull may demonstrate inflammation. Otoscopy is difficult in horses, and rarely diagnostic for otitis media–interna. Infusion of a small amount of saline across the ear drum, followed by withdrawal (transtympanic lavage) may allow for a diagnosis based on colour of fluid and presence of bacteria; bacterial culture of the fluid may demonstrate the causative organism. Endoscopy of the guttural pouch may show thickening and proliferation of the stylohyoid bone. Treatment involves prolonged administration of antimicrobial agents (several weeks), ideally

determined by culture. Additional supportive care, e.g. topical medication for corneal ulceration occurring secondary to a paralysed eyelid, may be required. Surgery to remove a portion of proliferative stylohyoid bone prior to fracture has been reported in an attempt to prevent stress fractures and subsequent neurological disease; however, long-term follow-up has so far not been reported. Prognosis is fair for recovery, even with neurological signs, unless secondary meningitis occurs.

See Bacterium, Ear, Endoscopy, Guttural pouch, Otoscopy, Nystagmus, Vestibular apparatus.

Otobius megnini ◀ *ō̱ tō bē ēs / meg nē nē, n.* ear tick. An important pest of livestock and horses throughout the western United States. Heavy infestations can result in skin irritation and rubbing. Infestation in the ears may be associated with severe muscle cramping and contraction, accompanied by prolapse of the third eyelid, sweating, pawing, and colic-like signs. Serum creatine kinase and aspartate transaminase levels may be elevated. Removal of ticks is curative.
See Tick.

Otorrhoea ◀ *ō̱ tō rē̱ ē, n.* discharge from ear, e.g. as occasionally seen in otitis.
See Ear, Otitis.

Otoscopy ◀ *ō̱ to̱ skē pē, n.* examination of ear canal. Cursory examinations are performed using an otoscope, a small, rigid light source. More thorough otoscopy of horse can only be carried out under general anaesthesia, but is still difficult because the ear canal of the horse is long, bony, narrow, and horizontal.

Ovarian ◀ *ō vă̱ rē ĕn, adj.* relating to ovaries.
See Ovary.

    O. hypoplasia ◀ *ō vă̱ rē ĕn / hī pō plā̱ zē ē, n.* (Turner's syndrome) bilateral condition resulting in underdeveloped ovaries, absence of follicles, and ovarian fibrosis. Mares are infertile. Condition has been described in numerous breeds. Affected

mares are often undersized, and have abnormal oestrous cycles, if they cycle at all. Other abnormalities include a small, flaccid uterus and cervix. Caused by chromosomal abnormality, generally an absence of one of the sex chromosomes; affected mares are designated XO. There is no treatment.
See Infertility, Ovary.

Ovariectomy ◀ *ō vă̱ rē eḵ tē mē, n.* (oophorectomy) surgical removal of ovary, e.g. to remove tumour, or bilaterally, to improve attitude and performance. In one study of mares in which bilateral ovariectomy has been performed for behavioural reasons, continuing signs of behavioural oestrus were detected in 35% of the mares.

Ovariohysterectomy ◀ *ō vă̱ rē ō his tē rek tēm ē, n.* removal of ovaries and uterus; rarely indicated in mares. Conditions which may necessitate the procedure include non-resolving pyometra, neoplasia, uterine rupture, or failure of normal development, with accumulations of secretions (segmental aplasia). Requires general anaesthesia; surgery is performed through a ventral midline incision.

Ovary ◀ *ō̱ vē rē, n.* female gonad; produces eggs. Horse has two ovaries, 4–8 cm long, roughly oval or bean-shaped, suspended in abdomen at end of oviducts, the termination of the Y-shaped uterus. Ovaries enlarge during the breeding season, and are smaller in anoestrous. Composed of a fibrous tissue mesh (stroma) in which fluid-filled follicles develop. Each follicle contains an egg (ovum). Ovary undergoes cyclic changes (oestrous cycle) related to development and release of egg and formation of corpus luteum. Ovary also produces the hormones oestrogen and progesterone. Conditions which affect ovaries include tumours (most common is granulosa-theca cell tumour), hypoplasia, and persistent ovarian follicles.
See Corpus, Follicle, Luteinizing hormone, Oestrogen, Oestrous cycle, Oviduct, Pituitary, Progesterone.

Overexertion ◀≋ *ō vē eks er shēn, n.* physical work to the state of exhaustion. Most horses will do this willingly, so prevention requires owner attentiveness, especially in hot or humid weather. Consequences of overexertion may include multiple organ failure, acid–base abnormalities, or rhabdomyolysis
See Exhausted horse syndrome.

Over-reaching ◀≋ *ō vē-rē ching, n.* problem with gait where toe of hind foot catches heel or pastern of front foot on same side. Over-reach boot may be worn on front foot to protect it. Various shoeing and trimming techniques are described to help prevent problem, especially rolling or squaring the toe of the hind foot.
See Gait.

Oviduct ◀≋ *ō vi dukt, n.* (Fallopian tube) one of a pair of narrow tubes through which egg (ovum) travels after it has been released from ovary. Connects to uterus, where ovum can be fertilized. Sperm from stallion travel up oviduct and fertilization takes place here. Fertilized egg then travels to uterus for implantation and development.

Ovulation ◀≋ *o vū lā shēn, n.* release of mature egg (ovum) from follicle of ovary.
See Oestrous cycle, Ovary, Ovum.

Ovum ◀≋ *ō vēm, n.* female reproductive cell or egg; released during ovulation from the ovary. Large cell with a thick, transparent outer membrane. Contains half of the genetic information needed for a viable embryo. Produced in ovarian follicle, and released into oviduct where is fertilized by male reproductive cell, the sperm. If ovum is not fertilized, it dies within 4–36 hours (reports vary) and disintegrates within oviduct; there is one report of fertilization occurring 7 days after ovulation.
See Chromosome, Fertilization, Ovary, Sperm.

Oxalate ◀≋ *oks ēl āt, n.* a salt of oxalic acid; may accumulate in certain plants, e.g. rhubarb. Excessive consumption of oxalates may result in kidney problems, or nutritional secondary hyperparathy-

roidism owing to interference with calcium absorption.
See Nutritional.

Oxfendazole ◀≋ *oks fen dā zōl, n.* anthelmintic drug of benzamidazole group. Occasionally used for treatment of strongyle (*Strongylus* and *Strongyloides*) infections. Several species of small strongyles have been reported to have developed resistance to oxfendazole.
See Anthelmintic, Benzamidazole, *Strongyloides, Strongylus* spp.

Oximetry ◀≋ *ok si mē trē, n.* non-invasive method of monitoring the percentage of haemoglobin that is saturated with oxygen. A pulse oximeter unit has a probe which is attached to a mucous membrane, such as in the nostril. In addition to percentage of haemoglobin saturation, the unit gives an audible signal for each pulse beat, a calculated heart rate and, in some models, a graphical display of the blood flow past the probe. Small, portable pulse oximeters may be used to obtain information about respiration, and to assess the peripheral circulation in horses undergoing field anaesthesia. Unfortunately, oximetry provides a fairly poor indication of the true circulatory status of horses; research has also shown that the accuracy and failure rates vary widely from model to model.
See Colic, Intestine, Oxygen.

Oxygen ◀≋ *ok si jēn, n.* (O_2) chemical element. Colourless, odourless gas; makes up about 20% of the air. Vital for aerobic respiration in mammals, oxygen in the air is breathed into lungs and attaches to molecules of haemoglobin, whereby it is transported to cells of body. Along with carbon and hydrogen, oxygen forms many of the most important molecules of living organisms (organic compounds). Lack of oxygen (hypoxia or anoxia) results in death of cells. For therapeutic purposes, oxygen gas is stored under pressure in metal cylinders; may be administered to horses during anaesthesia, or given to foals as part of neonatal care, especially in horses that suffer from various postnatal problems.

See Haemoglobin, Hypoxic ischaemic encephalopathy.

O. free radical see Free radical

Oxytetracycline see Tetracyclines

Oxytocin ◀ _ok_ si _tō_ sin, *n.* hormone produced by pituitary gland, stimulates muscular contractions of uterus during foaling, and stimulates flow of milk in mammary gland. Synthetic oxytocin may be given to mare in late pregnancy to induce foaling, and to assist in difficult deliveries. After foaling, may be administered to stimulate expulsion of placenta if it has not been expelled in normal fashion, usually by 3 hours post-foaling. Has also been administered to help relieve oesophageal obstruction, i.e. choke.
See Choke, Hormone, Mammary gland, Parturition, Pituitary, Placenta, Uterus.

Oxytropis **spp.** ◀ _ok_ si trop is / spē shēs, *n.*

toxic perennial plant native to the western United States and Canada.
See Locoweed.

Oxyuris equi ◀ _ok_ si _ŭr_ ris / _e_ kwī, *n.* (pinworm) species of parasitic worm which lives in large intestine of horse. Efficient life cycle that does not require migration through any organ tissue; eggs never leave the herd of horses. Female pinworms crawl out of the horse's rectum, deposit eggs and a sticky substance on the perianal region of the horse, and crawl back into the rectum. Infective pinworm eggs are ingested orally. In the colon, larvae develop through several stages; sexual maturity occurs in about 5 months. As horses move, eggs and adults go with them. As adult worms emerge from anus and lay eggs, this can cause irritation of the skin and anus. Signs include rubbing tailhead. Diagnosis by identification of eggs on skin around anus. Treated with commonly used anthelmintics.
See Worm.

P

P-wave ◀≀ *pē-wāv, n.* the initial part of the tracing of the heart's electrical activity, as measured by an electrocardiogram. The P-wave represents the spread of electrical activity over the atrium.

Pacemaker ◀≀ *pās mā kē, n.* **1)** the sinoatrial node – area of heart wall where impulses for regular beats originate; **2)** artificial pacemaker (device which produces impulses to make heart beat regularly) may be used if horse's heart suffers from a severe heart block (where no regular impulses are produced by the sinoatrial node – a bradydysrhythmia). This is very rare in horses.
See Atrioventricular block, Heart.

Packed cell volume ◀≀ *pakt / sel / vo lūm, n.* (PCV) percentage by volume of whole blood which is made up by red blood cells (haematocrit). Test performed by centrifugation of narrow tube containing whole blood sample to which anticoagulant has been added; centrifugation separates blood cells from serum, and packs blood cells into the bottom of the tube (hence, 'packed' cell volume). The volume of packed red blood cells, divided by the total volume of the blood sample, gives the PCV. Because a tube is used, the PCV can be calculated by measuring the lengths of the layers. Normal value in adult horses can vary, depending on altitude at which horse lives, or whether the horse has been recently exercised or stressed; typical adult horse PCV is in range 32–53%. PCV is high in dehydration; in anaemia, it will be low.
See Anaemia, Blood, Dehydration.

Pad ◀≀ *pad, n.* material (e.g. leather, plastic) interposed between the hoof and horseshoe to protect the horse's foot, to reduce impact on the foot, to change the angle of the hoof (e.g. wedge pad), or to prevent debris from accumulating in the hoof. Innumerable permutations of pads exist, and uses appear to be limited only by the imagination of the person employing them.

Pain ◀≀ *pān, n.* unpleasant sensation, ranging from mild discomfort to agony, often associated with some degree of tissue damage. Pain results from stimulation of specific nerve fibres that carry the pain impulses to the brain. Nerve fibres may be stimulated by injury, e.g. trauma or exposure to caustic chemicals, stretching, e.g. as occurs in the intestines in some cases of colic, or heat or cold. Pain-sensitive nerve fibres are not distributed evenly through body, e.g. the cornea is more heavily innervated than the liver. To a certain extent, and in certain circumstances, pain may be thought of as protective, especially as pertains to pain coming from the musculoskeletal system, because a painful sensation may tend to make a horse less likely to use the affected area, and perhaps less likely to further injure it. However, this is not without consequence, as when a horse bears excessive weight on one limb, it may result in breakdown and/or laminitis in the supporting limb.
See Laminitis, Nerve.

Painkiller ◀≀ *pān ki lē, n.* widely used colloquial term for an analgesic medicine given to reduce pain.
See Analgesic.

Palate ◀≀ *pa lēt, n.* upper surface (roof) of mouth, separating the oral and nasal cavities. Two main subdivisions:

1. Hard p. – the relatively hard, bony, anterior portion of the palate.
2. Soft p. – the movable muscular fold, enclosed in a mucous membrane, that is suspended from the rear of the hard palate. The soft palate completely divides the pharynx into oral and nasal compartments. The soft palate normally lies ventral to the epiglottis, except during swallowing, and allows for a direct and unimpeded passage of air through the pharynx when the horse breathes. The position of the soft palate is determined by a group of coordinated muscles that pull against each other. Soft palate may also be affected by conditions such as cysts, hypoplasia, and dorsal displacement.

See Dorsal displacement of soft palate.

Cleft p. ◀﹦ *kleft* / *pa lēt, n.* longitudinal split in roof of mouth, allows contents of mouth to enter nose. Congenital defect seen in foals from failure of roof of mouth to form properly in embryo, causes milk to run out of nostrils and coughing as foal suckles. Surgical repair has been attempted, with limited success.

See Congenital.

Palatopharyngeal arch ◀﹦ *pal at ō far in gē ēl* / *arch, n.* termination of the soft palate that covers the opening to the oesophagus. Displacement of the arch rostrally (towards the nose) has been reported as a congenital anomaly; mild cases may demonstrate respiratory noise at exercise, while more severe cases may have difficulty swallowing, coughing, or nasal discharge of food. Successful treatment has not been reported; severely affected horses may be euthanized.

Palmar ◀﹦ *par mē, adj.* descriptive of the palm of the human hand; the homologous surface of the equine forelimb (the 'back' part of the limb).

P. digital nerve ◀﹦ *par mē* / *dij it ēl* / *nerv, n.* paired superficial nerve that runs down the palmar surface of the horse's pastern, supplying sensation to the majority of the structures in the foot.

P. digital nerve block ◀﹦ *par mē* / *dij it ēl* / *nerv* / *blok, n.* commonly employed diagnostic anaesthetic technique for evaluating lameness. Small amount of local anaesthetic is deposited under skin; block eliminates pain arising from the majority of conditions causing lameness distal to the block site, including pain from navicular syndrome, ligament disease, and pain related to inflammation of the distal interphalangeal (coffin) joint.

Palmar n. ◀﹦ *par mē* / *nerv, n.* large paired nerve located medial and lateral to fetlock, abaxial to the sesamoid bones.

Palmar n. block ◀﹦ *par mē* / *nerv* / *blok, n.* commonly employed regional nerve block used for diagnostic anaesthesia of structures distal to the fetlock, including the pastern and foot. Also known as abaxial nerve block.

See Abaxial, Nerve.

Palpate ◀﹦ *pal pāt, v.* to touch or feel, especially as part of a physical examination of various tissues.

Palpation ◀﹦ *pal pā shēn, n.* touching or feeling, especially to examine the horse's body by touch, feeling for changes in size, hardness of tissues, etc.

Rectal p. ◀﹦ *rek tēl* / *pal pā shēn, n.* examination of the internal organs of the abdominal cavity by palpation, per rectum. Approximately 40% of the contents of the abdominal cavity can be examined per rectum, including the reproductive tract of the mare, various areas of the large and small colon, the border of the left kidney, and the border of the spleen.

Palpebra ◀﹦ *pal pi brē, n.* eyelid. Plural: palpebrae.

See Eye, Eyelid.

P. reflex see Reflex

Pan- ◀﹦ *pan, prefix,* all; including or involving all members.

Pancreas ◀﹦ *pan krē ēs, n.* large gland situated in abdomen near stomach and small intestine (duodenum). Has two glandular functions:

- Exocrine – acinar cells secrete digestive enzymes (pancreatic juice), which enter duodenum and help to break down food. Enzymes include amylase (breaks down carbohydrates), proteases (break down proteins) and lipases (break down fats). The exocrine secretion of the pancreas is alkaline owing to a high concentration of bicarbonate ions secreted by pancreatic duct cells, which helps neutralize stomach acid, and allows for efficient enzyme activity. Secretion is regulated by a hormone, secretin, which is released by the duodenum when fats and proteins are detected.

- Endocrine – produces several important hormones important in regulating metabolism, growth and development, and tissue function, including insulin, glucagon, and somatostatin. Insulin, produced in islets of Langerhans, is involved in regulation of glucose levels.

Disease of the pancreas is not common in the horse. Conditions include pancreatitis and neoplasia.
See Digestion, Enzyme, Glucose, Insulin, Pancreatitis, Small intestine.

Pancreatic ◀ɛ *pan krē a̱ tik, adj.* relating to the pancreas, e.g. pancreatic enzyme is one secreted by pancreas.

    P. duct ◀ɛ *pan krē a̱ tik / dukt, n.* duct conducting pancreatic enzymes to the duodenum; opens into the major duodenal papilla.
    See Pancreas, Papilla.

Pancreatitis ◀ɛ *pan krē ēt i̱t is, n.* inflammation of the pancreas. Acute pancreatitis is characterized by a fulminating syndrome of abdominal pain, gastric distension, and shock; acute disease has also been related to hypersensitivity to parasite migration, accompanied by diarrhoea, weight loss, and coronary band ulceration. Acute pancreatitis is rarely diagnosed in horses, and the prevalence may be underestimated for several reasons. Ante-mortem diagnosis is difficult on the basis of clinical and laboratory findings, the pancreas is not easily visualized by routine surgical approaches to the abdomen, and the pancreas is easily overlooked at necropsy, particularly if gastric rupture has occurred. Chronic pancreatitis may result in weight loss, colic, jaundice, high temperatures; secondary diabetes mellitus

may occur as a consequence of exocrine failure.

Pancytopenia ◀ɛ *pan sī tō pē nē ē, n.* abnormally low levels of all types of cells in the circulating blood, including erythrocytes, all types of white blood cells, and the blood platelets. Rarely seen in horses; may be caused by bone marrow abnormality (e.g. aplastic anaemia), neoplasia, radiation, drug toxicity, etc. Clinical remission in a case of suspected drug toxicity has been reported in one horse after treatment with glucocorticoids, androgens, and broad-spectrum antimicrobials; prognosis for horses with neoplasia is grave.
See Aplastic anaemia, Blood, Bone, Phenylbutazone, Radiation.

Pangola grass ◀ɛ *pan gō lē / gras, n.* aggressively growing tropical to subtropical grass with some tolerance for warm temperate climates, used as forage grass, cover crop, and for erosion control. Although primarily used for grazing, pangola can be made into hay and silage. No toxicity.

Panniculus reflex ◀ɛ *pa ni̱ kū lus / rē̱ fleks, n.* twitching of skin over flank and back caused by contraction of cutaneous trunci muscle, in response to pinprick or prod to back. Absence of reflex may indicate damage to spinal cord. If reflex is present for part of back, level at which reflex stops being present can be used to locate where spinal cord is damaged. Unfortunately, the test is not always reliable; some horses have poorly developed cutaneous trunci muscles, especially in the lumbar region, and these horses may not demonstrate the reflex when tested.
See Reflex, Spinal.

Pannus ◀ɛ *pa̱ nēs, n.* growth of blood vessels on, and growth of connective tissue below, the surface cells of the eye (corneal epithelium), usually as a result of chronic inflammation, e.g. a non-healing corneal ulcer. Also, the overgrowth of connective tissue on a joint surface as a result of chronic inflammation.
See Cornea, Eye, Joint.

Panophthalmitis ◀ *pa nof thal mī tis, n.* inflammation of all tissues of the eyeball; most commonly as a result of injury or infection. Affected eye is commonly painful, and sclera is inflamed and red. Eyelids are typically swollen and held shut (blepharospasm). Uveitis may result in cloudy humoral fluid in eye. Horse may have high temperature if affected by concurrent clinical disease. Prognosis is guarded, even with appropriate treatment (including anti-inflammatory and antibiotic medications, both systemic and topical); cases that do not respond to treatment may require enucleation.
See Eye.

Papilla ◀ *pa pi lē, n.* small, nipple-like projection or elevation, e.g. parotid papilla is fleshy bump on inner side of cheek where parotid salivary gland opens into mouth; lingual papillae (pl.) are elevations of the tongue that contain taste buds. Papillae exist in many anatomical locations; most are microscopic.
See Parotid.

Papilloma ◀ *pa pi lō mē, n.* wart; small, benign tumour of epithelium, such as may be seen on skin, conjunctiva of eye or mucous membrane; may be caused by virus.
See Benign, Virus.

Papillomatosis see Equine viral papillomatosis

Papillomavirus ◀ *pa pi lō mē vir ēs, n.* virus that has been isolated from warts and aural plaques, especially in young horses. The bovine papillomavirus has been suggested as being a cause of equine sarcoid in several studies; however, a causal link has not been established because inoculation of the bovine virus into healthy horses does not cause sarcoids.
See Aural, Equine sarcoid, Wart.

Para- ◀ *pa rē, prefix.* beside, beyond, accessory to, apart from, against.

Paracentesis ◀ *pa rē sen tē sis, n.* surgical piercing (e.g. with needle) of a fluid-filled cavity, in order to withdraw fluid, e.g. from abdomen, thorax, etc. May be performed to obtain sample for diagnosis, or to remove fluid as part of treatment.
See Abdomen, Thorax.

Paraffin see Liquid paraffin

Parafilaria multipapillosa ◀ *pa rē fi lǎ rē ē / mul ti pa pi lō zē, n.* parasitic filarid worm which causes nodules in skin of horse, especially on the head and upper forelimbs. Common in spring and summer in Russia and Eastern Europe, spread by biting flies, probably of *Haematobia* spp. Nodules may bleed profusely ('summer bleeding') and can become ulcerated or discharge pus. Horse does not appear to be affected unless nodules interfere with harness. No treatment is available; fly control may help reduce incidence of disease.

Paralysis ◀ *pē ra li sis, n.* loss of ability to move part (or all) of body, usually as a result of damage to its nerve supply. Damage to specific nerves is associated with characteristic signs that are pathognomonic for the condition, e.g. paralysis of suprascapular nerve causes partial dislocation of shoulder joint and wastage of muscles over shoulder blade ('sweeny'), or radial nerve paralysis, which results in an inability of the horse to extend the affected forelimb, or bear weight on it.
See Nerve, Nervous system, Sweeny.

Parameter ◀ *pē ra mi tē, n.* a measureable characteristic, e.g. blood parameters include red blood cell count, packed cell volume, haemoglobin concentration, white blood cell count. Also, a variable whose measure is related to a quantity or function that cannot itself be measured directly, e.g. blood pressure and pulse rate are parameters of cardiovascular function; the level of glucose in blood and urine is a parameter of carbohydrate metabolism; respiratory parameters include breathing rate and tidal volume.
See Blood, Respiratory.

Paranasal sinus see Sinus

Paraphimosis ◀╎ *pa rē fi mō sis, n.* displaced and ventrally prolapsed prepuce; in horses, the terms paraphimosis, priaprism, and penile paralysis are used almost interchangeably (albeit, from an etymological point of view, inappropriately) to refer to an inability to retract the penis into the prepuce owing to swelling and oedema, usually of both structures. In many cases, it is difficult to determine whether the primary cause of paraphimosis is penile or preputial; in most cases, both areas are involved. Has been observed following the use of phenothiazine tranquillizers, e.g. acepromazine, owing to stasis of blood in the erectile tissues of the penis, following castration, or following injury, e.g. mare kicking stallion. Immediate treatment is indicated, and involves reducing oedema (massage, cold water therapy), manually reducing penis into prepuce, holding the penis in the prepuce with packing material, or circumferential suture around the preputial orifice, and maintaining the moist condition of the penile mucosa with emollient and/or antibiotic creams or ointments. If condition persists for any length of time, gravity causes fluid to accumulate in the penis and may result in urinary obstruction, or permanent inability to retract penis, and/or impotence in stallions.
See Penis, Prepuce, Priapism.

Parapneumonic effusion ◀╎ *pa rē nū mon ik / ef ū̲ zhēn, n.* accumulation of fluid between layers of the membrane lining the lung and the chest cavity (pleura), as seen in cases of pleuropneumonia ('shipping fever') or pneumonia.
See Pleuritis/Pleuropneumonia, Pneumonia.

Parapox ovis virus ◀╎ *pa rē pox / ō̲ vis /vir̲ ēs, n.* inactivated virus that is marketed and sold as an immunostimulant for use in horses 4 months of age or older, especially as an aid in reducing upper respiratory disease, e.g. as caused by equine herpes virus types 1 and 4.
See Equine herpes virus.

Parascaris equorum ◀╎ *pa rēs ka̲ ris / e kwor̲ rēm, n.* (ascarid) rigid, large, heavy para-sistic roundworm found in small intestine of horses. Parasite has direct life cycle (i.e. no intermediate host); adult worms produce huge numbers of eggs, and environment can easily become severely contaminated if problem is unrecognized. Adult worms in intestines lay eggs, which are passed in the faeces, and mature to infective larvae in 1–6 weeks. Larvae are eaten by horse, then hatch and burrow into the walls of the intestine. Larvae migrate via the blood stream to the liver and lungs; lung larvae are then coughed up the trachea to the throat, and swallowed. In the intestines, larvae mature into egg-laying adults.

Signs of infection include lethargy, weight loss (as worms feed on intestinal contents), foul-smelling diarrhoea, colic, liver disease, and pot-bellied appearance. Young horses clinically affected with signs of lung problems, e.g. coughing, fever, pneumonia, bleeding lungs, and respiratory infection damage, should be routinely evaluated for the presence of ascarids. Poor growth and even death may follow severe cases. Adult ascarids living in the small intestine can occasionally cause colic, intestinal obstruction, ruptured bowel, and death. Control is by environmental management, e.g. cleaning pasture, and administration of antiparasitic compounds. Some clinicians have expressed concern that ivermectin-based compounds are less effective in the treatment of ascarid infections than are benzimidazole compounds, but both appear to be effective experimentally.
See Colic, Parasite, Roundworm.

Parasite ◀╎ *pa̲ rē sīt, n.* animal (or plant) which lives on or in body of another (the host) and benefits from doing so, without killing the host. Host does not benefit. Parasites are grouped in various fashions, including by species, or by site of occurrence (e.g. intestinal parasite, skin parasite). Most parasites are obligate, i.e. they cannot survive apart from their hosts, commonly because they have evolved to lose various organs needed to live independently. Many parasites have specialized reproductive systems and complex, multihost life cycles. Parasites affecting horses include:

- External parasites – such as lice, mites (e.g. causing demodectic, sarcoptic and psoroptic mange), stick-tight fleas, ticks.
- Internal parasites – such as round-worms (*Strongylus*, *Strongyloides*, *Parascaris*), tapeworms, lungworm, stomach worms (*Habronema*, *Oxyuris*, *Parafilaria*), liver flukes, bot fly larvae, warble fly larvae, etc.

See parasites under individual entries.

P. control ◀ *pa rē sīt / kon trōl, n.* use of management techniques, e.g. removal of faeces from pasture, and pharmaceutical products, e.g. regular treatment with anthelmintic drugs, to reduce numbers of parasites affecting host. Unfortunately, and in spite of much scientific work into the pathophysiology of parasitic infections and the effect of anthelmintics, very basic questions concerning parasite control remain unanswered, including questions as to whether adult horses need regular treatment at a set interval, and, if so, what variables might be most important in determining that interval.

Parasitic ◀ *pa rē si tik, adj.* related to or caused by parasites.

P. arteritis ◀ *pa rē si tik / art ē rī tis, n.* damage to arteries, especially as caused by *Strongylus vulgaris* larvae.

P. infection ◀ *pa rē si tik / in fek shēn, n.* invasion by and multiplication of parasites in or on the horse's body.

P. myositis ◀ *pa rē si tik / mī os ī tis, n.* primary parasitic infection of muscle, e.g. as cuased by *Sarcocystis* spp., or *Trypanosoma evansi.*

P. pneumonia ◀ *pa rē si tik / nū mō nē ē, n.* primary infection of the lungs with para-sites. May be seen in foals, e.g. as caused by infection with *Parascaris equorum*, or in adults, e.g. as caused by infection with *Dictyocaulus arnfieldi.*

See *Dictyocaulus arnfieldi*, *Parascaris*, Parasite, *Sarcocystis* spp., *Trypanosoma.*

Parasiticide ◀ *pa rē si ti sīd, n.* an agent or preparation used to destroy and kill para-sites, e.g. anthelmintic agents used in the treatment of intestinal parasitism.
See Parasite.

Parasitology ◀ *pa rē si to lo jē, n.* branch of medicine and biology concerned with parasites and the diseases they cause.
See Parasite.

Parasympathetic nervous system ◀ *pa rē sim pē the tik / ner vēs / sis tēm, n.* part of autonomic nervous system, nerves derived from the brain stem and the lower part of the spinal cord. Nerves supply various organs and tissues, including heart, smooth muscle, and many glands. In general, the parasympathetic nervous system acts to oppose the nerves of the sympathetic nervous system (that is, they help rest and digestion rather than promote fight or flight). Stimulation causes constriction of pupils, slowing of the heart rate, increased saliva production, increased digestive action (more enzymes secreted, intestinal motility increases), and blood vessel dilation.
See Autonomic nervous system, Sympathetic nervous system.

Parasympathomimetic ◀ *pa rē sim pē thō mi me tik, adj.* describes substance which mimics action of parasympathetic nervous system, e.g. physostigmine (acts to constrict pupil, increase intestinal motility, etc.).
See Parasympathetic nervous system.

Paratenon ◀ *pa rē ten ēn, n.* the loose connective tissue around a tendon when it is not contained in a sheath. Inflammation of the paratenon may be an occasional cause of lameness in horses; must be distinguished from tendon injury by ultra-sound.

Parathyroid ◀ *pa rē thī roid, adj.* beside thyroid gland (in neck); the parathyroid gland.

P. gland ◀ *pa rē thī roid / gland, n.* gland which lies beside thyroid gland in neck. The gland is responsible for the regulation of calcium in addition to secreting parathyroid hormone, which regulates calcium and phosphorus metabolism.

P. hormone ◀ *pa rē thī roid / hor mōn, n.* (PTH) hormone secreted by parathyroid gland. Important in maintenance of calcium levels in body; secreted in response to low

level of calcium in blood. PTH regulates the level of calcium in the blood by adjusting the activity of bone cells (osteoblasts and osteoclasts) and kidney cells. Through the action of PTH and vitamin D, the body maintains a constant level of calcium in the blood. PTH increases production of vitamin D, increases calcium absorption from intestine, mobilizes calcium from bone, increases calcium reabsorption in kidneys (so it is not lost in urine) and increases urinary phosphate excretion. Excessive secretion of PTH (hyperparathyroidism) is rarely seen; occurs because of imbalance of calcium and phosphorus in diet (high phosphorus, low calcium – nutritional secondary hyperparathyroidism). Excessive hormone causes calcium resorption from bones. Rarely, oversecretion may occur as result of tumour of parathyroid gland or secretion of similar hormone by malignant tumour elsewhere.
See Calcium, Nutritional secondary hyperparathyroidism, P. gland (above).

Paravertebral ◀ɛ *pa rē ver ti brūl, adj.* beside or near the bones of the spine.
    P. nerve block ◀ɛ *pa rē ver ti brūl /nerv / blok, n.* regional anaesthesia produced by injection of local anaesthetic around the spinal nerves where they exit the spinal column, e.g. to produce anaesthesia of the flank prior to standing laparotomy.
See Anaesthesia, Laparotomy, Nerve block, Spinal nerve, Spine.

Parenchyma ◀ɛ *pē reng ki mē, n.* essential functional tissue of an organ, as opposed to the connective tissue and supporting framework.

Parenteral ◀ɛ *pa ren tē rūl, adj.* not involving the alimentary tract. A medicine given by a parenteral route may be given under skin (subcutaneously), into muscle (intramuscularly), into blood stream (intravenously), into abdominal cavity (intraperitoneally), etc.
    P. support ◀ɛ *pa ren tē rūl / sēp ort, n.* intravenous nutrition that bypasses the intestines. Provides energy and protein to animals unable to sustain themselves because of disease, e.g. severe diarrhoea, prolonged

ileus, or intestinal obstruction. Parenteral nutrition of the horse requires considerable time, expense, and expertise, and is best administered in hospital settings.

Paresis ◀ɛ *pa rē sis, n.* weakness; slight or incomplete paralysis, e.g. as seen with injury, especially to limbs, secondary to nerve impingement from tumour growth, post-foaling, or in laryngeal dysfunction. See Ataxia, Brain, Paralysis.

Parietal ◀ɛ *pē rii tl, adj.* relating to the wall of a body cavity or organ.
    P. bones ◀ɛ *pē rii tl / bōns, n.* paired bones which make up sides and roof of cranium (part of skull).
See Skull.
    P. peritoneum ◀ɛ *pē rii tl / pe ri tē nē ēm, n.* the membrane attached to the wall of the abdominal cavity (as opposed to the visceral peritoneum, which is the membrane attached to the abdominal structures).
    P. pleura ◀ɛ *pē rii tl /plūr rē* the membrane attached to the inside of the chest wall (as opposed to the visceral pleura, which is the membrane attached to the lungs etc.).
See Pleura.

Parotid ◀ɛ *pē rot id, adj.* located near the ear; related to the parotid salivary gland.
    P. duct ◀ɛ *pē rot id / duct, n.* duct conducting saliva from the parotid salivary gland; travels with facial artery and vein and winds around the ventral mandible to reach the lateral side of the face, opening at the parotid papilla, adjacent to the second or third upper cheek tooth (2nd or 3rd premolar).
    P. salivary gland ◀ɛ *pē ro tid / sal īv ērē / gland, n.* paired glands that produce saliva, situated just below ear, behind jaw. Largest salivary glands in horse.
See Salivary gland.

Parrot mouth/jaw see Brachygnathism

Pars ◀ɛ *parz, n.* part or portion of a structure, especially of an anatomical structure.

Parturient ◀ɛ *par tūr rēēnt, adj.* relating to giving birth, e.g. parturient mare is one that is giving birth.
See Parturition.

Parturition ◄⁞ *par tŭr* <u>ri</u> *shēn, n.* process of giving birth; foaling. Normally occurs after approximately 11 months of gestation: 320–360 days of pregnancy.

Signs that foaling is about to happen include:

- Enlarged abdomen.
- Hollowing of flank.
- Discharge of yellowish fluid from mammary glands.
- Enlargement of udder, beginning a few weeks before foaling.
- Waxing of teats (exudation of waxy colostrum covers teats) usually up to 2 days before foaling.
- Ligaments around vulva and pelvis relax.
- Milk flow from teats (approximately 4 hours before foaling – if prolonged, colostrum may be depleted, and foal may need supplemental colostrum).
- Restlessness. Pre-parturient mares tend to leave other horses, become unfriendly, show mild signs of colic, may walk their stalls, or otherwise appear uncomfortable, usually within 24 hours of delivery.

Some mares may show none of these obvious signs prior to delivery.

Parturition itself is typically divided into three stages:

Stage 1: contractions of uterus start, cervix widens, mare is restless, with patchy sweating, may appear to have colic. The outer layer of the placenta (allantochorion) bursts and watery yellowish fluid is released from vulva ('breaking water'). Stage 1 ranges from 10 minutes to 6 hours, usually lasting about 1 hour.

Stage 2: the time from rupture of allantochorion until the foal is delivered. The mare lies on her side, and abdominal muscles contract to provide abdominal pressure. The thin white amnion appears at the vulva; if allantochorion fails to rupture, 'red bag' will be presented, which must be ruptured manually to prevent suffocation of foal. Foal is pushed out by abdominal contractions of mare, still covered in membrane (amnion). Normal presentation is with one foreleg positioned slightly ahead of the other, the foal's head positioned on top of the forelegs, the foal's back towards the mare's back, and the foal's hind legs stretched out behind. Any deviation from this position is considered abnormal (dystocia) and requires immediate veterinary assistance. The amnion may remain intact over the foal until delivered, and the foal will break the membrane with its forelegs. However, commonly, if the amnion remains intact, attendant help with the removal of the amnion is given to prevent suffocation. Newborn foal may lie with its hind legs remaining in the mare and the umbilical cord still attached for up to 30 minutes; if this occurs, the mare should not be disturbed. If mare stands, and foal is free of mare, mare will typically begin sniffing and licking foal.

Stage 3: placenta passed. Once passed, the placenta should be checked to make sure that it is intact, since retained portions of placenta can cause severe uterine infection. Stage 3 ranges from 5 minutes to 3 hours (average 1 hour). Any case in which the placenta is retained for more than 3 hours requires veterinary attention to assist in removal.

Foal should stand within an average of 30 minutes from birth, and suck within an average of 1 hour. Foal passes meconium (first stool) in an average of 2 hours, and urinates in an average of 8 hours.

See Allantois, Amnion, Chorion, Dystocia, Mammary gland, Meconium, Placenta, Uterus.

Passive (immunity) transfer ◄⁞ *pas iv* / (*im* <u>ū</u> *nit ē*) / *trans* <u>fĕ</u>, *n.* the transfer of *active* humoral immunity, in the form of antibodies, from one individual to another, especially from mare to newborn foal via first milk (colostrum), but also via serum transfusion. Foals are born immunologically naïve, and thus require antibodies obtained in the mare's colostrum to be able to fight off microbiological pathogens to which they may be exposed in the environment until such time as their own immune system is competent (starting at a few months after birth). Colostral antibodies can only be absorbed through the intestine in the first 24 hours after birth, hence the importance of making sure foals suck vigorously in that time period.

Failure of the newborn foal to receive adequate levels of antibodies via the mare's milk may occur as a result of separation of foal from mare, diseased foal (e.g. hypoxic–ischaemic encephalopathy), or inadequate production of colostrum by mare (e.g. as in fescue grass toxicity). Newborn foals should be tested for adequate passive transfer, normally considered as 800 mg/dl of IgG. Numerous tests are described. If failure of passive transfer has occurred, foal should receive transfer via serum transfusion.

Pastern ◀┊ *pas tēn*, *n.* part of lower leg between fetlock and foot. Conditions affecting pastern include trauma, osteoarthritis ('ringbone', so-named for the bony enlargement of the area in a 'ring' around the pastern), osteochondrosis, and various tendon and ligament injuries.
See Osteochondrosis, Ringbone.

> **P. joint** ◀┊ *pas tēn / joint*, *n.* (proximal interphalangeal joint) articulation between first and second phalanges. May be affected by osteoarthritis, trauma, fractures involving joint (e.g. from turning at high speeds), partial dislocation (subluxation: dorsal subluxation may be congenital in Arabian horses or related to suspensory ligament damage; palmar subluxation may be result of injury to supporting ligaments of pastern or sesamoidean ligaments, e.g. in foals leaping from heights).
> See Ligament, Subluxation.

Pasteurella **spp.** ◀┊ *pas tŭr ē lē / spē shēs*, *n.* species of Gram-negative bacteria. Rare cause of infection in horses; has occasionally been implicated in cases of infective endocarditis or neonatal septicaemia.
See Bacterium, Gram stain.

Patella ◀┊ *pa te lē*, *n.* (knee-cap) large bone in tendon (sesamoid bone) of quadriceps muscle where it runs over front of stifle joint. Articulates with femur in trochlear groove at front of femur; three patellar tendons insert on the tibia. In horse, patella has hook-shaped parapatellar cartilage on medial side. When horse is standing and bearing weight on one hind leg, the parapatellar cartilage on that leg hooks over the medial side of the trochlear groove so that the leg is held in extension without

muscular effort (part of the stay apparatus). Conditions which affect patella include chondromalacia (softening of the cartilage, diagnosed by radiographs or arthroscopy) and fracture (e.g. from direct kick on patella; causes pain, swelling and lameness). Upward fixation of the patella occurs when the patella, or the parapatellar cartilage, gets locked over top of trochlear groove by a patellar tendon. When this occurs, the limb becomes fixed and stretched out backwards: 'locked stifle'. Luxation of the patella occurs when the patella does not stay in trochlear groove; the condition may be congenital or acquired, especially in miniature horses.
See Cartilage, Congenital, Femur, Luxation, Patellar, Sesamoid bone, Stay apparatus, Stifle.

Patellar ◀┊ *pa te ē*, *adj.* relating to, or of, the patella.
See Patella.

> **P. ligament(s)** ◀┊ *pa te lē / li gē mēnt(s)*, *n.* any one of three ligaments, lateral, middle, or medial, that connect the patella to the proximal tibia. Normally, these ligaments allow the horse to lock its stifle, which enables it to stand with little muscular effort. Injection, surgical splitting, or transaction of the medial patellar ligament may be techniques employed to treat upward fixation of the patella.
> **P. reflex** see Reflex

Patent ◀┊ *pā tēnt*, *adj.* open, unobstructed, allowing unobstructed passage, e.g. a patent blood vessel. Also, apparent or evident; a patent infection is one in which the infectious agent can be shown in discharges of the patient, e.g. a patent parasitic infection may be demonstrated by presence of parasite eggs in faeces.
> **P. ductus arteriosus** see Ductus
> **P. urachus** see Urachus

Patho- ◀┊ *pa thō*, *prefix.* relating to disease or suffering.

Pathogen ◀┊ *pa thō jēn*, *n.* a producer of disease, most commonly in reference to a microorganism, e.g. bacterium, fungus, protozoon, virus, etc.
See Bacterium, Fungus, Protozoa, Virus.

Pathogenesis ◀ɛ *pa thō jen isis, n.* the development of a disease; the origin of a disease and the way by which disease develops in the body.

Pathogenic ◀ɛ *pa thō je nik, adj.* able to cause disease.
See Pathogen.

Pathognomonic ◀ɛ *pa thō gnē mon ik, adj.* describes a characteristic which is so obviously a feature of a particular disease that it allows the veterinary surgeon to make a diagnosis based on that characteristic, e.g. inappropriate hair growth is a pathognomonic sign for pituitary pars intermedia dysfunction (Cushing's disease).

Pathologist ◀ɛ *pē tho lēj ist, n.* one who interprets and diagnoses the changes in body tissue that are caused by disease.

Pathology ◀ɛ *pē tho lē jē, n.* a scientific study concerned with causes and nature of disease, and its processes, development, and consequences, i.e. how disease affects structures and functions of body and tissues; the anatomical or functional manifestations of a disease, e.g. the pathology of pleuropneumonia; departure or deviation from a normal condition, e.g. uterine pathology in infertile mares.

Pattern ◀ɛ *pa tn, n.* a definable characteristic relationship, e.g. the distribution or characteristic development of a disease; also, a characteristic routine, e.g. behavioural pattern.

PCR see Polymerase chain reaction

Pectoral ◀ɛ *pek trūl, n.* pertaining to the chest region. Pectoral muscles are the muscles of the chest.

Pedal ◀ɛ *pē dl, adj.* of the foot or feet.
See Foot.
   P. bone see Third: T. phalanx
   P. osteitis ◀ɛ *pē dl / os tē ī tis, n.* poorly defined, controversial, but still commonly diagnosed condition suggesting that observed lameness is as a result of chronic inflammation of third phalanx, presumably secondary to conditions including injury,

bruising, or penetrating foreign body. Diagnosis is commonly made by a combination of the clinical observation of lameness, response to hoof testers, and radiographic interpretation of bone lysis (osteolysis) in the third phalanx (coffin bone). Unfortunately, no particular changes correlate consistently with the clinical condition, and interpretation of the radiographs is subject to tremendous examiner variability (i.e. different examiners may interpret the same radiographs differently). Scintigraphy may assist in the diagnosis of inflammation of structures of the foot, or soft tissues therein.
See Inflammation, Scintigraphy, Third: T. phalanx.

Pediculosis ◀ɛ *pe di kū lō sis, n.* infestation with lice.
See Louse.

Pelvic ◀ɛ *pel vik, adj.* of, or related to, the pelvis.
   P. flexure ◀ɛ *pel vik / fleks ūr, n.* region of the large intestine, where the left ventral colon reflects upon itself to form the left dorsal colon. Common area of impaction (of ingesta, sand, etc.), which may result in colic.
   See Colic, Colon.

Pelvis ◀ ɛ *pel vis, n.* the arch-like frame of bones attached by the sacroiliac ligament to the sacrum of the spine, and with which the hind limbs of the horse are articulated at the hip joints (bony pelvis); forms a rigid girdle at the end of the abdominal cavity. The bony pelvis is made up of three pairs of connected bones:
- Pubis – pubic bones join together at pubic symphysis to form floor of pelvic cavity.
- Ilium – each ilium forms a joint with the sacrum of the spine; the point of the hip is a bony protruberance which can be felt under the skin, and is part of the wing of the ilium (also called tuber coxae).
- Ischium – the point of the buttock can be felt in the muscles of the rump, and is the rear part of the ischium (also called tuber ischium).

Together, the three bones of the pelvis

contribute to the acetabulum, a concave surface of the hip that forms the hip joint with the head of the femur.

Pelvic bones may be fractured, e.g. by trauma; pelvic fractures have also been identified in racing horses, presumably from the effects of hard galloping. Foaling trauma may induce pelvic injuries in mares. Signs of pelvic injury include lameness, swelling over hip area, and pain on palpation. Muscles may gradually atrophy over affected area in the event of fractures; there may be a marked asymmetry between two hip areas, especially when viewed from behind, and especially with fractures of the wing of the ilium.
See Hip.

Renal p. ◀⁞ _rē nūl_ / _pel vis_, *n.* a funnel-like structure of the kidney; the renal pelvis is the outlet in the kidney into which the tubules empty and which connects to the ureter.

Pemphigoid, bullous see Bullous pemphigoid

Pemphigus foliaceous ◀⁞ _pem fi gēs_ / _fō lē a shēs_, *n.* rare autoimmune skin disease, typified by crusting and matting of hair coat. No age or sex predilection; perhaps more prevalent in Appaloosa horses. Lesions typically begin on face or legs, and become more generalized. In some horses, only the coronary band is affected. Other clinical signs include weight loss, fever, lameness and lethargy. Diagnosis by skin biopsy; submitting biopsy with attached crusts is critical for accurate diagnosis. Disease is usually self-limiting in horses less than 1 year of age; in adult horses, treatment is generally difficult and unrewarding. Steroid therapy is a cornerstone of most therapy; chrysotherapy (gold salts) has also been used, but expense is considerable. Most adult cases are eventually euthanized owing to poor response to therapy, and inability to control lesions.
See Autoimmune disease, Biopsy, Blister.

Penicillin ◀⁞ _pe ni si lin_, *n.* the first antibiotic, discovered in 1928. It is a term for a large group of bactericidal antibiotics, originally derived from fungus (_Penicillium_). In common usage, the term penicillin usually refers to the natural penicillin G, which is provided in sterile suspension for intramuscular injection in horses. Penicillin interferes with formation of bacterial cell wall by inhibiting the enzyme that is responsible for forming cross-links, causing death of the cell as a result of inability to resist or maintain osmotic pressure. Active against many bacteria, especially Gram-positive bacteria e.g. _Staphylococcus_, _Streptococcus_ and _Clostridium_. Some bacteria are able to inactivate penicillin by secretion of penicillinase, and so are resistant to the antibiotic. Many penicillins have been chemically altered to increase their ability to kill bacteria. An example of such a drug is ampicillin sodium. Injections of penicillin commonly cause muscle soreness or swelling at the site of injection. Horses can get muscle necrosis and abscesses secondary to large injections of procaine penicillin G. Thus, many clinicians recommend that no more than 15 ml of penicillin be given at any one injection site. Various penicillins are used in horses, including:

- Benzathine p. – penicillin that is absorbed slowly into the circulation after intramuscular injection, and hydrolysed to benzylpenicillin in vivo. Commonly considered a 'long-acting' penicillin; however, studies have shown that the drug offers no advantage over procaine penicillin.
- Benzylpenicillin – the definitive form of pencillin. Given by intramuscular injection; poorly absorbed orally.
- Penicillin G – see Benzylpenicillin (above)
- Potassium p. – potassium salt of penicillin; can be given by intravenous administration.
- Procaine p. – combination of benzylpenicillin with the local anaesthetic agent procaine. The combination helps reduce the pain and discomfort associated with the large volume of penicillin required to treat horses. Reactions to the procaine contained in procaine penicillin are occasionally seen; affected horses typically undergo a transient period of excitement. Procaine penicillin should not be used in competition

horses since the procaine that is added to the suspension of penicillin as an anaesthetic cannot be differentiated from procaine or lidocaine that might be used illegally to desensitize a horse's lower limb.
See Antibiotic, Bacterium, Resistance.

Penicillinase ◀┊ *pe ni si li nāz, n.* enzyme produced by some bacteria which enables them to inactivate the antibiotic penicillin. These bacteria have resistance against penicillin (i.e. penicillin will not be effective as a treatment for an infection with these bacteria). Penicillinase-resistant penicillins have been synthesized, e.g. methicillin; however, there is widespread resistance even to these antibiotics.

Penis ◀┊ *pē nis, n.* organ of the male horse, used for copulation and urination. Made up largely of erectile tissue (tissue which can expand and become firm as a result of increased blood flow into the organ), with central duct (urethra) which carries both semen and urine. When not erect it is normally held within the prepuce. Horses may be affected by penile tumours, e.g. squamous cell carcinoma, warts, and traumatic accidents, especially during breeding activity (e.g lacerations from mare's tail hair, bruising from artificial vaginas, or injury from mare's kick).
See Breeding, Prepuce, Urethra.

Penrose drain ◀┊ *pen rōz / drān, n.* a latex tube used to drain fluid, e.g. Penrose drains may be placed below skin during surgery or wound repair to prevent accumulation of subcutaneous fluid.
See Drain.

Pentazocine ◀┊ *pen ta zō sēn, n.* opioid pain-relieving drug which has been used in treatment of colic. Uncommon; experimental colic models have shown that the drug has little analgesic effect.
See Colic, Flunixin meglumine, Xylazine.

Pentobarbital ◀┊ *pen tō bar bi tol, n.* (pentobarbitone) barbiturate drug, may be used for induction of anaesthesia (given by intravenous injection), or for treatment of convulsions, e.g. as occur in some cases of encephalitis; in large doses may be used for euthanasia.
See Anaesthesia, Barbiturate, Euthanasia.

Pentosan polysulphate ◀┊ *pen tō san / po lē sul fāt, n.* a semi-synthetic polysulphated polysaccharide which possesses anti-inflammatory and anti-arthritic properties, especially in vitro. Said to be chondroprotective (protective of cartilage). Not available in the United States.

Pentoxifylline ◀┊ *pen toks ifi lēn, n.* drug used to improve blood flow in human patients with circulatory problems to reduce aching, cramping, and tiredness in the hands and feet. It acts by decreasing the thickness (viscosity) of blood. It is is thought to work by improving the ability of red blood cells to change their shape (deformability). This effect would theoretically allow blood to flow more easily, especially in the small blood vessels of the hands and feet. In horses, pentoxifylline has been tried for several different uses where circulatory problems are suspected, including laminitis, navicular syndrome, placentitis, exercise-induced pulmonary hemorrhage ('bleeders'), and endotoxaemia. Unfortunately, the drug does not appear to have been very useful in horses in the conditions for which it has been studied. This may be at least partially because in humans it can take 2–4 weeks for the drug to have any effect. Also, in horses, there seems to be tremendous variability in how individual horses absorb the drug, which makes accurate and effective dosing essentially impossible.
See Endotoxaemia, Laminitis.

Peptic ulcer ◀┊ *pep tik / ul ser, n.* erosions or ulceration caused by acid, in any part of the gastrointestinal tract. Severe cases may perforate.
See Equine gastric ulcer syndrome.

Peptide ◀┊ *pep tīd, n.* organic molecule, made up of two or more amino acids. Large peptide molecules are referred to as polypeptides, or proteins.
See Amino acid, Protein.

Per ◄⧉ per, *prefix, prep.* to, for, or by each; for every.

> **P. os** ◄⧉ *per / os* , *adj.* orally; administered through the mouth.
>
> **P. rectum** ◄⧉ *per / rek tēm, adj.* through the rectum, i.e. examination per rectum is a rectal examination; some drugs or fluids may be given per rectum
> See Rectal, Rectum.

Peracute ◄⧉ *per rē kūt, adj.* very acute, sharp, or violent; describes a condition which is extremely sudden in onset.

Percussion ◄⧉ *per ku shēn, n.* diagnostic technique, involves tapping or striking the surface of the body and listening to sound produced, or feeling the sensation given to the fingers, in order to try to learn about the condition of the parts underneath, e.g. gas distension in the large intestines may produce an audible 'ping' when the abdomen is percussed; normal sinus is full of air and produces a resonant sound; if there is fluid in the sinus there may be a dullness detectable by percussion.
See Thorax.

Percutaneous ◄⧉ *per kū tā nē ēs, adj.* passed, done, or effected through the skin, e.g. percutaneous fine needle aspiration biopsy of a lymph node is performed by inserting needle through the skin into the lymph node.
See Biopsy, Lymph, Skin.

Perforation ◄⧉ *per for rā shēn, n.* development of hole(s) in an anatomical structure, e.g. perforation of intestine may occur when a sharp foreign body is swallowed and pierces the intestine wall.
See Intestines.

Performance ◄⧉ *per for mēns, n.* the way in which a horse does its job, judged by the success at which it carries out the discipline in which it participates, e.g. racing, jumping, dressage, endurance, etc. Complaints of poor performance are among the most common encountered in equine medicine; such complaints may have components that are both physiological, and pertain mostly to the horse (e.g. health, training, genetics, size, strength, diet, etc.), and psychological, and pertain to the horse as well as the rider (e.g. nervous horses, competition anxiety on the part of the owner, owner's unrealistic expectations, etc.). Some complaints of poor performance occur in the absence of clinical disease, and such complaints may be affected by almost any intervention in that they address the owner's concerns, even if there is no problem in the horse. Subtle performance problems may only occur during particular situations, e.g. jumping, or when gait is collected (e.g. as in certain dressage movements), which may complicate evaluation; some horses with performance problems may have multiple abnormalities. A typical clinical approach to diagnosis would include a thorough history, comprehensive physical examination, and laboratory evaluation. Lameness examination, exercise testing and endoscopic examination of the airway may also be helpful in establishing a diagnosis in some cases.

Pergolide mesylate ◄⧉ *per gol īd / mes ē lāt, n.* in humans, pergolide is commonly prescribed along with another medication to treat the symptoms of Parkinson's disease. Pergolide is in a class of medications called dopamine agonists. It works by acting in place of dopamine, a natural substance in the brain that is needed to control movement. In horses, pergolide has found widespread use in the treatment of pituitary pars intermedia dysfunction, a disorder of the equine pituitary gland. One of the problems in this disease is a loss of nerve function associated with dopamine, so giving drugs that improve the action of dopamine makes sense in these horses. Adverse effects of pergolide, such as loss of appetite, diarrhoea and colic are occasionally seen, but usually only when higher doses of the drug are given.
See Pituitary pars intermedia dysfunction.

Periapical ◄⧉ *pe ri ā pi kēl, adj.* pertaining to the tissues around the tip (apex) of tooth root, e.g. pus around tip of tooth root can be seen on radiograph as periapical 'halo' (bright area where bone has become thin or lost).
See Tooth.

Periarticular ◀┊ *pe ri ar ti kū lē, adj.* surrounding a joint, e.g. the periarticular tissues include the joint capsule and the synovial membrane.

Pericardial ◀┊ *pe ri kar dē ūl, adj.* of or pertaining to the pericardium; situated around the heart.

    P. effusion ◀┊ *pe ri kar dē ūl / ef ū zhēn, n.* collection of fluid or blood in the pericardial space (inside the pericardial sac), around the heart. Causes may include congestive heart failure and neoplasia, e.g. lymphosarcoma. Can be detected with ultrasound.

    P. fluid ◀┊ *pe ri kar dē ūl / flū id, n.* a watery, pale yellow fluid normally contained in the pericardium.

    P. sac ◀┊ *pe ri kar dē ūl/ sak, n.* the tough fibrous membrane that surrounds and protects the heart; pericardium.

Pericarditis ◀┊ *pe ri kar dī tis, n.* inflammation of pericardial sac (pericardium) which surrounds heart. Uncommon in horses. Various causes, including viral or bacterial infection, trauma, idiopathic (possibly immune-mediated, as is seen in humans), and tumour (e.g. mesothelioma, lymphosarcoma). Typically accompanied by fluid build-up in sac (pericardial effusion), which restricts movement of heart wall (tamponade); sac itself may become thickened and restrict heart movement. Clinical history usually includes recent respiratory tract infection. Clinical signs in affected horses include signs of systemic illness, e.g. fever, depression, anorexia, rapid breathing (tachypnoea), colic, weight loss, and ventral oedema. If there is restriction of heart muscle movement, additional signs may include muffled heart sounds, friction rubs, and jugular vein distension. Laboratory findings, if abnormal, may include elevated white blood cell counts, and elevated fibrinogen. Echocardiography is diagnostic; pericardial fluid samples may be obtained (pericardiocentesis) to establish the cause under ultrasound guidance. Treatment varies as to the cause and the duration of the problem; acute infectious cases that can be treated with antibiotics carry a better prognosis than do long-standing cases with chronic fibrin accumulation. The prognosis for neoplastic conditions is grave.

See Echocardiography, Electrocardiography, Heart, Oedema, Pericardium.

Pericardium ◀┊ *pe ri kar dē ēm, n.* tough membrane which loosely encloses heart, large veins, and arteries as they emerge from or enter heart. Has double inner serous coat (secretes a lubricating fluid to help heart move smoothly), one layer closely adhered to the heart, and the other on the inside of an outer fibrous layer.

See Heart, Pericarditis.

Perinatal ◀┊ *pe ri nā tl, adj.* occuring around the time of giving birth, foaling (just before or just afterwards).

See Parturition.

    P. asphyxia syndrome see Hypoxic ischaemic encephalopathy

Perineal ◀┊ *pe ri nē ūl, adj.* relating to the perineum.

    P. laceration ◀┊ *pe ri nē ūl / la ser ā shēn, n.* foaling injury, caused by foal's limb perforating tissue, and tearing tissue as foal is delivered at birth. Typically classified according to the degree of tissue damage:

- First degree p. laceration – tearing of the vulvar lips, involving only the skin and mucous membranes. Can be repaired immediately, using a Caslick's procedure, or left to heal if not extensive.
- Second degree p. laceration – tearing of the vulvar lips, through deeper tissues, including the vulvar musculature and body of the perineum; causes pneumovagina and inability to close vulva. Significant tissue bruising and oedema usually preclude an immediate surgical repair. After oedema and inflammation resolve, successful surgical repair can be effected.
- Third degree p. laceration – lacerations that damage all previously noted tissues, as well as vaginal roof, rectal floor, and the perineal tissues that lie between the vagina and rectum. Tissue trauma, faecal contamination of the vaginal vault, oedema and swelling preclude immediate surgical repair. After tissue healing has occurred the extent of tissue damage is assessed, and repair may be attempted.

Repair can be difficult, and multiple attempts may be required. Faeces must be kept soft for successful repair to occur. Some cases may result in infertility owing to extensive damage to reproductive tract; anal function may never be normal owing to disruption of muscular anal ring. In some cases, foal's foot may penetrate rectum and then return to normal position, resulting in recto-vaginal fistula.
See Fistula, Perineum.

Perineum ◀╎ *pe ri ne̱ ēm, n.* region between tail and scrotum or vulva, includes anus.

Perineural ◀╎ *pe ri nu̱r ēl, adj.* around, or alongside, one or more nerves. For example, perineural anaesthesia involves injection of an anaesthetic agent alongside a nerve (e.g. palmar digital nerve block); perineural fibromas are fibrous tumours that surround nerves.

    P. anaesthesia see Anaesthesia

Periodic ophthalmia see Equine recurrent uveitis

Periodontal ◀╎ *pe rē ō do̱n tl, adj.* covering or surrounding a tooth; periodontal structures include the cementum, the periodontal ligament, the bone of the alveolar process, and the gums.
See Tooth.

    P. ligament ◀╎ *pe rē ō do̱n tl / li̱ gē mēnt, n.* the fibrous connective tissue between tooth and tooth socket that attaches the tooth to the alveolus of the jaw.
    See Tooth.

Periodontitis ◀╎ *pe rē ō don ti̱ tis, n.* infection and inflammation of the periodontal structures. Thought to occur as result of inflammation of gums, secondary to impacted food around teeth. Packed food undergoes decay and fermentation by bacteria; infection and inflammation cause a breakdown of the periodontal tissues. As disease progresses, the gum begins to recede and forms a pocket, which worsens the problem of food packing. If unrecognized, eventually periodontal disease will destroy the structures, and result in tooth loss. Signs include dropping food from mouth, weight loss, smelly material around edges of gums, sore, red areas of the gums, halitosis, and, perhaps, poor performance. Painful, so treatment and examination may require local or general anaesthetic. Sustained-release antibiotics may be placed in the pocket to aid healing, with an overlying acrylic cover to protect the antibiotic and the pocket. Advanced cases may require tooth extraction.
See Tooth.

Periosteal ◀╎ *pe rē o̱s tēul, adj.* of, or relating to, the periosteum.
See Bone.

    P. stripping see P. transection (below)
    P. transection ◀╎ *pe rē o̱s tēul / tran se̱k shēn, n.* (hemicircumferential periosteal transection) surgical technique for the treatment of angular limb deformities in foals, whereby the periosteum is transected and elevated (e.g. on the lateral side of the distal radius). Said to increase bone growth on the side of the transection. At least one study has concluded that the procedure is no more effective than stall confinement and hoof trimming alone for correction of angular limb deformities.

Periosteum ◀╎ *pe rē o̱s tē ēm, n.* dense fibrous tissue which covers bones, except at the joints. Inner layer has ability to form new bone. Outer layer is tough and provides attachment for muscles, tendons and ligaments.
See Bone.

Periostitis ◀╎ *pe rē os ti̱ tis, n.* inflammation of periosteum, e.g. resulting from trauma, infection, strain. Irritation of periosteum causes new bone to be produced, which can be seen on radiographs.
See Bone, Periosteum, Sesamoiditis.

Periparturient ◀╎ *pe ri par tu̱r ē ēnt, adj.* occurring around the time of parturition.

    Postpartum p. haemorrhage ◀╎ *po̱st pa̱r tum / pe ri par tu̱r ē ēnt / he̱ mē rij, n.* bleeding from uterine blood vessels, especially the uterine arteries, following parturition. A significant cause of colic and death in older mares that have had multiple foals. Affected mares may be found dead, or show signs of acute blood loss, such as rapid heart rate (tachycardia), pale mucous membranes, or rapid, shallow breathing (tachypnoea). May be self-limiting in less severe cases, with the only sign being a haematoma of the broad ligament or uterine wall that is recognized on subsequent examination (e.g. at foal heat); in more severe cases, heroic efforts to save mare such as blood transfusions or fluid therapy may be successful, but are expensive.

Peripheral ◀﹤ *pe ri fē rŭl, adj.* near the surface of the body, or away from the centre.

P. ganglionopathy ◀﹤ *pe ri fē rŭl /gang glē ēn op ath ē, n.* see Fell pony immunodeficiency syndrome.

P. nervous system ◀﹤ *pe ri fē rŭl /ner vēs / sis tēm, n.* one of the two major divisions of the nervous system, consisting of the nerves that connect the brain and spinal cord (central nervous system) to the rest of the body.
See Nervous system.

P. neuropathy ◀﹤ *pe ri fē rŭl / nŭr op ēth ē, n.* inflammation, degeneration, or damage of nerves of the peripheral nervous system, e.g, as is seen in equine motor neuron disease.
See Equine motor neuron disease.

P. vasculature ◀﹤ *pe ri fē rŭl / vas kŭl ēt ŭr, n.* the blood vessels outside of the heart.

Peristalsis ◀﹤ *pe ri stal sis, n.* the synchro-nized and coordinated, progressive and rhythmic, contraction of the smooth muscles that moves food or liquid through the gastrointestinal (GI) tract in order to allow normal digestion, the absorption of nutrients, and the elimina-tion of waste material. Peristalsis is dependent upon the coordination between the muscles, nerves, and hormones in the digestive tract. May be affected by various conditions, e.g. exer-cise decreases peristalsis owing to epinephrine release, or colic, in which various pathologies may result in decreased intestinal movement.
See Alimentary tract, Diarrhoea.

Peritoneal ◀﹤ *pe ri tē nē ŭl, adj.* relating to the peritoneum.
See Peritoneum.

P. cavity ◀﹤ *pe ri tē nē ŭl / kav it ē, n.* the space

formed between the parietal and visceral layers of the peritoneum.

P. dialysis ◀﹤ *pe ri tē nē ŭl / dī al is is, n.* infu-sion of large volumes of polyionic fluid into the abdominal cavity, by gravitational flow, as a treatment for acute renal failure. Treatment works by virtue of the fact that the peritoneal membrane can act as a natural semi-permeable membrane; if a dialysis fluid is introduced into the peritoneal cavity, dialysis can occur by diffusion. Continuous flow peritoneal dialysis has also been reported.

P. fluid ◀﹤ *pe ri tē nē ŭl / flŭ id, adj.* straw-coloured, watery fluid normally contained within peritoneal cavity, usually present in small amounts. In disease, fluid may be changed in volume (e.g. high volume in hypoproteinaemia), colour (e.g. can become dark and blood-stained in colic), clarity (may become turbid if there are many cells present, e.g. peritonitis or neoplasia), protein content, etc. Sample obtained by abdomino-centesis may be useful in diagnosis of colic, peritonitis, etc.
See Colic, Hypoproteinaemia, Paracentesis, Peritoneum, Peritonitis.

P. lavage ◀﹤ *pe ri tē nē ŭl / lav arzh, n.* infu-sion of large volumes of polyionic fluid into the abdominal cavity, by gravitational flow. May be performed in cases of peritonitis, in an effort to remove infectious organisms and products of inflammation.

Peritoneum ◀﹤ *pe ri tē nē ēm, n.* thin serous membrane which lines abdominal wall (parietal peritoneum) and covers all the organs within the cavity (visceral perito-neum). Composed of a layer of mesothelium and supported by a thin layer of connective tissue. The peritoneum supports the abdominal organs; blood and lymphatic vessels, and nerves, travel through it.
See Abdomen, Peritoneal.

Peritonitis ◀﹤ *pe ri tē nī tis, n.* inflamma-tion of peritoneum. Characterized by secretion of fluid, increased blood flow to peritoneum and fibrin formation. Causes may be infectious, e.g. as result of bacte-rial infection (disseminated *Streptococcus equi* etc.), fungal or viral infection, or migrating parasites; or non-infectious, e.g.

trauma (after a rectal tear, during rectal examination, etc.), ruptured gastric ulcer, hepatic disease, chemicals, neoplasia. Clinical signs variable depending on causative factors, whether the disease is acute or chronic, and whether disease is localized or spread diffusely throughout peritoneum. Signs of acute diffuse peritonitis include fast heart rate, dullness, dehydration, weak pulse, abdominal pain; signs of shock (discoloured mucous membranes, delayed capillary refill time, etc.) appear in horses with septicaemia as a result of peritonitis. Signs of chronic or localized peritonitis include dullness, weight loss, abdominal pain, fever, diarrhoea, or intermittent colic; in chronic disease, fibrin formation can lead to adhesions between loops of intestine. Diagnosis includes examination of sample of peritoneal fluid, obtained by abdominocentesis. In such samples, the cell count and protein are generally high in infectious peritonitis; bacteria may also be seen and cultured. Cytology of fluid may be diagnostic for non-infectious causes, e.g. may show cancer cells. Blood tests, radiography (in foal), gastroscopy, laparoscopy, and rectal examination may also provide additional information. Treatment varies with severity of disease and cause. Broad-spectrum antimicrobial therapy is the cornerstone of care in infectious peritonitis, along with concurrent supportive care, e.g. intravenous fluids, non-steroidal anti-inflammatory drugs, nasogastric tube placement to relieve reflux from secondary ileus, peritoneal lavage, etc. Peritonitis secondary to other primary disease processes carries a more guarded prognosis, depending on whether the primary disease process can be treated effectively. See Adhesion, Fibrin, Inflammation, Peritoneal, Peritoneum.

Permethrin see Pyrethroid

Peroneal nerve ◀ *pe rē nē ŭl / nerv, n.* (fibular nerve) nerve of hind limb, innervates the digital flexor muscles. May be damaged by kick above lateral hock; signs include limb held behind animal slightly, with hock extended and fetlock and pastern flexed.

See Nerve.

P.n. block ◀ *pe rē nē ŭl / nerv / blok, n.* local anaesthetic nerve block of peroneal nerve; occasionally used in the diagnosis of hind limb lameness. Achieved by injection of a local anaesthetic into the groove between the tendons of long and lateral digital extensors on the hind limb, about 10 cm above the point of the hock, on the lateral side of the limb. Usually used in an effort to determine whether lameness is proximal or distal to the hock. Anaesthesia is obtained mainly over the plantar surface of the limb distal to the injection site, over the medial and lateral fetlocks, and the whole digit. Limbs blocked with this technique should be bandaged when the horse is trotted, to prevent damage from knuckling at fetlock. When combined with a block of the tibial nerve, this nerve block may be more effective at eliminating pain from the tarsus (hock) than intra-articular anaesthesia.

See Nerve, Nerve block, Stifle.

Peroneus tertius ◀ *pe rē nē ēs / ter shē ēs, n.* tendinous muscle of hind leg, important in stay apparatus. May be ruptured, e.g. from trauma, overextension of hock, etc. Pathognomonic sign of rupture is the ability to extend hock and flex stifle at same time. Horse usually lame but can bear weight. Clinical diagnosis may be confirmed by ultrasonography. Prognosis for full recovery is favourable with prolonged rest.

See Hock, Stay apparatus, Tendon, Ultrasonography.

Persistent ◀ *pē sis tēnt, adj.* continuing to exist; sometimes in spite of treatment, or tending to recur.

P. hymen see Hymen

P. pulmonary hypertension ◀ *pē sis tēnt / pul mēn rē / hī pē ten shūn, n.* a condition most often associated with perinatal asphyxia, whereby the pulmonary vascular resistance fails to decrease after birth, despite improved alveolar oxygenation and lung expansion. May be seen in association with conditions such as hypoxic ischaemic encephalopathy, patent ductus arteriosus, or following meconium aspiration. Treatment involves providing oxygen, and correcting accompanying respiratory acidosis. See under various conditions, Acidosis.

P. pupillary membrane ◀╪ *pē sis tēnt / pū pi lē rē / mem brān, n.* remnants of tissue from developing eye, caused by a failure of the vascular pupillary membrane to atrophy, as normally occurs in young foals. Seen as strands arising from iris and attaching to cornea or anterior lens. Normally associated with opacity of the contacted structure. Uncommon finding in horses' eyes; small peripheral lesions typically cause no problems and are not progressive; large lesions may interfere with vision if associated with a large cataract.
See Eye.

P. right aortic arch ◀╪ *pē sis tēnt / rīt / ā or tik / arch, n.* uncommon congenital condition in which the oesophagus is constricted between the foetal ligamentum arteriosum and the aorta; results in oesophageal dilation and dysphagia. Usually reported when foals change to a solid diet, but affected milk-fed foals have been observed to regurgitate milk through their nostrils. Surgical correction has been attempted; however, oesophageal narrowing resulting from fibrous tissue stricture resulted in an unsuccessful outcome.

Perspiration see Sweat

Peruvian horse sickness virus ◀╪ *pē rū vē ēn / hors / sik nis / vir ēs, n.* arthropod-borne virus (*Orbivirus*); occasional cause of encephalitis in endemic areas of South America. No vaccine; no treatment.
See *Orbivirus.*

Pessary ◀╪ *pe sē rē, n.* soluble tablet (e.g. of antibiotic) inserted into vagina; occasionally used in the treatment of conditions of female reproductive tract.
See Antibiotic, Vagina.

Petechiae ◀╪ *pe tē chē ē, n.* very small, round red or purple spots on skin or gum, caused by bleeding into skin or mucous membrane. Many disease conditions are associated with the formation of petechiae, including local injury and trauma, allergic reactions, autoimmune diseases, viral infections, blood clotting problems, purpura haemorrhagica, equine infectious anaemia, and thrombocytopenia.
See Equine infectious anaemia, Purpura haemorrhagica, Thrombocytopenia.

Petrolatum ◀╪ *pe trō lar tēm, n.* hydrocarbon-derived base for many of the ointments that are used on the skin of the horse. Petrolatum also has some effect as an emollient and protectant for the skin. Petrolatum has no known therapeutic properties. It is highly occlusive to the skin; for this reason, it is an effective emollient. Some people believe that applying petrolatum to a healing wound will help the wound grow hair; there is no scientific basis for such a belief.

Petroleum ◀╪ *pē trō lē ēm, n.* generic term for a naturally occurring complex mixture, primarily composed of hydrocarbons. Various petroleum products or distillates may be used as fuel (e.g. kerosene), or as carrier agents for insecticides. Horses usually will avoid petroleum-contaminated feed, but it may be consumed if horse is confined in an area which is contaminated with petroleum products, or by iatrogenic applications. Signs are of gastrointestinal or respiratory system dysfunction. Products are irritating to mucous membranes and may blister mouth and lips; ingestion causes salivation, colic, diarrhoea. Applied to skin, petroleum products can cause contact dermatitis, including hair loss and skin redness. Inhalation of droplets may cause coughing, depression, weight loss, fever, and rapid breathing. Treatment is supportive, e.g. gastrointestinal tract may be treated with laxatives, skin by bathing to remove products; treatment of respiratory disease (e.g. aspiration pneumonia from inadvertent nasogastric intubation with liquid paraffin) is generally unrewarding.
See Blister, Colic, Diarrhoea.

Petrous temporal bone ◀╪ *pe trēs / tem per ēl / bōn, n.* paired bones of skull, form sides of head; contains inner ear.
See Skull, Temporohyoid osteoarthropathy.

pH ◀╪ *pē / āch, n.* potential of hydrogen; a measure of degree of acidity or alkalinity of a solution, based on concentration of hydrogen ions. Logarithmic scale; pH of 7 is neutral, lower values are acidic, and higher values are alkaline. Normal blood

pH in adult horse is approximately 7.4.
See Acid, Alkali.

Phaeochromocytoma ◀ৈ *fā ō krō mō sī tō mē, n.* tumour of medulla of adrenal gland. May be non-functional or functional; usually unilateral and benign, although malignant tumours have been reported. Non-functional tumours do not secrete hormones, and are found incidentally at post-mortem, but may cause colic signs if tumours are sufficiently large. Functional tumours secrete catecholamines (e.g. epinephrine and norepinephrine), and are usually seen only in horses older than 12 years. Clinical signs of functional phaeo-chromocytoma include sweating, muscle tremors, dilated pupils, rapid heart rate, rapid breathing, colic, restlessness. Blood tests are generally non-specific, but may show acidosis, high potassium, or elevated blood glucose. Rupture of tumours has been described after trauma (e.g. kick). Surgery (adrenalectomy) would be cura-tive, but is difficult.
See Adrenal gland, Epinephrine.

Phaeohyphomycosis ◀ৈ *fā ō hī fō mī kō sis, n.* any of a group of opportunistic superfi-cial or deep tissue infections caused by various fungi that form hyphae and yeast-like cells in tissue. Identification of the specific causative organism requires fungal culture. Surgical excision, if possible, may be curative. Various phar-macological agents may be indicated for treatment, depending on culture.

Phagocyte ◀ৈ *fa gō sīt, n.* cell in body that ingests and destroys bacteria, other cells and foreign material; engulfs organism in cell cytoplasm and digests it. Phagocytes may circulate in blood or lymph, or be found in body tissues. Examples in horse include neutrophils in the circulation and macrophages in various tissues.
See Bacterium, Neutrophil, Macrophages.

Phagocytosis ◀ৈ *fa gō sī tō sis, n.* the process of digestion by cells, especially phagocytes, of solid substances, e.g. bacteria and foreign particles. Part of the horse's body defences. Antibodies can stimulate phagocytosis by macrophages

and other phagocytic cells by coating the pathogenic substance, as part of normal immune function.
See Antibody, Phagocyte.

Phalangeal ◀ৈ *fa lan jē ūl, adj.* of, or relating to, the phalanges.
See First phalanx, Third phalanx.

Phalanx ◀ৈ *fa langks, n.* each of the bones of the digits of the fore- or hind limbs. Horse has only one digit on each limb; each is made up of three bones (phalanges).
See First phalanx, Third: T. phalanx.

Phallectomy ◀ৈ *fa lek tēm ē, n.* surgical removal of the penis. Indicated when penis is extensively and permanently damaged, or in cases of extensive neoplasia. Stallions should be castrated several weeks prior to the procedure, so as to avoid post-operative complications secondary to erection.

Phallopexy ◀ৈ *fa lō pek sē, n.* (Bolz proce-dure) surgical technique for permanent retention of penis within prepuce, as an alternative to phallectomy. May be performed if nerves to penis are damaged so it cannot be retracted into prepuce normally; cannot be used if the penis is severely damaged, or if stallion is still capable of developing an erection.
See Paraphimosis, Penis, Prepuce.

Phantom ◀ৈ *fan tēm, n.* a breeding mount; semen can be collected from a stallion on a phantom [mare] for semen evaluation or artificial insemination.

Pharmaceutical ◀ৈ *far mē sū tik ēl, n/adj.* a prepared drug or medicinal substance used in the treatment of disease, pertaining to pharmacy or drugs.

Pharmacokinetics ◀ৈ *far mē kō kin et iks, n.* the movement of drugs in the body, which includes the processes of drug absorption, drug distribution, drug local-ization in tissues, followed by the biotransformation and ultimate excretion of the drug or drug metabolites; the study of such processes.

345

Pharmacology ◀∈ *far mē ko lē jē, n.* the study of how chemical substances (both synthetic and non-synthetic) interact with living organisms to produce a change in the function of all or part of that organism; the science dealing with all aspects of the actions of drugs (pharmaceuticals) on living tissues.

Pharyngeal ◀∈ *fa rin jē ūl, adj.* relating to, or in the region of, the pharynx.
See Pharynx.

Pharyngitis ◀∈ *fa rin jī tis, n.* inflammation of the pharynx. In horses, pharyngitis may be secondary to infection (e.g. equine influenza, strangles), from inflammation (e.g. from dust or allergy), or from trauma, (e.g. from prolonged nasogastric intubation). Signs depend on cause, but generally include nasal discharge, coughing, coughing on palpation of pharyngeal region, and, if severe, dysphagia (difficulty swallowing). Clinical diagnosis may be confirmed by endoscopy; pharynx may be red, mucus-covered, or, in chronic cases, covered with lymphoid follicles. Chronic inflammation of the pharynx, also referred to as lymphoid hyperplasia, is common in young horses, especially young performance horses from 2 to 3 years old. If infection is present, treatment is directed at eliminating the primary cause, e.g. antimicrobial therapy. Numerous anti-inflammatory medications and preparations may be administered for non-infectious causes, especially in chronic cases, including local and topical corticosteroids, and medications such as dimethylsulphoxide or glycerine-containing solutions administered topically, or by nebulizer; the myriad and diverse nature of the treatments reflects the fact that the condition is not clearly understood. Environmental management to reduce dust exposure or improve air flow is often helpful in affected horses.
See Equine influenza, Inflammation, Pharynx, Strangles.

Pharynx ◀∈ *fa ringks, n.* throat, area at back of mouth and nose where alimentary and respiratory tracts meet and cross. Has several areas:

- Nasopharynx – the dorsal part of the pharynx; the continuation of the nasal meatuses, separated from oropharynx by soft palate. Contains openings of the auditory tubes, and provides passage for air from nose to larynx.
- Oropharynx – the continuation of the oral cavity to the base of the epiglottis, at the back part of mouth; separated from nasopharynx by soft palate, provides passage for food from mouth to entrance of oesophagus.
- Laryngopharynx – the continuation of the oropharynx around the rostal parts of the larynx; the backmost part of pharynx. Continued itself as the oesophagus.

Disorders affecting the pharynx include rostral or dorsal pharyngeal collapse (perhaps owing to weakness of pharyngeal muscles, which allows tissues to collapse and obstruct airway, affecting performance and causing noise when horse breathes in), dorsal displacement of the soft palate, pharyngeal cyst (fluid-filled sac on pharynx wall present from birth, signs caused depend on size), paralysis (from damage to nerves, e.g. as may be caused by fungal infection of guttural pouch), botulism (horse is unable to swallow and food may return through nostrils or drop out of mouth), foreign body (may be inhaled or swallowed, horse has difficulty and pain with swallowing), compression from abscesses (e.g. in strangles), tumours (lymphoma is most common tumour), inflammation (pharyngitis). Congenital pharyngeal abnormalities in foals include choanal atresia/stenosis, and cleft palate. Diagnosis of specific conditions of pharynx may require endoscopy; treatment varies by cause.
See Botulism, Cyst, Dorsal, Endoscopy, Guttural pouch, Lymphoma, Palate, Pharyngitis, Stenosis, Strangles.

Phenobarbital ◀∈ *fē nō bar bi tol, n.* (phenobarbitone) drug used as anticonvulsant, e.g. to control seizures associated with hypoxic ischaemic encephalopathy in foals. Also has sedative properties (but not generally used for sedation in horse).
See Anticonvulsant, Hypoxic ischaemic encephalopathy, Seizure.

Phenol ◄⟨ *fē nol, n.* synthetic chemical; can also be obtained from coal tar; also known as carbolic acid. Phenol has a variety of pharmaceutical uses. It is a caustic agent and can be used to chemically cauterize wounds. It is a disinfectant that was commonly used years ago although other, more potent disinfectants have replaced phenol today. In dilute solutions, phenol is mildly anaesthetic and is used to help control itching. Its most important use is probably as a preservative for injectable drugs. In the horse, phenol is used in some over-the-counter hoof dressings, presumably for its disinfectant properties. Some liquid preparations rubbed on horses' legs for counterirritation have also contained phenol because it is irritating to the skin. See Antibacterial.

Phenothiazine ◄⟨ *fē nō thī ē zēn, n.* a group of tranquillizing medications with anti-psychotic action, thought to act by blocking dopaminergic transmission in the brain. Medications that have been used in horses include promazine, acepromazine, and fluphenazine. Also, an early anthelmintic drug, used in the mid twentieth century, now superseded by more effective drugs.
See Anthelmintic, Dopamine, Tranquilliser.

Phenotype ◄⟨ *fē nō tīp, n.* visible characteristics of animal resulting from a combination of inherited traits and the effect of the animal's environment, e.g. diet, housing, etc. (c.f. genotype, which is purely the inherited characteristics).
See Genotype, Heredity.

Phenylbutazone ◄⟨ *fē nīl bū tē zōn, n.* (PBZ) non-steroidal anti-inflammatory drug, used for treatment of painful muscle, tendon, joint, etc. conditions, e.g. laminitis, strained muscles and tendons, arthritis, etc.; also effective as an antipyretic (controls fever). PBZ is the most commonly administered non-steroidal anti-inflammatory pain-relieving drug for the horse in the United States; however PBZ is banned for use in horses in several member states of the EU due to concerns about

residues in horse meat, and it is much less commonly used in the UK and other EU countries than in the US. Available as a 1 g tablet, a paste and a pre-ground powder for oral administration to the horse as well as a sterile liquid for IV administration only (the drug is extremely irritating if injected in the muscle). Phenylbutazone has been demonstrated to be a safe and effective pain reliever for the horse at recommended dosages. Its side effects are similar to those of other non-steroidal anti-inflammatory drugs, e.g. aspirin.

PRECAUTIONS
In certain circumstances, caution may be advisable in using phenylbutazone (or any of the related drugs). Two types of adverse side effects have been reported in the horse: gastrointestinal and renal (of the kidney). These effects are most commonly reported in foals and ponies; adverse effects are rarely reported in adult large-breed horses. The reported gastrointestinal side effects of phenylbutazone are primarily ulcers. Ulcers are erosions of the surface of the mouth, stomach or intestines. Ulceration probably occurs as a result of some local effect of irritation from the drug when it is given orally. Ulcers are most commonly seen in foals that are maintained on phenylbutazone (or any other drug of the same class) for various conditions. Ulcers are rarely seen when phenylbutazone is given IV (and then only at very high doses). Renal side effects are usually associated with decreased water consumption. In horses with kidney disease, illness occurs because of a failure of the kidneys to remove the body's waste products. The use of phenylbutazone should be carefully monitored in horses that are dehydrated, debilitated (and not drinking well) or that have disease of the kidneys. Care should be taken when using phenylbutazone in combination with other drugs that have side effects related to the kidney, such as aminoglycoside antibiotics (e.g. gentamicin, amikacin).

Phenylbutazone does have an unwarranted reputation as being a dangerous drug in horses. Side effects from the use of phenylbutazone are extremely uncommon

at the routinely prescribed doses. Doubling the recommended dose increases the potential for side effects. However, recent research has shown that a commonly prescribed dose, 2 g twice daily, is not more effective than 2 g daily. The lower dose would presumably have a lower incidence of side effects. Phenylbutazone, as with all drugs, should be used according to your veterinarian's recommendations. It should not be used in horses intended for human consumption.
See Arthritis, Laminitis.

Phenylephrine ◀₹ *fe nī lef rēn, n.* a synthetic sympathomimetic agent; a vasoconstrictor (pressor) drug chemically related to epinephrine. Available as a sterile solution for parenteral injection. Can be given intranasally to reduce post-anaesthetic upper airway obstruction. Phenylephrine injections have also been used to reduce the size of the spleen in trying to manage nephrosplenic entrapment non-surgically.
See Nephrosplenic.

Phenytoin ◀₹ *fe ni tō in, n.* anticonvulsant and anti-arrhythmic drug, related to the barbiturates in chemical structure. Has been used to control seizures, e.g. as may be seen in hypoxic ischaemic encephalopathy, and to control cardiac glycoside-induced arrhythmias. Has also been used to treat stringhalt.
See Anticonvulsant, Hypoxic ischaemic encephalopathy, Seizure, Stringhalt.

Pheromone ◀₹ *fe rē mōn, n.* chemical substance secreted by animals, especially insects; act as molecular messengers, influencing behaviour of other members of the same species, especially to attract the opposite sex, e.g. mare produces pheromones when in oestrus.

Phimosis ◀₹ *fi mō sis, n.* inability of horse to protrude penis from prepuce owing to a constricted preputial ring. Congenital condition, but may also occur secondarily, e.g. because tumour or scarring narrows opening of prepuce.
See Penis, Prepuce.

Phonocardiography ◀₹ *fō nō kar dē o grē fē, n.* recording of heart sounds and murmurs as a graphical record (microphone placed on chest collects sound waves which are then converted to electrical energy and produce trace). Of some academic interest, but rarely used as diagnostic tool for heart conditions.
See Heart.

Phosphorus ◀₹ *fos fēr rēs, n.* (P) a mineral required for normal development of the skeleton of the horse as well as for various metabolic functions, as it is a principal component of adenosine triphosphate, the main source of energy at a cellular level. About 8% of the horse's phosphorus is contained in the bones and teeth. Its levels in the body are closely associated with calcium levels. The horse's body tries to maintain a relatively constant ratio between the two minerals. A deficiency of phosphorus produces problems with bone growth in young horses and softening of the bones in older ones, similar to those seen with calcium deficiencies. An excess of phosphorus causes calcium absorption by the horse's intestines to be decreased; clinically, this condition is called nutritional secondary hyperparathyroidism. The dietary requirements for phosphorus are generally supplied in a normal horse's diet. However, some attention must be paid to the balance between calcium and phosphorus in the diet, especially in growing foals. Ratios from 1:1 (calcium level:phosphorus level) to 6:1 can be fed with no adverse effects on the growing horse, as long as the absolute dietary requirements for phosphorus are met. Alfalfa (lucerne) hay tends to have high levels of calcium relative to phosphorus. Grains and brans tend to have higher phosphorus levels relative to calcium.
See Calcium, Hyperparathyroidism.

Photic ◀₹ *fō tik, adj.* relating to light.
  P. head-shaking ◀₹ *fō tik /hed-shā king, n.* idiopathic condition where horse shakes its head when exposed to bright sunlight; can make it dangerous to ride.
  See Head-shaking.

Photoallergy ◀€ *fō tō al ēj ē, n.* skin hypersensitivity reaction in which the allergen, usually an exogenous chemical compound, is activated by light. Subsequent exposures produce photoallergic skin conditions (photodermatitis).
See Photodermatitis, Photosensitization.

Photodermatitis ◀€ *fō tō der mēt ī tis, n.* skin reaction, caused by excessive exposure to ultraviolet light. UV light raises the energy level of light-absorbing molecules in the horse's body, which initiates damaging chemical processes that result in various manifestations of skin disease, especially in non-pigmented (pink) areas.

Photoperiod ◀€ *fō tō pér ē ēd, n.* the duration of the horse's daily exposure to daylight. Seasonal changes in photoperiod are responsible for controlling the mare's reproductive cycle. In broodmares, photoperiod is commonly managed artificially so as to induce oestrus earlier than would occur under normal conditions.
See Oestrus.

Photophobia ◀€ *fō tō fō bē ē, n.* fear, or avoidance, of light. Clinical sign of ocular discomfort, e.g. as seen in some cases of keratitis, or after eye has been dilated with drugs such as atropine.
See Atropine, Keratitis.

Photosensitization ◀€ *fō tō sen si tī zā shēn, n.* increased skin susceptibility to the deleterious effects of ultraviolet light because of a photoactive agent. Certain photodynamic chemicals in skin, which may be contacted, ingested (e.g. St John's wort, some clovers, or as a result of high levels of phylloerythrin), produced, or injected, increase the likelihood of the skin being damaged by ultraviolet light. Skin damage is seen in areas with little or no pigment and little hair growth, e.g. muzzle. Affected skin is usually swollen, and may blister, weep, or peel.
See Liver, Phylloerythrin, Skin.

Phototoxicity ◀€ *fō tō toks is it ē, n.* sunburn; occurs when unpigmented skin, not protected by hair (e.g. on muzzle or prepuce), is exposed to excessive amounts of sunlight. Skin damage from phototoxicity in pink-skinned animals predisposes to squamous cell carcinoma.
See Squamous.

Phrenic ◀€ *fre nik, adj.* relating to the diaphragm.
See Diaphragm.
> **P. nerve** ◀€ *fre nik / nerv, n.* large nerve which arises from spinal nerves of neck and innervates diaphragm.
> See Diaphragm.

Phthisis ◀€ *fthi sis, n.* wasting, shrinkage, especially of a body part.
> **P. bulbi** ◀€ *fthi sis / bul bī, n.* shrinkage of eyeball, e.g. as result of severe injury to eye.
> See Eye.

Phycomycosis see Pythiosis

Phylloerythrin ◀€ *fi lō e ri thrin, n.* chemical normally produced from breakdown of chlorophyll (pigment of green plants) by bacteria in large intestine. Normally excreted in bile by liver. May build up in body if liver is damaged or diseased; can result in photosensitization.
See Photosensitization.

Physical examination ◀€ *fiz ik ēl / eks am in ā shēn, n.* the process of investigating the horse's body for signs of disease or abnormality. Techniques involved in equine physical examination include auscultation, palpation, and observation.

Physical therapy see Physiotherapy

Physiology ◀€ *fi zē o lē jē, n.* the study of the normal mechanical, physical, and biochemical functions of living organisms.

Physiotherapy ◀€ *fi zē ō the rē pē, n.* treatment of injury or disease by physical and mechanical methods (e.g. massage, manipulation, heat, laser treatment). Physiotherapist may work alongside veterinary surgeon to treat muscle injuries, tendon and ligament problems, back problems, rehabilitation after operations, etc. The benefits of such therapeutic efforts are not well documented in horses.

Physis ◀ː *fī zis, n.* the portion of ends of a long bone that is concerned mainly with growth in length of the bone. The physis consists of four zones: zone of resting cartilage, zone of proliferating cartilage, zone of hypertrophy, and zone of calcification.
See Bone, Growth.

Physitis ◀ː *fī sī tis, n.* swelling around the physis (growth plate), especially of the distal radius and distal metacarpus in rapidly growing young horses. Cause commonly attributed to rapid growth, or calcium:phosphorus imbalance; however, the pathophysiology of the condition is not well-established. Swelling commonly occurs with no evidence of a clinical problem, and usually resolves without treatment. If physitis is associated with lameness, radiographs should be taken to evaluate the physis, to make sure that there are no significant problems within the growth plate. Physitis is usually managed conservatively (e.g. decreased exercise, evaluation of mineral balance in diet, and judicious use of non-steroidal anti-inflammatory agents), and usually resolves without complication. May occasionally occur in association with other orthopaedic problems, e.g. osteochondrosis, flexural deformities, etc.
See Bone, Flexural deformity, Osteochondrosis.

Physostigmine ◀ː *fī zō stig mēn, n.* drug obtained from calabar bean, from a leguminous African plant (*Physostigma venenosum*). Pharmacological effects similar to stimulation of parasympathetic nervous system (parasympathomimetic). Used to decrease intraocular pressure in the treatment of glaucoma, or in provocative testing for narcolepsy.
See Glaucoma, Narcolepsy, Parasympathetic nervous system.

Pia mater ◀ː *pī ē / mā tē, n.* the fine innermost vascular layer of the membranes covering the brain and spinal cord.
See Meninges.

Pica ◀ː *pē kē, n.* tendency to eat non-nutritive material. Horse may lick at unusual materials or eat substances such as faeces (coprophagy), wood (lignophagy), etc. Commonly attributed to lack of some dietary component; however, it has been difficult to correlate lack of any particular substance with pica. Nutritionists have found that horses have a true appetite for only three nutrients: energy, salt, and water. Horses do not typically express other nutritional deficiencies as pica; they do not appear to have any innate nutritional knowledge that would cause them seek ways to correct dietary imbalances. Pica is more likely an indication of curiosity or boredom than an indication of a dietary problem. However, an association has been made between a lack of dietary fibre and wood-chewing. Pica can become a habit.
See Coprophagy.

Picornavirus see Equine rhinovirus

Pigeon breast see *Corynebacterium*

Pigment ◀ː *pig mēnt, n.* any of the coloured substances found in tissues and fluids, e.g. bilirubin, haemoglobin (gives blood its colour), melanin (pigment found in hair, skin and eye).
See Haemoglobin, Melanin.
> **P. cell** ◀ː *pig mēnt / sel, n.* small cell containing coloured substances, e.g. the pigmented epithelial cells of the choroid and iris of the eye.

Pigmentation ◀ː *pig mēn tā shēn, n.* deposition of pigment resulting in colouring or discolouration of a tissue.
See Pigment.

Pigmenturia ◀ː *pig men tūr ēē, n.* coloured substances present in the urine. Seen especially as a feature of exertional myopathies, owing to the presence of myoglobin.

Pilocarpine ◀ː *pī lō kar pēn, n.* alkaloid drug extracted from leaves of tropical American shrub (*Pilocarpus* spp.); effects similar to stimulation of muscarinic receptors of the parasympathetic nervous system. May be used in the treatment of glaucoma to reduce intraocular pressure.
See Parasympathetic nervous system.

Pineal gland ◀┊ *pin ē al / gland, n.* small organ, shaped like a pine cone (hence its name), located at the roof of the third ventricle of the brain. The gland secretes the hormone melatonin, which communicates information about light in the environment to various parts of the body, especially the reproductive tract. This light-transducing ability of the pineal gland has led to the gland being called the 'third eye' by some.
See Melatonin.

Pinna ◀┊ *pi nē, n.* external part of ear.
See Ear.

Pinworm see *Oxyuris equi.*

Piperazine ◀┊ *pi pe rē zēn, n.* anthelmintic drug, from which numerous derivatives have been developed. Wide margin of safety, but less commonly used in horses than previously, as more effective broad-spectrum compounds have been developed. Effective especially against *Parascaris* spp. Rarely, signs of toxicity have been reported, including depression and incoordination; horses typically recover with supportive care.
See *Oxyuris equi, Parascaris equorum.*

Piroplasmosis see Babesiosis

Pituitary ◀┊ *pi tū i tē rē, n.* (hypophysis) endocrine gland at the base of brain, functionally connected to the hypothalamus of the brain. Produces hormones that regulate homeostasis, including hormones that regulate other endocrine glands (trophic hormones). In horses, the pituitary is typically divided into three lobes, the anterior (adenohypophysis), intermediate (pars intermedia), and posterior (neurohypophysis). The hypothalamus integrates both stimulatory and inhibitory signals to the pituitary gland by various mechanisms, both internal (e.g. autonomic inputs, sex steroids) and external (e.g. day length). Hormones secreted by the anterior pituitary include:
• Adrenocorticotrophic hormone (ACTH) – stimulates secretion of corticosteroids by cortex of adrenal gland.
• Follicle stimulating hormone (FSH) –

acts on ovary to stimulate growth of ovarian follicles.
• Growth hormone (somatotropin) – acts on many tissues, results in normal growth of body.
• Interstitial cell stimulating hormone (ICSH) – stimulates interstitial cells of testis to produce testosterone.
• Luteinizing hormone (LSH) – acts on ovary to initiate development of corpus luteum post-ovulation.
• Prolactin – stimulates secretion of milk from mammary glands.
• Thyroid stimulating hormone (TSH) – stimulates thyroid gland to produce thyroxine and tri-iodothyronine.
Hormones secreted by the posterior pituitary gland include:
• Antidiuretic hormone (ADH) – acts on kidney to increase water reabsorption.
• Oxytocin – stimulates contraction of smooth muscle of uterus and mammary glands.
The most common condition affecting the equine pituitary gland is pituitary pars intermedia dysfunction (Cushing's disease).
See hormones and other glands under separate entries, Gland, Hormone, Pituitary pars intermedia dysfunction.

Pituitary pars intermedia dysfunction ◀┊ *pi tū i tē rē / pars / in ter mē dē ē / dis fungk shēn, n.* (PPID, Equine Cushing's disease, Pituitary adenoma) syndrome caused by growth of the cells in the pituitary gland which generates melanocyte-stimulating hormone in the pars intermedia (PI) of the pituitary gland; one of the most common endocrine problems of older horses. Accumulated research suggests that PPID occurs as a result of a loss of inhibitory dopaminergic influence from the hypothalamus. Any breed or sex can be affected; Morgan horses and pony breeds appear to be at increased risk. Older horses, greater than 18 years of age, are most commonly affected; however, PPID may be seen in younger horses with no obvious clinical signs. Classic clinical signs include hirsutism (increased hair growth – inappropriate hair growth in an older horse is considered a pathognomonic sign of PPID) and weight loss. Other signs may include increased urination, non-healing wounds, laminitis, and mammary enlargement in mares.

DIAGNOSIS

Syndrome may be confirmed by one of several tests; the overnight low-dose dexamethasone suppression test is generally considered the 'best' test for PPID; however both false positive and false negative results have been reported. Another possible problem with testing for PPID is the effect of seasonality; affected horses may respond differently in the autumn and winter months, with an increased risk of false positives. Concerns have been expressed that the dexamethasone administration may cause laminitis, or make laminitis worse, in tested horses; however, this has not been observed in research studies. Elevated plasma adrenocorticotrophic hormone is also a commonly employed test for the diagnosis of PPID; however, the rate of release of ACTH by the pituitary gland varies throughout the day, and such variation can make the significance of a single plasma ACTH determination questionable. Preliminary studies suggest that a challenge test with domperidone may be accurate; however, more work needs to be done on a large number of horses to determine the true utility of this test.

TREATMENT

The most commonly used drugs to treat PPID are pergolide and cyproheptadine. Doses are based on extrapolations from human studies. Serotonin stimulates the release of ACTH from the pars intermedia of rats (this has not been studied in horses), and cyproheptadine, a serotonin antagonist, has been advocated for the management of PPID accordingly. However, pergolide, a dopaminergic agonist, is probably the most widely used drug for treatment of PPID. Pergolide has been reported to be a more effective treatment for PPID than cyproheptadine, both with regard to clinical response, and in returning dexamethasone suppression tests to normal. *Vitex agnus castus* (chaste berry) has also been tested; clinical and endocrinological criteria worsened in all

but one of the treated horses. The drug trilostane, a competitive 3-beta hydroxysteroid dehydrogenase inhibitor, has been used successfully to control clinical signs of Cushing's disease in dogs (a similar, but not identical, condition); one study reports successful use in horses, but further work is needed to confirm the drug's usefulness in treating PPID in horses. Other treatment is directed at associated clinical conditions, e.g. evaluating feed ration in underweight horses, treating concurrent laminitis, etc.

PROGNOSIS

Equine PPID is currently incurable. Unfortunately, it is not possible to demonstrate reliably that any treatment method allows for demonstrable clinical resolution or control of PPID. Clinical signs may wax and wane in individual horses, making even accurate clinical assessment of a response to treatment in one individual difficult. Furthermore, all horses are not affected equally by the disease.

See Adrenocorticotrophic hormone, Cyproheptadine, Dexamethasone, Laminitis, Pergolide mesylate.

Placenta ◀ *plē sen tē, n.* (afterbirth) organ in pregnant mammals which joins mother to offspring and allows transfer of substances (e.g. oxygen, nourishment, hormones) between blood stream of mother and offspring. Placenta of mare is made up of foetal membranes (chorion and allantois fused to form allantochorion) which are almost completely attached to uterine wall during pregnancy except at the cervix (diffuse attachment; seen in horses and pigs). Attachment is by tiny finger-like projections (microvilli) which bind closely to similar projections of the uterine wall. The attachment of the equine placenta is called epitheliochorial, which means that the foetal chorion is merely in contact with, but does not erode, the endometrium of the mare's uterus. Foetal blood travels to and from placenta via the umbilical cord. After approximately 100 days of gestation, pregnancy is maintained by placental progestins. The placenta is normally expelled at end of foaling (stage 3 of parturtion); it should always be exam-

ined to ensure that it has been completely expelled.
See Foetus, Parturition, Pregnancy, Progestin, Progesterone, Uterus.

Premature separation of p. ◀€ _pre_ mē tŭr / sep ē _rā_ shĕn / ov / plē _sen_ tē, n. early separation of the allantochorion of the placenta from the uterine wall during foaling. The allantochorion attaches to the uterine wall and allows the exchange of nutrients and waste back through the umbilical cord; normally, it breaks prior to the foal entering the birth canal.

When a velvety 'red bag' is seen hanging from the vulva, it means that a portion of the placenta has detached from the uterine wall prematurely, thereby reducing or eliminating the exchange of nutrients to the foetus that is still inside the mare. When recognized, prompt action to open the allantochorion and deliver the foal is required to prevent a weak or stillborn foal. Foals born under such circumstances should be watched carefully for signs of hypoxia or infection. Aetiology includes placentitis, and exposure of late pregnant mares to infected fescue grass.

Placental ◀€ plē _sen_ tl, adj. relating to placenta.

P. barrier see Barrier

P. insufficiency ◀€ plē _sen_ tl / in sēf _ish_ ĕn sē, n. abnormal condition of pregnancy, in which the placenta, its membranes, or the umbilical cord develop abnormally and affect the growth of the foetus; may result in abortion, or delivery of a premature or dysmature foal. Various conditions contribute to placental insufficiency, including fescue toxicosis, placentitis, twins (placenta may not be able to support two foetuses), or maternal illness.
See Abortion, Fescue grass, Placenta, Placentitis.

Placentation ◀€ pla sen _tā_ shĕn, n. the formation of the placenta in utero; also, the type or structure of the placenta.
See Placenta.

Placentitis ◀€ pla sen _tī_ tis, n. inflammation of the placenta, usually secondary to bacterial infection. A major cause of abortion in mares; rarely has long-term effects

on fertility. Numerous bacterial organisms may be implicated, including _Streptococcus equi_ subsp. _zooepidemicus, E. coli, Pseudomonas aeruginosa,_ as well as fungi such as _Aspergillus_ spp.; infection typically ascends through the posterior reproductive tract. Current treatment protocols for mares affected with placentitis are based largely on practitioner preference and experience. Specific therapies and rationales used to treat placentitis include various antimicrobial and anti-inflammatory agents, drugs used to relax uterine contractions (tocolytic agents, e.g. indomethacin, terbutaline), clenbuterol (to suppress uterine motility), pentoxyfylline (possibly increases erythrocyte flexibility, so as to facilitate blood flow), and progesterones (may act to inhibit gap junctions which may form in the uterus secondary to prostaglandins released during inflammation). Measuring serum relaxin levels may be useful in monitoring placental function.

Plantar ◀€ _plarn_ tē, adj. pertaining to the sole or caudal portion of the hind limb (c.f. palmar).

P. ligaments ◀€ _plarn_ tē / _li_ gē mĕnts, n. strong ligaments running down the caudal surface of the hock. Sprain or strain of the plantar ligament is called curb.
See Curb.

P. nerve block ◀€ _plarn_ tē / nerv / blok, n. nerve block of the medial and lateral plantar nerves to desensitize the digit in the horse; in the forelimb, it is called a palmar digital nerve block.

Plaque ◀€ plak, n. small, flat, disc-shaped formation or growth; may be raised above rest of tissue, e.g. as in describing raised areas seen in some allergic skin reactions; also, a film of mucus and bacteria on a tooth surface.

Aural p. see Aural

Plasma ◀€ _plaz_ mē, n. liquid part of blood, in which blood cells are suspended. Consists of approximately 95% water, with the remainder being dissolved or suspended substances, including anions such as chloride and bicarbonate, cations such as sodium, potassium, calcium and

magnesium, complex protein molecules (e.g. plasma proteins), dissolved nutrients (e.g. glucose), and fat particles.
See Blood, Serum.

P. cell ◀︎ _plaz mē / sel, n._ any of the antibody-secreting cells found in lymphoid tissue. Plasma cells are derived from B lymphocytes. Their production is stimulated by lymphokines, as well as reactions with specific antigens.

P. protein ◀︎ _plaz mē / prō tēn, n._ protein molecules, such as albumins, globulins, and blood-clotting proteins, which circulate in the blood plasma. Plasma proteins also hold fluid in blood vessels by osmosis.
See Blood, Osmosis, Serum.

Plasmid ◀︎ _plaz mid, n._ a self-replicating circle of DNA that is distinct from the chromosomal genome of bacteria. A plasmid contains genes normally not essential for cell growth or survival. One method of transfer of antibiotic resistance by bacteria is via transfer of plasmids.
See Resistance.

Plasmin ◀︎ _plaz min, n._ the primary enzyme of the fibrinolytic system that dissolves blood clots.

Plasminogen ◀︎ _plaz min ē jēn, n._ inactive precursor of plasmin; activated in response to blood stasis and high concentrations of thrombin, a clotting protein.

Plate ◀︎ _plāt, n._ **1)** lightweight shoe, typically made of aluminium, worn especially by racehorses; **2)** a thin, relatively flat, piece of bone, e.g. bone of skull.

Bone p. ◀︎ _bōn / plāt, n._ flat metal implant screwed to bone to provide support for healing fracture.

Platelet ◀︎ _plāt lit, n._ (thrombocyte) tiny disc-like body in blood; formed in bone marrow by break-up of large cells (megakaryocytes). Very important in blood clotting; helps in clotting by sticking to other platelets, and to damaged epithelium. Lack of platelets (thrombocytopenia) can result in poor blood clotting and is associated with haemorrhagic conditions.
See Blood, Bone, Clotting, Thrombocytopenia.

P.-rich plasma ◀︎ _plāt lit-rich / plaz mē, n._ Ultraconcentrate of platelets; contains high concentration of growth factors released when platelets exposed to thrombin. Has been used to augment ligament, bone; wound healing in humans; one report of use is suspensory desmitis in horses.

Pleura ◀︎ _plor rē, n._ thin serous membrane which lines thoracic wall (parietal pleura) and covers lungs (pulmonary pleura).
See Lung, Thorax.

Pleural ◀︎ _plor rūl, adj._ relating to the pleura.
See Pleura.

P. effusion ◀︎ _plor rūl / i fū zhēn n._ abnormal collection of fluid between the two layers of pleura. Volume and nature of pleural effusions vary depending on the condition, e.g. purulent effusions in pleuropneumonia, cellular effusions from tumours in thorax (e.g. lymphosarcoma), chylous effusions from damage to thoracic duct (which normally carries lymph through chest), serous effusions in heart failure.
See Lymphosarcoma, Pleura, Pleuritis, Thoracic.

P. fluid ◀︎ _plor rūl / flū id, n._ fluid which lies in small space between two layers of pleura, in the pleural space. Normally, the fluid in the pleural space transmits transpleural forces involved in normal respiration and acts as a lubricant between the two pleural membranes; the maintenance of the optimal volume and thickness of the pleural fluid is closely regulated.

P. space _plor rūl / spās, n._ between two layers of pleura is a potential space, the pleural space, which usually just contains a small amount of pleural fluid.

Pleuritis/Pleuropneumonia ◀︎ _plor ī tis/ plor rō nū mō nē ē, n._ inflammation of pleura (pleuritis) or of lung tissue and pleura (pleuropneumonia), most commonly as a result of extension of bacterial or viral infection of lungs (pneumonia) or lung abscesses, but also from chest trauma, rupture of the oesophagus, or penetrating wounds. Risk factors for development include prolonged transport (hence 'shipping fever'), respiratory disease, surgery, and systemic disease.

Risk factors appear to impair pulmonary defence mechanisms, and allow microorganism contamination of the lower airways to progress to infection. Infection is accompanied by inflammation of lung tissues; inflamed tissues leak fluid into the pleural space, which may then become infected. Clinical signs depend on extent and duration of disease; acute cases may have fever, lethargy, cough, shallow breathing, and stiff gait (from chest pain). Animal may grunt when chest is compressed. Auscultation of chest may reveal muffled lung sounds or friction rubs. Chronic cases may have intermittent fever, weight loss, and ventral or limb oedema; development of intrathoracic adhesions may prevent successful recovery in some cases. Diagnosis is based on clinical history, blood tests, aspiration of pleural fluid (thoracocentesis); ultrasound of chest will typically reveal fluid accumulation. Treatment involves removing excessive pleural fluid, by aspiration or continuous drainage; instituting antimicrobial therapy; administering non-steroidal anti-inflammatory drugs to control fever and, hopefully, help prevent adhesion formation; supportive care, as needed; treatment of other disease processes. Prognosis for recovery is good if the condition is recognized early; chronic cases may develop secondary complications, e.g. laminitis, pericarditis, or abscesses in the cranial thorax, that complicate prognosis. See Thoracocentesis, Ultrasonography.

Plexus ◀ _plek_ sēs, _n._ a structure in the form of a network, especially a network of nerves, lymphatic vessels or blood vessels, e.g. brachial plexus is a network of nerves which lies between the front leg and the chest and innervates the front leg.
See Nerve.

**Pneumocystis jirovecii (carinii)** ◀ nū mō _sis_ tis / j ē rō _ve_ chi (ka rē nē), _n._ saprophytic fungus; does not ordinarily cause disease; however, especially in immunocompromised horses, e.g. Arabian foals with combined immunodeficiency, infection with the organism most commonly results in interstitial pneumonia. Organism was previously called _Pneumocystis carinii_.

Pneumonia ◀ nū _mō_ nē ē, _n._ inflammation of lung tissue, accompanied by consolidation. Most commonly caused by infection with microorganisms. Viral (e.g. equine herpes virus), bacterial (e.g. _Rhodococcus equi_) and fungal (e.g. _Histoplasma, Cryptococcus_) pneumonias have been reported in horses; sometimes, primary infection by one organism may be complicated by secondary infection with another organism (e.g. secondary bacterial invasion during a primary viral pneumonia). Non-infectious causes include aspiration (e.g. secondary to choke), inadvertent iatrogenic administration of substances into lungs by nasogastric tube, or layrngeal or pharyngeal dysfunction (e.g. following laryngeal surgery, secondary to neuropathies caused by botulism or equine protozoal myelitis, or secondary to myopathies, such as vitamin E deficiency or megaoesophagus), inhalation of smoke, or migration of parasitic worm larvae (ascarids). Risk factors for the development of pneumonia include crowding (easy spread of disease), regular heavy exercise (inhalation of dirt and oral secretions, as well as exercise-induced pulmonary haemorrhage), transport (horse is unable to lower head and clear respiratory secretions), endotracheal intubation and general anaesthesia (introduce contaminants into respiratory tract, compression of lungs from prolonged recumbency, and impaired ability to clear lungs). Signs of pneumonia include difficulty breathing, rapid breathing, high temperature, cough and discharge from nose. Diagnosis involves auscultation, thoracic radiography (especially in foals) and ultrasound. Blood counts may reveal elevated leukocyte count and increased levels of fibrinogen, depending on extent of infection and inflammation. Transtracheal aspiration biopsy and/or bronchoalveolar lavage may assist in establishing causative agent; appropriate antimicrobial therapy may be determined by culture of samples obtained. Environmental management to prevent overcrowding and ensure good air circulation helps to prevent airway inflammation and reduce the spread of infectious disease.

Pneumonia is often seen in combination with inflammation of airways (bronchopneumonia) or pleura (pleuropneumonia). See Auscultation, Bronchoalveolar lavage, *Cryptococcus neoformans*, Equine herpes virus, *Histoplasma*, Percussion, Pleuritis, *Rhodococcus equi*.

Pneumothorax ◄ *nū mō thor aks, n.* presence of air within pleural space. Causes pleural pressure to be equal to atmospheric pressure (normally, pleural pressure is negative), and lungs collapse. May be:
- Open, e.g. following wound to chest wall, where air can enter and leave chest.
- Closed, e.g. following rupture of oesophagus or lung tissue, or lung abscess, and there is no external exit for air.
- Tension p. develops when air continuously enters the pleural cavity without being removed. In such cases, the pleural pressure can increase to above atmospheric pressure, collapse the lungs, impair inspiration, and become life threatening.

Signs of pneumothorax include dyspnoea (difficulty breathing) and tachypnoea (rapid breathing). Diagnostic techniques include auscultation, percussion (resonance increased), radiography and ultrasonography. In cases of open pneumothorax, the opening into the chest must be sealed (e.g. by suturing the wound, or wrapping the chest in plastic wrap) and air evacuated, before healing can occur. In closed and tension pneumothorax, air must be evacuated until the leak can be sealed.
See Auscultation, Percussion, Pleural, Radiography, Ultrasonography.

Pneumovagina ◄ *nū mō vē jī nē, n.* entry of air into vagina caused by poor conformation of vagina, or vaginal injury. Seen especially in thin mares, or older mares, where the lips of vulva and the vaginovestibular fold do not adequately seal the entrance to the vaginal vault. Can be exacerbated during oestrus, with relaxation of the perineal body. May result in uterine contamination and infertility if untreated and chronic. Treatment may involve Caslick's operation, or reconstruction of the perineal body, if severe. Many young racing fillies are routinely treated with a Caslick's procedure so as to avoid pneumovagina while running, under the belief that the condition causes decreased racing performance.
See Caslick, Vagina.

Pododermatitis ◄ *pō dō der mē tī tis, n.* (greasy heel, mud fever, cracked heel, foot rot) inflammation of that portion of the skin which continues downwards to and within the horny structure of the hoof. Signs include lameness, soreness on palpation, swelling, and heat in the affected area. Treatment involves cleaning affected area, and topical and systemic antimicrobial therapy.
See Dermatitis, Foot, Sole.
    Proliferative p. see Canker

Poikilocyte ◄ *poi ki lō sīt, n.* abnormally shaped red blood cell, may be seen as consequence of fragmentation of erythrocytes (cells that have been mechanically damaged in circulation, as may occur in infection, inflammation, and neoplasia, especially when sufficient damage to endothelial surfaces results in fibrin deposition), oxidative injury from exposure to endogenous or exogenous circulating toxins, immune-mediated damage, or some congenital abnormalities. Poikilocytes are not usually considered highly sensitive or specific indicators of disease.

Point ◄ *point, n.* in reference to an anatomical structure, a structure with a distinct 'V' shape, e.g. point of hock, point of elbow, etc.; a surface with a sharp end, as in enamel points which form on teeth.

Poison ◄ *poi zēn, n.* substance which causes illness or death when consumed, injected, inhaled, etc., especially by chemical means. Numerous poisons may affect horses, including those in plants (e.g. ragwort, yew, bracken), rat poisons, heavy metals, etc. Signs seen vary according to type of poison.
See poisons under separate entries.

Poll ◄ *pōl, n.* top of head, between ears.
    P. evil ◄ *pōl / ē vūl, n.* bacterial infection of

bursa on top of head, causes painful swelling on one or both sides of neck, especially as associated with *Brucella abortus* infection.
See Brucellosis, Bursa.

Pollakiuria ◀€ *po la kē ŭr rē ē, n.* rarely used term denoting abnormally frequent urination, e.g. as may be occasionally seen in cases of inflammation of bladder (cystitis).
See Cystitis, Urinate.

Polycystic renal disease ◀€ *po lē sis tik / rē nŭl / di zēz, n.* very rare condition in horse, where kidneys have many fluid-filled cystic sacs throughout the renal cortex and medulla. Affected horses lose weight and develop chronic renal failure.
See Kidney.

Polycythaemia ◀€ *po lē sī tē mē ē, n.* increase in red blood cell count; may be relative, owing to a decrease in plasma volume (e.g. dehydration), or absolute, owing to an increase in the number of red blood cells. Affected horses show lethargy and varying degrees of hypoxia because of inefficient circulation from increased blood viscosity and sludging in capillaries. Absolute polycythaemia may be appropriate (e.g. as may be seen in horses living at high altitude), or secondary to the chronic hypoxia that may accompany some cases of heart or lung disease, or inappropriate (e.g. from myeloproliferative neoplasias of bone marrow). Most horses with inappropriate polycythaemia have a poor prognosis; intermittent phlebotomy may temporarily alleviate the condition.
See Erythrocyte.

Polydactyly ◀€ *pol ē dak til ē, n.* congenital condition of foals characterized by the formation of supernumerary digits. Selected individuals may be treated by surgery, which may consist of osteotomy of the affected bones and amputation of the supernumerary digits.

Polydipsia ◀€ *po lē dip sē ē, n.* abnormally high water consumption. May be seen secondary to disease conditions, e.g. diarrhoea, diabetes, from excessive salt consumption, or as a psychogenic phenomenon, most likely as a result of boredom from stall confinement.
See Diabetes, Diarrhoea.

Polymerase chain reaction ◀€ *pol ē mē rāz / chān / rē ak shēn , n.* molecular biology technique, increasingly used in equine medicine for identification of various infectious agents, including many viruses and bacteria. The test employs an enzyme that assists in the replication of DNA (polymerase) to replicate a piece of DNA from the organism. As the reaction progresses, additional DNA produced by the technique also participates in the process of replicating more DNA (chain reaction). The replicated DNA can be used to identify the organism that produced it.

Polymethyl methacrylate ◀€ *pol ē mē thil / meth ak ril āt, n.* (PMMA) synthetic polymer that has been used in orthopaedic surgery to fix bone plates, and in hoof repair. PMMA beads impregnated with antibiotics have been used for the treatment of chronic infections, especially of bones (osteomyelitis).

Polymixin B ◀€ *po lē miks in / bē, n.* antibiotic with limited use in the horse because it is not well absorbed from the horse's gastrointestinal tract. Works by disrupting the structure of bacterial cell membranes. Polymixin B kills relatively few types of bacteria; however, it is very effective in killing the bacteria that are sensitive to it. Occasionally employed in the treatment of infectious diarrhoea, usually in hospital settings. Polymixin B is the antibiotic of choice for the treatment of bacterial infections caused by *Pseudomonas* spp., as may be seen most often in the eye, or the uterus of the mare. Polymixin B is frequently combined with bacitracin and neomycin, other antibiotics that increase the number of bacteria killed compared to each antibiotic alone, as well as with corticosteroid anti-inflammatory agents (see Corticosteroid). Several polymixins have been identified, named A, B, C, D, E, and M. Only B and E have any clinical use.

Polymorphonuclear cell ◀ *po lē morf ō nū klēē / sel, n.* white blood cell, nucleus of which has several lobes, e.g. neutrophil. See Neutrophil.

Polymyopathy ◀ *po lē mī op ath ē, n.* unusual condition characterized by slowly progressive gait stiffness. Rare; has been reported in an aged pony mare. Histology of muscle showed muscle fibre degeneration; cause unknown.

Polyneuritis equi ◀ *po lē nŭ rī tis / e kwī, n.* (previously, referred to as cauda equine neuritis) uncommon neurological disease of unknown cause, characterized by paralysis of the tail and anal sphincter muscle, as well as cranial and peripheral nerve damage. Appears to be more common in Europe, where the condition was first recognized. Evidence indicates that the condition may be an autoimmune disease. Two forms; acute signs include hyperaesthesia, especially of the head and tail regions; chronic signs include gradual paralysis of tail, bladder sphincter and anal sphincter, leading to urinary and faecal incontinence; faecal retention may cause colic. May also involve cranial nerves, causing signs such as drooping eyelids, lips and tongue, and difficulty swallowing. Hind legs may become weak; muscle atrophy and ataxia may also be present. Unfortunately, definitive diagnosis is at post-morten examination; cerebrospinal fluid analysis may show increased protein. No effective treatment for the condition is known; condition is slowly progressive, in spite of treatment. See Autoimmune disease, Cauda equina, Nerve, Paralysis.

Polyp ◀ *po lip, n.* small, usually benign, growth which protrudes from mucous membrane, usually attached by a stalk. In horse, may occasionally be found in nasal sinuses, nasal cavity, throat, bladder, etc. Signs may be seen if size or position mean that polyp interferes with normal function, e.g. polyp in throat may result in noise during breathing.

Polysaccharide storage myopathy ◀ *pol ē sak ē rīd / stor ij / mī op ē thē, n.* (PSSM) a common cause of exertional myopathy (tying-up) that is seen in a variety of horse breeds, especially including Quarter Horses and related breeds, and also including draught horses. The disease is characterized by an abnormal accumulation of sugar (polysaccharide) in muscle cells. Once inside the muscle cells, the muscles of PSSM horses make an abnormally increased amount of glycogen when compared to normal horses. However, the accumulated sugar may not be responsible for the clinical signs of disease; rather, the accumulated sugar may merely reflect an underlying metabolic problem. Signs of PSSM are as seen with other exertional myopathies, including muscle stiffness or cramping, pain and firmness on muscle palpation, muscle tremors, lameness, discoloured brownish urine (myoglobinuria), and weakness. Blood samples can be used to help determine the extent of muscle damage; two muscle proteins to measure muscle damage are creatine kinase (CK) and aspartate aminotransferase (AST). However, these tests are not specific for PSSM; CK and AST levels in the blood elevate with almost any muscle damage.

TREATMENT
When signs of disease occur, exercise should be stopped and the horse should be moved to a stall; affected horses should not be forced to walk. If the weather is cool, affected horses should be blanketed. If horses are sweating, the sweat should be removed; if dehydration occurs due to excessive sweating, fluids, oral and/or intravenous (depending on the degree of dehydration) should be provided. Electrolyte deficits may cause other clinical signs (e.g. synchronous diaphragmatic flutter) in severe cases. Sedative/analgesic and non-steroidal anti-inflammatory drugs may be indicated to help treat anxiety and/or pain. Once clinical signs subside, horses may be fed hay; once horses move freely, they may be turned out into a small area to exercise.

PREVENTION
After an episode, horses should be returned to work very gradually so as to prevent future episodes. Dietary manage-

ment is important in reducing the incidence of PSSM. The horse's diet should be modified to decrease the amount of insulin and sugar in the blood stream. Feeds that have high starch content, such as corn, wheat, oats, barley, and molasses, should be avoided; extra calories can be given in the form of fats, e.g. vegetable or corn oil, or rice bran. However, dietary changes alone appear to be only about 50% effective in managing PSSM cases. Thus, horses with PSSM should also be exercised daily. Exercise suppresses glucose uptake, increases glucose utilization, and improves muscle energy metabolism. If both diet and exercise are modified, as many as 90% of affected horses may remain free of clinical signs of disease. Muscle biopsy is often useful in determining the underlying cause of myopathies such as PSSM. Furthermore, PSSM appears to have a genetic basis. A genetic mutation, which appears to have its origin prior to the foundation of modern horse breeds, appears to be responsible for as much as 90% of the incidence of PSSM; the PSSM gene is dominant, and one genetic copy of the mutation can cause disease. A second genetic mutation appears to make PSSM even worse in Quarter Horses and related breeds. Genetic blood testing for PSSM is available.

See Aspartate aminotransferase, Creatine kinase, Exertional rhabdomyolysis, Glycogen, Myoglobinuria.

Polysulphated glycosaminoglycan ◀ *po lē sul f̱a̱ tid / glī ko̱s am ē no̱ glī kěn, n.* (PSGAG) pharmaceutical compound chemically similar to substances that occur in normal joint cartilage (mucopolysaccharides). Two preparations of PSGAG are available for the horse: both are sterile solutions. One solution is injected directly into joints and the other is given IM (intramuscularly). PSGAG inhibits enzymes that are released during joint inflammation in vitro. Experimentally, when horse's knee joints that have been inflamed by injecting a chemical into them are treated with PSGAG, protein levels in inflamed joints are reduced and the thickness (viscosity) of the joint fluid is increased. In the laboratory, but not necessarily in the living horse, PSGAG causes increased

production of hyaluronic acid by the lining cells of the joint membrane (synovial cells). It may also stimulate the synthesis of glycosaminoglycans by cartilage cells themselves. PSGAG has been evaluated extensively but its actual effects in the horse are still relatively poorly understood. Unfortunately, for all of the potential benefits that can be observed in the laboratory, the clinical benefits of PSGAG are more difficult to measure. PSGAG does appear to be an excellent anti-inflammatory drug when it is injected into joints that have been treated with a chemical to cause inflammation. However, PSGAG has not shown any obvious beneficial effects on healing when it is injected into joints in which there have been surgically created defects in the cartilage. The effects of injection of PSGAG into muscle are even less clear. It is likely that PSGAG does reach therapeutic concentrations in horse's joints when it is injected into the muscle. It is possible that it exerts some anti-inflammatory effect and that multiple joints may be affected by a single intramuscular injection. However, it is also likely that the effect on a particular joint will be less than if PSGAG is given directly into that joint. It is unlikely, however, that PSGAG given into the muscle has any significant effect on delaying the development of, or helping in the repair of, damaged, arthritic joints. There is no evidence whatsoever to suggest that routine administration of PSGAG to normal horses will prevent the development of joint problems such as osteoarthritis. PSGAG has been injected in the muscle and injected directly into tendons and ligaments after injuries to these structures. One large study showed no difference in the recovery of horses with tendon injuries treated with such injections compared to those not treated with PSGAG.

Dilute PSGAG solutions have also been used topically to treat eye inflammation in animals.

SIDE EFFECTS
Injections of PSGAG into horse's joints have been associated with inflammatory joint reactions, similar to allergic reactions

in the joint. These usually are self-limiting. They must be differentiated from joint infections, which are much more serious. PSGAG injections may also increase the potential for bacteria to cause joint infections, should bacteria be introduced into the joint by the injection process. The intramuscular use of PSGAG appears to be largely safe.

Polyuria ◄€ *po lē ŭr rē ē, n.* production of abnormally large volume of urine, e.g. seen in pituitary pars intermedia dysfunction, renal disease, or diabetes.
See various conditions.

Ponazuril ◄€ *pon az ŭr il, n.* antiprotozoal agent used for the treatment of the protozoan parasite *Sarcocystis neurona,* the parasite that causes equine protozoal myeloencephalitis (EPM) in horses. Ponazuril interferes with normal parasite division. It is provided as a paste for oral administration. In the field studies conducted for approval of ponazuril, eight animals were noted to have unusual reactions as recorded in daily observations. In the field study, two horses exhibited blisters on the nose and mouth at some point during the study, three animals showed a skin rash or hives for up to 18 days, one animal had loose stools throughout the treatment period, one had a mild colic on one day and one animal had a seizure while on medication. The association of these reactions to treatment was not established.

Pons ◄€ *ponz, n.* a rounded area located at the ventral surface of the brainstem. Cranial nerves V, VI, VII and VIII originate at the border of the pons.
See Brain.

Popped knee see Carpitis

Portal ◄€ *por tl, n./adj.* the point at which something enters the body, e.g. the portal of infection; relating to an entrance, usually in reference to area of liver where major blood vessels enter and leave.
See Liver.
    P. lobule ◄€ *por tl / lob ŭl, n.* mass of liver tissue; the centre has a portal canal and

several central hepatic veins are at the periphery.
See Liver.
P. vein ◄€ *por tl / vān, n.* large blood vessel which carries blood from intestines, spleen, stomach and pancreas to liver.
See Liver.

Portosystemic shunt ◄€ *por tō sis tem ik / shunt, n.* (portocaval shunt) very rare condition in which there is a blood vessel link directly from the portal vein to the vena cava, bypassing the liver. Circulating blood does not benefit from filtration by the liver, especially of ammonia. May be congenital or, more rarely, acquired. Clinical signs are of neurological dysfunction from hepatic encephalopathy. No treatment is available.
See Ammonia, Liver, Portal.

Position ◄€ *pē zi shēn, n.* a particular arrangement or location.
    Foetal p. ◄€ *fētl / pē zi shēn, n.* term used to describe orientation of foal relative to mare, especially during foaling, e.g. foal in dorsal position has spine uppermost.
    See Parturition, Presentation.

Positive ◄€ *poz it iv, adj.* affirming the presence of something that is suspected to be present, e.g. a positive test.

Post- ◄€ *pōst, prefix.* behind, after.

Post-anaesthetic myopathy ◄€ *pōst-an ēs thet ik / mī op ēth ē, n.* condition characterized by pain and swelling in local muscle groups following general anaesthesia. The weight of the horse puts muscle groups on the 'down' side of the horse under pressure; compression of those muscles, combined with low blood pressure during anaesthesia, apparently predisposes to the development of the condition. Condition resembles exertional rhabdomyolysis, with stiff gait, and myoglobinuria in severe cases; the recovery of affected horses is prolonged, and affected muscles are rigid and painful. Severe cases may have elevated and rising body temperatures (malignant hyperthermia). Adequate padding, proper positioning of the horse during surgery, and blood pressure moni-

toring can help prevent most incidents. Treatment of affected horses is supportive, especially involving intravenous fluid therapy; some cases may remain sore for several days, but severely affected horses may not recover.
See Exertional rhabdomyolysis, Hyperthermia, Myopathy.

Posterior ◀ᴺ *pos lé rē ē, adj.* towards tail end, further back, opposite of anterior.

Posthitis ◀ᴺ *pos thī tis, n.* inflammation of the prepuce (sheath). Various causes, including fly strike, bacterial infection, trauma, or disease such as coital exanthema. Sometimes accompanied by inflammation of the penis (balanoposthitis). Sheath swells from inflammation, and may be sore on palpation. Treatment is directed at the underlying cause, e.g. antimicrobials for bacterial infection. Non-steroidal anti-inflammatory drugs may help reduce swelling and pain. Local therapy, e.g. cold hydrotherapy, massage, and especially exercise, may help move fluid from sheath. If unresolved, sheath swelling can become chronic, and predispose to further infection.

Postileus ◀ᴺ *post il ē ēs, adj./n.* stasis of the gastrointestinal tract following surgery.
See Ileus.

Post-mating endometritis ◀ᴺ *pōst-mā ting / en dō met rī tis, n.* transitory, and possibly normal physiological, uterine infection and inflammation following breeding; estimates are that the condition may affect as many as 15% of mares intended for breeding. Semen and microorganisms introduced to the reproductive tract by the covering process, whether natural or artificial, are responsible for the inflammation. Most mares are able to clear their uterus within 24 hours, but some mares have impaired uterine clearance mechanisms, probably owing to a defect in uterine muscle function. Mares that are unable to conceive when covered by stallions known to be fertile should be suspected of having post-mating endometritis. The presence of uterine fluid based on ultrasound examination more than 24 hours following

covering is supportive of the diagnosis. Surgery to correct conformation defects of the reproductive tract may help prevent uterine contamination. Oxytocin administered 4–8 hours after covering assists uterine clearance. Uterine lavage with large volumes of warm isotonic solutions helps remove fluid and inflammatory products from the uterine lumen. Both oxytocin and uterine lavage may be used in combination. Infusion of antibiotic solutions into the uterine lumen is another common approach to treatment.
See Endometritis.

Post-mortem ◀ᴺ *pōst-mor tēm, n./adj.* occurring after death.
   P. change ◀ᴺ *pōst- mor tēm / chanj, n.* a change in the condition of the animal occurring after death, e.g. tissue autolysis.
   P. examination ◀ᴺ *pōst-mor tēm / igs am in ā shēn, n.* inspection of dead animal in an attempt to ascertain cause of death.

Postnatal ◀ᴺ *post nā tl, adj.* after the birth; the period of time immediately after foaling.
See Foal, Parturition.

Postoperative ◀ᴺ *pōst op er ēt iv, adj.* occurring after a surgical procedure.

Postpartum ◀ᴺ *post par tēm, adj.* (postparturient) occurring to mare in period immediately after foaling.
See Parturition.
   P. eclampsia see Lactation
   P. periparturient haemorrhage see Periparturient

Postural balance see Balance

Potassium ◀ᴺ *pē ta sē ēm, n.* (K) chemical element, important in maintenance of acid–base balance in body, and normal cell function. Present in all cells, high levels in muscle.
See Acid, Muscle.
   P. chloride ◀ᴺ *pē ta sē ēm / klor īd, n.* chemical compound KCl. Can be administered intravenously or orally (by paste or pill), to help combat electrolyte-related problems, e.g. solutions containing potassium chloride may be given intravenously to help combat

hypokalaemia. Concentrated solutions of potassium chloride, given under general anaesthesia, are considered an acceptable method of euthanasia.

P. iodide ◀᠅ *pē ta sē ēm / īo dīd, n.* white crystalline salt with chemical formula KI. Potassium iodide solutions are occasionally used to treat conditions characterized by the formation of abscesses or granulomas, e.g. sporotrichosis. It is also used as an expectorant in cough formulations to help liquify thick mucus in respiratory diseases. Applied to the skin, potassium iodide has mild antifungal properties. An old treatment for thrush, an infection of the horse's foot, involves applying potassium iodide to the foot and then pouring on liquid turpentine. The resulting acrid purple smoke is quite dramatic and the treatment does kill bacteria in the foot. However, this application of potassium iodide can burn the skin of the lower limb, so it should be used carefully, if at all.

P. penicillin see Penicillin.

P. permanganate ◀᠅ *po ta sē ēm / per man gĕn āt, n.* chemical compound KMnO$_4$. Has been used as a bactericidal and fungicidal agent.

Potential ◀᠅ *pō ten shŭl, n.* a possibility.

Action p. ◀᠅ *ak shŭn / pō ten shŭl n.* a positive and negative ionic discharge that moves along a cell membrane; action potentials carry information within and between cells, especially between neurons, and from neurons to muscle and glandular tissues.

Membrane p. ◀᠅ *mem brān / pō ten shŭl, n.* the electrical potential difference (measured in millivolts) across a cell's membrane. Kept stable by concentrations of ions, especially sodium and potassium. Cellular communication, especially among neurons, occurs because of changes in membrane potentials (action potentials). Disruptions in serum ion concentrations, e.g. as seen in exhaustion, or severe dehydration, result in neurological dysfunction because of their effects on membrane potentials.

See Exhausted horse syndrome.

Potomac horse fever ◀᠅ *pē tō mak / hors / fē vē, n.* (Equine monocytic ehrlichiosis) disease first described in the area around the Potomac River in Maryland, USA, in 1979; distributed widely in US and other countries. Caused by *Neorickettsia risticii*, previously called *Ehrlichia risticii*. Organism is transmitted by freshwater snail; after ingestion, the organism multiplies in the gastrointestinal tract, where it can cause colitis. Clinical signs of disease include fever, depression, oedema of the lower limbs or ventral abdomen, and inappetance; most cases develop diarrhoea. May cause laminitis or abortion in some horses. Early in the disease, the bacteria may occasionally be seen in circulating monocytes; a complete blood count may show an increased number of monocytes. Accurate diagnosis requires polymerase chain reaction testing of the blood or faeces. Paired blood samples can also be evaluated to measure the antibody levels produced in response to active infection. Treatment is with tetracycline antibiotics; affected horses respond rapidly to treatment. A vaccine is available; however, the efficacy of the vaccine is questionable.

See Abortion, Diarrhoea, Laminitis, Polymerase chain reaction.

Poultice ◀᠅ *pōl tis, n.* moist substance commonly applied to the limbs and hooves of the horse, typically made up of clay or other earthen materials mixed with many other substances such as glycerin, kaolin, boric acid, aloe vera and oils of such things as peppermint and wintergreen. Poultices may also be made of moist bran, cereal, flour, or herbs. Poultices are commonly used in an effort to help reduce limb swelling or foot soreness in horses. As the agents dry, it is possible that they tend to dehydrate the surface tissue or absorb surface fluid into them. The actual medical benefits of poultices are unknown. Poultices almost certainly do not 'draw out' tissue infections such as abscesses. Poultices do not penetrate tissue, and tissue is not permeable to poultice, which is good, since absorption of clay or other earthen materials into the circulation would presumably be very bad for the horse's health. Also, since no substance can move back and forth freely across body tissue, an osmotic effect on abscesses should not be possible. Thus poultices should not be able to bring fluid underneath the skin to the surface. In human medicine, poultices are generally warm, moist mixtures of such things as hot water and linseed meal, usually applied between layers of cloth or muslin. The purpose of a poultice is to keep the treated areas hot and moist; in this manner, poultices increase tissue heat, and may be soothing, but they may also cause some local skin irritation.

Povidone–iodine ◀≀ *po vi dōn - ī ō dēn, n.* iodophor disinfectant that destroys many microorganisms by local irritation and germicidal action; commonly used as topical antiseptic, presurgical scrub, and for general disinfection.

Pox see Horsepox

P-R interval ◀≀ *pē-ar / in tē vūl n.* in electrocardiography, the P-R interval is the time (in seconds) from the beginning of the P wave (indicating the onset of atrial depolarization) to the beginning of the QRS complex (indicating the onset of ventricular depolarization). The P-R interval is longer with high vagal tone. A prolonged P-R interval may be a sign of impaired atrioventricular node conduction, e.g. as seen in various atrioventricular blocks.
See Atrioventricular, Electrocardiography.

Precipitation ◀≀ *pre si pi tā shēn, n.* the formation of a solid in a solution, as a result of a chemical reaction; separation, as occurs with a fine suspension of solid particles in a liquid, e.g. crystals and cells which fall to the bottom (gravitate) of a tube of urine sample.
  P. tests *pre si pi tā shēn / tests, n.* laboratory tests, e.g. radial immunodiffusion and immunoelectrophoresis, used to detect the presence of antibody–antigen complexes. Tests are possible because antibodies in solution react with soluble substances to form a precipitate. Dilutions of antigen and antibody in aqueous solution are combined until a precipitation reaction occurs and visible particles accumulate.
  See Antibody, Antigen, Electrophoresis, Radial, Urine.

Predictive value ◀≀ *pri dik tiv / val ū, n.* a measure (percentage) of the times that the value of a test (positive or negative) is the true value.
- Positive p.v – the percentage of all positive tests that are true positives. If a test has a high positive p.v., the likelihood that a horse testing positive has the disease for which it is being tested is high.
- Negative p.v. – the percentage of all negative tests that are true negatives. If a test has a high negative p.v., the likelihood that a horse testing positive does not have the disease for which it is being tested is high.

Predispose ◀≀ *prē dis pōz, v.* to make more likely, make an animal more susceptible to particular condition, e.g. obese horses are predisposed to developing laminitis.
See Laminitis

Prednisolone ◀≀ *pred ni so lōn, n.* the active metabolite of prednisone; a synthetic adrenal corticosteroid, commonly available as a tablet for oral ingestion, and in solution in ophthalmic preparations. Methylprednisolone acetate, a synthetic derivative of prednisolone, is commonly used for intra-articular injections into inflamed joints. Commonly used as anti-inflammatory drug, and to treat allergic conditions, e.g. recurrent airway obstruction. Prednisolone tablets have excellent bioavailability in horses and are preferred over prednisone when such therapy is indicated.
See Methylprednisolone, Prednisone, Recurrent airway obstruction.

Prednisone ◀≀ *pred ni sōn, n.* synthetic corticosteroid drug with a glucocorticoid effect; converted by the liver into prednisolone, its active metabolite. Orally administered prednisone has poor efficacy in horses because it is poorly absorbed and the active metabolite, prednisolone, is rarely produced.

Pregnancy ◀≀ *preg nēn sē, n.* the state of carrying a developing embryo or foetus within the mare; lasts 320–360 days (approximately 11 months). Clinical signs

of pregnancy include cessation of oestrous cycle, gradual enlargement of abdomen, development of mammary tissue, and behavioural changes.
See Embryo, Foetus, Oestrous cycle, Uterus.

P. test ◀╎ _preg nēn sē_ / _test_, _n_. one of several diagnostic tests to determine if mare is pregnant. Various techniques may be used in mare:

- Ultrasonography – probe inserted into rectum, and uterus scanned transrectally. May be used from day 11 (but more accurate a few days later) to end of pregnancy. However, effective imaging of the foetus is only possible up to about days 60–80 of gestation. Foetal gender may be most easily determined from days 60–70. Probe applied to flank (transabdominal ultrasound) may be used from day 60 of pregnancy, depending on size of mare. Allows maximum visualization of foetus and placenta.

- Progesterone sampling – hormone progesterone is secreted by corpus luteum. Elevated progesterone in a sample collected during the period of the next expected oestrus (20 days after last oestrus) indicates pregnancy. For a random sample from a mare, the more appropriate test for pregnancy is the Mare Pregnancy Test (MPT) based on the PMSG level.

- Rectal palpation – can detect pregnancy from 18–21 days post-conception; foetus is more easily detected as it enlarges.

- Equine chorionic gonadotrophin testing (pregnant mare serum gonadotrophin) – hormone produced by endometrial cups of the uterus of pregnant mare can be detected in serum sample from days 35–120. Can get false positive results (i.e. test indicates mare is pregnant but she is not) because endometrial cups persist even if foetus is lost.

- Cuboni test – based on detection of oestrogens in the mare's urine based on fluorescence of urine. Positive predictive value of approximately 90% after 100 days gestation; rate 100% after 150 days gestation.

- Oestrone sulphate test – hormone produced by foetus; sharp rise in serum after 60 days gestation, with peak levels

by 80 days gestation. Before 60 days a false positive can be obtained owing to oestrus. Test is considered an indicator of foetal viability after 44 days gestation. In faeces, oestrone sulphate can be detected after approximately 4 months (day 120 of gestation).
See Chorionic, Corpus, Oestrogen, Oestrone sulphate, Progesterone, Rectal, Ultrasonography.

Pregnant ◀╎ _preg nēnt_, _adj_. of a mare, carrying a foetus (or more than one).
See Pregnancy.

P. mare serum gonadotropin see Equine chorionic gondaotrophin

Prehension ◀╎ _prē hen shēn_, _n_. the act of grasping or seizing, especially of food with the mouth. In horses, the lips are prehensile.
See Lip, Tooth.

Premature ◀╎ _pre mē tŭr_, _adj_. born after a gestation period of less than the normal time; describes foal born before 320 days of gestation. Premature foals are generally of small size/weight, with floppy ears, and a soft, silky coat. They are generally slow to rise and suck, poor at maintaining normal body temperature (get cold easily), may have difficulty breathing (owing to immature lungs) and may be more susceptible than usual to infections, e.g. diarrhoea, respiratory infections. Neonatal intensive care units at referral hospitals have enabled premature foals that would have been previously unable to live to survive and thrive; however, such care is expensive. Intensive support of the immune, respiratory, digestive, musculoskeletal and circulatory systems is frequently indicated in premature foals.
See Pregnancy.

P. ventricular contraction see Ventricular

Premaxilla ◀╎ _prē maks il ē_, _n_. paired bones that form the front of the upper jaw and which contain the incisor teeth.

Premolar ◀╎ _prē mō lē_, _n_. designating one of the teeth between the molars and canine teeth, or between molars and incisors

when canine teeth are not present. Horse has three premolars on each side in top and bottom jaws. Unlike molars, premolars are preceded by deciduous teeth. When deciduous premolars are retained, i.e. they are not shed normally, they are referred to as 'caps'.
See Dentition, Tooth.

Prepubic tendon ◀≣ *prē pū bik / ten dēn, n.* the terminal tendon of the rectus abdominus muscle; where the muscle attaches to pubic bone of pelvis.

> **Ruptured p.t.** ◀≣ *rup tūrd / prē pū bik / ten dēn, n.* prepubic tendon may be ruptured in pregnant mare; this occurs more commonly in older, multiparous mares, and in draught breeds. Cause unclear; may relate to the weight of the foetus and foetal membranes, especially in cases of foetal abnormality (e.g. hydrops amnion). Rupture is often preceded by severe swelling under abdomen; rupture may result in cranial displacement of the mammary glands, or a palpable defect in the abdominal wall once swelling subsides. Condition is also painful, and clinical signs may be mistaken for acute colic. Affected mares walk stiffly, and may assume a 'sawhorse' stance because the loss of ventral muscle tension makes the pelvis unable to maintain its normal relationship with the spine. If late term, foaling is usually induced; supportive slinging of the abdomen may allow mare to carry foal to term if rupture is not too severe. Foaling must then be assisted. Surgical repair may be possible post-foaling in some instances, using a mesh; other affected mares may be euthanized if defect is irreparable or if expense of surgery is prohibitive.

See Pregnancy.

Prepuce ◀≣ *pre pūs, n.* ventral skin fold of male horse which forms sheath for penis (equivalent of human foreskin). Invagination of skin is a double fold, so is able to cover erect penis. The prepuce may be affected by various conditions, including habronemiasis infection, or neoplasia.
See Habronemiasis, Penis.

Prescription ◀≣ *pri skrip shēn, n.* an order for a medication or other medical inter-

vention. Prescriptions usually contain information as to the drug being prescribed, appropriate dosage interval, duration of dosing, and potential side effects.

Presentation ◀≣ *pre sēn tā shēn, n.* in obstetrics, the position of the foetus in the uterus relative to the birth canal, o.g. anterior presentation (head first, which is normal), or posterior presentation (hind end presented first).
See Parturition, Position.

Pressor ◀≣ *pre sē, n.* an agent that acts to constrict blood vessels and narrow their openings (vasoconstrictor); e.g. cold, stress, phenylephrine, or epinephrine. Also, increasing (or tending to increase) blood pressure.

Pressure ◀≣ *presh ē, n.* the force per unit area.

> **Blood p.** see Blood
> **Colloid oncotic p.** ◀≣ *kol oid / on kot ik / presh ē, n.* the difference between the osmotic pressure exerted by plasma proteins (colloid osmotic pressure) and that exerted by tissue fluid proteins.
> **Colloid osmotic p.** ◀≣ *kol oid / oz mot ik / presh ē, n.* osmotic pressure exerted by plasma proteins. Plasma proteins are colloids; colloids are particles that are so small and light that they do not settle in solution; the movement of blood is enough to keep the plasma proteins in suspension.
> **Partial p.** ◀≣ *par shūl / presh ē, n.* the pressure which a gas would have if it alone occupied the volume. Two common examples are the arterial gas measurements of:
> - P.p. carbon dioxide – measures how much carbon dioxide is dissolved in the blood and how well carbon dioxide is able to move out of the body.
> - P.p. oxygen – measures the pressure of oxygen dissolved in the blood and how well oxygen is able to move from the lungs into the blood.

Pressure bandage ◀≣ *presh ē / ban dij, n.* limb bandage applied in an attempt to control or prevent swelling, often using an elastic adhesive wrap. Care must be taken when employing such bandages so that they are not applied too tightly, or left in place for excessive time, so as to avoid complications from loss of blood supply (tourniquet-like action).

Pressure sore ◀ _presh ē_ / _sor_, _n._ a chronic ulcer of the skin caused by prolonged pressure, e.g. as may be seen in prolonged recumbency. Also known as a bedsore, or a decubitus ulcer.

Priapism ◀ _prī a pizm_, _n._ persistent erection of penis in stallion, without sexual arousal. In horses, the terms paraphimosis, priapism, and penile paralysis are used almost interchangeably (albeit, from an etymological point of view, inappropriately) to refer to an inability to retract the penis into the prepuce owing to swelling and oedema, usually of both structures. May occur following administration of phenothiazine tranquillizers.
See Paraphimosis, Penis, Phenothiazine.

Primary ◀ _prī mē rē_, _n._ first, as in order of time; principal. For example, the primary immune response is the immune response to the first challenge by a particular antigen; the primary teeth are the first teeth to develop in the foal.

Primidone ◀ _pri mi dōn_, _n._ a barbiturate anticonvulsant drug, metabolized in the liver to form two active metabolites, including phenobarbital. May be used to control seizures in foal associated with hypoxic ischaemic encephalopathy.
See Anticonvulsant, Hypoxic ischaemic encephalopathy, Seizure.

Primigravida ◀ _prī mi gra vi dē_, _n._ describes mare which is pregnant for first time.
See Pregnancy.

Primipara ◀ _prī mē pē rē_, _n._ describes a mare which has borne one foal.
See Pregnancy.

Probiotics ◀ _prō bī o tiks_, _n._ living micro-organisms, which upon digestion in certain numbers, exert health benefit beyond inherent basic nutrition; sold to promote or improve normal digestive function, speed up recovery from diarrhoea, etc. While probiotics may eventually have a role in equine medicine, at present it is not clear which, if any, organisms possess probiotic properties in the horse's digestive tract, have clinical effect, or can survive processing and storage.
See Bacteria, Diarrhoea.

Procaine ◀ _prō kān_, _n._ local anaesthetic drug, used primarily to reduce pain on injection of penicillin, i.e. procaine penicillin G.
See Penicillin.

Process ◀ _prō ses_, _n._ **1)** projecting part or prominence, especially as seen on a bone, e.g. extensor process of third phalanx. **2)** a naturally occurring progressive series of changes, generally gradual, that follow one another in a relatively predictable way, and which lead toward a particular result, e.g. the process of growth, or digestion; a naturally occurring, and usually continuous, activity or function, e.g. life processes such as breathing and blood circulation.
See Third: T. phalanx.

Progesterone ◀ _prō jes tē rōn_, _n._ female steroid sex hormone, $C_{21}H_{30}O_2$, that is produced by corpus luteum of ovary after ovulation to prepare the endometrium for implantation. Functions to protect embryo: reduces frequency of uterine contractions, changes secretions of uterus so that embryo is nourished. Later, progesterone produced by the placenta during pregnancy prevents rejection of the developing embryo or foetus, from about day 70 of gestation. Blood test for level of progesterone may be used as indicator of pregnancy at the appropriate time.
See Corpus, Ovary, Pregnancy, Uterus.

Progestin ◀ _prō jes tin_, _n._ (progestogen) general term for a group of hormones (5-alpha-pregnanes) that have biological effects similar to progesterone. Naturally produced by placenta during pregnancy; serve for maintainance of pregnancy. Near the end of gestation, blood progestin levels are approximately 100 times those of progesterone. Synthetic progestins (e.g. altrenogest) are commonly used in repro-

ductive and behavioural management of mares.
See Placenta, Progesterone.

Progestogen see Progestin

Prognosis ◄⸿ *prog nō sis, n.* likely outcome of a disease, i.e. forecast of prospect of recovery or return to full function.

Programmed cell death see Death

Progressive ethmoid haematoma see Ethmoid

Prokinetic ◄⸿ *prō kin et ik, adj.* stimulating movement or motility. Prokinetic agents, e.g. neostigmine or lidocaine, may be used to promote gastrointestinal motility with varying degrees of success, e.g. in the treatment of ileus.

Prolactin ◄⸿ *prō lak tin, n.* hormone produced by pituitary in mare in pregnancy and after foaling; under negative feedback control of dopamine, from the hypothalamus. Stimulates growth of mammary gland tissue and secretion of milk in late pregnancy. Concentrations in mares and stallions vary with the seasons, and are higher in summer than in winter; physiological function of prolactin in stallions is, as yet, unknown.
See Mammary gland, Milk, Pregnancy.

Prolapse ◄⸿ *prō laps, n.* displacement of organ or part of organ from its normal position, e.g. prolapse of uterus is where uterus is displaced through the vagina post-partum (rare in mares); prolapsed rectum may occur with diarrhoea, especially secondary to excessive straining.
See Uterus.

Proliferative ◄⸿ *prō lif er ēt iv, n.* characterized by rapid and repeated production or division, especially as in a mass of cells.
  P. arthritis see Arthritis
  P. enteropathy see Enteropathy, *Lawsonia intracellularis*

Promazine ◄⸿ *prō mē zēn, n.* phenothiazine antipsychotic and sedative drug; related to acepromazine. Has been used to tran-

quillize horses; an oral formulation has been available. Somewhat inconsistent in its effects and so not commonly used.
See Sedative.

Prophylaxis ◄⸿ *prō fi lak sis, n.* treatment to prevent disease, e.g. vaccination, quarantine, etc.
See Vaccine.

Propranolol ◄⸿ *prō pra no lol, n.* drug which blocks beta-adrenoreceptors of sympathetic nervous system (beta-blocker). Results in lower heart rate, may be used in treatment of certain dysrhythmias, e.g. ventricular tachycardia, especially those that are unresponsive to other medications.
See Heart, Sympathetic nervous system, Ventricular.

Proprioception ◄⸿ *prō prē ō sep shēn, n.* sense of perception of the position of the body, especially limbs and head; the sense that tells the body whether it is moving with required effort, as well as where the various body parts are located relative to each other. Proprioceptive stimuli originate in receptors imbedded in the joints, tendons, muscles, and labyrinth of the ear, and send impulses to cerebellum of brain. If there is a defect in the proprioceptive system, horse may appear incoordinated or ataxic, e.g. as may be seen with cervical stenotic myelopathy. Proprioception is assessed by various means, e.g. walking horse over uneven terrain, e.g. up and down slopes, or by blindfolding.
See Brain.

Proptosis see Exophthalmos

Prostaglandin ◄⸿ *pros tē glan din, n.* any of group of naturally occurring fatty acids that occur in cells and have hormone-like effects, e.g. regulate secretion of acid by stomach wall, stimulate contraction of smooth muscle of uterus. Synthetic prostaglandins are widely used for control of the mare's reproductive cycle, especially to lyse the corpus luteum of the mare's ovary. Prostaglandin is normally released by the mare's uterus when it is time for her to come back into heat; giving prostaglandins to the mare mimics the natural process. However, for injectable prostaglandins to be effective, the corpus luteum must be mature. Therefore, the drug will not work properly until at least 4 or 5 days after the last day of the mare's heat cycle. Clinical uses of prostaglandin in horses include:

1. To end situations where the corpus luteum persists.
2. To shorten the interval between heat cycles and allow for earlier re-covering.
3. To try to control the time of ovulation.
4. To help treat uterine infections by inducing heat.
5. To abort the foetus during pregnancy.

Certain synthetic prostaglandins (e.g. fenprostalene) have been used for elective birth inductions. Non-steroidal anti-inflammatory drugs (NSAIDs) block the effects of prostaglandins and thereby may promote the formation of gastric ulcers.

PRECAUTIONS
Prostaglandins can be absorbed through human skin and could cause abortion or bronchial spasms in people. Pregnant women and asthmatics should handle the drugs carefully. If they get on the skin, they should be washed off immediately with soap and water.

SIDE EFFECTS
After horses have been given prostaglandin, sweating, mild diarrhoea and colic signs have been observed. These signs are usually transient and disappear within an hour. Clinical experience suggests that these signs may be seen more frequently with dinoprost than with fluprostenol or other synthetic prostaglandins, although the effects seem to be dose-dependent. Low-dose prostaglandin use on consecutive days in horses has been studied, and seems to be as effective, with fewer side effects.
See Oestrous cycle, Parturition, Pregnancy, Uterus.

Prostate gland ◀≷ *pros tāt / gland, n.* accessory sex gland of male, lies around neck of bladder where it intersects with the pelvic urethra. Secretes milky fluid into urethra on ejaculation. Fluid increases seminal volume, and contains several alkaline secretions, including protein, citric acid, and zinc, the function of which is unclear. See Accessory sex gland, Semen, Sperm, Urethra.

Prosthetic ◀≷ *pros thet ik, n/adj.* an artifical replacement, especially of a body part. Prosthetic ocular implants may be used after enucleation of the eye, to maintain the outline of the globe. Prosthetic limbs have been constructed for some horses following amputation, e.g. in valuable stallions, or in mares carrying valuable foals.

Protease ◀≷ *prō tēs, n.* an enzyme that breaks down proteins into their component peptides. Important digestive enzymes; matrix metalloproteinases have been shown to be important in the pathogenesis of laminitis.
See Laminitis, Matrix metalloproteinase.

Protein ◀≷ *prō tēn, n.* any of a large group of nitrogen-containing organic compounds, made up of amino acids arranged into polypeptide chains which are then folded into specific molecules (proteins). Proteins are the basic building blocks from which tissue is made. Proteins also make up some of the hormones and all of the enzymes of the horse's body. Eighty per cent of the horse's structure is protein (after the fat and water are removed). Protein is being used constantly by the horse. Even though the horse's body reuses some of its own protein, and although bacteria present in horse's large intestine can synthesize some of the amino acids necessary to make up proteins, a steady supply must be available in the diet to replace some of what is lost or used up. Growing horses are more sensitive to protein needs than are adult horses. If protein is restricted in the diet in foals, growth is restricted as well. In adult horses, inadequate protein can cause decreased appetite, loss of body tissue and poor hoof and coat growth.

Excessive protein intake by horses appears to cause no obvious harm. However, there are studies that suggest that excessive protein intake may be associated with decreased performance. Exercising horses do not require supplemental protein, and extra protein does not make a horse stronger. Protein in excess of dietary requirements is merely burned as fuel or converted to fat. Digesting protein requires much work by the horse's body and giving a horse an excessive amount of protein is an expensive and inefficient way of giving extra calories.

Most horse's diets supply more than ample amounts of protein. Additional protein may be needed by horses for growth and lactation if these horses are fed certain poor-quality grasses or hays. However, rations based on alfalfa (lucerne), or other legume hays, generally supply plenty of protein for horses of all ages and metabolic requirements.
See Amino acid.

Protein-losing enteropathy see Enteropathy

Proteinuria ◀⁞ *prō tēn ŭr rē ē*, *n.* presence of protein in urine. Proteinuria is strongly indicative of damage to kidney tubules; such damage allows the large protein molecules to pass through the glomerular filtration system, e.g. as seen in glomerulonephritis.
See Blood, Glomerulonephritis, Kidney, Urine.

Proteoglycan ◀⁞ *prō tē ō glī kēn*, *n.* polysaccharide molecule that contains both protein and glycosaminoglycans. Proteoglycans are a primary component of the extracellular cartilage matrix, i.e. they are the 'filler' substance that exists between cartilage cells. Loss of proteoglycans occurs in osteoarthritis. Proteoglycans are also important components of tendons, ligaments, and dermis.
See Osteoarthritis.

Proteus spp. ◀⁞ *prō tē ēs / spē shēs*, *n.* genus of Gram-negative bacteria. Commonly found in soil, but also in the intestines. Can act as an opportunistic pathogen, e.g. *Proteus* may be associated with infections of the urinary and reproductive tracts, and may colonize the surface of granulation

tissue in healing wounds.

Prothrombin ◀⁞ *prō throm bin*, *n.* one of the plasma protein components of the blood that create the clotting mechanism, factor II. Synthesized in the liver, and converted to thrombin during blood clotting as part of blood clotting cascade.
See Clotting, Thrombin.
  P. time ◀⁞ *prō throm bin / tīm*, *n.* test used to assess the horse's body's ability to clot blood; time taken for clot to form in blood plasma sample after addition of tissue thromboplastin (factor III). Increased prothrombin time may be seen e.g. when the liver is damaged, with subsequent impairment in its ability to make clotting factors. If the p. time increases, it shows that the liver is not functioning normally.
  See Clotting.

Protozoa ◀⁞ *prō tē zō ē*, *n.* group (phylum) of simple organisms, made of a single cell but with no cell wall; larger than bacteria. Several protozoan parasites can cause disease in horses, including *Babesia*, *Cryptosporidium*.
See organisms under separate entries.

Proud ◀⁞ *prŏd*, *adj.* raised above the surrounding area (chiefly British usage).
  P. cut ◀⁞ *prŏd / kut*, *n.* colloquial term, used in US to describe male horses that maintain stallion-like behaviour post-castration; in UK terms are usually reversed ('cut proud'). Commonly said to be result of failure to remove adequate testosterone-producing tissue at castration, e.g. not castrated 'high enough' up the testicular cord. However, there is no testosterone-producing tissue other than the male gonads so, if they are removed, undesirable stallion-like behaviour post-castration is most likely to be the result of the horse's personality or poor training.
  See Cut.
  P. flesh ◀⁞ *prŏd flesh*, *n.* excessive growth of granulation tissue; 'exuberant' granulation tissue that protrudes from surface of healing wound. Can interfere with healing because of inability of epithelial cells to cover tissue, especially in areas subjected to much movement, e.g. over a joint.
  See Granulation.

Proximal ◀€ _prok si mūl, adj._ situated nearer to centre of body; as opposed to distal, e.g. proximal interphalangeal joint is the joint between first and second phalanges, nearer the centre of the body, whereas the distal interphalangeal joint is joint between second and third phalanges, relatively further from the centre of the body.

P. enteritis see Duodenitis–proximal jejunitis

P. phalanx ◀€ _prok si mūl / fa langks, n._ the most proximal bone of the phalanges; the largest bone of the pastern. Articulates with metacarpal or metatarsal bone to form the metacarpophalangeal or metatarsophalangeal (fetlock) joint in the front or hind limb, respectively.

P. sesamoid bone ◀€ _prok si mūl / ses ēm oid / bōn, n._ one of two paired bones at the posterior aspect of the fetlock joint.
See Sesamoid.

P. suspensory ligament ◀€ _prok si mūl / sēs pens ēr ē / li gē mēnt_ – that aspect of the suspensory ligament nearest the carpus. Common site of injury in sport horses.
See Suspensory ligament.

Prunus ◀€ _prū nēs, n._ genus of trees, some of which contain cyanogenic glycosides in seeds, e.g. cherries, peaches, apricots, almonds, and cherry laurel. Can be occasional cause of poisoning.
See Cherry.

Pruritus ◀€ _prū rī tēs, n._ itching. Sign of many skin conditions, e.g. allergic dermatitis (e.g. _Culicoides_ hypersensitivity), or parasitic skin conditions (e.g. mange). Horse demonstrates pruritis by biting at skin, or rubbing on fences, partitions, etc.

Prussic acid see Cyanide

Pseudohermaphrodite ◀€ _sū dō her ma fro dīt, n._ horse with gonads of one sex and external genitalia that resemble those of opposite sex.
See Hermaphrodite, Intersex.

Pseudohyperparathyroidism ◀€ _sū dō hī pē pa rē thī roi dizm, n._ rare paraneoplastic syndrome (i.e. a condition in which the clinical signs result from the secretion of a substance by a tumour) caused by secretion of hormone similar to parathyroid hormone. Typically results in high levels of calcium in blood. Has been reported as being associated with various neoplasias, including squamous cell carcinoma of various sites, as well as lymphosarcoma.
See Hyperparathyroidism, Lymphosarcoma, Parathyroid, Squamous.

Pseudomonas ◀€ _sū dō mō nēs, n._ genus of Gram-negative bacteria. Some species can cause disease in horses, especially _P. aeruginosa_, which has caused endometritis, secondary infection of burns, placentitis, pericarditis, and infectious keratitis. May be transmitted venerally by infected stallions. Treatment of infections is with appropriate antibiotic therapy, as determined by bacterial culture and sensitivity.
See Culture, Keratitis, Pericarditis, Placentitis, Uterus, Venereal.

Psoroptes ◀€ _so rop tēz, n._ genus of mange mites; causes psoroptic mange. Species which affect horses include _P. equi_ (body louse), and _P. cuniculi_ (in ears).
See Mange.

Psyllium ◀€ _sil ē um, n._ (hydrophilic mucilloid) fibre source made from the outer portion of psyllium seeds. Psyllium attracts large amounts of water to it and therefore has some effect as a stool softener. In horses, psyllium is commonly used in an effort to prevent or remove accumulations of sand from the intestine. Horses can inadvertently eat sand when they pull hay or grass from the ground when they are fed in areas of sandy soil. It has also been recommended as a treatment for some types of impaction colics (constipation). However, some research suggests that giving psyllium is no more effective at removing sand than preventing the horse from having further access to sand, whereby the horse will remove the sand on its own. Psyllium supplementation is no substitute for good management – that is, horses may still accumulate considerable amounts of sand while being given psyllium. Doses are variable, and not based on experimental data; however, there is general agreement that psyllium should not be fed continuously. Feeding psyllium for more than three consecutive weeks is not harmful, but if psyllium is provided to the horse constantly, the horse's intestinal tract may begin to digest it and thus render it ineffective. There are anecdotal reports of excessive gas in some horses receiving psyllium.

Pterydium aquilinum see Bracken fern

Ptosis ◀ᴇ *tō sis, n.* drooping of upper eyelid. May be seen in conditions affecting peripheral nerves, e.g. Horner's syndrome or paralysis of facial nerve (cranial nerve VII).
See Facial, Horner's syndrome.

Ptyalism ◀ᴇ *tī ē liz ēm, n.* excessive salivation. Many causes, including chemical irritation (e.g. from treated wood that is chewed by horses), stomatitis, inflammation of the tongue (glossitis), foreign body in mouth, or difficulty swallowing (dysphagia). Ingesting the fungal toxin slaframine, found in fungal-infected red clover, also causes ptyalism. Specific therapy is usually not indicated; the problem usually resolves when the primary problem is identified.
See Red clover, Slaframine.

Puberty ◀ᴇ *pū bē tē, n.* period when animal reaches sexual maturity and secondary sex characteristics start to develop: fillies typically reach puberty between 12 and 15 months of age. Stallions are considered to have reached puberty when an ejaculate contains 1×10^8 total sperm, with a progressive motility of 10%; on average, puberty in stallions occurs at about 67 weeks of age.

Pubic ◀ᴇ *pū bik, adj.* relating to the pubis.
See Pubis.
 P. symphysis ◀ᴇ *pū bik / sim fi sis, n.* the point of junction between the two pubic bones.

Pubis ◀ᴇ *pū bis, n.* paired bone of bony pelvis (os coxae); the smallest of the three

parts that make up the bony pelvis. Ventral surface is for muscular attachment; medial border joins the opposite bone at pubic symphysis. Cranial part joints the ilium and ischium to form the acetabulum; caudal part joints the ischium to form the inner border of the obturator foramen.
See Pelvis.

Pulmonary ◀ᴇ *pul mēn rē, adj.* relating to the lungs.
See Lung.
 P. alveolus see Alveolus
 P. artery ◀ᴇ *pul mēn rē / ar tē rē, n.* large blood vessel which carries deoxygenated blood from right ventricle of heart to lungs; the only artery in the horse's body that carries deoxygenated blood.
 See Heart, Lung.
 P. atresia ◀ᴇ *pul mēn rē / ēt rē si ē, n.* rarely occurring condition, characterized by failure of lung development, in combination with various cardiac defects. Observed primarily in neonatal Arabian foals.
 P. congestion ◀ᴇ *pul mēn rē / cēn jes chēn, n.* excessive accumulation of blood or fluid in the lungs. May occur after heavy exercise in unfit horse, or when horse has been recumbent some time, where lung on the underside of the body cannot expand owing to weight of overlying tissues.
 See Lung.
 P. contusion ◀ᴇ *pul mēn rē / kēn tū zhēn, n.* bruising of the lung, e.g. as may be caused by blunt trauma to the thorax.
 See Lung.
 P. emphysema see Emphysema
 P. function tests ◀ᴇ *pul mēn rē / fungk shēn / tests, n.* diagnostic measurements to assess lung function in horses with lung disease. Various tests include measurements of lung volume, changes in pleural pressure, arterial blood gas measurements, and airflow analysis.
 See Lung.
 P. hypertension ◀ᴇ *pul mēn rē / hī pē ten shēn, n.* increased blood pressure in arteries of lungs; in horse, usually seen in left-sided congestive heart failure, e.g. when left atrioventricular valve of heart is not functioning properly, allowing pressure to build up in lung blood vessels. P. hypertension occurring during heavy exercise (as a result of

high cardiac output and increased blood viscosity) may be a causal factor in exercise-induced pulmonary haemorrhage (EIPH). P. hypertension may lead to fluid leaving blood vessels and entering lung tissue (pulmonary oedema).

Persistent p. hypertension is a condition arising from persistent foetal blood circulation; seen when foal fails to adapt to extrauterine environment. Affected foals are in hypoxaemic respiratory failure, and respiratory acidosis. Diagnosis is by multiple serial blood gasses. Treatment is directed at correcting hypoxaemia (i.e. oxygen therapy) and acidosis.
See Heart, Lung, P. oedema (below).

P. insufficiency ◀⁞ *pul men re / in suf ish en se*, *n.* the backward (retrograde) flow of blood through the pulmonary valve into the right ventricle during diastole; may be acute or chronic. Clinically significant p. insufficiency is rarely recognized; most commonly occurs with pulmonary hypertension and left-sided heart failure.

P. oedema ◀⁞ *pul men re / i de me*, *n.* accumulation of fluid in lungs. May occur as result of severe allergic reaction (anaphylaxis), congestive heart failure (from pulmonary hypertension), pneumonia, etc. Signs of p. oedema depend on severity, but include rapid shallow breathing or frothy discharge from nose. Severe cases, e.g. as seen in cases of shock and hypoxia, may demonstrate incoordination and weakness, and low body temperature, which may progress to collapse and death as result of lack of oxygen in blood. Diagnosis involves auscultation and radiography; successful treatment requires identification and correction of primary cause(s).
See Allergy, Auscultation, Heart, Lung, Pneumonia, P. hypertension (above), Radiography.

P. valve ◀⁞ *pul mon re / valv*, *n.* (pulmonic valve) semilunar valve in heart between right ventricle and pulmonary artery; controls blood flow to the lungs.
See Heart.

Pulp ◀⁞ *pulp*, *n.* soft or soggy tissue (especially dental tissue, e.g. pulp of tooth is soft central portion where nerves and blood vessels are).
See Tooth.

Pulpitis ◀⁞ *pulp it is*, *n.* inflammation of the pulp of a tooth. Not commonly recognized as a problem in normal horses; may be caused by excessive iatrogenic removal of tooth crown.

Pulse ◀⁞ *puls*, *n.* the rhythmic contraction and expansion of an artery in response to the surge of blood from the beating heart. In horses, the pulse is commonly measured at various superficial locations, including the digital arteries behind the pastern (i.e. the digital pulse, the quality of which is often assessed in lameness diagnosis; pulse is typically increased – i.e. the pulsations are stronger and more obvious – in conditions such as laminitis or hoof abscess); the facial artery, just lateral to the eye; or the mandibular artery, where it passes under the horse's jaw, along the curve of the musculature. There is also a pulse, although far weaker, in veins. The jugular pulse is the rhythmic pulsation of the jugular vein, along the ventral neck, travelling from the heart towards the head. The jugular pulse is not commonly seen in normal horses unless the head is below the heart; in standing horses, the jugular pulse can reflect cardiac abnormalities (e.g. cardiac insufficiency).
See Artery, Heart, Jugular.

P. diagnosis ◀⁞ *puls / di eg no sis*, *n.* diagnostic technique in traditional medical practices, especially Chinese medicine. Character and quality of pulse are assessed, and purported to indicate various disease states. Scientific support for pulse diagnosis is lacking.

P. oximeter ◀⁞ *puls / oks e me te*, *n.* see Oximetry.

P. quality ◀⁞ *puls / kwo lit e*, *n.* a subjective assessment of the strength of the pulse.
Weak pulse may be seen in shock, or in cases of low blood pressure. Increased pulse may indicate inflammation.

P. rate ◀⁞ *puls / rat*, *n.* peripheral assessment of heart rate. Normally 30–50 beats per minute in adult horses; athletic animals tend to have a lower resting heart rate. Rate is higher in foals; normal rate 60–80 in newborn foal increases to 130 in a few hours. Rate decreases as horse ages.
See Artery, Heart, Jugular.

Punch biopsy see Biopsy

Puncture ◀⦂ _pungk_ tūr, _n._ the act of piercing or penetrating, especially in reference to a wound.

Pupil ◀⦂ _pū_ pūl, _n._ opening in centre of iris of eye, regulates the amount of light that enters the eye by varying size; tends to be open (dilated) in poor light, and smaller (constricted) in bright light. Normal pupil in horse is a horizontal elliptical shape; both eyes should be symmetrical. Pupil reacts to autonomic nervous system input; can be dilated with medication, to enable examination of back of eye.
See Eye.
    Pupillary light reflex see Reflex

Purgative ◀⦂ _per_ gē tiv, _noun/adj._ (laxative) substance which causes evacuation of faeces, e.g. liquid paraffin; the action of such a substance.

Purpura haemorrhagica ◀⦂ _per pŭ_ rē / he mē _ra_ ji kē, _n._ disease characterized by severe oedema and haemorrhages in the skin and mucous membranes that result in the appearance of purplish spots or patches (purpura). Associated with previous or concurrent respiratory tract infection, especially with _Streptococcus equi_ ('strangles'). Caused by the formation of antibody–antigen complexes that are deposited in small blood vessels and cause inflammation of blood vessel walls (vasculitis). Clinical disease can range from a mild, short-term reaction to a severe and fatal form. Blood and fluid escape from inflamed blood vessels, resulting in patches of bleeding (ecchymoses) seen in mucous membranes (e.g. gums), and oedema of limbs, sometimes severe. Intense vasculitis can cause areas of skin to be sloughed off as cells die from lack of oxygen. Severe disease may involve the respiratory, cardiac, renal, and gastrointestinal systems. Diagnosis from clinical signs and history of respiratory infection; immune function testing (e.g. Coombs' test) may reveal antigen–antibody reactions; IgA titres to _S. equi_ may be elevated. Skin biopsy shows typical vasculitis. Treatment is with corticosteroid therapy; treatment may be prolonged,

depending on severity of condition. Concurrent antibiotic, intravenous fluid, and non-steroidal anti-inflammatory drug therapy may also be indicated, as well as supportive care to control limb oedema. Prognosis for recovery depends on the severity of the insult.
See Antibody, Antigen, Biopsy, Streptococcus.

Purulent ◀⦂ _pūr_ ūl ēnt, _adj._ containing, discharging, or consisting of pus, e.g. purulent discharge is one which contains pus.
See Pus.

Pus ◀⦂ _pus_, _n._ thick opaque liquid, often yellowish-white, often with offensive smell, produced in infected tissue and abscesses. Composed of white blood cells, necrotic tissue and cellular debris, and often containing bacteria when pus is the result of an infectious process, e.g. _Streptococcus equi_ infection.
See Abscess, Bacterium, Leukocyte, Serum.

Pustular dermatitis ◀⦂ _pus_ tūl ē / _der_ mē _ti_ tis, _n._ skin disease characterized by the formation of pustules. May be seen as a feature of dermatitis of various causes, from viral infections, from autoimmune conditions (e.g. lupus erythematosus), or from drug eruptions.
See Pustule.

Pustule ◀⦂ _pus_ tūl, _n._ small raised elevation of the skin, or spot, containing pus.
See Pus.

Pyaemia ◀⦂ _pī_ ē mē ē, _n._ septicaemia caused by pus-forming microorganisms in the blood, e.g. from abscess. Bacteria are spread by the blood stream to all areas of body; multiple secondary abscesses may develop.
See Abscess, Bacterium, Pus.

Pyelonephritis ◀⦂ _pī_ e lō ne _frī_ tis, _n._ inflammation of kidney, both renal pelvis (where ureters and blood vessels enter – pyelitis) and functional kidney tissue (nephritis); rare in horses. In foal, may occur secondary to septicaemia; in adult horses, the condition has been associated with urolithiasis, recurrent bacterial infection of bladder (cystitis), or bladder paralysis. Signs include fever, depression, anorexia and weight loss. Unlike lower urinary tract infections, pyelonephritis is not typically associated with alterations in passing urine, such as more frequent or difficult urination; instead, signs such as haematuria or pyuria are more common, resulting in urine appearing abnormal. Diagnosis includes urinalysis, urine culture, cystoscopy, ultrasonography, rectal palpation and blood tests. Treatment is by lengthy course of appropriate antibiotics; cases in which only one kidney is affected may be treated by nephrectomy if antibiotic therapy is unsuccessful. Successful treatment of bilateral pyelonephritis is unusual, most likely because the disease is often not diagnosed until chronic and irreversible renal changes have occurred.

See Cystitis, Kidney, Rectal, Urinalysis, Ultrasonography.

Pyloric ◀̇ *pī lor ik, adj.* pertaining to that part of the stomach from which the intestine leads (the pylorus).

    P. sphincter ◀̇ *pī lor ik /sfingk tēr, n.* muscle at the beginning of small intestine; prevents intestinal contents from re-entering the stomach when the small intestine contracts, and regulates passage of food into the duodenum.

    P. stenosis ◀̇ *pī lor ik / sten ō sis, n.* thickening and hypertrophy of the sphincter muscle of the pylorus. Pyloric stenosis may begin as prolonged muscular spasm, which may lead to muscular hypertrophy and complete obstruction. Occurs primarily as a congenital problem in foals. Aquired pyloric stenosis can occur secondary to neoplasia or gastric ulceration. Clincal signs are of colic, salivation, and grinding teeth; complete obstruction can cause gastric reflux. Gastroscopy assists in diagnosis; surgery, e.g. gastrojejunostomy, may be indicated in some cases.

Pylorus ◀̇ *pī lor rēs, n.* the opening of the stomach into the small intestine (duodenum).

See Duodenum, Stomach.

Pyogranulomatous ◀̇ *pī ō gran ū lō mēt ēs, adj.* a chronic inflammatory process characterized by the formation of granulation tissue and pus. Typical reaction of the body in dealing with indigestible substances, e.g. foreign bodies. Principal cells in such reactions are macrophages and lymphocytes. Pyogranulomatous reactions have been reported to occur in many types of infections, in many different tissues, including infections caused by various parasites, fungi, and bacteria.

Pyometra ◀̇ *pī ō mē trē, n.* accumulation of pus within uterus. Uncommon in mares. May not affect mare's reproductive cycle; chronic cases may have prolonged oestrus. Infection appears to require combination of chronic endometritis and cervical dysfunction. Diagnosis is made by observation of uterine discharge (when present), and rectal palpation; ultrasound assists in differentiating pyometra from uterus enlarged by pregnancy. Treatment is by uterine lavage to remove fluid; lavage fluids may contain combinations of isotonic fluids, DMSO, or antibiotics. Successful treatment may be difficult; hysterectomy may be recommended to eliminate problem. Commonly results in infertility of mare.

See Pus, Uterus.

Pyospermia ◀̇ *pī ō sper mēē, n.* presence of white cells in the semen. The presence of pyospermia indicates possible infection and/or inflammation in the male reproductive tract.

Pyramidal disease see Buttress foot

Pyrantel ◀̇ *pī rēn tēl, n.* (pyrantel pamoate, pyrantel tartrate) anthelmintic drug. Drug is available as a paste for oral administration, a liquid for administration via nasogastric intubation, and a pelleted formulation that is given daily in the feed. Pyrantel causes paralysis of intestinal parasites. The parasites are then removed from the body by normal intestinal movements. Pyrantel is effective for control of the majority of equine intestinal parasites, including strongyles, *Oxyuris*, *Parascaris* and *Anoplocephala*, but has no effect against bots. Pyrantel is the only deworming agent that has demonstrated effectiveness against *Anoplocephala*, the equine tapeworm; the dose must be doubled to achieve this effect. Pyrantel is considered safe for all horses at up to twenty times overdose. Resistance to pyrantel is reported.

See *Anoplocephala*, Anthelmintic, Benzimidazole, *Oxyuris equi*, *Parascaris equorum*, Resistance, *Strongylus* spp.

Pyrethrin ◄⁞ *pī reth rin, n.* a pair of natural organic compounds that have potent insecticidal activity; contained in the seed cases of the perennial plant pyrethrum (*Chrysanthemum cinerariaefolium*). Biodegradable and considered to be among the safest of the insecticide and insect repellent compounds known.

Pyrethroid ◄⁞ *pī rē throid, n.* synthetic chemical compound similar to the natural chemical pyrethrins; permethrin is a commonly used pyrethroid in horses. Common ingredient in insecticides and insect repellents used in horses. Relatively safe; excessive exposure associated with reversible neurotoxicity.

Pyridoxine ◄⁞ *pī rid oks ēn, n.* vitamin B-6.
See Vitamin B-6.

Pyrimethamine ◄⁞ *pi ri meth ē mēn, n.* drug that may be used for the treatment of equine protozoal myeloencephalitis, typically in combination with a sulphur-trimethoprim combination antibacterial drug. Drug interferes with folic acid synthesis, which is necessary for normal DNA and RNA synthesis by the organism. Treatment for protozoal myeloencephalitis must often be continued for several months. Pyrimethamine comes as a tablet for oral administration to the horse; the two products, sulphur-trimethoprim and pyrimethamine, may also be mixed together into an oral liquid or paste.

Pyrrolizidine ◄⁞ *pī rō li zi dēn, n.* poisonous alkaloids named for their inclusion of a pyrrolizidine nucleus (a pair of linked pyrrole rings). Found in some plants, especially the Boraginaceae, Compositae, and Leguminosae families, e.g. ragwort, comfrey, and *Senecio* spp. Alkaloid metabolites are toxic to the liver. Signs of toxicity include weight loss (often acute), icterus, diarrhoea, ventral oedema, and central nervous system signs (circling, head pressing) from hepatic encephalopathy. Blood panels show elevated liver enzymes; liver biopsy is diagnostic. No specific treatment; however, affected horses can recover if hepatic damage is not too severe.
See Ragwort, *Senecio* spp.

Pythiosis ◄⁞ *pi thē ō sis, n.* (phycomycosis) tropical and subtropical skin infection caused by fungal-like organisms of *Pythium* spp; in horses, especially *P. insidiosum*. Organism can be found in cooler environments as well as warmer ones; infections have been reported over a wide range, including Australia, the Pacific islands, Asia, southern United States, and Central and South America. Disease is characterized by the formation of cutaneous, subcutaneous, lymphatic and intestinal tumour-like masses, with fistulas and a serosanguineous discharge; small, hard, coral-like masses called 'kunkers' are a feature of pythiosis in horses. Chronic cases, involving bones and lungs, have been reported. Large lesions are often pruritic. Disease occurs mostly in the summer months, especially after periods of high rainfall. Occurrence commonly associated with grazing in stagnant water; however, the infection may also be acquired after contact with soil and grass containing infectious organisms. Most equine cases apparently occur through open wounds in contact with water or grass, especially wounds of the extremities. Diagnosis is through examination of impression smears, biopsy, or culture; an ELISA test has been developed for *Pythium insidiosum*. Surgical removal of the lesions is common, but has a high rate of recurrence owing to incomplete removal of the organisms from affected tissues; complete surgical excision of limb lesions may be difficult without permanently scarring limbs because of relative lack of skin on the equine extremity. The use of drugs such as sodium iodide, itraconazole, and amphotericin B in treating pythiosis has been limited because of cost, poor success rate, and high toxicity. Immunotherapy has been reported to have been used successfully in a few equine cases. The prognosis for complete recovery is guarded.

***Pythium* spp.** see Pythiosis

Pyuria ◄∈ *pī ŭr ē ē, n.* pus in the urine. See Pus.

Q

QRS Complex ◀ *kū / ar / es / kom pleks, n.* the tracings in an electrocardiographic record that represent ventricular activity of the heart.

Q-T interval ◀ *kū – tē / in tē vūl, n.* in electrocardiography, the time between the start of the Q wave and the end of the T wave in the heart's electrical cycle. The faster the heart rate, the shorter the Q-T interval. If abnormal, there is a possibility of arrythmias.
See Arrhythmia.

Quadriceps ◀ *kwo dri seps, n.* the large muscles of the thigh which help move and support the stifle joint.

Qualitative ◀ *kwo li tēt iv, adj.* in reference to a diagnostic test, the determination of the existence of a tested parameter in a tested sample or population. Qualitative tests are usually reported in terms of positive, negative, or suspect.

Quantitative ◀ *kwon ti tē tiv, adj.* in reference to a diagnostic test, the determination of the absolute or relative abundance of a tested parameter in a sample or population. Quantitative tests are reported in measured units.

Quarantine ◀ *kwo rēn tēn, n.* all necessary procedures associated with the prevention of importation of unwanted microorganisms into an area, especially by restricting movement of an animal, or holding it in isolation for a period of time to ensure freedom from diseases and/or external parasites. May be used to treat individual animals on a premises to prevent the spread of disease, for animals newly introduced to premises, or prior to importation into a foreign country in an effort to prevent introduction of diseases.

Quarter ◀ *kwor tē, n.* the lateral or medial aspect of the hoof wall.
See Hoof.

    Q. crack ◀ *kwor tē / crak, n.* a gap or fissure in the hoof quarter. Quarter cracks may start on the ground surface, or at the coronary band, and extend to a variable distance. Such cracks may cause lameness if they involve the sensitive structures of the hoof. Various repair techniques are described, usually in combination with horseshoe manipulations done in an attempt to relieve stress on the hoof wall.
    See Hoof.

Queensland itch ◀ *kwēnz land / ich, n.* pruritic skin condition, as described in Australia; caused by allergic reaction to biting midges, e.g. *Culicoides* spp.
See *Culicoides* spp.

Quercus **spp.** see Oak

Quid ◀ *kwid, v.* in horses, a chewed portion of food that has been dropped from the mouth. Various causes, including tooth loss, inability to swallow, paralysis of tongue.
See Tongue, Tooth.

Quinidine sulphate ◀ *kwi ni dēn / sul fāt, n.* drug used to treat heart rhythm abnormalities, e.g. atrial fibrillation. Works by blocking the fast inward sodium current. At higher heart rates, the effect of the drug increases, while at lower heart rates the effect of the drug decreases. Derived from quinine, which was itself originally derived from the bark of the cinchona tree.
See Atrial, Heart.

Quinsy ◀ _kwin_ zē, *n.* inflammation or abscess of tonsilar tissues. Obscure term for infection with *Streptococcus equi* (strangles).
See Abscess, Strangles.

Quittor ◀ _kwi_ tor, *n.* chronic purulent inflammation of a collateral cartilage of the foot, most commonly affecting a forelimb. Commonly results from injury over or penetrating wound into one of the collateral cartilages of third phalanx. Cartilage becomes necrotic; pus produced which drains from sinus at top of coronary band. Horse may be lame, with swelling above hoof; in long-term cases hoof shape may become deformed. Treatment is by surgical excision of the draining tracts and necrotic cartilage, and appropriate aftercare. The prognosis for recovery is good with complete removal of tissue, assuming no secondary complications, such as osteomyelitis of the third phalanx or infection of the distal interphalangeal (coffin) joint.
See Foot.

R

R wave 🔊 *ar / wāv, n.* the initial positive or upward tracing of the QRS complex on an electrocardiogram. Caused by activation of the ventricles.

Rabies 🔊 *rā bēz, n.* zoonotic disease caused by rabies virus (genus *Lyssavirus*). Uncommon in horses; where it occurs, usually transmitted to infected horse by bite from rabid wild carnivore or bat (i.e. one infected with rabies). Reservoir hosts are skunks, racoons, bats and foxes. Is not endemic in UK, Ireland, Australia or New Zealand at present. Virus infects and replicates in muscle cells, and may remain in muscle for weeks or months. Virus then infects peripheral nerves and progresses to the central nervous system, where it replicates rapidly. Incubation period can vary from as few as 9 days to as long as 1 year, depending on factors such as the location of bite (direct inoculation into nerve causes a more rapid course of disease) and amount of virus inoculated. Signs variable; no signs are pathognomonic. Affected horses may be lame, or may die suddenly. Initial signs of hyperaesthesia, ataxia, anorexia, behavioural changes, paralysis, or colic have been reported. Neurological signs are typically classified into one of three forms:

1. Cerebral form (furious form) is typified by photophobia (dislike of bright light), aggressiveness, hydrophobia (fear of water), hyperaesthesia, muscle tremors, and convulsions.
2. Brainstem form (dumb form) is characterized by depression, anorexia, head tilt, circling, incoordination, drooling, pharyngeal paralysis, blindness, urinary incontinence and self-mutilation.
3. Spinal form (paralytic form) is typified by ascending paralysis, ataxia, lameness, and self-mutilation.

Diagnosis is difficult ante-mortem, but rabies should be considered as a differential diagnosis in endemic areas in horses with rapidly progressing neurological disease. Fluorescent antibody testing of hair follicles of facial skin may reveal viral antigens, but test may be falsely negative. Post-mortem examination of the brain is diagnostic. No treatment is available; horses in endemic areas are usually vaccinated to prevent rabies. Notifiable disease.
See Notifiable disease, Paralysis, Pharynx, Spinal, Virus.

Racing plate 🔊 *rā sing / plāt, n.* light aluminium horseshoe, typically worn by flat track racing and some jump racing horses.

Radial 🔊 *rā dē ūl, adj.* relating to radius. See Radius.

    R. immunodiffusion 🔊 *rā dē ūl / im ū nō dif ū shēn.* a quantitative immunodiffusion test in which an agar gel contains evenly distributed antigen (or antibody). Test sample diffuses into the gel from a well, resulting in a circular line of precipitation around the sample well. The diameter of the precipitin ring is proportional to the concentration of the antigen (or antibody) present in the test sample. When the diameter of the test specimen precipitin ring is compared to known standards, it is possible to reach a relatively insensitive estimation of the concentration of specific antigen or antibody.

    R. nerve 🔊 *rā dē ūl / nerv, n.* large nerve of front leg, innervates extensor muscles of elbow, knee and foot, and allows the horse to bear weight on its leg. Has sensory fibres on front and outside of leg.
See Elbow, Humerus.

R. nerve paralysis ◀⁞ *rā dē ūl / nerv / pē ra li sis, n*. r. nerve may be damaged by trauma, e.g. fracture of humerus, pressure from recumbency during general anaesthesia, etc. Signs of damage include inability to bear weight on affected leg, dropped (low) elbow position, scuffing of toe, foot knuckled over. Prognosis depends on degree of insult; if nerve is severed, prognosis is grave; however, horses with nerve damage from pressure may recover with time.
See Elbow, Humerus.

Radiation ◀⁞ *rā dē ā shēn, n*. energy emitted as electromagnetic waves (includes light, X-rays) or stream of subatomic particles (e.g. alpha and beta particles produced by radioactive material). Two types:
- Ionizing r. – energy that is powerful enough to remove electrons from atoms (i.e. to form ions). Includes X-rays, and alpha and beta particles.
- Non-ionizing r. – energy that may excite, but not remove, electrons. Includes visible light, radio waves, infrared light, and ultraviolet light.

See Ion, X-ray.

Radical ◀⁞ *rad ik ēl, n/adj*. atom or group of atoms with an unpaired electron; see Free radical. Also, describes a treatment or procedure designed to remove all diseased tissue, or the root of disease (e.g. a radical surgical procedure).

Radioactive ◀⁞ *rā dē ō ak tiv, adj*. describes physical material that emits ionizing radiation.
See Radiation.

Radiocarpal joint ◀⁞ *rā dē ō kar pūl / joint n*. joint between radius and carpal bone; the most proximal joint of carpus. Common site of chip fracture in racing horses.
See Carpus.

Radiofrequency hyperthermia ◀⁞ *rā dē ō frē kwēn sē / hī pē ther mē ē, n*. use of electromagnetic waves with a frequency in the 10s to 100s of megahertz range (radio waves) to induce heat in tissue. Sometimes used in the treatment of localized

neoplasia in horses, e.g. squamous cell carcinoma.
See Equine sarcoid, Squamous.

Radiograph ◀⁞ *rā dē ō grarf, n*. visible image produced on sensitive film or plate by a particular type of ionizing radiation (X-rays). More commonly known as an X-ray.
See Radiation, Radiography, X-ray.

Radiography ◀⁞ *rā dē o grē fē, n*. examination of internal structures of body by use of non-destructive ionizing radiation (X-rays). Machine artificially produces a stream of X-rays, which pass through body, and are recorded on sensitive film or plate placed at an angle to the stream. Depending on the density of the tissue examined, more or less radiation will pass through. Radio-opaque structures, e.g. bone and enteroliths, stop the majority of the radiation, and appear white on radiographs. Radiolucent tissue, e.g. fatty tissue, tendon and muscle, stop relatively little of the radiation, and so appear relatively darker, if at all, on radiographs. Radiographic examination may be facilitated by the use of radio-opaque contrast material, e.g. iodine compounds, that may be injected into blood stream to assess blood supply to lower limb (e.g. venogram), ingested to highlight interference with passage through the gastrointestinal tract (e.g. barium swallowed to show blockage in intestine of foal, or oesophageal stricture in adult horses), or infused locally to trace the source of a draining tract (fistulogram).
See X-ray.

> **Digital r.** ◀⁞ *dij it ēl / rā dē o grē fē , n*. radiographic examination that involves recording information electronically, as opposed to on sensitive film. Images are obtained quickly (no film development required) and can be manipulated. Expensive; may not offer diagnostic advantage over good quality plain film radiography.

See X-ray.

Radioisotope ◀⁞ *rā dē ō ī sō tōp, n*. version of an element with an unstable nucleus; emits radiation as it decays to a stable

form. Various radioisotopes may be used in examination by scintigraphy.
See Scintigraphy.

Radiotherapy ◀ *rā dē ō the rē pē, n.* treatment of disease, e.g. cancer, using ionizing radiation. Ionizing radiation damages cells non-specifically, so radiation treatment must be carefully localized. Not widely used in horses, but may be used for tumours of eye. Radioactive material may also be implanted within body (brachytherapy), e.g. in treatment of skin tumours.
See Brachytherapy, Radiation.

Radius ◀ *rā dē ĕs, n.* large bone of the forearm. Paired with the short ulna, with which the radius fuses below elbow, to form elbow joint with humerus proximally; articulates with the proximal row of carpal bones to form the knee joint (carpus) distally.
See Carpus, Elbow, Ulna.

Ragwort ◀ *rag wert, n.* (*Senecio jacobea*) yellow-flowered plant, widespread in UK and Europe; may contain pyrrolizidine alkaloids which cause chronic liver failure if eaten. Plant not very palatable to horse, but may be eaten if grazing is restricted or plant wilted, e.g. in hay. Signs of poisoning, which may not appear for months after plant is eaten, include weight loss, dullness, nervous signs (e.g. yawning, incoordination, blindness, head-pressing), skin changes (e.g. photosensitization), jaundice. Diagnosis by liver biopsy.
See Biopsy, Liver, Photosensitization, Pyrrolizidine.

Rain scald/rash/rot see Dermatophilosis

Rale ◀ *rarl, n.* abnormal rattling breathing sound heard on auscultation of chest of horse, especially in horses with lung disease. May be described with reference to intensity (e.g. loud or small), origin (e.g. tracheal, pulmonary, or pleural), or quality, as in:
- Dry r. – a crackling lung sound; more commonly heard in conditions without excessive mucus production, e.g. recurrent airway obstruction.
- Moist r. – a wet lung sound; reflects the presence of fluid in the air passages.
See Auscultation, Crackle, Lung, Pneumonia.

Ramus ◀ *rā mĕs, n.* branch of an anatomical structure, e.g. bone or nerve. For example, the mandibular ramus is the vertical part of the lower jaw bone (mandible).
See Mandible.

Randomized study ◀ *ran dēm īzd / stud ē, n.* a comparative study in which patients are assigned randomly (by chance) to separate treatment groups. The best scientific clinical trials are randomized, controlled, and blinded.

Ranitidine ◀ *ra ni ti dēn, n.* antihistamine that is most commonly used for the treatment of stomach ulcers in the horse. Available in pill form for oral administration; normally dosed three times daily. Reduces secretion of acid by stomach.
See Antihistamine, Equine gastric ulcer syndrome, Stomach.

Rash ◀ *rash, n.* a skin eruption; colloquial term used to describe reddening of skin or spots on skin.
See Dermatitis, Skin.

Rasp ◀ *rarsp, n./v.* coarse file; to make smoother with a coarse file. Horse's teeth may be rasped (floated) when sharp enamel points develop from uneven wear of teeth.
See Tooth.

Rate ◀ *rāt, n.* measure of speed or frequency relative to another specified quantity; e.g. heart rate is number of beats in a given time (usually a minute), pregnancy rate is number of mares from a population which become pregnant in a certain period.

Ratio ◀ *rā shē ō, n.* mathematical relationship of one substance to another, e.g. albumin:globulin ratio is amount of albumin in blood relative to globulin, (usually 2:1, i.e. for every two molecules of albumin there is one of globulin).

Rattlepod ◀⁙ _ra_ tl pod, *n*. (*Crotalaria* spp.) genus of plants occurring in USA, S. Africa, Australia. White pea flowers are followed by papery inflated pods in which the small seed rattles about if it is shaken. May contain pyrrolizidine alkaloids which accumulate in the liver and produce long-term damage that may be fatal. Generally not eaten by horse, but may be present in hay or may be eaten if little other forage available.
See Liver, Pyrrolizidine.

Rauwolfia ◀⁙ *rő* _wūl_ *fē ē*, *n*. genus of evergreen trees and shrubs. Plants contain a number of bioactive chemicals. Reserpine, a drug used for behaviour-modifying effects in horses, is a *Rauwolfia* alkaloid.
See Reserpine.

Reabsorption ◀⁙ *rē ab* _sorp_ *shēn*, *n*. the act or process of absorbing again, e.g. as is performed by the renal tubules of the kidneys in the process of regulating important molecules such as glucose, proteins, or sodium. These reabsorbed molecules return to the blood. Not to be confused with resorption – see that entry.
See Glucose, Kidney, Protein, Renal, Sodium.

Reaction ◀⁙ *rē* _ak_ *shēn*, *n*. response to chemical or physical stimulus. For example:
- Adverse r. – an unwanted or harmful reaction, especially following the administration of a drug.
- Allergic r. – the hypersensitive response of the horse's immune system to a substance, e.g. insect bite, or inhaled allergen.
- Chemical r. – change or transformation resulting from a substance decomposing, combining with other substances, or interchanging constituents with other substances.

Reactive oxygen species ◀⁙ *rē* _ak_ *tiv* / _ok_ *si jēn* / *spē shēs*, *n*. any of a number of highly reactive forms of oxygen. Highly unstable and highly interactive with other molecules. Can be harmful to tissues. Normally form as a by-product of oxygen metabolism, and have important roles in cell signalling. Normally controlled by various enzymes and antioxidant molecules, e.g. vitamin C. Reactive oxygen species play a role in the pathogenesis of conditions such as diarrhoea, muscular damage, colitis, recurrent airway obstruction, and spinal cord injuries.
See Free radical, various disease conditions, Vitamin C.

Reagent ◀⁙ *rē* _ā_ *jēnt*, *n*. substance used to cause chemical reaction, e.g. as in various diagnostic tests in order to detect, measure, produce, etc. other substances.

Receptor ◀⁙ *ri* _sep_ *tē*, *n*. A molecule within a cell or on a cell surface to which a substance (such as a hormone or a drug) selectively binds, causing a specific physiological effect in the cell. Innumerable examples of specific receptors exist, e.g. receptors on liver cells respond to insulin by causing increased conversion of glucose to glycogen.
See Insulin, Liver.

Reciprocal mechanism ◀⁙ *re* _si_ *prē kŭl* / _me_ *kē nizm*, *n*. anatomical specialization of horse's hind leg whereby the stifle and tarsus (hock) are forced to move in unison, e.g. the tarsus is locked if stifle joint is also locked; if stifle joint is extended or flexed, tarsus is also extended or flexed. Brought about by a combination of ligamentous structures, which run from above stifle joint to below tarsus, including the peroneus tertius. Along with the stay and the locking mechanism of the patella in the stifle, the reciprocal mechanism allows the horse to stand for much longer periods than other domestic animals, with little muscular effort.
See Patella, Peroneus tertius, Stay apparatus, Stifle, Tarsus.

Reconstructive surgery ◀⁙ *rē kon* _struk_ *tiv* / _serjē_ *rē*, *n*. surgery that is done to reshape or rebuild (reconstruct) a part of the body, especially a part that has been changed by injury, e.g. skin grafting to cover a large wound on a lower limb.

Rectal ◀⁙ _rek_ *tŭl*, *adj*. of, relating to, or situated near the rectum.
See Rectum.

R. examination ◀╎ _rek_ tūl / ig _za_ mi _nā_ shĕn, _n._ diagnostic technique where veterinary surgeon inserts arm into rectum to examine a portion of the abdominal cavity. About 40% of the equine abdomen can be examined rectally, and it is sometimes possible to feel changes in various structures, including the intestinal tract, reproductive structures, blood vessels (e.g. iliac artery), left kidney, lymph nodes, urinary tract, and spleen. Used especially in diagnosis of colic, and in diagnostic procedures involving the reproductive tract (e.g. pregnancy diagnosis).
See Colic, Pregnancy.

R. mucosal biopsy ◀╎ _rek_ tūl / mū kō zūl / _bī_ op sē, _n._ diagnostic procedure by which sample of the mucosal lining of rectum is collected for histological examination. Various techniques for collection. May assist in the diagnosis of some intestinal conditions, e.g. chronic inflammatory bowel disease or neoplasia.
See Chronic inflammatory bowel disease, Endoscope.

R. palpation see Palpation

Rectourethral ◀╎ _rek_ tō ŭr ē thrūl, _adj._ pertaining to the rectum and the urethra. Congenital rectourethral fistula is a rare condition of colts, usually associated with other defects such as atresia ani.
See Atresia ani.

Rectovaginal ◀╎ _rek_ tō vē _jī_ nūl, _adj._ pertaining to the rectum and the vagina (of the mare).
See Rectum, Vagina.

R. fistula ◀╎ _rek_ tō vē _jī_ nūl / _fis_ tū lē, _n._ hole through vaginal wall into rectum, does not extend all the way to the perineum. Occasionally seen in mares post-foaling, caused by foal's foot tearing through vaginal wall and into rectum, then retracting. Faeces can enter vagina through the resulting fistula and cause bacterial infection of reproductive tract, or signs of colic caused by faecal impaction. May also be seen as a rare congenital defect in fillies, typically associated with other congenital abnormalities such as atresia ani. Tears may be repaired surgically.
See Atresia, Parturition, Rectum, Vagina.

Rectum ◀╎ _rek_ tĕm, _n._ the terminal part of the large intestine; ends at anus. Faeces are formed in colon and pushed into rectum by intestinal contractions. Distension of rectum stimulates nerves which results in passing of faeces (defecation).
See Faeces, Large intestine.

Rectus abdominus ◀╎ _rek_ tēs / ab _do_ mi nēs, _n._ large paired muscle which forms ventral abdominal wall. Attaches to pelvis by prepubic tendon.
See Abdominal, Muscle, Prepubic tendon.

Recumbent ◀╎ ri _kum_ bĕnt, _adj._ lying down.

Recumbency ◀╎ ri _kum_ bĕn sē, _n._ clinical term used to describe state of an animal that is lying down and unable to rise, either through disease or general anaesthesia. Usually described relative to body position:
- Dorsal r. – lying down on back.
- Lateral r. – lying down on side.
- Sternal r. – sitting up on the chest, with legs tucked underneath the body (a.k.a. ventral recumbency).

Recurrent ◀╎ ri kur ēnt, _adj._ **1)** occurring or appearing again or repeatedly, e.g. recurrent airway obstruction. **2)** in anatomy, turning in a reverse direction, e.g. recurrent laryngeal nerve.
See Recurrent airway obstruction, Recurrent largyneal nerve.

Recurrent airway obstruction ◀╎ ri _kur_ ēnt / _ăr_ wā / ob _struk_ shĕn, _n._ (RAO, COPD, chronic small airway disease, broken wind, heaves) common respiratory condition of horses, especially middle-aged horses (over 10 years of age). No breed predilection; familial tendency has been identified. Disease characterized by reversible periods of airway obstruction, with accumulation of neutrophils, mucus, and bronchial spasm. Underlying cause is thought to be allergic (hypersensitivity reaction), especially allergies to inhaled dust, fungal spores, and/or pollen. Allergic reaction causes an increase in lung resistance, an increase in respiratory effort, secretion of mucus into the air passages, and inflammation. Disease process results in obstruction of airways. Previously called chronic obstructive pulmonary disease (COPD); however, the condition in horses differs significantly from COPD in humans and such terminology is now felt to be inappropriate in describing the disease in horses.

CLINICAL SIGNS
Depend on severity of reaction and length of time horse is exposed to allergens; ranging from exercise intolerance, cough, and nasal discharge in mildly affected horses to persistent cough, nasal discharge, increased respiratory rate, weight loss, and increased respiratory effort (abdominal lift as abdominal muscles help to push air out may result in 'heave line' from enlargement of abdominal muscles). Affected horses rarely have fever.

DIAGNOSIS
By history of seasonal disorder, especially associated with changes in husbandry, along with clinical signs. Auscultation may demonstrate wheezes and rales. Endoscopy typically may show mucopurulent exudate in trachea. Examination of tracheal aspirate obtained by aspiration biopsy, or bronchoalveolar lavage, shows nonseptic inflammation. Pulmonary function tests show decreased lung compliance and increased lung resistance. Arterial blood gas analysis may show arterial hypoxaemia. Skin testing for allergens appears to be of little use.

TREATMENT
Changing management to avoid exposure to allergens is a crucial part of therapy. Stabled horses may be allowed more access outdoors; however, horses that develop recurrent airway obstruction associated with dusty pastures may benefit from more time in stable. Dust control is crucial to management; dusty hay may be soaked in water prior to feeding, and air circulation may be improved using fans. Medical management includes corticosteroid therapy; inhalant therapy appears to be particularly effective. Bronchodilators, e.g. clenbuterol, may help relax smooth muscles and open airways.

Anticholinergics, e.g. atropine, can be used diagnostically (affected horses breathe more easily after administration), but may cause ileus if used therapeutically. Antimicrobials may be used if microorganisms are identified on diagnostic aspirates, or if there are signs of concurrent infections. Antihistamines were once widely used in treatment, but would appear to have little use based on the known pathogenesis.

PREVENTION
Once a horse has been identified as suffering from recurrent airway obstruction, it will always be predisposed to the condition. Attempts should be made to reduce exposure to dust and other allergens, and to improve air circulation. Prophylactic use of medications such as inhaled corticosteroids may be indicated for horses that become severely affected. See Airway, Allergy, Auscultation, Bronchoalveolar lavage.

Recurrent laryngeal nerve ◀ *ri kur ĕnt / la rin jē ŭl / nerv, n.* nerve that innervates the laryngeal muscles. The nerve runs an indirect route, descending from the spinal cord down into the thorax, before turning up between the trachea and oesophagus to supply the muscles of the larynx. The anatomical position of the nerve makes it subject to damage from perivascular injections of irritant substances. However, in many cases, the cause of damage to the nerve is unknown; many cases of idiopathic degeneration occur.
See Laryngeal.

Recurrent laryngeal neuropathy ◀ *ri kur ĕnt / la rin jē ŭl / nŭr ro pĕ thĕ, n.* damage to recurrent laryngeal nerve, primarily the left nerve, resulting in failure of muscles to hold larynx open fully during breathing, commonly resulting in noise on inspiration, particularly at speed, and exercise intolerance. Cause is unknown; nerve fibre degeneration has been recognized in weanlings. There is some evidence that the condition is heritable. Treatment is by surgery, either by prosthetic laryngoplasty or laryngeal reinnervation surgery.
See Laryngeal, Larynx.

Red bag ◀≀ *red/ bag, n.* colloquial term for premature separation of the placenta prior to or during a mare's foaling. Infrequent; when recognized, prompt action to open the allantochorion (the 'red bag') is required to prevent weak or stillborn foal.
See Placenta.

Red blood cell (RBC, erythrocyte) see Erythrocyte

Red clover ◀≀ *red / klō vē, n.* (*Trifolium pratense*) biennial clover; lives for about two years before dying off unless it is allowed to re-seed itself. Grows to 30–38 cm in height with 19–25 mm diameter rose-purple to magenta flowers. Can be infected with a fungus (*Rhizoctonia leguminocola*) that produces an alkaloid that causes excessive salivation ('slobbers').
See Slaframine.

Red maple ◀≀ *red / mā pl, n.* (*Acer rubrum*) tree found mainly in the eastern United States. Fresh leaves are non-toxic; however, dried or wilted leaves are poisonous. Poisoning more common in late summer and autumn. Blood cells are damaged by as yet unidentified toxin, causing a haemolytic anaemia, methaemoglobinaemia, and Heinz body formation. Signs of poisoning include loss of appetite, dullness, weakness, and increased heart and respiratory rates. Most characteristic signs are intense icterus, and a brown colour of the gums and the urine. If severe, horse will become comatose in 4–5 days; naturally occurring fatality rate is approximately 60%. May recover in 7–14 days with milder exposure. Treatment is supportive, e.g. fluid therapy, nasogastric intubation with intestinal adsorbents (e.g. activated charcoal), and corticosteroids to stabilize blood cell membranes.
See Erythrocyte, Haemoglobin.

Red worm ◀≀ *red worm, n.* colloquial name for *Strongylus* spp. parasitic worms.
See *Strongylus* spp., Worm.

Reefing ◀≀ *rē fing, n.* surgical reduction of the extent of a tissue, by excising a portion of it and repairing the resultant wound with sutures. In horses, term is most commonly used to describe reduction of the prepuce, e.g. as may be indicated for the treatment of neoplasias such as squamous cell carcinoma.
See Squamous.

Reflex ◀≀ *rē fleks, n.* involuntary muscle action or movement in response to stimulus; does not require conscious control. Normal reflex needs intact sensory nerve supply to transmit the stretching of receptors, and intact motor nerve supply for the muscle to contract. Reflexes may sometimes be tested as part of assessment of nervous system.
Significant reflex actions include:

- Corneal r. – reflex involving trigeminal (fifth cranial; sensory) and facial (seventh cranial; motor) nerves. Any stimulus to the cornea (e.g. pain, touching) leads to reflex closure of the eye. May be used to test for depth of general anaesthesia.
- Cough r. – reflex involving the laryngeal and vagus (tenth cranial) nerves. Stimulation of air passages by dust or other foreign particles produces a cough; cough removes the foreign material from the respiratory tract.
- Menace r. (blink r.) – involves optic (second cranial; sensory) and facial (seventh cranial; motor) nerves. Reflex occurs after sudden stimulation of visual system (e.g. by threatening eye with finger); stimulus leads to reflex closure of the eyelids. Must be interpreted with caution, e.g. neonatal foals may lack a menace reflex until they learn that objects directed at their eyes are threatening. The clarity of the eye and the contrast of the menacing object with its surroundings are other important considerations in interpreting this menace reflex, e.g. horses with complete cataracts lack a menace response – however, the lack of response is understandable.
- Palpebral r. – involuntary neuromuscular action of horse (as well as most animals with eyelids), that closes eyelids to protect the eye from contact in response to a stimulus, e.g. pain, or touching. Involves trigeminal (fifth

cranial; senses the touch) and facial nerve (seventh cranial; moves the eyelid). May be used to test for depth of general anaesthesia.

- Pupillary light r. – reduction of the size of the pupil in response to light. This reflex involves optic (first cranial; sensory) and oculomotor (third cranial; motor) nerves. Two types of papillary light reflex are noted:
  1. Direct pupillary light r. – the pupil constricts in response to light shone in the same eye.
  2. Consensual (indirect) pupillary light r. – the pupil of one eye constricts in response to light shone in the other eye.

  Several patterns of response are possible, e.g. if the optic nerve in one eye is damaged, that eye will lack a direct pupillary light reflex but the consensual reflex is likely to be intact.

- Patellar r. – a stretch reflex, whereby the stifle joint extends rapidly in response to sharp tap on patellar tendon. Involves sensory and motor pathways of the femoral nerve. May be tested occasionally in foals but can only be tested when animal is in lateral recumbency.

- Righting r. – postural reaction that returns the horse to sternal recumbency after being placed on its back or side. A normal righting reflex depends on normal vestibular, visual and proprioceptive functions.

- Suck r. – primitive reflex of newborn foals; foals are stimulated to suck by contact around the mouth. Suck reflex disappears as horse ages.

See Cranial nerve, Facial, Patella, Reflex, Trigeminal nerve.

R. arc see Arc

Reflux ◀ː *rē fluks, v.* to flow back or return, e.g. the reflux of stomach contents through a nasogastric tube, as may occur in some cases of small intestinal obstruction or enteritis.
See Enteritis.

R. oesophagitis ◀ː *rē fluks / ē sof ēg it is, n.* inflammation of the oesophagus caused by reflux of gastic secretions. May be a feature of equine gastric ulcer syndrome.

See Enteritis, Equine gastric ulcer syndrome.

Regeneration ◀ː *rē jen ē rā shēn, n.* the ability to grow back, as with certain tissues, e.g. liver tissue may be able to regenerate and return to normal function if the horse is removed from a source of liver toxicosis.

Regional ◀ː *rē jēn ēl, adj.* pertaining to, or limited to, a certain area.

R. anaesthesia see Anaesthesia, Nerve block
R. anatomy see Anatomy
R. limb perfusion ◀ː *rē jēn ēl / lim / per fū zhēn, n.* technique for the regional delivery of high concentrations of antibiotics. Involves administration of an antimicrobial solution into the blood vessels of a selected portion of the limb that has been isolated from the systemic circulation by controlled application of a tourniquet.

Regurgitation ◀ː *ri ger ji tā shēn, n.* flow in the opposite direction from normal. Regurgitation of food material from the stomach is very rare in horses, and usually only seen in terminal stages of grass sickness or extremely severe colic with gastric rupture; term also used to describe backwards flow through faulty heart valve, e.g. mitral valve regurgitation.
See Colic, Grass sickness, Heart.

Rehydration ◀ː *rē hī drā shēn, n.* restoration of normal fluid and electrolyte levels, e.g. after dehydration, by oral means (e.g. drinking or nasogastric tube), or intravenous fluid therapy.
See Dehydration, Fluid.

Rejection ◀ː *rē jek shēn, n.* an immune response whereby a foreign tissue, such as a skin graft, is attacked by the immune system of the organism receiving such tissue (i.e. by antibodies, T cells, and macrophages).

Relaxin ◀ː *ri lak sin, n.* hormone produced by the placenta during pregnancy, starting at approximately day 80. Thought to act synergistically with progesterone to maintain pregnancy. Causes softening of cervix

and relaxation of joint between pubic bones of pelvis, so that foaling is facilitated. Has also been used as a biochemical marker of placental insufficiency, foetal viability, and pregnancy determination in horses.
See Cervix, Hormone, Parturition, Pelvis, Pregnancy.

Remodelling ◀: *rē modl ing, n.* the simultaneous resorption and deposition of bone tissue. In normal bone remodelling, the two processes occur in equilibrium, and function to repair and replace bone as part of normal metabolism. Bone also remodels in response to the stresses placed upon it (Wolff's law), e.g. the cortices of the metacarpal bones thicken in racing horses in response to the stresses caused by running round turns.
See Wolff's law.

Renal ◀: *rē nūl, adj.* relating to kidney.
See Kidney.

    R. insufficiency see Insufficiency
    R. tubular acidosis ◀: *rē nūl /tūb ū lē / as id ō sis, n.* rare disorder of kidney function of unknown cause in which the blood filtering structures in the kidney are impaired; causes production of urine that is more acid than normal. Clinical signs in affected horses include anorexia, ataxia, heart rhythm abnormalities and weight loss. Blood testing shows metabolic acidosis and electrolyte abnormalities, e.g. hyperchloraemia. Treatment with intravenous fluid therapy and bicarbonate may help correct clinical condition; long-term oral bicarbonate therapy is required for clinical management. Prognosis guarded; recurrence is common, especially with associated kidney disease.
    See Kidney.

Reperfusion ◀: *rē pē fū shēn, n.* restoration of blood flow to tissue after it has suffered ischaemia or a loss of blood supply.

    R. injury ◀: *rē pē fū shēn / in jē rē, n.* damage to tissue caused when blood supply returns to the tissue after a period of ischaemia. Clinically relevant problem especially when surgically correcting intestinal displacements, torsions, or entrapments that have compromised circulation to affected portions of the bowel.

Reproduction ◀: *rē prē duk shēn, n.* the process of generating offspring; duplicating. Term may be used for mammals and also for simpler organisms, e.g. bacteria, fungi, etc. In horses, depends on production of egg (ovum) by ovaries of mare, production of sperm by testes of stallion, mating of fertile stallion and mare at end of oestrus, and sperm travelling through female reproductive tract to oviduct where it fuses with egg to form embryo. Embryo must attach to wall of uterus; develops there into foetus, which is then born as a foal after gestation period of 320–360 days.
See Embryo, Foetus, Oestrus, Ovary, Ovum, Pregnancy, Sperm, Testis.

Reproductive system ◀: *rē prē duk tiv / sis tēm, n.* the male and female organs that are responsible for the process of reproduction, i.e. penis and testicles in male; uterus and ovaries in female.

Repulse ◀: *ri puls, v.* drive back; e.g. to repulse a foal is to push a foal back into uterus to correct positioning of leg during foaling; to repulse a tooth is to extract a tooth from the root side, by addressing the root with an instrument, either from the sinus, or from a hole drilled into the mandible, usually under general anaesthesia.
See Parturition, Tooth.

Resection ◀: *rē sek shēn, n.* surgical procedure to remove all or part of an organ or tissue, e.g. intestinal resection during colic surgery.

Reserpine ◀: *rē sē pīn, n.* alkaloid human antipsychotic drug that has been occasionally employed in horses for longer term behavioural modification (up to several days; possibly a week or more). Works as a sympatholytic agent. Therapeutic and toxic doses are close; signs of toxicity include depression, profuse sweating, colic, diarrhoea, and AV block. No specific antidote is available for toxicity; the drug can be easily detected in laboratory screening tests.
See Sympatholytic.

Resistance ◀⁞ *ri zis těns, n.* the ability to withstand something; opposition to something. Specifically, in clinical context:

- Disease r. – the natural ability of an animal to withstand invasion by a disease-causing organism.
- Drug r. – the ability of bacterium, parasite, etc. to be unaffected by drug (i.e. antibiotic resistance, anthelmintic resistance). Drug resistance may be promoted by treatment of animals with inadequate doses of drug, for treatment for too short a time, or simply from a population being exposed to the agent over time. Continued pressure from the drug selects for individuals that are resistant, so that eventually the population is largely unaffected. Some types of drug resistance can be passed from one organism to its offspring, e.g. by plasmids in bacteria. Organisms also develop specific strategies to inactivate drugs, e.g. β-lactamase enzymes produced by some bacteria inactivate penicillin. Anthelmintic and antibiotic resistances are serious problems in horses, as well as in all mammalian species.

See Anthelmintic, Antibiotic, Plasmid.

Resonance ◀⁞ *re zě něns, n.* sound produced by hollow cavity during percussion, e.g. of chest or gas-filled bowel. Resonance will be reduced by changes to cavity, e.g. presence of fluid.
See Percussion.

> **Magnetic r.** see Magnetic resonance imaging

Resorption ◀⁞ *ri sorp shěn, n.* the process of losing substance. When a substance is resorbed, it is broken down and assimilated back into the body, especially as pertains to bone, as part of the process of bone metabolism, or as to the loss of a foetus in early gestation without apparent clinical signs. Not to be confused with Reabsorption – see that entry.

Respiration ◀⁞ *re spi rǎ shěn, n.* the process by which an organism with lungs exchanges gas with its environment (breathing), taking oxygen in air into lungs and removing carbon dioxide from body;

at a cellular level, respiration is the oxidative process by which the chemical energy of organic molecules is released in a series of steps that involve the consumption of oxygen and the release of carbon dioxide and water.
See Carbon dioxide, Lungs, Oxygen.

Respiratory ◀⁞ *re spě rě trě, adj.* concerned with respiration, breathing, or the lungs.
See Respiration.

> **Acute r. distress syndrome** (ARDS) see Acute respiratory distress syndrome
> **R. acidosis** see Acidosis
> **R. alkalosis** see Alkalosis
> **R. distress** ◀⁞ *re spě rě trě / dis tres, n.* (dyspnoea) difficulty breathing, e.g. owing to blockage of airway or a variety of lung diseases. Affected horses are tachypnoeic. Typically results in hypoxaemia (low oxygen levels in blood).
> **R. insufficiency** see Insufficiency
> **R. rate** ◀⁞ *re spě rě trě / rāt, n.* the number of breaths taken in a unit of time; typically, the number of breaths per minute. In horses, the respiratory rate is most commonly taken by counting the number of times the horse's chest expands and falls per minute (or counting for 15 seconds, and multiplying by 4). Normal resting respiratory rate in a horse is 12–20 breaths per minute; the rate normally increases with exercise. At high speed, the respiratory rate is equal to the stride rate, that is, the horse breaths with each stride when he is running; the limb movement itself expands and contracts the lungs. In foals, the respiratory rate is 40–60 breaths per minute in the first 5 minutes after birth, slowing to 30–40 breaths per minute after a few hours. Respiratory rate may be normal, abnormally fast (tachypnoea), abnormally slow (bradypnoea), or nonexistent (apnoea).
> **R. sound** ◀⁞ *re spě rě trě / sǒnd, n.* noises made by breathing; noise by air as it moves through airways can be heard by auscultation of the respiratory tract. Various diseases of the respiratory tract may result in differences in the intensity, quantity, or quality of sounds; an absence of sounds may also occur, e.g. with consolidation of lung tissue, as may be seen in severe pneumonia, or when there is fluid in chest cavity, as in pleuritis. Different sounds may be heard:

crackle, wheeze, rale, creaking, friction rubs, etc.

See Pleuritis, Pneumonia, Rale.

R. system ◀ *re spē rē trē / sis tĕm, n.* the organs and tissues which work together to allow breathing (i.e. the exchange of oxygen and carbon dioxide) to take place. Includes upper and lower respiratory tract, a functioning nervous system (including the vagus nerve, cranial nerve X, and the respiratory centre of brain). Also involves muscles, i.e. the diaphragm and, to a lesser extent, the muscles between ribs (intercostal muscles). See Blood, Diaphragm, Heart, R. tract (below).

R. tract ◀ *re spē rē trē / trakt, n.* passages through which air enters and leaves the body, i.e. nasal cavities, pharynx, larynx, trachea, bronchi, bronchioles and alveoli of lungs. Divided into two parts:

- Upper r. t. – the upper portion of the air passages; includes nasal cavities, pharynx.
- Lower r. t. – the lower portion of the air passages, as they leave the head; includes larynx, trachea, bronchi, bronchioles, and the alveoli of the lungs.

See parts under separate entries.

Resting ◀ *res ting, adj.* not active, e.g. the resting heart rate is the rate when the animal is not exercising. Also, the posture taken by a standing horse when its weight is borne on three limbs, allowing the other limb to relax.

R. behaviour see Behaviour

Resuscitation ◀ *ri su si tā shĕn, n.* restoration of life functions, e.g. breathing and regular heart beat, in animal near to death, as may be seen when an animal is in ventricular fibrillation, or in a foal after difficult birth, where breathing has stopped. Principles involved in resuscitation involve attention to the 'ABCs':

- A – Airway – ensure airway is not obstructed.
- B – Breathing – if horse is not breathing, oxygen can be provided via endotracheal tube or mask; artificial ventilation may be provided by respirator, or chest compression.
- C – Circulation – regular pressure applied to chest to stimulate heart beat.

Various pharmaceuticals may also be employed to stimulate and support the cardiovascular system, e.g. epinephrine, dobutamine, intravenous fluids.

Most of the information used for resuscitation, especially in neonatal foals, comes from human medical research and clinical medicine.

See Endotracheal, Heart, Ventricular.

Retain ◀ *ri tān, v.* held or kept in, e.g. retained fluids.

R. foetal membranes see Placenta

Reticulocyte ◀ *re ti kū lō sīt, n.* immature red blood cell, has cytoplasm which contains remnants of RNA which can be revealed with staining. Rarely seen in horses. Usually only seen in severe, chronic anaemia; equine bone marrow usually responds to blood loss by increased erythropoiesis.

See Bone, Erythrocyte.

Reticuloendothelial system ◀ *re ti kū lō en dō thē lē ūl / sis tĕm, n.* part of the immune system; phagocytic cells able to ingest microorganisms, e.g. bacteria, or colloidal particles. Made up primarily of macrophages and monocytes that are present in reticular connective tissue, a loose connective tissue that supports the lymphoid organs, e.g. bone marrow, lymph nodes, thymus, and spleen.

See Immunity, Macrophage, Phagocytosis.

Retina ◀ *re ti nē, n.* the light-sensitive, highly vascular, layer of cells at back of eye; the sensory membrane of the eye. Contains light-sensitive cells (rods and cones) which convert light energy to impulses which are transmitted via optic nerve to brain.

See Eye.

Retinal ◀ *re ti nūl, adj.* of, or pertaining to, the retina.

See Eye, Retina.

R. atrophy ◀ *re ti nūl / a trē fē, n.* shrinkage in size of retina. Localized areas of retinal atrophy are relatively common findings in ophthalmic examinations of horses, usually in the tapetum, recognized as oddly shaped

pigmented areas; cause is generally unknown. More generalized areas of atrophy, with retinal detachment, are sometimes encountered; those eyes are blind. Progressive r. a. is a rare, bilateral disease of the retina that has been reported in Thoroughbred horses, causing blindness. Appears as an increase in reflectivity of the tapetum, with areas of pigment loss elsewhere. No treatment.
See Eye, Retina, Tapetum.

R. detachment ◀┊ *re* ti *nūl* / di *tach* mĕnt, *n.* separation of retina from back of eye. Most commonly the result of trauma (blunt trauma or penetrating wounds), neoplasia, or chronic inflammation (uveitis); may also be idiopathic, with no known underlying cause. In foal, is reported as congenital condition.
See Eye, Retina, Uveitis.

R. haemorrhage ◀┊ *re* ti *nūl* / *he* mē rij, *n.* bleeding from blood vessels of retina; occasionally seen in otherwise normal newborn foals, presumably secondary to birth trauma. May be seen in adult horses in association with a variety of conditions, including trauma, encephalitis, blood clotting abnormalities, and parasitic infections.
See Clotting, Eye, Retina.

Retinoscopy ◀┊ *re* ti nos kop ē, *n.* technique used in ophthalmic examination, whereby reflections from the retina are viewed in order to determine the refractive index of the eye. Retinoscope projects a beam of light into the eye, and the movement of the illuminated area on the retinal surface is observed. May help in selection of lens implants in selected cases.

Retro- ◀┊ *re* trō, *prefix.* behind, backward.

Retrograde ◀┊ ret rō *grād, adj.* moving or tending to move backwards, usually in reference to flow of a liquid.

R. cystogram ◀┊ ret rō *grād* / *sis* tō gram, *n.* a radiographic examination of the bladder, whereby contrast material is injected into the bladder (the contrast material flowing backwards relative to normal urine flow).

R. ejaculation ◀┊ ret rō *grād* / ē *jak* ū lā shĕn, *n.* the retrograde flow of sperm into the bladder during ejaculation. Reported as an occasional cause of infertility in stallions.

Retroperitoneal ◀┊ *re* trō per it ō nē ēl, *adj.* behind the peritoneum, e.g. the kidneys are located behind the peritoneum, under the back muscles.
See Kidney.

Retropharyngeal ◀┊ *re* trō fĕr *an* jē ŭl, *adj.* behind the pharynx, e.g. the retropharyngeal lymph nodes are behind pharynx in the tissues at the back of the throat.
See Lymph, Pharynx.

Retrospective study ◀┊ ret rō *spek* tiv / *stud* ē, *n.* a study looking back in time, so that the outcomes have occurred to the participants before the study commences.

Retrovirus ◀┊ ret rō *vir* ēs, *n.* any virus belonging to the viral family *Retroviridae*. Retroviruses are RNA viruses, but integrate themselves into the host's DNA. Cause equine infectious anaemia in horses.
See Equine infectious anaemia.

Rhabdomyolysis see Exertional rhabdomyolysis

Rhabdomyosarcoma ◀┊ *rab* dō *mī* ō sar kō mē, *n.* rare malignant tumour of skeletal muscle. Diagnosis by biopsy; prognosis poor.

Rhinitis ◀┊ rī *nī* tis, *n.* inflammation of nasal passages, especially with discharge. Inflammation is seen from a variety of causes, including bacterial, viral or fungal infection, allergy, etc. Signs vary according to cause and severity of insult, but may include discharge from nose (watery to purulent), sneezing, nosebleed (epistaxis), head-shaking.
See Epistaxis, Nasal.

Rhinopneumonitis ◀┊ *rī* nō *nū* mo *nī* tis, *n.* acute, febrile disease of the respiratory tract caused by Equine herpes viruses 1 and 4.
See Equine herpes virus.

Rhinosporidiosis ◀┊ *rī* nō spor idē ō sis, *n.* rare fungal skin infection endemic in India and Argentina; has been reported on occasion in the southern US. Thought to require a portal of entry through a wound, then exposure to stagnant water. Clinical signs are of respiratory distress: wheezing, sneezing, nasal discharge and bleeding from the nose (epistaxis). Fungal polyps may be visible in the nostrils, or on endoscopic examination of the upper air passages. Cytological or histological examination is diagnostic; treatment is by surgical excision, however recurrence is common.

Rhinovirus see Equine rhinovirus

Rhodococcus equi ◀◌ *rō dō ko kēs / e kwī, n.* Gram-positive rod-shaped bacterium, causes pneumonia, diarrhoea, abscesses in lungs and abdomen, septic arthritis, etc. in foals. Bacterium is widespread in environment and thrives in horse manure; can become endemic on some farms. There appears to be a relationship between the number of bacteria in the environment and the number of infections. Bacteria may multiply in, and be shed from, intestines of foals without causing clinical disease, but such multiplication is an important form of dissemination and propagation of the organism. Disease typically peaks in foals 6–12 weeks of age, coincident with the decline of maternal antibodies obtained by passive transfer. Signs of infection depend on site, pneumonia is most common; may be acute (high temperature, difficulty breathing, coughing, discharge from nose) or chronic (temperature, dullness, gradual weight loss, difficulty breathing, coughing). Affected foals may be seriously ill before they are recognized clinically. The signs of disease are not distinct from other causes of pneumonia; diagnosis of pneumonia is from clinical signs, blood tests, and thoracic radiography. Bacteria may be identified from culture of fluid from trachea, obtained by endoscopy or transtracheal aspiration biopsy. Treatment is typically by combination of a macrolide antibiotic (erythromycin or azithromycin) and rifampin. Administration of *R. equi* antibody by plasma infusion to healthy foals has been recommended as a prophylactic treatment.
See Abscess, Arthritis, Diarrhoea, Passive (immunity) transfer, Pneumonia, Serology.

Rhododendron ◀◌ *rō dō den drēn, n.* large genus of flowering plants; leaves contain a glycoside called grayanotoxin which binds to sodium ion channels in cell membranes. Various clinical signs all related to failure of cell membrane signalling, including diarrhoea, muscular weakness, impaired vision, bradycardia, hypotension (caused by vasodilation) and atrioventricular block; cardiovascular effects may be lethal. Dyspnoea, depression, and recumbency develop; death may occur in 24–48 hours.

Rhonchus ◀◌ *rong kēs, n.* (dry rale) a whistling or snoring sound heard on auscultation of the chest, e.g. when bronchus is partially obstructed, e.g. by thick mucus.
See Rale, Respiratory.

Rhythm ◀◌ *ri thēm, n.* regular repeated pattern; in medicine, pertains to a repeated pattern in a biological process, e.g. rhythm of heart is the pattern of heart beats.
See Heart.

Rib ◀◌ *rib, n.* each of a set of curved bones on either side of chest; set forms wall of thorax and protects heart and lungs. Ribs articulate with spine dorsally; first eight or nine ribs attach ventrally to sternum via a cartilage extension (costal hyaline cartilage); subsequent ribs join on to adjacent cartilage ('false' ribs). Last pair or two of ribs are 'floating', with no ventral attachment. Most horses have 18 pairs of ribs.
See Spine, Thorax.

Riboflavin ◀◌ *rī bō flā vin, n.* vitamin B-2.
See Vitamin B.

Ribonucleic acid ◀◌ *rī bō nū klā ik / a sid, n.* (RNA) a nucleic acid that plays numerous crucial roles in the processes of translating genetic information from deoxyribonucleic acid (DNA) into proteins. Similar to DNA in structure, however RNA is usually single-stranded (DNA is double-stranded). RNA also contains the genetic code for some types of virus, e.g. retroviruses.
See Deoxyribonucleic acid, Protein, Retrovirus, Virus.

Rice bran ◀≀ *rīs / bran, n.* the hard outer layer of the rice kernel, a by-product of the rice milling process. Contains 12–13% oil; 0.45 kg of rice bran has approximately the same amount of caloric energy as 0.59 kg oats or approximately 250 ml of corn oil, and it is highly digestible (at least 85%). Because of its energy density, rice bran may be a useful source of calories for horses engaging in heavy aerobic exercise (e.g. endurance horses). It is also a good calorie source for horses in which a lower carbohydrate level is desirable, e.g. in horses with insulin resistance.
See Bran, Insulin resistance.

Ricin ◀≀ *rīs in, n.* toxic component of castor bean (*Ricinus communis*). Toxin inhibits protein synthesis. Causes colic and diarrhoea after ingestion of plant, and especially seeds. If horses are clinically ill after ingestion, survival is unlikely.

Rickettsia ◀≀ *rik et sē ē, n.* genus of Gram-negative bacteria that is an obligate cellular parasite. Life cycle depends on entry, growth, and replication inside host cells. *Rickettsia* spp. carried as parasites by many arthropods (ticks, fleas, and lice). In horses, *Rickettsia* spp. cause Potomac horse fever and equine ehrlichiosis. The parasite responsible for these diseases is carried in freshwater snails. Effective vaccine prophylaxis for *Rickettsia* infections is unavailable, although vaccines exist; the organisms·are very sensitive to tetracycline antibiotics.
See Anaplasmosis, Potomac horse fever.

Rifampin ◀≀ *rīf am pin, n.* antibiotic used most commonly in the treatment of pneumonias in foals caused by the bacterium, *Rhodococcus equi*. Available as a pill for oral administration. In humans, it is commonly used in the treatment of tuberculosis. Rifampin is almost always given in combination with erythromycin, or a related antibiotic, azithromycin. The two drugs given together increase the effectiveness over what is seen when each drug is given alone. Bacterial resistance to rifampin alone occurs rapidly, which is why it is almost always given in combination with other drugs. Softening of the stool can be seen in foals treated with rifampin, and affected foals should be monitored closely. Sometimes severe diarrhoea develops in treated foals, in which case the drug must be discontinued. Rifampin can also cause a harmless reddish discoloration of the foal's urine.
See Erythromycin, *Rhodococcus equi*.

Rig see Cryptorchid

Righting reflex see Reflex

Rigidity ◀≀ *ri ji di tē, n.* inflexibility, stiffness. May be seen as a clinical sign, e.g. in foals with hypoxic ischaemic encephalopathy, or adult horses with tetanus.
See Hypoxic ischaemic encephalopathy, Tetanus.

Rigor mortis ◀≀ *ri gē / mor tis, n.* stiffening of muscles of dead body, resulting from the depletion of ATP and the production of rigor complexes between actin and myosin in muscle tissue. Occurs within 24 hours of death and lasts for up to 2 days.

Rima glottidis ◀≀ *rē mē / glo ti dis, n.* opening between the two vocal cords and the arytenoid cartilages, in larynx. Widened by laryngeal muscles when animal breathes heavily, e.g. during exercise. Laryngeal disease (e.g. laryngeal paralysis) prevents full opening of the rima glottidis, resulting in obstruction to airflow.
See Laryngeal, Larynx.

Ring ◀≀ *ring, n.* circular structure; an anatomical structure having a circular opening. A ring on the hoof is a ridge around hoof that may indicate an alteration in hoof growth rate, possibly secondary to a period of disease, e.g. fever; the inguinal ring is a roughly circular opening in the abdominal wall muscle through which the spermatic cord passes in stallions.
See Hoof, Inguinal.

Ringbone ◀≀ *ring bōn, n.* osteoarthritis of the distal limb, characterized by growth of new bone (exostosis) in a 'ring' around the pastern area. May occur in proximal inter-

phalangeal joint (high ringbone) or distal interphalangeal joint (low ringbone). Exostosis of joint capsule or ligament attachments is sometimes described as 'non-articular' ringbone, i.e. not involving joint. May also develop secondary to injury to pastern area, or infection. Signs include hard swelling of pastern, lameness, pain on manipulation of the distal limb. Regional nerve blocks, e.g. abaxial sesamoid block, typically abolish lameness. Clinical diagnosis confirmed by radiography. Treatment may involve the use of non-steroidal anti-inflammatory drugs, intra-articular injections with substances such as corticosteroids, polysulphated glycosaminoglycan, or hyaluronan, and/or hoof trimming and shoeing manipulations (e.g. elevated heel or rolled toe). Severely affected cases may return to soundness following surgical arthrodesis. Prognosis for soundness is generally guarded, and affected by the extent of the disease and the use of the horse.
See Arthrodesis, Corticosteroid, Hyaluronan, Pastern, Radiography.

Ringer's solution ◀╎ *ring ēz / sē lŭ shēn, n.* sterile solution of sodium chloride, potassium chloride and calcium chloride in water. Electrolytes are in same concentration as in body fluids (isotonic). Can be used for intravenous fluid replacement; topically, may be used in lavage solutions to treat wounds.

> **Lactated r. s.** ◀╎ *lac tā tid / ring ēz / sē lŭ shēn, n.* (Hartmann's solution) is Ringer's solution modified by the addition of lactate. Lactate buffers the fluids, which mitigates changes in pH. This is the most commonly used fluid for intravenous fluid therapy in horses, e.g. animals in shock, after operation, with fluid loss from diarrhoea. (Named after Sidney Ringer, British physiologist 1835–1910.)

See Electrolyte, Isotonic.

Ringworm see Dermatophytosis

Roach back see Kyphosis

Roaring ◀╎ *ror ring, n.* colloquial term used to describe noise made during breathing. Especially noted when larynx is not opened properly or is obstructed, as most commonly occurs in laryngeal paralysis.
See Laryngeal, Larynx.

Robert Jones bandage ◀╎ *rob ēt / jōnz / ban dij, n.* bulky bandage used to apply compression to limb, and to restrict mobility. Can be used in conjunction with splinting as first aid for selected fractures, in order to allow for transport to surgical facility for repair.

Rocker-/Roller-toed shoe ◀╎ *rok ē- / ro lē- / tōd / shū, n.* horseshoe in which the toe has been bent up (rocker), or bevelled (roller), theoretically to ease or speed up breakover at the end of the horse's stride. Often employed in the treatment of such conditions as limb interference, or lower limb arthritis (e.g. ringbone). However, there is a remarkable consensus of scientific information that such shoes do not speed breakover.
See Interfering, Ringbone.

Romifidine ◀╎ *rom if id ēn, n.* α_2-adrenoceptor agonist sedative and analgesic drug used in horses. Sedation is shallower and shorter-lived than that obtained with detomidine, but longer than that obtained with xylazine.
See Detomidine, Xylazine.

Ross River virus ◀╎ *ros / ri vē / vir ēs, n. Alphavirus* (same virus class as Getah virus); the most common mosquito-borne virus in continental Australia, and also occurring in New Guinea, Fiji, and Samoa. Has not been documented as a cause of clinical disease in horses; however, horses with clinical signs of musculoskeletal disease have also tested serologically positive for the virus.

Rostral ◀╎ *ros trūl, n.* towards nose (front of head), e.g. the rostral maxillary sinus.

Rotavirus ◀╎ *rō tē vī rēs, n.* RNA virus with five genera. One of the most common viruses infecting newborn foals; the most common cause of foal enteritis in major breeding centres around the world.

Transmitted through ingestion of faeces; virus affects intestinal cells, resulting in poor digestion and malabsorption of nutrients, leading to a hyperosmotic diarrhoea. Signs include lethargy, depression, and decreased suckling. Infected foals may pass large quantities of watery faeces, which can result in dehydration; average duration of diarrhoea is approximately 3 days. Several foals may be affected at same time; mortality is low. Fluid therapy is the cornerstone of treatment, to prevent dehydration. Diarrhoea is also a risk factor for the development of gastric ulcers; regular cleansing is crucial to prevent skin scalding in the perianal area, and application of emollient ointments may be beneficial. An equine rotavirus vaccine is available and may help reduce incidence and severity of the disease; however, good husbandry and hygiene practices, e.g. preventing overcrowding, keeping premises clean, are the main factors in helping to reduce the incidence and spread of the disease. See Diarrhoea, Virus.

Round ligament see Ligament

Roundworm ◀ _rŏnd werm, n._ parasitic worm, phylum Nematoda. Those affecting horses include _Oxyuris, Strongylus, Strongyloides, Parascaris,_ etc. Roundworms have cylindrical body and are distinct from flatworms, e.g. tapeworms.
See worms under separate entries.

Rupture ◀ _rup tŭr, n./v._ break, burst, tear, as in:

- Ruptured bladder – may occur in foal during foaling.
- Ruptured prepubic tendon – may occur in heavily pregnant mare.
See Bladder, Prepubic tendon.

Russian knapweed ◀ _rush ĕn / nap wĕd, n._ (_Centaurea repens_) noxious creeping perennial weed found in western United States. Emerges in early spring, quickly flowers in May to June, and maintains its flowers through the summer into autumn. It is poisonous to horses, causing nigropalladial encephalomalacia ('chewing disease'). Normally a horse will not consume the plant unless there is a shortage of food, but it is readily consumed in dried form in hay. Repin, a principal sesquiterpene lactone, is the toxic agent. There is no cure for the disease once the horse is affected.
See Nigropalladial encephalomalacia, Yellow star thistle.

Ryegrass staggers ◀ _rī grars / sta gerz, n._ condition seen in horses grazing pastures predominantly of perennial ryegrass (_Lolium perenne_) infested by a ryegrass fungal endophyte, _Neotyphodium lolii,_ that grows within the leaves, stems and seeds. Signs include muscle spasms, loss of muscle control, incoordination, stiff gait, muscle tremor, collapse. Signs usually begin 7–14 days after horses start grazing on infected pastures. Movement and handling may make clinical signs worse; horses recover spontaneously in 1–2 weeks if they are removed from infected pastures.

S

ST-T wave ◀€ *es tē tē / wāv, n.* in electrocardiography, that portion of the tracing that reflects repolarization of the ventricles. See Electrocardiography.

Sac ◀€ *sak, n.* soft-walled anatomical pouch, cavity, organ or structure; often fluid filled.

> Hernia s. *her nē ē / sak, n.* the pouch of peritoneum that herniates through the abdominal wall in horses with umbilical hernias.
> See Hernia.
> Lacrimal s. ◀€ *la kri mūl / sak, n.* bag-shaped upper end of the nasolacrimal duct of the eye.
> See Lacrimal apparatus.

Sacculectomy ◀€ *sak ū lek tēm ē, n.* removal of the laryngeal saccules, with or without removal of the vocal cords. The procedure is sometimes recommended for the treatment of laryngeal hemiplegia; the rationale for treatment is to treat an adhesion between the thyroid and arytenoid cartilages, which should theoretically limit the collapse of the arytenoid cartilages during exercise. May be performed in the standing horse, usually with the aid of a surgical laser; can also be performed under general anaesthesia via an incision into the larynx (laryngotomy).
See Larynx, Laryngeal.

Sacral ◀€ *sā krūl, adj.* of, or relating to, the sacrum.
See Sacrum.

Sacroiliac joint ◀€ *sā krō i lē ak / joint, n.* joint where sacrum attaches to ilium of pelvis (one joint on each side of sacrum). The sacrum is the bottom of the spine; the ilium is the largest bone in the pelvis. The sacroiliac joint is roughly ovoid in shape, with its long axis angled to the midline. The joint is the pelvic attachment to the axial skeleton; the articular surface of the sacrum is attached tightly to the ilium by a number of short, strong ligaments. It helps transfer the muscular forces of the hind limb to the spinal column. Normally, movement of the sacroiliac joint is limited. Problems that occur within the region of the sacroiliac joint include osteoarthritis, stress fractures of the wing of the ilium, and inflammation of the sacroiliac ligaments (desmitis). Clinical signs of problems with the sacroiliac joint include hind limb weakness, decreased performance and quality of movement, behavioural changes, reluctance to work on the bit, frequent hind limb lead changes, trouble performing lateral movements, difficulty with flying lead changes, refusal to jump, or difficulty shoeing the hind limbs. Disease can be progressive, and insidious in onset. Damage to joint, resulting in subluxation, may result in tilted pelvis and an asymmetry of the tuber sacrale, i.e. when horse is observed from behind, hip on affected side looks lower (hunter's bump). Infiltration of local anaesthetic into the region can aid in diagnosing sacroiliac problems; scintigraphy can highlight areas of inflammation. Radiography of the area requires general anaesthesia, and there are many variations of normal that can make accurate interpretation of radiographs difficult. Treatment includes exercise to increase the strength of the gluteal and hind limb muscles. Local injections of sclerotic agents are sometimes recommended. The prognosis for full return to function after sacroiliac joint injury is generally poor, depending on the extent of sacroiliac osteoarthritis or desmitis; most horses with sacroiliac joint injury will be sound enough to turn out, or able to perform low level exercise.

See Cartilage, Desmitis, Hunter's bump, Ilium, Ligament, Pelvis, Sacrum, Skeleton, Tuber.

Sacrum ◀ *sā krēm, n.* triangular, wedge-shaped bone, part of spine, made of five fused vertebrae between lumbar vertebrae and spine. Attached to pelvis (at sacroiliac joints) and forms roof of pelvic cavity.

See Pelvic, Pelvis, Sacroiliac joint, Spine.

Saddle-sore ◀ *sa dl / sor, n.* skin damage, e.g. an open sore (ulcer), caused by pressure from badly fitting saddle. Treatment involves topical antimicrobial and anti-inflammatory medication, and a period of rest to allow time for the sore to heal. Proper saddle fitting is important in prevention.

See Ulcer.

Sagittal ◀ *sa ji tēl, adj.* shaped like an arrow; describes a vertical plane running through the body from front to back, parallel to the median (mid-sagittal) plane of the body.

    S. groove ◀ *sa ji tēl / grŭv, n.* a groove that runs across the articular surface of the first phalanx, from front to back. First phalanx fractures often travel distally, beginning at the sagittal groove.

    See Skull.

    S. suture ◀ *sa ji tēl / sŭ tŭr , n.* the suture uniting the two parietal bones of the skull. A sagittal plane is said to run in the direction of the sagittal suture.

    See Suture.

St John's wort ◀ *sēnt jonz wert, n.* (*Hypericum perforatum*) common, shrubby pasture plant with clusters of yellow flowers with long, oval petals. Wide range of distribution, including temperate and subtropical regions of North America, Europe, Turkey, Russia, India and China. Contains hypericin, a chemical which can cause photosensitization when eaten. May also cause problems when found in hay. Signs of toxicity include inflammation of unpigmented areas of the skin, soreness, reddening, and peeling of the affected area(s); the tongue and mouth may also be affected. Horses should not be pastured where the plant is plentiful; affected animals should be kept out of the sun.

See Photosensitization.

Saline ◀ *sā lin, adj.* containing salt, or of the nature of salt.

• S. solution is a solution of salt (sodium chloride) in water. Normal saline (physiological saline, saline solution) is a 0.9% solution and is isotonic with plasma (i.e. has same osmotic pressure as plasma). There are many topical uses for saline, e.g. rinsing the eye of debris to facilitate examination; intravenous saline solution is the fluid of choice in animals with ruptured bladder.

• Hypertonic s. is a fluid for intravenous administration that has a higher degree of saltiness (tonicity) than that of the blood. The immediate effect of intravenous hypertonic saline is to expand the volume of fluid in the blood vessels, by drawing in water through osmosis. As such, it may be useful for the treatment of conditions such as haemorrhagic or endotoxic shock (e.g. as may occur with enteritis), where there has been fluid loss or cardiovascular system compromise, or in the treatment of brain swelling (draws fluid out of the brain). However, this effect of hypertonic saline is short-lived, as the electrolytes quickly redistribute in the extracellular spaces. As such, the administration of hypertonic saline should be considered an emergency first aid procedure to support the cardiovascular system, and must be followed quickly by volumes of isotonic fluids. Hypertonic saline dressings have also been advocated for the use of infected or draining wounds (act to dessicate bacteria).

See Bladder, Pressure, Shock.

Saliva ◀ *sa lī vē, n.* watery, alkaline fluid secreted into mouth by three sets of salivary glands and other smaller glands in the mouth. Equine saliva is 99% water and 1% salts (e.g. bicarbonate) and proteins. Horse saliva does not contain digestive enzymes (unlike that of humans and other herbivores). Saliva secretion is stimulated

by the mechanical action (scratching) of the food against the mucous membranes of the oral cavity; up to 38 litres may be produced by a horse in 24 hours. Mixed with food during chewing, saliva helps food to be formed into a bolus for swallowing, and lubricates passage of bolus down oesophagus into stomach
See Salivary gland, Swallow.

Salivary ductus see Ductus

Salivary duct fistula see Fistula

Salivary gland ◀≀ *sĕ l̲i̲ vĕ rĕ / gland, n.* any of the three major exocrine glands which secrete saliva into the mouth. The three pairs of primary glands are:
• Parotid – fills the space between the caudal border of the mandible, the wing of the atlas, and the base of ear. Duct follows facial artery and vein, winds around the ventral border of the mandible, and opens into mouth by the 2nd or 3rd upper cheek teeth.
• Mandibular – at angle of jaw, deep to the parotid gland. Duct opens into mouth under tongue, a few cm caudal to the incisors.
• Sublingual – under tongue, from the level of the chin to about the third cheek tooth. Short duct opens into mouth under tongue.
Duct of parotid gland can be injured as it lies close to skin surface. Salivary glands may become inflamed; ducts, especially of parotid gland, may occasionally be blocked by stone (calculus, sialolith). Congenital atresia of the parotid duct has been reported; injury may rarely cause a stricture or fistula.
See Atresia, Fistula, Gland, Saliva, Sialolith, Stricture.

Salivation ◀≀ *sa li v̲ā̲ shĕn, n.* production/ secretion of saliva. Conditions characterized by excessive salivation include ingestion of irritant substances, or injury to, or a foreign body in, the mouth.
See Salivary gland, Swallow.

Salmonella ◀≀ *sal mĕ n̲e̲ lĕ, n.* genus of Gram-negative, rod-shaped bacteria. The genus contains two species; only one, *S.*

enterica, has ever been associated with equine disease (salmonellosis). *S. enterica* includes at least six subspecies with over 2,000 serovars, all of which are potentially able to cause disease. However, the vast majority of disease-causing salmonella organisms come from only one subspecies, *S. enterica* subsp. *enterica;* of this subspecies, only a few serovars consistently cause disease, and epidemic strains appear and disappear periodically. Different serovars may be 'host adapted' or 'non-host adapted'; host-adapted serovars, e.g. *S. abortus equi,* produce systemic infections, whereas non-host adapted serovars tend to cause enterocolitis (salmonellosis). Important *S. enterica* subsp. *enterica* serovars that have been identified as causing disease in horses include:
• S. Abortus equi: causes systemic infections, and abortions in mares. Rare (has not been reported in the United States since at least 1978; no other current reports are available).
• S. Agona.
• S. Anatum.
• S. Newport – caused death of many horses in UK in 1976; increasing frequency in the twenty-first century.
• S. Typhimurium.
(Named after Daniel Salmon, American veterinary surgeon 1850–1914.)
See Abortion, Salmonellosis, Serovar.

Salmonellosis ◀≀ *sal mĕ ne l̲ō̲ sis, n.* disease caused by *Salmonella* bacteria. Most common route of infection is oral, e.g. by consumption of contaminated food or water, or by ingestion of faeces from infected animals; infection by inhalation is theoretically possible. Most disease outbreaks of salmonellosis have occurred in hospitalized horses; the source of infection is often uncertain, but nosocomial (hospital-based) infections are a problem. Clinically normal horses can shed the bacteria (especially in the summer) and pose a risk to other animals; the prevalence of *Salmonella* bacteria in clinically normal horses is not definitely known, with various studies, conducted with various methodologies on different populations of horses, indicating prevalence rates of 0.8–70%. Other livestock, especially cattle, can also be carriers; salmonellosis also has zoonotic potential. Pasture and water are also potential sources of infection, as the bacteria can persist in the environment for years. The development of clinical disease (salmonellosis) in foals and adult horses is assisted by predisposing factors such as recent surgery, change of diet, deworming, recent history of colic, transportation, heavy exercise, or hospitalization (i.e. 'stress'). Normal intestinal bacterial flora appear to make horses more resistant to salmonellosis; thus, the association of salmonellosis and diarrhoea may be as much of an effect (the diarrhoea interferes with normal bacterial flora, resulting in overgrowth of the *Salmonella* bacteria) as a cause. Upon ingestion, non-host adapted bacteria must survive the passage through the intestinal tract before either lodging in the epithelial cells of the intestines or elaborating proteins; bacteria cause an acute inflammatory response that causes a massive influx of leukocytes, and causes the intestines to secrete fluid. Host-adapted bacteria cause bacteraemia and systemic disease, usually without enteritis.

Disease has range of severity:

- Inapparent infections – symptomless carrier state: animal sheds bacteria in faeces, is not ill, but may become ill if stressed.
- Mild disease – horse may have mild fever, poor appetite, mild diarrhoea. These infections are most often self-limiting; affected horses usually recover in a few days, but bacteria may be present in faeces for up to several months, and thus be a source of infection for other animals.
- Acute diarrhoea and enterocolitis – dullness and poor appetite, profuse watery diarrhoea with malodorous faeces, severe dehydration, colic, weight loss; loss of plasma protein through damaged intestinal wall may result in fluid swelling of limbs or below abdomen (oedema). This is the form of the disease that is most commonly associated with salmonellosis. Laminitis is a frequent sequela. May result in death.
- Septicaemia – enterocolitis can progress

to bacteraemia where bacteria invade blood stream, spread to rest of body, and can cause infections in joints, liver, kidney, and heart. Less common in adult horses than in foals.
- Abortion – has been causes by S. Abortus-equi (equine paratyphoid). Abortion usually occurs with other clinical signs, e.g. fistulous withers, septicaemia, or arthritis.

DIAGNOSIS
Diagnosis is suggested by clinical signs of illness of varying severity, diarrhoea, and colic (abdominal pain). Blood tests are not diagnostic but may show changes consistent with enteritis (e.g. low neutrophil count, low total protein, dehydration). Bacterial isolation of *Salmonella* from faecal samples provides a definitive diagnosis; serial samples are required, as bacteria are present intermittently. Polymerase chain reaction (PCR) tests are sensitive, but can result in false positives; serological testing is possible, but not generally available.

TREATMENT
The cornerstone of therapy is large volumes of fluid replacement. Treatment with antimicrobial drugs is controversial in enteritis; they have not been shown to speed the course of recovery, and they can damage the normal intestinal flora. Antimicrobial therapy is more clearly indicated in cases of bacteraemia/septicaemia. Treatment of the effects of bacterial endotoxin includes non-steroidal anti-inflammatory agents (especially flunixin meglumine); oral smectite helped reduce the frequency and duration of diarrhoea in one study. Oral plasma may be administered to help bind endotoxin. Probiotic products have not proved helpful in managing clinical cases. Icing the feet has been recommended as a preventive treatment for laminitis. Treated animals should be isolated from other animals; supportive care, e.g. clean, comfortable bedding, fresh water, etc., should be mandatory.

PREVENTATIVE MEASURES
Prevention is difficult; given the ubiquitous nature of the bacteria, it is unlikely that exposure can be totally prevented.

However, reducing oral exposure to faecal material, and good husbandry practices (e.g. fresh feed, clean water, clean bedding, etc.) are likely to be of benefit in preventing disease.

When attending infected horses, clothes and equipment should be cleaned or changed prior to attending other horses. No vaccine is available to prevent salmonellosis. Note: Salmonellosis is an important zoonotic disease, i.e. it can be spread to humans. More than 1 million cases of salmonella diarrhoea, 15,000 hospitalizations, and 400 human deaths occur annually in the United States as a result of *Salmonella* infections.
See Bacteraemia, Diarrhoea, Enteritis, Laminitis, Polymerase chain reaction, Salmonella, Zoonosis.

Salpingitis ◀︎ *sal pin jī tis, n.* inflammation of oviduct (Fallopian tube); thought to be caused by ascending uterine infection after parturition, as has been described in mares with contagious equine metritis. Can cause infertility in mare, or sterility if bilateral.
See Oviduct.

Salt ◀︎ *sawlt, n.* essentially, a chemical compound formed by replacing the hydrogen ions of an acid with metallic ions; in common usage, the white crystalline compound composed of sodium chloride (NaCl). Salts are needed in the diet for many important functions, including helping regulate body fluids, to keep a constant acid–base balance, and to help generate electrical action potentials in nerves and muscle. Exercise increases the requirement for various body salts, thus supplemental salts (usually containing mixtures of sodium chloride, potassium chloride and calcium salts) are commonly given to horses that sweat heavily during exercise (e.g. endurance racing horses). Supplemental salt is commonly given to horses via free-choice salt blocks placed in the stable or pasture (trace mineral salt blocks, composed mostly of sodium chloride, with small amounts of trace minerals added, can be offered similiarly), but loose salt can be added to rations if desired. However, most commercially prepared feeds add enough salt to fulfil the horse's normal dietary requirement. Horses will generally consume all the salt they need provided it is available in some form or other. However, some horses like the taste of salt, and will consume quantities far greater than their dietary needs; this is not harmful, assuming that they have free access to water, since eating excessive amounts of salt increases water intake, as well as urine production.

Salter-Harris fracture ◀︎ *Sawl ter-Har is / frak tŭr, n.* a system used to describe fractures of the growth plate (epiphysis) in foals. Five types are described, depending on the involvement of the growth plate and epiphysis, and the degree of separation from the underlying bone.

Sand ◀︎ *sand, n.* fine granular material formed from gradual breakdown of rocks. In the US, used for the floor of some stables (very rare in UK), and in the footing of many riding arenas.
   S. colic ◀︎ *sand / kol ik, n.* colic related to the ingestion of sand. Horse may eat sand while grazing on very sandy soil or paddocks, especially if pasture is poor, or if they are fed directly from the ground rather than from troughs. Ingested sand can build up in the large intestine, and can cause irritation resulting in diarrhoea. With sufficient accumulation, sand can cause blockage of the large intestine, resulting in colic. Diagnosis includes rectal examination (may be able to palpate impaction); when faeces is placed in a container of water, sand will separate and fall to the bottom of the container. Sand will be eliminated from the large intestine if the horse is denied further access to it; psyllium hydrophilic muciloid has gained a reputation as being the treatment of choice for sand colic, although it has not been shown that treatment with psyllium is more effective than simply removing the horse from sand. See Colic, Diarrhoea, Psyllium.

Sandcrack ◀︎ *sand krak, n.* vertical crack in wall of hoof, may start at ground surface and extend upwards, or start at coronary band and extend downwards. Numerous causes, including injury to coronary band,

poor foot care, poor quality horn; the root cause of many hoof cracks is unknown. If crack is through full thickness of hoof, or into the coronary band, sensitive tissues may become involved and cause the horse to be lame. Myriad techniques are described for repair, including lacing, drilling, acrylic patches, etc. Protective boots, proper hoof trimming, and attention to good environmental conditions (e.g. clean, dry stabling) are also necessary.
See Foot, Hoof, Quarter.

Sanguineous ◀ *san gwi nēs, n.* bloody, or involving blood, e.g. a sanguineous discharge is one containing blood.
See Blood.

Saprophyte ◀ *sap rō fit, n.* microorganism (e.g. a fungus) that takes nourishment from dead organic matter. Certain saprophytic fungi, e.g. *Microsporum gypseum,* can occasionally cause skin infections in horses (dermatophytosis).
See Dermatophytosis, *Microsporum* spp.

Sarcocystis **spp.** ◀ *sar kō sis tis / spē shēs, n.* genus of coccidian protozoa. Have two host life cycles, with a definitive and an intermediate host. The horse serves as an intermediate host for at least two species, *S. equicanis* and *S. fayeri,* and is an occasional aberrant host for *S. neurona* (the coccidian parasite that causes equine protozoal myelitis – see that entry). Dogs are definitive hosts for both species that are specific to the horse. The horse ingests oocysts found in the faeces of the definitive host; tissue cysts containing the parasite develop in muscles of the horse; definitive host eats infected muscle to complete the cycle. In most horses, the cysts in the muscle are not clinically significant; cases of granulomatous muscle disease have been reported. Successful treatment with trimethoprim-sulpha and pyrimethamine has been described.
See Equine protozoal myeloencephalitis, Parasite, Protozoa.

Sarcoid see Equine sarcoid

Sarcoidosis ◀ *sar koi dō sis, n.* see Granulomatous: G. disease. Term should

perhaps be avoided because of confusion with equine sarcoid.

Sarcoma ◀ *sar kō mē, n.* malignant tumour, develops from tissue of connective tissue origin (e.g. cartilage, bone, muscle, blood vessels, lymphoid tissue). Different types named according to specific tissue type, including:
• Chondrosarcoma – tumour that develops from cartilage.
• Osteosarcoma – tumour that develops from bone.
• Rhabdomyosarcoma – tumour that develops from muscle.
Sarcomas tend to grow rapidly and metastasize to other parts of body. Soft tissue sarcomas, even if localized, tend to have poorly defined margins, tend to infiltrate locally, and tend to recur after surgical excision. The wide surgical excisions needed to remove soft tissue sarcomas are not always possible in horses, especially when such tumours are located on the head or distal limbs. Fortunately, sarcomas are relatively uncommon in horses.

Sarcoptes scabei ◀ *sar kop tēz / skā bē ī, n.* species of parasitic mite, cause of sarcoptic mange (scabies); burrows into skin where it causes irritation and pruritis. *Sarcoptes* mites are not specific to their main host; various mange mites appear to be genotypically identical, and can survive on any horse.
See Mange, Sarcoptic mange.

Sarcoptic mange ◀ *sar kop tik / mānj, n.* (scabies) itchy skin condition (mange) caused by mite, *Sarcoptes scabei.* Rare in horses.
See Mange, *Sarcoptes scabei.*

Saucer fracture see Dorsal

Scab ◀ *skab, n.* a crust discharged from, and covering, a healing skin wound; composed of coagulated blood, tissue fluids, pus, skin debris, etc.

Scabies see Sarcoptic mange.

Scalping ◀ *skal ping, n.* gait problem where the toe of the forefoot hits the pastern or the cannon bone of the hind limb on the same side. Usually addressed by various shoeing measures, e.g. shortening toe of the forefoot. Protective boots on the hind limbs may help prevent injury. Term less commonly used in the UK.

Scan ◀ɛ *skan, v./ n.* to examine and/or produce image(s) of all or part of body, for diagnostic purposes; various diagnostic techniques produce 'scans', e.g. ultrasonography, scintigraphy or computed tomography.
See Computed tomography, Scintigraphy, Ultrasonography.

Scapula ◀ɛ *ska pū lē, n.* (shoulder blade) large triangular flat bone at top of front leg, lies against the lateral chest wall, attached by muscles and ligaments; many muscles involved in movement of front leg are attached to the scapula. Distal end has bulb-shaped glenoid cavity, into which head of humerus fits to form shoulder joint. Rarely, the scapula may be fractured, e.g. from a fall; fractures can occur at any point on the bone. Longitudinal fractures have been surgically repaired; fractures into the joint carry a poor prognosis. The glenoid area may be affected by osteochondrosis or osteoarthritis. Damage to the scapula and the suprascapular nerve results in sweeny.
See Osteochrondrosis, Osteoarthritis, Shoulder, Sweeny.

Scar ◀ɛ *skar, n.* (cicatrix) mark left on skin or other tissue as a result of injury and subsequent repair. Made of fibrous connective tissue, without normal skin adnexa; forms when normal skin is unable to cover injured subcutaneous tissue owing to tissue loss, poor wound healing, or as a result of second intention healing. In horses, minor scars tend not to be a significant issue, as they are covered by hair growth. Scar in muscle can occasionally cause functional impairment, e.g. as seen in fibrotic myopathy.
See Fibrotic myopathy, Fibrous tissue, Wound healing.

Schirmer tear test ◀ɛ *sher mē / tér / test, n.* (STT) commonly used method for testing tear production. A small strip of special absorbent paper is placed inside lower eyelid (in conjunctival sac) and left for 1 minute; length of wet part of paper is measured in millimetres; units of measurement are mm/min. There are actually two Schirmer tests: STT1 is done without local anaesthesia, and measures basal and reflex tearing, while STT2 is done with local anaesthesia, and theoretically measures basal levels of tearing only. The test should be performed prior to manipulation of the eye, to minimize reflex tearing. The STT is not a routine part of the ocular examination of horses, because defects in tear production of horses are exceedingly rare. The STT value in horses is much greater than in small animals; there also appears to be wide variability in the STT in normal horses and ponies. Theoretically, if lower than normal, the STT would indicate an abnormality of tear production, e.g. such as might occur with damage to cranial nerve VII, or in keratoconjunctivitis sicca (e.g. as has been reported after trauma to cranial nerves V or VII, from mandibular or hyoid bone fractures, or locoweed poisoning). (Named after Rudolf Schirmer, German ophthalmologist 1831–1896.)
See Keratoconjunctivitis sicca, Lacrimal apparatus.

Schwannoma ◀ɛ *skwan ō mē, n.* a tumour of the peripheral nervous system that arises in the nerve sheath; generally benign, although malignant tumours have been reported. Can occur in or on a variety of structures. Surgical removal, when possible, is usually curative.
See Sheath.

Sciatic nerve ◀ɛ *sī a tik / nerv, n.* largest nerve of the hind limb; starts at the lumbosacral spinal cord and passes behind hip joint and runs down between biceps and semitendinosus muscles; gives branches to many muscles of hind leg. May rarely be damaged by intramuscular injections in rump, especially in foals; the large muscle mass of the adult horse's hind limb protects the nerve from inadvertent injections. Damage results in difficulty flexing the stifle, and knuckling of the fetlock joint.
See Intramuscular, Nerve.

Scintigraphy ◀ *sin ti grē fē, n.* (bone scan) diagnostic imaging technique based on the detection of radiation emitted by radioactive substances – many radiopharmaceuticals use technetium (Tc-99m) – injected into the horse's body. Scintigraphy primarily shows inflammation in the area being investigated, as opposed to anatomical imaging, e.g. as is done by radiography. Areas of inflammation will usually cause increased concentration of the radioactive tracer, because the tracer moves out of inflamed blood vessels into surrounding issues. This often results in the appearance of a 'hot-spot', i.e. a localized increase in the accumulation of the radionucleide. The accumulation of the tracer is then imaged using a gamma camera (a scintillation counter) and a computer is used to produce the image. Can be used to diagnose areas of active inflammation that may not be apparent on radiography, e.g. stress fractures, navicular disease, and in evaluation of dental problems (to identify which tooth is diseased).
See Navicular syndrome, Stress.

Scirrhous ◀ *ski rēs, adj.* hard and swollen.
    S. cord ◀ *ski rēs / kord, n.* hard swelling of spermatic cord caused by infection with bacteria after castration. Area is swollen and horse may be stiff as result of pain. Signs include fever and lameness. Occasional cases may resolve with antimicrobial therapy; often requires surgery to remove the infected cord remnant.
    See Castration, Spermatic cord.

Sclera ◀ *sklé rē, n.* white coat of the eyeball, made of tough connective tissue, and covering approximately 80% of the posterior surface of the eye. Continues cranially with the cornea, and posteriorly with the external sheath of the optic nerve.
See Eye.

Sclerosis ◀ *skle rō sis, n.* abnormal hardening of body tissue; usually the result of an inflammatory process. Examples:
• Bone s. – hardening of bone. Shows up on radiographs as an area that is whiter than the surrounding bone. Detection of sclerosis of the third carpal bone may be significant in preventing injury to the carpus in racing horses; horses with chronic disease of the navicular bone typically have sclerosis in that bone.
• Nuclear s. – increased density of the lens causing a grey–blue haze; often mistaken for a cataract.
See Cataract.

Scoliosis ◀ *sko lē ō sis, n.* deformity where spine is curved laterally. Rare; may be seen as congenital abnormality in foals, associated with vertebral malformations.
See Congenital, Spine.

Scours ◀ *skōēs n.* colloquial term for diarrhoea, especially in foals.
See Diarrhoea.

Scratches see Dermatitis

Scrotal ◀ *skrō tl, adj.* of, or relating to, the scrotum.
See Scrotum.
    S. hernia see Hernia

Scrotum ◀ *skrō tēm, n.* sac of skin which contains the testicles, epididymis, and the first portion of the vas deferens. Under skin is a thin muscular layer (tunica dartos) which can function in thermoregulation of the testicles by expanding or contracting the scrotal skin. Lined by tunica vaginalis, a thin double-layered pouch which is an extension of the peritoneum, and which covers the testicles.
See Peritoneum, Testes, Tunica.

Seasonal ◀ *sē zēn ūl, adj.* occurring in periods related to the seasons of the year. Mares are seasonal breeders, that is, they have a period of regularly occurring oestrous cycles, in the spring, summer and early autumn, followed by a period of sexual inactivity (anoestrus). Horses with pituitary pars intermedia dysfunction (equine Cushing's) have a seasonal period in the late autumn and winter where routine diagnostic tests are not reliable. Some diseases have seasonal incidence, e.g. equine viral encephalitis, or *Onchocerca*

cervicalis infections, which occur during the warm months when mosquitoes are prevalent.
See Encephalitis, Oestrus, *Onchocerca*, Pituitary pars intermedia dysfunction.

Seatworm see *Oxyuris equi*

Seaweed ◀ℰ *sē wēd, n.* one of any number of large marine algae; has been used as food for horses, especially as a vitamin and mineral supplement. May contain high levels of iodine; however, the concentration of other vitamins and minerals in seaweed is so low it makes essentially no contribution to fulfilling the mineral requirements of a horse when fed at recommended levels.
See Iodine.

Sebaceous ◀ℰ *si bā shēs, adj.* related to an oily or fatty secretion.
   S. cyst ◀ℰ *si bā shēs / sist, n.* cyst filled with sebaceous material; formed by dilation of a sebaceous gland as a result of obstruction of its excretory duct. Commonly seen in horses; usually treated by surgical excision.
   S. gland ◀ℰ *si bā shēs / gland, n.* small holocrine gland in skin, secretes oily substance (sebum) through hair follicles. Sebum acts as lubricant for hair and skin.
   See Gland, Holocrine, Skin.

Seborrhoea ◀ℰ *se bē rē ē, n.* a chronic inflammatory skin disorder that affects sebaceous glands, resulting in either greasy skin, dry flakes, or greasy scales in the coat (or all three). Results from abnormal keratinization. In horses, primary seborrhoea has been occasionally reported, especially of the mane and tail; however, seborrhoea is most commonly secondary to a variety of skin disorders, including external parasites, infectious dermatitis, immunological reactions, poor nutrition, and drug reactions. If there is an identifiable underlying cause, it should be treated, and the seborrhoea will resolve; clipping the coat, and the use of topical antiseborrhoeic shampoos can help control the condition, or help hasten its resolution.
See Keratin, Sebaceous, Skin.

Second ◀ℰ *sek ēnd, n.* coming next after the first place in order. In medicine, the term usually indicates *increasing* severity, e.g. a second-degree burn, second-degree atrioventricular block, etc.
See Burn, Heart.
   S. generation ◀ℰ *sek ēnd / jen ē rā shēn, n.* medications developed from an earlier form of the medication; in equine medicine, especially as pertains to antibiotics. Second (and subsequent) generations of an antibiotic tend to have a broader spectrum of activity, and are subject to less bacterial resistance than are earlier forms.

Secondary ◀ℰ *se cēn drē, adj.* used to describe a condition which occurs as result of another (primary) condition. For example, a secondary bacterial infection may result following a primary infection by a virus; the primary problem of a diet low in calcium and high phosphorus causes the problem of nutritional secondary hyperparathyroidism; infection with *Streptococcus equi* (strangles) may rarely result in a secondary infectious myositis.
See Hyperparathyroidism, Myositis, Primary, Strangles.

Secrete ◀ℰ *si krēt, v.* to create and release substance, as from cell, gland, etc., for a specific purpose; many secretions are important in bodily functions, e.g. the pancreas secretes digestive juices; the pituitary gland secretes various hormones.
See Gland, Secretion.

Secretion ◀ℰ *si krē shēn, n.* a substance that is produced by a gland, usually for a specific purpose. Secretions may be released into the blood (e.g. insulin, by the pancreas), into spaces (e.g. bile, by the liver, into the digestive tract) or onto the body surfaces (e.g. sweat); the process of elaborating secretions.
See Bile, Gland, Insulin, Liver, Pancreas, Sweat.

Sedation ◀ℰ *si dā shēn, n.* medication, usually administered via an injection, which reduces the horse's awareness of its surroundings, but does not cause the horse to be unconscious (anaesthetized).

Sedative ◀ᴇ *se dē tiv, n.* drug which has a calming effect; in horses, examples include acepromazine, romifidine, detomidine, and xylazine. Commonly used to calm animals for short-term surgical procedures, to assist in performing tasks to which the horse objects, e.g. loading in trailer, clipping.

Sediment ◀ᴇ *se di mēnt, n.* solid matter that settles to the bottom of a liquid. For example, urine s. is solid material that settles to the bottom of a urine sample. Urine sediment may contain cells, bacteria, crystals, casts, all of which can be examined, and possibly associated with clinical disease.
See Urinalysis.

Sedimentation ◀ᴇ *se di men ṯā shēn, n.* the settling out of the solid particles from a liquid, e.g. as of the urine crystals that are found normally in an equine urine sample, or of parasite eggs in a faecal sample. This will happen if the liquid is left undisturbed; the process can be speeded up by centrifugation (spinning sample at high speed in centrifuge).
See Centrifuge, Sediment.

Seedy toe see White line

Seizure ◀ᴇ *sē zher, n.* violent, uncontrollable contractions of muscles associated with abnormal electrical activity in brain or part of brain; may occur in epilepsy, or as a result of some poisonings, e.g. chlorinated hydrocarbon or strychnine, or with conditions such as tetany.
See Epilepsy, Tetany.

Selenium ◀ᴇ *se lē nē ēm, n.* trace mineral that, among other things, functions as an antioxidant in the body. Important for normal muscle function; works in close association with vitamin E. Selenium deficiencies are reported to occur in areas where the soil is lacking in selenium, particularly in some areas of the United States, e.g. the Great Lakes region and the Eastern, Gulf and Northwestern coasts. Selenium deficiency is commonly referred to as white muscle disease. Selenium toxicity is also seen, primarily in areas of the United States such as the Rocky Mountains or Great Plains, where selenium levels in the ground are high: plants can accumulate high levels of selenium in these areas. Signs of toxicity include lameness that is often confused with laminitis, rough and brittle coat and swelling of the coronary band. Therapeutically, selenium is commonly combined with vitamin E in preparations advocated for treatment of exertional rhabdomyolysis. Experimental evidence for the effectiveness of this combination at preventing exertional rhabdomyolysis is lacking; many horses that have been previously diagnosed with the condition appear to have problems with carbohydrate metabolism (e.g. polysaccharide storage myopathy) that would not be responsive to selenium supplementation.
See Exertional rhabdomyolysis, Polysaccharide storage myopathy, Vitamin E, White muscle disease.

Self-mutilation syndrome ◀ᴇ *self / mū til ā shēn / sin drōm, n.* unusual behavioural disorder of horses; mostly seen in stallions. A repetitive behaviour that may involve the production of endogenous opioids. Affected horses bite their flanks, chest, tail, and limbs; most show this behaviour daily. Can lead to considerable skin damage; there is no consistently effective treatment. Castration may help some stallions; chemical agents that have been tried include fluphenzine, amitriptyline, and megoestrol acetate.
See Opioid.

Semen ◀ᴇ *sē mēn, n.* fluid discharged by male at ejaculation to fertilize female ovum. Contains sperm (from the testicles) and secretions of accessory sex glands (seminal vesicles, bulbourethral glands and prostate). Semen sample may be collected for assessment as part of examination of stallion for breeding soundness. Average values and ranges for stallion semen are:
- Volume – 70 ml (range from 30–250 ml).
- pH – 7.2–7.7. Increased pH can be associated with contamination of the ejaculate with soap or urine, or inflam-

matory lesions of the genitourinary tract, e.g. from infections of the accessory sex glands.
- Sperm concentration – 120 x 10⁶ cells/ml (range 30–600 x 10⁶ cells/ml).
- Total sperm per ejaculate – 7–10 x 10⁹/ml.
- Progressive motility – greater than 60%.
- Morphology – greater than 60% normal.

See Sperm.

Semilunar valve ◀ *se mē lŭ nē / valv, n.* one of two valves of the arteries leaving the heart: the aortic valve (between left ventricle and aorta) and pulmonary valve (between right ventricle and pulmonary artery). Valves prevent blood from flowing back into the heart when the heart is relaxing (diastole). Cusps of valves are roughly half-moon shaped, hence the name.
See Heart.

Seminal ◀ *se mi nŭl, n.* relating to semen.
See Semen.

   S. vesicle ◀ *se mi nŭl / ve si kŭl, n.* paired, long, pouch-shaped gland; lies above bladder in stallion and secretes many components of semen during ejaculation.
   See Ejaculate, Semen, Sperm, Urethra.

Seminiferous tubules ◀ *se min if ē rēs / tū būlz, n.* microscopic tubular structures in the testes that contain the germinal cells that produce sperm.
See Sperm, Testes.

Seminoma ◀ *se mi nō mē, n.* tumour of germinal cells of testes; most common testicular tumour in stallions, although, in general, testicular tumours are rare. May invade other tissues locally, and spread to distant tissues (metastasis) may also be seen. Treatment is by castration, after inspection of the abdomen for metastases.
See Testes.

Senecio **spp.** ◀ *sen es ē ō / spē shēs, n.* plant genus that is the most common cause of pyrrolizidine alkaloid toxicity worldwide,

especially *S. jacobea* (ragwort), but also *S. vulgaris* (groundsel).
See Pyrrolizidine, Seneciosis.

Seneciosis ◀ *sen es ē ō sis, n.* toxicity caused by ingestion of plants of the genus *Senecio*, which causes signs of ascites, liver enlargement and degeneration, cellular necrosis and cirrhosis. Disease has worldwide distribution, and, as such, is characterized by various names, including 'walking disease' in the United States; 'walking about disease' or 'Kimberly horse disease' in Australia; 'Winton disease' in New Zealand; 'Pictou disease' in Nova Scotia; 'Zdar disease' in the Czech Republic; 'Schwienberger disease' in Germany; and 'Dunziekte' in South Africa. Plants of *Crotalaria* (rattlepod) and *Heliotropium* spp. may have similar hepatotoxic properties, and their effects are often included under the umbrella term 'seneciosis'.
See Pyrrolizidine.

Sensitivity ◀ *sen si ti vi tē, n.* **1)** in reference to a medical test, sensitivity refers to the percentage of horses that test positive for a disease in a group of horses that have the disease (no test has 100% sensitivity, because some false negatives will occur); the minimum detection limit of a laboratory test; **2)** the degree to which a pathogen is susceptible to a drug (i.e. a bacterium that is killed by an antibiotic is sensitive to that antibiotic).
See Antibiotic.

Sensitization ◀ *sen si ti zā shēn, n.* the development, over time, of an immune reaction. The first exposure to an allergen sensitizes the horse (i.e. it causes an immune response); once sensitized, subsequent exposure causes exaggerated immune response which results in clinical signs of allergy.
See Allergy, Antigen, Hypersensitivity, Immunity.

Sepsis ◀ *sep sis, n.* infection of the blood stream; presence of disease-causing bacteria (bacteraemia) and/or their toxins (toxaemia) in blood. In adults, sepsis is most commonly associated with absorption of bacterial

endotoxins from the gastrointestinal tract (e.g. in colic or enteritis); clinical disease is as often caused by the absorbed toxins as it is the bacteria. In foals, the primary site of infection is often unknown, although it is frequently attributed to the umbilical remnant ('navel ill'). Sepsis is generally associated with clinical signs of systemic (bodywide) disease, such as fever, depression and loss of appetite; may be life-threatening, and lead to septic shock. Signs of sepsis include increased heart rate, rapid breathing, dark mucous membranes with delayed capillary refill time (sometimes with a toxic ring around the teeth), red (injected) sclera, and fever. In severe cases, coagulation disorders may occur (e.g. disseminated intravascular coagulation). Treatment generally includes antibacterial therapy, intravenous fluid support, and anti-inflammatory agents.
See Bacterium, Disseminated, Endotoxin, Enteritis, Septicaemia, Shock, Toxaemia.

Septal defect see Defect

Septic ◄፝ _sep_ tik, adj. related to sepsis, i.e. caused by infection or the toxins produced by infectious agents, e.g. bacteria or fungi. Examples include:
- S. arthritis – bacterial infection within a joint.
- S. pericarditis – bacterial infection in the heart sac.
- S. shock – shock accompanied by systemic infection (especially by bacteria).

See Arthritis, Bacterium, Pericarditis, Shock.

Septicaemia ◄፝ _sep_ ti _sē_ _mē_ _ē_, n. (blood poisoning) the systemic disease caused by sepsis; disease especially caused by the spread of bacteria, and bacterial toxins, in the blood stream.
See Sepsis.

Septicaemic ◄፝ _sep_ ti _sē_ mik, adj. describes a systemic infection caused by presence of disease-causing microorganisms circulating in the blood; refers to a whole body infection.
See Septicaemia.

Septum ◄፝ _sep_ tēm, n. partition between two cavities. Examples include:
- Nasal s. – the partition between the nostrils.
- S. pellucidum – thin wall of brain tissue which separates the lateral ventricles of the brain.
- Ventricular s. – the partition between chambers (ventricles) of the heart.

See Heart.

Sequela ◄፝ _sē_ kwe lē, n. (pl. sequelae) disease or condition which occurs as consequence of disease or injury.

Sequestrum ◄፝ si _kwe_ strēm, n. a piece of dead bone that has become detached from living bone as a result of necrosis. Can be seen especially following wounds that have exposed bone, e.g. to the cannon bone. The presence of a sequestrum results in clinical signs of swelling, heat, persistent drainage and non-healing wounds; the sequestrum can often be detected with radiographs. Surgical removal of the dead bone fragment is curative.

Seroconversion ◄፝ _sé_ rō kon _ver_ zhēn, n. development of antibodies (e.g. to bacterium or virus) in serum, in response to infection or vaccination; time for conversion can vary, depending on the agent provoking the immune response. Serological techniques are used to detect antibody levels.
See Antibody, Serology, Vaccine.

Serology ◄፝ _sé_ _ro_ lē jē, n. the science of serum, its properties and reactions; testing of levels of antibodies and antigens in blood serum.
See Antibody, Serum.

Seroma ◄፝ _sē_ _rō_ mē, n. swelling caused by the localized accumulation of serum. In horses, most commonly seen after fall or trauma, especially in the hind limb, over or behind the quarters, or in the pectoral region; can also occasionally develop secondary to surgical closure of wounds. Swelling may be remarkably large and fluctuant. Most seromas, even if large, will resolve over a few weeks; the horse's body will reabsorb the fluid. Surgical drainage

will also resolve a seroma; however, simple needle drainage is usually inadequate, as the seroma refills; use of a surgical drain to facilitate continuous drainage is generally required. May be associated with lameness if there has been significant trauma to deeper structures.
See Drain.

Serotype see Serovar

Serovar ◀€ *sēr ō vē*, *n*.a grouping of microorganisms, e.g. *Salmonella* bacteria, or viruses, that is based on identification of distinct antigens on the cell surface. Serovars allow organisms to be classified at the subspecies level; this is particularly important when trying to follow the epidemiology of disease. Also called serotype.
See *Salmonella*.

Sertoli cell ◀€ *ser tō lē* / *sel*, *n*. testicular cells lining the testicular tubules; function to nurture the developing sperm cells. Tumour which develops from these cells is a rare form of testicular cancer in horses; treated by castration. Malignant Sertoli cell tumours, with metastasis, have been reported. (Named after Enrico Sertoli, Italian physiologist and histologist 1842–1910.)
See Sperm, Testes.

Serum ◀€ *sé rēm*, *n*. clear, non-cellular yellow liquid which remains after blood or plasma has clotted; serum is blood without the cells and clotting factors.
See Antibody, Anticoagulant, Blood, Fibrinogen.
    S. albumin see Albumin
    S. neutralization test ◀€ *sé rēm* / *nū trē līz ā shēn* / *test*, *n*. test used for determining level of antibody in blood, by antibody's ability to neutralize a toxin or antigen, e.g. may be used to establish that a vaccine has stimulated an immune response.
See Antibody, Antigen, Immunity, Vaccine.
    S. protein ◀€ *sé rēm* / *prō tēn*, *n*. the total amount of protein in the blood. Serum protein is made up of albumin and globulin. Changes in serum protein levels (elevations or decreases) can be caused by many conditions, including inflammation, immune reactions, renal disease, enteritis, etc.
See Albumin, Globulin.
    S. sample ◀€ *sé rum* / *sarm* pl, *n*. aliquot of blood serum used for conducting various blood tests (e.g. enzyme assays, levels of antibodies, electrolyte levels, blood glucose). Blood is collected into tube with no anticoagulant, sample allowed to stand, blood clots and serum is separated from clot. Serum is sent to laboratory for analysis.
    S. sickness see Theiler's disease

Sesamoid bone ◀€ *se sē moid* / *bōn*, *n*. small bone which lies within tendon, especially where tendon angles (e.g. posterior fetlock joint, the insertion of the deep flexor tendon into the distal phalanx). In horse, principal sesamoid bones are:
- Proximal sesamoid bones – paired bones at back of fetlock joint, attached by ligaments to cannon bone and proximal phalanx. Conditions affecting the bones are various fractures, sesamoiditis, and trauma. Clinical signs of injury to the proximal sesamoid bones include swelling, heat, pain on palpation, and lameness, depending on the extent of injury. Diagnosis of conditions affecting the proximal sesamoid bones is primarily by a combination of clinical signs and radiography; scintigraphy can highlight focal areas of inflammation. Detailed examination of bone and soft tissue can be achieved with magnetic resonance imaging.
- Distal sesamoid bone – the navicular bone.
See Fetlock, Ligament, Magnetic resonance imaging, Navicular, Navicular syndrome, Scintigraphy, Sesamoiditis, Suspensory apparatus.

Sesamoidean ligaments ◀€ *se sē moid ē ēn* / *li gē mēnts*, *n*. three sets of ligaments which connect the proximal sesamoid bones to the proximal and middle phalanges. The sesamoidean ligaments function as a tight band to support the fetlock; part of the stay apparatus. Three sets of distal sesamoidean ligaments are described by their appearance to the naked eye; from superficial to deep, the distal sesamoidean ligaments are:
- Straight sesamoidean ligament.

- Oblique sesamoidean ligament.
- Cruciate (cross-shaped) sesamoidean ligament.

Two other sets of ligaments connect the sesamoid bones to other bones:

- Collateral s.l. – medial and lateral ligaments that connect the proximal sesamoid bone to the distal cannon bone.
- Short s.l. – small sesamoidean ligaments connecting the proximal sesamoid bone to the proximal phalanx.

Sesamoidean ligaments can be injured during the course of athletic activity. Lameness is the most common presenting sign; swelling is generally difficult to detect because the structures are not superficial. Diagnosis of injury is made by ultrasonography; prolonged rest is the primary course of treatment.
See Phalanx, Sesamoid bone, Stay apparatus.

Sesamoiditis ◀﹦ _se sē moi dī tis_, *n.* inflammation of proximal sesamoid bones; sesamoiditis is a common but potentially confusing radiographic diagnosis, especially in Thoroughbred racehorses, and in yearlings prepared for the sales. The pathogenesis is poorly understood but the condition seems associated with the stress of high-speed exercise in young racing horses. Trauma to, or inflammation in, ligaments around sesamoid bone (sesamoidean ligaments) or suspensory ligament may result in production of enthesophytes ('bone spurs'); the condition does not appear to occur as a result of disruption in the blood supply to the bone. Clinical signs include heat in the affected area of the posterior fetlock joint, pain on palpation or flexion, swelling and lameness. Ultrasonography is helpful for evaluation of the associated soft tissues; diagnosis is made by radiography. Unfortunately, a precise diagnosis of sesamoiditis can be somewhat confusing, as some individuals may overinterpret the significance of the presence of blood vascular channels in the sesamoid bones. Vascular canals with parallel sides and less than 2 mm in width are most likely to be normal. However, young horses with enlarged vascular canals, especially if they occur only in one

limb, have a decreased likelihood of racing successfully. Treatment of sesamoiditis typically involves rest; anti-inflammatory therapies, e.g. non-steroidal anti-inflammatory drugs, bandaging, cold hydrotherapy, are also commonly employed.
See Ligament, Sesamoid bone, Sesamoidean ligaments, Suspensory apparatus.

Setaria spp. ◀﹦ _set ar ē ē / spē shēs_, *n.* thin, nematode worms that live in the horse's stomach. Aberrant migration can occur into the eye and cause severe ocular inflammation, with signs including photophobia, tearing (epiphora), and corneal oedema. Successful surgical removal of a parasite from an affected eye has been reported. Anti-inflammatory and antiparasitic medications are indicated for medical treatment.

Seton ◀﹦ _sē tĕn_, *n.* material such as thread, wire, or gauze that is passed through tissues in order to form a sinus or fistula and increase drainage of fluids or pus; the surgical instrument used to pass such material. Technique not commonly used in modern veterinary practice, as more effective drainage techniques (e.g. via the arthroscope) are currently used.
See Drain.

Sex chromosome see Chromosome

Sexual dimorphism see Dimorphism

SGOT see Aspartate aminotransferase

SGPT see Alanine aminotransferase

Shaft ◀﹦ _sharft_, *n.* main long part of a columnar structure, e.g. of a long bone (the diaphysis), or the penis.
See Bone, Penis.

Shaker foal syndrome see Botulism, *Clostridium*

Shear mouth ◀﹦ _shér / mőth_, *n.* condition arising when cheek teeth are worn at a steep angle, e.g. when lower jaw is very narrow in relation to upper jaw. Sharp points or edges form on teeth, which are

typically treated by various dental procedures (e.g. rasping or floating teeth).
See Floating, Tooth.

Sheared heels ◀﹦ *shérd / hēlz, n.* displacement of one heel bulb proximally relative to the adjacent heel bulb; thought to occur as result of increased impact on one side of the foot, causing the hoof wall on the affected side to become compressed and assume a steeper angle (i.e. the wall becomes straighter) . Lameness has been attributed to this condition, but a number of sound horses also have sheared heels. If lameness occurs, it is likely to be because of bruising of the heel, or damage to the sensitive laminae in the hoof. Although selective trimming (e.g. lowering the high heel), in conjunction with fitting some form of horseshoe that provides rigid support (e.g. a bar shoe), is often carried out, such trimming and shoeing does not always return the hoof to a more normal conformation, especially if the changes are chronic.
See Conformation, Foot.

Sheath ◀﹦ *shēth, n.* an enveloping connective tissue which encloses and protects another structure. (Also colloquial term for prepuce – the prepuce sheaths the penis.) Types of sheath include:
- Myelin s. – the fatty layer surrounding the axons of some nerves (e.g. the white matter of the spinal cord); provides electrical insulation to facilitate travel of nerve impulses. In the peripheral nervous system, myelin is produced by Schwann cells.
- Nerve s.– the thin membranous covering that forms the myelin sheath around the axons of peripheral nerves; the neurilemma.
- Tendon s. – a synovial membrane sleeve that surrounds a tendon, especially where it runs over a joint.

See Myelin, Nerve, Prepuce, Spinal, Synovial, Tendon, Tissue.

Shigellosis ◀﹦ *shi ge lō sis, n.* name for sleepy foal disease (*Actinobacillus equuli* infection – in the past this bacterium was named *Shigella equirulis*).
See *Actinobacillus*, Sleepy foal disease.

Shin ◀﹦ *shin, n.* the dorsal cannon bone (metacarpus and metatarsus).
See Cannon.

Shivering ◀﹦ *shi vē ring, n.* involuntary slight shaking of body; reflex response to cold, fever, fear, or excitement. Shivering is a hypothalamic response to the sensation of cold; it is the body's attempt to increase body temperature by creating muscle activity (in humans, heat production can be increased by up to four times by shivering). Fever activates shivering if the body feels cold.
See Hypothalamus, Thermoregulation.

Shivers ◀﹦ *shi vēs, n.* chronic nervous or neuromuscular syndrome in horses; has been recognized for centuries, primarily in draught horse and Warmblood breeds. Shivers affects horses of all ages, primarily in one or both hind limbs and the tail. Clinical signs are of periodic, involuntary spasms of the muscles in the pelvic region, hind limbs and tail, of varying degrees of severity. Spasms may be increased when hind limbs are lifted (e.g. by a farrier), or when the horse is made to move backwards. Mildly affected horses may be able to perform athletic functions normally; severely affected animals may be hesitant to lie down, or may fall over. As the disease progresses, gradual and progressive atrophy of the muscles of the hind limbs occurs, which can progress to more generalized muscle atrophy. The exact cause is, as yet, undetermined; a familial tendency is suspected, however there is no genetic test for the disease. The disease may rarely resolve spontaneously; it may improve with rest, but signs typically return when work is resumed. Unfortunately, in many affected horses, the disease is slowly progressive and may result in inability to perform, with death/euthanasia the outcome as a consequence of continual muscle cramping and muscle wastage. There is currently no specific treatment for shivers. It has been suggested that shivers is related to polysaccharide storage myopathy (PSSM) and that dietary treatment of affected horses with high-fat, low-carbohydrate diets may be helpful; however, studies have not shown benefit from such dietary adjustments, and not all horses with shivers have PSSM.

See Polysaccharide storage myopathy.

Shock ◀€ *shok*, *n.* emergency medical condition caused by a failure of blood flow to the body. May occur as result of loss of blood (e.g. severe bleeding) or body fluids (e.g. severe dehydration, burns), or loss of normal control over circulation. Shock may result in release of substances which complicate and worsen the situation; disseminated intravascular coagulation is a serious, and often fatal, problem associated with end-stage shock. Tissues can be damaged by loss of blood supply. Several types of shock are described, including:

- Anaphylactic shock – sudden, severe, life-threatening allergic reaction; causes release of substances, e.g. histamine, which cause blood vessels to dilate so that blood pressure drops rapidly, and also causes constriction of air passages. Vasodilation allows for fluid leakage into tissues, which lowers blood volume and leads to collapse of the systemic circulation (circulatory shock); leakage of fluid into lungs can cause pulmonary oedema. Constriction of air passages and pulmonary oedema can result in respiratory distress.
- Cardiogenic shock – shock caused by primary failure of pumping action of heart, e.g. from valve failure, cardiomyopathy, or abnormal heart rhythms. Uncommon in horses.
- Endotoxic shock – bacterial toxins from damaged intestine (e.g. in obstructed small intestine) enter blood stream, and cause a strong inflammatory response from the body, which contributes to septic shock. Blood pressure falls rapidly.
- Hypovolaemic shock – loss of blood or fluid (e.g. severe bleeding, severe burn, diarrhoea, cantharidin toxicity) results in heart being unable to pump enough blood to the body. Blood vessels to less essential areas (e.g. the gastrointestinal tract) constrict in an attempt to maintain blood supply to heart and brain. Organs may be damaged through lack of oxygen, failure to remove carbon dioxide and other waste products, etc.
- Septic shock – may be seen when an overwhelming infection leads to low blood pressure and low blood flow. Failure of blood flow can damage vital organs.

Clinical signs of shock include rapid breathing, rapid heart rate, shaking and shivering, weak peripheral pulse, dry, pale, or dark mucous membranes, with delayed capillary refill time (depending on stage of shock), and cold extremities. Shock is a veterinary emergency. Horses should be kept warm and quiet. Intravenous fluid therapy is a mainstay of treatment; large volumes (as much as 100 litres daily) may be required. Antimicrobial therapy may be necessary in septic shock; vasopressors may help maintain blood pressure. Corticosteroids, or, in severe anaphylactic shock, epinephrine, may be indicated to combat allergic reactions.

See Allergy, Cantharidin, Circulation, Colic, Disseminated, Heart.

Shock wave see Extracorporeal shock wave therapy

Shoe boil see Capped

Shoeing ◀€ *shū ing*, *v.* applying horseshoes to hooves; ordinarily preceded by trimming the hoof. Specialized skill, primarily carried out by farriers. In UK, shoeing can only be legally performed by qualified person.

See Horseshoe.

Shoulder ◀€ *shŏl dē*, *n.* joint of forelimb, between glenoid of scapula (shoulder blade) and head of humerus; area of front leg around the scapula, and associated muscles. The horse's shoulder is attached to, and supports the weight of, the front end by sheets of muscle, ligament, and tendon; unlike humans, horses do not have collar bones. Shoulder joint primarily only flexes and extends; the horse is largely unable to adduct or abduct its forelimbs. Lameness of the shoulder, although a common concern, especially among riders, is actually relatively rare. Conditions affecting the shoulder joint include osteochondrosis and bone cysts. Fractures or luxations of the scapula are uncommon; however, when fractures involve the joint surfaces, the prognosis for soundness is poor. Sweeny is a condition characterized by muscle atrophy secondary to trauma to the suprascapular nerve.

See Bone, Osteochondritis dissecans, Fracture, Humerus, Luxation, Scapula, Sweeny.

S. angle ◀ː *shŏl dē / ang gĕl, n.* angle made by the intersection of a line formed by palpable spine of the scapula, with a line at the level of the point of the shoulder, parallel to the ground. Shoulder angle is said to affect the horse's movement and jumping ability. It is an important consideration when evaluating equine conformation; a sloping shoulder (that is, a shoulder with a more acute angle) is generally considered more desirable than an upright shoulder, as a sloping shoulder allows for greater stride length, allows for more room for a horse to tuck its legs when jumping, and is associated with higher levels of performance in dressage and jumping horses.

See Scapula.

Point of the s. – firm, palpable prominence, surrounded by muscle, at the distal end of the spine of the scapula, at the cranial aspect of the horse's torso.

Shunt ◀ː *shunt, v/n.* to turn or move aside or onto another course. In medicine, a shunt is a passage, which may be normal, abnormal or surgically created, that allows blood or other fluid to move from one part of the body to another.

Arteriovenous s. ◀ː *ar tĕ rē ō vē nĕs / shunt, n.* special lamellar blood vessels which move blood from artery to vein, bypassing the hoof. AV shunts appear to be an adaptation that allows horses' hooves to tolerate long periods of cold without thermal damage. When the brain detects that the hooves are in danger of thermal damage, the arteriovenous shunts open to allow warm arterial blood to the surface, supplying energy and preventing hypothermia (the opposite may happen in hot climates). It was once thought that laminitis was a disturbance in the control of the AV shunts; this contention has not been supported by scientific investigations.

See Arteriovenous.

Portosystemic s. ◀ː *por tō sis tem ik / shunt, n.* congenital failure of hepatic circulation caused by a failure of the circulatory system of the foetal liver to adapt. Normally, placental blood bypasses the foetal liver and goes directly into the circulation via the ductus venosus, a foetal blood vessel. If the ductus venosus fails to close, an intrahepatic shunt persists, thereby partially or completely allowing blood from the intestine to bypass the liver, and mix directly with the general circulation.

See Hepatic encephalopathy.

Pulmonary s. ◀ː *pul mĕn rē / shunt, n.* when there is normal perfusion to an alveolus, but ventilation fails to supply the affected area of the lung. May be seen in neonatal foals as part of hypoxic ischaemic encephalopathy, or in adult horses under general anaesthesia.

See Hypoxic ischaemic encephalopathy.

Sialoadenitis ◀ː *sī a lō den itis, n.* acute inflammation of a salivary gland. May occur as a primary disease, e.g. from ascending bacterial infections, or secondary to conditions such as rabies, equine herpes virus infections, or infection with *Streptococcus equi.* Clinical signs include swollen glands, pain on palpation, anorexia, and increased salivation (ptyalism). Bacterial culture and cytological examination of aspirates from the salivary glands may be helpful for diagnostic purposes. Treatment of primary disease typically consists of anti-inflammatory drugs, and antimicrobial therapy, as indicated. Identification of the primary cause of disease is important with secondary sialoadenitis.

See Equine herpes virus, Ptyalism, Rabies, Strangles, *Streptococcus.*

Sialocoele ◀ː *sī a lō sēl, n.* (salivary cyst) cystic swelling of salivary gland resulting from blockage of duct, either as result of injury or because of sialolith (stone).

See Salivary gland, Sialolith.

Sialolith ◀ː *sī a lō lith, n.* a salivary calculus. Uncommon problem in the horse; said to occur more often in donkeys. Most often occurs in the rostral portion of the parotid salivary duct, usually as

smooth, oval single stones, although multiple stones may be present. Stones most often form in concentric layers around a central nidus (e.g. of plant matter). Surgical removal, usually via a transoral approach, is curative. Surgical wounds are usually left to heal by second intention.
See Calculus.

Sickle hock see Hock

Sidebone ◀€ _sīd bōn, n._ ossification (changing to bone) of collateral cartilages of foot. Seen more commonly in heavy horses (e.g. draught horses); may be associated with trauma. Can be palpated as prominent, hard enlargement just above coronary band on the lateral or medial aspects of the foot. Not typically associated with lameness. Can be demonstrated by radiography.
See Foot.

Side effect ◀€ _sīd / i fekt, n._ undesirable effect of drug or treatment, e.g. aminoglycoside antibiotics can cause side effects such as damage to the nerves of the ear or kidneys; the anti-inflammatory drug phenylbutazone can cause side effects such as stomach irritation, gastric ulcers, and kidney damage.

Siderocyte ◀€ _si dē rō sīt, n._ red blood cell containing iron in a form other than haemoglobin. Rare; may be seen blood sample from horse with equine infectious anaemia.
See Equine infectious anaemia, Erythrocyte, Haemoglobin, Iron.

Sign ◀€ _sīn, n._ evidence or indication of disease, e.g. change in breathing, swelling, high temperature, etc. In common usage, the terms sign and symptom overlap to a considerable degree.

Signalment ◀€ _sig nēl ment, n._ that part of the medical history pertaining to the animal's age, sex and breed.
See History.

Silage ◀€ _sī lij, n._ cut green (high-moisture) feed that is stored under anaerobic conditions. Any type of plant can be used to make silage; most common are maize (corn) and alfalfa (lucerne). Good nutrient content, although tends to be low in vitamin D. As the green feed ferments, it acidifies from the action of anaerobic bacteria, and kills bacteria, moulds, and yeasts; properly made and stored, it can be kept for years. Poorly stored silage (not packed properly, allowing oxygen to get in) may be unpalatable, or contain mould or bacteria; there are reports of botulism in horses that have been fed poor silage. Horses may initially object to the acidic taste. Silage is a wet feed; on a nutritional basis, approximately 3 kg of good quality silage equals 1 kg of good quality dry feed.

Silver ◀€ _sil vē, n._ metallic element, symbol Ag. Has the highest electrical and thermal conductivity of any metal.
S. nitrate ◀€ _sil vē / nī trāt, n._ soluble silver compound with chemical formula $AgNO_3$. Silver nitrate is sometimes used as a cauterizing agent, for example to remove granulation tissue or warts, or as a styptic, to help stop small areas of haemorrhage.
See Granulation, Wart.
S. sulphadiazine ◀€ _sil vē / sul fē dī az ēn, n._ sulpha drug; most commonly used in people to prevent and treat infections of second- and third-degree burns. Kills many bacteria; comes as a cream, and is applied once or twice daily. In horses, one study concluded that it prevented granulation tissue formation in healing wounds (but did not otherwise speed wound healing); test tube studies have found the medication effective at killing fungi responsible for fungal keratitis, but tests have not been conducted on live horses.
See Granulation, Keratitis, Wart.

Sinew ◀€ _si nū, n._ old name for tendon.
See Tendon.

Sinoatrial node ◀€ _sī nō ā trē ūl / nōd, n._ the pacemaker tissue of the heart (generates the impulses that cause the heart to beat rhythmically); located in the right atrium of the heart, near the entrance of the cranial vena cava. If the sinoatrial node does not function properly (sinoatrial block or sinoatrial arrest) heart rhythm will be irregular (dysrhythmia). Irregular heart rhythms may be heard with a stethoscope; they may be further demonstrated by electrocardiography.

See Dysrhythmia, Electrocardiography, Heart.

Sinus ◀╎ *sı̄ nēs*, *n.* a term that has two discrete meanings in equine physiology.

1) Recess or cavity within the body (numerous sinuses exist in the horse's body), usually filled with either blood (venous sinus) or air.

- Venous sinus – a wide, blood-filled channel, especially one that does not have the coating of an ordinary blood vessel. Several venous sinuses can be found in the brain, e.g. the cavernous sinus – a venous channel between the layers of dura mater of the brain. The transverse facial venous sinus, located on the side of the horse's face, below the eye, is an alternative site for blood collection in horses.

In common usage, the term sinus is most often a reference to any of the three pairs of air-filled paranasal sinuses in the horse's head (one of each of the pairs lies on either side of the head). These sinuses connect with the nasal cavity, and are lined with a specialized layer of tissue (mucoperiosteum). They are:

- Frontal sinuses – paired sinuses that ccupy the dorsal skull, between the eyes, divided by a bony septum (wall). These sinuses communicate with the inside of the nasal conchae, and there form the concho-frontal sinuses. The frontal sinuses drain into the nasal passages via the caudal maxillary sinus.
- Maxillary sinuses – spaces within maxilla, above the upper tooth roots, lined with mucous membrane and usually filled with air. In horse, divided into front (rostral) and back (caudal) sections; these sections do not communicate. All other sinuses of the horse communicate with the nasal chambers via the caudal maxillary sinus. Roots of the last three cheek teeth lie within caudal sinus. If lining of sinus becomes inflamed (e.g. in viral or bacterial infection, tooth infection) fluid or pus may

build up in sinus and cause discomfort. See Maxilla, Sinusitis, Tooth.

- Sphenopalatine sinuses – paired small sinuses medial to the caudal maxillary sinuses.

See Sinusitis, Skull, Tooth.

2) A small group of cells in the upper right atrium of the heart; contain special 'pacemaker' cells that generate the heartbeat. The following terms are used to describe the heartbeat:

- S. bradycardia – a regular, but unusually slow, heartbeat. Can be the result of many things, including good physical fitness (e.g. in racing horses), effect of some medications, and some forms of atrioventricular block. Most commonly seen in older performance horses.
- S. rhythm – the normal rhythm of the beating heart.
- S. tachycardia – a regular, but unusually fast, heartbeat. Usually the result of excitement or exercise. Sustained tachycardia in resting horses generally reflects some cardiac abnormality.

S. arrhythmia see Arrhythmia

Sinusitis ◀╎ *sı̄ nēs ītis*, *n.* inflammation of sinus (airspace within the facial bones), especially the maxillary and the frontal sinuses, most commonly owing to an infection within the spaces. In horses, sinusitis is commonly divided into primary and secondary sinusitis; primary causes include infection, cysts, trauma (e.g. penetrating wound) and, rarely, tumour (especially squamous cell carcinoma). Secondary sinusitis subsequent to tooth disease is more common in older horses (roots of the last three cheek teeth lie within maxillary sinus). Sinuses normally drain into nasal cavity, but inflammation results in accumulation of discharge. This accumulation causes pain and swelling, and successful resolution of the condition often requires drainage of the sinus. Signs of sinusitis include discharge (may contain pus or blood) from nostril, usually unilateral, swelling of affected side of the face, pain, muffled sounds on percussion, nose bleeds (epistaxis), and foul smell. Useful diagnostic techniques include endoscopy,

radiography (especially to obtain image of tooth roots), biopsy, and magnetic resonance imaging. Primary sinusitis, e.g. as may be seen following respiratory disease, may respond to appropriate antimicrobial therapy; however, flushing the sinus, via a cathether placed through a small hole in the adjacent bone, is often necessary. Chronic sinusitis with underlying pathology requires treatment of the primary cause, e.g. extraction of an infected tooth. Surgical removal of masses (e.g. ethmoid haematoma) can be achieved through a bone flap; the prognosis for recovery depends on the primary cause.
See Biopsy, Endoscopy, Radiography, Sinus, Tooth.

Skeleton ◀ _ske_ li _tēn_, _n_. framework of bones and cartilage which give the horse's body its shape and support. A horse's skeleton has an average of approximately 210 bones.
- Appendicular s. – the part of the skeleton containing the skull, spine, and ribs.
- Axial s. – the part of the skeleton containing the forelimbs, shoulders, hind legs, and pelvis.
See Bone.

Skin ◀ _skin_, _n_. tissue which forms outer covering of body; largest organ of body. Functions include:
- Protection against pathogens.
- Protection from water loss – skin is relatively impermeable, so horse does not lose significant amounts of body water through the skin under normal conditions.
- Elimination of some wastes – sweat contains small amounts of waste material, e.g. urea; a minor function, especially when compaired to other functions.
- Temperature regulation – the skin's blood supply is much greater than needed to satisfy its metabolic requirements. This allows for use of the skin vasculature to control energy loss by radiation, convection and conduction. Blood vessels can dilate to increase heat loss; constriction of skin blood vessels preserves heat. The erector pili muscles elevate hair to provide an insulating barrier.

- Protection against ultraviolet radiation.
- Synthesizes vitamin D.
- Detection of stimuli, e.g. heat, cold, pain, touch.

Skin is composed of three layers; epidermis, dermis, and subcutis.
- Epidermis – outermost part, made of five sublayers of cells. The cells gradually migrate outwards, as the superficial layers are shed, becoming flatter as they move towards the surface. Eventually, epithelial cells form a horny layer that is shed regularly. Epidermal cells also contain melanocytes, the pigment-producing cells. (Hoof wall, the horny laminae, and other horny hoof structures are all of epidermal origin, but are much harder than skin because they contain keratin, a specialized protein.)
- Dermis – forms structural support for epidermis; it is the thickest of the three layers of the skin. The dermis functions to regulate body temperature and to supply the epidermis with blood; in addition, much of the body's water supply is stored within the dermis. It is composed primarily of two proteins, collagen, which gives skin strength and resilience, and elastin, which gives skin its elasticity. The dermis contains blood vessels, nerves, lymphatics, as well as most of the specialized structures and cells of the skin, including sweat glands, sebaceous glands, and hair follicles.
- Subcutis – the third layer of the skin (subcutaneous layer), made up of a network of fat and collagen cells. The subcutis acts to conserve body heat, and also acts as a shock-absorber to protecting the inner organs from trauma. Fat is stored in the subcutis. Blood vessels, nerves, lymph vessels, and hair follicles also cross through the subcutis.
Skin may be affected by infection with various pathogenic microorganisms, neoplasia (equine sarcoid is most common, followed by squamous cell carcinoma), and allergy; traumatic wounds to the skin are frequent occurrences in horses.
See Collagen, Connective tissue, Equine sarcoid, Hair, Hoof, Keratin, Melanoma, Sebaceous, Sweat gland, Thermoregulation, Vitamin D.

S. flap ◀ₑ *skin /flap, n.* a grafting technique whereby a portion of skin is moved from one part of the body to another without interrupting its blood supply; also, used to describe a moveable piece of skin that is partially detached from the skin surface, usually as a result of trauma.

S. graft ◀ₑ *skin / graft, n.* surgical transplantation of skin to cover large wounds. Full-thickness skin grafts are not commonly done in horses; the thickness of equine skin usually causes skin to die before it can be revascularized.

See Graft.

Skull ◀ₑ *skul, n.* bony structure which forms the framework of the head; encloses brain, protects structures of the head against injury, provides attachment for muscles, supports teeth, forms nasal cavities. The fixed distance between the eyes is necessary for stereoscopic vision; the fixed position of the ears allows the brain to help distinguish the direction and distance from which sounds come. The skull consists of 34 bones (not considering the hyoid bones). It also contains four cavities:

- Cranial cavity – encloses and protects brain; supports several sense organs (e.g. ears, eyes).
- Orbital cavity – surrounds and protects eye.
- Oral cavity – the passageway into the respiratory and digestive systems
- Nasal cavity – leads into the respiratory system, and includes the paranasal sinuses. The nasal cavity also contains the mucous membrane-lined ethmoturbinate bones (turbinate bones) that filter and warm inspired air.

Although there are numerous smaller bones, the major bones of the skull are:

- Incisive bones (premaxilla) – the upper jaw; where the upper incisors attach.
- Nasal bones – cover the nasal cavity.
- Maxillary bones – the upper portion of the jaw.
- Mandible – lower portion of the jaw; the largest bone in the skull. Formed from paired bones which fuse at the mandibular symphysis.
- Orbit – bones rimming the eye.
- Frontal bones – create the forehead of the horse.

- Temporal bones – found behind the ears.

See Brain, Mandible, Nasal, Tooth.

Slab fracture ◀ₑ *slab / frak tŭr, n.* vertical break in bone through its length, so that a flat piece (slab) of bone is broken off. May be seen in the cubiodal bones of the carpus and the distal tarsal bones. Usually repaired surgically, with lag screw fixation, especially in the forelimb.

See Carpal, Fracture.

Slaframine ◀ₑ *sla frē mēn, n.* toxin elaborated by the fungus *Rhizoctonia leguminicola*; causes disease of red clover. Toxin is parasympathomimetic, and produces excessive salivation. Toxicosis most often occurs in the spring and early summer. Treatment is by removal from infected pastures; mowing pastures will control fungal growth.

See Red clover.

Slap test ◀ₑ *slap / test, n.* test developed in an effort to assess function of nerves of larynx, e.g. in diagnosis of laryngeal hemiplegia. Side of chest is slapped just behind top of shoulder blade while larynx is palpated or watched through endoscope. It was hypothesized that in normal horses, the laryngeal cartilage on side of larynx opposite to side of chest slapped would move outward (abduct) briefly; however, most studies have shown that the test is unable to differentiate between normal horses and horses with the moderate to severe muscle changes characteristic of laryngeal hemiplegia, thus making it essentially useless as a diagnostic test.

See Endoscopy, Laryngeal, Larynx.

Sleep ◀ₑ *slēp, n.* period of rest for the horse's body and mind; horse is immobile, consciousness and body functions are at least partially suspended, but animal can respond to external stimuli. Horses achieve a level of sleep while standing, but true deep, restful sleep ('paradoxical sleep') can only be achieved by lying down. Horses can sleep lying in sternal recumbency (i.e. chest area upright, resting on breastbone), or flat on their sides. Foals lie down frequently; they spend approximately half of their day sleeping until they reach 3 months of age. Adult horses require approximately 3 hours of sleep in each 24 hour period; the required sleep occurs in many short intervals, lasting about 15 minutes each. Variables that affect the length and type of sleep include diet, temperature, workload, gestation and gender. Sleep is important for normal welfare of horse, but exact function is not completely understood.

Putting to s. see Euthanasia

S. deprived ◀ऽ *slēp / dip rīvd, adj.* if a horse is not allowed to lie down, after several days it will become sleep deprived, from lack of sleep. Signs of sleep deprivation include sudden collapse. This condition is commonly misdiagnosed as narcolepsy. In herds, some horses sleep while others watch for predators. Horses kept totally alone may not sleep well, because their instincts are to be alert for danger in their surroundings.
See Narcolepsy.

Sleeping sickness see Encephalitis

Sleepy foal disease ◀ऽ *slē pē / fōl / di zēz, n.* colloquial term for disease caused by infection in foal by bacteria *Actinobacillus equuli* and *A. haemolyticus*. Infection is thought to be acquired via a contaminated umbilicus, by inhalation, or by ingestion. Initial clinical signs include high temperature, lethargy (sleepiness), and diarrhoea; as disease progresses meningitis, pneumonia, purulent nephritis, septicaemica and septic polyarthritis may follow. Good husbandry procedures, e.g. clean birthing environment, and assuring that the newborn foal has adequate intake of colostrums, can help reduce the incidence of infection. Treatment is with appropriate antimicrobial drugs and supportive care (e.g. intravenous fluids, supplemental oxygen, plasma transfusions). Generally fatal if untreated; successful treatment usually depends on early recognition.
See Septicaemia.

Sling ◀ऽ *sling, n.* device made of synthetic fibre strap or ropes used to support horse in standing position. Most slings have a sheet of material to pass under abdomen, and straps in front of the chest and behind the hindquarters. The sling is supported from above, e.g. attached to ceiling beam. May be used in the treatment of conditions where the horse is unable to stand on its own, e.g. certain leg fractures, or neurological conditions.
See Fracture.

Slobbers ◀ऽ *slob erz, n.* colloquial term for excessive salivation.
See Ptyalism, Red clover, Slaframine.

Slough ◀ऽ *sluf, v.* to shed or cast off. Said of necrotic tissue or membranes, such as skin affected by immune-mediated conditions (e.g. pemphigus) or photosensitization, or the intestinal lining in severe cases of colitis.
See Colitis, Pemphigus foliaceus, Photosensitization.

Small intestine ◀ऽ *smawl / in tes tin, n.* part of alimentary tract between stomach and large intestine (joins large intestine at ileocaecal junction). Consists of duodenum, jejunum and ileum; approximately 21.3 m long, and can accommodate approximately 55 litres of ingesta. Intestinal wall is made up of smooth muscle lined by specialized mucosa. Continues the digestive process, and acts to transport food to large intestine, which is main site for bacterial fermentation of food in horse. Various pancreatic enzymes help digest the food; carbohydrates digest sugars and starches and proteases break proteins down into their constituent amino acids. Bile, which continuously flows from the liver as a consequence of the horse's lack of a gall bladder, emulsifies fats (breaks them into smaller units). Fluid is secreted by intestine lining and added to contents, e.g. the emulsified fats are suspended in the fluid as they pass along to large intestine; passage of ingesta through the small intestine can take as little as 30–60 minutes. Around 50–70% of carbohydrate digestion and absorption, and almost all amino acid absorption, occurs in the small intestine. Conditions affecting small intestine include enteritis (inflammation causes fever, colic, anorexia, and diarrhoea),

ulceration, obstruction (blockage), entrapment, volvulus (twisting), muscular spasm. Painful conditions of small intestine result in colic.
See Colic, Diarrhoea, Digestion, Large intestine, Liver, Pancreas.

Small strongyles see Cyathostome, Cyathostomosis

Smear ◀ᴇ *smēr, n.* diagnostic technique whereby a sample, e.g. of blood or bacterial cells, is obtained by some method (e.g. centesis or direct impression) and spread on a glass slide for microscopic examination.

Smectite ◀ᴇ *smek tīt, n.* group of clay minerals, including bentonite, that tend to swell when exposed to water. Smectites have been advocated for administration to horses with diarrhoea of various causes because of their water-absorbing capacity; can bind *Clostridium difficile* toxins A and B, *Clostridium perfringens* enterotoxin and endotoxin in vitro; however, this capability has not been demonstrated in the living horse.
See *Clostridium*, Diarrhoea.

Smegma ◀ᴇ *smeg mē, n.* secretion of sebaceous glands of prepuce, combined with exfoliated epithelial cells, skin oils, moisture and bacteria that can accumulate within prepuce; may form a smelly deposit. Smegma in stallions should be cleaned out prior to covering to prevent contamination of the mare's reproductive tract.
See Prepuce, Sebaceous.

Smell ◀ᴇ *smel, n.* odour of a particular substance or thing; the sensation that results when olfactory receptors in the nose are stimulated by certain chemicals in gaseous form. Information pertaining to smell is transmitted to the brain by the olfactory (first cranial) nerve.

Smoke inhalation ◀ᴇ *smōk / in hē lā shēn, n.* breathing in of smoke, e.g. during stable fire. Three primary mechanisms lead to injury of the respiratory tract in smoke inhalation:

- Thermal damage, usually restricted to the upper air passages.
- Asphyxiation, resulting from lack of ambient oxygen owing to consumption by fire, and the production of gases such as carbon monoxide (CO) and cyanide from combustion of plastics, polyurethane, wool, silk, nylon, nitriles, rubber, and paper products.
- Pulmonary irritation from chemicals in smoke. Irritants can cause direct tissue injury, acute bronchospasm, and activation of inflammatory pathways.

Upper airways are particularly affected, and irritation can cause enough swelling to occlude the pharynx. In severe cases lungs may be damaged and oedematous, and small airways can become blocked by dead bronchial and inflammatory cells; horse may develop pneumonia. Affected horses may have fever, cough, ocular discharge (from conjunctival irritation), difficulty breathing, and stridor; signs of toxicity include dullness, incoordination, and collapse. Time required for healing of the respiratory tract depends on the severity of the insult. The upper respiratory tract tends to recover more rapidly (2–4 weeks) than the lower respiratory tract. Severe cases may require months to recover; scar tissue may form in the lungs of some severely affected horses, resulting in chronic respiratory problems.

Snake bite ◀ᴇ *snāk / bīt, n.* envenomation bite by any one of several species of venomous snake; venom introduced into animal by fangs of snake. In UK, only venomous snake is adder (*Vipera berus*), which may cause a painful swollen area, but death from bite is unlikely. Other countries have more venomous snakes, e.g. tiger snake and brown snake in Australia, rattlesnakes in USA. Many snake bites are 'dry' (defensive), with little or no venom injected: rapid swelling and pain suggest venom injection. Venom is absorbed within a period ranging from 30 seconds to several minutes. Most bites occur on the muzzle (curious horses look down at the snakes, and are bitten on the muzzle); bites on the legs and torso are also seen. Clinical signs of snake bite include swelling at the site of the bite; the

swelling can be dramatic, depending on the amount of venom received. Antibiotics are indicated to prevent limb infections; non-steroidal anti-inflammatory agents may help reduce fever, pain, and swelling. The use of steroidal anti-inflammatory agents is controversial. Bandaging of limbs may help control swelling; severe cases of bites on the muzzle may require maintaining a patent airway by tracheostomy. Asphyxiation from massive throat swelling might necessitate a tracheotomy in rare cases. Tetanus prophylaxis is recommended. Cutting an incision on the bite and suction is not recommended, nor is icing of the bite, nor is a tourniquet. Snake bites are rarely fatal to horses, but complications of severe bites (mostly massive swelling and infection) can be difficult to manage, and occasionally result in death. Antivenin is rarely used in treatment and is cost-prohibitive.
See Antivenin.

SNAP test ◀¿ *abbr. /test, n.* membrane-based ELISA test for adequacy of passive transfer in foals.
See Passive (immunity) transfer.

Sneeze ◀¿ *snēz, n./v.* involuntary, spasmodic, explosive expulsion of air through nostrils; triggered by irritation of lining of nasal cavity, e.g. by dust, inflammation (e.g. in infection with equine influenza virus), etc. When irritating particles contact the nasal mucosa, they trigger the production of histamine. Histamine stimulates nerve cells in the nose, which then signal the brain to trigger the sneeze. Sneezing is a reflex response that involves the muscles of the face, throat, and thorax.

Social behaviour see Behaviour

Soda lime ◀¿ *sō dē / līm, n.* mixture of calcium, potassium, sodium hydroxide and water. Used in anaesthetic machine circuits to absorb carbon dioxide from gas breathed out by animal, so that anaesthetic gas can be recycled.
See Anaesthetic machine, Carbon dioxide.

Sodium ◀¿ *sō dē ēm, n.* (Na) chemical element; highly reactive metal in elemental form. Important in body as sodium ion (Na⁺). Major cation (positive ion; 90–95% of all positively charged ions) in body fluids. Numerous important functions, including helping to maintain fluid balance, aiding in nerve conduction and muscle contraction, and maintaining normal heart rhythm. The sodium level in the horse's body is controlled by the kidneys.

S. gluconate ◀¿ *sō dē ēm / glū kō nāt, n.* treatment that has been recommended for aorto-iliac thrombosis. Given by IV infusion; no scientific evidence of effectiveness.

S. iodide ◀¿ *sō dē ēm / ī ō dīd, n.* white, crystalline salt with chemical formula NaI. Sodium iodide solutions have been used to treat conditions characterized by abscesses, e.g. pulmonary abscesses; also reported to be a good treatment for sporotrichosis, but limited scientific evidence of effectiveness.
See Abscess, Sporotrichosis.

S. hyaluronate see Hyaluronan
S. penicillin see Penicillin
S. thiosulphate ◀¿ *sō dē ēm / thī ō sul fāt, n.* compound that has been recommended for treatment of arsenic toxicity; questionable efficacy.

Sodium bicarbonate ◀¿ *sō dē ēm / bī kar bē nāt, n.* chemical compound; formula NaHCO₃; may be added to intravenous fluids in treatment of metabolic acidosis (bicarbonate ion helps to correct acidosis). 'Milkshakes' of sodium bicarbonate solutions have been administered to racing horses by nasogastric tube 4 to 6 hours before racing to produce a metabolic alkalosis. This is purported to prevent tying-up, and to delay fatigue by causing increased buffering for lactic acid produced by anaerobic muscular activity. The procedure is banned in most racing jurisdictions, and tested for by examining levels of carbon dioxide in the blood (horses receiving such treatment may have elevated carbon dioxide levels). There is good evidence that the procedure does not do what it is intended to do.
See Acidosis.

Soft palate ◀¿ *soft / pa lit, n.* elongated, muscular structure that forms the division

between the oral and nasal portions of the pharynx. During normal breathing, its posterior border lies underneath the epiglottis. In this position, there is maximum air flow. Except when swallowing, the free border of the soft palate remains under the epiglottis. (Horse does not breathe through mouth when exercising hard.) Conditions affecting the soft palate are diagnosed by a combination of clinical signs (most conditions result in abnormal noise during breathing and may affect performance) and endoscopy, and include dorsal displacement, clefts, hypoplasia, cysts, cicatrices and iatrogenic defects of the soft palate created by improper or overly aggressive surgical procedures.
See Cyst, Larynx, Salivary gland.

Solanum see Deadly nightshade

Sole ◀ː *sōl*, *n*. the underside of hoof; usually somewhat concave. When the horse steps, the foot changes in shape, partly because of the concavity of the sole. When the hoof lands, it spreads, and the concavity decreases. A fully loaded hoof contacts the ground along the wall, most of the sole, the bars, and the frog; to some degree, solar contact may be attenuated by placement of a shoe along the hoof wall. Solar trauma (sole bruise) is a commonly diagnosed cause of lameness. The sole may also be damaged by penetrating wounds (e.g. from nails), which can cause inflammation and/or infection in underlying structures (e.g. deep digital flexor tendon, digital cushion, digital synovial sheath, navicular bursa, third phalanx). Signs of penetrating wound vary depending on the depth of penetration and the structure affected, but include presence of object embedded in sole, lameness, abscess, and, in severe cases, swelling above foot. Diagnosis of sole-related problems involves use of hoof testers to find area of pain, careful paring away of horn of sole to find abscesses, or site of wound penetration, and radiography.

A thin sole is one that lacks adequate depth to protect the underlying structures from trauma. Normal sole is 1.25–1.9 cm thick. The most common cause of thin sole

is aggressive trimming; excessively wet conditions may soften sole and cause loss of horn and thinning.
See Deep: D. digital flexor tendon, Digital, Foot, Laminitis, Navicular bursa, Third: T. phalanx.

Somatotropin ◀ː *sō mat ō trō pin*, *n*. (growth hormone; equine somatotropin; eST) a protein hormone secreted by the pituitary gland that stimulates growth; each animal produces its own specific somatotropin that is active in its own species. A synthetic freeze-dried eST produced by recombinant DNA technology is available in some countries (Equi-Gen®), and has been advocated for various indications, including improving growth rate in foals, improving stallion reproductive performance, for wound healing, and for the treatment of tendon injuries. Unfortunately, studies show that eST does not increase foal growth, it may increase seminal volume but does not appear to alter sperm quality, pituitary gonadotrope function or testicular testosterone secretion, does not appear to affect wound healing, and has a negative effect on the biomechanical properties of injured equine superficial flexor tendon in the early phases of healing.
See Growth.

Somerekzem see *Culicoides* spp.

Soporific ◀ː *so por ri fik*, *adj./n*. inducing sleep; substance or drug which induces sleep, e.g. a sedative.
See Sedative.

Sore ◀ː *sor*, *n./adj*. open area of damage or disease on skin or mucous membrane, e.g. an ulcer; painful, aching, sensitive, or hurting, e.g. sore mouth, or sore back.

Soring ◀ː *sor ing*, *n*. a process of intentionally causing pain to a horse's front legs and hoofs to enhance a 'gaited' horse's movement (e.g. a Tennessee Walking Horse) for the show ring. The practice is against the law in the United States.

Sound ◀ː *sōnd*, *n./adj*. as a noun, auditory effect produced by a given cause, e.g.

- Heart s. – noise caused by closure of heart valves and turbulence of blood flow, and heard on auscultation.
- Intestinal s. – noise caused by contraction of intestinal smooth muscle; borborygmi.

As an adjective, in good condition, without serious defect (e.g. a sound horse).

Soundness ◀ː _sōnd_ nis, _n._ the condition of being free from defects or flaws; as applies to horse, typically refers to the suitability of horse to be used for a particular function, e.g. breeding, riding, racing.

    S. examination ◀ː _sōnd_ nis / ig za mi _nā_ shĕn, _n._ (commonly called 'vetting') is a thorough physical examination, usually performed by an experienced veterinary surgeon, evaluating whether a horse is free from serious defects that may interfere with the ability of that horse to perform its intended function. Such exams typically focus on the musculoskeletal system, although various parameters of other systems, such as heart and lung function, sight, nervous system function, etc., are usually also thoroughly evaluated.

    Breeding s. examination ◀ː _brē_ ding / _sōnd_ nis / ig za mi _nā_ shĕn, _n._ is examination of the mare or stallion for the specific purpose of determining the likelihood that the animal being examined is fertile. In stallions, such exams may include palpation of the testes, ultrasound examination, and semen evaluation. In mares, such exams may include rectal palpation of the reproductive tract, ultrasound examination, bacterial culture of the uterus, uterine cytology, etc.

Spasm ◀ː _spa_ zĕm, _n._ sudden, involuntary contraction of muscle; often persistent and often accompanied by pain. Spasm occurs secondary to a variety of causes, including various diseases, strain or injury to the muscle or nearby tissues, circulatory impairment, or disturbances in body chemistry (e.g. electrolyte abnormalities). Spasms may be confined to one muscle, or group of muscles (e.g. a muscle twitch), or they may be severe and generalized, as occur in convulsions. Spasm of intestinal smooth muscle is considered one cause of colic.

See Colic, Muscle.

Spasmodic colic see Colic

Spasmolytic ◀ː _spaz_ mō _li_ tik, _n._ (antispasmodic) a medication which reduces spasm of smooth or skeletal muscle. The drug n-butylscopolammonium bromide is a spasmolytic agent of smooth muscle used in the treatment of spasmodic colic; methocarbamol is a spasmolytic agent of skeletal muscle that works by depressing the central nervous system.

See Colic, Muscle, Spasm.

Spasticity ◀ː _spas_ _ti_ si _tē_, _n._ a state of increased muscular tone resulting in spasmodic tightening and shortening of a muscle, especially muscles of limbs or back. Affected horses move stiffly, with less-than-normal joint flexion; may be exacerbated by neurological tests, e.g. if horse walks up and down slope. May be seen in disease of cerebellum (e.g. cerebellar abiotrophy), conditions associated with low blood calcium (e.g. transit tetany, lactation tetany), equine protozoal myelitis, cervical vertebral stenotic myelopathy, or some plant poisonings (e.g. ryegrass staggers).

See Cerebellum, Cervical vertebral stenotic myelopathy, Equine protozoal myeloencephalitis, Ryegrass staggers, Spasm, Tetany.

Spavin ◀ː _spa_ vin, _n._ old term given to many disorders of hock joint (tarsus). These include:

- Blind s. (also termed occult spavin) – lameness related to the distal tarsal joint without external signs of bony enlargement or radiographic signs of osteoarthritis (e.g. exostosis). Diagnosis confirmed by local anaesthetic injections into affected joint(s).
- Bog s. – swelling of the tibiotarsal joint. May occur as consequence of numerous conditions, including trauma, exercise-related stress, osteoarthritis, or osteochondrosis.
- Bone s. – osteoarthritis of one or both of the distal tarsal joints.
- Blood s. – bleeding into the tibiotarsal joint. Typically occurs as a result of trauma.

See Bog spavin, Bone, Osteoarthritis, Osteochondrosis, Tarsus.

Specific gravity ◄⁐ *spē si fik / gra vi tē, n.* ratio of the density of a substance to another substance used as a standard, especially the density of water. Commonly evaluated as part of urinalysis. Water has specific gravity of 1; normal specific gravity of horse's urine is 1.030–1.060, but varies considerably depending on the horse's state of hydration. Abnormalities in specific gravity of urine may indicate disease of the kidneys.
See Urinalysis.

Specimen ◄⁐ *spe si min, n.* tissue, blood, or fluid, e.g. urine, taken for laboratory testing.

Speculum ◄⁐ *spe kū lēm, n.* instrument used to open a body cavity or orifice to allow for inspection of the interior.
  Dental s. ◄⁐ *den tūl / spe kū lēm, n.* a metal device used to open the horse's mouth to allow for examination and treatment of the oral cavity.
  Vaginal s. *vē ji nūl /* ◄⁐ *spe kū lēm, n.* a tube or device used to facilitate visual examination and/or treatment of the vagina and cervix in mare.
  See Vagina.

Speedy-cutting ◄⁐ *spē dē-ku ting, n.* (interfering) gait problem where hoof of one forelimb hits medial aspect of lower leg or hoof of other forelimb. Can cause injury; may be prevented to some extent by horse wearing boot over hoof. Foot flight that predisposes to speedy-cutting can be influenced by toe-out conformation.
See Gait, Hoof.

Sperm ◄⁐ *sperm, n.* (*abbr.* for spermatozoon) microscopic male reproductive cell; has oval-shaped head, which contains the genetic material, a body, which contains the energy-producing mitochondria, and a long tail, which propels cell by whip-like lashing movements of its flagella. Sperm is modified by capacitation before fusing with ova (egg) at fertilization to form the embryo. Sperm is produced in testes of stallion; released into semen at ejaculation by muscular contraction. Normal daily sperm production is 7–8 x 10^9 cells per day; it takes 8–11 days for sperm to pass from the testes to the exterior. Normal semen contains approximately 1–5 x 10^9 sperm per ml. Abnormalities of sperm, which may be found during examination of semen sample, include poor motility, abnormality of head or tail, head detached from tail, low numbers of sperm – such abnormalities typically depress fertility. Frequent collection may assist in the reduction of such abnormalities.
See Capacitation, Fertilization, Semen, Testes.

Spermatic cord ◄⁐ *sper ma tik / kord, n.* structure resembling a cord, which connects testis to the inguinal ring; comprised of ductus deferens, blood vessels, nerves, cremaster muscle, connective tissue, and lymphatics. Spermatic cord is cut during castration. Torsion of spermatic cord can occur, whereby testis rotates on vertical axis; may result in permanent damage to testis if blood supply is occluded.
See Castration, Ductus, Testes, Torsion.

Spermatogenesis ◄⁐ *sper ma tō jen is is, n.* the process of producing sperm.
See Sperm.

Spermatozoon see Sperm

Spherocyte ◄⁐ *sfe rō sīt, n.* spherical erythrocyte (red blood cell) with no lighter-coloured central area (unlike the erythrocytes of most species, which appear doughnut-shaped owing to central area of pallor). May occasionally be seen in samples from animals with immune-mediated anaemia; however, identification may be difficult in equine blood, as normal horse's red blood cells often lack an obvious central area.
See Anaemia, Erythrocyte.

Sphincter ◄⁐ *sfingk tē, n.* ring-shaped muscle that relaxes or tightens to open or close a passage or opening in the body. Examples include:
- Anal s. – muscular ring that controls passage of faeces through the anus.
- Pyloric s. – muscular ring that controls passage of ingesta from stomach into small intestine

- Urethral s. – muscular ring that controls the retention and release of urine from the bladder.

See Anus, Pylorus.

Spina bifida ◀€ *spī nẽ / bi fi dẽ, n.* extremely rare congenital defect of development of spine; has been seen in newborn miniature horse foals. In spina bifida, the backbone does not form properly, so spinal cord or covering layers (meninges) may protrude through defect.

See Meninges, Spinal, Spine.

Spinal ◀€ *spī nūl, adj.* of, or relating to, the spine (backbone). Also, colloquially used as a noun to describe injecting an anesthetic beneath the arachnoid membrane that surrounds the spinal cord (a 'spinal').

See Spine.

S. accessory nerve ◀€ *spī nūl / ak ses ẽr ẽ / nerv, n.* cranial nerve XI.

See Cranial nerve.

S. canal ◀€ *spī nūl / kẽ nal, n.* the space that houses the spinal cord and spinal nerves throughout the length of the vertebral column; formed by the alignment of each vertebral foramen (the hole in the body of each vertebra). Spinal cord lies within the canal.

See Spinal, Spine, Vertebra.

S. column ◀€ *spī nūl / kol ẽm, n.* the axial skeleton, consisting of an articulated series of vertebrae, connected by ligaments, and spaced by fibrocartilage discs, which extends from the neck to the tail, protecting the spinal cord; backbone.

S. cord ◀€ *spī nūl / kord, n.* part of central nervous system within spinal canal; extending from the base of the skull (as a continuation of the brain) through the vertebrae of the spinal column, ending around 5th–6th lumbar vertebra. On cross-section, the spinal cord is made up of an H-shaped core of grey matter (consisting of nerve cell bodies, or neurons), glial cells (astroglia and oligodendrocytes), capillaries, and short nerve cell extensions/processes (axons and dendrites), surrounded by white matter (composed of myelinated nerve cell processes, or axons, which carry nerve impulses between neurons), covered by three protective membranes (meninges) and enclosed within the vertebrae. At regular intervals along length are spinal nerves, which emerge from each side of the cord (42 pairs in horse). Damage to spinal cord will result in failure of nervous impulses to reach brain, and failure of nervous impulses from brain to reach organs and legs; complete disruption of spinal cord function causes paralysis. Other conditions which can affect spinal cord include cervical vertebral stenotic myelopathy (wobbler syndrome), inflammation (myelitis), infection and tumours. Signs of spinal cord problems include incoordination (ataxia) and proprioceptive defects.

See Central nervous system, Cervical vertebral stenotic myelopathy, Nerve, Proprioception, Spinal.

S. nerve ◀€ *spī nūl / nerv, n.* any of paired nerves which arise from spinal cord along its length; 42 pairs in horse. Each nerve is attached to the cord by a dorsal (upper) and ventral (lower) root; dorsal roots are afferent (carry sensory information), and ventral roots are efferent (carry impulses away from the spinal cord to structures such as muscles or glands) which join together to form a single nerve inside the spinal canal, prior to passing through the intervertebral foramen. Spinal nerves carry information from all over the body to the spinal cord and relay commands from the brain and spinal cord back to the body. Injuries to the spinal cord can be located to a certain extent by establishing which spinal nerves are affected, as lesions of one or more nerve roots result in typical patterns of neurological deficits.

See Nerve, Spinal.

S. stenosis ◀€ *spī nūl / ste nõ sis, n.* narrowing of the spinal canal.

See Cervical vertebral stenotic myelopathy, Stenosis.

S. tap ◀€ *spī nūl / tap, n.* diagnostic procedure used to collect cerebrospinal fluid for evaluation or diagnosis of disease, e.g. for equine protozoal myelitis, meningitis, etc. Two sites are used for spinal taps in horses: the cisterna magna, at the base of the skull (requires general anaesthesia), and the lumbosacral space (can be performed in standing horse).

See Nerve, Spinal.

Spine ◀❬ *spīn*, *n*. backbone, vertebral column; the horse's spine is typically separated into regions, e.g. the cervical spine, thoracic spine, etc. Also, a sharp, rigid process or appendage, e.g. the dorsal spine (dorsal spinous process) of a vertebra. See Vertebral.

Spirochaete ◀❬ *spī rō kēt*, *n*. long, coiled or spiral, free-living bacterium; includes genera *Leptospira* (in horses, associated with abortion and some cases of uveitis) and *Borrelia* (cause of Lyme disease). See *Leptospira* spp., Lyme disease.

Spleen ◀❬ *splēn*, *n*. Soft, dark red, large organ on the left side of the abdomen, behind the stomach. The spleen produces lymphocytes, filters the blood, stores blood cells, and destroys old blood cells. The horse's spleen is normally about 1–1.2 m long, 20 cm wide and 10 cm thick. Approximately 80% of the spleen's contents are red blood cells; these stored cells are not measured on routine blood counts, thus diagnoses of anaemia based on single blood counts are highly suspect. When horses start to exercise, contraction of the musculature surrounding the spleen squeezes additional red blood cells into the circulatory system, increasing the oxygen-carrying capacity of blood, as well as the capacity of the horse to exercise. Splenic contraction may be caused by injection of phenylephrine; such therapy may be indicated for correction of some cases of nephrosplenic entrapment. Splenic enlargement (splenomegaly) can occur secondary to barbiturate anaesthesia, in lymphoma or other neoplastic conditions, or in diseases such as anthrax, equine infectious anaemia or Potomac horse fever.
See Anthrax, Barbiturate, Equine infectious anaemia, Erythrocyte, Immunity, Lymphoma, Nephrosplenic, Potomac horse fever, Tumour.

Splenomegaly ◀❬ *splēn ō meg ēl ē*, *n*. enlargement of the spleen.
See Spleen.

Splint ◀❬ *splint n*. **1)** a device used to maintain a body part in a fixed position; a splint may be applied to an injured limb (e.g. fracture or severe tendon or ligament injury) to immobilize and protect the limb, especially prior to surgical repair. **2)** as pertains specifically to horses, inflammation of the interosseous ligament between a splint bone and the cannon bone (third metacarpal or metatarsal bone, on front or hind limb, respectively). Splints most commonly develop in young horses with immature musculoskeletal systems; often associated with stress from excessive exercise or poor conformation. Clinical signs include swelling at the site of inflammation, heat, and pain on palpation; lameness may be a feature of cases with more extensive inflammation. Pain and lameness usually resolve spontaneously over 4–8 weeks; however, numerous treatments, e.g. cold therapy, topical and systemic anti-inflammatory agents, local corticosteroid injections, low-intensity laser therapy, and extracorporeal shock wave therapy, may be recommended. Acute swelling may result in permanent bony enlargement (exostosis – a 'splint') as a consequence of inflammation of surrounding bone, with subsequent new bone formation; after resolution of the acute condition, such swellings are rarely associated with future problems. Surgical removal of the exostosis is sometimes contemplated for cosmetic reasons; however, such surgery is not always successful, as inflammation of the treated area subsequent to the surgery may merely promote the formation of additional new bone.
See Exostosis, Ligament, Splint bone.

Splint bone ◀❬ *splint / bōn*, *n*. paired, thin bones on lateral and medial aspects of front and hind cannon bones. The splint bones are vestigial second and fourth metacarpal and metatarsal bones, in front and hind limbs, respectively, remaining from when primitive horses had five toes. Each has rounded head dorsally and small button ventrally (ventral tip can be felt through skin two-thirds of way down cannon bone). Splint bone is attached to cannon bone by intraosseous ligament; inflammation of the intraosseous ligament causes 'splints'. The bone may also be fractured, e.g. as may be seen associated with inflammation of the suspensory ligament, from a kick from another horse or from interference or speedy-cutting; fracture causes lameness, pain, swelling. Severely comminuted or open fractures may form a sequestrum, with local discharge. Clinical diagnosis of fracture or 'splints' is confirmed by radiography. Surgical removal of the distal fragment of a fractured splint bone is commonly recommended in racing horses with such injuries.

See Cannon, Ligament, Metacarpals, Metatarsals, Sequestrum, Speedy-cutting, Splint.

Spondylitis ◀ᴇ *spon di lī tis, n.* inflammation of the vertebrae (bones of spine). Pathological lesions tend to affect multiple vertebral locations; lesions may be from infections (e.g. in foals from *Rhodococcus equi* infections), or from the strain of athletic endeavours. Some horses with isolated lesions may have no apparent clinical signs. The disease is not necessarily associated with domestication and riding; erosive spondylitis is now documented to have occurred in many prehistoric horse specimens, and in mammalian species at least 40 million years old. Clinical signs may include stiffness, cervical or back pain, unwillingness to work, and lameness. Radiology of affected areas may demonstrate bony pathology; scintigraphic examination may reveal areas of increased radionuclide uptake. Cases associated with bacterial infection have resolved with prolonged courses of antimicrobials.

> **Ankylosing s.** ◀ᴇ *ang ki lōs ing / spon di lī tis, n.* is inflammation of the vertebrae with bony fusion (ankylosis).
> See Ankylosis, Inflammation, Scintigraphy, Spine, Vertebra.

Spondylosis ◀ᴇ *spon di lō sis, n.* degenerative changes in vertebrae, with fusing of joints between vertebrae of spine. New bone may be formed on the ventral surfaces of the spine, especially on cervical or thoracic vertebrae. Clinical signs may include stiffness, cervical or back pain, and unwillingness to work. Radiographic findings in chronic cases may include lysis

of vertebral endplates and sclerosis, and vertebral subluxation; scintigraphic examination may reveal areas of increased radionuclide uptake. Ultrasonographic examination of the back may reveal findings such as vertebral malalignment and destruction of intervertebral discs, widened disc spaces, paravertebral abscesses, and atrophy of adjacent musculature. No effective treatment once chronic changes are present.

See Scintigraphy, Spine, Spondylitis, Vertebra.

Sporadic ◀ᴇ *spo ra dik, adj.* describes condition which occurs at irregular intervals; occurring in no pattern or order in time. Also, isolated or unique, i.e. not endemic or epidemic, as in a sporadic disease outbreak.

See Endemic, Epidemic.

Sporotrichosis ◀ᴇ *spo rō tri kō sis, n.* skin disease caused by soil fungus (*Sporothrix schenckii*); usually introduced via a skin wound. Occurs especially in southern Canada, parts of Europe, South Africa and USA. Disease typically presents as multiple lumps, abscesses, or ulcers of a single limb, beginning near the hoof. Limb swelling is common, as is lameness. In chronic cases, the infection can invade the lymphatic system, resulting in firm cords that extend towards the horse's trunk, and lymphangitis. Clinical diagnosis is obtained by histological examination of fluid from the lesions, and skin biopsies; the presence of cigar-shaped yeasts strongly suggests the presence of the organism. Definitive diagnosis is by fungal culture or fluorescent antibody testing on skin biopsy material. Serological detection of serum antibodies indicates exposure, but not necessarily infection. Treatment for sporotrichosis usually involves the administration of at least one of several iodine-based products. The disease has zoonotic potential, so good hygiene procedures (e.g. gloves) should be followed so as to prevent cross-infection when treating infected animals. Months of treatment may be required for resolution; stopping treatment too early may result in relapse. Sporotrichosis can be a chronic, debili-

tating disease in the horse but cure is possible. However, early, accurate diagnosis and treatment are essential to prevent irreversible damage.
See Iodine, Lymphangitis, Zoonosis.

Sprain ◀€ *sprān, n.* injury to a ligament from violent contraction or excessive stretch, e.g. of the suspensory ligament, or of ligaments associated with joints. Damage to ligament results in desmitis (inflammation) from which recovery can be slow as blood supply within ligament is poor; typical signs include swelling, soreness on palpation of the affected ligament, and lameness. The analogous injury to a tendon or muscle is a strain.
See Ligament, Strain, Tendon.

Squamous ◀€ *skwā mẽs, adj.* scaly; characterized by scales.
   S. cells ◀€ *skwā mẽs / sels, n.* flat cells with an irregular shape. Squamous cells make up the surface of the skin, and the linings of structures such as the oesophagus, vagina, and rectum.
   S. cell carcinoma ◀€ *skwā mẽs / sel / kar si nō mē, n.* neoplasia which develops from squamous cells. Reportedly the second most commonly diagnosed tumour of the horse (after equine sarcoid); as many as 20% of the diagnosed equine neoplasms are squamous cell carsinomas. The average age at which horses are diagnosed with this cancer is approximately 8–14 years; however, horses as young as 1 year old, and older than 30 years, have been affected. Risk factors include increased exposure to ultraviolet radiation (i.e. dry, sunny climate) and lightly pigmented, pink-skinned areas of the horse (e.g. vulva, prepuce, penis, third eyelid, and cornea). Squamous cell carcinomas of the skin originate from epidermal cells; usually locally invasive but slow to metastasize, although as many as 18% of horses with the cancer may have metastasis, especially to regional lymph nodes. The tumours usually initially arise as discrete, solitary lesions, but adjacent skin is soon involved. Early lesions tend to be small, and superficial areas of reddening or ulceration; some nodules may initially be covered with normal skin. As the disease progresses, the epidermis is destroyed and ulceration, proliferation, and

necrosis occur as the lesion grows. In early cases, medical therapy, e.g. 5-fluorouracil cream, or cisplatin injections, may be curative; surgery may also be curative in instances where medical therapy may not be possible (e.g. removal of the third eyelid where chemotherapeutic agents may be irritating to the eye, or local excision of small lesions of the penis, where application of topical medicines may not be tolerated). Corneal tumours may require superficial keratectomy, radiation therapy, or chemotherapy; the prognosis is guarded with corneal lesions, as recurrence is not unusual. With extensive lesions and metastasis, the prognosis is grave.
See Tumour.

Stable fly ◀€ *stā būl / flī, n.* (*Stomoxys calcitrans*) biting fly, resembling common houseflies in both size and appearance. An annoying pest; feeds by sucking blood from horse. Lays eggs in horse dung. Important in the mechanical transmission of diseases such as trypanosomiasis (e.g. Surra), and equine infectious anaemia. Also serves as intermediate host for *Habronema*.
See Equine infectious anaemia, Surra, *Trypanosoma*.

Staggers ◀€ *sta gerz, n.* colloquial description for a disease characterized by an unsteady swaying gait, frequent falling, incoordination, and ataxia.
See Ataxia, Ryegrass staggers.

Stain ◀€ *stān, n.* dye, combination of dyes, or other colouring material used to colour tissue or microorganisms (e.g. bacteria, fungi), so that they can be seen and identified more easily in microscopic examination. Examples of stains used in veterinary medicine include:
- Diff-Quik® (a modified Wright–Giemsa stain for staining a variety of smears).
- Giemsa (shows up protozoan blood parasites, e.g. babesiosis).
- Gram stain – used in identification of bacteria.
- Haematoxylin and eosin – H & E; used for staining sections of tissue.
- Wright's stain – commonly used in the examination of peripheral blood smears, as well as of bone marrow aspirates.

- Ziehl–Neelsen – shows up several characteristic red-staining acid-fast bacteria, such as *Mycobacterium* species.
See Gram stain, Wright's stain.

Stale ◀€ *stāl*, *n.* colloquial term for urination.
See Urinate.

Stallion ◀€ *stal yēn*, *n.* adult, sexually mature, male horse.

Stallion ring ◀€ *stal yēn / ring*, *n.* rubber device placed over the stallion's penis to discourage masturbating. If a stallion ring is too tight, or fits poorly, it can cause penile injury, scars, and strictures, which may result in inability of stallion to maintain an erection.
See Stallion.

Staphylectomy ◀€ *sta fi lec tē mē*, *n.* surgical operation involving resection of the posterior part of the soft palate. May be performed as a treatment for dorsal displacement of the soft palate.
See Dorsal, Soft palate.

Staphylococcus ◀€ *sta fi lō ko kēs*, *n.* genus of approximately 50 different species and subspecies of Gram-positive cocci bacteria, commonly present on skin and in upper airways. *Staphylococcus* infections are generally opportunistic, i.e. one or more risk factors must be present before disease can occur. Risk factors favouring bacterial growth and infection include surgery, trauma (including such things as intra-articular injections), other infections, skin lesions (e.g. ulcers), and immune system incompetence. The bacteria are usually divided based on their ability to produce coagulase; most major *Staphylococcus* pathogens are coagulase positive. Clinical disease can vary from mild local infections to systemic infections and toxaemia; diagnosis can usually be confirmed with bacterial culture. Treatment depends on the site and severity of the infection, and the sensitivity of the bacteria to antimicrobials. Topical therapy (e.g. cleansing, and topical antibacterial therapy) may be sufficient to treat superficial wound infections; more severe infections may require tech-

niques such as regional limb perfusion or high doses of broad-spectrum antibiotics, in addition to supportive care. Prevention of staphylococcal infections involves good husbandry practices, prompt attention to local wounds, judicious use of antibiotics, proper disinfection of equipment, and proper technique when invasive procedures are performed. As the infections have zoonotic potential, humans should take appropriate precautions when working around infected animals. The two most important species that are associated with disease in horses are:

- *Staphylococcus aureus* – the most important *Staphylococcus* pathogen of the horse. Common cause of wound and surgical infections, and infection of almost any tissue; conditions associated with *S. aureus* infections include cellulitis, skin infections, septic arthritis, tenosynovitis, metritis, lymphangitis, pleuropneumonia, and sinusitis.
  - ○ **Methicillin-resistant** *S. aureus* (MRSA) are an emerging and important cause of nosocomial (hospital) infections. These bacteria are resistant to most antibiotics, including all penicillins, and they are a potential source of zoonotic infection.
- *Staphylococcus intermedius* – infections tend to be similar to those caused by *S. aureus*, but are less common.
See Abscess, Folliculitis, Mastitis, Pus.

Stapling ◀€ *stā pling*, *v.* use of stainless steel staples to repair skin wounds or in intestinal surgery, e.g. for intestinal closure or anastomosis. In skin repair, cosmetic results may not be as acceptable as in closure of wounds with fine sutures, and staples cannot be used in areas with significant skin tension. In intestinal surgery, stapling allows more rapid repair than with traditional suturing techniques, so surgery time is reduced: an important factor in survival of horse.
See Anastomosis, Colic.

Stasis ◀€ *stā sis*, *n.* stagnation or inactivity, especially of flow of fluid within body.
  Gastrointestinal s. ◀€ *gas trō in tes tin ēl / stā sis*, *n.* stagnation of intestinal motility, e.g. as

may be seen in grass sickness, with various causes of colic, or peritonitis; ileus.
See Colic, Grass sickness, Ileus, Peritonitis.
Venous s. ◀⬩ *vē nĕs / stā sis, n.* stagnation of blood in the venous system of the body. Results in impaired circulation and oedema; clinically, may cause skin ulceration, or can result from conditions where tissue circulation is impaired, e.g. intestinal strangulation.

Stay apparatus ◀⬩ *stā / a pē rā tĕs, n.* anatomical arrangement of muscles, ligaments and tendons which allows horse to remain standing for long periods (in combination with locking mechanism of the patella (kneecap) and reciprocal mechanism of hind limb). The stay apparatus allows the limbs to be 'locked' with little muscular effort; this allows the horse to be perpetually ready to run away from danger, real or perceived.
See Ligament, Patella, Reciprocal mechanism, Tendon.

Steatitis ◀⬩ *stā ē tī tis, n.* inflammation of adipose (fatty) tissue. Rare condition, usually reported in foals, associated with selenium and/or vitamin E deficiency. Has also been seen in older horses, associated with selenium and/or vitamin E deficiency, but also as occurring with other problems such as panniculitis or pancreatitis. Signs include fever, lethargy, weight loss (sometimes severe), colic, and weakness. Areas of hardened fat can be felt under skin. Diagnosis can be made by biopsy; radiography may show calcification of tissues such as the nuchal ligament. Prognosis poor.
See Selenium, Vitamin E.

Stem ◀⬩ *stem, n.* stalk-like supporting structure, e.g. brainstem.
See Brain.

Stem cell ◀⬩ *stem / sel, n.* an unspecialized cell that can produce other cells that eventually make up specialized tissues and organs (e.g. tendon or ligament). Stem cells can be found at different stages of foetal development and are present in a wide range of adult tissues, e.g. adipose tissue, bone marrow, or

blood. Of most interest in equine medicine are pluripotent stem cells, which are able to generate almost all body cell types (but which cannot themselves form a whole functioning organism). In principle, some of the horse's own stem cells can be harvested and injected into a diseased or damaged region (e.g. of a tendon) to produce new cells. Various applications of stem cell therapies are available for the treatment of tendon and ligament injuries in horses; however, it has yet to be demonstrated that such therapies provide benefits over conventional therapy (e.g. rest and controlled rehabilitation). However, stem cell therapy is being intensively investigated and offers a potential revolution in medical treatment for diseases and disorders where tissue function is abnormal.

Stenosis ◀⬩ *ste nō sis, n.* narrowing of passage, vessel or opening in body (e.g. a heart valve).
  Aortic s. ◀⬩ *ā or tik / ste nō sis, n.* narrowing of the aorta as it exits the heart; rare congenital defect. Can cause increased pressure in heart and cardiac failure.
  See Heart.
  Choanal s. ◀⬩ *kō ā nĕl / ste nō sis, n.* narrowing of the airways where nasal cavities enter nasopharynx. May be seen as congenital problem. There is no effective treatment, and the narrowing of the air passages can impair athletic performance.
  See Congenital, Nasal, Nasopharynx.
  Vertebral s. ◀⬩ *ver ti brĕl / ste nō sis, n.* narrowing of the vertebral foramen; causes cervical vertebral stenotic myelopathy.
  See Cervical vertebral stenotic myelopathy.

Stereotype (Stereotypy) *ster ē ĕ tīp, n.* in behavioural science, a stereotypy, or fixed action pattern, is a repetitive pattern of behaviour that serves no obvious purpose; an innate, pre-programmed response that is repeated when an animal is exposed to a stimulus. Examples of sterotypes in horses include self-mutilation syndrome, weaving, and crib-biting.
See Crib-biting, Self-mutilation syndrome, Weave.

Sterile ◀≀ _ste ríl, adj._ **1)** infertile, incapable of reproducing; **2)** free from living microorganisms (bacteria, fungi, viruses, etc.), e.g. sterile instruments are used for operations to prevent them from introducing infection into operating site.

Sterilization ◀≀ _ste ri lī zā shēn, n._ **1)** the process of making an animal unable to reproduce, especially by castration in male, or by ovariectomy (removal of ovaries) or ovariohysterectomy (removal of ovaries and uterus) in female; **2)** destruction of all microorganisms, including vegetative forms and spores, by use of heat (e.g. in autoclave), radiation, filtration, or chemicals.
See Autoclave, Castration, Ovariectomy.

Sternum ◀≀ _ster nēm, n._ breastbone; canoe-shaped bone to which first eight ribs attach. At birth, the sternum is made up of seven bony segments called sternebrae; the last two segments fuse at approximately 2 months of age, but the others never fuse completely. Sternum forms ventral border of chest wall. The ventral surface of the sternum has a prominent keel-like crest which can be felt in living horses (unlike the flat surface of sternum in ruminants). The cranial extremity of the sternum is the cartilagenous manubrium, which is distinctly palpable; the caudal attachment is the xiphoid process, which is wide, and nearly circular, and gives attachement to the diaphragm dorsally and to the transverse abdominal muscle and the linea alba ventrally. Bone marrow may be obtained from the sternebrae for biopsy, or bone for grafting; there are occasional reports of pneumothorax from such procedures.
See Cartilage, Pneumothorax, Rib.

Steroid ◀≀ _ste roid, n._ A class of molecules that contain a similar chemical core, consisting of four interconnected carbon rings. Steroids are lipids, based on the cholesterol molecule. Steroids naturally function as hormonal messengers in the body. Various synthetic versions of steroids are administered as drugs. Different classes of steroids have different functions, including:

- Sex steroids (including testosterone, oestrogen).
- Corticosteroids produced by cortex of adrenal gland (e.g. cortisone). Corticosteroids are used to treat inflammation, pain, and swelling.
- Anabolic steroids are drugs which are used clinically to encourage tissue growth or recovery.

See Adrenal gland, Corticosteroid, Oestrogen, Testosterone.

Stertor ◀≀ _ster tē, n._ snoring, sonorous sound made during breathing; term may be used to describe the sound caused by partial obstruction of upper airway, e.g. as seen in laryngeal paralysis, strangles. The term stridor is more commonly used to describe such sounds.
See Laryngeal, Strangles, Stridor.

Stethoscope ◀≀ _ste thē skōp, n._ an instrument used to transmit low-volume sounds (e.g. the heartbeat, or intestinal or lung sounds) to the ear of the listener. A stethoscope typically consists of two earpieces connected by means of flexible tubing to a diaphragm; the diaphragm is placed against the horse at various locations, depending on the structure being examined.
See Heart, Respiratory.

Stifle ◀ ≀ _stī fúl, n._ joint of upper hind leg between the femur, patella, and the tibia; the joint proximal to the hock, analogous to human knee joint. Kneecap (patella) is a small bone at the front of the joint that lies between two (trochlear) ridges of the femur; cartilage discs (the medial and lateral menisci) lie between femur and tibia within the joint and act as shock absorbers. Several important ligaments stabilize the stifle joint, including medial and lateral collateral ligaments, cruciate liagments, meniscal ligaments, and the patellar ligaments. Major conditions affecting joint include osteochondritis, bone cysts, ligament injuries, problems with patella (luxation, fixation, fracture), damage to menisci, and osteoarthritis. Stifle-related problems may sometimes be seen on radiographs. Ultrasonography allows imaging of the subcutaneous

tissue, the medial, middle and lateral patellar ligaments, the medial and lateral collateral ligaments, the femoral trochlear ridges, and the menisci; cruciate ligaments cannot be visualized in a standing horse. Treatment of stifle problems includes intra-articular injections for osteoarthritis; surgical procedures of the stifle joint are typically performed arthroscopically.
See Arthroscope, Bone, Femur, Ligament, Meniscus, Osteochondrosis, Patella, Tibia, Ultrasonography.

Stillbirth ◀ᴇ _stil berth_, _n._ delivery of fully formed dead neonate, usually defined as being from a gestation of at least 300 days. Causes may be infection (e.g. with equine herpes virus), placentitis, or dystocia, where foal dies before it can be delivered.
See Dystocia, Equine herpes virus, Placentitis.

Stimulant ◀ᴇ _sti mū lĕnt_, _n._ substance which temporarily causes increased physiological activity, e.g. a respiratory stimulant might be given to a newborn foal to encourage breathing.

Stitch ◀ᴇ _stich_, _v._ to suture; to sew up a wound or surgical cut.
See Suture.

Stomach ◀ᴇ _stu mĕk_, _n._ enlarged, muscular organ; the initial organ of digestion. Food enters the proximal portion of the stomach from oesophagus through the lower oesophageal sphincter; the proximal portion of the stomach acts as a reservoir for food by first relaxing, then later emptying as a consequence of increased pressure which moves the digested food from the stomach through the pyloric sphincter into the small intestine. The degree of relaxation of the stomach is affected by the size of the meal; the equine stomach is relatively small, thus it is more natural for horses to eat small amounts more frequently throughout the day rather than a few large meals. The upper one-third of the stomach is called the oesophageal region, or squamous mucosa; this region has no glands and is covered by a stratified squamous epithelium similar to that which covers the oesophagus. The lower two-thirds of the stomach is called the glandular region; this region contains glands that continually secrete hydrochloric acid, pepsin, bicarbonate and mucus. A sharp line of demarcation (margo plicatus) separates the squamous mucosa from the glandular mucosa, and can be easily visualized on endoscopy. Conditions which affect the stomach include impaction (blockage with food, bedding), rupture (e.g. in impactions that do not resolve, or in grass sickness), ulceration, tumours.
See Colic, Digestion, Equine gastric ulcer syndrome, Grass sickness, Large intestine, Oesophagus, Small intestine.
   S. tube see Nasogastric
   S. worm see _Habronema_

Stomatitis ◀ᴇ _stō mē tī tis_, _n._ inflammation of any of the mucous membranes of the mouth; includes inflammation of gums (gingivitis), inflammation of tongue (glossitis), etc. May be due to dental disease or various infections, e.g. equine viral arteritis, vesicular stomatitis. Signs may include unwillingness to eat, salivation, dropping food from mouth.
See Equine viral arteritis, Gingivitis, Glossitis, Tooth, Vesicular stomatitis.

Stone see Calculus

Strabismus ◀ᴇ _stra biz mēs_, _n._ eye deviated from normal position. Rare in horses; appears to occur most commonly in Appaloosas, associated with night blindness. May be congenital, associated with microphthalmos and facial abnormalities, or caused by various conditions, including trauma, tumour or abscess in eye socket.
See Eye, Oculomotor nerve.

Strain ◀ᴇ _strān_, _n._ injury to muscle and/or tendon from violent contraction or excessive stretch. Damage to tendon results in tendinitis (inflammation), resulting in clinical signs of heat, swelling, soreness on palpation, and lameness (colloquial term for a tendon strain with swelling is 'bowed tendon'). Recovery from strains can be slow as blood supply within tendon is

poor. The equivalent injury to a ligament is a sprain.
See Muscle, Sprain, Tendinitis.

Strangles ◀€ _strang gŭlz, n._ one of the most ubiquitous infections of the equine airway; first described in 1251. Strangles is an infection of the upper airways (nose and pharynx) and associated lymph nodes with the bacterium _Streptococcus equi_; in some cases, the infection can be disseminated to lymph nodes throughout the body. Can occur in horses of any age, but seen most commonly in herds of young horses, and the disease is often more severe in younger animals. Transmission is direct (horse to horse) or indirect (via such things as contaminated stables, water sources, feeders, tack, or the clothing and equipment of handlers), by contact with purulent discharges. Disease outbreaks usually begin with the introduction of a new horse incubating or carrying the disease (especially in the guttural pouches) and shedding the organism in nasal secretions; the bacteria do not appear to persist in the environment. Bacteria infect horse by entering mouth or nose and attaching to local lymph nodes and the pharyngeal epithelium. Bacteria rapidly spread to regional lymph nodes (e.g. the submandibular lymph nodes) where the bacteria are attacked by neutrophils; the horse's response to infection ultimately results in the abscesses characteristic of the disease. Signs include high temperature starting 3–14 days after exposure, loss of appetite, difficulty swallowing (dysphagia), depression, inflammation of the pharynx and larynx, discharge from nose (may be watery initially, then turns purulent), difficulty breathing, noise when breathing (stridor) caused by swelling of the airways, as well as accumulation of discharge. The characteristic feature of the disease is lymphadenopathy; lymph nodes of neck and throat typically become hot, swollen and painful within a week of infection, beginning as a hot, painful oedema, with oozing of serum, and progressing to a soft, fluctuant swelling that ultimately bursts after a few days or weeks. Enlargement of lymph nodes may result in obstruction of the respiratory tract, which gives the disease its name (i.e. the horses have difficulty breathing as if they were being strangled). Metastatic spread of infection to elsewhere in body may cause other signs, e.g. pneumonia, colic, fever, weight loss. Purpura haemorrhagica is an immune-mediated complication of strangles, caused by the deposition of antigen–antibody complexes in blood vessels (vasculitis). Diagnosis is from typical clinical signs; the _Streptococcus equi_ bacteria can be isolated by direct culture of purulent material, polymerase chain reaction testing of nasal swabs or washes, or detected by serological tests (e.g. ELISA). Treatment for individual horses depends on the stage and severity of disease. Many horses with strangles require no care beyond supportive care while the disease runs its course. In outbreaks, early antibiotic therapy, especially penicillin (considered the antibiotic of choice), instituted at the first signs of disease, or prophylactically in animals that appear normal, can prevent focal abscess formation; however, animals so treated are susceptible to reinfection because such treatment prevents the formation of protective antibodies. Once lymph node enlargement is seen, antibiotic therapy is probably not indicated; such therapy merely prolongs the enlargement and rupture of the characteristic abscesses. Instead, topical treatments to promote maturation of the abscess, e.g. hot packs, are commonly prescribed, though are not necessarily clinically important. Surgical drainage of the abscesses is common, although it is important to wait until the abscess is mature prior to drainage. Non-steroidal anti-inflammatory drugs may help control fever, and improve appetite and demeanour. Disseminated infections are treated with systemic antimicrobials and supportive care; purpura haemorrhagica is treated with antimicrobials and corticosteroids. Disease outbreaks may be controlled by isolating affected horses, and separating horses that have not been exposed from the rest of the herd; strict hygiene of handlers is important to prevent transmission (bacterium does not spread through air, unlike respiratory viruses). Several vaccines are available but none has yet been shown to give comprehensive protection. Complications from vaccination, including injection site swelling and abscesses with intramuscular vaccines, or vaccine strain infection from intranasal vaccines, have been reported. Nasal shedding from previously infected animals lasts 2–3 weeks in most individuals; persistent, inapparent infections of the guttural pouches can result in horses becoming carrier animals that can shed the bacteria for years. Inapparent infections can be eliminated by local treatment of the guttural pouches after such animals are identified.

See Lymph, Pneumonia, Purpura haemorrhagica, *Streptococcus*.

> **Bastard s.** ◀︎ *bar* stēd / *strang* gŭls, *n*. term used to describe metastatic abscessation of the *S. equi* bacteria that cause strangles. The organism may potentially spread to any tissue of the body, either by the blood, or through lymphatic channels. Common sites of infection include the lung, mesentery (causing internal abscesses), liver, kidneys, and brain. Diagnosis can be difficult, but a previous history of strangles infection is highly suggestive. Blood counts often show elevations in white blood cells; fibrinogen levels can be dramatically elevated. Treatment is with prolonged courses of antibiotics. The contention that antibiotic therapy causes bastard strangles has no scientific support.
>
> **Colorado s.** see *Corynebacterium*

Strangulation ◀︎ *strang* gŭ *lā* shēn, *n*. constriction of all or part of a tissue so as to cut off the flow of blood or other fluid through it. A strangulated hernia is one where blood supply to the contents is constricted by the small size of the opening through which contents have protruded; intestines become strangulated in torsion of large intestine, or by pedunculated lipomas. Strangulations are emergencies; strangulated tissues very quickly become necrotic, and affected animals usually die if untreated.

See Colic, Hernia, Lipoma.

Stranguria/Strangury ◀︎ *strang* gŭ rēē / *strang* gŭ rē *n*. slow, painful urination; straining to urinate. Has been seen in adult horses associated with colon ulceration and abdominal abscess, with urolithiasas, or inflammation of the urethra (urethritis); in foals, may reflect a congenital defect, e.g. ectopic ureter, or ruptured bladder.

See Bladder, Ureter, Urethra, Urethritis, Urolith.

Stratum ◀︎ *strar* tēm, *n*. in medicine, describes a layer of tissue, e.g. as of the various layers of the skin, hoof, brain, or retina.

Straw ◀︎ *straw*, *n*. the dry stalk of a cereal plant, after the nutrient grain or seed has been removed, commonly used as stable bedding. Straw can also be fed to horses; however, because of its poor nutrient profile, supplementary calories must be added (e.g. grain). The high fibre content increases the risk of intestinal impaction.

Street nail ◀︎ *strēt* / *nāl*, *n*. surgical procedure for the treatment of deep penetrating wounds of the hoof. Technique involves following wound tract to its base, aggressively debriding infected tissue and allowing for subsolar drainage. Wound typically treated with medicated dressings and protective plate until sole keratinizes. Prognosis is guarded; successful outcome depends on how rapidly the wound is recognized, which structures are affected, and to what degree.

Streptococcus ◀︎ *strep* tō *ko* kēs, *n*. genus of spherical, facultatively anaerobic, Gram-positive bacteria; form chains which look like strings of beads under microscope. Individual species of *Streptococcus* are often classified based on their breakdown of red blood cells (haemolysis) in a culture plate; however, some of the bacteria are non-haemolytic. Alpha haemolysis is caused by a reduction of iron in haemoglobin, which gives a greenish cast to the culture medium. Beta haemolysis is complete rupture of red blood cells, which shows up as a distinct, clear, and wide area around the bacterial colonies being cultured on blood agar;

most of the significant equine pathogens are β-haemolytic. *Streptococcus* spp. are subdivided into alphabetically designated serological groups based on specific carbohydrates in cell wall (Lancefield grouping; Lancefield group C *streptococci* are of most importance in equine medicine). *Streptococcus* species have zoonotic potential; cross-infections between horses and humans are frequently reported in the human medical literature. *Streptococcus* species which affect horses include:

- *Streptococcus* subsp. *equi* – the most clinically significant streptococcal bacterium of horses; causes strangles.
- *Streptococcus equisimilis* – largely a commensal organism of the equine skin; occasionally isolated from various skin conditions, including ulcerative lymphangitis and dermatitis of the lower limbs. Has also occasionally been found in abscessed lymph nodes and aborted placentas.
- *Streptococcus pneumoniae* – non-haemolytic streptococcus occasionally isolated from healthy horses, as well as horses with respiratory disease, especially foals with pneumonia.
- *Streptococcus equi.* subsp. *zooepidemicus* – largely a commensal organism of the equine respiratory tract, can rarely act as an opportunistic pathogen and cause secondary infections after viral infections, heat stress, or tissue injury (e.g. wounds). May also cause intrauterine infections or placentitis; it is one of the most common bacteria isolated from infections of the mare's reproductive tract.

Penicillins are usually the drugs of choice for treatment of streptococcal infections of horses. Several vaccines are available for the prevention of *S. equi* infections; their use is somewhat controversial, as no vaccines have been shown to effectively prevent the strangles disease caused by the organism.
See Abscess, Commensal, Gram stain, Penicillin, Strangles.

Streptomycin ◀ᴇ *strep tō mī sin, n.* antibiotic; the first of the aminoglycoside class of drugs to be discovered, produced by the soil fungus *Streptomyces*. Has some activity against many Gram-negative (e.g. *Leptospira*) and some Gram-positive bacteria; bacterial resistance is a common problem. Is sometimes combined with procaine penicillin G in an effort to provide a broader spectrum of coverage.

Stress ◀ᴇ *stres, n.* as pertains to medicine, the term stress refers to a physical or psychological stimulus that can produce mental or physiological reactions. It is the horse's total response, in terms of behavioural reactions, as well as of physical parameters (e.g. increased heartbeat, sweating), to the demands or pressures of its environment. Many neurotransmitter systems are activated by stress; stress also releases glucocorticoids. In general, the chemical substances released during stress are protective and adaptive for the animal; however, prolonged stress is thought to contribute to ill-health. Stressful situations for a horse include weaning, transport, introduction to a new group of horses, removal from a familiar place, over-exercising, surgery, illness. Also, stress is an applied force or system of forces that tends to strain or deform all or part of a body, e.g. the stress applied to a suspensory ligament when the horse is running can disrupt the ligament, causing injury.
See Surgery, Suspensory ligament, Weaning.

    S. fracture ◀ᴇ *stres / frak tŭr, n.* damage to bone from repeated physical stress, e.g. galloping on hard ground. Tough cortex of bone suffers tiny breaks (microfractures) which can cause pain and lameness. In stress fractures, there is disruption of cortical bone and pain but no crack going through a bone. Most commonly seen in young Thoroughbred racing horses, especially in cannon bone (bucked shin; dorsal cortical stress fracture), but also the tibia, humerus and pelvis. May not be visible on radiograph; can often be diagnosed using scintigraphy. Rest is crucial for resolution of most stress fractures; various treatments are advocated for the resolution of bucked shins.
See Bone, Bucked shin, Cannon, Dorsal, Humerus, Pelvis, Scintigraphy, Tibia.

    S. leukogram ◀ᴇ *stres / lŭ kō gram, n.* white blood cell count that is typical of a physiological stress response; thought to result largely from increases in plasma glucocorticoids. In horses with stress leukograms the white blood cell count may be as high as 20,000 cells/ml, made up predominately of neutrophils. Additionally, the lymphocyte count is typically normal to low (< 2,000 cells/ml)

Stricture ◀ _strik tŭr_, _n._ abnormal narrowing of passage or duct in body. Examples include:
- Urethral s. – narrowing of the urethra with scar tissue, e.g. as may be caused by damage to urethra by passage of urinary calculus.
- Oesophageal s. – narrowing of the oesophagus with scar tissue, as may be caused by oesophageal damage from choke or nasogastric intubation.

See Choke, Urethra, Urolithiasis.

Stride ◀ _strīd_, _n._ a single long step; a single, cyclical, coordinated movement of the four legs, finished when the legs return to their initial relative position. A stride of a single limb has an anterior (cranial) phase, i.e. the half of the stride when the limb is in front of the print of the opposite foot, and a posterior (caudal) phase, i.e. the half of the stride when the limb is behind the print of the opposite foot. The stride of a single limb is further subdivided into: 1) landing, when the hoof touches the ground and begins to bear the horse's body weight; 2) loading, when the horse's body moves over the hoof (and the fetlock reaches its lowest point); 3) stance, a transitional phase between loading and unloading of the horse's weight, where the fetlock is at a level equivalent to that of the limb at rest; 4) breakover, where the hoof leaves the ground; and 5) swing, where the limb moves through the air, and prepares for landing. Shortening of the different phases of stride may be seen in different types of lameness and this may help in diagnosis of lameness.

Stridor ◀ _strī dē_, _n._ term used to generally describe noisy breathing; in horses, commonly heard during exercise in cases of laryngeal hemiplegia.
See Laryngeal.

Stringhalt ◀ _string hawlt_, _n._ disease that results in an exaggerated flexion of one or both hind legs; hyperflexion can vary from mild, intermittent spasmodic lifting and rapid grounding of the foot (especially when the horse is turned sharply, or backed), to extreme hyperflexion where the foot touches the abdomen. Disease of adult horses; uncommon in foals. Cause unknown, however peripheral neuropathies have been identified in nerves of the hind limbs of affected horses. Some cases have been associated with plant toxicities (e.g. lathyrism). Diagnosis is generally made clinically, but can be confirmed by electromyography. Sometimes resolves spontaneously; tenotomy of the lateral digital extensor tendon, with partial myectomy, has been reported to help some horses, but not all cases respond (which may not be surprising, since the condition affects nerves). Large doses of thiamine (vitamin B1) have been tried on some horses; the anticonvulsant drug phenytoin is of use in treating some horses. Although the disease is considered to be an unsoundness, some mildly affected horses are still able to work and perform normally.

> **Australian s.** ◀ _Os trā lē ĕn_ / _string hawlt_, _n._ stringhalt, possibly associated with an ingested toxin. Signs may vary from mild to severe, as per all types of stringhalt; muscle wasting of the gaskin muscles is common. Laryngeal paralysis may also be seen. An Australian pasture weed, Cat's ear (_Hypochoeris radicata_) has been associated with many outbreaks of stringhalt, as have other plants, such as Dandelion (_Taraxacum officinale_); this association has not been confirmed by laboratory testing. Cases typically occur in late summer months in Australia, and may happen more frequently in dry pasture conditions. Horses will usually recover if they are removed from the incriminated plants; recovery can vary from a few days to over one year. Treatment of affected horses with the anticonvulsant drug phenytoin has been reported to relieve clinical signs and speed recovery. Surgery to remove the lateral digital extensor tendon in the hind leg is a treatment option for some horses. Pasture management may be the best option for minimizing the chance of exposure to the implicated plants.

Stroke ◀ *strōk, n.* in human medicine, stroke is sudden loss of brain function caused by a blockage or rupture of a blood vessel to the brain. Horses appear to be rarely affected by strokes; however, brain infarcts have been reported rarely, with signs of depression, incoordination, dysphasia, seizure, and head tilt. Most horses diagnosed with stroke are probably suffering from the sequela of head trauma, or from stylohyoid fractures secondary to inner ear infection; or a sudden severe attack, e.g. sunstroke, heat stroke (see Heat).
See Ear, Infarct.

Stroke volume *strōk / vol ūm, n.* the amount of blood ejected from each ventricle at each heart beat; typically measured in millilitres (the heart stroke is a single complete beat).

Stroma ◀ *strō mē, n.* the supportive framework of a tissue or organ; distinct from the parenchyma, which has the important functional elements.
See Parenchyma.

    Stromal abscess see Cornea

Strongyle see Cyathostome, *Strongylus* spp.

Strongyloides ◀ *strong gī loi dēz, n.* (intestinal threadworm) genus of parasitic nematode intestinal worm. *Strongyloides westeri* found in small intestine of foals; can infect foals as young as five days of age. Larvae are ingested, or penetrate foal's skin, then migrate through the lungs and small intestines; life cycle can be completed in as little as two weeks. Foals develop immunity to the parasite in 60–90 days and eliminate adult worms. Contrary to common belief, the worm is not responsible for the diarrhoea of foals often seen at the mare's foal heat; it usually does not cause any disease at all. However, heavy infestation may cause diarrhoea. Prevention is by deworming the mare prior to foaling, to help reduce parasite burden. Treatment of foals with diarrhoea is with most commonly used anthelmintics.
See Diarrhoea, Worm.

Strongylus spp. ◀ *strong gī lēs / spē shēs, n.* (redworm, large strongyle) genus of parasitic intestinal nematode worms. Younger horses, and horses that have not been previously exposed to parasites, are more susceptible to infection; older horses acquire some immunological resistance to parasitic disease. Life cycle is direct. Infection with *Strongylus* worms is most problematical when horses graze together on contaminated pastures. Infected horses pass strongyle eggs in their faeces, and contaminate the environment; under certain circumstances, eggs can survive in the environment for up to 2 years. Within 1–3 weeks after the larvae are passed, they mature to the infective stage of the larvae called an L3. In moist conditions, L3 larvae can survive for approximately 5 weeks up to several months. Under any circumstances, the horse ingests the infective L3 larvae while grazing. The L3 continues on a migration path that varies with each worm species. Three species found in horses:

1. *Strongylus vulgaris* – L3 larvae shed their sheaths into the small intestine, and then enter the caecum, where they continue to develop. Next, they migrate through the large intestine into blood vessels, causing damage and inflammation. Damage to blood vessels may cause thrombi (clots) to form, which can block blood flow to various segments of the intestines, causing ischaemia. After several months in the blood vessels, the larvae return via the blood stream to the caecum and colon, complete the maturation to adulthood, and begin producing eggs.

2. *Strongylus edentatus* – L3 larvae bore into the walls of the intestine and enter the veins that lead to the liver. The larvae develop in the liver for about 8 weeks; larval activity may cause hepatitis. After about 2 months, larvae leave the liver and migrate throughout the horse's abdomen. In about 11 months, adults return to the large intestines and lay eggs.

3. *Strongylus equinus* – L3 larvae leave the caecum and travel to the liver, pancreas, and other parts of the abdomen; larval migration can cause pancreatitis, peri-

tonitis, or hepatitis. Larvae return to the large intestines after about 9 months to begin laying eggs.

Clinical signs associated with heavy infestation of *Strongylus* worms include loss of weight, fever, loss of appetite, colic (interference with blood supply, peritonitis, intestinal motility affected), diarrhoea, anaemia (through blood loss into intestines), poor coat, lethargy. Severe infections with *Strongylus vulgaris* can cause colic, enteritis, torsion, rupture of the intestines, and death. Diagnosis of the presence of strongyles can be determined by a faecal flotation; faecal culture allows for the maturation of the larvae and the subsequent identification of the parasites. Unfortunately, there is no reliable correlation between faecal egg count and parasitic burden in individual animals. Treatment is with anthelmintic agents, e.g. pyrantel pamoate, ivermectin, fenbendazole; parasite resistance, especially to several anthelmintics of the benzimidazole family, is problematical. Individual parasite control programmes should be designed with the assistance of a veterinarian; no single deworming schedule works for all regions and all conditions. Prevention and control of infection important; involves planned use of anthelmintics and picking up droppings from pasture. Pastures should also not be overgrazed; fresh manure should not be spread across pastures, as this disseminates the contamination.
See Anaemia, Anthelmintic, Colic, Diarrhoea, Peritonitis, Worm.

Strychnine ◀︎ *strik nēn, n.* alkaloid plant toxin; used as a pesticide, particularly for killing small rodents. Toxin binds to synaptic membranes and antagonizes the effects of a major inhibitory neurotransmitter, resulting in hyperexcitability and lack of nervous system control. Strychnine poisoning is rarely reported in horses; accidental poisoning of horse is theoretically possible. Signs of overdose include convulsions and rapid death.

Stud ◀︎ *stud, n.* **1)** a stallion that is kept for breeding; a stable or farm where stallions are kept. **2)** Also, a metal device that is screwed or driven into the bottom of a horseshoe in order to provide traction over muddy or deep footing, especially in jumping horses or polo ponies. Although perhaps obvious in intent, the actual benefits of such devices are unknown; limb interference with a studded horseshoe can cause severe injury.

> **S. book** ◀︎ *stud / bŭk, n.* the register in which the names and parentage of all of the animals that constitute a particular breed are kept.

Styptic ◀︎ *stip tik, n.* describes astringent substance used to stop bleeding by making the tissues contract rapidly, e.g. silver nitrate.

Sub- ◀︎ *sub-, prefix.* under, almost, less than, somewhat.

Subacute ◀︎ *sub ēk ūt, adj.* decribes a condition which is between acute and chronic, in terms of rapidity of onset, as well as duration of condition.
See Acute, Chronic.

Subchondral bone cyst see Bone

Subcutaneous ◀︎ *sub kū tā nē ĕs, adj.* beneath the skin, or placed beneath the skin, e.g. a subcutaneous injection deposits the drug just below the skin. A subcutaneous abscess is one that is just below the skin.
See Skin.

> **S. calcaneal bursa** see Bursa
> **S. emphysema** see Emphysema

Subluxation ◀︎ *sub luks ā shĕn, n.* partial dislocation of joint, e.g. of shoulder joint in suprascapular nerve paralysis.

> **Chiropractic s.** ◀︎ *kī rō prak tik / sub luks ā shĕn, n.* is a term used by some chiropractors to refer to bones, especially bones of the vertebral column, being 'out of place', thereby interfering with normal bodily functions, especially of the nervous system. The chiropractic subluxation is the defining term of the human chiropractic profession; however, no such lesion has ever been demonstrated, nor has it been demonstrated how such lesions are identified, or if they can be corrected, nor have such lesions ever been associated with any clinical condition in any species.

See Chiropractic, Luxation, Suprascapular nerve.

Submandibular ◀ _sub_ man _di_ bū lē, _adj._ located beneath, or close to, the lower jaw (i.e. the mandible). Submandibular lymph nodes (affected in strangles) are situated below the jaw.
See Lymph, Strangles.

Subpalpebral ◀ _sub pal_ pi brēl, _n._ – underneath the eyelid.
   S. lavage ◀ _sub pal_ pi brēl / _lav arzh_, _n._ method of medicating the horse's eye, e.g. as in cases of severe corneal ulceration where horse will not allow medication, or for continuous delivery of medication. Latex tubing is surgically placed from the conjunctival sac through the upper eyelid; the tube is extended onto the head or neck and secured. Medication can then be delivered through the tube.

Subsolar abscess ◀ _sub sō lē_ / _ab ses_, _n._ an abscess that occurs beneath the sole of the horse's hoof.
See Abscess.

Suck reflex see Reflex

Sucralfate ◀ _su krūl fāt_, _n._ medication made up of aluminium hydroxide and type of sugar. When given orally, sucralfate adheres to proteins, e.g. as may occur at the site of a gastric ulcer. Often given to foals with stomach ulcers, in conjunction with drugs such as ranitidine or omeprazole.
See Equine gastric ulcer syndrome, Omeprazole, Ranitidine, Stomach.

Sudan grass ◀ _sŭ dan_ / _grars_, _n._ (_Sorghum_ spp.) a species of grasses raised especially for grain; the grasses are native to tropical and subtropical regions of East Africa. The plant has since been grown in Southern Europe, South America, Central America, North America and Southern Asia, as a forage crop for animals, or as a cover crop. Sudan grasses and hybrids may contain cyanogenic glycosides that can cause two problems – nitrate toxicity and prussic acid (cyanide) toxicity. The extent of the glycoside accumulation problem depends on growing and handling conditions of the plant.

Sudden death see Death

Sugar ◀ _shü gē_, _n._ any of a group of sweet crystalline substances; an essential structural component of living cells and an energy source for horses. The term includes simple sugars with small molecules, as well as complex macromolecular substances. Important sugars include glucose (a monosaccharide), sucrose (a white, crystalline disaccharide with wide use as a sweetener – often the colloquial term 'sugar' refers to sucrose), fructose (sugar contained in many fruits), etc. Glucose is the primary source of energy for the horse.
See Carbohydrates, Glucose.

Sugar beet ◀ _shü gē_ / _bēt_, _n._ (_Beta vulgaris_) root vegetable, grown for extraction of sugar. After extraction of the sugar, dried beet pulp may be fed to horses; some horses object to the taste. Beet pulp is approximately 10% crude protein and 18% crude fibre; nutritionally, beet pulp is roughly between a forage and a high-energy feed, e.g. a grain. Generally soaked before feeding out of fear that it can become impacted and cause obstruction of oesophagus (choke); there is no scientific support for the notion that dried beet pulp is dangerous to horses, although the practice is harmless, and soaking may improve palatablity. The leafy parts of the sugar beet plant (sugar beet tops) are high in oxalic acid and nitrates, which could conceivably cause poisoning in horses if sufficient amounts were eaten.
See Choke, Nitrate, Oxalate.

Sulpha see Sulphonamide

Sulphonamide ◀ _sul fo nē mīd_, _n._ any of a group of antibacterial drugs (sulpha drugs) that contain an $-SO_2NH_2$ group (a sulphone group connected to an amine group). Work by competitively inhibiting folic acid synthesis in various microorganisms; bacteriostatic (prevent growth rather than kill bacteria). Many strains of bacteria have developed resistance to sulphonamides, especially to agents that have been used singly; thus, they are generally used in combination, or in combination with other antimicrobial agents (e.g. trimetho-prim). The routine use of sulphonamides has been often replaced by more effective and less toxic antibiotics, especially in more severe infections. Sulphonamides are concentrated by the kidney in the urine, and are widely used to treat infections of the urinary tract.

Note: The International Non-proprietary Name (sulfa-) has superseded the original UK form (sulpha-).
See Antibacterial, Bacteriostatic.

Sulphur ◀⦂ *sul fē, n.* (S) non-metallic element, best known in yellow crystalline form. Sulphur-containing amino acids are found in abundance in hoof and hair, as well as many connective tissues; most horse feeds contain sufficient sulphur to meet dietary requirements. At one time, sulphur compounds were widely used as purgatives.

    Lime-sulphur ◀⦂ *līm* / *sul fē, n.* a mixture of calcium polysulphides formed by reacting calcium hydroxide with sulphur. Possibly the earliest synthetic chemical used as a pesticide. Can be applied by spraying, sponging, or dipping, especially as a topical treatment for various skin conditions, e.g. mange, fungal dermatitis.

Summer sore see Habronemiasis

Sunburn ◀⦂ *sun bern, n.* inflammation of the skin that develops in response to exposure to ultraviolet (UV) radiation, especially in non-pigmented skin. Ingestion of plant toxins of various origins (photosensitization) is often the underlying cause.
See Photosensitization.

Superficial ◀⦂ *sŭ pē fish ūl, adj.* of, or relating to, the surface.

    S. digital flexor tendon see Tendon

    S. keratectomy ◀⦂ *sŭ pē fish ūl* / *ke rē tek tom ē, n.* surgical removal of a thin portion of the cornea; may be performed as a biopsy technique, or as a treatment for certain corneal conditions, e.g. squamous cell carcinoma.
See Biopsy, Cornea, Squamous.

    S. skin scraping ◀⦂ *sŭ pē fish ūl* / *skin* / *skrā ping, n.* diagnostic technique for evaluation of various skin conditions, e.g. mite infesta-

tions. Scalpel blade is coated in mineral oil, and scraped across the skin; a smear is made, and examined. Limited use in horses, since mite infestations are uncommon in horses.
See Mite, Smear.

    S. wound ◀⦂ *sŭ pē fish ūl* / *wŭnd, n.* a skin injury that does not extend into the deeper tissue. Treatment typically includes cleansing and bandaging; antibiotics are generally not necessary for most superficial wounds.

Supernumerary ◀⦂ *sŭ pē nū mē rē, adj.* more than the usual number, especially as applies to teeth. Horses may rarely have supernumerary teeth. It is thought that an extra tooth forms when the small mass of foetal tissue that develops into a tooth (tooth germ) splits in half. Can affect incisors or the cheek teeth; the supernumerary teeth may erupt either beside or behind them. Supernumerary teeth need to be removed only if they interfere with the horse's health and dental function. When they are a problem, clinical signs include nasal discharge, facial swelling (from sinus infections), performance problems (especially related to bit evasion), and difficulty eating.
See Sinus, Tooth.

Supplement ◀⦂ *sup lim ēnt, n.* by definition, a supplement is something that is provided to complete something else, to make up for a deficiency or to extend or strengthen the whole [horse]. Supplements that are provided to the horse's diet purport to do most or all of these things. Without question, the most common deficiency seen in the horse is a lack of adequate calories in the diet. Horses are often not given enough feed for the work that is required of them. As such, horses that work hard may need more feed than is routinely given to them. However, there is a big difference between the chemical energy supplied by calories, and the less tangible concept of 'feeling energetic'. It is this latter concept that concerns many horse owners, thus, there are many supplements marketed to horse owners that claim to 'help' the horse with perceived deficiencies in energy. Most of these contain a variety of vitamins, minerals or proteins. If horses are calorie-deficient – lacking in enough fuel to run their bodies – they lose weight, are in poor condition and may not feel energetic. However, these are not helped by any amount of supplemental vitamins or minerals. Furthermore, it is very difficult to create a diet of normal horse feed that supplies enough calories for their systems to run but that is also deficient in protein, vitamins and minerals. Vitamins, minerals and protein all have important functions in the horse. However, providing *more* of any of these substances than is necessary for a particular function will not cause the horse to perform that function better.

Dietary protein supplements are also commonly given to horses; however, adult horses have fairly low protein requirements and protein in excess of dietary requirements is merely digested by the horse and converted to energy. Thus protein supplements are mostly just relatively expensive sources of supplemental energy for the horse. Claims that supplements perform functions such as 'improving bloom', 'improving disposition', 'lengthening attention span', 'boosting the immune system', or 'eliminating toxins' are medically meaningless – some are actually ridiculous, e.g. there are no 'toxins' circulating in the horse's body that need to be removed, and no evidence that products that claim to do so have any effect whatsoever. Furthermore, a 'boosted' immune system isn't necessarily a good thing; allergies and autoimmune conditions are two diseases characterized by a 'boosted' immune system.

Supplements are also promoted by stating what the individual ingredients are and how they are used in the horse. Then, either directly or by implication, the horse owner is led to believe that the horse may not be getting enough of that ingredient. For example, the statement: 'This supplement contains fourteen amino acids. If any one of them is deficient in the diet, the horse's protein needs will not be fulfilled' is undoubtedly true. However, protein- or amino acid-deficient diets are essentially never reported as problems in the horse. Thus, supplementation with amino acids is rarely, if ever, required. Similar examples can be given for vitamins, minerals and electrolytes, the other most commonly supplemented substances. In fact, horses are well equipped to satisfy the vast majority of their metabolic needs on a simple diet of forage, salt, and water. Additional supplements are rarely necessary.

Support ◀ *sē port, v.* to bear the weight of; to hold in position so as to keep [an anatomical structure] from falling, sinking, slipping, or being overloaded.
 S. bandage ◀ *sē port / ban dij, n.* bandage placed on the horse's lower limb, typically in an effort to resist the downward movement of the fetlock joint when the horse bears weight. The elastic effect of such bandages is supposed to help assist limb movement and prevent injury.
 S. phase ◀ *sē port / fāz, n.* during the stride, the time in which a limb is bearing weight. Also called stance phase.
 See Stride.

Supportive ◀ *sēp or tiv, adj.* treatment given to prevent, control, or relieve complications of disease and disease side effects, e.g. intravenous fluids, non-steroidal anti-inflammatory drugs. Supportive care is not specific to any disease, but is given to improve the horse's comfort and quality of life until such time that the disease process can be cured, or the disease process is eliminated by the horse's natural defences.

Suppuration ◀ *su pŭ rā shēn, n.* production or discharge of pus, e.g. as in strangles abscesses, etc.
See Abscess, Pus, Strangles.

Suppurative ◀ *su pŭ rēt iv, adj.* describes disease characterized by the formation of pus.
See Abscess, Pus, Strangles.

Suprascapular nerve ◀ *sŭ prē ska pū lē / nerv, n.* nerve above the scapula.
See Scapula, Shoulder, Sweeny.

Supraspinous bursa see Bursa

Surfactant ◀ *ser fak tēnt, n.* substance that, when dissolved in an aqueous solution, reduces the surface tension of a liquid. Surfactants are present in lungs, where they act to reduce surface tension of fluids in air sacs (alveoli) of lungs, so that air sacs can open easily. In premature foals, surfactant may not be present in lungs; this may be a cause of difficulty in breathing. Surfactants are also present in sweat, where they allow the sweat to spread more easily over the body, assisting more thorough cooling. Dioctyl sodium sulfosuccinate (DSS) is a surfactant that is sometimes administered via nasogastric tube for the treatment of intestinal impactions that cause colic; the surfactant action helps break down faecal material.
See Dioctyl sodium sulphosuccinate, Lung, Premature, Sweat.

Surgery ◀ *ser jē rē, n.* the branch of veterinary medical science that treats disease or injury by operative procedures using specialized instruments, i.e. cutting, removing diseased tissue, or repairing of tissue, etc.

Surgical ◀ *ser ji kēl, adj.* of, or relating to, or involved in surgery, e.g. a surgical instrument is one used in surgery. May also be used to describe a condition that is amenable to treatment by surgery, especially as opposed to treatment with medicine only, e.g. a surgical colic is a serious intestinal condition that can only be relieved by an operation.
See Colic, Surgery.
  S. diathermy see Diathermy

Surra ◀ *sor ē, n.* chronic disease caused by the protozoan parasite *Trypanosoma evansi*; endemic in some areas of Africa (e.g. Sudan); can affect a wide range of hosts including horses, and causes a wasting disease. Parasite has direct life cycle with no intermediate host and is transmitted by biting insects (e.g. genus *Tabanus*). Incubation period is from 5 days to 2 months; clinical signs of disease include fever, weakness and lethargy, petechial haemorrhages of the eyelids, nostrils and anus, oedema (with swellings of the legs, chest and abdomen), urticaria and skin eruptions, progressive weight loss, anaemia, and jaundice. After clinical signs begin, death may occur in 2 weeks to 4 months. Treatment in horses includes diminazene aceturate (3.5mg/kg); no vaccination is available. Control of surra can be difficult as there is no specific vector and a wide range of hosts.
See *Trypanosoma*, Wasting.

Susceptible ◀ *sē sep tib ūl, adj.* the state of being easily affected; said especially of microorganisms in relation to antibacterial medications (e.g. susceptibility testing). Horses in disease states may be susceptible to secondary complications.

Suspensory apparatus ◀ *sē spen sē rē / a pē rā tēs, n.* anatomical association with the main function of preventing the fetlock joint from sinking into the ground when the horse bears weight. Made up of the suspensory ligament, the sesamoid bones, and the sesamoidean ligaments.
See Sesamoid, Sesamoidean ligaments, Suspensory ligament.

Suspensory ligament ◀ *sē spen sē rē / li gē mēnt, n.* (SL) large fibrous structure made up primarily of collagenous tendon fibres, with a few residual muscle fibres (the number of muscle fibres varies between individual horses and between breeds). The ligament travels down behind the cannon bone, between the knee and the fetlock in the foreleg (originating from the distal row of carpal bones), and between the hock and the fetlock in the hind leg (originating primarily from the proximal metatarsus, with a few attachments on the distal row of tarsal bones). Two-thirds of the way down the metacarpus (or metatarsus) the SL divides into medial and lateral branches; these branches attach to the outside surface of the sesamoid bones at the fetlock joint. From there, the ligament continues as lateral and medial extensor branches; these branches ultimately insert on the common digital extensor tendon (at the front of the pastern).
  Along with the sesamoid bones and distal sesamoidean ligaments, the suspen-

sory ligament forms the suspensory apparatus; the main function of the suspensory ligament is to resist the sinking of the fetlock during the weight-bearing phase of the stride, and to assist in its return to normal position when the limb is not bearing weight. Injuries to the suspensory ligament are common in athletic horses; they can occur in both the fore and hind limbs and can become chronic, even potentially ending a horse's competitive career. Overloading of the ligament, as can occur from chronic overuse, or acute overload, may lead to tearing of the collagenous tendon fibres, as well as the small blood vessels associated with the muscle fibres. The tearing of the collagen fibres produces the characteristic signs of inflammation: heat, swelling, pain and loss of function. Injuries to the suspensory ligament include avulsion of bone at the origin of the suspensory ligment, inflammation and tearing of the proximal ligament, the body, or its branches, and total breakdown of the suspensory apparatus (especially in racing horses). The chance of a return to full function is related primarily to the degree of initial injury; local and systemic anti-inflammatory therapy (e.g. ice, cold hosing, bandaging, non-steroidal anti-inflammatory drugs, rest) are important in the days immediately after injury; by keeping the initial inflammatory reaction minimized, the amount of damaged tissue that has later to be removed and remodelled is reduced. Controlled rehabilitation is the cornerstone of successful recovery. Various additional therapies have been advocated, including injections of substances such as stem cells, bone marrow, and corticosteroids; extracorporeal shock wave therapy; low-intensity laser and magnetic therapy; various surgeries; innumerable shoeing and trimming interventions. The existence of so many diverse and unrelated therapies indicates that no therapy is likely to be totally satisfactory.

Suture ◀⣿ _sů_ tŭr, _v/n_. **1)** the process of joining two surfaces or edges (as in a wound, or surgical cut) together in a line, by sewing; any of the materials used to perform such a process. **2)** in anatomy, a suture is the line of junction, e.g. an immovable joint between bones, as seen between bones of skull, or the junction of fibres of the lens of the eye.

S. material ◀⣿ _sů_ tŭr / _mē_ _té_ rē ŭl, _n_. thread used for stitching wounds or surgical cuts. May be absorbable (dissolves after a period of time; e.g. subcutaneous sutures placed under the skin will ultimately be absorbed by the horse's body) or non-absorbable (does not dissolve, may have to be removed; most commonly used to join skin surfaces); may be a single thread (monofilament) or several threads (braided). No material is perfect for all situations; material has to be chosen to suit requirements for strength (e.g. abdominal incisions are typically closed with large sutures, so that they can resist the strain put on the healing tissue by the abdominal musculature), ease of tying, knot strength, how much reaction it will cause, etc.

S. pattern ◀⣿ _sů_ tŭr / _pat_ _n_, _n_. design of suture placement. Various suture patterns are described, and chosen according to tissue being repaired, e.g. skin, intestinal wall, muscle, tendon, etc.

Swab ◀⣿ _swob_, _n/v_. a small piece of absorbent material, usually made of cotton or gauze, used to soak up fluids during surgery; a small piece of cotton or gauze attached to a stick or wire used for collecting samples, especially for culture and identification of microorganisms (e.g. bacteria, fungi, etc.; a culture swab). Also, to take a specimen from (a horse) using a swab.

Swallow ◀ ⣿ _swo_ _lō_, _v_. to cause food or drink to pass from mouth into pharynx and then into oesophagus. In order to swallow non-liquids, bolus of food is softened by chewing, moved through the mouth by the action of the tongue. In the back of the mouth, the bolus is squeezed against the hard palate, and the kinetic energy given by the tongue to the bolus moves the bolus into and through the pharynx. In the pharynx, reflex contractions of the pharyngeal muscles push the bolus down into the oesophagus and on into the stomach. Difficulty with swallowing may result from nerve damage

(especially the hypoglossal, glossopharyngeal nerves), obstruction of pharynx by foreign body, inflammation or pain.
See Cranial nerve, Larynx, Oesophagus, Pharynx.

Swamp fever see Equine infectious anaemia

Sway back see Back

Sway test ◀≀ *swā / test, n.* test used to assess neurological function, especially the awareness of position of limbs (proprioception). Two people are needed for the sway test. One person walks the horse; the other person takes the tail and tries to pull the horse to one side. Normally, horses will allow themselves to be pulled once, and slightly, before correcting themselves. Horses with neurological abnormalities, e.g. cervical vertebral malformation, do not know where their limbs are, and thus will allow themselves to be pulled over, and off balance, repeatedly.
See Cervical vertebral stenotic myelopathy, Proprioception.

Sweat ◀≀ *swet, n / v.* the fluid secreted by sweat glands in skin (perspiration); to excrete such fluid through the skin. Sweat contains water, salts (e.g. sodium chloride), small amounts of urea, lactic acid, proteins (the presence of which are responsible for sweat 'lathering' in horses; the proteins act as surfactants to promote the spread of sweat over the skin area, hence increasing evaporation), calcium, chloride, and potassium. Horses sweat more than any other domestic animal; it is their principal method of cooling (by evaporation). However, they also lose considerable amounts of electrolytes in their sweat, which can lead to metabolic problems in heavily exercising horses (e.g. exhausted horse syndrome, 'thumps'). Sweat also has an excretory function.
See Exhausted horse syndrome, Skin, Thermoregulation, Thumps.

Sweat gland ◀≀ *swet / gland, n.* a long, coiled, hollow tube of cells found in the skin, which produces sweat through a duct to the skin surface, where it opens into a pore. Stimulated to secrete sweat by the sympathetic nervous system. There are two types of sweat glands in horses (as in other mammals):
- Eccrine – produce watery secretion for cooling horse.
- Apocrine – larger; produce sweat containing protein molecules (especially latherin) which act as surfactants to promote the spread of sweat over the skin area, hence increasing evaporation, and produce the foaming sweat (lather) seen in horses that have exercised hard.

The ceruminous glands (that produce ear wax) and the mammary glands (that produce milk) are modified sweat glands.
See Epinephrine, Gland, Sweat, Sympathetic nervous system.

Sweeny ◀≀ *swē nē, n.* (var. **sweeney, swinny**) condition of musculoskeletal system characterized by damage to nerve associated with muscles of shoulder (suprascapular nerve). May be damaged by trauma where it passes over shoulder blade (scapula); was once common in draught horses. Signs of damage to nerve include partial dislocation of shoulder joint (popping) when leg bears weight, and wastage of muscles over shoulder blade (spine of shoulder blade becomes prominent). Can resolve spontaneously over months; surgery to decompress the suprascapular nerve by cutting a notch in the spine of the scapula has been tried, with limited success.

Sweet itch see *Culicoides* spp.

Symbiosis ◀≀ *sim bī ō sis, n.* an interaction of two different organisms which live in close association that is of benefit to both (as opposed to parasitism, where the host does not benefit).

Sympathetic nervous system ◀≀ *sim pē the tik / ner vēs / sis tēm, n.* part of autonomic (not consciously controlled) nervous system that is concerned with body functions under stress; nerve fibres are derived from thoracic and lumbar spinal cord and innervate heart, smooth muscle and glands. Involved in 'flight or

fight' response; the sympathetic nervous system of the horse responds to a sudden or dangerous stimulus by involuntary responses such as stimulating heart to beat fast, reducing intestinal motility and digestion, reducing flow of saliva, opening up airways (bronchi), dilating pupils of eye, diverting blood to vital organs (away from skin and intestines to heart, brain, leg muscles). Most actions of sympathetic nervous system are antagonized by parasympathetic nervous system.
See Autonomic nervous system, Parasympathetic nervous system.

Sympatholytic ◀ᴇ *sim pē thō li tik, adj.* having the effect of decreasing or inhibiting the activity of the sympathetic nervous system. Sympatholytic drugs may act indirectly, by interfering with the storage, release, or synthesis of norepinephrine (e.g. reserpine decreases norepinephrine storage), or directly, by binding to, but not activating, specific receptor sites (e.g. α-adrenergic blocking agents such as xylazine or detomidine).
See Detomidine, Norepinephrine, Reserpine, Xylazine.

Symptom ◀ᴇ *simp tēm, n.* indication of disease as felt and reported by patient. Strictly speaking, the term cannot be applied to animals; instead, the term 'sign' is used to describe indications of disease (a sign is noticed by someone else, e.g. the veterinarian). In common usage, the terms sign and symptom overlap to a considerable degree.
See Sign.

Synapse ◀ᴇ *sī naps, n.* the site where neurons communicate with each other. A synapse is a small gap between individual neurons. Axon terminals of a neuron sending a message (the presynaptic neuron) release chemical neurotransmitters (e.g. acetylcholine, epinephrine) which diffuse across the synapse and cause changes in the membrane of the adjacent cell (e.g. another nerve cell, or cells of an endocrine gland).

Synchronous diaphragmatic flutter ◀ᴇ *sing krō nēs / dī ēf rēm at ik / flut ē, n.* ('thumps')

condition characterized by movements of the flanks in synchrony with the heart beat. Associated with acid–base or electrolyte imbalances, especially calcium deficiency, but also magnesium, potassium, and chloride, e.g. as may be seen following prolonged endurance riding with excessive sweating, or secondary to transit or lactation tetany from calcium loss. The electrolyte losses appear to increase the irritability of the phrenic nerve such that, when electrical activity causes the heart to beat, it also causes the nerve to fire, resulting in a vigorous, audible contraction of the diaphragm. The condition usually passes with rest; administration of calcium-containing solutions quickly resolves the problem. Prevention is by assuring adequate water and electrolyte consumption, especially during exercise.
See Tetany.

Syncope ◀ ᴇ *sing kē pē, n.* (fainting) temporary loss of consciouness. Rare in horses; most commonly seen context of a temporary failure of the systemic circulation with transient lack of blood flow to the brain (cerebral hypoxia). Has been reported, especially in ponies, following stretching of the neck; has been seen in horses related to airway obstruction (e.g. by a subepiglottic cyst) or heart block.

Syndrome ◀ ᴇ *sin drōm, n* group of clinical signs of disease or conditions that occur together that, assessed together, suggest the presence of a certain disease, or an increased chance of developing that disease. The use of the term 'syndrome' usually indicates that the cause of the particular (medical) situation is not known or poorly understood; when a cause is discovered the syndrome is more precisely referred to as a disease.

Synergism ◀ ᴇ *si nē jizm, n.* combination of actions of two entities (e.g. chemical substances, organisms), which produce a greater total result than the sum of their independent effects, e.g. in drug therapy, where the combined action of two drugs is greater than when the two agents are used independently (e.g. a bronchodilator and an inhaled corticosteroid in horses with recurrent airway obstruction). See Recurrent airway obstruction.

Synostosis ◀€ *sī nos tō sis, n.* joining together of adjacent bones by means of osseous union. May be normal, e.g. the synostosis between the paired frontal bones of the skull, or abnormal, e.g. as a congenital abnormality of vertebrae, especially of the thoracolumbar spine, where some bones are fused together (uncommon). See Spine, Vertebra.

Synovia ◀€ *sī nō vē ē, n.* sticky, viscous, transparent yellowish fluid found in joint cavities, bursae and tendon sheaths. Secreted by synovial membrane. Acts as lubricant, helping to smooth and cushion movement within joint or synovial sheath, or to cushion movement over a structure (e.g. as a bursa). Synovia is also nutritive to cartilage cells in joints. See Bursa, Joint, Synovial, Tendon.

Synovial ◀€ *sī nō vē ūl, adj.* relating to, or secreting, synovia.

   S. fistula ◀€ *sī nō vē ūl / fis tū lē, n.* an abnormal opening between a tendon sheath and a joint. Clinical signs are of a distended tendon sheath; may be difficult to distinguish from tenosynovitis clinically. Contrast radiography confirms diagnosis; surgical closure of the fistula is curative. See Tenosynovitis.

   S. fluid ◀€ *sī nō vē ūl / flŭ id, n.* a lubricating, cushioning, and nutritive fluid secreted by a synovial membrane, e.g. in a joint, bursa, or tendon sheath. Synovial fluid contains various components, including synovin (mucin), hyaluronan, and a small amount of mineral salts. It is slightly yellow in colour, transparent, alkaline, and viscous (resembling the white of an egg).

   S. fluid analysis ◀€ *sī nō vē ūl / flŭ id / ēn al is is, n.* centesis of a synovial structure and cytological examination of the fluid; used to assess abnormalities of synovial structures (e.g. an infected joint).

   S. hernia ◀€ *sī nō vē ūl / her nē ē* cystic structure that arises owing to herniation of the synovial membrane through a defect in the fibrous capsule of a joint or tendon sheath.

Pressure over the affected structure will allow the fluid to be reduced; clinical diagnosis can be confirmed by contrast radiography. Surgery is an effective treatment, but may not be warranted, as most synovial hernias are cosmetic defects only. See Joint, Tendon.

   S. joint ◀€ *sī nō vē ūl / joint, n.* the most common of three types of joints in the skeleton, lined with a (synovial) membrane which secretes a lubricating fluid. Synovial joints achieve movement at the point of contact of the articulating bones. See Joint.

   S. membrane ◀€ *sī nō vē ūl / mem brān, n.* layer of connective tissue that lines the cavities of joints, tendon sheaths and bursae; produces synovial fluid. Injury or inflammation of the s. membrane causes synovitis. See Synovitis.

   S. sheath ◀€ *sī nō vē ūl / shēth, n.* sheath of synovial membrane surrounding certain tendons, e.g. the deep digital flexor tendon as it passes over the metacarpo-/metatarsophalangeal (fetlock) joint; s. sheaths produce synovial fluid to facilitate movement of the tendon through the sheath.

Synovitis ◀ €*sī nō vī tis, n.* inflammation of synovial membrane, i.e. lining of tendon sheath, lining of joint, lining of bursa. May be caused by trauma, infection, injury, etc. Inflammation typically results in secretion of fluid, and swelling. Some of these swellings have been given traditional names, e.g. bog spavin in the tarsus (hock) or windgall (windpuff) in the metacarpo-/metatarsophalangeal joint (fetlock). Diagnosis by clinical signs; centesis of swelling will reveal fluid for cytological analysis. Treatment depends on cause e.g. rest and injections of anti-inflammatory compounds in inflammatory conditions, or antibiotics for synovial infections.

Syringe ◀€ *si rinj, n.* instrument for injecting (e.g. drugs) or withdrawing fluid (e.g. blood sample) from body. Consists of tube with a plunger at one end and a narrow opening the other; at the narrow end of most syringes, a needle can be attached.

System ◀ *sis tēm, n.* a group of physiologically or anatomically related organs or parts that typically work together, e.g. the respiratory system has many parts (lungs, trachea, larynx, diaphragm, nasal passages, etc.) working together to allow gaseous exchange in body.
See various systems, including Cardiovascular, Endocrine, Musculoskeletal, Nervous, Respiratory.

Systemic ◀ *sis te mik, adj.* affecting or relating to the whole body (as opposed to affecting a specific organ or body part).

S. circulation ◀ *sis te mik / ser kū lā shēn, n.* the circulation of blood throughout the horse's body.

S. infection ◀ *sis te mik / in fek shēn, n.* any infection in which the causative microorganism has spread widely throughout the horse's body.
See Septicaemia.

S. treatment ◀ *sis te mik / trēt mēnt, n.* a treatment that impacts on the entire body as a system, as opposed to a treatment directed at one isolated region (local treatment). For example, an intravenous injection of corticosteroids would be a systemic treatment; an injection of corticosteroids into a joint would be a local treatment.

Systemic lupus erythematosus ◀ *sis te mik / lū pēs / e ri thē mē tō sēs, n.* auto-immune condition which can affect all parts of body (although not all organ systems may be affected in one individual). Rare in horses; two cases have been reported in the equine medical literature. Signs include scaling of skin, anaemia, alopecia (hair loss), polyarthritis (arthritis of more than one joint), destruction of blood platelets (thrombocytopenia), high temperature, lymphadenopathy, and weight loss. Laboratory tests confirm autoimmune disease (e.g. Coomb's test). Treatment is with high doses of corticosteroids; prognosis grave.
See Arthritis, Autoimmune disease, Thrombocytopenia.

Systole ◀ *sis tē lē, n.* the time period during which the heart is contracting; more specifically referring to the left ventricle of the heart when it contracts. Blood is forced out of heart into pulmonary artery and aorta during systole.
See Heart.

Systolic ◀ *sis to lik, adj.* of, or relating to, contraction of heart (systole).

• S. murmur – murmur which is heard during contraction of heart. Systolic murmurs may be further subdivided as left-sided (mitral regurgitation, or the normal murmur heard in some horses caused by ejection of blood from the ventricles) or right-sided (e.g. tricuspid regurgitation, or ventricular septal defect).

• S. pressure – the maximum arterial pressure during contraction of the left ventricle of the heart.

See Heart, Mitral valve, Tricuspid valve, Ventricular.

T

T3 see Tri-iodothyronine

T4 see Thyroxine

T cell ◀: *tē / sel, n.* lymphocyte (white blood cell), originates in bone marrow. 'T' stands for thymus, which is where the cells mature. T cells are responsible for cell-mediated immunity. They may directly kill cells, e.g. virus-infected cells, foreign cells, or cancer cells, or they may produce chemicals called lymphokines that activate tissue macrophages which will kill the cells. Various types of T cells exist:
- T helper cells – cells that divide rapidly and secrete small proteins (cytokines) to regulate ('help') the immune response. T helper cells fall into two main classes:
  o T helper cells that activate other T cells, and promote cellular inflammatory responses.
  o T helper cells that stimulate B cells to make antibodies (the humoral immune response).
- Suppressor (regulatory) T cells – T cells that reduce or suppress the immune response of B cells or of other T cells to an antigen. Required for self-tolerance and control of immune function.
- Cytotoxic T cells and natural killer cells – T cells that cause the death of cells that are infected with various pathogens (e.g. viruses), or of cells that are otherwise damaged or dysfunctional (e.g. cancer cells).

See B lymphocyte, Immunity, Lymphocyte, Thymus.

Tabanus ◀: *ta bēn ĕs, n.* genus of biting, bloodsucking flies of the Tabanidae family; includes horseflies and deerflies. Can cause irritability, local skin irritation from bites, dermatitis, and may act as vector to transmit disease.

Tachycardia ◀: *ta kē kar dē ē, n.* abnormally fast heart rate. Normal rate is 28–48 beats per minute in adult horse; higher in foals. May be physiological response, e.g. in response to increased need for oxygen in tissues during exercise, or pathological, e.g. as result of defect in heart muscle, e.g. atrial tachycardia (where the heart's electrical impulse comes from somewhere in the atria) or ventricular tachycardia (where the heart's electrical impulse comes from somewhere in the ventricles; often occurs in life-threatening situations).
See Atrial, Heart, Ventricular.

Tachypnoea ◀: *ta kip nē ē, n.* abnormally fast rate of breathing. Normal rate is 8–20 breaths per minute; higher in foals; lower in athletic animals. May be seen after heavy exercise, or in diseases of upper or lower respiratory tract, e.g. pneumonia, upper airway obstruction.
See Breathing, Pneumonia, Respiratory.

Taenia (coli) ◀: *tā en ē ē (kō lī), n.* band-like thickenings of the outer longitudinal layer of the external muscular layer of the equine colon. Common site for enterotomy.

Tail ◀: *tāl, n.* the posterior part of the horse, composed of coccygeal vertebrae and associated muscles and nerves.
   T. rubbing ◀: *tāl / ru bing, n.* scraping the tail, e.g. against a fence or stable wall; typically in response to skin irritation, e.g. fly bites, pinworm (*Oxyuris equi*) infestation.

445

Tallebudgera horse disease see Crofton weed

Talus ◄⁞ *tal ēs, n.* large bone of tarsus (hock); most of the motion in the tarsal joint occurs from the movement of the tibia over the talus (tarsocrural joint). See Tarsocrural joint, Tarsus, Tibia.

Tamponade ◄⁞ _tam_ *pē nard, n.* compression of the heart caused by blood or fluid accumulation in the space between the myocardium (the muscle of the heart) and the pericardium (the outer covering sac of the heart), e.g. following rupture of aortic root. Movement of heart muscle is restricted, heart sounds muffled; may result in heart failure and death. See Heart.

Tapetum ◄⁞ *tap it ēm, n.* the iridescent membrane of the choroid of the eye; reflects light, allowing improved night vision.

Tapeworm ◄⁞ _tāp_ *werm, n.* flat, ribbon-like, segmented, parasitic worm of a group of worms called flatworms, or cestodes. Infestation in horses is relatively common, but rarely causes clinical signs; however, severe infestation is associated with colic (especially intussusception), and inflammation and ulceration around the ileocaecal valve. Three species infest horses: *Anoplocephala perfoliata* (caecal tapeworm) is the most common species; *Anoplocephala magna* (largest species, located in the posterior small intestine), and *Paranoplocephala mamillana* (smallest species, located in the anterior small intestine and occasionally in the stomach) are uncommon. Tapeworms have indirect life cycle (i.e. they require an intermediate host; the horse is the definitive host; intermediate hosts are oribatid mites). Horses accidentally ingest orbatid mites as they feed; these mites contain immature tapeworms. The immature stages of tapeworms develop inside the horse into adult tapeworms in approx. 2 months; tapeworm eggs pass in horses' faeces and are ingested by mites. Diagnosis by detection of eggs in faeces is not reliable, that is, a lack of tapeworm eggs does not mean that tapeworms

are not present in the horse; infestations may be best determined by examining faecal sample after treatment for tapeworms. Treatment is typically by double-dosing of pyrantel compounds; praziquantel has also been used for control, however it is not specifically labelled for horses in the US, but it is available for such purposes in the UK. See Colic.

Tar ◄⁞ *tar, n.* dark brown liquid obtained from distillation of pine wood or coal; a complex chemical mixture, containing substances such as cresol, creosol, guaiacol, naphthalene, paraffin, phenol, toluene, and xylene. Widely used historically for various conditions, now available in shampoos to treat dermatitis and, possibly, to help repel insects, e.g. in *Culicoides* hypersensitivity (sweet itch). See *Culicoides*.

Tarsal ◄⁞ _tar_ *sūl, adj.* of, or relating to, the tarsus (hock). See Tarsus.

   T. bone ◄⁞ _tar_ *sūl / bōn, n.* any of six (occasionally seven) bones of tarsus (hock), arranged in three rows:
- Proximal – tibial tarsal (talus; the majority of the motion of the tarsus occurs around the articular surface of the talus), fibular tarsal (calcaneus – largest bone, can feel this as point of hock).
- Central tarsal (scaphoid).
- Distal – 1st and 2nd tarsals (fused), 3rd tarsal, 4th tarsal.

See Tarsus.

   T. joints ◄⁞ _tar_ *sūl / joints, n.* the articulations between the various bones of the tarsus. See Tarsus.

   T. sheath ◄⁞ _tar_ *sūl / shēth, n.* the synovial sheath around the deep flexor tendon in the hind limb of the horse, at the posterior aspect of the tarsus (hock). See Tarsus.

Tarsocrural joint ◄⁞ _tar_ *sō krūr ēl joint, n.* the articulation between the tibial tarsal bone (talus) and the tibia. See Talus, Tarsus, Tibia.

Tarsometatarsal joint ◄⁞ _tar_ *sō met ē* _tar_ *sūl / joint, n.* the joint between the distal row of tarsal bones and the third metatarsal bone. Common site of osteoarthritis (bone spavin). Area is frequently injected with various anti-inflammatory agents, especially for the treatment of hind limb lameness.

Tarsorrhaphy ◀≀ *tar sor ĕfē, n.* an operation to diminish the size of the opening between eyelids; indicated to protect the cornea in conditions such as selected cases of corneal ulceration, to protect the eye from drying (e.g. in cases of facial paralysis), following corneal surgery to protect the globe, or following eyelid surgery to prevent movement of the eyelids during healing.

Tarsus ◀≀ *tar sēs, n.* (hock) complex joint in hind limb between tibia and cannon bone (metatarsal). Made up of six tarsal bones and four main joints:

- Tarsocrural joint, between talus and tibia – where most movement occurs. Conditions which affect this joint include effusion ('bog spavin'), infection, osteochondrosis and luxation (grave prognosis).
- Proximal intertarsal joint (talocalcaneal-centroquatral joint), between the proximal (talus and calcaneus) and central tarsal bones. May be affected by osteoarthritis (bone spavin), or fracture.
- Distal intertarsal joint, between central and distal (second, third, and fourth) tarsal bones. May be affected by fracture and osteoarthritis (bone spavin).
- Tarsometatarsal joint, between distal tarsal (second, third, and fourth) bones and metatarsal (cannon) bone.

The tarsus is a common site of injections of therapeutic substances, e.g. corticosteroids. The two most distal tarsal joints are those most commonly affected by problems, e.g. osteoarthritis; those two joints are the most commonly injected, accordingly. Considerable effort has gone into attempting to determine the degree of communication between the two joints, and anatomical studies routinely show that a significant percentage of horses have such communication. In addition, it has been shown that corticosteroid medication placed in the tarsometatarsal joint diffuses into the distal intertarsal joint. In some horses, the distal tarsal joints are routinely injected for 'maintenance', or in an attempt to prevent joint problems; there is no medical basis for such therapy.

See Bog spavin, Bone, Luxation, Osteoarthritis, Osteochondrosis, Tarsal.

Tartar see Calculus

Taste ◀≀ *tāst, n.* the sensation that results when nerve receptors in the tongue and throat (taste buds) are stimulated to send information about the chemical composition of a soluble stimulus to the brain. Studies have shown that the sense of taste in horses is probably not as important as the sense of smell; behavioural responses that are triggered primarily by taste are difficult to distinguish from responses caused by smell.

Taxus see Yew

Taylorella equigenitalis ◀≀ *tā lor re lē / e kwi je ni tā lis, n.* Gram-negative coccobacillus bacterium; causative agent of contagious equine metritis.
See Contagious equine metritis.

Tear ◀≀ *tēr u, n.* clear, slightly salty, watery liquid secretion of lacrimal gland of eye. Moistens and lubricates eye.
See Eye, Lacrimal apparatus.

Tear duct see Nasolacrimal duct

Teasing ◀≀ *tē zing, n.* reproductive management technique using stallion, and occasionally, aggressive gelding, to establish if mare is ready to mate (i.e. in oestrus). Teaser horse is held near mare (may be separated by board, fence, etc.) and mare's reaction is observed. If in oestrus, mare will typically lean towards teaser, 'wink' vulva (rhythmically evert the clitoris), urinate, or show other signs of sexual receptivity. Teasing has also been used as a method for libido enhancement in some stallions.
See Breeding, Oestrus, Vasectomy.

Teat ◀< *tēt, n.* nipple of mammary gland of mare. Each teat has two papillary ducts through which milk passes when mare feeds foal.
See Mammary gland.

Teeth see Tooth

Telemetry ◀< *ti le mē trē, n.* the process by which measured quantities (e.g. strides, heartbeats, forces of acceleration) from the horse are transmitted to a data collection point (receiver) for recording and processing. Mostly used for research purposes; can be used for recording electrocardiogram in exercising horse.
See Electrocardiography.

Telogen ◀< *tel ō jĕn, n.* the resting phase of the hair growth cycle; lasts until hair shedding beings, and new hair growth begins (anagen).
See Anagen, Hair.

Temperament ◀< *tem prē mĕnt, n.* animal's nature; the innate aspect of an individual horse's personality. A horse's temperament may affect how it responds to different situations, and may also be affected by management, environment, diet, etc.
See Behaviour.

Temperature ◀< *tem pri tŭr, n.* degree of heat or cold, as measured on scale: Celsius (°C) or Fahrenheit (°F); a somatic sensation of heat or cold. In veterinary medicine, the term is most commonly used in the context of body temperature (core temperature), the measure of heat of an animal's body. In horses, the temperature is normally measured rectally. Normal temperature in horse is 37.0–38.3 °C (roughly 99.5–101 °F). May be elevated (hyperthermia, fever, pyrexia) owing to infection, inflammation, heat exhaustion, or after exercise; may be low (hypothermia) in certain ill foals (e.g. septicaemia), with some poisonings, coma, and in end-stage disease.
See Colic, Infection, Inflammation.

Temporal ◀< *tem pē rŭl, adj.* of, or relating to, the sides of the head ('temples'); relating to the sides of the skull behind the orbit.

T. bone see Petrous temporal bone
T. teratoma see Dentigerous

Temporohyoid osteoarthropathy ◀< *tem pē rō hī oid / ost ē ō ar throp ĕth ē, n.* early disease of middle ear associated with behavioural changes, e.g. head tossing or rubbing; typically progresses to signs associated with vestibular disease, e.g. ataxia, head tilt. Radiography of affected bones may be diagnostic; endoscopy of guttural pouch may show involvement of hyoid bones. Antibiotics may be curative if initiated early; surgical treatment by partial removal of the stylohyoid bone has been performed in chronic cases.

Temporomandibular joint ◀< *tem pē rō man di bū lē / joint, n.* (TMJ) joint of jaw, between mandible (bone of lower jaw) and temporal bone. Moves by action of muscles of mastication; has wide range of movement so allows lateral movement of lower teeth against upper teeth for grinding food. Disease of the temporomandibular joint is uncommon in horses according to most authorities, although some practitioners may commonly make a diagnosis of problems with the joint.

Tendinitis (tendonitis) ◀< *ten di nī tis, n.* inflammation of tendon; usually caused by acute or chronic injury. Damage can vary from mild inflammation with stretching of tendon fibres, to tendon fibre rupture, or even complete tendon rupture. Fibre rupture is typically accompanied by bleeding within tendon which can be detected by ultrasonography. Clinical signs of tendinitis include swelling, soreness on palpation, and lameness. Diagnosis is based on clinical history, and typical clinical signs; confirmed by ultrasonography. Numerous treatments have been proposed for tendinitis, including cold or hot water therapy, bandaging, wrapping in anti-inflammatory substances (e.g. dimethyl sulphoxide), and non-steroidal anti-inflammatory drugs; pin-firing and blistering; various physical modalities, including extracorporeal shock wave therapy, low-intensity laser therapy, application of magnets, or therapeutic ultrasound; intratendinous injections of

substances such as stem cells, polysulphated glycosaminoglycans or hyaluronan; and various surgeries, especially including tendon splitting or stabbing, with or without ultrasound guidance. All therapies are given in conjunction with a variable period of rest and controlled rehabilitation, which is probably the most important of any of the proposed interventions. The existence of so many treatments for one condition mostly reflects the fact that no treatment appears to be totally satisfactory, or is demonstrably superior to any other treatment. Disrupted tendon fibres heal by the formation of granulation tissue, which then gradually forms into a more disorganized fibrous tissue that lacks the strength of normal tendon, and probably predisposes to future injury, especially at high speed activities (e.g. racing).
See Tendon.

Tendon ◀⠷ _ten_ _dēn_, _n._ tough band of fibrous connective tissue which attaches muscle to bone. Contraction of muscle pulls on tendon to flex or extend a joint. Tendon is composed of bundles of parallel collagen fibrils (long thin fibres) in a mucopolysaccharide matrix; in chemical composition, it is similar to articular cartilage. Tendon composition is different between regions, which apparently reflects different biomechanical loading in those regions.

    T. sheath ◀ _ʒten_ _dēn_ / _shēth_, _n._ in some areas, the tendon is surrounded by a synovial membrane, the tendon sheath, especially where a tendon passes over a joint surface, e.g. the superficial digital flexor tendon where it passes behind the metacarpophalangeal (fetlock) joint. Tendon sheath produces a lubricating synovial fluid so that tendon can move easily, with little friction.
    See Collagen, Muscle, Synovial.

Tenectomy ◀⠷ _te_ _nek_ _tē_ _mē_, _n._ surgical removal of piece of tendon.
- Cunean t. – removal of a portion of the cunean tendon, over the medial aspect of the tarsus. Was once commonly used in the treatment of osteoarthritis of intertarsal joint (bone spavin).

- Long digital extensor t. – removal of a portion of the long digital extensor tendon over the lateral aspect of the tarsus. Sometimes recommended for the treatment of stringhalt.
See Osteoarthritis, Stringhalt.

Tenesmus ◀⠷ _ti_ _nez_ _mēs_, _n._ straining to pass faeces or urine, especially straining which is long, continuous, or ineffective, e.g. in a horse with urethral blockage by urolithiasis.
See Urolithiasis.

Tenoscopy ◀ _ʒten os kop ē_, _n._ examination and treatment of lesions in a tendon sheath using a fibreoptic scope; e.g. tenoscopy has been used to break down and flush out the foreign material, fibrin, and other debris in the sheath that results from septic tenovitis, or to remove fibrous masses from the sheath that result in lameness.

Tenosynovitis ◀ _ʒte_ _nō_ _sī_ _nō_ _vī_ _tis_, _n._ inflammation of tendon and associated synovial sheath. In horse, most commonly seen in the flexor tendon sheath of the distal limb. May be seen from tendon injury and inflammation, or in infections, e.g. through infection from puncture wounds. Condition typically causes lameness, swelling, and pain on palpation. Clinical diagnosis is confirmed by local anaesthesia; analysis of synovial fluid from sheath can help determine whether condition is primarily inflammatory or infectious. Radiography (including contrast radiography, injecting contrast medium into sheath) is occasionally helpful; ultrasonography provides the most detailed evaluation of the affected area. The tendon sheath can also be examined with an arthroscope (tenoscopy) under general anaesthesia; treatment, such as removal of adhesions, can also be performed. Other common treatments include rest, bandaging, regional limb perfusion (in cases of infection), and injection of anti-inflammatory substances such as corticosteroids or hyaluronan (in cases of primary inflammation).
See Corticosteroid, Hyaluronan, Regional.

Tenotomy ◀﹔ *te* <u>*no*</u> *tē mē, n.* surgical transection of a tendon. Procedures used in equine veterinary medicine include:

- Biceps brachii t. – transection of the biceps tendon. Has been advocated for the treatment of bicipital bursitis, tendonitis, and humeral osteitis. (See Bursa.)
- Deep digital flexor t. – transection of the deep digital flexor tendon. Sometimes recommended for the treatment of severe cases of laminitis. One study that looked at long-term follow-up was unable to find a difference in outcome between those horses that did and did not receive DDF tenotomies. (See Laminitis.)
- Semitendinosus t. – transection of the tendon of the semitendinosus muscle of the hind limb. Has been recommended for treatment of fibrotic myopathy. (See Fibrotic myopathy.)
- Superficial digital flexor t. – transection of the superficial digital flexor tendon. Has occasionally been recommended for treatment of severe flexural deformity of fetlock. Sometimes contracture of surrounding soft tissue precludes a successful outcome, even with SDF tenotomy.

See Flexural deformity, Laminitis, Tendon.

Tension ◀﹔ <u>*ten*</u> *shēn, n.* the physical condition of being strained or stretched.

    T. pneumothorax see Pneumothorax

Teratogenic ◀﹔ *te* <u>*ra*</u> *tō* <u>*je*</u> *nik, adj.* describes substance or factor which can cause deformity or malformation in a developing foetus or embryo. Substances such as griseofulvin or ionizing radiation are potentially teratogenic.

Teratoma ◀﹔ *te rē* <u>*tō*</u> *mē, n.* benign growth made up of different types of tissue, e.g. hair, teeth, bone, cartilage; caused by the growth of independent germ cells. Most common in ovary and testis (especially if not descended; they are most often seen in cryptorchid horses); teratoma is the most common testicular neoplasm of the horse. See Cryptorchid, Ovary, Testes.

    Temporal t. see Dentigerous

Terminal apnoea see Apnoea

Termination ◀﹔ *ter mi* <u>*nā*</u> *shēn, n.* ending, often used as term for elective ending of pregnancy (abortion). Most commonly and easily done by prostaglandin injection in early pregnancy.
See Abortion.

Test ◀﹔ *test, n.* a procedure for the critical evaluation of something. Innumerable tests are used in equine medicine, especially for the diagnosis of disease and monitoring of treatment (diagnostic tests), e.g. blood cell count, measurement of antibody levels (e.g. immunofluorescent antibody test), urine pH; for lameness evaluation (e.g. flexion test), or for normal organ function (e.g. kidney or liver function tests).
See tests under individual entries.

Testes ◀﹔ <u>*tes*</u> *tēz, n.* (singular: testis; testicle) pair of oval reproductive glands of male, contained within scrotum. Testes function as exocrine glands to produce sperm, and as endocrine glands to produce sex hormones (e.g. testosterone and oestrogen). Sex hormones function to facilitate spermatogenesis, development of typical secondary sex characteristics of stallion (e.g. cresty neck), and to stimulate libido. The testes lie outside the abdominal cavity and are normally 4–6 °C below body temperature; the lower temperature is required for normal sperm production. The testicles may be raised or lowered to help maintain appropriate temperature by the cremaster muscle. Size varies between breeds. The tubular compartment of the testes is composed of tightly coiled seminiferous tubules lined with germinal epithelium, from which the sperm cells are formed. Tubules straighten at their ends to form the rete testis, from which several ducts enter the epididymis, where sperm collects prior to ejaculation. Between the tubules is the interstitial tissue, made up of Leydig cells, blood vessels, lymphatic vessels, and connective tissue; interstitial tissue produces sex hormones. Testes are surrounded by strong tunics of fibrous tissue (tunica vaginalis, tunica albuginea).

See Epididymis, Leydig cell, Scrotum, Sperm, Testosterone, Tunica.

Testicular ◀₹ *tes ti kū lē, adj.* of, or relating to, the testis or testes.
See Testes.

    T. haematoma ◀₹ *tes ti kū lē / hē mē tō mē, n.* blood-filled swelling within testis, most commonly results from injury, e.g. kick. Usually quite painful on palpation and results in scrotal enlargement. Degree of damage can be evaluated with ultrasonography. Prognosis for return to normal testicular function is guarded depending on the degree of tissue damage.

    T. neoplasia ◀₹ *tes ti kū lē / nē ō plā zē ē, n.* tumour of testicular tissue; rare in stallions, although the true incidence in male horses is unknown because so many are castrated at an early age. Can be classified as: germinal (e.g. seminomas, teratomas, or embryonal carcinomas), non-germinal (e.g. interstitial cell and Sertoli cell tumours), or secondary (e.g. lipomas and mast cell tumours). Treatment is by castration; testicular tumours are locally invasive, and can metastasize, so evaluation of abdomen for cancer spread is commonly performed at the time of castration. Most common testicular neoplasia is a teratoma.

    T. torsion ◀₹ *tes ti kū lē / tor shēn, n.* rotation of testis on the spermatic cord; can lead to twisting of spermatic cord and ischaemia of testis. If twists up to 180° (partial torsion), there are usually no signs and fertility is usually not affected; may be a developmental defect in the descent of the testis. Twists of 360° (complete torsion) can occur, especially in Standardbreds and Thoroughbreds, and blood supply to testis will be impaired. Clinical signs are of acute colic, with swelling of testis and cord, especially during exercise or after covering. Treatment consists of emergency castration of the affected testicle to prevent changes from overheating in the other testicle; attempts to resolve the torsion by untwisting it and tacking it in place with sutures have met with variable success, presumably because of subsequent difficulties in the ability to raise and lower the testicle normally. Even if testicle can be saved, the prognosis for fertility of the affected testicle is poor.

Testosterone ◀₹ *tes to stē rōn, n.* primary male sex hormone produced by interstitial cells of testis. With other androgens, testosterone stimulates descent of testes from abdomen, development of secondary sex glands, male secondary sexual characteristics and libido, and facilitates spermatogenesis. Measurable levels of testosterone in mares are an indication of a granulosa-theca cell tumour of the ovary.
See Granulosa-thecal cell.

Tetanus ◀₹ *te tē nēs, n.* (lockjaw) condition caused by toxin produced by bacterium, *Clostridium tetani*. *C. tetani* found worldwide in soil, especially cultivated soil, as spores; spores can contaminate wounds and produce an exotoxin in anaerobic conditions (i.e. no oxygen). Toxin affects nervous system. Muscle spasm, stiff gait, rigid posture ('sawhorse stance'), raised tailhead, flared nostrils, upright ears, stiff jaw; hyperaesthesia and prolapse of the third eyelid, especially following stimulation around the head, are common clinical signs. Signs in all areas may become more pronounced in response to a sudden stimulus, e.g. loud noise, tap on head. As the disease progresses the muscles become so rigid and stiff that the horse may fall and not be able to get up again. Convulsions may occur and death is caused by paralysis of the breathing muscles. Diagnosis is made by typical clinical signs: demonstrating toxin in blood or *Clostridium tetani* in wounds is extremely difficult. Treatment regimens vary, but commonly include providing a quiet, safe environment, parenteral penicillin (to eliminate bacteria), tranquillizers and muscle relaxants, and tetanus toxoid and tetanus antitoxin to neutralize toxin. Recovery is possible, especially in milder cases. The prognosis appears to be best for horses that (1) have been vaccinated, (2) responded to phenothiazine tranquillizers, and (3) do not become recumbent over 24–48 hours. Prevention is by vaccination with tetanus toxoid. The exact vaccine interval has not been determined, however, common recommendations include two doses 4–6 weeks apart (from 6 months of age), with booster at 1 year, and then every 1–2 years. Tetanus toxoid vaccine is also commonly given as a component of many multivalent vaccines.

See Antitoxin, *Clostridium*, Vaccinate.

T. antitoxin ◀ *te tē nĕs / an tē tok sin, n.* an antibody injection that can be given to provide short-term immunization against the toxin of the tetanus bacterium. Tetanus antitoxin provides immediate protection but this protection only lasts for 3 weeks. Injection of tetanus antitoxin has been associated with the development of Theiler's disease in some horses 1 to 3 months before the onset of signs of disease.

See Antitoxin, Theiler's disease, Vaccinate.

T. toxoid ◀ *te tē nĕs / toks oid, n.* vaccine against tetanus in which the tetanus toxin has been modified so that it is no longer toxic, but can still stimulate an antibody response. Tetanus toxoid vaccine promotes a long-lasting immunity in species in which duration of immunity has been studied (not including the horse).

See Toxoid, Vaccinate.

Tetany ◀ *te tē nē, n.* intermittent muscular stiffening and spasms, most commonly as a result of low blood calcium, but also magnesium. Signs include rapid breathing, thumping sounds from chest caused by spasm of diaphragm, sweating, stiff gait or incoordination. Can result in recumbency, convulsions and death if calcium deficiency not corrected.

See Calcium.

Lactation t. see Lactation

Transport t. ◀ *trans port / te tē nē, n.* low levels of calcium and/or magnesium as a result of stress, e.g. through transport or prolonged physical exertion.

Tetracyclines ◀ *te trĕ sī klins, n.* a group of antibiotics that work by interfering with the ability of some growing or multiplying bacteria to make proteins, thereby inhibiting their growth. Tetracyclines kill a wide variety of bacteria and are employed for the treatment of many equine diseases, e.g. Potomac horse fever (equine monocytic ehrlichiosis). Oxytetracycline, the most widely used form of tetracycline, is supplied as a sterile liquid for IV or IM administration in the horse. The IM route is not commonly used, however, because it tends to make horses' muscles sore at the site of injection. Tetracyclines are also administered to foals with tendon contractures early in life. Some foals will be observed to develop limb deformities early in life characterized by knuckling over at the fetlock joint or standing on the toes. Tetracycline is used here for its ability to bind calcium; this causes muscle and tendon relaxation. After large doses of tetracyclines, contracted tendons are frequently observed to relax in affected foals. Tetracyclines are also available in ophthalmic preparations that are sold over the counter for the treatment of eye infections. When given intravenously, rapid administration of tetracycline has caused animals to collapse. This is because it rapidly binds up body calcium, which is needed for normal muscle function, including heart muscle activity. This same effect is not seen when the drug is given slowly. Tetracycline is relatively nontoxic. Some veterinary surgeons are reluctant to use tetracycline in the horse, however, apparently because of a report in 1973 that the drug caused colitis and severe diarrhoea in the horse. As the use of the drug has become more widespread this complication has not been commonly reported, and the drug is generally considered safe.

Tetralogy of Fallot ◀ *te tra lĕ jē / ov / fa lō, n.* combination of four congenital heart defects: malposition of the aorta over both ventricles, ventricular septal defect, pulmonic stenosis, and right ventricular hypertrophy. Causes obvious signs of heart failure early in foal's life. (Named after Etienne-Louis Arthur Fallot, French physician 1850–1911.)

See Heart.

Thalamus ◀ *tha lĕ mĕs, n.* one of two large ovoid structures at base of cerebrum of brain. Receives sensory information from body and relays stimuli to and from cerebral cortex.

See Brain.

Theiler's disease ◀€ *tī lerz / di zēz, n.* (acute hepatic necrosis, serum hepatitis, serum sickness) acute liver failure. Most commonly associated with the use of equine serum products, especially tetanus antitoxin, but has also been seen without the use of such products; in such cases, an infectious organism is suspected. Clinical signs include depression, anorexia, and icterus; laboratory tests show elevations in liver enzymes; liver biopsy is not specific for the disease, but shows changes of acute hepatic cellular necrosis with inflammatory infiltrates. There is no specific therapy for Theiler's disease; supportive therapy is given as required, e.g. intravenous fluids, minimizing stress, sedatives to control hepatic encephalopathy. Horses can recover from Theiler's disease, especially if they survive the first week of the disease. Outbreaks may be seasonal, especially in summer and autumn; disease is unreported in some parts of the world. (Sir Arnold Theiler first described disease in 1918, in South Africa, following vaccination of horses against African Horse Sickness.)

Thelazia spp. ◀ €*thel az iē / spē shēs, n.* (eyeworm) group of parasites that can occasionally parasitize the eyes of horses. Horses are infected primarily by *T. lacrymalis*. The face fly, *Musca autumnalis*, is the vector. Female worms lay larvae into the ocular secretions (tears and mucus); the larvae are ingested by the fly and become infective in 2–4 weeks. Infective larvae emerge and are deposited in the host's eye by the fly during feeding. Development of sexually mature worms takes 10–11 weeks. Infestations are usually associated with the warm season, when flies are most active. Can cause localized irritation and dermatitis; conjunctivitis and inflammation of the eyelids (blepharitis) are also common. In more severe cases, signs such as keratitis, corneal ulceration, and corneal scarring may develop. Treatment is by surgical removal (usually under local anaesthesia); topical application of organophosphate compounds has also been effective. Fenbendazole at 10 mg/kg once daily for 5 days is an effective treatment. Environmental measures to control

flies, e.g. clean stables, keeping conditions as dry as possible, are important for control.

Therapeutic ◀€ *the rē pū tik, adj.* having or exhibiting powers of healing; pertaining to the treatment of disease. Something that is considered therapeutic is generally also considered healthy.

> **T. blood monitoring** ◀€ *the rē pū tik / blud / mon it ēr ing, n.* term used for measuring the blood level of some drugs during therapy; a way to determine the optimum dose of a certain drug, or to avoid toxicity, e.g. monitoring the levels of aminoglycoside antibiotics in animals with compromised or immature kidney function. Most drugs do not need to be monitored in this fashion; improvement in clinical signs is usually adequate to tell if a dose is appropriate.
>
> **T. shoeing** ◀€ *the rē pū tik / shŭ ing, n.* widely used term to broadly describe the use of any number of farriery techniques to treat problems of the feet, e.g. bar shoe used with trimming to protect sore heels.
> See Horseshoe.

Therapy ◀€ *the rē pē, n.* any measure used to treat disease; examples include:

- Gene t. – experimental medical technique whereby genes are inserted into an individual's cells and tissues to treat a disease. The technique is currently being investigated in horses to treat joint problems.
- Physical t. – the use of exercises and physical methods (e.g. massage, applications of heat) to treat or rehabilitate disease, especially of the musculoskeletal system.
- Supportive t. – treatment or nursing care given in addition to specific therapy, e.g. providing warmth, fluid therapy, etc.

Thermography ◀€ *ther mo grē fē, n.* diagnostic technique in which a heat-sensing infrared camera is used to record the surface heat on the skin, which is recorded as one or more computer images (thermogram(s)). Has been advocated for the detection of inflammation, e.g. in tendonitis; however, the technique has not found wide acceptance in veterinary

medicine, possibly owing to cost, as well as difficulty in interpretation.
See Tendinitis.

Thermometer ◀╏ *ther mo mi tĕ, n.* instrument used to measure temperature. Most commonly used veterinary thermometer consists of glass tube containing an organic liquid (e.g. alcohol) which expands when heated (mercury-in-glass thermometers are becoming rarer, and some countries have banned their medical use); electronic digital thermometers are finding increasing application. In horses, taking body temperature with a thermometer is usually done rectally: typically, the thermometer is maintained in place for at least 1 minute to ensure an accurate measurement.

Thermoregulation ◀╏ *ther mō re gū lā shĕn, n.* maintenance of body temperature within narrow limits, regardless of environmental temperature, so that the body functions normally. Horses have various thermoregulatory mechanisms, to adapt to heat and cold. Heat is a particular problem for horses: because a large metabolic heat load is generated as a consequence of muscular work during exercise, various thermoregulatory mechanisms must be activated in order to prevent an excessive and potentially dangerous rise in body temperature. These mechanisms include losing heat by sweating, increasing blood flow to skin (where heat can dissipate) by increasing heart rate, dilating blood vessels of skin, and rapid breathing; maintenance of body heat in cold conditions is achieved by mechanisms such as shivering, and growth of a thick hair coat. The horse's foot has an elegant thermoregulatory mechanism to help prevent cold injury; the testes have their own thermoregulatory apparatus to help maintain the lower temperatures required for spermatogenesis. Failure of thermoregulation can lead to serious consequences, e.g. heat stroke in horses that are overworked in hot, humid conditions, or transported in poorly ventilated, hot trailers. The condition anhidrosis arises from a failure of sweating, resulting in increased core body temperature.

See Anhydrosis, Coat, Heat: H. stroke, Sweat, Temperature, Testes.

Thiabendazole ◀╏ *thī ē ben dē zōl, n.* anthelmintic compound of the benzimidazole group; also has antifungal properties. No longer as widely used as previously because of widespread parasite resistance and the development of more effective products.
See Anthelmintic, Benzimidazole, Resistance.

Thiamine see Vitamin B1

Thiaminase ◀╏ *thī am in ās, n.* an enzyme that destroys thiamine; active agent in bracken fern toxicity.
See Bracken fern.

Thigh ◀╏ *thī, n.* part of hind leg between hip and stifle joint.
   T. bone see Femur

Thiopental ◀╏ *thī ō pen tl, n.* (thiopentone) strong, rapid and short-acting barbiturate drug sometimes used for induction of anaesthesia after initial sedation (e.g. with xylazine). Comes as hygroscopic powder that is reconstituted and given by intravenous injection.
See Anaesthesia, Xylazine.

Third ◀╏ *therd, adj.* as pertains to anatomy, the last of a group of three; occurring between the second, but before the fourth, in a series of similar structures.
   T. cranial nerve ◀╏ *therd / krā nē ūl / nerv, n.* oculomotor nerve.
   See Cranial nerve.
   T.-degree burn see Burn
   T. eyelid ◀╏ *therd / ī lid, n.* (nictitating membrane) inner membrane of the eye; an inner eyelid made up of cartilage covered in conjunctiva; may be pigmented or non-pigmented (appears more obvious when non-pigmented). Moves laterally across eye from medial canthus. Examination may be facilitated by applying pressure to eyeball through the upper eyelid. Conditions which affect third eyelid include tumours (especially squamous cell carcinoma in non-pigmented eyelid), conjunctivitis, tetanus (causes prolapse of the third eyelids, especially on stimulation). May also appear

prominent if there is pressure from a growth, abscess, etc. near or in eye.

T. eyelid flap ◀€ *therd / ī lid / flap, n.* surgical procedure where the third eyelid is used as a flap to cover corneal lesions, especially corneal ulcers. Provides protection to the cornea and may help bring blood vessels to lesion to promote healing.

See Conjunctivitis, Eye, Squamous.

T. heart sound ◀€ *therd / hart / sŏnd, n.* low-frequency vibration of the heart caused by the end of rapid ventricular filling.

T. metacarpal bone ◀€ *therd / met ē kar pūl / bōn, n.* (cannon bone). Largest bone of the distal forelimb.

T. phalanx ◀€ *therd / fa langks, n.* (pedal bone; coffin bone) most distal bone of the fore- or hind limb; contained within hoof. Analogous to tip of finger or toe in human. Forms coffin joint with second phalanx and navicular bone. Extensor tendons attach to extensor process (on dorsal surface), flexor tendons attach to palmar surface. Conditions affecting the third phalanx include bruising; laminitis; fracture of the margin, body, or wing (typically from trauma, e.g. kicking or racing on hard ground); osteochondrosis and/or fracture of the extensor process; and infection, e.g. from foreign body penetrating through foot. Conditions involving the third phalanx typically result in obvious lameness; acute fractures involving joint surfaces usually cause more severe lameness, and may result in osteoarthritis. Diagnosis is by clinical examination, pain in response to examination with hoof testers; nerve blocks can confirm that the foot is the location of lameness; radiography confirms fracture.

See Bruise, Extensor, Foot, Laminitis, Osteochrondrosis.

T. ventricle ◀€ *therd / ven trik ĕl, n.* narrow space between the right and left halves of the thalamus and between the lateral ventricles in the brain; contains cerebrospinal fluid.

Thirst ◀€ *therst, n.* the physiological need to drink water; arises from a relative lack of body fluids, or from an increased concentration of body salts. Thirst is influenced by diet and state of hydration, e.g. thirst increases in hot weather or after hard work, as a way of maintaining fluid balance in body.

Thoracic ◀€ *thor ra sik, adj.* of or relating to thorax/chest.

See Thorax.

T. cavity ◀€ *thor ra sik / kav it ē, n.* the cavity in the body enclosed laterally by the ribs, and dorsally by the thoracic spine, between the diaphragm and the neck, and containing the lungs and heart.

T. duct ◀€ *thor ra sik / dukt, n.* the major lymphatic vessel of the body that drains lymph from the entire lymphatics of abdomen, hind legs and part of thorax and empties into venous system in the thorax (returning lymph to blood circulation). May rarely be damaged (e.g. from trauma), resulting in lymphatic fluid collecting in chest (chylothorax).

See Lymphatic.

T. spine ◀€ *thor ra sik / spīn, n.* relating to the vertebrae found at the level of the ribs and chest.

See Rib, Spine.

T. vertebra ◀€ *thor ra sik / ver ti brē, n.* one of 18 bones which make up the spine of the thoracic region. Have tall spinous process which form the withers rostrally, and which are attached to the ribs. Form dorsal part of wall of thoracic cavity.

See Vertebra.

Thoracocentesis ◀€ *thor ra sō sen tē sis, n.* withdrawal of fluid from pleural space by centesis; technique aids in diagnosis of conditions of the thoracic cavity, and is used for fluid drainage in conditions with excessive accumulation of fluid in the thorax (e.g. pleuropneumonia, heart failure, thoracic neoplasia). Usually performed in bottom third of chest, between 6th, 7th, or 8th ribs (in the intercostal space), on left or right side; site of centesis may be determined by ultrasound. Normal horses will have small amount of straw-coloured, clear, watery fluid; various conditions cause increased amounts of fluid, with various accumulations of cells.

See Centesis, Pleural, Thorax.

Thoracolumbar ◀€ *thor ra sō lum bē, adj.* of or relating to the region of the spine where the thoracic and lumbar areas meet. The t. vertebrae are the vertebrae of the thoracic and lumbar regions.

See Thoracic, Lumbar.

Thoracotomy ◀ᘿ _tho rē ko tē mē, n._ surgical operation in which the thoracic cavity is opened. Rarely performed in horses; however, open thoracotomies may occasionally be performed to facilitate chest drainage in horses with severe pleuropneumonia.
See Pleuritis/Pleuropneumonia.

Thorax ◀ᘿ _thor raks, n._ chest; the division of the body between the neck and abdomen. Walls made up of ribs, sternum and thoracic vertebrae; diaphragm separates it from abdomen. Lined by parietal pleura; two pleural sacs contact each other on the median plane to form the mediastinum, then reflect back to cover the diaphragm, turning cranially to cover the ribs. Pleural fluid lubricates the movement of the lungs inside the thoracic cavity. Contents of the thorax include heart, trachea, bronchi, lungs, oesophagus, thymus.
See Bronchus, Diaphragm, Heart, Lung, Mediastinum, Oesophagus, Pleura, Rib, Trachea.

Thoroughpin ◀ᘿ _thu rē pin, n._ fluid swelling of tendon sheath of deep digital flexor tendon (tarsal sheath) as it passes behind tarsus. Seen as swelling either side of Achilles tendon, usually unilateral, above point of hock. Usually not associated with lameness, and most treatments are for cosmetic purposes (e.g. in show horses). May be associated with acute inflammation of tendon and tendon sheath (acute tenosynovitis); in such cases, the horse may be lame. Can become chronic if tendon sheath becomes thickened with fibrous tissue.
See Tenosynovitis.

Threadworm ◀ᘿ _thred werm, n._ name for very thin parasitic worms. The term has been liberally used to apply to several species of worms, including intestinal worms, e.g. _Oxyuris, Strongyloides westerii, Parascaris equorum_, as well as _Onchocerca cervicalis_ (neck threadworm).
See _Oxyuris equi._

Thrill ◀ᘿ _thril, n._ an abnormal fine tremor or vibration felt by palpation; may occur in the respiratory system, caused by turbulence of air in narrow airway (e.g. partially blocked by mucus), or in the cardiovascular system, caused by turbulent blood flow (e.g. caused by damaged heart valve).

Throat ◀ᘿ _thrōt, n._ the passage to the stomach and lungs, at the back of mouth, containing the pharynx and larynx.
See Larynx, Pharynx.
  T. latch ◀ᘿ _thrōt / lash, n._ the soft area under the throat where the head and neck are joined; the place where a harness throat latch fits, or across which the throat latch of the bridle is fastened.

Thrombin ◀ᘿ _throm bin, n._ enzyme in blood plasma formed from prothrombin during blood clotting. Catalyses conversion of soluble fibrinogen to insoluble fibrin.
See Clotting, Fibrinogen.

Thrombocyte ◀ᘿ _throm bō sīt, n._ platelet; the component of blood that aids in clotting.
See Platelet.

Thrombocytopenia ◀ᘿ _throm bō sī tō pē nē ē, n._ condition of abnormally low levels of platelets in blood. Most laboratories consider thrombocytopenia to be when platelet counts are less than 100,000 per μl of serum. May rarely be related to lack of production in bone marrow (e.g. bone marrow failure secondary to neoplasia), or from toxicities caused by drug or toxin poisoning; may also be related to an increased use of circulating platelets, e.g. in massive haemorrhage, or from coagulation disorders such as disseminated intravascular coagulation (DIC). More commonly, thrombocytopenia results from excessive destruction of platelets, e.g. immune-mediated thrombocytopenic purpura, from destruction caused by antibodies produced against platelets: this may be secondary to infection (e.g. equine infectious anaemia, anaplasmosis), drug, disease (e.g. renal failure), or of unknown cause (idiopathic). Clinical signs related to failure of blood clotting include

bruising, petechial and ecchymotic haemorrhages on mucous membranes (e.g. gums), nosebleed (epistaxis), prolonged bleeding from wounds or after intravenous injections, or blood in faeces. Diagnosis by platelet count on blood smear; detection of underlying cause important for treatment. Treatment of primary disease, If possible, is crucial for resolution; treatment of immune-mediated thrombocytopenia involves corticosteroid therapy.
See Anaplasmosis, Clotting, Disseminated, Epistaxis, Equine infectious anaemia, Petechiae.

Thrombocytosis ◀ː _throm bō sī tō sis, n._ an increase in the number of circulating platelets. May occur in conjunction with neoplasia of the bone marrow, following acute or chronic inflammation, or after acute haemorrhage. Mild thrombocytosis may be seen after exercise, from splenic contraction. Most non-neoplastic thrombocytosis is not associated with any abnormal clinical signs.

Thromboembolism ◀ː _throm bō em bē lizm, n._ obstruction of blood vessel by blood clot which became dislodged from site of formation. May rarely be seen in adult horses, where blood clots caused by _Strongylus vulgaris_ can travel to the intestines, causing areas of intestinal ischaemia and colic (thromboembolic colic). Thromboembolism may sometimes affect the horse's brain, the thrombus travelling via the carotid arteries. The clinical signs in such horses depend on the part of brain affected, and may include seizures, abnormal gait, circling, blindness, etc. Diagnosis by analysis of cerebrospinal fluid and increase in eosinophils in blood sample.
See Clotting, _Strongylus_ spp.

    Aorto-iliac t. ◀ː _ā or tō il ē ak_ / _throm bō em bē lizm, n._ thromboembolism of the terminal aorta; typically causes chronic bilateral hind limb lameness. Can often be detected by rectal examination; confirmed by transrectal ultrasonography.

    Septic t. ◀ː _sep tik_ / _throm bō em bē lizm, n._ thromboembolism associated with a site of infection, e.g. _Strep. equi_ infection; can be a predisposing factor for bacterial endocarditis in horses.
See Endocarditis.

Thrombophlebitis ◀ː _throm bō fli bī tis, n._ inflammation of a vein secondary to the formation of a blood clot. Most commonly caused by prolonged intravenous catheterization, e.g. as may be necessary in hospitalized horses receiving prolonged intravenous fluid therapy.

Thrombosis ◀ː _throm bō sis, n._ formation or presence of a blood clot within blood vessel. In the horse, thrombosis may occur in the aorta (aorto-iliac thrombosis) and cause hind limb lameness, or after chronic thrombophlebitis.
See Clotting, Thromboembolism, Thrombophlebitis.

Thrombus ◀ː _throm bēs, n._ blood clot formed within blood vessel or a chamber of the heart; may cause obstruction of affected structure.

Thrush ◀ː _thrush, n._ infection of the soft tissues of the foot, especially the frog, or the sulcus of the frog, with various microorganisms. Most common clinical sign is black, foul-smelling material in the sulcus of the frog. Associated with unhygienic stabling conditions. May extend into sensitive areas of foot, in which case horse may be lame.
See Foot.

Thumps ◀ː _thumps, n._ (synchronous diaphragmatic flutter) noise associated with diaphragm contracting in a synchronous manner with each heart beat.
See Synchronous diaphragmatic flutter, Tetany.

Thymus ◀ː _thī mēs, n._ lymphoid organ in chest (in cranial mediastinum of thorax). Large in foal and up until puberty, then size and activity gradually decline with age. Important role in maturation of T cells.
See T cell, Thorax.

Thyroid ◀ː _thī roid, adj._ shaped like a shield; pertaining to the thyroid gland or the region of the thyroid gland.

T. adenoma ◀€ _thī roid / a dēn ō mē, n._ benign tumour of the thyroid gland. Most commonly seen in older horses; tumour typically does not affect function of the thyroid gland.

T. adenocarcinoma ◀€ _thī roid / ad ēn ō kar si nō mē, n._ malignant tumour of the thyroid gland. Uncommon; diagnosis by biopsy. No specific treatment; prognosis poor.

T. cartilage ◀€ _thī roid / kar ti lij, n._ large cartilage of larynx, can be felt at upper end of trachea. One end of vocal folds attaches to cartilage.
See Larynx.

T. gland ◀€ _thī roid / gland, n._ ductless (endocrine) gland with two lobes, situated either side of larynx. Secretes hormones (thyroxine and tri-iodothyronine) which affect growth, development and metabolism. Control of hormone secretion quite complex: stimulated to secrete hormones by thyroid-stimulating hormone (TSH, thyrotropin), produced by pituitary gland. Secretion of thyrotropin-releasing hormone (TRH) by hypothalamus stimulates secretion of TSH. Lack of secretion by gland is termed hypothyroidism; oversecretion is termed hyperthyroidism. Both are uncommon in horses. The thyroid gland also produces calcitonin, which participates in control of calcium and phosphorus homeostasis and has significant effects on bone physiology.
See Calcitonin, Hyperthyroidism, Hypothyroidism, Pituitary, Thyroxine, Tri-iodothyronine.

T. hormones ◀€ _thī roid / hor mōnz, n._ thyroxine and tri-iodothyronine; hormones which affect growth, development and metabolism. It is likely that all of the cells in the horse's body are targets for thyroid hormones.
See Thyroxine, Tri-iodothyronine.

T.-releasing hormone ◀€ _thī roid-ril ēs ing / hor mōn, n._ (TRH) the hormone that ultimately controls the circulating level of thyroid hormones. Thyroid-releasing hormone is secreted by hypothalamic neurons and causes release of thyroid-stimulating hormone (TSH) by the anterior pituitary. Secretion of thyroid-releasing hormone (and hence, TSH and circulating hormones) is inhibited by high blood levels of thyroid hormones in a negative feedback loop.

See Negative, T.-stimulating hormone (below).

T.- stimulating hormone ◀€ _thī roid-stim ū lā ting / hor mōn, n._ (TSH; thyrotropin) hormone secreted by cells in the anterior pituitary called thyrotrophs; receptors for TSH are found on epithelial cells in the thyroid gland. TSH stimulates the thyroid gland to synthesize and release thyroid hormones. TSH secretion is primarily controlled by thyroid-releasing hormone. A thyroid stimulation test using TSH would be an ideal way to assess equine thyroid function, and is used in other species; unfortunately an equine TSH product is generally not available for such use.
See Pituitary, T. gland (above), T.-releasing hormone (above).

Thyroxine ◀€ _thī rok sēn, n._ (T4, tetra-iodothyronine) hormone secreted by thyroid gland, contains iodine. In peripheral tissues, much T4 loses an iodine ion to become tri-iodothyronine (T3), a more active form. Acts as catalyst in body and has many effects: increases metabolic rate, increases metabolism of carbohydrates, fats and proteins, promotes breakdown of liver glycogen, promotes the formation of glucose from volatile fatty acids, and increases cellular oxygen consumption. Also important in growth and development, reproduction, and for resistance to infection. It is difficult to make an accurate assessment of equine thyroid gland function. Single blood tests are not necessarily accurate reflections of the horse's thyroid status; levels vary considerably during a 24-hour period. In addition, other factors, including the administration of drugs, and systemic diseases, affect the blood levels of thyroxine, and may falsely affect the results of blood tests. A synthetic version of thyroxine, levothyroxine (l-thyroxine) is commonly given to horses for a variety of reasons, many of which are not necessarily supported by scientific data.
See Hyperthyroidism, Hypothyroidism, Thyroid, Tri-iodothyronine.

Tibia ◀€ _ti bē ē, n._ long bone of hind leg; articulates proximally at the stifle, with the femur and patella, and distally at the tarsus (hock), with the talus.
See Stifle, Tarsus.

Tibial ◀€ _ti bē ūl, adj._ of, or relating to, the tibia.

    T. fracture ◀€ _ti bi ūl / frak tŭr, n._ break of tibia, usually as result of trauma. Uncommon; prognosis poor with most tibial fractures, especially if displaced or in adult horses.

    T. nerve ◀€ _ti bē ūl / nerv, n_ nerve of hind limb, runs down medial surface of leg over tibia. Gives branches to the extensor muscles of the hock and the flexor muscles of the digit. May rarely be injured; signs include flexion of hock and knuckled fetlock.

    T. nerve block ◀€ _ti bē ūl / nerv / blok, n._ local anaesthetic block of t. nerve. May be blocked, along with the peroneal nerves, to desensitize the hock and distal structures, as part of lameness evaluation (if area supplied by nerve is anaesthetized and lameness or pain are no longer evident, then pain or lameness arise from that area).

    See Nerve block.

Tick ◀€ _tik, n._ small parasitic, blood-sucking arachnid of the suborder Ixodides, superfamily Ixodoidea. The ticks are larger than the mites. There are two families: Argasidae (soft ticks) and Ixodidae (hard ticks); those which affect horses are primarily of family Ixodidae. Attaches to skin, penetrates skin with mouthparts and sucks blood, body swells as feeds. Usually drops off host at end of feeding. Ticks may harm horses by: 1) bites, which may become secondarily infected; 2) sucking blood, with secondary anaemia, 3) transmitting disease, e.g. viral encephalitis, babesiosis, and 4) causing paralysis. Not generally a major problem in UK.

See _Babesia_, Encephalitis.

tid _abbr._ 'for three times a day', used to give dosage for frequency of drug administration in prescriptions.

Tiludronate ◀€ _til ūd rēn āt, n._ a member of a class of drugs known as bisphosphonates. These drugs bind to active bone cells called osteoclasts. Normally, bone is an active tissue, and new bone is constantly being made and replaced. Osteoclasts help remove bone. By binding to osteoclasts, tiludronate favours bone production instead of bone removal. As such, bisphosphonates find wide application in human medicine, for the treatment of conditions such as osteoporosis. In Europe, tiludronate is available in a preparation for intramuscular adminstration in horses, and the drug has been imported for use in horses in the United States. It has been used to treat horses where increased bone activity is suspected, such as suspensory ligament disease, inflammation of the bone of the hoof, and disease of the navicular bone. There is one study that supports its use for the treatment of disease of the navicular bone. The more widespread use of tiludronate, and other drugs of this class, in the United States will await more studies to demonstrate the drug's true usefulness.

Timothy grass ◀€ _tim ēth ē / grars, n._ (_Phleum pratense_), an abundant perennial grass native to most of Europe except for the Mediterranean region, and grown especially in the western United States as a hay crop. Compared to legume hays, timothy hay is higher in fibre and phosphorus, but lower in protein, calories, and calcium.

Tincture ◀€ _tink tŭr, n._ drug dissolved in alcohol and water for use as medicine, e.g. tincture of iodine.

Tipped vulva see Vulva

Tissue ◀€ _ti shǔ, n._ a collection of interconnected cells united together to perform similar function. Many different types in body, including:

- Adipose t. – fat tissue; connective tissue made up of fat cells.
- Connective t. – the material that holds together various body structures; composed of cells embedded in a matrix (gel, elastic fibres, liquid, or inorganic minerals). Cartilage, tendons, ligaments and blood vessels are each made up entirely of various types of connective tissue.
- Fibrous t. – term usually used to refer to tissue deposited at a wound site, which is initially rich in blood vessels (granulation tissue) but later becomes avascular, and tissue made up of

bundles of white collagen fibres, with rows of connective tissue cells interposed (e.g. scar).

- Granulation t. – a specialized tissue, rich in capillaries, created by the body as a response to injury (see Wound).
- Muscle t. – type of connective tissue that has the ability to contract, either voluntarily or involuntarily. Three types: striated, smooth, or cardiac (see Muscle).
- Scar t. – type of connective tissue that results from the normal wound healing process. Scar tissue is composed mostly of collagen, and lacks normal epithelial structures. It provides a means of tissue repair, but is not as elastic or as strong as normal, uninjured tissue.
- Soft t. – any body tissue other than cartilage, bone or teeth, e.g. muscle, tendons, ligaments, synovial tissue, fascia, and other structures such as nerves, blood vessels and fat.

See under separate headings.

T. culture ◀€ *ti shŭ / kul tŭr, n.* growing various tissues in a laboratory; requires a specially prepared medium. Mostly used for research purposes.

Titrate ◀€ *tī trāt, v.* to gradually increase (or decrease) the dose of a drug; to determine level of a component in solution by titration.
See Titration.

Titration ◀€ *tī trā shēn, n.* the adjustment of the drug dosage to a desired effect; a method, or the process, of using a standard solution to determine the strength of another solution, e.g. by causing a reaction that results in a clear end-point, e.g. colour change, agglutination. In biochemical tests, titration may be used to determine the level of antibodies in blood sample; serial dilutions are used and test discovers at which dilution antibodies can still be detected.

Titre ◀€ *tī tē, n.* the degree of a dilution of a substance, especially as pertains to antibodies, in test solution; titres reflect the level of antibody response, i.e. the strength of the solution being tested. While titres may be measured as a means of deter-

mining an antibody response, e.g. to infection, unfortunately there is no clear correlation between measurable antibody titres and disease protection.

Tobramycin ◀€ *tō brē mī sin, n.* aminoglycoside antibiotic, active against Gram-negative bacteria, especially *Pseudomonas aeruginosa.* Used especially as topical treatment for eye conditions where *P. aeruginosa* isolated (e.g. corneal ulcer, bacterial keratitis). Can be used systemically; however, expense limits its widespread use.

Tocopherol ◀€ *to ko fē rol, n.* vitamin E; primarily serves the horse's body as an antioxidant.
See Antioxidant, Vitamin E.

Toe ◀€ *tō, n.* front part of hoof.

T. clip ◀€ *tō / klip, n.* triangular-shaped projection drawn from a metal horseshoe placed at the toe; intended to help secure shoe, and prevent slipping.

T. dragging ◀€ *tō / dra ging, n.* failure to lift front part of hoof of hind leg clear of ground when moving; common sign of hind limb problem. May be caused by problems with the nervous system (e.g. cervical vertebral malformation), musculoskeletal system (e.g. navicular disease, back problem, osteoarthritis of the tarsus), or secondary to infections (e.g. scirrhous cord).
See Navicular syndrome, Scirrhous.

T. extension ◀€ *tō / eks ten shēn, n.* application of an acrylic or metal plate to the toe. Used to help correct contractural deformities in foals. Toe extension increases forces on the deep digital flexor tendon and helps stretch contracture, and helps prevent knuckling and excessive wear on toe.

T. grab ◀€ *tō / grab, n.* metal prominence (calk) used to increase traction at the toe of a horseshoe. Has been associated with limb injuries in US racing horses; not permitted in the UK.
See Calkin.

Toe-in ◀€ *tō-in, adj.* (pigeon-toed) foot conformation, where toes are pointed more towards midline. Tends to result in forelimb movement whereby feet are thrown to the outside of the body (US: paddling; UK: dishing).

Toe-out ◄≀ *tō-owt, adj.* (splay-footed) foot conformation where toes are pointed more away from midline. Tends to result in forelimb movement where feet are thrown under the body (US: winging; UK: plaiting).

Togavirus *see* Eastern equine encephalitis, Venezuelan equine encephalitis, Western equine encephalitis

-tomy ◄≀ *tĕ mē, suffix* incision; cutting, as in a surgical operation, e.g. laparotomy is cutting into abdomen, thoracotomy is cutting into thorax.

Tongue ◄≀ *tung, n.* fleshy, flexible muscular organ, attached to floor of mouth. The principal organ of taste, aids in prehension, chewing and swallowing (moves food to cheek teeth for chewing, forms chewed food into bolus for swallowing and moves bolus to back of mouth). Surface of tongue has taste buds which detect chemical components of food such as salt, sweet, etc. Conditions which affect tongue include injuries (e.g. lacerations), foreign bodies and paralysis (e.g. from damage to hypoglossal nerve, botulism).
See Hypoglossal nerve.

    T. tie ◄≀ *tung tī, n.* a band made of cloth or leather used to tie down a horse's tongue; commonly used to try to prevent dorsal displacement of soft palate.
    See Dorsal.

Tonic ◄≀ *to nik, v./n.* of or relating to or producing normal tone in muscles or tissue; an old term used in reference to a liquid preparation, usually given with the intent of restoring health, refreshing, or invigorating the body.

    Tonic–clonic seizure ◄≀ *to nik-klo nik / sē zhŭr, n.* seizure marked by loss of consciousness, falling, stiffening, and jerking. This is the classic sign of a generalized motor seizure.

    T. muscle contraction ◄≀ *to nik / mu sŭl / kon trak shĕn, n.* a sustained muscular contraction, as is necessary for maintaining posture.

Tonometry ◄≀ *to no mē trē, n.* measurement of pressure within eyeball (intraocular pressure). Used in diagnosis of various eye diseases, e.g. glaucoma causes an increase in intraocular pressure; uveitis causes a decrease in intraocular pressure.
See Eye, Glaucoma, Uveitis.

Tooth ◄≀ *tūth, n.* (pl. teeth) hard, enamel-coated, bone-like structure in mouth used for grasping and chewing of food, and for attack or defence. Adult horse normally has between 36 and 44 teeth: 12 front teeth (incisors), up to 28 cheek teeth (3 or 4 premolars, and 3 molars) and 4 canine teeth (tusks). Toughest substance of tooth is very hard enamel, covers dentine, a hard yellowish substance which forms the bulk of the tooth. Innermost part is the pulp cavity which contains blood vessels and nerves. This gradually fills with dentine. Chewing surface has a cavity (infundibulum) lined with cement. The horse teeth are called hypsodont; roughly, they are folded teeth covered by cement and enamel, with rings and ridges of enamel surrounded by cement and dentine on the chewing (occlusal) surfaces. As the tooth wears down from chewing, the former fill with secondary dentine. The tooth has crown above gum level and root below gum, embedded in socket (alveolus) in bone; attaches to soft tissue with outer layer of cement. The reserve crown is very long in the young horse, and it lies embedded in the bones of the skull. When the erupted crown wears (approximately 2–3 mm per year), it is refilled with new tooth. As horse ages, teeth are worn down by chewing. Horses may suffer discomfort and damage to tongue or cheeks if teeth wear unevenly and sharp enamel points form. Age of horse can be estimated fairly accurately by the pattern of eruption of teeth (dentition) up until 5 years of age. After 5 years of age, various techniques, e.g. examining structures visible on biting surface of incisors (e.g. dental cups), angle of incisor teeth, Galvayne's groove, may be used to provide an estimate of the horse's age. However, several studies have shown that such a method of estimation in horses beyond 5 years of age is relatively inaccurate. Teeth are named either by their type and loca-

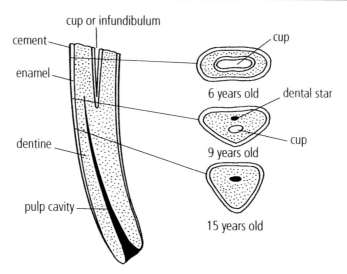

Section through the incisor tooth, showing approximate stages of wear

tion (e.g. upper right third premolar) or by a modified triadan three-digit system. See Dentition, Triadan three-digit system, modified.

Wolf t. ◄᠈ *wulf / tŭth, n.* vestigial premolar tooth, so-named because it resembles the tooth of a wolf. Up to approximately one-third of all horses are born with as many as four wolf teeth; most of those having only one or two, most likely on the upper jaw. Wolf teeth are equally common in male and female horses. Problems in the bitting of the horse are often attributed to wolf teeth, although as the teeth typically have shallow roots, and are far back in the mouth, how they can interfere with the horse's bit contact is hard to understand. Regardless, wolf teeth are commonly removed.

Topical ◄᠈ *to pi cēl, adj.* on the surface of the body; applied to the skin. Topical medication is applied directly to the part of the body it is intended to treat, e.g. eye ointments, skin creams, etc.

T. anaesthesia see Anaesthesia

Torsion ◄᠈ *tor shēn, n.* a twisting, especially of the bowel or the testicle, along its long axis, in a clockwise or counter-clockwise direction, resulting in a spiral or helical configuration. Torsion cuts off the blood supply to the affected area, and so rapidly results in tissue death (ischaemic

necrosis). Associated with severe colic pain. Torsion is different from volvulus (intestinal rotation), although clinically both conditions result in severe pain. See Volvulus.

Tourniquet ◄᠈ *tor ni kā, n.* constricting band (e.g. a bandage, rope or rubber strap) applied tightly to a limb; used to apply pressure to artery and vein, either to reduce blood loss (e.g. after injury, or during surgery), or to facilitate therapeutic techniques such as regional limb perfusion. Tourniquets may be applied to the equine limb for as long as two hours without damaging tissue from lack of blood supply.

See Regional.

Toxaemia ◄᠈ *tok sē mē ē, n.* presence of poisonous substances (toxins) in blood. For example, toxins absorbed into blood stream from an area of bacterial infection may spread to rest of body and can have effects on various organ systems, e.g. heart, kidneys, liver, etc.

Toxicology ◄᠈ *tok si ko lē jē, n.* study or branch of medicine concerned with the nature, effects and detection of poisons (substances that can cause damage, illness, or death to organisms, usually by chemical reaction), and the treatment of poisoning.

Toxin ◀ℰ *tok sin, n.* a substance, produced or released by a living organism (e.g. bacteria or other microorganisms), that can cause illness, injury, or death. For example, exotoxins are produced by bacteria and released (e.g. tetanus toxin); endotoxins are part of the bacterial cell membrane of certain Gram negative bacteria and are only released when bacteria break down; mycotoxins are toxins elaborated by fungi.
See Bacterium, Endotoxin, Exotoxin, Mycotoxin, Tetanus.

Toxoid ◀ℰ *tok soid, n.* vaccine in which toxin has been modified so that it is no longer toxic, but can still stimulate an antibody response, e.g. tetanus toxoid used as vaccine to protect against *Clostridium tetani* toxin.
See Tetanus, Vaccine.

Trace mineral ◀ℰ *trās / mi ner ūl, n.* mineral/chemical element needed in very small amounts in diet for animal's health. Examples include cobalt, copper, iodine, iron, magnesium, manganese, selenium, zinc. Many trace minerals are needed in such small quantities that naturally occurring deficiencies are unknown.
See Mineral, and under individual entries.

    T.-m. salt ◀ℰ *trās-mi ner ūl / sawlt, n.* salt combined with small amounts of trace minerals; often provided as a free-choice block. Typical mixtures generally consist of approximately 98% sodium chloride, with added minerals such as zinc, manganese, copper, or iodine. Trace-mineral salt typically does not contain calcium or phosphorus. These products do not typically supply enough minerals for growing horses, or for mares in late pregnancy or lactation.

Trachea ◀ℰ *trē kē ē, n.* windpipe, tube which carries air from larynx to main bronchi and removes air expelled from lungs. Wall of tube strengthened and supported by C-shaped rings of cartilage. Lined by mucous membrane with special ciliated surface: cilia act to sweep mucus and foreign material to pharynx where can be swallowed. Tracheal inflammation (tracheitis) is a common primary problem,

especially in stabled horses. Horses may occasionally inhale foreign bodies that lodge in trachea. Primary tracheal diseases in horses are uncommon; however, congenital collapse (rings flattened from birth) has been seen rarely in horses, ponies, and miniature horses. Most tracheal problems are secondary to injury or trauma (e.g. from kicks, or running into fences) and cause airway obstruction. If the mucous membrane of the trachea is injured, air may leak, leading to regional or generalized subcutaneous emphysema, which is easily indented with thumb pressure, and crackles when palpated. Most common clinical sign of a tracheal problem is cough.
See Cilium.

Tracheitis ◀ℰ *tra kē ī tis, n.* inflammation of the trachea. Common primary problem, especially in stabled horses, and may be seen secondary to a variety of infections and inflammatory conditions of the upper and lower airways, e.g. pneumonia, recurrent airway obstruction.
See Pneumonia, Recurrent airway obstruction.

Tracheostomy ◀ℰ *tra kē os tē mē, n.* surgery in which an artificial opening (stoma) is made in trachea to help breathing, e.g. as may be required for upper respiratory tract obstruction or severe cases of laryngeal paralysis. May be temporary or permanent. The surgical opening itself may also be called a tracheostomy.
See Larynx, Trachea.

Tracheotomy ◀ℰ *tra kē o tē mē, n.* cutting into the trachea; surgical procedure in which artificial opening (stoma) is made in trachea (tracheostomy).
See Trachea.

Tract ◀ℰ *trakt, n.* anatomical passage or path, e.g. alimentary tract, urinary tract; a bundle of nerve fibres within the central nervous system.
See Alimentary tract, Central nervous system, Urinary.

Traction ◀ ℰ *trak shēn, n.* the concept of achieving grip, e.g. a heel calk may be applied to a horseshoe in an effort to increase traction; application of constant pull on part of body to overcome muscular contraction or displacement of fracture, e.g. in returning broken bone to correct position and alignment prior to surgical fixation with bone screws and plates. See Calkin, Fracture.

Tranquillizer ◀﹕ _trang_ kwi _lī_ zĕr, n. a medication administered for a calming effect; commonly given before procedure which may cause anxiety, e.g. prior to wound repair, or to facilitate various handling procedures. Examples of tranquillizers commonly used in horses include acepromazine, butorphanol, detomidine, and xylazine. See Various entries.

Transfusion ◀﹕ trans _fū_ zhĕn, n. administration of whole blood or blood products (e.g. red blood cells, plasma, platelets) directly into blood stream.
  Blood t. ◀﹕ _blud_ / trans _fū_ zhĕn administration of whole blood components into blood stream. Used in treatment of severe blood loss (haemorrhage); blood must come from compatible donor (see Blood type). 5–10 litres may be collected from adult donor, sodium citrate used as anticoagulant, blood administered through filter, very slowly at first while monitoring for adverse reactions. Adverse reactions include increased heart and respiratory rate, fever, weakness, diarrhoea, abdominal pain, anaphylaxis, shock, fluid in lungs (pulmonary oedema). If adverse reaction occurs, transfusion must be stopped and intravenous crystalline fluids and epinephrine may be administered. See Anaphylaxis, Blood, Haemorrhage.
  Plasma t. ◀﹕ _plaz_ mĕ / trans _fū_ zhĕn, n. administration of blood plasma. Commonly performed in neonatal foals with suspected or confirmed failure of passive transfer of maternal immunoglobulins, or with neonatal septicaemia; commercially available.

Transillumination ◀﹕ _trans_ il _ŭm_ in _ā_ shĕn, n. the transmission of light through tissues of the body for the purposes of examination; commonly used to examine the equine eye. The eye can be examined by transillumination with light from an ophthalmoscope, or even a penlight.

Transit tetany see Tetany

Transitional cell ◀﹕ _tran zi_ shĕn _ŭl_ / sel, n. a cell with varying shape depending on whether the tissue of which it is a component is being stretched. Transitional cells can stretch without breaking apart; the primary cell type of the urinary bladder.
  T. c. carcinoma ◀﹕ _tran zi_ shĕn _ŭl_ / sel / _kar_ si _nō_ mĕ, n. malignant tumour of lining of urinary tract (transitional epithelium), especially of bladder. Rare in horse; clinical signs in affected horses include acute onset of bleeding into urine (haematuria).

Transphyseal bridging ◀ ﹕_tranz_ fiz ē _ŭl_ / _brij_ ing, n. surgical technique for the treatment of angular limb deformities, e.g. carpus valgus or carpus varus. A metal staple (or screws and a wire) is placed across the epiphysis and secured. This prevents normal physeal growth on the side on which the device has been placed. Normal physeal growth occurs on the untreated side; when the leg has straightened, the implant is removed. See Carpus, Developmental orthopaedic disease.

Transplant ◀﹕ _trans_ plarnt, v./n. the procedure of grafting a donor's tissues or organs into or onto a patient's body. Organ transplant from one individual to another is not performed in horses; skin transplants grafts are occasionally performed, especially autografts (skin from elsewhere on body transplanted to cover a wound on lower limb). See Graft.

Transtracheal aspirate ◀ ﹕_tranz_ trāk ē _ŭl_ / _asp_ ir _āt_, n. diagnostic technique used to investigate causes of respiratory disease. Cannula is introduced into trachea on the ventral neck; catheter is passed through cannula to the level of the tracheal bifurcation. A large volume of sterile saline solution is injected through the catheter and immediately withdrawn. The fluid aspirate is examined for cells and the presence of infectious agents; fluid samples can be cultured for microorganisms.

Transudate ◄╎ *tran sū dāt, n.* a blood filtrate; a fluid that passes through a membrane, e.g. the wall of a blood vessel, which filters out most of the protein and cellular elements, yielding a watery solution. Causes of transudates include increased pressure in veins and capillaries, e.g. where venous drainage is blocked, which forces fluid through the vessel walls, or from low levels of protein in the serum (hypoproteinaemia), which causes a decrease in plasma colloid oncotic pressure. Transudated fluid may accumulate in tissues and cause swelling (oedema). See Hypoalbuminaemia, Pressure.

> **Modified t.** ◄╎ *mo di fīd / tran sū dāt, n.* transudate with an elevated protein content, usually as a result of inflammation, or owing to accumulation of high-protein hepatic lymphatic fluid.

Trauma ◄╎ *traw mē, n.* wound or injury to living tissue caused by outside force, e.g. impact, kick, surgery.

Traumatic ◄╎ *traw ma tik, adj.* relating to a physical wound or injury, e.g. traumatic arthritis is inflammation of a joint secondary to joint trauma.

> **T. arthritis** see Arthritis

Tread ◄╎ *tred, n.* old term for an injury caused to coronet of foot by shoe of opposite foot (or by second horse, if being worked in pair). See Foot.

Treatment ◄╎ *trēt mēnt, n.* the medical or surgical management of a patient; providing care by procedures or interventions for the purpose of relieving illness, injury, disease, or pathological condition.

Trephine ◄╎ *tri fīn, v./n.* surgical procedure to remove small circle of bone from skull. In horse most frequently performed to facilitate drainage from sinus in sinusitis, also allows administration of antibiotics into sinus; the instrument with which a trephine operation is performed. See Sinusitis.

Triadan three-digit system, modified ◄╎ *trī ad ēn / thrē-dij it / sis tēm, mod if*

īd, n. system of dental nomenclature. In this system, each tooth is given a three-digit number which identifies the position of the tooth, and whether it is a primary or permanent tooth. The first number reflects the quadrant in which the tooth is located; numbers 1–4 are used to identify the quadrant for permanent teeth, starting with 1 in the upper right quadrant, and moving counter-clockwise; numbers 5–8 are used for the temporary dentition, starting with 5 in the upper right quadrant. The second and third digits are used to identify the specific tooth number; the left lower third premolar is tooth '307' (the seventh tooth in the left lower quadrant, beginning at the central incisor and counting caudally). The next-to-last molar on the right mandible is labelled '410'.

Triamcinolone ◄╎ *trī am si nē lōn, n.* long-lasting synthetic corticosteroid agent, used to treat inflammation of various tissues. Available in various preparations, e.g. for topical use on inflamed skin, or for intra-articular administration in cases of arthritis. See Corticosteroid.

Trichiasis ◄╎ *tri kī ē sis, n.* condition where eyelashes grow inwards. Can cause irritation of cornea. Seen especially in foals, or after injury to eyelids in adult horses. Foals can often be treated by infiltrating eyelids with a solution such as procaine penicillin G; adult horse may require surgical correction (blepharoplasty). See Eye, Eyelash.

Trichophyton ◄╎ *trī kō fī ton, n.* genus of fungus of the family Moniliaceae; causes dermatophytosis (ringworm). *T. equinum* and *T. mentagrophytes* most commonly affect horses. See Dermatophytosis.

Tricuspid valve ◄╎ *trī kus pid / valv, n.* (right atrioventricular valve) heart valve with three cusps, lies between right atrium and ventricle. The tricuspid valve is the inflow valve of the right ventricle; it closes when the ventricle squeezes blood out into the lungs, and then opens to allow blood to flow into the ventricle. Insufficiency of valve can occur, e.g. in bacterial endocarditis, rupture of chorda tendinae (which hold cusps in place), prolapse of floppy valve, etc. Signs of insufficiency include heart murmur (especially on right side of chest), poor performance if insufficiency severe. Diagnosis by clinical signs of exercise intolerance and auscultation of heart murmur; confirmed by echocardiography. See Heart, Valve.

Trifolium see Clover

Trigeminal nerve ◀ *trī je mi nūl / nerv, n.* cranial nerve V. Contains primarily sensory fibres for much of head, and some motor branches for muscles of chewing (mastication). Trigeminal nerve has three branches: mandibular, maxillary, ophthalmic. Deficit of sensory fibres results in loss of sensation from head and loss of facial reflexes, such as closure of eyelid, flicking of ear in response to touch; these functions also require intact facial nerve, and so loss of the sensory function of the trigeminal nerve may be clinically inapparent. Deficit in motor fibres results in wasting of muscles of mastication, drooling, open jaw, difficulty with chewing (or inability to chew). Damage to nerve may be caused by tumour or inflammation, e.g. secondary to equine protozoal myelitis or botulism, or from idiopathic nerve fibre degeneration.
See Cranial nerve, Facial, Head-shaking, Reflex.

> **T. neuralgia** ◀ *trī je mi nūl / nū ral jē, n.* is sensitivity of the fifth cranial nerve, especially to light. Extreme sensitivity to light stimulates the trigeminal nerve, making the horse's nose itch or twitch. In response, the horse rubs its nose or shakes its head.

Tri-iodothyronine ◀ *trī - ī ō dō thī ro nēn, n.* (T3) thyroid hormone, higher activity than thyroxine. Acts as catalyst in body and has many effects: increases metabolic rate, increases metabolism of carbohydrates, fats and proteins, important in growth and development, reproduction and resistance to infection. Single blood tests are not necessarily accurate reflections of the horse's thyroid status; levels vary considerably during a 24-hour period. In addition, other factors, including the administration of drugs, and systemic diseases, affect the blood levels of tri-iodothyronine, and may falsely affect the results of blood tests.
See Thyroid, Thyroxine.

Trimethoprim ◀ *trī me thō prim, n.* bacteriostatic antibacterial drug, most commonly used in combination with sulfonamide (combination may be called potentiated sulphonamide). Works by inhibiting synthesis of the DNA nucleotide thymidine; this inhibition starves the bacteria of nucleotides necessary for DNA replication. Active against many Gram-positive and Gram-negative bacteria; combining trimethoprim with a sulfa drug increases (potentiates) the effectiveness of each drug. Because the combination of drugs is relatively inexpensive and is given orally, it is popularly used in the treatment of many different types of infections of the horse.
See Sulphonamide.

Trismus ◀ *triz mēs, n.* inability to open mouth fully; typically caused by spasm of jaw muscles. May be seen as early sign of tetanus, resulting in common name of 'lockjaw'.
See Tetanus.

Trocar ◀ *trō kar, n.* hollow cylinder (cannula) with a sharply pointed instrument which fits inside. Used to pierce body cavity, especially the abdomen; pointed part is removed so that tube can allow fluid or gas to escape, e.g. for drainage of fluid from abdominal cavity (e.g. in peritonitis), or as a procedure to relieve gas from distended large bowel in colic caused by excessive accumulation of gas.
See Abdominocentesis, Colic.

Trochanter ◀ *tro kan tē, n.* any of three prominences (greater, lesser and third trochanters) on thigh bone (femur) to which muscles attach.
See Femur.

Trochanteric bursitis ◀ *tro kan tik / ber sī tis, n.* (whirlbone lameness) lameness

caused by inflammation of bursa (fluid-containing sac) beneath tendon of gluteal muscle, where it passes over part of femur (greater trochanter). May occur after a fall. Causes lameness, pain when pressure applied over hip area or outside of foot put to ground when walking.
See Bursa, Femur, Gluteal.

Trochlea ◀€ *trok lē ē, n.* an anatomical structure that resembles a pulley. For example, the patella slides in the trochlea of the distal femur; the tibia articulates with the trochlea of the talus.

Trochlear nerve ◀€ *trok lē ē / nerv, n.* cranial nerve IV. Important in control of extraocular muscles to maintain normal position of eyeball (with cranial nerves III and VI); if damaged, eyeball turns medially.
See Cranial nerve.

Trombicula ◀€ *trom bi kū lē, n.* (harvest mite, chigger) genus of mite. Larvae of *Trombicula autumnalis* are parasitic, come off pasture in autumn and cause skin irritation, especially on face and neck, heels and ventral abdomen. Dermatitis is characterized by intense pruritis caused by larval mites injecting digestive juices into the skin while feeding. Larvae fall off after feeding; cases usually resolve spontaneously assuming no reinfestation. Head-shaking has been associated with infestation of *Trombicula* mites in a few instances. Significant problem in horses; widely distributed in Europe, North America, and occasionally in Australia and the Far East. Infected animals may be treated with organophosphate compounds; environmental control of heavily infested pastures with miticides may be indicated.

Tropicamide ◀€ *tro pi kē mīd, n.* acetylcholine blocking agent sometimes used in examination of eye; given as drops, acts to dilate pupil (mydriatic) so as to facilitate examination of back of eye. Note: it is important to assess pupillary light reflex prior to using mydriatic agents to examine the eye.
See Eye.

Trot ◀€ *trot, v./n.* two-beat gait of horse, faster than walk but slower than canter; each diagonal pair moves forward together, and alternately. Lameness evaluation is most commonly done at the trot.
See Gait.

Trypanosoma ◀€ *tri pa nō zō mē, n.* genus of unicellular parasitic protozoa. Adult stage is a single-celled organism with elongated shape, and usually a flagellum; lives in blood or lymphatics of animals. Larval stages usually live in insect host, usually spread by insect bite. Examples that affect horses include *T. equiperdum* (causes dourine, transmitted venereally); also *T. congolense, T. brucei, T. vivax, T. evansi,* which can cause intermittent fever, weight loss, swelling of legs, and cloudiness of cornea associated with diseases such as nagana.
See Dourine, Nagana.

Trypsin ◀€ *trip sin, n.* proteinase enzyme involved in digestion of proteins; acts to hydrolyse proteins into smaller peptides or amino acids, which is required for the uptake of protein in the food by the alimentary tract. Secreted as trypsinogen by pancreas and activated in small intestine by another enzyme (enterokinase).

TSH see Thyroid: T. stimulating hormone

Tube ◀€ *tūb, n.* hollow cylindrical conduit, used to hold or conduct substances (e.g. liquid paraffin).
Endotracheal t. see Endotracheal
Stomach t. see Nasogastric

Tuber ◀€ *tū bē, n.* an anatomical prominence, especially of a bone.
T. coxae ◀€ *tū bē / kok sē, n.* protruding part at front of pelvis, forms point of horse's hip. Important site of muscle attachment for hind limb. May be broken in fall or as result of very fast galloping in young racehorses; may not result in obvious lameness, but affected hip is typically dropped when compared to other hip. Surgical methods for treatment of hip fractures have not been developed in horses. Common site of collection of bone marrow or bone cells for grafting.
See Pelvis.

T. ischii ◄⁞ *tū bē / i shē, n.* (pins) protruding part at hindmost part of pelvis, in buttock region of horse near the joint of the hip (acetabulum); not visible in horses that are in good body condition. Important site of muscle attachment for hind limb. Uncommon site of pathology in horses; rare site of fracture.

T. sacrale ◄⁞ *tū bē / sāk rar lā, n.* paired medial prominence of the dorsal aspect of the ilium, close to the sacroiliac joint on the midline; situated opposite the tuber coxae. The two tuber sacrale can be easily palpated at the top of the horse's back. The tuber sacrale is normally watched closely during lameness examination for asymmetry of movement; tuber sacrale may be made more prominent owing to subluxation of sacroiliac joint (hunter's bump).
See Pelvis, Sacroiliac joint.

Tuberculosis ◄⁞ *tū ber kū lō sis, n.* disease caused by *Mycobacterium tuberculosis*, *M. bovis*, or *M. avium*. Very rare in horses. Typical clinical signs are related to the site of infection, but can include neck stiffness owing to vertebral osteomyelitis of bones of neck, with weight loss, pneumonia, and intermittent fever. Septic arthritis and granulomatous synovitis have been reported in one instance of *M. avium* infection, and bilateral ocular tuberculosis has been reported in another. Prognosis is grave in tuberculosis; successful treatment has not been reported; in general, the condition is recognized too late for treatment to be effective.

Tubular water dropwort ◄⁞ *tū bū lē / wor tē / drop wert, n.* (*Oenanthe fistulosa*) poisonous plant of Umbellifera family typically found in wet areas. Toxic component oenathin is less poisonous than hemlock water dropwort (*Oenanthe crocata*); classified as a vulnerable plant in UK, as numbers have been decreasing in the past decade.

Tumour ◄⁞ *tū mē, n.* (neoplasm, cancer, growth) growth or swelling caused by uncontrolled cell multiplication. May be classified according to site, tissue of origin (e.g. carcinomas arise from epithelial cells, sarcomas arise from connective tissue, and lymphoma is a tumour of lymphatic cells),

and whether benign or malignant. Benign tumours grow relatively slowly, do not invade into other tissues (that is, they are generally well circumscribed), and do not spread by metastasis to distant parts of the body. If they can be removed they do not usually recur. Malignant tumours grow relatively rapidly, may invade into other tissues locally, and may spread to other parts of the body by metastasis. Some tumours are more malignant than others; fortunately, malignant tumours in horses are rare, compared to other domestic mammalian species. Causes of tumours include ionizing and ultraviolet radiation (e.g. squamous cell carcinoma in pink-skinned horses), genetic predisposition (e.g. melanomas in grey horses), viruses (e.g. some cases of equine sarcoid); very often cause of tumour is unknown. Clinical signs of a tumour will vary depending on site, degree of malignancy, metastasis, etc. Treatment varies according to tumour type.
See individual tumours under separate entries, Metastasis, Radiation.

Tumour necrosis factor ◄⁞ *tū mē / nek rō sis / fak tē, n.* (TNF) a cytokine produced in various parts of the body. TNF is important in stimulating leukocytosis, fever, and necrosis (death) of some tissues, e.g. neoplastic cells. TNF has been described as the body's natural form of chemotherapy; TNF is also an inflammatory mediator, e.g. in osteoarthritis.
See Cytokine, Osteoarthritis.

Tumoural calcinosis see Calcinosis circumscripta

Tunica ◄⁞ *tū nik ē, n.* an enveloping or covering membrane or layer of body tissue.

> **T. albuginea** ◄⁞ *tū nik ē / al bū gin ē ē, n.* thick, tough, flexible membrane surrounding the corpus cavernosa of the penis, as well as the testicles.

> **T. intima** ◄⁞ *tū nik ē / in tē mē, n.* the innermost, or deepest, layer of a tubular blood vessel.

> **T. vaginalis** ◄⁞ *tū nik ē / vaj in ar lis, n.* the double layered pouch, which originates from the peritoneum, that covers each testis.

Turn-out syndrome ◀≀ *tern ŏt / sin drōm, n.* (adrenal exhaustion, hypoadrenocorticism) condition most commonly related to stopping long-term corticosteroid therapy; has been most commonly described in racing horses in the United States; in the UK horses in training cannot be administered corticosteroids. Regardless, the condition is poorly documented in horses and the dosage of corticosteroids required to produce the problem is unknown. Typical signs include a history of depression, inappetance, poor performance, weight loss, and poor hair coat. Adrenal gland typically atrophies from corticosteroid effects to decrease adrenocorticotrophic hormone (ACTH) secretion by pituitary gland. May also be related to stress associated with training. Diagnosis is confirmed by ACTH stimulation test. Treatment involves rest and supplementation with glucocorticoids, especially prednisolone; glucocorticoids are ultimately slowly withdrawn as adrenal function is restored.
See Adrenal gland, Adrenocorticotrophic hormone, Corticosteroid, Prednisolone.

Turner's syndrome see Ovarian

Twin ◀≀ *twin, n.* one of two foals or foetuses of same pregnancy. In horses, twins usually result from fertilization of two eggs from a double ovulation, rather than splitting of one egg to form identical twins. Appears to be more common in Thoroughbreds than in other breeds. Common cause of spontaneous abortion. If two embryos are in the same horn, one of the embryos has a 50–60% likelihood of reabsorbing or dissolving on its own by 40 days of pregnancy; spontaneous resorption is very uncommon when the embryos lie in separate horns. Of twin conceptions present after 40 days of pregnancy, about 80% will subsequently abort both foetuses, most often after the eighth month of pregnancy. Only approximately 10–15% of mares with twin pregnancies will deliver two live foals at term. With late-term abortion, mares can develop severe complications including birth-related trauma, illness, infection, laminitis, and decreased fertility for subsequent breeding. Twin pregnancy is apparently undesirable in horses. When twin foals are delivered, there is a high risk of losing both foals during the first two weeks of life. The combined birth weight of the twins equals the size of one normal, single foal, and the twins never catch up to normal weight and size. Twins can be recognized by rectal ultrasonography at approximately two weeks post-insemination. Management typically includes either terminating both pregnancies prior to 35 days (e.g. by prostaglandin injection) or by manual reduction of one of the twins prior to approximately 25 days gestation (approximately 90% success rate in delivering one healthy foal at term). Other methods of twin reduction include transvaginal ultrasound-guided aspiration (results are highly variable, depending on age of the gestation and the ability of the veterinarian) and transabdominal ultrasound-guided injection (approximately 30% success in producing normal, healthy foals). Craniocervical dislocation, i.e. dislocation of the first cervical vertebrae from the cranium, through a flank incision, has been successful at eliminating one twin at between days 65 and 110 of gestation. Mares which produce twins once are likely to produce twins again. Unfortunately, there is no good way to prevent or minimize twin pregnancies; early recognition and removal of one embryo is the best management option.
See Fertilization, Foetus, Pregnancy.

Twist ◀≀ *twist, n.* (volvulus, torsion) lay term for a kink, or a segment of intestine that has formed a spiral, resulting in signs of colic. Horses with colic are commonly walked so as to prevent them from lying down and 'twisting' their intestine; in fact, intestinal volvulus and torsion ('twists') are among the most painful colics, and the 'twist' precedes signs of colic pain.
See Colic, Torsion, Volvulus.

Twitch ◀ ≀ *twich, n.* **1)** short, uncontrolled jerky muscular motion, e.g. reflex movement of third eyelid. **2)** a device used for restraining horses by placing pressure on the upper lip. Several different types are available, including those consisting of a loop of rope or chain attached to a handle and twisted onto the lip, or small hinged devices that clamp onto the lip. While the exact mechanism of action is uncertain, various explanations have been advanced to explain how twitches work, including inducing high levels of endorphins and distraction due to a noxious stimulus.

Tying-up see Exertional rhabdomyolysis

Tympanic ◀ *tim pa̱ nik, adj.* drum-like or relating to a drum; associated with the eardrum.
See Ear.

> **T. bulla** ◀ *tim pa̱ nik / bū lē, n.* thin-walled, bony capsule within temporal bone which contains middle and inner ear.
> See Ear.

> **T. membrane** ◀ *tim pa̱ nik / mem brān, n.* ear drum; thin, translucent membrane which stretches across ear canal, forming division between outer and middle ear. Vibrates as sound waves pass down ear canal, vibrations are passed though auditory ossicles (tiny bones) to inner ear where they are converted to nerve impulses.
> See Ear.

Tympanitic ◀ *tim pē ni̱ tik, adj.* bell- or drum-like as result of being distended by air or other gas, e.g. caecum filled with gas in colic.

Tympany ◀ *tim pē nē, n.* distension of cavity with air or gas. Has been especially described as related to distension of the guttural pouch. Tympany of the large bowel is a cause of colic; gas-distended bowel may sometimes be auscultated or percussed in certain cases.

Tyzzer's disease ◀ *tī zerz / di zēz, n.* acute inflammation and necrosis of liver caused by Gram-negative bacterium, *Clostridium piliformis*. Infection caused by foal eating spores in contaminated soil or faecal matter; the disease appears to be prevalent in certain regions and farms, most likely as a result of pathogenic bacteria from the faeces of carrier mares contaminating soil and bedding. Most commonly seen in young foals, 1–6 weeks of age. May cause sudden death, or rapid onset of signs such as depression, high temperature, loss of appetite, with progression to recumbency, seizures, coma, death in 24–48 hours. Most commonly fatal; successful treatment with large doses of penicillin, and supportive care, has been described. Disease occurs sporadically and is not very contagious. (Ernest Tyzzer [1875–1965] described the disease in 1917.)

U

Uasin Gishu disease see Equine viral papular dermatitis

Udder ◀ฅ *u dẽ, n.* mammary organ (gland) of mare, between hind legs. Has two halves, each with a teat.
See Mammary gland.

Ulcer ◀ฅ *ul sẽ, n.* any eroded area of skin, mucous membrane or organ surface, caused by disintegration and loss of surface layer of cells. Ulcers may have physical or chemical causes, or be due to failure of blood supply or to infection. Ulcers may be described as to their location (e.g. right dorsal colon ulcer) or aetiology (e.g. decubitus ulcer). For example:
• Corneal u. – see Cornea
• Decubitus u. – an ulcer caused by arterial occlusion, typically from prolonged pressure, such as may be seen when a horse is in prolonged recumbency, especially seen in locations such as the point of the hip, shoulder, or elbow, where there is little underlying muscle.
• Gastric u. – see Equine gastric ulcer syndrome
• Peptic u. – ulceration of the mucous membrane of the oesophagus, stomach, or duodenum. Associated with increased acid levels.
• Perforating u. – an ulcer that penetrates the entire thickness of an organ, such as the wall of the stomach or intestine.
• Right dorsal colon u. – ulcer of the right dorsal colon; clinical signs typically include intermittent low-grade colic, weight loss, diarrhoea, hypoproteinaemia, and ventral oedema. Generally associated with non-steroidal anti-inflammatory drug (NSAID) toxicosis. Medical management (withdraw NSAID drugs, sucralfate, anti-ulcer drugs such as omeprazole or ranitidine) is successful if condition diagnosed prior to ulcer perforation.
See Inflammation, Non-steroidal anti-inflammatory drug.

Ulcerative ◀ฅ *ul sẽ rẽ tiv, adj.* pertaining to, or characterized by, the formation of ulcers.
See Ulcer.
U. colitis ◀ฅ *ul sẽ rẽ tiv / ko lī tis, n.* chronic inflammation of the colon that produces ulcers. Rarely diagnosed ante-mortem; clinical signs include weight loss and diarrhoea. Poor prognosis.
U. keratitis see Keratitis
U. lymphangitis ◀ฅ *ul sẽ rẽ tiv / lim fan jī tis, n.* a severe cellulitis, with draining ulcerative lesions and involving cutaneous lymph vessels of one or more limbs, most commonly caused by the bacterium *Corynebacterium pseudotuberculosis*, but also by many other bacteria; mixed infections have also been described. Infection thought to be caused by contamination of abrasions or wounds; insects, e.g. common fly (*Musca domestica*) can act as vectors; also associated with poor hygiene. Horse to horse transmission is possible, but uncommon. Environmental conditions which cause disease have not been determined. Legs develop fluid swelling and nodules which form into ulcers which abscess, ulcerate, and drain. Bacterial culture may help identify infective organism(s). Treatment is with broad spectrum antimicrobial therapy; exercise, bandaging, massage, hydrotherapy, and drainage of abscesses may be useful adjuncts to assist in fluid removal. The condition is rarely fatal; however, it can cause acute lameness, and, if not resolved, debilitation and disfigurement of the affected limb(s).
See Lymphatic.

Ulna ◀︎ _ul_ nē, n. bone of forearm, extends halfway down radius to which it is fused at lower end. Fusion prevents rotation of limb. A fully developed ulna is rarely seen in Shetland ponies, but is associated with congenital distal limb abnormalities; the ancestors of the modern horse also had complete ulnas. The proximal elbow is part of the elbow joint, together with radius and humerus. The ulna is most easily palpable at point of elbow (olecranon). The most common condition affecting the ulna is fracture, commonly following kick or fall. Clinical signs depend on extent of fracture and involvement of joint surfaces; signs include pain, lameness, swelling, horse stands with elbow lower than normal, crepitus. Surgical treatment may be required; some non-articular fractures heal uneventfully with conservative management.
See Elbow, Radius.

Ulnar ◀︎ _ul_ nē, adj. of the ulna.
See Ulna.

U. carpal bone ◀︎ _ul_ nē / kar pēl / bōn, n. the large carpal bone located laterally in the proximal row of carpal bones.
See Carpus.

U. nerve ◀︎ _ul_ nē / nerv, n. nerve which runs obliquely down the palmar aspect of front leg; innervates flexor muscles and sensory for skin of back of front leg.

U. nerve block ◀︎ _ul_ nē / nerv / blok, n. nerve block used in lameness evaluation. Block is performed approx. 10 cm proximal to the carpus, on the caudal aspect of the forearm. Block desensitizes skin of lateral limb distal to the fetlock, and at least partially blocks the structures of the carpus, as well as the proximal suspensory ligament.

U. neurectomy ◀︎ _ul_ nē / nŭr _ek_ tēm ē, n. transection of the ulnar nerve. Has been occasionally used in cases of intractable pain, e.g. in the treatment of accessory carpal bone fractures that have healed poorly. In such cases, it is best considered a salvage procedure, and such horses are unsafe for riding.
See Flexor, Nerve block.

Ultrasonography ◀︎ _ul_ trē sē _no_ grē fē, n. technique using high frequency sound waves (1–5 megahertz) to produce images of body structures; most useful for soft tissues. In horse ultrasonography finds wide application, including in diagnosis of heart problems (echocardiography); examination of tendons and ligaments of lower leg; examination of kidneys (using rectal probe); examination of the female reproductive tract to facilitate breeding, to evaluate pathological conditions, for pregnancy diagnosis (using rectal probe, can be used from day 12 of pregnancy); examination of the contents of the abdominal cavity, including the liver, spleen, bladder, and segments of bowel (e.g. in colic diagnosis); detection of umbilical abscesses in foal; detection of testicular abnormalities; and examination of the eye and associated structures.
See under separate headings.

Ultrasound ◀︎ _ul_ trē sőnd, n. very high frequency sound (1–5 megahertz) used in ultrasonography to produce image of soft tissues. Ultrasound images are produced by the following steps:

1. The generator (ultrasound machine) produces an electrical pulse and sends it to a transducer.
2. The transducer, or probe, changes the electrical pulse into a sound pulse and sends it into the body. This is done using a piezoelectric crystal, which expands and contracts from the electrical pulse, producing a sound wave.
3. The sound wave travels through the first body tissue until it hits an interface, which is where two different tissues, or areas of different composition, e.g. fluid in a tendon, are found next to each other.
4. At the interface, some of the sound wave will be reflected back (echo) and some will continue to travel through the next tissue.
5. The part that is reflected back, the echo, is picked up by the transducer and changed into an electrical pulse.
6. The electrical pulse is then sent to the computer/display.
7. Depending on the time it takes an electrical pulse to make the round trip into the body, and the intensity of the electrical pulse (which is related to the tissue or area that is encountered), a

computer determines where on the display screen to make a dot and what shade of grey, from light to dark, it should be.

8. The operator reads the information that appears on the screen.

See Ultrasonography.

Ultraviolet ◀︎ _ul trĕ vī ē lĕt, n./adj._ light waves (electromagnetic radiation) with wavelength shorter than violet light. Sunlight has an ultraviolet component; exposure to this can trigger development of some skin tumours, especially in pink-skinned horses, e.g. squamous cell carcinoma in unpigmented tissues such as the vulva or prepuce. Important in conversion of vitamin D to active form. Examination of skin with ultraviolet light may assist in the diagnosis of some fungal infections (Wood's lamp).

See Squamous, Wood's lamp.

Umbilical ◀︎ _um bi li kĕl, adj._ of, or related to, the umbilicus.

See Umbilicus.

U. abscess ◀︎ _um bi li kĕl / ab ses, n._ infection in remnant of umbilical cord. Typically causes firm, painful swelling of the umbilical remnant and surrounding body wall, with drainage from the umbilicus; many foals have fever. Infection may spread to other parts of body and cause conditions such as septicaemia, septic arthritis (joint ill), or pyelonephritis. Diagnosis by clinical signs; complete blood count may show increase in white blood cells; ultrasonography can help determine the extent of the problem. Treating the umbilical remnant with disinfectants (e.g. povidone–iodine) may help prevent the problem; however, the problem can occur even in foals that have been so treated.

See Arthritis, Pyelonephritis, Ultrasonography.

U. arteries ◀︎ _um bi li kĕl / ar ter iz, n._ paired arteries that carry deoxygenated blood from the foetus to the placenta in the umbilical cord. Trauma and infection can result in changes to the umbilical arteries; detected by ultrasound as part of umbilical abscess. May require surgical removal in such cases.

U. cord ◀︎ _um bi li kĕl / kord, n._ long flexible tube which connects foetus to placenta, contains three blood vessels (two arteries and a vein) in soft substance called Wharton's jelly. Allows for exchange of nutrients and oxygen between mare and foetus. Cord naturally breaks after birth, approx. 3 cm from foal's abdominal wall; stump shrivels away. Cord passes through opening in abdomen (umbilical ring); this ring normally closes in first week of foal's life. The umbilical cord can occasionally twist and reduce blood flow to the foetus, which may result in abortion; long umbilical cords increase the risk of abortions and stillbirths in horses (the length of the cord increases directly relative to the mare's age and the length of the non-pregnant uterine horn). The cord also may get caught round foal's leg or neck and cause dystocia.

See Abortion, Dystocia.

U. hernia see Hernia

U. tape ◀︎ _um bi li kĕl / tāp, n._ cotton tape, about 1 cm wide, with finished edges. Occasionally used to tie off an umbilicus in foals, or for purse-string suturing, such as used to hold replaced uterine prolapse.

See Uterine.

U. vein ◀︎ _um bi li kĕl / vān, n._ blood vessel that carries oxygenated blood from the placenta to the growing foetus. Trauma and infection can result in changes to the umbilical arteries; detected by ultrasound as part of umbilical abscess. May require surgical removal in such cases.

Umbilicus ◀︎ _um bi lī kĕs, n._ navel; point where umbilical cord entered abdomen of foetus.

Underrun heel see Heel

Unilateral ◀︎ _ū ni la tĕr ĕl, adj._ having to do with one side of the body, e.g. a unilateral nasal discharge occurs out of only one nostril.

Upper ◀︎ _up ē, adj._ being further up, literally or figuratively (e.g. upper eyelid or upper jaw); being cranial, oral, or rostral in position.

U. airway ◀︎ _up ē / ar wā, n._ the passages of the respiratory system that extend from the nostrils to the larynx.

See U. respiratory tract (below).

U. motor neuron ◄⁞ *up ē / mō tē / nŭr ōn, n.* motor nerve pathway that begins in the brain and ends at a peripheral motor neuron. Disease of, or damage to, upper motor neurons removes central control from the peripheral nerve.

U. respiratory tract ◄⁞ *up ē / re spē rē trē / trakt, n.* the part of the respiratory system that includes the nose, nasal passages, the nasopharynx, and the larynx; some anatomists also include the upper portions of the bronchial tree. Inflammation and infection of the upper respiratory tract is common in horses, causing signs of coughing, serous or mucoid nasal discharge, and pain or cough on manual compression of the larynx, pharynx and trachea.

U. urinary tract ◄⁞ *up ēr / ŭr in ē rē / trakt, n.* the kidneys and ureters. Infection in the upper urinary tract most commonly affects the kidneys (e.g. pyelonephritis). See Pyelonephritis.

Upward fixation (of patella) see Patella

Urachus ◄⁞ *ŭr rā kēs, n.* foetal structure which connects the bladder to the umbilicus. Formed as the allantoic stalk during foetal development. Usually closes at birth or shortly thereafter.

Patent u. ◄⁞ *pā tēnt / ŭr rā kēs, n.* failure of the urachus to close after birth. In affected foals, urine may be detected leaking from the umbilicus; however, this may be a normal finding in foals up to 5 to 7 days of age. Persistence of a patent urachus can result in localized infection, with swelling and pain on palpation; can progress to septicaemia if untreated. Ultrasonography can help determine the extent of the problem. Affected foals should be monitored; the condition is not a surgical emergency. Time and medical treatment should be considered before engaging in a surgical procedure. See Umbilical.

Uraemia ◄⁞ *ŭr rē mē ē, n.* abnormally high level of nitrogenous waste products in blood; more commonly referred to as azotaemia. Usually an indication of kidney disease; in common usage, the term refers to the syndrome of chronic renal failure. Due to inadequacy of glomerular filtration, in conditions such as acute tubular necrosis or chronic renal failure, indicators of kidney function determined in serum chemistry tests, especially the serum urea (usually measured as blood urea nitrogen, BUN) and creatinine, rise to high levels. However, other nitrogenous compounds present in small amounts may produce most of the toxic effects seen in uraemia; BUN and creatinine measurements do not correlate well with clinical signs of uraemia, which include depression and chronic diarrhoea. See BUN, Kidney, Urea.

Urea ◄⁞ *ŭr rē ē, n.* nitrogen-containing organic compound, formed in liver from amino acids and compounds of ammonia; the end-product of protein metabolism. Filtered from blood by kidneys and excreted in urine. Urea is often included in cattle feeds as a source of non-protein nitrogen that can be used by bacteria in the cow's rumen to produce protein; in horses, urea cannot be converted in this fashion, since most of the urea is absorbed by the stomach and small intestines and excreted before it can get to the bacteria in the horse's large intestine. See Kidney, Liver.

Ureter ◄⁞ *ŭr ri tē, n.* narrow tube which connects kidney to bladder; has wall made of fibrous tissue with some smooth muscle. See Bladder, Incontinent, Kidney.

Ectopic u. ◄⁞ *ek top ik / ŭr ri tē, n.* an abnormally located terminal portion of the ureter; uncommon. No sex or breed predilection. May be asymptomatic, or may cause urinary incontinence. Unilateral or bilateral cases may occur; some cases may also present with hydroureter (dilated fluid filled ureter) or hydronephrosis (dilated kidney). Ureterovesicular anastomosis may be indicated in unilateral cases that have no signs of ascending urinary tract infection or hydronephrosis, and in cases where the condition is bilateral. Surgery to remove the affected kidney has been successful in some cases with more extensive involvement of the upper urinary tract, e.g. hydronephrosis.

Urethra ◄⁞ *ŭr rē thrē, n.* tube which drains bladder; passes from neck of bladder to external orifice. In female horses, the urethra is short, and opens just posterior to the vulva, carrying only urine. In male horses, the urethra passes from bladder into pelvis and curves around the pelvis ventrally into penis; vas deferens joins ureter near pelvis, so in stallion it serves as a conduit for both urine and semen.

Urethral ◄⁞ *ŭr rē thrūl, adj.* of, or relating to, the urethra.

    U. calculus ◄⁞ *ŭr rē thrūl / kal kū lūs, n.* stone which has passed into, or formed in, urethra that causes urethral obstruction. Uncommon; almost exclusively in male horses. Signs include pain, straining to urinate, bloody urine dripping from end of penis and onto hind limbs. If untreated may result in bladder rupture or perforation of urethra. Rectal, ultrasound, and endoscopic examinations are usually diagnostic. Catheterization may allow opening of urinary tract; calculus may be removed with endoscopic basket, but surgical removal, usually via urethrotomy, is often necessary. Ulcers are common at the site of obstruction.
See Urethrotomy, Urolith

    U. extension ◄⁞ *ŭr rē thrūl / eks ten shĕn, n.* surgical technique for the treatment of urovagina (urine pooling) in mare. The surgery creates an extended tunnel from the opening of the urethra to the vestibule.

    U. fossa ◄⁞ *ŭr rē thrūl / fo sē, n.* small pouch in end of glans penis of stallion into which end of urethra projects as urethral process. U.f. is one of sites from which swabs are taken to detect venereal diseases, e.g. contagious equine metritis. Smegma can accumulate in the urethral fossa, causing surprisingly large concretions, and, rarely, urinary tract obstruction.
See Contagious equine metritis, Penis, Venereal.

    U. process ◄⁞ *ŭr rē thrūl / prō ses, n.* the free end of urethra in male horse; protrudes from end of penis in urethral fossa.
See Penis.

Urethritis ◄⁞ *ŭr ri thrī tis, n.* infection and/ or inflammation of urethra, may be result of trauma, or primary bacterial infection. Swelling may reduce flow of urine; bleeding may be seen, and can cause

bleeding into the semen (haemospermia) in breeding stallions. Treatment involves systemic antibiotics and rest from sexual activity in stallions; corticosteroid anti-inflammatory agents have occasionally been used. In rare cases, urethrostomy, with packing of the urethra with antibiotics and corticosteroids, may be required.

Urethrostomy ◄⁞ *ŭr ri thro stē me, n.* surgical operation in male horse whereby an artificial excretory opening is created in the urethra, usually in the perineal region (i.e. before urethra bends forward to enter penis). Has occasionally been performed to provide relief from chronic urethral obstruction, or in cases where distal penis is destroyed, e.g. from injury or neoplasia (e.g. squamous cell carcinoma), usually in conjunction with penile amputation.
See Urethra.

Urethrotomy ◄⁞ *ŭr ri thro tē mē, n.* incision into the urethra, usually in the perineal area at the level of the ischium. Ischial urethrotomy is sometimes performed in male horses to provide a portal for endoscopic examination, or access to the urethra and/or bladder for the treatment of uroliths (e.g. for manual manipulation and removal of stones), lavage, or endoscopic exam and associated surgeries. Ischial urethrotomies are typically allowed to heal by second intention.

Urinalysis ◄⁞ *ŭr ri na li sis, n.* laboratory analysis of urine sample; used in the diagnosis of various diseases, especially those of the urinary tract. Tests performed include urine specific gravity (normal 1.030–1.060), pH (normal 7.5–8.5), glucose, fluid analysis and cytology, looking for casts, bacteria, cells, especially red or white blood cells, but also neoplastic cells, protein, and colour.

Urinary ◄⁞ *ŭr ri nē rē, adj.* of urine, pertaining to urine.

    U. calculus see Urolith

    U. incontinence ◄⁞ *ŭr ri nē rē / in kon tin ēns, n.* the inability to hold urine in the bladder. Uncommon in horses; conditions causing urinary incontinence include urolithiasis,

cystic calculus, equine herpes virus neurological infections, and ectopic ureter.
See under various conditions.

U. tract ◄⁞ _ŭr_ ri _nē rē_ / _trakt, n._ the organs of the horse's body that produce and discharge urine; the kidneys, ureters, bladder, and urethra.

U. tract infections (UTI) ◄⁞ _ŭr_ ri _nē rē_ / _trakt_ / in _fek shēn, n._ infection of the urinary tract, most commonly with bacteria. UTIs are relatively uncommon in horses, but are more common in mares than in male horses, presumably because the mare's urinary tract is much shorter and much more vulnerable to contamination (e.g. from activities such as breeding).

Urinate ◄⁞ _ŭr_ ri _nāt, v._ (micturate) void or pass urine from bladder; urine, which is formed in the kidneys, is passed every few seconds through the ureters into the bladder, where it collects until voided. During the act of urination, the urine passes from the bladder to the outside via the urethra. The act of urination involves relaxation of muscular bladder sphincter and contraction of muscles in bladder wall.
See Bladder.

Urine ◄⁞ _ŭr_ rin, _n._ yellowish liquid, containing water and waste products such as urea (end product of protein metabolism) and electrolytes. Produced by kidneys and discharged from bladder via urethra. Horse normally produces 2–10 litres per day; production may vary greatly according to amount of water drunk, amount of work done, diet, temperature, etc. Exogenous substances, e.g. many drugs, are also eliminated by the kidney and excreted in urine.

U. pooling see Urovagina

U. scald ◄⁞ _ŭr_ rin / _skawld, n._ chemical irritation (dermatitis) of the perineal area (in females), and/or the hindlegs, by urine. Most commonly seen secondary to urinary incontinence, e.g. from paralysis due to equine herpes virus infection. Secondary infection of the skin (dermatitis) is relatively common. Petrolatum-based ointments applied to the affected area(s) may help provide some protection.

U. specific gravity ◄⁞ _ŭr_ rin / _spē sif_ ik / _gra_ vi _tē, n._ laboratory test that measures the concentration of particles in the urine. Requires clean urine sample. Specific gravity measures the kidney's ability to concentrate or dilute urine in relation to plasma. Water has a specific gravity of 1.000; urine is a solution of minerals, salts, and compounds dissolved in water, thus the specific gravity is greater than 1.000. The more concentrated the urine, the higher the urine specific gravity. Various substances, including glucose, protein, or dyes used in diagnostic tests, that are excreted into the urine will increase the specific gravity. If none of these abnormal substances are present in the urine, the kidney will produce concentrated urine with a high specific gravity for two primary reasons, 1) dehydration and 2) increased secretion of antidiuretic hormone (ADH), secondary to things such as trauma, stress, surgery, and secondary to the administration of some drugs. On the other hand, in conditions such as renal failure, the kidney cannot normally concentrate urine, and the urine specific gravity will be low.

Urogenital system ◄⁞ _ŭr_ rō _je_ ni _tēl_ / _sis tēm, n._ the organs of the urinary system and their associated genital structures. In mare includes kidneys, ureters, bladder, urethra, ovaries, uterus, cervix, vagina, vulva. In stallion includes kidneys, ureters, bladder, urethra, testes, scrotum, vas deferens, accessory sex glands, penis. Also called genitourinary system. Closely linked anatomically, so diseases or conditions affecting urinary organs can affect reproductive organs (and vice versa), e.g. in mares, poor genital conformation can lead to urovagina, which can then lead to infertility.
See under separate headings.

Urolith ◄⁞ _ŭr_ rō _lith, n._ (urinary calculus) hard crystalline structure which forms in urine, may form in kidney, ureter, and especially bladder (cystic calculus). In horse usually made up of calcium carbonate. If form in kidney or ureter, uroliths can cause renal obstruction with secondary kidney failure; signs include weight loss, anorexia, depression, ulcers in mouth. Cystic calculi may cause urine dribbling, straining to urinate, or protrusion of penis. Diagnosis involves blood

tests to determine kidney function, urinalysis, rectal palpation (can occasionally feel stones in bladder or ureters), ultrasonography, endoscopic examination of bladder (cystoscopy). Surgical removal may be curative, although stones can return; urinary acidification is commonly recommended (with uncertain effectiveness) to prevent or treat problem. If secondary kidney disease is end-stage, treatment is not rewarding.
See Kidney, Ultrasonography, Urinalysis.

Urolithiasis ◀┊ *ŭr rō li thī ā sis, n.* presence of uroliths in the urinary tract, i.e. bladder, kidneys, ureters, or urethra.
See Urolith.

> **Sabulous urolithiasis** ◀┊ *sa bū lēs / ŭr rō li thī ā sis, n.* accumulation of large amounts of crystalline material in the bladder. Usually a secondary problem from neurological problems that cause difficulty emptying bladder, e.g. equine herpes virus neurological disease. Affected horses typically have neurological signs, e.g. ataxia, hind limb weakness. Typically treated by bladder lavage with large amounts of polyionic fluid. Cystoscopy can help assess adequacy of flush. Prognosis is poor unless primary condition resolves.

Uroperitoneum ◀┊ *ŭr rō pe ri to nē ēm, n.* presence of urine in abdominal cavity. Most commonly caused by bladder rupture (e.g. from trauma, especially in male foals after parturition, or following difficult foaling); may also rarely be caused by congenital defects (e.g. ureteral abnormality) or damage to urachus. Uncommon in adult horses, but may be seen in male horses with urethral obstruction. Clinical signs include depression, poor appetite, distension of abdomen, fast heart rate and breathing; usually little or no urine passed normally. Diagnosis by analysis of peritoneal fluid (usually high creatinine relative to serum creatinine level); dye (e.g. fluorescein) placed in bladder may be recovered in peritoneal fluid. Affected animals can suffer from severe metabolic disturbances, characterized by increased potassium (hyperkalaemia), decreased sodium (hyponatraemia), decreased chloride (hypochloraemia) and presence of urea in the blood (azotaemia); correction of such abnormalities prior to surgical repair is critical.
See Bladder.

Urospermia ◀┊ *ŭr rō sper mē ē, n.* contamination of ejaculated semen with stallion's urine. Can be diagnosed by colour and appearance; laboratory tests for creatinine and urea nitrogen are diagnostic in less obvious cases. Cause is generally unknown; treatment is usually unrewarding, and the intermittent nature of the problem in some horses can make determining treatment success difficult. Collection following urination may help reduce or prevent contamination; the bladder can be emptied by catheterization prior to breeding, if necessary.

Urovagina ◀┊ *ŭr rō vē ji nē, n.* urine pooling in the vagina. Generally the result of abnormalities of perineal conformation. Can cause infertility. A variety of medical and surgical techniques are described to correct this problem, e.g. Caslick's operation.
See Caslick.

Urticaria ◀┊ *er ti că rē ē, n.* (hives; nettle rash) skin condition characterized by sudden development of oedematous, raised patches, most often on head, neck and chest area. Associated with allergy, e.g. to penicillin, vaccines, pollen, insect bites, bacterial infection, etc. Causes may be exogenous, e.g. contact dermatitis, or endogenous, and immune mediated, e.g. after ingestion or absorption of allergens; seasonal occurrence may be seen in some horses. Precise cause often not determined. May resolve spontaneously; administration of corticosteroid drugs generally provides relief within 12–24 hours. Antihistamines are commonly prescribed, but are of questionable value. Intradermal skin testing may be of some value in determining basis for allergies in some individuals.
See Allergy, Antihistamine, Corticosteroid.

Uterine ◀┊ *ū tē rīn, adj.* of, or relating to, the uterus.
See Uterus.

U. abscess ◄ *ū tē rīn / ab ses, n.* pus-filled swelling in uterine wall, rare, may occur following difficult foaling (dystocia) or uterine infection (metritis). Can be recognized by ultrasound. See Dystocia, Metritis.

U. adhesion ◄ *ū tē rīn / ad hē zhēn, n.* abnormal sheet or band of fibrous tissue which forms inside or outside uterus. Intrauterine adhesions join folds of the uterine lining (endometrium) and may occur following injury or inflammation of uterine lining, causing infertility or problems during foaling (dystocia). Diagnosis may be made by ultrasound, or hysteroscopy. Extrauterine adhesions may be seen following uterine compromise, e.g. uterine torsion, or secondary to inflammation in the abdominal cavity, e.g. peritonitis. Treatment of intrauterine adhesions via endoscopic surgery may be recommended; extrauterine adhesions generally cannot be treated until they are recognized at abdominal surgery. See Hysteroscopy, Peritonitis, Ultrasound.

U. artery ◄ *ū tē rīn / ar tē rē, n.* the paired arteries of the uterus; the primary blood supply to the uterus and the developing foetus. The uterine artery enlarges greatly during pregnancy. Rupture of the u. artery is an occasional complication of foaling, and can result in haematoma of the broad ligament, or death of the mare if haemorrhage is uncontrollable.

U. body ◄ *ū tē rīn / bo dē, n.* looking forward from the rear of the horse, the uterus is roughly shaped like the capital letter 'T'. The vertical line of the 'T' would represent the uterine body.

U. cyst see Cyst

U. fluid ◄ *ū tē rīn / flū id, n.* accumulation of liquid in the uterus. Volumes of fluid within the uterus lumen are evaluated by ultrasound; quality of the fluid is commonly graded from I to IV according to degree of echogenicity. The degree of echogenicity is correlated with amount of cellular debris and white blood cells in the fluid. Grade I fluid has large quantities of neutrophils; grade IV has very few neutrophils. Clinical determinations of the quality and quantity of uterine fluid have been used to assess the effectiveness of various therapeutic procedures in endometritis; management of excessive uterine fluid pre-breeding, via

uterine lavage or oxytocin administration, is commonly done to help improve reproductive efficiency.

U. horn ◄ *ū tē rīn / horn, n.* one of the pair of tubular extensions from the uterine body. Looking forward from the rear of the horse, the uterus is roughly shaped like the capital letter 'T'. The horizontal lines on either side of the vertical line of the 'T' (representing the uterine body) are the uterine horns. Normal site of foetal implantation.

U. laceration ◄ *ū tē rīn / la sē ā shēn, n.* tearing of the uterus, usually associated with dystocia, fetotomy, or uterine torsion. May be partial thickness, or complete (uterine rupture). Most partial thickness lacerations may be managed conservatively; uterine rupture may require more aggressive intervention. See U. rupture (below).

U. lavage ◄ *ū tē rīn / lav arzh, n.* washing out of the uterus, generally with balanced polyionic solutions (e.g. lactated Ringer's solution). Uterine lavage is a commonly performed technique in reproductive medicine that may be performed pre- or post-insemination, in an effort to remove excessive uterine fluid that may interfere with successful fertilization and implantation, post-foaling, to remove debris and haemorrhage from the postpartum uterus, or to assist in the management of pyometra.

U. prolapse ◄ *ū tē rīn / prō laps, n.* displacement of uterus from its normal position; uncommon in horses. Most commonly occurs within a few hours of foaling, but may occur after several days postpartum. A medical emergency; often fatal, as a result of complications such as peritonitis, uterine laceration, rupture of uterine artery, or systemic shock. Difficult foaling, abortion, or retention of placenta are significant risk factors. Pain and straining make management difficult; the prolapsed uterus should be protected, e.g. in plastic bag, and elevated to the level of the vulvar aperture to reduce tension on uterine vessels and oedema formation. Reduction of prolapsed uterus is relatively easy, when compared to cattle; tranquillizers or epidural anaesthesia may be necessary to facilitate replacement, and general anaesthesia may be required in some individuals. Uterine lavage, or distension with polyionic fluids, may help uterus return to normal position and prevent metritis; purse-string sutures in the vulva to retain the uterus may occasionally be required. See Dystocia.

U. rupture ◀ *ū tē rīn / rup tūr, n.* tear in wall of uterine body; various causes, including difficulty foaling (dystocia), hydrops amnion, foetal mutation, uterine torsion, foal putting foot through uterus at delivery, or possibly even violent movement of the foetus in utero. Clinical signs of uterine rupture can be vague and colic-like; some cases are asymptomatic. It is possible for the uterus to repair itself in some cases; other, more severe, cases are complicated by herniation of the viscera through the uterus. Abdominocentesis of affected mares will yield large quantities of serous fluid. Small tears may be managed with systemic antibiotics, non-steroidal anti-inflammatory drugs, fluid therapy, as necessary, and oxytocin (to promote uterine involution). Surgical repair may be necessary in larger tears, often via ventral midline incision. See Dystocia, U. torsion (below).

U. torsion ◀ *ū tē rīn / tor shēn, n.* rotation of the mare's uterus on its axis; an uncommon, but serious, complication of late gestation mares, generally occurring in the last 2 months of gestation. Most common sign is a mild to moderate colic, which usually responds to analgesics; the severity of clinical signs is related to the amount of torsion and the degree of vascular compromise. Rectal examination provides a definitive diagnosis; the direction of the rotation can often be determined by palpating the ovarian pedicle and uterine ligaments. The method of correction depends on stage of gestation and value of the animal. If the torsion occurs at foaling it will cause a dystocia; manual turning of the foetus through the cervix is often possible. It may

also be possible to roll the mare and correct the torsion (various techniques are described); however, such techniques can occasionally result in uterine rupture. Surgical techniques for correction include standing flank laparotomy and ventral midline approach under general anaesthesia. Caesarian section may be indicated in selected cases to save the foal. See Colic, Dystocia.

Uterus ◀ *ū tē rēs, n.* (womb) T-shaped, hollow, muscular organ in mare in which the fertilized ovum implants, and which then holds the developing foetus and embryo. Composed of uterine body with two uterine horns; each horn ends in oviduct. Body ends distally in narrow neck (cervix), which opens into vagina.

Uvea ◀ *ū vē ē, n.* pigmented, blood vessel-rich layer of eye, made up of iris, ciliary body and choroid. The uvea contains the majority of the eye's blood. See Eye.

Uveitis ◀ *ū vē ī tis, n.* inflammation of uvea. Causes include injury to any part of the eye (e.g. as may be seen secondary to corneal ulceration), parasitic infection, viral infection, or immune mediated. Usually affects one eye. Condition can be acute or chronic/recurrent (equine recurrent uveitis):

- Acute: signs include pain, poor vision, spasm of eyelid, lacrimation, dislike of bright light, swelling of eyelids, redness of eye, cloudy cornea, small pupil, etc.
- Chronic: signs include those of acute uveitis, but may also include blindness, cloudy cornea, pus in anterior chamber (hyphaema), fixed irregular pupil, cataract, lens luxation, small eyeball (phthisis bulbi), etc.

See Equine recurrent uveitis, Eye, Uvea.

V

V/Q ratio see Ventilation

V–Y plasty ◀ᴇ *vē–wī / plas tē, n.* cosmetic surgical technique whereby a 'V'-shaped incision is made, and closed as a 'Y.' Allows for relief of a small amount of tension on a wound edge, or in scar revision.

Vaccinate ◀ᴇ *vak si nāt, v.* to produce immunity by administering a vaccine, with the aim of preventing or combating infection. In horses, administration of vaccines is most commonly by deep intramuscular injection or intranasal administration.
See Immunity, Vaccine.

Vaccine ◀ᴇ *vak sēn, n.* antigenic preparation of one or more pathogens, either killed or weakened (i.e. altered in some way to render them relatively harmless), or of a portion of the pathogen's structure. When administered to the horse, either by the intramuscular or intranasal routes, a vaccine stimulates the horse's immune system to produce antibodies or cellular immunity against the antigens of the vaccine, thereby protecting the horse against the pathogen without causing disease. Upon exposure to the pathogen, vaccine-provoked antibody responses allow horses to neutralize infection more readily, and thereby prevent or attenuate disease. Several types of vaccines are available for use in horses:

- Inactivated vaccines – include bacterins, toxoids, and inactivated viral vaccines. These are the most common vaccines in current use in equine medicine. They are made up of microorganisms that have been inactivated using heat or chemicals, while still preserving their ability to provoke an immune response. Such vaccines are safe in almost every animal (they cannot cause disease) and stable in storage. However, they typically require multiple and regular boosters, and often need adjuvants to increase their immunogenicity. They may also be more likely to cause reactions than other vaccines; these vaccines are also not good at eliminating virus-infected cells, because they do not provoke a good cell-mediated immunity.

- Inactivated protein subunit vaccines – contain components of bacterial cell walls that induce protective immunity. These vaccines cannot cause disease; they have also been associated with fewer injection reactions than whole-organism inactivated products. Examples in equine medicine are tetanus toxoid vaccines and M-protein vaccines against *Streptococcus equi* (strangles) infection.

- Modified live viral and bacterial spore vaccines for intramuscular administration – vaccines that consist of attenuated (weakened) microorganisms that replicate in laboratory conditions; serial replications cause mutations in the microorganisms that prevent them from causing disease. These vaccines cause immune responses similar to those occurring with natural infections, but without causing disease. These vaccines do not require an adjuvant because they typically cause a strong immune response. Examples in equine medicine include vaccines against equine influenza and equine viral arteritis.

- Modified live viral and bacterial vaccines for intranasal administration – examples in equine medicine include the vaccine against *S. equi* (strangles) infection.

- Recombinant vectored vaccines – involve the use of viruses or bacteria that have been genetically engineered to act as carriers of foreign deoxyribonucleic acid (DNA), e.g. canarypox-vectored vaccines for the prevention of West Nile virus infection.
- Deoxyribonucleic acid (DNA) vaccines – involve inoculating naked DNA that is then taken up by cells. These cells then produce antigenic proteins, in the same fashion as occurs in natural infections. DNA vaccines stimulate both humoral and cell-mediated immunity. A DNA vaccine is licensed in horses for the prevention of West Nile virus infection.

Most vaccines are given as an initial course of two injections, 3–4 weeks apart, followed by boosters (timing will vary with different vaccines, and with potential exposure of the individual horse). Vaccines used in horses include:

- Equine herpes virus 1 and 4.
- Equine influenza.
- Tetanus.
- Rabies.
- Potomac horse fever.
- Equine encephalitis (Eastern, Western, Venezuelan).
- *S. equi* (strangles).

Some pathogens, especially viruses, can undergo antigenic shift or drift, by which their antigenic make-up changes; others have different variants that are antigenically distinct. This at least partially explains why vaccines may not give total protection against a strain of the virus; outbreaks of disease may occur even in vaccinated animals.
See Antibody, Antigen, Equine herpes virus, Equine influenza, Potomac horse fever, Strangles, Tetanus, Rabies.

Vagina ◀┊ *vē ji̱ nē*, n. (birth canal) the passage from vulva to cervix in mare, approximately 20 cm long. Muscular walls, with mucous membrane lining.

    Artificial v. ◀┊ *art if ish ūl / vē ji̱ nē*, n. device used for semen collection for purposes of semen evaluation and artificial insemination. Several types are available, but the general design is a hard outer cylinder containing a clean inner liner. The liner is normally filled with warm water at a specific temperature that mimics that of the mare, in order to encourage ejaculation as well as to maximize semen output (semen output is reduced beyond a narrow temperature range). The inner liner typically also contains a filter to separate the semen from the gel fraction.

Vaginal ◀┊ *ve ji̱ nūl, adj.* of, or pertaining to, a vagina; relating to or resembling a sheath.
See Vagina.

    V. bruising ◀┊ *vē ji̱ nūl / brū zing*, n. bleeding within vaginal walls during foaling. May be seen as dark areas of haemorrhage (ecchymoses) inside the vulvar lips or in vaginal walls; rarely, bruising may be severe enough to cause a blood-filled swelling (haematoma).
See Haematoma, Parturition.

    V. ring ◀┊ *vē ji̱ nūl / ring*, n. the reflection of the parietal peritoneum through the deep inguinal ring. Part of inguinal canal. The terms inguinal and scrotal hernia refer to passage of intestinal loops through the vaginal ring. Laparoscopic peritoneal flap hernioplasty has been recommended as a method of anatomically closing the vaginal ring to protect mares with a history of strangulated inguinal hernias against future herniation.
See Inguinal.

    V. sac see Tunica

Vaginitis ◀┊ *va ji ni̱ tis*, n. inflammation and/or infection of vagina or vestibule, often in association with infection and inflammation of the uterus (metritis). Commonly associated with pneumovagina; may be seen following foaling, especially following dystocia, or mating. Signs typically include vaginal discharge; can result in breeding difficulties. Specific diseases associated with vaginitis include coital exanthema (equine herpes virus 3) and dourine. Treatment may involve Caslick's procedure to correct pneumovagina; local or systemic antibiotic therapy may be indicated in certain infections.
See Caslick, Dourine, Equine herpes virus, Pneumovagina.

Vagus ◀┊ *vā gēs*, n. cranial nerve X. Long, efferent nerve of parasympathetic branch of autonomic nervous system. Arises from medulla of brain, passes down jugular furrow of neck, into chest, and continues through diaphragm into abdomen. Supplies pharynx, heart, oesophagus, bronchi, stomach, duodenum, liver. Essential for normal function of respiratory and gastrointestinal tracts. See Autonomic nervous system, Cranial nerve, Parasympathetic nervous system.

Valerian root ◀℥ *val ār ēēn / rŭt, n.* valerian products are made from the root of a tall, wispy plant, which is grown to decorate gardens but also grows wild in damp grasslands. Its umbrella-like heads top grooved, erect, and hollow stems. Its dark green leaves are pointed at the tip and hairy underneath. Small, sweet-smelling white, light purple, or pink flowers bloom in early summer. Valerian is native to the Americas, Asia, and Europe. The plant became particularly popular in Europe from the seventeenth century and has been used for insomnia, anxiety and restlessness. Its most well researched use is as a calming or tranquillizing agent to help people sleep. Products containing valerian root may show up in blood or urine tests and constitute 'forbidden substances' under the rules of many equestrian sporting organizations.

Valgus ◀℥ *val gēs, n.* bent outward, away from midline. Used to describe angular limb deformity in which lower limb is angled outwards from midline, most commonly noted at the carpus or fetlock in young foals; c.f. varus. See Carpus, Fetlock, Growth.

Valve ◀℥ *valv, n.* fold of tissue in a hollow organ or tubular structure which ensures that fluid flows only in one direction, e.g. in heart, vein, lymphatic vessels. See Heart, Lymphatic, Vein.

Valvular ◀℥ *val vū lē, adj.* relating to valves, or possessing valves. See Valve.

    V. disease ◀℥ *val vū lē / diz ēz, n.* disease of the heart valves. Post-mortem surveys indicate that vegetative and nodular diseases of equine heart valves are more common than are recognized clinically, affecting up to 25%

of horses. Common cause of heart murmur. The significance of valvular disease in individual horses may be difficult to determine; it may only mean that a small percentage of cardiac function is lost. V. disease is probably of more importance in racing horses than in more sedentary individuals.

V. endocarditis ◀℥ *val vū lē / en dō kar dī tis, n.* (valvulitis) inflammation of heart valve. Typically associated with bacterial infection. Most commonly affects horses less than 3 years of age, although any age or breed can be affected. Vegetative lesions may develop on a valve and make it unable to close completely, resulting in murmur and retrograde flow (some blood flows back the wrong way). Most frequent signs are continuous or intermittent fever, rapid breathing (tachypnoea), rapid heart rate (tachycardia), and cardiac murmur, generally harsh and loud. Complete blood count may show elevations in leukocyte count or fibrinogen. Diagnosis may be confirmed by ultrasound examination of the heart and heart valves. Blood culture may occasionally help identify causative organism(s). Treatment is with appropriate antibiotics, typically for weeks. Prognosis is guarded. Lesions of the mitral or aortic valve typically carry a grave prognosis because of permanent valvular damage; the high pressures that pass through these damaged valves can lead to volume overload and congestive heart failure, even if the endocarditis resolves. Dislodgement of vegetative lesions can result in embolism. Clinical condition may be monitored by resolution of clinical signs, improvements in complete blood cell count parameters, and return to normal of the heart structures as seen on ultrasound. See Embolism, Heart.

V. prolapse ◀℥ *val vū lē / prō laps, n.* drooping down or abnormal bulging of a valve's cusps backward during the contraction of the heart, e.g. of the mitral valve into the atrium. Typically recognized on echocardiography, especially affecting aortic valve or left atrioventricular (mitral) valve; prolapse of the mitral valve is suspected to be the most common cause of mid-systolic murmurs in horses. May not cause significant problems of regurgitation; more severe cases, where valvular prolapse occurs secondary to rupture of the chordae tendinae, may be

accompanied by respiratory distress and severe heart murmurs.
See Heart.

Valvulitis see Valvular

Varicocele ◀︎ *va rik ō sēl, n.* an abnormally distended pampiniform plexus of the testis; disturbs the normal exchange of heat between testicular artery and vein; causes abnormalities in sperm formation in humans and rams, but horses with varicoceles have been shown to have normal ejaculations. Usually occur unilaterally, and are not painful. Treatment generally not required.

Varicose ◀︎ *va rik ōs, adj.* abnormally swollen or knotted; term applied especially to veins. Vaginal varicose veins are not uncommon in mares, and may rupture in late-term pregnancy, resulting in bleeding from the vulvar lips.
See Vagina, Vulva.

Varus ◀︎ *vă rēs, n.* bent inward, towards midline. Used to describe angular limb deformity in which lower limb is angled inwards from midline, most commonly noted at the carpus or fetlock in young foals, c.f. valgus.
See Fetlock, Growth.

Vascular ◀︎ *vas kū lē, adj.* pertaining to blood vessels, or describing tissue that is well supplied with blood.
See Blood.
    V. resistance ◀︎ *vas kū lē / rēz is tinz, n.* term that is used to define the force opposing the flow of blood that must be overcome to push blood through the circulatory system. Vasoconstriction increases vascular resistance.
See Blood.

Vasculitis ◀︎ *vas kū lī tis, n.* inflammation of blood vessel(s). Inflammation of blood vessel walls causes them to become permeable, allowing fluid to leave vessel; causes oedema. May be caused by some viruses, e.g. equine herpes virus 1, equine viral arteritis, or as an immune-mediated phenomenon subsequent to bacterial infections, e.g. *S. equi* (purpura haemorrhagica).

Treatment of vasculitis may not be necessary in mild cases; more severe cases may require treatments such as compression bandaging, exercise, and corticosteroid therapy to combat vascular inflammation.
See Equine herpes virus: EVH-1, Equine viral arteritis, Oedema, Purpura haemorrhagica, *Streptococcus*.

Vas deferens ◀︎ *vas / de fē renz, n.* duct, small tube, which carries spermatozoa from each testis to urethra.
See Ductus, Sperm, Testes.

Vasectomy ◀︎ *va sek tē mē, n.* operation in which vas deferens are cut, and a small portion of them removed, so that horse is sterile (as sperm can no longer travel to urethra). Horse still has normal male hormones. Operation may be performed on colt to produce teaser stallion, which can be used to assess whether mare is ready to mate with stallion (i.e. is in oestrus). However, problems with safety and spread of venereal disease when a vasectomized animal is used for teasing limit its use. Has also been used for control of feral horse populations.
See Breeding, Oestrus.

Vasoconstriction ◀︎ *vā zō kon strik shēn, n.* constriction or narrowing of blood vessels; may lead to decrease in blood flow to tissue. May be caused by activity of sympathetic nervous system or by exogenous substances, e.g. epinephrine, ergot alkaloids.
See Epinephrine, Ergot, Sympathetic nervous system.

Vasoconstrictor ◀︎ *vā zō kon strik tē, n.* substance which causes constriction of blood vessels, e.g. epinephrine, ergot alkaloids.
See Epinephrine, Ergot, Sympathetic nervous system.

Vasodilation ◀︎ *vā zō dī lā shēn, n.* (vasodilatation) widening of, or relaxation of, smooth muscular walls in blood vessels; may lead to an increase in blood flow to tissue. May be generalized or localized, in response to various chemical agents (e.g. alpha blockers such as yohimbine), or during the process of inflammation, from

inflammatory mediators such as histamine.
See Histamine, Inflammation, Yohimbine.

Vasodilator ◀┊ *vā zō dī lā tē, n.* substance which causes dilation of blood vessels, e.g. histamine, yohimbine.
See Histamine, Inflammation, Yohimbine.

Vasomotor ◀┊ *vā zō mō tē, n.* relating to the nerves and muscles that cause the blood vessels to constrict or dilate.

Vasopressin see Antidiuretic hormone

Vector ◀┊ *vek tē, n.* a live carrier (usually arthropod, e.g. mosquito or tick) which spreads an infective agent from one host to another. Examples of vectors which transmit disease to horses include ticks which spread babesiosis, *Culicoides* midges which spread African horse sickness, mosquitoes which spread equine infectious anaemia or West Nile virus. Two groups of vectors, which spread disease in different ways:

- Biological v. – vector, usually an arthropod, in which infecting organism multiplies before it is passed to another host; essential to the normal development of the pathogenic organism.
- Mechanical v. – vector which transmits a pathogen to a susceptible individual but which is not part of the pathogen's life cycle, and is not necessary for the development of the pathogen.

See African horse sickness, Babesiosis, Equine infectious anaemia, West Nile virus.

Vein ◀┊ *vān, n.* blood vessel which carries blood towards the heart; all veins except the pulmonary vein carry deoxygenated

TABLE OF SOME MAJOR VEINS OF THE HORSE

Vein	Tissues from which vein transports blood	Notes
Cardiac (Coronary)	Heart	Several; most open into coronary sinus, which itself opens into right atrium; a few small coronary veins open directly into the right artrium, and others into the left atrium and ventricles.
Facial	Head and Face	Prominent vein of face which crosses the ventral border of the mandible, and ascends across the face.
Jugular	Head	Prominent bifurcation at the angle of the mandible; runs in jugular furrow either side of neck; primary site for intravenous injection and catheter placement.
Lateral Thoracic	Lateral chest wall	Can be used for IV catheter placement.
Median	Forelimb	Palpable on medial forearm.
Portal	Stomach, Intestines, Spleen	Carries blood to liver; blood contains various products of digestion and numerous white blood cells.
Hepatic	Liver	Opens into posterior vena cava.
Pulmonary	Lungs	Usually 7–8 in number in horse; open into right atrium. Take oxygenated blood from lungs to left side of heart; the only veins that carry oxygenated blood.
Vena Cava, Anterior	Head, Neck, Forelimbs, Thorax	
Vena Cava, Posterior	Abdomen, Hind Limbs	Lies posterior to the peritoneal cavity; parallels aorta in abdomen; passes through diaphragm via caval fossa.

blood. Generally, veins carry blood at low pressure, thus, they have thinner walls than do arteries, with outer fibrous layer, middle muscular and elastic layer and inner elastic membrane with flattened epithelial cells. Flow through veins is typically controlled by valves to prevent retrograde blood flow. Veins often lie parallel to corresponding artery (which takes blood from heart to tissues). See table of major veins.
See Blood, Circulation.

Vena cava ◀┊ _vē nē_ / _kā vē_, _n._ one of two large veins, open into right side of heart, returning deoxygenated blood from tissues.
- Anterior v.c. – the anterior (or cranial) vena cava brings blood from the head region, front legs, and upper chest to the heart.
- Posterior v.c. – the posterior (or caudal) vena cava carries blood from the areas of the abdomen and hind legs to the heart.
See Vein.

Venereal ◀┊ _ve né rē ūl_, _adj._ pertaining to, relating to, or transmitted by sexual contact. Examples of equine venereal diseases include equine herpes virus 3, contagious equine metritis, equine viral arteritis, and bacterial infections by agents such as _Klebsiella pneumoniae_ or _Pseudomonas aeruginosa_. Control of venereal diseases depends on identification of infected animals by techniques such as identification of pathogens in swabs of urethra, urethral fossa, penile sheath or pre-ejaculatory fluid of stallion, or serology; removal of infected animals from breeding programmes, treating infected animals where possible, and, in selected cases, vaccination. Animals previously shown to have venereal diseases should be shown to be free of infective organisms prior to being used for breeding.
See Contagious equine metritis, Equine herpes virus: EHV-3, Equine viral arteritis, _Klebsiella_ spp., _Pseudomonas_.

Venezuelan equine encephalitis ◀┊ _ve ni zwā lēn_ / _e kwin_ / _en ke fē lī tis_, _n._ (VEE) infection of brain and other nervous tissue by _Alphavirus_ (same virus genus that causes Eastern and Western equine encephalitis); one of the most important veterinary and human pathogens of Central and South America, and Mexico. Has made occasional incursions into United States, but not endemic. Transmission cycle normally centres around rats and mosquitoes (_Culex cedecci_ is thought to be the most important vector in its spread). In epizootics, virus spreads to birds, where virus amplifies. Virus also replicates well in infected horses, which serve as a reservoir of infection (unlike other alphavirus infections of horses); several species of mosquitoes from 11 genera have been implicated in epidemic outbreaks of the disease; ticks may also be able to transmit virus. Virus is very neuroinvasive; young animals are especially susceptible. First indication of infection is fever; fever may resolve by the time that neurological signs become apparent. Neurological signs are caused by inflammation of the brain; signs include profound depression (leading to the common name 'sleeping sickness'), incoordination, head pressing, blindness, irregular gait, circling, and leaning against walls, or standing with hind legs crossed. No specific treatment. Horses affected with VEE are less likely to die than those affected with Eastern equine encephalitis; terminally diseased horses become recumbent, comatose, and may also seizure. Virus is inactivated by common disinfectants; mosquito control is important to minimize spread of disease. Vaccine is available but lack of sustained and widespread vaccination programmes in endemic areas perpetuates the disease.
See Eastern equine encephalitis, Western equine encephalitis.

Venogram ◀┊ _ven ō gram_, _n._ contrast radiographic technique used by some for visualization of the venous circulation in horses affected with laminitis. The utility of procedure is undocumented.
See Laminitis, Radiography.

Venom ◄ᵉ *ven ēm, n.* a poison, especially one secreted by an animal such as a snake or arthropod. Venoms are complex mixtures that include enzymes, lipids, amino acids, and proteins. Crotalid venom causes severe tissue reactions in horses that are bitten by such snakes (e.g. rattlesnakes).

Venous ◄ᵉ *vē nēs, adj.* full of, characterized by, or relating to veins. See Vein.

V. return ◄ᵉ *vē nēs / ri tern, n.* the flow of blood back to the heart. In normal conditions, the venous return equals the cardiac output.

V. thrombosis ◄ᵉ *vē nēs / throm bō sis, n.* thrombus formation in a vein. Serious problem in horses with septicaemia, or may also occur secondary to prolonged intravenous catheterization.
See Septicaemia, Thrombus, Vein.

Ventilation ◄ᵉ *ven ti lā shēn, n.* the process by which oxygen and carbon dioxide are exchanged between the lungs and the air; also refers to the use of a machine (a ventilator) to carry out this process in a horse that cannot breathe on its own, e.g. during general anaesthesia, by means of endotracheal tube and rebreathing bag of anaesthetic machine. Also, the flow of air throughout a building, e.g. stables; adequate ventilation is important to help maintain health of the horse's respiratory tract.
See Anaesthetic.

V.–perfusion imbalance ◄ᵉ *ven ti lā shēn-per fū shēn / im bal ēns, n.* a mismatch between ventilation of the lungs and blood perfusion. Occurs in various disease states, especially in neonatal foals with compromised lung function (e.g. as seen in pneumonia); typically results in hypoxaemia.

V. perfusion ratio ◄ᵉ *ven ti lā shēn-per fū shēn / rā shē ō, n.* (V/Q ratio) the ratio between ventilation of the lungs (V) and perfusion of blood (Q). The ratio is an indication of the adequacy of gas exchange in the lung
See Anaesthetic, Pneumonia.

Ventral ◄ᵉ *ven trŭl, adj.* underside of body or part of body; towards the belly. Opposite: dorsal.

V. hernia see Hernia

Ventricle ◄ᵉ *ven tri kēl, n.* a cavity of a body part or organ, especially of the heart or brain. Right ventricle of the heart pumps blood into pulmonary arteries; the left ventricle, the larger of the two, pumps blood into aorta, to be distributed to the body. Brain has four fluid-filled ventricles; ventricles also occur in the larynx.
See Brain, Heart.

Ventricular ◄ᵉ *ven tri kū lē, adj.* of, or relating to, the ventricles, especially of ventricles of the heart.
See Heart.

V. fibrillation ◄ᵉ *ven tri kū lē / fi bri lā shēn, n.* a condition in which the ventricles contract in rapid and unsynchronized rhythms, and thus cannot pump blood into the body. Generally a terminal state of heart, and not normally seen clinically; no heart sounds, no pulse, and electrocardiograph shows chaotic movements of trace line owing to uncoordinated contraction of individual fibrils. Treatment is usually impossible; depolarizers do not work on the large body of the horse, and injections of cardiac stimulants such as epinephrine do not correct the problem.
See Electrocardiography, Heart.

Premature v. contraction ◄ᵉ *pre mē tŭr / ven tri kū lē / kēn trakt shēn, n.* (PVC) a type of irregular heart beat in which the ventricle contracts prior to its normal time. Can occur normally as an isolated incident, especially in horses that are recovering from exercise; may also be associated with an irritable area of the ventricle, as may be seen with disease of heart muscle. Normal rhythm is interrupted by a premature beat, followed by a compensatory pause, and resumption of normal rhythm. The heart sounds with the premature beat are generally decreased; the compensatory beat is usually loud. Electrocardiographs show odd-shaped QRS complexes. Four or more concurrent PVCs are considered ventricular tachycardia.
See Electrocardiography, Heart, QRS complex, V. tachycardia (below).

V. septal defect ◄ᵉ *ven tri kū lē / sep tēl / dē fekt, n.* (VSD) a defect in the wall separating the left and right sides of the heart (the interventricular septum); allows blood to flow from left ventricle to right. The defect is

usually found at the base of the interventricular septum, just below the aortic root. The most common congenital cardiac defect of horses. The clinical signs seen in animals with a VSD depend on the size of the defect, and the effect of the defect on haemodynamics. Large defects will result in volume overload of the ventricles and can cause congestive heart failure, with signs of increased and difficult respiration (tachypnoea and dyspnoea) from pulmonary oedema, with or without pneumonia. Smaller defects may not be seen until animals turned out to pasture; these foals may show exercise intolerance compared to their pasture mates. Murmurs from VSDs may be detected in foals as an incidental finding during physical examination. Horses with very small defects may seem quite normal, and only show exercise intolerance at the start of an athletic career; horses with small VSDs that do not perform strenuous exercise may not be clinically affected. VSDs may also occur concurrently with more severe cardiac defects such as tetralogy of Fallot. No specific treatment is available; successful surgical treatment has not been reported in horses.
See Echocardiography, Heart, Tetralogy of Fallot.

V. tachycardia ◀€ *ven tri kū lē / ta kē kar dē ē, n.* abnormally rapid heart rhythm that originates from a ventricle; may be paroxysmal or sustained. Has been reported as a complication of systemic diseases, e.g. babesiosis; more commonly, v. tachycardia is caused by disease of heart muscle, e.g. congestive heart failure or myocardial fibrosis; in such cases, the ventricles contract independently of sinus node impulses. Auscultation of heart will reveal a rapid heart rhythm (greater than 60 beats per minute); peripheral pulse may be weak or variable. Diagnosis confirmed by electrocardiography. Treatment is directed at reversing the underlying cause of disease, if possible. Has been reported in horses recovering from colic surgery; no medication may be required in such horses. Antiarrhythmic drugs, e.g. quinidine, may be required in some cases, especially those with primary cardiac disease. The prognosis is likely to be poor unless the underlying disease can be treated; when v. tachycardia occurs because of a primary cardiac condition, it usually indicates severe disease.
See Electrocardiography, Heart.

Ventriculectomy ◀€ *ven tri kū lek tēm ē, n.* surgical removal of the mucous membrane lining of the laryngeal ventricle. May be performed during the surgical treatment of laryngeal hemiplegia, although generally not as the sole procedure.
See Laryngeal.

Ventriculocordectomy ◀€ *ven tri kū lō kor dek tēm ē, n.* surgical removal of the mucous membrane lining of the laryngeal ventricle and the vocal fold (vocal cord). Transendoscopic, laser-assisted ventriculocordectomy in the standing horse has been reported as a successful treatment for left laryngeal hemiplegia in a group of horses.
See Laryngeal.

Venule ◀€ *ve nūl, n.* a small vein, especially any vein that connects larger veins to capillaries.
See Vein, Capillary.

Vermicide ◀€ *ver mi sīd, n.* chemical substance which kills intestinal worms; anthelmintic.
See Anthelmintic.

Verminous ◀€ *ver mi nēs, adj.* of, related to, or caused by, vermin (various species regarded as pests or nuisances, especially those associated with diseases. In horses, used especially to describe internal parasitism.

V. aneurysm ◀€ *ver mi nēs / a nŭr rizm, n.* sac formed by pathological dilation of wall of artery supplying intestines, e.g. the cranial mesenteric artery. Occasionally seen in association with v. arteritis, on post-mortem examination.
See Aneurysm, V. arteritis (below).

V. arteritis ◀€ *ver mi nēs / ar tē rī tis, n.* inflammation of arteries caused by migration of *Strongylus vulgaris* larvae. Arteries supplying intestines, e.g. cranial mesenteric artery, may be affected; blood supply to intestines can be affected and result in signs of colic.
See *Strongylus* spp.

Vertebra ◀ ⟨ _ver_ ti brē, _n._ an individual bone of the spinal column. Cylindrical body with a hole in the middle, which forms protective cover for spinal cord. On the mid-dorsal line, spinous processes arise from midline of arch, reaching their maximum height at the 4th or 5th thoracic vertebra. These processes incline caudally until about the 16th thoracic vertebra (the anticlinal, or diaphragmatic, vertebra). On either side of the spinous processes is a groove in which lies the deep spinal musculature, formed by the vertebra and the transverse processes, which protrude on either side like wings. Articular and mammillary processes articulate with the vertebrae in front and behind. There are five types of vertebrae in the horse:

1. Cervical vertebrae – normally 7 in number. The first cervical vertebra is called the atlas. The second cervical vertebra is called the axis.
2. Thoracic vertebrae – normally 18 in number, although some Arabian horses may have only 17 thoracic vertebrae; Przewalski's horses may have as many as 19 thoracic vertebrae.
3. Lumbar vertebrae, normally 6 in number, although some Arabian horses may have only 5 lumbar vertebrae.
4. Sacral vertebrae – normally 5 in number; these vertebrae are fused to form the sacrum.
5. Coccygeal vertebrae – the vertebrae of the tail, normally 15–21 in number.

See Spinal.

Vertebral ◀ ⟨ _ver_ ti brūl, _adj._ of, or relating to, the vertebrae or spinal column.

V. column ◀ ⟨ _ver_ ti brūl / _ko_ lēm, _n._ backbone, spine; the flexible supporting column of vertebrae separated by discs and bound together by ligaments. Made up of cervical, thoracic, lumbar, sacral, and coccygeal vertebrae. Each vertebra separated from neighbours by cartilaginous disc. Provides bony cover for spinal cord and provides muscle attachments over length of body. Viewed from the side, the v. column appears as a series of curves.

See Intervertebral, Vertebra.

V. formula ◀ ⟨ _ver_ ti brūl / _form_ ū lē, _n._ the normal number of vertebrae in a horse (or any animal). The vertebral formula in most horses is $C_7T_{18}L_6S_5C_{15-21}$.

V. fusion ◀ ⟨ _ver_ ti brūl / _fū_ zhēn, _n._ surgical technique for the treatment of cervical vertebral stenotic myelopathy.

See Cervical vertebral stenotic myelopathy.

V. stenosis see Cervical vertebral stenotic myelopathy

Vesicle ◀ ⟨ _ve_ si kēl, _n._ small fluid-filled elevation of skin or mucous membrane, e.g. in mouth; small, membranous fluid-filled pouch, e.g. seminal vesicle.

Vesicovaginal reflux (urine pooling) see Urovagina

Vesicular ◀ ⟨ _ve si kū lē, adj._ characterized by the formation of small, fluid-filled elevations of the skin or mucous membranes (vesicles).

Vesicular stomatitis ◀ ⟨ _ve si kū lē / stō mē ti_ tis, _n._ viral disease of horses, pigs and cattle; in pigs and cattle may be confused with foot and mouth disease (which does not affect horses). Caused by two distinct serotypes of the genus *Vesiculovirus* (Indiana and New Jersey), of the family Rhabdovirus. The disease was first reported in the United States in 1916. The primary method of transmission is via arthropod insects; however, the life cycle of the virus, and the natural host reservoir, are still unknown. Occasional outbreaks have affected horses in the southwestern United States, beginning in the late spring, and continuing through late autumn, in association with increased numbers of arthropods. The risk of contracting the disease is less when animals have access to shelter, as opposed to only being at pasture. The virus attaches to epithelial cells; following an incubation period of 3–7 days, clinical signs appear. Typical signs are of raised, whitened vesicles, sometimes filled with fluid. Vesicles rupture and leave large ulcerations and erosions, resulting in difficulty eating. Crusts or scabs may also appear on the muzzle, ventral abdomen, coronary band, prepuce, and udder. Lesions must be differentiated from sunburn, trauma, other viral infections (e.g. equine viral arteritis), cantharidin toxicosis, and autoimmune conditions such as

pemphigus foliaceous. Diagnosis is by one of three methods: 1) antibody detection through serological tests, 2) virus isolation, or 3) detection of viral genetic material by polymerase chain reaction testing (PCR). The disease typically has a short course and is self-limiting; no specific treatment is available. Endemic in South and Central America, Mexico, and in one area of southwestern USA. No vaccine is currently available; affected individuals should be isolated, and infected premises quarantined, until the disease resolves.
See Cantharidin, Equine viral arteritis, Pemphigus foliaceous.

Vessel ◀ː _ve_ _sĕl_, *n.* tube through which blood or other bodily fluid flows, e.g. blood vessel, lymphatic vessel.
See Blood, Lymphatic.

Vestibular apparatus ◀ː _ves_ _ti_ _bū_ _lĕr_ / *a* _pē_ _rā_ _tĕs_, *n.* the functional apparatus of the inner ear; associated with balance and proprioception (positioning of limbs and head). The vestibular apparatus is made up of the saccule, utricle and semicircular canals. Receptors in inner ear transmit information about position and balance to brain (vestibular nuclei and cerebellum).
See Ear, Proprioception.

Vestibular disease ◀ː _ves_ _ti_ _bū_ _lĕ_ / *di* _zēz_, *n.* any condition in which there is damage to vestibular apparatus, causing lack of balance. May be unilateral or bilateral; can be associated with inflammation of inner ear or injury to head; the primary cause is temporohyoid osteopathy, which may lead to pathological fracture of the petrous temporal bone secondary to fusion of the temporohyoid joint. Signs include circling, unsteady walk, leaning, head tilt, nystagmus (flickering of eyes), inability to walk straight. Acute onset vestibular disease is relatively uncommon in horses. Diagnosis is by clinical signs; endoscopy of guttural pouches and radiography may demonstrate fracture or osteopathy. Medical treatment involves antibiotic therapy and non-steroidal anti-inflammatory drugs; surgical options include partial stylohyoidectomy. The prognosis for full return to function is fairly good in most

cases of vestibular disease, although cranial nerve deficits, e.g. facial paralysis, may persist. Still, horses that survive their initial episodes remain at risk for subsequent fractures because of irreversible bony changes.
See Paralysis, Temporohyoid osteoarthropathy.

Vestibule ◀ː _ves_ _li_ _būl_, *n.* any body space or cavity, especially occurring at entrance to another structure or organ, e.g. vaginal vestibule.

Vestibulocochlear nerve ◀ː _ves_ _ti_ _bū_ _lō_ _kok_ _lē_ _ē_ / *nerv,* *n.* cranial nerve VIII. Two branches: vestibular branch supplies vestibular apparatus (concerned with balance); cochlear branch (acoustic or auditory nerve) supplies cochlea (concerned with hearing). Nerve may be damaged from pathological fracture secondary to temporohyoid osteopathy; damage to nerve may cause vestibular disease.
See Cranial nerve, Ear, Temporohyoid osteoarthropathy, Vestibular disease.

Vetch see Hairy vetch

Veterinary ◀ː _vet_ _rin_ _rē_, *adj.* relating to diseases of animals, and their treatments.

Viborg's triangle ◀ː _vī_ _borgz_ / _trī_ *ang* _gĕl_, *n.* area of the horse's upper neck through which the guttural pouch may be approached for surgical intervention. Bounded rostrally by the vertical border of mandible, dorsally by the tendinous insertion of sternomandibularis muscle, and ventrally by the linguofacial vein.

Vice ◀ː _vīs,_ *n.* term sometimes used to describe behaviours in horses that are considered abnormal; controversial, as the term 'vice' implies immorality on the part of the horse. Often related to poor management or boredom. Conditions so-named include crib-biting, wind-sucking, weaving, wood-chewing, kicking, shying. Detrimental affects of such behaviours on the health of the horse may be difficult to document.
See under separate headings, Soundness.

Videoendoscopy ◀ː _vid_ _ē_ _ō_ *en* _do_ _skēp_ _ē,_ *n.* endoscopy that is performed using a video camera located in the tip of the endoscope. Technique used to evaluate airway function in horse moving on treadmill; some surgical procedures of the upper airway can be performed using videoendoscopy. See Endoscopy.

Villus ◀ _vi_ lĕs, n. (pl. villi) tiny, hair-like projection, generally occurring on the surface of a mucous membrane, as in intestinal or synovial cells (of joints). Seen on surface of cell, e.g. on cells lining small intestine, where they increase surface area, and the absorptive ability of intestine, accordingly.

Vincristine ◀ _vin_ kris tīn, n. alkaloid compound with anti-cancer, immunosuppressive, and stimulatory effects on thrombocytes. In horses, has been used to treat immune-mediated thrombocytopenia, and lymphosarcoma.
See Lymphosarcoma, Thrombocytopenia.

Vinegar ◀ _vin_ ig ĕ, n. clear liquid, consisting chiefly of acetic acid, obtained by fermentation of various substances. Vinegar infusions have been used to treat endometritis; vinegar added to the horse's diet is an unproven folk remedy for the prevention of enteroliths, as well as for the prevention of fly strikes.
See Endometritis, Enterolith.

Viraemia ◀ _vī_ rĕ mē ĕ, n. presence of virus in blood stream. Highest levels of viraemia generally occur early in infection, as virus spreads through body.
See Virus.

Viral ◀ _vī_ rŭl, n. of, or pertaining to, viruses; caused by virus, e.g. viral infection.
V. **abortion**. see Equine herpes virus
V. **arteritis** see Equine viral arteritis
V. **isolation** ◀ _vī_ rŭl / ī sĕl ā shĕn, n. test for identification of viral agent of infection. Based on inoculating a clinical specimen on to cells growing in culture, then detecting and identifying viruses by techniques such as polymerase chain reaction (PCR), fluorescent antibody testing, or electron microscopy.
See Polymerase chain reaction, Virus.

V. **keratitis** see Keratitis
V. **respiratory disease** ◀ _vī_ rŭl / re spē rē trē / di zĕz, n. any disease of the respiratory tract caused by a virus, e.g. equine influenza. See Equine influenza, Polymerase chain reaction, Virus.

Virulence ◀ _vi_ rŭ lĕns, n. the degree of pathogenicity of a microorganism. Virulence is relative to the severity of disease produced, and the ability of the microorganism to invade the tissues of the host.

Virus ◀ _vī_ rĕs, n. infective agent, smaller than a bacterium (can be seen using electron microscopy), that cannot grow or reproduce outside of a living cell. Viruses infect living cells by injecting genetic material into the cells, and use the chemical machinery of the cells to keep themselves alive, and to reproduce. Viruses contain either deoxyribonucleic acid (DNA) or ribonucleic acid (RNA) as their genetic material; RNA viruses have an enzyme called reverse transcriptase that permits the usual sequence of DNA-to-RNA to be reversed so the virus can make a DNA version of itself. Most viruses are enclosed in protein coat; some have an outer membranous envelope. Many different families, classified according to type of genetic material (RNA, DNA), shape (cubical, complex, helical), whether they have envelope or not. Many different viruses infect horses, including:
- Reovirus – RNA virus causing African horse sickness.
- Adenovirus – DNA virus causing acute upper respiratory disease, especially in Arabian foals with combined immunodeficiency.
- Herpes viruses – DNA viruses causing respiratory, venereal and neurological disease, and abortions.
- Retrovirus – RNA virus causing equine infectious anaemia.
- Orthomyxovirus – family of RNA viruses causing equine influenza.
- Picornavirus – RNA virus causing upper respiratory disease (rhinovirus).
- Togavirus – RNA virus causing equine viral arteritis.

- Alphavirus – RNA viruses causing equine viral encephalitis (eastern, western and Venezuelan).
- Rhabdovirus – RNA virus causing rabies.
- Rotavirus – RNA virus causing neonatal diarrhoea.

Most viral infections of horses are ultimately self-limiting; it would seem counterproductive for a virus to consistently kill its host. Some viruses, e.g. equine herpes virus, maintain a subclinical presence in the host. Antibiotic agents are ineffective against viruses. Some antiviral agents are available, e.g. acyclovir has been used in topical treatment of viral keratitis and systemically, albeit controversially, for the treatment of neurological disease caused by equine herpes virus.

See viral infections under separate headings; see also Deoxyribonucleic acid, Ribonucleic acid, Titre.

Virus neutralization ◀€ *vi rēs / nŭ trēl īz ā shēn, n.* test that detects antibodies that can neutralize the infectiveness of a virus. To perform the test, serial dilutions of blood serum are mixed with a reference strain of a virus, and incubated. This allows any antibody in the serum to neutralize the virus. These dilutions are then inoculated onto cell culture and the presence or absence of viral growth is observed. The highest dilution (otherwise stated, the least amount of antibody), is the titre. The test is highly sensitive and very specific; however, such tests are costly, and require trained personnel.
See Titre.

Viscera ◀€ *vi sē rē, n.* soft internal organs of the body, including heart, lungs, spleen, intestines, liver, kidneys, etc.

Visceral ◀€ *vi sē rŭl, adj.* having to do with the viscera; pertaining to the major internal organs.
   V. pain ◀€ *vi sē rŭl / pān, n.* pain originating from internal body organs. In horses, especially associated with intestinal problems, e.g. as caused by distension, inflammation of intestinal lining, impaired blood supply (e.g. strangulation), or spasm. Horse responds to visceral pain with clinical signs

of colic, including pawing ground, looking at flank, kicking at abdomen, rolling, sweating, etc.
See Colic.

Viscosupplementation ◀€ *vi skō sup lim ēn tā shēn, n.* a treatment option for osteoarthritis of a joint; involves the injection of hyaluronan, which occurs naturally in synovial fluid.
See Hyaluronan, Synovial.

Vision ◀€ *vi zhēn, n.* sight; the ability to see. Problems with vision can be associated with defects of the eye, optic nerve or part of brain associated with vision (visual cortex). Vision problems may be bilateral or unilateral, complete (causing blindness), or partial (e.g. small cataracts), or subclinical, causing no obvious deficits in the overall ability to see, yet still being demonstrable on ophthalmological examination. Many causes of problems with vision, including injury to eye or head, cataract, or bacterial infection. Assessment of vision by ophthalmoscopic examination, including response of pupils to light, menace reflex, or assessment of the ease with which a horse moves through obstacle course.
See Cataract, Eye, Ophthalmoscope.

Vitamin ◀ €*vi tē min, n.* a general term used to describe a variety of unrelated organic compounds that occur in most foods in small amounts. They are necessary for the normal metabolic functions of the body, acting as coenzymes or cofactors in reactions within body. With the exception of vitamin E, vitamin deficiencies are not known to exist naturally in the horse. Normally, the horse's body (unlike that of humans) provides all of its own vitamins, by synthesis from its own system, by exposure to sunlight, and by absorption of vitamins produced by the bacteria that live in the gastrointestinal tract. There appears to be little need for vitamin supplementation in the horse, according to most studies. However, most vitamins are available in relatively inexpensive forms and they are widely supplemented, presumably because of a general perception that since vitamins are essential for life, more is probably better. Vitamins are typically classified as:

1. Fat-soluble – those vitamins (A, D, E, and K) that are absorbed along with dietary fat. Fat-soluble vitamins are not normally excreted in the urine and tend to be stored in the body in moderate amounts.

2. Water-soluble – those vitamins (B and C) that are soluble in water and are not stored in the body.

Vitamin A ◀€ _vi_ tē min / ā, n. fat-soluble vitamin derived entirely from carotenoid pigments found in plants. Vitamin A maintains the normal structure and function of the epithelial cells, and is also needed for normal bone growth. It has a well-defined role in maintaining normal vision. Vitamin A is also needed for normal reproductive function in both males and females. Deficiencies of vitamin A are not known to occur naturally in horses; in diets that are _made_ deficient in vitamin A, the first changes are to the epithelial surfaces. Surfaces become dryer and less resilient; their mucus-secreting capacity becomes reduced. As epithelial surfaces lose their normal capabilities, the potential for infection increases. Night blindness and excessive tear formation are ocular signs of vitamin A deficiencies. Reproductive efficiency is also greatly reduced.

It has been said that if the feed given to a horse has the colour green in it, there is sufficient vitamin A for the needs of the horse. The relative content of vitamin A in feed is roughly equal to the amount of the colour green in the feed; the greener the feed, the more vitamin A it has. Additionally, a 3–6 month supply of vitamin A is stored in the liver of the horse. Vitamin and mineral supplements commonly contain vitamin A; however, adding vitamin A supplements to mineral mixtures rapidly destroys the vitamin. Vitamin A is one of the few vitamins that can cause toxicity. Fortunately, the dosages required for toxicity are quite large. The signs of toxicity are similar to those of deficiencies.
See Vitamin.

Vitamin B ◀€ _vi_ tē min / bē, n. the B-vitamins are a whole group of vitamins with a variety of metabolic functions in the horse. They are found in plentiful supply in horse feed. The microorganisms of the horse's digestive tract also manufacture B-vitamins in large amounts. In normal circumstances, these two sources provide more than enough of the B-vitamins needed to meet the horse's requirements. However, B-vitamins are among the most commonly supplemented vitamins in the horse, possibly because of the fact that in humans, B-vitamin deficiencies occasionally occur. B-vitamins are commonly given as a supplement to horses when they are in disease states; they are not stored in the horse's body for long periods of time. Chronic disease or decreased food intake may be considered reasons to provide B-vitamin supplementation to a horse. It is virtually impossible (and extremely expensive) to determine that a horse might be deficient in a specific B-vitamin, and supplements are relatively cheap; hence, they are frequently given 'just in case' something might be needed. It is commonly thought that B-vitamins can serve as an appetite stimulant; however, experimental evidence with B-vitamins has shown no effect in stimulating the horse's appetite. Sterile 'vitamin B-complex' solutions are available for IM injection in the horse. These products typically contain vitamins B-1, B-2, B-3, B-6, pantothenic acid and B-12. Warnings on the label suggest caution because administration of vitamin B-1 has resulted in anaphylactic (allergic) shock in some animals.

Vitamin B-1 ◀€ _vi_ tē min / bē-1, n. (thiamine) important in the production of energy by the cells of the horse's body. Present in high levels in plant products, such as hay. Easily destroyed by heat and cooking, so thiamine may have to be added back to heat-processed feeds to restore pre-processing levels. Intestinal bacteria produce a great deal of thiamine. It is impossible to give a horse a normal diet that is thiamine deficient. Primary dietary thiamine deficiencies have only been seen in horses with experimentally produced diets. However, secondary deficiencies of thiamine have been associated with the ingestion of plants that produce enzymes that break down thiamine or have anti-thiamine activity, e.g. bracken fern (see Bracken fern). Signs of thiamine deficiency include loss of appetite, weight loss, haemorrhage of the gums and heart rate abnormalities. Thiamine toxicity is very unlikely if the vitamin is given orally. A dose of one thousand times that which is recommended appears to be safe. High doses of thiamine have been injected into the horse in an effort to provide 'natural' tranquillization, indeed, some work done in Australia suggested that horses given thiamine seemed to be less excitable while walking to the racetrack. However, other studies have been unable to repeat this effect. A negative side effect of thiamine is reported to be anaphylactic (allergic) shock. This effect is reportedly seen more often when the vitamin is given intravenously (IV). Excessive blood levels of thiamine are prohibited by racing associations.

Vitamin B-2 ◀ _vi tē min / bē-2, n._ (riboflavin) important for normal metabolic activity in the horse; provided in high levels in horse feed and produced by the bacteria of the horse's intestines. Neither deficiencies nor toxicities of vitamin B-2 have ever been reported in the horse.

Vitamin B-3 ◀ _vi tē min / bē-3, n._ (niacin) important for energy production in all cells of the horse's body. As with all B-vitamins, the horse's normal intake and intestinal production appear to provide vast amounts of vitamin B-3 for the horse. Vitamin B-3 can also be manufactured from the amino acid tryptophan in the horse's tissues. Specific deficiencies or toxicities have not been reported in the horse.

Vitamin B-6 ◀ _vi tē min / bē-6, n._ a generic term for three similar compounds that have equal vitamin activity: pyridoxal, pyridoxine and pyridoxamine. No dietary requirements for these have been established in the horse and their precise functions are not known. Ample levels are provided from the normal sources in the

horse. Deficiencies or toxicities of vitamin B-6 are unknown.

Vitamin B-7 see Biotin (also known as vitamin H)

Vitamin B-12 ◀ _vi tē min / bē-12, n._ (cyanocobalamin) the only B-vitamin that is not found in large amounts in the horse's feed. However, synthesis of vitamin B-12 by the intestinal bacteria of the horse is more than adequate to meet the horse's needs, even when extremely low amounts of the vitamin are supplied in the diet. Vitamin B-12 is needed for red blood cells to mature. There are no reports of vitamin B-12 deficiencies or toxicities in the horse. Vitamin B-12 is available as a sterile solution for IM or IV injection at a variety of concentrations. It is commonly used in an effort to pep up or 'build blood' in horses that are deemed to be inadequate in these areas. There has been no observed response to vitamin B-12 injections in experimental situations. Injected B-12 is removed rapidly from the blood by the kidney and liver.
See Vitamin.

Vitamin C ◀ _vi tē min / sē, n._ (ascorbic acid) found in high levels in many vegetable compounds (like hay). It has a variety of important metabolic functions. Like vitamin E and the trace mineral, selenium, vitamin C is also an anti-oxidant. Although sometimes recommended for treatment of various conditions, especially arthritis, Vitamin C deficiencies are unknown in horses because horses synthesize it in their bodies. In humans, a deficiency of vitamin C causes scurvy, a condition characterized by weakness, anaemia, spongy gums and a tendency towards bruising and bleeding. Supplemental vitamin C has no known beneficial effects in the horse.
See Anti-oxidant, Selenium, Vitamin, Vitamin E.

Vitamin D ◀ _vi tē min / dē, n._ formed in the tissues of the horse by the action of the sun's rays on a by-product of the body's cholesterol. Because vitamin D levels are related to exposure to the sun, very little exposure to the sun is required to produce

adequate levels of vitamin D, and as horses tend to be exposed to adequate sunlight, it is very difficult to make a horse deficient in vitamin D. Vitamin D is stored in all tissues of the horse's body. It helps to maintain calcium and phosphorus levels in the body. Accordingly, vitamin D deficiencies, on the rare occasions that they are seen, occur in growing animals and show up as abnormalities of bone formation (rickets). Vitamin D toxicity has been reported in horses. Most commonly it is associated with eating the wild Jasmine plant (*Cestrum diurnum*), although there are also reports of horses being given too much vitamin D in their diets. Signs of toxicity are stiffness and soreness, inappetance, weight loss, excessive drinking and urination and calcification of the kidneys. The prognosis for recovery from vitamin D toxicosis is poor.
See Vitamin, Jasmine.

Vitamin E ◄; *vi tē min / ē, n.* (alpha-tocopherol) a fat-soluble vitamin necessary in the diet of the horse for normal reproduction, normal muscle development, normal red blood cell function and a variety of other biochemical functions. It is found in high levels in cereals, fresh pasture, wheatgerm oil and various grains. Vitamin E is also an anti-oxidant. Because of its antioxidant properties, vitamin E is frequently administered as treatment of or prevention for acute or chronic equine exertional rhabdomyolysis, also known as tying-up, myositis or azoturia. Theoretically, vitamin E would help prevent further degrading of muscle cells. Typically, it is combined with selenium, a trace mineral, for treatment or prevention of this condition. No scientific evidence exists to support the effectiveness of this treatment for rhabdomyolysis, and most research suggests that rhabdomyolysis is caused by other factors, many of which appear to be genetic. Deficiencies of vitamin E are associated with equine motor neuron disease, a condition characterized by incoordination and muscle twitching. The condition is usually seen in horses that have inadequate access to green forage. Vitamin E is also available in various ointments and oils for application to wounds in the horse,

as well as in various hoof dressings. There is no evidence that vitamin E has any effect in these areas. Application of vitamin E to the surface of a wound does not decrease the formation of scar tissue, nor does it increase the speed of, or the amount of, hair re-growth.
See Anti-oxidant, Equine motor neuron disease, Exertional rhabdomyolysis, Selenium, Vitamin.

Vitamin H see Biotin

Vitamin K ◄; *vi tē min / kā, n.* fat-soluble compound, essential for formation of prothrombin which is needed for normal blood clotting. High amounts of vitamin K occur in alfalfa (lucerne) hay. Vitamin K deficiencies are not known to occur in horses. Vitamin K is the antidote for warfarin toxicity.
See Clotting, Vitamin, Warfarin.

Vitex agnus castus ◄; *vī teks / a gnēs / kas tēs, n.* (Chasteberry) – plant that has been suggested as a treatment for equine pituitary pars intermedia dysfunction. The fruit and seeds of the plant contain oils that appear to help the action of dopamine. This mechanism of action would mirror that of the drug pergolide, although, as with all herbal products, it would be difficult to administer a consistent dose. In horses, there is a report of chasteberry being effective for the treatment of equine Cushing's disease in a lay equine publication. However, one well-conducted study at the University of Pennsylvania concluded that chasteberry was not effective at treating equine Cushing's disease. The common name of the plant arises from the fact that historians say that monks chewed chaste tree parts to make it easier to maintain their celibacy.

Vitiligo ◄; *vi ti lī gō, n.* loss of pigment from skin, especially around eyes, muzzle and lips; not associated with inflammation. Most commonly seen in Arabian horses, but also in other breeds; possibly hereditary basis. Results from destruction of cells which produce pigment (melanocytes), cause unknown. No treatments have been shown to be effective; however, anecdotal reports of response to mineral supplementation, especially to copper, exist.

Vitrectomy ◀€ *vi̱ trek te̱m e̱, n.* surgical removal of the vitreous humour of the eye. Has been described as a treatment for equine recurrent uveitis. The procedure appears to be more commonly performed, and more widely accepted, in Europe than elsewhere, perhaps reflecting a difference in the manifestation of the disease.
See Equine recurrent uveitis.

Vitreous ◀€ *vi̱ tre̱ e̱s, adj.* glass-like in appearance or texture. The vitreous (sometimes referred to as the vitreous humour) is a soft gelatinous material that fills the back of the eye, and sits behind the lens.
See Eye.

Vocal cord ◀€ *vo̱ ke̱l / kord, n.* one of paired mucous membrane folds (vocal folds) of the lining of larynx covering the vocal ligament and underlying vocalis muscle. These folds form thin bands which vibrate in the flow of air though the larynx and produce various vocalizations (neigh, whinny, etc.), the nature of which can also be altered in nose and mouth.
See Larynx, Vocalization.

Vocalization ◀€ *vo̱ ke̱l i̱z a̱ she̱n, n.* communication by making sounds. There are six recognized equine sounds: scream, squeal, nicker, whinny, snort and blow. Of these, whinnies are considered to have the highest potential for communication, perhaps being the horse's equivalent of a dog's bark.

Voice box see Larynx

Volar ◀€ *vo̱ le̱, adj.* located on the same side as the sole of the foot; the back (flexor) surface of forelimb.
See Palmar.

Volatile anaesthesia see Anaesthesia

Volatile fatty acid (VFA) see Fatty acid

Volume ◀€ *vol u̱m, n.* amount of three-dimensional space occupied by substance. Various volumes are considered in horses:

- Blood v. – total amount of blood in body. Depending on the breed, 6–10% of the body weight is blood (Arabians and Thoroughbreds tend to be higher; draught horses tend to be the lowest).
- Packed cell v. – percentage by volume of whole blood which is made up by red blood cells.
- Stroke v. – the volume of blood ejected by one ventricle of the heart with each contraction; typically measured in millilitres. Stroke v. is a measure of the effectiveness of ventricular contraction.
- Tidal v. – volume of gas entering or leaving the lungs when a normal breath is taken.

V. deficit ◀€ *vol u̱m / def is it, n.* an imbalance in bodily fluid volume, where there is loss of fluid from the body that cannot be adequately replaced by intake of water. The major causes of v. deficits are: (1) inadequate fluid intake, and (2) excessive fluid loss, e.g. from diarrhoea, or loss through burns or wounds. Since water is able to move freely between the cellular compartments, a volume deficit in the extracellular fluid also causes a fluid deficit in the cells (cellular dehydration), leaving cells without adequate water to function normally.

V. of distribution ◀€ *vol u̱m / ov / dist rib u̱ she̱n, n.* a mathematical term describing the fluid volume through which a drug is distributed in the horse's body. Determined by the ability of the drug to cross biological membranes and reach the tissues; that ability is determined by the characteristics of the drug (e.g. lipid solubility, molecular size).

Volvulus ◀€ *vol vu̱ le̱s, n.* obstruction of intestine or stomach caused by the bowel twisting upon itself; causes clinical signs of severe colic and obstruction of blood supply (strangulation) which can be rapidly fatal.
See Colic, Strangulation.

Vomit ◀€ *vo̱ mit, v./n.* to eject stomach contents through mouth/nose; material ejected during vomiting. Because of the oesophageal sphincter where the oesophagus enters the stomach, it is almost impossible for a horse to vomit. In addition, the oesophagus meets the stomach at an angle which further prevents food or liquid from moving towards the oral cavity. It is also likely, based on evidence from pharmacological studies, that the vomiting reflex is poorly developed in horses. Vomiting may rarely be seen after gastric rupture, which destroys the structural integrity of the stomach, allowing for liquid to pass back up the oesophagus.

von Willebrand's disease ◀ː *fon* / <u>*wi*</u> *le brandz* / *di* <u>*zēz*</u>, *n.* congenital, extrinsic platelet defect that results in dysfunction of blood platelets. The disease is characterized by a deficiency of von Willebrand factor (vWF), a glycoprotein that is involved in platelet adhesion to blood vessel walls – the initial stage of blood clotting. Disease has been rarely reported in Quarter Horses and Thoroughbreds; affected horses experience bleeding, especially following surgery or trauma. Recurrent nosebleeds (epistaxis) may be observed. Prevention is directed at minimizing injury and avoiding the use of drugs that suppress platelet function (e.g. non-steroidal anti-inflammatory drugs and sulphonamides). Fresh blood or fresh or frozen plasma transfusions may help control bleeding episodes. Affected animals should not be used for breeding. (Named after Erik Adolf von Willebrand, Finnish doctor 1870–1949.)

Vulva ◀ː <u>*vul*</u> *vē, n.* external part of female genitalia; opening to vagina. Two vulvar lips (labia) cover clitoris. Vulvar trauma may occur from breeding or foaling injuries. Vulva can be affected by tumours, especially melanoma in old grey mares and squamous cell carcinoma in pink-skinned horses. Several venereal diseases may cause vulvar changes, e.g. equine herpes virus 3, the virus that causes coital exanthema, a disease characterized by blisters and erosions on vulva. Poor conformation of the vulva, e.g. as seen in aged broodmares, is often an indication for surgical reduction of the vulvar aperture (Caslick's operation). Tipped v. is conformation of vulva where anus is recessed relative to the dorsal opening of the vulva, and vulvar lips slope, allowing the vulvar opening to become more horizontal. This can result in aspiration of faecal material, leading to vaginitis, metritis, and infertility. This is also typically addressed by Caslick's operation to reduce the vulvar aperture.
See Caslick, Equine herpes virus: EHV-3, Leiomyoma, Melanoma, Squamous.

Vulvoplasty see Caslick

W

W-plasty ◀€ *dub ūl ū / plas tē, n.* cosmetic surgical technique designed to improve the cosmetic appearance of a scar. Involves creating a series of zigzag incisions across a scar that, when closed, results in a suture line resembling a series of Ws.

Walk ◀€ *wawk, n./v.* the slowest gait of horse, or to move at that gait. Walk is a gait of four evenly spaced beats, with no suspension phase. Each foot is moved in turn (e.g. left hind, left fore, right hind, right fore); the horse will always have three feet on the ground, and one foot in the air, except during the moment when weight is transferred from one foot to another. See Gait.

Walking disease see Pyrrolizidine, Seneciosis

Wall ◀€ *wawl, n.* a surrounding or enveloping structural layer. Walls may be seen surrounding organisms (e.g. the body wall), cavities (e.g. abdominal wall or thoracic wall), hollow organs (e.g. intestinal wall), structures (e.g. hoof wall), masses of material such as pus (e.g. the wall of an abscess), or microorganisms (e.g. bacterial cell wall).

Wall-eye ◀€ *wawl / ī, n.* a combination of white and blue pigment in the iris (lacks normal brown pigment) with a normal brown corpora nigra. See Eye.

Walnut see Black walnut

Wanderer ◀€ *won der rē, n.* term sometimes used to describe foal which has suffered lack of oxygen at or around birth. See Hypoxic ischaemic encephalopathy.

Warbles ◀€ *wor būls, n.* cutaneous nodules caused by larval stages of large warble flies *Hypoderma bovis* and *H. linatum* (the flies look like a bee). More common in cattle; horse is occasional dead-end host; especially seen in horses that are housed with cattle. Adult flies lay eggs on hair, larvae burrow into skin and migrate into subcutaneous tissues of neck, trunk, chest and abdomen. A painful swelling develops over the larva; the swelling will become an open wound as a breathing pore for the larva is formed (breathing pore is pathognomonic). Occasional aberrant migration may cause neurological signs; rupture of nodules can cause anaphylaxis. Treatment is by enlarging breathing pore and removing larva, excising the entire nodule, or by allowing larva to fall out spontaneously. Pour-on insecticides may be used as a preventative; cattle in endemic areas should also be treated.

Warfarin ◀€ *wor fē rin, n.* anticoagulant compound; synthetic derivative of coumarin, a chemical found in some plants. Has been used especially as a rodenticide; kills rats and mice by preventing clotting of blood; however, second-generation compounds have been developed for this purpose because of acquired resistance. May rarely cause poisoning in horses; clinical signs are of bleeding from various areas, e.g. bloody diarrhoea, nosebleeds, lameness from bleeding in joints. Warfarin was previously used in the treatment of navicular disease, when it was hypothesized that the condition was related to a vascular problem, but toxicity was sometimes seen in treated horses and that pathogenesis has since been discarded. Treatment is by eliminating source of toxicity; vitamin K, especially vitamin K_1, is a swift and specific antidote.

Wart ◀€ *wort*, *n.* raised fleshy or hard growth on skin.
See Equine viral papillomatosis, Papilloma.

Wasting ◀€ *wās ting*, *v./adj.* loss of body strength, mass, or vitality (cachexia); decrease in size caused by disuse or disease (atrophy).

> **W. disease** ◀€ *wās ting / di zēz*, *n.* any disease characterized by cachexia, that is, by reduction in body strength or mass, especially intestinal malabsorption syndromes.
> See Atrophy, Cachexia, Malabsorption.

Water ◀€ *wor tē*, *n.* clear, odourless, tasteless compound; chemical formula H_2O. Liquid between 0 and 100 degrees Celsius. Binary chemical, essential to all known living organisms. The most abundant molecule on the surface of the Earth; approximately 70–75% of the Earth's surface is either liquid or solid water, with additional water occurring in the atmosphere as a vapour. Horses should always have access to clean, fresh water. Water consumption varies depending on climate, moisture content of food, the amount of physical work being done, body size, and in times of metabolic need, e.g. lactation. Water is also a solvent, and is used for bathing and cleansing horses and their equipment.

> **W. balance** ◀€ *wor tē / bal ēns*, *n.* the balance between water intake and excretion such that the plasma osmolality remains constant. Hormonal control of water balance is primarily through secretion of antiduretic hormone (ADH) by the hypothalamus and by its action on the kidneys; when the need for water cannot be met by renal conservation, thirst is stimulated.
> See Antidiuretic hormone, Hypothalamus.
> **W. deprivation test** ◀€ *wor tē / dep riv ā shēn / test*, *n.* diagnostic test whereby horse is denied access to water for a period of time. The test is used to see whether increased drinking in a horse (polydipsia) is caused by a behavioural problem or is a result of a central or renal problem. The normal response to water deprivation is the concen-

tration of urine; abnormal animals fail to concentrate their urine. The test should not be performed in animals that are dehydrated or azotaemic.

W. sac see Allantois, Chorion.
W. soluble ◀€ *wor tē / sol ū būl*, *adj.* capable of being dissolved in water.

Water hemlock ◀€ *wor tē / hem lok*, *n.* (*Cicuta maculata*) erect perennial plant growing to 2.4 m tall, found on the edges of lakes, marshes and streams. Umbelliferae family (similar to cowbane). Plant contains cicutoxin; extremely poisonous if eaten. Animals have been poisoned by drinking water standing in small pools where the plant has been trampled and the roots crushed. Poisoning is most common when the plant is young, somewhat succulent, and growing rapidly. Signs of toxicity include dilated pupils, colic, convulsions, death.

Wave mouth ◀€ *wāv / möth*, *n.* condition that occurs when at least two of the cheek teeth are higher than the others. When viewed from the side, the grinding surfaces of the teeth are thus aligned in a wave-like pattern, rather than a straight line. Cause is unknown; may be addressed by dental interventions (e.g. lowering of high cheek teeth), but significance to horse's health is questionable.
See Tooth.

Wax ◀€ *waks*, *n.* colloquial term for accumulation of dry milk (including colostrum) seen at end of teat in mares, usually approximately 48 hours before foaling ('waxing-up').
See Parturition.

Weakness ◀€ *wēk nis*, *n.* a bodily state: a lack of physical strength, vigour, or energy. In horses, weakness may be characterized by a reluctance to rise, or difficulty in rising, a shuffling, slow, gait, eating slowly, or postural adjustments. Weakness can occur as a result of disease of many body systems, including toxaemias, upper and lower motor neuron diseases, cachexia, etc. Depending on the condition, weakness may be a constant feature of disease, or episodic, that is, weakness may come and go, and vary from mild to severe in the same animal (e.g. as seen in conditions such as hypokalaemic periodic paralysis, equine motor neuron disease, polysaccharide storage myopathy, certain cardiac arrhythmias, or atrioventricular block). See various disease conditions.

Wean ◀ *wēn*, *v.* to separate the foal from the mare from whom it has been nursing, and to substitute other food for the mare's milk.

Weaning ◀ *wē ning*, *n.* the act of separating the foal from the mare, discontinuing the feeding of foal by mare, and providing alternative sources of nutrition. Gradual process in natural conditions; usually completed by time foal is 10–11 months old, (i.e. before birth of next foal). In managed horses, age of weaning is often by 5–6 months of age, although earlier weaning has been reported to increase growth rate.

Weanling ◀ *wēn ling*, *n.* a newly weaned foal, typically approximately 6 months of age.

Weave ◀ *wēv*, *v.* to repeatedly shift weight from one front leg to the other and swing head from side to side; considered a behavioural abnormality by some, but may simply be an adaptation to housing conditions, e.g. to boredom from confinement within stable.

Web ◀ *web*, *n.* term used to describe the width of the bar of a horseshoe, e.g. 'wide-web' shoes are made from a wider piece of metal than are normal horsehoes.

Wedge ◀ *wej*, *n.* a shape that is triangular in cross-section.

    W. pad ◀ *wej / pad*, *n.* a pad that is interposed between the heels and the horseshoe, to elevate and, hopefully, cushion heels. Often, and sometimes controversially, prescribed to change alignment of the hoof–pastern axis, and for various conditions affecting the horse's heel, including low heels and navicular syndrome. See Hoof.

    W. ostectomy ◀ *wej / os tek tē mē*, *n.* removal of a wedge-shaped piece of bone, followed by stabilization with bone plates and screws. May occasionally be recommended for the treatment of severe angular limb deformities.

    W. shoe ◀ *wej / shŭ*, *n.* shoe that is thicker at the heels than at the toe; also called a swelled heel shoe.

    W. test ◀ *wej / test*, *n.* diagnostic test occasionally performed in lameness examinations. To perform this test, the foot is placed on a wooden wedge, and the contralateral limb is lifted and held for approximately 1 minute. The horse is immediately trotted and examined for lameness. Theoretically, tension caused on limb structures from standing on the wedge will exacerbate lameness, e.g. elevating the toe may cause increased tension in the deep digital flexor tendon or surrounding ligaments, thereby causing pain and lameness if these structures have been injured.

Weight ◀ *wāt*, *n.* a measure of heaviness. Horse's weight is usually measured in kilograms or pounds. Much individual variation, depending on type, age, breed, and condition.

- W. gain is an increase in heaviness, generally as a result of excessive calorific intake, inadequate exercise, or both. Excessive weight gain has been associated anecdotally with various developmental abnormalities in foals; excessive gain in horses may predispose them to conditions such as laminitis.

- W. loss is a decrease in heaviness. May be the result of inadequate calorific intake (e.g. poor quality feed, low in pecking order in herded horses), increased metabolic demands (e.g. heavy exercise, lactation), or various disease conditions (e.g. parasitic infestations, dental disease, gastrointestinal or renal disease). Weight loss may be chronic, or can occur rapidly in the face of systemic infections (e.g. septicaemia).

Western blot ◀ *wes tēn / blot*, *n.* a diagnostic technique for identifying proteins in a complex mixture; separated proteins are transferred from a gel medium to a protein-binding nitrocellulose sheet for analysis. In horses, is used especially for the diagnosis of equine protozoal myelitis. The test is very sensitive, but not specific; strong negative predictive value.

Western equine encephalitis ◀ː _wes tēn_ / _ek wīn_ / _en ke fē lī tis, n._ (WEE) infection of brain and other nervous tissue by Alphavirus (same virus genus that causes Eastern and Venezuelan equine encephalitis); at least two variants have been reported. Occurs primarily in North America, but also South America. Life cycle involves transmission between birds or rodents, and mosquitoes; does not cause clinical disease in these hosts. Mosquitoes (especially _Culex tarsalis_) are the primary vector; disease prevalence is increased with moist conditions that favour mosquito reproduction. _Culex tarsalis_ does not occur in South America; thus, disease prevalence is lower than in North America. Clinical signs depend on the degree of exposure and the virulence of the virus strain; typical signs in affected horses include fever, depression, and nervous system signs including incoordination, grinding of teeth (bruxism), head pressing, hyperexcitability, blindness, circling, seizures. Severe depression seen with some infections gives rise to common name of 'sleeping sickness'. Treatment of affected horses is supportive; unlike horses affected with Eastern equine encephalitis, horses affected with WEE commonly survive. The disease is not contagious; horses do not produce enough circulating virus (viraemia) to infect mosquitoes. Zoonotic potential; virus can also cause encephalitis in humans. In USA, vaccination and protective immunity from subclinical exposure has made disease uncommon in horses.
See Eastern equine encephalitis, Venezuelan equine encephalitis.

West Nile virus ◀ː _west_ / _nīl_ / _vī rēs, n._ (WNV) Flavivirus infection, first seen in United States in 1999, where it caused an epizootic outbreak beginning in New York state, ultimately spreading across the United States. Virus is transmitted by ticks or mosquitoes from avian or mammalian host; virus is amplified in vector species; birds are the primary reservoir hosts. Oral transmission is also possible. The virus has a predilection for infection of nervous system tissues; in epizootic outbreak, horses affected with West Nile virus demonstrated a variable combination and severity of clinical signs. Signs including trembling of the muscles of the neck and face; trembling can become severe, and affect the limbs and trunk, causing gait abnormalities. Personality changes (hyperexcitablity or apprehension) and sleep-like activity may occur in affected individuals. Ataxia in affected horses may progress to recumbency, with accompanying cranial nerve abnormalities. Approximately 30% of infected horses progress to paralysis of one or more limbs. Seizures and coma are rare. Treatment is supportive; no specific treatments are supported by evidence of effectiveness. Many horses will show improvement within a few days of onset of clinical signs; horses that show rapid improvement will often go on to a full recovery; horses that progress to paralysis or recumbency typically do not recover. Diagnosis is by serology based on detection of an IgM antibody response; no specific signs distinguish WNV infection from other neurological diseases. Several vaccines are available for prevention; the recommended interval of vaccination may vary depending on disease prevalence. Vaccination, protective immunity from subclinical exposure, and decreased viral virulence with spread through the population has made the disease less common, or less severe, in horses in the United States with each passing year.

Wet gangrene see Gangrene

Wheal ◀ː _wē ūl, n._ suddenly formed, raised area of skin, as seen with allergic reactions, e.g. urticaria. A wheal-and-flare reaction is an immediate reaction to an injected allegen, especially as seen in response to intradermal allergy testing. In response to the allergen, a wheal appears, surrounded by an area of skin redness (the 'flare').
See Urticaria.

Wheat ◀ː _wēt, n._ (_Triticum aestivum_) cereal plant grown widely throughout the world.

Not used extensively in animal feeds because of high cost. Should be cracked, coarsely ground or steam-flaked before feeding to horses because of small, hard kernels that make digestion difficult. Higher in energy density than maize (corn); about 2.5 times more energy dense than oats; wheat is less palatable to horses than are maize (corn) and oats. Wheat contains gluten, which gives it a sticky consistency; fears that wheat can form a sticky mass in the intestines are not supported by research, but general recommendations are that wheat should make up no more than 50% of any grain mix.

W. bran ◀ *wēt / bran, n.* outer layer or the grain kernel of wheat, removed during the milling process; commonly fed to horses in North America, especially as a home remedy for colic prevention (no evidence that it is effective in this regard, and wheat bran has been shown not to have a laxative effect in horses). Wheat bran is fluffy and low density, so contains much less digestible energy than does maize (corn) or oats, but is a source of dietary fibre. High phosphorus content resulted in nutritional disease in horses fed bran rations in the nineteenth century (nutritional hyperparathyroidism). Typically fed as a warm mash, combined with hot water; feeding as such does not improve digestibility.

Wheeze ◀ *wēz, n./v.* abnormal respiratory sound heard on auscultation of air passages; to make a whistling sound while breathing. Described as a hoarse whistling sound during breathing, especially during expiration. For wheezing to occur, some portion of the airway must be narrowed or obstructed, e.g. in bronchopneumonia or recurrent airway obstruction. See Bronchopneumonia, Recurrent airway obstruction.

White blood cell see Leukocyte
W. b. c. count ◀ *wīt / blud / sel / kŏnt, n.* laboratory test to determine the number and types of white blood cells (leukocytes) in the blood. WBC counts are included in most general blood tests, and are used to investigate the underlying cause of various diseases, including infection, allergy, and neoplasia.

White clover see Clover

White line ◀ *wīt / līn, n.* the part of the hoof where the wall joins the sole, as seen on the underside of hoof. Important marker for farrier, as horseshoe nails must be driven outside white line to avoid damaging sensitive parts of foot. See Foot.
W. l. disease ◀ *wīt / līn / di zēs, n.* condition characterized by progressive hoof wall separation occurring in the non-pigmented horn of the hoof, where the stratum medium (middle layer of the hoof capsule) joins the laminar horn. Typically involves the toe and quarters. The name is actually a misnomer; the white line is not involved. Cause is unknown, but may be an opportunistic infection following trauma to the hoof, or bleeding from laminar tearing (e.g. as might be caused by bruising), or laminitis, with secondary infection (i.e. condition may occur from the inside out). Other causes that have been associated with the condition include moist environmental conditions, abnormal hoof mechanics (e.g. long toe), and improper nutrition. In mild cases, horses may not show clinical signs; in more advanced cases, horses will be clinically lame, with massive undermining and separation of the hoof wall. Affected foot has crumbly whitish, greyish or brown material or powdery areas at the white line area of toe, and soreness to hoof testers; hoof may produce hollow sound when tapped. Condition may be discovered during routine hoof trimming; extent of disease is evaluated by radiography. Treatment involves removal of the undermined hoof wall, and providing support to the hoof while the affected hoof area grows out. Various chemical and antibiotic preparations have been applied to the exposed hoof tissue; however, treatment success has been reported from simply debriding the affected area(s) with a steel brush until good horn attachment is recognized. Called various names, including seedy toe, hoof or stall rot, hollow foot, yeast infection, candida, wall thrush, and (incorrectly) onychomycosis (condition is not necessarily caused by a fungus). See Foot, Laminitis.

White muscle disease ◄ _wīt_ / _mu_ _sēl_ / _di_ _zēs_, _n._ disease of foals caused by a dietary deficiency of the trace element, selenium. See Nutritional.

White snakeroot ◄ _whīt_ / _snāk_ _rŭt_, _n._ (_Eupatorium rugosum_) erect, herbaceous, perennial plant widely distributed through wooded areas of USA. Toxic agent is tremetone, which is at peak concentrations in summer and autumn. Can cause poisoning if eaten; toxin concentrates in milk. Signs of toxicity include trembling, incoordination, sweating, laboured breathing, stiffness, sluggish movements, death.

Whole blood transfusion see Transfusion

Whorl ◄ _werl_, _n._ a spiral arrangement of hairs, occurring on head, neck, and body. Positions of various whorls are commonly marked on certificates and passports for equine identification.

Whorlbone (Whirlbone) lameness see Trochanteric bursitis.

Wild jessamine see Jasmine

Wind ◄ _wind_, _n._ breath; lay term for breathing, respiration.

Windgall/Windpuff ◄ _wind gawl/wind puf_, _n._ colloquial term (windpuff more common in US) used to describe a soft synovial fluid swelling of joint or tendon sheath in or around fetlock joint. May occur with no other clinical signs; when secondary to damage to, or infection of, tendon or joint surface, affected horse is commonly lame. Centesis of affected area may help reveal underlying cause; ultrasound or radiography of affected area may reveal associated structural damage. Treatment is directed according to cause. Drainage and injection of asymptomatic windgalls with corticosteroid compounds is common for cosmetic reasons, but may be unrewarding, as condition frequently recurs.

Windpipe ◄ _wind pīp_, _n._ trachea; the cartilaginous, mucus membrane-lined tube that carries air from throat to lungs. See Trachea.

Windswept ◄ _wind swept_, _adj._ colloquial term sometimes used to describe foals with multiple angular limb deformities; the limbs of such foals may seem as if they have been blown to the side by the wind.

Wind-sucking ◄ _wind-_ _su_ _king_, _v._ noise made by horse when crib-biting; term may also be used to describe pneumovagina, where air enters vagina when vulvar lips are parted. See Crib-biting, Pneumovagina.

Wing ◄ _wing_ _n._ in anatomy, a structure that resembles a wing in appearance, function, or position relative to a main body, e.g. the wings of the third phalanx (coffin bone), or the ilium. Term is also occasionally used to describe either of the palmar or plantar processes of the second (middle) phalanx (short pastern bone).

    W. fracture ◄ _wing_ / _frak_ _tŭr_, _n._ break of the wings of the third phalanx, or the palmar/plantar processes of the middle phalanx. Prognosis depends on the extent of the injury, especially if the fracture is comminuted or extends into the joint. Wing fractures of the palmar/plantar processes are most common in hind legs of horses that make rapid turns, e.g. polo ponies, or cutting or reining Quarter Horses. Bone fractures typically cause sudden, severe lameness; swelling may be associated with fractures of the middle phalanx. Diagnosis by clinical examination, e.g. painful response to hoof testers with wing fractures of the coffin bone. Radiography confirms extent of injury. Treatment may involve rest, supportive shoeing, cast immobilization, or surgery, depending on location and extent of injury.

Winging ◄ _wing_ _ing_, _n._ path of foot flight whereby the hooves deviate across midline. May cause limb interference. Associated with a toed-out position of the foot at rest. See Interference.

Wink ◄ _wingk_, _v._ colloquial term used to describe eversion of lips of vulva; commonly displayed by mares in heat (oestrus). See Oestrus.

Winton disease see Pyrrolizidine, Seneciosis

Withers ◀ *wi thēz, n.* the highest part of the back in the horse, located between the shoulder blades, at junction of neck and back. Formed by the dorsal spinous processes of 3rd–9th thoracic vertebrae. Highest point of the withers is used for measuring height of horse.
See Height.

Wobbler syndrome see Cervical vertebral stenotic myelopathy

Wolf tooth ◀ *wŭlf / tŭth, n.* small rudimentary premolar, in front of first large cheek tooth. Not always present, but counted as first premolar when present. Removal may be recommended prior to bitting/bridle training; however, there is no evidentiary basis for such recommendations. May also be shed spontaneously. See Dentition.

Wolff's law ◀ *wŭlfz / lor, n.* a concept that states that bone in a healthy individual will adapt to the loads that are placed on it. The shape of the horse's cannon bone (metacarpus or metatarus) changes during training in response to the stresses placed on it; Wolff's law may also have relevance in the pathogenesis of navicular disease. (Developed by the German anatomist/surgeon Julius Wolff [1835–1902] in the nineteenth century.)
See Navicular syndrome.

Womb ◀ *wŭm, n.* colloquial term for uterus.
See Uterus.

Wood chewing ◀ *wŭd / chŭ ing, n.* behaviour commonly seen in stabled horses; no apparent breed, age, or sex predilection. May be seen more commonly when horses are exposed to soft woods (e.g. pine and fir, but also plywood and particle board) but is seen in horses kept outdoors as well. May also increase with cold, wet weather. May be a normal adaptation to the boredom of stable confinement, but undesirable owing to damage caused to facilities. Can become habitual, and some

horses seem to like the taste of wood. Wood chewing increases when normal chewing activity is reduced, e.g. in horses which have no access to pasture, or horses that are fed pelleted rations instead of hay. May also occur secondary to protein deficiency or lack of dietary fibre. Changes in husbandry practices (e.g. allowing more contact with other horses) or housing (e.g. allowing access to pasture, or providing toys such as balls or plastic jugs) may help correct problem; muzzling, covering stable with electrified wire or applying unpleasant flavourings to wood may help reduce incidence of problem, but does not relieve the underlying boredom, and may cause injury (e.g. mouth lacerations from exposed metal edges) or ulcers (from chemical injury).

Wood's lamp ◀ *wŭdz / lamp, n.* diagnostic tool used in dermatology, whereby an ultraviolet light is shone on the skin; the skin is then observed for fluorescence. May occasionally demonstrate fungal skin infections (dematophytosis); however, only a few fungal pathogens of equine skin fluoresce, and topical therapy may cause false-positive reactions.

Worm ◀ *werm, n.* as used in veterinary medicine, term used to describe any of the various invertebrate helminth parasites which spend a part of their life cycle in the intestines. Includes roundworms (nematodes), tapeworms (cestodes) and flukes (trematodes). Important parasitic worms in horses include:

- Intestinal roundworms: *Strongylus* spp., *Parascaris equorum, Strongyloides westeri, Oxyuris equi.*
- Tapeworms: *Anoplocephala perfoliata, Anoplocephala magna, Paranoplocephala mamillana.*
- Lungworm: *Dictyocaulus arnfieldi.*
See under individual entries.

Wound ◀ *wŭnd, v./n.* to cause injury to living tissue; compromise to the integrity of any living tissue. Myriad causes, including trauma (e.g. accident, kick, tear from barbed wire, puncture from nail, etc.), infection, or ulcer. Surgical wounds may be created in the course of operations by veterinary surgeons. Various methods of classification include:

- Acute w. – typically caused by trauma, occurring immediately after injury. Acute wounds may be additionally subdivided using terms such as:
  o Abrasions – where the skin surface is rubbed away, e.g. as may occur from falling on hard or abrasive surfaces.
  – Avulsions – where an entire structure is pulled away, e.g. an avulsed tooth.
  o Contusions (bruises) – where blunt trauma damages underlying tissues without breaking skin.
  o Cuts – slicing wounds made by objects, generally resulting in even skin edges, e.g. from surgical instruments, wire, nails, or sharp edges.
  o Lacerations (tears) – slicing wounds that result in uneven or jagged wound edges.
  o Punctures – deep, narrow wounds typically produced by objects such as nails.
- Chronic w. – typically associated with the presence of a long-term condition, e.g. skin damage caused by prolonged recumbency (decubitus ulcer).
- Closed w. – occurring where skin has not been compromised, but underlying tissues have been damaged (e.g. closed fractures).
- Open w. – where the skin has been compromised, and underlying tissues are exposed.

W. contraction ◀ᴇ *wǔnd / kon trak shēn, n.* process by which open skin wounds reduce in size owing to skin movement secondary to shortening of wound fibroblasts. Contraction works best in areas where the skin is comparatively loose, e.g. in the pectoral or gluteal regions. In areas where wound contraction cannot bring skin edges together, e.g. owing to excessive skin loss or wound tension, scar results. Wound contraction stops when surface cells contact other cells, or when skin tension equilibrates, or when excessive granulation tissue prevents tissue contraction.

W. dehiscence see Dehiscence

Wound healing ◀ᴇ *wǔnd / hē ling, n.* the equine body's natural process of regener-ating tissues of dermal and epidermal origin to restore normal function. A set of events that occurs in a predictable fashion, but over a variable time period, depending on things such as the size and nature of wound, the site on the body (e.g. healing is typically delayed over exposed bone), contamination, and infection. Wound healing is typically divided into three phases:

1. Inflammatory phase – removal of debris and bacteria by phagocytosis and release of factors that cause cell migration and tissue proliferation.
2. Proliferative phase – tissue repair phase characterized by formation of new blood vessels (angiogenesis), deposition of tissue proteins (initially by proliferation of fibroblasts, which then excrete substances such as collagen), formation of granulation tissue (granulation), covering of the wound with epithelial cells (epithelialization), and wound contraction.
3. Remodelling phase – removal and remodelling of collagen along lines of tension, and removal of unnecessary cells by apoptosis. The remodelling phase may last for a year or longer.

Wounds that do not heal appropriately may result in chronic, open wounds, or excessive amounts of scar tissue.

Healing of skin wounds may be described by the manner by which the integrity of the injured skin is restored:

- First intention w. h. – describes the process by which wounds heal without the intervention of granulation tissue, e.g. when skin edges are reunited directly, e.g. by suturing (stitching).
- Second intention w.h. – describes the process by which a wound closes when skin edges cannot be directly reunited. In second intention healing, granulation tissue forms at the base and sides of the wound, and fills the wound defect. Epithelial cells migrate to cover the granulation tissue; however, the resulting scar lacks normal skin structures such as sweat and oil glands, and hair follicles. Second intention healing can be problematical if granulation tissue develops to such a level that skin

cannot cover it (proud flesh), e.g. as may occur in unattended wounds, or in wounds occurring over mobile surfaces, e.g. over joints.

- Delayed primary w.h. (third intention w.h.) – method of wound closure in wounds that are badly contaminated. Wound closure is performed after a few days, once contamination, inflammation, and infection have been controlled.

See Granulation, Skin.

Wound tension ◀ᴈ *wûnd* / <u>*ten*</u> *shēn, n.* stretching or straining on the edges of the wound. Wound tension results in delayed or prolonged healing, and is an important factor in wound dehiscence. Numerous suturing and cosmetic surgical techniques have been developed to help decrease wound tension.

Wright's stain ◀ᴈ *rītz* / *stān, n.* staining technique occasionally used for examination of blood smears. Blood cells stained by Wright's method show four major staining properties that allow the cell types to be distinguished: basophilia (affinity for methylene blue), azurophilia (affinity for the reddish-purple oxidation products of methylene blue, called azures), acidophilia (affinity for eosin), and neutrophilia (affinity for a complex of dyes in the mixture, which are pale lilac). Erythrocytes bind eosin and appear orange to pink, nuclei are purplish-blue, basophilic granules are very dark bluish-purple, eosinophilic granules red to red–orange, neutrophilic granules reddish-brown to lilac, platelets are violet to purple, and lymphocyte cytoplasm stains pale blue. (Named after American pathologist James Homer Wright, 1869–1928, who discovered the staining technique in 1902.)

Wry ◀ᴈ *rī, adj.* bent or twisted in shape, especially to one side.

W. neck ◀ᴈ *rī* / *nek, n.* contracted state of neck muscles, resulting in abnormal position of foetus at foaling, with head bent backwards; causes difficulty in foaling (dystocia).
See Dystocia.

W. nose ◀ᴈ *ri* / *nōz, n.* congenital abnormality of nose, where rostral maxilla is twisted, resulting in one side shorter than the other.

X

X chromosome ◀ᴇ *eks / krō mē zōm, n.* one of the two sex-determining chromosomes. Females have two X chromosomes. X chromosome abnormalities (e.g. X chromosome monosomy, i.e. missing an X chromosome from a pair) have been rarely described in horses. See Chromosome.

X-ray see Radiograph

Xanthochromic ◀ᴇ *zan thō krom ik, adj.* having a yellowish discolouration, especially pertaining to cerebrospinal fluid, e.g. as especially seen in many cases of equine herpes virus encephalomyelitis. See Equine herpes virus.

Xenograft ◀ᴇ *zen ō grarft, n.* a surgical graft of tissue from one species onto a different species. Xenografts obtained from pigs have been occasionally used in wound management in horses.

Xerosis ◀ᴇ *zi rō sis, n.* dryness of the skin. Caused by a lack of water content in the skin; the skin must be more than 10% water in order for it to have a normal appearance and texture.

Xxterra™ ◀ᴇ *eks tē rē, n.* a trademarked product advertised as a 'natural' treatment for various skin cancers of the horse. Two of the primary components of the product are extracts of the plant bloodroot (*Sanguinaria canadensis*) and high concentrations of zinc chloride ($ZnCl_2$). The plant root contains an alkaloid (sanguinarine) principally used in dental products; it has also been shown to suppress blood vessel growth experimentally. While bloodroot itself has no known anticancer properties, high concentrations of zinc chloride are caustic, and have been used to remove such things as warts in people. See Zinc.

Xylazine ◀ᴇ *zī lē zēn, n.* a short-acting sedative and potent analgesic drug for horses, especially for relief of abdominal pain (colic). Some clinicians feel that if a horse's abdominal pain cannot be controlled by xylazine, the problem most likely will require surgery to correct. Xylazine is also a relaxant of skeletal muscle; as such, it can reduce the respiratory rate, as is seen in natural sleep. Care should be taken in using xylazine in horses with depressed respiration, accordingly. After the drug is given to the horse, the horse's head drops within a very short time, indicating that it is sedated. Xylazine is often used in combination with other drugs when putting a horse under general anaesthesia for surgery. Xylazine comes as a sterile liquid for intravenous or intramuscular administration; its effects are dose related. Xylazine is also used to cause chemical ejaculation in stallions that may have difficulty being collected under normal circumstances. In large doses, xylazine can cause a horse to become unsteady. It is particularly important to note that even when horses are sedated with large doses of xylazine, they can still react to stimuli. Horses have been observed to kick out quickly, even while sedated with relatively large doses of this drug. Horses intended for use in shows must not have traces of xylazine in their systems. After dosage with xylazine, it is common to observe a heart rhythm abnormality known as second degree AV (atrioventricular) block. This is best described as the heart having a regular pattern, characterized by the heart rhythm slowing down and then skipping a beat. This usually disappears within a few minutes of administration of the drug and is not a health threat to the horse. Caution in giving the drug to horses with heart problems would be advisable, however. Sweating is also common after administration of xylazine. This is an effect of the drug on sweat glands and is not a sign of an abnormal or dangerous response.

Xylocaine see Lidocaine

Xylose (D-xylose) ◄ *zy lōz, n.* a wood sugar with the chemical formula $C_5H_{10}O_5$. In horses, xylose has been used to test for intestinal malabsorption. In a solution given by nasogastric tube after fasting, xylose peaks in the blood plasma after approximately 90 min, and helps distinguish normal from abnormal absorption by the intestines.
See Malabsorption.

Y

Y chromosome ◀ᛃ *wī / krō mō zōm, n.* male sex chromosome. In normal male animal there is a pair comprising one Y chromosome and one X chromosome in each cell. See Chromosome.

Yawning ◀ᛃ *yor ning, v.* in humans, yawning is an involuntary inspiration with open mouth. However, horses do not appear to breathe in when they yawn, so the root cause is speculative. Most commonly, it is a normal behaviour. However, yawning is one of several clinical signs in 'Kimberly horse disease', also known as 'walk about disease' (*Crotolaria* spp. grows in the Kimberly region of northeastern W. Australia). Yawning may also be seen with oral pain, after bit removal (possibly related to stretching the jaw muscles), in chronic abdominal pain or liver disease. The exact cause of horse yawning is unknown, although it is fairly certain that the trigger is not the same as in humans, which is a response to transient drops in blood oxygen levels. See Pyrrolizidine, Seneciosis.

Yearling ◀ᛃ *yeer ling, n.* a horse or pony of either sex that is between 1 and 2 years old.

Yeast ◀ᛃ *yēst, n.* an inexact term that is generally used to describe one of the two largest groupings of fungi (the other being moulds). Yeasts are single-celled organisms that occasionally cause disease in horses.

> **Brewer's y.** ◀ᛃ *brŭ wēs / yēst, n.* the yeast that grows during the fermentation process during the manufacture of beer. Brewer's yeast provides some protein and amino acids, although it is generally too expensive to be used as a protein supplement. Instead,

brewer's yeast is mainly used as a source of supplemental B-vitamins.

Yellow body see Corpus

Yellow fat disease see Steatitis

Yellow oleander ◀ᛃ *ye lō / ō lē an dē, n.* (*T. peruviana*) a perennial branched shrub or tree native to tropical America (Hawaii and the southern United States) that is a potential source of cardiac glycoside poisoning in horses.

Yellow star thistle ◀ᛃ *ye lō / star / thi sēl, n.* (*Centaurea solstitialis*) plant occurs in western USA, S. America (particularly Argentina), Australia, where the plants are abundant. If eaten for several months yellow star thistle causes softening or dissolution and cell death (necrosis) of parts of brain (substantia nigra and globus pallidus); the resultant pathology is called nigropalladial encephalomalacia. Clinical signs, which develop in association with the development of brain lesions, include yawning, continuous movement of the tongue, violent head tossing, depression, inability to eat, excessive muscle tone, grinding teeth, lips drawn back. The exact toxin has not yet been identified. No known treatment. Euthanasia is eventually necessary.

Yellow sweet clover ◀ᛃ *ye lō / swēt / clō vē, n.* although not toxic itself, yellow sweet clover hay is a legume hay that contains coumarin. If not cured properly, coumarin can be converted by moulds to dicoumarol, which has strong anti-blood clotting properties. The problem is most common in cattle, but has been described in horses. Affected animals show signs of excessive haemorrhage, but the problem can be successfully treated with blood transfusions and/or injections of vitamin K.

Yew ◀ᷤ *yū, n.* (*Taxus* spp.) horses are highly susceptible to poisoning by yew trees. Yew is a common ornamental plant in North America; it is the most poisonous native tree in Britain. Contains alkaloid, taxine, which depresses heart function if plant is eaten. Affected animals may show incoordination, nervousness, diarrhoea, difficulty breathing or convulsions. Horse dies almost immediately, diagnosed by finding traces of leaves in stomach at post-mortem examination. There is no effective treatment.

Yohimbine ◀ᷤ *yō him bēn, n.* yohimbine is the principal alkaloid of the bark of the West African tree *Pausinystalia yohimbe* Pierre (formerly *Corynanthe yohimbe*), family Rubiaceae (Madder family). The drug is a selective competitive α2-adrenergic receptor antagonist. As such, it has been used as a reversal agent for sedative α2-adrenergic receptor agonist drugs, such as xylazine or detomidine, for example, after routine examination procedures.

Yolk sac ◀ᷤ *yōk / sak, n.* foetal membrane that arises from foetal midgut. Has rich blood supply, provides nourishment for foetus up to 30 days' gestation, then replaced by true placenta. See Foetus, Placenta.

Yucca ◀ᷤ *yuk ē, n.* yucca is a feed supplement obtained from a cactus-like plant that is purported to be for the relief of arthritic conditions of the horse. Most preparations are combined with anise, the seed that gives the flavouring to black liquorice. Herbal pharmacy texts provide no indication as to why yucca should be beneficial in the treatment of arthritis, or in the relief of arthritis signs.

Z

Z plasty ◀ *zed* / *plas* tē, *n*. in wound repair, a technique of creating two equal triangular skin flaps that are undermined and transposed to gain skin length, to help with wound closure, e.g. to dilate a constricted orifice or to relieve tension on sutured wounds.

Zearalenone ◀ *ze* ral ē nōn, *n*. a fungal toxin (mycotoxin) produced by the fungus *Fusarium* spp., with oestrogenic properties (causes oestrus); horses eating contaminated grain (usually corn) may develop fertility problems; occasional deaths reported.

Zdar disease see Pyrrolizidine, Seneciosis

Zinc ◀ *zingk*, *n*. a blue–white metallic element, many of whose salts are used in medicine; necessary in trace amounts in the horse's body; essential part of many cellular enzymes; plays an important role in protein synthesis and cell division. See Trace mineral.
   Z. chloride ◀ *zingk klor* īd, *n*. a caustic zinc salt that has been used, in concentrations of approximately 20%, for the treatment of warts in humans. Found in high concentrations in 'natural' products intended for skin tumour treatment in horses.
   Z. deficiency ◀ *zingk* / *de* fi shēn sē, *n*. experimentally, lack of dietary zinc can cause reduced appetite, poor growth and skin lesions in several species. Naturally occurring zinc deficiencies have not been reported in horses.
   Z. oxide ◀ *zingk* oks īd, *n*. also called white zinc, zinc oxide is used topically as an astringent and protectant in various skin conditions, e.g. to protect from sun exposure.
   Z. sulphate turbidity test ◀ *zingk* / *sul* fāt / ter bi di tē / *test*, *n*. serum test used to assess whether foal has acquired antibodies from mare via first milk (colostrum) in period immediately after foaling. The test estimates the serum immunoglobulin IgG based on its precipitation when the foal's blood serum is added to a zinc-containing solution; results in approximately 1 hour. The test appears to have adequate sensitivity, that is, it can detect IgG in serum; however, its specificity is poor, that is, there is a high number of false positive tests. Accordingly, positive test results should generally not be taken as an indication for treatment; rather, such results should be confirmed with a more sensitive test.
See Antibody, Colostrum, Immunoglobulin, Neonatal.
   Z. toxicity ◀ *zingk* / *tok* si si tē, *n*. high levels of zinc in pasture may occur from industrial contamination. High levels of zinc may cause signs, especially in foals or yearlings, including anaemia, enlargement of ends of long bones, stiffness, lameness and weight loss. Rare.

Zoonosis ◀ *zō* ō nō sis, *n*. animal disease transmissible to humans under natural conditions. Equine zoonotic diseases include, but are not limited to, viral equine encephalomyelitis, Hendra virus (Australia, 1994), Borna virus (Germany), rabies, salmonellosis, glanders, anthrax, brucellosis and leptospirosis, dermatophytosis ('ringworm').
See Encephalomyelitis, Rabies.

Zootoxin ◀ *zō* ō toks in, *n*. a toxic substance of animal origin, such as snake, spider or scorpion venom.

Zygomatic arch ◀ *zī* gō ma tik / *arch*, *n*. a bony structure of the skull, formed by the frontal process of the zygomatic bone, and

the zygomatic processes of the temporal and frontal bones; together these structures form the external prominence of the cheek.
See Frontal, Skull, Petrous temporal bone, Zygomatic bone.

Zygomatic bone ◀ zi $gō$ ma tik / $bōn$, $n.$ a small, irregularly triangular bone, located on the side of the horse's face, between the lacrimal bone dorsally, and the maxilla ventrally.

Zygomycosis ◀ zi $gō$ mi $kō$ sis, $n.$ a rarely seen, localized subcutaneous fungal infection caused by several fungi in the class Zygomycetes, characterized by granulation tissue, itching, and necrotic, draining tracts.

Zygote ◀ zi $gōt$, n the fertilized ovum (egg); the cell formed by the union of the female and male gamete (egg and sperm, respectively).
See Fertilization.